Constitutional and Administrative Law

Pearson

At Pearson, we have a simple mission: to help people make more of their lives through learning.

We combine innovative learning technology with trusted content and educational expertise to provide engaging and effective learning experiences that serve people wherever and whenever they are learning.

From classroom to boardroom, our curriculum materials, digital learning tools and testing programmes help to educate millions of people worldwide – more than any other private enterprise.

Every day our work helps learning flourish, and wherever learning flourishes, so do people.

To learn more, please visit us at **www.pearson.com/uk**

Constitutional and Administrative Law

Second edition

Roger Masterman and Colin Murray

Pearson

Harlow, England • London • New York • Boston • San Francisco • Toronto • Sydney • Dubai • Singapore • Hong Kong
Tokyo • Seoul • Taipei • New Delhi • Cape Town • São Paulo • Mexico City • Madrid • Amsterdam • Munich • Paris • Milan

PEARSON EDUCATION LIMITED
KAO Two
KAO Park
Harlow CM17 9NA
United Kingdom
Tel: +44 (0)1279 623623
Web: www.pearson.com/uk

First published 2013 (print and electronic)
Second edition published 2018 (print and electronic)

© Pearson Education Limited 2013, 2018 (print and electronic)

ISBN: 978-1-292-14425-2 (print)
         978-1-292-14427-6 (PDF)
         978-1-292-14426-9 (ePub)

British Library Cataloguing-in-Publication Data
A catalogue record for the print edition is available from the British Library

Library of Congress Cataloging-in-Publication Data

Names: Masterman, Roger, author. | Murray, Colin (Colin R. G.), author.
Title: Constitutional and administrative law / Roger Masterman and Colin Murray.
Other titles: Exploring constitutional and administrative law.
Description: Second edition. | Harlow, England ; New York : Pearson, 2018. |
   Includes index.
Identifiers: LCCN 2018008837| ISBN 9781292144252 (print) | ISBN 9781292144276
   (PDF) | ISBN 9781292144269 (ePub)
Subjects: LCSH: Constitutional law--Great Britain--Outlines, syllabi, etc. |
   Administrative law--Great Britain--Outlines, syllabi, etc.
Classification: LCC KD3930 .M37 2018 | DDC 342.41--dc23
LC record available at https://urldefense.proofpoint.com/v2/url?u=https-3A__lccn.loc.
gov_2018008837&d=DwIFAg&c=0YLnzTkWOdJlub_y7qAx8Q&r=Q1huLr_hfN5hBmNklTyEbqNk
qKPJUy4ujVI9zNDFILM&m=oSsxL0CBub-dEeizF0FwW9ZTkpCjPynyeP58INjnmks&s=HM4Kquy
J8ZhqRRVB7lVrrKTCtDAkZBhCKbp4ss2Yn34&c=

A catalog record for the print edition is available from the Library of Congress

10 9 8 7 6 5 4 3 2 1
22 21 20 19 18

Cover image © @Yuri_Arcurs/DigitalVision/Getty Images

Print edition typeset in 9.5/12pt ITC Galliard Pro by SPi Global
Printed by Ashford Colour Press Ltd, Gosport

NOTE THAT ANY PAGE CROSS REFERENCES REFER TO THE PRINT EDITION

Brief contents

Preface to the second edition   xiii
Acknowledgements   xvi
Table of cases   xvii
Table of statutes   xxxii

Part I
Constitutional regulation in the absence of a codified constitution   1

1 The purposes and characteristics of constitutions   2
2 The domestic sources of the UK constitution   21
3 The United Kingdom Constitution and international legal orders   55
4 Law, politics and the nature of the United Kingdom Constitution   98

Part II
The theory and practice of the United Kingdom Constitution   121

5 Parliamentary sovereignty   122
6 The rule of law   182
7 Separation of powers   221

Part III
Central government in the United Kingdom   253

8 The executive   254
9 Parliament (I): the House of Commons   285
10 Parliament (II): the House of Lords   315
11 The United Kingdom Supreme Court and the office of Lord Chancellor: towards an independent judicial branch?   340

Part IV
Decentralised government in the United Kingdom   357

12 The United Kingdom's devolution arrangements   358
13 Devolution and the United Kingdom Constitution   393

Part V
Accountability (I): responsibility, scrutiny, openness and good administration   429

14 Principles of political accountability   430
15 Parliamentary scrutiny of government   451
16 The Parliamentary Ombudsman   468
17 Freedom of information   485

Part VI
Accountability (II): the courts   505

18 Judicial review of administrative action – theory, procedure and remedies   506
19 Judicial review of administrative action – grounds for review   541
20 The European Convention on Human Rights   595
21 The Human Rights Act 1998   647
22 Political freedoms and democratic participation   688

Index   720

Contents

Preface to the second edition   xiii
Acknowledgements   xvi
Table of cases   xvii
Table of statutes   xxxii

Part I
Constitutional regulation in the absence of a codified constitution   1

1 The purposes and characteristics of constitutions   2

Chapter outline   2
The nature and purpose of constitutions   2
Characteristics of constitutions – does the United Kingdom have a constitution?   4
The content of constitutions   8
Forms of constitutions   12
The United Kingdom Constitution   15
Practice questions   19
Further reading   19

2 The domestic sources of the UK Constitution   21

Chapter outline   21
Introduction: a constitution built using different materials   21
Legal sources of the constitution   22
Non-legal sources of the constitution   40
Conclusion   51
Practice questions   53
Further reading   53

3 The United Kingdom Constitution and international legal orders   55

Chapter outline   55
Introduction: External sources of constitutional law?   55
Public international law   57
The European Union   74
Brexit: The UK's Withdrawal from the European Union   89
Conclusion   95
Practice questions   96
Further reading   96

4 Law politics and the nature of the United Kingdom Constitution   98

Chapter outline   98
Introduction: the relationship between law and politics   98
Two competing ideas of constitutionalism   102
Judges and political questions   108
The differing responses of law and politics illustrated   115
Conclusion: the legalisation of the United Kingdom Constitution?   118
Practice questions   119
Further reading   119

Part II
The theory and practice of the United Kingdom Constitution   121

5 Parliamentary sovereignty   122

Chapter outline   122
Introduction   122
Diceyan orthodoxy: the legally unlimited power of Parliament   123
Parliamentary sovereignty: a legal or political construct?   126
Can Parliament impose limitations upon its own legislative competence?   133
Can Parliament amend the primary legislative process?   139
The relationships between primary legislation and other sources of law   148
The Human Rights Act 1998   163
The influence of – and the UK's exit from – the European Union   167
Brexit: reclaiming sovereignty   176
Conclusion   179
Practice questions   180
Further reading   180

6 The rule of law   182

Chapter outline   182
Introduction   182
The rule of law's domain   183
The core rule of law   187
The extended rule of law   199
The substantive rule of law   215
Conclusion   218
Practice questions   219
Further reading   219

7 Separation of powers   221

Chapter outline   221
Introduction   221
The theory and aims of separation of powers   223

Governmental institutions and functions   227
Separation of powers in the United Kingdom Constitution (I):
a partial division of functions?   236
Separation of powers in the United Kingdom (II):
partially separated institutions?   239
Constitutional checks and balances   246
Conclusion   249
Practice questions   250
Further reading   251

Part III
Central government in the United Kingdom   253

8 The executive   254

Chapter outline   254
Introduction   254
From absolute monarchy to the modern executive   255
The composition and role of the modern executive   265
Conclusion   282
Practice questions   283
Further reading   284

9 Parliament (I): the House of Commons   285

Chapter outline   285
Introduction: Parliament   285
The composition of the House of Commons   287
The role and functions of the House of Commons   293
The pre-eminent House of Parliament   302
The question of 'elective dictatorship'   304
Towards a rebalancing of executive/legislative relations?   306
Electoral systems and electoral reform   307
The review of Westminster constituency boundaries   312
Conclusion   313
Practice questions   314
Further reading   314

10 Parliament (II): the House of Lords   315

Chapter outline   315
Introduction   316
The composition of the House of the Lords   316
The Role of the House of Lords   324
Reform of the House of Lords   331
Conclusion   338
Practice questions   338
Further reading   339

11 The United Kingdom Supreme Court and the office of Lord Chancellor: towards an independent judicial branch? 340

Chapter outline 340
Introduction 340
The apex of the United Kingdom judicial system prior to the Constitutional Reform Act 2005 341
The pressure for institutional reform of the judiciary 346
The Constitutional Reform Act 2005 349
Conclusion 355
Practice questions 355
Further reading 356

Part IV
Decentralised government in the United Kingdom   357

12 The United Kingdom's devolution arrangements 358

Chapter outline 358
Introduction 358
From union to devolution 359
Devolution in practice: Scotland 367
Devolution in practice: Wales 375
Devolution in practice: Northern Ireland 381
Conclusion 389
Practice questions 390
Further reading 391

13 Devolution and the United Kingdom Constitution 393

Chapter outline 393
Introduction 393
The subordinate nature of the devolved legislatures 394
The English/West Lothian question 410
Tackling the English/West Lothian question 415
Conclusion 425
Practice questions 426
Further reading 426

Part V
Accountability (I): responsibility, scrutiny, openness and good administration   429

14 Principles of political accountability 430

Chapter outline 430
Introduction 430
Political and legal accountability distinguished 432

Open government and effective accountability   434
Individual ministerial responsibility   436
Sanctions and effectiveness   442
Conclusion   449
Practice questions   449
Further reading   450

15 Parliamentary scrutiny of government   451

Chapter outline   451
Introduction   451
Scrutiny in Parliament   453
Reforming parliamentary scrutiny: the Wright reforms   461
Assessing parliamentary scrutiny of government   463
Conclusion   465
Practice questions   466
Further reading   466

16 The Parliamentary Ombudsman   468

Chapter outline   468
Introduction   468
The work of the Parliamentary Ombudsman   470
Remedies and redress   477
Efficiency and effectiveness   480
Conclusion   483
Practice questions   483
Further reading   484

17 Freedom of information   485

Chapter outline   485
Introduction   485
The Freedom of Information Act 2000   488
Assessing the impact of the Freedom of Information Act   499
Conclusion   502
Practice questions   503
Further reading   503

Part VI
Accountability (II): the courts   505

18 Judicial review of administrative action – theory,
procedure and remedies   506

Chapter outline   506
Introduction   506
Judicial review's constitutional role   507
Procedural elements of judicial review   516
Remedies available under judicial review   536
Conclusion   539

Practice questions   539
Further reading   540

19 Judicial review of administrative action – grounds for review   541

Chapter outline   541
Introduction   542
Illegality   544
Irrationality   558
Procedural impropriety   567
Legitimate expectations   584
Conclusion   592
Practice questions   593
Further reading   594

20 The European Convention on Human Rights   595

Chapter outline   595
Introduction   595
The nature of human rights   596
The development of the ECHR and associated institutions   609
The rights and freedoms protected under the ECHR   617
Human rights and trade-offs under the ECHR   632
Conclusion   644
Practice questions   645
Further reading   645

21 The Human Rights Act 1998   647

Chapter outline   647
Introduction   647
From civil liberties to human rights   648
Incorporating the Convention   651
The HRA and legislation   660
Employing the Convention rights under the HRA   673
Towards A Bill of Rights for the United Kingdom?   681
Conclusion   684
Practice questions   686
Further reading   686

22 Political freedoms and democratic participation   688

Chapter outline   688
Introduction   688
Freedom of expression   690
Freedom of assembly   699
Liberty   708
Voting rights   713
Conclusion   717
Practice questions   718
Further reading   718

Index   720

Preface to the second edition

The United Kingdom's constitutional and administrative law remains among the most dynamic, complex and exciting subjects that law students will encounter during the course of their studies. It is also, unfortunately, an often misunderstood area of law which, groaning under the weight of hundreds of years of constitutional history, can seem surrounded by pitfalls and booby traps for the unwary. This book attempts to navigate those obstacles. We have set out to place constitutional and administrative law in its historical, political and social context. To this end, while our focus is the core principles underpinning the UK's constitutional edifice and the operation of those institutions through which it is animated, we have sought to highlight the vitality and topicality of this field of study through a focused contemporary lens.

The first step to negotiating some of constitutional law's potential pitfalls is to keep in mind the purpose of the law that conditions public bodies and their relationships with individuals and with each other. Constitutional law will always be tasked with demarking the powers of public bodies, *enabling* them to act in certain ways and simultaneously *disabling* them from acting in others. This book holds this duality at its heart, from its study of the building blocks of the UK's system of government, to its review of constitutional principles, to its efforts to understand how administrative law operationalises these concepts.

We have built a number of features into the text which we hope will assist the process of demystifying some of the more arcane aspects of the UK Constitution. In certain sections, we focus on particular situations in order to illuminate how constitutional law and legal principles influence the operation of, and relationships between, public bodies in the UK, or to draw comparison between the UK and other legal systems. In others, we examine key cases that have shaped our understanding of the constitution and the role of institutions and actors within it. We also rely in places on diagrams and representative images to help the reader to master complex constitutional ideas. Throughout this book, readers will be confronted with 'thinking points', asking them to relate what they are reading to other parts of the book or to contemporary developments.

The fall-out from the June 2016 referendum on the UK's membership of the European Union – which resulted in a 51.9 per cent to 48.1 per cent vote in favour of leaving the Union[1] – provided the backdrop to the preparation of the second edition of this text. The UK Constitution has long been described as enjoying a greater fluidity than those systems in which a written constitutional document establishes and sets down the core features of government, but the 'Brexit' referendum prompted a period of constitutional flux that will continue for years to come. In constitutional terms, the apparently binary in–out question posed on EU membership raises questions – not only for the UK's relationship with the EU and the status of EU laws in the constitution – but for our

---

[1] On a turnout of 72.2 per cent of the registered UK electorate.

understanding of the concepts on which the constitution rests, including the division of powers between national-level institutions of government, the territorial dimension of the constitution and perhaps also for the integrity of the Union itself. In short, the prospect that Brexit might precipitate a fundamental realignment of the UK constitutional order is a realistic one.[2]

In the first instance, notions of 'sovereignty' provided much of the driving force behind the decision to leave the EU. The notion that the UK could 'take back control' ceded to the EU provided a compelling justification for many who voted to leave. But where, domestically, would that 'control' reside once repatriated? For some, restoring the 'lost' sovereignty of *Parliament* – the constitutional concept on which the UK Constitution rests and the principle most clearly challenged by EU membership[3] – provided a motivation (Chapter 5). And yet, as the European Union (Withdrawal) Bill 2017 (the so-called 'Great Repeal Bill') indicates, the repatriation of powers from the EU will see the executive branch of government – rather than the legislature – empowered to determine which EU-derived laws will ultimately remain on the UK statute book (Chapter 7).

Constitutional principle, however, can only provide one perspective from which to examine the changes in train as a result of the Brexit referendum, as for many others the vote to leave represented – or came to represent – something else: an empowerment of the *people* (or electorate). This notion of *popular* sovereignty – the sovereignty of the people – most certainly resonates in the UK Constitution (Chapter 5), but rests upon a less secure footing as a matter of constitutional principle, and poses questions relating to (among other things) the status of referendums in the UK Constitution (Chapter 5) and the role of MPs as representatives or as delegates of the electorate (Chapter 9).

None of this should be taken to suggest that significant change has not *already* taken place. Indeed the period since the referendum result has seen occasionally frenetic constitutional activity. The resolution of the question of whether prerogative or legislation should provide the appropriate means to trigger Article 50 of the Lisbon Treaty (which would precipitate the UK's exit from the EU) provides a case in point. In a constitution in which incremental change has frequently provided a defining characteristic, the speed with which this question was addressed and acted upon – via decisions in the High Court (November 2016) and Supreme Court (January 2017), the enactment of the European Union (Notification of Withdrawal Act) 2017 (March 2017) and the Prime Minister's triggering of Article 50 in March 2017 – is worthy of note in itself.

While Brexit-related change provides perhaps the most significant series of issues tackled across this new edition, notable constitutional changes have also taken place – or are mooted – across numerous areas of the constitution. This new edition has been comprehensively updated to address developments including: the 2017 general election and proposed changes to Westminster parliamentary constituency boundaries; the Strathclyde proposals on the powers of the House of Lords; the 2014 Scottish Independence Referendum and changes to the fabric of the devolutionary arrangements; the Independent Commission on Freedom of Information; and the Conservative Party's mooted replacement of the Human Rights Act 1998 with a British Bill of Rights. Alongside updated developments in the fields of judicial review and human rights adjudication, significant cases receiving

---

[2] For our immediate post-referendum reaction see: R. Masterman and C. Murray, 'A House of Cards?' UK Const. L. Blog, 4 July 2016.

[3] See pp.167–76 for discussion and analysis.

dedicated examination in this edition include the *Miller* decisions,[4] *R (Evans)* v *Attorney General*,[5] *HS2*,[6] and *R (UNISON)* v *Lord Chancellor*.[7] Finally, a completely new chapter (Chapter 22) on political freedoms and democratic participation provides further detail regarding a number of core liberties (including freedom of expression and the right to vote) and their role in supporting participation in the political process.

Much as we could continue to augment or alter our analysis on an almost daily basis, publication deadlines impose unnatural cut-off points. This account examines legal developments up to November 2017, although the website and twitter feed – @mastermanmurray – which accompany this book attempt to bring the reader up-to-date on more recent developments.

With all of these features in mind, we should emphasise to readers that this textbook is certainly not the work of the writers alone. All aspects of the book are the product of a series of collaborations. Our respective colleagues and students at Durham and Newcastle Universities (and beyond) have often acted (perhaps unknowingly) as sounding boards for our ideas. Those to whom our gratitude is particularly due include Alan Greene, Kathryn Hollingsworth, Josh Jowitt, Lucinda Maer, Jo Murkens, Gavin Phillipson, Hélène Tyrrell, Se-shauna Wheatle and Thomas Yeon. We cannot guarantee that we have avoided all of the hazards lurking within constitutional law, but if we have, it is in no small part due to the advice and input of these individuals.

We are also extremely grateful to all the efforts of the team at Pearson for bringing this project to completion. We remain grateful to Zoë Botterill, the commissioning editor with whom the idea for this textbook was first developed, and Owen Knight, who oversaw publication of the first edition. For this edition, Melanie Carter and Cheryl Stevart have been models of unobtrusive and constructive encouragement.

Finally, and most importantly, we would like to thank our families – and in particular Laura, Rufus and Evie, and Aoife and Aoibhlínn – for their love, support and toleration during the research and production of this book.

Roger Masterman, Durham
Colin Murray, Newcastle

November 2017

---

[4] [2016] ECHR 2768 (Admin); [2017] 1 All ER 158 (HC) and [2017] UKSC 5; [2017] 2 WLR 583 (SC).

[5] [2015] UKSC 21; [2015] AC 1787.

[6] *R (Buckinghamshire CC)* v *Secretary of State for Transport* [2014] UKSC 3; [2014] 1 WLR 324.

[7] [2017] UKSC 51; [2017] 3 WLR 409.

Acknowledgements

We are grateful to the following for permission to reproduce copyright material:

Extract on page 158 from *Thoburn v Sunderland City Council* [2002] EWHC 195 (Admin); [2003] QB 151, [62]; Extract on page 129 from *Jackson v Attorney-General* [2006] 1 AC 56, [159] (Baroness Hale). See also [113] (Lord Hope); Extract on page 158 from *Thoburn v Sunderland City Council* [2003] QB 151, 186; Extract on page 159 from *Thoburn v Sunderland City Council* [2003] QB 151,187; Extract on page 160 from *Thoburn v Sunderland City Council* [2003] QB 151, 187; Extract on page 163 from *Jackson v Attorney-General* [2006] 1 AC 56, [159] (Baroness Hale). See also the comments of Lord Steyn, [102]; Extract on page 230 from *R v Secretary of State for the Home Department, exparte Fire Brigades Union* [1995] 2 AC 513, 567 (Lord Mustill); Extract on page 522 from *R v Panel on Takeovers and Mergers, ex parte Datafin plc.* [1987] QB 815, 835–836 (Sir John Don-aldson MR); Extract on page 531 from *R v Secretary of State for Foreign and Commonwealth Affairs, ex parte World Development Movement* [1995] 1 WLR 386; Extract on page 535 from *Roy v Kensington and Chelsea Family Practitioner Committee* [1992] 1 AC 624, 654 (Lord Lowry). 630; Extract on page 542 from *Council of Civil Service Unions v Minister for the Civil Service* [1985] AC 374. See below, p. 140; Extract on page 544 from *Council of Civil Service Unions v Minister for the Civil Service* [1985] AC 374, 410; Extract on page 550 from *R v Criminal Injuries Compensation Board, ex parte A* [1999] 2 AC 330, 345; Extract on page 555 from *Padfield v Minister of Agriculture, Fisheries and Food* [1968] AC 997, 1030; Extract on page 556 from *R v Inner London Education Authority, ex parte Westminster City Council* [1986] 1 WLR 28, 46–47; Extract on page 559 from *Council of Civil Service Unions v Minister for the Civil Service* [1985] AC 374, 410–11; Extract on page 565 from *R (Rogers) v Swindon NHS Primary Care Trust* [2006] EWCA Civ 392; [2006] 1 WLR 2649 (Court of Appeal) at [58]; Extract on page 565 from *R (Rogers) v Swindon NHS Primary Care Trust* [2006] EWCA Civ 392; [2006] 1 WLR 2649 (Court of Appeal) at [63]; Extract on page 566 from *Council of Civil Service Unions v Minister for the Civil Service* [1985] AC 374, 410; Extract on page 568 from *R (Osborn) v Parole Board* [2013] UKSC 61; [2014] 1 AC 1115, [67]-[71] (Lord Reed); Extract on page 579 from *R (Osborn) v Parole Board* [2013] UKSC 61; [2014] 1 AC 1115, [82] (Lord Reed); Extract on page 588 from *Council of Civil Service Unions v Minister for the Civil Service* [1985] AC 374, 401; Extract on page 592 from *Council of Civil Service Unions v Minister for the Civil Service* [1985] AC 374, 419.

Table of cases

A v HM Treasury [2010] UKSC 2; [2010] 2 AC 534 *30, 219*

A v Secretary of State for the Home Department [2004] UKHL 56; [2005] 2 AC 68; [2005] 2 WLR 87; [2005] 3 All ER 169 *105, 327, 643, 668, 670*

A v United Kingdom (2009) 49 EHRR 29 *643, 685*

A, B and C v Ireland (2011) 53 EHRR 13 *621, 636, 640*

Abdi and Nadarajah v Secretary of State for the Home Department; [2005] EWCA Civ 1363 *585, 587*

Adams v Scottish Ministers 2004 SC 665; IH (2 Div); affirming in part 2003 SC 171; 2003 SLT 366 *403*

Agricultural Sector (Wales) Bill, Re [2014] UKSC 43; [2014] 1 WLR 2622 *400*

Al Rabbat v Westminster Magistrates' Court [2017] EWHC 1969 (Admin) *70*

Alinak v Turkey (Application no. 40287/98 [2005]) *695*

Al-Jedda v United Kingdom (2011) 53 EHRR 23 *71, 619*

Al-Khawaja and Tahery v United Kingdom (2009) 49 EHRR 1 *657*

Al-Skeini v United Kingdom (2011) 53 EHRR 18 *619, 639, 644*

Anderson v Gorrie [1895] 1 QB 668 *192*

Animal Defenders International v United Kingdom [2013] 57 EHRR 21 *635, 636, 699*

Animal Defenders (judicial review) [2006] EWHC 3069; [2007] EMLR 6 *698*

Anisminic Ltd v Foreign Compensation Commission [1969] 2 AC 147; [1969] 2 WLR 163; [1969] 1 All ER 208; HL *153, 154, 212–214, 550*

Anufrijeva v Southwark LBC [2003] EWCA Civ 1406; [2004] QB 1124; [2004] 2 WLR 603; [2004] 1 All ER 833 *677*

Arthur JS Hall & Co v Simons [2002] 1 AC 615; [2000] 3 WLR 543; [2000] 3 All ER 673 *192, 207*

Assange v Swedish Prosecution Authority [2012] UKSC 22; [2012] 2 AC 471 *152*

Associated Provincial Picture Houses Ltd v Wednesbury Corp [1948] 1 KB 223; [1947]; 2 All ER 680 *248, 476, 479, 558–560, 562–566, 592*

Association of British Civilian Internees (Far East Region) v Secretary of State for Defence [2003] EWCA Civ 473; [2003] QB 1397; [2003] 3 WLR 80 *567, 589, 590*

Aston Cantlow and Wilmcote with Billesley Parochial Church Council v Wallbank [2003] UKHL 37; [2004] 1 AC 546; [2003] 3 WLR 283; [2003] 3 All ER 1213 *676*

Attorney-General for Canada v Attorney General for Ontario [1937] AC 326 *59*

Attorney-General for Jersey v Holley [2005] UKPC 23; [2005] 2 AC 580; [2005] 3 WLR 29; [2005] 3 All ER 371 *40*

Attorney-General of Hong Kong v Ng Yuen Shiu [1983] 2 AC 629; [1983] 2 WLR 735; [1983] 2 All ER 346 *585*

Attorney-General of New South Wales v Trethowan [1932] AC 526, PC (Aus) *138, 139*

Attorney-General v De Keyser's Royal Hotel Ltd (1920) AC 508 *36, 149*

Attorney-General v Fulham Corporation [1921] 1 Ch 440 *546*

Attorney-General v Guardian Newspapers Ltd [1987] 1 WLR 1248 *691, 693, 699*

Attorney-General v Jonathan Cape Ltd [1976] QB 752; [1975] 3 WLR 606; [1975] 3 All ER 484 *43, 47, 693*

Attorney-General v London and Home Counties Joint Electricity Authority [1929] 1 Ch 513 *552*

Attorney-General v *Observer Ltd* [1990] 1 AC 109 *693*

Austin v *Commissioner of Police for the Metropolis* [2009] UKHL 5; [2009] 1 AC 564 *707, 711*

Austin v *United Kingdom* (2012) 55 EHRR 14 (GC) *712*

AXA General Insurance Ltd, v *Lord Advocate (Scotland)* [2011] UKSC 46; [2012] 1 AC 868; [2011] 3 WLR 871; 2012 SC (UKSC) 122 *140, 152, 403, 405–407*

Bank Mellat v *HM Treasury* [2013] UKSC 38; [2014] AC 700 *584*

Banković v *Belgium* (2007) 44 EHRR SE5 *618, 619*

Barnard v *National Dock Labour Board* [1953] 2 QB 18; [1953] 2 WLR 995; [1953] 1 All ER 1113 *548*

Beatty v *Gillbanks* (1882) LR 9 QBD 308; *649, 689, 700–702, 707*

Beauchamp (Earl) v *Madresfield* (1872) LR 8 CP 245 *288*

Begum v *London Borough of Tower Hamlets* [2003] UKHL 5; [2003] 2 AC 430; [2003] 2 WLR 388; [2003] 1 All ER 731 *551*

Belfast City Council v *Miss Behavin' Ltd* [2007] UKHL 19; [2007] 1 WLR 1420; [2007] 3 All ER 1007 *674*

Belfast Corporation v *O.D. Cars* [1960] AC 490; [1960] 2 WLR 148; [1960] 1 All ER 65 *402*

Belgian Linguistic Case (1979–80) 1 EHRR 252 *631, 637*

Bellinger v *Bellinger* [2003] UKHL 21; [2003] 2 AC 467; [2003] 2 WLR 1174; [2003] 2 All ER 593 *669*

Benkharbouche v *Secretary of State for Foreign and Commonwealth Affairs* [2017] UKSC 62 *177*

Bici v *Ministry of Defence* [2004] EWHC 786 (QB) *192*

Board of Education v *Rice* [1911] AC 179 *569*

Boddington v *British Transport Police* [1999] 2 AC 143; [1998] 2 WLR 639; [1998] 2 All ER 203 *344*

British Broadcasting Corportation v *Johns* [1965] Ch 32 *149*

British Oxygen Co Ltd v *Minister of Technology* [1971] AC 610; [1969] 2 WLR 892; [1970] 3 WLR 488; [1970] 3 All ER 165 *556, 557*

British Railways Board v *Pickin* [1974] AC 765; [1974] 2 WLR 208; [1974] 1 All ER 609 *140, 144, 162, 512*

Bromley London Borough Council v *Greater London Council* [1983] 1 AC 768; [1982] 2 WLR 92; [1982] 1 All ER 153 *113, 114, 547, 548, 553, 554*

Broniowski v *Poland* (2006) 43 EHRR 1 (GC) *637*

Brown v *Stott* [2003] 1 AC 681; [2001] 2 WLR 817; [2001] 2 All ER 97 *160*

Bulmer Ltd v *J Bollinger SA* [1974] Ch 401; [1974] 3 WLR 202; [1974] 2 All ER 1226 *88*

Burden v *United Kingdom* (2008) 47 EHRR 38 *656*

Burmah Oil Co v *Lord Advocate* [1965] AC 75; [1964] 2 WLR 1231; [1964] 2 All ER 348 *149, 201*

Bush (George W) v *Gore (Al)* 531 US 98 (2000) *49*

Cadder v *HM Advocate (Scotland)* [2010] UKSC 43; [2010] 1 WLR 2601; 2011 SC (UKSC) 13 *202, 406–408*

Campbell and Fell v *United Kingdom* (1985) 7 EHRR 165 *245*

Campbell v *MGN Ltd* [2004] UKHL 22; [2004] 2 AC 457; [2004] 2 WLR 1232; [2004] 2 All ER 995 *663, 680, 695*

Carltona Ltd v *Commissioners of Works* [1943] 2 All ER 560 *38, 47, 270, 278, 548, 549*

Casado Coca v *Spain* (1994) 18 EHRR 1 *695*

Case of Proclamations (1611) 12 Co Rep 74 *127*

Case of Ship Money (1637) 3 St Tr 825 *127*

Champion v *Chief Constable of Gwent* [1990] 1 WLR 1 *714*

Cheney v *Conn* [1968] 1 WLR 242; [1968] 1 All ER 779 *63, 140*

Chester v *Bateson* [1920] 1 KB 829 *521*

Christian Institute v *Scottish Ministers* [2016] UKSC 51; [2016] HRLR 19 *405*

Clark v *University of Lincolnshire and Humberside* [2000] 1 WLR 1988; [2000] 3 All ER 752 *535*

Communist Party of Germany v *Federal Republic of Germany, Application No.250/57 (1957) 0 697*

Congreve v *Home Office* [1976] QB 629; [1976] 2 WLR 291; [1976] 1 All ER 697 *34*

Connors v *United Kingdom* (2005) 40 EHRR 9 *634, 640*

Cooper v *Wandsworth Board of Works* (1863) 143 ER 414 *569*

Corporate Officer of the House of Commons v *Information Commissioner* [2008] EWHC 1084 (Admin); [2009] 3 All ER 403 *502*

Costello-Roberts v *United Kingdom* (1995) 19 EHRR 112 *621*

Council of Civil Service Unions v *Minister for the Civil Service* [1985] AC 374; [1984] 3 WLR 1174; [1984] 3 All ER 935 *59, 248, 520, 521, 542, 544, 559, 566, 568, 585, 588, 592, 714*

Cream Holdings Ltd v *Banerjee* [2004] UKHL 44; [2005] 1 AC 253; [2004] 3 WLR 918; [2004] 4 All ER 617 *660*

Cyprus v *Turkey* (2002) 35 EHRR 30 *613*

Davidson v *Scottish Ministers:* [2004] UKHL 34; 2005 1 SC (HL) 7; [2004] HRLR 34 *246*

Day v *Savadge* (1614) Hob 85 *162*

De Wilde, Ooms and Versyp v *Belgium (No. 1)* (1979–80) 1 EHRR 373 *347*

Dean of Ely v *Bliss* (1842) 5 Beav 574 *134*

Department for Education and Skills v *Information Commissioner and the Evening Standard* (EA/2006/0006) *494, 503*

Derbyshire County Council v *Times Newspapers Ltd:* [1993] AC 534; [1993] 2 WLR 449; [1993] 1 All ER 1011; HL; affirming [1992] QB 770 *650, 691*

Dimes v *Proprietors of the Grand Junction Canal* (1852) 3 HLC 759 *571*

Director of Public Prosecutions v *Haw* [2007] EWHC 1931 (Admin); [2008] 1 WLR 379 *549*

Director of Public Prosecutions v *Jones* [1999] 2 AC 240; [1999] 2 WLR 625; [1999] 2 All ER 257 *704, 344*

Douglas v *Hello! Ltd* [2000] EWCA Civ 353; [2001] QB 967; [2001] 2 WLR 992; [2001] 2 All ER 289 *660, 695*

Dr. Bonham's Case (1609) 8 Coke Reports 113b; 77 ER 646 *128, 162*

Dred Scott v *Sandford* 60 US 393 (1857) *226*

Duffy, Re [2008] UKHL 4 *561*

Duncan v *Jones* [1936] 1 KB 218 *701–703*

Duport Steels Ltd v *Sirs* [1980] 1 WLR 142; [1980] 1 All ER 529 *237, 250*

E v *Secretary of State for the Home Department* [2004] EWCA Civ 49; [2004] QB 1044; [2004] 2 WLR 1351 *551*

Eckle v *Germany* (1983) 5 EHRR 1 *678*

Ecuador v *Occidental Exploration & Production Co* [2005] EWCA Civ 1116; [2006] QB 432; [2006] 2 WLR 70; [2006] 2 All ER 225 *64, 65*

Edinburgh and Dalkeith Railway Co v *Wauchope* (1842) VIII Clark & Finnelly 710 *140*

Edwards v *Attorney-General of Canada* [1930] AC 124 *401, 402*

Egan v *Basildon Borough Council* [2011] EWHC 2416 (QB) *196*

Ellen Street Estates v *Minister of Health CA* [1934] 1 KB 590 *134–136*

Entick v *Carrington* (1765) 19 St Tr 1029 *193–198, 215, 649*

Erbakan v *Turkey, Application No.59405/00 (2006) 0 698*

Evans v *Information Commissioner* [2012] UKIT 340 (AAC) *498*

Evans v *Information Commissioner* [2012] UKUT 313 (Upper Tribunal) *43, 499*

Felixstowe Dock & Railway Co v *British Transport Docks Board* [1976] 2 Lloyd's Rep 656; [1976] 2 CMLR 655 *168*

Findlay v *United Kingdom* (1997) 24 EHRR 221 *346, 347*

Fitzpatrick v *Sterling Housing Association Ltd* [2001] 1 AC 27; [1999] 3 WLR 1113; [1999] 4 All ER 705 *666*

Fletcher's Application, Re [1970] 2 All ER 527 *475*

Franklin v *Minister of Town and Country Planning* [1948] AC 87; [1947] 2 All ER 289 *573*

Frodl v Austria (2011) 52 EHRR 5 *631, 637*

Fuentes Bobo v Spain (2001) 31 EHRR 50 *627*

Gallagher v Lynn [1937] AC 863 *401, 402*

Garland v British Rail Engineering Ltd [1983] 2 AC 751; [1982] 2 WLR 918 *65*

Ghaidan v Godin-Mendoza [2004] UKHL 30; [2004] 2 AC 557; [2004] 3 WLR 113; [2004] 3 All ER 411 *26, 235, 666, 669, 680, 716*

Gillan v United Kingdom (2010) 50 EHRR 45 *614, 685*

Glimmerveen and Hagenbeek v The Netherlands (1982) 4 EHRR 260 *697*

Godden v Hales (1686) 11 St Tr 1165 *127*

Goldsmith v Bhoyrul [1998] QB 489 *691*

Greens and MT v United Kingdom (2011) 53 EHRR 21 *289*

Guardian News and Media v Incedal and Bouhadjar [2014] EWCA Crim 1861 *209*

Gunduz v Turkey (2005) 41 EHRR 5 *629*

Guzzardi v Italy (1981) 3 EHRR 333 *623*

H v Lord Advocate [2012] UKSC 24; [2013] 1 AC 413 *160*

Handyside v United Kingdom [1976] ECHR 5; (1976) 1 EHRR 737 ; (1979) 1 EHRR 737 *627, 633, 695*

Hannover, von v Germany (2006) 43 EHRR 7 *638*

Hatton v United Kingdom (2002) 34 EHRR 1 *628*

Hirst v United Kingdom (2006) 42 EHRR 41 *25, 289, 616, 631, 635, 637, 671, 713, 715, 716*

HM Treasury v Mohammed Ahmed see A v HM Treasury *0*

HM's application for Judicial Review [2014] NIQB 43 *668*

Hoekstra, Van Rijs, et al v HM Advocate (No.2) 2000 JC 387; 2000 SLT 602 *113*

Hoffman-La Roche v Secretary of State for Trade and Industry [1975] AC 295; [1974] 3 WLR 104; [1974] 2 All ER 1128 *521*

Hogan v Information Commissioner (EA/2005/0026) *493*

Horsnell v Boston BC [2005] EWHC 1311 (QB) *579*

HTV v Price Commission [1976] ICR 170 *539*

Hutchinson v United Kingdom [2017] ECHR 65; Application No. 5759208/08, 17 January 2017 (GC) *637*

Imperial Tobacco, Petitioner [2010] CSOH 134; 2010 SLT 1203 *160*

Inland Revenue Commissioners v National Federation of Self Employed and Small Businesses Ltd [1982] AC 617; [1981] 2 WLR 722; [1981] 2 All ER 93 *527, 529, 532*

International Transport Roth GmbH v Secretary of State for the Home Department [2002] EWCA Civ 158; [2003] QB 728; [2002] 3 WLR 344 *180*

Ireland v United Kingdom (1979–80) 2 EHRR 25 *611, 621, 635*

Jackson v Attorney General see R (on the application of Jackson) v Attorney General *0*

Jones v Ministry of the Interior of Saudi Arabia and Others [2006] UKHL 26; [2007] 1 AC 270; [2006] 2 WLR 1424; [2007] 1 All ER 113 *68*

Kay v Commissioner of Police for the Metropolis [2008] UKHL 69; [2008] 1 WLR 2723 *703*

Kay v Lambeth LBC [2006] UKHL 10; [2006] 2 AC 465; [2006] 2 WLR 570; [2006] 4 All ER 128 *644, 659, 680*

Kaye v Robertson [1991] FSR 62 *649, 650*

Kennedy v Charity Commission [2014] UKSC 20; [2015] AC 455 *500, 563, 566*

Kennedy v Information Commissioner [2014] UKSC 20; [2015] AC 455 *694*

Kingsley v United Kingdom (2002) 35 EHRR 10 *581*

Kulkarni v Milton Keynes Hospital NHS Trust [2009] EWCA Civ 789; CA (Civ Div); reversing [2008] EWHC 1861 (QB); [2008] IRLR 949 *580, 581*

Kuwait Airways Corp v Iraqi Airways Co [2002] UKHL 19; [2002] 2 AC 883; [2002] 2 WLR 1353; [2002] 3 All ER 209 *66*

Lange v *Atkinson, 28 October 1999* PC, Unreported *345*

Lawless v *Ireland (No.3)* (1979–80) 1 EHRR 15 *642, 643*

Lingens v *Austria* (1986) 8 EHRR 407 *695*

Lion Laboratories v *Evans* [1985] QB 526 *692*

Litster v *Forth Dry Dock & Engineering Co Ltd* [1990] 1 AC 546; [1989] 2 WLR 634; [1989] 1 All ER 1134 *169*

Liversidge v *Anderson* [1942] AC 206 *105*

Lloyd v *McMahon* [1987] AC 625; [1987] 2 WLR 821; [1987] 1 All ER 1118 *570, 575*

Locabail (UK) Ltd v *Bayfield Properties Ltd* [2000] QB 451; [2000] 2 WLR 870; [2000] 1 All ER 65 *572*

Local Government Board v *Arlidge* [1915] AC 120 *569*

Local Government Byelaws (Wales) Bill, Re [2012] UKSC 53; [2013] 1 AC 792 *400*

Loizidou v *Turkey* (1997) 23 EHRR 513 *618*

M v *Home Office* [1994] 1 AC 377; [1993] 3 WLR 433; [1993] 3 All ER 53 HL; affirming [1992] QB 270; [1992] 2 WLR 73; [1992] 4 All ER 97 *38, 188, 189, 198, 236, 237, 242, 243, 246, 259*

Macarthys Ltd v *Smith* [1979] 1 WLR 1189; [1979] 3 All ER 325; [1979] ICR 785 *168, 169, 176*

MacCormick v *Lord Advocate* 1953 SC 396; 1953 SLT 255 *361*

Madzimbamuto v *Lardner Burke* [1969] 1 AC 645; [1968] 3 WLR 1229; [1968] 3 All ER 561 *129*

Magyar Helsinki Bizottság v *Hungary* [2016] All ER (D) 02 (Dec); Application No.18030/11, 8 November 2016 *500*

Malone v *Commissioner of Police of the Metropolis* [1979] Ch 344; [1979] 2 WLR 700; [1979] 2 All ER 620 *196, 197, 234, 649, 650*

Malone v *United Kingdom* (1985) 7 EHRR 14 *198, 205*

Manchester City Council v *Pinnock* [2010] UKSC 45; [2011] 2 AC 104 *658, 659*

Manuel v *Attorney General* [1983] Ch 77; [1982] 3 WLR 821; [1982] 3 All ER 822 *47, 49*

Marais v *France, Application No.31159/96* (1996) 0 *697*

Marbury v *Madison* 5 US (1 Cranch) 137 (1803) *11, 14, 133, 225*

Marsh v *Arscott* (1982) 75 Cr App Rep 211 *709*

Martin v *Lord Advocate* [2010] UKSC 10; 2010 SC (UKSC) 40; 2010 SLT 412 *403, 406*

Martin, C and Oxford City Council v *Information Commissioner* (EA/2005/0026 AND 0030) *493*

Maxwell v *Department of Trade and Industry* [1974] QB 523; [1974] 2 WLR 338; [1974] 2 All ER 122 *580*

McCann v *United Kingdom* (1996) 21 EHRR 97 *624, 639*

McCartan Turkington Breen v *Times Newspapers* [2001] 2 AC 277; [2000] 3 WLR 1670; [2000] 4 All ER 913 *160, 694*

McCawley v *King, The* [1920] AC 691, PC (Aus) *29*

McDonald v *McDonald* [2016] UKSC 28; [2016] 3 WLR 45 *667, 679*

McFarlane v *Relate Avon Ltd* [2010] EWCA Civ 880; [2010] IRLR 872 *208*

McGonnell v *United Kingdom* (2000) 30 EHRR 289 *240, 347–349*

McInnes v *Onslow Fane* [1978] 1 WLR 1520; [1978] 3 All ER 211 *578, 579*

McKerr, Re [2004] UKHL 12; [2004] 1 WLR 807; [2004] 2 All ER 409 *674*

McKinney's Application, Re [2006] NICA 15 [35] *277*

McLaren v *Home Office* [1990] ICR 824; [1990] IRLR 338 *280*

Minister of Health v *King, The (on the Prosecution of Yaffe)* [1931] AC 494 *544*

Moohan v *Lord Advocate* [2014] UKSC 67; [2015] AC 901 *163, 659, 717*

Moonen v *Board of Film and Literature Board* [2000] 2 NZLR 9 *655*

Mortensen v *Peters* (1906) 14 SLT 227 *150*

Mosley v *News Group Newspapers Ltd* [2008] EWHC 1777 (QB); [2008] EMLR 20 *629*

Mosley v *United Kingdom* (2011) 53 EHRR 30 *628, 629*

Mouvement Raëlien Suisse v *Switzerland* (2013) 56 EHRR 14 *696*

Murphy v *Ireland* (2003) 38 EHRR *699*

N v *Secretary of State for the Home Department* [2005] UKHL 31; [2005] 2 AC 296; [2005] 2 WLR 1124; [2005] 4 All ER 1017 *657*
Nakkuda Ali v *Jayaratne* [1951] AC 66 *569*
Neilson v *Laugharne* [1981] QB 736 *517*
Norwood v *United Kingdom* (2005) 40 EHRR SE11 *697*

O'Reilly v *Mackman* [1983] 2 AC 237; [1982] 3 WLR 1096; [1982] 3 All ER 112 *533, 535*
Oberschlick v *Austria* (1995) 19 EHRR 389 *695*
Öcalan v *Turkey* (2005) 41 EHRR 45 *618, 619*
Occidental Petroleum v *Ecuador see Ecuador Occidental Exploration & Production Co* 0
Open Door Counselling Ltd and Dublin Well Woman Centre v *Ireland* (1993) 15 EHRR 244 *627*
Otto-Preminger Institute v *Austria* (1995) 19 EHRR 34 *629*

P, Re [2008] UKHL 38; [2009] 1 AC 173 *658*
Padfield v *Minister of Agriculture, Fisheries and Food* [1968] AC 997; [1968] 2 WLR 924; [1968] 1 All ER 694 *552, 555*
Pavel Ivanov v *Russia, Application No.35222/04* (2007) 0 *697*
Pedro v *Diss* [1981] 2 All ER 59 *188*
Pepper v *Hart* [1993] AC 593; [1992] 3 WLR 1032; [1993] 1 All ER 42 *39, 190, 345*
PF and EF v *United Kingdom* [2010] ECHR 2015 *639*
Pham v *Secretary of State for the Home Department* [2015] UKSC 19; [2015] 1 WLR 1591 *79, 175, 567*
Phillips v *Eyre* (1870) LR 6 QB 1 *153, 201*
Pickin v *British Railways Board see British Railways Board* v *Pickin* 0
Pickstone v *Freemans Plc* [1989] AC 66; [1988] 3 WLR 265; [1988] 2 All ER 803 *169*
Plattform 'Ärzte für das Leben' v *Austria* (1988) 13 EHRR 204 *706*

Poplar Housing & Regeneration Community Association Ltd v *Donoghue* [2001] EWCA Civ 595; [2002] QB 48; [2001] 3 WLR 183; [2001] 4 All ER 604 *665*
Porter v *Magill* [2001] UKHL 67; [2002] 2 AC 357; [2002] 2 WLR 37; [2002] 1 All ER 465 *554, 556, 573, 574, 581*
Prince's Case (1606) 8 Co Rep 1a 505 *140*
Procola v *Luxembourg* (1996) 22 EHRR 193 *348, 349*

R (A and B) v *Secretary of State for Health* [2017] UKSC 41 *218*
R (A) v *B (Investigatory Powers Tribunal: Jurisdiction)* [2009] UKSC 12; [2010] 2 AC 1; [2010] 2 WLR 1; [2010] All ER 1149 *212*
R (Al Rawi) v *Secretary of State for Foreign and Commonwealth Affairs* [2006] EWCA Civ 1279;[2007] 2 WLR 1219 *522*
R (Alconbury Investments) v *Secretary of State for the Environment, Transport and the Regions* [2001] UKHL 23; [2003] 2 AC 295 *219*
R (Bailey) v *London Borough of Brent Council* [2011] EWHC 2572 (Admin) *218*
R (Ben Hoare Bell Solicitors) v *Lord Chancellor* [2015] EWHC 523 (Admin); [2015] 1 WLR 4175 *518, 555*
R (Bourgass) v *Secretary of State for Justice* [2015] UKSC 54; [2016] AC 384 *549*
R (Buckingham CC) v *Secretary of State for Transport (HS2)* [2014] UKSC 3; [2014] 1 WLR 324 *7, 27, 160, 161, 175, 177, 181*
R (Buglife) v *Natural England* [2011] EWHC 746 (Admin) *533*
R (Cart) v *Upper Tribunal* [2011] 2 WLR 36; [2010] EWCA Civ 859 *206*
R (Chester) v *Secretary of State for Justice* [2013] UKSC 63; [2014] AC 271 *671, 715, 716*
R (Corner House Research) v *Secretary of State for Trade and Industry* [2005] EWCA Civ 192; [2005] 1 WLR 2600 *518*

R (Edison First Power Ltd) v Secretary of State For Environment, Transport & Regions [2000] EWHC (Admin) 317 546

R (Evans) v Attorney-General [2015] UKSC 21; [2015] 1 AC 1787 157, 158, 160, 163, 212–214, 497, 499, 715

R (Gentle) v Prime Minister [2008] UKHL 20; [2008] 1 AC 1356 658

R (Haw) v Secretary of State for the Home Department [2006] EWCA Civ 532; [2006] QB 780 705

R (Howard League for Penal Reform) v Lord Chancellor [2014] EWHC 709 (Admin) 184

R (Keyu) v Secretary of State for Foreign and Commonwealth Affairs [2015] UKSC 69, [2015] 3 WLR 1665; [2016] AC 1355 67, 567, 658, 659

R (Laporte) v Chief Constable of Gloucester-shire [2006] UKHL 55; [2007] 2 AC 105 700, 701, 706

R (Lewis) v Redcar & Cleveland BC [2007] EWHC (Admin) 3166; [2008] ACD 38 574

R (McClure) v Commissioner of Police for the Metropolis [2012] EWCA Civ 12 712

R (Miller) v Secretary of State for Exiting the European Union [2016] EWHC 2768 (Admin) 17, 21, 28, 92, 100, 351

R (Miller) v Secretary of State for Exiting the European Union [2017] UKSC 5; [2017] 2 WLR 583 21, 28, 37, 60, 61, 79, 92, 93, 100, 131, 132, 149, 150, 160, 177, 178, 181

R (Moseley) v Haringey LBC [2014] UKSC 56; [2014] 1 WLR 3947 577

R (National Secular Society) v Bideford Town Council [2012] HC 175 (Admin); [2012] 2 All ER 1175 420

R (New College London) v Secretary of State for the Home Department [2013] UKSC 51; [2013] 1 WLR 2358 38

R (Nicklinson) v Ministry of Justice [2014] UKSC 38; [2015] AC 657 672

R (on the application of A) v Secretary of State for the Home Department [2006] EWHC 526 (Admin) 585, 587

R (on the application of Abbasi) v Secretary of State for Foreign and Commonwealth Affairs [2002] EWCA Civ 1598; [2003] UKHRR 76 521, 588, 590

R (on the application of Al-Haq) v Secretary of State for Foreign and Commonwealth Affairs [2009] EWHC 1910 (Admin) 530

R (on the application of Ali) v Secretary of State for the Home Department [2003] EWHC 899 538

R (on the application of Al-Jedda) v Secretary of State for Defence [2007] UKHL 58; [2008] 1 AC 332; [2008] 2 WLR 31; [2008] 3 All ER 28 71

R (on the application of Al-Rawi) v Secretary of State for Foreign and Commonwealth Affairs [2006] EWCA Civ 1279; [2008] QB 289; [2007] 2 WLR 1219 522

R (on the application of Al-Skeini) v Secretary of State for Defence [2007] UKHL 26; [2008] 1 AC 153; [2007] 3 WLR 33; [2007] 3 All ER 685 619

R (on the application of Animal Defenders International) v Secretary of State for Culture, Media and Sport [2008] UKHL 15; [2008] 1 AC 1312; [2008] 2 WLR 781; [2008] 3 All ER 193 165, 627, 658, 661, 699

R (on the application of Anufrijeva) v Secretary of State for the Home Department [2003] UKHL 36; [2004] 1 AC 604; [2003] 3 WLR 252; [2003] 3 All ER 827 576, 583

R (on the application of Asha Foundation) v Millennium Commission [2003] EWCA Civ 88 583

R (on the application of Bancoult) v Secretary of State for Foreign and Commonwealth Affairs (No 2) [2008] UKHL 61; [2009] 1 AC 453; [2008] 3 WLR 955; [2008] 4 All ER 1055 36, 149, 589

R (on the application of Bancoult) v Secretary of State for the Foreign and Commonwealth Office [2001] QB 1067; [2001] 2 WLR 1219 546

R (on the application of BAPIO Action Ltd) v Secretary of State for the Home Department [2008] UKHL 27; [2008] 1 AC 1003; [2008] 2 WLR 1073; [2009] 1 All ER 93; HL; affirming [2007] EWCA Civ 1139; [2008] ACD 7 575, 577, 578, 583

R *(on the application of Beer* v *Hampshire Farmers Markets Ltd* [2003] EWCA Civ 1056; [2004] 1 WLR 233 *524, 680*

R *(on the application of Begum)* v *Denbigh High School Governors 2* [2006] UKHL 15; [2007] 1 AC 100; [2006] 2 WLR 719; [2006] 2 All ER 487 *674, 675*

R *(on the application of Bhatt Murphy)* v *Independent Assessor* [2008] EWCA Civ 755 *591, 593*

R *(on the application of Boyle)* v *Haverhill Pub Watch* [2009] EWHC 2441 *526*

R *(on the application of Bradley)* v *Secretary of State for Work and Pensions* [2008] EWCA Civ 36; [2009] QB 114; [2008] 3 WLR 1059; [2008] 3 All ER 1116; [2008] Pens. L.R. 103; CA (Civ Div); reversing in part [2007] EWHC 242 (Admin) *479, 480*

R *(on the application of Brooke)* v *Parole Board* [2008] EWCA Civ 29; [2008] 1 WLR 1950; [2008] 3 All ER 289 *246*

R *(on the application of Buglife: The Invertebrate Conservation Trust)* v *Medway Council* [2011] EWH 746 (Admin) *533*

R *(on the application of Campaign for Nuclear Disarmament)* v *Prime Minister* [2002] EWHC 2777 (Admin) *64*

R *(on the application of Cart)* v *Upper Tribunal* [2009] EWHC 3052 (QB); [2010] 2 WLR 1012; [2010] 1 All ER 908 *152*

R *(on the application of Chester)* v *Secretary of State for Justice* [2010] EWCA Civ 1439; [2011] 1 WLR 1436; [2011] UKHRR 53 *289, 716*

R *(on the application of Chief Constable of the West Midlands)* v *Birmingham Magistrates Court* [2002] EWHC 1087 *549*

R *(on the application of Condliff)* v *North Staffordshire Primary Care Trust* [2011] EWCA Civ 910; [2012] 1 All ER 689; (2011) 121 BMLR 192 *641*

R *(on the application of Condron)* v *National Assembly for Wales* [2006] EWCA Civ 1573 *573*

R *(on the application of Corner House Research)* v *Serious Fraud Office* [2008]

UKHL 60; [2009] 1 AC 756; [2008] 3 WLR 568; [2008] 4 All ER 927 HL; reversing [2008] EWHC 714 *63, 210, 211, 271, 341, 509*

R *(on the application of Countryside Alliance)* v *Attorney General* [2007] UKHL 52; [2008] 1 AC 719; [2007] 3 WLR 922; [2008] 2 All ER 95 *607*

R *(on the application of Daly)* v *Secretary of State for the Home Department* [2001] UKHL 26; [2001] 2 AC 532; [2001] 2 WLR 1622; [2001] 3 All ER 433 *564*

R *(on the application of Dixon)* v *Secretary of State for the Environment, Food and Rural Affairs* [2002] EWHC 831 (Admin) *195*

R *(on the application of Doy)* v *Commissioner for Local Administration* [2001] EWHC Admin 361 *475*

R *(on the application of European Roma Rights Centre)* v *Immigration Officer, Prague Airport* [2004] UKHL 55; [2005] 2 AC 1; [2005] 2 WLR 1; [2005] 1 All ER 527 *68*

R *(on the application of Evans)* v *Lord Chancellor* [2011] EWHC 1146 (Admin); [2012] 1 WLR 838; [2011] 3 All ER 594 *207, 583*

R *(on the application of Evans)* v *Secretary of State for Defence* [2010] EWHC 1445 (Admin); [2011] ACD 11 *528, 529*

R *(on the application of F and Thompson)* v *Secretary of State for the Home Department* [2010] UKSC 17; [2011] 1 AC 331; [2010] 2 WLR 992; [2010] 2 All ER 707 *671*

R *(on the application of Farrakhan)* v *Secretary of State for the Home Department* [2002] EWCA Civ 606; [2002] QB 1391; [2002] 3 WLR 481; [2002] 4 All ER 289 *522*

R *(on the application of Ghai)* v *Newcastle City Council* [2010] EWCA Civ 59; [2011] QB 591; [2010] 3 WLR 737 *551*

R *(on the application of Gillan)* v *Commissioner of Police of the Metropolis* [2006] UKHL 12; [2006] 2 AC 307; [2006] 2 WLR 537; [2006] 4 All ER 1041 *205*

R *(on the application of Greenfield)* v *Secretary of State for the Home Department*

[2005] UKHL 14; [2005] 1 WLR 673; [2005] 2 All ER 240 *677*

R (on the application of Horvath) v *Secretary of State for the Environment, Food and Rural Affairs* [2007] EWCA Civ 620 *366*

R (on the application of Hurley and Moore) v *Secretary of State for Business Innovation and Skills* [2012] EWHC (Admin 201; [2012] HRLR 13 *537*

R (on the application of Jackson) v *Attorney General* [2005] UKHL 56; [2006] 1 AC 262; [2005] 3 WLR 733; [2005] 4 All ER 1253, HL; affirming [2005] EWCA Civ 126; [2005] QB 579 *28, 35, 99, 122, 126, 133, 139, 143–147, 178–181, 214, 217, 230, 239, 250, 262*

R (on the application of Jackson) v *Attorney General* [2006] 1 AC 56 *125, 129, 163, 181*

R (on the application of Jenkins) v *Marsh Farm Community Development Trust* [2011] EWHC 1097 *526*

R (on the application of Kambadzi) v *Secretary of State for the Home Department* [2011] UKSC 23; [2011] 1 WLR 1299; [2011] 4 All ER 975 *585*

R (on the application of Lewis) v *Persimmon Homes Teesside Ltd* [2008] EWCA Civ 746; [2009] 1 WLR 83, CA (Civ Div); reversing in part [2007] EWHC 3166 (Admin); [2008] ACD 38 *573, 574, 575*

R (on the application of Mahmood) v *Secretary of State for the Home Department* [2001] 1 WLR 840; [2000] EWCA Civ 315 *563*

R (on the application of Mayor and Citizens of the City of Westminster) v *Mayor of London* [2002] EWHC 2440 (Admin) *553*

R (on the application of McDonald) [2011] UKSC 33; [2011] 4 All ER 881 *218*

R (on the application of Mohamed, Binyan) v *Secretary of State for Foreign and Commonwealth Affairs* [2008] EWHC 2048 (Admin); [2009] 1 WLR 2579 *184*

R (on the application of Mohamed, Binyan) v *Secretary of State for Foreign and Commonwealth Affairs* [2009] EWHC 2549 (Admin); [2009] 1 WLR 2653 *209*

R (on the application of Mohamed, Binyan) v *Secretary of State for Foreign and*

Commonwealth Affairs [2010] EWCA Civ 65; [2011] QB 218; [2010] 3 WLR 554; [2010] 4 All ER 91 *209*

R (on the application of Molinaro) v *Royal Borough of Kensington and Chelsea* [2001] EWHC Admin 896; [2002] BLGR 336 *552*

R (on the application of Nasseri) v *Secretary of State for the Home Department* [2009] UKHL 23; [2010] 1 AC 1; [2009] 2 WLR 1190; [2009] 3 All ER 774 *674*

R (on the application of PKK) v *Secretary of State for the Home Department* [2002] EWHC 644 (Admin) *534*

R (on the application of ProLife Alliance) v *BBC* [2003] UKHL 23; [2004] 1 AC 185; [2003] 2 WLR 1403; [2003] 2 All ER 977 *217, 236, 696*

R (on the application of ProLife Alliance) v *British Broadcasting Corporation* [2013] EHRLR 651 *697*

R (on the application of Purdy) v *Director of Public Prosecutions* [2009] UKHL 45; [2010] 1 AC 345; [2009] 3 WLR 403; [2009] 4 All ER 1147 *205, 210*

R (on the application of Q) v *Secretary of State for the Home Department* [2003] EWCA Civ 364; [2004] QB 36; [2003] 3 WLR 365; [2003] 2 All ER 905 *245*

R (on the application of Quark Fishing Ltd) v *Secretary of State for Foreign and Commonwealth Affairs* [2005] UKHL 57; [2006] 1 AC529; [2005] 3 WLR 837; [2006] 3 All ER 111 *261*

R (on the application of Rogers) v *Swindon NHS Primary Care Trust* [2006] EWCA Civ 392; [2006] 1 WLR 2649 *565*

R (on the application of S) v *Secretary of State for the Home Department* [2006] EWCA Civ 1157; CA (Civ Div); affirming [2006] EWHC 1111 (Admin) *116, 117*

R (on the application of Secretary of State for the Home Department) v *Humberside Police Authority* [2004] EWHC 1642 (Admin) *531*

R (on the application of Secretary of State for the Home Department) v *Mental Health* [2007] EWHC 2224 (Admin); [2008] MHLR 212 *561*

R (on the application of Shoesmith) v
OFSTED [2011] EWCA Civ 642; IRLR
679 *554, 577*

R (on the application of Southall) v *Secretary
of State for Foreign and Commonwealth
Affairs* [2003] EWCA Civ 1002 *47*

R (on the application of Ullah) v *Special
Adjudicator* [2004] UKHL 26; [2004] 2
AC 323; [2004] 3 WLR 23; [2004] 3 All
ER 785 *656*

R (on the application of West) v *Lloyd's of
London* [2004] EWCA Civ 506; [2004] 3
All ER 251 *524*

R (on the application of West) v *Parole Board*
[2002] EWCA Civ 1641; [2003] 1 WLR
705 *579*

R (on the application of Wilkinson) v *Inland
Revenue Commissioners* [2005] UKHL
30; [2005] 1 WLR 1718; [2006] 1 All
ER 529 *667*

R (on the application of Woolas) v
Parliamentary Electoral Court [2010]
EWHC 3169 (Admin); [2012] QB 1;
[2011] 2 WLR 1362 *291*

R (Osborn) v *Parole Board* [2013] UKSC 61;
[2014] 1 AC 1115 *568, 579, 651*

R (Plantagenet Alliance) v *Secretary of State
for Justice* [2014] EWHC 1662; [2015] 3
All ER 261 *530, 578*

R (ProLife Alliance) v *British Broadcasting
Corporation* [2002] EWCA Civ 297;
[2002] 3 WLR 1080; [2003] UKHL 23;
[2004] 1 AC 185 *697*

R (Public Law Project) v *Lord Chancellor*
[2016] UKSC 39; [2016] 3 WLR
387 *29*

R (Quila) v *Secretary of State for the Home
Department* [2011] UKSC 48; [2012] 1
AC 621 *658*

R (Quintaville) v *Secretary of State for Health*
[2003] UKHL 13; [2003] 2 AC 687 *39*

R (Reilly & Hewstone) v *Secretary of State for
Work and Pensions* [2014] EWHC 2182
(Admin) *202*

R (Reilly & Hewstone) v *Secretary of State
for Work and Pensions* [2016] EWCA Civ
413; [2016] 3 WLR 1641 *202*

R (Reilly & Wilson) v *The Secretary of State
for Work and Pensions* [2013] UKSC 68;
[2013] 3 WLR 1276 *201*

R (SG) v *Secretary of State for Work and
Pensions* [2015] UKSC 16; [2015] 1 WLR
1449 *66*

R (Smith) v *Parole Board* [2005] UKHL 1;
[2005] 1 WLR 350 *579*

R (UNISON) v *Lord Chancellor* [2017]
UKSC 51; [2017] 3 WLR 409 *157, 206,
207, 211*

R v A [2001] UKHL 25; [2002] 1 AC 45;
[2001] 2 WLR 1546; [2001] 3 All ER 1
665, 666, 669

R v Barnsley MBC Ex p. Hook [1976] 1 WLR
1052; [1976] 3 All ER 452 *578*

R v Blackwell [2006] EWCA Crim 2185 *190*

*R v Board of Visitors of Hull Prison Ex p. St
Germain (No.2)* [1979] 1 WLR 1401;
[1979] 3 All ER 545 *533, 580*

*R v Bow Street Metropolitan Stipendiary
Magistrate Ex p. Pinochet (No. 3)* [2000]
1 AC 147; [1999] 2 WLR 827; [1999] 2
All ER 97 *72, 73, 345*

*R v Bow Street Metropolitan Stipendiary
Magistrate Ex p. Pinochet Ugarte (No.2)*
[2000] 1 AC 119; [1999] 2 WLR 272;
[1999] 1 All ER 577 *571, 572*

R v C [2004] EWCA Crim 292; [2004] 1
WLR 2098; [2004] 3 All ER 1 *203, 204*

R v Cambridge Health Authority Ex p. B
[1995] 1 WLR 898; [1995] 2 All ER 129
109, 511, 562

R v Chambers [2008] EWCA Crim 2467
204, 205

R v Chaytor [2010] UKSC 52; [2011] 1 A.C.
684 *191*

*R v Chief Constable of North Wales Police, Ex
p. Evans* [1982] 1 WLR 1155 *508*

*R v Chief Constable of Sussex Ex p.
International Trader's Ferry Ltd* [1999]
2 AC 418; [1998] 3 WLR 1260; [1999]
1 All ER 129 *566, 567*

*R v Chief Constable of the Thames Valley
Police Ex p. Cotton* [1990] IRLR 344 *575*

R v Chief Rabbi Ex p. Wachmann [1992] 1
WLR 1036; [1993] 2 All ER 249 *523*

R v Cockerton [1901] 1 QB 726 CA *420*

R v Cole [2008] EWCA Crim 3234; (2009)
173 CL & J 39 *573*

*R v Commissioner for Local Administration
Ex p. Croydon London Borough Council*
[1989] 1 All ER 1033 *559, 560*

R v *Commissioner of Police of the Metropolis Ex p. Parker* [1953] 1 WLR 1150; [1953] 2 All ER 717 *569*

R v *Criminal Injuries Compensation Board Ex p. A* [1999] 2 AC 330; [1999] 2 WLR 974 *550*

R v *Darnel* (1627) 3 State Tr 1 *24*

R v *Derbyshire CC Ex p. Noble* [1990] I.C.R. 808 *519*

R v *Devon County Council Ex p. Baker* [1995] 1 All ER 73 *586*

R v *Director of Public Prosecutions Ex p. Bull* [1999] 1 WLR 347; [1998] 2 All ER 755 *530*

R v *Director of Public Prosecutions Ex p. Kebilene* [2000] 2 AC 326; [1999] 3 WLR 972; [1999] 4 All ER 801 *648, 667*

R v *Director of Public Prosecutions Ex p. Manning* [2001] QB 330; [2000] 3 WLR 463 *560*

R v *Felixstowe Justices Ex p. Leigh* [1987] QB 582; [1987] 2 WLR 380; [1987] 1 All ER 551 *209*

R v *Football Association Ex p. Football League* [1993] 2 All ER 833 *523*

R v *Gaming Board for Great Britain Ex p. Benaim* [1970] 2 QB 417; [1970] 2 WLR 1009; [1970] 2 All ER 528 *576*

R v *Gough* [1993] AC 646; [1993] 2 WLR 883; [1993] 2 All ER 724 *571, 574*

R v *Halliday ex parte Zadig* [1917] A.C. 260 *30, 521*

R v *Hampden* (1637) 3 State Tr 826 *24, 255*

R v *Higher Education Funding Council Ex p. Institute of Dental Surgery* [1994] 1 WLR 242; [1994] 1 All ER 651 *581, 582*

R v *HM Advocate* [2002] UKPC D 3; [2004] 1 AC 462; [2003] 2 WLR 317; 2003 SC (PC) 21 *160, 406*

R v *HM Queen in Council Ex p. Vijayatunga* [1990] 2 QB 444; [1989] 3 WLR 13; [1989] 2 All ER 843; CA (Civ Div); affirming [1988] QB 322; [1988] 2 WLR 106; [1987] 3 All ER 204 *539*

R v *HM Treasury Ex p. Smedley* [1985] QB 657; [1985] 2 WLR 576; [1985] 1 All ER 589 *528, 529*

R v *Horncastle* [2009] UKSC 14; [2010] 2 AC 373; [2010] 2 WLR 47; [2010] 2 All ER 359 *657–659*

R v *Horseferry Road Magistrates Court Ex p. Bennett* [1994] 1 AC 42; [1993] 3 WLR 90; [1993] 3 All ER 138 *210, 341*

R v *Howell* [1982] QB 416 *701, 707*

R v *Inland Revenue Commissioners Ex p. MFK Underwriting Agencies* [1990] 1 WLR 1545; [1990] 1 All ER 91 *591*

R v *Inland Revenue Commissioners Ex p. Preston* [1985] AC 835; [1985] 2 WLR 836; [1985] 2 All ER 327 *534, 542*

R v *Inland Revenue Commissioners Ex p. Rossminster Ltd* [1980] AC 952; [1980] 2 WLR 1; [1980] 1 All ER 80 *194, 195, 200*

R v *Inner London Education Authority Ex p. Westminster City Council* [1986] 1 WLR 28; [1986] 1 All ER 19 *556*

R v *Inspectorate of Pollution Ex p. Greenpeace Ltd (No.2)* [1994] 4 All ER. 329 *530*

R v *IRC, ex parte Rossminster* [1980] AC 952 *715*

R v *Jockey Club Ex p. Aga Khan* [1993] 1 WLR 909; [1993] 2 All ER 853 *523*

R v *Jones (Margaret) and Others* [2006] UKHL 16; [2007] 1 AC 136; [2006] 2 WLR 772; [2006] 2 All ER 741 *67, 69, 72, 73*

R v *Jordan* [1967] Crim LR 483 *151*

R v *K* [2001] UKHL 41; [2002] 1 AC 462 *40*

R v *Keyn* (1876) L.R. 2 Ex D 63 *56, 68*

R v *Lambert* [2001] UKHL 37; [2002] 2 AC 545; [2001] 3 WLR 206; [2001] 3 All ER 577 *666*

R v *Legal Aid Board Ex p. Duncan* [2000] COD 159 *207*

R v *Local Commissioner for Local Government Ex p. Liverpool City Council* [2001] 1 All ER 462 *469*

R v *Lord Chancellor Ex p. Witham* [1998] QB 575; [1998] 2 WLR 849; [1997] 2 All ER 779 *109, 140, 154–157, 159, 206, 207, 231, 232, 248, 651*

R v *Lyons* [2002] UKHL 44; [2003] 1 AC 976; [2002] 3 WLR 1562; [2002] 4 All ER 1028 *62, 63, 152*

R v *Medical Appeal Tribunal Ex p. Gilmore* [1957] 1 QB 574; [1957] 2 WLR 498; [1957] 1 All ER 796 *153*

R v Ministry of Agriculture, Fisheries and Food Ex p. Hamble (Offshore) Fisheries Ltd [1995] 2 All ER. 714 *586, 587*

R v Ministry of Defence Ex p. Smith [1996] QB 517; [1996] 2 WLR 305; [1996] 1 All ER 257 *563*

R v Monopolies and Mergers Commission Ex p. Argyll Group [1986] 1 WLR 763; [1986] 2 All ER 257 *527*

R v Morley (1760) 2 Burr 1041 *212*

R v North and East Devon Health Authority Ex p. Coughlan [1999] EWCA Civ 1871; [2001] QB 213; [2000] 2 WLR 622; [2000] 3 All ER 850 *585–588, 590–592*

R v Offen [2001] 1 WLR 253; [2001] 2 All ER 154 *160*

R v Panel on Takeovers and Mergers Ex p. Datafin Plc [1987] QB 815; [1987] 2 WLR 699; [1987] 1 All ER 564 *522–524*

R v Parliamentary Commissioner for Administration Ex p. Dyer [1994] 1 WLR 621; [1994] 1 All ER 375 *476*

R v R [1992] 1 AC 599; [1991] 3 WLR 767; [1991] 4 All ER 481 *202–204*

R v Safi (Ali Ahmed) and others [2003] EWCA Crim 1809; [2004] 1 Cr App R 14 *116*

R v Secretary of State for Education and Employment Ex p. Begbie [2000] 1 WLR 1115 *588–590, 592*

R v Secretary of State for Employment Ex p. Equal Opportunities Commission [1995] 1 AC 1; [1994] 2 WLR 409; [1994] 1 All ER 910 *531*

R v Secretary of State for Foreign and Commonwealth Affairs Ex p. Rees-Mogg [1994] QB 552; [1994] 2 WLR 115; [1994] 1 All ER 457 *59, 60, 528*

R v Secretary of State for Foreign and Commonwealth Affairs Ex p. World Development Movement Ltd [1995] 1 WLR 386; [1995] 1 All ER 611 *547, 548*

R v Secretary of State for Foreign and Commonwealth Affairs, ex parte World Development Movement [1995] 1 WLR 386 *531*

R v Secretary of State for Health Ex p. United States Tobacco International Inc [1992] QB 353; [1991] 3 WLR 529; [1992] 1 All ER 212 *586*

R v Secretary of State for the Environment Ex p. Hammersmith and Fulham LBC [1991] 1 AC 521; [1990] 3 WLR 898; [1990] 3 All ER 589 *109, 562*

R v Secretary of State for the Environment Ex p. Kirkstall Valley Campaign Ltd [1996] 3 All ER 304 *573*

R v Secretary of State for the Environment Ex p. Nottinghamshire CC [1986] AC 240; [1986] 2 WLR 1; [1986] 1 All ER 199 *109, 562*

R v Secretary of State for the Environment Ex p. Rose Theatre Trust [1990] 1 QB 504; [1990] 2 WLR 186; [1990] 1 All ER 754 *529, 530*

R v Secretary of State for the Home Department Ex p. Al-Fayed [1998] 1 WLR 763; [1997] 1 All ER 228 *583*

R v Secretary of State for the Home Department Ex p. Anderson [2002] UKHL 46; [2003] 1 AC 837; [2002] 3 WLR 1800; [2002] 4 All ER 1089 *249*

R v Secretary of State for the Home Department Ex p. Brind [1991] 1 AC 696; [1991] 2 WLR 588; [1991] 1 All ER 720 *566, 650, 673, 693, 694*

R v Secretary of State for the Home Department Ex p. Bugdaycay [1987] AC 514; [1987] 2 WLR 606; [1987] 1 All ER 940 *564*

R v Secretary of State for the Home Department Ex p. Doody [1994] 1 AC 531; [1993] 3 WLR 154; [1993] 3 All ER 92 *549, 576–578, 582*

R v Secretary of State for the Home Department Ex p. Fire Brigades Union [1995] 2 AC 513; [1995] 2 WLR 464; [1995] 2 All ER 244 *37, 149, 230, 345, 510, 513, 549, 715*

R v Secretary of State for the Home Department Ex p. Hargreaves [1997] 1 WLR 906; [1997] 1 All ER 397 *587*

R v Secretary of State for the Home Department Ex p. Hindley [2000] UKHL 21; [2001] 1 AC 410; [2000] 2 WLR 730; [2000] 2 All ER 385 *527, 557*

R v Secretary of State for the Home
Department Ex p. Hosenball [1977] 1
WLR 766; [1977] 3 All ER 452 *47*

R v Secretary of State for the Home
Department Ex p. Khan (Asif Mahmood)
[1984] 1 WLR 1337; [1985] 1 All ER 40
586, 588

R v Secretary of State for the Home
Department Ex p. Leech (No.2) [1994] QB
198; [1993] 3 WLR 1125; [1993] 4 All
ER 539 *109, 651*

R v Secretary of State for the Home
Department Ex p. Northumbria Police
Authority [1989] QB 26; [1988] 2 WLR
590; [1988] 1 All ER 556 *35*

R v Secretary of State for the Home
Department Ex p. Pierson [1998] AC 539
152, 153

R v Secretary of State for the Home
Department Ex p. Simms [2000] 2 AC
115; [1999] 3 WLR 328; [1999] 3 All ER
400 *99, 155–157, 159, 211, 239, 248, 546,
651, 691, 715*

R v Secretary of State for the Home
Department Ex p. Tarrant [1985] QB
251; [1984] 2 WLR 613; [1984] 1 All ER
799 *580*

R v Secretary of State for the Home
Department Ex p. Venables [1998] AC
407; [1997] 3 WLR 23; [1997] 3 All ER
97 *238, 249, 554*

R v Secretary of State for the Home
Department, Ex p. Cheblak [1991] 1 WLR
890 *708*

R v Secretary of State for the Home
Department, ex parte Northumbria Police
Authority [1989] QB 26 *705*

R v Secretary of State for Transport Ex p.
Factortame Ltd (C-213/89) [1990] 2
Lloyd's Rep 351; [1990] ECR I-2433;
[1990] 3 CMLR 1 *171*

R v Secretary of State for Transport Ex p.
Factortame Ltd (No.1) [1990] 2 AC 85;
[1989] 2 WLR 997; [1989] 2 All ER
692; [1989] 3 CMLR 1; HL; affirming
[1989] 2 CMLR 353 *169, 170, 173, 174,
176, 181*

R v Secretary of State for Transport Ex p.
Factortame Ltd (No.2) [1991] 1 AC 603;
[1990] 3 WLR 818; [1991] 1 All ER 70
*88, 162, 167, 171–174, 177, 181, 247, 406,
512*

R v Secretary of State for Transport Ex p.
Richmond upon Thames LBC (No.4)
[1996] 1 WLR 1460; [1996] 4 All
ER 903; CA (Civ Div); affirming
[1996] 1 WLR 1005; [1996] 4 All ER
93 *581*

R v Shayler [2002] UKHL 11; [2003] 1 AC
247; [2002] 2 WLR 754; [2002] 2 All
ER 477 *434, 435, 691*

R v Somerset CC Ex p. Fewings [1995] 1
WLR 1037; [1995] 3 All ER 20; CA (Civ
Div); affirming [1995] 1 All ER 513 *198,
541, 553, 555*

R v Sussex Justices Ex p. McCarthy [1924] 1
KB 256 *570*

R v Swale Borough Council Ex p. Royal Society
for the Protection of Birds [1991] JPL 39
533

R v Tower Hamlets London Borough Council
Ex p. Chetnik Developments Ltd [1988] AC
858; [1988] 2 WLR 654; [1988] 1 All ER
961 *555*

R. (on the application of DR) v Head Teacher
of St George's Catholic School Head Teacher
[2002] EWCA Civ 1822; [2003] BLGR
371 *534*

Rabone v Penine Care NHS Trust [2012]
UKSC 2; [2012] 2 AC 72; [2012] 2 WLR
381 *658, 678*

Rayner (JH) (Mincing Lane) Ltd v
Department of Trade and Industry [1990]
2 AC 418; [1989] 3 WLR 969; [1989] 3
All ER 523 *96*

Recovery of Medical Costs for Asbestos Diseases
(Wales) Bill, Re [2015] UKSC 3; [2015]
1 AC 1016 *400, 405*

Redmond-Bate v Director of Public
Prosecutions [2000] HRLR 249 *706*

Reference re Amendment of the Constitution
of Canada [1981] 1 SCR 753 *46, 47*

Reynolds v Times Newspapers Ltd [2001] 2
AC 127; [1999] 3 WLR 1010; [1999] 4
All ER 609 *345, 691*

Ridge v Baldwin [1964] AC 40; [1963] 2
WLR 935; [1963] 2 All ER 66 *513, 569,
570, 576, 577*

Ringeisen v Austria (No.1) (1979–80) 1
EHRR 455 *347*

Roberts v *Hopwood* [1925] AC 578
113, 552

Robinson v *Secretary of State for Northern Ireland* [2002] UKHL 32; [2002] NI 390 *160, 382*

Roose v *Parole Board* [2010] EWHC 1780 (Admin) *580*

Roy v *Kensington and Chelsea and Westminster Family Practitioner Committee* [1992] 1 AC 624; [1992] 2 WLR 239; [1992] 1 All ER 705 *535*

S (A Child) (Identification: Restriction on Publication), [2004] UKHL 47; [2005] 1 AC 593; [2004] 3 WLR 1129; [2004] 4 All ER 683 *628*

S v *L (No.2)* [2012] UKSC 30; 2013 SC (UKSC) 20 *667*

Saadi v *Italy* (2009) 49 EHRR 30 *622*

Şahin v *Turkey* (2007) 44 EHRR 5 *630*

Salvesen v *Riddell* [2013] UKSC 22; [2013] HRLR 23 *405*

Schenck v *United States* (1919) 249 US 47 *696*

Schmidt v *Secretary of State for Home Affairs* [1969] 2 Ch 149; [1969] 2 WLR 337; [1969] 1 All ER 904 *585*

Scoppola v *Italy (No.3)* [2012] ECHR 868 *637, 638, 716*

Scott v *Scott* [1913] AC 417 *209*

Secretary of State for Defence v *Guardian Newspapers Ltd* [1985] AC 339 *28*

Secretary of State for Education and Science v *Tameside MBC* [1977] AC 1014; [1976] 3 WLR 641; [1976] 3 All ER 665 *109, 114, 559, 560*

Secretary of State for the Home Department v *AF* [2009] UKHL 28; [2010] 2 AC 269; [2009] 3 WLR 74; [2009] 3 All ER 643 *642, 666*

Secretary of State for the Home Department v *MB* [2007] UKHL 46; [2008] 1 AC 440; [2007] 3 WLR 681; [2008] 1 All ER 657CA (Civ Div); reversing [2006] EWHC 1000 *217*

Sejdia v *Bosnia and Herzegovina* [2009] ECHR 2122 *630*

Shaw v *DPP* [1962] AC 220 *39, 234*

Sheffield and Horsham v *United Kingdom* [1998] 2 FLR 928; (1999) 27 EHRR 163 *628*

Short v *Poole Corp* [1926] Ch 66 *558*

Shrewsbury and Atcham BC v *Secretary of State for Communities and Local Government* [2008] EWCA Civ 148; [2008] 3 All ER 548 *38, 39*

Sim v *Stretch* [1936] 2 All ER 1237 *692*

Smith and Grady v *United Kingdom* (2000) 29 EHRR 493 *563*

Smith v *Scott* [2007] CSIH 9; 2007 SC 345; 2007 SLT 137 *289, 671, 716*

Soering v *United Kingdom* (1989) 11 EHRR 439 *621*

Somerville v *Scottish Ministers* [2007] UKHL 44; [2007] 1 WLR 2734; 2008 SC (HL) 45; 2007 SLT 1113; HL; reversing in part [2006] CSIH 52; 2007 SC 140; 2007 SLT 96 *160, 406*

South Bucks DC v *Porter* [2003] UKHL 33; [2004] 1 WLR 1953; [2004] 4 All ER 775 *582*

South Hetton Coal Co. v *North Eastern News Association Ltd* [1894] 1 QB 133 *692*

Spackman v *Plumstead Board of Works* (1885) L.R. 10 App Cas 229 *569*

Starrs v *Ruxton* 2000 JC 208; 2000 SLT 42 *348, 349*

Steel v *United Kingdom* (1998) 28 EHRR 603 *707*

Stockdale v *Hansard* (1839) 9 A & El *140*

Sugar v *British Broadcasting Corporation* [2012] UKSC 4 *490, 492*

Sunday Times v *United Kingdom* (1979–80) 2 EHRR 245 *205, 626, 636, 650*

SW v *United Kingdom* (1996) 21 EHRR 363 *203*

T and V v *United Kingdom* [2000] 2 AllER 1024 (Note); (2000) 30 EHRR 121 *249*

Taylor v *Brighton Borough Council* [1947] KB 736; [1947] 1 All ER 864 *545*

Taylor v *Chief Constable of Thames Valley Police* [2004] EWCA Civ 858; [2004] 1 WLR 3155; [2004] 3 All ER 503 *188*

Taylor v *New Zealand Poultry Board* [1984] 1 NZLR 394 *214*

Theodore v *Duncan* [1919] AC 696 *545*

Thoburn v *Sunderland City Council (Metric Martyrs)* [2002] EWHC 195 (Admin); [2003] QB 151; [2002] 3 WLR 247; [2002] 4 All E.R. 156 *7, 13, 14, 24, 158–160, 174, 175, 177, 248*

Thomas v *Sawkins* [1936] 1 KB 249 *701, 702*

Tomašic v *Croatia* [2012] MHLR 167 *637*

Town Investments Ltd v *Department of the Environment* [1978] AC 359; [1977] 2 WLR 450; [1977] 1 All ER 813 *258, 262*

Triquet v *Bath* (1764) 97 ER 936 *56, 67*

Tyrer v *United Kingdom* (1979–80) 2 EHRR 1 *631, 635*

Vauxhall Estates Ltd v *Liverpool Corp* [1932] 1 KB 733 *136*

Vereinigung Demokratischer Soldaten Österreichs and Gubi v *Austria* (1994) 20 EHRR 56 *696*

VgT Verein gegen Tierfabriken v *Switzerland* (2001) 34 EHRR 159 *698, 699*

Vo v *France* (2005) 40 EHRR 259 *623*

Waddington v *Miah* [1974] 1 WLR 683; [1974] 2 All ER 377 *202*

Watkins v *Secretary of State for the Home Department* [2006] UKHL 17; [2006] 2 AC 395; [2006] 2 WLR 807; [2006] 2 All ER 353 *28, 157*

Watkins v *Woolas* [2010] EWHC 2702 (QB) *291*

Whaley v *Lord Advocate* [2007] UKHL 53; 2008 SC (HL) 107; 2007 SLT 1209; 2008 SCLR 128 *521*

Whaley v *Lord Watson* 2000 SC 340; 2000 SLT 475 *140, 403*

Wheeler v *Leicester City Council* [1985] AC 1054; [1985] 3 WLR 335; [1985] 2 All ER 1106 *553, 649*

White and Collins v *Minister of Health* [1939] 2 KB 838; [1939] 3 All ER 548 *545, 551*

Wilson v *First County Trust Ltd (No.2)* [2003] UKHL 40; [2004] 1 AC 816 *161*

Wiseman v *Borneman* [1971] AC 297; [1969] 3 WLR 706; [1969] 3 All ER 275 *583*

Wood v *Commissioner of Police of the Metropolis* [2009] EWCA Civ 414; [2010] 1 WLR 123; [2009] 4 All ER 951 *198*

X Ltd v *Morgan Grampian* [1991] 1 AC 1; [1990] 2 WLR 1000; [1990] 2 All ER 1 *218*

X, Re [2017] NIFam 12 *385*

YL v *Birmingham City Council* [2007] UKHL 27; [2008] 1 AC 95; [2007] 3 WLR 112; [2007] 3 All ER 957 *676*

YL v *Birmingham City Council and Southern Cross* [2007] UKHL 27;[2007] 3 WLR 112 (House of Lords) *525, 534*

Youssef v *Secretary of State for Foreign and Commonwealth Affairs* [2016] AC 1457; [2016] UKSC 3 *594*

Z v *United Kingdom* [2001] 2 FLR 612; (2002) 34 EHRR 3 *639*

Table of statutes

Statutes

Access to Justice Act 1999 *207*
Acquisition of Land (Assessment of Compensation) Act 1919 *135, 136*
    s. 7 *135, 136*
Act of Settlement 1701 *9, 16, 45, 128, 161, 244, 262, 341, 346*
    s. 2 *262*
Act of Union 1706 (Scotland) *16, 27, 159, 161, 257, 360*
Act of Union 1800 (Ireland) *27*
Agricultural Marketing Act 1931 *555*
Agricultural Marketing Act 1958 *555*
Animal Health Act 1981 *195*
    s. 34(4) *195*
Anti-terrorism, Crime and Security Act 2001 *327, 398, 454, 670, 709*
    Pt IV *670*
    s. 23 *670*
Appellate Jurisdiction Act 1876 *16, 134, 241, 244, 317*
    s. 6 *241, 244*
Appellate Jurisdiction Act 1887 *317, 318, 344*
    s. 2 *318*
Assembly Members (Reduction of Numbers) Act (Northern Ireland) 2016 *383*
    s. 1 *383*

Baths and Washhouses Acts 1846 and 1847 *546*
Bill of Rights 1689 *9, 16, 24, 25, 34, 36, 128, 140, 159, 161, 190, 191, 244, 256, 300, 692*
    Art. 1 *25*
    Art. 2 *25*
    Art. 3 *34*
    Art. 4 *24, 34, 300*
    Art. 6 *34*
    Art. 9 *140, 161, 190, 191*
    Art. 11 *24*
    Art. IX *692*
Bill of Rights Act (New Zealand) 1990 *655*
Bishopric of Manchester Act 1947 *317*
    s. 2 *317*
Bishoprics Act 1878 *317*
    s. 5 *317*
Boundary Commissions Act 1992 *312*
    s. 2 *312*
British Nationality Act 1981 *583*
    s. 44 *583*
Broadcasting Act 1990 *3, 697*
Broadcasting Act 1996 *3*

Charter of Human Rights and Responsibilities 2006 (Victoria) *655*
Charter of Rights and Freedoms (1982) (Canada) *137*
    s. 2 *137*
    ss 7–15 *137*
    s. 33(1) *137*
Chequers Estate Act 1917 *42, 266*
Child Poverty Act 2010 *43*
Children and Young People (Scotland) Act 2014 *405*
    Pt 4 *405*
Children's Commissioner for Wales Act 2001 *378*
Cities and Local Government Devolution Act 2016 *419*
Civil Partnership Act 2004 *3*
Claim of Rights Act 1689 (Scotland) *161*
Colonial Laws Validity Act 1865 *138*
    s. 5 *138*

Communications Act 2003 *3, 165,* 698
  s. 319(2)(g) *698*
  s. 321 *698*
  s. 321(2) *698*
  s. 321(2)(g) *698*
  s. 321(7) *698*
Communications Act 2005 *661*
Companies Act 2006 *522*
  Pt 28 *522*
Constitutional Reform Act 2005 *17, 23, 134,*
  161, 218, 228, 240, 241, 243–245, 249, 267,
  316, 320, 321, 339–344, 349, 350, 352–356
  Pt 4 *354*
  Pt III *228, 241*
  s. 1 *218*
  s. 2(1) *350*
  s. 3(1) *245, 249, 267, 350*
  s. 3(5) *350*
  s. 3(6) *350*
  s. 4 *350*
  s. 7 *350*
  s. 7(2) *350*
  s. 9 *353*
  s. 17 *350*
  s. 18 *321, 350*
  s. 23(2) *352*
  s. 23(6) *352*
  s. 24(a) *352*
  ss 25–31 *354*
  s. 33 *244*
  s. 40 *352*
  s. 40(4)(b) *353*
  s. 63 *354*
  s. 64 *354*
  s. 137 *352*
  s. 146 *134*
  Sch. 6 *350*
  Sch. 18 *134*
Constitutional Reform and Governance Act
  2010 *23, 37, 53, 60, 61, 96, 279, 280, 282,*
  284, 448, 492, 501, 714
  Pt 1 *37*
  Pt 2 *37, 61, 96*
  Pt I *714*
  s. 5(5) *282*
  s. 7(2) *282*
  s. 8(5) *282*
  s. 15 *280*
  s. 20(1) *60*
  s. 20(4) *60*
  s. 20(8) *60*
  Sch. 7 *492*
Consumer Protection Act 1987 *3, 94*
Contempt of Court Act 1981 *149, 650, 692*
  s. 10 *692*
Corporation Tax (Northern Ireland) Act
  2015 *388*
Counter-Terrorism Act 2008 *584*
  Sch. 7 *584*
Courts Act 2003 *192*
  s. 32 *192*
Crime and Courts Act 2013 *354, 517, 711*
  s. 22 *517*
  s. 57(2) *711*
  Sch. 13, Pt 4 *354*
Criminal Justice Act 1988 *73*
  s. 134 *73*
Criminal Justice and Courts Act 2015 *507,*
  512, 518, 535, 539
  s. 84 *535*
  s. 88(3) *518*
Criminal Justice and Public Order Act 1994
  3, 704
Criminal Law Act 1967 *69, 709*
  s. 3 *69, 709*
Criminal Procedure (Scotland) Act 1995
  406
Crown of Ireland Act 1542 *361*
Crown Proceedings Act 1947 *243, 259*
  s. 1 *259*
  s. 2 *259*
  s. 21 *259*

Damages (Asbestos-related Conditions)
  (Scotland) Act 2009 *403*
Dangerous Dogs Act 1991 *28, 130*
Defamation Act 1996 *149, 320, 345*
Defence of the Realm Act 1842 *36*
Defence of the Realm Act 1914 *30, 56, 709*
Defence of the Realm Act 1915 *56*
Defence of the Realm Consolidation Act
  1914 *30*
  s. 1(1) *30*
Deregulation and Contracting Out Act
  1994 *278*
  Pt 2 *278*
Diplomatic Privileges Act 1964 *190*
Disability Discrimination Act 1995 *26*
'Dog Act' *29*
Duties in American Colonies Act 1765 *652*

Electoral Registration and Administration
   Act 2013 313
   s. 6 *313*
Employment Protection (Consolidation) Act
   1978 *531*
Employment Rights Act 1996 *279*
   s. 191 *279*
Equal Pay Act 1970 *169*
Equality Act 2010 *27, 30, 537, 630*
   s. 149 *537*
European Communities Act 1972 *16, 27, 78,
   79, 86, 89, 90, 92, 94, 151, 158, 159, 161,
   167–169, 172, 174, 175, 177, 178, 233, 512,
   567, 656*
   s. 2(1) *78, 167, 169, 175*
   s. 2(2) *90*
   s. 2(4) *167–169*
   s. 3 *656*
   s. 3(1) *79*
European Convention on Human Rights
   Act 2003 (Ireland) *655*
European Parliamentary Elections Act 1999
   143, 325
European Union (Amendment) Act 2008 *86*
European Union (Notification of
   Withdrawal) Act 2017 *27, 51, 89, 93, 176*
   s. 1(2) *176*
European Union (Withdrawal) Bill 2016 *94*
   Clause 2 *94*
   Clause 7 *94*
European Union (Withdrawal) Bill 2017
   178, 233
   Clause 1 *178*
European Union Act 2011 *175, 177*
   s. 18 *175, 177*
European Union Referendum Act 2015 *90,
   132*
   s. 1(4) *90*

Financial Services and Markets Act 2000
   472
Fixed-Term Parliaments Act 2011 *6, 17, 45,
   50, 149, 265, 266, 283, 289, 290, 314, 334,
   466*
   s. 1 *45, 265*
   s. 1(3) *289*
   s. 2 *265, 266*
   s. 2(1) *289, 290*
   s. 2(2) *290*
   s. 3 *290*

Food and Environment Protection Act 1985
   398
Foreign Compensation Act 1950 *153, 213*
   s. 4(4) *153*
Freedom of Information (Scotland) Act
   2002 *490, 492, 497*
   s. 30 *492*
   s. 52 *496*
Freedom of Information Act 2000 *3, 25, 44,
   118, 157, 163, 213, 267, 436, 455, 485–504,
   675, 692*
   Pt IV *494*
   Pt V *494*
   s. 1 *490, 502*
   s. 1(1) *490*
   s. 1(1)(a) *490*
   s. 1(6) *490*
   s. 2 *491*
   s. 2(2)(b) *491*
   s. 3 *675*
   s. 5 *489*
   s. 11(1) *490*
   s. 12(1) *490*
   s. 14(1) *491*
   s. 14(2) *491*
   s. 17 *494*
   s. 18 *490, 494*
   s. 19 *490*
   s. 19(1)(c) *490*
   s. 20 *490*
   s. 21 *493*
   s. 22 *491*
   s. 23 *493*
   s. 24 *491*
   s. 26 *492*
   s. 27 *492*
   s. 29 *492*
   s. 31 *492*
   s. 32 *494, 500*
   s. 34 *455, 494*
   s. 35 *491, 493, 497*
   s. 36 *492*
   s. 37 *491*
   s. 41 *494*
   s. 44 *494*
   s. 45 *494*
   s. 47 *490, 494*
   s. 51 *495*
   s. 52 *495*
   s. 53 *44, 157, 163, 213, 496, 498*

s. 53(1)(b) *496*
s. 53(2) *496*
s. 53(3) *498*
s. 53(6) *498*
s. 54(3) *495*
s. 55 *495*
s. 57 *495*
s. 58(1)(a) *495*
s. 58(1)(b) *495*
s. 58(2) *495*
s. 59 *495*
Sch. 1 *675*
Sch. 3 *495*

Gender Recognition Act 2004 *669*
Government of Ireland Act 1914 *142, xiv*
Government of Ireland Act 1920 *146, 363*
Government of Wales Act 1998 *3, 26, 159,*
    353, 375–377, 379, 418
s. 2(1) *375*
s. 22(1) *376*
s. 56(1) *376*
s. 80(1) *377*
Government of Wales Act 2006 *26, 353, 355,*
    377–381, 400, 401, 683
Pt 2 *378*
Pts 2–4 *355*
s. 45(1) *378*
s. 81 *683*
ss 93–102 *379*
s. 94 *683*
s. 99 *400*
ss 103–16 *379*
s. 108 *683*
s. 112 *400*
s. 154 *401*
s. 158 *683*
Sch. 5 *379*
Sch. 7 *380*
Sch. 7A *381*
Greater London Authority Act 1999 *3, 417*
Greater London Authority Act 2007 *417*

Habeas Corpus Act 1640 *708*
Habeas Corpus Act 1679 *649, 708*
Health (Wales) Act 2003 *378*
Health and Social Care Act 2008 *676*
s. 145 *676*
Herring Fishery (Scotland) Act 1889 *150*
s. 7 *150*

Higher Education Act 2004 *306, 415, 511*
s. 53 *415*
Highways Act 1980 *710*
s. 137 *710*
House of Commons Disqualification Act
    1975 *3, 45, 245, 267, 277, 288*
s. 1 *245, 288*
s. 1(1)(b) *277*
s. 4 *45*
Sch. 1 *245, 288*
House of Lords (Expulsion and Suspension)
    Act 2015 *321*
s. 1(1) *321*
House of Lords Act 1999 *17, 288, 316, 319,*
    321, 322, 330, 331, 453
s. 3 *288*
House of Lords Reform Act 2014 *321*
s. 1(1) *321*
s. 2(1) *321*
s. 3(1) *321*
s. 4(5) *321*
Housing Act 1925 *135, 136*
Housing Act 1936 *545*
s. 74 *545*
s. 75 *545*
Housing Act 1988 *665*
Housing Act 1996 *472*
Housing Grants, Construction and Regen-
    eration Act 1996 *526*
ss 126–128 *526*
Human Rights Act 1998 *3, 11, 17, 25, 29,*
    62, 109, 111, 112, 116–118, 151, 152, 154,
    157, 159, 161, 163–167, 181, 198, 216, 217,
    235, 239, 245, 247, 248, 346, 348, 394,
    406, 426, 482, 499, 525, 543, 567, 574,
    592, 605, 617, 623, 632, 646–687, 690,
    694, 695, 697, 698, 705, 706, 710, 714,
    716, 717
s. 1 *652, 654, 664*
s. 1(1) *164, 235, 694*
s. 2 *652, 656, 659, 664, 668*
s. 2(1) *167, 656, 658, 659*
s. 3 *166, 661, 663–670, 686, 694, 706*
s. 3(1) *164, 166, 235, 500, 663, 667–669,*
    671, 674, 683
s. 4 *165, 661, 663, 664, 666, 668–670, 674,*
    686, 694, 706
s. 4(2) *152, 248, 668, 674*
s. 4(4) *164*
s. 4(6) *152, 164, 165, 248, 668, 670*

s. 4(6)(a) *668*
s. 6 *164, 248, 661, 664, 668, 673, 674, 677–680, 694*
s. 6(1) *663, 673*
s. 6(2) *674*
s. 6(2)(a) *673*
s. 6(3) *675*
s. 6(3)(a) *663, 675, 706*
s. 6(3)(b) *164, 675*
s. 6(5) *676*
s. 6(6) *673, 674*
s. 7 *677*
s. 7(1)(a) *678*
s. 7(1)(b) *679*
s. 7(3) *678*
s. 7(5)(a) *679*
s. 7(7) *677*
s. 8(2) *676*
s. 8(3) *677*
s. 10 *165, 661, 668, 672, 673*
s. 10(1)(a) *672*
s. 10(1)(b) *672*
s. 10(2) *672*
s. 11 *664*
s. 11(1) *705*
s. 11(2) *705*
s. 12 *652, 660, 694, 695*
s. 12(3) *660*
s. 13 *652, 660*
s. 19 *165, 661*
s. 19(1) *662*
s. 19(1)(a) *661*
s. 19(1)(b) *165, 661, 698*
s. 21 *623*
s. 21(1)(f) *664*
s. 22(3) *678*
Human Rights Act 2004 (Australian Capital Territory) *655*
Hunting Act 2004 *28, 29, 143, 145, 148, 331, 413*

Immigration Act 1971 *47, 522*
s. 3(5)(b) *522*
Immigration and Asylum Act 1999 *270*
s. 60(9)(a) *270*
Income Tax Act 2007 *373*
s. 6(2) *373*
International Criminal Court Act 2001 *70*
Interpretation Act 1978 *267*
Ireland Act 1949 *27*

Irish Church Act 1869 *135*
Irish Free State (Constitution) Act 1922 *27*

Jobseekers (Back to Work Schemes) Act 2013 *201*

Larceny Act 1916 *149*
Legal Aid and Advice Act 1949 *206*
Legal Aid, Sentencing and Punishment of Offenders Act 2012 *207*
Legislative and Regulatory Reform Act 2006 *33*
s. 1(2) *33*
s. 3(2) *33*
s. 18 *33*
Life Peerages Act 1958 *318, 322*
Limitation Act 1980 *532*
s. 2 *532*
s. 5 *532*
Local Democracy, Economic Development and Construction Act 2009 *421*
s. 107F *421*
Local Government Act 1972 *553*
s. 120(1)(b) *553*
Local Government Act 1974 *472*
Local Government Act 2000 *3, 419*
Local Government and Public Involvement in Health Act 2007 *472*
Local Government Finance Act 1992 *43*
Localism Act 2011 *420*
s. 1(1) *420*

Magistrates' Courts Act 1980 *709*
s. 1 *709*
Magna Carta 1215 *16, 24, 25, 159, 161, 184, 244*
Clause 39 *24, 184*
Marine and Coastal Access Act 2009 *398*
Marriage (Same Sex Couples) Act 2013 *3*
Matrimonial Causes Act 1973 *3, 669*
Mental Health Act 1983 *561, 568*
s. 3 *568*
ss 65–79 *568*
s. 72(1)(b) *561*
Merchant Shipping Act 1894 *170*
Merchant Shipping Act 1988 *169–172, 177, 512*
s. 14(1) *169*
s. 14(7) *170*
Military Service Acts 1916–1918 *56*

Ministerial and other Salaries Act 1975 *32, 41, 267*
   s. 1B(1) *32*
Misuse of Drugs Act 1971 *666*

National Health Service Reorganisation Act 1973 *472*
Northern Ireland (Emergency Provisions) Act 1978 *694*
Northern Ireland (St Andrews Agreement) Act 2006 *388*
Northern Ireland Act 1998 *3, 26, 137, 157, 160, 353, 382–387, 389, 395, 400, 401, 683, 684*
   s. 1 *137*
   s. 1(2) *395*
   s. 4(5) *384*
   s. 6 *683*
   s. 11 *400*
   s. 18(2) *385*
   s. 18(5) *386*
   s. 22(1) *385*
   s. 23(2) *385*
   s. 24 *683*
   s. 32(3) *389*
   s. 33 *383*
   s. 34 *383*
   s. 42(1) *384*
   s. 63(3) *384*
   s. 81 *683*
   s. 83 *401, 683*
   s. 16A(5) *385*
   s. 16A(6) *385*
   s. 16B(2) *385*
   Sch. 2 *386*
   Sch. 3 *386*
Northern Ireland Constitution Act 1973 *387*

Official Secrets Act 1911 *281, 435, 693*
   s. 2 *435, 693*
   s. 2(1) *435*
Official Secrets Act 1989 *281, 435, 693*
Overseas Development and Co-operation Act 1980 *547*
   s. 1 *547*
   s. 1(1) *547*

Parliament Act 1911 *16, 26, 28, 29, 45, 50, 141–148, 247, 289, 300, 302, 303, 316, 324, 328, 329, 331, 334, 453*
   s. 1 *50, 141*
   s. 1(1) *142*
   s. 1(2) *141, 324*
   s. 2 *141*
   s. 2(1) *142, 143, 145–147, 303, 324, 329*
   s. 4 *143*
   s. 7 *45, 141, 289*
Parliament Act 1949 *16, 26, 28, 29, 141–148, 247, 300, 302, 303, 325, 334, 338, 453*
   s. 1 *325*
   s. 2(1) *303*
Parliament Acts *28, 29*
Parliamentary Commissioner Act 1967 *469, 470, 473, 474, 476–479*
   s. 1(2) *469*
   s. 1(3) *469*
   s. 2 *469*
   s. 5(1) *473*
   s. 5(1)(a) *474, 475*
   s. 5(1)(b) *475*
   s. 5(2) *470, 473*
   s. 6(1) *474*
   s. 7(1) *476*
   s. 7(2) *476*
   s. 7(4) *477*
   s. 8(1) *476*
   s. 8(2) *476*
   s. 9 *476*
   s. 10(1) *477*
   s. 10(2) *477*
   s. 10(3) *478*
   s. 12(3) *474*
   Sch. 2 *473, 474*
   Sch. 3 *474*
Parliamentary Constituencies Act 1986 *312*
   s. 2 *312*
Parliamentary Standards Act 2009 *501*
Parliamentary Voting System and Constituencies Act 2011 *132, 276, 287, 312, 313, 326*
   s. 1(3) *312*
   s. 1(7) *312*
   s. 1(8) *312*
   s. 8 *132*
   s. 10 *312*
   s. 11 *287, 313*
Petition of Right 1628 *161, 255*
Police Act 1964 *35*
Police and Criminal Evidence Act 1984 *3, 702, 709*

s. 17(6) *702*
s. 24 *709*
Police Reform and Social Responsibility Act
2011 *420, 705*
Pt III *705*
s. 142 *705*
s. 143(2) *705*
Political Parties, Elections and Referendums
Act 2000 *291*
Pt I *291*
Prevention of Terrorism Act 2005 *641*
s. 2 *641*
Prison Act 1952 *155*
s. 47(1) *155*
s. 52(1) *155*
Protection of Freedoms Act 2012 *495*
ss 105–108 *495*
Protection of Wild Mammals (Scotland) Act
2002 *403, 413, 521*
Public Bodies Act 2011 *279, 418*
Sch. 1 *279*
Sch. 2 *279*
Public Interest Disclosure Act 1998 *692*
Public Order Act 1936 *709*
s. 5 *709*
Public Order Act 1986 *692, 703, 704, 706,
710, 711*
Pt II *703*
Pt III *692*
s. 1 *703*
s. 2 *703*
s. 3 *703*
s. 4 *703*
s. 4A *703*
s. 5 *703, 710, 711*
s. 11 *703*
s. 11(1) *703*
s. 11(3) *703*
s. 11(4) *703*
s. 11(7) *703*
s. 12 *703*
s. 12(1) *703*
s. 12(4) *704*
s. 13 *704, 706*
s. 14 *703*
s. 14(1) *704*
s. 14(4) *704*
s. 14A *704*
s. 14A(1) *704*
s. 14A(4) *704*

s. 14A(9) *704*
s. 14B *704*
s. 14C *704*
s. 16 *703, 704*
Public Processions (Northern Ireland) Act
1998 *561*
Public Services Ombudsman (Wales) Act
2005 *378, 472*

Race Relations Act 1965 *151*
Race Relations Act 1976 *26, 553*
s. 17 *553*
Recall of MPs Act 2015 *300*
Referendums (Scotland and Wales) Act 1997
367
Reform Act 1832 *288, 513*
Reform Act 1867 *513*
Reform Act 1884 *513*
Regional Assemblies (Preparations) Act
2003 *418*
Regional Development Agencies Act 1998
418
Regulation of Investigatory Powers Act
2000 *212*
Rent Act 1977 *666, 680*
s. 3 *680*
Representation of the People Act 1832 *25,
159*
Representation of the People Act 1867 *159*
Representation of the People Act 1884 *159,
288*
Representation of the People Act 1918 *25,
159, 288*
Representation of the People Act 1928 *16,
127, 159, 288*
Representation of the People Act 1969 *16,
127, 159, 288*
Representation of the People Act 1983 *6, 28,
159, 288, 291, 671, 716*
Pt III *291*
s. 1 *288*
s. 3 *671*
s. 3A *288*
s. 3(1) *716*
s. 123 *291*
Road Traffic Act 1988 *3*

Scotland Act 1978 *132*
Scotland Act 1998 *3, 26, 50, 130, 131, 137,
157, 159, 160, 312, 348, 352, 367–374, 376,*

395, 396, 400–408, 410, 412, 413, 418,
421, 521, 683
s. 1(2) *368*
s. 1(3) *368*
s. 2(2) *368*
s. 23(1) *374*
s. 28(7) *130, 395, 396, 407, 408, 413*
s. 28(8) *50*
s. 29 *396, 406, 683*
s. 29(2) *404*
s. 30 *369, 408*
s. 30(2) *371*
s. 33(1) *400*
s. 35(1) *400*
s. 45(2) *374*
s. 46(3) *374*
s. 46(4) *374*
s. 47(2) *374*
s. 47(3)(e) *374*
s. 53(1) *374*
s. 53(2) *374*
s. 56 *374*
s. 57 *683*
s. 57(2) *374*
ss 57–58 *406*
s. 63A *410*
s. 73 *372*
s. 86 *312, 421*
s. 101 *401, 402*
s. 101(2) *401*
s. 102(2)(b) *405*
s. 80C *373*
Sch. 5 *369, 370*
Sch. 6 *400*
Sch. 6.1(f) *400*
Sch. 6.10 *400*
Sch. 6.22 *400*
Scotland Act 2012 *367, 371, 373, 374, 376,*
390, 407
s. 10 *371*
ss 16–22 *374*
s. 35 *407*
s. 36 *407*
Scotland Act 2016 *50, 51, 131, 135, 367,*
372–374, 376, 380, 390, 397, 409
s. 1 *135, 409*
s. 2 *50, 51, 131, 397*
ss 3–10 *372*
s. 16 *373*
s. 17 *373*

s. 18 *373*
ss 22–35 *372*
s. 40 *372*
s. 50 *372*
s. 53 *372*
s. 57 *374*
Scottish Elections (Reduction of Voting
Age) Act 2015 *288*
Scottish Independence Referendum (Franchise) Act 2013 *409*
s. 2 *409*
Scottish Independence Referendum Act
2013 *409*
s. 1(2) *409*
s. 1(5) *409*
Scottish Parliament (Constituencies) Act
2004 *368*
Scottish Public Services Ombudsman Act
2002 *472*
Senior Courts Act 1981 *526, 527, 531, 532,*
536, 538, 539
s. 31 *531, 536*
s. 31(1)(a) *536*
s. 31(1)(b) *538*
s. 31(2B) *536*
s. 31(3) *527*
s. 31(4) *538, 539*
s. 31(6) *532*
s. 31(6)(a) *532*
s. 31(6)(b) *532*
Septennial Act 1715 *289*
Serious Organised Crime and Police Act
2005 *271, 704, 705*
s. 128 *271*
ss 132–138 *704*
s. 136 *705*
Sex Discrimination Act 1975 *26, 65*
Sexual Offences (Amendment) Act 1976 *203*
s. 1 *203*
Sexual Offences (Amendment) Act 1992
190, 204
s. 1 *190, 204*
Sexual Offences (Amendment) Act 2000
143, 330
Sexual Offences Act 2003 *671*
State Immunity Act 1978 *73*
s. 20 *73*
Statute of Proclamations 1539 *33*
Statute of Wales Act 1284 *27, 360*
Statutory Instruments Act 1946 *32, 231*

Succession of the Crown Act 2013 *262*
    s. 1 *262*
    s. 2 *262*
Suicide Act 1961 *672*
    s. 2 *672*
Supreme Court Act 1981 *154, 155, 231, 244, 346*
    s. 11(3) *244*
    s. 130 *154, 155, 231*

Taxes Management Act 1970 *194, 195, 200*
    s. 20C *194*
Terrorism (Temporary Provisions) Act 1984 *694*
Terrorism Act 2000 *205, 709, 714*
    s. 41 *709*
Terrorism Act 2006 *692*
    s. 1 *692*
Terrorist Asset-Freezing etc Act 2010 *31*
Theft Act 1968 *191*
    s. 17 *191*
Trading with the Enemy Act 1914 *56*
Transport (London) Act 1969 *113, 547*
    s. 1 *113, 547*
Transport (Wales) Act 2006 *378*
Tribunals and Inquiries Act 1992 *581*
Tribunals and Inquiries Act 1992
    Sch. 1 *581*

Tribunals and Inquiries Act 1992
    s. 10 *581*
Tribunals, Courts and Enforcement Act 2007 *157*
    s. 42 *157*

Union with Ireland Act 1800 *135, 361, 362*
United Nations Act 1946 *27, 30, 31*
    s. 1(1) *31*

Wales Act 2014 *378, 380*
    s. 4(1) *378*
    ss 8–14 *380*
    s. 15 *380*
    s. 18 *380*
Wales Act 2017 *131, 380, 397, 400, 410*
    s. 1 *410*
    s. 2 *397*
    ss 5–8 *380*
    s. 17 *380*
War Crimes Act 1991 *143, 325*
War Damage Act 1965 *201*
Welfare Reform Act 2012 *327, 328, 398*
Welfare Reform and Work Act 2016 *43*
Welsh Church Act 1914 *xiv, 142*
Youth Justice and Criminal Evidence Act 1999 *665*
    s. 41 *665*

Table of EU Legislation

Contains:

- Treaties and Conventions
- Regulations
- Directives

Table of Treaties and Conventions

1949 Treaty of London (Statute of the Council of Europe) *56*
1951 Treaty Establishing the European Coal and Steel Community (Treaty of Paris) *76*
    Preamble *75*
1951 Treaty of Paris *77*
1957 Treaty establishing the European Community (EC Treaty) see (Treaty of Rome)

1957 Treaty of Rome *75, 77, 168*
1957 Treaty of Rome Art. 119 *169*
1957 Treaty of Rome Art. 177 *170*
1965 European Social Charter (1965) 529 UNTS 89 *617*
1986 Single European Act *75, 77, 81*
1992 Treaty of the European Union (TEU) (Maastricht) *75, 77, 80*
    Art. 5.2 *74*
1997 Treaty of Amsterdam *76, 76*

2001 Treaty of Nice *76, 77*

2007 Treaty of Lisbon; Treaty on European
Union (TEU) *76, 77*
  Art. 1 *79, 90*
  Art. 2 *80*
  Art. 4(3) *87*
  Art. 13 *80*
  Art. 14(1) *83, 84*
  Art. 14(2) *83*
  Art. 15(1) *81*
  Art. 15(5) *81*
  Art. 15(6) *81*
  Art. 16(1) *82*
  Art. 16(4) *82*
  Art. 16(8) *82*
  Art. 17(1) *84*
  Art. 17(2) *84*
  Art. 17(7) *81, 84*
  Art. 19(1) *85*
  Art. 50 *17, 92~~95, 100, 176*
  Art. 50(2) *93*

2009 Treaty of Lisbon; Treaty on the
Functioning of the European Union
(TFEU) *79, 81*
  Arts. 206–207 *85*
  Art. 226 *83*
  Art. 234 *83, 84*
  Art. 236 *81*
  Art. 253 *84*
  Art. 254 *84*
  Art. 258 *84, 86*
  Art. 259 *86*
  Art. 263 *83, 86*
  Art. 265 *86*
  Art. 267 *86*
  Art. 288 *86, 87*
  Art. 289 *83*
  Art. 314 *83*
  Protocol 2 *83*

2012 Brighton Declaration (19 April 2012)
615, 645, 646

2013 Treaty on Stability, Coordination and
Governance in the Economic and Monetary Union *81, 85*

European Convention on Human Rights
1950 *16, 56, 63, 151, 374, 394, 404, 567,
592, 593, 595, 596, 600, 603, 605, 610,
644, 648~~652, 654, 655, 662, 664, 667,
668, 673, 679, 682, 684~~687*
  Art. 1 *616, 618, 619*

Arts 2–12 *655*
Art. 2 *622, 623, 638~~641, 678, 711*
Art. 2(2) *624*
Art. 3 *116, 620~~622, 635, 639,
  640, 657*
Art. 4 *620*
Art. 5 *71, 454, 620, 622, 623, 641~~643,
  670, 708, 710~~712*
Art. 5(1) *712*
Art. 5(1)(c) *710*
Art. 5(4) *579, 709*
Art. 6 *62, 208, 349, 406, 568, 573, 574,
  620, 625, 657, 658, 665*
Art. 6(1) *208, 238, 245, 346~~348, 483,
  574*
Art. 7 *203, 622*
Art. 7(1) *202*
Art. 8 *29, 198, 405, 525, 563, 614, 625,
  628, 629, 634, 636, 640, 641, 660, 663,
  665, 666, 671, 672, 677, 680*
Art. 9 *625, 629, 656, 659, 675*
Art. 10 *205, 277, 330, 499, 625~~627, 629,
  659~~661, 690, 694, 695, 697~~699,
  705*
Art. 10(2) *628, 696, 711*
Art. 11 *29, 626, 699, 705, 706, 711, 714*
Art. 12 *626*
Art. 13 *656*
Art. 14 *630, 643, 655, 659, 666, 670*
Art. 15 *620, 632, 634, 642, 643, 670*
Art. 21 *616*
Art. 23 *616*
Art. 27 *614*
Art. 28 *614*
Art. 29 *614*
Art. 33 *613*
Art. 34 *613, 677, 678*
Art. 35 *613*
Art. 43 *614*
Art. 46 *616, 683*
Art. 56 *610*
Protocol 1 *261, 405, 626*
Protocol 1
Art. 2 *630, 631, 655*
Protocol 1
Art. 3 *631, 635, 637, 713, 715, 716*
Protocol 4
Art. 2 *711*
Protocol 6 *623*
Protocol 11 *609, 611, 612*

Protocol 12
Art. 1 *630*
Protocol 13 *623*
Protocol 13
Art. 1 *655*
Protocol 14 *609, 612~~614, 616,*
645, 646
Protocol 15
Art. 4 *615*
European Convention on Human Rights
and Fundamental Freedoms, 3 September
1953, 213 UNTS 222 *600*

EU Regulations

Reg. 998/2003 *87*
Reg. 717/2007 *87*
Reg. 267/2012 *87*

EU Directives

Directive on Professional Qualifications
2005/36/EC *87*
Directive on combating the sexual abuse and
sexual exploitation of children and child
pornography 2011/92/EU *161*

Table of Internation Legislation

Access to Information Act 1982 (Canada)
487
Access to Official Information Act 1978
(Netherlands) *487*
Australian Freedom of Information Act
1982 *487*

Belfast Good Friday Agreement (10 April
1998) *684*
s. 6 *684*

Canadian Charter of Rights and Freedoms
1982 *11, 165, 654*
s. 33 *653*
Charter of the United Nations (26 June
1945) 1 UNTS XVI *70, 71*
Art. 25 *70*
Art. 103 *71*
Constitution of Austria *9*
Art. 8(a) *9*
Constitution of Croatia 1990 *52*
Constitution of Germany (Grundgesetz or
Basic Law) *8, 15, 52, 125*
Art. 22 *9*
Art. 25 *58*
Arts. 38–53 *10*
Art. 59 *58*
Arts. 62–69 *10*
Art. 79 *14*
Arts. 92–104 *10*
Constitution of India 1950 *608*
Constitution of Japan Art. 9 *8*
Constitution of Lebanon *9*

Art. 1 *9*
Art. 2 *9*
Constitution of the Kingdom of Thailand *8*
s. 79 *8*
Constitution of the Netherlands *58*
Art. 66 *58*
Constitution of The Republic of South
Africa 1996 *5, 8, 15, 165*
Preamble *8*
Constitution of the United States of
America 1787 *5, 6, 15, 52, 224, 652, 654*
First Amendment *9, 11, 696*
Fifth Amendment *11*
Sixth Amendment *11*
Art. I *10, 225*
Arts. I–III *14*
14th Amendment *226*
Art. I, s. 7 *226*
Art. II *10, 225*
Art. II, s. 1, cl. 2 *49*
Art. II, s. 2 *226*
26th Amendment *14*
27th Amendment *14*
Art. III *10, 225*
Art. V *226*

Egyptian Provisional Constitution
2011 *52*

Finland Publicity of Documents Act 1951
487
French Declaration of the Rights of Man
and of the Citizen 1789 *599*

International Convention against Torture and other Cruel, Inhuman or Degrading Treatment or Punishment 1984 *73*

International Covenant on Civil and Political Rights 1966 *56*

International Covenant on Economic, Social and Cultural Rights, 16 December 1966, 993 UNTS 3 *56, 600, 617*

Ireland Freedom of Information Act 1997 *487*

New Zealand Official Information Act 1983 *487*

New Zealand Bill of Rights Act 1990 *11, 653, 654*

OECD, Convention on Combating Bribery of Foreign Public Officials in International Business Transactions (17 December 1997) 37 ILM 1 *63*

Statute of the International Court of Justice *67*
Art. 38.1(b) *67*

Treaty of London 1839 Art. VII *57*

United States Bill of Rights 1792 *125, 165, 599*

Universal Declaration on Human Rights (UDHR) UN General Assembly Resolution 217 A (III), UN Doc. A/810 (10 December 1948) *58, 600, 610*

US Freedom of Information Act 1966 *487*

Vienna Convention on Diplomatic Relations (1961) 500 UNTS 95 *67, 189*

Vienna Convention on the Law of Treaties (1969) 1155 UNTS 331 *62*
Art. 2(1)(a) *58*

Table of SIs

Civil Legal Aid (Remuneration) (Amendment) Regulations 2015 (SI 2015/898) *518*

Civil Procedure Rules 2000 (SI 2000/2092) *518~~520, 526, 532~~534, 536~~538*
rule 54 *526*
rule 54.1(2)(a) *519*
rule 54.1(2)(a)(i) *520*
rule 54.2 *536*
rule 54.3(1) *538*
rule 54.3(2) *538*
rule 54.4 *518*
rule 54.5(1) *532*
rule 54.5(1)(a) *533*
rule 54.5(5) *532*
rule 54.5(6) *532*
rule 54.12 *518*
rule 54.19(2) *537*
rule 54.20 *534*

Civil Service (Amendment) Order in Council 1995 *281*
art 3(3) *281*

Commissioner for Complaints (Amendment) (Northern Ireland) Order (SI 1997/1758) *472*

Commissioner for Complaints (Northern Ireland) Order (SI 1996/1297) *472*

Defence of the Realm (Consolidation) Regulations 1914 *30*
reg 14B *30*

Employment Equality (Sexual Orientation) Regulations (SI 2003/1661) *30*

Equality Act (Sexual Orientation) Regulations (SI 2007/1263) *30*

European Communities (Recognition of Professional Qualifications) Regulations (SI 2007/2781) *87*

Gambling (Geographical Distribution of Casino Premises Licences) Order 2007 (Draft) *328*

Greater London Authority Elections (Expenses) Order (SI 2000/789) *328*

Higher Education (Higher Amount) Regulations (SI 2010/3020) *537*

Ministerial and Other Salaries Act
    1975 (Amendment) Order 2011
    (SI 2011/1689) *32*

National Assembly for Wales (Legislative
    Competence) (Agriculture and
    Rural Development) Order
    (SI 2009/1758) *379*
    art 2 *379*
Northern Ireland Act 1998 (Amendment of
    Schedule 3) Order (SI 2010/977) *388*

Ombudsman (Northern Ireland) Order
    (SI 1996/1298) *472*

Scotland Act 1998 (Modification of Sched-
    ule 5) Order 2013 (SI 2013/242) *408*
Sexual Offences Act 2003 (Remedial) Order
    (SI 2012/1883) *671*
South Georgia and South Sandwich Islands
    Order (SI 1985/449) *261*
Supreme Court Fees (Amendment) Order
    (SI 1996/3191) *154*
    art 3 *207*

Terrorism (United Nations Measures) Order
    (SI 2001/3365) *30*
Terrorism Act 2000 (Remedial) Order
    (SI 2011/631) *614*

Part I
Constitutional regulation in the absence of a codified constitution

Chapter 1
The purposes and characteristics of constitutions

'[Constitutions are] codes of norms which aspire to regulate the allocation of powers, functions, and duties among the various agencies and officers of government, and to define the relationship between these and the public.'

S. E. Finer, V. Bogdanor and B. Rudden, *Comparing Constitutions* (Clarendon Press, 1995) p. 1.

Chapter outline

This introductory chapter begins by examining the key purpose of a constitution; the definition and allocation of governmental power. Following this – using examples – it proceeds to illustrate the various functions that such devices are meant to perform and the differing forms that constitutions can take. The chapter then goes on to introduce the UK constitution, noting its key characteristics and comparing them with those of constitutions elsewhere.

The nature and purpose of constitutions

The central purpose of a constitution is to regulate and allocate governmental power within a state. A constitution establishes the key institutions of government; it grants power to them, distributes power between them, and governs the ways in which the institutions of government interact with each other. A constitution also controls the way in which those institutions might exercise their powers, and determines how those powers might be exercised in relation to the individuals who reside within that state. Constitutions are therefore, as the quote which opens this chapter suggests, a distinctive species of legal norms (rules) which are concerned with the government and governance of the state within which they apply.

Key issues

- Constitutions are concerned with the allocation and regulation of governmental powers within a state. A constitution will – typically in liberal democracies – divide governmental power between three core branches of the state: the executive, the legislature and the judiciary.
- Constitutional law is therefore the body of law that determines the exercise and control of governmental power between both the institutions of government and between those institutions and the individual.

Described in the abstract, constitutions shoulder enormous responsibility: they control, in effect, the mechanisms by which we are to be governed, the composition of the various components of government and the nature of the relationship(s) between individuals and the machinery of the state. Constitutional law, therefore, should not be thought of as an esoteric subject only of interest to political or legal philosophers (although it is obviously of interest to both of those groups), for the reason of its considerable *practical* significance. Even from the brief definition of a constitution given above, we can discern a number of general characteristics of constitutions that can clearly be seen to influence government in practice. Constitutions can be seen to allocate governmental power. In liberal democracies, this allocation will typically be between three distinct arms, or branches, of government – the legislature, the executive and the judiciary – each of whom exercise specific activities under the authority vested in them by the constitution.[1] First, the constitution may typically empower a parliament – the legislature – to enact rules for the governance of the country in the form of legislation (otherwise known as statutes). In the UK, parliamentary legislation deals with a number of issues of obvious significance to the government of the country; for instance, legislation governs who may be eligible to stand for election as a Member of Parliament,[2] the powers of the police,[3] what legal rights the individual may be able to assert against the state,[4] what structures of local – or sub-national – government should exist,[5] and so on. But legislation also governs a huge range of topics which affect us on a daily basis (in many cases, perhaps, without our really appreciating it); for example, statute law regulates such diverse activities as whom we can marry or enter into a civil partnership with,[6] road safety,[7] our rights as consumers,[8] and the regulation of broadcast media,[9] to give but a few examples.

The second branch of the state is the executive branch, typically referred to as the government. The constitution governs not only which individuals should comprise the executive branch, but also how the various roles associated with executive functions should be exercised. For example, constitutional rules concern the appointment of a Prime Minister, and influence who the Queen should appoint as her Ministers of the Crown. Hence, in the constitution of the UK, it is generally the case that the leader of the largest political party in the House of Commons will hold the office of Prime Minister, while those people who are recommended to the Queen by the Prime Minister will act as government ministers.[10] Rarely a day goes by without some mention of the activities of the executive in the press. Frequently, for example, we will read about, or see television coverage of, ministers answering questions in Parliament. They do so not out of courtesy, but because the constitution requires Ministers of the Crown to present themselves to Parliament to explain their policies, successes and failings. So the government is both created by, and regulated by, constitutional norms.

---

[1] See Chapter 7.
[2] House of Commons Disqualification Act 1975.
[3] See e.g. Police and Criminal Evidence Act 1984; Criminal Justice and Public Order Act 1994.
[4] See e.g. Human Rights Act 1998; Freedom of Information Act 2000.
[5] See e.g. Scotland Act 1998; Government of Wales Act 1998; Northern Ireland Act 1998; Greater London Authority Act 1999; Local Government Act 2000.
[6] Matrimonial Causes Act 1973; Civil Partnerships Act 2004; Marriage (Same Sex Couples) Act 2013.
[7] Road Traffic Act 1988.
[8] Consumer Protection Act 1987.
[9] Broadcasting Act 1990; Broadcasting Act 1996; Communications Act 2003.
[10] See pp. 265–72.

Finally, the judiciary is tasked with determining the outcome of legal disputes, including those between private individuals or bodies, and those between the individual and the executive. Constitutional rules govern the legal mechanisms by which disputes between individuals, or with the state itself, might be resolved fairly and finally. Again, hardly a day goes by without the press reporting on the progress or outcome of a criminal trial or decision made against the government in judicial review proceedings. Therefore, the constitution provides an institutional structure for the impartial resolution of legal disputes and constitutional rules tell us when – and on what grounds – we might challenge decisions taken by public officials.

In sum, the constitution therefore tells us which bodies should exercise governmental power, and how those bodies should be composed. The constitution grants power to those bodies, and provides mechanisms that govern how their powers might be exercised. Further, the constitution provides structures and procedures to resolve disputes of law between the individual and the state, or between private bodies or individuals.

Characteristics of constitutions – does the United Kingdom have a constitution?

Key issues

Though at the outset of this chapter a working definition of a constitution was offered, there is a disagreement over the precise meaning of the term. At the heavily prescriptive end of the spectrum, some authors argue that a 'constitution' must satisfy a series of specific characteristics – for instance, that it must be immune from amendment or repeal through the ordinary legislative process – in order to be worthy of the name. Others (as with our working definition) consider that the term 'constitution' may be applied to the general system of rules and conventions applicable to government and governmental powers. While at the least prescriptive end of the spectrum some consider that the constitution is simply the result of 'what happens' in the course of a country's governance.

While constitutions may take different forms – an issue addressed below – there are certain key characteristics that constitutions are argued to possess. The academic writer F. F. Ridley has categorised what he argues to be the central characteristics of a constitution as follows:

(1) [A constitution] establishes, or constitutes, the system of government. Thus it is prior to the system of government, not part of it, and its rules cannot be derived from that system.

(2) [A constitution] therefore involves an authority outside and above the order it establishes. This is the notion of constituent power . . . In democracies that power is attributed to the people, on whose ratification the legitimacy of a constitution depends and, with it, the legitimacy of the governmental system.

(3) [A constitution] is a form of law superior to other laws – because (i) it originates in an authority higher than the legislature which makes ordinary law and (ii) the authority of the legislature derives from it and is thus bound by it. The principle of hierarchy of law generally (but not always) leads to the possibility of judicial review of ordinary legislation.

(4) [A constitution] is entrenched – (i) because its purpose is generally to limit the powers of government, but also (ii) again because of its origins in a higher authority outside the system. It can thus only be changed by special procedures, generally (and certainly for major change) requiring reference back to the constituent power.[11]

Let us address each of these characteristics in turn.

1. A constitution must be prior to a government

First, Ridley suggests that a constitution must be in existence prior to the formulation of a government. If we accept that a constitution provides the grounds on which a government can be created, then this suggestion would appear to make logical sense. The rules of the constitution, in other words, the rules that provide for the very creation of a government, must be agreed to and in place *before* the actual formulation of a government. A legitimate government is one which is created subject to the specifications of the constitution, in turn, as Ridley argues, 'a constitutional order derives its legitimacy from the constituent act which establishes it.'[12]

2. The force of a constitution can be traced to the notion of constituent power

Secondly, the normative force of a constitution is to be attributed to something other than the system of government established; in other words, a higher source of authority than that wielded by the government itself. In a democracy, Ridley argues, a constitution owes its authority, ultimately, to the people who – collectively – endorse its terms and therefore its legitimacy. The Constitution of the United States of America 1787 perhaps reflects this sentiment best in its famous opening passage:

> *We the People of the United States,* in order to form a more perfect Union, establish Justice, ensure Domestic Tranquility, provide for common Defence, promote the general Welfare, and secure the Blessings of Liberty to ourselves and our Posterity, do ordain and establish this Constitution for the United States of America.[13]

3. A constitution is superior to the ordinary law

Thirdly, as the authority of the legislature (and of the executive and judiciary) must ultimately derive from the constitution, then the powers of those branches of government may not exceed the powers granted by the constitution itself. As a result, the constitution is of a higher status of authority than the laws, rules and regulations, and judgments passed, by those arms of government who owe their authority to the constitution. As a result, the constitution both empowers, and as importantly *limits,* the power exercisable by the branches of government.

---

[11] F. F. Ridley, 'There is no British constitution: A dangerous case of the emperor's clothes' (1988) 41 *Parliamentary Affairs* 340, 342–3.

[12] Ibid., 343.

[13] Emphasis added. See also: the preamble to the Constitution of The Republic of South Africa 1996.

4. A constitution must be entrenched

And finally, Ridley argues that a constitution must be entrenched, that is, must be protected from amendment or repeal by those who temporarily hold governmental power at the request of the electorate. Constitutions, it is suggested, should have longevity, and should not be susceptible to legislative revision in the same way that ordinary laws may be. It should be remembered that the idea of limited government – the notion that those who govern us should not possess entirely unfettered power – lies at the heart of constitutions, and therefore, of constitutionalism.

An overly prescriptive definition?

On this reading perhaps, Ridley's assertions may seem entirely uncontroversial. Applying his own definition, Ridley concludes that the UK has no constitution, at least not in any meaningful sense of the word. This is primarily because, in the UK, Parliament, and not the constitution, is sovereign.[14] As a result of the doctrine of parliamentary sovereignty – which holds that parliamentary legislation is the highest law of the land and that Parliament can make, or unmake, any law – Ridley argues that any of the UK's 'so-called constitutional arrangements may be changed by Parliament by simple majority vote.'[15] As a result, the UK lacks what Ridley argues to be the defining characteristics of a constitution, namely, a superior body of 'constitutional' rules, largely immune from legislative interference, which determine how a government should be composed and how it should operate.

However, Ridley's definition of a constitution may appear – especially to a student with even a passing familiarity with the British, or UK, system of government – to be highly, perhaps overly, prescriptive. First, Ridley's conclusion would appear to suggest that there is no stable body of rules which govern how an administration (or government) should be formed, and how its powers should be exercised. To say that this body of rules is entirely absent the UK's system of government would be misleading; elections to the House of Commons are governed by primary legislation[16] and we have already, for instance, encountered the conventional rule that the leader of the party able to command a majority in the House of Commons will ordinarily be appointed by the Queen to the office of Prime Minister. Once in office, a government's power is not unfettered; the law relating to judicial review places restrictions on the exercise of governmental power.[17]

Ridley would further suggest that we have not given our consent to the system of government established. While the UK constitution does not contain a grand declaration such as that found in the opening lines of the Constitution of the United States of America, that is not to say that government in the UK is not carried out on behalf of the electorate. As a result of regular general elections to Parliament, which determine both whom will represent us in the legislature, and which party (or parties) will form a government, our consent to the system of government is given, albeit indirectly. Therefore, as one leading constitutional commentator has declared, 'even in the British system, constituent power – the power to make and alter constitutional contracts – rests with "the people"'.[18]

---

[14] For a more detailed analysis of the doctrine of parliamentary sovereignty, see Chapter 5.

[15] F. F. Ridley, 'There is no British constitution: A dangerous case of the emperor's clothes' (1988) 41 *Parliamentary Affairs* 340, 350–1.

[16] See, for instance, Representation of the People Act 1983 (governing who is eligible to vote); Fixed Term Parliaments Act 2011 (governing when general elections should be held).

[17] See Chapters 18 and 19.

[18] M. Loughlin, *Foundations of Public Law* (OUP, 2010) p. 224 .

Ridley's thesis regarding the lack of a distinction between 'constitutional' and 'ordinary' law would also appear to be open to question. '[C]onstitutional statutes', in other words legislation recognised as having an especial significance for the powers of government or the rights of individuals, have been identified in judicial decisions by UK courts.[19] In addition, the importance of 'constitutional' reform and innovation has been recognised by the creation of a series of parliamentary committees with a specific mandate to scrutinise the operation of governmental structures and processes, and the implications of proposed amendments to them.[20]

Finally, Ridley's analysis would also suggest that there is no guarantee of longevity and stability in the UK Constitution, as can arguably be found in those systems with entrenched constitutional orders. While the legal entrenchment of specific statutory provisions is not a feature of the UK system of government, many of its fundamental features can be traced back many centuries.[21]

As we will examine in greater detail in the chapters that follow, each of Ridley's suggestions may be open to question. For present purposes, however, Ridley's highly specific definition of a constitution illustrates but one of a number of varying analyses of what a constitution is, or should be. Other definitions, which – as we will see – may lend themselves more readily to the UK's unique constitutional arrangements, are less dogmatic.

A less prescriptive definition of a constitution than that offered by Ridley suggests that:

> A country's constitution is simply the set of rules and common understandings [relating to the composition and conduct of government] that currently exist.[22]

On this definition, provided by Anthony King, less emphasis is placed on the necessity for a constitution to exist prior to the creation of a government, or for the constitution itself to be entrenched in some way. Ridley argued that a constitution 'establishes, or constitutes, the system of government'. By contrast, King argues that the system of government *is* the constitution. The constitution – on King's definition – should still be regarded as being binding in some way, as it includes 'rules' relating to the composition and conduct of government. Similarly, King's definition hints at the requirement of consent, mentioning the '*common* understandings' that underpin the operation of the constitution. But perhaps the crucial difference between Ridley and King's definitions is that while the former emphasises rigidity and stability, the latter appears to accommodate the potential for flexibility and change.

An even less prescriptive definition of a constitution, as suggested by the academic J. A. G. Griffith, suggests that:

> The constitution is no more and no less than what happens. Everything that happens is constitutional. And if nothing happened that would be constitutional also.[23]

---

[19] *Thoburn* v *Sunderland City Council* [2002] EWHC 195 (Admin); [2003] QB 151 (on which, see pp. 158–60). See also the recognition of 'fundamental principles' of the constitution in *R (Buckingham CC)* v *Secretary of State for Transport* [2014] UKSC 3; [2014] 1 WLR 324, [207] (on which see: P. Craig, 'Constitutionalising Constitutional Law: *HS2*' [2014] PL 373).

[20] See for instance, the House of Lords Select Committee on the Constitution and The House of Commons Public Administration and Constitutional Affairs Select Committee.

[21] On which see Chapter 5.

[22] A. King, *The British Constitution* (OUP, 2007) p. 3. See also the definition given in the quotation at the opening of this chapter (S. E. Finer, V. Bogdanor and B. Rudden, *Comparing Constitutions* (Clarendon Press, 1995) p. 1).

[23] J. A. G. Griffith, 'The Political Constitution' (1979) 42 MLR 1, 19. See further Chapter 4.

For Griffith then, the constitution is not seemingly defined by the structure of rules, practice and custom which govern how government *should* be composed and how government *should* operate. Rather, the constitution is defined, purely and simply, by what *does* happen.

Thinking Point . . .

The *Oxford English Dictionary* defines 'constitution' as '[t]he body of principles according to which a state *or* organisation is governed'. Constitutions not only regulate countries but also companies, political parties, societies, trades unions, associations and so on.

Hence, there are different ways in which to go about defining what is a constitution, or what is constitutional. As we will see, elements of each of the three explanations of what a constitution is will be seen in the following analysis and explanation of the UK Constitution. At this stage it is sufficient to simply note that there are various ways in which the words 'constitution' and 'constitutional' can be interpreted. It follows from this that the characteristics of individual constitutions will also vary from state to state, and it is to the content and form of some of those constitutions that we now turn.

The content of constitutions

Key issues

Though constitutions may typically deal with three core issues – the establishment of the branches of government, the delineation of their powers and the provision of individual rights – there is considerable variance between constitutions as to how, and in how much detail, these central functions are addressed. The content of a constitution may therefore tell us as much about a state's history or aspirations as it does about its system of government.

The content of constitutions across the world varies; each is inevitably shaped by the circumstances which give rise to the drafting and implementation of a particular instrument, or to the emergence and development of a particular rule or practice of governance. Drawn up in the aftermath of the Second World War, for example, the Constitution of Germany – the *Grundgesetz* or Basic Law – is according to its preamble 'animated by the resolve to serve world peace as an equal partner in a united Europe.'[24] The modern Constitution of the Republic of South Africa is aspirational in its tone – reflecting the intentions of its framers to distance themselves from the discriminatory apartheid regime – and setting down the intention that the constitution would 'lay the foundations for a democratic and open society in which government is based on the will of the people and every citizen is equally protected by law.'[25] The Constitution of the United States – with its famous system of checks and balances – reflects the commitment of the founders to a system of limited government, under which governmental power should not be exercised unsupervised.[26] Constitutions might further set down various characteristics of the state, from whether[27]

---

[24] See also the commitment to pacifism in Article 9 of the Constitution of Japan.
[25] Preamble to the Constitution of the Republic of South Africa.
[26] S. E. Finer, V. Bogdanor and B. Rudden, *Comparing Constitutions* (Clarendon Press, 1995), p. 15.
[27] For example, Section 79 of the Constitution of the Kingdom of Thailand 2007.

or not[28] there should be a state religion, to the extent of the territory to which the constitution applies.[29]

Rather than being declared by written instrument, many of the fundamental principles of the UK Constitution have developed and solidified over time. In the UK, the central doctrine of parliamentary supremacy emerged out of the Glorious Revolution of 1688, and was confirmed by the Bill of Rights 1689 and Act of Settlement 1701. These developments effectively ended the lengthy power struggle between parliamentary and monarchical power in the historical constitution, placing political and legal power firmly in the hands of Parliament.[30] As Adam Tomkins has written:

> If the Bill of Rights established that Parliament could lay down the terms and conditions on which England was to continue as a monarchy, the Act of Settlement, which followed in 1701, established that Parliament could also control the very identity of the monarch, by altering, if it wished, the line of succession.[31]

As the experience in the UK illustrates, core principles of government might emerge over time, as a result of events or of constitutional actors' responses to those events. This points to an important lesson; as Anthony King reminds us, 'constitutions . . . are never – repeat, *never* – written down in their entirety.'[32]

While the primary task of a constitution may be to establish and regulate a system of government, the topics covered by constitutions may go considerably beyond what is thought necessary to fulfil this task, from carefully describing the appearance of the national flag[33] or national coat of arms,[34] to nominating the adoption of a national animal (which is 'always attractive, but rarely edible'[35]). All constitutions are therefore individual – or 'autobiographical and idiosyncratic'[36] – and as such should be examined in the light of the circumstances which gave rise to their creation as well as the more contemporary situations in which they apply.

Just as the content of written constitutions may vary, so may their length. Some constitutions are incredibly long and detailed – as might be imagined to be necessary to effectively document every potential exercise of governmental power in a state. The German Basic Law, for instance, extends to some 22,000 words. Others are relatively brief, as is the case in perhaps the most famous of constitutional documents, the Constitution of the United States of America. As the American constitutional scholar Mark Tushnet has written:

> The written United States Constitution is old, short and difficult to amend. Adopted in 1789 and amended only 27 times since, the Constitution and its amendments do not reach 6,000 words in length.[37]

To put the brevity of the United States' Constitution in context, this opening chapter, simply attempting to describe what it is that constitutions do in practice, is some 8,000

---

[28] For example, the First Amendment to the Constitution of the United States.

[29] Articles 1 and 2 of the Constitution of Lebanon.

[30] See Chapter 5 esp. at pp. 128–9; E. Wicks, *The Evolution of a Constitution: Eight Key Moments in British Constitutional History* (Hart Publishing, 2006) ch. 1.

[31] A. Tomkins, *Public Law* (Clarendon Press, 2003) p. 44.

[32] A. King, *The British Constitution* (OUP, 2007) p. 5.

[33] Article 22 of the German Basic Law.

[34] Article 8a of the Austrian Constitution (on which, see A. King, *The British Constitution* (OUP, 2007) p. 7).

[35] S. E. Finer, V. Bogdanor and B. Rudden, *Comparing Constitutions* (Clarendon Press, 1995) p. 6.

[36] Ibid., p. 7.

[37] M. Tushnet, *The Constitution of the United States of America: A contextual analysis* (Hart Publishing, 2000) p. 1.

words in length. The United States Constitution is able to provide the basis for an entire system of democratic, federal, government, using fewer words.

So, to recap, while there may be different ways of explaining what we understand a constitution to be, and while the content and specificity of constitutions may vary considerably, we can still say with a degree of certainty that there are certain key functions that a constitution should fulfill. A constitution should:

- establish the central (and possibly sub-national) structure(s) of government;
- define and delimit the powers exercisable by government; and
- define the relationships between individuals and the state.

Each of these tasks will be introduced in turn.

Establishing the central structures of government

Constitutions will make provision for the various structures of government that should exist in a state. The idea of government comprising a legislative, executive and judicial branch has already been introduced, and is clearly evident in, for example, the opening Articles of the Constitution of the United States of America. Article I provides that there shall be a legislative branch (otherwise known as Congress) comprising the Senate and the House of Representatives. Article II provides that the executive power shall be held and exercisable by the President. While Article III provides that judicial power shall be exercised by a Supreme Court. Similarly, the German Basic Law makes provision for a federal legislature,[38] executive[39] and constitutional court and judicial branch.[40]

Beyond this, a constitution may specify that the state government should adhere to a certain division of functions between national and regional levels. For example, the constitution may require the state to be federal in structure (as in the United States and Germany). Federal systems divide governmental power between the federal (national) and state (regional) institutions of government. By contrast, unitary states (such as the UK) – while they may comprise different regional components, to whom governmental power may be delegated – are ultimately governed by one structure of central government.[41]

Defining and delimiting the powers exercisable by government

The relationships between the three branches of government – often explained through the theory of separation of powers – are also governed by the constitution. The doctrine of separation of powers – discussed in more detail in relation to the UK Constitution in Chapter 7 – holds that governmental activities should be carried out by the legislative, executive and judicial branches of government, each of which should exercise specific individual functions, and each of which may exercise a role in scrutinising the functions carried out by the other branches. Such powers of scrutiny and restraint are frequently referred to as systems of constitutional 'checks and balances' and emphasise the notion inherent in constitutionalism that governmental power should be limited in some way rather than being unfettered.

---

[38] Articles 38–53 of the German Basic Law.
[39] Articles 62–69 of the German Basic Law.
[40] Articles 92–104 of the German Basic Law.
[41] For further discussion – including analysis of quasi-federal nature of the UK, post-devolution – see Chapters 12 and 13.

The degree to which each of the branches of government may intervene in the activities of the others may, however, vary between states. Although not explicitly provided for by the Constitution of the United States, for example, the Supreme Court is able to judicially review the actions of the executive and legislative branches, and is empowered to strike down measures that contravene the provisions of the constitution.[42] In the UK, however, courts do not exercise similar powers of constitutional review, and are not permitted to invalidate legislative measures in this way, as a result of the doctrine of parliamentary sovereignty.[43] This is not to say, however, that no such 'checks and balances' exist in the UK; Parliament, for example, is able to scrutinise the activities of the executive and must give its consent before the government's legislative proposals become law, while the courts possess jurisdiction to judicially review the use of executive discretionary powers.[44]

Defining the relationships between individuals and the state

As well as regulating the relationships between branches of government, constitutions will frequently regulate the relationships between the individual, or individuals, and the state. In addition to providing for an independent judicial branch to determine disputes of law between the state and the individual (for example, criminal trials and judicial review proceedings) or between individuals themselves (for example, proceedings in tort or contract law perhaps), a constitution will often provide a list of legal, constitutional, rights inherent in the individual with which the state may not interfere, or which may only be interfered with by law on limited, specified, grounds. Such 'Bills of Rights' are common features of constitutional documents across the globe. The most famous Bill of Rights is, again, perhaps that found in the first ten amendments to the Constitution of the United States of America which make provision for, *inter alia,* the freedom of assembly, expression and religion (the First Amendment),[45] due process of law (the Fifth Amendment),[46] and the right to a fair trial (the Sixth Amendment).[47] Further examples can be found in the Canadian Charter of Rights and Freedoms 1982, the New Zealand Bill of Rights Act 1990, and of course, the UK's own Human Rights Act 1998.[48]

---

[42] *Marbury* v *Madison* 5 US (1 Cranch) 137 (1803).

[43] See Chapter 5.

[44] See Chapters 15, 18 and 19.

[45] 'Congress shall make no law respecting an establishment of religion, or prohibiting the free exercise thereof; or abridging the freedom of speech or of the press; or the right of the people peaceably to assemble, and to petition the government for a redress of grievances.'

[46] 'No person shall be held to answer for a capital or other infamous crime unless on a presentment or indictment of a grand jury, except in cases arising in the land or naval forces, or in the militia, when in actual service, in time of war or public danger; nor shall any person be subject for the same offence to be twice put in jeopardy of life or limb; nor shall be compelled in any criminal case to be a witness against himself, nor be deprived of life, liberty, or property, without due process of law; nor shall private property be taken for public use without just compensation.'

[47] 'In all criminal prosecutions, the accused shall enjoy the right to a speedy and public trial, by an impartial jury of the state and district wherein the crime shall have been committed, which district shall have been previously ascertained by law, and to be informed of the nature and cause of the accusation; to be confronted with the witnesses against him; to have compulsory process for obtaining witnesses in his favor, and to have the assistance of counsel for his defence.'

[48] On which, see Chapter 21.

Forms of constitutions

Key issues

- Constitutions are typically categorised as either being written (otherwise referred to as codified or documentary constitutions) or unwritten (otherwise known as non-codified constitutions).
- Written constitutions may also be entrenched, meaning that they are either immune, or are protected, from amendment by way of the ordinary legislative process.
- The status of a constitution will condition whether a set process exists for its amendment or whether it is open to incremental, or organic, change over time.
- A constitution's status may also determine how it is to be interpreted and given effect to by those actors to whom it applies.

It has become commonplace to draw a distinction between two typical types of constitution – those that are said to be 'written' and those that are categorised as 'unwritten'. This categorisation is slightly misleading, as the suggestion that a constitution is 'unwritten' gives the impression that it exists entirely in the realm of convention, practice and tradition and that it contains nothing that is actually written down in a legal document of some sort. It is suggested therefore that codified and non-codified provide a more accurate encapsulation of the two main forms of constitution. A codified constitution will contain the vast majority of a state's constitutional rules in one written document. A non-codified constitutional system, such as exists in the UK, may not have a specific document titled 'The Constitution', but may nevertheless contain constitutional rules that are written down in one way or another – in legislative measures, codes of practice, and so on. As the contemporary constitutional and political commentator Anthony King has written:

> . . . the fact that Britain lacks a capital-C Constitution is far less important than is often made out. On the one hand, large chunks of Britain's small-c constitution *are* written down. On the other, large and important chunks of other countries' capital-C Constitutions are *not* written down.[49]

The vast majority of the world's constitutions are codified in nature. In the United States, Canada, South Africa, Germany, France and Australia – to give but a few examples – we can point to documents that can be identified as 'the Constitution'. Non-codified constitutions, by contrast, are only found in a small number of modern democracies: Israel, New Zealand, and the UK.

One advantage of the written, or codified, form of constitutions would appear to be certainty, at least as to the source of the rules that govern the creation and operation of the system of government. If all of the constitutional rules of a state are to be found by making reference to one, easily identifiable, source, then – while they may be linguistically unclear, or make reference to concepts we may not readily understand – at least we know where to find them. As Dicey – the famous constitutional commentator with

---

[49] A. King, *The British Constitution* (OUP, 2007) p. 5.

which every student of the law becomes familiar – commented on the Constitution of the United States:

> The articles of this constitution fall indeed far short of perfect logical arrangement, and lack absolute lucidity of expression; but they contain, in a clear and intelligible form, the fundamental law of the Union.[50]

By contrast, the student or commentator seeking the UK or – as Dicey then referred to it – English constitution would have a more difficult search on their hands:

> He may search the statute-book from beginning to end, but he will find no enactment which purports to contain the articles of the constitution; he will not possess any test by which to discriminate laws which are constitutional or fundamental from ordinary enactments.[51]

Yet, as King notes, the difference in substance between the two forms of constitution may be overstated, since even in countries with a codified constitution, not all of the rules of government may be written down.

The UK Constitution cannot be found in one single document. This is for the reason that the basis of the UK system of government, and the respective powers of its component parts, are to be found in a range of differing legal and political sources. Statute, convention, judicial precedent and international treaty obligations may all be seen to exert constitutional influence on the UK's system of governance, and, as a result, may cumulatively be said to provide us with the content of the constitution.[52] If we adopt King's definition of a constitution, such a diversity of sources of authority should prove no obstacle to concluding that a constitution does exist in the UK; taken as a whole this range of legal and political authority provides a 'set of rules and common understandings' that underpin our system of government.

Entrenchment and amendment

It is common for constitutions to be entrenched, that is, insulated from amendment or repeal through the ordinary legislative process. This is because constitutions are not only the source of governmental power, but are also designed to restrain the exercise of governmental power, to enshrine as a higher form of law certain fixed principles of government held to be so fundamental that they should be placed out of the reach of temporary majorities. Entrenchment is a mechanism that is utilised to protect a constitution from amendment or repeal through the ordinary legislative process. While a fully entrenched constitution would bring with it certainty and stability, it may also, on account of its age, reflect political values and aspirations that do not reflect those of contemporary society. It is for this reason that even entrenched constitutions provide special mechanisms, in other words mechanisms outside the ordinary legislative process, to allow for their own amendment.

For example, as has been noted, the United States' Constitution occupies a status above ordinary statute law and may only be amended following endorsement by a special, two-thirds, majority of Congress (the federal legislature) and with the consent of

---

[50] A. V. Dicey, *Introduction to the Study of the Law of the Constitution* (Liberty Fund, 1982) p. cxxvii.

[51] Ibid., p. cxxvii. Although, on the latter point, now see the discussion of *Thoburn* v *Sunderland City Council* [2002] EWHC 195 (Admin); [2003] QB 151, pp. 158–60.

[52] See Chapters 2 and 3.

three-quarters of the States. It is for this reason that Mark Tushnet noted that the United States' Constitution is 'hard to amend'; the last successful amendment – the 27th – was passed in 1992,[53] with the 26th amendment passed in 1971.[54]

Similarly, amendments to the German Basic Law – under Article 79 – require the support of two-thirds of the votes cast in the federal legislature (*Bundestag*) as well as two-thirds of the votes cast in the federal council representing the regions, or Länder (*Bundesrat*). Amendments to the division of the German Federation into Länder, or to the principles of federalism on which the Basic Law is based, are prohibited under Article 79. As a result, the system of federal government is fully entrenched in the Basic Law, and could only be overturned by a complete abandonment of the Basic Law itself.

By contrast, and as will be seen in later chapters, entrenchment is a legal impossibility in the constitution of the UK. Again, the reasons for this can be traced to the doctrine of parliamentary sovereignty, which holds that, as a result of Parliament's omnipotence, Parliament can do anything, including repealing the enactments of previous Parliaments.[55] While this may point towards a lack of permanence in our constitutional arrangements – of the type sought by Ridley – it allows the constitution of the UK to be more responsive to contemporary needs and conditions, and ensures that we are not necessarily bound to adhere to rules which may have been decided upon hundreds of years ago.

Constitutional interpretation and unwritten constitutional norms

Even in those systems that maintain codified constitutions, the written words to be found in the document itself cannot provide a complete picture of how the constitution itself operates and has been applied in practice. A codified constitution, in and of itself, will therefore only provide a limited insight into the constitutional law of a state. Judicial interpretation of how the constitution operates, and political practice, is as informative as the bare text of the constitutional document or statute under examination. As Munro notes, constitutional instruments – no matter how comprehensive or precisely worded – only provide a 'framework' around and under which government operates and will over time become 'overlaid with judicial interpretation and political practices.'[56]

Principles of judicial interpretation will shape how constitutional rules will take effect. For example, the doctrine of 'political questions' as found in the jurisprudence of the United States Supreme Court holds that certain issues are most appropriately resolved by the elected branches of government – the President and Congress – rather than by courts. The doctrine of 'political questions' can be traced back to the opinion of Marshall CJ in *Marbury* v *Madison*, where the Chief Justice noted that the Supreme Court's power was 'solely, to decide on the rights of individuals . . . Questions in their nature political . . . can never be made in this court.'[57] As a result, the 'political questions' doctrine affects how the separation of powers outlined in Articles I–III of the Constitution comes into effect in practice.

---

[53] The 27th Amendment holds that any law passed altering the salaries of members of Congress shall not take effect until the Congressional term after its passage.

[54] The 26th Amendment standardised the voting age across the United States at 18 years.

[55] See Chapter 5. See, for example, *Thoburn* v *Sunderland City Council* [2002] EWHC 195; [2003] QB 151, 181(Laws LJ): 'Parliament cannot bind its successors.'

[56] C. Munro, *Studies in Constitutional Law* (2nd edn) (Butterworths, 1999) p. 3.

[57] *Marbury* v *Madison* 5 US (1 Cranch) 137 (1803), 168.

Constitutional practice – in other words, the activities of legal and political actors within a system of government – provides further evidence of the requirements of a constitution. The requirement that Ministers of the Crown in the UK should present themselves to Parliament to give an account to Parliament, for example, has already been introduced. This obligation forms a part of the doctrine of Ministerial Responsibility to Parliament, one of the many conventions, or non-legal rules, of the UK Constitution.[58] The nature of ministerial responses to parliamentary questions, and their responses to political pressures exerted by the opposition parties, will provide an insight into the specific requirements – the content – of ministers' constitutional obligations.

The United Kingdom Constitution

Key issues

- Many of the world's documentary constitutions have been adopted following a significant societal upheaval, such as the conclusion of a war, or in the aftermath of a revolution. The UK Constitution – by contrast – has developed over time and has been shaped by political and societal events and change.

- The UK Constitution is therefore famously regarded as being unwritten (or non-codified) and can be regarded as being an amalgam of documentary and non-documentary sources.

Thinking Point . . .

Jennings likens the development of the constitution to the building, and renovation, of a house:

> [t]here has been a constant process of invention, reform, and amended distribution of powers. The building has been constantly added to, and partially reconstructed, so that it has been renewed from century to century; but it has never been razed to the ground and rebuilt on new foundations. (W. I. Jennings, *The Law and the Constitution* 4th edn, University of London Press, 1952, p. 8.)

Understood as such, the UK constitution has been, and remains, in a near-constant state of flux.

Experience tells us that many other constitutions across the globe have been forged in the aftermath of some enormous political and legal disturbance or other catastrophe, such as the creation of a new state following the achievement of independence, or following a revolution or war. For example, the Constitution of the United States, agreed to in 1789, was the product of the embryonic United States of America severing itself from Britain. As we have already seen, the Constitution of the Federal Republic of Germany was drawn up and implemented in 1949 following the Second World War, while the South African constitution was implemented following the end of apartheid in 1996. By contrast, the

---

[58] See pp. 41–51.

constitution of the UK is said to have developed 'organically'[59] rather than having been designed and specifically implemented in response to some momentous event or upheaval. It is not strictly true to say therefore, as Mr Podsnap did in Charles Dickens' *Our Mutual Friend,* that the constitution has been bestowed upon us by fate or by chance.[60] Significant constitutional developments have been the product of careful thought and design – the UK's entry into the European Community[61] and the devolution of power from Parliament to devolved administrations in Scotland, Wales and Northern Ireland[62] to give two examples. It is perhaps more realistic to describe the UK Constitution as being the product of events, and of political and legal responses to them: as the famous writer Ivor Jennings observed, '[t]he British constitution has not been made but has grown'.[63] Some of the most important landmarks in the shaping of the constitution – each of which are discussed in the chapters which follow – are highlighted in the box below.

Key debates
Constitutional landmarks

1215	Magna Carta declared liberties of feudal England and placed certain limitations on the arbitrary power of the King
1689	Bill of Rights secured the legal supremacy of Parliament over the Monarch
1701	Act of Settlement regulated the line of succession to the Throne
1707	Acts of Union between England and Scotland to create the United Kingdom of Great Britain
1876	Formalisation of the Judicial functions of the House of Lords under the Appellate Jurisdiction Act
1911	The Passage of the Parliament Act 1911 ensures legal supremacy of House of Commons over the House of Lords
1928	The Franchise is extended to all men and women over the age of 21 by the Representation of the People Act
1949	Powers of House of Lords limited further by the Parliament Act 1949
1951	UK ratifies European Convention on Human Rights
1966	Right of individual petition to the European Court of Human Rights permitted
1969	Franchise extended to all those over the age of 18
1972	Entry of the United Kingdom into the European Economic Community (EEC)
1975	Continued membership of the EEC endorsed at the UK's first national referendum
1999	Devolution of power to Scotland, Wales and Northern Ireland following endorsement at referendums in those territories

---

[59] See e.g. R. Stevens, 'A loss of innocence: Judicial independence and the separation of powers' (1999) 19 OJLS 365, 397.

[60] Charles Dickens, *Our Mutual Friend,* ch. 11: 'We Englishmen are very proud of our constitution, Sir. It was bestowed on us by providence. No other country is so favoured as this country.'

[61] See pp. 74–89.

[62] See Chapters 12–13.

[63] W. I. Jennings, *The Law and the Constitution* (5th edn) (University of London Press, 1967) p. 8.

1999	Removal of the majority of the hereditary peers from the House of Lords
2000	Full implementation of the Human Rights Act 1998
2009	Establishment of the United Kingdom Supreme Court – and abolition of the judicial functions of the House of Lords – following the enactment of the Constitutional Reform Act 2005
2011	The passage of Fixed-Term Parliaments Act terminates the power of the Prime Minister to dictate when to hold a general election
2014	Referendum on Scottish independence held (with 44.7 per cent of Scottish voters in support of Scotland becoming an independent country, 55.3 per cent against)
2016	UK-wide referendum on the UK's continued membership of the European Union (with 51.9 per cent voting in favour of leaving the EU, 48.1 per cent to remain)
2017	UK Government triggers Article 50 of the Lisbon Treaty, beginning the process by which the UK will leave the European Union
2019	Conclusion of two-year period of withdrawal mandated by Article 50 (29 March 2019) – UK exits the European Union?

It is, at least in part, for this reason that the constitution of the UK is, famously, said to be unwritten (although, as we have seen, it is more accurate to refer to it as non-codified). This does not mean that it exists only in the ether – although certain parts of it might certainly be argued to – more that it cannot be found in one single written document. Instead the constitution of the UK is an amalgamation of the laws, practices, customs and institutions that, taken as a whole, comprise our system of government. The House of Lords Select Committee on the Constitution has defined the UK Constitution as:

> . . . the set of laws, rules and practices that create the basic institutions of the state, and its component and related parts, and stipulate the powers of those institutions and the relationship between the different institutions and between those institutions and the individual.[64]

The High Court decision in *R (Miller)* v *Secretary of State for Exiting the European Union* provides a more detailed account of how these varying sources of rule combine to create a *de facto* constitutional system:

> The United Kingdom does not have a constitution to be found entirely in a written document. This does not mean there is an absence of a constitution or constitutional law. On the contrary, the United Kingdom has its own form of constitutional law, as recognised in each of the jurisdictions of the four constituent nations. Some of it is written, in the form of statutes which have particular constitutional importance . . . Some of it is reflected in fundamental rules of law recognised by both Parliament and the courts. There are established and well-recognised legal rules which govern the exercise of public power and which distribute decision-making authority between different entities in the state and define the extent of their respective powers. The United Kingdom is a constitutional democracy framed by legal rules and subject to the rule of law.[65]

---

[64] House of Lords Select Committee on the Constitution, *Reviewing the Constitution* (First Report of Session 2001–2002), HL 11, July 2001, [20].

[65] *R (Miller)* v *Secretary of State for Exiting the European Union* [2016] EWHC 2768 (Admin), [18].

While the form of the UK Constitution may differ from written constitutions elsewhere, considerable similarities can be found between its object and purpose and that of many codified constitutions. It nonetheless has a number of notable characteristics. So far, a number of the distinctive features of the UK Constitution have been alluded to. It is worth drawing these characteristics together, before embarking on a more detailed analysis of the sources and nature of that constitution:

- The UK Constitution is non-codified and can be found in various written (statutes, judicial decisions) and unwritten (conventions, practices or customs) sources.
- The main structures of national government in the UK are Parliament, the executive and the courts (although limited power has been devolved to institutions in Scotland, Wales and Northern Ireland).
- The dominant characteristic of the UK Constitution is that of the sovereignty of Parliament.
- The UK Constitution is not entrenched, and can be modified through ordinary parliamentary legislation (or indeed through judicial decision or a change in political practice).
- The UK Constitution contains mechanisms designed to hold government to account both through Parliament (through, for instance, parliamentary questions) and in the courts (through the judicial review jurisdiction).

Although some of these assertions may not immediately strike the reader as being self-evident, they nevertheless should hopefully also give the impression that a number of the core features of a constitutional order *are* present in the UK system of government.[66] The purpose of this book is to examine in more detail the institutions of government in the UK, the laws, rules and practices that regulate their activities, and the relationship between the individual and the state, with the aim of establishing how far the amalgamation of these central features can be said to:

- establish the central structure(s) of government;
- define and delimit the powers exercisable by government; and
- define the relationships between individuals and the state.

The aim of this book is not only to chart the central features of the UK's system of government, but also to ask how effectively that system operates in a constitutional sense.

The book is divided into six substantive parts. *Part I* examines the nature of constitutions, the sources of the UK Constitution, and the relationships between law and politics that are central to the operation of the constitution in practice. *Part II* examines the constitutional theories that underpin the UK Constitution, namely, the doctrine of parliamentary sovereignty, the rule of law and the separation of powers. In *Part III* we examine the structures of central – or national – government that exist in the UK, before turning, in *Part IV,* to examine the devolved institutions in Northern Ireland, Scotland and Wales.

---

[66] Though for the suggestion that the UK lacks a formal constitution (and discussion of the consequences of that finding in the context of the relationship between UK laws and European legal norms) see: Lord Neuberger, 'The British and Europe' Cambridge Freshfields Annual Law Lecture 2014, 12 February 2014, esp. [26]–[33].

Parts V and VI are concerned with accountability and the mechanisms by which the powers of government are subjected to scrutiny. *Part V* is focused on primarily political means of holding government to account and considers parliamentary scrutiny of government, the Parliamentary Ombudsman and the promotion of openness through the Freedom of Information Act. *Part VI* meanwhile, examines the legal ability of the courts to supervise the exercise of executive action through judicial review and to uphold the rights of the individual against the state.

Having looked briefly at some of the key features of constitutions overseas, and introduced some of the central characteristics of the UK Constitution, we now turn to examine the sources of the UK Constitution.

Practice questions

1. Which definition of the term 'constitution' do you find most persuasive, and why?
2. What benefits flow from the existence of a written, entrenched constitution?
3. *'The flexibility and fluidity of the United Kingdom's Constitution is arguably its greatest strength, and its most significant weakness.'*
   Discuss.

Further reading

Three classic commentaries can be found in **W. Bagehot,** *The English Constitution* (first published in 1867), **A. V. Dicey,** *An Introduction to the Study of the Law of the Constitution* (first published in 1885) and **W. I. Jennings,** *The Law and the Constitution* (first published in 1933). Each exists in multiple editions and reprints, most of which are worthy of consultation. More recent, and frequently more accessible, commentaries – taking into account the significant attempts to reform and reshape the constitution in recent decades – can be found in **A. King,** *The British Constitution* (OUP, 2007) and **V. Bogdanor,** *The New British Constitution* (Hart Publishing, 2009). A particularly concise account can be found in **Martin Loughlin's,** *The British Constitution: A Very Short Introduction* (OUP, 2013).

Valuable comparative material and analysis can be found in **S. E. Finer, V. Bogdanor and B. Rudden,** *Comparing Constitutions* (OUP, 1995). Hart Publishing's *Constitutional Systems of the World* provides a series of easily digestible and contextual assessments of an ever-growing number of jurisdictions written by leading commentators. Details can be found at **http://www.bloomsburyprofessional.com/uk/series/constitutional-systems-of-the-world/**

Those interested in the interpretation of constitutions by the courts may wish to consult **J. Goldsworthy,** *Interpreting Constitutions: a Comparative Study* (OUP, 2006).

The case against the existence of a British constitution is forcefully made in **F. F. Ridley, 'There Is No British Constitution: a Dangerous Case of the Emperor's Clothes'** (1998) 41 *Parliamentary Affairs* 340. Effective rejoinders can be found in ch. 1 of **A. King,** *The British Constitution* (OUP, 2007) and ch. 2 of **E. Barendt,** *An Introduction to Constitutional Law* (Clarendon Press, 1998).

Chapter 2
The domestic sources of the UK constitution

'[The UK constitution's] essence is strong with the strength of modern simplicity; its exterior is august with the Gothic grandeur of a more imposing age.'

Walter Bagehot, *The English Constitution* (2nd edn, first published 1872, OUP, 1961) 9.

Chapter outline

In most countries a codified constitution explains the overarching relationship between individuals and the state and establishes a coherent hierarchy of authoritative sources of law. The absence of a codified UK Constitution means that constitutionally significant rules can be found in a range of legal sources including statutes, statutory instruments, the Royal Prerogative and judicial decisions. There is even a prominent role for political under-standings, known as conventions. This chapter compares the operation of the UK Consti-tution to the codified constitutions adopted in most other liberal democracies and introduces constitutional debates which will be developed in later sections of this book.

Introduction: a constitution built using different materials

The previous chapter explained the nature and role of constitutions in liberal democracies in general and in the UK in particular. But describing certain features of a country's gov-ernance arrangements as 'constitutional', as Sir Stephen Sedley says, 'presupposes the exist-ence of a constitution'.[1] The UK's 'uncodified constitution', which has 'evolved over time and continues to do so',[2] is unique in terms of the diversity of sources of constitutionally significant rules. In the words of eight justices of the Supreme Court in *Miller*:

> [T]he United Kingdom does not have a constitution in the sense of a single coherent code of fundamental law which prevails over all other sources of law. Our constitutional arrangements have developed over time in a pragmatic as much as in a principled way, through a combination of statutes, events, conventions, academic writings and judicial decisions.[3]

---

[1] S. Sedley, 'The Sound of Silence: Constitutional Law without a Constitution' (1994) LQR 270, 270.

[2] HM Government, *The Cabinet Manual: A Guide to Laws, Conventions and Rules on the Operation of Government* (Cabinet Office, 2011) 9.

[3] *R (Miller)* v *Secretary of State for Exiting the European Union* [2017] UKSC 5; [2017] 2 WLR 583, [40].

In order to study UK constitutional law, therefore, we need to establish how to find it. Codified constitutions, such as the US Constitution, alleviate this difficulty by establishing in a single source the core rules by which lawful authority is constituted, the most important powers the branches of government are able to exercise (such as making laws) and the key restraints upon those powers (such as individual rights).

Without the platform provided by a codified document, the UK's 'organic' constitution can present itself as a confused tangle of legal rules and political understandings. Moreover, some of these rules appear to be so ancient as to place serious question marks over their continued relevance within a modern system of government. On becoming Prime Minister in 2007, Gordon Brown even considered resolving this lack of clarity by drafting a new constitution.[4] Nothing came of the proposal, and many commentators have agonised over what might be lost in such a transition.[5] Academics seeking to explain the present jumble of rules have frequently compared the UK Constitution to a centuries-old, but frequently refurbished, building. Walter Bagehot, one of the most famous constitutional commentators of the Victorian era, turned to this metaphor in the quote which opens this chapter. Whereas a codified constitution enshrines the prevailing political consensus at the time of its adoption as constitutional law, Bagehot emphasised that there is no single architect behind the UK Constitution.[6] Instead, as the UK's constitutional order developed, new rules were constructed to reflect new political ideas. Old rules were either retained, demolished or refurbished depending upon their utility. Our task in this chapter is to establish and test the materials used in this construction.

Legal sources of the constitution

Key issues

- The UK has not codified its major constitutional provisions into a single document and entrenched these rules as 'higher-order' law. Anyone studying the UK's system of government must therefore assess ordinary legal provisions to determine which have constitutional significance.

- Acts of Parliament (or statutes) are the highest form of law which can be produced within the UK governance order, and as a result are often the source of rules explaining how the UK's institutions of government interact with each other and with individuals subject to their authority. Some statutes give the UK Government the authority to produce secondary legislation (which consists of Orders in Council and statutory instruments). These measures allow ministers to make law with little parliamentary oversight.

- The Crown Prerogative (also known as the Royal Prerogative) contains ancient rules dating from the era of absolute monarchy which remained in place even after Parliament's law-making supremacy was established. These powers fall into two categories:

  1. The monarch's personal prerogatives: constitutional functions which the monarch nominally performs in person (such as appointing the Prime Minister).

---

[4] HM Government, *The Governance of Britain* (HMSO, 2007) Cm. 7170, 62.
[5] See N. Barber, 'Against a Written Constitution' [2008] PL 11 and V. Bogdanor and S. Vogenauer, 'Enacting a British Constitution: Some Problems' [2008] PL 38.
[6] See A. King, *Does the United Kingdom still have a Constitution?* (Sweet and Maxwell, 2001) 99–101.

2. Government-exercised prerogative powers: powers exercised by ministers in the name of the crown (such as deploying the armed forces or entering treaties).

- The UK's courts can issue judgments which establish constitutionally significant rules as a matter of common law. Their rulings are also a source of information on how the judiciary will exercise their own constitutional functions (including interpreting legislation and holding government to account).

Much of the UK Constitution is constructed out of legal rules which have been generated by authoritative law-making sources. These rules can be found in statutes and statutory instruments (both produced by Parliament), decisions upon legal cases (produced by the courts) and in the prerogative powers (powers left over from the era of absolute monarchy). Some of this mass of rules have constitutional significance. Part of the challenge facing scholars of the UK's uncodified constitution is to assess what new legal rules, from amongst the volume of new legislation and case law produced each year, affect the constitution. We therefore need to understand how these sources of law interact to enable us to assess the significance of particular developments.

Thinking Point . . .

Spotting legal rules which have constitutional significance is proving to be increasingly challenging. The Law Commission (a statutory body which reviews the laws of England and Wales) has noted how, in 1965, Parliament generated 7,567 new pages of statute and statutory instruments. By 2005, the volume of new legislative material produced annually stood at approximately 15,200 pages. See Law Commission, *Post-Legislative Scrutiny* [2006] EWLC 302, Appendix C.

Constitutionally significant Acts of Parliament

Acts of Parliament (also known as statutes) are the most important form of law which can be created by the UK's legislature, the Westminster Parliament. According to traditional accounts of the UK Constitution, since the constitutional upheavals of 1688 no legal rule has been able to supersede a statute other than a more recent statute. We will examine the basis for this status in Chapter 5,[7] but for now it is essential to appreciate that the UK's courts will not ordinarily question the validity of Acts of Parliament. The legal status of statutes has meant that many of the most important constitutional changes in modern UK history have been effected by their enactment, even though very few are explicitly described as being constitutional enactments.[8] In this section, we explain what is meant by a 'constitutionally significant' statute. Our approach builds upon *obiter dicta* comments by Laws LJ, a senior judge who defined a statute as 'constitutional' if it 'conditions the legal

---

[7] See pp. 123–6.

[8] For example, the Constitutional Reform Act 2005 and the Constitutional Reform and Governance Act 2010. See D. Feldman, 'The Nature and Significance of "Constitutional" Legislation' (2013) 129 LQR 342, 349.

relationship between citizen and state in some general, overarching manner' or 'enlarges or diminishes the scope of what we would now regard as fundamental constitutional rights'.[9] This section is not intended to provide an exhaustive list of constitutional statutes and many of the featured statutes will be considered in greater depth in later chapters. Instead, it considers how a range of statutes have 'overarching' influence upon interactions between the individual and the state and also between the different elements of the state, and between the UK and international legal orders.

Thinking Point . . .

An effort to catalogue every potentially constitutionally significant legislative provision would be doomed to fail. For example, every change to the substantive criminal law alters what activities individuals can undertake, and might therefore be said to affect the relationship between the individual and the state.

(i) Statutes regulating the relationship between the individual and the state

Some statutes alter the relationship between the individual and the state, for example by increasing or decreasing the powers of the state or by introducing or removing rights enjoyed by individuals. These statutes often mark flashpoints in constitutional history. Magna Carta 1215, for example, was a compact forced upon King John at a time of weakness by powerful landowners. King John disregarded many of the promises contained in Magna Carta as soon as his authority was strong enough to do so. Nonetheless, for centuries Magna Carta continued to hold a symbolic value. Although it was in no way a modern charter of human rights, Hersch Lauterpacht appreciated its importance as an early rejection of absolute power; 'The vindication of human liberties does not begin with their complete and triumphant assertion at the very outset. It commences with their recognition in *some* matters, to *some* extent, for *some* people, against *some* organ of the State'.[10] Magna Carta required that monarchs show lawful authority for their actions and established that justice should be impartially administered in the courts.[11] By the seventeenth century these provisions were again rallying cries as the Atlantic Isles were racked by civil wars.[12] In the run up to these wars, King Charles I imprisoned opponents without trial[13] and levied taxes without Parliament's authority.[14] But with the defeat of the King's forces in battle, and again in the Revolution of 1688, Parliament asserted its constitutional dominance. This process culminated in a statute, the Bill of Rights 1689 which reaffirmed some constitutional restrictions which monarchs had long sought to circumvent, including the right to trial by jury[15] and the requirement of Parliament's permission to impose taxes.[16] Most importantly of all, the Bill of Rights asserted that the power to make or repeal laws in

---

[9] *Thoburn* v *Sunderland City Council* [2002] EWHC 195 (Admin); [2003] QB 151, [62].

[10] H. Lauterpacht, *An International Bill of the Rights of Man* (Columbia UP, 1945) 56–7.

[11] Magna Carta 1215, Clause 39.

[12] For further information, see pp. 255–60.

[13] *R* v *Darnel* (1627) 3 State Tr 1.

[14] *R* v *Hampden* (1637) 3 State Tr 826.

[15] Bill of Rights 1689, Article 11.

[16] Ibid., Article 4.

England (in the era prior to the creation of the UK in 1707) rested with Parliament and not with the monarch.[17]

Not that this seventeenth-century Parliament was a democratically elected body, with representatives chosen on the basis of a popular vote. The ability to vote for Members of Parliament (MPs) was restricted to 'elite groupings' within the population, defined on the basis of their gender and the scale of their property holdings.[18] Universal suffrage, which presumes that all adult citizens of a state should be able to elect law-making representatives, would not become a feature of the UK Constitution until the twentieth century, through statutory reform of restrictions on voting. In the early nineteenth century roughly one in ten adults in the UK could vote. From 1832 onwards the property-based restrictions upon the electorate were progressively lowered in a series of statutes known as the Representation of the People Acts. It was not until the Representation of the People Act 1918 that property qualifications for voters were removed. Men over the age of 21, and for the first time women, although not until they reached the age of 30 (age qualifications for voting were not equalised until 1928), were able to vote in parliamentary elections simply on the basis of being UK nationals resident in the UK. Restrictions on voting age would be relaxed again in 1969, when all resident UK nationals of age 18 or older were permitted to vote.[19]

Although the UK became a democracy through these statutes, it would not be until the close of the twentieth century that Human Rights Act (HRA) 1998 brought modern statement of human rights into force within the UK's domestic legal systems. Until this time, the remaining elements of statutes such as Magna Carta and the Bill of Rights continued to carry the burden of protecting the individual. As we shall see in Chapter 21, however, the HRA 1998 now provides for a comprehensive statement of civil and political rights, relegating the ancient statutes providing scattered rights to background importance.[20] In enacting the HRA, Parliament demonstrated that its legislation remains central to determining the relationship between the individual and the state.

Thinking Point . . .

In the same era as the HRA 1998, Tony Blair's New Labour government also enacted the Freedom of Information Act 2000, which gave individuals the ability to request information held by public bodies, in order to encourage open government and well informed public debate. This statute is examined in Chapter 17.

(ii) Statutes organising (and regulating the relationship between) government institutions

Many constitutionally significant statutes establish the basis on which particular public authorities operate and the relationship between different public authorities.[21] The Bill of Rights itself saw the Houses of Parliament exert their control over the monarchy by setting out the order of succession in the event of the monarch's death. The order of succession

---

[17] Ibid., Articles 1 and 2.
[18] *Hirst* v *UK* (2006) 42 EHRR 41, [59].
[19] For further information, see p. 271.
[20] See pp. 648–51.
[21] See D. Feldman, 'The Nature and Significance of "Constitutional" Legislation' (2013) 129 LQR 342, 347.

would thereafter be altered by Parliament in the Act of Settlement 1700, establishing Parliament's primacy over the monarchy within the UK Constitution.

The Parliament Acts of 1911 and 1949 provide further examples of statutes regulating the interaction between important institutions under the UK Constitution, together establishing that the unelected House of Lords cannot ordinarily veto legislation passed by the elected House of Commons.[22] Just as significant, the statutes establishing devolved administrations for Scotland, Wales and Northern Ireland (the Scotland Act 1998, the Government of Wales Acts 1998 and 2006 and the Northern Ireland Act 1998) stipulate how the devolved administrations operate, how they are funded and what powers they possess.[23] This legislation also affirms the ultimate supremacy of the Westminster Parliament over the devolved assemblies.[24]

Thinking Point . . .

The powers of local authorities are stipulated in the Local Government Acts 1972 and 2000, but these statutes are frequently omitted from lists of 'constitutionally significant' legislation, perhaps indicating how little consideration is often given to local government activity, despite its impact on the UK's populace. See HM Government, *The Cabinet Manual: A Guide to Laws, Conventions and Rules on the Operation of Government* (Cabinet Office, 2011) 2.

(iii) Statutes regulating the relationship between private individuals

Statutes can also give rights to individuals which they can assert not only against the state but also against other private actors. Such statutes are exemplified by the legislation enacted to prevent people from discriminating against others in fields such as employment or provision of services on the basis of personal attributes, spearheaded by the Sex Discrimination Act 1975 and the Race Relations Act 1976. More recently Parliament also introduced protection against discrimination on the basis of a person's disability under the Disability Discrimination Act 1995.

These measures, dealing primarily with relations between private individuals (although also applying to the policies of public authorities), may not at first seem *constitutionally* significant when compared to some of the statutes that are considered above. For those facing discrimination on the basis of protected characteristics, they are of vital importance. As Baroness Hale asserted in *Ghaidan* v *Godin-Mendoza*,[25] these measures amount to an important affirmation by the state of the equal dignity of people:

> [A] guarantee of equal treatment is . . . essential to democracy. Democracy is founded on the principle that each individual has equal value. Treating some as automatically having less value than others not only causes pain and distress to that person but also violates his or her dignity as a human being.[26]

---

[22] For further information, see pp. 324–31.

[23] For further information, see pp. 367–88.

[24] For further information, see pp. 394–6.

[25] *Ghaidan* v *Godin-Mendoza* [2004] UKHL 30; [2004] 2 AC 557.

[26] Ibid., [132].

We will return to this case in Chapter 21,[27] but such is the importance of the constitutional principle of equal treatment that the disparate pieces of disability discrimination legislation were merged under the Equality Act 2010, modernising and simplifying the protections against discrimination on the basis of protected characteristics (including race, gender, disability, sexual orientation age and religion). The Act applies within England, Wales and Scotland, but only certain elements cover Northern Ireland (which maintains its own anti-discrimination legislation).

(iv) Statutes altering the geographical extent of the UK

The present structure of the UK is also the product of constitutional statutes which, from the Middle Ages onwards, drew different parts of the Atlantic Isles together into one country.[28] The Statute of Wales Act 1284 formally annexed Wales as part of England. Scotland and Ireland did not give up their national governance structures until much later. Scotland entered into Union with England (and Wales) in the early eighteenth century. The treaty which established the union of the two states was brought into effect through the Act of Union 1706. Ireland subsequently joined the Union at the turn of the nineteenth century through the Act of Union 1800. This composition of the Union was not destined to last. Much of Ireland gained its independence from the UK as a result of the Irish War of Independence waged between 1918 and 1921. Only six counties in the North-East of Ireland, where the majority of the population descended from settlers from Great Britain, remained part of the UK. It was left for Acts of Parliament, the Irish Free State (Constitution) Act 1922 and Ireland Act 1949, to mark this change.[29]

(v) Statutes bringing the UK into other legal orders

Statutes have also brought the UK into international and supra-national legal orders, allowing the legislation or judicial decisions of these orders (such as the United Nations or the European Union) to have an impact within the legal systems of the UK. This means that such orders can provide legitimate sources of legal obligations within the UK's domestic legal systems. After the Second World War, Parliament passed the United Nations Act 1946, giving the government the ability to implement UN Security Council resolutions within the UK's legal systems by statutory instrument. Thereafter, the European Communities Act 1972 ratified a treaty by which the UK joined the organisation which would become the European Union. The Supreme Court has explicitly affirmed that this is a 'constitutional' statute.[30] What Parliament gives, however, Parliament can also explicitly take away. The passage of the European Union (Notification of Withdrawal) Act 2017 authorised Theresa May's Government to trigger the Brexit process.[31]

(vi) 'Ordinary' and 'constitutional' statutes compared

With these Acts of Parliament in mind, it is important to remember that a legal rule is not constitutionally significant simply because it is found in a statute. Some statutes, for

---

[27] See pp. 666–7.

[28] For further information, see pp. 359–66.

[29] See pp. 361–2.

[30] See *R (Buckinghamshire County Council)* v *Secretary of State for Transport* [2014] UKSC 3; [2014] 1 WLR 324, [78]–[79] (Lord Reed).

[31] For further information, see pp. 89–94.

example the Dangerous Dogs Act 1991, can regulate dog ownership whereas others, such as the Representation of the People Act 1983, determine the electorate for parliamentary elections. The latter is qualitatively more important for the UK's governance order. Having said that, traditional UK constitutional theory rejects the idea of 'ranking' the legal value of different statutes according to their subject matter.[32] As almost all statutes are passed in the same way (with the exception of those passed under the Parliament Acts[33]) none are in formal terms more important than others, meaning that later statutes involving seemingly mundane subject matter can affect earlier legislation which was considered constitutionally significant when passed. Lord Bingham has nonetheless maintained that, 'in the absence of a codified constitution', the courts determine what constitutes 'ordinary' and 'constitutional' law and that in spite of Laws LJ's efforts 'these terms are incapable of precise definition, the outcome of such argument in other than clear cases would necessarily be uncertain'.[34]

Thinking Point . . .

The litigation relating to the triggering of the UK's withdrawal from the European Union saw the Divisional Court place considerable emphasis on the constitutional statutes doctrine as setting up special rules of statutory interpretation (*R (Miller)* v *Secretary of State for Exiting the European Union* [2016] EWHC 2768 (Admin), [82]–[85]). The Supreme Court, however, made little reference to this approach, perhaps indicating a lack of appetite for this reasoning in light of the difficulties associated with it (*R (Miller)* v *Secretary of State for Exiting the European Union* [2017] UKSC 5; [2017] 2 WLR 583, [67]).

In the UK context, describing a statute as being of 'constitutional' importance currently carries limited legal significance (although this could change should the courts become more willing to identify statutes as 'constitutional'[35]) beyond the issue of implied repeal.[36] This lack of a formal division between laws which are constitutionally significant and those which are not sometimes makes it difficult to identify the former:

Key debates
Legal Battles over the Hunting Act 2004

Since the introduction of the ban on fox hunting in England through the enactment of the Hunting Act 2004, the ban has been challenged in several important cases for constitutional law. *R (Jackson)* v *Attorney-General* [2005] UKHL 56; [2006] 1 AC 262 saw pro-hunting campaigners challenge the procedure by which this legislation was passed. They argued that all legislation passed under the Parliament Act 1949, thereby becoming law without the

---

[32] See *Secretary of State for Defence* v *Guardian Newspapers Ltd* [1985] AC 339, 369 (Lord Roskill).
[33] For further information, see pp. 324–30.
[34] *Watkins* v *Secretary of State for the Home Department* [2006] UKHL 17; [2006] 2 AC 395, [26].
[35] D. Feldman, 'The Nature and Significance of "Constitutional" Legislation' (2013) 129 LQR 342, 358.
[36] For further information, see pp. 158–61.

approval of the House of Lords, was invalid as the 1949 Act (purporting to vary the terms of the earlier Parliament Act 1911) was a form of subordinate legislation that exceeded its powers. The *manner* in which the legislation was enacted therefore produced a constitutional debate. Ultimately, the House of Lords rejected this claim, with Lord Bingham's leading judgment declaring that legislation passed under the Parliament Acts was primary legislation and that the courts would not question it on procedural grounds (para. 25).

R (Countryside Alliance) v *Attorney-General* [2007] UKHL 52; [2008] 1 AC 719 involved a further challenge to the 2004 Act, based upon claims that the restrictions on hunting undermined the human rights of hunt supporters (specifically the right to private and family life under Art. 8 ECHR and freedom of association under Art. 11 ECHR, brought into UK law through the HRA 1998). The constitutional issue at the heart of this case was therefore whether the 2004 Act infringed the human rights of those involved in hunting. Lord Bingham accepted that the 2004 Act interfered with the freedom of association of those involved in hunting, but ultimately ruled that the interference was proportionate to legitimate aims (para. 46) and therefore rejected the claim.

Lord Birkenhead, Lord Chancellor in the aftermath of the First World War, explained that under the UK Constitution 'in the eye of the law the legislative document or documents which defined [the constitution] occupied precisely the same position as a Dog Act or any other Act, however humble its subject-matter' (*McCawley* v *The King* [1920] AC 691, 704). The Hunting Act 2004 is perhaps the best example of Lord Birkenhead's 'Dog Act', demonstrating how even a narrowly focused statute has the potential to assume constitutional significance. The courts' unwillingness to label particular statutes as being of 'constitutional' significance is the natural consequence of the uncodified nature of the UK's Constitution. Depending upon factors such as the drafting of its provisions, its subject matter and the context of its enactment any new statute could be a 'constitutional' law.

Secondary (or delegated) legislation

(i) The relationship between primary and secondary/delegated legislation

Some Acts of Parliament delegate the power to make 'secondary legislation' to particular ministers. The power to create secondary legislation is very attractive to the executive as it gives ministers the discretion to develop legal rules giving effect to their policies with little parliamentary oversight. Under the UK Constitution statutory instruments and Orders in Council created under Acts of Parliament are both examples of secondary legislation.[37] Just as statutes can contain many sections, any piece of secondary legislation can contain numerous regulations. Because, as we shall see, secondary legislation is not subject to the thorough legislative process required of Acts of Parliament, pieces of secondary legislation can be struck down by the courts.[38]

The constitutional significance of a particular piece of secondary legislation depends upon the terms of its 'parent' Act of Parliament (the statute which gives government ministers the ability to make statutory instruments). For example, at the outset of the First World War, the UK Government was not sure that it had listed all of the powers it would

---

[37] HM Government, *The Cabinet Manual: A Guide to Laws, Conventions and Rules on the Operation of Government* (Cabinet Office, 2011) 9.
[38] See *R (Public Law Project)* v *Lord Chancellor* [2016] UKSC 39; [2016] 3 WLR 387, [27].

ultimately need to maintain wartime security in the Defence of the Realm Act 1914. Nonetheless, if an emergency arose which required new powers, officials wanted to avoid having to pilot an entirely new statute through Parliament. The government therefore asked Parliament for a broad power 'during the continuance of the present war to issue regulations for securing the public safety and the defence of the realm'.[39] Using this power the wartime administration drafted regulations which enabled it to intern (detain without trial) people believed to be of 'hostile origin or associations'.[40] These provisions undermined long-standing individual liberties and were challenged by one of the internees in *ex parte Zadig*.[41] The courts, reluctant to undermine the war effort, accepted these broad powers. But one Law Lord, Lord Shaw, highlighted the constitutional implications of this secondary legislation; 'Against [these] regulations . . . nothing can stand. No rights, be they as ancient as Magna Carta, no laws, be they as deep as the foundations of the Constitution: all are swept aside by the generality of the power vested in the Executive to issue "regulations".'[42]

Thinking Point . . .

Depending upon the terms of the parent statute, secondary legislation can also be used to enhance protections for individuals. Prior to the passage of the Equality Act 2010, discrimination against individuals on the basis of sexual orientation was prohibited by statutory instruments (the Employment Equality (Sexual Orientation) Regulations 2003 and the Sexual Orientation Regulations 2007).

The First World War was not the last occasion on which UK governments have sought to assume powers with serious human rights and civil liberties implications through statutory instruments, and the courts have become more rigorous in their policing of these measures:

Key case
A v *HM Treasury* [2010] UKSC 2; [2010] 2 AC 534
(Supreme Court)

As part of international efforts to tackle terrorist financing developed in the immediate prelude to, and aftermath of, the Al Qaeda attacks of 11 September 2001, the United Nations Security Council adopted a regime which froze assets belonging to listed individuals and organisations suspected of funding international terrorism (including SCR 1373 (2001)). The UK brought this regime into effect in domestic law through the Terrorism (United Nations Measures) Order 2001, SI 2001/3365, passed under section 1 of the United Nations Act 1946. Further statutory instruments amended this regime over much of the next decade.

---

[39] Defence of the Realm Consolidation Act 1914, s. 1(1).
[40] Defence of the Realm (Consolidation) Regulations 1914, Reg. 14B.
[41] *R v Halliday* [1917] AC 260.
[42] Ibid., 289.

Several individuals challenged the asset-freezing orders imposed upon them. As Lord Hope affirmed in the Supreme Court's decision, these orders seriously curtailed the human rights of the affected individuals (at [60]):

Designated persons are effectively prisoners of the state. I repeat: their freedom of movement is severely restricted without access to funds or other economic resources, and the effect on both them and their families can be devastating.

The claimants argued that the UK Government could not impose such 'devastating' restrictions on individuals on the basis of statutory instruments. They asked the courts to strike down this delegated legislation on the basis that it exceeded the authority of the parent statute (the United Nations Act 1946). The Supreme Court upheld this claim (Lord Hope, at [61]):

I would hold that, by introducing the reasonable suspicion test as a means of giving effect to SCR 1373 (2001), the Treasury exceeded their powers under section 1(1) of the 1946 Act. This is a clear example of an attempt to adversely affect the basic rights of the citizen without the clear authority of Parliament.

Although the statutory instruments were struck down, Parliament subsequently enacted the Terrorist Asset-Freezing etc. Act 2010, re-imposing many of the restrictions previously in place (but this time under statutory authority).

(ii) The creation of secondary/delegated legislation

The attraction of secondary legislation is that it provides government with a speedy means of implementing policy by comparison to the often prolonged process of enacting primary legislation. When circumstances require rapid government responses the speed and flexibility of skeletal parent legislation which is subsequently fleshed out by regulations can prove very attractive, as the following example from the US demonstrates:

Insight
The Paulson plan in the US and the 2008 banking crisis

One prominent example of an attempt by an executive to gain a delegation of sweeping powers to make law (underlined by a budget of $700 billion) came in the original 'Paulson plan' advanced by the US Treasury Secretary Hank Paulson to address the banking crisis in the autumn of 2008. The US Government initially proposed a short piece of primary legislation which would grant it sweeping powers to purchase bad debts from banks in order to stabilise them, including the following provision (s. 2(b)(5) Legislative Proposal for Treasury Authority to Purchase Mortgage Related Assets (US Congress, 20 September 2008)):

The Secretary is authorized to take such actions as the Secretary deems necessary to carry out the authorities in this Act, including, without limitation . . . issuing such regulations and other guidance as may be necessary or appropriate to define terms or carry out the authorities of this Act.

As the Paulson plan shows, powers delegated by primary legislation can be very broad. The proposed legislation was essentially a request by the US Government for the power to make any secondary legislation it felt necessary to administer a massive $700 billion purchase of assets.

The Paulson plan was an extreme example of secondary legislation being proposed as a means to flesh out specific powers which had been granted to a government in broad terms under primary legislation. More often such measures are used to update the law. For example, in the 1970s Parliament updated the arrangements for the salaries payable to government ministers through the Ministerial and Other Salaries Act 1975. However, Parliament also accepted a provision that would allow ministerial salaries provided under this legislation to be periodically adjusted by means of secondary legislation.[43] In 2011, an Order in Council, issued by the then government under this power, altered the salaries payable to ministers under the 1975 Act.[44]

Parliament has much less input into secondary legislation than it has in relation to statutes. The 'parent' Act of Parliament explains the process by which such secondary legislation is made. Orders in Council which are not also statutory instruments do not require any parliamentary approval and become law once formally approved by the Queen at a Privy Council meeting.[45] For statutory instruments, the Statutory Instruments Act 1946 allows for two alternate mechanisms for creating statutory instruments. The more heavily employed mechanism, applying to some four-fifths of statutory instruments, is the 'negative resolution procedure', whereby the piece of secondary legislation automatically becomes law 40 days after the government proposes it unless a majority of legislators call a debate on the measure and oppose it.[46] The remainder of the thousands of statutory instruments made every year are approved by Parliament under the 'positive resolution procedure'. This procedure requires that a majority of legislators support the statutory instrument in a vote in the House of Commons.[47] Measures which are needed urgently can therefore enter force as soon as a vote can be held, with the positive procedure also allowing a parliamentary debate upon controversial pieces of secondary legislation.

Even under the positive procedure there is often limited scrutiny of law-making process. Parliament maintains a Joint Standing Committee on Statutory Instruments which examines whether statutory instruments which are not subject to full debate exceed the powers provided by their parent Act of Parliament. But the work of one committee is not always adequate to the task of scrutinising so much secondary legislation.[48] Moreover, the high volume of secondary legislation employed as government ministers attempt to rapidly bring new policies into force, makes it very hard to keep pace with developments in certain areas of law. Even specialist non-governmental organisations, like the Children's Legal Centre, have highlighted the risks inherent when laws can be easily and quickly altered; 'It is frequently the case that secondary legislation and guidance are overlooked in the process of scrutiny, although their impact on the day-to-day operation of the law is as significant as the primary statute'.[49]

(iii) Legislative Reform Orders

'Henry VIII clauses' are a particularly controversial form of delegated legislation. The name derives from that monarch's attempts to secure a royal power to legislate without

---

[43] Ministerial and Other Salaries Act 1975, s. 1B(1).
[44] Ministerial and Other Salaries Act 1975 (Amendment) Order 2011, SI 2011/1689.
[45] HM Government, *The Cabinet Manual: A Guide to Laws, Conventions and Rules on the Operation of Government* (Cabinet Office, 2011) 9.
[46] Statutory Instruments Act 1946, s. 6(1).
[47] Ibid.
[48] See D. Greenberg, 'Dangerous Trends in Modern Legislation' [2015] PL 96, 98.
[49] The Law Commission, *Post-Legislative Scrutiny (Report)* [2006] EWLC 302, [4.11].

the involvement of Parliament. In the later years of his reign he pressurised Parliament into enacting the Statute of Proclamations 1539, which allowed him to personally issue proclamations repealing or altering Acts of Parliament. Although the Statute of Proclamations was repealed in 1547, soon after Henry's death, so-called Henry VIII clauses became a feature of the UK Constitution when modern Acts of Parliament began to grant government ministers the power to alter Acts of Parliament by means of secondary legislation.

The Labour Governments in power from 1997 to 2010 made increasing use of such provisions to fast-track changes to legislation, culminating in the Legislative and Regulatory Reform Act 2006, which allowed ministers to make secondary legislation with the purpose of 'removing or reducing any burden, or the overall burdens, resulting directly or indirectly for any person from any legislation'.[50] This power to use delegated legislation to change statutes is potentially sweeping. For example, using a statutory instrument to repeal all the statutes relating to the gathering of evidence in criminal law would 'reduce a burden' upon the efforts of the police to arrest suspected criminals. Permitting the government to alter such constitutionally significant statutes through measures which are habitually rushed through Parliament with little scrutiny would therefore greatly increase the power of the executive. When the legislative proposal was first published the opposition nicknamed it the 'Abolition of Parliament Bill'.[51] Political and media pressure forced the government to restrict the power to alter statutes using delegated legislation (known as Legislative Reform Orders) with safeguards. The Act establishes a list of conditions which must all be fulfilled if the power is to be used:

(a) the policy objective intended to be secured by the provision could not be satisfactorily secured by non-legislative means;

(b) the effect of the provision is proportionate to the policy objective;

(c) the provision, taken as a whole, strikes a fair balance between the public interest and the interests of any person adversely affected by it;

(d) the provision does not remove any necessary protection;

(e) the provision does not prevent any person from continuing to exercise any right or freedom which that person might reasonably expect to continue to exercise;

(f) the provision is not of constitutional significance.[52]

The last of these safeguards in particular protects important constitutional statutes against alteration by statutory instrument. This marks the increasing relevance of the concept of a 'constitutional' statute in the UK's legal systems, even if there remains no clear definition of such a provision. Legislative Reform Orders can be passed under the negative or positive procedure, but the most far-reaching require an extended version of the positive procedure which involves a consultation process and the extensive involvement of parliamentary committees.[53] The UK governance order, however, has yet to grapple with the question of what types of measure are too important to enact by way of secondary legislation.[54]

---

[50] Legislative and Regulatory Reform Act 2006, s. 1(2).
[51] S. Kalitowski, 'Rubber Stamp or Cockpit? The Impact of Parliament on Government Legislation' (2008) 61 *Parliamentary Affairs* 694, 701.
[52] Legislative and Regulatory Reform Act 2006, s. 3(2).
[53] Ibid., s. 18.
[54] See D. Greenberg, 'Dangerous Trends in Modern Legislation' [2015] PL 96, 106.

> ## Thinking Point . . .
>
> In 2010 the then Lord Chief Justice, Lord Judge, made his views on Legislative Reform Orders clear, stating that 'the powers of the executive have indeed increased, are indeed increasing, when many believe they ought to be diminished, and I suggest that . . . Henry VIII clauses should be confined to the dustbin of history'. Lord Judge, *Mansion House Speech to Her Majesty's Judges* (13 July 2010) 6.

The Royal (or Crown) Prerogative

(i) A remnant of the monarch's historic powers

The Royal Prerogative (also known as the Crown Prerogative) remains a source of authority for executive actions independent of statutes. Historically, the prerogatives of the Crown were powers which were exercised directly by the monarch. One of the most important factors driving the civil wars of the seventeenth century was the clash between the Crown and Parliament as to which wielded supreme law-making power. When Parliament's authority was finally imposed on the monarchy by the Bill of Rights 1689, this statute expressly abolished several of the most controversial prerogative powers claimed by seventeenth-century monarchs, including removing their power to create new courts[55] and preventing them from levying taxes[56] or maintaining an army without Parliament's approval.[57] From this Act onwards Parliament could abolish or curtail the operation of prerogative powers, but some of these powers remain in place to this day.

Sir William Blackstone, writing almost a century after the enactment of the Bill of Rights, offers one reason why important powers, such as the ability to declare war, remained in the hands of the Crown after 1689. The prerogative powers, according to Blackstone, were 'wisely placed in a single hand by the British constitution, for the sake of unanimity, strength, and dispatch'.[58] If the country was, for example, invaded, it may take some time to summon Parliament if the legislature was responsible for declaring war. Entrusting the power to declare war and to deploy the military to the Crown would ensure that speedy arrangements could be made for national defence. No new prerogative powers can be created once Parliament established its supremacy in 1689, thereby obliging government ministers to seek *statutory* authority for any new powers. When the Court of Appeal rejected an attempt by government in the mid-1970s to increase the TV licensing fee without Parliament's approval, Roskill LJ declared that '[i]f the Secretary of State wishes to put his position in this respect beyond all argument, he should seek the necessary Parliamentary powers – if he can obtain them'.[59] Confusingly, however, although new prerogative powers cannot be created, no definitive list exists of all of the prerogative powers that existed in the seventeenth century, or those which are still in force. To establish the existence of a prerogative power, the government has to point to historical common law acceptance of the power and ascertain whether any intervening statute has supplanted the power.

---

[55] Bill of Rights 1689, Article 3.
[56] Ibid., Art. 4.
[57] Ibid., Art. 6.
[58] W. Blackstone, *Commentaries on the Laws of England* (1ˢᵗ edn, Clarendon Press, 1765–69) vol. I, 250.
[59] *Congreve* v *Home Office* [1976] QB 629, 657–8.

That, at least, is the theory. The case of *ex parte Northumbria Police Authority*[60] involved a dispute between the Northumbria Police Authority and the central government over the equipping of Northumbria Police. The Police Authority, seeking to prevent the government from issuing its officers with crowd control equipment which it regarded as unsafe, pointed to its statutory power to equip the force under the Police Act 1964. The government argued that this power existed alongside a prerogative power of the Crown to take steps necessary 'to keep the peace', even though there was no reference to such a power in two centuries of textbooks and case law. Surprisingly, the Court of Appeal did not consider that this lack of evidence for the existence of the prerogative undermined the government's case, with Nourse LJ declaring that '[the] scarcity of reference in the books to the prerogative of keeping the peace within the realm does not disprove that it exists. Rather, it may point to an unspoken assumption that it does'.[61] The Court of Appeal's acceptance of the existence of a prerogative power in this case, despite the lack of supporting authority, exemplifies some of the uncertainty inherent in an uncodified constitution.

(ii) The monarch's 'personal prerogatives' (or 'reserve powers')

Over time, monarchs passed the execution of many of their prerogative powers to government ministers. Nevertheless, some powers continued to be exercised directly by the reigning monarch, either because of the ceremonial importance of these functions or because of the monarch's position as a politically neutral constitutional actor.[62] In these roles the monarch receives advice from politically neutral civil servants. First, the Queen personally assents to all statutes becoming law. This power is effectively a 'rubber-stamp', as once a Bill passed by Parliament is presented to the monarch constitutional convention dictates that '[t]he Royal Assent will follow automatically'.[63] The second group of personal prerogatives relate to the office of Prime Minister and the Cabinet. The Prime Minister remains, in constitutional terms, the monarch's representative in Parliament. This theoretically gives her the power to choose any parliamentarian of her choice as Prime Minister and to dismiss a Prime Minister from office at will. Nonetheless these powers are exercised on the guiding principle that no monarch will intervene unless a Prime Minister is unable to command the confidence of the House of Commons (that is, being able, at least, to pass pieces of legislation vital to the running of the country, such as the budget).[64]

(iii) The prerogative powers exercised by the government

Beyond the personal prerogatives, a range of prerogatives are exercised by government ministers in the name of the Crown. These powers continue to provide the basis for many important government actions. In 2004, the Public Administration Select Committee

---

[60] *R v Secretary of State for the Home Department, ex parte Northumbria Police Authority* [1988] 1 All ER 556.
[61] Ibid., 575.
[62] For further information, see pp. 258–9.
[63] *Jackson v Attorney-General* [2005] UKHL 56; [2006] 1 AC 262, [134] (Lord Rodger).
[64] For further information, see pp. 262–3.

listed the main powers which the government then recognised as covered by prerogative.[65] These included:

'Foreign policy' prerogatives	'Domestic policy' prerogatives
The making of treaties	Appointment/dismissal of ministers
Recognising other states and governments (including appointing/receiving ambassadors)	Pardoning of offenders
Declaring war or peace	Granting charters to universities, charities and professional organisations
Control over the deployment of the armed forces overseas	Control over the domestic disposition of the armed forces
The issue/withdrawal of passports	

The exercise of these powers can be subject to debate in Parliament, which in particular will have to approve the financing of any exercises of the prerogative. The use of the powers is moreover reviewable in the courts, under the judicial review jurisdiction which we will examine in Chapter 18.[66]

Thinking Point . . .

Judicial review of the operation of the prerogative is a relatively recent constitutional development. Only in **Bancoult** did the House of Lords affirm that an Order in Council made under the prerogative, is 'an exercise of power by the executive alone' and therefore subject to challenge through judicial review. *R (Bancoult)* v *Secretary of State for Foreign and Commonwealth Affairs* [2008] UKHL 61; [2009] 1 AC 453, [35] (Lord Hoffmann).

Controversial exercises of prerogative powers to conclude international treaties and to deploy UK armed forces gave rise to pressure, particularly within Parliament, to create a statutory basis for these government activities. Statutes are superior to the prerogative in UK constitutional law and ever since the Bill of Rights 1689 legislation has restricted the range of prerogative powers. One famous example of this was evidenced at the height of the First World War, when the government seized De Keyser's Hotel in London to use as the Headquarters of the expanding Royal Flying Corps. The government claimed that this action was taken under the prerogative, and that therefore compensation did not have to be provided, in spite of statutory provisions under the Defence Act 1842 which detailed conditions on the compulsory seizure of land for defence purposes. The House of Lords affirmed that the government could not rely on the prerogative as it had been superseded by statute. Lord Atkinson declared:

> [W]hen a statute is passed . . . it abridges the Royal Prerogative while it is in force to this extent: that the Crown can only do the particular thing under and in accordance with the statutory provisions, and that its prerogative power to do that thing is in abeyance.[67]

---

[65] Public Administration Select Committee, *Taming the Prerogative: Strengthening Ministerial Accountability to Parliament* (2004) HC 422, 6–7.

[66] See pp. 521–2.

[67] *Attorney-General* v *De Keyser's Royal Hotel* (1920) AC 508, 539.

In other words, once a statute covers the exercise of a government function, prerogative powers cannot be employed by the government to circumvent that statute's operation.[68] The ambit of the prerogative has therefore been shrinking across the centuries, as no new prerogative powers can be created and many of the existing prerogative powers have been replaced by statutory powers. In 2010, for example, Parliament passed the Constitutional Reform and Governance Act, which replaced the important prerogative powers relating to the civil service with statutory arrangements[69] and also imposed statutory rules regarding the ratification of treaties.[70]

Thinking Point . . .

As the Supreme Court's majority judgment in **Miller** noted, '[i]t is inherent in its residual nature that a prerogative power will be displaced in a field which becomes occupied by a corresponding power conferred or regulated by statute'. This statement of legal principle was important in the context of this case because Theresa May's Government was arguing that it could use prerogative powers over international relations to begin the process of withdrawing the UK from the European Union notwithstanding the impact on statutory rights and obligations (*R (Miller)* v *Secretary of State for Exiting the European Union* [2017] UKSC 5; [2017] 2 WLR 583, [48]).

The common law

(i) The end of the 'ancient constitution'

The common law develops on the basis of judicial precedents, which derive their authority from their being the product of reasoned legal argument. Sir Edward Coke, a seventeenth-century judge, considered that over time the latticework of authorities which accumulated in any area of law gave rise to a system which displayed 'the perfection of reason'.[71] A century and a half later another judge, Sir William Blackstone, lauded the system of precedent based on existing judicial decisions for preventing judges from simply following their personal opinions 'where the same points come again in litigation'.[72] For these writers the courts were guardians of the 'ancient constitution', preserving it through their jurisprudence.[73] From the 1600s to 1800s legislation granting new powers to government was relatively infrequent, supplementing powers largely derived from common law or the Royal Prerogative under the ancient constitution.

By contrast the philosopher Thomas Hobbes, whose writings in the seventeenth century had a significant impact on the development of the UK's Constitution, offered a simple riposte to claims of the 'perfection' of the common law. He argued that '[it] is not Wisdom, but Authority that makes a Law'.[74] As the authority to make statutes (the supreme form of

---

[68] See also *R* v *Secretary of State for the Home Department, ex parte Fire Brigades Union* [1995] 2 AC 513.

[69] Constitutional Reform and Governance Act 2010, Part 1.

[70] Ibid., Part 2.

[71] E. Coke, *Institutes of the Laws of England* (15th edn, first published 1628, E. and R. Brooke, 1794) vol. I, Section 97b.

[72] W. Blackstone, *Commentaries on the Laws of England* (1st edn, Clarendon Press, 1765–69) vol. I, 69.

[73] J. Pocock, 'Burke and the Ancient Constitution – A Problem in the History of Ideas' (1960) 3 *Historical Journal* 125, 129.

[74] T. Hobbes, *A Dialogue Between a Philosopher and a Student of the Common Laws of England* (University of Chicago Press, 1971) 55.

domestic law) is vested in Parliament, it follows from Hobbes' argument that the courts are constrained by the need to respect the will of Parliament. As the tasks performed by government expanded in the 1900s, many of the ancient bases for government action were supplanted by statute. Parliament's increasing legislative activity in the Victorian era over-wrote the ancient constitution and reduced the prominence of the courts as constitutional actors. Later chapters will evaluate the contemporary constitutional relationship between the courts and Parliament, but for now, perhaps the best that can be said is that neither now claims a monopoly on 'wisdom' when it comes to law making. Instead, as Professor Roscoe Pound recognised over a century ago, 'crudity and carelessness have too often characterized . . . law-making both legislative and judicial. They do not inhere necessarily in the one any more than in the other'.[75]

Thinking Point . . .

Bentham's criticisms of the common law (and Blackstone's writings in particular) can still resonate with many law students. The common law, for Bentham, was no better than a 'game' of trumps. In court a small legally-trained elite battled to outdo each other by citing ever more obscure and ancient authorities. For Bentham the outcome of this game decided the case, seemingly without reference to the principles at issue. See J. Bentham, *A Fragment on Government* (1st edn, first published 1776, W. Harrison ed., Blackwell, 1948) *Finis,* para. 27.

(ii) Case law as a source of constitutional rules

The importance of the common law as constitutional source may have declined since the nineteenth century, but some constitutional rules are still based upon judicial decisions. The decision in *M* v *Home Office,*[76] for example, established that all ministers exercising statutory powers must respect court orders regarding such actions. Without this case, no other legal rule asserts the constitutional principle that government obeys court orders 'as a matter of necessity' and not 'as a matter of grace'.[77] Similarly, the decision in *Carltona* v *Commissioners of Works*[78] is also constitutionally significant, providing legal authority for permitting junior ministers and civil servants to exercise powers allocated by statute to senior ministers ('Secretaries of State'). Without the courts' permission for government departments to be managed in this way, some writers maintain that 'public administration would break down'.[79]

The common law not only explains how government powers should be exercised, it also provides the basis for some essential powers, known as 'third-source' powers. As the name indicates, these powers derive not from statute, or from the prerogative (the first and sec-ond sources of powers).[80] Instead, as Richards LJ has explained, they 'are normal powers (or capacities and freedoms) of a corporation with legal personality'.[81] In other words, the

---

[75] R. Pound, 'Common Law and Legislation' (1907–1908) 21 *Harvard LR* 383, 406.

[76] *M* v *Home Office* [1994] 1 AC 377. For further information, see pp. 243 and 259.

[77] Ibid., 395.

[78] *Carltona* v *Commissioners of Works* [1943] 2 All ER 560. For further information, see p. 270.

[79] C. Turpin, 'Deportation: The *Carltona* Principle' (1990) 49 CLJ 380, 380.

[80] *R (New College London)* v *Secretary of State for the Home Department* [2013] UKSC 51; [2013] 1 WLR 2358, [28] (Lord Sumption).

[81] *Shrewsbury and Atcham Borough Council* v *Secretary of State for Communities and Local Government* [2008] EWCA Civ 148; [2008] 3 All ER 548, [73].

common law treats public bodies as being corporate bodies, possessing powers to act in a manner which is 'a necessary and incidental part of the ordinary business of government'.[82] Therefore, NHS Trusts and Academy Groups do not have to point to specific statutory or prerogative authority allowing them to enter contracts for the supply of stationery or catering, such contracts are treated as necessary elements of their operations.[83] But public bodies can only act in such ways when they are ancillary to their statutory or prerogative powers, and cannot be used to circumvent applicable laws or rights.[84]

(iii) Case law as a source of interpretative principles

Beyond case law which grants powers or explains their operation much constitutional jurisprudence relates to how statutes are interpreted. In this regard, the courts' role is 'to ascertain and give effect to the true meaning of what Parliament has said in the enactment',[85] something which poses particular difficulties if the literal wording of a provision is vague and if important constitutional issues are at stake.

If a statutory provision's meaning is ambiguous judges ordinarily seek to interpret it in accordance with Parliament's intention or in conformity with the legislation's purpose. Such approaches are intended to deflect criticisms that unelected judges are free to tamper with the meaning of Parliament's legislation as they choose. Nonetheless, this task is seemingly superhuman, obliging judges to establish the aggregate intention of all legislators involved in making a provision while suppressing their personal views on whether a particular interpretation is appropriate.[86] By the 1970s, senior members of the judiciary openly acknowledged that it was nonsensical to believe that judges had no personal input into law making when they exercised their interpretative function (for Lord Reid – then the senior Law Lord – 'we do not believe in fairy tales any more'[87]). Consequently, in the case of *Pepper* v *Hart*,[88] the House of Lords accepted that the courts could turn to parliamentary materials, and in particular statements by the legislation's promoter (often a minister) as to its meaning, in order to resolve ambiguities.[89] *Pepper* v *Hart* therefore fits the mould of constitutional case law, explaining what tools the judiciary can employ in carrying out its constitutional role of interpreting statutory provisions.

In cases involving issues of constitutional importance (such as human rights) the judiciary is often willing to employ special rules of interpretation, even if it means departing from Parliament's stated intention behind legislation. These presumptions can exert a powerful influence on statutory interpretation. With regard to the criminal law, for example, judges have recognised that only Parliament has the legitimacy to develop new criminal offences, and that it is not open to them to extend the reach of the criminal law (even if offences are still based upon the common law) because of the implications for the liberty of the individual.[90] Parliament's intention would therefore seem to be particularly important

---

[82] Ibid., [49] (Carnwarth LJ).

[83] See J. Harris, 'The Third Source of Authority for Government Action' (1992) 109 LQR 626.

[84] See Select Committee on the Constitution, *The Pre-emption of Parliament* (2013) HL Paper 165, para. 61–62.

[85] *R (Quintaville)* v *Secretary of State for Health* [2003] UKHL 13; [2003] 2 AC 687, [8] (Lord Bingham).

[86] See D. Feldman, 'Statutory Interpretation and Constitutional Legislation' (2014) 130 LQR 473, 477.

[87] J. Reid, 'The Judge as Lawmaker' (1972) 12 *JSPTL* 22, 22.

[88] *Pepper* v *Hart* [1993] AC 593.

[89] Ibid., 616 (Lord Bridge).

[90] For an earlier and contrary approach, see *Shaw* v *DPP* [1962] AC 220.

when criminal legislation is at issue.[91] The judges have, nonetheless, been willing to assert constitutional presumptions to restrict the extent to which statutes can interfere with safeguards protecting individual liberty. In such instances, prosecutors would have to establish unambiguous legislative authority enabling a conviction if they are to rebut these presumptions. For example, the courts have sought to protect the principle that when an individual is charged with a serious criminal offence the prosecution must establish criminal intent, a presumption which 'can only be displaced by specific language'.[92]

Non-legal sources of the constitution

Key issues

- The UK's Constitution is often described as a 'political' rather than a 'legal' constitution. This is, in part, explained by the degree to which it consists of political rather than legal rules (although it also relates to the fact that, as we saw in the last section, even when legal rules are at issue they remain subject to reform on the basis of a simple parliamentary majority).
- Constitutional rules which are political in nature are known as constitutional conventions. They can cover subject matter every bit as important as constitutionally significant laws, but are not enforceable in court.
- Constitutional conventions often developed as political rules, rather than legal ones, because they were not considered suitable subject matter for litigation. If these political rules were legalised, this would dramatically increase the involvement of the courts in matters of political controversy and, therefore, could risk politicising the judiciary.

The sources examined above illustrate that, for all the talk of the UK's 'unwritten' constitution, much of the constitution is governed by established legal rules. Other areas of the UK's Constitution, however, are regulated not by legal rules but by political understandings. Further areas are addressed by legal rules which are outdated. The operation of these rules is only sustained because of similar political understandings. These political understandings are known as constitutional conventions.

Although it is misleading to describe the UK's Constitution as 'unwritten', the prominence of these political understandings mean that the statutory provisions, case law and prerogative powers we have examined to date do not tell the full story of constitutional sources. The UK Constitution involves the interaction between legal and political rules. The relative importance of conventions to the UK's Constitution moreover distinguishes the UK from countries which have codified their most important constitutional rules into 'higher-order' constitutional law. Constitutional conventions, together with Parliament's ability to change constitutional law by enacting new statutes in the ordinary way, affirm for Griffith that the UK Constitution is 'political' in nature, and capable of 'changing from day to day'.[93]

---

[91] See *Attorney-General of Jersey* v *Holley* [2005] UKPC 23; [2005] 2 AC 580, [22] (Lord Nicholls).

[92] *R* v *K* [2001] UKHL 41; [2002] 1 AC 462, [32] (Lord Steyn).

[93] J. Griffith, 'The Political Constitution' (1979) 42 MLR 1, 19. On this point see below, pp. 98–108.

The role of constitutional conventions

(i) What are constitutional conventions?

Mid-Victorian constitutional writers Walter Bagehot and A. V. Dicey were the first to emphasise the discrepancies between the UK's theoretical constitutional arrangements and how the constitution operated in reality. Bagehot noted the apparent significance of the Crown as a matter of law, with ministers exercising their office on behalf of the monarch and the monarch having to accept ('assent to') legislative proposals before they could take effect as law. He nonetheless concluded that the monarch's role within the UK's Constitution amounted to little more than a 'dignified' smokescreen, maintained to promote loyalty to the state amongst the then poorly educated majority of the UK population. Even in the mid-Victorian era, the 'efficient' reality of the UK Constitution was that the monarch assented to statutes as a matter of course and that only the parliamentarian able to control a stable majority in the House of Commons could be Prime Minister.[94]

Dicey built on Bagehot's analysis, explaining that this disconnect between constitutional theory and reality was the product of what he described as 'conventions of the constitution'.[95] These conventions were non-legal rules of conduct guiding the actions of, and relationships between, politicians and officials under the UK Constitution. These rules operate not only to cover the gaps in the framework of constitutional laws, they also explain the modern function of legal rules which, on their face, have become dated. In the words of Sir Ivor Jennings, one of the mid-twentieth century's leading constitutional writers, 'they provide the flesh which clothes the dry bones of the law; they make the legal constitution work; they keep it in touch with the growth of ideas'.[96]

(ii) Some significant conventions

Several examples illustrate how important conventions are to the UK Constitution. First, even after Parliament assumed supreme law-making power in the late-seventeenth century, the monarch retained a number of prerogative powers. As we have seen, these included the ability to reject legislation and to declare that the UK was at war with other countries. These arrangements placed considerable authority in the hands of a hereditary monarch. However, as Parliament developed and the monarch's parliamentary representatives (government ministers) became more important, the monarch became less able to exercise these powers. The last time a monarch refused to assent to legislation was in 1708, when Queen Anne rejected the proposed Scottish Militia Bill. Meanwhile, many of the prerogative powers came to be exercised by ministers who were accountable to the electorate. Over time these political arrangements became accepted features of the UK's Constitution, despite their lack of legal status, and royal involvement in these activities became 'ceremonial'.[97]

Another prominent constitutional convention relates to the very existence of government ministers. Whilst such offices are referred to in Acts of Parliament such as the Ministerial and Other Salaries Act 1975 (setting out salaries for government ministers according to

---

[94] W. Bagehot, *The English Constitution* (2nd edn, first published 1872, OUP, 1961) 4–7.

[95] A. Dicey, *An Introduction to the Study of the Constitution* (8th edn, first published 1915, Liberty Fund, 1982) 277.

[96] I. Jennings, *The Law and the Constitution* (5th edn, University of London Press, 1959) 81–2.

[97] See HM Government, *The Cabinet Manual: A Guide to Laws, Conventions and Rules on the Operation of Government* (Cabinet Office, 2011) 7.

rank) and the Chequers Estate Act 1917 (providing an official country residence, Chequers, for the use of the Prime Minister), they were not created by statutes. Ministerial offices simply evolved from the earlier position of royal advisers, with eighteenth-century monarchs needing advisers capable of commanding a parliamentary majority to pass legislation.[98]

A further group of conventions relate to the relationship between the executive and legislature. As the composition of the House of Commons developed to reflect the will of the people due to the electoral reforms of the nineteenth century, the personal relationship between the monarch and Prime Minister became less important. Queen Victoria, for example, was obliged to appoint William Gladstone as Prime Minister fully four times despite her deep personal dislike of him. On each of these occasions Gladstone was best placed, due to the large number of Members of Parliament belonging to the Liberal Party he led, to command a majority in Parliament. However, when he lost his majority midway through a Parliament in 1886 (with the defection of a large number of Liberal Party MPs due to his efforts to introduce self-government to Ireland) he was obliged to resign. This was an early example of the convention that the government will resign if it loses the confidence of the House of Commons.[99] These examples by no means provide a comprehensive list of constitutional conventions (we will meet many other examples in the course of this book), but they do serve to illustrate the importance of conventions to the UK Constitution and also the manner in which conventions develop to reflect changing constitutional relationships.

Conventions, laws and practices

(i) Distinguishing conventions from laws

Dicey found it difficult to divide laws and conventions rationally. They could not be divided in terms of subject matter or their relative importance, as so many areas of the UK Constitution are governed by a mixture of laws and conventions.[100] Laws were also not clearer than conventions, for many conventions could be explained with as much precision as legal rules. He concluded that the only way to divide these rules was on the basis that, being *political* understandings, conventions were not enforceable in court.[101] In other words, whether constitutional conventions are upheld (and the penalties for breach) are entirely matters for the political process and will not provide a basis for a legal challenge in the courts.

Dicey's view was criticised by Sir Ivor Jennings, who was unimpressed by assertions that some constitutional rules are enforceable and others not in the absence of a rationale for this distinction. He argued that laws and conventions were in fact very similar, as both rested on the general acquiescence of affected parties.[102] If a convention is not accepted by political actors (perhaps because it is out of date), they will simply ignore it when they make decisions. Likewise, for Jennings, civil unrest in response to a law can lead to its repeal. For example, in 1990 the introduction of the Poll Tax to fund local government was hotly contested. Following widespread public discontent with the operation of the tax, including

---

[98] Ibid., 32.

[99] Ibid., 14.

[100] A. Dicey, *Introduction to the Study of the Law of the Constitution* (8th edn, first published 1915, Liberty Fund, 1982) 293.

[101] Ibid., 292.

[102] I. Jennings, *The Law and the Constitution* (5th edn, University of London Press, 1959) 117.

riots in Trafalgar Square, Parliament passed the Local Government Finance Act 1992 which replaced the 'Poll Tax' with a council tax system. For Jennings, a lack of acquiescence undermines a law in the same manner as conventions.

Thinking Point . . .

Not all laws are necessarily court enforceable. In Jennings' time he was able to point to statutory duties which were only enforceable by application to ministers. Such measures have given way to long-term statutory 'targets' which remain aspirational until a future delivery date and are open to repeal ahead of that date. The 2020 child poverty action targets introduced in the Child Poverty Act 2010, for example, were repealed by the Welfare Reform and Work Act 2016.

Jennings' critique focuses heavily upon exceptional cases. Legal rules are presumed to be court-enforceable, whereas many conventions are insufficiently definite for court enforcement.[103] Furthermore, whilst every convention requires continued acquiescence by affected individuals, only the principle behind law requires acceptance. Provided that a law is made in a legitimate way, for example, by enacting an Act of Parliament, it remains enforceable until it is repealed.[104] Jennings, however, posited a further important consideration in dividing laws and conventions. He argued that observers should be able to point to reasons explaining why a convention was adopted rather than a law; 'if a convention continues because it is desirable in the circumstances of the constitution, it must be created for the same reason'.[105] This is a valuable addition to Dicey's criteria of enforceability as it provides some information as to the *nature* of a constitutional convention. Many conventions, including collective cabinet responsibility, which protects the confidentiality of cabinet discussions,[106] developed as non-legal rules specifically to keep politically contentious decisions out of the courts.[107]

Key case

Evans v Information Commissioner [2012] UKUT 313 (Upper Tribunal)

Prince Charles has, for many years, written letters to ministers informing them of his views on various issues of public policy in his distinctive handwriting (the correspondence consequently became known as the 'black-spider memos'). Evans, a journalist investigating whether the Prince sought to influence ministerial decisions, issued a Freedom of Information request seeking access to this correspondence. In attempting to block the release of the correspondence the UK Government maintained that constitutional conventions protected Charles' activity.

→

---

[103] See C. Munro, *Studies in Constitutional Law* (Butterworths, 1999) 65–6.
[104] Ibid., 70.
[105] I. Jennings, *The Law and the Constitution* (5th edn, University of London Press, 1959) 136.
[106] HM Government, *The Ministerial Code* (Cabinet Office, 2018) 3.
[107] See *Attorney-General v Jonathan Cape* [1975] QB 752, 770.

→

The Upper Tribunal sought to unpack this claim, beginning with a useful explanation of the nature of constitutional conventions within the UK's system of government (at [66]-[67]):

'What are constitutional conventions? The first thing to stress is that they are not law. They are not enforced by courts. For example, there is a convention that an incumbent Prime Minister must resign if, after a general election, another party has won a majority in the House of Commons. But no-one can seek to enforce this in the courts – there is no law which says that such a Prime Minister must resign. Because it is a constitutional convention, however, a Prime Minister who broke it could be said to have acted unconstitutionally . . . The second thing to stress is that the major constitutional conventions are core elements in the United Kingdom's parliamentary democracy.'

The Upper Tribunal then carefully defined the operation of some of the conventions constraining the monarchy's role within the UK's constitutional order (at [87]):

'Our constitution reconciles monarchy and democracy through fundamental constitutional mechanisms under which (1) state power is exercised by and in the name of the monarch in accordance with the advice of ministers, and (2) the monarch is entitled to be consulted, to encourage, and to warn, but so long as ministers are in office their advice must be followed. In order to ensure that these fundamental mechanisms are not put in doubt, it is not until a long time has passed that details of how they operated in any particular instance can be revealed.'

Having laid this groundwork the Upper Tribunal proceeded to apply Jennings' test for determining the existence of a convention, focusing on the need for there to be a good reason for developing the protections surrounding the monarch's communications with ministers to the heir to the throne (at [106]):

'In our view . . . there is an overwhelming difficulty in suggesting that there is good reason for regarding advocacy correspondence by Prince Charles as falling within a constitutional convention. It is . . . the constitutional role of the monarch, not the heir to the throne, to encourage or warn government. Accordingly it is fundamental that advocacy by Prince Charles cannot have constitutional status. . . . [T]he communication of encouragement or warning to government has constitutional status only when done by the monarch.'

On this conclusion any suggestion that the information should be restricted to protect a constitutional convention collapsed, and the Upper Tribunal permitted the release of some of Prince Charles' advocacy correspondence. The Attorney-General subsequently vetoed the release of this correspondence under s. 53 FOIA 2000 on the grounds that it could damage the position of monarchy, sparking a fresh round of litigation which we examine in depth in Chapter 6 (p. 213).

(ii) Distinguishing conventions from 'practices'

There are a large number of political understandings which apply to constitutional actors in the UK which do not attain the status of constitutional conventions. Conventions can be distinguished from such inferior non-legal 'practices' by their normative force (the degree to which actors feel bound to follow their terms). Like conventions, practices are ordinarily followed by political actors, but they do not impose obligations and departing from them could not be characterised as 'unconstitutional'. Government should therefore be able to change or abandon a practice without having to engage in a constitutional debate, but in many instances the boundary between conventions and practices is tricky to identify:

Key debates
Gerry Adams resigns as MP

MPs are formally prevented, under House of Commons resolutions dating back to 1624, to resign their seat in the Commons. Under the Act of Settlement of 1701, however, MPs were prohibited from holding Crown Offices (this requirement does not apply to ministers). From the mid-eighteenth century onwards a practice therefore developed of 'utilising the appointment to certain Crown stewardships for the sole purpose of enabling Members to vacate their seats' (Select Committee to Inquire into Issue of Writ for Attercliffe Division, and Law and Practice in reference to Vacating of Seats in the House of Commons (1894) HC 278, 56). Two such stewardships, over the Chiltern Hundreds and the Manor of Northstead, nominally remain Crown Offices. For centuries MPs seeking to leave the Commons (other than standing down at a General Election) have been appointed to one of these offices.

In 2011, Gerry Adams, leader of Sinn Fein, wished to resign his seat (Belfast West) in order to pursue election to the Republic of Ireland's legislature. Sinn Fein, being an Irish Republican party, refuses to take the oath of allegiance to the Crown (much less accept Crown Offices). The Prime Minister informed Parliament that Adams had, by 'tradition', accepted the Stewardship of the Manor of Northstead (David Cameron, MP, HC Debs, vol. 522, col. 290 (26 January 2011)). Although Adams denied that he had accepted the appointment, he held the office from January to April 2011 (see John Bercow, MP, HC Debs, vol. 522, col. 404 (26 January 2011)).

This imbroglio shows how difficult it is to determine whether a political understanding is a constitutional convention or a mere practice. On the practice side of the argument, although what David Cameron describes as a 'tradition' was followed, Crown Office appointments seem to be an administrative mechanism without practical significance. Moreover, Cameron's being 'pleased that tradition has been maintained' does not imply that government ministers felt bound by the rule. In favour of Crown Office appointments being a convention, however, Cameron declares that they constitute 'the only way to retire from this House', affecting a clear constitutional issue (the composition of the Commons). The Crown-offices rule is backed up by House resolutions and even mentioned in statute as one way of being disqualified from being an MP (House of Commons Disqualification Act 1975, section 4). Together with the fact that ultimately Adams was appointed to this Office over his objections, it is arguably a constitutional convention that taking a Crown Office is the only means of resigning as an MP.

Jennings regarded practices as potential constitutional conventions. The difference, as Jennings emphasised, is that constitutional actors following a mere practice do not consider themselves to be bound by the rule.[108] The difference is illustrated by considering the length of time between elections. Although the maximum time limit between general elections is five years,[109] between 1945 and 2010 most parliamentary terms did not last longer than four years. Although during this period the electorate might have expected a general election to be called roughly every four years, Prime Ministers such as Gordon Brown and John Major did not call elections until the full five-year limit had expired. They were not bound by any putative practice of holding elections more regularly.

---

[108] I. Jennings, *The Law and the Constitution* (5th edn, University of London Press, 1959) 136.
[109] Parliament Act 1911, s. 7. See also the Fixed-Term Parliaments Act 2011, s. 1.

Practices can transform into conventions if their validity is respected by political actors over an extended period. For example, the Prime Minister has, since 1902, been a member of the elected House of Commons and not the House of Lords. This practice became increasingly important as the UK developed into a democracy. Nonetheless, as late as Neville Chamberlain's resignation as Prime Minister in 1940, many senior members of the Conservative Party argued that Lord Halifax, and not Winston Churchill, should take his place. Roy Jenkins wrote in his biography of Winston Churchill that, had Lord Halifax sought it, there was 'little doubt that he could have secured the appointment'.[110] Today, by contrast, with the legitimacy of the UK's system of government resting on democratic elections to the House of Commons, it would be politically unthinkable for the Prime Minister to not be an MP, demonstrating how this practice has hardened into a convention.

The significance that Jennings attributes to affected parties showing continued respect for a rule over a period of time before it can be recognised as a convention raises the issue of how long it takes for conventions to develop. If a rule is agreed between affected parties, it can attain the status of a convention instantaneously. An instantaneous convention is likely to develop when a rule reflects political consensus on a specific issue or is necessary to underpin a new constitutional development. For example, confusion surrounded whether a government was constitutionally obliged to gain House of Commons consent for combat deployments of the UK Armed Forces for many years, in light of contradictory precedents.[111] The Coalition Government ended this confusion by accepting that it would treat itself as being bound by a convention requiring a Commons vote on deployments 'except when there is an emergency and such action would not be appropriate'.[112] This convention has been followed ever since, indicating that the explicit acceptance by affected parties that a binding rule applies can be a more important element for the recognition of a convention than historic practice.

(iii) Constitutional conventions and the courts

As constitutional conventions are political and not legal rules, the courts cannot order political actors to follow them. A breach of a convention can accurately be described as unconstitutional but not illegal. Nonetheless, this seemingly insurmountable obstacle has not dissuaded some claimants from seeking judicial recognition of constitutional conventions as a means of enhancing the political pressure on governments. The Canadian case of ***Reference re Amendment of the Constitution of Canada***[113] provides the best example of the potential impact of judicial recognition that a convention has been breached. One of the constitutional safeguards established when Canada gained independence from the UK was an understanding that the constitution would not be amended without the consent of the provinces. When the Canadian Parliament pushed through constitutional reforms supported by only two of the ten Provinces, opponents began litigation on the basis that this understanding had the status of a constitutional convention. The court ruled that, even though this rule had no legal value, in spite of its importance and long standing, efforts by government to act without

---

[110] R. Jenkins, *Churchill: A Biography* (Macmillan, 2001) 584.

[111] See C. Murray and A. O'Donoghue, 'Towards Unilateralism? House of Commons Oversight of the Use of Force' (2016) 65 ICLQ 305, 320–25.

[112] G. Young, MP, HC Deb., vol. 525, col. 1066 (10 Mar 2011).

[113] *Reference re Amendment of the Constitution of Canada* [1981] 1 SCR 753.

such consent 'would be unconstitutional in the conventional sense'.[114] This ruling added political weight to the arguments of the opponents of the proposed constitution, and the government was obliged to renegotiate important provisions.

The UK courts have been slow to follow this Canadian example. When opponents of the UK's European Union membership sought judicial recognition that a constitutional convention existed that required that major constitutional changes receive the consent of the UK electorate through a referendum, the Court of Appeal refused to be drawn into this territory: 'We recognise that a political case can be made for Parliament requiring a referendum before enacting the necessary legislation but that it seems to us is a matter for political judgment and not for the courts'.[115] Likewise, in *Manuel* v *Attorney-General*,[116] Slade LJ refused to develop a rule of interpretation whereby statutes would be interpreted, where possible, in line with established constitutional conventions:

> This court would run counter to all principles of statutory interpretation if it were to purport to vary or supplement the terms of [an Act of Parliament] by reference to some supposed convention, which . . . is not incorporated in the body of the Statute.[117]

Despite these assertions, we cannot assume that constitutional conventions will never impact upon judicial decisions in UK courts, for in other cases judges have interpreted statutory powers generously in light of the operation of conventions. In *ex parte Hosenball*, for example, Lord Denning linked his broad interpretation of the Home Secretary's power to deport foreign nationals under the Immigration Act 1971 to the convention that, '[i]f a mistake is made, it is the Home Secretary who will be responsible to Parliament'.[118] The existence of relevant conventions has also, in particular cases, affected the development of common law rules. For example, the convention regarding ministerial accountability to Parliament for the actions of civil servants[119] influenced Lord Greene MR's decision to reject claims that certain civil servants had acted without lawful authority in *Carltona* v *Commissioners of Works*.[120] Conventions therefore occupy a singular position in the UK Constitution; they cannot supply the basis for a legal action, but their existence can affect the outcome of such an action. This awkward proposition requires some explanation, and is best illustrated by the following case:

Key case

Attorney-General v *Jonathan Cape* [1976] QB 752 (Court of Appeal, Civil Division)

Collective cabinet responsibility provides that cabinet meetings are confidential, allowing ministers to debate issues of public interest freely and then, even if they lose the argument in cabinet, follow the agreed government approach in public without loss of face. In the 1970s,

---

114 Ibid., 909.

115 *R (Southall)* v *Secretary of State for Foreign & Commonwealth Affairs* [2003] EWCA Civ 1002, [14].

116 *Manuel* v *Attorney General* [1983] ch. 77.

117 Ibid., 107.

118 *R* v *Secretary of State for Home Affairs, ex parte Hosenball* [1977] 1 WLR 766, 782.

119 For further information, see pp. 276–8.

120 *Carltona* v *Commissioners of Works* [1943] 2 All ER 560.

however, a new threat to this convention emerged: the publication of ministerial diaries. Some of the first diaries to be published by a former minister were those belonging to Richard Crossman. Crossman, a Cabinet minister in Harold Wilson's 1960s Labour Government, died in the early 1970s and his family sought to publish his diaries.

Many of Crossman's former colleagues were still active politicians who believed that their careers cold be harmed if details of their personal views in controversial cabinet discussions became public. The Attorney-General therefore sought an injunction preventing the diaries' publication. This legal challenge to publication, however, faced a serious problem. As collective cabinet responsibility is a constitutional convention, it cannot serve as the basis of a legal claim. As Lord Widgery CJ would state in his decision in the case (at 765), 'a true convention [is] . . . an obligation founded in conscience only'.

Despite this finding, Lord Widgery did accept (at 770) that collective cabinet responsibility 'is an established feature of the English form of government, and it follows that some matters leading up to a Cabinet decision may be regarded as confidential'. He was influenced by the convention's existence to develop the common law doctrine of breach of confidence so that it would, at least for a period of time, protect the confidentiality of Cabinet deliberations (at 770):

> To leak a Cabinet decision a day or so before it is officially announced is an accepted exercise in public relations, but to identify the Ministers who voted one way or another is objectionable because it undermines the doctrine of joint responsibility.

Although the Attorney-General secured an extension of the tort of breach of confidence in light of the constitutional convention, he nonetheless lost the case. The first volume of Crossman's diaries were over a decade old, and the Court of Appeal was unconvinced (at 771) that its publication 'would in any way inhibit free and open discussion in Cabinet hereafter'. Today, accounts by former ministers of their time in government are commonplace, but there remains a tension between them and the convention of collective cabinet responsibility. Whereas former ministers often wish to publish their diaries as quickly as possible (to cash in on their relevance to contemporary political debate), the convention is intended to protect the confidentiality of controversial discussions. Therefore, under the Ministerial Code (HM Government, *The Ministerial Code* (Cabinet Office, 2018) para. 8.10), which provides a non-statutory explanation of the convention, '[f]ormer Ministers intending to publish their memoirs are required to submit the draft manuscript in good time before publication to the Cabinet Secretary'.

Codifying constitutional conventions

(i) The risks associated with constitutional conventions

The extensive role played by constitutional conventions is one of the defining features of the UK Constitution. This reliance on moral or political obligations, however, means that the courts cannot require political actors to respect important rules. In the political debate as to whether an actor has broken a convention, the rule-breaker is potentially able to claim that the rule had not attained the status of a convention or that the obligation was unclear. Joseph Jaconelli does not regard this as a weakness of conventions, but as inevitable given their political nature:

> Constitutional conventions, like all conventions, are 'self-policing'. Furthermore, short-term personal interest often inclines those who occupy governmental positions in the direction of violating the standards that they set. Yet, ultimately each party political actor must conduct himself in the

realisation that he is helping to shape a social rule. As he acts, so too may those of the opposite political persuasion when they, in their turn, attain office.[121]

Conventions are not, moreover, unique to the UK Constitution. The need to keep law 'in touch with the growth of ideas'[122] applies to any system of government reliant upon long-standing constitutional arrangements, no matter how highly legalised. This is illustrated by the conventions underpinning the 'electoral college' system employed in US presidential elections:

Key debates
Conventions and the US Electoral College

Under Article II, Section 1, Clause 2 of the US Constitution the US President and Vice-President are not chosen on the basis of the overall number of votes received for particular candidates (the popular vote), but on the basis of the number of votes attained in the 'Electoral College'. Each of the 50 US States (and the District of Columbia) appoints a number of electors to the college based on the number of seats it has in both Houses of Congress (i.e. roughly proportionate to the size of its electorate).

The US Constitution does not oblige states to link the choice of Electors to the popular vote. Instead, all US States decided to link the selection of their electors to a popular vote from the 1820s onwards, despite the lack of constitutional obligation upon them to do so.[123] In the US presidential election in 2000, Al Gore won on the popular vote (scooping the largest number of votes for President when the votes of every elector in the US were added together) but George W. Bush received a majority in the Electoral College. During litigation arising out of this disputed result,[124] the Supreme Court (at 104) explained that:

> The individual citizen has no federal constitutional right to vote for electors for the President of the United States unless and until the state legislature chooses a statewide election as the means to implement its power to appoint members of the electoral college.

In other words, the US Constitution includes no legal obligations on the US States to tie their choice of electors to the popular vote. Instead, they are obliged to do so as a result of a constitutional convention. At law, the court continued (at 104), '[t]he State . . . after granting the franchise in the special context of Article II, can take back the power to appoint electors'.

(ii) Turning constitutional conventions into laws

The courts have rejected suggestions that constitutional conventions can ever 'harden' into common law rules which attract legal penalties if breached.[125] Nonetheless, it is possible for government to provide official definitions of conventions or for Parliament to enact statutes which operate in place of conventions. Such acts can be described, respectively, as the political and legal codification of conventions. Examples exist of conventions being

---

[121] J. Jaconelli, 'Do Constitutional Conventions Bind?' (2005) 64 CLJ 149, 176.

[122] I. Jennings, *The Law and the Constitution* (5th edn, University of London Press, 1959) 82.

[123] See J. Wilson, 'American Constitutional Conventions: the Judicially Unenforceable Rules that Combine with Judicial Doctrine and Public Opinion to Regulate Political Behavior' (1992) 40 *Buffalo LR* 645, 650).

[124] *George W. Bush* v *Al Gore* (2000) 531 US 98.

[125] See *Manuel* v *Attorney – General* [1983] Ch. 77, 107.

replaced by similar statutory rules which carry legal force. Often, such statutes are enacted in response to particularly egregious breaches of the existing convention. Prior to 1909, the unelected House of Lords had respected a convention whereby the elected House of Commons was solely responsible for the raising of taxation. However, that year the Liberal Government sought to introduce taxes on land which would have impacted heavily on large landowners. The House of Lords rejected the budget, a decision which was deeply unpopular with the majority of the electorate. With the standing of the House of Lords weakened as a result of this constitutional crisis the Liberal Government enacted legislation stripping the House of Lords of its legal ability to veto or delay 'Money Bills'.[126]

The Money Bills convention thereby became law. In legalising political rules, however, their inherent flexibility is lost. This development can be intended by constitutional actors. When the Liberal Democrats insisted on the enactment of the Fixed-Term Parliaments Act 2011 as a condition for entering the Coalition Government, their intention was to prevent the bigger coalition partner, the Conservatives, from using the convention that the monarch will always grant the Prime Minister's request for a dissolution of Parliament to call an election at a time of electoral advantage. In the long run, however, attempting to replace many of the existing constitutional conventions with legal rules would risk further involving the courts in what have hitherto been political disputes (with the risk that the judiciary will be politicised as a result). As one select committee noted with regard to the conventions applicable to Parliament, '[e]ven if an adjudicator could be found, the possibility of adjudication would introduce uncertainty and delay into the business of Parliament'.[127] These concerns were clearly at work in the devolution elements of the Supreme Court's decision in *Miller*:

Key case

R (Miller) v Secretary of State for Exiting the European Union [2017] UKSC 5; [2017] 2 WLR 583 (Supreme Court)

When the devolved legislatures in Scotland, Wales and Northern Ireland were created in 1998, the UK Government agreed to what became known as the Sewel Convention, under which it would 'proceed in accordance with the convention that the UK Parliament would not normally legislate with regard to devolved matters except with the agreement of the devolved legislature' (Office of the Deputy Prime Minister, *Devolution Memorandum of Understanding and Supplementary Agreements* (2001) Cm 5240, para. 13). In the aftermath of the Scottish Independence Referendum in 2014 Westminster legislated to enhance devolution to Scotland, including statutory recognition that 'the Parliament of the United Kingdom will not normally legislate with regard to devolved matters without the consent of the Scottish Parliament' in section 2 of the Scotland Act 2016 (inserting this new provision as section 28(8) of the Scotland Act 1998). The Scottish Government argued that, because Brexit would alter the competences of the devolved institutions (see below, pp. 367–75), this newly 'legalised' constitutional convention required the Scottish Parliament to consent to any Westminster legislation authorising the UK's withdrawal from the EU.

---

[126] Parliament Act 1911, s. 1.
[127] Joint Committee on Conventions, *Conventions of the UK Parliament* (2006) HL 265-I, [279].

The Supreme Court's majority first identified that the Sewel Convention had developed to cover a range of types of legislation (at [140]): 'devolved legislatures have passed legislative consent motions not only when the UK Parliament has legislated on matters which fall within the legislative competence of a devolved legislature, but also when the UK Parliament has enacted provisions that directly alter the legislative competence of a devolved legislature or amend the executive competence of devolved administrations'. The convention could therefore potentially cover any legislation triggering Brexit. In reaching this conclusion the majority judges, it should be noted, were not simply recognising that a convention existed, they were seemingly adopting a particularly broad interpretation of its scope.

The majority nonetheless refused to countenance any suggestion that the Scotland Act 2016 had translated the Sewel Convention into a legal rule (at [148]):

> [T]he UK Parliament is not seeking to convert the Sewel Convention into a rule which can be interpreted, let alone enforced, by the courts; rather, it is recognising the convention for what it is, namely a political convention, and is effectively declaring that it is a permanent feature of the relevant devolution settlement. That follows from the nature of the content, and is acknowledged by the words ("it is recognised" and "will not normally"), of the relevant subsection. We would have expected UK Parliament to have used other words if it were seeking to convert a convention into a legal rule justiciable by the courts.

The Court therefore maintained that as the rule was a convention it had no role in legally enforcing it; the consent of the devolved legislatures was not a legal prerequisite for the UK Parliament to authorise Brexit. Section 2 of the Scotland Act would therefore seem to add little by way of constitutional protection for the devolution arrangements. Indeed, it would seem to have little impact whatsoever; statutory codification did not, in this case, amount to legalisation. When the European Union (Notification of Withdrawal) Act 2017 was subsequently passed, the UK Government ultimately sidestepped even the constitutional convention, claiming that the triggering of Brexit did not, of itself, engage the Sewel Convention.

The UK's reliance on constitutional conventions does not keep its courts isolated from all matters of political controversy, it merely ensures that some overtly political disputes are resolved by political, not legal, processes. In an effort to keep such disputes out of the courts, some of the UK's most prominent constitutional conventions are 'codified' in non-statutory form. Codification, but not *legalisation,* has the advantage of clarifying these conventions' meaning but not transferring related disputes to the courts' jurisdiction. *The Ministerial Code,* for example, is a document which is not legally binding, but which contains authoritative statements explaining the operation of the conventions of collective cabinet responsibility[128] and individual ministerial responsibility[129] which govern ministerial conduct.[130]

Conclusion

Dicey described constitutional law as 'a sort of maze in which the wanderer is perplexed by unreality, by antiquarianism, and by conventionalism'.[131] Although Dicey has been

---

[128] For further information, see pp. 273–4.
[129] For further information, see pp. 436–7.
[130] HM Government, *The Ministerial Code* (Cabinet Office, 2018) 3 and 22.
[131] A. Dicey, *An Introduction to the Study of the Constitution* (8th edn, first published 1915, Liberty Fund, 1982) cxxix.

accused of making such statements to ensure that he would be regarded as a 'pioneering scholar',[132] perhaps his empathy towards the bewilderment of students studying the UK Constitution goes some way to explaining the continuing importance of his work a century after his death. The mixture of ancient prerogative powers, centuries of statutory material, case law and constitutional conventions, makes for a diverse set of constitutional sources and ensures that the UK Government's authority 'differs quite radically from governments in states with Constitutions whose powers are granted, and therefore limited by their constitution'.[133] Although this plethora of constitutional sources may appear impenetrable, it speaks to the UK's fortunes as a country since its creation. For Colin Munro, codified constitutions are 'rites of passage',[134] providing a break from the past in the aftermath of an event like a war (as with the German *Grundgesetz* of 1949, concluded after Nazi Germany's defeat in the Second World War) or revolution (like Egypt's Provisional Constitution of 2011, following the overthrow of President Mubarak during the 'Arab Spring'), or at the creation of new states (like the Constitution of Croatia, concluded when Croatia broke away from Yugoslavia in 1990). Instead, the UK Constitution is the product of centuries of reform of existing governance arrangements which have featured no 'radical break with the old constitutional order'.[135] To return to the building metaphor which introduced this chapter, the UK Constitution has been 'constantly added to, patched, and partially re-constructed, so that it has been renewed from century to century; but it has never been razed to the ground and rebuilt on new foundations'.[136]

Although the UK Constitution's development has been unique, the distinctiveness of the end result can be overstated. First, the creation of a codified constitution is unlikely to greatly clarify or further legitimate the UK's governance order. Between 1787 and 1788, some of the leading figures involved in the drafting of the US Constitution defended its terms in articles known as the *Federalist Papers*. These articles cautioned that, despite the new Constitution, 'a nation of philosophers is as little to be expected as the philosophical race of kings wished for by Plato'.[137] In all countries with codified constitutions experts are still required to articulate constitutional claims. Second, constitutional conventions are likely to develop over time in any long-standing constitutional regime. The UK Constitution is distinct, not because conventions exist, but because so many are operative. Third, particularly in countries with constitutions which are difficult to amend, some statutes which are distinct from 'the Constitution' are likely to assume constitutional significance. For Mark Tushnet 'the "efficient" constitution of the United States . . . can be found in various written forms, but the document called the US Constitution is only one, and not the most important, of them'.[138] The UK's Constitution, in function if not in form, therefore differs little from comparable national constitutions; the domestic sources we have studied construct and delimit exercises of official power. They do not, however, operate in isolation and in the next chapter we examine external contributions to the UK's Constitution.

---

[132] A. Simpson, *Human Rights and the End of Empire: Britain and the Genesis of the European Convention* (OUP, 2001) 33.

[133] D. Oliver, *Constitutional Reform in the United Kingdom* (OUP, 2003) 6.

[134] C. Munro, *Studies in Constitutional Law* (Butterworths, 1999) 4.

[135] N. Barber, 'Against a Written Constitution' [2008] PL 11, 11.

[136] I. Jennings, *The Law and the Constitution* (5th edn, University of London Press, 1959) 8.

[137] J. Madison, *The Federalist,* No. 49 (2 February 1788). Available at: www.constitution.org/fed/federa49 .htm.

[138] M. Tushnet, *The Constitution of the United States of America* (Hart, 2009) 1.

Practice questions

1. *'Unwritten constitutions can be just as good as written ones, and in some respects may be better, because they can be updated more easily. But they do need to be nurtured and valued.'*

   (R. Hazell, 'Constitutional Reform in the United Kingdom: Past, Present and Future' in C. Morris, J. Boston and P. Butler, *Reconstituting the Constitution* (Springer, 2011) 83, 95)

   Has the constitutionally significant legislation enacted by governments in office since 1997 succeeded in 'nurturing' the UK's Constitution?

2. *'With . . . treaties we are modifying the prerogative [under the provisions of the Constitutional Reform and Governance Act 2010]; with the Civil Service we are replacing the prerogative basis of the Civil Service with an entirely statutory basis.'*

   (Joint Committee, *The Draft Constitutional Renewal Bill: Evidence* (2008) HC 551-II, 323 (Jack Straw, MP))

   Explain the interaction of statutory and prerogative powers where they appear to apply to similar subject matter in light of this statement.

3. *'It would be virtually impossible to codify all the present conventions of the British constitution, especially those which relate to political parties, or the Cabinet, even if it could be decided which of them still exist or ought to be revived.'*

   (J. Baker, 'Our Unwritten Constitution' (2010) 167 *Proceedings of the British Academy* 91, 111)

   Evaluate whether it would be desirable and practicable to codify the UK's constitutional conventions.

Further reading

In this chapter, we have attempted to trace the sources of the UK's uncodified constitution. This may at times seem a frustrating task (especially when the UK is compared to those countries which maintain a codified constitution) but for Nicholas Barber (**N. Barber, 'Against a Written Constitution'** [2008] *Public Law* 11–18) the effort is worthwhile. Barber sets out a brief and accessible case as to why the UK's current constitutional arrangements have produced a stable system of government and why any effort at codification has the potential to destabilise these arrangements. One of the disadvantages of these arrangements is that a considerable amount of 'constitutional clutter' remains within the UK system, with the Crown Prerogative providing perhaps the best example of such clutter. Colin Munro (**C. Munro, *Studies in Constitutional Law*** (Butterworths, 1999) 255–91) delivers a punchy (if now dated) summary of the role played by the prerogative within the constitution.

Parliament is the engine room of the UK's Constitution, and Susanna Kalitowski (**S. Kalitowski, 'Rubber Stamp or Cockpit? The Impact of Parliament on Government Legislation'** (2008) 61 *Parliamentary Affairs* 694–708) provides an invaluable insight into not only the law-making process, but also the potential for delegated legislation to undermine the extended procedure often involved in making Acts of Parliament. The prominence of Parliament (and its ability to make new constitutionally significant legislation on a simple majority vote) is but one feature, however, which leads commentators to describe the UK's Constitution as being 'political' in nature. The other key feature is the prominence of constitutional conventions. Joseph Jaconelli's research (**J. Jaconelli, 'Do Constitutional Conventions Bind?'** (2005) 64 *Cambridge Law Journal* 149–76) focuses on the long-established prominence these political rules within the UK's Constitution, whilst Lord Wilson (**R. Wilson, 'The Robustness of Conventions in a Time of Modernisation'** [2004] *Public Law* 407–420) helps the reader to understand their ongoing significance amid the increasing legalisation of the constitution.

Chapter 3
The United Kingdom Constitution and international legal orders

'In the past . . . we might give way to insular feelings of superiority over foreign breeds . . . We [now] have to consider the state of the world as it is today and will be tomorrow and not in outdated terms of a vanished past.'

Harold Macmillan, Britain, the Commonwealth and Europe (September 1962).

Chapter outline

The UK's Constitution is not an island, insulated from external influences. In considering the sources of constitutional law, we cannot ignore the influence of public international law and international legal orders to which the UK belongs. This chapter therefore examines the relationship between the UK's legal systems, public international law in general, and specific treaties which are highly significant for the UK's legal systems, such as the European Convention of Human Rights (ECHR) and the treaties governing the operation and organisation of the European Union (EU).

Introduction: External sources of constitutional law?

Until relatively recently in the UK's constitutional history, commentators devoted little time to international sources for domestic constitutional rules. This insularity is painfully evident in the first part of the quote by then Prime Minister, Harold Macmillan, which opens this chapter. Domestic law was accepted as the source of the UK's governance structures and of the rules governing the relationship between these institutions and the individuals subject to them, whereas international law governed the relationship between sovereign states. This is not to say that international law did not, historically, have a profound impact upon life in the UK. The UK entered the First World War in 1914, for example, on the pretext of upholding a treaty affirming Belgium's neutrality, breached by Germany's invasion.[1] Nonetheless, as writers pointed out at the time, 'the mere fact of England being at war with a foreign country does not place English territory in a state of war'.[2]

---

[1] Treaty of London 1839, Art. VII. See A. Oakes and R. Mowat, 'The Great European Treaties of the Nineteenth Century' (OUP, 1918) p. 141.

[2] T. Baty and J. Morgan, *War: Its Conduct and Legal Results* (John Murray, 1915) pp. 7–8.

> ## Thinking Point . . .
>
> As the works of Bagehot and Dicey attest, until the conclusion of the First World War most constitutional commentators continued to refer to England, as opposed to the UK, when discussing the country's constitution. Such writings give credence to the view that, for much of its history, the UK itself has been regarded as an imperial project (a 'Greater England'). See I. Ward, *The English Constitution: Myths and Realities* (Hart, 2004) pp. 142–5.

Instead, to enable it to prosecute the war, the UK Government had to persuade Parliament to pass acts such as the Defence of the Realm Acts 1914 and 1915, the Military Service Acts 1916–18 and the Trading with the Enemy Act 1914. New legal obligations could only be imposed within the UK's legal systems by domestic legislation, and under the doctrine of dualism (which we will cover in detail below), if the UK Government concludes an international agreement requiring changes to domestic legal obligations, it will have to persuade Parliament to enact legislation to that effect.

The treatment of domestic and international law as separate has had a profound impact upon constitutional thought in the UK, with Thomas lamenting that 'British lawyers have long been educated according to the orthodoxy that international law norms *per se* play a minimal role in resolving domestic litigation'.[3] But this supposedly neat divide was illusory. For hundreds of years, the domestic courts have had to address cases regarding the application of international law within domestic legal systems, from assessing the protections available to diplomats[4] to resolving questions of jurisdiction regarding collisions at sea.[5] After the Second World War, as states became increasingly interconnected and even interdependent, the domestic impact of international law increased to such a degree that, by the mid-1970s, Sir Leslie Scarman (not yet elevated to the House of Lords, but already one of the UK's most prominent judges) felt able to declare that 'international affairs are no longer only the business of sovereign states'.[6] As evidence to support this contention, he pointed to the UK's signing and ratifying regional treaties alongside other states in Europe, including the European Convention on Human Rights (ECHR) and the treaties which established (and have since expanded) the supra-national organisation now known as the European Union (EU). In 2007, Gordon Brown, newly appointed as Prime Minister, was eager to set out his constitutional vision. He did so in a policy document (a 'Green Paper'), which outlined a central role for international instruments in the UK's existing constitutional settlement:

> The post-war settlement also saw the growth in international organisations and international conceptions of rights. The establishment of the United Nations in 1945 led to the Universal Declaration of Human Rights (1948), which in turn inspired two major UN human rights treaties, the International Covenant on Civil and Political Rights and the International Covenant on Economic, Social and Cultural Rights (both 1966); the UK is party to each. The Treaty of London (1949) created the Council of Europe, which now has 47 member states and works to promote democracy, human rights and the rule of law. Under its auspices, the European Convention on Human Rights (1950) was drafted principally by British lawyers. And in 1973, the UK joined

---

[3] K. Thomas, 'The Changing Status of International Law in English Domestic Law' (2006) 53 NILR 371, 372.

[4] *Triquet* v *Bath* (1764) 97 ER 936.

[5] *R* v *Keyn* (1876) 2 Ex D 63.

[6] L. Scarman, *English Law – The New Dimension* (Steven & Sons, 1974) p. 10.

the European Economic Community (now the European Union) and became a part of a multinational political structure.[7]

In this chapter we will outline the importance of international law as a source of the rights and duties of individuals within the UK's Constitution. The chapter will first address the impact of general rules of international law upon the UK's Constitution. It will than tackle the fraught issue of the UK's membership of the EU and the role that EU law will continue to play in the UK's legal systems until Brexit (the UK's withdrawal from the EU, demanded by the majority of voters in a nationwide referendum in June 2016) takes effect. This chapter does not stand alone; later chapters will expand upon its themes, with Chapter 5 on parliamentary sovereignty examining the issue of clashes between rules produced by the domestic and international legal orders within the UK Constitution, and Chapters 20 and 21 evaluating the UK's relationship with the ECHR.

Public international law

Key issues

- Domestic legal systems have to explain their relationship with international law and when international law can have legal effects before domestic courts. The interrelationship between domestic and international law can be explained in terms of the theories of monism and dualism.

- International treaties (agreements concluded between states or groups of states) do not ordinarily have effects within the UK's domestic legal systems unless they are incorporated into domestic law by Act of Parliament.

- Customary international law, by contrast, can be applied by the courts within the domestic legal systems. Some rules of customary international law are so fundamental that no state can lawfully depart from them. These are known as *jus cogens* norms.

Rival approaches to international law within domestic legal systems

Constitutions establish how their domestic institutions can reach agreements with other states or international bodies and outline how their domestic legal orders treat international law. These rules amount to 'filters', of varying strengths, which condition the application of international law within domestic legal systems.[8] At one end of this spectrum is monism, which in its pure form recognises no distinction between national and international law, enabling international law to affect rights and obligations within domestic legal systems. At the other end of the spectrum is dualism, which filters international law out of the domestic legal order by maintaining that international and domestic law are separate. From the outset, it is important to recognise that no state's constitutional arrangements fully reflect these pure approaches to international law. Nonetheless, these distinctions provide a start point from which to evaluate how particular states treat clashes between international and domestic law:

---

[7] HM Government, *The Governance of Britain* (TSO, 2007) Cm. 7170, 13–14.
[8] D. Feldman, 'The Internationalization of Public Law and its Impact on the United Kingdom' in J. Jowell and D. Oliver (eds), *The Changing Constitution* (7th edn, OUP, 2011) 132, 136.

[T]he difference in response to a clash of international law and domestic law in various domestic courts is substantially conditioned by whether the country concerned is monist or dualist. I say 'substantially' conditioned, because in reality there is usually little explanation or discussion of these large jurisprudential matters in the domestic court hearing. The response of the court to the problem is often instinctive rather than explicitly predicated.[9]

Labelling a legal system as monist or dualist can produce an 'instinctive', often not fully rationalised, approach to international law by domestic courts.

(i) Monism

The Netherlands and Germany are commonly identified as adopting a monist approach, with their constitutions recognising that international law is effective within their legal systems. In such systems, the internalisation of international law within the domestic legal order is a mark of a state's commitment to the principles underpinning international law, allowing them to constrain domestic law. Monist interpretations of international law have emphasised that this approach extends international law's protections to individuals. This became increasingly important as international law developed after the Second World War to impose constraints on the way states treated individuals. Writing shortly after the UN adopted the Universal Declaration of Human Rights[10] Hersch Lauterpacht believed that individuals, as much as states, would become the subjects of international law, which had hitherto been characterised by an 'insistence on the respect owed by one sovereign State to another'.[11]

Although the Dutch and German Constitutions are both broadly monist, they nonetheless treat international law differently within their domestic hierarchies of legal norms. In the Netherlands, Article 66 of the Constitution provides that treaty provisions have supremacy over both prior and subsequent national law. This powerful position of international law is, however, balanced by the Dutch legislature's extensive control over the process of treaty approval. The Dutch legislature must approve treaties before the Dutch Government is able to ratify them. This safeguard limits the risk of the Netherlands accepting obligations under treaties which would conflict with domestic constitutional law. Article 25 of the German *Grundgesetz* (the 'Basic Law', or Constitution) provides that rules of customary international law are part of the country's federal law which takes precedence over other domestic law. By contrast, under Article 59 of the Basic Law, whilst treaties concluded by Germany have a status equal to Federal statutes, they will have no effect within the German legal system if they are contrary to the Basic Law's provisions.

Thinking Point . . .

The term 'treaty' covers any 'international agreement concluded between States in written form and governed by international law' (Vienna Convention on the Law of Treaties (1969) 1155 UNTS 331, Article 2(1)(a)). It can be applied to any international legal instrument fitting this definition, even if that instrument describes itself as an 'agreement', 'convention', 'protocol', 'covenant', etc.

---

[9] R. Higgins, *Problems and Process: International Law and How We Use It* (OUP, 1994) p. 206.
[10] UN General Assembly Resolution 217 A (III), UN Doc. A/810 (10 December 1948).
[11] H. Lauterpacht, *International Law and Human Rights* (London: Stevens, 1950) p. 70.

(ii) Dualism

Dualism separates international and domestic legal orders. In its purest form dualism prevents rules of international law from having any effect within domestic law unless they have been incorporated into the domestic order. The UK is usually cited as an example of a dualist legal order, although this epithet rather simplifies its constitutional arrangements. As Feldman explains, dualist systems can be justified for both principled and pragmatic reasons:

> The principled reason is the desire to uphold constitutional guarantees, including the Rule of Law, and keep in the hands of the nations the democratic control of and accountability for national law and policy, in order to maintain the legitimacy of politics and public law in the state. The pragmatic reason is that international obligations may be contrary to the national interest and may derail important national objectives.[12]

As we have seen, in monist states domestic constitutional protections and democratic control over law making are also highly prized, but they are secured by mechanisms such as legislative and judicial oversight of treaty provisions. Historically, any such protections were lacking within the UK Constitution. The executive was free to conclude international agreements as it chose because the management of foreign policy was part of the Royal Prerogative. Although a constitutional convention known as the Ponsonby Rule[13] provided that Parliament had to be informed that a treaty had been concluded and given 21 days in which to debate its substance before the executive ratified it, the executive's control of Parliamentary procedure meant that few treaties were even subjected to a vote. Given the lack of safeguards regarding the adoption of treaties, it is not surprising that the courts maintained the dualist idea that such international agreements should not have any effect within the UK's domestic legal systems. As Lord Atkin asserted in a Privy Council decision relating to the effect of international law within the then British Empire:

> It will be essential to keep in mind the distinction between (1.) the formation, and (2.) the performance, of the obligations constituted by a treaty, using that word as comprising any agreement between two or more sovereign States. Within the British Empire there is a well-established rule that the making of a treaty is an executive act, while the performance of its obligations, if they entail alteration of the existing domestic law, requires legislative action. Unlike some other countries, the stipulations of a treaty duly ratified do not within the Empire, by virtue of the treaty alone, have the force of law. If the national executive, the government of the day, decide to incur the obligations of a treaty which involve alteration of law they have to run the risk of obtaining the assent of Parliament to the necessary statute or statutes.[14]

As a corollary of treaties not having an effect in UK law without further legislation, the courts historically refused to consider challenges to the validity of treaties concluded by the UK Government.[15] In decision in *ex parte Rees-Mogg*, prominent Euro-sceptic Lord Rees-Mogg initiated a judicial review of the UK's signing of the Treaty of the European Union. The Court, however, found that there was 'insufficient ground to hold that Parliament has by implication curtailed or fettered the Crown's prerogative to alter or add to

---

[12] D. Feldman, 'The Internationalization of Public Law and its Impact on the United Kingdom' in J. Jowell and D. Oliver (eds), *The Changing Constitution* (7th edn, OUP, 2007) 132, 137–8.

[13] See Arthur Ponsonby, MP, HC Deb., vol. 171, cols 2001–2004 (1 April 1924).

[14] *Attorney-General for Canada* v *Attorney-General for Ontario* [1937] AC 326, 347.

[15] *Council of Civil Service Unions* v *Minister for the Civil Service* [1985] AC 374, 418 (Lord Roskill).

the [competences of the EU]'.[16] When it came to considering Brexit the Supreme Court gave this question more thought, but *ex parte Rees Mogg* illustrates how recently they offered no meaningful constraint upon treaty making.[17]

The executive's control over treaty making, however, was only part of the reason for the prevalence of dualism amongst common law legal systems. Lord Scarman claimed that a more pervasive factor was an attitude of common law superiority which he regarded as a hangover from the era of the British Empire:

> [D]espite its world-wide expansion, [the common law] learnt surprisingly little from other legal systems. Paradoxically, now that its days of expansion are over, it is more open to foreign influence and challenge than when it strode the world as part of the British colossus: perhaps, in the shadow of that colossus, no other system had a chance.[18]

If dualism indeed rests on such shaky foundations then the judiciary could potentially reverse this long-held position regarding international law. Lord Scarman was one of the first judges to recognise that the UK's traditional constitutional theory faced a profound 'challenge from overseas' in the later part of the twentieth century.[19] If the principled basis for dualism is to prevent the executive from creating obligations binding upon individuals in the UK without the legislature's assent, then requiring Parliament to assent to treaties, as monist states do, would facilitate a shift in doctrine. The Constitutional Reform and Governance Act 2010, which established a legal basis for parliamentary oversight of the Crown's treaty-making power, is therefore a significant development.[20] This legislation, however, does not require parliamentary debate and approval of every treaty. It merely requires that, for a treaty to be ratified, the House of Commons must not reject it within 21 days of its being presented to Parliament.[21] A rejection in the House of Lords is essentially treated as advisory.[22] Even after a Commons rejection, the legislation gives ministers a further opportunity to explain the government's reasons for supporting ratification (which starts the 21 day countdown again).[23] This rather convoluted process is summarised in Figure 3.1.

Under the Act, this process of Commons rejection followed by Government re-explanation can continue indefinitely. However, as commentators have pointed out, these provisions do not require ministers to make allowance in parliamentary schedules for a debate.[24] Nor do they require Parliament to take positive steps to approve every treaty that the UK Government agrees (a simple failure to reject suffices). Parliament now exercises oversight of treaty making in much the same way it oversees statutory instruments approved under the 'negative' approval process (see Chapter 2[25]). It remains to be seen whether the courts could

---

[16] *R v Secretary of State for Foreign and Commonwealth Affairs, ex parte Rees-Mogg* [1994] QB 552, 567 (Lloyd LJ).

[17] *R (Miller) v Secretary of State for Exiting the European Union* [2017] UKSC 5; [2017] 2 WLR 583, [85]–[89] (Lord Neuberger).

[18] L. Scarman, *English Law – The New Dimension* (Steven & Sons, 1974) p. 10.

[19] Ibid., p. 9.

[20] J. Barrett, 'The United Kingdom and Parliamentary Scrutiny of Treaties: recent reforms' (2011) 60 ICLQ 225, 236.

[21] Constitutional Reform and Governance Act 2010, s. 20(1).

[22] Ibid., s. 20(8).

[23] Ibid., s. 20(4).

[24] See Joint Committee, *Joint Committee on the Draft Constitutional Renewal Bill: Evidence* (2008) HC 551–II, 331 (Lord Norton of Louth).

[25] See pp. 31–2.

accept that unincorporated treaties, concluded after the 2010 Act entered force, could have some domestic legal status in light of Parliament's strengthened oversight function.

Thinking Point . . .

Prior to these reforms, the Ponsonby Rule operated as a constitutional convention, meaning that the Constitutional Reform and Governance Act 2010, Part 2, provides a contemporary example of a statute 'legalising' a convention (see Chapter 2, pp. 49–51). The operation of these statutory provisions in some respects emulates the workings of the previous convention, which has now been 'superseded and formalised'. See *R (Miller)* v *Secretary of State for Exiting the European Union* [2017] UKSC 5; [2017] 2 WLR 583, [58] (Lord Neuberger).

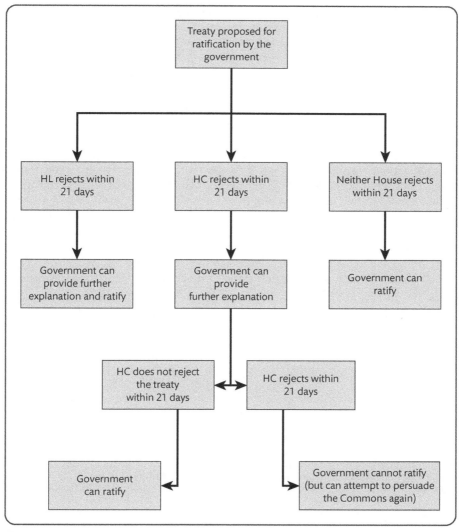

Figure 3.1 Process of treaty approval

The legal effect of treaties within the United Kingdom Constitution

(i) 'Incorporated' treaties

Treaties are binding international agreements, concluded between two or more states, which are governed by rules of international law.[26] They can be limited in scope, requiring the parties to undertake a 'single enterprise' (for example, a treaty ending a war), or they can be 'law-making', setting out rules governing future conduct by states party to the treaty, and even individuals within their jurisdiction.[27] States enter treaties with each other on the basis that, by agreeing to act in a particular way, they will secure advantages for themselves and their citizens. Feldman summarises the trade-off that states make:

> States surrender part of their autonomy in exchange for the benefits of co-operation, allowing them to pursue objectives unattainable without coordination. International organizations can help to maintain peace, bolster social or economic stability, and foster free trade and open markets. At the same time, co-operation has significant costs for states. They must take account of internationally agreed objectives and values in their internal decision-making. Sometimes they must subordinate their own interests to those of other states.[28]

When the UK Government agrees to a treaty this, of itself, creates no rights or obligations within the UK's legal systems. International and domestic law are theoretically sealed compartments; for a treaty to take effect within the domestic legal structure it is necessary for Parliament to legislate to incorporate its provisions into domestic law.

Even after a treaty has been 'statutorily incorporated', the courts have maintained a dualist approach to such treaties, declaring that it is not the treaty but the statute which creates obligations within domestic law. This approach to treaties, ensuring the primacy of statutes, rests heavily on A. V. Dicey's writings. When Dicey set out his view of Parliament as a sovereign body, free from constraint in its law making, he explicitly rejected assertions that statutes 'are invalid if they are opposed to the principles of morality or to the doctrines of international law'.[29] The case of *Lyons*[30] concerned whether Article 6 ECHR's standard of a fair hearing applied in the law of England and Wales even before Human Rights Act (HRA) 1998 entered force bringing elements of the ECHR into UK law. Dismissing these claims, Lord Hoffmann was even reluctant to describe the HRA as an incorporating statute:

> [I]t is firmly established that international treaties do not form part of English law and that English courts have no jurisdiction to interpret or apply them . . . Parliament may pass a law which mirrors the terms of the treaty and in this sense incorporates the treaty into English law. But even then, the metaphor of incorporation may be misleading. It is not the treaty but the statute which forms part of English law.[31]

---

[26] Vienna Convention on the Law of Treaties (1969) 1155 UNTS 331.

[27] See I. Brownlie, *Principles of Public International Law* (OUP, 2008) pp. 12–13.

[28] D. Feldman, 'The Internationalization of Public Law and its Impact on the United Kingdom' in J. Jowell and D. Oliver (eds), *The Changing Constitution* (7th edn, OUP, 2007) pp. 132, 132–3.

[29] A. Dicey, *An Introduction to the Study of the Constitution* (8th edn, first published 1915, Liberty Fund, 1982) p. 19.

[30] *R v Lyons* [2002] UKHL 44; [2003] 1 AC 976.

[31] Ibid., [27].

Lord Hoffmann's statement illustrates the commitment of some judges to segregating the domestic legal systems from international legal orders.

(ii) 'Unincorporated' treaties: presumption against enforceability

If the practical effect of Dicey's dualist approach to international law was 'to bequeath . . . a legal culture of resistance to the use of international law before domestic courts',[32] this applies particularly to claims reliant upon unincorporated treaties. In *Lyons,* for example, the House of Lords ultimately found that the ECHR, unincorporated at the time of Lyons' conviction, could not influence the application of clear statutory rules. For Lord Hoffmann, the foundations of such claims 'rest upon sand'.[33] Through much of the twentieth century the courts, reliant upon Dicey, displayed considerable reluctance to attribute any legal effect to unincorporated treaties. For example, the claimant in *Cheney* argued that the UK's arsenal of nuclear weapons breached the Geneva Conventions, and that it was therefore illegal for the Government to levy taxes to pay for such weapons. The Geneva Conventions were treaties which the UK had signed and ratified, but the relevant provisions had not been incorporated into domestic law. Ungoed-Thomas J quickly dismissed this argument:

> What the statute itself enacts cannot be unlawful, because what the statute says and provides is itself the law, and the highest form of law that is known to this country. It is the law which prevails over every other form of law, and it is not for the court to say that a parliamentary enactment, the highest law in this country, is illegal.[34]

Even where public officials claim to be acting in accordance with the requirements of unincorporated international treaties, the courts have been reluctant to hold them to account on the basis of such claims. In *Corner House Research,* the Director of the Serious Fraud Office had claimed that his actions, in stopping an investigation into an arms deal, were in line with the provisions of an unincorporated treaty, the OECD Convention on Bribery.[35] Lord Bingham, although finding it unnecessary to determine this issue in the case, did conclude that it would be 'unfortunate if decision-makers were to be deterred from seeking to give effect to what they understand to be the international obligations of the UK by fear that their decisions might be held to be vitiated by an incorrect understanding'.[36] Under this approach to unincorporated treaties:

> [I]f domestic legislation clearly conflicts with a treaty obligation which has not been statutorily incorporated into domestic law, the courts are constitutionally bound to give effect to the domestic provision, even though this involves a breach of the state's obligations in international law.[37]

---

[32] M. Hunt, *Using Human Rights Law in English Courts* (Hart, 1997) p. 11.

[33] *R v Lyons* [2002] UKHL 44; [2003] 1 AC 976, [39].

[34] *Cheney v Conn* [1968] 1 WLR 242, 247.

[35] OECD, Convention on Combating Bribery of Foreign Public Officials in International Business Transactions (17 December 1997) 37 ILM 1.

[36] *R (Corner House Research) v Serious Fraud Office* [2008] UKHL 60; [2009] 1 AC 756, [44].

[37] M. Hunt, *Using Human Rights Law in English Courts* (Hart, 1997) p. 7.

To illustrate the impact of this approach, consider the *CND* case:

Key case

R (Campaign for Nuclear Disarmament) v Prime Minister [2002] EWHC 2777 (Admin) (High Court, Administrative Division)

Simon Brown LJ noted (at [1]) that this judicial review was 'nothing if not topical'. It followed the United Nations Security Council's issuing of Resolution 1441, which was billed as a 'final opportunity' for Saddam Hussein's regime to disarm weapons of mass destruction it was then believed to possess. Although the Resolution warned Iraq of serious consequences if it failed to comply, the Campaign for Nuclear Disarmament brought an action seeking that the courts issue an advisory declaration that the Resolution was not a sufficient basis for lawful military action under international law. Simon Brown LJ refused to countenance this suggestion (at [36]):

> Should the court declare the meaning of an international instrument operating purely on the plane of international law? In my judgment the answer is plainly no. All of the cases relied upon by the applicants in which the court has pronounced upon some issue of international law are cases where it has been necessary to do so in order to determine rights and obligations under domestic law.

Richards J (at [61]) further explained the 'basic rule' regarding the relationship between treaties and domestic law:

> The basic rule is that international treaties do not form part of domestic law and that the national courts have no jurisdiction to interpret or apply them . . . The same basic rule must in my view apply to an instrument such as Resolution 1441 which has been made under an international treaty and has been negotiated in the same way as a treaty.

But he proceeded to acknowledge (at [61]) that the basic rule was not all encompassing, and there were situations when the domestic courts would have to interpret rules of international legal instruments:

> By way of exception to the basic rule, situations arise where the national courts have to adjudicate upon the interpretation of international treaties e.g. in determining private rights and obligations under domestic law and/or where statute requires decisions to be taken in accordance with an international treaty; and in human rights cases there may be a wider exception.

(iii) 'Unincorporated' treaties: exceptions to the standard presumption

Richards J's acknowledgement in *CND* that even unincorporated treaties could have an impact in domestic law shows that, for the UK courts, dualism's exclusion of international law is a presumption and not a fixed rule. His judgment points towards circumstances in which the presumption can be set aside, which we shall consider in turn.

A. Where Private Parties assume obligations under treaties

In *Occidental Exploration & Production Co.* the Court of Appeal went so far as to accept that an unincorporated treaty could, in particular circumstances, affect the interests of private parties in a dispute in the English courts. The case involved a commercial arbitration, conducted on the basis of rules contained within a Bilateral Investment Treaty (an agreement between two states to implement specific rules regarding cross-border investments) between the United States and Ecuador. The Court concluded that, in the context of assessing an arbitration that had been entered with the consent of both parties, it did have the jurisdiction to consider the treaty, as it was simply 'being asked to interpret [the treaty's] scope in order to give effect to the rights and duties contained in the agreement to arbitrate. That in our view satisfies . . . the criterion for jurisdiction identified in the CND case'.[38]

B. Where a statute is enacted in light of the UK's international obligations

Even Dicey accepted that statutes relating to the subject matter of the UK's international obligations would be presumed by the courts, in the case of any ambiguity, to conform to the requirements of those instruments.[39] Thus Lord Diplock, deciding the case of *Garland*, considered it a general principle of constitutional law that:

> [T]he words of a statute passed after the Treaty has been signed and dealing with the subject matter of the international obligation of the United Kingdom, are to be construed, if they are reasonably capable of bearing such a meaning, as intended to carry out the obligation, and not to be inconsistent with it.[40]

Garland involved a dispute over benefits for retired employees of a subsidiary of British Railways. Retired female employees were not entitled to the same benefits as retired male employees, and challenged this discrimination on the basis of the Sex Discrimination Act 1975. The terms of this Act, however, did not provide a clear basis for claims involving retirement schemes. Lord Diplock, invoking the above rule of construction, determined that the 1975 Act had to be read in line with the UK's EEC Treaty obligations, permitting the claimants to succeed.

This exception to the general rule that international law does not, of itself, have a domestic effect has in recent decades reduced the UK courts' reluctance to engage with international law. Moreover, the late-twentieth century marked a new departure for the UK's legal systems. Parliament, quite simply, began enacting an unprecedented volume of legislation which drew upon rules of international law into domestic law. Lord Bingham, writing extra-judicially, noted some areas in which international law impacted upon the UK's legal systems:

> [T]hey are aviation law, commercial and intellectual property law, criminal law, employment and industrial relations law, environmental law, European treaties, family and child law, human rights law, immigration and asylum law, immunities and privileges, international organizations, jurisdiction, law of the sea, treaties and finally, warfare and weapons law. In recent years the British courts have ruled on questions arising in most of these areas.[41]

In interpreting this increasingly broad range of statutes enacted in light of the UK's international obligations, the courts must temper the common law's historic dualism by considering the underlying international instruments. The step change in international

---

[38] *Ecuador* v *Occidental Exploration & Production Co.* [2005] EWCA Civ 1116; [2006] 2 WLR 70, [46].
[39] A. Dicey, *An Introduction to the Study of the Constitution* (8th edn, first published 1915, Liberty Fund, 1982) pp. 19–20.
[40] *Garland* v *British Rail Engineering Ltd* [1983] 2 AC 751, 771.
[41] T. Bingham, *The Rule of Law* (Allen Lane, 2010) p. 119.

law's prominence within the UK's domestic legal systems may well have profound consequences for dualism's old orthodoxy. As Singh has pointed out, a general presumption seems to be developing which requires that domestic legal rules, including those of common law,[42] should ordinarily be interpreted in light of the UK's international obligations even if they are not statutorily incorporated.[43]

C. Where international obligations contextualise rights and obligations

Some senior judges have bridled against orthodox dualism's restrictive approach to unincorporated treaties, especially where human rights are at issue. In *SG* Lord Kerr mouthed the ancient pieties that where unincorporated agreements are at issue it is 'open to domestic courts to refuse to allow such treaties to have any influence'.[44] But he proceeded to explain why, with regard to human rights treaties, he would regard it as equally possible that the courts would find the international instrument highly influential:

> [W]here the claimed right is directly relevant to the domestic issue to be decided, then recourse to the standards that the international instrument exemplifies is not only legitimate, it is required. How, otherwise, are we to acquire a true understanding of the proper contours and content of the right under discussion? This is not applying an unincorporated international treaty directly to domestic law. It is merely allowing directly relevant standards to infuse our thinking about what the content of the domestic right should be.[45]

In other words, even unincorporated international treaties relating to rights provide a source of inspiration that domestic judges can draw upon in shaping how they approach cases before them. Lord Kerr's approach could be interpreted as an assault on Parliament's ability to choose what international obligations to incorporate into domestic law.[46] But an open discussion of sources of judicial thinking is undoubtedly preferable to treating unincorporated treaties as an unmentionable clandestine influence. It remains the constitutional function of judges to interpret the meaning of legal provisions and Parliament, after all, can vitiate outcomes of the process of interpretation with which it disagrees.

The legal effect of customary international law within the United Kingdom Constitution

(i) The historical approach to customary international law: the 'incorporation' model

Although the approach of the UK courts to treaties illustrates the influence of dualism this, however, tells only part of the story of international law's role within the UK Constitution. Before the proliferation of treaty making in the modern era much of international

---

[42] See *Kuwait Airways Corp.* v *Iraqi Airways Co.* [2002] UKHL 19; [2002] 2 AC 883, [114] (Lord Steyn).

[43] R. Singh, 'The Use of International Law in the Domestic Courts of the United Kingdom' (2005) 56 NILQ 119, 122.

[44] *R (SG)* v *Secretary of State for Work and Pensions* [2015] UKSC 16; [2015] 1 WLR 1449, [261].

[45] Ibid.

[46] P. Sales and J. Clement, 'International Law in Domestic Courts: The Developing Framework' (2008) 124 LQR 388, 421.

law consisted of customary rules regarding relations between states. These customary rules amounted to established modes of conduct, widely accepted as binding upon states even though they were not based on a formal agreement. For example, practices on the exchange and safe treatment of diplomats existed for centuries before they were codified in a treaty.[47] Customary international law remains an important basis for international obligations, with the Statute of the International Court of Justice stating that part of the court's function is to decide disputes in accordance with 'international custom, as evidence of a general practice accepted as law'.[48] For state practice to be accepted as customary international law it must be generally observed and states must act in this way because they regard the practice as legally binding. Where such customary obligations are at issue, distinguished legal authorities have long maintained that they form part of the common law. In his eighteenth-century account of English law, William Blackstone accepted that 'the law of nations . . . is here adopted in its full extent by the common law, and is held to be part of the law of the land'.[49] If we consider this statement to relate solely to customary international law,[50] Blackstone's opinion was supported by cases such as *Triquet* v *Bath,* in which Lord Mansfield accepted that customary rules of international law relating to diplomatic privileges formed an operative part of the common law and could be determined on the basis of 'the practice of different nations and the authority of writers'.[51]

(ii) The courts as gatekeepers: the 'transformation' model

More recently, however, the courts have been more reticent towards claims that customary international law is without question part of domestic law (as opposed to a source that domestic courts can draw upon).[52] Lord Mance has carefully constrained the presumption that customary international law 'once established, can and should shape the common law', by recognising that this presumption will only take effect 'whenever it can do so consistently with domestic constitutional principles, statutory law and common law rules which the courts can themselves sensibly adapt'.[53]

One problem with assertions of a distinct role for customary international law within domestic law, hinted at by the 'once established' element of Lord Mance's presumption, is the difficulty the courts have in identifying whether or not states consider themselves bound by an emerging practice. If they do not, then the practice in question does not constitute international law. But as Brownlie, a former Chairman of the International Law Commission, has recognised, numerous sources can be used to determine whether a practice is consistently applied and generally accepted by states, from diplomatic correspondence, to press releases, international and national judicial decisions and national legislation (to name but some of the possible sources).[54] Where a developing rule of customary international law is at issue this diversity of sources can require the domestic courts to undertake

---

[47] Vienna Convention on Diplomatic Relations (1961) 500 UNTS 95.
[48] Statute of the International Court of Justice, Art. 38.1(b).
[49] W. Blackstone, *Commentaries on the Laws of England* (1st edn, Clarendon Press, 1765–69) Vol. IV, 67.
[50] R. Singh, 'The Use of International Law in the Domestic Courts of the United Kingdom' (2005) 56 NILQ 119, 124.
[51] *Triquet* v *Bath* (1764) 97 ER 936, 938.
[52] *R* v *Jones (Margaret)* [2006] UKHL 16; [2007] 1 AC 136, [11].
[53] *Keyu* v *Secretary of State for Foreign and Commonwealth Affairs* [2015] UKSC 69; [2016] AC 1355, [150].
[54] I. Brownlie, *Principles of Public International Law* (OUP, 2008) pp. 6–7.

an extensive review of state practice and academic commentary to determine whether a rule of customary international law exists.[55] In controversial cases this process can draw the courts into the difficult task of choosing between conflicting examples of state practice, decisions of international tribunals and academic opinions regarding the position of customary international law.

Thinking Point . . .

Academic sources, whilst useful, are not, of themselves a sufficient basis for declaring a practice to constitute a rule of customary international law according to the English courts. See *R* v *Keyn* (1876) 2 Ex D 63, 202 (Cockburn CJ).

The *Jones* v *Ministry of Interior* case, in which the claimant alleged that he had been tortured whilst held in custody in Saudi Arabia and sought damages from the Saudi government in the courts of England and Wales, provides a good example of how difficult it can be for judges to accurately assess the limits of customary international law. Lord Bingham summarised the conflicting international law rules which confronted the House of Lords in this case:

> The issue turns on the relationship . . . between two principles of international law. One principle, historically the older of the two, is that one sovereign state will not, save in certain specified instances, assert its judicial authority over another. The second principle, of more recent vintage but of the highest authority among principles of international law, is one that condemns and criminalises the official practice of torture, requires states to suppress the practice and provides for the trial and punishment of officials found to be guilty of it.[56]

The House of Lords rejected Jones' claim, concluding that the first of these international law concepts, state immunity, prevented the court from considering the case. Customary international law banning torture may have been developing rapidly, but the Court found itself unable to conclude that it currently operated to displace the rules of state immunity.[57] Lord Hoffmann's judgment illustrates how difficult the Court found it to reach this conclusion, which placed it out of step with the approach taken to similar overseas torture claims by the US courts and prominent experts on international law:

> Although, as Professor Cassese says, the [successful claims of torture survivors before the US courts] may be 'meritorious' as 'a practical expedient for circumventing the [US Foreign Sovereign Immunities Act]' . . . and were . . . described by Judges Higgins, Kooijmans and Buergenthal in the *Arrest Warrant* case . . . as a 'unilateral exercise of the function of guardian of international values', they are in my opinion contrary to customary international law and the Immunity Convention and not in accordance with the law of England.[58]

This passage not only indicates the process of how judges assess the terms of customary international law (with Lord Hoffmann considering the works of expert writers on

---

[55] See, for example, *R (European Roma Rights Centre)* v *Immigration Officer at Prague Airport* [2004] UKHL 55; [2005] 2 AC 1, [24]–[27] (Lord Bingham).

[56] *Jones* v *Ministry of Interior for the Kingdom of Saudi Arabia and Others* [2006] UKHL 26; [2007] 1 AC 270, [1].

[57] Ibid., [34] (Lord Bingham).

[58] Ibid., [99].

international law and the practice of domestic courts in other jurisdictions regarding overseas torture claims), but also affirms that such rules can have a place within the domestic legal system. The courts act as gatekeepers, determining which rules of customary international law operate within the domestic legal system and the meaning of these rules within domestic law.

Thinking Point . . .

The responsibility of domestic courts for the process of transforming rules of customary international law into domestic legal rules can mean that approaches to international law diverge in different legal systems, creating 'US international law', 'UK international law' or 'German international law' depending on how the approaches adopted by different jurisdictions diverge; A. Roberts, 'Comparative International Law? The Role of National Courts in International Law' (2011) 60 ICLQ 57, 74.

In carrying out this role the courts have to decide whether to 'transform' a rule of international law into a rule of common law on the basis of considerations such as whether it conflicts with existing rules within the domestic legal system (including rules contained in statutes, common law and the royal prerogative). As O'Keefe states, 'customary international law is applicable in the English courts only where the constitution permits'.[59] The following case provides a good example of the courts carrying out this evaluation:

Key case

R v Jones (Margaret) [2006] UKHL 16; [2007] 1 AC 136 (House of Lords)

During the invasion of Iraq in 2003 protesters entered military bases in the UK in order to voice their opposition to the war and to peacefully disrupt operations. Several were arrested and charged with criminal damage and aggravated trespass. They claimed that as they were acting to prevent an act of aggression illegal under international law, they enjoyed a defence under s. 3 of the Criminal Law Act 1967, which made it legal to use reasonable force to prevent the commission of a crime.

The House of Lords heard the issue as a question of general public importance. Lord Bingham did accept (at [22]) the appellant protesters' contention that war crimes could be punished as breaches of the criminal law in force in England and Wales:

> It would seem to me at least arguable that war crimes, recognised as such in customary international law, would now be triable and punishable under the domestic criminal law of this country irrespective of any domestic statute. But it is not necessary to decide that question, since war crimes are something quite distinct from the crime of aggression.

All crimes under international law are not, however, assimilated into domestic law automatically. In the absence of legislation the courts will be very reluctant to recognise new criminal offences. Having considered a range of international offences that had been assimilated into

---

[59] R. O'Keefe, 'Customary International Crimes in English Courts' [2001] BYBIL 293, 335.

domestic law by statute, Lord Bingham (at [28]) refused to allow 'international acts of aggression' to be treated as an offence without an Act of Parliament recognising it as such:

> It would be anomalous if the crime of aggression, excluded (obviously deliberately) from the [International Criminal Court Act 2001], were to be treated as a domestic crime, since it would not be subject to the constraints (as to the need for the Attorney General's consent, the mode of trial, the requisite *mens rea,* the liability of secondary parties and maximum penalties) applicable to the crimes which were included.

The elements of the crime could not be ascertained with sufficient certainty without further development of the law, and the Court refused to supply elements through common law (a long-standing UK constitutional principle being that new criminal offences require legislation, see Chapter 6, pp. 202–4). On the basis of this ruling the High Court subsequently blocked an attempted private prosecution of former Prime Minister Tony Blair for the 'crime of aggression' for leading the UK into the Iraq War; *Al Rabbat* v *Westminster Magistrates' Court* [2017] EWHC 1969 (Admin), [24] (Lord Thomas).

The shift to 'transformation' model may appear to imply that the domestic courts have become more reluctant to enforce principles of customary international law. In reality, however, the degree to which international dealings are covered by legal rules has increased exponentially since the courts in the eighteenth century expounded the 'incorporation' approach. This fact necessitates the more active approach by the courts in reconciling these rules with domestic law. As writers such as de Londras point out, in the large volume of recent cases requiring the courts to consider questions of international law, '[t]he superior courts of the United Kingdom . . . [have] demonstrated a notably internationalist bent in recent years'.[60]

Hierarchies of norms within international law

The previous sections have examined the impact of international law on legal relationships within the UK's legal systems. Not all international law, however, is of equal importance. Some treaties and some rules of customary international law constitute 'higher-order' legal rules (sometimes described as higher-order norms of international law). This creates an added level of complexity for the domestic courts in determining the position of international law on particular issues and the degree to which it is applicable within domestic law.

(i) Hierarchies between treaties?

In response to international law's ineffectiveness at constraining states in the first half of the twentieth century, the Charter of the United Nations (UN) was signed in 1945.[61] The UN Charter purported to create a global legal order (with UN Security Council Resolutions potentially being binding upon UN members[62]) superior to UN member states' other international obligations:

---

[60] F. de Londras, 'Dualism, domestic courts, and the rule of international law', in M. Sellers and T. Tomaszewski (eds), *The Rule of Law in Comparative Perspective* (Springer, 2010) 217, 225.
[61] *Charter of the United Nations* (26 June 1945) 1 UNTS XVI.
[62] Ibid., Art. 25.

In the event of a conflict between the obligations of the Members of the United Nations under the present Charter and their obligations under any other international agreement, their obligations under the present Charter shall prevail.[63]

For many decades the divisions in the UN apparatus brought about by the Cold War stymied its activities. Since the 1990s, however, the UN has become more active, and in light of this increased activity the supposed primacy of the UN Charter has posed difficult questions for the UK's domestic courts.

Subsequent to the invasion of Iraq in 2003, the UN Security Council authorised the UK to use its military as part of a multi-national force to maintain security and stability in Iraq[64] (although, in doing so, the Security Council did not legitimate the invasion of Iraq, which was the immediate cause of this instability[65]). In the course of this UN-authorised mission, the UK military was responsible for human rights abuses against Iraqi civilians. Al-Jedda (a dual national of Iraq and the UK) was held for several years without trial by UK forces on suspicion of involvement with terrorism in Iraq. He claimed that this detention breached his right to liberty (Article 5 ECHR), but the UK Government sought to exclude the claim on the basis that the UK's obligations under the ECHR are of subordinate importance to its obligations under the UN Charter, and that, because UK forces were acting under a UN mandate, they were absolved of human-rights responsibility.[66] In addressing this question, the House of Lords found itself 'deep inside the realm of international law'.[67] The court indicated that, in dismissing this appeal, it would consider the UN Charter to be superior in effect to the ECHR (although several judges made it clear that this reasoning was not the *ratio* behind their decision).[68] This last caveat would prove to be important, for in 2011 the European Court of Human Rights rejected the House of Lords' approach in *Al-Jedda*,[69] refusing to accept that the ECHR conflicted with Article 103 UN Charter because respect for human rights was embedded within the Charter itself:

> In the light of the United Nations' important role in promoting and encouraging respect for human rights, it is to be expected that clear and explicit language would be used were the Security Council to intend States to take particular measures which would conflict with their obligations under international human rights law.[70]

This dispute, and the ultimate vindication of Al-Jedda's human rights, indicates that the UK courts do not simply have to assess the implications of international law for the UK's legal systems, which would be difficult enough, they also often have to ascertain which of multiple international legal orders should take precedence within domestic law on a given issue.

---

[63] Ibid., Art. 103.

[64] UN Doc. No. S/RES/1511 (16 Oct. 2003), para. 13 and UN Doc. No. S/RES/1546 (8 June 2004), para. 10.

[65] *R (Al-Jedda)* v *Secretary of State for* Defence [2007] UKHL 58; [2008] 1 AC 332, [23] (Lord Bingham).

[66] Ibid., [3].

[67] Ibid., [55] (Lord Rodger).

[68] Ibid., [34] (Lord Bingham).

[69] *Al-Jedda* v *United Kingdom* (2011) 53 EHRR 23.

[70] Ibid., [102].

(ii) *Jus cogens* norms under customary international law

Some rules of international law are so important that states cannot depart from them or restrict their operation by adopting treaties which stand contrary to these rules. Within the hierarchy of international laws these rules, known as *jus cogens* norms, outrank treaties and other rules of customary international law. Some states have adapted their domestic laws to enable the prosecution of individuals who use positions of power in other states to offend against these pre-emptory rules on which the entire system of international law is based. These states apply what is known as 'universal jurisdiction' where a breach of one of these rules is at issue.

Thinking Point . . .

Jus cogens is Latin for 'compelling rule'. The reaction against the two world wars saw the rule against international aggression develop into a *jus cogens* norm by the middle of the twentieth century. This meant that states generally accepted that an aggressive attack by one state on another was not simply a breach of international law, but an attack on the concept of international law. See *R v Jones (Margaret)* [2006] UKHL 16; [2007] 1 AC 136, [12]–[14] (Lord Bingham).

The recognition of *jus cogens* rules exemplifies the increasing reach of international law. The basis for applying international law to criminalise particular activities, even if they occur solely within the territory of another state, is linked to the abuses of state power which took place during the Second World War:

> Since the Nazi atrocities and the Nuremberg trials, international law has recognised a number of offences as being international crimes. Individual states have taken jurisdiction to try some international crimes even in cases where such crimes were not committed within the geographical boundaries of such states.[71]

The most prominent *jus cogens* norms relate to activities such as aggressive wars, torture and genocide. Where such norms are at issue before the domestic courts in the UK, they can displace other rules of international law and even influence the interpretation of statutes:

Key case

R v Bow Street Metropolitan Stipendiary Magistrate, ex parte Pinochet (No. 3) [2000] 1 AC 147 (House of Lords)

General Augusto Pinochet, the former President of Chile, arrived in the UK for medical treatment in 1998. The military seized power in Chile through a coup in 1973 and installed Pinochet as President. Under his regime, large numbers of suspected opponents were murdered, tortured or simply disappeared. Spanish judicial authorities, alleging that Pinochet had

---

[71] *R v Bow Street Metropolitan Stipendiary Magistrate, ex parte Pinochet (No. 3)* [2000] 1 AC 147, 189 (Lord Browne-Wilkinson).

conspired in these acts, requested his extradition to stand trial in Spain. Most of the charges had no relation to Spanish citizens, but the Spanish judicial authorities nonetheless asserted that, because of the *jus cogens* nature of the offence of torture in international law, they had jurisdiction to try Pinochet.

A seven-judge House of Lords panel accepted that former heads of state, such as General Pinochet, had immunity from criminal prosecution for acts done in their official capacity as head of state (known as immunity *ratione materiae*), under rules of customary international law incorporated into domestic law through section 20 of the State Immunity Act 1978 (see Lord Saville, 265). However, the Law Lords recognised that torture was an international crime against humanity and a *jus cogens* norm and that after the International Convention against Torture and other Cruel, Inhuman or Degrading Treatment or Punishment 1984 came into effect in 1988 there had been a universal jurisdiction in all states party to the Convention to either extradite or punish a public official who had committed torture. Parliament had enacted section 134 of the Criminal Justice Act 1988 to bring this jurisdiction into effect in the UK. In the light of that universal jurisdiction a majority accepted that states party to the Convention (including the UK) could not have intended that immunity could continue to apply to former heads of state involved in torture. This is aptly summarised by Lord Phillips (at 289):

> International crimes and extra-territorial jurisdiction in relation to them are both new arrivals in the field of public international law. I do not believe that state immunity *ratione materiae* can coexist with them. The exercise of extraterritorial jurisdiction overrides the principle that one state will not intervene in the internal affairs of another. It does so because, where international crime is concerned, that principle cannot prevail. An international crime is as offensive, if not more offensive, to the international community when committed under colour of office. Once extraterritorial jurisdiction is established, it makes no sense to exclude from it acts done in an official capacity.

Therefore, the House of Lords ruled that torture could not constitute one of the official functions of a head of state and that Pinochet could be extradited on the basis of alleged acts of torture (as this, unlike murder, was a crime for which universal jurisdiction applied), at least with regard to those instances which took place after the ratification of the Torture Convention in 1988. Pinochet, however, would never be extradited. Citing the former President's failing health, Jack Straw, the then Home Secretary, permitted him to return to Chile on medical grounds.

Jus cogens therefore challenge domestic courts tasked with determining how these norms fit alongside existing constitutional standards (the task which gave the House of Lords such difficulty in *Jones* v *Ministry of Interior*, above[72]). They could even upset long-standing hierarchies within domestic law.[73] In *ex parte Pinochet* the House of Lords interpreted the State Immunity Act 1978 in light of the need to respect the *jus cogens* prohibition upon torture. If *jus cogens* really are fundamental and binding upon states, in the future the UK's judiciary could find themselves obliged to apply these norms, even in the face of contrary UK statutes.

---

[72] See pp. 68–9.

[73] G. Teubner, 'The King's Many Bodies: The Self-Deconstruction of Law's Hierarchy' (1997) 31 *Law & Society Review* 763, 763.

The European Union

Key issues

- The European Union (EU) has developed as a supranational body responsible for extensive fields of law making with the UK as one of its 28 member states.
- In order to operate this supranational body the treaties establishing the EU created a number of institutions:

    1. The European Council provides overall strategic direction to the EU, whilst the Council of Ministers and the European Parliament are together responsible for most day-to-day law making in the EU.

    2. The European Commission ensures that the policies of the EU are carried into effect.

    3. The Court of Justice acts as a final arbiter on whether the member states and EU institutions are fulfilling their responsibilities under the treaties.

- Laws made under the EU treaties (for the purposes of this brief overview, regulations and directives) can have legal effects within the domestic legal systems of the UK.

The development of the EU

International law is not simply made up of general rules applying to all states or treaties concluded between individual states. States can agree to become members of international organisations such as the United Nations, the International Labour Organization or the World Trade Organization, and in doing so agree to act in accordance with the rules of such organisations. In the aftermath of the Second World War one organisation has expanded, in terms of its powers, remit and membership, past the point where it is merely international in scope. The EU, today made up of 28 member states, is a *supranational* organisation. In a wide range of policy areas member states have not simply agreed to act as required by the treaties on which the EU is based, but have passed broad law-making power to EU institutions. But this account of the EU's role also acknowledges a limitation upon the organisation; it can only gain or extend competences over areas of law if its member states agree, by treaty, to transfer these competences:

> Under the principle of conferral, the Union shall act only within the limits of the competences conferred upon it by the Member States in the Treaties to attain the objectives set out therein. Competences not conferred upon the Union in the Treaties remain with the Member States.[74]

Thinking Point . . .

Describing an organisation as 'international' emphasises the primacy of member state consent in its operations. Describing the EU as 'supranational' invites controversy, because it emphasises that member states have ceded the capacity to make certain areas of law to the EU. Less flatteringly, one writer has described the EU as 'some sort of ambiguous non-state polity'; J. Shaw, 'Europe's Constitutional Future' [2005] PL 132, 133.

---

[74] Treaty of the European Union (TEU), Art. 5.2.

This short introduction to the EU is intended to explain why so many states chose to pass some of their law-making functions to this supranational body and to look at the fundamental features of how it exercises this authority, before we turn to discuss the UK's impending withdrawal.

(i) A brief history of the EU

The so-called European Project has never lacked ambition. It began life as an agreement between six countries in Western Europe to pool coal supplies and steel production, the raw ingredients of industrial economies. At the time, it was thought that sharing these resources would not simply prevent war between the countries involved, but that it would provide 'the basis for a broader and deeper community among peoples long divided by bloody conflicts'.[75]

With the success of the European Coal and Steel Community (ECSC) European statesmen, eager to maintain economic growth in the post-war era, turned to more ambitious goals. If such important resources could be traded across their borders without trade barriers, how much more economic growth could be achieved if goods, services, labour and capital could flow between their countries to where they were required? And so, in 1957, Belgium, the Netherlands, Luxembourg (the 'Benelux countries'), the Federal Republic of Germany, France and Italy established the European Economic Community (EEC).[76]

Over the next 30 years the EEC progressively broadened its membership (with the UK joining in 1973). The EEC's institutions generated and applied laws intended to remove barriers to the flows of goods, services, labour and capital and thereby establish a functioning single market.[77] But it became increasingly evident that the benefits of co-operation between states could be extended far beyond the factors of production. To realise these benefits the EEC would have to expand beyond its avowedly 'economic' focus. Individuals, for example, were able to travel between the members of the EEC without visas if they were 'workers' or if they were accessing 'services' in other member states. But the European Project could extend more benefits to Europeans if it could treat them as citizens, rather than simply as producers and consumers. In 1992, the member states therefore agreed to transfer further areas of law-making competence to the EEC.[78] This name, however, no longer reflected the expanded role of the organisation. It was renamed the European Union (EU), marking the organisation's shift in competence from purely economic integration to pursuing aspects of political integration. When this change in role occurred, the EU had only 12 member states, with a population of fewer than 360 million people. Just 12 years later, in 2004, it had expanded to 25 member states. It would grow again, reaching 28 states in 2013. More countries have applied for membership. In 2017, the EU's population is 510 million (although fewer than 400 million are EU citizens). The change in membership of the EU and its predecessors is charted in Figure 3.2.

This expansion into central and eastern European states, once under the influence of (and in the case of Latvia, Lithuania and Estonia, part of) the USSR, made it increasingly difficult for the EU to exercise its law-making competence. The Maastricht Treaty of 1992

---

[75] Treaty Establishing the European Coal and Steel Community (Paris, 18 April 1951), Preamble.
[76] Treaty of Rome 1957.
[77] Single European Act 1986.
[78] Maastricht Treaty 1992.

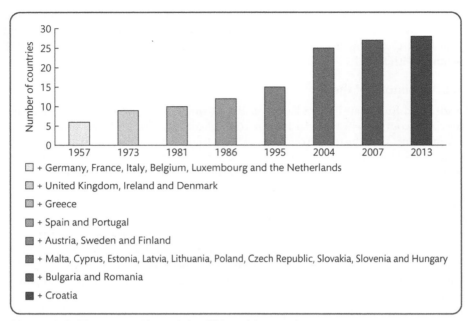

Figure 3.2 The expansion of the EU and its predecessors

maintained that many areas of law making required unanimous agreement by the EU member states. A series of treaties was agreed which gradually transformed the EU's law-making process (as well as granting the EU some new competences), much of which now occurs on the basis of population-weighted majority support by EU member states, even if some states object (a process known as qualified majority voting).[79]

A rough outline of changes in the treaty structure underpinning the competences which member states have transferred can be seen in Figure 3.3. The width of each box indicates the period of time a treaty was in force for and the depth indicates how broad the competences of Europe are in each field. Colour continuities between boxes indicate common areas of competence. As this diagram shows, the range of the EU's competences (represented by the breadth of the 'European Union' box) far outstrips the range of competences originally enjoyed by the ECSC (represented by the breadth of the 'European Coal and Steel Community' box). By the early years of the twenty-first century the original 'economic' aspects of the EU's activity were encapsulated by the first area of EU area of competence (or 'pillar' in the jargon of the EU), the 'European Community' pillar. In 2002 this pillar also subsumed the competences exercised under the original ECSC Treaty when it elapsed after fifty years in operation. This pillar was the longest established part of the European Project and hence, by the early the twenty-first century, this pillar was by far the broadest and best developed area of EU competence. Treaties from the 1980s onwards had granted, and subsequently extended, EU competences in new fields, ultimately known as 'Police and Judicial Co-operation' (which dealt primarily with common criminal justice measures and institutions) and 'Foreign and Security Policy' (which dealt primarily with the external relations of the EU as a whole, including areas such as trade policies with non-member states). In other words, the EU was gaining an increasing range of

---

[79] Treaty of Amsterdam 1997, Treaty of Nice 2001, Treaty of Lisbon 2007.

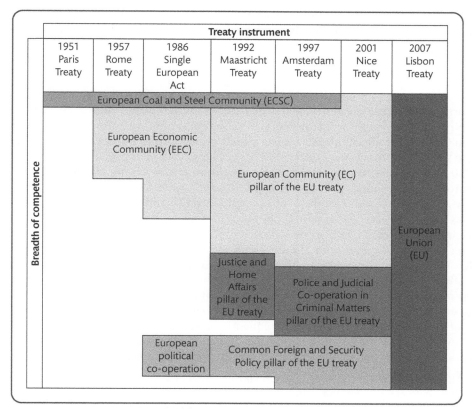

Figure 3.3 The expanding competences of EU institutions

competences in new fields, and performing functions that had traditionally been exercised in these fields by its member states alone. Elements within the EU believed that the time had come to adopt a European constitutional treaty, extending the powers of the EU in all three pillars.

In 2005, however, these ambitious plans were rejected by voters in a series of Referendums across Europe. Following the shock of this rejection, which indicated that Europe's peoples were not ready to accept such a dramatic extension of the European Project, the Lisbon Treaty was agreed in 2007. This Treaty, which entered into force in 2009, was not primarily intended to extend the EU's competences but to reorganise its institutional arrangements. Instead of three pillars, with different levels of involvement by the Court of Justice and European Parliament depending upon the area of competence in question, all areas of EU activity were now to be managed under the same rules. To combat concerns that the EU had lost touch with European citizens, for example, some of the most important reforms aimed to enhance the EU's direct accountability by enhancing the role of the European Parliament.[80] This very brief history demonstrates that the changes in the EU's membership and competences have never happened uniformly. But across Europe states

---

[80] See J. Snell, '"European Constitutional Settlement", an Ever Closer Union, and the Treaty of Lisbon: Democracy or Relevance?' (2008) 33 *EL Rev* 619, 619.

and their populations enjoyed tangible benefits by allowing various policy decisions to be made at the EU level, and these benefits fuelled the EU's growth, both in membership and competence.

(ii) The UK's accession to the EU

The UK remained outside the project for 15 years after the EEC was founded. Mired in efforts to dismantle the British Empire in the 1950s and early 1960s, and fearful that joining the EEC might jeopardise its trade and relationship with the United States and with Commonwealth countries, it opted instead to establish the European Free Trade Area with some of the other states on the EEC's periphery. Today it is easy to forget that in the 1950s and early 1960s trade with Commonwealth countries was roughly twice as import-ant to the UK economy as trade with the EEC's founder states.[81]

Ministers in office during the 1960s soon decided that this approach was an error. The UK's trade imbalance with the EEC worsened through the 1960s, with the UK importing much more from EEC member states than it exported to them. The result was the devalu-ation of the UK's currency in 1966.[82] Faced with intractable economic decline, the UK Government's requests for association with the EEC became increasingly desperate as the 1960s progressed. Nonetheless, relishing his role at the centre of this increasingly powerful organisation, the French President Charles de Gaulle repeatedly blocked UK entry. It was not until 1972, after de Gaulle had been ousted from power, that the UK's request to join was finally accepted. Parliament subsequently passed the European Communities Act (ECA) 1972, although by a mere eight votes (setting the pattern for the UK's uncertain relationship with the EU).[83] Section 2 of the ECA 1972, as amended, provides:

> All such rights, powers, liabilities, obligations and restrictions from time to time created or arising by or under the Treaties, and all such remedies and procedures from time to time provided for by or under the Treaties, as in accordance with the Treaties are without further enactment to be given legal effect or used in the United Kingdom shall be recognised and available in law, and be enforced, allowed and followed accordingly . . . [84]

This provision allowed laws generated by the EU institutions to alter rights and obligations in the UK 'without further enactment'. This applied not only to EU laws which had been in force before the UK joined but also to any laws that were subsequently created by these institutions. By conceding that they were to be a source of law within the UK without further enactment, Parliament had effectively created an exception to the operation of dualism within the UK Constitution. Only in the aftermath of the June 2016 Referendum on EU membership did the UK Supreme Court fully explain this legislation in terms of introducing a new source of UK law:

> Many statutes give effect to treaties by prescribing the content of domestic law in the areas covered by them. The 1972 Act does this, but it does considerably more as well. It authorises a dynamic process by which, without further primary legislation (and, in some cases, even without any domestic legislation), EU law not only becomes a source of UK law, but actually takes precedence

---

[81] See N. Ferguson, *Empire: How Britain Made the Modern World* (Penguin, 2003) p. 361.

[82] I. Ward, *A Critical Introduction to European Law* (CUP, 2003) p. 87.

[83] See I. Ward, *The English Constitution: Myths and Realities* (Hart, 2004) pp. 125–39.

[84] European Communities Act 1972, s. 2(1).

over all domestic sources of UK law, including statutes. This may sound rather dry or technical to many people, but in constitutional terms the effect of the 1972 Act was unprecedented.[85]

Lord Scarman, however, had recognised the significance of this constitutional shift as early as the mid-1970s. No longer would law students simply learn about statutes, the royal prerogative and the common law as sources of authority for government actions; he appreciated that they would also have to learn about this 'potent new source of English law'.[86] This new source of law was supported by section 3(1) of the ECA 1972, which provided that authoritative interpretation of the meaning of EU law would be provided by the Court of Justice, the EU's judicial institution:

> For the purpose of all legal proceedings any question as to the meaning or effect of any of the treaties or as to the validity, meaning or effect of any EU instrument . . . shall be for determination as such in accordance with the principles laid down by . . . the European Court.

Again, Lord Scarman immediately recognised the significance of this provision, which acknowledges the existence of 'a court uncontrolled by Parliament'.[87] This court could, and would, develop the EU's competences by interpreting the European treaties in light of their underlying purposes. Before the passing of the ECA 1972 the Court of Justice had already established that European law was an autonomous 'legal system',[88] permitting it to expand the EU's competences even without the UK's express agreement. But even such dramatic developments have been accommodated within the UK's governance order, with the courts continuing to 'view the United Kingdom as independent, Parliament as sovereign and European law as part of domestic law because Parliament has so willed'.[89]

The current structure and operation of the European Union

(i) The EU's role under the Lisbon Treaty

The Lisbon Treaty of 2009 is, in reality, two treaties. The first (and shorter) treaty, the Treaty on European Union (TEU), sets out the principles upon which the EU is based and explains the institutions which now make up this supranational body. The second, the Treaty on the Functioning of the European Union (TFEU), enumerates the competences enjoyed by these institutions. This means that neither of the treaties stands without reference to the other.

The Lisbon Treaty did not dramatically increase the EU's competences but it did substantially reorganise its institutions to enable it to continue to effectively implement its powers in the wake of two decades of membership expansion. The EU's core aim is set out in direct terms in Article 1 TEU; to forge 'an ever closer union among the peoples of Europe'. As we have seen, the EU's more narrowly focused predecessors, such as the

---

[85] *R (Miller)* v *Secretary of State for Exiting the European Union* [2017] UKSC 5; [2017] 2 WLR 583, [60] (Lord Neuberger).

[86] L. Scarman, *English Law – The New Dimension* (Steven & Sons, 1974) p. 22.

[87] Ibid., p. 21.

[88] Case 6/64, *Flaminio Costa* v *ENEL* [1964] ECR 585, 593.

[89] *Pham* v *Secretary of State for the Home Department* [2015] UKSC 19; [2015] 1 WLR 1591, [80] (Lord Mance).

EEC, sought to foster a common economic marketplace. But since the Maastricht Treaty of 1992, the EU's goal of forging a closer relationship between its member states has extended into other areas of life. As Article 2 TEU now states:

> The Union is founded on the values of respect for human dignity, freedom, democracy, equality, the rule of law and respect for human rights, including the rights of persons belonging to minorities. These values are common to the Member States in a society in which pluralism, non-discrimination, tolerance, justice, solidarity and equality between women and men prevail.

The EU today has, therefore, changed out of recognition from its beginnings. As Habermas asserts, the original aims of the leaders who first established the European Project in the 1950s were to put an end to warfare between the states of western Europe and to try to constrain the rise of post-war Germany,[90] now seem anachronistic. Instead, the European Project stumbled over the aim of making the peoples of Europe collectively better off and more integrated. This change of focus of itself spawned the successive amendments to the treaties and the complex web of EU institutions which we will now turn to analyse.

(ii) European Union institutions

The EU has established a range of institutions to manage its competences. Many liberal democracies divide up the key functions of law making, law implementation and adjudication between different institutions (see Chapter 7).[91] The status of the EU, however, as a supranational institution with different competences in different areas of law making (on some issues supplementing, on others replacing and on still others not affecting the competences of national institutions), does not lend itself to such a structure. Article 13 TEU outlines seven main EU institutions:

EU institution	Location
The European Council	Brussels
The Council of the European Union	Brussels
The European Parliament	Alternates between Strasbourg and Brussels
The European Commission	Brussels
The Court of Justice of the European Union	Luxembourg
The European Central Bank	Frankfurt
The Court of Auditors	Luxembourg

A thorough evaluation of the roles of, and interrelationship between, all of these institutions is beyond the scope of this brief outline of the EU and the impact of its law-making role on the UK's Constitution.[92] There follows instead an overview of the composition and role of the first five of these institutions, drawing upon both the TEU and the TFEU.

---

[90] J. Habermas, 'Why Europe Needs a Constitution', in R. Rogowski and C. Turner (eds), *The Shape of the New Europe* (CUP, 2006) pp. 25, 26.

[91] See pp. 223–7.

[92] For a fuller account, see S. Peers 'The EU's Political Institutions', in C. Barnard and S. Peers (eds) *European Union Law* (OUP, 2017) pp. 37–70.

> ## Thinking Point . . .
>
> This account does not cover EU arrangements that the UK is not involved in (such as the European Monetary Union, the 'Eurozone') and relevant institutions (like the European Central Bank). In 2013, a new treaty, the Treaty on Stability, Coordination and Governance in the Economic and Monetary Union, entered force to attempt to reform the rules affecting the Eurozone in light of the ongoing financial crisis. As the UK is not a member of the Eurozone, it has not signed this treaty. See European Scrutiny Committee, *Treaty on Stability, Coordination and Governance: Impact on the Eurozone and the Rule of Law* (2012) HC 1817-I.

1. The European Council

The heads of government or heads of state of EU member states meet once every six months as the European Council to discuss the future of the European Project, including key issues such as negotiating new treaties and expansions of EU membership and to appoint important figures such as the President of the European Commission. The fact that the European Council is made up of the elected leaders of the member states supplies some democratic legitimacy for its actions. Until the Single European Act of 1986, the operation of the European Council was not governed by the treaties. Since the Lisbon Treaty of 2009, however, its central role within the European Project has been recognised, with the European Council gaining its own President under Article 15(6) TEU (a post that had previously rotated between the member state representatives). The President, currently Donald Tusk, holds the largely administrative position of organising and chairing European Council meetings. Within this position, however, lies the important strategic role of setting the agenda for such meetings.

Setting the scene
Key roles of the European Council

- *Strategic Control of the European Union*: Art. 15(1) TEU provides that '[t]he European Council shall provide the Union with the necessary impetus for its development and shall define the general political directions and priorities thereof'. Although it is not involved in the day-to-day law making in the EU, it is the forum in which the leaders of the member states debate the major challenges facing the EU.

- *Appointment of key EU Officials*: Art. 15(5) and Art. 17(7) TEU respectively give the European Council the responsibility for selecting, by qualified majority voting (see below), the President of the European Council and nominating the President of the European Commission.

2. The Council of the European Union (also known as the Council of Ministers)

If the European Council provides the EU with its strategic vision, the Council of Ministers is one of the bodies responsible for the day-to-day task of implementing that vision. The similarity of name is not accidental, for it is again made up of government ministers from the member states. Its composition varies according to the topic at issue (Article 236 TFEU lists the different configurations). If the issue concerns foreign policy, for example, foreign ministers of all of the member states will convene as the Foreign Affairs Council. By contrast, if an economic or budgetary issue is at stake, the 27 finance ministers will convene as the Economic and Financial Affairs Council.

Together with the European Parliament the Council of Ministers acts as the legislative centre of the EU. Because any new EU legislation must be passed by the Council, it represents the interests of the member state governments in the EU's law-making process. Again, this permits some level of democratic accountability as electorates in each member state can hold their governments to account for their voting record in the Council. This, however, is far from an ideal situation given the limited public understanding of the Council's activity (even though, under Article 16(8) TEU, all meetings on draft legislation are heard in public).

Two mechanisms cover most of the law making in the Council. Some measures (often involving controversial issues such as harmonisation of taxation or social security) require a unanimous decision by all 28 representatives, but most are approved by a process known as qualified majority voting (QMV). The expansion of the EU's law-making role has gone hand-in-hand with the increased use of QMV, because it prevents individual states from vetoing legislative proposals. The Lisbon Treaty saw the extension of QMV to cover areas such as immigration and border controls, preventing single states from vetoing reforms. The UK, it must be noted, has refused to give up its veto powers in these areas so easily, as explained by Parliament's European Scrutiny Committee:

> Under the Lisbon Treaty, the national veto over EU proposals in police and criminal justice matters is abolished, while the UK is not bound by such laws unless it decides to 'opt in' to them. Such an opt in arrangement existed prior to the Lisbon Treaty in relation to EU laws concerning asylum, immigration and judicial co-operation in civil matters, and continues to apply in this field under the Lisbon Treaty.[93]

Under the simplified QMV system adopted under Article 16(4) TEU, the process requires that at least a 55 per cent majority of state representatives on the Council support a measure and that those supporters represent a 65 per cent majority of EU citizens as a whole. This requirement of a double majority is intended to prevent the large states in the EU from ignoring the wishes of smaller states. A measure can only be blocked if opposed by at least four states.

Setting the scene
Key roles of the Council of Ministers

Creation of legislation and co-ordination of the EU budget. Under Art. 16(1) TEU, '[t]he Council shall, jointly with the European Parliament, exercise legislative and budgetary functions. It shall carry out policy-making and coordinating functions as laid down in the Treaties'. It is therefore one half of the ordinary law-making process, alongside the European Parliament.

3. The European Parliament

The European Parliament as a directly elected assembly did not come into being until 1979. Since then it has operated as the EU institution with the greatest claim upon democratic legitimacy. The 736 Members of the European Parliament (MEPs) are elected for five-year terms from all of the member states, with larger states returning the largest number of MEPs, but smaller states are over-represented per head of population to ensure that

---

[93] European Scrutiny Committee, *Sixth Report: The Work of the Committee in 2008–9* (2010) HC 267.

their concerns are not marginalised. Under the Lisbon Treaty arrangements (Article 14(2) TEU), for example, Germany has 96 MEPs, whereas Malta has just 6 MEPs. This means, however, that one German MEP represents roughly 860,000 people, compared to 73,000 people for each Maltese MEP.

For much of the Parliament's life, however, it has been little more than a talking shop. Despite its name, its legislative powers were limited and electorates (particularly in the UK) have been apathetic to its existence. In the 2014 European Parliament elections, for example, turnout across the UK stood at just under 36 per cent. This lack of interest in the Parliament belies its increased importance under the Lisbon Treaty. Under the 'ordinary legislative procedure', established as the standard method of law making in most fields by Article 289 TFEU, measures must pass both the Council of Ministers and receive Parliament's assent before they can enter force. Even with these reforms, however, the European Parliament does not initiate legislation (which remains the purview of the Commission) even if it can scrutinise and block proposals. As a result of concerns over the level of democratic deficit resultant from the European Parliament's atypical powers, the treaties have also expanded the say of national legislatures within EU law making.[94] If enough national legislatures issue a 'reasoned opinion' regarding a Commission proposal which they believe infringes the principle of subsidiarity (in short, which impinges upon domestic competences or provides insufficient leeway for national differences) then the Commission is subject to a 'yellow card' obliging commissioners to give a reasoned response for maintaining, changing or withdrawing their proposal. If more than half of legislatures object, an 'orange card' requires that a proposal be immediately voted upon by European Parliament and Council.[95]

Setting the scene
Key roles of the European Parliament

- *Approval of legislation.* In line with its role as the directly elected EU institution, Art. 14(1) TEU provides that '[t]he European Parliament shall, jointly with the Council, exercise legislative and budgetary functions'. The Parliament must therefore approve most legislative proposals which pass the Council of Ministers before they can have legal effect.

- *Oversight of the Commission.* Under Art. 14(1) TEU the Parliament has the responsibility for approving the Council's candidate for President of the Commission (and also for approving the President's nominations for Commissioner). It can also, under Art. 234 TFEU, pass motions formally censuring the Commission. If such a motion passes with a two-thirds majority, the Commission is obliged to resign.

- *Approval of the budget.* Under Art. 314 TFEU the European Parliament must approve the annual budget for the running of the EU and can request amendments.

- *Establishing inquiries and instigating litigation.* The Parliament has the ability to establish inquiries to investigate 'alleged contraventions or maladministration in the implementation of Union law' under Art. 226 TFEU. This scrutiny function is backed up by its ability to bring the other institutions before the Court of Justice under Art. 263 TFEU.

---

[94] K. Auel, and C. Neuhold, 'Multi-arena players in the making? Conceptualizing the role of national parliaments since the Lisbon Treaty' (2016) 24 *Journal of European Public Policy* 1.

[95] TFEU, Protocol 2.

4. The European Commission

If the Council of Ministers and the European Parliament share the law-making function in most areas of EU law, the European Commission can be likened to the UK's civil service. Its role is largely the bureaucratic task of managing the operation of the European Project and ensuring that EU law is correctly applied by the member states. At present, there is one Commissioner per member state, although the Lisbon reforms make provision to reduce this if the member states agree to do so. What sets the Commission apart from national bureaucracies, however, is its independent capacity to use its extensive enforcement powers and the fact that it has sole responsibility for proposing new legislative initiatives. Although the President of the Commission (currently Jean-Claude Juncker) is nominated by the European Council (Article 17(7) TEU) and approved, together with his fellow Commissioners, by the Parliament (Article 14(1) TEU), on a day-to-day basis the Commission operates independently of the wishes of the member states or their electorates. Only if a two-thirds majority in the Parliament censure the Commission is it forced to resign (Article 234 TFEU). This insulation from such concerns allows the Commission to sustain the European Project, even to the point of initiating unpopular actions to ensure that EU law is fulfilled.

Setting the scene

Key roles of the European Commission

- *Management of the EU.* Art. 17(1) TEU sets out the Commission's wide managerial remit, whereby, '[t]he Commission shall promote the general interest of the Union and take appropriate initiatives to that end. It shall ensure the application of the Treaties, and of measures adopted by the institutions pursuant to them. It shall oversee the application of Union law under the control of the Court of Justice of the European Union. It shall execute the budget and manage programmes. It shall exercise coordinating, executive and management functions, as laid down in the Treaties'.

- *Legislative proposals.* Under Art. 17(2) TEU most EU legislation is proposed by the Commission to the Council of Ministers and European Parliament.

- *Commission enforcement proceedings.* In terms of teeth to back up its managerial role, under Art. 258 TFEU the Commission regularly institutes enforcement proceedings before the Court of Justice against member states which fail to fully implement EU law.

5. The Court of Justice of the European Union

The Court of Justice of the European Union is made up of not one, but two, important tribunals. The more important is the European Court of Justice (ECJ) which operates as the final court on matters of EU law, and the lesser tribunal is the European General Court (EGC) which hears many actions brought by individuals and member states at first instance (and which can be appealed to the ECJ). Both courts are made up of 28 judges, one appointed by each member state (although they fulfil their role independent of their state). These judges are arranged into panels to hear cases. The qualifications required by the TEU for judicial candidates for each court reflect the hierarchy between the courts; ECJ judges must be qualified to take 'the highest judicial office' (Article 253 TFEU) in their member states whilst EGC judges must be qualified for 'high judicial office' (Article 254 TFEU) in their country.

The court has played a pivotal role in the history of the EU. When other institutions have at times been deadlocked, the court's 'bold approach . . . to the scope of its jurisdiction'[96] has often provided the innovation necessary to resolve such stalemates. As Francis Jacobs (a former Advocate General of the Court) has recognised, many of these innovations have subsequently been 'given treaty expression'.[97] One of the best examples of the Court's expansive jurisprudence can be seen in the field of the Common Commercial Policy (CCP). In *ERTA* the member states and the Commission squared-off over who had the competence to conclude a road transport agreement with non-members. The Court conclude that 'the system of internal Community measures may not . . . be separated from that of external relations',[98] and that where 'Community rules are promulgated for the attainment of the objectives of the Treaty, the Member States cannot, outside the framework of the Community institutions, assume obligations which might affect those rules or alter their scope'.[99] For Cremona, this decision 'heralded a decade in which the Court of Justice delineated both the extent and the nature of external Community competence'.[100] Much of the EU's current CCP competence, now built into the treaties,[101] therefore began with this jurisprudence. This willingness of the Court to interpret EU treaty provisions in light of the underlying principles of EU law can be unsettling for member states. The UK, which as we saw above is not part of the Eurozone,[102] did not sign the Treaty on Stability, Coordination and Governance in the Economic and Monetary Union 2012, which is aimed to bring stability to the single currency by ensuring greater convergence between the economic policies of Eurozone members. But Prime Minister David Cameron was still obliged to assure the House of Commons that 'we will watch this matter closely and that, if necessary, we will take action, including legal action, if our national interests are threatened by the misuse of the institutions'.[103] In other words, the Prime Minister was concerned that the Court would, in his words 'misuse' its role to extend some of the new treaty's conditions to the UK.

Setting the scene
Key roles of the Court of Justice of the European Union

The Guardian of the Treaties. Under Art. 19(1) TEU the function of the Court of Justice is to 'ensure that in the interpretation and application of the Treaties the law is observed'. Exercising this function dynamically, the Court has been a very important vehicle for the European Project, establishing the supremacy of EU law over national law and using its interpretive power to circumvent obstacles to law making in important fields such as trade policy.

→

---

[96] F. Jacobs, *The Sovereignty of Law: The European Way* (CUP, 2007) p. 44.

[97] Ibid., p. 45.

[98] Case C-22/70 *Commission of the European Communities* v *Council of the European Communities (ERTA)* [1971] ECR 262, [19].

[99] Ibid., [22].

[100] M. Cremona, 'External Relations and External Competence; the Emergence of an Integrated Policy' in P. Craig and G. De Burca (eds), *The Evolution of EU Law* (OUP, 1999) 137, 139.

[101] TFEU, Articles 206–207.

[102] See p. 81.

[103] HC Deb., vol. 539, col. 678 (31 January 2012).

The Court of Justice hears three main types of case:

1. *Enforcement proceedings.* The European Commission (under Art. 258 TFEU) or member states (under Art. 259 TFEU) can challenge an alleged failure of another member state to fulfil its obligations under EU law.

2. *Judicial review.* Under Articles 263 and 265 TFEU the court can hear actions brought by member states, EU institutions or private individuals challenging the legality of an EU institution's action or failure to act.

3. *Preliminary rulings.* Any national tribunal dealing with a case involving an aspect of EU law enforceable within the domestic legal system can request an authoritative ruling from the court as to the meaning of EU law under Art. 267 TFEU.

The European Union's legal measures

We have already seen that the parameters of the competence of the EU are set by the treaties upon which it is based (now the TEU and the TFEU). Major changes to these competences would require a new treaty, which would also, in the UK context, require that the ECA 1972 be updated (such an update occurred in the European Union (Amendment) Act 2008, adding the Lisbon Treaty to the list of EU treaties which the UK had adopted into domestic law). Individuals can rely upon the provisions of the treaties within their domestic legal system (provided they are clear and precise, unconditional and confer a specific right upon an individual):

> [T]he Community constitutes a new legal order of international law . . . the subjects of which comprise not only Member States but also their nationals. Independently of the legislation of Member States, Community law not only imposes obligations on individuals but is also intended to confer upon them rights which become part of their legal heritage.[104]

The Court of Justice has subsequently affirmed that individuals must, within their domestic legal systems, be able to 'obtain redress when their rights are infringed by a breach of [EU] law'.[105] The treaties, however, are often vague and do little more than sketch the limits on the EU's competence with regard to particular issues. As we saw above, the Council of Ministers and European Parliament therefore have the power to approve legislative measures proposed by Commission. These measures are the life-blood of EU law, giving effect to the treaties' aspirations. Together they build what is called the *acquis communautaire* (the body of EU law). In this brief overview we will introduce the two most important forms of EU legislation, regulations and directives.

(i) Regulations

In 2016, the EU created 1,216 regulations. These measures are extremely useful for EU law-makers as, under Article 288 TFEU, each is 'binding in its entirety and directly applicable in all Member States'. Direct applicability means that, immediately upon the adoption of a regulation, it operates within the domestic law of a member state, as if its own

---

[104] Case C-26/62, *NV Algemene Transport – en Onderneming Van Gend en Loos* v *Netherlands Inland Revenue Administration* [1963] ECR 1, 12.
[105] Case C-6/90 and C-9/90, *Francovich and Bonafaci* v *Italy* [1991] ECR I-5357, [33].

legislature had produced the measure. EU regulations impose legal rules in spheres as diverse as mobile phone roaming charges,[106] trade with Iran,[107] and even the movement of pets within the EU.[108]

(ii) Directives

In 2016, the EU created 41 directives. As with regulations, Article 288 TFEU stipulates that directives which apply to a member state are binding 'as to the result to be achieved', but by contrast to regulations these measures 'leave to the national authorities the choice of form and methods' by which they are brought into force in national law. The reason for this latitude is to allow national parliaments to debate and give effect to directives (often on controversial issues) in their own terms. For example, the Directive on Professional Qualifications[109] requires the transferability of many professional qualifications across the EU, but for some professions it allows member states, should they wish, to impose aptitude tests or adaptation periods. The UK brought the directive into domestic law, and set out the aptitude tests it would require, through a statutory instrument.[110]

This leeway does not create merely presentational differences, as many directives are mere frameworks and they enable member states to legitimately transpose varying standards within their national law (within the limits of possible interpretations of the directive). Directives therefore enhance the flexibility of EU law, creating a situation in which 'different authoritative orders overlap, compete and collaborate'.[111] The latitude built into directives presupposes that if the national solution inadequately transposes the directive into domestic law, the national courts and the Court of Justice will accept challenges to the measure. This is known as 'indirect effect', a concept first outlined in the *von Colson* case, where the Court of Justice drew upon the duty of all member states, now contained in Article 4(3) TEU to 'take any appropriate measure, general or particular, to ensure fulfilment of the obligations arising out of the Treaties or resulting from the acts of the institutions of the Union'.[112] The concept ensures that the member states cannot neglect their duty to faithfully transpose EU directives and thereby ensures a measure of consistency (if not uniformity) across the EU. It is 'indirect' because this outcome is generated by judicial interpretation of the domestic legislation (if necessary dramatically departing from the literal meaning of such legislation).

A European legal system?

(i) UK judges as EU judges

The UK's entry into the supranational European Project impacted upon more than just law making, it also altered the constitutional role of UK judges. Where EU law is at issue, the UK's courts have effectively become domestic branches of the Court of Justice, tasked with

---

[106] Regulation (EC) No. 717/2007.

[107] Regulation (EU) No. 267/2012.

[108] Regulation (EC) No. 998/2003.

[109] Directive 2005/36/EC.

[110] The European Communities (Recognition of Professional Qualifications) Regulations 2007, SI 2007/2781.

[111] M. Wind, 'The European Union as a polycentric polity: Returning to a neo-medieval Europe' in J. Weiler and W. Wind, *European Constitutionalism Beyond the State* (CUP, 2003) 103, 127.

[112] Case C-14/83 *Sabine von Colson and Elisabeth Kamann* v *Land Nordrhein-Westfalen* [1984] ECR 1891.

ensuring that individuals can enforce their EU-protected interests (even, when EU law is clear, doing so without directly involving the Court of Justice[113]). This has prompted a shift in the courts' approach to the interpretation of legislation, as foreseen by Lord Scarman:

> If we stay in the [European Union], I would expect to see its principles of legislation and statutory interpretation and its conception of an activist court whose role is to strengthen and fulfil the purpose of statute law replace the traditional attitudes of English judges and lawyers to statute law and the current complex style of statutory drafting.[114]

Whilst this chapter has examined how EU law came to operate as a source of law within the domestic legal systems of the UK, we have yet to address where EU law fits within the hierarchy of sources of law, and particularly its relationship with parliamentary sovereignty. Lord Denning was one of the first judges to grasp the significance of EU law as a new autonomous source of law within the UK Constitution. In the *Bulmer* case[115] he declared that:

> The Treaty does not touch any of the matters which concern solely England and the people in it. These are still governed by English law. They are not affected by the Treaty. But when we come to matters with a European element, the Treaty is like an incoming tide. It flows into the estuaries and up the rivers. It cannot be held back, Parliament has decreed that the Treaty is henceforward to be part of our law. It is equal in force to any statute.[116]

Prescient though this recognition of the importance of EU law was at the time, there remains an inescapable problem with Lord Denning's statement. Sources cannot be said to be equally important in a constitution. Sooner or later rules originating from the different, supposedly equal, sources will come into conflict and the courts will have to decide which source is superior. For now it suffices to note that, for as long as the UK remains within the EU, even statutes can be disapplied where they conflict with EU law.[117] We will revisit such conflicts when we evaluate the concept of parliamentary sovereignty in Chapter 5.[118]

(ii) Diversity amid harmonisation

One final point must be emphasised before we leave this topic. The UK's courts only act as 'EU courts' in so far as an issue falls within the competence of the EU, and the EU has exercised that competence. During the later years of the twentieth century, many legal theorists presented the convergence of the European legal systems as the natural impact of the 'European project', with the harmonisation of rules being agreed even outside the EU's remit. Ambitious expeditions set out, for example, to forge harmonised rules of 'European private law'.[119] In the main, however, these expeditions have returned empty handed. The predicted convergence of European legal systems, into 'one great legal family with uniform or strongly similar rules in many areas',[120] remains unrealised.

---

[113] Case C-283/81, *Srl CILFIT and Lanificio di Gavardo SpA* v *Ministry of Health* [1982] ECR 3415, [16].

[114] L. Scarman, *English Law – The New Dimension* (Steven & Sons, 1974) p. 26.

[115] *Bulmer Ltd* v *Bollinger SA* [1974] Ch. 401.

[116] Ibid., 418.

[117] *R* v *Secretary of State for Transport, ex parte Factortame* (No. 2) [1991] 1 AC 603.

[118] See pp. 67–76.

[119] See European Commission 'A More Coherent European Contract Law – An Action Plan' COM(03)68 final.

[120] G.-R. de Groot, 'European Education in the 21st Century', in B. De Witte and C. Forder (eds), *The Common Law of Europe and the Future of Legal Education* (Kluwer, 1992) 7, 11.

Legal systems across Europe exist on the basis of fundamentally distinct common law and civil law models. As Legrand argues, it is almost impossible to harmonise such distinct models which maintain a very different legal ethos:

> [I]f one forgoes a surface examination at the level of rules and concepts to conduct a deep examination in terms of legal *mentalités,* one must come to the conclusion that legal systems, despite their adjacence within the [EU], have not been converging, are not converging and will not be converging.[121]

Worse, given that all of the legal systems of Europe developed as specific responses to the 'economic and political histories of the polities which they order',[122] piecemeal harmonisation of limited areas of law is likely to have unintended knock-on consequences in other areas. When the EU encounters such difficulties within one of its competences, it has the means to navigate such issues not through imposing uniformity, but by permitting member state legal systems to maintain their distinctiveness through tools such as directives. Friction between the EU and the member states often arises when, in a controversial field, the EU institutions (frequently the Commission) wish to impose greater harmonisation than the member states desire. It falls to each member state's domestic courts to help in the process of mitigating such tensions under the ultimate oversight of the Court of Justice.

Brexit: The UK's Withdrawal from the European Union

Key issues

- Brexit is a compound term describing a British-Exit from the European Union. It has become the defining contemporary constitutional issue since the UK electorate voted to support withdrawal from the EU in a referendum in June 2016.

- In the aftermath of the referendum result, David Cameron resigned as Prime Minister and was replaced by Theresa May after a leadership contest within the Conservative Party. Her attempts to manage the notification of withdrawal from the EU by Royal Prerogative were blocked in the Supreme Court.

- Following parliamentary authorisation for withdrawal in the European Union (Notification of Withdrawal) Act 2017, Theresa May has pursued a policy of negotiating a Free Trade Agreement with the EU alongside repealing the ECA 1972. This process remains ongoing at the time of writing.

The Brexit referendum

On 23 June 2016, a UK-wide referendum was held on the following question: 'Should the United Kingdom remain a member of the European Union or leave the European Union?'[123] By a majority of 52 per cent to 48 per cent, UK voters backed Brexit, the UK's withdrawal from the EU. The reasons behind the Brexit vote were myriad, but much of the Leave campaign was characterised by anxieties over the direction of the EU project

---

[121] P. Legrand, 'European Systems are not Converging' (1996) 45 ICLQ 52, 61–2.
[122] C. Joerges, 'The Challenge of Europeanization in the Realm of Private Law' (2004) *14 Duke J of Comparative and Intl Law* 149, 150.
[123] European Union Referendum Act 2015, s.1(4).

and its impact upon the UK's constitution, encapsulated in the Leave slogan 'Take back control'. This slogan has multiple legal-constitutional aspects. First, it speaks to concerns that the expansion of the EU's powers since UK membership had last been approved by a referendum in 1975 amounted to a loss of national sovereignty. David Cameron himself had kicked off the referendum campaign with a renegotiation of the UK's position in the EU on the basis that:

> [W]e do not want to have our country bound up in an ever closer political union in Europe. We are a proud and independent nation, with proud, independent, democratic institutions that have served us well over the centuries. For us, Europe is about working together to advance our shared prosperity and security; it is not about being sucked into some kind of European superstate – not now, not ever.[124]

This was not a ringing endorsement of the European Project. Even though David Cameron secured assurances from the European Council that the UK would not be bound by the principle of 'ever closer union',[125] his much-trumpeted renegotiation of this issue in early 2016 backfired. He was making much out of staving off a threat supposedly lurking in the wording of the treaties which in reality did not exist. Read in context, 'an ever closer union *among the peoples of Europe*' under Article 1 TEU does not speak to increased political integration or a European superstate. Instead, the Leave campaign harnessed the attention devoted to the issue to highlight the very real expansion of EU competences over the preceding 40 years (although not emphasising that Parliament had approved the treaties granting those new competences).

Second, 'Take back control' also plays upon the extent to which EU institutions make law for the UK. Hundreds of statutory instruments are passed annually under the ECA 1972 to give effect to EU law,[126] with a conservative estimate identifying 'that on average around 9 per cent of all statutory instruments originate in Brussels'.[127] And it must be remembered that many aspects of EU law are directly effective, preventing domestic institutions from altering their terms, creating anxieties about EU law overriding parliamentary sovereignty.[128] The volume of EU law contributed to 'the often tense relationship' between the EU and the UK.[129] In other words, many voters, even if they accepted that benefits accrued from harmonising legal rules affecting issues within the EU's competence, struggle to reconcile these benefits with the loss of national freedom of action. The Leave campaign was in particular able to connect popular concerns over levels of immigration into the UK to the UK's obligation under EU law to permit freedom of movement to EU citizens, in spite of David Cameron's renegotiation securing a so-called 'emergency brake' restricting the ability of EU citizens to claim in-work benefits.[130]

Third, 'Take back control' speaks to anxieties about the nature of EU law making. The EU came late to direct democratic input into its law making. Although the Lisbon Treaty strengthened the role of the European Parliament, and indeed national legislatures

---

[124] HC Debs, vol. 605, col. 925 (3 February 2016).

[125] European Council, *The United Kingdom and the European Union* (19 February 2016) Annex I, 16.

[126] European Communities Act 1972, s. 2(2).

[127] Lord Triesman, HL Debs., vol. 683, col. WA184 (29 June 2006).

[128] European Scrutiny Committee, *UK Government's Renegotiation of EU Membership: Parliamentary Sovereignty and Scrutiny* (2015) HC 458, para. 132.

[129] I. Ward, *A Critical Introduction to European Law* (CUP, 2003) pp. 45–6.

[130] European Council, *The United Kingdom and the European Union* (19 February 2016) Annex I, 19-24.

(through the 'yellow' and 'orange' card warning mechanism over controversial Commission proposals) these reforms had yet to displace the popular conception of the EU as a faceless bureaucracy. Again, David Cameron's renegotiation only served to highlight concerns over the EU's supposed democratic deficit:

> I also wanted to strengthen the role of this House and all national Parliaments, so we now have a proposal in the texts that if Brussels comes up with legislation that we do not want, we can get together with other Parliaments and block it with a red card.[131]

The European Council did accede to Cameron's request to institute a 'red card' procedure, but it did not amount to a veto by national legislatures over Commission proposals.[132] Moreover, the Leave campaign emphasised the Court of Justice's capacity to invalidate domestic measures (including Acts of Parliament) which conflicted with EU law.

Fourth, part of the EU's mission is to redistribute resources between member states so as to improve the general standard of living. This fed into the campaign as a narrative whereby the UK was a net-contributor state and other countries were net-beneficiary states from the EU budget, and that by 'Taking back control' of the money that the UK contributed to the EU budget Parliament would be able to use these funds to directly benefit the UK population. Leaving aside that indirect benefits flow to the UK from the EU's budgetary arrangements (raising living standards in countries like Romania enables its citizens to buy more cars made in the UK or to send more students to UK universities) the Leave campaign was once again advancing a narrative that the UK's domestic institutions are best placed to respond to the UK population's needs.

Fifth, the Leave campaign questioned whether the benefits of EU membership really necessitated the UK's membership of a supra-national institution. It posited that the UK need only conclude a bi-lateral Free Trade Agreement with the EU to maintain existing trade arrangements and that doing so would amount to an international, rather than supra-national, relationship. It maintained that such an arrangement would allow the UK to escape the jurisdiction of the Court of Justice.

Following the Brexit vote, David Cameron resigned and the task of turning this ambition into a reality fell to his successor as leader of the Conservative Party, Theresa May. When her administration outlined its Brexit strategy in a White Paper in 2017 it spoke to the antimonies which undermined the UK's EU membership; 'Whilst Parliament has remained sovereign throughout our membership of the EU, it has not always felt like that'.[133]

The aftermath of the referendum: in search of the feeling of sovereignty

Whether or not readers find these claims compelling, their ascendency within the UK's public discourse in the aftermath of the Brexit referendum heralded a constitutional turning point. The referendum legislation did not specify the steps that the UK Government would take in the aftermath of the result. Although in legal terms this meant that the

---

[131] HC Debs, vol. 605, col. 925 (3 February 2016).

[132] European Council, *The United Kingdom and the European Union* (19 February 2016) Annex I, 17-18.

[133] T. May, *The United Kingdom's Exit from and New Partnership with the European Union* (2017) Cmnd. 9417, para. 2.1.

referendum was advisory in nature, David Cameron had informed Parliament what would happen following a vote for Brexit:

> For a Prime Minister to ignore the express will of the British people to leave the EU would be not just wrong, but undemocratic . . . If the British people vote to leave, there is only one way to bring that about, namely to trigger Article 50 of the Treaties and begin the process of exit, and the British people would rightly expect that to start straight away.[134]

Following Cameron's resignation, Theresa May's administration had to put into action its interpretation of the will of the people as expressed in the referendum vote. Article 50(1) TEU asserts that any EU member state can decide to withdraw from the EU 'in accordance with its own constitutional requirements'. The meaning of this provision is, however, unfortunately enigmatic in the context of the UK's uncodified constitutional arrangements.

The UK Government maintained that Article 50, as a change in the UK's treaty arrangements, could be triggered by exercise of the royal prerogative. Its reasons for seeking to by-pass Parliament at this stage of the process were two-fold: first, ministers were concerned that MPs (who had by overwhelming majority backed remaining within the EU) would seek to frustrate or delay the Brexit process; and, second, they considered that the referendum vote supplied the necessary democratic legitimacy for managing the initial phases of withdrawal through the prerogative.[135] But even within the Conservative Party senior politicians, including the former Attorney-General Dominic Grieve, questioned this approach:

> [T]he *acquis communautaire* . . . is about the conferring of private legal rights on individuals in this country which have the force of statute. . . . [T]he idea that those should simply be revoked by our exit without parliamentary approval troubles me very much and appears to me to be an abdication of the responsibility of this House.[136]

The courts therefore became embroiled in settling the issue of what the UK constitution required to trigger Article 50. In *Miller* the Divisional Court resolved the issue in part by relying on the 'constitutional statutes' doctrine;[137] the ECA 1972 was such an important statute that it could only be altered by the express terms of another statute.[138] The judgment provoked a storm of criticism in sections of the media which backed Brexit; the *Daily Mail* headline screamed that the judges were 'Enemies of the People'.[139]

In these fraught circumstances the Government's appeal against this decision was leap-frogged directly to the Supreme Court, to be heard before a special eleven-judge panel. For the eight judges of the majority, two issues were determinative. The first was that, as Dominic Grieve had warned Parliament, the rights and obligations of private parties would be altered by Brexit. Second the majority recognised that EU law-based rights will be affected from the moment the Article 50 process is initiated:

> If ministers give Notice without Parliament having first authorised them to do so, the die will be cast before Parliament has become formally involved. . . . [T]he bullet will have left the gun before Parliament has accorded the necessary leave for the trigger to be pulled.[140]

---

[134] HC Debs, vol. 606, col. 24 (22 February 2016).

[135] D. Davis, HC Debs, vol. 614, col. 61 (5 September 2016).

[136] D. Grieve, HC Debs, vol. 614, col. 52 (5 September 2016).

[137] See pp. 158–61.

[138] *Miller* v *Secretary of State for Exiting the European Union* [2016] EWHC 2768 (admin); [2017] 1 All ER 158, [88] (Lord Thomas).

[139] J. Slack, 'Enemies of the People' *Daily Mail* (4 November 2016).

[140] *R (Miller)* v *Secretary of State for Exiting the European Union* [2017] UKSC 5; [2017] 2 WLR 583, [94] (Lord Neuberger).

Unless ministers could point to a statute in which 'Parliament "squarely confront[ed]" the notion that it was clothing ministers with the far-reaching and anomalous right to use a treaty-making power to remove an important source of domestic law and important domestic rights' the Supreme Court majority would not allow them to trigger Article 50 on this basis.[141] Not even the referendum result altered this position; 'unless and until acted on by Parliament, its force is political rather than legal'.[142] If the circumstances of the *Miller* case were highly-charged, the Supreme Court majority's decision itself breaks little new ground; the position affirms the centrality of Parliament within the UK's constitutional order. In light of the intense interest in the judgment the majority needed to present a united front, and these circumstances fostered a cautious approach which coalesced around grounds which all eight judges in the majority could agree upon.

In handing the keys to the Brexit process to Parliament, the Supreme Court could be confident that it was not precipitating a constitutional crisis. As was noted in the *Miller* decision, the Commons had already passed a motion recognising 'that this House should respect the wishes of the United Kingdom as expressed in the referendum on 23 June'.[143] In response to the judgment ministers swiftly introduced a two-clause Bill inviting Parliament to give them the power to issue a notification of withdrawal pursuant to Article 50. As the Supreme Court had noted, the referendum's significance might have been political, but it was no less important for that; most remain-supporting MPs accepted the legislation on the basis that they could not challenge the will of the electorate as expressed in the referendum. Less than two months after the *Miller* judgment the European Union (Notification of Withdrawal) Act 2017 came into force. Two weeks later, on 29 March 2017, Theresa May used the power granted to her by Parliament to notify the European Council of the UK's decision to leave the EU, in accordance with Article 50(2).

The on going process of withdrawing from the EU

In the words of the Supreme Court majority in *Miller,* '[a] complete withdrawal represents . . . as significant a constitutional change as that which occurred when EU law was first incorporated in domestic law by the 1972 Act'.[144] The legislative process of extricating the UK from the EU is, however, anything but simple. The effects of EU law extend across whole areas of rights and obligations, from trade law, to intellectual property, to employment relationships. Not only does the UK have to shut off the 'conduit pipe'[145] connecting it to EU law by repealing the ECA 1972, it must translate the EU law which has already flowed through that pipe into the UK's domestic legal systems into a form of UK law. Nor is it simply a matter of translation, for much of that law is intertwined with EU institutions. All of these measures will have to be re-examined and adapted to accommodate new domestic institutions taking the place of their EU counterparts. At the time of writing, Parliament is in the midst of making this shift a reality in the form of the European Union (Withdrawal) Bill (with further legislation to come substituting new domestic law in key areas currently within the EU's competence), which is proceeding in parallel to

---

[141] Ibid., [87].
[142] Ibid., [124].
[143] HC Debs, vol. 618, col. 336 (7 December 2016).
[144] *R (Miller)* v *Secretary of State for Exiting the European Union* [2017] UKSC 5; [2017] 2 WLR 583, [81] (Lord Neuberger).
[145] Ibid., [65].

negotiations with the EU under the two-year timeframe established by Article 50(3). The complexity of this twin-track approach, to be completed by March 2019, is stretching the capacity of the UK civil service. Following the loss of her parliamentary majority after the June 2017 general election, it is also a task that will stretch Theresa May's ability to manage the House of Commons.

The European Union (Withdrawal) Bill is before the Commons at the time of writing and makes provision for the repeal of the ECA 1972. On one level, the process of repeal is parliamentary theatre; the ECA makes provision for implementing the UK's treaty obligations (which will no longer exist once the withdrawal process has been completed). The bigger challenge is converting the body of EU law currently operative within UK law into a form of domestic law. This is necessary to prevent gaps in the law from appearing at the point of Brexit, but it is also complex. EU law presupposes EU institutions to manage it, and references to such institutions in transposed law must be altered. Moreover much EU law is directly applicable within the UK's domestic legal systems, and has not, therefore, been subject to existing UK legislation. The Bill therefore proposes a continuation clause, maintaining its effect until such time as Parliament chooses to alter it.[146]

The UK Government is also eager to immediately alter some areas substantive rules to fit its post Brexit policy priorities. According to the Government, some alterations will be tackled by delegated legislation passed under a future European Union (Withdrawal) Act, whereas major policy changes will be effected by new legislation.[147] Such claims are, however, inherently controversial. The Bill proposes to give ministers Henry VIII powers[148] to alter legislation enacting EU law (for example, the Consumer Protection Act 1987) by statutory instrument, with their judgement determining whether a change really is minor.[149] The House of Lords' Constitution Committee questioned these proposals:

> We accept that the Government will require some Henry VIII powers in order to amend primary legislation to facilitate the UK's withdrawal from the European Union, but they should not be granted lightly, and they must come with commensurate safeguards and levels of scrutiny. We do not believe that the Government has engaged with the need for such safeguards.[150]

Ministers need some delegated law-making powers in order to manage Brexit, but much of the legislative battle to come will likely focus on the level of parliamentary scrutiny over such powers (and whether consequent statutory instruments will need to be affirmed by the Commons and Lords).

Whilst the mechanisms making EU law a source of domestic law are being repealed the UK has to negotiate both its exit with the EU and the terms of its future relationship. As a matter of domestic law, all that is necessary for withdrawal would be the repeal of the ECA 1972. But undertaking such a course prior to the completing of the Article 50 TEU process would breach the UK's obligations under EU law and undermine hopes of close relations with the EU after Brexit. At the time of writing attempting to forecast the shape of those negotiations would be an exercise in speculation, but it suffices to note that the same forces driving the referendum debate are shaping disagreements over the shape of the future

---

[146] European Union (Withdrawal) Bill 2016, cl. 2.
[147] T. May, *Legislating for the United Kingdom's withdrawal from the European Union* (2017) Cm. 9446, para. 1.21.
[148] See pp. 32–4.
[149] European Union (Withdrawal) Bill 2016, cl. 7.
[150] Constitution Committee, *European Union (Withdrawal) Bill 2017: Interim Report* (2017) HL 19, para. 48.

relationship. The UK could seek membership of the European Economic Area (the EEA), which covers countries including Norway and Iceland, to secure some of the benefits of economic integration. But in doing so the UK would have to adhere to broad areas of EU law (including free movement of labour) and would find itself under the jurisdiction of the European Free Trade Area Court, a judicial body which usually follows Court of Justice jurisprudence. Given the prospect of these restrictions on the UK's sovereignty, without the say over new Commission proposals that EU member states enjoy, the Brexit Secretary has dismissed EEA membership as 'the worst of all outcomes'.[151]

The UK Government is instead pursuing a bespoke Free Trade Agreement with the EU, in line with countries like Switzerland and Canada.[152] Concerns over sovereignty come to the fore in this position. As Theresa May told the 2016 Conservative Party Conference, she wanted 'free trade, in goods and services' between the UK and the EU, but only on the basis of 'an agreement between an independent, sovereign United Kingdom and the European Union'.[153] Such Agreements, however, are often painstakingly slow to negotiate and need to be approved by both the EU and all of its remaining member states. And its terms would likely require the UK to maintain regulatory standards that were harmonised with the EU (the 'red-tape' so loathed by Euro-sceptics). The EU also has reason to be cautious of rushing into making such a deal; if the UK secures a favourable trade deal having left the EU this could spur movements in other EU member states seeking to follow the UK's example.[154] If the UK Government does not get an outcome from negotiations that it can accept then the UK will adopt a position of trading with the EU under World Trade Organization rules, with the Prime Minister repeatedly insisting that 'no deal for the UK is better than a bad deal for the UK'.[155] In such a scenario the UK would escape the constraints of EU law, but potentially at the cost of subjecting UK exporters to invidious barriers to trade. In an increasingly globalised world, the independence of sovereign states is not necessarily all it is cracked up to be.

Conclusion

International law and, for now, EU law constitute significant sources of legal rules and general principles within the UK's constitutional order, and that it is impossible to understand the UK's current constitutional arrangements without understanding its interactions with these legal orders. Brexit does not seek to fully seal the UK Constitution from these influences, but it does seek to assert an expression of national sovereignty; more say by UK institutions over whether and how external sources play a role in the UK Constitution. Theresa May's Government has, since initiating the withdrawal process under Article 50 TEU, been determined to substitute supranational arrangements (the UK being part of the EU) for international agreements (the UK doing deals with the EU). With regard to

---

[151] D. Davis, HC Debs, vol. 628, col. 286 (7 September 2017).

[152] T. May, *The United Kingdom's Exit from and New Partnership with the European Union* (2017) Cmnd. 9417, para. 8.1.

[153] T. May, 'Britain after Brexit: A Vision of a Global Britain' (2 October 2016).

[154] International Trade Committee, UK Trade Options Beyond 2019 (2017) HC 817, para. 60.

[155] T. May, *The United Kingdom's Exit from and New Partnership with the European Union* (2017) Cmnd. 9417, para. 12.3.

external sovereignty, striking agreements with the EU and other partner states will create binding obligations upon the UK to maintain certain standards in its domestic law. As for internal sovereignty, the enormity of the task of legislating for Brexit is already seeing Parliament delegate considerable law-making authority to ministers. As the post-Brexit arrangements take shape, entire areas of repatriated competences might well be transferred to the devolved legislatures. As Gordon warns, 'any expectation that Brexit could herald a glorious restoration of sovereignty in the UK emerges as a false promise based on a flawed premise'.[156]

Practice questions

1. *'The position would . . . seem to be that an alleged breach of Part 2 of the [Constitutional Reform and Governance] Act could, in principle, be justiciable, but courts are likely still to be reluctant to interfere with the exercise of the power when the issue involves policy concerning foreign relations.'*

   (J. Barrett, 'The United Kingdom and Parliamentary scrutiny of treaties: recent reforms' (2011) 60 ICLQ 225, 242)

   Evaluate Barrett's claim, and whether, in light of it, the reforms enacted under Part 2 of the Constitutional Reform and Governance Act 2010 have had any meaningful impact.

2. *'Treaties, as it is sometimes expressed, are not self-executing. Quite simply, a treaty is not part of English law unless and until it has been incorporated into the law by legislation.'*

   (*J. H. Rayner (Mincing Lane) Ltd* v *Department of Trade and Industry* [1990] 2 AC 418, 500 (Lord Oliver))

   Evaluate whether claims that unincorporated treaties cannot affect legal obligations within the UK's domestic legal systems remain valid.

3. *'The idea of a "post-national constitutionalism" does not . . . appeal to everyone. It has certainly met with a mixed reception in the United Kingdom. We, it is commonly said, have been the "awkward partner" in the "new" Europe.'*

   (I. Ward, *The English Constitution: Myths and Realities* (Hart, 2004) p. 134)

   Evaluate why the UK's constitutional framework struggled to accommodate EU membership.

Further reading

This chapter examines the sources of law which, although they originate outside the UK legal systems, can (and sometimes must) be drawn upon by the UK courts. Only in the last few decades would this issue have warranted more than a few lines in a textbook upon the UK Constitution, for as Katherine Thomas (**K. Thomas, 'The Changing Status of International Law in English Domestic Law'** (2006) 53 *Netherlands International Law Review* 371–398) explains, these decades have seen a profound shift in the relationship between international and domestic law in the UK. Her work provides a thorough analysis of the relevant case law and theoretical underpinnings of the relationship, whilst Jill

---

[156] M. Gordon, 'The UK's Sovereignty Situation: Brexit, Bewilderment and Beyond . . . ' (2016) 27 KLJ 333, 335.

Barrett's readers (**J. Barrett, 'The United Kingdom and Parliamentary Scrutiny of Treaties: Recent Reforms'** (2011) 60 *International and Comparative Law Quarterly* 225–245) will find an extensive analysis of how the UK Parliament has tackled the increasing volume of international agreements involving the UK by legalising parliamentary involvement in the treaty ratification process under the Constitutional Reform and Governance Act 2010. Moving from treaties to customary international law, Anthea Roberts (**A. Roberts, 'Comparative International Law? The Role of National Courts in International Law'** (2011) 60 *International and Comparative Law Quarterly* 57–92) provides a valuable account of the challenges faced by national courts in transposing the rules of customary international law (and especially *jus cogens* norms).

We thereafter addressed the EU and its impact on the UK legal system. In the context of this basic outline of a complex and supranational legal order, further reading is best directed towards understanding the EU institutions. Paul Craig (**P. Craig, 'The Treaty of Lisbon: Process, Architecture and Substance'** (2008) 33 *European Law Review* 137–166) unpacks the changes to the institutional structure and law-making processes of the EU brought about by the Lisbon Treaty and compares them to the proposals under the abandoned European Constitutional Treaty. This analysis is complemented by the work of Jukka Snell (**J. Snell, '"European Constitutional Settlement", an Ever Closer Union, and the Treaty of Lisbon: Democracy or Relevance?'** (2008) 33 *European Law Review* 619–642), who analyses the necessity of democratic input to legitimise the operations of EU competences. As for the implications of Brexit for the UK Constitution, it is worth reading Michael Gordon's short response in the aftermath of the June 2016 referendum (**M. Gordon, 'The UK's Sovereignty Situation: Brexit, Bewilderment and Beyond . . . '** (2016) 27 *King's Law Journal* 333–343).

Remember that this chapter is only intended to introduce the UK Constitution's external sources. We will return to consider the EU specifically when we investigate parliamentary sovereignty (Chapter 5) and evaluate the incorporation of the ECHR into the UK Constitution (Chapters 20 and 21).

Chapter 4
Law, politics and the nature of the United Kingdom Constitution

'The constitution of the United Kingdom lives on, changing from day to day for the constitution is no more and no less than what happens. Everything that happens is constitutional. And if nothing happened that would be constitutional also.'

J. A. G. Griffith, 'The Political Constitution' (1979) 42 *Modern Law Review* 1, 19.

Chapter outline

This chapter examines the interplay between law and politics in the UK Constitution, highlighting that, in many ways, the study of the UK Constitution is a study of politics as much as a study of law. Two alternative readings of the UK Constitution will be introduced. First, we will consider the 'political' constitution as outlined by J. A. G. Griffith, before moving on to look at the contrasting ideas associated with common law constitutionalism. Each model envisages a particular role for the courts within the constitution. Courts in the 'political' constitution play a limited role, secondary to that of elected politicians. By contrast, common law constitutionalism envisages a more active role for the judges in holding elected politicians to account, envisaging the common law as articulating the fundamental guiding principles of the constitution. Each theory will be examined against the track record of recent decisions in the contested area of human rights protection. Finally, and as a precursor to the more detailed treatment of constitutional reform to follow, the suggestion that the UK Constitution is slowly becoming more legal than political will be introduced.

Introduction: the relationships between law and politics

Key issues

Questions of law and politics are intertwined in the UK Constitution; they cannot, therefore, be compartmentalised and considered separately of each other. Decisions taken by elected officials in pursuance of a political agenda may give rise to legal action to be resolved in the courts. Judicial decisions may, in turn, prompt debate in Parliament, and a change in the law. This law may, in turn, govern action taken by officials which is subsequently challenged in the courts, and so on. The relationship between law and politics in the constitution is both symbiotic and multifaceted.

The relationships that exist between the law and politics are central to any discussion of the UK Constitution. Law and politics cannot be considered in complete isolation of each other in this sphere. The two are intimately entangled and enjoy a symbiotic relationship; as a result, a study of the constitution which focuses solely on law or politics to the exclusion of the other would be impoverished. We have already seen that the UK Constitution is not codified, and that many of the rules and practices relating to the conduct of government in the UK are not legally enforceable. Constitutional conventions and the customs associated with the conduct of parliamentary proceedings are perhaps the prime examples of this type of rule; each has constitutional status, though neither is enforced by the ordinary courts.[1]

To characterise the constitution as being an entirely legal entity, therefore, would be misleading. To similarly characterise disputes, or adjudication, over the constitutional effects of law as lacking a political dimension would be similarly mistaken. In reality, the study of the UK Constitution is as much a study of *political* relationships and dynamics as it is a study of law in the formal sense. This is for the reason that many of the concepts which are seen as being central to an understanding of the UK Constitution can be seen to have both legal and political characteristics, both of which should be examined in order to achieve a complete appreciation of the constitution itself. Take for instance what is arguably the most fundamental principle on which the UK Constitution is based, parliamentary sovereignty.[2] In its legal sense, the sovereignty doctrine holds that Parliament can make, or indeed unmake, any law. As a result, Parliament holds the supreme legal authority within the constitution, and appears to hold a legal power which, in theory at least, can be utilised in order to achieve any aim whatsoever. The *exercise* of this theoretically limitless power is, however, restrained in practice by the contemporary political priorities and values of the time. So while in theory at least Parliament may possess the legal power to legislate in any manner of outlandish and/or draconian ways – for instance to command that all blue-eyed babies be put to death[3] – the potential political cost of its so doing will, it is hoped, exercise a restraining influence to prevent this unfettered legal power from being invoked to cause manifest injustice.[4] In this very basic sense then, the interplay between law and politics can be demonstrated. As a matter of legal doctrine, Parliament's sovereignty is unfettered. As a matter of practical politics, there are in fact many issues on which Parliament would not legislate in order to avoid potential public unrest.[5]

Thinking Point . . .

Using parliamentary sovereignty as his example, Ivor Jennings reminds that in constitutional affairs the gap between theory and practice is often wide: 'De Lolme's remark that Parliament can do anything except make a man into a woman and a woman into a man is often quoted.

→

---

[1] See pp. 40–51.

[2] On which, see Chapter 5.

[3] L. Stephen, *The Science of Ethics* (Smith, Elder and Co., 1882) p. 143 (cited in T. R. S. Allan, *Law Liberty and Justice: the Legal Foundations of British Constitutionalism* (Clarendon Press, 1993) p. 130. Cf. J. Goldsworthy, *The Sovereignty of Parliament: History and Philosophy* (Clarendon Press, 1999) pp. 259–72.

[4] For judicial recognition of the ability of political realities to restrain Parliament's theoretically unlimited power, see: *R v Secretary of State for the Home Department, ex parte Simms* [2002] 2 AC 115, 131 (Lord Hoffmann); *R (Jackson) v Attorney-General* [2006] 1 AC 262, [159] (Baroness Hale).

[5] A. V. Dicey, *Introduction to the Study of the Law of the Constitution* (Liberty Fund, 1982) pp. 24 and 26.

> But, like many of the remarks which de Lolme made, it is wrong . . . Though it is true that Parliament cannot change the course of nature, it is equally true that it cannot in fact do all sorts of things. The supremacy of Parliament is a legal fiction, and legal fiction can assume anything.' (I. Jennings, *The Law and the Constitution* (5th edn) (University of London Press, 1959) p. 170) This gap is bridged in part by the prevailing political values and debates reflected in Parliament's legislative output.

Those elements of governmental activity which are more visible in the day-to-day operation of the constitutional system also display legal and political dynamics. In the operation of judicial review of executive action[6] – the mechanism by which government is most frequently brought before the courts – for instance, the legal and political dimensions of the constitution can be seen at a more practical level. In the event that a legal dispute comes before the courts involving the government as a party to the proceedings – whether as a result of the activities of a Secretary of State or of a local government official – that dispute can be said to have a political dimension. Though the mechanism for the resolution of the dispute (the court), and the grounds on which the dispute is resolved (the law), are obviously legal in character, the dispute will often have arisen as a result of the actions, or inaction, of a political actor exercising, or purporting to exercise, legal powers. The resolution of that dispute, in the sense that it may condition the future exercise of governmental powers by other ministers or officials, will also have a political outcome. And, assuming that the subject matter of the case involves the legal extent of power conferred on the minister or official by statute, the resolution of the dispute will be conditioned by legally enforceable rules that were initially proposed and debated in Parliament, by politicians.

Key debates

R (Miller) v Secretary of State for Exiting the European Union

The *Miller* adjudication – *R (Miller) v Secretary of State for Exiting the European Union* [2016] EWHC 2768 (Admin) and [2017] UKSC 5 – highlights interrelationships between law and politics particularly well. The processes by which the UK will leave the European Union are inherently political; the decision to leave rests upon the expressed preference of a majority of those voting in a UK-wide referendum and the UK's future relationship with the EU will be primarily determined by elected representatives seeking to negotiate the specific parameters of that relationship in respect of trade, immigration, security co-operation, and many, many other matters besides. The *Miller* adjudication was, by contrast, focused upon a discrete element of this far broader process.

Miller concerned a challenge to the government's position that the decision to notify the European Union of the UK's intent to leave (under Article 50 of the Treaty of Lisbon) could be taken by the executive alone, on the basis of its prerogative powers. The claimants effectively argued that the prerogative could not be used to 'diminish or abrogate rights' (such as those arising under EU law) unless Parliament had allocated by statute that power to the government

---

[6] On which see Chapters 18 and 19.

(which the claimants contended Parliament had not done). In the High Court's decision in *Miller*, the Court therefore emphasised that:

'. . . the court in these proceedings is only dealing with a pure question of law. Nothing we say has any bearing on the question of the merits or demerits of a withdrawal by the UK from the European Union; nor does it have any bearing on government policy, because government policy is not law. The policy to be applied by the executive government and the merits and demerits of withdrawal are matters of political judgement to be resolved through the political process. The legal question is whether the executive government can use the Crown's prerogative powers to give notice of withdrawal ([5]).'

A similar sentiment was evident in the lead judgment of Lord Neuberger in the Supreme Court:

'It is . . . worth emphasising that this case has nothing to do with issues such as the wisdom of the decision to withdraw from the European Union, the terms of withdrawal, the timetable or arrangements for withdrawal, or the details of any future relationship with the European Union. Those are all political issues which are matters for ministers and Parliament to resolve ([3]).'

Neither court sought to deny that its decision would have political implications, or that its judgment formed part of a much broader series of decisions relating to the UK's exit from the European Union, rather both attempted to highlight that the justiciable question to be determined was whether – as a matter of UK constitutional law – the executive alone held the power to formally begin the process of withdrawal.

In other words, the relationships between law and politics are not simply of a one-dimensional nature. In fact, the interplay between law and politics can take a number of differing forms, with the examples given so far providing only a brief glimpse of the many differing ways in which law and politics can and do interact. As Adam Tomkins has written, in addressing the relationships between the law and politics:

[W]e could be concerned with any of the following: (1) the relationship between legal and political *institutions* – between courts and legislatures, for example, or between the bar and political parties; (2) the relationship between legal and political *actors* – between barristers and politicians, or between judges and civil servants, for example; (3) the relationship between *academic disciplines*, that is between political science and law as they are taught and studied in universities; (4) the relationship between legal and political theories – between jurisprudential questions such as the obligation to obey the law and questions of political philosophy such as democracy and the common good; and (5) the relationship between legal and political values (or prejudices), which could in itself mean either one (or both) of two things – a relationship between a legal value and a different political value (between, say, individual privacy and national security) or a relationship between a legal perception of a value and a different political perception of the same value (between, say a lawyer who thought that fair administration required the giving of reasons and a politician who thought that fair administration required decision-makers to make decisions as speedily as possible). To make matters more complicated we might be concerned about any number of these alternatives in combination . . . [7]

In short then, the relationships between law and politics are numerous, multifaceted, and complicated.

---

[7] A. Tomkins, 'In Defence of the Political Constitution' (2002) 22 OJLS 157, 166. See also: M. Loughlin, *Sword and Scales: An Examination of the Relationship between Law and Politics* (Hart Publishing, 2000) ch. 14.

So the study of the UK Constitution is not simply a study of the law, nor is it simply a study of politics, it is a study of both. While later chapters of this book will examine the relationships between governmental institutions, governmental actors and indeed between government and the individual, this chapter seeks to outline the relevance of the interplay of law and politics to the shape and nature of the constitution more broadly and to high-light a number of controversies that will be returned to in subsequent chapters. We have already found that the constitution is uncodified, and that its sources can be found in a multitude of rules and practice of contemporary, historic and international origins, now we will examine some of the debates centring on the question of whether law, or politics, is or should be the dominant force in our constitutional arrangements.

Two competing ideas of constitutionalism

Key issues

Two polarised schools of thought dominate debate over the nature of the UK Constitution. Those who view the constitution as being predominantly 'political' in character emphasise the importance of democratic government, and regard the political process as the most important check on (and facilitator of) governmental power. By contrast, legal constitutionalists suggest that government takes place within the regulatory framework provided by the law. As a result, those who fall in the latter camp argue that the courts and the legal process provide a more effective counter-balance to the powers of government.

A. V. Dicey has been described as having the status of a 'guru'[8] for constitutional lawyers in the UK; new editions of Dicey's *Introduction to the Study of the Law of the Constitution* were being described as the 'classical' exposition of the constitution less than twenty years after its first publication.[9] His genius was organisational, for he was the first person to produce a convincing account of how constitutional principles mapped onto the operation of the constitution. Jeffrey Jowell has reduced Dicey's balancing of principles to the following formula:

> Although [Dicey] regarded Parliamentary sovereignty as the primary principle – one that could override the Rule of Law – he recognized that, ideally, Parliament and all public officials should respect the Rule of Law as a quality that distinguished a democratic from a despotic constitution.[10]

This statement highlights Dicey's inner conflict as to the relationship between these principles. Elsewhere, he saluted the common law as the font of civil liberties under the constitution.[11] This 'paradox'[12] at the centre of Dicey's constitution gave rise to different

---

[8] A. W. B. Simpson, *Human Rights and the End of Empire: Britain and the Genisis of the European Convention* (OUP, 2001) p. 33.

[9] R. Blackburn, 'Dicey and the Teaching of Public Law' [1985] PL 679, 688.

[10] J. Jowell, 'The Rule of Law and its Underlying Values' in J. Jowell and D. Oliver (eds), *The Changing Constitution* (6th edn, OUP, 2007) p. 5.

[11] A. Dicey, *Introduction to the Study of the Law of the Constitution* (Liberty Fund, 1982) p. 115.

[12] K. D. Ewing and C. A. Gearty, *The Struggle for Civil Liberties* (OUP, 2000) p. 21.

constitutional schools of thought, with very different outlooks on the proper relationship between the courts and Parliament.

The political constitution

In Chapter 1 we encountered the work of the constitutional scholar J. A. G. Griffith. Griffith, it will be recalled, argued that a constitution is defined, not by a prescriptive catalogue of specific characteristics, but is characterised, purely and simply, by how a system of government, and the actors within that system, operate in practice. Griffith argued, in his seminal article, 'The Political Constitution'[13] that the realities of day-to-day political practice lay at the heart of the UK's constitutional arrangements. Further to this, Griffith expressed a strong preference for a system in which governmental accountability was secured through the operation of the political process, rather than in the courtroom. Important decisions, he argued, should be taken by elected and removable politicians so that the ability of the electorate to participate (albeit indirectly) in the business of government be preserved.

Griffith did not argue that there should be *no* meaningful role for judges within the constitutional framework; rather, he suggested that the role of courts should be strictly limited. As a result, Griffith offered broad support for the role of courts as part of the criminal justice process and for the role of courts in ensuring that 'public authorities do not exceed their legal powers'.[14] His preference was for a positivistic approach to the law;[15] courts should therefore seek to apply the law passed by Parliament in as literal a manner as was possible, rather than seek to give meanings to the words of statutes that may not have been intended by the legislature.[16] Griffith was therefore deeply sceptical of a judicial branch able to influence – and worse still, override – judgments taken by elected officials on matters of public controversy. Judges – unelected, unrepresentative and unaccountable – he argued, should not possess the power to displace decisions taken by elected representatives. The role of the judges – and of law – in this regard was therefore of secondary importance to the process of politics. As a result, Griffith argued, 'the principle function of the judiciary is to support the institutions of government as established by law' rather than to drive – or indeed to resist – radical social change.[17] Griffith's view of the constitution, therefore, can be placed within the school of thought that views the law – not as a potential brake on political activity or political change – but as a facilitator of effective government and of societal development.

Griffith wrote 'The Political Constitution' in the late 1970s when a number of high-profile legal commentators were seeking to advance legal change which would have seen a significant increase in legal regulation within the constitution. Lord Hailsham – the future Lord Chancellor under Margaret Thatcher's government – had published a book arguing against the powers of an over-mighty executive branch (in his words an 'elective dictatorship') and proposing various legal limitations on the powers of governments including a Bill of Rights.[18] Meanwhile, the judge Lord Scarman had given a series of

---

[13] J. A. G. Griffith, 'The Political Constitution' (1979) 42 MLR 1.
[14] Ibid., 15.
[15] Ibid., 19.
[16] See J. Steyn, Does Legal Formalism Hold Sway in England? (1996) *Current Legal Problems* 43.
[17] J. A. G. Griffith, *The Politics of the Judiciary* (5th edn) (Fontana Press, 1997) p. 343.
[18] Lord Hailsham, *The Dilemma of Democracy* (Collins, 1978).

influential lectures in which he proposed an entrenched constitution and Bill of Rights, a Supreme Court and limitations on the sovereign power of Parliament.[19] The legal philosopher Ronald Dworkin had also published his work, *Taking Rights Seriously,* in which he suggested that in 'hard cases' – that is, disputes which cannot be readily determined under a clear, pre-existing, legal rule – judges should rely on external 'principles' in order to guide their resolution of the problem.[20] Each of these authors provoked fierce criticism from Griffith, who saw revitalising and reforming the political process – not handing further power to the judges,[21] or employing methods of judicial reasoning which departed from literal methods of interpretation[22] – as the solution to crises of accountability. Griffith argued:

> I am . . . much more concerned to create situations in which groups of individuals may make their political claims and seek to persuade governments to accept them. I therefore want greater opportunities for discussion, more open government, less restriction on debate, weaker Official Secrets Acts, more access to information, stronger pressure from backbenchers, changes in the law of contempt of court.[23]

The democratic process was therefore at the core of Griffith's understanding of the constitution. While Griffith did not necessarily trust the judgments of politicians any more than he trusted the decisions of judges, the fact that the electorate might participate in the appointment and the removal of politicians made the *process* of decision-making by elected officials preferable to decision-making by unelected judges.[24] While debate and argument in both legal and political fora thrive on disagreement, the characteristics of each process are markedly different. As we have already seen, the electorate is able to exercise a choice over who is elected to govern on our behalf. By contrast, the electorate has no say over the appointment of the judiciary. Political decision-making is, in theory, open to accommodate the wide and varying viewpoints of political parties, interest groups and campaigners, and individuals. By contrast, the world of legal argument is – mostly[25] – limited to the viewpoints of the parties to the case. Participation in the political process is free, while bringing a case before a court will incur significant financial cost. Decision-making in the political realm is frequently able to benefit large numbers of people. Decisions of courts are less frequently – though not always of course – of benefit to those other than the victorious party to the case.[26] Decisions taken by courts frequently give the impression that there is one right answer to whatever dispute is before them,

---

[19] Lord Scarman, *English Law – The New Dimension* (Stevens and Sons, 1974).

[20] R. Dworkin, *Taking Rights Seriously* (Duckworth, 1977).

[21] J. A. G. Griffith, 'The Political Constitution' (1979) 42 MLR 1, 14.

[22] Ibid., 12.

[23] Ibid., 18.

[24] R. Bellamy, *Political Constitutionalism: A Republican Defence of the Constitutionality of Democracy* (CUP, 2007) p. 164 : '. . . the test of a political process is not so much that it generates outcomes we agree *with* as that it produces outcomes that we can all agree *to*, on the grounds that they are legitimate'.

[25] Though in recent years the appearance of third-party interveners (otherwise known as *amicus curiae,* literally meaning 'friend of the court') in litigation has become a far more regular occurrence. See for disucussion: S. Hannett, 'Third Party Intervention: in the Public Interest?' [2003] PL 128; M. Arshi and C. O'Cinneide, 'Third Party Intervention: the Public Interest Re-Affirmed' [2004] PL 69.

[26] While judicial decisions may accommodate disagreement in the form of dissenting judgments, this is of no immediate benefit to the losing party to the legal dispute.

rather than a number of (perhaps equally valid) alternatives. As a result, it is easy to see why Griffith held an ideological preference in favour of matters of political controversy being determined, as far as possible, by elected politicians. As Tomkins has observed, the democratic credentials of Parliament, and other elected bodies, will always outweigh those of the courts.[27]

Griffith's work provided an important corrective for studies of the constitution that neglected the interplay between law and politics, and his scepticism of the extension of judicial power at the expense of open political argument continues to be seen in the work of a number of more contemporary commentators on the UK Constitution.[28]

Common law constitutionalism

The UK Constitution retains many 'political' characteristics in the sense envisaged by Griffith. Institutions comprised of elected officials – the Westminster Parliament, the devolved Parliament in Scotland and Assemblies in Northern Ireland and Wales, and local government – clearly exercise significant influence within our system of government. The ability of Parliament to hold the government to account, and of the electorate to participate in determining the composition of Parliament, both play a central role in our democratic system.[29] Increasingly however, the ability of elected officials to act absent the supervisory jurisdiction of the courts has become limited. The growth in judicial power *vis-à-vis* that of the democratic branches of government – evidenced most obviously in the development and expansion of the judicial review jurisdiction since the 1950s[30] – has prompted constitutional scholars to introduce alternative explanations of the balance of governmental powers within the constitution. The development of the judicial review jurisdiction has led to judicial interventions in the business of 'politics' on a much more regular basis, and with considerably more influence, than countenanced for much of the twentieth century.[31] As advocates of the 'political constitution' regard judges' involvement in matters of political controversy as highly questionable – particularly where the dispute in question is one of social policy over which rational people are likely to disagree – alternative justifications were advanced seeking to legitimise this expanded judicial role. The most persuasive is the theory of common law, or legal, constitutionalism.

---

[27] A. Tomkins, *Our Republican Constitution* (Hart, 2005) p. 10: 'Politics is able both democratically and effectively to stop government, to check the exercise of executive power, to hold it to account. The courts, no matter what their powers and what their composition, will always find it more difficult.'

[28] See, for instance, R. Bellamy, *Political Constitutionalism: a Republican Defence of the Constitutionality of Democracy* (CUP, 2007); K. D. Ewing, 'The Human Rights Act and Parliamentary Democracy' (1999) 62 MLR 79; A. Tomkins, 'In Defence of the Political Constitution' (2002) OJLS 157. The 'Judicial Power Project' undertaken by the think tank Policy Exchange (since 2015) seeks to examine the 'proper scope of the judicial power within the constitution' and is motivated by a concern that 'judicial overreach increasingly threatens the rule of law and effective, democratic government.' For detail see: https://judicialpowerproject.org.uk/.

[29] See Chapters 9 and 15.

[30] On which, see Chapters 18 and 19.

[31] Compare, for instance, the House of Lords decision in the case of *Liversidge* v *Anderson* [1942] AC 201 with the more recent case of *A* v *Secretary of State for the Home Department* [2004] UKHL 56; [2005] 2 AC 68.

Thinking Point . . .

Scepticism over the courts' influence over issues of policy is most keenly seen in debates over the extent of judicial protections afforded to human rights. Rights to expression, privacy, life, association and so on are argued to be inherently uncertain, open to a multitude of interpretations and frequent qualification. Political constitutionalists therefore suggest that permitting judges to apply such rights in practice effectively allows the courts to unduly influence the shape and direction of many fields of public policy.

Adam Tomkins, in his book *Our Republican Constitution,* has outlined what he refers to as the 'six tenets of legal constitutionalism':

(1) Law is an activity that is not only distinctive from but also superior to politics.

(2) The principal arena in which the activity of law takes place is the courtroom.

(3) Individuals should, as far as possible, remain free of interference by the government.

(4) Where government interference is unavoidable, it should be limited and justified by reason.

(5) Both the extent of and the justification for government interference are questions of law for the judges to determine.

(6) The law should control government through the enforcement of specific rules and general principles of legality (such as human rights).[32]

When considering these characteristics, it should be remembered that Tomkins, in putting forward his conception of the republican democratic traditions of the UK's constitutional system, is critical of theories of common law, or legal, constitutionalism.[33] Nevertheless, Tomkins' criteria provide a useful starting point when considering the characteristics that distinguish legal constitutionalism from the ideas associated with the political constitution. While advocates of legal constitutionalism might concede that – as a result of its composition – the judicial branch cannot make claim to match the democratic characteristics of an elected legislature, they would nevertheless argue that the law, and the legal process, make a valuable and legitimate contribution to a system of government. They would argue that the intimate forum of the courtroom makes law a more responsive decision-making tool when considering *individual* interests, rather than those of society as a whole. They would also suggest that certain characteristics of the judicial decision-making process – its relative rationality, stability and predictability – provide an invaluable counterpoint to the politically-driven and partisan deliberations which often take place in Parliament. The dissociation of the court process from the controversies of party politics is in fact one of the characteristics that, legal constitutionalists would argue, makes the law the perfect tool with which to resolve disputes, with the law's dispassionate approach said to ensure a just outcome. Proponents of common law constitutionalism would further suggest that certain values (for instance inalienable human rights[34]) or principles (such as the rule of law[35]) are so central to any system of government which purports to call itself democratic

---

[32] A. Tomkins, *Our Republican Constitution* (Hart Publishing, 2005) p. 11.
[33] Ibid., pp. 11–31.
[34] On which see Chapter 20.
[35] On which see Chapter 6.

that they should be realised in law as *enforceable* standards rather than mere political aspirations or claims – as a result, should government wish to legitimately interfere with these rights or principles, then it should offer compelling justification for so doing.

Many, in fact, go further, indicating that as a result of these characteristics, instead of merely complementing the democratic law-making process, the common law's decision-making techniques are *superior* to those of the political process; for instance, T. R. S. Allan has argued:

> ... there is an important sense in which common law is superior to statute. As a body of evolving principle, the common law provides stability and continuity. Its settled doctrines and assumptions, though always open to reconsideration and challenge, constitute a framework into which legislation must be fitted.[36]

In short then, legal constitutionalists envisage politics as a discipline which is not only distinct from law, but which should also be constrained by the 'straightjacket' of the law's regulatory framework.[37]

'Red light' and 'green light' approaches to legal power

Theories which emphasise the centrality of politics or law to the constitution are broadly consonant with the contrasting theories of administrative law famously put forward by Harlow and Rawlings in their work, *Law and Administration*.[38] Harlow and Rawlings invoked the metaphor of a set of traffic lights in order to demonstrate the dominant characteristics of the two competing theories of administrative law – the law relating to the administration of government. The two approaches were the 'red light' and 'green light' theories of public administration. In short, red-light theory sees government subject to, and constrained by, law. By contrast, green-light theory sees law more as a tool of effective and efficient government.

It might be helpful at this stage to consider how the competing schools of constitutional thought relate to these two competing models of public administration (Table 4.1). Griffith's political constitution emphasises that the role of law and of the courts should be secondary to the role of politics and of political debate. Laws, a body of rules that may be subject to constant change and revision, exist in order to facilitate the political objectives of the elected representatives that from time to time exercise power on behalf of the electorate. Law, therefore, exists in order to facilitate the business of government, nothing more, and nothing less. Griffith's model therefore falls squarely into the green-light school.

By contrast, legal constitutionalists place emphasis on the law as exercising a constraining force over government. Governmental power should only be exercised within the constraints of the law. Importantly, those constraints might include values and principles that should be immune from interference by the government or, at the very least, should require government to advance cogent reasons before the courts in order to argue that an interference be legitimate. Legal constitutionalism therefore falls squarely within the 'red light' school of thought.

---

[36] T. R. S. Allan, *Law, Liberty and Justice: The Legal Foundations of British Constitutionalism* (OUP, 1993) p. 79. See also: T. R. S. Allan, *The Sovereignty of Law: Freedom, Constitution and Common Law* (OUP, 2013); J. Laws, *The Common Law Constitution* (CUP, 2014).

[37] M. Loughlin, *Sword and Scales: An Examination of the Relationship between Law and Politics* (Hart Publishing, 2000) p. 5.

[38] C. Harlow and R. Rawlings, *Law and Administration* (3rd edn) (CUP, 2009) ch. 1.

Table 4.1 Competing schools of constitutional thought

The political/'green-light' constitution	The legal/'red-light' constitution
Facilitating role of law	Restraining role of law
Positivistic	Common law based
Procedural rule of law	Substantive rule of law
Limited judicial role	Active judicial role
Conflict and debate	Certainty and predictability
Ever-changing	Relatively stable
No inherent 'human rights'	Judicially enforceable 'human rights'

Thinking Point . . .

Martin Loughlin – in his book *Public Law and Political Theory* (Oxford: Clarendon Press, 1992) – has applied the terms 'normativist' and 'functionalist' as alternatives to the 'red light'/'green light' categorisation of approaches to public law. The normativist (red-light) school 'is rooted in a belief in the ideal of the separation of powers and in the need to subordinate government to law'. The functionalist (green-light) school, by contrast, 'views law as part of the apparatus of government . . . its focus is upon law's regulatory and facilitative functions and therefore is orientated to aims and objectives and adopts an instrumentalist social policy approach' (p. 60).

Judges and political questions

Key issues

- The interplay between law and politics is frequently played out in the courtroom, with the judiciary determining whether executive discretion has been exercised in accordance with the requirements of the law. The extent to which this supervisory jurisdiction permits judges to interfere with the policy choices of elected representatives is a matter of some controversy.

- Disagreement over the legitimate extent to which judges should be able to supervise decisions taken by elected representatives coalesces around a number of issues. First, there is dissent over whether law, and the judges, are appropriately placed to resolve (policy) questions to which many – equally legitimate – answers exist. Second, there is disagreement over whether the judges are institutionally capable of acting as neutral arbiters of the public interest. Finally, there is occasional disquiet concerning overly political statements made by judges.

Having introduced competing theories as to whether judges should be able to adjudicate over difficult matters of political disagreement, it is important to clarify what we mean when we make reference to 'political questions'. The following section will therefore provide us with a working definition of a political question, will examine the idea of the political neutrality of the judiciary, and will finally consider some examples of cases which have engaged with matters of political controversy.

What is a 'political' question?

The relationship between law and politics, when played out in the courtroom, frequently involves the judicial determination of disputes which originate in the political realm – in other words in the actions or inactions of elected politicians or of public officials acting on their behalf. In this descriptive sense, the courts are clearly engaged with resolving disputes that can be said to be 'political' in origin. When commentators argue that courts are making 'political decisions', or that the courts have become politicised, it is frequently being suggested that courts are making decisions that they are ill-suited to make, or – more bluntly – that they simply should not make. A 'political question' in its pejorative sense is therefore a decision that the courts should not take, an issue which is best taken by elected officials. For Griffith, whose notion of society was that it was based on – and indeed thrived on – conflict, a 'political decision' was therefore any decision of public importance on which people were likely to disagree. Griffith wrote:

> '[B]y political I mean those cases which arise out of controversial legislation or controversial action initiated by public authorities, or which touch on important moral or social issues.'[39]

Admittedly, this definition of a political question is a broad one. Nevertheless, for our purposes it provides a flavour of the type of decision in which judicial involvement is seen by some as being unsatisfactory. It is easy to imagine, for instance, reasonable people disagreeing over a whole range of issues that are relevant to the regulation of society and the governance of the country; education,[40] healthcare[41] and financial policy[42] to name an obvious few.

The increase in litigation involving claims of individual rights – both prior to[43] and following the implementation of the Human Rights Act 1998[44] – has gone some way towards increasing the frequency with which courts are being asked to play a role in resolving 'political' disputes (in both a descriptive and pejorative sense). For those sceptical of judicial involvement in the resolution of such political disagreements, issues relating to human rights present significant difficulties.[45]

The problem, critics argue, with asking judges to determine questions of rights has two distinct aspects. Each poses a democratic objection to the judicial determination of questions of rights. The first is direct. Critics such as Griffith suggest that requiring judges to determine questions of human rights asks judges to take decisions on public policy which should rightly be taken by elected (and removable) politicians. Some commentators therefore suggest that judicial determination of questions of fundamental, or human, rights, amounts to asking judges to determine outcomes to:

> . . . controversial questions of social policy over which sincere, intelligent, well-meaning people disagree – questions about where to draw the line when it comes to abortion, privacy, free speech,

---

[39] J. A. G. Griffith, *The Politics of the Judiciary* (5th edn) (Fontana Press, 1997) p. 7.

[40] See, for example, *Secretary of State for Education and Science* v *Tameside MBC* [1977] AC 1014.

[41] See, for example, *R* v *Cambridge Health Authority, ex parte B* [1995] 2 All ER 129.

[42] See, for example, *Nottinghamshire County Council* v *Secretary of State for the Environment* [1986] AC 240; *R* v *Secretary of State for the Environment, ex parte Hammersmith and Fulham London Borough Council* [1991] 1 AC 521.

[43] See, for example, *R* v *Secretary of State for the Home Department, ex parte Leech (No. 2)* [1994] QB 198; *R* v *Lord Chancellor, ex parte Witham* [1998] QB 575.

[44] See pp. 651–81.

[45] For a more detailed coverage of the judicial role in the protection of human rights, see Chapters 20 and 21.

police powers, religious practices, how refugee claimants are to be treated, who can marry, and much else.[46]

Judicially enforced Bills of Rights therefore allow 'judges to unsettle decisions made in the political arena by the people's representatives and thereby frustrate the democratic process.'[47] This difficulty is obviously heightened in those jurisdictions – for example, the United States – in which the courts are permitted to strike down legislation passed by the elected legislature in the event that it is held to contravene the protections afforded to individual rights by the constitution.[48]

The second objection is less direct and asserts that the impartiality of courts is eroded by requiring them to determine questions of rights, that is, legal standards that are generally phrased in relatively vague terms and open to multiple (equally legitimate) interpretations. Take the 'right to life' for instance, and ask at what point in time that right should be recognised in the gestation and birth of a child. Should it be at the point of conception? At the point when a heartbeat is first discernable in a foetus? At the point at which medical standards determine that – should the baby be born prematurely – it would stand a reasonable chance of survival? Or should the right to life only be recognised as applying from the point of birth onwards? Each of these readings of the right to life might be more or less persuasive, dependent on your point of view, but each might also legitimately fall within your own interpretation of the point at which 'life' begins and therefore the point at which the right to life becomes applicable. The point that critics of judicially enforced rights therefore make, is that giving effect to such vague standards requires judges to depart from the positivistic legal method that allows the intentions of the legislature to be respected and instead allows them – in giving meaning to the content of rights – to essentially give effect to their own preferences, proclivities and world view.[49] And if a judge is giving indirect effect to his or her own preferences through adjudication, then how can judicial neutrality be regarded as anything other than a pretence?

A final, related objection might also be made to the judicial resolution of human rights issues: the unsuitability of the judges as arbiters of the public interest. As Griffith argued, 'the solution to [the perceived failures of politicians, or of politics itself] should not lie with the imprecisions of Bills of Rights *or* the illiberal instincts of judges'.[50] It is to the latter accusation that we now turn.

---

[46] J. Allan, 'A Defence of the Status Quo' in T. Campbell, J. Goldsworthy and A. Stone, *Protecting Human Rights: Instruments and Institutions* (OUP, 2003) p. 190. See also M. Loughlin, *The Idea of Public Law* (OUP, 2003) p. 129: 'Rights adjudication is intrinsically political; it requires judges to reach a determination on the relative importance of conflicting social, political and cultural interests in circumstances in which there is no objective – or even consensual – answer'.

[47] K. D. Ewing, 'The Bill of Rights Debate: Democracy or Juristocracy in Britain?' in K. D. Ewing, C. A. Gearty and B. A. Hepple, *Human Rights and Labour Law: Essays for Paul O'Higgins* (Mansell, 1994) p. 156.

[48] See for discussion: J. Waldron, 'The Core of the Case Against Judicial Review' 115 *Yale Law Journal* 1346; A. M. Bickel, *The Least Dangerous Branch: the Supreme Court at the Bar of Politics* (Bobbs-Merrill, 1962). In the UK, there is no general power for judges to invalidate Acts of Parliament. The limited exceptions to this rule fall in the sphere of EU law – on which see the discussion at pp. 169–76 below – and in the ability of the higher courts to declare Acts incompatible with the Convention Rights as given effect by the Human Rights Act 1998 – on which see Chapter 21.

[49] See, for example, Justice Antonin Scalia 'The Bill of Rights: Confirmation of Extent Freedoms or Invitation to Judicial Creation?' in G. Huscroft and P. Rishworth (eds), *Litigating Rights: Perspectives from Domestic and International Law* (Hart Publishing, 2002) p. 23; J. Allan, 'A Defence of the Status Quo' in T. Campbell, J. Goldsworthy and A. Stone, *Protecting Human Rights: Instruments and Institutions* (OUP, 2003) p. 183.

[50] J. A. G. Griffith, 'The Political Constitution' (1979) 42 MLR 1, 14 (emphasis added).

The politics of the judiciary

We have already seen that, in the course of carrying out their role as adjudicators and arbiters of legal disputes, the courts may have to engage with subject matter that can be described as politically contentious. The ability of the judicial branch to determine such disputes is underpinned by the related ideas of judicial independence and impartiality. In short, the judges are able to fairly adjudicate over issues which may be politically controversial, and determine them in accordance with the requirements of the law, because they themselves have no overt political disposition. In the words of the former Court of Appeal judge Laws LJ, the courts have 'no programme, no mandate, no popular vote'.[51] The agenda of the judiciary – by contrast with the efforts of politicians to further particular moral or ethical causes – is, in theory at least, to apply the law and to adjudicate impartially upon those disputes which come before the courts.

The independence of the judiciary requires that the judges be detached from the open, and manifestly partial, debates of the political process. As we will see when we examine the issue of separation of powers in the UK Constitution, various mechanisms seek to uphold and preserve the idea that the judges are politically neutral.[52] The most obvious of these for the present discussion is perhaps the convention that all judges resign any membership of a political party upon appointment to the bench. The independence of the judiciary therefore seeks to ensure that legal disputes are determined by a body of decision-makers who are free to decide cases impartially, and based on the requirements of the law, rather than in pursuance of a party-political agenda, or because a particular outcome would be more cost-effective, or more popular with the electorate.

However, a number of commentators have argued that judicial independence is something of a myth that cannot be sustained upon closer examination of the record of the judiciary in determining questions of political controversy. Griffith, in perhaps his most famous work, *The Politics of the Judiciary,* challenged the idea of the neutrality of the courts, arguing that, as a result of the composition of the senior judiciary, the collective opinions of the courts – manifested in their decisions – were generally conservative and resistant to ideas of radical change. This sense of inherent conservatism stemmed from the lack of diversity among the senior judiciary, which was (and indeed is) largely male, white, Oxbridge-educated, and drawn from the ranks of the bar. As a result, Griffith argued that, the senior judiciary had 'by their education and training and the pursuit of their profession as barristers, acquired a strikingly homogenous collection of attitudes, beliefs and principles, which to them represent the public interest.'[53] As a result of this homogenous set of views, judges had – Griffith argued – consistently displayed conservative tendencies in their decisions on industrial relations, civil liberties, and in judicial review litigation.

The lack of diversity among the senior judiciary remains a problematic issue;[54] until the appointment of Lady Black to the Supreme Court in October 2017, Lady Hale had been the first, and only, woman judge to sit in the apex court since her appointment in 2004. The figures in Tables 4.2 and 4.3 – showing the composition of the senior judiciary in July

---

[51] Sir John Laws, '*Wednesbury*' in C. Forsyth and I. Hare (eds), *The Golden Metwand and the Crooked Cord: Essays on Public Law in Honour of Sir William Wade* (Clarendon Press, 1998) p. 190.

[52] See pp. 243–6.

[53] *The Politics of the Judiciary* (5th edn) (Fontana Press, 1997) p. 295. See also T. C. Hartley and J. A. G. Griffith, *Government and the Law* (2nd edn) (Weidenfeld and Nicolson, 1981) p. 181.

[54] For a recent, and wide-ranging, contribution to the literature see: G. Gee and E. Rackley (eds), *Debating Judicial Appointments in an Age of Diversity* (Routledge, 2017).

Table 4.2 The composition of the senior judiciary in England and Wales by gender*

	Male	Female	Total
Heads of Division**	5	0	5
Lords Justices of Appeal	29	9	38
High Court judges	76	21	97

* Statistics taken from the website of the Judiciary of England and Wales: **https://www.judiciary .gov.uk/publications/judicial-statistics-2017/** – dated July 2017.

** The five Heads of Division are: the Lord Chief Justice of England and Wales (head of the judiciary in England and Wales, and senior judge in the Criminal Division of the Court of Appeal); the Master of the Rolls (senior judge of the Civil Division of the Court of Appeal); the President of the Queen's Bench Division of the High Court; the President of the Family Division of the High Court; and the Chancellor of the High Court (the senior judge in the Chancery division of the High Court).

Source: Crown copyright

Table 4.3 The composition of the senior judiciary in England and Wales by ethnicity*

	Unknown	White	BAME	Total
Heads of Division	3	2	0	5
Lords Justices of Appeal	10	29	0	39
High Court judges	12	89	5	106

* Statistics taken from the website of the Judiciary of England and Wales: **https://www.judiciary .gov.uk/publications/judicial-statistics-2017/** – dated Jul 2017 (the relatively high proportion of those in the 'unknown' category is reflective of the fact that the information is provided on a voluntary basis).

Source: Crown copyright

2017 – illustrate that the contemporary senior judiciary remains predominantly male and white. Increasingly, however, Griffith's thesis on the politics of the judiciary appears dated. In spite of the persistence of concerns relating to the diversity of the bench,[55] the supposed inherent conservative bias of the senior judiciary no longer rings as true as it might once have done, and the judiciary in the early twenty-first century seems equally susceptible to criticism on the grounds of excessive liberalism as for a natural inclination towards conservatism.[56] In part this may be due to the influences of common law constitutionalism and human rights adjudication the emphasis each places on the protection of individual liberty, in part perhaps it may simply be due to the increasing frequency with which politically contentious disputes make their way before the courts.

---

[55] See, for instance, E. Rackley, 'In Conversation with Lord Justice Etherton: Revisiting the Case for a More Diverse Judiciary' [2010] PL 655; T. Etherton, 'Liberty, the Archetype and Diversity: A Philosophy of Judging' [2010] PL 727.

[56] See, for instance, the various charges made against the judiciary in the context of their implementation of the Human Rights Act 1998, most notably the suggestion that the judges have consistently elevated the rights of individuals above the interests of society at large. For commentary, see H. Fenwick, G. Phillipson and R. Masterman, 'The Human Rights Act in Contemporary Context' in H. Fenwick, G. Phillipson and R. Masterman, *Judicial Reasoning under the UK Human Rights Act* (CUP, 2007).

The determination of political questions

Though judges may occasionally make intemperate comments on matters of controversy extra-judicially,[57] indications of apparently *overt* political motivation are infrequent in judicial decision-making. One notorious example, however, arose in the 1925 case of *Roberts* v *Hopwood.* In **Roberts,** the House of Lords struck down the decision of Poplar Borough Council to impose a minimum wage of £4 per week on the ground that it was an unreasonable – and therefore illegal – exercise of the council's discretionary powers. The minimum wage was to be payable to both men and women, and the Law Lords' disquiet on that particular point was evident throughout their judgments.[58] In perhaps the most (in)famous passage from the House of Lords' decision, Lord Atkinson stated that:

> The council would, in my view, fail in their duty [to reasonably administer public funds] if . . . they . . . allowed themselves to be guided in preference by some eccentric principles of socialistic philanthropy, or by a feminist ambition to secure the equality of the sexes in the matter of wages in the world of labour.[59]

For Lord Atkinson, the fact that the council had considered gender equality as one of the aims of the minimum wage policy was, in part at least, one of the characteristics of the decision that made it offensive to their duty to administer public funds in a reasonable manner. Yet, if public bodies and elected politicians cannot make decisions based on political ideology – whether that ideology be feminism, socialism, conservatism or indeed any other viewpoint – then their freedom to act in accordance with their democratic mandate will be severely hampered. *Roberts* v *Hopwood* is among a notorious minority of judicial decisions apparently blatantly displaying the political prejudices of the judges. However, it is by no means the only judicial decision in which the ability of an elected body to carry out its manifesto commitments has been halted by the courts.

Bromley LBC v *Greater London Council* concerned a dispute over the ability of the Greater London Council (GLC) to impose an increase in rates across London boroughs in order to fund a reduction in fares on London's public transport system.[60] The council acted pursuant to the provisions of the Transport (London) Act 1969, under s. 1 of which its general duty was to develop the 'integrated, efficient and economic transport facilities and services for Greater London'. The GLC had been elected on the back of a manifesto commitment to reduce fares on London public transport by 25 per cent, and in order to fund the reduction the GLC was going to increase rates in all London boroughs by 6.1p in the pound. The Labour-controlled GLC directed that boroughs make the increase. The Conservative-controlled London Borough of Bromley applied for judicial review of the decision. The High Court rejected Bromley's application, but on appeal to the Court of Appeal the application was granted, and the actions of the GLC declared to be *ultra vires.* The GLC appealed to the House of Lords.

---

[57] In one notable example, the Scottish judge Lord McCluskey was required to stand down from the bench hearing a particular trial after writing in a Sunday newspaper that the Human Rights Act 1998 amounted to 'a field day for crackpots, a pain in the neck for judges and legislators and a goldmine for lawyers' (*Scotland on Sunday,* 2 February 2000). On which see: *Hoekstra, van Rijs et al* v *HM Advocate (No. 2)* 2000 SLT 605. And see further J. A. G. Griffith, *The Politics of the Judiciary* (5th edn) (Fontana Press, 1997) pp. 12–13.

[58] R. Stevens, *The English Judges: Their Role in the Changing Constitution* (Hart Publishing, 2005) p. 23.

[59] *Roberts* v *Hopwood* [1925] AC 578, 594 (Lord Atkinson).

[60] *Bromley LBC* v *Greater London Council* [1983] 1 AC 768. For commentary see: A. Tomkins, *Public Law* (Clarendon Press, 2003) pp.178–9.

The House of Lords found that the GLC had acted illegally by failing to appropriately balance the interests of the users of the London transport system with those of the rate-payers by whom the financial burden of the reduction in fares would have been shouldered. As a result, the Law Lords endorsed Bromley's argument that the use of the word 'economic' in the Transport (London) Act should be taken to suggest that the transport system in Greater London should be run according to 'ordinary business principles' and not, therefore, at a deficit that would have to be supplemented by rate-payers. The fact that the GLC's policy had been endorsed by many of those rate-payers was largely irrelevant. Lord Wilberforce stated that:

> It makes no difference on the question of legality . . . whether the impugned action was or was not submitted to or approved by the relevant electorate: that cannot confer validity on *ultra vires* action.[61]

Bromley is clearly therefore evidence of the political process operating within the confines of the law, as determined by the courts. It is evidence of a legal constitutional – or red-light – approach to constitutional governance. Naturally, Griffith found the decision an unjustifiable inroad by the courts into the realm of political decision-making:

> It is surely no more the function of the judiciary to tell the GLC where the public interest lay in its spending of public money than it is the function of the judiciary to make similar judgments about spending by the departments of the central government. The application of the doctrine of the fiduciary duty in this case was gross interference by the judiciary in the exercise of political responsibility of an elected local authority.[62]

The difficulty of course with Griffith's position is that it holds the potential to reduce the supervisory role of the courts to almost vanishing point. If it is illegitimate for the courts to restrain the actions of elected officials where those actions involve determining where the public interest should lie, or have been endorsed in a manifesto, or engage a topic on which reasonable people are likely to disagree, then the role of the courts is reduced to the point at which it becomes meaningless to talk of effective legal supervision of government by the courts. As we will see in Chapter 6, such a position would be entirely incompatible with the ideal of the rule of law.

In practice, however, the approach of the courts has not been as one-sided as Griffith might suggest. In *Secretary of State for Education* v *Tameside*[63] the House of Lords held that it was not unreasonable (and as such, not unlawful) for a Conservative-controlled local authority to resist the directions of the Labour Government to make selective grammar schools within their jurisdiction comprehensive. One of the circumstances which the House of Lords considered relevant in coming to their decision was that the Conservative council had recently been elected, having promised during the election campaign to maintain the area's grammar schools. As Lord Salmon outlined:

> The Conservative party having won the election in Tameside on May 6 [1976] the authority *rightly* considered that they had a mandate from the electors to preserve the Tameside grammar schools – the question as to whether or not the grammar schools were to be preserved having been one of the chief issues in the election.[64]

---

[61] Ibid., 814 (see also Lord Diplock and Lord Brandon at 829–31 and 853 respectively).
[62] J. A. G. Griffith, *The Politics of the Judiciary* (5th edn) (Fontana Press, 1997) p. 129.
[63] *Secretary of State for Education* v *Tameside MBC* [1977] AC 1014.
[64] Ibid., 1067 (emphasis added).

These cases are just a very brief selection of the many judicial review decisions in which the aims and objectives of political parties have been engaged in decisions before the courts. The detailed legal bases on which the cases were resolved by the judges have been deliberately avoided in order to illustrate the difficulties of balancing the sometimes conflicting imperatives of upholding the law and of democratic government. Just as a judicial approach that routinely ignored the policy objectives of political actors would illegitimately stifle the ability of elected officials to respond to the will of the electorate, an approach which saw action taken pursuant to a manifesto commitment as effectively non-justiciable would run the risk of excusing or legitimising behaviour which would otherwise be held to contravene the law. As we will see when we come to examine judicial review in more detail,[65] while individual cases may waver towards one or the other of these two extremes, the general pattern of judicial decision-making attempts to tread a careful line between the two.

The differing responses of law and politics illustrated

Key issues

- It is not the function of courts to either routinely challenge, or routinely support, decisions made by elected officials. It is the role of courts to apply the law. From time to time, however, the discharge of this constitutional function may seem to result in 'conflict' between courts and politicians.

- It is important to appreciate that the regulatory role of the courts is not – as politicians may occasionally contend – motivated by a desire to thwart certain policy objectives or to deliberately, and maliciously, obstruct the business of government. The role of the courts is to independently ensure that government acts in accordance with the requirements of the law.

While the constitutional role of the judiciary is to adjudicate, impartially, all decisions that come before the courts, the frequency with which the government, in its various guises, appears before the courts – particularly in judicial review proceedings – gives rise to the impression that the government and the judges are in some way in conflict with each other. While it is true to say – as the former Law Lord, Lord Steyn has done – that the government and the judges 'are not on the same side,'[66] and it is equally true to say that palpable tensions may arise from time to time between courts and the executive,[67] it is not true to say that the courts consistently and as a matter of routine attempt to present obstacles to prevent the government from acting or carrying its policies into effect. Certainly, the government is found on occasion by the courts not to have acted in accordance with the requirements of the law; equally certainly it is found to have acted in accordance with the law. It is typically the former, rather than the latter, that attracts attention.

---

[65] See Chapters 18 and 19.
[66] Lord Steyn, 'Democracy, the Rule of Law and the Role of the Judges' [2006] EHRLR 243, 248; A. W. Bradley, 'Relations between Executive, Judiciary and Parliament: an Evolving Saga?' [2008] PL 470, 476.
[67] On which, see A. Le Sueur, 'The Judicial Review Debate: from Partnership to Friction' (1996) 31 *Government and Opposition* 8; I. Loveland, 'The War Against the Judges' (1997) 68 *Political Quarterly* 162.

As outlined above, the judicial determination of questions concerning potential human rights violations has been the subject of academic criticism. In practice, the judicial determination of alleged rights violations has provoked a degree of discord between politicians and the courts.

Key debates

The 'Afghan hijackers' case

On 10 May 2006, Sullivan J, handed down the decision of the High Court in the case of *R (S)* v *Secretary of State for the Home Department*.[68] The case concerned nine Afghan citizens who, in February 2000, had hijacked an aeroplane in Afghanistan and travelled to the UK aboard that plane in order to escape the oppressive rule of the Taliban. The nine applicants were convicted of offences relating to the hijacking of the aeroplane.[69] The proceedings before Sullivan J related to applications made by the applicants against a decision of the Home Secretary not to grant them asylum in the UK. Reviewing the decision of the Home Secretary, the Immigration Adjudication Panel had determined, in June 2004, that the nine should not be returned to Afghanistan as a result of the real risk to their safety that their return would pose. The Panel relied on the established principles of Art. 3 of the European Convention on Human Rights (the prohibition of torture), as given effect under the Human Rights Act 1998. As a result of this finding, the Home Secretary should have followed the published Home Office policy, and granted the claimants 'discretionary leave' to remain in the UK for a period of six months. Alternatively, it was open to the Home Secretary to appeal the findings of the Immigration Appeal Tribunal. Instead of taking either of these avenues, the Home Secretary did nothing.

The proceedings before Sullivan J therefore concerned an application made by the claimants seeking (i) a declaration that, in failing to grant them 'discretionary leave' to remain in the UK, the Home Secretary had acted unlawfully, and (ii) a mandatory order requiring the Home Secretary to grant the discretionary leave initially ordered by the Immigration Appeals Tribunal. Sullivan J found in favour of the applicants, endorsing their submission that 'it was an abuse of power for the [Home Secretary] to deliberately delay making a decision and to prevaricate until such time as he had in place a policy which would enable him to reach a decision refusing the claimants discretionary leave'.[70]

For present purposes, it is unnecessary to go into greater detail on the legal grounds on which Sullivan J found in favour of the applicants. Instead, it is responses of politicians to the decision that are of interest, for they demonstrate how the differing objectives and institutional roles of judges and politicians give rise to conflict and, potentially, to misunderstandings regarding the role of the courts.

The then Prime Minister, Tony Blair, in an extraordinary abandonment of the recognised rules of syntax, criticised Sullivan J's decision, saying:

We can't have a situation in which people who hijack a plane, we're not able to deport back to their country. It's not an abuse of justice for us to order their deportation, it's an abuse of common sense frankly to be in a position where we can't do this.[71]

---

[68] [2006] EWHC 1111 (Admin).

[69] Although those convictions were subsequently quashed by the Court of Appeal, as a result of judicial misdirection at the criminal trial (see *R* v *Safi (Ali Ahmed) and others* [2003] EWCA Crim 1809), no retrial was ordered as at the time the convictions were quashed, seven of the nine had served their full sentences.

[70] [2006] EWHC 1111 (Admin), [59].

[71] 'Afghans Who Fled Taliban by Hijacking Airliner Given Permission to Remain in Britain', *Guardian*, 11 May 2006.

The Home Secretary at the time, John Reid, added:

> When decisions are taken [by the courts] which appear inexplicable or bizarre to the general public, it only reinforces the perception that the system is not working to protect or in favour of the vast majority of ordinary decent hard-working citizens in this country.[72]

In their categorisation of this particular decision as 'an abuse of common sense', 'inexplicable' and 'bizarre', leading members of the Government openly suggested that Sullivan J's decision was 'based on a perverse interpretation of human rights law'[73] and therefore entirely without legitimate basis. In fact, as even the brief outline of the facts given above demonstrates, Sullivan J's decision simply required the Home Secretary to comply with the findings of the Immigration Appeals Tribunal, something which – had he followed the published Home Office policy – he should already have done!

Unsurprisingly, the government appealed against the decision. Perhaps also unsurprisingly, the Court of Appeal upheld the decision of Sullivan J. In giving its unanimous judgment, the Court of Appeal noted:

> We commend the judge [Sullivan J] for an impeccable judgment. The history of this case . . . has attracted a degree of opprobrium for those carrying out judicial functions. Judges and adjudicators have to apply the law as they find it, not as they wish it to be.[74]

In many respects, the responses of legal and political actors to this particular controversy could hardly have been further apart.

The *Afghan Hijackers* case is just one of a number of human rights disputes that have caused tension between the judges and elected politicians in recent years.[75] Subsequent reviews of the enforcement of the Human Rights Act by the courts – conducted by the Department for Constitutional Affairs,[76] and the Joint Parliamentary Committee on Human Rights[77] – were broadly supportive of the approach taken by the courts to the interpretation and application of the Human Rights Act. The response of the Joint Committee on Human Rights to the *Afghan Hijackers* episode, for instance, showed a degree of restraint not immediately evident in the responses of Cabinet ministers. The Joint Committee wrote:

> In our view high level ministerial criticism of court judgments in human rights cases as an abuse of common sense, or bizarre or inexplicable, only serves to fuel public misconceptions of the Human Rights Act and of human rights law generally.[78]

---

[72] 'Stop meddling, top judges tell Blair and Reid', *Daily Mail*, 31 May 2006.

[73] Joint Committee on Human Rights, *The Human Rights Act: The DCA and Home Office Reviews* (32nd Report, 2005–2006), HL 278/HC 1716 (14 November 2006), [14].

[74] *R (S) v Secretary of State for the Home Department* [2006] EWCA Civ 1157, [50].

[75] For a general survey, see H. Fenwick, R. Masterman and G. Phillipson, 'The Human Rights Act in Contemporary Context' in H. Fenwick, R. Masterman and G. Phillipson (eds), *Judicial Reasoning under the UK Human Rights Act* (CUP, 2007).

[76] Department of Constitutional Affairs, *Review of the Implementation of the Human Rights Act* (July 2006).

[77] Joint Committee on Human Rights, *The Human Rights Act: The DCA and Home Office Reviews* (32nd Report, 2005–2006), HL 278/HC 1716 (14 November 2006).

[78] Joint Committee on Human Rights, *The Human Rights Act: The DCA and Home Office Reviews* (32nd Report, 2005–2006), HL 278/HC 1716 (14 November 2006), [21].

These reports, however, did little to quell popular disquiet over the Human Rights Act, prompting the Conservative Party to commit – in 2006 – to its abolition or reform.[79] The 2015 General Election saw the return of a Conservative majority administration committed to the replacement of the Human Rights Act with a British Bill of Rights.[80] Following the June 2016 Brexit referendum, the Government reiterated this commitment[81] and the Conservative Party's 2017 general election manifesto committed to a re-examination of the UK's human rights framework on completion of the 'Brexit' negotiations.

Conclusion: the legalisation of the United Kingdom Constitution?

The purpose of this chapter has been to introduce some of the debates that will underpin discussions of the institutions of government, their powers and functions and the relationships between them that will be covered in more detail in later chapters. The final issue to be raised concerns the legalisation of the constitution, namely the suggestion that the constitution is in a period of transition, making it significantly more reliant on legal rules and regulation than it has hitherto been. The enactment of the Human Rights Act 1998, the devolution statutes, the Freedom of Information Act 2000, the development of common law constitutional principles and of judicial review, the influence of European laws and other related developments have all contributed to a growing sense that the UK Constitution is more reliant on legal norms and regulation than ever before.[82] Although 'politically contentious' to many, 'law has come to be viewed as establishing a cordon within which politics is conducted.'[83] Of course, the UK Constitution continues to display elements of the political constitution – its ultimate preference for the sovereignty of *Parliament* rather than of the constitution or the courts, its continued reliance on conventions, and so on. The arguments analysed in this chapter have occasionally indicated that the debate is one of polar, and irreconcilable, opposites. Yet, in reality, the UK Constitution displays an (occasionally uneasy) balance between political and legal mechanisms of control, with both playing an important role in the discharge, and regulation, of governmental functions. As Dawn Oliver has written:

> The middle way that is evolving, then, is based on recognition that the courts have an important, rather political role, in giving effect to constitutionally significant legislation and in developing the common law.[84]

---

[79] 'Cameron promises UK Bill of Rights to replace Human Rights Act', *Guardian,* 26 June 2006.

[80] The Conservative Party Manifesto, 2015.

[81] House of Commons Justice Committee, Oral Evidence, The Work of the Secretary of State HC 620, 7 September 2016, Q78-Q91. See pp. 681–4.

[82] Prior to the 2015 General Election, a number of issues relating to this sense of constitutional legalisation were being examined by the House of Commons Political and Constitutional Reform Select Committee (see for instance: *A New Magna Carta?* (HC 463), 10 July 2014; *The Constitutional Role of the Judiciary if there were a Codified Constitution* (HC 802), 14 May 2014). The Committee was not re-constituted in the 2015 Parliament.

[83] M. Loughlin, *Sword and Scales: an Examination of the Relationship between Law and Politics* (Hart Publishing, 2000) p. 232.

[84] D. Oliver, *Constitutional Reform in the United Kingdom* (OUP, 2003) pp. 388–9.

This 'middle way' (or 'amber light' approach to constitutional regulation[85]) values the restraining and facilitating functions of the law, and – as such – sees the courts as having a distinctive constitutional function alongside (rather than in competition with) the elected arms of government.[86] The relationships between law and politics, and the tensions that exist between legal and political actors, are therefore a thread running through the constitution as a whole. This chapter has attempted to highlight some of the significant aspects of this complex set of relationships, as we progress into later chapters the thread will be unravelled and particular strands examined in greater detail.

Practice questions

1. Should judges decide political questions?

2. *'Politics is able both democratically and effectively to stop government, to check the exercise of executive power, to hold it to account. The courts, no matter what their powers and what their composition, will always find it more difficult.'*

   (A. Tomkins, *Our Republican Constitution* (Hart, 2005) p. 10)

   Critically assess this viewpoint.

3. *'The United Kingdom Constitution is in transition; the rule-based, judicially-enforced, constitution is slowly consigning the flexible, "political" constitution to history.'*

   Discuss.

Further reading

While this chapter has drawn heavily on the work of **J. A. G. Griffith,** his contributions are by no means the only significant works in this field. Nonetheless, two of his most important pieces – **'The Political Constitution'** (1979) 42 *Modern Law Review* 1 and **The Politics of the Judiciary** (5th edn) (Fontana Press, 1997) – remain insightful, readable and provocative in equal measure. **Richard Bellamy's Political Constitutionalism: a Republican Defence of the Constitutionality of Democracy** (CUP, 2007) is a contemporary partner to the former.

Two excellent articles examine Griffith's scholarship in some depth. **Graham Gee's** piece, **'The Political Constitutionalism of J. A. G. Griffith'** (2008) *Legal Studies* 20 examines the influence of Griffith's work on constitutional thought, arguing that his account retains currency in contemporary constitutional discourse. **Graham Gee and Grégoire C. N. Webber** use Griffith's 1979 piece as the starting point for their article **'What is a Political Constitution?'** ((2010) 30 *Oxford Journal of Legal Studies* 273) which examines whether Griffith's 'model' of the constitution is descriptive or normative, and how it maps onto the 'real world' UK Constitution. A collection of short papers marking Griffith's contribution to public law scholarship – commissioned after his death in 2010 – can be found in the

---

[85] On which see: M. Taggart, 'Reinvented Government, Traffic Lights and the Convergence of Public and Private Law' [1999] PL 124.

[86] See also: R. Masterman and J. E. K. Murkens, 'Skirting Supremacy and Subordination: The Constitutional Authority of the United Kingdom Supreme Court' [2013] PL 800.

January 2014 issue of the journal *Public Law*. The papers cover a diverse range of topics including Parliament and legislation, local government, and administrative law.

Perhaps the most comprehensive accounts of the liberal legal – or common law – model of constitutionalism can be found in **T. R. S. Allan**'s, *Law, Liberty and Justice: the Legal Foundations of British Constitutionalism* (Clarendon Press, 1993) and his more recent work *The Sovereignty of Law: Freedom, Constitution and Common Law* (OUP, 2013). **T. Poole, 'Back to the Future? Unearthing the Theory of Common Law Constitutionalism'** (2003) 23 *Oxford Journal of Legal Studies* 435 provides a shorter, critical, account.

Part II
The theory and practice of the United Kingdom Constitution

Chapter 5
Parliamentary sovereignty

'The concept of Parliamentary Sovereignty which has been fundamental to the constitution of England and Wales since the 17th Century . . . means that Parliament can do anything.'

Jackson v *Attorney-General* [2005] UKHL 56, [159] (Baroness Hale).

Chapter outline

This chapter examines the doctrine of parliamentary sovereignty, the commonly used shorthand for the legal supremacy attributed to Acts of Parliament within the hierarchy of norms in the UK's constitutional system. The characteristics of the doctrine will be examined, alongside its historical origins and the crucial distinction between the idea of legal sovereignty and that of political or popular sovereignty. We will then go on to examine potential limitations on Parliament's legislative power, before examining and assessing contemporary challenges to the orthodox model of legal sovereignty.

While the doctrine of legal sovereignty undoubtedly forms the backbone of the UK's Constitution, it should be considered alongside the principle of the rule of law and – to a lesser extent – that of separation of powers. Both are considered in the chapters which follow.

Introduction

The opening chapter to this book outlined how the idea of *limited* government was central to an understanding of constitutions, and of constitutionalism. Examining the constitution of the UK on these terms presents us with something of a paradox, for its most fundamental principle – the principle of parliamentary *sovereignty* – is representative of *unlimited* legal power.

At its most straightforward, the doctrine of parliamentary sovereignty is an encapsulation of the legally unlimited power of Parliament to enact legislation; the ability of Parliament to enact legislation concerning any topic, in any form of words, at any time of its choosing. So fundamental is the idea of parliamentary sovereignty that Vernon Bogdanor has used it to distil that entire constitution into a mere eight words: 'what the Queen in Parliament enacts is law.'[1] This phrase is worth dwelling on, as it is at once accurate and misleading. It is accurate in the sense that it effectively conveys the idea that primary

---

[1] V. Bogdanor, *Politics and the Constitution: Essays on British Government* (Dartmouth, 1996) p. 5.

legislation enacted by Parliament is the highest source of legal – and constitutional – authority in the UK. It is also accurate in its (implicit) suggestion that laws may change over time, should Parliament determine a change to be necessary.

However, Bogdanor's neat dilution of the constitution is also slightly disingenuous. First, it seems to deny that other sources of law might have a constitutional status of sorts or, at the very least, be of constitutional importance. As we have already seen, the common law and the laws of the European Union (at least during the term of the UK's membership), among other sources, can be described as having constitutional significance.[2] Secondly, it also disregards the importance of the non-legal rules of the constitution. While it is undeniable that primary legislation possesses a superior normative authority to conventions, the crucial role of the latter in constitutional practice has also already been demonstrated and should not be understated, or indeed ruled out completely.[3] Bogdanor's over-simplification of the constitution therefore provides us with a salient lesson; while the basic premise of parliamentary sovereignty might well appear to be 'simple and clear',[4] we should be careful to remember that even the most straightforward rule might be open to contrasting interpretations.

This chapter explores the meaning and interpretation of the central concept of parliamentary sovereignty. Understanding the doctrine of sovereignty is an integral aspect of appreciating the development of, and distribution of powers within, the constitution and the reach and influence of the idea of parliamentary sovereignty can be seen throughout our constitutional arrangements – from the division of power between the three 'branches' of government to the specific grounds on which courts might review the decisions of governmental bodies. As a result, parliamentary sovereignty should not be thought to be a standalone topic, but one which forms the cornerstone of our constitutional arrangements and reaches far into the day-to-day realities of our constitutional governance.

Diceyan orthodoxy: the legally unlimited power of Parliament

Key issues

- A. V. Dicey is arguably most renowned for his influential work on parliamentary sovereignty. There are two dimensions to the classic Diceyan reading of parliamentary sovereignty. The positive aspect holds that Parliament possesses unlimited law-making power. The negative aspect holds that no other body has the authority to challenge the validity of an Act of Parliament.

- Two important points flow from this understanding of Parliament's legislative power. The first is that – on this account – there is no distinction between constitutional and ordinary laws; all Acts of Parliament are of the same legal value. The constitution is the cumulative result of legislative (and judicial) decisions rather than a precursor to legislative and judicial action. The second is that entrenchment is a legal impossibility; Parliament cannot bind its successors.

---

[2] See Chapters 2–3.
[3] See Chapter 2.
[4] H. W. R. Wade, 'The Basis of Legal Sovereignty' (1955) CLJ 172, 172.

The concept of parliamentary sovereignty – alternatively referred to as parliamentary supremacy[5] – is an expression of the legally unlimited power of Parliament. Its most famous advocate was Albert Venn Dicey, whose account of sovereignty resounds to this day. In his seminal text, *An Introduction to the Study of the Law of the Constitution*, Dicey noted:

> The principle of parliamentary sovereignty means neither more nor less than this, namely, that Parliament . . . has, under the English constitution, the right to make or unmake any law whatever; and, further, that no person or body is recognised by the law of England as having a right to override or set aside the legislation of Parliament.[6]

Dicey's definition of the parliamentary sovereignty doctrine can be seen has having two distinct aspects: the positive and the negative.

1. The positive aspect – Parliament can 'make or unmake any law'[7]

The positive dynamic of Dicey's definition of legal sovereignty holds that Parliament can enact, or repeal, *any* law. Hence, Parliament can enact, annul or amend primary legislation, and is subject to no legal limitations concerning the content of legislation, what form that legislation should take and so on.

If, indeed, there is 'no law which Parliament cannot change',[8] it follows that no one statute is any more important than any other piece of primary legislation; there is therefore no distinction between 'constitutional' and 'ordinary' law as all statutes are of equal validity. 'The constitution' – on Dicey's account – is therefore synonymous with, and a result of, the ordinary law of the land.

It further follows that the idea of entrenchment – or protection from future repeal – of a statute or its provisions is therefore seemingly impossible within this constitutional framework. If no statute is more fundamental than any other statute, and all statutes can be repealed or amended via the ordinary legislative process, then it follows that Parliament cannot pass legislation that is protected from future amendment or repeal. In other words, Parliament cannot bind or impose limitations upon itself, for to do so would be to surrender the unlimited power that is characteristic of a legally sovereign institution.

2. The negative aspect – '[n]o person or body . . . [possesses] a right to override or set aside the legislation of Parliament'[9]

While in systems operating under a written, entrenched, constitution, a supreme or constitutional court might possess power to invalidate legislation that contravenes the terms of the constitution, no such power is available to courts in the UK. As a result, primary legislation is not only the highest source of law recognised in our constitutional system, but also, on Dicey's account, immune from interference or revision by any body other than Parliament itself.

---

[5] For discussion of important distinctions between 'sovereignty', on the one hand, and 'supremacy', on the other, see p. 132.
[6] A. V. Dicey, *Introduction to the Study of the Law of the Constitution* (Liberty Fund, 1982) pp. 3–4.
[7] Ibid., p. 3.
[8] Ibid, p. 37.
[9] Ibid., p. 4.

Taken together, the positive and negative aspects illustrate the legally unlimited power of Parliament. As we have already seen, in other constitutional jurisdictions, the power of the legislature might be legally or constitutionally inhibited in some way. The legislature may not, for example, be able to dispense with, or abolish, the system of federalism set down by the constitution.[10] Alternatively, it might not be able to pass legislation which breaches fundamental human rights principles.[11] This is not the case in the UK. In theory at least, the legal power of Parliament to legislate on *any* subject, for *any* place and in *any* terms is unfettered. The vast potential of this unlimited power was perhaps best captured by Ivor Jennings:

> . . . Parliament may remodel the British constitution, prolong its own life, legislate ex post facto, legalise illegalities, provide for individual cases, interfere with contracts and authorise the seizure of property, give dictatorial powers to the Government, dissolve the United Kingdom or the British Commonwealth, introduce communism or socialism or individualism or facism, entirely without legal remedy.[12]

As a result of this power, it has been suggested that Parliament could, should it so wish, legislate in order to achieve any manner of (potentially outlandish, irrational or immoral) things. (As Wade noted, in attempting to rationalise this theoretically unbridled legislative power '[a]ll writers on sovereignty are bound to deal in improbable examples'.[13]) It has, for instance, been suggested that parliamentary sovereignty would permit Parliament to legislate to the effect that all babies with blue eyes should be killed.[14] Similarly, it has been suggested that Parliament could legislate to deprive Jews of their British nationality, to dissolve marriages between blacks and whites, to confiscate the property of all women with red hair,[15] or – rather more prosaically perhaps – to outlaw smoking on the streets of Paris.[16] Parliament has not as a matter of fact legislated in order to achieve *any* of these particular aims and as a result we should be careful to avoid being side-tracked by a battle of examples, hypothetical or not, for the reason that:

> One no more demonstrates [that the powers of the UK Parliament are unlimited] by pointing to a wide range of legislative objects than one demonstrates the contrary by pointing to matters on which Parliament has not, in fact, ever legislated.[17]

In practice, as we will see, the contemporary state of parliamentary sovereignty is more nuanced and complex than Dicey's initial synopsis would appear to suggest. While senior judges remain able to refer to legal sovereignty as providing the 'bedrock'[18] of the constitution, 'the more deeply the subject is explored, the more one is inclined to suspect that the bedrock will turn out to be quicksand'.[19]

---

[10] For instance, in the German constitution.

[11] As under the United States Bill of Rights.

[12] W. I. Jennings, *The Law and the Constitution* (4th edn) (University of London Press, 1952) p. 142.

[13] H. W. R. Wade, 'The Basis of Legal Sovereignty' (1955) CLJ 172, 173.

[14] L. Stephen, *The Science of Ethics* (Smith, Elder and Co., 1882), p. 143 (cited in T. R. S. Allan, *Law Liberty and Justice: the Legal Foundations of British Constitutionalism* (Clarendon Press, 1993) p. 130.

[15] F. A. Mann, 'Britain's Bill of Rights' (1978) 94 LQR 512, 513.

[16] W. I. Jennings, *The Law and the Constitution* (4th edn) (University of London Press, 1952) p. 154.

[17] H. Calvert, *Constitutional Law in Northern Ireland: a Study in Regional Government* (Stevens & Sons, 1968) p. 14.

[18] *Jackson v Attorney-General* [2006] 1 AC 56, [9] (Lord Bingham).

[19] H. W. R. Wade, 'The Basis of Legal Sovereignty' (1955) CLJ 172, 173.

Thinking Point . . .

On the extent of a sovereign Parliament's legislative power Leslie Stephen wrote: 'If a legislature decided that all blue-eyed babies should be murdered, the preservation of blue-eyed babies would be illegal; but legislators must go mad before they could pass such a law, and subjects be idiotic before they could submit to it' (*The Science of Ethics* (London: Smith, Elder and Co., 1882), p. 143). Stephen draws out two important points relating to the potentially draconian deployment of Parliament's legislative powers. First, a majority of legislators must support the passage of the measure. Second, in order to be effective, the legislation (and legislature) must enjoy the (broad) support of the electorate.

Parliamentary sovereignty: a legal or political construct?

Key issues

The doctrine of parliamentary sovereignty relates to the *legal* powers of Parliament. However, the links between the legal doctrine and the political dimensions of Parliament's power are undeniable. Historically, the legal supremacy of Parliament was the result of lengthy political battles between the crown and the legislature and to this day the ability to enact legislation is a power vested collectively in those political actors who are Members of Parliament. As a result of this latter point, it might be said that the political process conditions how the legislative powers of Parliament are to be deployed; does it follow that the political process might be regarded as a limitation on parliament's sovereignty?

The origins of the sovereignty doctrine

The fact that the UK Constitution is not governed by a written document specifying the powers and functions of the various actors within the constitution presents us with something of a problem.[20] From where – if not from such a constitutional instrument – does the sovereignty of Parliament originate? It cannot be an entrenched constitutional document, for no such thing exists in the UK polity. It cannot be in legislation, for the 'powers of Parliament are not expressed in an Act of Parliament.'[21] And if sovereignty were to be 'a construct of the common law'[22], then it might reasonably be supposed that, in one way at least, the courts would be superior to Parliament.

A democratic foundation?

It is clear that for some contemporary commentators, the importance of parliamentary sovereignty lies in the preference it displays for democratic government – that is, government by elected and accountable officials – over government by non-elected officials.[23] There is a

---

[20] This issue will be returned to in Chapter 7, on separation of powers.

[21] W. I. Jennings, *The Law and the Constitution* (4th edn) (University of London Press, 1952) p. 149.

[22] *R (Jackson)* v *Attorney-General* [2005] UKHL 56; [2006] 1 AC 262, [102] (Lord Steyn).

[23] C. A. Gearty and K. D. Ewing, 'Rocky Foundations for Labour's new rights' (1997) EHRLR 146, 148; A. Tomkins, *Our Republican Constitution* (Hart Publishing, 2005) Ch. 1.

clear line of contemporary constitutional thought that suggests that Parliament should be the dominant force in the constitution, as a result of the regular elections that are held to determine a significant proportion (though not all) of its membership. Parliament *is* the dominant legal force in the UK, because its democratic credentials mean it *should* occupy that position. Indeed, for the modern reader, the notion that the membership of the House of Commons – the pre-eminent chamber of the UK Parliament[24] – is determined by a general election provides an obvious explanation for its dominant political position in the constitution. However, Parliament during – for instance – the nineteenth century did not possess the same democratic mandate that the Parliament of the twenty-first century can make a claim to today:[25] the franchise was not extended to all adults over the age of 21 until the passing of the Representation of the People Act 1928, and not to all adults over the age of 18 until the implementation of the Representation of the People Act 1969. As a result, while arguments rooted in democracy might provide a justification for the *continued* relevance of the sovereignty doctrine, they cannot of themselves explain its origins. To provide a partial account of the answer to that particular question, a brief historical survey is required.

Monarch versus Parliament

The interplay between the legal and political dynamics of the constitution is once again amply illustrated by the seventeenth-century struggles between Parliament and the monarchy which, in part at least, gave rise to the idea of the supremacy of Parliament within the constitutional structure, and in turn to the *legal* notion of legislative supremacy. The seventeenth century saw the resolution of a lengthy series of disputes over where ultimate constitutional authority should reside. The main players in this dispute were the monarch and Parliament.[26] The central legal question at issue was:

> . . . whether the King was above the law (as the divine rights theory so beloved by the Stuarts would suggest) or whether the law was above the King and able to impose enforceable limits upon him.[27]

Prior to the English civil war and the events of the so-called Glorious Revolution of 1688 – the overthrow by parliamentarians of the Catholic monarch James II of England (James VII of Scotland) and his replacement by the Protestant monarchs William and Mary – the supremacy of parliamentary legislation over other sources of law was by no means as clear as Dicey's account of sovereignty would have us believe. The monarch, for instance, claimed the ability to legislate by way of proclamation,[28] to levy taxation without parliamentary sanction,[29] and the prerogative to unilaterally suspend laws.[30] Each, of course, posed a particular threat to the power and authority of Parliament which – since the fourteenth century – had slowly developed from a body which assisted much of the revenue-raising activities of the

---

[24] On which see Chapter 9, pp. 302–4.

[25] J. Goldsworthy, *The Sovereignty of Parliament: History and Philosophy* (OUP, 1999) Ch. 5.

[26] For two accessible accounts see: A. Tomkins, Public Law (Clarendon Press, 2003) ch. 2; E. Wicks, *The Evolution of a Constitution: Eight Key Moments in British Constitutional History* (Hart Publishing, 2006) Ch. 1. For a more detailed coverage, see J. Goldsworthy, *The Sovereignty of Parliament: History and Philosophy* (OUP, 1999).

[27] E. Wicks, *The Evolution of a Constitution: Eight Key Moments in British Constitutional History* (Hart Publishing, 2006) p. 19.

[28] See e.g. *The Case of Proclamations* (1611) 12 Co Rep 74.

[29] See e.g. *The Case of Ship Money* (1637) 3 St Tr 825.

[30] See e.g. *Godden* v *Hales* (1686) 11 St Tr 1165.

monarch into a body through which much of the business of government was conducted. Add to this a power claimed by the common law courts to 'controul' the exercise of legislative power by Parliament and the question of where primary legal authority resided at this time appears even more confused.[31]

The Glorious Revolution ended the uncertainty, with the Bill of Rights 1689 and Act of Settlement 1701 forming the foundations of the modern constitution.

Insight
Key features of the Bill of Rights 1689

- Provided that the monarch may not suspend or execute laws without the consent of Parliament.
- Made it unlawful for the monarch to use the prerogative in order to levy taxes.
- Prevented the monarch from raising a standing army without the consent of Parliament.
- Guaranteed free elections to Parliament.
- Provided that the freedom of speech of Members of Parliament should be protected.
- Held that Parliament should meet frequently.

Insight
Key features of the Act of Settlement 1701

- Prescribed that the Crown should pass to descendants of Princess Sophia of Hanover.
- Provided that future monarchs should be of the established Church of England.
- Provided the foundations of judicial independence (that judges should hold office during good behaviour and can be removed only on an address of both Houses of Parliament).
- Held that a Royal pardon cannot serve as a defence to parliamentary impeachment.

Taken together, the two instruments established the ultimate supremacy of Parliament over the competing source of constitutional authority in the state, the monarch:

> If the Bill of Rights established that Parliament could lay down the terms and conditions on which England was to continue as a monarchy, the Act of Settlement, which followed in 1701, established that Parliament could also control the very identity of the monarch, by altering, if it wished, the line of succession.[32]

The combined effect of these two pieces of legislation was to cement the transition from monarchical to parliamentary government. The Bill of Rights 1689 and Act of Settlement 1701 saw the power of the monarch reduced to a shadow of its former self,[33] and saw the idea of divine right consigned to history; in the struggles between Crown and Parliament for constitutional supremacy, Parliament emerged the clear victor.

---

[31] *Dr Bonham's Case* (1609) 8 Coke Reports 113b; 77 ER 646.
[32] A. Tomkins, *Public Law* (Clarendon Press, 2003) p. 44.
[33] See pp. 255–64.

The distinction between legal and political sovereignty

There is perhaps something of a logical leap between Parliament asserting its political and legal primacy over the monarchy, and the suggestion that Parliament is legally sovereign. Put another way, there is some distance between the assertion that an Act of Parliament should be treated as being superior to other sources of law, and the suggestion that an Act of Parliament can, legally, do anything. To say that Parliament's legislative power is in effect legally unfettered, is not to say that Parliament's power is subject to no limitations whatsoever. The concept of legal sovereignty is therefore slightly misleading. While Dicey's account of sovereignty holds that Parliament may theoretically legislate in order to achieve any aim, and that no other body enjoys the right to set aside that legislation, it does not suggest that Parliament's power is subject to no constraints whatsoever. Dicey acknowledged that his idea of sovereignty was a *legal* one,[34] but that it nevertheless was the 'dominant characteristic of our political institutions'.[35] As Dicey therefore recognised, Parliament's legislative power is only exercisable in practice subject to the prevailing political conditions in which Parliament carries out its business. As a result, he argued that there are 'many enactments . . . which Parliament never would and (to speak plainly) never could pass'.[36] Dicey seemed to acknowledge that the political process possesses the ability to temper the potential absolutism of Parliament's legal power. Having said that, the orthodox position of the courts – should the political process be unable to prevent Parliament enacting legislation which may be widely regarded as being Draconian, immoral, or simply ridiculous – has traditionally been clear:

> It is often said that it would be unconstitutional for the United Kingdom Parliament to do certain things, meaning that the moral, political and other reasons against doing them are so strong that most people would regard it as highly improper if Parliament did those things. But that does not mean that it is beyond the power of Parliament to do those things, if Parliament chooses to do any of them the courts could not hold that Act of Parliament invalid.[37]

This strand of thinking resonates in the contemporary constitution: as Baroness Hale recognised in the *Jackson* decision, 'the constraints upon what Parliament can do are political and diplomatic rather than constitutional'.[38] However, as we will see later in this chapter, and in the next, there is a clear – and perhaps growing – undercurrent to contemporary constitutional thought which suggests that such an absolutist reading of parliamentary sovereignty is incompatible with the demands of constitutionalism and the rule of law.[39]

Parliamentary sovereignty, in the sense that Dicey envisaged the doctrine, was manifestly a legal device. As a result, it 'denotes only an absence of legal limitations, not the absence of *all* limitations or, a more appropriate word, inhibitions on Parliament's actions'.[40] It follows from this that we should be careful to distinguish between the apparent lack of *legal* restraints on Parliament's legislative power, and those *political* factors which may prevent Parliament from legislating to unjust or wicked effect. A good introductory illustration of the relationship between these two dynamics of sovereignty can be found in the experience of devolution to Scotland.

---

[34] A. V. Dicey, *Introduction to the Study of the Law of the Constitution* (Liberty Fund, 1982) p. 24.

[35] Ibid., p. 3.

[36] Ibid., p. 26.

[37] *Madzimbamuto* v *Lardner-Burke* [1969] 1 AC 645, 723.

[38] *Jackson* v *Attorney-General* [2006] 1 AC 56, [159] (Baroness Hale). See also [113] (Lord Hope).

[39] See pp. 179–80.

[40] C. Munro, *Studies in Constitutional Law* (2nd edn) (Butterworths, 1999) p. 135 (emphasis added).

Key debates

The distinction between legal sovereignty and political sovereignty illustrated

The experience of devolution to Scotland provides a useful comparison when considering ideas of legal and political – or popular – sovereignty. Devolution to Scotland, Wales and Northern Ireland and its consequences for the constitution of the UK is considered further in Chapters 12 and 13. In short, devolution is the *delegation* of power from a central legal authority – the Parliament at Westminster – to a subordinate body, for the purposes of our example, the Scottish Parliament.[41]

Devolution and sovereignty: the orthodox legal position

In orthodox legal terms, devolution can be presented consistently with the idea of parliamentary sovereignty, as power *delegated,* by statute, from Westminster, rather than *divided,* constitutionally, between Westminster and the devolved institutions.[42] The apparent retention of Westminster's sovereign powers is made plain in the terms of s. 28(7) of the Scotland Act 1998 – the provision which outlines the legislative competence of the Scottish Parliament – which provides:

> This section does not affect the power of the Parliament of the United Kingdom to make laws for Scotland.

As a result of this, and applying the orthodox approach to parliamentary sovereignty, should the Westminster Parliament wish to legislate in an area of devolved competence, or restrict the exercise of that competence, it would be possible for it to do so by simply enacting subsequent legislation to that effect. In effect, orthodox theory holds that the Westminster Parliament maintains an ability to legislate irrespective of the powers delegated to the Scottish Parliament. In practice however, and from the establishment of the devolved institutions in Scotland, a constitutional convention (the Sewel convention) has presented a barrier to this possibility.

Devolution and sovereignty: the political dimensions

Under orthodox – Diceyan – theory, the Scotland Act 1998 is an ordinary statute, with the exact same constitutional status and susceptibility to repeal as the Dangerous Dogs Act 1991. The Scotland Act 1998 however is notably different from most other primary legislation in at least one important respect; it was passed in order to give effect to widespread demand for devolved government[43] following a referendum at which its objectives were endorsed by almost 75 per cent of the Scottish electorate. As a result, it has been argued that the Scotland Act, by contrast with other Acts of Parliament *not* specifically endorsed by referendum, possesses an 'extra validity' which might be said to distinguish it from those other enactments. Bogdanor, for one, therefore, suggested that in order to repeal or significantly and regressively amend the scheme of devolution, the consent of the Scottish electorate would have to be similarly obtained.[44] As a result, the 'political entrenchment' of the Scotland Act

---

[41] V. Bogdanor, *Devolution in the United Kingdom* (OUP, 1999) pp. 2–3.
[42] As would be the case in a federal system.
[43] See the Scottish Constitutional Convention, *Scotland's Parliament, Scotland's Right* (1995), and the discussion at pp. 362–6.
[44] See also B. Hadfield, 'The United Kingdom as a Territorial State' in V. Bogdanor, *The British Constitution in the Twentieth Century* (OUP/British Academy, 2003) p. 626.

1998 would place a *de facto,* if not *de jure,* restriction on Parliament's ability to legislate in order to limit the powers available to the institutions of devolved government.[45]

In spite of Parliament's legal ability to unilaterally legislate in an area of devolved competence following the creation of the Scottish Parliament, a further political limitation on this particular power has emerged by way of convention. Under what is known as the Sewel convention – named after the member of the House of Lords who initially proposed it – the Parliament of the UK will not ordinarily legislate on a devolved issue affecting Scotland unless the consent of the Scottish Parliament is gained in advance via what has become known as a legislative consent motion. The memorandum of understanding, agreed between the UK government and the three devolved administrations, reads as follows on this point:

> The UK Government will normally proceed in accordance with the convention that the UK Parliament would not normally legislate with regard to devolved matters except with the agreement of the devolved legislature.

Though the Sewel Convention was formalised in statute by s. 2 of the Scotland Act 2016 (and also in the Wales Act 2017), the Supreme Court confirmed in the *Miller* decision that the convention remains operative as a *'political* restriction on the activity of the UK Parliament', and as such would not be judicially-enforced.[46]

Devolution and sovereignty: the consequences

While Parliament's legal sovereignty formally remains unscathed, we should not underestimate the practical effect of these political limitations. As Bogdanor has argued:

> It is then in constitutional theory alone that full legislative power remains with Westminster. It is in constitutional theory alone that the supremacy of Parliament is preserved. For power devolved, far from being power retained, will be power transferred; and it will not be possible to recover that power except under pathological circumstances . . . [47]

A further illustration of a potential political limitation on Parliament's legislative capacity can be found in the use of referendums in the UK.

Key debates

The status of referendums in United Kingdom constitutional law

The orthodox theory of parliamentary sovereignty holds that Parliament's legislative power cannot be subject to external limitations. As such, the electorate, cannot – via a referendum – *compel* Parliament to legislate in a particular manner. It follows from this that Referendums are non-binding as a matter of law (House of Lords Select Committee on the Constitution, *Referendums in*

→

---

[45] As will be addressed in what follows, the Scotland Act 1998 has also been recognised, at common law, as a 'constitutional statute' (a statute which will not be susceptible to implied repeal). For discussion see pp.158–61.

[46] *R (Miller)* v *Secretary of State for Exiting the European Union* [2017] UKSC 5; [2017] 2 WLR 583, [145] (emphasis added).

[47] V. Bogdanor, *Devolution in the United Kingdom* (OUP, 1999) p. 291.

the United Kingdom (2009–2010), HL 99, [197]). However, as was recognised in the Supreme Court decision in *Miller* it is open to Parliament to stipulate a particular consequence if a certain threshold is met: '[t]he effect of any particular referendum must depend on the terms of the statute which authorises it' ([2017] UKSC 5; [2017] 2 WLR 583, [118]). The scheme of devolution contained in the Scotland Act 1978 – for instance – was only to come into force if over 40 per cent of the electorate voted in its favour at a referendum (with only 32.9 per cent doing so). Section 8 of the Parliamentary Voting System and Constituencies Act 2011 required that the Alternative Vote system be adopted for general elections (on which see pp. 310–12) if a majority supported such a move (again, the statutory requirement was not met, with only 32.1 per cent voting to support the change).

By contrast with these examples, the European Union Referendum Act 2015 was silent as to the consequences of the June 2016 referendum. Ministers' statements as to the effect of the referendum were, unsurprisingly, inconsistent. As was also recognised in the Supreme Court's *Miller* decision, ministerial statements of intent *cannot* resolve the question of as a matter of law: '[w]hether or not they are clear and consistent, such public observations, wherever they are made, are not law: they are statements of political intention. Further, such statements are, at least normally, made by ministers on behalf of the UK government, not on behalf of Parliament.' ([119]). In short, as the Supreme Court further noted in *Miller,* unless acted upon by Parliament, the force of the referendum was 'political rather than legal' [124].

So while a compelling case can be made that the 2016 referendum was not legally binding, it is undoubted however, that the political weight which attaches to the majority vote – via a UK-wide plebiscite – in favour of leaving the EU is considerable. It would therefore be difficult for any government (in the short term aftermath of the vote or in the absence of a material change of circumstance) to reverse or avoid this outcome. While the outcome of the Brexit referendum may not impose a legal obligation on Parliament to legislate, it is clear that MPs have proceeded since June 2016 as if subject to a *de facto* obligation to respect the outcome of the vote.

If we are to take seriously the restrictions placed on the idea of Parliament's legal power due to the influence of a political authority of some sort then perhaps the label of *sovereignty* is something of a misnomer. As the leading critic of Dicey, Ivor Jennings, wrote:

> If [we are to acknowledge a source of political authority that may restrict Parliament's legislative latitude] legal sovereignty is not sovereignty at all. It is not supreme power. It is a legal concept, a form of expression which lawyers use to express the relations between Parliament and the courts. It means that the courts will recognise as law the rules which Parliament makes by legislation . . . [48]

In other words, Jennings argued that the concept of legal sovereignty was only a label used to describe the relationship between constitutional actors, rather than an encapsulation of a potentially limitless legislative power. Jennings, as a result, preferred the phrase 'legislative supremacy' as a more accurate description of the status of Acts of Parliament as norms within the UK's constitutional hierarchy.[49]

Jennings' assessment provides us with a salient reminder: Parliament does not exercise its legislative power in the abstract, and for recognition of the supposed supremacy of parliamentary legislation we must look to the responses of other constitutional actors. It should always be remembered that while it is the role and duty of Parliament to legislate,

---

[48] W. I. Jennings, *The Law and the Constitution* (4th edn) (University of London Press, 1952) p. 144.
[49] Ibid., p. 149.

it is the role and duty of the courts to interpret and apply legislation passed by Parliament: as Lord Nicholls stated in the House of Lords decision in *Jackson v Atttorney-General,* '[t]he proper interpretation of a statute is a matter for the courts, not Parliament. This principle is as fundamental in this country's constitution as the principle that Parliament has exclusive cognisance (jurisdiction) over its own affairs.'[50] Implicit in this function is the ability of the courts to determine what measures should be recognised as having the force of law, and – more specifically in the UK context – what should be recognised as having the authority that attaches to an *Act of Parliament.* In other words, as Wade has written, 'it is always for the courts, in the last resort, to say what is a valid Act of Parliament'.[51]

In order to begin explaining the relationship between Parliament and the courts more fully, it is worth examining one of Dicey's core propositions – the question of whether Parliament can impose limitations on itself – in more detail.

Thinking Point . . .

In his *dicta* in **Jackson,** Lord Nicholls echoed sentiments expressed in the United States Supreme Court in *Marbury* v *Madison* 5 US (1 Cranch) 137 (1803). In that case – albeit one decided by a court giving effect to a written constitutional document – the court determined that 'it is emphatically the province and duty of the Judicial Department to say what the law is'. We shall return to the idea that the constitutional functions of 'legislator' and 'interpreter' should be carried out by different institutions when we examine separation of powers in Chapter 7.

Can Parliament impose limitations upon its own legislative competence?

Key issues

- Dicey denied that Parliament can place legal limitations on its own power; no Act of Parliament may be insulated from repeal or amendment by an Act yet to be passed. The idea that any statute might be either expressly repealed or – in the event of a conflict – repealed by the necessary implication of a subsequently passed Act reinforces the suggestion that Parliament cannot bind itself. Dicey's conception of sovereignty is referred to as being 'continuing', meaning that each Parliament enjoys the exact same legal powers as its predecessors.

- An alternative theory – 'self-embracing sovereignty' – advances the suggestion that Parliament possesses the ability to place certain limitations on itself. Under the theory of self-embracing sovereignty a Parliament may find itself bound to adhere to previous enactments pertaining to the manner in which legislation is enacted, and the form that that legislation might take.

The legislative powers of the UK Parliament are not limited by the terms of a written constitution, but are its powers restricted by the decisions of previous Parliaments? Is the Parliament elected in 2017 bound to adhere to decisions enacted in legislation by Parliaments in, for example, 1900, 1979, or 2005? On Dicey's account, the answer would be a

---

[50] *Jackson v Attorney-General* [2005] UKHL 56; [2006] 1 AC 262, [51] (Lord Nicholls).
[51] H. W. R. Wade, 'The Basis of Legal Sovereignty' (1955) CLJ 172, 189.

conclusive 'no'. Following each general election a new Parliament is created with the exact same powers (i.e. sovereign powers) as the previous Parliament, the Parliament before that, and so on. This idea is referred to as 'continuing sovereignty', with the only limitation on Parliament being that it cannot limit its own power.[52] The question of whether Parliament might impose limitations on itself exposes some of the circularity of the debates over the nature of legal sovereignty; if Parliament really is sovereign – if it really can legally achieve *anything* – then why, it might reasonably be asked, can it not bind itself?

The orthodox responses

(i) Express repeal

The evidence in favour of the notion that one Parliament is not bound to adhere to the legislative directions of a previous Parliament can be found in both legislative and judicial decisions. The legislative evidence in favour of the orthodox reading of continuing sovereignty can be found in the numerous occasions on which Parliament has enacted legislation that expressly overrules or invalidates a previous enactment, either in whole or in part. This process is known as express repeal. As Maugham LJ noted in the leading case of *Ellen Street Estates* v *Minister of Health:*

> If in a subsequent Act Parliament chooses to make plain that an earlier statute is being to some extent repealed, effect must be given to that intention just because it is the will of the legislature.[53]

In practice, many Acts of Parliament include a section entitled 'repeals' which will provide a list of specific provisions of previous enactments that are to be invalidated. To give a brief example: the Constitutional Reform Act 2005, among other things, abolished the Appellate Committee of the House of Lords and established a Supreme Court for the UK. In order to do so, it was necessary for Parliament to repeal the Appellate Jurisdiction Act 1876 – the Act that previously regulated the appellate jurisdiction of the House of Lords – in its entirety. As a result, the Constitutional Reform Act 2005 contained a provision indicating that it was Parliament's express intention that the Appellate Jurisdiction Act 1876 should be repealed.[54]

(ii) Implied repeal

Evidence in favour of Parliament's continued freedom of legislative action can also be found on the judicial record in cases concerning what is known as implied repeal. Where two pieces of legislation, on the same topic, are in apparent conflict with each other, it is the role of the courts to determine which should apply. In the event of such a clash, the courts have held that the most recent legislation will be enforced, and that the older instrument will be taken to have been repealed by implication. As Lord Langdale stated in *Dean of Ely* v *Bliss:*

> If two inconsistent Acts be passed at different times, the last must be obeyed, and if obedience cannot be observed without derogating from the first, it is the first which must give way . . . Every Act is made either for the purpose of making a change in the law, or for the purpose of better declaring the law, and its operation is not to be impeded by the mere fact that it is inconsistent with some previous enactment.[55]

---

[52] H. W. R. Wade, 'The Basis of Legal Sovereignty' [1955] CLJ 172, 175.
[53] *Ellen Street Estates* v *Minister of Health* [1934] 1 KB 590, 597.
[54] Constitutional Reform Act 2005, s. 146 and sch. 18.
[55] *Dean of Ely* v *Bliss* (1842) 5 Beav 574, 582.

To give a straightforward example; say, for instance, that an Act of Parliament passed in 1990 provided that the mandatory sentence for committing the crime of treason should be 20 years' imprisonment. An Act then passed in 2013 provides that the mandatory sentence for committing the crime of treason should be 25 years' imprisonment (though in so doing makes no explicit reference to the terms of the earlier Act). In a dispute over which Act should apply, the courts will enforce the later of the two statutes and, in the event of a conviction, impose a sentence of 25 years' imprisonment. In such cases, it is taken by the courts to be a necessary implication of Parliament having legislated to achieve a specific effect that any earlier, conflicting legislation should no longer be operable. In other words, Parliament will be taken to have impliedly repealed a provision simply 'by enacting a provision which is clearly inconsistent with [a] previous Act'.[56]

Can an Act of Parliament be protected from future repeal?

Constitutional measures that, in other jurisdictions, are protected from repeal or amendment via the ordinary legislative process are referred to as being entrenched. The idea of entrenchment is not obviously compatible with the idea of continuing sovereignty; if the Parliament of today is not bound to adhere to the legislative decisions of previous Parliaments then protecting a statute or its provisions from repeal would seem to be legally impossible. This has not, however, prevented legislation from being enacted by Parliament which purports to apply in perpetuity. The Union with Ireland Act 1800, for example, provided that the Churches of England and Ireland should be united 'for ever'. This supposedly undoable union of churches was nonetheless undone when the Church of Ireland was disestablished by the Irish Church Act 1869.[57] A more recent example can be found in the provisions of the Scotland Act 2016, s. 1 of which declares that the Scottish Parliament and Scottish Government are a 'permanent part of the United Kingdom's constitutional arrangements'.[58]

The question of whether an earlier Act of Parliament might control the effects of a later Act of Parliament was addressed in the case of *Ellen Street Estates* v *Minister of Health*:

Key case
Ellen Street Estates v *Minister of Health [1934] 1 KB 590*

In **Ellen Street Estates**, the Court of Appeal was confronted with two apparently contradictory provisions relating to compensation for landowners following the compulsory purchase of their land by a public authority. The first piece of legislation – the Acquisition of Land (Assessment of Compensation) Act – had been passed in 1919. The second, the Housing Act, was passed in 1925. On its face, the dispute appeared to be a straightforward application of the doctrine of implied repeal. Section 7 of the Acquisition of Land (Assessment of Compensation) Act 1919, however, provided:

> The provisions of the Act or order by which the land is authorised to be acquired, or of any Act incorporated therewith, shall, in relation to the matters dealt with in this Act, have effect subject

---

[56] *Ellen Street Estates* v *Minister of Health* [1934] 1 KB 590, 595–6 (Scrutton LJ).
[57] The political and legal union with Ireland was also subsequently undone following the Anglo-Irish Treaty of 1921.
[58] See 409–10.

> to this Act, and so far as inconsistent with those provisions shall cease to have effect or shall not have effect.
>
> The purported effect of s. 7 was that future legislation should only take effect subject to its provisions, and that future inconsistent legislation would be of no legal effect. Section 7 of the Acquisition of Land (Assessment of Compensation) Act therefore attempted to insulate the 1919 statute from repeal by suggesting that future legislation which was inconsistent with it would be of no legal effect.
>
> The court's decision reinforced the orthodox – or Diceyan – approach to sovereignty.[59] Holding that the 1925 Act would apply, Maugham LJ noted that:
>
>> The legislature cannot, according to our constitution, bind itself as to the form of subsequent legislation, and it is impossible for Parliament to enact that in a subsequent statute dealing with the same subject-matter there can be no implied repeal.[60]
>
> The Court of Appeal therefore held that the later Act would apply, and the attempt by the 1919 statute to entrench itself was of no legal effect.

Some confusion has been seen to result from the particular choice of wording used by Maugham LJ, specifically in his suggestion that no Act of Parliament can specify the 'form' which subsequent legislation should take in order to effect a valid repeal. This finding is frequently used in support of the proposition that Parliament may not seek to legally restrict itself in *any* way. At first glance, this conclusion appears to be consistent with the idea of continuing sovereignty and, therefore, with Dicey's suggestion that 'a sovereign power cannot, while retaining its sovereign character, restrict is own powers by any particular enactment'.[61] However, this conclusion also makes no acknowledgement of the fact that the extent of one purported limitation may be trivial by comparison with another.

A departure from the orthodoxy: self–embracing sovereignty

By contrast with the assertion of advocates of continuing sovereignty that Parliament's legislative power might not be restricted in *any* way, a competing school of thought advances the proposition that Parliament can in fact place certain limitations on the use of its own powers. Considered in the abstract for instance, a procedural restriction on the use of a particular power – a stipulation that a specified legislative process is adhered to in order to effect change to pre-existing legislation – does not necessarily preclude that the amending power might be exercised. Rather, it imposes a limitation of process which would simply require a specified formula to be followed in order that a purported repeal might be effective. The theory of self-embracing sovereignty – sometimes referred to as the 'new' view of sovereignty – suggests that sovereignty might be subject to such limitations for the reason that 'the "legal sovereign" may impose legal limitations upon itself, because its power to change the law includes the power to change the law affecting itself'.[62]

For illustrative purposes, it is necessary to consider the differing types of limitation that might be placed on the legislative power of Parliament.

---

[59] See also *Vauxhall Estates* v *Liverpool Corporation* [1932] 1 KB 733, 743 (Avory J): 'no Act of Parliament can effectively provide that no future Act of Parliament can interfere with its provisions'.

[60] *Ellen Street Estates* v *Minister of Health* [1934] 1 KB 590, 597 (Maugham LJ).

[61] A. V. Dicey, *Introduction to the Study of the Law of the Constitution* (Liberty Fund, 1982) p. 24.

[62] W. I. Jennings, *The Law and the Constitution* (4th edn) (University of London Press, 1952) p. 148.

(i) Limitations on the manner of enactment of future legislation

Such a limitation would specify that a certain legislative procedure ought to be adopted before a particular legislative provision might come into effect or might be effectively repealed. For instance, a statutory provision which declared that 'this section might only be repealed following a two-thirds majority vote in each House of Parliament' would require a specific process to be adopted in order to achieve a valid repeal. Similarly, a statutory requirement that a referendum be held on a particular subject prior to effective legislative action on that topic would also impose a requirement that a particular manner of legislative process be adopted. An example of the latter can be found in s. 1 of the Northern Ireland Act 1998, which stipulates that:

> It is hereby declared that Northern Ireland in its entirety remains part of the United Kingdom and shall not cease to be so without the consent of a majority of the people of Northern Ireland voting in a poll held for the purposes of this section . . .

On the terms of s. 1, the government of the UK (with the agreement of the government of Ireland) should not lay before Parliament any legislative proposal which would see Northern Ireland leave the UK unless that end had been approved by referendum held in accordance with the Northern Ireland Act.[63]

(ii) Limitations on the form which future legislation ought to take

Such a limitation would specify that a particular form of words ought to be adopted in order to repeal a legislative measure. For example, a limitation of form might require an express repeal in order to legitimately override a particular measure. Perhaps the most well-known measure designed to limit the form in which future legislation be expressed in order to take effect can be found in s. 33(1) of the Canadian Charter of Rights and Freedoms, commonly referred to as the 'notwithstanding clause'. Section 33(1) provides:

> Parliament or the legislature of a province may expressly declare in an Act of Parliament or of the legislature . . . that the Act or a provision thereof shall operate notwithstanding certain of the substantive protections afforded by the Charter.[64]

By including an express provision indicating that the Act should take effect 'notwithstanding' the protections afforded by the Charter, the Canadian Parliament and provincial legislatures are able to effectively suspend the operation of the Charter in respect of that particular piece of legislation.

Limitations of manner and form effectively place procedural hurdles in the way of Parliament achieving certain legislative objectives. Those objectives might still be achieved, so long as the requirements of the specified procedures are adhered to. As such, manner and form restrictions are limitations of process rather than substance.

---

[63] The suggestion made by Bogdanor (V. Bogdanor, *Devolution in the United Kingdom* (OUP, 1999) p. 291) – discussed at pp. 130–1 – that a referendum would be required to endorse any proposed legislative repeal or significant and regressive amendment of the Scotland Act 1998 would amount, for instance, to a politically-imposed limitation on the manner in which legislation should be passed.

[64] Namely, the protections provided under s. 2 and ss. 7–15 of the Charter of Rights and Freedoms 1982.

(iii) Limitations on the substance or content of future legislation

A limitation on the content of future legislation however poses more difficulties. A limitation which would preclude Parliament legislating on a particular topic, or to achieve a particular aim – no matter what the manner and form adopted – would amount to a substantive restriction on the legal powers of a Parliament. No legislature could therefore make a realistic claim to exercise sovereign power in the event of such a limitation being effective. While restrictions of manner and form might well be argued to be consistent with the idea of a legislature exercising sovereign power, a limitation of substance could not be so easily defended.

Self-embracing sovereignty in practice

Self-embracing sovereignty recognises a material difference between the internal rules which govern Parliament's legislative *procedures* and those which regulate its legislative *competence*. Heuston formulates the idea of self-embracing sovereignty in the following way:

(1) Sovereignty is a legal concept: the rules of which identify the sovereign and prescribe its composition and functions are logically prior to it.

(2) There is a distinction between rules which govern, on the one hand, (a) the composition, and (b) the procedure, and, on the other hand, (c) the area of power, of a sovereign legislature.

(3) The courts have jurisdiction to question the validity of an alleged Act of Parliament on grounds 2(a) and 2(b), but not on ground 2(c).

(4) This jurisdiction is exercisable either before or after the Royal Assent has been signified – in the former case by way of injunction, in the latter by way of declaratory judgment.[65]

Manner and form requirements relate to a Parliament's internal procedures rather than to the legislature's ability to legislate to achieve a specific end. The theory of self-embracing sovereignty therefore posits that Parliament *may* limit its own power, not by placing substantive restrictions on the topics on which legislation might be passed, but through the procedural limitation of making the validity of future legislation contingent on certain manner and form requirements.

The Australian case of *Trethowen* is frequently raised in support of the suggestion that Parliament could subject itself to manner and form requirements.

Key case

Attorney-General for New South Wales v *Trethowen [1932] AC 526*

Section 5 of the Colonial Laws Validity Act 1865 provided that:

> . . . every Representative Legislature shall, in respect to the Colony under its jurisdiction, have . . . full power to make laws respecting the Constitution, Power and Procedure of such legislature; provided that such laws shall have been passed in such manner and form as may from time to time be required by any [legislative measure] for the time being in force in the said colony.

---

[65] R. F. V. Heuston, *Essays in Constitutional Law* (2nd edn) (Stevens and Sons, 1964) pp. 6–7.

> The legislature of New South Wales, operating under the provisions of the 1865 Act, enacted legislation in 1929 which required that any future bill which purported to abolish the Legislative Council could not be granted Royal Assent unless and until it had been endorsed by referendum.
>
> In 1930 the legislature – acting to give effect to the commitments of a new government – enacted a measure which purported to repeal the 1929 Act, and a further measure which purported to abolish the Legislative Council. Neither had been endorsed by way of referendum.
>
> An injunction was sought in order to prevent the bills being granted Royal Assent. The Judicial Committee of the Privy Council held that the Act of 1929 was binding as to the manner and form required of a legislative instrument purporting to abolish the Legislative Council.

The difficulty of applying *Trethowen* in the domestic context is that it is a case concerning an explicitly limited legislature, rather than a legislature purporting to exercise sovereign powers, such as that at Westminster.[66] Jennings was nonetheless able to countenance the idea of the UK Parliament placing limitations on its own power for the reason that he approached the subject from a different perspective to that adopted by Dicey. Instead of regarding sovereignty as a description of the extent of Parliament's power, Jennings – as has already been touched on – saw the notion of legal sovereignty as convenient shorthand for the power relationship between Parliament and the courts. Instead of attempting to deny the possibility that a truly sovereign power might be limited in some way, Jennings looked to the reactions of other constitutional actors. Jennings asked, 'what might the courts recognise as a valid use of Parliament's legislative power?' Or put another way, 'what will the courts recognise as statute law?'

Can Parliament amend the primary legislative process?

Key issues

- Primary legislation is enacted when a Bill is approved by the House of Commons and House of Lords and is granted the Royal Assent. An exception to this rule exists as a result of the Parliament Acts, which provide that in certain circumstances a Bill might be put forward for Royal Assent despite having been rejected by the House of Lords.

- The status of legislation enacted under the Parliament Acts procedure was the subject of the House of Lords 2006 decision in *Jackson* v *Attorney-General*. The House of Lords found in *Jackson* that measures enacted under the Parliament Acts procedure had the status of primary legislation, and in so doing directly (and indirectly) addressed a series of fundamental questions relating to parliamentary sovereignty.

Dicey noted that a law is 'any rule which will be enforced by the courts.'[67] We have already seen, however, that Acts of Parliament are but one of a number of sources of legal rules which will be enforced by the judiciary.[68] The doctrine of parliamentary sovereignty holds

---

[66] C. Munro, *Studies in Constitutional Law* (2nd edn) (London: Butterworths, 1999) pp. 158–9.
[67] A. V. Dicey, *Introduction to the Study of the Law of the Constitution* (Liberty Fund, 1982) p. 4.
[68] See Chapters 2 and 3.

that *Acts of Parliament* occupy a position at the top of the hierarchy of legal rules to which the courts will give effect. When, and on the orthodox account *only* when, the three con- stituent parts of Parliament work together in order to enact legislation – i.e. when a legis- lative measure is passed by the House of Commons, House of Lords and is granted the Royal Assent – then an Act of Parliament is passed. Other parliamentary decisions – for instance, resolutions of the House of Commons[69] – will not be acknowledged by the courts as possessing a similar force to that carried by an Act of Parliament. Secondary, or dele- gated, legislation is not immune from judicial review and is susceptible to being struck down by the courts.[70] Similarly, legislative instruments passed by bodies other than Par- liament – for example, legislation passed by the devolved legislatures[71] – will not carry the legal authority that attaches to primary legislation enacted by the Westminster Parliament.

In order to distinguish between those decisions that should carry the authority of pri- mary legislation and decisions which carry a lesser authority, the courts look for evidence that the legislative measure has been enacted. Such evidence was historically found by looking to something known as the parliamentary roll (the official record of proceedings in Parliament):[72]

> . . . if from that it should appear that a bill has passed both Houses and received the Royal Assent, no Court of Justice can inquire into the mode in which it was introduced into Parliament, nor into what was done previous to its introduction, or what passed in Parliament during its progress in its various stages through both Houses.[73]

The most obvious contemporary evidence will be that the vast majority of Acts of Parlia- ment will bear the following words of enactment:

> Be it enacted by the Queen's most Excellent Majesty, by and with the consent of the Lords Spiritual and Temporal, and Commons, in this present Parliament assembled, and by the authority of the same, as follows: -

If the customary words of enactment are present, then it is not for the courts to question the process by which such legislation was adopted or otherwise question the authority which attaches to the Act; '. . . it is not for the court to say that a parliamentary enact- ment, the highest law in this country, is illegal.[74] As a result, for instance, the House of Lords refused to entertain the suggestion that Parliament had been fraudulently misled into enacting a particular statute in *British Railways Board* v *Pickin*.[75] The courts are concerned only with the enforcement of the end result – the Act of Parliament – the processes and procedures by which the Act came to be on the statute book are matters for Parliament itself.[76]

---

[69] *Stockdale* v *Hansard* (1839) 9 A & E 1.

[70] For an example, see *R* v *Lord Chancellor, ex parte Witham* [1998] QB 575.

[71] *Whaley* v *Lord Watson of Invergowrie* [2000] SLT 475, 481–2; *AXA General Insurance Ltd* v *HM Advocate* [2011] UKSC 46; [2012] 1 AC 868, [43]-[47].

[72] *The Prince's Case* (1606) 8 Co Rep 1a 505.

[73] *Edinburgh and Dalkeith Railway Co.* v *Wauchope* (1842) VIII Clark & Finnelly 710, 725.

[74] *Cheney* v *Conn* [1968] 1 All ER 779, 782.

[75] *British Railways Board* v *Pickin* [1974] AC 765.

[76] See also Bill of Rights 1689, Article 9: 'That the Freedome of Speech and Debates or Proceedings in Parlyament ought not to be impeached or questioned in any Court or Place out of Parlyament' (on which see p. 172).

Can Parliament redesign itself?

To suggest, however, that primary legislation can *only* be enacted on the assent of the House of Commons, the House of Lords and the monarch would be an over-simplification. Since 1911, a process has existed which permits the House of Commons to propose for Royal Assent a Bill that has not been consented to by the House of Lords. This procedure can be found in the Parliament Acts of 1911 and 1949.

Insight
The enactment of the Parliament Act 1911

The circumstances which gave rise to the implementation of the Parliament Act 1911 involved a legislative impasse between the House of Commons and the House of Lords. Prior to the enactment of the Parliament Act 1911, the House of Lords' powers to delay or reject legislative proposals passed to it from the Commons were considerable. As Rhodri Walters has pithily put it:

> [t]he Lords' powers over public legislation, other than bills of supply [which, by convention, the Lords did not interfere with], were unfettered. If the Lords disliked any provisions in a bill, they could amend them; if they disliked a bill in its entirety, they could reject it outright.[77]

While the powers of the House of Commons at this time were increasingly bolstered by a democratic mandate, those of the House of Lords, composed almost entirely of hereditary peers, could not be claimed to be similarly supported by the popular vote. In the period preceding the passing of the Parliament Act, the Lords' effective power of legislative veto was 'invariably' deployed for political purposes, as the Conservative-dominated upper house sought to 'frustrate measures laid before it by Liberal administrations'.[78]

The rejection by the House of Lords of Lloyd George's so-called 'People's Budget' of 1909 proved to be the final straw for an elected government repeatedly thwarted by the largely hereditary Lords. In the face of a threat by the Liberal government to persuade the King to pack the House of Lords with Liberal Peers, the House of Lords was persuaded to accept a reduction to its legal powers, and gave its consent to what became the Parliament Act 1911.

The central provisions of the Parliament Act 1911 achieved the following:

- the Lords' powers of delay over Money Bills – that is, bills which only concern taxation by central government or certain issues relating to public finances[79] – were set at one month;[80]

- the power of the Lords to veto public bills (other than Money Bills or Bills purporting to extend the life of Parliament beyond five years) was replaced with a mere power to delay legislative proposals;[81] and

- the maximum life of a Parliament was reduced from seven to five years.[82]

---

[77] R. Walters, 'The House of Lords' in V. Bogdanor (ed.), *The British Constitution in the Twentieth Century* (OUP/British Academy, 2003) p. 191.

[78] Ibid.

[79] Parliament Act 1911, s. 1(2).

[80] Parliament Act 1911, s. 1.

[81] Parliament Act 1911, s. 2.

[82] Parliament Act 1911, s. 7.

The previously-held ability of the House of Lords to veto legislative proposals was, as a result of the Parliament Act 1911, done away with in favour of a mere power of delay. The effect of the Parliament Act 1911, therefore, was to provide a procedure under which Public Bills (other than a Money Bill or an instrument purporting to extend the life of Parliament beyond five years) that had been rejected by the House of Lords could be delayed for only two years before being presented for royal assent. By the Parliament Act 1949 – itself an Act passed without the consent of the upper house – the House of Lords' power of delay was reduced yet further, to one year.

Section 2(1) of the Parliament Act (as amended), provides as follows:

> If any Public Bill (other than a Money Bill or a Bill containing any provision to extend the maximum life of Parliament beyond five years) is passed by the House of Commons in two successive sessions (whether of the same Parliament or not), and, having been sent up to the House of Lords at least one month before the end of the session, is rejected by the House of Lords in each of those sessions, that Bill shall, on its rejection for the second time by the House of Lords, unless the House of Commons direct to the contrary, be presented to His Majesty and become an Act of Parliament on the Royal Assent being signified thereto, notwithstanding that the House of Lords have not consented to the Bill . . .

As a result, under the terms of s. 2(1) any Public Bill other than (a) a Money Bill or (b) a Bill which purports to extend the life of a Parliament beyond five years may – following its rejection in two successive sessions by the upper house – become an 'Act of Parliament'. The Lords' power of delay in respect of such Bills stands at one year. The Lords' power of delay over Money Bills stands at only one month.[83] The Parliament Acts severely curtailed the powers of the House of Lords, transforming it from a House of veto into a House of deliberation and revision.[84] The democratic primacy of the House of Commons was – as a result of the Parliament Acts – matched by its legal primacy.[85]

Under the Parliament Acts procedure, the House of Commons enjoys considerable power to pass (or threaten to pass) legislation which has not been endorsed by the House of Lords. Having said that, the Parliament Acts procedure has been used relatively sparingly.

Key statutes

Acts passed under the Parliament Act 1911

- Welsh Church Act 1914
- Government of Ireland Act 1914
- Parliament Act 1949

---

[83] Parliament Act 1911, s. 1(1).
[84] See generally R. Walters, 'The House of Lords' in V. Bogdanor (ed.), *The British Constitution in the Twentieth Century* (OUP/British Academy, 2003).
[85] For further discussion, see Chapter 9, pp. 302–4.

Key statutes

Acts passed under the Parliament Act as amended

- War Crimes Act 1991
- European Parliamentary Elections Act 1999
- Sexual Offences (Amendment) Act 2000
- Hunting Act 2004

An Act passed utilising the Parliament Acts procedure has not been assented to by the House of Lords. As a result, it will bear the following words of enactment:

> BE IT ENACTED by the Queen's most Excellent Majesty, by and with the advice and consent of the Commons in this present Parliament assembled, in accordance with the provisions of the Parliament Acts 1911 and 1949, and by the authority of the same, as follows: – [86]

The Parliament Acts procedure poses a number of difficult questions for our understanding of the doctrine of parliamentary sovereignty. Foremost among those questions are two of crucial significance:

- Does an Act passed under the Parliament Acts procedure – that is, an Act passed without the consent of the House of Lords – enjoy the same legal status as an Act passed by all three elements of Parliament acting in accord? And, if so:
- How could an Act passed under the Parliament Acts procedure – that is, a legislative body specifically *limited* by the explicit terms of s. 2(1) of the Parliament Act – enjoy the same legal status as an Act passed by the sovereign legislature enacting legislation under the orthodox manner and form?

Both questions arose for consideration in the case of *Jackson* v *Attorney General*.[87]

Jackson v Attorney-General

The validity of the Parliament Acts procedure was the question at issue in the case of *Jackson* v *Attorney-General*. The *Jackson* litigation was brought as a consequence of the prohibition on hunting with dogs brought about by the Hunting Act 2004. The Hunting Act – a particularly controversial piece of legislation to many – had been passed using the Parliament Acts procedure; it had been endorsed by the House of Commons, and rejected by the House of Lords.

The arguments

The challenge brought by Jackson questioned the validity of the Hunting Act 2004; as Lord Bingham summarised however, 'the real question turns on the validity of the 1949

---

[86] Parliament Act 1911 (as amended), s. 4. See, for example, *Jackson* v *Attorney-General* [2005] UKHL 56; [2006] 1 AC 262, [3].

[87] *Jackson* v *Attorney-General* [2005] UKHL 56; [2006] 1 AC 262.

[Parliament] Act and that in turn depends on the true effect of the 1911 [Parliament] Act'.[88] This was for the reason that the argument advanced by Jackson ran as follows:

(1) That the Parliament Act 1911 – in setting down a procedure for enacting legislation without the consent of the House of Lords – provided for a new way of making *delegated* legislation.

(2) That, as the 1949 Parliament Act had been enacted under this legislative procedure, it was delegated – not primary – legislation.

(3) That the Parliament Act 1949 was therefore susceptible to invalidation by the courts.

(4) That because it was impossible for delegated legislation to expand on the powers allocated under the parent statute, the Parliament Act 1949 was *ultra vires* (or, in other words, that the 1911 Act could not be utilised in order to modify itself).

(5) That, as a result, each Act passed under the Parliament Acts as amended in 1949 was not only delegated legislation, but also invalid as each had been purportedly implemented under the void terms of the 1949 amendment.

By contrast, the Attorney-General, who presented the case for the Government, argued that the Parliament Acts created a new method of creating – as per the language of s. 2(1) – an 'Act of Parliament'.[89] That the Parliament Acts procedure designated a valid procedure for the enactment of primary legislation was borne out by the acceptance – over a period of more than 50 years – by constitutional actors of the validity of the Parliament Act 1949, and those Acts subsequently enacted under its provisions.[90] Ultimately, in this field, the Attorney-General argued, 'questions of law blend into those of political fact'.[91]

The argument of the applicants was technical and legalistic. In many ways, it could be described as Diceyan; the applicants argued that Parliament – a body which *necessarily* comprised monarch, Commons and Lords – enjoyed the power within the constitution to enact primary legislation. The Attorney-General's argument – by comparison – was prepared to countenance that our understanding of 'Parliament' was more flexible, and that Parliament could redefine itself in order to enact valid primary legislation. In other words, the Government's argument contended that, so long as the manner and form requirements of the Parliament Acts were adhered to, then the Commons and monarch – acting alone – could enact primary legislation.

The courts' jurisdiction

As we have already seen, courts in the UK enjoy no general power to invalidate primary legislation.[92] The applicants, of course, argued that the Parliament Act 1949 and the Hunting Act 2004 were both pieces of *delegated* legislation. But it is clear that regardless of this submission, both the Court of Appeal and House of Lords felt a 'sense of strangeness'[93] at being asked to investigate the validity of instruments that, at first glance appear to be, and on closer inspection actually are, *Acts of Parliament*. In answering the question of whether the courts had jurisdiction to entertain the arguments put forward, differing answers were given. The Court of Appeal noted that, in hearing the appeal, it was exercising a 'constitutional'

---

[88] *Jackson* v *Attorney-General* [2005] UKHL 56; [2006] 1 AC 262, [1].

[89] *Jackson* v *Attorney-General* [2005] UKHL 56; [2006] 1 AC 262, 268.

[90] Ibid., 269.

[91] Ibid.

[92] See e.g. *Pickin* v *British Railways Board* [1974] AC 765.

[93] *Jackson* v *Attorney-General* [2005] UKHL 56; [2006] 1 AC 262, [27] (Lord Bingham).

jurisdiction, and openly acknowledged that in so doing it was operating in an entirely unprecedented manner.[94] Lord Bingham, in the House of Lords, opted for an alternate explanation, drawing attention to the uncertainty that would arise if the House of Lords did not hear the case, and if the important arguments raised by the applicants were effectively left unanswered.[95] The question was not, as Lord Bingham put it, whether enacted legislation was valid (which would be in breach of the standard account of sovereignty), but rather whether the measures at issue were 'enacted legislation' at all.[96] Such an analysis fits neatly with the account of continuing sovereignty given above; it is a valid question for the courts to ask whether legislation that is required to be passed in a particular manner and form has, in practice, been implemented according to the required manner and form.

The findings of the Appellate Committee of the House of Lords

The decision of the House of Lords in *Jackson* is in many ways complicated. It is a lengthy decision of the Appellate Committee; eight of the nine judges gave substantive speeches and across some 195 paragraphs offer a range of significantly differing perspectives on the contemporary status of parliamentary sovereignty.

At its most straightforward however, the finding in *Jackson* is a simple one: the 1949 Parliament Act and the Hunting Act 2004 are both valid pieces of primary legislation enjoying the same legal status as Acts adopted by Parliament as traditionally construed. The Appellate Committee found that the purpose of the Parliament Act was to limit the legal powers of the House of Lords to obstruct legislative proposals that had been endorsed by a majority of members in the House of Commons (rather than, as the applicants had contended, to extend the powers of the House of Commons).[97] The effect of this limitation in practice was to create a 'parallel' method of creating primary legislation (rather than, as the applicants had argued, to create a method of enacting delegated legislation).[98] And finally, the House of Lords found that the only limitations on the use of the Parliament Act to pass legislation, were those expressly referred to in s. 2(1) of the 1911 Act (in other words, the Appellate Committee also rejected the applicant's suggestion that the Parliament Act included the implied limitation that the Act could not be employed in order to amend itself by further limiting the House of Lords' powers of delay).

The reach of the Parliament Acts procedure

In addition to the central finding that an Act passed under the Parliament Acts procedure was valid primary legislation, discussion in the *Jackson* decision turned to the reach of the legislative changes that might be possible under this alternative legislative procedure. The Court of Appeal had found that use of the Parliament Acts procedure was limited by (a) the express provisions of the Act itself (i.e. the limitation that it applied to any public bill other than a money bill or a bill that purported to extend the life of Parliament beyond five years) and (b) by the implied restriction that the procedure could not be used to give effect to 'fundamental constitutional change'.[99]

---

[94] *R (Jackson)* v *Attorney-General* [2005] QB 579, [12], where the then Lord Chief Justice acknowledged that the court was acting as a 'constitutional court' and that there was 'no precise precedent' for its so doing.
[95] *Jackson* v *Attorney-General* [2005] UKHL 56; [2006] 1 AC 262, [27] (Lord Bingham).
[96] Ibid.
[97] Ibid., [25] (Lord Bingham).
[98] Ibid. [24], [26] (Lord Bingham); [64] (Lord Nicholls); [94] (Lord Steyn).
[99] *R (Jackson)* v *Attorney-General* [2005] QB 579, [45] and [100].

On the latter point, the House of Lords departed from the findings of the Court of Appeal. By contrast, the House of Lords found that the *only* legislative objective that could not be achieved by legislation enacted under the Parliament Acts procedure was that stated in s. 2(1) of the 1911 Act; the House of Commons and Monarch, acting without the consent of the House of Lords, cannot legislate in order to extend the life of Parliament beyond five years. As a result of the fact that the Parliament Acts procedure was designed to effect constitutional change – by placing limits on the powers of the House of Lords – and as a matter of fact *had* been used to implement constitutional change – for instance in allowing the enactment of the Government of Ireland Act[100] – Baroness Hale was able to conclude that 'history . . . clearly indicates that it was always contemplated that the procedure might be used to bring about constitutional change'.[101] Any distinction therefore between the 'constitutional change' already brought about using the procedure and the 'significant constitutional change' envisaged by the Court of Appeal was likely to be arbitrary, and had no foundation in either the Act itself or in its past uses.

So while, under the Parliament Acts procedure, an executive-dominated House of Commons might not be able to insulate itself from the popular will by extending the life of a Parliament beyond five years, the potential range of legislative ambitions that could be achieved without obtaining the consent of the House of Lords is undoubtedly extensive. As Lord Hope noted, legislative competence is only exercisable subject to the demands, pressures and potential repercussions of the political process:

> . . . a conclusion that there are no [implied] legal limits to what can be done under section 2(1) does not mean that the power to legislate which it contains is without any limits whatsoever. Parliamentary sovereignty is an empty principle if legislation is passed which is so absurd or so unacceptable that the populace at large refuse to recognise it as law.[102]

A minority of the Law Lords felt a degree of discomfit with the potential range of this (effectively executive-exercised) legislative power, and were prepared to countenance the emergence and imposition of formal legal constraints on Parliament's legislative abilities.[103]

The implications of *Jackson*

The technical outcome of the *Jackson* decision is relatively straightforward; Acts passed utilising the Parliament Acts procedure are good law and of an equal validity to Acts passed when all three components of Parliament are in accord. Just as revealing as the technical legal result of the case, perhaps, are the unspoken implications of the decision and the clear difficulties faced by the Law Lords in their attempted reconciliation of legal doctrine and political fact.

Turning to the latter, the House of Lords' decision in *Jackson* tacitly acknowledged that it would have been an outrageous result politically for the courts to suddenly declare that a legislative instrument that had been on the statute book for over 50 years – namely, the Parliament Act 1949 – was not in fact an 'Act of Parliament' at all. Lord Nicholls perhaps came closest to acknowledging this by referring to the practice of the relevant political actors, stating that 'both Houses of Parliament have unequivocally and repeatedly

---

[100] Which had sought to provide for devolved government for Ireland prior to the severing of the Union in 1922.
[101] *Jackson* v *Attorney-General* [2005] UKHL 56; [2006] 1 AC 262, [157]. Also [31] (Lord Bingham).
[102] Ibid., [120] (Lord Hope).
[103] pp. 161–3.

recognised the validity and effectiveness of the 1949 Act'.[104] The suggestion presented by the Attorney-General in argument before the Appellate Committee, that political fact and legal theory are almost indistinguishable in this case, is as a result, hard to disagree with.

Turning back to one of the issues covered earlier in this chapter, it also seems to be implicit in the decision in *Jackson* that manner and form restrictions are legitimate. Of the nine Law Lords, Lord Steyn and Baroness Hale said as much explicitly. Lord Steyn noted that:

> The word Parliament involves both static and dynamic concepts. The static concept refers to the constituent elements which make up Parliament: the House of Commons, the House of Lords, and the Monarch. The dynamic concept involves the constituent elements functioning together as a law-making body. The inquiry is: has Parliament spoken? The law and custom of Parliament regulates what the constituent elements must do to legislate: all three must signify consent to the measure. But, apart from the traditional method of law making, Parliament acting as ordinarily constituted may functionally redistribute legislative power in different ways.[105]

On Steyn's account, the effect of the Parliament Acts was to 'functionally redistribute legislative power' in a way that permits the House of Commons and the monarch in certain circumstances – acting absent the consent of the House of Lords – to enact primary legislation. Baroness Hale meanwhile, was similarly prepared to countenance that Parliament might limit itself in respect of the manner and form in which legislation is enacted, saying:

> . . . if Parliament is required to pass legislation on particular matters in a particular way, then Parliament is not permitted to ignore these requirements when passing legislation on those matters, nor is it permitted to remove or relax those requirements by passing legislation in the ordinary way.[106]

While other members of the panel were not quite so enthusiastic in their endorsement of limitations of manner and form,[107] it is nonetheless implicit in the House of Lords, decision in *Jackson* that such limitations can be – either as a matter of legal doctrine, a recognition of political reality, or a combination of both[108] – effective. The difficulty faced by the House of Lords in attempting to reconcile the two occasionally disparate threads of constitutional principle and constitutional practice is best evidenced in the apparently contradictory words of Lord Hope:

> It is impossible for Parliament to enact something which a subsequent statute dealing with the same subject matter cannot repeal. But there is no doubt that, in practice, and as a matter of political reality, the 1911 Act did have that effect.[109]

It is at this point that it is worth returning to the question posed above; how could an Act passed under the Parliament Acts procedure – that is, a legislative body specifically *limited* by the explicit terms of s. 2(1) of the Parliament Act – enjoy the same legal status as an Act passed by the sovereign legislature enacting legislation in the orthodox manner?

---

[104] *Jackson* v *Attorney-General* [2005] UKHL 56; [2006] 1 AC 262, [68] (Lord Nicholls). Also [113] (Lord Hope).

[105] Ibid., [81] (Lord Steyn).

[106] Ibid., [163] (Baroness Hale).

[107] Ibid., [113] (Lord Hope); [174] (Lord Carswell).

[108] Ibid., [113] (Lord Hope).

[109] Ibid., [113] (Lord Hope).

The Parliament Acts – and their interpretation by the House of Lords in the *Jackson* decision – present us with a difficulty; we are asked to attribute the characteristics of legislation passed by a *sovereign* parliament, to legislation passed under a parallel mechanism which is explicitly *limited* in its scope. We can perhaps only accept this, if we also accept – as Lord Steyn and Baroness Hale clearly did – that Parliament *can* effectively redefine itself for the purposes of enacting legislation.

So, if Parliament can redefine itself in this way, and the courts will accept legislation passed by Parliament so redefined, then we must also accept that in order to enact legislation in a particular manner (in other words without the consent of the House of Lords) Parliament is bound by the provisions of the Parliament Acts in order for that legislation to be valid. As a result, the 1949 Act was valid because it complied with the manner and form requirements set down by the 1911 Parliament Act. Similarly, the Hunting Act 2004, and each of the other Acts passed under the amended Parliament Acts procedure were also validly enacted because they too were in compliance with the amended manner and form requirements prescribed by the 1949 Act. The manner in which the Parliament of 2004 enacted the Hunting Act was controlled by the procedure set down by the Parliament of 1949: Parliament, in order to legislate absent the consent of the House of Lords, is bound to adhere to the manner and form requirements set down by the Parliament Acts. And if the manner and form requirements of the Parliament Acts are – for the time being – apparently effective and policed by the courts, then surely it is open to Parliament to impose other comparable limitations on itself. Now, of course, a contemporary Parliament could explicitly repeal the Parliament Acts. As a result, it might be said that the Diceyan (continuing) view of the sovereignty of Parliament has been preserved. But for the period during which the Parliament Acts remain on the statute book it seems that the courts will only permit Parliament to legislate in the absence of the consent of the House of Lords on the terms that the Parliament Acts prescribe.

The relationships between primary legislation and other sources of law

Key issues

- As a result of the sovereignty of Parliament, primary legislation is superior to other sources of law, including the common law, international law and competing constitutional principles.
- It should not be forgotten, however, that it is the constitutional function of the courts to interpret and apply the law. In doing so, the courts have articulated a number of interpretative presumptions – for instance, to presume that Parliament will intend to legislate in a way which is compatible with the UK's treaty obligations – that may condition how statutes take effect.
- Such interpretative presumptions have given rise to the recognition, at common law, of constitutional rights and constitutional statutes.

The processes of express and implied repeal govern the interrelationships between statutes. But given that statutes are only one of a number of sources of law within the constitution, the courts have had to articulate the relationships between statute and those other sources of law that are effective within the constitution. Given the supremacy of statute law the constitutional orthodoxy places primary legislation at the pinnacle of this hierarchy of norms.

Primary legislation and common law

As a result of the supremacy of primary legislation over other domestic sources of law, an Act of Parliament will be superior to the common law and will be taken to override judicially made law in the event of a clash between the two. As Dicey noted, the common law is 'in short, subordinate . . . carried on with the assent and subject to the supervision of Parliament'.[110]

As a result, Parliament might legislate in order to regulate activity previously governed only by the common law or in order to bring certainty or clarity to areas of the common law. The Larceny Act 1916, Contempt of Court Act 1981 and Defamation Act 1996, to give only three well-known examples, each apply in areas previously governed almost exclusively by the common law. Equally, it is less common, though by no means unheard of, for individual judicial decisions to be reversed by statute.[111]

Primary legislation and prerogative

Statute is similarly superior to prerogative. The 1920 House of Lords decision *De Keyser's Royal Hotel* clearly indicates that primary legislation will therefore override any pre-existing prerogative power:

> when . . . a statute, expressing the will and intention of the King and of the three estates of the realm, is passed, it abridges the Royal Prerogative while it is in force to this extent: that the Crown can only do the particular thing under and in accordance with the statutory provisions, and that its prerogative power to do that thing is in abeyance.[112]

Abridgement or curtailment of the prerogative may 'be by express words or . . . by necessary implication'.[113] As an illustration of this abridgement in practice, on the implementation of the Fixed-Term Parliaments Act 2011, the prerogative of dissolution was rendered inoperable by the provisions of the Act.[114] Prerogative cannot be used to 'change English common or statute law'[115] and nor can it be used to 'frustrate the will of Parliament expressed in a statute.'[116] The primacy of legislation in this field is a direct consequence of the sovereignty of Parliament and the logical necessity of the 'residual' nature of prerogative power.[117] This residual character is also evident in the inability of prerogatives to be expanded; as Diplock LJ argued in 1964:

> . . . it is 350 years and a civil war too late for the Queen's courts to broaden the prerogative. The limits within which the executive government may impose obligations or restraints upon citizens of the United Kingdom without any statutory authority are now well settled and incapable of extension.[118]

---

[110] A. V. Dicey, *Introduction to the Study of the Law of the Constitution* (Liberty Fund, 1982) p. 18.

[111] For example, *Burmah Oil* v *Lord Advocate* [1965] AC 75 was reversed by the War Damages Act 1965.

[112] *Attorney-General* v *De Keyser's Royal Hotel* (1920) AC 508, 539.

[113] *R (Miller)* v *Secretary of State for Exiting the European Union* [2017] UKSC 5; [2017] 2 WLR 583, [48].

[114] pp. 289–90.

[115] *R (Bancoult)* v *Secretary of State for Foreign and Commonwealth Affairs (No. 2)* [2008] UKHL 61; [2009] AC 453, [44]; *R (Miller)* v *Secretary of State for Exiting the European Union* [2017] UKSC 5; [2017] 2 WLR 583, [50].

[116] *R* v *Secretary of State for the Home Department, ex parte Fire Brigades Union* [1995] 2 AC 513.

[117] *R (Miller)* v *Secretary of State for Exiting the European Union* [2017] UKSC 5; [2017] 2 WLR 583, [48].

[118] *British Broadcasting Corporation* v *Johns* [1965] Ch. 32, 79.

> **Thinking Point . . .**
>
> While it is clear that prerogative may be 'curtailed' by statute, an uncertainty persists as to whether this curtailment is permanent. The language chosen by the court in *De Keyser's Royal Hotel* – indicating that the prerogative is placed in 'abeyance' while the overriding statute is operative – seems to hint at the possibility that the prerogative might be in future resurrected in the event that the curtailing statute is repealed without replacement. The Supreme Court decision in *Miller* does not remove this uncertainty, with the majority suggesting that, '[i]f prerogative powers are curtailed by legislation, they may *sometimes* be reinstated by the repeal of that legislation, *depending on the construction of the statutes in question.*' (*R (Miller)* v *Secretary of State for Exiting the European Union* [2017] UKSC 5; [2017] 2 WLR 583, [112] (emphasis added)).

Primary legislation and international law

The relationship between the national laws of individual states and international law is conditioned by the constitution or constitutional rules of the individual state in question. A straightforward distinction can be drawn between those states whose constitutional rules prescribe that international law standards and treaty obligations binding the state are effectively a part of the national law and should be given effect to as such by national courts and those states whose systems recognise international law and treaty obligations as a distinct body of law which should only take effect in the domestic legal system following statutory incorporation of the specific treaty or rule of international law. As we have already seen, the former states are known as monist systems and the latter, including the UK, are known as dualist.[119]

The dualism doctrine flows from the legislative sovereignty of Parliament. As parliamentary sovereignty holds that no source of law can be of a higher authority than primary legislation, it stands to reason that international law should not be given higher status in domestic courts. As the conduct of foreign relations (including the signing of treaties) is a matter for the government, then any legal obligations arising out of accession to a treaty – while binding on the state as a matter of international law – cannot be given effect in domestic law on that basis alone. It is the function of Parliament – and not the executive – to legislate. As a result, the orthodox position is that '[c]ourts cannot hold [a] statutory provision void, disapply it, ignore it or otherwise render it of no effect on the ground that it contravenes a treaty to which the UK is signatory or otherwise breaches general principles of international law'.[120]

In *Mortensen* v *Peters*,[121] a case concerning the prohibition of a particular method of fishing in the Moray Firth area under s. 7 of the Herring Fishery (Scotland) Act 1889, the captain of a Norwegian fishing boat was prosecuted for contravening the prohibition, despite the fact that the activity did not occur in British territorial waters, under international law. The High Court of Justiciary noted that:

> In this court we have nothing to do with the question whether the legislature has or has not done what foreign powers may consider a usurpation. Neither are we a tribunal sitting to determine whether an Act of [Parliament] is [outside its powers] as in contravention of generally acknowledged principles of international law. For us an Act of Parliament . . . is supreme and we are bound to give effect to its terms.[122]

---

[119] Chapter 3, pp. 58–61.
[120] M. Hunt, *Using Human Rights Law in English Courts* (Hart Publishing, 1997) p. 7.
[121] *Mortensen* v *Peters* (1906) 14 SLT 228.
[122] *Mortensen* v *Peters* (1906) 14 SLT 228.

Specific bodies of international law have been given effect in the UK constitution via statute. The influences of the laws of the European Union (via the European Communities Act 1972) and the European Convention on Human Rights (via the Human Rights Act 1998) are discussed further below.[123]

Thinking Point . . .

International law has – when given domestic effect via primary legislation (in statutes such as the European Communities Act 1972 and the Human Rights Act 1998) – had a significant impact on the domestic legal system. Even in such instances – where the means of giving effect to those extra-jurisdictional norms are consistent with the sovereignty-respecting doctrine of dualism – the *extent* to which those norms might influence domestic law has proven politically controversial and fuelled calls for Brexit as well as underpinning the Conservative Party's case for a British Bill of Rights.

Primary legislation and 'constitutional' principle

We will see in the following chapters that while the constitutional principles of the rule of law[124] and separation of powers[125] both have a role to play in the UK Constitution, neither have – to date – been regarded as being of such fundamental importance as to displace the validity of an Act of Parliament.[126] Similarly, while constitutional protections for individual rights may empower courts to strike down legislation in other jurisdictions, the judiciary in the UK does not have such power. This much is evident from the case of *R v Jordan*.

Key case
R v Jordan [1967] Crim LR 483

The applicant had been imprisoned for 18 months after having been found guilty of offences under the Race Relations Act 1965. He applied for a writ of habeas corpus on the basis that, as it imposed unjustified restrictions on his right of freedom of speech, the Act was invalid. The court rejected the application holding that the grounds advanced in support of it were completely unarguable; Parliament was sovereign, and the courts had no competence to question the validity of enacted primary legislation.

It should be noted that the decision in *Jordan* pre-dated the implementation of the Human Rights Act 1998. While the Human Rights Act permits scrutiny of Acts of Parliament on human rights grounds, it does not empower courts to strike down or invalidate Acts which contravene human rights standards.[127] In the event that a court finds that it is impossible

---

[123] See pp. 163–7 and pp. 167–79.
[124] Chapter 6.
[125] Chapter 7.
[126] See esp. at pp. 211–14.
[127] For discussion and analysis, see pp. 668–73 and Chapter 21.

to interpret legislation in a way that is compatible with the Convention rights protected by the Act, it may issue a declaration of incompatibility.[128] Declarations of incompatibility are, however, not binding as a matter of law and can result in only political pressure for legislative change.[129]

The interpretation of primary legislation

Interpretative technique and interpretative presumptions

We have already seen that while it is the role of Parliament to act as legislator, it is the role and duty of the courts to interpret and apply legislation in practice.[130] Respect for the sovereign authority of Parliament can be seen in the processes of judicial reasoning adopted by courts seeking to apply statutes to real-life situations. In his book, *Constitutional Theory*, Geoffrey Marshall described the link between sovereignty and statutory interpretation as follows:

> Parliament, in the United Kingdom . . . is the sovereign master. Its instructions are subject to no constitutional reservations and this, perhaps, gives rise to a belief in the sanctity of the exact words of the statute.[131]

As a result, the literal approach to statutory interpretation – that is, the search for, and application of, the natural meaning of statutory wording – dominated the judicial interpretation of statutes for much of the twentieth century.[132]

Increasingly, however, the courts have begun to deploy contextual methods of interpretation, recognising – as Lord Steyn did in *Pierson* – that, 'Parliament does not legislate in a vacuum. Parliament legislates for a European liberal democracy founded on the principles and assumptions of the common law.'[133] The rigidity of the literal approach to statutory construction is militated by a number of interpretative presumptions that might be employed by the judges, especially where the language employed by the statute is unclear or gives rise to an ambiguity. For instance, the courts will assume that Parliament intends to legislate compatibly with the UK's obligations under international law:

> . . . there is a strong presumption in favour of interpreting English law (whether common law or statute) in a way which does not place the United Kingdom in breach of an international obligation.[134]

The courts will also assume that a domestic statute is not to apply outside the jurisdiction unless express words to that effect are used. Similarly, the courts will further assume that

---

[128] Human Rights Act, s. 4(2).
[129] Human Rights Act, s. 4(6).
[130] *R (Cart)* v *Upper Tribunal* [2009] EWHC 3052, [37].
[131] G. Marshall, *Constitutional Theory* (Clarendon Press, 1971) p. 74.
[132] J. Steyn, 'Does legal formalism hold sway in England?' (1996) 49 *Current Legal Problems* 43; R. Stevens, 'Judges, politics, politicians and the confusing role of the judiciary' in K. Hawkins (ed.), *The Human Face of Law: Essays in Honour of Donald Harris* (Clarendon Press, 1997).
[133] *R* v *Secretary of State for the Home Department, ex parte Pierson* [1998] AC 539, 587 (Lord Steyn). See also *AXA General Insurance Ltd* v *HM Advocate* [2011] UKSC 46; [2012] 1 AC 868, [153].
[134] *R* v *Lyons* [2002] UKHL 44, [27]. See also *Assange* v *Swedish Prosecution Authority* [2012] UKSC 22; [2012] 2 AC 471.

a statute is not to be enforced retroactively unless specific words mean that such an effect was the clear intention of Parliament – as was noted in *Phillips* v *Eyre*:

> . . . the courts will not ascribe retrospective force to new laws affecting rights unless by express words or necessary implication it appears that such was the intention of the legislature.[135]

Express statutory wording may, however, displace such presumptions.[136]

Thinking Point . . .

The application of statute law by the judicial branch is not a mechanical exercise; as H. L. A. Hart wrote: ' . . . in the vast majority of cases that trouble the courts, neither statutes nor precedents in which the rules are allegedly contained allow of only one result. In the most important cases there is always a choice. The judge has to choose between alternative meanings to be given to the words of a statute or between rival interpretations of what a precedent "amounts to". It is only the tradition that judges "find" and do not "make" law that conceals this, and presents their decisions as if they were deductions smoothly made from clear pre-existing rules without intrusion of the judge's choice' (H. L. A. Hart, *The Concept of Law* (2nd edn) (Clarendon Press, 1997), p. 12).

Even acknowledging that the judicial interpretation of statute allows for a degree of judicial discretion – or as Hart termed it, 'choice' – the courts have maintained that the *application* of statute law remains an overriding imperative. As a result, examples of overt judicial disobedience to statutes are few and far between. A potential example of such 'disobedience' can be found in the decision of the House of Lords in *Anisminic* v *Foreign Compensation Commission*.[137]

Key case

Anisminic Ltd v Foreign Compensation Commission [1969] 2 AC 147

By the 1950 Foreign Compensation Act, Parliament created a Commission which would be responsible for the compensation of British nationals who had been deprived of their property by the administrations of other states. Section 4(4) of the 1950 Act provided that, 'The determination by the Commission of any application made to them under this Act shall not be called into question in any court of law.' As a result of the plain language of the Act, it seemed that determinations made by the Commission could not be appealed against, or be the subject of an application for judicial review. Such provisions are, for obvious reasons, known as 'ouster clauses'.[138]

---

[135] *Phillips* v *Eyre* (1870) LR 6 QB 1, 23.

[136] *R* v *Secretary of State for the Home Department, ex parte Pierson* [1998] AC 539, 587 (Lord Steyn).

[137] For such an interpretation see H. W. R. Wade and C. F. Forsyth, *Administrative Law* (10th edn) (OUP, 2009) pp. 615–16 (cf. T. R. S. Allan, *Constitutional Justice: A Liberal Theory of the Rule of Law* (OUP, 2001) pp. 210–13).

[138] See also *R* v *Medical Appeal Tribunal, ex parte Gilmore* [1957] 1 QB 574 (CA).

> The case was brought by Anisminic Ltd, whose assets had been sequestrated by the Egyptian authorities in the run up to the Suez crisis of 1956. Anisminic had made a claim before the Foreign Compensation Commission. The claim had been rejected.
>
> In spite of the apparently clear language of s. 4(4) the House of Lords decided that its jurisdiction was not in fact excluded. By a 3:2 majority the House held that to exclude the jurisdiction of the courts completely would run the risk that decisions of the Compensation Commission that would otherwise be regarded as *ultra vires* would have to stand. As Lord Reid stated:
>
>> Statutory provisions which seek to limit the ordinary jurisdiction of the court have a long history. No case has been cited [in argument] in which any other form of words limiting the jurisdiction of the court has been held to protect a nullity. If the draftsmen or Parliament had intended to introduce a new kind of ouster clause so as to prevent *any* inquiry . . . I would have expected to find something much more specific than the bald statement that a determination shall not be called into question in any court of law.[139]

The difficult relationship between ouster clauses and the rule of law – the constitutional principle that might be interpreted to require *all* governmental activity to be subject to the supervisory role of the courts – is returned to in the following chapter.[140]

Common law rights and the principle of legality

The judicial expectation that Parliament might achieve certain objectives if and only when its intention is made *explicit* in primary legislation has solidified into an important tool of statutory interpretation in the UK. Prior to the enactment of the HRA, the judicial recognition of 'common law rights' enabled the courts to provide a degree of protection to the rights of the individual where those rights were threatened by less than clear statutory language. Central to the development of this interpretative tool was the decision in *R v Lord Chancellor, ex parte Witham*:

Key case

R v Lord Chancellor, ex parte Witham [1998] QB 575

*R v Lord Chancellor, ex parte **Witham*** [1998] QB 575 concerned the common law right of access to a court.[141] The facts of ***Witham*** were as follows: acting under s. 130 of the Supreme Court Act 1981, the Lord Chancellor sought by order, a type of secondary legislation, to increase the fees payable for the issuing of a writ, and to remove the exemption from such payment enjoyed by those litigants in person who received income support.[142] The applicant, who was unemployed and on income support, had intended to commence proceedings for defamation. Without the exemption – from which he would previously have benefited – he could not afford to begin the proceedings and his right of access to the courts would be denied. He brought an application for judicial review, contending that the Lord Chancellor had acted outside the powers conferred by the Supreme Court Act 1981.

---

[139] *Anisminic Ltd v Foreign Compensation Commission* [1969] 2 AC 147, 170 (Lord Reid).
[140] See pp. 212–13.
[141] *R v Lord Chancellor, ex parte Witham* [1998] QB 575.
[142] Supreme Court (Fees) Amendment Order 1996.

The court found that the right of access to a court was a 'fundamental constitutional right'[143] recognised by the common law, which could not be limited other than by express wording in primary legislation or by secondary legislation whose parent legislation provided for the power to make such restriction; 'general words', Laws J indicated, 'will not suffice' for this purpose.[144] As the wording of the s. 130 of the Supreme Court Act 1981 provided a general power to levy fees,[145] and did not provide the Lord Chancellor power to deny those who could not otherwise afford to commence litigation access to the courts. Laws J concluded his judgment by adding:

Access to the courts is a constitutional right; it can only be denied by the government if it persuades Parliament to pass legislation which specifically – in effect by express provision – permits the executive to turn people away from the court door. That has not been done here.[146]

The High Court found in favour of the applicant, and issued a declaration that the order purported to be made by the Lord Chancellor was *ultra vires*.

Laws J's finding amounted to a common law (and therefore judicially-imposed) restriction on the form in which legislation might be expressed. The House of Lords subsequently applied similar reasoning in *R v Secretary of State for the Home Department, ex parte Simms*.

Key case

R v Secretary of State for the Home Department, ex parte Simms [2000] 2 AC 115

The two applicants in *Simms* were both in prison after having been convicted of murder. Both protested their innocence. The Court of Appeal had refused their applications to appeal against their convictions, and the applicants had been involved in discussions with a number of journalists who had become interested in their cases.

The prison authorities refused to authorise future visits by the journalists unless they agreed to sign undertakings not to use any material gained through the prisoner interviews for professional purposes. The journalists refused to make the undertakings.

The prison authorities acted pursuant to rules implemented by the Home Secretary under s. 47(1) of the Prison Act 1952. Section 47(1) permitted the Secretary of State to make rules – by way of statutory instrument[147] – for, *inter alia,* 'the regulation and management of prisons . . . and for the treatment, employment, discipline and control of persons required to be detained therein'.

→

---

[143] *R v Lord Chancellor, ex parte Witham* [1998] QB 575, 586.

[144] Ibid., 581.

[145] Section 130 of the Supreme Court Act 1981, so far as is relevant, provided:

(1) The Lord Chancellor may by order under this section prescribe the fees to be taken in the Supreme Court, other than fees for while he or some other authority has power to prescribe apart from this section.

(2) The concurrence of the Treasury shall be required for the making of any order under this section; and in addition – (a) the concurrence of the Lord Chief Justice, the Master of the Rolls, the President of the Family Division and the Vice-Chancellor or of any three of them, shall be required for the making of any such order not relating exclusively to fees to be taken in connection with proceedings in the Crown Court . . .

(3) Any order under this section shall be made by statutory instrument, which shall be laid before Parliament after being made.

[146] *R v Lord Chancellor, ex parte Witham* [1998] QB 575, 586.

[147] Prison Act 1952, s. 52(1).

The relevant rules provided that 'visits to inmates by journalists or authors in their professional capacity should generally not be allowed' in the absence of a written undertaking not to utilise information gained from the visit in a professional capacity.

The applicants applied for judicial review arguing that the rules were a disproportionate interference with their right to freedom of speech, and, as a result, were unlawful. The High Court granted their application. In turn, the Court of Appeal granted the appeal of the Home Secretary. The applicants appealed to the House of Lords.

The House of Lords unanimously found in favour of the applicants holding the rules to be unlawful to the extent that they amounted to a disproportionate interference with the prisoners' rights of freedom of expression. Lord Steyn gave the leading speech, in which he highlighted the intrinsic value to be found in freedom of expression,[148] and the added value brought by journalists in bringing miscarriages of justice to light.[149] But it is Lord Hoffmann's articulation of the 'principle of legality' that has become 'canonical'.[150] It is worth repeating in full:

> Parliamentary sovereignty means that Parliament can, if it chooses, legislate contrary to fundamental principles of human rights . . . But the principle of legality means that Parliament must squarely confront what it is doing and accept the political cost. Fundamental rights cannot be overridden by general or ambiguous words. This is because there is too great a risk that the full implications of their unqualified meaning may have passed unnoticed in the democratic process. In the absence of express language or necessary implication to the contrary, the courts will therefore presume that even the most general words were intended to be subject to the basic rights of the individual.[151]

In *Simms*, as in *Witham*, the courts therefore held secondary legislation purporting to restrict constitutional rights to be unlawful, in circumstances where the relevant parent (primary) legislation had failed to provide what was deemed to be a sufficiently specific enabling power.

Thinking Point . . .

Something of a difficulty of this emergent constitutional rights jurisprudence lay in the failure of the courts to fully articulate the range and parameters of these newly recognised rights. Extra-judicially, Lord Cooke of Thorndon attempted to list those rights which the common law recognised as 'constitutional'; he included: '. . . the right of access to a court; the right of access to legal advice; and the right to communicate confidentially with a legal adviser under the seal of legal professional privilege . . . [the right of] participation in the democratic process, equality of treatment, freedom of expression, religious freedom . . . [and] the right to a fair trial (Lord Cooke of Thorndon, 'The Road Ahead for the Common Law' (2004) 53 ICLQ 273, 276–7).

---

[148] *R v Secretary of State for the Home Department, ex parte Simms* [1999] AC 115, 126.
[149] Ibid., 127–30.
[150] H. W. R. Wade and C. F. Forsyth, *Administrative Law* (10th edn) (OUP, 2009) p. 22.
[151] *R v Secretary of State for the Home Department, ex parte Simms* [1999] AC 115, 131.

Mere months after the decision of the House of Lords in *Simms,* the Human Rights Act came into force in England and Wales,[152] and the emergence of a common law jurisprudence of human rights was somewhat stifled.[153] Given that the HRA laid down in statute a defined catalogue of rights, set out the means by which they might be asserted against public bodies and deployed in statutory interpretation, and provided for remedies in the event of a breach, it was unsurprising to find that the HRA came to provide the primary mechanism through which human rights disputes made their way before the courts. The continuing importance of rights recognised at common law should not go ignored however. In the light of political disquiet over the domestic influence of the jurisprudence of the European Court of Human Rights (manifested most clearly in Conservatives' calls for a British Bill of Rights[154]), the Supreme Court has emphasised that the common law remains a vital – and complementary – tool of rights protection.[155] But more importantly, for the purposes of our coverage of parliamentary sovereignty, the interpretative tools established in *Witham* and *Simms* have been deployed, and expanded upon, in subsequent judicial decisions.

Two important decisions of the UK Supreme Court have served to illustrate that the principle of legality can be deployed in order to protect both rights existent at common law *and* the (potentially more far reaching) values that attach to the rule of law.[156] In *R (UNISON)* v *Lord Chancellor,*[157] the Supreme Court unanimously struck down a statutory instrument significantly increasing the court fees payable in respect of Employment Tribunal cases on the basis that the provision under which the instrument was made (s. 42 of the Tribunals, Courts and Enforcement Act 2007) did not explicitly confer a power to limit the common law right of access to the courts.[158] The Supreme Court decision in *Evans* – the background to which we introduced in Chapter 2 – serves to illustrate *explicitly* that the principle of legality might be employed in defence of constitutional principles, as well as common law rights, against legislative intrusions.[159] In *Evans,* Lord Neuberger employed the principle of legality to limit the circumstances under which the power of 'ministerial override' found in s. 53 of the Freedom of Information Act 2000 might be deployed.[160] In his judgment,[161] Lord Neuberger – arguing that s. 53 fell far short of reaching the level of clarity required by the principle of legality[162] – sought to interpret the legislation in a way which was compliant with the rule of law (specifically on the basis that a 'decision of a judicial body should be final and binding and should not be capable

---

[152] The rights given effect by the Human Rights Act had been effective since the establishment of devolved administrations in Scotland (in May 1999) and Northern Ireland (in December 1999) under the terms of the Scotland Act 1998 and Northern Ireland Act 1998.

[153] *Watkins* v *Secretary of State for the Home Department* [2006] UKHL 17; [2006] 2 AC 395, [62].

[154] pp.pp. 681–4.

[155] See below at p. 651 and R. Masterman and S. Wheatle, 'A Common Law Resurgence in Rights Protection?' [2015] EHRLR 57.

[156] On which see Chapter 6.

[157] *R (UNISON)* v *Lord Chancellor* [2017] UKSC 51; [2017] 3 WLR 409.

[158] Ibid., [87].

[159] *R (Evans)* v *Attorney-General* [2015] UKSC 21; [2015] 1 AC 1787, [51]-[59].

[160] On which see Chapter 17, pp. 496–500.

[161] With which Lords Kerr and Reed agreed. Lord Mance and Baroness Hale – also finding for Evans – decided the case on the basis of the 'reasonableness' of the reasons provided by the Attorney-General for deployment of the veto power.

[162] *R (Evans)* v *Attorney-General* [2015] UKSC 21; [2015] 1 AC 1787, [58]

of being overturned by a member of the executive'[163]), significantly (and controversially) curtailing the scope of the s. 53 power in the process. While we will return to the *Evans* decision in the following chapter, it suffices for present purposes to note that deployment of the principle of legality in order to ensure the compliance of 'general or ambiguous' provisions of primary legislation with the rule of law holds the *potential* to amount to a notable incursion into Parliament's primary legislative power.[164]

Constitutional statutes

In the High Court decision in *Thoburn* v *Sunderland City Council,* Laws LJ further developed the reasoning he first deployed in *Witham,* arguing that the common law had come to recognise the existence of 'constitutional statutes'.[165] *Thoburn* – sometimes referred to as the *Metric Martyrs case* – concerned a clash between European Union law and the provisions of a domestic statute. The domestic statute determined that goods could be sold following measurement on the imperial system (i.e. in pounds and ounces) or the metric system (i.e. in grams and kilograms). The European measure (given effect in domestic law as a result of the European Communities Act 1972) required that the metric system be the primary means of measurement from 1 January 2000. The relationship between European Union law and the laws of the UK – and how this clash between an Act of a supposedly sovereign legislature and the rules of an alien legal authority was resolved – is addressed more fully below.[166] For present purposes, it is the observations of Laws LJ on the 'constitutional' status of some Acts of the UK Parliament that are material.

In *Thoburn,* Laws LJ argued that the common law had not only come to a point where it could be said to recognise constitutional *rights* but has also come to a point where constitutional *statutes* could be seen to exist:

> In the present state of its maturity the common law has come to recognise that there exist rights which should properly be classified as constitutional or fundamental . . . from this a further insight follows. We should recognise a hierarchy of Acts of Parliament: as it were 'ordinary' statutes and 'constitutional' statutes. The two categories must be distinguished on a principled basis. In my opinion a constitutional statute is one which (a) conditions the legal relationship between citizen and State in some general, overarching manner, or (b) enlarges or diminishes the scope of what we would now regard as fundamental constitutional rights . . . '[167]

Key debates
What is a 'constitutional statute'?

According to Laws LJ in *Thoburn* v *Sunderland City Council* a 'constitutional statute' is an Act which **either** (a) Conditions the legal relationship between the individual and the state in some way; **or** (b) Enlarges or diminishes the scope of fundamental constitutional rights. By

---

[163] Ibid., [115].

[164] For discussion and analysis see: M. Elliott, 'A Tangled Constitutional Web: The Black-Spider Memos and the British Constitution's Relational Architecture' [2015] PL 539; R. Ekins and C. Forsyth, *Judging the Public Interest: The Rule of Law vs. The Rule of Courts* (Policy Exchange, 2015).

[165] *Thoburn* v *Sunderland City Council* [2003] QB 151; [2002] 1 CMLR 50.

[166] See pp. 174–5.

[167] *Thoburn* v *Sunderland City Council* [2003] QB 151, 186.

way of illustrating the legislative instruments that he felt lay within the scope of this definition, Laws LJ gave a series of examples of 'constitutional statutes':

- Magna Carta 1297
- The Bill of Rights 1689
- The Act of Union with Scotland 1706
- The Representation of the People Acts 1832–2000
- The European Communities Act 1972
- The Human Rights Act 1998
- The Scotland Act 1998
- The Government of Wales Act 1998

At first glance, Laws LJ's definition of a constitutional statute seems to neatly encapsulate those statutes whose subject matter falls within the range of topics we have covered so far in this book, and the list of examples provided also points to a body of legislation which covers core constitutional topics. If we consider Laws LJ's definition a little more carefully, however, it is obvious that it has the potential to cover a much wider range of legislation than would appear to be the case at first glance. A statute 'which conditions the relationship between the individual and the state in some general, overarching manner' could arguably see the many statutory provisions on criminal liability, for instance, fall within Laws LJ's definition. Similarly, *any* statute touching on a right recognised by the common law – such as freedom of expression or the right of access to a court – would arguably be of constitutional status. As a result, all legislation dealing with contempt of court, defamation, legal aid, and so on might also be 'constitutional' under Laws LJ's test. While this might not be objectionable in principle, it is certainly the case that Laws LJ's definition has the potential to be of much wider significance than the 'core' constitutional examples given in *Thoburn* would suggest.

The recognition of a category of statute which has a constitutional status of some sort clearly runs counter to Dicey's suggestions that all statutes are of equal validity and that the constitution is simply a product of the ordinary law of the land. Laws LJ's conception of a constitutional statute was not, however, simply a label used to categorise statutes by subject matter; constitutional status brought with it a degree of insulation from the orthodox process of implied repeal. As Laws LJ continued:

> Ordinary statutes may be impliedly repealed. Constitutional statutes may not. For the repeal of a constitutional Act or the abrogation of a fundamental right to be effected by statute, the court would apply this test: is it shown that the legislature's *actual* – not imputed, constructive or presumed – intention was to effect the repeal or abrogation? I think the test could only be met by express words in the later statute, or by words so specific that the inference of an actual determination to effect the result contended for was irresistible. The ordinary rule of implied repeal does not satisfy this test.[168]

Constitutional statutes, on the basis of this reasoning, are therefore protected from implied repeal; as a result, the effective repeal of such a statute might only be achieved through the use of express words. While this might be thought of as the logical – and incremental – extension of the rule in **Witham** and **Simms** that constitutional rights might only be limited by way of an express repeal,[169] it certainly also constitutes an inroad into the

---

[168] *Thoburn* v *Sunderland City Council* [2003] QB 151, 187.
[169] P. Craig, 'Constitutionalising Constitutional Law: *HS2*' [2014] PL 373, 387.

Diceyan reading of Parliament's sovereign power and might be thought of as demonstrative of the limited power of the common law to permit a degree of entrenchment.[170] As Laws LJ noted, recognition of a category of statute which enjoys 'constitutional' status:

> . . . gives us most of the benefits of a written constitution, in which fundamental rights are accorded special respect. But it preserves the sovereignty of the legislature and the flexibility of our uncodified constitution.[171]

On the terms examined above, the limitation imposed requires that constitutional statutes may only be repealed through the use of express language. The extent of this inroad into parliamentary sovereignty, however, should not be overstated; all that is required of Parliament is the adoption of wording which clearly illustrates its intent.[172] In other words, this is a judicial, common law-imposed, limitation of form rather than substance.[173]

Since the decision of the High Court in *Thoburn* the term 'constitutional statute' has been seen to infiltrate the subsequent jurisprudence of our highest courts. The Human Rights Act 1998 for instance – one of the statutes explicitly highlighted by Laws LJ in *Thoburn* – has on numerous occasions been described as having a constitutional status or explicitly referred to as a 'constitutional statute' by the higher courts.[174] Similarly, the constitutional status of the devolution Acts – notably the Northern Ireland Act 1998[175] and Scotland Act 1998[176] – has been invoked in order to justify particular judicial interpretations of their provisions.

The Supreme Court decision in *R (Buckinghamshire County Council)* v *Secretary of State for Transport*[177]– the HS2 decision – now provides a weighty endorsement for the existence of a hierarchy of statutes within the UK constitutional order.[178] The dispute at issue concerned the Government's decision to develop a high speed rail service (HS2) between London and the West Midlands, Manchester and Leeds, and specifically concerned whether the chosen decision-making process (a hybrid bill[179]) was compliant with the level

---

[170] On which see J. Young and D. Campbell, 'The Metric Martyrs and the Entrenchment Jurisprudence of Lord Justice Laws' [2002] PL 399.

[171] *Thoburn* v *Sunderland City Council* [2003] QB 151, 187.

[172] The judgments of Lord Neuberger and Lord Hughes in *R (Evans)* v *Attorney-General* [2015] UKSC 21; [2015] 1 AC 1787 illustrate that there is considerable scope for disagreement over what might amount to sufficiently clear legislative language.

[173] On the point that *Parliament* might also determine that a piece of legislation should benefit from similar, constitutional, status see: G. Phillipson, 'EU Law as an Agent of National Constitutional Change: *Miller* v *Secretary of State for Exiting the European Union*' (2017) 36 *Yearbook of European Law* 1, 42–8 (cf. *Thoburn* v *Sunderland City Council* [2003] QB 151, 184–185).

[174] See, for example, *McCartan Turkington Breen* v *Times Newspapers* [2001] 2 AC 277, 297 (Lord Steyn); *Brown* v *Stott* [2001] 2 WLR 817, 835 (Lord Bingham), 839 (Lord Steyn); *R* v *Offen* [2001] 1 WLR 253, 276 (Lord Woolf).

[175] *Robinson* v *Secretary of State for Northern Ireland* [2002] UKHL 32, [11] (Lord Bingham).

[176] *R* v *HM Advocate* 2002 SC (PC) 21, 60; *Sommerville* v *Scottish Ministers* 2007 SC 140, [47]; *Imperial Tobacco Ltd, Petitioner* [2010] CSOH 134, [3]-[7]; *H* v *Lord Advocate* [2012] UKSC 24; [2013] 1 AC 413, [30]-[31]. And see: F. Ahmed and A. Perry, 'The Quasi-Entrenchment of Constitutional Statutes' (2014) 73 CLJ 514.

[177] *R (Buckinghamshire County Council)* v *Secretary of State for Transport* [2014] UKSC 3; [2014] 1 WLR 324.

[178] See also *R (Miller)* v *Secretary of State for Exiting the European Union* [2017] UKSC 5; [2017] 2 WLR 583, [67].

[179] *R (Buckinghamshire County Council)* v *Secretary of State for Transport* [2014] UKSC 3; [2014] 1 WLR 324, [57]: 'a hybrid bill proceeds as a public bill, with a second reading, committee report and third reading, but with an additional select committee stage after the second reading in each House, at which objectors whose interests are directly and specifically affected by the bill (including local authorities) may petition against the bill and be heard.'

of public participation required by EU Directive 2011/92/EU. While the court was of the view that the proposed process *was* compliant with the Directive – finding for the Government on the basis that the hybrid bill process allowed for the consideration of views of both elected representatives and those who would be affected by the HS2 development – the Justices were concerned by arguments for the claimants which appeared to run contrary to the 'long-established constitutional principles governing the relationship between Parliament and the courts, as reflected . . . in article 9 of the Bill of Rights 1689.'[180] The judges' unease related to being drawn into assessing whether the domestic legislative *process* was compliant with EU law; as we have already seen the courts have – pursuant to Article 9 of the Bill of Rights 1689 – long-held that legislative process is a matter for Parliament alone.[181] On the broad question of whether EU law was capable of reaching so deeply into domestic constitutional arrangements the relevant extract from the judgment of Lords Neuberger and Mance is worth repeating in full as, though obiter, it was agreed to by all seven members of the court:

> The United Kingdom has no written constitution, but we have a number of constitutional instruments. They include Magna Carta, the Petition of Right 1628, the Bill of Rights and (in Scotland) the Claim of Rights Act 1689, the Act of Settlement 1701 and the Act of Union 1707. The European Communities Act 1972, the Human Rights Act 1998 and the Constitutional Reform Act 2005 may now be added to this list. The common law itself also recognises certain principles as fundamental to the rule of law. It is, putting the point at its lowest, certainly arguable (and it is for United Kingdom law and courts to determine) that there may be fundamental principles, whether contained in other constitutional instruments or recognised at common law, of which Parliament when it enacted the European Communities Act 1972 did not either contemplate or authorise the abrogation.[182]

As the court found in favour of the Government, the Supreme Court did not hear full argument on this specific issue, but – in the context of potential conflict between two constitutional instruments[183] – recommended Laws LJ's 'penetrating discussion' in *Thoburn* and suggested that the enactment of the European Communities Act 1972 would not necessarily impliedly repeal constitutional instruments passed at an earlier point in time.[184]

A residual common law limitation on sovereignty?

Our study of the courts' responses to parliamentary legislation again presents us with something of a paradox: to identify the substance of *Parliament's* sovereign power, we must look to the decisions of the *courts*. As T. R. S. Allan has written:

> . . . legislation obtains its force from the doctrine of parliamentary sovereignty . . . whose detailed content and limits are . . . of judicial making. Parliament is sovereign because the judges acknowledge its legal and political supremacy.[185]

---

[180] *R (Buckinghamshire County Council) v Secretary of State for Transport* [2014] UKSC 3; [2014] 1 WLR 324, [78]

[181] See p. 140. And see *Wilson v First County Trust Ltd (No. 2)* [2003] UKHL 40; [2004] 1 AC 816, [53]-[55].

[182] *R (Buckinghamshire County Council) v Secretary of State for Transport* [2014] UKSC 3; [2014] 1 WLR 324, [207].

[183] On which see: P. Craig, 'Constitutionalising Constitutional Law: *HS2*' [2014] PL 373, 387–388.

[184] *R (Buckinghamshire County Council) v Secretary of State for Transport* [2014] UKSC 3; [2014] 1 WLR 324, [207]-[208].

[185] T. R. S. Allan, *Law, Liberty and Justice: The Legal Foundations of British Constitutionalism* (Clarendon Press, 1993) p. 10.

As preceding sections have shown, the courts' interpretative powers should not be understated in terms of their constitutional significance. Does it follow from this that there might be circumstances in which the courts might refuse to recognise the legal and political supremacy of Parliament's actions? A number of responses might be given to this particularly thorny question.

Prior to the Glorious Revolution the courts seemed to claim the ability to control the exercise of legislative power by Parliament. As Coke LJ (in)famously suggested in *Dr Bonham's Case*:

> . . . in many cases, the common law will controul Acts of Parliament, and sometimes adjudge them to be utterly void: for when an Act of Parliament is against common right or reason, or repugnant, or impossible to be performed, the common law will controul it, and adjudge such Act to be void.[186]

Since then, however, this supposed common law limitation on the legislative ability of Parliament has been conspicuous only through its lack of use. In the 1974 House of Lords decision in *Pickin* v *British Railways Board* Lord Reid was able to suggest that:

> In earlier times many learned lawyers seem to have believed that an Act of Parliament could be disregarded in so far as it was contrary to the law of God or the law of nature or natural justice, but since the supremacy of Parliament was finally demonstrated by the Revolution of 1688 any such idea has become obsolete.[187]

The evidence in favour of Coke's assertion which post-dates the Glorious Revolution is indeed thin – no court in modern times has attempted to 'strike down' an Act of Parliament.[188] That has not, however, prevented a number of senior judges and other supporters of the ideas associated with common law constitutionalism[189] invoking Lord Coke's *dicta* in recent times. Foremost among those judges – 'common law radicals' as the authors of one leading text have labelled them[190] – is the former Lord Chief Justice of England and Wales, Lord Woolf. In an influential 1995 article, Lord Woolf suggested that if Parliament were to do the 'unthinkable' then 'the courts would also be required to act in a manner which would be without precedent'.[191] He continued, adding that, 'there are even limits on the supremacy of Parliament which it is the courts' inalienable responsibility to identify and uphold.'[192]

Lord Woolf's remarks are, at first glance, seemingly entirely contradictory to Dicey's idea of legislative sovereignty. The implication of these comments is that Parliament's sovereignty will be respected by the courts, but only up to a point. The question which flows from this of course is: where does that point lie? At what point might the courts determine that a legislative decision no longer carries the authority which makes it immune from judicial review? The short – but unsatisfactory – answer is that we can only guess. For present

---

[186] *Dr Bonham's Case* (1609) 8 Coke Reports 113b; 77 ER 646, 653. See also *Day* v *Savadge* (1614) Hob 85, 97 (Hobart CJ).

[187] *Pickin* v *British Railways Board* [1974] AC 765, 782 (Lord Reid).

[188] Though see the (current) ability of courts to 'disapply' domestic statutory provisions on the basis of incompatibility with directly-effective EU laws following *R* v *Secretary of State for Transport, ex parte Factortame (No. 2)* [1991] 1 AC 603 (pp. 167–79).

[189] See Chapter 4, pp. 105–7 for an introduction to this school of thought.

[190] See C. Turpin and A. Tomkins, *British Government and the Constitution* (7th edn) (CUP, 2011) pp. 86–95.

[191] Lord Woolf, 'Droit Public – English Style' [1995] PL 57, 69.

[192] Ibid.

purposes, some of the 'improbable examples' given in the opening sections of this chapter might allow us to gain a little purchase on this particular hypothetical, while the speech of Baroness Hale from the House of Lords' decision in *Jackson* provides a tangible example:

> The courts will treat with particular suspicion (or might even reject) any attempt to subvert the rule of law by removing governmental action affecting the rights of the individual from all judicial scrutiny.[193]

A more recent hypothetical can be found in the judgment of Lord Hodge in the Supreme Court decision in *Moohan*:

> '[if] a parliamentary majority abusively sought to entrench its power by a curtailment of the franchise or similar device, the common law, informed by principles of democracy and the rule of law and international norms, would be able to declare such legislation unlawful'.[194]

It should be stressed at this point that both sets of remarks were *obiter*, and therefore do not establish any enforceable precedent. However, both illustrate the tension that undoubtedly exists between the theoretically limitless legislative ability of Parliament and the values of the rule of law. This tension will be returned to and examined more thoroughly in the following chapter.[195]

Thinking Point . . .

While no court in modern times has sought to overtly strike down primary legislation on common law grounds, some commentators see the expansive use of the principle of legality as tantamount to a judicial power to invalidate legislation. Ekins and Forsyth have thus argued that Lord Neuberger's approach to s. 53 of the Freedom of Information Act in *Evans v Attorney General* 'effectively . . . excised the section from the statute book' (*Judging the Public Interest: The Rule of Law vs. The Rule of Courts* (Policy Exchange, 2015), p. 4).

The Human Rights Act 1998

Though our coverage of statutory interpretation has focused upon techniques of construction that have been judicially-developed, and articulated through the case-by-case processes of the common law, it is clear that Parliament can also enact legislative provisions which directly effect how statute law is to be interpreted (*and* in so doing impact upon our orthodox understandings of parliamentary sovereignty). A prime example can be found in the provisions of the Human Rights Act 1998. While the Human Rights Act 1998, and the substantive rights to which it affords protection, will be the subject of a later chapter,[196] the relationship between the Act and the doctrine of parliamentary sovereignty is worth addressing at this stage in order to address the relationship between the Act and other primary legislation.[197] In summary, the

---

[193] *Jackson* v *Attorney-General* [2006] 1 AC 56, [159] (Baroness Hale). See also the comments of Lord Steyn, [102].

[194] *Moohan* v *Lord Advocate* [2014] UKSC 67; [2015] AC 901, [35].

[195] Chapter 6.

[196] Chapter 21.

[197] For a dedicated treatment of this issue see A. Young, *Parliamentary Sovereignty and the Human Rights Act* (Hart Publishing, 2009).

Human Rights Act provides a statutory protection for certain of the rights found in the European Convention on Human Rights.[198] There are two main strands to this statutory protection. First, the Act places all public bodies – which include persons exercising 'functions of a public nature'[199] – under an obligation to act compatibly with the Convention rights.[200] A court or tribunal is a 'public authority' for the purposes of s. 6 of the Act, though Parliament is not. As a result, the courts find themselves under an obligation to act compatibly with the Convention rights;[201] Parliament – by contrast – is under no such obligation. As a result, and consistently with the idea of legislative sovereignty, Parliament may legislate incompatibly with the Convention rights if it so chooses, notwithstanding the obligations placed on other public bodies by the Act.

Secondly, the Act directs that *all* legislation, both primary and secondary, be interpreted and given effect 'so far as it is possible to do so' in a way which is compatible with the Convention rights.[202] In the event that no such interpretation is possible – for instance, where the necessary amendment would stray beyond the parameters of interpretation into statutory *amendment*[203] – the higher courts are able to issue a 'declaration of incompatibility' under s. 4(4) of the Act. Such a declaration – again, seemingly consistent with the idea of sovereignty – is non-binding and does not affect the 'validity, continuing operation or enforcement of the provision in respect of which it is given.'[204]

Nevertheless, the Human Rights Act poses something of a quandary for the orthodox reading of parliamentary sovereignty. Government Ministers responsible for piloting the Human Rights Bill through Parliament were able to claim that it would have no implications whatsoever for our traditional understanding of parliamentary sovereignty.[205] However, it is clear that, in its application, the Human Rights Act does subtly affect our understandings of the doctrine in operation. In one sense, the Human Rights Act seems to be an ordinary piece of legislation; in spite of its apparent 'constitutional' objectives, it appears to be susceptible to repeal or amendment by future enactments in just the same way as other Acts of Parliament. On its face at least, it makes no attempt to insulate itself from future repeal of amendment. Equally, however, it appears not to impliedly repeal inconsistent legislation that pre-dates its coming into effect. But at the same time, the Human Rights Act also seeks to exert an influence over legislation which post-dates its coming into effect, that is, legislation not passed – or perhaps even contemplated – at the time at which the Human Rights Act was brought into being. Each will be addressed in turn.

---

[198] Section 1(1) Human Rights Act 1998.
[199] Section 6(3)(b) Human Rights Act 1998.
[200] Section 6 Human Rights Act 1998.
[201] The extent of this obligation is considered further at pp. 679–81.
[202] Section 3(1) Human Rights Act 1998.
[203] The precise extent of the courts' interpretative powers under s. 3(1) are discussed in full at pp. 663–8.
[204] Section 4(6) Human Rights Act 1998.
[205] See, for example, HC Debs, vol. 306, col. 772, 16 February 1998 (Jack Straw MP).

Key debates
The Human Rights Act and parliamentary sovereignty:

1. The basic account

The Human Rights Act 1998 is a statutory Bill of Rights. By contrast with the United States' Bill of Rights, the Canadian Charter of Rights and Freedoms or the protections afforded in the South African Constitution, the Human Rights Act is a relatively weak instrument: it is not constitutionally entrenched, nor does it provide for a judicial power to invalidate statutes that contravene the protections it affords. Instead, as we have seen, the most a court can do is to make a (non-binding, non-enforceable) declaration to the effect that the legislation in question is incompatible with the Convention rights. The issue of a declaration of incompatibility will not necessarily result in legislative change remedying the supposed incompatibility; a declaration under s. 4 places no *legal* obligation on either ministers to initiate such change, or on Parliament to pass legislation to similar effect.[206] Instead, the declaration of incompatibility relies on *political* pressure, with the assumption being that rather than support or defend legislative provisions judicially determined to contravene human rights standards the elected branches of government will take legislative steps to amend or repeal the legislation in question.[207]

While the declaration of incompatibility mechanism seems not to affect the idea of sovereignty, legally construed, it is by no means the only provision of the HRA to attempt to insulate parliamentary sovereignty from potential dilution. The interpretative provision – s. 3(1) – also contains the disclaimer that its use does not affect the 'validity, continuing operation or enforcement' of any primary legislation interpreted in order to achieve Convention compatibility. Similarly, while public authorities fall under an obligation to act compatibly with the Convention rights, Parliament falls under no such obligation. As a result, the ability of Parliament to legislate in direct or, indeed, flagrant contravention of the Convention rights is seemingly preserved. Political restraints are again preferred to legal measures. Upon introducing draft legislation to Parliament, the responsible minister must make a statement of compatibility – indicating that the bill does not contravene the Convention rights given effect by the Human Rights Act.[208] Even if, however, there is a doubt over whether the proposed measure can be regarded as being Convention compatible the minister remains entitled to indicate that he or she wishes to proceed with the Bill.[209]

As a result, the then Lord Chancellor, Lord Irvine of Lairg QC, was able to describe the Human Rights Bill during the parliamentary debates as having been 'carefully drafted and designed to respect our traditional understanding of the separation of powers'.[210] Reduced to its bare minimum, this can be taken to mean that under the provisions of the Human Rights Act, while the reach and range of judicial review has been extended, the judges have no power

→

---

[206] Section 4(6) Human Rights Act 1998.

[207] The HRA puts in place a mechanism to allow for timely remedial responses to declarations of incompatibility: s. 10.

[208] Section 19 Human Rights Act 1998.

[209] Section 19(1)(b) Human Rights Act. For an example of a statute passed in the absence of a s. 19 statement of compatibility, see the Communications Act 2003 and the subsequent decisions of the House of Lords in *R (Animal Defenders International)* v *Secretary of State for Culture, Media and Sport* [2008] UKHL 15; [2008] 1 AC 1312 and European Court of Human Rights in *Animal Defenders International* v *United Kingdom* (2013) 57 EHRR 21 (for discussion see pp. 661–2).

[210] HL Debs, vol. 582, col. 1228 (3 November 1997).

to overturn statutes. As Jack Straw MP, then Home Secretary, also outlined during the parliamentary debates on the Human Rights Bill:

> 'The sovereignty of Parliament must be paramount. By that, I mean that Parliament must be competent to make any law on any matter of its choosing. In enacting legislation, Parliament is making decisions about important matters of public policy. The authority to make those decisions derives from a democratic mandate. Members of this place possess such a mandate because they are elected, accountable and representative . . . To allow the courts to set aside Acts of Parliament would confer on the judiciary a power that it does not possess, and which would draw it into conflict with Parliament . . .'[211]

On its face therefore, the Human Rights Act preserves the sovereignty of Parliament and eschews the 'strong form judicial review'[212] which permits the invalidation of legislation under constitutional Bills of Rights.

2. The Human Rights Act and implied repeal

There are two distinct dynamics to any discussion of the Human Rights Act and the doctrine of implied repeal. In the first instance, the Human Rights Act does not seem to impliedly overrule pre-existing legislation that is incompatible with the Convention rights. Nor is the Human Rights Act susceptible to repeal by future Acts of Parliament which are incompatible with the Convention rights. This is most probably for the reason that Convention-incompatible legislation does not actually conflict with the terms of the Human Rights Act itself and as a result, the orthodox doctrine of implied repeal does not apply. The Human Rights Act also seems to be immune from implied repeal by subsequent inconsistent legislation for the reason that, as we have already seen, it is regarded as being a 'constitutional statute'[213] and can only be repealed through the use of express statutory words to that effect.

In terms of the doctrine of implied repeal then, the Human Rights Act is simultaneously weaker and stronger than other legislation; it does not appear to repeal prior inconsistent legislation, nor is it impliedly repealed by subsequent inconsistent legislation. However, the relationship between the Human Rights Act and other primary legislation is a complex one, and in one important sense, the Human Rights Act is very much superior to other statutory measures.

3. The influence of the Human Rights Act over primary legislation 'whenever enacted'

The interpretative provision of the Human Rights Act – s. 3 – applies to all primary and secondary legislation, and directs that legislative provisions should be interpreted in a way which is compatible with the Convention rights so far as it is possible for the courts to do so. The Human Rights Act therefore controls the way in which both past and future legislation is to take effect through the ability of the courts – via s. 3(1) – to interpret legislation (no matter when that legislation was passed relative to the Human Rights Act) as far as possible to be compatible with the Convention rights. The precise nature and effects of this interpretative role are examined in full in Chapter 21, but for present purposes it is sufficient to acknowledge that the controlling influence of the Human Rights Act 1998 over legislation which post-dates its enactment might be regarded as a substantial constraint on Parliament's legislative power. Section 3(1) permits clear statutory language to be effectively modified in order to achieve a

---

[211] HC Debs, vol. 306, col. 772 (16 February 1998).
[212] See for a discussion, M. Tushnet, 'New Forms of Judicial Review and the Persistence of Rights- and Democracy-Based Worries' (2003) 38 *Wake Forest Law Review* 813, esp. 819–33.
[213] See pp. 158–61.

Convention-compliant interpretation and as such marks a radical departure from the literal techniques of statutory interpretation that derive from the orthodox reading of sovereignty. Such is the wide ranging potential for the Human Rights Act to affect the interpretation, and therefore the effect, of legislation that the former Law Lord Lord Cooke has asked; how '[c]an the United Kingdom Parliament . . . [continue to] be classified as sovereign if, by virtue of an earlier Act of Parliament, it was powerless to achieve its intention, however clearly articulated?'[214]

The influence of – and the UK's exit from – the European Union

Key issues

- The UK's membership of the European Union has amounted to a significant challenge to the orthodox reading of parliamentary sovereignty. Membership of the European Union, which requires the acceptance of a form of law which claims superiority over the laws of national legal systems, stands in apparent opposition to the principle that Parliament's legislative sovereignty renders it the highest legal authority recognised by the constitution.

- Initially seeking to reconcile conflicting EU and domestic laws through interpretative means, the *Factortame (No. 2)* decision eventually accepted that UK courts were empowered to 'disapply' provisions of domestic statutes which were incompatible with directly-effective EU norms. The apparent loss of domestic 'sovereignty' to European institutions provided a motivating factor underpinning the June 2016 vote in favour of leaving the European Union. Whether Brexit will result in the resurrection of a more Diceyan approach to parliamentary sovereignty however is very much open to doubt.

Membership of the European Union

The UK joined the European Economic Community – as it then was – on 1 January 1973. In order to give domestic effect to the obligations arising out of the treaties regulating the European Community, Parliament passed the European Communities Act 1972 (ECA). As we have seen, s. 2(1) of the ECA 1972, as amended, provides that directly effective provisions of Community law should be enforceable by courts in the UK,[215] with s. 2(4) of the ECA adding that 'any enactment passed or to be passed . . . shall be construed and have effect subject to the foregoing provisions of this section'.

The difficulties arising out of the UK's membership of the European Community for our understandings of sovereignty were therefore twofold. First, s. 2(1) of the ECA provided that future provisions of European Community law would become effective as a matter of

---

[214] Lord Cooke of Thorndon, 'The Myth of Sovereignty' (2007) 11 *Otago Law Review* 377, 380.

[215] Section 2(1) provides: 'All such rights, powers, liabilities, obligations and restrictions from time to time created or arising by or under the Treaties, and all such remedies and procedures from time to time provided for by or under the Treaties, as in accordance with the Treaties are without further enactment to be given legal effect or used in the United Kingdom shall be recognised and available in law, and be enforced, allowed and followed accordingly; and the expression "enforceable EU right" and similar expressions shall be read as referring to one to which this subsection applies.'

domestic law 'without further enactment'. As a result, 'rights, powers, liabilities' which were not yet a part of Community law – but which would become so in the future – would be translated into the domestic legal system without Parliament specifically legislating to give effect to them. This amounted to something of a weakening of the system of dualism which had previously appeared to require specific legislative action in order to give domestic legal effect to obligations arising out of a treaty. Secondly, s. 2(4) suggested that domestic legislation not yet passed at the time of accession was to take effect subject to the requirements of Community law. As a result, the prospect arose that – in a clash between a provision of Community law and a statute subsequently passed in the UK – the ordinary process of repeal would not be operative and the UK Parliament would find itself constrained by the provisions of the 1972 Act.

These difficulties were compounded – and made far more problematic for the Diceyan understanding of sovereignty – by the fact that European Community law had been held by the European Court of Justice to be superior to the national laws of member states.[216] As we saw above, Dicey did not countenance that another institution or collection of norms might be legally superior to the law as enacted by Parliament. How then, was a clash between the two forms of supposedly superior law (a UK statute and a directly effective European Community norm) to be resolved? Should the established principles of parliamentary sovereignty be held to apply – and the UK court hold that the domestic statute took precedence – then the UK would run the risk of enforcement proceedings before the European Court of Justice, which would, in turn uphold the supremacy of European Union law. Should the domestic court allow the European norm to take precedence, then the idea of Parliament's sovereignty would appear to be turned on its head, with the norms of another legal entity overriding those of a supposedly sovereign legislature.

Reconciliation through interpretation?

Initially, the response from the domestic courts was – perhaps unsurprisingly – a little confused. In *Felixstowe Dock and Railway Co.* v *British Transport Docks Board* Lord Denning appeared to endorse a Diceyan view of sovereignty, stating that once a bill had entered the statute book, 'that will dispose of all discussion about the Treaty [of Rome]. These courts will then have to abide by the statute without regard to the Treaty at all'.[217] An alternate approach emerged from the decision of the Court of Appeal in *Macarthys Ltd* v *Smith*.[218]

Key case
Macarthys Ltd v *Smith [1979] ICR 785*

Macarthys concerned a dispute over equal pay. The applicant (a woman) had been employed as the manager of a warehouse stockroom and contended that she was entitled to receive the same salary as her predecessor in the post (a man). The relevant domestic legislation – the

---

[216] See Case 6/64, *Costa* v *ENEL* [1964] ECR 585: '. . . the member states have limited their sovereign rights, albeit within limited fields, and have thus created a body of law which binds both their nationals and themselves' (on which see P. Craig, 'Constitutionalising Constitutional Law: *HS2*' [2014] PL 373, 376–377). See also Case 11/70, *International Handelsgesellschaft* [1970] ECR 1125.

[217] *Felixstowe Dock and Railway Co.* v *British Transport Docks Board* [1976] 2 CMLR 655, 664–665.

[218] *Macarthys Ltd* v *Smith* [1979] ICR 785.

Equal Pay Act 1970 – was worded in a way which suggested that equality of pay might be due to two workers employed in the same position contemporaneously, but that it might not be due to two employees who – though occupying the same position – were not employed at the same time. The relevant provision of EC law – Art. 119 of the treaty – provided that 'men and women should receive equal pay for equal work'.

The majority of the Court of Appeal – Lawton and Cumming-Bruce LJJ – determined that it was unnecessary to refer to Art. 119 of the EEC Treaty as an aid to construction for the reason that the relevant domestic legislation – the Equal Pay Act 1970 – was clear. However, as Art. 119 was of direct effect, the majority were unsure of the precise relationship between the rules of the two jurisdictions and referred the matter to the European Court of Justice.

In the minority, Lord Denning stated, with a surprising degree of certainty given his comments in the **Felixstowe** case, that:

> In construing our statute, we are entitled to look at the Treaty as an aid to its construction: and even more, not only as an aid but as an overriding force. If on close inspection it should appear that our legislation is deficient – or it is inconsistent with Community law – by some oversight of our draftsmen – then it is our bounden duty to give priority to Community law. Such is the result of section 2(1) and (4) of the European Communities Act 1972.[219]

Following a reference to the European Court of Justice, Lord Denning's approach was shown to be correct.[220]

So while *Macarthys* demonstrated that the UK's obligations under EU law could be relied on in order to construe otherwise clear statutory provisions,[221] *and* that those obligations should be prioritised in the event of a clash, the outcome was not as 'constitutionally dangerous'[222] as it might have been had the court been asked to declare the Equal Pay Act invalid; instead, the court simply 'did not apply' the relevant provisions.[223] For a more radical judicial response to a question concerning how to respond to an irreconcilable difference between a domestic statute and provision of Community law, we had to wait until the *Factortame* litigation.

The voluntary acceptance of a limitation on sovereignty? The *Factortame* litigation

The *Factortame* litigation was the result of a conflict between primary legislation and directly applicable principles of European Community law that could not be remedied by way of interpretation.

The relevant domestic legislation

The domestic legislation in question – the Merchant Shipping Act 1988 – provided that in order to fish in British waters, fishing vessels should be registered in Britain. In order to be so registered, fishing vessels ought to be – under s. 14(1) – 'British owned'. For the

---

[219] *Macarthys Ltd* v *Smith* [1979] ICR 785, 789.
[220] *Macarthys Ltd* v *Smith* [1981] 1 QB 180.
[221] An approach subsequently applied in *Pickstone* v *Freemans* [1989] AC 66 and *Litster* v *Forth Dry Dock and Engineering Co. Ltd [1990] 1 AC 546. and Engineering Co Ltd* [1990] 1 AC 546.
[222] T. R. S. Allan, 'Parliamentary Sovereignty: Lord Denning's Dexterous Revolution' (1983) 3 OJLS 22, 27.
[223] Ibid.

purposes of the Act, 'British owned' meant that the vessel in question should either be owned by a British citizen resident in the UK, or by a company, 75 per cent of whose directors and shareholders ought to be British.[224]

The litigants

The litigation was brought by a group of predominantly Spanish companies which – under the previous regime for the registration of fishing vessels[225] – had been permitted to register boats as British, and to fish in British waters. As a result of the changes brought about to the conditions for registration the companies were not eligible for re-registration under the Merchant Shipping Act 1988. The financial implications for the affected fishing companies were potentially catastrophic.

The questions of law

Factortame argued that the Merchant Shipping Act 1988 was incompatible with directly effective provisions of Community law, including the right not to be discriminated against on the basis of nationality. *Factortame* therefore sought a declaration that the Merchant Shipping Act was incompatible with EC law, and that it was invalid as a result. While the grant of such a declaration would seem to be the natural consequence of accepting the superior status of EC law in those areas in which it applied, it would also amount to an unprecedented challenge to the Diceyan construction of parliamentary sovereignty.

Factortame (No. 1)

The Divisional Court referred the question of compatibility to the European Court of Justice under Art. 177 of the EEC Treaty and granted an interim injunction suspending application of the Merchant Shipping Act pending resolution of the substantive question of EU law by the ECJ. The Court of Appeal, on the Secretary of State's appeal, quashed the injunction, finding that the domestic statute should be upheld.[226] Lord Donaldson, Master of the Rolls, found that – as the answer to the substantive question of EC law was by no means clear – there existed 'no juridical basis upon which interim relief can be granted by the British courts'.[227] Factortame appealed to the House of Lords.

The only relevant issue considered by the House of Lords in *Factortame (No. 1)* was whether the courts enjoyed jurisdiction to suspend the application of a domestic statute – as the Divisional Court had attempted to – by way of an interim injunction in circumstances where there was a potential, though unconfirmed, inconsistency between a domestic statute and directly-effective provisions of EC law.[228] Lord Bridge – giving the only substantial speech in the House of Lords – was not persuaded that domestic courts were so empowered, either as a matter of national or EC law, and sought clarification in the form of a preliminary ruling from the ECJ.

---

[224] Section 14(7) Merchant Shipping Act 1988.
[225] Governed by the Merchant Shipping Act 1894.
[226] *R v Secretary of State for Transport, ex parte Factortame (No. 1)* [1989] 2 CMLR 353.
[227] Ibid., [20].
[228] *R v Secretary of State for Transport ex parte Factortame (No. 1)* [1990] 2 AC 85, 135.

The response from the European Court of Justice

In separate proceedings, the ECJ considered (a) the substantive question concerning the compatibility (or otherwise) of the scheme established under the Merchant Shipping Act with the protections afforded under EC law and (b) the question of whether, as a matter of EC law, national courts should have competence to set aside provisions of domestic legislation in order to give effect to directly effective rights in EC law.

As to the first of those decisions, the ECJ found that the scheme established under the Merchant Shipping Act contravened the requirements of Community law on the basis that it was discriminatory on the basis of nationality.[229] In answering the second issue,[230] the ECJ referred to its earlier decision in *Simmenthal* in which it had noted that:

> . . . in accordance with the principle of the precedence of Community law, the relationship between the provisions of the Treaty and directly applicable measures of the institutions on the one hand and the national law of the member states on the other is such that those provisions and measures . . . by their entry into force render automatically inapplicable any conflicting provisions of . . . national law.[231]

The outcome of the case, as far as the position of the ECJ was concerned, was that the relevant provisions of the Merchant Shipping Act should be ineffective, and that in order to give effect to directly-effective Community norms, domestic courts should be competent to set aside national laws that were incompatible with Community law. The question for the House of Lords following these decisions of the ECJ was whether this requirement might be squared with domestic constitutional doctrine.

Factortame (No. 2)

The outcome of *Factortame (No. 2)* was that the House of Lords 'disapplied' provisions of the Merchant Shipping Act 1988 in so far as they were incompatible with the directly-effective requirements of Community law.[232] Clearly, this was an unprecedented modification of the orthodox reading of the sovereignty doctrine. In the House of Lords, Lord Bridge made the most obvious attempts to address the issue of sovereignty. He noted that suggestions had been made that permitting domestic courts to 'override' national legislation on the basis of the supremacy of European law would amount to 'a novel and dangerous invasion by a Community institution of the sovereignty of the United Kingdom Parliament'.[233] This view, he argued, was a 'misconception'.[234] Lord Bridge explained that, as the supremacy of European Community law was a principle 'well established in the jurisprudence of the European Court of Justice long before the United Kingdom joined the Community' it was wrong to portray the outcome of the *Factortame (No. 2)* litigation as an attack on national sovereignty.[235] Instead, Lord Bridge explained that, 'whatever limitation on its sovereignty

---

[229] Case C-246/89R, *EC Commission* v *United Kingdom* [1989] ECR 3125.

[230] Case C-213/89, *R* v *Secretary of State for Transport, ex parte Factortame* [1990] 3 CMLR 1.

[231] Case 106/77, *Amministrazione delle Finanze dello Stato* v *Simmenthal SpA* [1978] ECR 629; [1978] 3 CMLR 263, [17].

[232] On the distinction between 'disapplication' and 'invalidation' see: A. Young, '*Benkharbouche* and the future of disapplication', UK Const L Blog (24 October 2017).

[233] *R* v *Secretary of State for Transport, ex parte Factortame (No. 2)* [1991] 1 AC 603, 658.

[234] Ibid.

[235] Ibid., 658–9.

Parliament accepted when it enacted the European Communities Act 1972 was entirely voluntary.'[236] In *Factortame (No. 2)* the House of Lords appeared to tacitly acknowledge that Parliament's legislative ability had been limited in some way by accession to the European Community; the established principles of implied repeal seemed not to operate as Community law – given effect through an Act passed in 1972 – was not overridden by an Act passed by Parliament in 1988. Sovereignty had clearly been limited in some way, but the Law Lords declined to expand upon the precise nature of the limitation imposed.

Key debates
Interpreting Factortame (No. 2)

Opinions vary on the effect of the decision of the House of Lords in *Factortame (No. 2).* While Lord Bridge was the only of the five Law Lords to address the issue of sovereignty explicitly, he offered little explanation as to why Parliament appeared suddenly to be able to do the one thing that it had been traditionally argued to be unable to do; namely, bind itself as regards the substance of legislation.[237] Instead, as we have seen, Bridge simply resorted to suggesting that upon the UK's accession to the European Community the principle of the supremacy of Community law was 'well established' and that, as a result, 'whatever limitation' was imposed by Parliament as a result of the European Communities Act had been 'entirely voluntary'.[238] Wade's accusation that in *Factortame (No. 2)* the House of Lords collectively turned a blind eye to issues of constitutional theory is, in many ways, fully justified.[239] As a result, many efforts have subsequently been made to explain the constitutional implications of *Factortame (No. 2).*

1. A legal revolution?

As a result of the unprecedented findings of the House of Lords in *Factortame (No. 2),* H. W. R. Wade contended that a 'revolution' in our constitutional fundamentals had taken place. Wade noted that 'the rule of recognition is itself a political fact which the judges themselves are able to change when they are confronted with a new situation which so demands'.[240] In deciding *Factortame (No. 2),* Wade suggested that such a change had occurred, as 'the established rule about conflicting Acts of Parliament, namely that the later Act must prevail, was evidently violated' as a result of the Merchant Shipping Act of 1988 having been 'disapplied' on the authority of the European Communities Act 1972.[241] As such an eventuality was supposedly – under the orthodox Diceyan approach – 'constitutionally impossible', Wade felt it fair to describe what had happened as a 'constitutional revolution'.[242] Citing the speech of Lord Bridge, Wade argued that in voluntarily accepting a limitation on its sovereignty '[h]e takes it for granted that Parliament can "accept" a limitation of its sovereignty which will be effective both for the present and for the future. It is a statement which could hardly be clearer: Parliament can bind its successors'.[243] 'If that is not revolutionary', Wade concluded, 'constitutional lawyers are Dutchmen'.[244]

---

[236] Ibid., 659; *Amministrazione delle Finanze dello Stato* v *Simmenthal SpA* [1978] ECR 629; [1978] 3 CMLR 263.
[237] I. Loveland, *Constitutional Law, Administrative Law and Human Rights: a Critical Introduction* (4th edn) (OUP, 2006) p. 483.
[238] *R* v *Secretary of State for Transport, ex parte Factortame Ltd* (No. 2) [1991] 1 AC 603, 659 (Lord Bridge).
[239] H. W. R. Wade, 'Sovereignty – Revolution or Evolution?' (1996)112 LQR 568, 575.
[240] Ibid., 568, 574.
[241] Ibid., 568, 568.
[242] Ibid.
[243] Ibid., 572.
[244] Ibid.

2. The evolution of a rule of statutory construction?

T. R. S. Allan, however, saw little evidence of a revolution having taken place. Allan argued that in the **Factortame** decision, the House of Lords simply applied settled constitutional doctrine to a new set of circumstances. Just because the courts acknowledged that the UK's membership of the European Community amounted to a legitimate curtailment of legislative sovereignty did not mean – Allan argued – that the courts would necessarily accept *all* such purported restrictions as valid. As Allan notes, '[t]he principle of "voluntary acceptance" by Parliament of limits on sovereignty must clearly be confined to the present context. Whether or not such voluntary acceptance of limits would be permitted in another context would depend on the circumstances: the reasons for and against such limits would have to be weighed'.[245] The fundamental distinction between Wade and Allan's viewpoints is that while Wade is able to suggest that the rule of recognition is a matter of 'political fact',[246] Allan argues that this cannot be the case for the reason that the political dynamics of the constitution cannot be divorced in their entirety from its legal characteristics. Hence, the legal reasons underpinning the courts' recognition of the authority of a particular statute are equally as important to the rule of recognition as a political fact:

> Legal reasons are usually understood to ground a legitimate judicial decision by invoking settled doctrine or principle: they serve to justify it by explaining the sense in which it was required by the standards of the existing legal order. A revolution occurs, or is cemented, only when a new source of authority is acknowledged, or fundamental rule adopted, which is *not* justified by the existing order, from which the courts have for whatever reason withdrawn their allegiance.[247]

Allan therefore argues that 'talk of revolution falsely implies that the courts' role is merely to accept, on grounds of expediency, whatever the politicians decide.'[248] Instead, Allan saw **Factortame (No. 2)** as an application of 'accepted constitutional principle'[249] in novel circumstances. As a result, 'revolutions of the kind suggested [by Wade] turn out, on analysis, to be only examples of evolution after all'.[250]

3. The application of the rules of a separate and distinct legal jurisdiction?

An alternative view is proffered by Adam Tomkins, who has argued that in implementing European legal norms the courts are now operating in what might be called a European jurisdiction. Tomkins argues that when applying the rules of European Union law, courts are no longer applying simple rules of domestic law. As a result, the rules that would ordinarily guide their application of the law – including the rule of parliamentary sovereignty – no longer apply. Instead, the courts are operating a jurisdiction which is governed by the law of the European Union, in which the supremacy of European Union law over that of the member states will apply. Tomkins explains:

> Since 1 January 1973 there have been two legal systems operating in this country, not one, and the doctrine of the legislative supremacy of statute is a doctrine known to only one of those two systems . . . European Community law is . . . a new legal order that is to be enforced by the same courts as enforce domestic law. They may be the same courts, but they are not enforcing the same law.'[251]

→

---

[245] T. R. S. Allan, 'Parliamentary Sovereignty: law, politics and revolution' (1997) 113 LQR 443, 447.
[246] H. W. R. Wade, 'Sovereignty – Revolution or Evolution?' (1996) 112 LQR 568, 574.
[247] T. R. S. Allan, 'Parliamentary Sovereignty: law, politics and revolution' (1997) 113 LQR 443, 444 (emphasis in the original).
[248] Ibid., 443, 451.
[249] Ibid., 443, 445.
[250] Ibid., 443, 447.
[251] A. Tomkins, *Public Law* (Clarendon Press, 2003) p. 118.

As a result of the European Communities Act 1972, the two jurisdictions – the European and the domestic[252] – operate in parallel. Tomkins' view finds support in the opening paragraph to Lord Bridge's speech in *Factortame (No. 2)* where His Lordship outlines what was effectively the key distinction between the decisions in *Factortame (No. 1)* and *Factortame (No. 2)*:

> '. . . when this appeal first came before the House last year . . . your Lordships held that, *as a matter of English law,* the courts had no jurisdiction to grant interim relief in terms which would involve either overturning an English statute in advance of any decision of the European Court of Justice that the statute infringed Community law or granting an injunction against the Crown. It became necessary to seek a preliminary ruling from the European Court of Justice as to whether *Community law* itself invested us with such jurisdiction.[253]

In those circumstances where European law applies, it will prevail over domestic law. In those areas where it does not, no authority is recognised as having higher legal status than an Act of Parliament. As a result, on Tomkins' account, the doctrine of legislative supremacy survives unscathed:

> Parliament may make or unmake any law whatsoever, and under *English law* nobody may override or set aside a statute.[254]

4. The controlling influence of the common law: *Thoburn* v *Sunderland City Council*

In the case of *Thoburn,* however, Laws LJ offered an alternative reading of why the European Communities Act 1972 continues to exert an influence over how subsequently passed domestic legislation takes effect. The facts of this particular case have already been introduced, so for present purposes, it is the discussion of the relationship between European law and national law that is relevant. First, Laws LJ held that the doctrine of implied repeal did not operate in the context of the *Metric Martyrs* case: the clash was between the domestic weights and measures instrument and the provisions of EU law regarding the weight and measurement of goods for sale, rather than between the domestic weights and measures provisions and the European Communities Act 1972. As will be recalled from the earlier discussion, implied repeal traditionally operates when statutory provisions *on the same topic* are found to be in conflict. As a result, subsequent domestic instruments regarding weights and measurements were not inconsistent – strictly speaking – with the provisions of the European Communities Act 1972.[255]

Laws LJ also found that the terms of the 1972 Act continued to exert an influence over how subsequently passed primary legislation should take effect. This influence was not, however, a result of Parliament having bound itself by passing the ECA in 1972; such an outcome was, Laws LJ noted, an impossibility.[256] Nor was it the necessary consequence of the European Court of Justice's doctrine of the supremacy of European law.[257] Instead, Laws LJ explained,

---

[252] Taken here to include the three technically separate jurisdictions of England and Wales, Scotland and Northern Ireland.

[253] *R* v *Secretary of State for Transport, ex parte Factortame Ltd* (No. 2) [1991] 1 AC 603, 658 (Lord Bridge) (emphasis added).

[254] A. Tomkins, *Public Law* (Clarendon Press, 2003) p. 118 (emphasis added).

[255] *Thoburn* v *Sunderland City Council* [2003] QB 151, 180–1.

[256] *Thoburn* v *Sunderland City Council* [2003] QB 151, 184–5.

[257] *Thoburn* v *Sunderland City Council* [2003] QB 151, 184–185. It should be noted that Laws LJ also denied that the Parliament of the UK could bind *itself* as to the manner and form of future legislation. As we have already seen however – at pp. 158–61 – it is explicit in the decision in *Thoburn* that the common law might impose such limitations on Parliament.

any limitation to which Parliament found itself subject governing the relationship between national law and the laws of the European Community was a result of the common law. More specifically, the reason advanced for the continued effectiveness of the provisions of the European Communities Act 1972 (and its immunity from implied repeal) was that it is 'by force of the common law, a constitutional statute'.[258]

5. The European Union Act 2011

Persistent (and politicised) uncertainty over the event to which Parliament remained legally sovereign in relation to matters falling within the ambit of EU law led the 2010–15 Coalition Government to introduce the European Union Act 2011, s. 18 of which provides:

> Directly applicable or directly effective EU law (that is, the rights, powers, liabilities, obligations, restrictions, remedies and procedures referred to in section 2(1) of the European Communities Act 1972) falls to be recognized and available in law in the United Kingdom *only by virtue of that Act* or where it is required to be recognized and available in law by virtue of any other Act.

In other words, the authority which attaches to European Union law in the UK Constitution does so, not as a result of the *sui generis* nature of EU law, nor as a result of the constraining influence of the common law, but *only* as a result of the direction of an Act of Parliament. As Lord Mance recognised in *Pham* v *Secretary of State for the Home Department* [2015] UKSC 19; [2015] 1 WLR 1591, [76]: 'European law is part of United Kingdom law only to the extent that Parliament has legislated that it should be.' EU law therefore enjoys superior status over national laws, purely and simply because *Parliament* permits it to enjoy that status.

In spite of the undoubted – if unclear – limitation placed on Parliament's legislative power by the ECA 1972 and the UK's membership of the European Union it remains possible to answer the question 'does Parliament remain legally sovereign?' in the affirmative. First, in enacting the 2011 European Union Act, Parliament had sought to clarify that the influence of EU law over the constitution was the express result of statutory authorisation. Second, this attempted legislative clarification was accompanied – in the Supreme Court's *HS2* decision – by Lord Reed's indication that conflicts between EU norms and domestic law 'cannot be resolved simply by applying the doctrine developed by the Court of Justice of the supremacy of EU law, since the application of that doctrine in our law itself *depends* upon the 1972 Act.'[259] As we touched upon above, the *HS2* decision indicated that the overriding capacity of EU law in all fields of competence was not a matter of unquestioning assumption, but of judicial judgment. For Lord Reed – with whom all of the remaining justices agreed – conflicts between EU and domestic laws therefore fall 'to be resolved by our courts as an issue arising under the constitutional law of the United Kingdom'.[260] And finally, Parliament – ultimately – retained the legal power to withdraw the UK from the EU; as Jeffrey Goldsworthy suggested in 1999, 'Parliament remains sovereign so long as it retains its authority to withdraw Britain from the European Community by enacting

---

[258] *Thoburn* v *Sunderland City Council* [2003] QB 151, 186.

[259] *R (Buckinghamshire County Council)* v *Secretary of State for Transport* [2014] UKSC 3; [2014] 1 WLR 324, [79] (emphasis added).

[260] Ibid. See further M. Elliott, 'Constitutional Legislation, European Union Law and the Nature of the United Kingdom's Contemporary Constitution' (2014) 10 *European Constitutional Law Review* 379.

express and unambiguous words to that effect.'[261] At the time Goldsworthy made these remarks, the UK's exit from the European Union appeared to be an unlikely prospect. Times change. By March 2017, 52 per cent of the voting electorate had endorsed leaving the EU, Parliament had passed the European Union (Notification of Withdrawal) Act 2017, and the Prime Minister had triggered the process – under Article 50 of the Lisbon Treaty – which would precipitate the UK's departure from the EU.

Thinking Point. . .

While **Factortame** appeared to suggest that legislation post-dating the 1972 Act would not impliedly repeal inconsistent and directly effective provisions of EU law, the question of whether Parliament was competent to legislate in express words to override EU law was left unaddressed. Divergent views amongst the judiciary were evident. First, as Lord Denning noted in his dissenting judgment in the Court of Appeal decision in *Macarthys* v *Smith*: 'If the time should come when our Parliament *deliberately* passes an Act with the intention of repudiating the Treaty or any provision in it or *intentionally* of acting inconsistently with it and says so in *express* terms then I should have thought that it would be the duty of our courts to follow the statute of our Parliament' (*Macarthys* v *Smith* [1979] ICR 785, 789 (Lord Denning) (emphasis added)). However, Lord Denning's comments should be contrasted with the more recent view of Bingham LJ in the Court of Appeal in **Factortame (No. 1),** who observed that for the period of the UK's membership of the European Union 'the duty of the national court is to give effect to [applicable European Union law] in *all circumstances*' (*R* v *Secretary of State for Transport, ex parte Factortame (No. 1)* [1989] 2 CMLR 353, [30] (emphasis added)). That Parliament retains competence to legislate notwithstanding the requirements of EU law is put beyond doubt by s. 1(2) of the European Union (Notification of Withdrawal) Act 2017; '[t]his section has effect despite any provision made by or under the European Communities Act 1972.'

Brexit: reclaiming sovereignty?

'Taking back control' of the UK's laws was one of the core messages of the campaign to leave the European Union. Though the debates over the UK's membership of the EU primarily engaged with the notion of *national* sovereignty – that is, a broader sense of the appropriate division of powers between national and international institutions – the specific issue of Parliament's *legislative* sovereignty (or perceived sovereignty) was a relevant concern to many who voted in the 2016 referendum.[262] The dilemma at the heart of the *Factortame* litigation – the question of how the law-making capacities of two supposedly sovereign bodies of law might be reconciled – provided a clear illustration of an *external* influence on Parliament's legislative power, interpreted by some as a dilution (or limitation) of Parliament's sovereignty. The actions of the Parliament of 1972 (in joining the EEC) had undoubtedly impacted upon those of the Parliament wishing to implement the Merchant

---

[261] J. Goldsworthy, *The Sovereignty of Parliament: History and Philosophy* (OUP, 1999) p. 15. See also: *The United Kingdom's Exit from and new Partnership with the European Union*, Cm. 9417 (February 2017), [2.1].

[262] Mike Gordon has referred to the Leave campaign as being possessed by 'sovereignty hysteria' in its 'pursuit of a romantic return to a mythical constitutional past' (see M. Gordon, 'The UK's Sovereignty Situation: Brexit, Bewilderment and Beyond. . . ' (2016) KLJ 333, 334 and 342).

Shipping Act of 1988. The consequence of this decision was to permit a domestic court to, for the first time, 'disapply' a domestic statute on the basis of an incompatibility with law originating from an alternative source of authority.[263] In the light of this, attempts to explain the impact of the **Factortame** decision had sought to do so by reference to *internal* characteristics of the UK constitution, including the common law (Laws LJ),[264] the rule of recognition (Wade),[265] the interpretative power of courts (Allan, *HS2*)[266] and the legislative capacity of Parliament itself (Lord Bridge, Tomkins, European Union Act 2011, *HS2*).[267] An explanation of the domestic influence of EU law that was couched in the language and principles of domestic constitutional law was able to maintain the dominant position of Parliament with the legal order, *and* uphold the jurisdictional integrity required by the doctrine of dualism. Attempts to suggest that the influence of EU law in the domestic context rested on the autonomous – and *external* – doctrines of direct effect and the supremacy of EU laws[268] were therefore effectively dismissed as heretical.[269]

Given this track record, it was entirely unsurprising that the majority reasoning in the Supreme Court decision in *Miller*[270] sought to affirm relatively orthodox principles including the superiority of primary legislation over prerogative, the status of the Sewel convention as a political inhibition, and the (slightly vague) proposition that significant constitutional change should ordinarily be the product of primary legislation.[271] This trend continued as the majority emphasised the position of the European Communities Act 1972 as the 'source of EU law'[272] in the UK legal system. The 'unprecedented' effect of the 1972 Act, the majority found, was to authorise 'a dynamic process by which, without further primary legislation . . . EU law not only becomes a source of UK law, but actually takes precedence over all domestic sources of law, including statutes.'[273] However, this was, the majority continued, but 'one sense' in which EU could be taken to have domestic effect. Strikingly, the judges continued by suggesting that:

> . . . in a more fundamental sense and, we consider, a more realistic sense, where EU law applies in the United Kingdom, *it is the EU institutions which are the relevant source of that law* . . . so long as [the 1972] Act remains in force, the EU Treaties, EU legislation and the interpretations placed on these instruments by the Court of Justice are *direct sources* of UK law.[274]

---

[263] A power which persists during the period prior to the UK's formal departure from the EU (*Benkharbouche* v *Secretary of State for Foreign and Commonwealth Affairs* [2017] UKSC 62, [78]: '. . . a conflict between EU law and English domestic law must be resolved in favour of the former, and the latter must be disapplied.')

[264] *Thoburn* v *Sunderland City Council* [2003] QB 151.

[265] H. W. R. Wade, 'Sovereignty – Revolution or Evolution?' (1996) 112 LQR 568.

[266] T. R. S. Allan, 'Parliamentary Sovereignty: law, politics and revolution' (1997) 113 LQR 443; *R (Buckinghamshire County Council)* v *Secretary of State for Transport* [2014] UKSC 3; [2014] 1 WLR 324.

[267] *R* v *Secretary of State for Transport, ex parte Factortame Ltd (No. 2)* [1991] 1 AC 603; A. Tomkins, *Public Law* (Clarendon Press, 2003); European Union Act 2011, s. 18; HS2: as above.

[268] Case 26/62, *Van Gend en Loos* [1963] ECR 1; Case 6/64, *Costa* v *ENEL* [1964] ECR 585

[269] *Thoburn* v *Sunderland City Council* [2003] QB 151, 181–185.

[270] *R (Miller)* v *Secretary of State for Exiting the European Union* [2017] UKSC 5; [2017] 2 WLR 583. The facts and primary findings of the Supreme Court's decision in *Miller* are covered at pp. 92–3.

[271] On which see K. Ewing, 'Brexit and Parliamentary Sovereignty' (2017) 80(4) MLR 711.

[272] *R (Miller)* v *Secretary of State for Exiting the European Union* [2017] UKSC 5; [2017] 2 WLR 583, [61].

[273] Ibid., [60].

[274] Ibid., [61] (emphasis added).

At the point at which the process of leaving the EU was about to begin in earnest, there is an irony in the majority's finding that during the UK's membership, EU law amounted to an '*independent* and overriding source of domestic law'.[275] The Supreme Court acknowledged the 1972 Act as being the 'conduit pipe'[276] through which EU flows into the domestic system (acknowledging also that the repeal of the 1972 would stop that flow[277]). But in declaring that – during the period within which the ECA remains operable – EU law amounts to a 'direct' and 'independent' source of law emanating from the EU institutions seems to attribute an *external* dynamic to the sovereignty debate that many actors and commentators have been hitherto reluctant to concede.[278] Whether, this acknowledgment will in time reveal itself as underpinning a 'softening of constitutional dualism' remains to be seen.[279]

It might be thought that much of this debate is moot, given that the UK's formal exit from the EU looks set to occur in 2019. But the experience of the UK's membership of the EU serves to illustrate a number of important points relating to the *future* operation of the doctrine of parliamentary sovereignty. First, it indicates that Parliament might legislate – in general terms – in order to give an external, and *dynamic,* source of law effect in the domestic legal order. Second, it indicates that – subject to the maintenance of this legislative direction – an external body of laws might be given practical precedence over competing domestic laws, and that courts might give effect to that precedence by 'disapplying' the competing domestic provisions, whenever enacted. Finally, EU membership also illustrates that any such 'voluntary acceptance' of a limitation on Parliament's sovereignty may well be temporal, and can be ended by an indication of clear legislative intent.

But even in the light of this latter point, it does not necessarily follow that a resurgence of Diceyan orthodoxy will be the result of the UK's departure from the EU. While EU membership has posed the most obvious challenge to the Diceyan understanding of parliamentary sovereignty, parallel developments have indicated that bald statements of Parliament's unlimited legislative capacity must give way to rather more qualified assessments. Of course, it remains possible to state – as Lord Bingham did in the *Jackson* decision – that:

> . . . the bedrock of the British constitution is, and in 1911 [when the first Parliament Act was passed] was, the supremacy of the Crown in Parliament . . . Then, as now, the Crown in Parliament was unconstrained by any entrenched or codified constitution. It could make or unmake any law it wished.[280]

---

[275] Ibid., [65] (emphasis added). On this point see J. E. K. Murkens, 'Mixed Messages in Bottles: the European Union, Devolution and the Future of the Constitution' (2017) 80 MLR 685, 686–690.

[276] *R (Miller)* v *Secretary of State for Exiting the European Union* [2017] UKSC 5; [2017] 2 WLR 583, [65].

[277] Repeal of the European Communities Act 1972 is one of the core objectives of the European Union (Withdrawal Bill) 2017 (cl. 1 as introduced).

[278] For forceful criticism of the Supreme Court's reasoning on this particular point see M. Elliott, 'The Supreme Court's judgment in *Miller*: in Search of Constitutional Principle' (2017) 76 CLJ 257.

[279] T. Poole, 'Devotion to Legalism: On the Brexit case' (2017) 80(4) MLR 696, 710.

[280] *Jackson* v *Attorney-General* [2005] UKHL 56; [2006] 1 AC 262, [9].

But the ongoing absence of codified constitutional limitations on legislative power does not mean that Parliament's sovereignty can necessarily be seen as absolute.[281] Political limitations on the legislative capacity of Parliament – in the light of conventional limitations such as the Sewel convention – amount to more than hypothetical restraints, whose effects cannot merely be summarily dismissed as lacking in legal force. The advent of rights recognised by the common law and the development of a hierarchy of statutes within the domestic legal order has resulted in a change in the courts' approach to implied repeal and undoes at least one of the core threads of Diceyan orthodoxy by acknowledging that not all statutes are of equal constitutional importance. The courts' development (and deployment) of the principle of legality – as we will see in the chapter that follows – may well now function to permit competing imperatives (as required by the rule of law or separation of powers) to temper legislation impacting upon those constitutional fundamentals. In combination, and in spheres *almost wholly unaffected* by the UK's membership of the EU, political developments and judicial decisions are increasingly 'defining the limits' of Parliament's legislative power.[282] Though Parliament may be in the process of securing the UK's withdrawal from the EU, our understanding of the doctrine of legal sovereignty is unlikely to return to its pre-1972 state.

Conclusion

Does Dicey's conception of legal sovereignty retain any credibility? Undoubtedly it does.[283] But, as students of a constitution that has undergone (occasionally radical) change since Dicey's era we should recognise his encapsulation of parliamentary sovereignty for what it is; the view of one (admittedly influential) commentator that should be understood as a construct of its time. We have already seen that the constitution itself is something of a fluid concept that has shown itself able to develop. In order to achieve a full appreciation of the idea of parliamentary sovereignty, and its relevance in the contemporary constitution, we should appreciate that concept in the same light; as a foundational constitutional concept, but also as an idea that has been subject to development and modification over the course of time.

Sovereignty is therefore perhaps best understood, as Jennings noted, as an expression of the power relationships between courts and Parliament. The legal and political developments that have taken place since Dicey first wrote *An Introduction to the Study of the Law of the Constitution* have made those power relationships far more multi-faceted, and therefore far more complex, than Dicey's account of sovereignty would seem to acknowledge. The steady expansion of the role of the courts, the acceptance of international influences into our legal order, implementation of legislation designed to implement specific popular demands and the enactment of legislation which seeks to exercise a pervasive influence across statutory provisions whenever enacted, among other things, have all taken their toll on Dicey's monolithic view of legal sovereignty. For the contemporary reader, Dicey's rather one-dimensional account of sovereignty can only offer a partial account of the multidimensional relationships between the courts and Parliament. As a result, it has

---

[281] *Ibid.*, [104].
[282] *Ibid.*, [107].
[283] See Lord Neuberger, 'Who are the masters now?' Lord Alexander of Weedon Lecture, 6 April 2011; K. Ewing, 'Brexit and Parliamentary Sovereignty' (2017) 80(4) MLR 711.

become commonplace to read that sovereign power is now effectively divided between institutions.[284] As Lord Steyn suggested in Jackson, it remains the case that parliamentary sovereignty can be described as the '*general* principle of our constitution',[285] but our constitution is by no means as 'uncontrolled' as the notion of unlimited legislative power would suggest.[286] Sovereignty in the modern day constitution, Steyn argued, was effectively divided between Parliament, the devolved administrations and the courts.[287]

We noted at the beginning of this chapter that in order to achieve a full appreciation of the contemporary status of parliamentary sovereignty, that doctrine should be considered in parallel with the idea (or ideal) of the rule of law; at its most basic, the idea that government be conducted according to the requirements of the law. Dicey acknowledged that the rule of law existed in parallel with the notion of legal sovereignty, but on the orthodox account the latter was clearly in the ascendancy. The steady evolution of the idea of sovereignty has arguably seen the traditional emphasis on the unlimited legal power of Parliament slowly concede ground to the 'nascent idea that a democratic legislature cannot be above the law.'[288] The roots of this idea lie firmly in the constitutional principle to which we now turn – the rule of law.

Practice questions

1. Compare and contrast the views of parliamentary sovereignty as put forward by Dicey and Jennings. Which do you think is best reflected in the relevant case law?

2. '*Even in the light of the Supreme Court's* Miller *judgment, the precise implications of EU membership for the doctrine of parliamentary sovereignty remain uncertain.*'

   Discuss.

3. '*In its present state of evolution, the British system may be said to stand at an intermediate stage between parliamentary supremacy and constitutional supremacy.*'

   (*International Transport Roth GmbH v Secretary of State for the Home Department* [2002] EWCA Civ 158; [2003] QB 728, [71] (Laws LJ))

   Discuss.

Further reading

The classic work in this area is of course to be found in **A. V. Dicey**'s *Introduction to the Study of the Law of the Constitution* (Liberty Fund, 1982). A powerful alternative account is provided by Dicey's leading critic – and advocate of the new view of sovereignty – **W. Ivor Jennings** in *The Law and the Constitution* (4th edn) (University of London Press, 1952). Both perspectives are analysed in H. W. R. Wade's now classic article '**The Basis of Legal Sovereignty**' (**H. W. R. Wade, 'The Basis of Legal Sovereignty'** (1955) *Cambridge Law Journal* 172).

---

[284] See for instance C. J. S. Knight, 'Bi-Polar Sovereignty Restated' (2009) 68 CLJ 361.

[285] *Jackson* v *Attorney-General* [2005] UKHL 56; [2006] 1 AC 262, [102] (emphasis added).

[286] Ibid.

[287] Ibid.

[288] Sir John Laws, 'Illegality and the Problem of Jurisdiction' in M. Supperstone and J. Goudie (eds), *Judicial Review* (2nd edn) (Butterworths, 1997), [4.17].

Perhaps the most extensive treatment of sovereignty by a contemporary scholar is to be found in the work of **Jeffrey Goldsworthy.** His books *The Sovereignty of Parliament: History and Philosophy* (Clarendon Press, 1999) and *Parliamentary Sovereignty: Contemporary Debates* (CUP, 2010) combine to produce a detailed defence of the doctrine. Goldsworthy's work, however, should be contrasted with that of Trevor Allan who makes a powerful argument that the rule of law, and not the doctrine of sovereignty, should be regarded as the core value of the UK Constitution: **T. R. S. Allan,** *Law, Liberty and Justice: the Legal Foundations of UK Constitutionalism* (Clarendon Press, 1993).

The decision of the House of Lords in *Jackson* v *Attorney General* has been the subject of a number of academic articles and commentaries. Among the best are: **J. Jowell, 'Parliamentary Sovereignty under the New Constitutional Hypothesis'** [2006] PL 562 and **T. Mullen, 'Reflections on** *Jackson* v *Attorney General*: **Questioning Sovereignty'** (2007) 27 LS 1. The development of a hierarchy of constitutional and other statutes is critiqued in **F. Ahmed and A. Perry, 'Constitutional Statutes'** (2017) 37 OJLS 461 and provides the backdrop to Paul Craig's excellent analysis of the *HS2* decision (**P. Craig, 'Constitutionalising Constitutional Law:** *HS2* ' [2014] PL 373).

The relationship between sovereignty and the Human Rights Act 1998 is examined at length in **Alison Young's** *Parliamentary Sovereignty and the Human Rights Act* (Hart Publishing, 2009), and in **Nicholas Bamforth's** earlier – and shorter – **piece of the same name** ([1998] PL 572). The difficult boundary between judicial interpretation and legislation – and the constitutional implications of legislative review under the Human Rights Act 1998 – receive their most sustained coverage in **Aileen Kavanagh's,** *Constitutional Review under the UK Human Rights Act* (CUP, 2009).

The impact of European Union law in the *Factortame* era is examined through the perspective of Wade's 'revolutionary' thesis and T. R. S. Allan's 'evolutionary' account: **H. W. R. Wade, 'Sovereignty – Revolution or Evolution?'** (1996) 112 LQR 568; **T. R. S. Allan, 'Parliamentary Sovereignty: Law, Politics and Revolution'** (1997) 113 LQR 443. Unsurprisingly, Brexit and the *Miller* decisions have prompted a flurry of academic commentaries and critiques. The July 2017 issue of the *Modern Law Review* ((2017) 80(4) MLR) includes provoking analyses from **Thomas Poole, Jo Murkens, Keith Ewing and Nicholas Aroney. Mark Elliott's** essay, **'The Supreme Court's judgment in** *Miller*: **in search of constitutional principle'** ((2017) 76 CLJ 257), questions whether the decision – in the context of earlier decisions such as *HS2* – is defensible from the perspective of constitutional principle, finding it to veer between 'muscular but ill focused constitutional assertiveness and unwarranted activism' (259). A partial response to some of Elliott's arguments – and important discussion of the relationship between national and EU laws – can be found in **'***R (Miller)* v *Secretary of State for Exiting the European Union*: **Thriller or Vanilla?' by Alison Young** ((2017) 42 EL Rev 280).

Chapter 6
The rule of law

'A person may be said not to be in favour of the rule of law if he is critical of the Queen, the Commissioner of the Metropolitan Police, the Speaker of the House of Commons or Lord Denning . . . '

J. A. G. Griffith, 'The Political Constitution' (1979) 42 *Modern Law Review* 1, 15.

Chapter outline

The phrase 'rule of law' is used frequently in public debate, and is often relied upon for support by all sides in arguments over public policy. This chapter examines the nature of this disputed concept and assesses some of the most important interpretations of it. Assessing the value a system of government places upon the rule of law is vital to understanding the role of the courts within that system. The broader the conception of the rule of law which operates within a particular constitutional order, other factors notwithstanding, the more powerful the courts will be as constitutional actors. We must therefore place the rule of law in the context of other important concepts which form part of the UK Constitution, especially parliamentary sovereignty. Later chapters of this book will build upon this theoretical overview of the courts' role in upholding the rule of law by examining the day-to-day operation of the courts' judicial review jurisdiction.

Introduction

The rule of law is a concept without any universally accepted definition. Indeed, the term might be better thought of as representing a range of interlinked ideas rather than as a single concept. Confusion is inevitable when a jumble of distinct ideas are lumped together under a shared epithet, especially when commentators who subscribe to different conceptions of the rule of law frequently criticise each other for subverting the 'true' rule of law. This difficulty is highlighted by the legal academic J. A. G. Griffith in the quote which opens this chapter. When he claims that people are said to oppose the rule of law if they are 'critical of the Queen, the Commissioner of the Metropolitan Police, the Speaker of the House of Commons or Lord Denning',[1] he is not making a substantive claim about the content of the rule of law but decrying the frequently sloppy use of the term in public discourse. Such uses of the term 'rule of law' contribute 'nothing but an empty slogan to the course of debate'.[2] Sometimes the rule of law is used as an antonym for lawlessness,

---

[1] J. Griffith, 'The Political Constitution' (1979) 42 MLR 1, 15.
[2] K. Ewing and C. Gearty, *The Struggle for Civil Liberties* (OUP, 2000) p. 10.

implying that a society which is rule-bound respects the rule of law. As a constitutional idea, however, the rule of law does not exist to regulate the conduct of private individuals, but of government; public officials can only act on the basis of lawful authority.

Students therefore find themselves in the difficult position of having to separate purely rhetorical claims upon the rule of law from meaningful accounts of the concept and its implications for the UK Constitution. Furthermore, amid empty sloganeering and divergent accounts of what the rule of law *ought* to mean, students have to divine which conception of the rule of law best matches *current* practice within the UK's governance order and understand how that practice changes in the hands of individual judges. Those about to embark on the study of the rule of law should nonetheless take heart from Lord Bingham, the UK's senior Law Lord from 2000 to 2008, who candidly admitted in the preface to his book, *The Rule of Law,* that even at the end of his distinguished judicial career he continued to worry that although 'the expression was constantly on people's lips, I was not sure what it meant, and I was not sure that all those who used the expression knew what they meant either, or meant the same thing'.[3]

The rule of law's domain

Key issues

- The *rule of law* is not, of itself, a law. It is instead a contested constitutional concept, which different judges and commentators define in different ways in accordance with what they perceive to be its role and importance relative to other constitutional principles.

- A. V. Dicey was one of the first constitutional commentators to set out his vision of the rule of law. He regarded the rule of law as requiring little more than that the government be able to point to legal authority for its actions and that the government not receive special privileges in court.

- Later legal theorists, such as Lon Fuller, sought to expand on the basic requirement that government be able to identify *any* legal authority for its action, arguing that for laws to be legitimate they would have to possess particular qualities (like clarity and non-retroactivity).

- Other theorists have suggested that Fuller's efforts were insufficient, being directed towards the *form* and not the *substance* of laws. Ronald Dworkin suggested that legal systems must secure substantive goals, including respect for human rights, if they are to respect the rule of law. Marxist theorists go even further, suggesting that the rule of law should be employed to produce substantive equality between members of a society.

One label, many ideas

It may seem ironic that there is no accepted legal definition of the rule of law. But this is because, rather than being a *law* in itself, the rule of law is instead a political concept underpinning ideas of limited government and constitutionalism. The meaning of the term, as with all political concepts, is therefore open to debate. Different interpretations of the term that emerge from that debate may be embodied in particular aspects of a constitutional system, with different implications for the operation of government and the development and enforcement of the law.

---

[3] T. Bingham, *The Rule of Law* (Allen Lane, 2010) vii.

> ## Thinking Point . . .
>
> The courts have generally taken a dim view of vague claims based on nothing more than an invocation of the words 'rule of law', demonstrating that it is a principle which conditions how laws work, but not a law in its own right; *R (Howard League for Penal Reform)* v *Lord Chancellor* [2014] EWHC 709 (Admin), [53] (Cranston J).

(i) Dicey's account of the rule of law

As is so often the case, A. V. Dicey is credited with being the first person to recognise the significance of the rule of law in the UK Constitution. Of course, the idea of a government limited by the requirement that it point to lawful authority for its actions long predated Dicey.[4] In ancient Athens, for example, Aristotle argued that government officials should be obliged to point to lawful sources of their powers. Letting 'the law rule', he considered, would prevent arbitrary exercises of official power, whereas in the absence of law 'passion perverts the minds of rulers, even when they are the best of men'.[5] Dicey, however, was the first person to package some of the elements which we today associate with the rule of law under this title and to present it as the main counter-balance to parliamentary sovereignty within the UK Constitution.[6]

At well over a century's remove from the first edition of his *Introduction to the Study of the Law of the Constitution* in 1885, it is easy to envisage Dicey as a neutral commentator, and to regard his text as a faithful (if now dated) description of the UK Constitution. In reality, however, he wrote with the agenda of preserving the UK's Victorian governance order against change.[7] His agenda can be seen in two key tenets of his version of the rule of law. First, he considered that the principle required that any laws empowering public officials to act in a manner which affects the interests of private persons must be clear and specific:

> [N]o man is punishable or can be lawfully made to suffer in body or goods except for a distinct breach of law . . . In this sense the rule of law is contrasted with every system of government based on the exercise by persons in authority of wide, arbitrary or discretionary powers of constraint.[8]

This statement draws upon clause 39 of Magna Carta 1215, which provides (in modern English) that '[n]o freeman shall be taken, imprisoned, outlawed, banished or in any other way harmed except by the lawful judgment of his peers and by the law of the land'.[9] Indeed, the courts continue to draw inspiration from this provision.[10]

Second, Dicey believed that any law affecting relations between private persons and public officials must be administered by ordinary courts. He worried that specialist

---

[4] Ibid., 3–10.

[5] Aristotle, *The Politics* (Stephen Everson (ed.), CUP, 1988) 78 (Bk III, Ch. XVI, 1287a).

[6] See H. Arndt, 'The Origin of Dicey's Concept of the "Rule of Law"' (1957) 31 Australian LJ 117.

[7] See J. McEldowney, 'Dicey in Historical Perspective – a Review Essay' in J. McAuslan and J. McEldowney, *Law, Legitimacy and the Constitution* (Sweet & Maxwell, 1985) 39, 56.

[8] A. Dicey, *An Introduction to the Study of the Constitution* (8th edn, first published 1915, Liberty Fund, 1982) p. 110.

[9] Magna Carta 1215, clause 39.

[10] *R (Binyam Mohamed)* v *Secretary of State for Foreign and Commonwealth Affairs* [2008] EWHC (Admin) 2048; [2009] WLR 2579, [147] (Thomas LJ).

administrative law, in which tribunals dealt specifically with cases involving the state, might lead to such tribunals treating claims by government officials with undue leniency:

> We mean . . . when we speak of the 'rule of law' as a characteristic of our country, not only that with us no man is above the law, but . . . that here every man, whatever be his rank or condition, is subject to the ordinary law of the realm and amenable to the jurisdiction of the ordinary tribunals.[11]

Dicey believed that if he could embed these ideas at the centre of public debate on the UK's Constitution, then governments would not be able to introduce legislation proposing special tribunals or the granting of broad discretionary powers to ministers and government officials without provoking public outcry or even restrictive interpretation by the courts. But his rigid requirements could not be reconciled with the need for flexibility as the state expanded during the first half of the twentieth century to provide education, healthcare, old age pensions, benefit payments and social housing. As the welfare state developed, Parliament granted more powers to conduct these programmes to an expanding bureaucracy, supported by the very administrative tribunals which Dicey had so vigorously opposed. These developments faced vigorous opposition from some lawyers schooled in Dicey's views,[12] but Parliament continued to accept the need for new measures in these areas, and the courts accepted (as Dicey instructed) that a sovereign Parliament could make such laws.[13]

A new generation of legal theorists, led by Sir Ivor Jennings, therefore challenged Dicey's vision of the rule of law as outmoded. For these writers Dicey 'was concerned not with the clearing up of the nasty industrial sections of the towns, but with the liberty of the subject. In terms of powers, he was concerned with police powers, and not with other administrative powers'.[14] In short, they believed that Dicey's obsession with the supposed dangers of the discretionary powers of officials and specialist tribunals no longer reflected the reality of the UK Constitution. Even Dicey, in his later writings, recognised the failure of his efforts to constrain the discretionary powers of the executive using the rule of law. In 1915, when the UK government had assumed wide-ranging discretionary powers to enable it to conduct the First World War, he accepted that the 'ancient veneration' for his interpretation of the rule of law was in rapid decline.[15] New conceptions of the rule of law therefore emerged in the twentieth century to respond to the increasing complexity of governance in liberal democracies.

(ii) Modern conceptions of the rule of law

Philosophers have long questioned whether laws must be constrained by any inherent moral values if a legal system is to be legitimate. One school of thought holds that laws, of themselves, are neither good nor evil but simply rules by which society is organised to guide human conduct. This school is known as legal positivism and was particularly influential upon Dicey's thinking. Freed from some of Dicey's Victorian baggage, this 'thin'[16] conception of the rule

---

[11] A. Dicey, *An Introduction to the Study of the Constitution* (8th edn, first published 1915, Liberty Fund, 1982) p. 114.

[12] See, for example, Lord Hewart, *The New Despotism* (Ernest Benn, 1929).

[13] See J. Willis, 'Delegation of Legislative and Judicial Powers to Administrative Bodies: A Study of the Report of the Committee on Ministers' Powers' (1932) 18 Iowa LR 150.

[14] I. Jennings, *The Law and the Constitution* (5th edn, University of London Press, 1959) p. 311.

[15] A. Dicey, *An Introduction to the Study of the Constitution* (8th edn, first published 1915, Liberty Fund, 1982) lv.

[16] J. Goldsworthy, 'Legislative Sovereignty and the Rule of Law' in T. Campbell, K. Ewing and A. Tomkins (eds), *Sceptical Essays in Human Rights* (OUP, 2001) 61, 64–5.

of law could be usefully restated as a positivist ideal that public officials must point to a legal basis for their actions. After all, even Jennings acknowledged that Dicey's requirements remained important when applied to police powers (and by implication to fields of government action which can undermine important individual interests).

Thinking Point . . .

In Chapter 2, we examined Jeremy Bentham's clashes with William Blackstone over the nature of law and the role of judges. Bentham's writings provided much of the groundwork for Dicey's positivist approach to the rule of law. See above, pp. 37–8.

One difficulty which many theorists have with this account (we call it the 'core' rule of law) is that it recognises that a law can be valid even if its substance cannot be considered morally 'good'. In the light of the abuses of the powers of the state in the hands of Fascist and Communist regimes, theorists including Lon Fuller re-evaluated the rule of law. Fuller argued that all laws operative within a legal system must respect a range of formal qualities (like clarity of law, non-retroactivity of law and consistent application of law) if the system as a whole could be said to comply with the rule of law. He believed that respect for these formal qualities (which we bundle together as the 'extended' concept of the rule of law) would induce an 'inner morality' within a legal system.[17] They would prevent governments from abusing their power by arbitrarily interfering with the lives of individuals without lawful authority. Joseph Raz, however, was not so confident that such formal qualities would suffice to create a 'good' legal system:

> A non-democratic legal system, based on the denial of human rights, on extensive poverty, on racial segregation, sexual inequalities, and racial persecution may, in principle, conform to the requirements of the rule of law better than any of the legal systems of the more enlightened Western democracies . . .[18]

Simply because legislation is clear and applies to conduct which occurs after it comes into force does not prevent it from being a vehicle for repressive government. Much of the legislation promoting racial discrimination in apartheid-era South-Africa, for example, respected Fuller's criteria, but this did not make such laws morally justifiable. Raz therefore concluded that, whilst respect for the rule of law might be a necessary quality for the operation of a legitimate legal system, the rule of law did not hold all of the answers to whether a system was 'good'.

Under a third approach to the principle, some theorists went further than Fuller by attributing substantive, and not simply procedural, requirements to the concept of the rule of law. Whereas *procedural* values apply to the manner in which a law is made or an official decision is reached, *substantive* values constrain the outcomes of the decision- or law-making process (we therefore call this the 'substantive' rule of law). Writers such as Gustav Radbruch argued that positivist accounts of law had allowed the German legal system to be subverted to the Nazi's cause. He maintained that '[t]here are fundamental principles

---

[17] See L. Fuller, *The Inner Morality of Law* (2nd edn, YUP, 1969).
[18] J. Raz, *The Authority of Law* (OUP, 1979) p. 211.

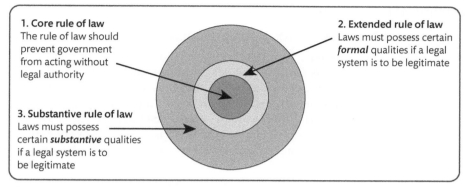

1. **Core rule of law**
The rule of law should prevent government from acting without legal authority

2. **Extended rule of law**
Laws must possess certain *formal* qualities if a legal system is to be legitimate

3. **Substantive rule of law**
Laws must possess certain **substantive** qualities if a legal system is to be legitimate

Figure 6.1 Different conceptions of the rule of law

of humanitarian morality which are part of the very concept of . . . Legality. Laws which transgress these principles for that reason lack legal character and should be denounced as such by judges and lawyers'.[19] Ronald Dworkin took up this challenge, asserting that, for a legal system to be legitimate legal rules within that system must respect values such as human rights.[20] Other substantive values have been coupled to the rule of law, from the protection of property interests[21] to the maintenance of state welfare provision.[22] This approach could provide a basis for judges, acting in the name of the rule of law, to deny legal effect to measures which undermined such requirements. Raz, unsurprisingly, repeated that the rule of law is not the only hallmark of a 'good' legal system, and that these approaches amounted to a 'perversion' of the concept.[23]

Since the mid-twentieth century, the UK Constitution has seen increasing competition between these different visions of the rule of law. The remainder of this chapter examines the relationship between these different approaches, as represented in Figure 6.1, and the degree to which each applies to the UK Constitution.

The core rule of law

Key issues

- A. V. Dicey proposed an account of the rule of law involving two key elements:

   1. Public officials and private actors are formally equal before the law;

   2. Public officials must never act without legal authority.

- Neither of these ideas was fully embedded in the UK's legal systems at the time of Dicey's writings, but such has been the influence of Dicey that constitutional actors have, over time, developed the constitution to better adhere to them.

- Today, these features are recognised as fundamental elements of a positivist account of the rule of law, but for many writers they amount to only the core of a broader concept.

---

[19] D. Dyzenhaus, *Hard Cases in Wicked Legal Systems: Pathologies of Legality* (2nd edn, OUP, 2010) p. 16.
[20] See R. Dworkin, *Taking Rights Seriously* (Duckworth, 1977) p. 46.
[21] See J. Waldron, *The Rule of Law and the Measure of Property* (CUP, 2012) p. 45.
[22] See M. Horwitz, 'The Rule of Law, an Unqualified Human Good?' (1977) 86 Yale LR 561, 566.
[23] J. Raz, *The Authority of Law* (OUP, 1979) p. 210.

Equality before the law

(i) No inherent privileges for public officials

At its heart, Dicey's conception of the rule of law was intended to ensure that public officials were accountable to the courts for their exercise of public functions: '[E]very official, from the Prime Minister down to the constable or collector of taxes, is under the same responsibility for every act done without legal justification as any other citizen'.[24] If government was able to isolate itself from the scrutiny of the courts which oversaw private legal relationships, Dicey feared that public officials would be able to abuse their powers. His writings therefore sought to embed the notion in English legal consciousness that relations between private legal persons were no different from relations between private individuals and public officials unless a law had granted some special power to the official.

The notion that official actors are not inherently special is reflected in a decision from the early 1980s, *Pedro* v *Diss*.[25] PC Diss was a police officer in plain clothes who, finding Ya Ya Pedro standing in a doorway, grabbed hold of him whilst attempting to establish whether it was his house. Pedro fought back, and was convicted of assaulting a police officer. Appealing against this conviction, however, Pedro asserted that PC Diss's attempt to detain him was illegal (as PC Diss had no reasonable basis for suspecting him of a criminal offence and the house belonged to his brother). The Court of Appeal granted this appeal, with Lord Lane CJ asserting that PC Diss's actions amounted to an illegal detention. As PC Diss therefore lacked legal authority for his actions, his status as a police officer did not warrant any special treatment by the courts.[26] In short, *Pedro* v *Diss* establishes that '[o]nce they go beyond their specified powers, the police have no special privileges'.[27] This decision accords with liberal-democratic understandings of the equal worth of individuals (encapsulated in the idea of 'one-person-one-vote' at elections, as we discussed in Chapter 2[28]). Indeed, in deciding a later case which required that police officers provide reasons to individuals before they would be able to lawfully arrest them, Sedley LJ rooted this requirement in the need for 'respect for the dignity of the individual'.[29] Unless there is a justification for the use of their special powers of arrest (a legal basis for acting), police officers are unable to interfere with other individuals.

In spite of such examples, Dicey was presenting an idealised view of the position of public authorities in the UK Constitution. As late as the 1990s government ministers continued to assert special privileges against being bound by court orders. In *M* v *Home Office*,[30] Home Office officials proceeded with the deportation of M, a Zairean asylum seeker, despite a High Court injunction ordering them not to do so. M's deportation in these circumstances was a mistake; the Home Office's legal representatives had misunderstood the High Court's direction. What happened next imbued the case with constitutional significance. Upon learning of M's deportation, Garland J ordered that he be returned to the UK immediately. The Home Office maintained that this ruling was not legally binding upon the Home Secretary and ignored the High Court. M's lawyers challenged this decision, arguing that attempts by government officials to ignore an injunction constituted a contempt of court.

---

[24] A. Dicey, *An Introduction to the Study of the Constitution* (8th edn, first published 1915, Indianapolis: Liberty Fund, 1982) p. 114.

[25] *Pedro* v *Diss* [1981] 2 All ER 59.

[26] Ibid., 64.

[27] J. Waldron, *The Law* (Routledge, 1990) p. 38.

[28] See above p. 25.

[29] *Taylor* v *Chief Constable of Thames Valley Police* [2004] EWCA Civ 858; [2004] 1 WLR 3155, [58].

[30] *M* v *Home Office* [1994] 1 AC 377.

> ## Thinking Point . . .
>
> Carol Harlow and Richard Rawlings conclude that the existence of such general Crown priv-ileges at the time of Dicey's writings on equality before the law 'somewhat undercut' his aspirations; C. Harlow and R. Rawlings, *Law and Administration* (CUP, 2009), p. 9.

The courts ultimately accepted that it was possible to issue binding injunctions against ministers (who could also be found in contempt of court). Lord Templeman explained this finding on the basis of the principle of equality before the law:

> [T]he argument that there is no power to enforce the law by injunction or contempt proceedings against a minister in his official capacity would, if upheld, establish the proposition that the execu-tive obey the law as a matter of grace and not as a matter of necessity, a proposition which would reverse the result of the Civil War.[31]

> ## Thinking Point . . .
>
> Lord Templeman is drawing upon the idea that the civil wars of the seventeenth century were fought (in part) to prevent assertions of absolute (i.e., legally unrestrained) authority by the monarchy. See Chapter 8, pp. 259–60.

The House of Lords' decision in *M* v *Home Office* therefore realised an important aspect of Dicey's principle of equality before the law as a presumption within the UK Constitution over 100 years after he had expounded the idea. As for M, soon after being returned he fled from Zaire for Nigeria. Thereafter neither the UK Government nor his legal repre-sentatives were able to trace his whereabouts.[32] Constitutional principles matter for indi-vidual lives.

(ii) Exceptional Privileges

Equality before the law is a *general* principle operative within the UK Constitution. None-theless, statutes have permitted qualifications to the principle's operation in relation to groups such as diplomats, judges and parliamentarians. This list is by no means comprehen-sive, for as we have seen all police constables are granted special powers in the performance of their duties. Nonetheless, the following examples serve to illustrate some justifications for departing from the general rule against special privileges.

A. Diplomatic immunity

One group controversially excluded from the operation of domestic law are diplomats. Diplomatic immunity is designed to protect diplomats being hounded by law enforcement officers in a host state or 'framed' for criminal offences. This provides an important pro-tection for British embassy staff operating in countries with tense relations with the UK. Diplomatic immunity is secured by an international treaty, the Vienna Convention on

---

[31] Ibid., 395.
[32] Ibid., 402.

Diplomatic Relations 1961, which was incorporated into domestic law in the UK under the Diplomatic Privileges Act 1964. Under this Act members of diplomatic missions and their family members are immune from prosecution, arrest or detention. Should a protected individual be accused of a criminal act, they can only be prosecuted if their own state agrees to a request from the UK Government that diplomatic immunity be waived. This has led to cases where some diplomats disregard domestic law with impunity, with examples ranging from unpaid fines for road traffic violations to incidents such as the Libyan Embassy shooting (when Libya refused to allow the UK to prosecute diplomats accused of shooting dead a police officer outside its London Embassy in 1984).[33] Diplomatic immunity therefore constitutes an exception to the operation of equality before the law which sometimes takes on great significance but which is accepted because of 'its practical utility'.[34] For as long as the UK dispatches its diplomats to countries with uneasy relations with the UK, this exception to the ordinary operation of equality before the law will be maintained.

B. Immunity relating to parliamentary proceedings

Members of Parliament enjoy various privileges which operate to protect parliamentary proceedings from interference. Many of these protections developed during the seventeenth century in response to efforts by the Stuart monarchs to constrain Parliament's freedom of action. Parliament polices abuses of these privileges for itself, excluding the jurisdiction of the ordinary courts. The most important of these privileges protects the ability of MPs to participate freely in parliamentary proceedings, and is enshrined in the Bill of Rights 1689: '[T]he Freedom of Speech and Debates or Proceedings in Parliament ought not to be impeached or questioned in any Court or Place out of Parliament'.[35] This privilege carries with it the risk of abuses of ordinary law. For example, MPs might make disclosures in Parliament which would constitute defamation or break the criminal law if spoken in any other forum. During House of Lords debates in 2006 Lord Campbell-Savours claimed false allegations by a woman, whom he named, had led to the imprisonment of a man for sexual assault for three years.[36] Had his actions not been covered by parliamentary privilege, this disclosure would have breached the criminal offence which shields the identity of people who report to the police that they have been subjected to a sexual offence.[37]

Thinking Point . . .

In 1641 King Charles I attempted to detain five members of the House of Commons for speaking out against him in Parliament, precipitating the civil wars of the 1640s. Episodes like this were of pivotal importance to the enactment of the protection contained within Bill of Rights 1688, Art. 9. See *Pepper* v *Hart* [1993] AC 593, 638 (Lord Browne-Wilkinson).

---

[33] See S. Sutton, 'Diplomatic Immunity and the siege of the Libyan People's Bureau' (1985) PL 193.
[34] J. Brown, 'Diplomatic immunity: state practice under the Vienna Convention on Diplomatic Relations' [1988] ICLQ 53, 54.
[35] Bill of Rights 1689, Art. 9.
[36] Lord Campbell Savours, HL Deb, vol. 685, col. 868 (19 October 2006). See also *R* v *Blackwell* [2006] EWCA Crim 2185.
[37] Sexual Offences (Amendment) Act 1992, s. 1.

Lord Campbell-Savours was highlighting what he saw as the unfairness involved in the law of complainant anonymity, and it might be argued that the Bill of Rights was designed to protect such freedom of debate. Even if he did not need to name the woman involved in the case to make his point, the publicity sparked by his decision to do so pushed government into reconsidering the law.[38] Other parliamentarians, however, have sought to rely on parliamentary privilege to protect them from prosecution for offences of false accounting relating to their parliamentary expense claims:

Key case

R v Chaytor [2010] UKSC 52; [2011] 1 AC 684 (Supreme Court)

Three former Labour MPs (David Chaytor, Elliot Morley and Jim Devine) and one Conservative peer (Lord Hanningfield) were charged with false accounting under section 17 of the Theft Act 1968 with regard to false parliamentary expenses claims (David Chaytor, the first named defendant, being charged with making claims for IT services which had not been supplied and rent payments which had never been made). All raised the issue, before their trial, of whether their actions were protected by parliamentary privilege rendering them immune to prosecution (being subject instead to the disciplinary jurisdiction of Parliament).

Having firstly recognised (at [14]) that the importance of the Bill of Rights' Article 9 'cannot be overestimated', the Court of Appeal examined the relationship between the principle of equality before the law and the exceptional privilege granted to Members of Parliament, with Lord Judge CJ asserting (at [42]) that:

> We are all equally subject to the law. It must be applied equally to every citizen, including members of Parliament. Any asserted immunities or exemptions against criminal proceedings asserted on their behalf must therefore be justified by reference to some further, over-arching principle, and they can only begin to come into contemplation in the context of the performance by Parliament of its core constitutional functions.

In the Supreme Court, Lord Phillips recognised (at [24]) that the key issue was 'whether business of this nature amounts to proceedings in Parliament, within the meaning of Article 9, or is otherwise privileged from scrutiny in the criminal courts because it falls within the exclusive cognisance or jurisdiction of Parliament'. Having identified that these were special privileges, the Supreme Court noted that Parliament had made no effort to assert the privileges on behalf of its members (see Lord Clarke, [131]). In other words, the privilege of immunity from prosecution was interpreted narrowly (in light of its purpose to protect parliamentary functions) so that it impinged upon the principle of equality before the law to the least degree possible. With the rejection of this defence, all four parliamentarians changed their pleas to guilty and were subsequently imprisoned.

C. Judicial immunity relating to court proceedings

The courts of England and Wales historically asserted that judicial independence required judges' absolute immunity from liability for actions in court. This principle was firmly established in the late nineteenth century, a time when judges, confronted by individuals representing themselves in court, feared that they would be at risk of defamation action if

---

[38] Lord Goldsmith, HL Deb, vol. 688, col. 109 (9 January 2007).

they criticised such individuals.[39] The leading case in the era was *Anderson* v *Gorrie*,[40] which arose after the claimant was imprisoned subject to onerous bail conditions by three judges of the Supreme Court of Trinidad and Tobago, headed by Sir John Gorrie. A report into these actions was highly critical of two of the three judges, resulting in one of them being dismissed. Not satisfied by being vindicated by this report, Anderson sought to recover damages before the English courts on the basis that these judges had maliciously abused their position. His claim was dismissed by the Court of Appeal, with Lord Esher MR concluding that 'no action lies for acts done or words spoken by a judge in the exercise of his judicial office, although his motive is malicious and the acts or words are not done or spoken in the honest exercise of his office'.[41] A judge acting in bad faith, he noted, could be removed from office by resolution of both Houses of Parliament. He justified this alternative to a right of civil action against judges on the basis that, 'if such an action would lie the judges would lose their independence, and that the absolute freedom and independence of the judges is necessary for the administration of justice'.[42]

Thinking Point . . .

Judicial immunities were eventually codified by statute, with the effect that under s. 32 of the Courts Act 2003 judges in lower courts do not enjoy immunity if they do not act in good faith or exceed their jurisdiction.

Later courts extended protections against civil action to cover 'all those directly taking part' in court proceedings.[43] As Lord Hoffmann recognised , '[t]he policy of this rule is to encourage persons who take part in court proceedings to express themselves freely', on the basis that the interests of justice would be undermined if individuals involved in a case feared that their statements could form the basis of a legal action against them.[44] Instead of being able to bring civil action against such individuals, different protections for the administration of justice exist in terms of offences like contempt of court. The courts have explicitly linked the maintenance of these immunities to the demands of the administration of justice (for example, removing immunity from negligence suits from advocates in the case of *Arthur J S Hall* v *Simons*).[45] As Lord Hope declared in that case, in a conclusion that applies to any of the privileges which we have examined in this section, '[a]ny immunity from suit is a derogation from a person's fundamental right of access to the court which has to be justified'.[46]

---

[39] See P. Polden, 'Doctor in Trouble: *Anderson* v *Gorrie* and the Extension of Judicial Immunity from Suit in the 1890s' (2001) 22 JLH 37.
[40] *Anderson* v *Gorrie* [1895] 1 QB 668.
[41] Ibid., 671.
[42] Ibid., 670.
[43] *Arthur J S Hall* v *Simons* [2002] 1 AC 615, 740 (Lord Hobhouse).
[44] Ibid., 697.
[45] Ibid., 697.
[46] Ibid., 710.

Government by law

(i) Government actions require authority

Dicey's writings assert that government must point to legal authority for its actions. He admitted that many of the laws in force in the UK in the 1800s were neither good nor lenient, in that they involved substantive infringements of individual liberties, especially if the individuals in question were poor, religious dissenters or political radicals. Nevertheless, he maintained that even in this era this requirement of the rule of law operated to restrict 'arbitrary power'.[47] The idea that public authorities cannot act in the absence of lawful authority is therefore the shoot from which the UK's public law has grown. As the economist Friedrich Hayek declared, this core principle makes it possible for a person 'to foresee with fair certainty how the authority will use its coercive powers in given circumstances, and to plan one's life accordingly'.[48]

These ideas did not originate with Dicey. As early as the seventeenth century the philosopher John Locke had recognised that when a constitutional order respects the requirement of government by law, this will carry benefits for both the government (by maintaining the legitimate basis by which they exercise authority) and private individuals (by constraining the exercise of government power).[49] Nonetheless, in order to establish that this conception of the rule of law was deep-rooted in the UK's legal systems, Dicey turned to case law which exemplified the courts' readiness to accept that exercises of power by public authorities needed to be justified by law and not simply by official claims that their actions were necessary. One of the most famous cases he identified as evidence for the respect for this principle was *Entick* v *Carrington,* still acclaimed as 'the most famous of all English civil liberties cases':[50]

Key case

Entick v *Carrington (1765) 19 St Tr 1029 (Court of Common Pleas)*

During a period when the UK Government faced popular unrest fomented by the radical John Wilkes, Parliament passed draconian legislation permitting government agents to raid premises given the issue of a 'general warrant'. John Entick was a London-based supporter of Wilkes, and his printing presses were used to produce pamphlets spreading Wilkes' opposition to government policy.

Entick's property was raided by government agents acting with the permission of a general warrant and his papers and printing equipment were removed. The time-limited legislation which permitted such warrants, however, had been allowed to lapse. Despite not having been convicted of any wrongdoing, Entick had lost his valuable papers and presses. He therefore brought an action for trespass against Nathan Carrington, one of the government agents who had raided his home.

---

[47] A. Dicey, *An Introduction to the Study of the Constitution* (8th edn, first published 1915, Liberty Fund, 1982) p. 111.

[48] F. Hayek, *The Road to Serfdom* (Routledge, 1944) p. 54.

[49] J. Locke, *Two Treatises of Civil Government* (first published 1690, Everyman's Library, 1961) Book II, Ch. IX, para. 137.

[50] K. Ewing and C. Gearty, *The Struggle for Civil Liberties* (OUP, 2000) p. 30.

Carrington raised the defence that ministerial authorisation for the raid was sufficient to make the raid legal, even in the absence of legislative authority, given the threat that radical activity posed to the state. Lord Camden CJ rejected this defence. He asserted (at 1066) that:

> By the laws of England, every invasion of private property, be it ever so minute, is a trespass. No man can set his foot upon my ground without my license, but he is liable to an action, though the damage be nothing; which is proved by every declaration in trespass, where the defendant is called upon to answer for bruising the grass and even treading upon the soil. If he admits the fact, he is bound to show by way of justification, that some positive law has empowered or excused him.

Lord Camden concluded that such an exorbitant exercise of state power required clear justification under common law or statute. As Carrington could point to no such lawful basis for his actions, the Court awarded Entick substantial damages.

Entick v *Carrington* continues to be cited as 'a ringing endorsement of the rule of law and of the system of democratic government' and as authority for the proposition that '[t]he executive cannot simply assert interests of state or the public interest and rely upon that as a justification for the commission of wrongs'.[51] Government by law, however, is such a narrow concept that ministers eventually became adept at circumventing it.

(ii) The limitations of government by law

The idea that requiring the government to identify legal authority for its actions will prevent the government from acting in excess of its powers has two major weaknesses. Firstly, officials may be able to rely upon statutes which provide it with broad discretionary authority to satisfy the requirement of lawful authority. Secondly, individuals subject to unauthorised government action have to be able to show that their legally protected interests have been affected in order to gain a remedy before the courts. The ability of the public authorities to rely on legislation which provides for very broad powers was highlighted in the case of *ex parte Rossminster*:

Key case

R v *Inland Revenue Commissioners, ex parte Rossminster [1980] AC 952 (House of Lords)*

The Inland Revenue Commissioners (IRC) raided the premises of Rossminster Ltd without offering explanation and seized documents. The raid was conducted under section 20C of the Taxes Management Act 1970, which permitted the IRC to conduct searches of property and seize and remove anything found there which they believed may be required as evidence of tax frauds without having to specify the nature of the offence or the perpetrator (provided that a warrant had been obtained from a Circuit Court Judge).

---

[51] *Bici* v *Ministry of Defence* [2004] EWHC 786 (QB), [86] (Elias J). See also T. Endicott, 'Was *Entick* v *Carrington* a landmark?' in A. Tomkins and P. Scott (eds), *Entick* v *Carrington: 250 Years of the Rule of Law* (Hart, 2015) p. 109.

In the Court of Appeal Lord Denning accepted that 'government under the law' required that such a power be used specifically and did not allow officials to conduct a random trawl through all documentation. Permitting the actions of the Revenue under a general reading of the legislation would allow it to be used as an 'instrument of oppression' in some hands and would be incompatible with contemporary moral standards. He concluded that (at 972):

> Once great power is granted, there is a danger of it being abused. Rather than risk such abuse, it is, as I see it, the duty of the courts so to construe the statute as to see that it encroaches as little as possible upon the liberties of the people of England.

The House of Lords reversed this decision, even though it accepted (as Lord Scarman acknowledged at 1022) that this power constituted 'a breath-taking inroad upon the individual's right of privacy and right of property'. He rejected comparisons to *Entick* v *Carrington*, with the case turning on whether the Taxes Management Act 1970 authorised the IRC's behaviour:

> The positive law relied on in this case is the statute. If the requirements of the statute have been met, there is justification [for the IRC's actions]: but, if they have not, there is none.

Lord Wilberforce concluded that the minimal requirements of the statute had been met and that the courts had no duty or power to impede the working of legislation (at 998):

> [W]hile the courts may look critically at legislation which impairs the rights of citizens and should resolve any doubt in interpretation in their favour, it is no part of their duty, or power, to restrict or impede the working of legislation, even of unpopular legislation; to do so would be to weaken rather than to advance the democratic process.

The *Rossminster* decision demonstrated what many public officials had long known, that central government could mitigate the impact of the restriction imposed on its actions by the principle of government by law by pushing legislation through Parliament which allowed for broad discretionary powers. Such legislation remains common. For example, Parliament granted government with broad powers to slaughter infected livestock under the Animal Health Act 1981. In 2001, when foot and mouth disease ravaged the UK's livestock herds, the government used its powers under the 1981 Act to slaughter over a million infected animals. The Dixons were dairy farmers who lost their animals. The government used some of their land to burn the infected carcasses of their slaughtered animals, but refused to compensate the Dixons for this use of their land on the basis that the 1981 Act granted it broad powers for the disposal of carcases without providing for compensation for land use.[52] The High Court dismissed the Dixons' claim that this action was unlawful: 'The regulatory and other constraints imposed under the 1981 Act are very broad and a conclusion as to necessity and what is necessary and what is reasonably incidental must be made in the light of the overall structure of the Act'.[53] In such cases government by law as implemented does not, therefore, appear to impose any requirements of quality upon the law. It simply requires that the public authority be able to point to some positive law which authorises its actions.

---

[52] Animal Health Act 1981, s. 34(4).
[53] *R (Dixon)* v *Secretary of State for the Environment, Food and Rural Affairs* [2002] EWHC 831 (Admin), [19] (Jack Beatson QC).

Thinking Point . . .

Although some cases continue to turn on the issue of whether any authority exists for a legal action (see, for example, *Egan* v *Basildon Borough Council* [2011] EWHC 2416 (QB), [69]–[70] (Edwards-Stuart J)), if this marked the extent of the rule of law's requirements then the concept will often have little practical impact.

A further issue constrained the operation of the rule of law within the UK Constitution for much of the twentieth century. The Diceyan conception of the rule of law does not require that public authorities identify positive law which authorises all of their actions, but only for their actions which infringe recognised private interests. In *Entick* v *Carrington*, Ewing and Gearty argue, 'personal liberty was protected because of the happy coincidence of personal interests and property rights'.[54] Although Dicey was once willing to trust the courts to identify relevant interests of individuals which were worthy of protection,[55] the courts subsequently struggled to recognise important personal interests, like a right to privacy, as having such legal value. Cases such as *Malone* v *Metropolitan Police Commissioner* called into question the notion that the courts would be alive to the need to identify private interests worthy of legal protection (at least without Parliament's approval for doing so):

Key case

Malone v *Metropolitan Police Commissioner [1979] Ch 344 (High Court, Chancery Division)*

The claimant, an antiques dealer, was charged with handling stolen property. During the trial it emerged that the applicant's telephone had been tapped by the police (acting on the authority of a warrant issued by the Home Secretary). Following his acquittal of the criminal charges, Mr Malone brought civil proceedings, seeking to establish that the tapping of his telephone had been unlawful on the basis that the government enjoyed no statutory or common law authority permitting it to carry out this type of surveillance.

Megarry V-C acknowledged that there was very little authority on the issue of the legality of phone tapping in English law (at 356):

It was common ground that there was no English authority that in any way directly bore on the point. The only English authorities that could be adduced related to arguments for and against the right not to be tapped that the plaintiff claimed for his telephone lines, but did not decide it. The absence of any authority on the point is something that has to be borne in mind; but it certainly does not establish that no such right exists.

He proceeded, however, to rule that the lack of positive law governing the tapping of phones meant that there was nothing to restrain the government in this activity (at 357):

[A]part from certain limited statutory provisions, there was nothing to make governmental telephone tapping illegal; and the statutory provisions of themselves assume that such tapping is not in other respects illegal. That being so, there is no general right to immunity from such tapping.

---

[54] K. Ewing and C. Gearty, *The Struggle for Civil Liberties*, (Oxford: OUP, 2000) p. 30.
[55] A. Dicey, *An Introduction to the Study of the Constitution* (8th edn, first published 1915, Liberty Fund, 1982) p. 115.

England, it may be said, is not a country where everything is forbidden except what is expressly permitted: it is a country where everything is permitted except what is expressly forbidden.

He distinguished this case from cases, such as *Entick* v *Carrington,* which involved physical searches of a property (at 369):

The reason why a search of premises which is not authorised by law is illegal is that it involves the tort of trespass to those premises: and any trespass, whether to land or goods or the person, that is made without legal authority is prima facie illegal. Telephone tapping by the Post Office, on the other hand, involves no act of trespass.

Having recognised that trespass did not protect Mr Malone's interest, Megarry V-C refused to recognise an actionable right to privacy in its stead on the basis (at 372) that 'it is no function of the courts to legislate in a new field'.

Malone evidences the severe limitations of government by law when the courts refuse to recognise interests infringed by unauthorised government activities as being legally action-able. It appeared that, if a claimant could not identify a legally recognised right which has been infringed by the government, judges following the lead of Megarry V-C would not properly evaluate whether officials could point to authority for their actions. A major shift in legal culture would be required if the rule of law was to be restored to centre-stage within the UK Constitution.

Tackling the limitations of the core rule of law

(i) Re-evaluating equality before the law

One problem, at the heart of cases such as *Malone* v *Metropolitan Police Commissioner,* was the failure of the courts to approach the idea of equality before the law as requiring that activities performed by public authorities should not ordinarily be beyond the authority of the courts. Instead, Megarry V-C seemed to treat equality before the law as a rule by which the courts should treat public authorities in the same way as private individuals. This approach undermined the core rule of law's requirement that the government must identify legal authority for its actions, requiring instead that affected individuals be able to establish that the officials had broken a particular law. Government, in spite of all its power, would be no more subject to restrictions as to the use of that power than private individuals.

Nonetheless, it is difficult to place the blame for this misapplication of the principle of equality before the law solely at the feet of Megarry V-C. A judiciary heavily schooled in Dicey was simply repeating some of the flawed elements in his own writings in a way which undermined his conception of the rule of law. As Dicey insisted, '[a] colonial governor, a secretary of state, a military officer, and all subordinates, though carrying out the com-mands of their official superiors, are as responsible for any act which the law does not authorise *as is any private and unofficial person*'.[56] This passage conflates private individuals with public officials, stating that both must point to legal authority for any of their actions. This is the opposite conclusion to that reached by Megarry V-C in *Malone* (that both private persons and public authorities were merely obliged to avoid breaching any laws).

---

[56] Ibid., p. 114 (emphasis added).

But both approaches commit the fundamental mistake of treating private and public bodies in the same way. Only when the courts confronted such mistakes could the damage done to the rule of law by decisions such as *Malone* be repaired. Not long after the decision in *M* v *Home Office,* Sir John Laws restated the requirements of equality before the law:

> Public bodies and private persons are both subject to the rule of law; nothing could be more elementary. But the principles which govern their relationships with the law are wholly different. For private persons, the rule is that you may do anything you choose which the law does not prohibit . . . But for public bodies the rule is opposite, and so of another character altogether. It is that any action to be taken must be justified by positive law.[57]

The virtue of this approach is that it shifts the attention away from the issue of the affected interests of the private individual (which is arguably more relevant to the question of the remedies available to the individual whose interests are affected by the state) and returns the focus to whether the public authority can point to some source of lawful authority for its actions.

(ii) Judicial identification of private interests

Malone also spurred arguments for incorporating the European Convention of Human Rights (ECHR) into the UK's domestic legal systems in order to counter the common law's limitations as a defence of important individual interests. Many commentators regarded the passage of the Human Rights Act (HRA) 1998 as supporting the rule of law by enumerating the interests that the courts were obliged to protect. Whilst later chapters will be devoted to this topic, consider for now the outcome when, having lost his claim before the English courts, Mr Malone took his case to the European Court of Human Rights. There he claimed that the laws regarding phone tapping did not adequately protect the right to privacy he supposedly enjoyed under Article 8 ECHR.[58] The Strasbourg Court found that this interest had been infringed, because 'telephone conversations are covered by the notions of "private life" and "correspondence" within the meaning of Article 8', making up for the deficiency of the common law.[59] Phone tapping was deemed a contravention of Article 8 in this case on the basis that domestic law failed to limit the power and therefore did not provide 'the minimum degree of legal protection to which citizens are entitled under the rule of law in a democratic society'.[60] *Malone* helped to reset how the UK courts approached the requirement that officials act on the basis of lawful authority. Looking back at the case in a lecture in the late 1990s, Sir Stephen Sedley marvelled at how, little over a decade earlier, the common law had 'dumbly accepted' official phone tapping in the absence of such authority.[61]

Thinking Point . . .

If *Entick* v *Carrington* is regarded narrowly as a defence of property interests then it makes sense that Megarry V-C would approach *Malone* differently, when no such interests were at stake in that case; P. Scott, '*Entick* v *Carrington* and the Legal Protection of Property' in A. Tomkins and P. Scott (eds), *Entick* v *Carrington: 250 Years of the Rule of Law* (Hart, 2015) 131, 133.

---

[57] *R* v *Somerset County Council, ex parte Fewings* [1995] 1 All ER 513, 524.
[58] *Malone* v *UK* (1985) 7 EHRR 14.
[59] Ibid., [64].
[60] Ibid., [79].
[61] S. Sedley, *Freedom, Law and Justice* (London: Sweet & Maxwell, 1999) 11. See also *Wood* v *Commissioner of Police for the Metropolis* [2009] EWCA Civ 414; [2010] WLR 123, [21] (Laws LJ).

The continued significance of the core rule of law

Many writers conclude that the core rule of law envisages a very restricted role for the courts within the UK Constitution, by which they simply police the existence of legal authority for actions by public officials and endeavour to maintain equality of treatment between individuals and the state in the administration of justice. If these aspirations are limited, they are, at least, relatively uncontroversial. Even the Marxist historian E. P. Thompson declared that, 'the inhibitions upon power imposed by law seem to me . . . a true and important cultural achievement'.[62] In reaching this conclusion, Thompson regarded the rule of law in its core sense as being necessary to prevent rulers from exercising their power by arbitrary discretion.[63] Useful though this conception of the rule of law may be, however, it does not require that laws promulgated be *good* laws (embodying characteristics which would be considered at least desirable in a liberal democracy such as respect for human rights). The core rule of law is therefore not a particularly inspiring prospect. The former East German dissident Bärbel Bohley spoke for many who had resisted Communist rule in East Germany when she concluded after the fall of the Berlin Wall that '[we] wanted justice but we got the rule of law instead'.[64] She was not arguing that transposing a legal order embodying the core rule of law was not an improvement upon a Communist legal system which had not respected the idea of government by law, but nonetheless found this to be something of an anti-climax when compared to the hopes of those who had opposed the East German regime. And yet, despite this lack of excitement, Adam Tomkins maintains that the core rule of law is what, 'as a matter of British constitutional law, is what is meant by "the rule of law"'.[65] Tomkins maintains that conceptions of the rule of law which go beyond this core are not established features of the UK Constitution. To evaluate this claim, we have to consider how others have sought to broaden the rule of law, and how the UK's institutions of government have engaged with their ideas.

The extended rule of law

Key issues

Some theorists argue that Dicey's vision of the rule of law, whilst important, was too limited in its scope to ensure that a legal system would be 'good'. They proposed extending the rule of law to protect a range of important considerations covering the manner in which laws operate and the legal system they operate within. This sub-topic will address some of these extensions to the rule of law:

1. Laws should not be retroactive but should only apply to conduct from the date of their enactment.
2. Laws must be sufficiently clear and stable to guide conduct, allowing individuals to adapt their conduct to ensure compliance with the law.

→

---

[62] E. Thompson, *Whigs and Hunters* (Pantheon, 1975) p. 265.
[63] See D. Cole, '"An Unqualified Human Good": E.P. Thompson and the Rule of Law' [2001] 28 JLS 177.
[64] See J. Elster (ed), *Retribution and Reparation in the Transition to Democracy* (CUP, 2006) p. 11.
[65] A. Tomkins, 'The Role of the Courts in the Political Constitution' (2010) 60 UTLJ 1, 7.

3. The legal system must be operated in a fair manner, allowing all individuals whose legal interests are threatened access to appropriate tribunals and requiring all officials involved in a legal system (not simply judges, but also police and prosecutors) to exercise their discretions fairly.

Theorists supporting these aims, however, disagree as to whether they should be mandatory or simply desirable features of a legal system.

Government under the law

By the late twentieth century the core rule of law had been swamped by the weight of the executive discretion required to manage the welfare state. Statutes which granted broad discretion to public officials, like the Taxes Management Act 1970, which we examined in the context of *ex parte Rossminster* above,[66] provided sufficient authority for official searches of premises to satisfy the requirements of the core rule of law despite the fact that it imposed no meaningful safeguards against abuses of power. Lon Fuller responded to this challenge by reconsidering the underlying principle of the rule of law.[67] He argued that for a measure to accord with the rule of law, it would have to exhibit certain qualities. Extending the 'core' rule of law, Fuller suggested that the validity of a law may be called into question if it did not display these qualities, which largely concerned the operation of a particular measure rather than its substance. Although theorists differ in the exact qualities they believe are required for a legal order to respect the extended rule of law, over the following pages we are going to examine some of Fuller's key requirements: that laws should be prospective and not retroactive, should be general in their operation, should be sufficiently clear and stable to guide conduct and should be subject to a consistent and impartial system of justice. In assessing whether the UK Constitution conforms to the extended rule of law we must consider whether Parliament has respected these requirements in its law making and whether judges have been willing to uphold these requirements in their interpretation of statutes.

Non-retroactivity of law

(i) Non-retroactivity and legislation

One of the more uncontroversial principles that proponents of an extended rule of law advance is that law should not be retroactive in its operation. If Parliament passed a law in 2012 which introduced a criminal offence banning smoking in public places, and stating that the offence would apply to any instance of such behaviour from 2005 onwards, this would provide an example of a law taking retroactive effect. Retroactively enacting legislation to change the lawfulness of an activity that has already occurred is anathema to the idea that law exists to guide conduct. Such laws prevent people from knowing whether their activity is legal or not.

The courts have therefore developed long-standing interpretive presumptions against legislation having this effect. In 1865 unrest erupted at Morant Bay in Jamaica, then a UK

---

[66] See above, pp. 194–5.
[67] L. Fuller, *The Inner Morality of Law* (2nd edn, YUP, 1969).

colony. Governor Eyre declared martial law in the area affected by the 'rebellion', allowing suspension of the ordinary criminal justice process and the trial of captured individuals by military justice. Under martial law, Eyre ordered the arrest and extra-judicial killing of hundreds, even rounding up political opponents from areas of the island not affected by the rebellion and transporting them to areas where martial law applied. At the end of his term as governor he arranged for the island's legislature to pass an Indemnity Act, prohibiting legal challenges to these actions. Appalled by this apparent abuse of power, prominent individuals instituted a private prosecution on Governor Eyre's return to the UK.[68] In his judgment in *Phillips* v *Eyre*, Willes J stated that '[t]he general principle of legislation by which the conduct of mankind is to be regulated ought to deal with future acts and ought not to change the character of past transactions carried on upon the faith of the then existing law'.[69] He nonetheless accepted that retrospective legislation may be justified in circumstances where other important public interests were at stake and concluded that the rebellion had demanded 'prompt and speedy action for the maintenance of law and order', even if such actions exceeded the Governor's powers.[70] The validity of the Indemnity Act was therefore upheld, and because it indemnified Eyre's actions in Jamaica they could not be actionable in English courts. Although the prosecution failed, the injustice of Indemnity Acts highlighted by this case contributed to the reluctance of later governments to employ them following emergency situations.

Later cases have, however, provided further examples of circumstances in which Parliament is willing to flout this principle and retroactively alter the law. During 1942, at the height of the Second World War, retreating UK Armed Forces, acting under prerogative powers,[71] destroyed a Burmah Oil refinery to prevent it falling into the hands of Japanese forces. After the war, the company received an *ex gratia* payment of less than a sixth of the value of the refinery as compensation. The company brought an action seeking the full value of the refinery, on the basis that the prerogative power was exercisable only on the basis of the payment of full compensation. The courts found in favour of Burmah Oil,[72] but this was to prove a pyrrhic victory. Alarmed by the potential liabilities for similar claims, Parliament passed the War Damages Act 1965, preventing not only claims for *future* damage caused by the armed forces but also claims *for damage that had already occurred*. Thus, having won its case, Burmah Oil was deprived of its victory by retrospective legislation.

Controversial Acts of Parliament continue to push at the boundaries of what constitutes non-retroactivity and the appellate courts have hitherto respected the validity of such legislation. Under the 2010–15 Coalition Government the Department for Work and Pensions introduced a scheme whereby jobseekers would have to undertake work for private employers to be able to access unemployment benefits.[73] Two affected individuals brought a legal action which successfully challenged the legality of benefit deductions imposed for refusal to participate in this scheme.[74] Even before this litigation had concluded, however, Parliament enacted the Jobseekers (Back to Work Schemes) Act 2013 to retrospectively validate the withholding of benefits under the impugned regulations. This statute was

---

[68] *Phillips* v *Eyre* (1870) LR 6 QB 1.
[69] Ibid., 23.
[70] Ibid., 16.
[71] See above pp. 34–7.
[72] *Burmah Oil* v *Lord Advocate* [1965] AC 75.
[73] Jobseeker's Allowance (Employment, Skills and Enterprise Scheme) Regulations 2011.
[74] *R (Reilly & Wilson)* v *The Secretary of State for Work and Pensions* [2013] UKSC 68; [2013] 3 WLR 1276.

immediately challenged as an affront to the rule of law. In her High Court decision Lang J accepted this challenge:

> Parliament's undoubted power to legislate to overrule the effect of court judgments generally ought not to take the form of retrospective legislation designed to favour the Executive in ongoing litigation in the courts brought against it by one of its citizens, unless there are compelling reasons to do so. Otherwise it is likely to offend a citizen's sense of fair play.[75]

Although this analysis has since been upheld by the Court of Appeal the existence of a clearly worded statute limited the remedy available to the claimants to a declaration of incompatibility recognising the breach of their right to a fair hearing.[76] The claimants have not been able to recover their lost benefits.

The courts exercise particular caution in relation to retroactive criminal law, with Lord Reid declaring in *Waddington* v *Miah*[77] that 'it is hardly credible that any government department would promote, or that Parliament would pass, retrospective criminal legislation'.[78] This common law principle is supported by Article 7(1) of the ECHR, which requires that '[n]o one shall be held guilty of any criminal offence on account of any act or omission which did not constitute a criminal offence under national or international law at the time when it was committed.'

(ii) Non-retroactivity and the common law

The principle of non-retroactivity seems like a simple one, whereby it is presumed that no law should alter the legality of an act after its occurrence (a presumption with particular force if such a law seeks to reclassify a past act as criminal). A problem arises, however, in reconciling this principle with the operation of a common law legal system. When judges change the existing interpretation of a law such an alteration would appear to have retroactive implications for the parties engaged in the case. Judges have therefore, in certain cases, stayed the retroactive effect of their decisions,[79] with the Supreme Court recognising that '[t]here are now a considerable number of dicta to the effect that the court has a general inherent power to limit the retrospective effect of its decisions'.[80] Where they refuse to do so the implications can be particularly serious in cases involving the alteration of some aspect of criminal law, as evidenced by the case of *R* v *R* early in the 1990s.[81]

A woman left her husband intending to divorce him, but whilst she was staying with her parents he forced his way into their home and attempted to rape her. He was convicted, but appealed on the basis of a common law exception to the offence of rape, whereby 'the husband cannot be guilty of rape committed by himself upon his lawful wife [as she has]

---

[75] *R (Reilly & Hewstone)* v *Secretary of State for Work and Pensions* [2014] EWHC 2182 (Admin), [83] (Lang J).

[76] *R (Reilly & Hewstone)* v *Secretary of State for Work and Pensions* [2016] EWCA Civ 413; [2016] 3 WLR 1641, [99].

[77] *Waddington* v *Miah* [1974] 2 All ER 377.

[78] Ibid., 379.

[79] See Lord Rodger, 'A Time for Everything under the Law: Some Reflections on Retrospectivity' (2005) 121 LQR 57, 77.

[80] *Cadder* v *Her Majesty's Advocate* [2010] UKSC 43, [58] (Lord Hope).

[81] *R* v *R* [1992] 1 AC 599.

given herself up in this kind'.[82] In support of his contention that this exception remained in force, the husband asserted that the statutory definition at the time of his actions described rape as 'having *unlawful* intercourse with a woman without her consent'.[83] He argued that this provision implied that an exceptional type of lawful non-consensual intercourse existed, and that this applied to his conduct.

The appellate courts dismissed these arguments. Having asserted that the wording of the Sexual Offences Act (Amendment) was inconsequential (the word unlawful being 'mere surplusage'[84]), Lord Keith asserting that the common law had moved on from the era in which a marital exemption to rape had been acceptable:

> The common law is . . . capable of evolving in the light of changing social, economic and cultural developments. [The marital exemption] reflected the state of affairs in these respects at the time it was enunciated. Since then the status of women, and particularly of married women, has changed out of all recognition . . .[85]

Whilst the desirability of this outcome is impossible to dispute, the House of Lords spent rather less time addressing the issue of whether they had retro actively changed the criminal law to achieve the desired result. To answer this charge, the Law Lords referred back to the decision of Lord Lane CJ in the Court of Appeal, who ruled that '[t]his is not the creation of a new offence, it is the removal of a common law fiction which has become anachronistic and offensive and . . . it is our duty having reached that conclusion to act upon it'.[86]

This outcome did not, however, dissuade the convicted husband from applying to the European Court of Human Rights on the basis that the interpretation adopted by the House of Lords amounted to a retroactive extension of the criminal law. The European Court agreed with the UK courts that the development of the common law did not amount to retroactive criminal law-making, prohibited under Article 7 ECHR, but was in this case '*a reasonably foreseeable development of the law*'.[87] The court's emphasis of whether the development of the common law was foreseeable 'with appropriate legal advice'[88] did not, however, conclude litigation on the supposed 'marital rape' exemption. Instead, in the case of *R v C*,[89] a husband who in 2002 was convicted of raping his wife whilst they were married (between 1967 and 1971) claimed that his prosecution in these circumstances constituted an abuse of process. The Court of Appeal rejected his appeal, ruling that '[t]his appellant knew perfectly well that to rape his wife was wrong, and that his marriage certificate did not entitle him to force his unwanted sexual attentions on her, nor did he suggest that he believed that he would be immune from prosecution if he did so'.[90]

This assertion, and indeed this line of authorities, sees the courts grappling to reconcile their decisions with the principle of non-retroactivity. When the House of Lords decided *R v R* on the basis that the common law kept pace with social change, the Law Lords essentially ruled that, although no previous case had reported this development, the

---

[82] M. Hale, *History of the Pleas of the Crown* (1st edn, 1736).

[83] Sexual Offences (Amendment) Act 1976, s. 1.

[84] *R v R* [1992] 1 AC 599, 623 (Lord Keith).

[85] Ibid., 616.

[86] Ibid., 611.

[87] *SW & CR v UK* (1996) 21 EHRR 363, 402.

[88] Ibid., 401.

[89] *R v C* [2004] EWCA Crim 292.

[90] Ibid., [26] (Judge LJ).

marital rape exemption had already lapsed by the time of this offence. The case itself, as Judge LJ insisted above, merely marked the moment when a fiction was 'finally dissipated'. We must nonetheless accept that judges do alter the law by their decisions and that these decisions have retroactive effect for not simply the parties involved (like the defendant in *R v R*) but also for other individuals to whom the law applies (like the defendant in *R v C*). Non-retroactivity is not, therefore, an absolute value to be protected within a legal system. Some forays into retroactivity are acceptable dependent upon the nature of the case and the degree of uncertainty or upheaval produced (the 'reasonably foreseeability' test).

Thinking Point . . .

The identities of the defendants in *R v R* and *R v C* were concealed not to protect them but to protect, under section 1 of the Sexual Offences (Amendment) Act 1992, complainants who shared their surnames.

Clarity and stability of law

A second guiding precept of the extended rule of law is that laws must be sufficiently clear to guide conduct, especially where they carry criminal penalties for their breach. In common with the presumption against retroactivity, Fuller maintained that individuals must be able to ascertain their legal rights and obligations at any given time in order for the law to guide their conduct. In this regard, a law which is unclear in its effect can dissuade individuals from certain activities out of fear that they may be unlawful (having what is often described as a 'chilling effect' upon such conduct).

One overarching problem in this regard is the sheer complexity of the system of laws in operation in the UK's legal systems, which can render it very difficult for individuals to ascertain their liabilities even with appropriate legal advice. This problem is exemplified by the case of *R v Chambers,* in which the defendant was convicted of evading customs duty on imports. However, just before judgment was to be handed down against him on appeal, it was discovered that the regulations he was convicted under had been replaced by new statutory instruments, under which he was not guilty. Toulson LJ acknowledged the systemic issue raised by this case:

> It is a maxim that ignorance of the law is no excuse, but it is profoundly unsatisfactory if the law itself is not practically accessible. To a worryingly large extent, statutory law is not practically accessible today, even to the courts whose constitutional duty it is to interpret and enforce it.[91]

He identified the reason for this threat to the viability of the legal system as lying in the volume of legislation (much of it secondary legislation) over recent decades and the fact that the law regarding many subjects existed as a 'patchwork' of primary legislation, secondary legislation and case law, resulting in an unsatisfactory situation in which 'the courts are in many cases unable to discover what the law is, or was at the date with which the court is concerned, and are entirely dependent on the parties for being able to inform them what were the relevant statutory provisions which the court has to apply'.[92]

---

[91] *R v Chambers* [2008] EWCA Crim 246, [64].
[92] Ibid., [64].

The ongoing failure of governments to consolidate the law affecting particular issues means that cases like *Chambers* are unlikely to constitute isolated aberrations, because, as Lord Bingham concluded, '[i]t seems that legislative hyperactivity has become a permanent feature of our governance'.[93] There is every indication, however, that the courts will not back down under this principle, particularly where criminal offences are at issue. As Baroness Hale has recognised:

> [A] major objective of the criminal law is to warn people that if they behave in a way which it prohibits they are liable to prosecution and punishment. People need and are entitled to be warned in advance so that, if they are of a law-abiding persuasion, they can behave accordingly.[94]

The general common law principle requiring clarity of law has received powerful reinforcement since the UK joined the ECHR. In cases such as *Sunday Times* v *UK*,[95] the European Court of Human Rights has been willing to find entire areas of law (in this case the law of contempt of court) insufficiently clear to guide conduct. In this case the newspaper was prevented by the then Attorney-General from publishing a series of articles regarding the side-effects of the drug thalidomide on unborn foetuses, on the basis that individuals affected by the drug were at the time seeking compensation before the courts. Article 10 ECHR requires that interferences with such rights must be 'prescribed by law' if they are to be acceptable. In *Sunday Times* the European Court concluded that the laws of contempt of court, under which the Attorney-General sought to prevent the newspaper's articles, were too vague to constitute justifiable restrictions of this right:

> [A] norm cannot be regarded as a 'law' unless it is formulated with sufficient precision to enable the citizen to regulate his conduct; he must be able, if need be with appropriate advice – to foresee to a degree that is reasonable in all the circumstances, the consequences which a given action may entail.[96]

This did not amount to a requirement that law be absolutely certain, or ascertainable without legal advice (as this would impose 'excessive rigidity'[97] upon a legal system). Nonetheless, in other cases Strasbourg has linked the condition of 'sufficient clarity to guide conduct' directly to the rule of law.[98] Lord Bingham fleshed out this reasoning behind the principle in the case of *Gillan* (relating to the use by police officers of enhanced powers under the Terrorism Act 2000 to search protesters involved in a demonstration against the arms trade):

> The lawfulness requirement in the Convention addresses supremely important features of the rule of law. The exercise of power by public officials, as it affects members of the public, must be governed by clear and publicly accessible rules of law. The public must not be vulnerable to interference by public officials acting on any personal whim, caprice, malice, predilection or purpose other than that for which the power was conferred. This is what, in this context, is meant by arbitrariness, which is the antithesis of legality.[99]

---

[93] T. Bingham, *The Rule of Law* (Allen Lane, 2010) p. 40.

[94] *R (Purdy)* v *Director of Public Prosecutions* [2009] UKHL 45; [2010] 1 AC 345, [59]. See also, [40] (Lord Hope).

[95] *Sunday Times* v *UK* (1979–80) 2 EHRR 245.

[96] Ibid., [49].

[97] Ibid., [49].

[98] *Malone* v *UK* (1985) 7 EHRR 14, [67].

[99] *R (Gillan)* v *Metropolitan Police Commissioner* [2006] UKHL 12; [2006] 2 AC 307, [34].

The idea that 'people should know, or at least be able to find out, what the law is' is therefore part of the UK's commitment to the rule of law.[100] It builds on the idea of 'government by law' by requiring that people be able to assess the law that affects their interests and actions (from the individual to the largest company). The operation of this principle clearly benefits each of these legal persons in allowing them to plan their affairs. But alongside this intrinsic benefit for each individual, the principle carries an extrinsic benefit for society as a whole. Lord Bingham regarded this concept as the bedrock upon which the UK's economy is founded; 'No one would choose to do business, perhaps involving large sums of money, in a country where the parties, rights and obligations were vague or undecided'.[101] That said, if stability of law is over-emphasised as a virtue, judges will find themselves trapped by existing precedents and unable to develop novel understandings of law in response to the needs of society.[102]

The legal process must be fair

Just as the two facets of the 'extended' rule of law above can be seen as building upon the principle of 'government by law' (part of the 'core' rule of law), the extended concept also has implications for the idea of 'equality before the law'. Equality before the law might, however, be satisfied on the basis that all parties are subject to the same legal process. The extended rule of law goes beyond this, requiring that a legal system display certain qualities, including a commitment to allowing individuals to access the courts, that the judiciary be impartial and their decisions open to scrutiny and that all officials with a role in the legal system exercise their discretion fairly. Without these marks of an independent legal system rules can be so malleable as to be devoid of meaning.[103]

(i) Access to the courts

An impartial judiciary is undoubtedly important to the rule of law, but only if supported by measures which allow individuals without sufficient private funds to access the legal system. In the 1940s, alongside state provision of healthcare and education, Clement Atlee's Government introduced the Legal Aid and Advice Act 1949. This Act provided support for most individuals facing criminal prosecution or engaged in various types of civil action, allowing them to receive independent legal advice and representation. Increasing costs, however, have spurred efforts to both restrict legal aid and impose higher court fees. These restrictions to access to the justice system have been challenged by the courts in rule-of-law terms: 'Without . . . access, laws are liable to become a dead letter, the work done by Parliament may be rendered nugatory, and the democratic election of Members of Parliament may become a meaningless charade'.[104]

The courts have found that some of these efforts conflicted with the extended rule of law's requirement that the legal process must be accessible. For example, *ex parte Witham*[105]

---

[100] Lord Neuberger, 'Access to Justice' (3 July 2017) para. 6. Available at: https://www.supremecourt.uk/docs/speech-170703.pdf.

[101] T. Bingham, *The Rule of Law* (Allen Lane, 2010) p. 38.

[102] J. Grant, 'The Ideals of the Rule of Law' (2017) 37 OJLS 383, 400–401.

[103] See *R (Cart)* v *Upper Tribunal* [2011] 2 WLR 36; [2010] EWCA Civ 859, [37] (Sedley LJ).

[104] *R (UNISON)* v *Lord Chancellor* [2017] UKSC 51; [2017] 3 WLR 409, [68] (Lord Reed).

[105] *R* v *Lord Chancellor, ex parte Witham* [1998] QB 575.

involved a challenge by an individual to a statutory instrument[106] which increased court fees and removed exemptions from fee payments of individuals claiming income support. Laws J struck down this statutory instrument, asserting that the new rules it contained threatened the 'constitutional right' of access to justice for individuals earning low incomes.[107] More recently, Laws LJ characterised efforts by the Ministry of Justice to restrict legal aid funding on the basis that the claims at issue were likely to be embarrassing for the Government as 'frankly inimical to the rule of law'.[108] The Supreme Court took up this baton in *UNISON,* quashing a statutory instrument which dramatically increased fees applicable to Employment Tribunals and Employment Appeal Tribunals on the basis that it violated '[t]he constitutional right of access to the courts [which] is inherent in the rule of law'.[109]

In response to legal aid reforms, beginning with restrictions on an individual's choice of legal representative under the Access to Justice Act 1999, the courts have accepted statutory restrictions upon the legal support provided by the state.[110] The courts have been reluctant to use access to justice to impose spending requirements on the ministry of justice. The concept does not, in one former Lord Chief Justice's analogy, imply a right to a 'Rolls-Royce service', it would suffice that access to the courts did not break down between London and Nottingham.[111] As Jackson LJ explained in public comments upon the Coalition Government's policy of reducing legal aid expenditure,[112] '[t]he extent of public funding which can be devoted to legal aid is of course a matter for Parliament, not for the judiciary to decide'.[113] The debate over when fee structures or legal aid rules inhibit access to justice, and therefore trigger heightened judicial scrutiny of legislation, looks set to continue.

(ii) Impartial and open adjudication

That the judiciary must be impartial in their dealings with parties before the courts is central to Dicey's core conception of equality before the law. Indeed, the centrality of an impartial judiciary to the peaceful resolution of disputes regarding rights and obligations has been noted by commentators writing long before Dicey. In the seventeenth century, the philosopher Thomas Hobbes recognised that corrupt or partial judges 'deter men from the use of judges and arbitrators, and consequently . . . [are] the cause of war'.[114] Hobbes' warning continues to exert considerable influence over contemporary judges, and his dictum is deeply embedded in accounts of the judicial role:

> The court . . . has essentially to make a decision between two conflicting parties and determining their respective rights *inter se* . . . The public interest does not normally come into it save in so far as the provision of a system of civil dispute resolution and the enforcement of civil rights is a necessary part of a society governed by the rule of law not by superior force.[115]

---

[106] Supreme Court Fees (Amendment) Order 1996, Art. 3.
[107] *R v Lord Chancellor, ex parte Witham* [1998] QB 575, 585.
[108] *R (Evans) v Lord Chancellor* [2012] 1 WLR 838; [2011] EWHC 1146 (Admin), [25] (Laws LJ).
[109] *R (UNISON) v Lord Chancellor* [2017] UKSC 51; [2017] 3 WLR 409, [66] (Lord Reed).
[110] See *R v Legal Aid Board, ex parte Duncan* [2000] COD 159, [460].
[111] Justice Select Committee, *The Work of the Lord Chief Justice: Oral Evidence* (2010) HC 521-I, 2 (Lord Judge).
[112] Legal Aid, Sentencing and Punishment of Offenders Act 2012.
[113] R. Jackson, 'Legal Aid and the Costs Review Reforms' (5 September 2011). Available at: https://www .judiciary.gov.uk/announcements/1-legal-aid-and-the-costs-review-reforms/.
[114] T. Hobbes, *Leviathan,* (first published 1651, Dover Publications, 2006) ch. XV.
[115] *Arthur J S Hall v Simons* [2002] 1 AC 615, 744 (Lord Hobhouse).

Judges, therefore, should never sit in cases where they have a personal or financial interest in the outcome of the case, if doing so would mean that it would appear to external observers that the process was unfair. Indeed, this is guaranteed by the requirement under Article 6 ECHR that tribunals dealing with civil disputes and criminal charges must be independent and impartial.[116] Whilst we will examine safeguards underpinning judicial independence more fully as an aspect of the separation of powers,[117] at this point it is, however, necessary to contrast judicial independence and complete judicial neutrality. Beyond preventing personal or financial interests biasing a judge as to the outcome of a case, judges are not blank slates, and they bring their own opinions on matters of public policy into the courtroom with them (if constrained by their judicial oath to administer the law 'without fear or favour, affection or ill-will').[118] Provided that an expert judge does not exhibit clear favouritism towards one side in the administration of his duties, human imperfection remains a feature of all systems of adjudication:

> Lawyers . . . whose practice is in these fields of public law, of public authorities and their powers, will need to know as much as they can about the general sympathies and antipathies of individual judges. The idea that judges can be politically neutral in such cases has never been true. Although to speak of bias or prejudice in this context is a misuse of language, judges differ in their view of where the public interest lies.[119]

In *McFarlane* v *Relate Avon Ltd*,[120] the claimant (a relationship counsellor) was dismissed by his employer when he refused to provide counselling on sexual relations to same-sex couples on the basis of his belief as a Christian that such activity was sinful. He claimed his dismissal discriminated against him on grounds of his belief. This claim was rejected by the Employment Tribunal and the Employment Appeal Tribunal. When permission to appeal to the Court of Appeal was refused, McFarlane obtained a witness statement supporting his claim from Lord Carey of Clifton, a retired Archbishop of Canterbury. In this statement, Lord Carey called for the establishment of a special judicial panel to hear such cases.[121] Laws LJ forcefully rejected such suggestions as incompatible with maintaining an impartial justice system, as 'the law must firmly safeguard the right to hold and express religious belief; equally firmly, it must eschew any protection of such a belief's content in the name only of its religious credentials. Both principles are necessary conditions of a free and rational regime'.[122]

The fairness and impartiality of the judiciary cannot, however, be established by individuals subject to a legal system unless court proceedings are open to the public and the reasoning behind judicial decisions is published. These extensions to the core idea of equality before the law are neatly encapsulated within the requirement in Article 6 ECHR that civil and criminal proceedings must be conducted by 'fair and *public* hearing'. Political philosophers have long recognised the virtue of open court processes. As Jeremy Bentham stated in the early nineteenth century:

---

[116] Article 6(1) ECHR.
[117] See below, pp. 346–9.
[118] T. Allan, *Constitutional Justice* (OUP, 2001) p. 62.
[119] J. Griffith, 'The Brave New World of Sir John Laws' (2000) 63 MLR 159, 159.
[120] *McFarlane* v *Relate Avon Ltd* [2010] EWCA Civ 880; [2010] IRLR 872.
[121] Ibid., [17].
[122] Ibid., [25].

In the darkness of secrecy, sinister interest and evil in every shape have full swing. Only in proportion as publicity has place can any of the checks applicable to judicial injustice operate. Where there is no publicity there is no justice.[123]

From the early twentieth-century senior judges such as Lord Shaw quoted Bentham with approval to ward off challenges to open justice, and the public administration of justice became a general rule at work within the UK's legal systems.[124] When exercising their discretion, courts have asserted that they may depart from the rule insofar as was necessary to protect the requirements of justice in a case.[125] More broadly, statutes have permitted limitations on the public reporting of cases to protect the identities of children or, as we have seen, complainants in rape cases. These exceptions, however, may have spurred government claims that other important considerations, particularly security concerns and intelligence co-operation with other countries, should be protected from disclosures by courts.

The issue came to a head in the high profile case of **Binyam Mohammed,** in which the claimant was a UK resident detained by the US Government at Guantánamo Bay on suspicion of involvement in international terrorism.[126] The UK Government sought to maintain the secrecy of evidence relating to intelligence exchanges between the US and the UK which indicated that the UK security services had knowledge of the ill treatment suffered by Mohammed whilst he was held without trial. Finding for Mohammed, the Divisional Court emphasised the importance of open court proceedings to the rule of law:

> In our view . . . a vital public interest requires, for reasons of democratic accountability and the rule of law in the United Kingdom, that a summary of the most important evidence relating to the British security services in wrongdoing be placed in the public domain in the United Kingdom.[127]

Taken to an extreme, restrictions in the interests of national security could lead to secret criminal trials of anonymous defendants, but to date the Courts have sought to limit the impact of such reporting restrictions to preserve a broad measure of open justice.[128]

Thinking Point . . .

Some tribunals which deal with sensitive intelligence, such as the Special Immigration Appeals Commission and the Proscribed Organisations Appeals Commission, are permitted by statute to sit in closed session and hear secret evidence. See A. Kavanagh, 'Special Advocates, Control Orders and the Right to a Fair Trial' (2010) 73 MLR 836.

---

[123] J. Bentham, *Rationale of Judicial Evidence* (Hunt & Clarke, 1827) Vol. 1, c. 10.

[124] *Scott* v *Scott* [1913] AC 417, 477.

[125] See *R* v *Felixtowe Justices, ex parte Leigh* [1987] QB 582, 593 (Watkins LJ).

[126] *R (Binyam Mohamed)* v *Secretary of State for Foreign and Commonwealth Affairs* [2009] EWHC (Admin) 2549.

[127] Ibid., [105] (Thomas LJ). This decision was upheld by the Court of Appeal; [2010] EWCA Civ 158; [2010] 3 WLR 554.

[128] *Guardian News and Media* v *Incedal and Bouhadjar* [2014] EWCA Crim 1861, [17] (Gross LJ).

(iii) Consistent operation of official discretion

Consistent and impartial application of the law is threatened if all stages of the criminal justice process are not fair. In the case of *ex parte Bennett,* this general principle was shown to even extend to issues such as how a prisoner is brought into the jurisdiction. Bennett, an individual who was alleged to have committed criminal offences in England was traced to Republic of South Africa. After collusion between the South African and UK police, he was kidnapped and returned to England, where he was arrested. Bennett claimed the police should have used the ordinary extradition process, and sought a judicial review of the magistrates' decision to commit him for trial. The House of Lords accepted that this case involved an abuse of process by the police, contrary to the rule of law, and ordered that the trial be stopped. As Lord Griffiths asserted, however, this breach of the rule of law did not result from unfairness in the forthcoming trial, but from the manner in which the police had sought to circumvent the established extradition procedures:

> In the present case there is no suggestion that the appellant cannot have a fair trial, nor could it be suggested that it would have been unfair to try him if he had been returned to this country through extradition procedures. If the court is to have the power to interfere with the prosecution in the present circumstances it must be because the judiciary accept a responsibility for the maintenance of the rule of law that embraces a willingness to oversee executive action and to refuse to countenance behaviour that threatens either basic human rights or the rule of law.[129]

Various public officials involved in the criminal and civil justice systems can potentially exercise their discretion in a manner which is unfair. Although such discretion is necessary, particularly where decisions by officials such as prosecutors 'intrude into areas which are particularly sensitive or controversial',[130] the courts have been eager to promote openness in such exercises of discretion. The reasoning behind this requirement of the rule of law, for Fuller, was to prevent 'a discrepancy between the law as declared and as actually administered'.[131] Requiring prosecutors to be able to explain, for example, the reasoning behind a decision not to prosecute individuals in particular cases makes it more difficult for unscrupulous officials to apply the criminal law differently between comparable groups of individuals, thereby helping to maintain public faith in the criminal justice process.[132]

Sensitive cases, however, provide wide scope for disagreement as to what constitutes unacceptable exercises of prosecutorial discretion. The case of *Corner House Research,* for example, involved the 'Al Yamamah' arms deal between BAE Systems and Saudi Arabia. Allegations surfaced that in order to secure this lucrative contract, BAE Systems had bribed Saudi officials. The Serious Fraud Office (SFO) launched an investigation into these claims, which was abruptly halted in December 2006, after Saudi officials informed the UK government that intelligence co-operation regarding counter-terrorism would be jeopardised if the investigation continued. Corner House Research, a pressure group, challenged this decision by the Director of the SFO, arguing that it constituted an abuse of discretion. This claim was upheld before the Divisional Court, on the basis that Saudi Arabia's threatened

---

[129] *R v Horseferry Road Magistrates Court, ex parte Bennett* [1994] 1 AC 42, 61–2.

[130] *R (Purdy) v Director of Public Prosecutions* [2009] UKHL 45; [2010] 1 AC 345, [46] (Lord Hope).

[131] L. Fuller, *The Inner Morality of Law* (2nd edn, YUP, 1969) p. 81.

[132] See *R (Purdy) v Director of Public Prosecutions* [2009] UKHL 45; [2010] 1 AC 345, [53] (Lord Hope).

withdrawal of intelligence co-operation had undermined the independent exercise of judgment required by prosecuting authorities:

> [T]he Director and Government failed to recognise that the rule of law required the decision to discontinue to be reached as an exercise of independent judgment, in pursuance of the power conferred by statute. To preserve the integrity and independence of that judgment demanded resistance to the pressure exerted by means of a specific threat.[133]

The Government appealed directly to the House of Lords. The Law Lords, upholding this appeal, were cautious about casting an 'extended' requirement of the rule of law, such as prosecutorial independence, as an absolute as opposed to desirable attribute of a legal system. As Baroness Hale asserted, there were very good reasons for the Director's decision to halt the investigation; 'The withdrawal of Saudi security co-operation would indeed have consequences of importance for the public as a whole. . . . "National security" in the sense of a threat to the safety of the nation as a nation state was not in issue here. Public safety was'.[134]

Parliamentary sovereignty and the extended rule of law

(i) The interpretive presumptions protecting the extended rule of law

Statutes have frequently introduced new legal rules which conflict with elements of the extended rule of law to serve other public interests. We have already considered examples of this, such as legislation which has limited the ability of the media to openly report details of certain cases. It therefore appears that the courts regard the elements of the 'extended' rule of law as desirable, but not essential, aspects of the UK's legal systems. They are important interests which the courts strongly presume will be respected by public officials, but which may be outweighed by other important interests in particular cases (such as the concern for public safety which swayed Baroness Hale's decision in *Corner House Research*). Ultimately, in a system grounded in parliamentary sovereignty, they can be abrogated by Acts of Parliament. Nonetheless, the courts have over several centuries, made it clear that they will apply constitutional presumptions in their interpretation of Acts of Parliament which attempt to tamper with the 'extended' rule of law.[135]

Thinking Point . . .

As we saw with clashes between parliamentary sovereignty and human rights, the courts were willing to impose an interpretive presumption ('the principle of legality') to protect the 'basic rights of the individual' against erosion by generally worded statutory provisions (*R v Secretary of State for the Home Department, ex parte Simms* [1999] 3 All ER 400, 412 (Lord Hoffmann)). Interpretive presumptions surrounding the rule of law operate in a similar manner. See Chapter 5, pp. 156–7.

---

[133] *R (Corner House Research)* v *Serious Fraud Office* [2008] EWHC 714 (Admin), [170].
[134] *R (Corner House Research)* v *Serious Fraud Office* [2008] UKHL 60; [2009] 1 AC 756, [53].
[135] *R (UNISON)* v *Lord Chancellor* [2017] UKSC 51; [2017] 3 WLR 409, [78] (Lord Reed).

In certain cases, where the interests at issue are particularly important, the reinterpretations imposed by the courts have radically departed from the literal meaning of particular statutes. Perhaps the most important facet of the extended rule of law (as all other elements depend upon it) is the requirement that access to the courts is not unfairly restricted. For centuries the ordinary courts have been particularly reluctant to follow a statutory provision which seeks to 'oust' (remove) a case from their jurisdiction without establishing an alternate system of fair tribunals, unless that provision is phrased in clear and express terms.[136] This rule of constitutional interpretation was particularly controversial after 1945, as governments responsible for an expanding welfare state sought to exclude the jurisdiction of the courts from oversight of certain government actions. The courts ultimately challenged this practice in *Anisminic Ltd v Foreign Compensation Commission*.[137] Compensation payable to UK companies which had their property seized by foreign governments was administered by the Foreign Compensation Commission. Although the Foreign Compensation Act stated that the Commission's 'determinations will not be called into question in any court of law',[138] Anisminic Ltd sought to challenge a Commission decision to deny it compensation in the courts. The House of Lords, accepting that the Commission had mistakenly failed to compensate Anisminic Ltd, refused to deny the company justice on the basis of the ouster clause. The majority asserted that, as the Commission had erred with regard to its jurisdiction, the court would not accept that it had issued a valid determination covered by the ouster.[139] As Allan asserts, '[b]y suitably deft, if subtle, linguistic analysis the statutory barrier to judicial review was neatly circumvented'.[140] The Court's language may have been subtle, but the clear message was that judges would, in such cases, defend their jurisdiction.

Even after *Anisminic,* ouster clauses can still be found in UK legislation. The courts have accepted their operation in particular fields (notably, under the Regulation of Investigatory Powers Act 2000 (RIPA),[141] regarding oversight of the security services) provided that appropriate independent tribunals are in place in their stead. Identifying RIPA's terms as 'an unambiguous ouster' in *obiter dicta* comments, Lord Brown did not seek to question this provision but instead acknowledged that 'there is no constitutional . . . requirement for any right of appeal from an appropriate tribunal'.[142] Such comments nonetheless indicate that, unless the elements of the extended rule of law are expressly abrogated by a clear Act of Parliament, the courts will not lightly subordinate them to other interests. This issue was at the heart of the Supreme Court's *Evans* decision, which has been presented as a 'constitutional-blockbuster':[143]

---

[136] See, for example, *R v Morley* (1760) 2 Burr 1041.
[137] *Anisminic v Foreign Compensation Commission* [1969] 2 AC 147.
[138] Foreign Compensation Act 1950, s. 4(4).
[139] See *Anisminic v Foreign Compensation Commission* [1969] 2 AC 147, 171 (Lord Reid).
[140] T. Allan, *Constitutional Justice* (OUP, 2001) p. 210.
[141] Regulation of Investigatory Powers Act 2000, s. 67(8).
[142] *R (A) v B* [2009] UKSC 12; [2010] 2 AC 1, [23].
[143] M. Elliott, 'A Tangled Constitutional Web: The Black-Spider Memos and the British Constitution's Relational Architecture' [2015] PL 539, 539.

Key case

R (Evans) v Attorney General [2015] UKSC 21; [2015] 1 AC 1787 (Supreme Court)

When we left the **Evans** case in Chapter 2 (pp. 43–4) the Upper Tribunal had rejected the UK Government's arguments that a constitutional convention prevented Prince Charles' corres-pondence from being released under the Freedom of Information Act 2000. Having lost that case the Attorney-General vetoed disclosure of the letters under Freedom of Information Act 2000, section 53, on the basis that he had 'reasonable grounds' for maintaining that non-dis-closure would not be unlawful. This decision was subject to a judicial review ultimately heard by a seven-judge Supreme Court panel.

The principles of parliamentary sovereignty and the rule of law are difficult to reconcile on the basis of that summary. Either the Supreme Court could refuse to quash the Attor-ney-General's decision as being in line with his broad statutory power, or it could confront the statutory veto as a means of circumventing a judicial decision. The multiple judgments in this case speak to disagreements between the panel of judges not only over how to resolve the case but over the method by which to reach a conclusion. For Lord Neuberger the case was about weighty constitutional principles, and the rule of law plays a prominent role in his judgment (at [52]); it is 'fundamental to the rule of law that decisions and actions of the execu-tive are . . . reviewable by the court at the suit of an interested citizen'. Ultimately this principle required the reinterpretation of section 53 to restrict the circumstances in which the ministerial veto could be used (at [115]):

> [A] decision of a judicial body should be final and binding and should not be capable of being overturned by a member of the executive. . . . [T]he relevant legislative instrument, the FOIA 2000, through section 53, expressly enables the executive to overrule a judicial decision, but only "on reasonable grounds", and the common law ensures that those grounds are limited so as not to undermine the fundamental principle, or at least to minimise any encroachment onto it.

Reasonable grounds, for Lord Neuberger, could not include disagreement with the Upper Tribunal's reasoning. Other judges (even a faction in the majority, which reached the same outcome in favouring release) baulked at this proposition. For the two dissenting judges, Lord Wilson and Lord Hughes, it was of little importance that the Attorney-General's attempt to circumvent a judicial decision was objectionable if he had a statutory power enabling him to act in this way. Both thought that the path taken by Lord Neuberger undermined the clear meaning of a statutory provision (see [168], (Lord Wilson)):

> How tempting it must have been for the Court of Appeal . . . to seek to maintain the supremacy of the astonishingly detailed . . . decision of the Upper Tribunal in favour of disclosure of the Prince's correspondence! But the Court of Appeal ought (as, with respect, ought this court) to have resisted the temptation. For, in reaching its decision, the Court of Appeal did not in my view interpret section 53 of FOIA. It re-wrote it. It invoked precious constitutional principles but among the most precious is that of parliamentary sovereignty, emblematic of our democracy.

As Mark Elliott concluded, the 'interpretive' approach adopted by the majority in **Evans** 'is comparable to the radical implications that the House of Lords' judgment in **Anisminic** had for the [Foreign Compensation Act's] ouster provision' (M. Elliott, 'A Tangled Constitutional Web: The Black-Spider Memos and the British Constitution's Relational Architecture' [2015] PL 539, 547). For all the effort that went into protecting the confidentiality of Prince Charles' correspondence, the letters released at the end of this legal battle turned out to contain no explosive revelations. The constitutional principles at work came to overshadow the relative triviality of the substantive issue at stake.

(ii) Beyond interpretation: overturning statutes in conflict with the extended rule of law

Advocates of 'common law' supremacy advocate the possibility of the courts overriding statute on the basis of its conflicting with fundamental common law principles such as aspects of the rule of law. The view enjoys some support in Commonwealth jurisprudence, where courts have been willing to recognise limits to the discretion of sovereign legislatures. In New Zealand, for example, Cooke J asserted that he did not believe that even the supposedly sovereign New Zealand Parliament could override certain fundamental common law rights. He asserted that some rights and common law principles 'presumably lie so deep that even Parliament could not override them'.[144]

Emboldened by this assertion, in the mid-1990s some judges began to argue, in extrajudicial writings, that should the UK Parliament legislate in a manner fundamentally at odds with the rule of law the courts should be prepared to find such statutes invalid: '[T]here are even limits on the supremacy of Parliament which it is the courts' inalienable responsibility to identify and uphold . . . They are no more than are necessary to enable the Rule of Law to be preserved'.[145] More recently other senior judges have responded to this rallying cry by raising the possibility of the courts invalidating statutes on the basis of the rule of law in their decisions. Some judges have been particularly vocal about the need to protect the impartial administration of justice. In *Jackson* Lord Steyn made it clear that he considered that the courts should act to constrain the supremacy of Parliament if it ever attempted to restrict the role of the ordinary courts in the absence of an alternate system of impartial tribunals:

> In exceptional circumstances involving an attempt to abolish judicial review or the ordinary role of the courts, the . . . Supreme Court may have to consider whether this is a constitutional fundamental which even a sovereign Parliament acting at the behest of a complaisant House of Commons cannot abolish.[146]

It should be remembered, however, that in cases such as *Evans* and *Anisminic* interpretations of a statute which move away from its literal terms can often suffice to protect 'constitutional fundamentals' without the need to take the totemic step of formally striking down a statute.

The increasing role of the extended rule of law in the UK Constitution

The extended rule of law enlarges the reach of the principle, but sometimes at the expense of diluting it. Whereas the core rule of law covers *necessary* aspects of a legal system, the elements of the extended rule of law are better characterised as *desirable* features of a legal system which indicate that the system is 'legally in good shape'.[147] These are therefore important features of a legal system, but features which can, in some cases, give way to other pressing policy considerations. Even with this caveat in place, the elements of the extended rule of law are being increasingly litigated, with the courts developing

---

[144] *Taylor* v *New Zealand Poultry Board* [1984] 1 NZLR 394.
[145] Lord Woolf, '*Droit Public* – English style' [1995] PL 57, 69.
[146] *R (Jackson)* v *Attorney-General* [2005] UKHL 56, [102].
[147] J. Finnis, *Natural Law and Natural Rights* (OUP, 1980) p. 270.

interpretative rules to buttress these principles against other public policy interests. This championing of the extended rule of law carries with it the possibility that government officials will not lightly seek to circumvent these principles and that even Parliament will take note of the consequences for the extended rule of law. The courts may not have more than flagged up the potential for these elements of the rule of law to coalesce into absolute values which not even statutes can transgress, but by holding out such a possibility, they have made Parliament increasingly wary of disregarding these principles.

The substantive rule of law

Key issues

- The rule of law, in its core and extended guises, focuses not on the subject matter of laws but on procedural aspects of their operation.
- Some commentators argue that this is inadequate, as laws can be enacted in clear and express terms permitting government officials to undertake unjust actions, ranging up to the commission of genocide. Under the narrower conceptions of the principle, such actions would not necessarily conflict with the rule of law.
- Others consider that such arguments confuse the rule of law with other desirable values within a legal system, such as social, economic, political and civil rights.

The limitations of procedural conceptions of the rule of law

(i) Formal equality and narrow conceptions of the rule of law

When Dicey explained his vision of the rule of law, he appeared to accept that the principle did not prevent laws from operating in a harsh or discriminatory manner. Considering Acts of Indemnity, which, as we have seen, retroactively protected government officials from legal action, he recognised that they allowed for 'the legalisation of illegality'.[148] Nonetheless, Dicey accepted that the ultimate sovereignty of Parliament extended to permit such repressive legislation.[149] Such limited conceptions of the rule of law's requirements do not restrict the substance of legislation. The conception of equality embodied in Dicey's rule of law is one of 'formal equality', requiring that everyone be judged according to the same law (even if that law may, of itself, be discriminatory).

A further problem with Dicey's vision of the rule of law was his preoccupation that the legal system should operate to secure no more than 'procedural' and 'corrective' justice, providing remedies where the state acted, without legal justification, in a manner which damaged the legally protected interests of individuals. Thus *Entick* v *Carrington*, where the courts ordered that government officials pay compensation to a radical printer for the tort of trespass to his property, fits perfectly within Dicey's conception of a properly functioning

---

[148] A. Dicey, *An Introduction to the Study of the Constitution* (8th edn, first published 1915, Liberty Fund, 1982) p. 145.
[149] Ibid., p. 145.

legal system. By the later years of the twentieth century some senior judges, like Lord Scarman, began re-examining the ideas of procedural justice operating within the UK's legal systems, and questioning whether the core or extended rule of law actually undermined efforts to prioritise the redistribution of resources to poorer members of society:

> A law of torts, a land law, and a family law, conceived on common law principles however admirable in substance, cannot effectively protect the general public or the weak, the poor, the aged and the sick. To satisfy the conscience of the nation the state has had to move into the empty spaces of the law . . . and there to make provision for society as a whole, and for those not strong enough to provide for themselves. Thus the welfare state is challenging the relevance, or at least the adequacy, of the common law's concepts and classifications.[150]

For Lord Scarman, the procedural conceptions of the rule of law which had historically operated within the UK Constitution may well be 'necessary' for a good society, but they are not 'sufficient' to maintain one.[151] For some constitutional commentators, the solution to the perceived conflict between promoting substantive and formal equality has been to radically reconceive the rule of law.

(ii) Towards substantive equality as part of the rule of law?

Thinking Point . . .

Sir Stephen Sedley (a now-retired Court of Appeal Judge) has highlighted the criticisms of procedural justice by writers such as Anatole France, who (writing in the context of late nineteenth-century France) lambasted 'the majestic even-handedness of the law, which forbids rich and poor alike to sleep under bridges, to beg in the streets and to steal bread'. S. Sedley, *Freedom, Law and Justice* (Sweet & Maxwell, 1999) 39, citing A. France, *Le Lys Rouge* (1894), Ch. 7.

The dramatic expansion of the welfare state in the UK in the aftermath of the Second World War, including the provision of social housing, social security payments, the National Health Service and the extension of state-funded education could all be considered to be examples of the UK Government moving into the 'empty spaces of the law' identified by Lord Scarman. These developments would ultimately be supported by the enumeration of civil and political rights in the UK's domestic legal systems under the HRA 1998. The problem for legal theorists became how to adapt the UK's legal systems, founded on rule of law principles which emphasised procedural fairness, to facilitate these efforts to ensure substantive equality of means or, at least, equality of opportunity.

For the International Congress of Jurists, in its Declaration of Dehli of 1959, these extensions of the government's remit in liberal democracies were instrumental in radically expanding the rule of law:

> [T]he Rule of Law is a dynamic concept for the expansion and fulfilment of which jurists are primarily responsible and which should be employed not only to safeguard and advance the civil and political rights of the individual in a free society, but also to establish social, economic,

---

[150] L. Scarman, *English Law – the New Dimension* (Steven & Sons, 1974) p. 70.
[151] See J. Waldron, 'The Rule of Law in Contemporary Liberal Theory' (1989) 2 *Ratio Juris* 79, 93.

educational and cultural conditions under which his legitimate aspirations and dignity may be realized.[152]

To other writers associating such goals with the rule of law overburdens the concept. Jeffrey Jowell maintains that substantive human rights, whether socio-economic or civil and political in nature, might well be worthy of protection, but this does not mean they should be subsumed into an ever-expanding rule of law, with the effect of divorcing that concept from any intelligible substance it might have. The rule of law, Jowell insists, is of unique significance and not a catch-all term for 'all good things' within a legal system.[153]

Thinking Point . . .

The distinction between civil and political rights and socio-economic rights is examined in Chapter 20, pp. 596–609, but the former concept acts as short hand for the interests once described as 'civil liberties' (like freedom of expression, religion and association) whereas the latter encompasses state provision of services (like healthcare and education).

As we have seen, the UK's courts have increasingly emphasised procedural protections under the rule of law in recent decades. When it comes to procedural rights such as access to the courts, many judges have emphasised their importance as an element of the rule of law, and in cases like *Jackson,* judges like Lord Steyn have even asserted that the courts could challenge statutes which threaten such interests.[154] By contrast, alive to Jowell's concern not to overburden the rule of law, many domestic judges have been reluctant to subsume substantive civil and political and socio-economic rights within the concept. Accepting a substantive conception of the rule of law could extend the judiciary's role with regard to government decision-making and resource allocation (a role which many judges consider to be beyond their competence to perform).[155] Judges often, therefore, continue to apply substantive rights standards not on the basis that they are inherent features of the common law, but to the extent required to give effect to legislation like the HRA 1998.[156]

Thinking Point . . .

Judges are not monolithic in their outlook. Some judges (particularly before the HRA 1998 was enacted) did reach decisions on the basis of 'fundamental rights' inherent within the common law, and more recently others have re-emphasised the role of the common law in protecting human rights (See R. Masterman and S. Wheatle, 'A Common Law Resurgence in Rights Protection?' [2015] EHRLR 57). See Chapter 21, pp. 648–51.

---

[152] International Congress of Jurists, *The Rule of Law in a Free Society* (N. Marsh (ed.), 1960) p. 3.

[153] J. Jowell, 'The Rule of Law and Its Underlying Values' in J. Jowell and D. Oliver (eds), *The Changing Constitution* (7th edn, OUP, 2011) 11, 22.

[154] See above, p. 214.

[155] See *R (Prolife Alliance) v British Broadcasting Corporation* [2004] 1 AC 185, at 240 (Lord Hoffmann). See also J. King, 'The Justiciability of Resource Allocation' (2007) 70 MLR 197.

[156] See, for example, *Secretary of State for the Home Department v MB* [2007] UKHL 46, [71] (Baroness Hale).

In an era of sustained cut-backs in public-service provision, judges will continue to be asked to reflect upon proposed cuts on the basis of substantive conceptions of the rule of law.[157] In this context Baroness Hale has played a leading role in advancing more substantive conceptions of the rule of law. Her dissenting judgment in *McDonald*[158] is illustrative. The claimant was a woman in her late 60s suffering from severely limited mobility as a result of an incapacitating stroke and reliant upon care assistance provided by her local council. Seeking to cut costs, the council sought to withdraw night-time care from the claimant, instead providing incontinence pads. Whilst four of the Supreme Court judges dismissed the claim that this decision was irrational on the narrow basis set out in argument before the court, Baroness Hale took the opportunity 'to address the question which we might have been asked'.[159] She regarded the provision of incontinence pads as irrational on the basis that they were inadequate to the claimant's needs: '[a] person in her situation needs this help during the day as well as during the night and irrespective of whether she needs to urinate or to defecate'.[160] Her conclusion explicitly linked her decision to a moral core within the legal system:

> In the United Kingdom we do not oblige people who can control their bodily functions to behave as if they cannot do so, unless they themselves find this the more convenient course. We are, I still believe, a civilised society.[161]

Baroness Hale's concern that the disabled claimant receives a level of care provision adequate to her needs is therefore steeped in the idea of substantive equality of treatment as the hallmark of 'a civilised society'. In response, Lord Brown strongly objected to Baroness Hale's characterisation of the care provision as irrational.[162] Baroness Hale, however, has continued to draw upon rule of law concepts in further dissenting judgments in cases involving public-spending implications. Questioning the imposition of charges on pregnant women from Northern Ireland seeking NHS abortions in other parts of the UK, she decried the policy as 'inconsistent with the principle of equal treatment which underlies so much of our law'.[163] Her substantive approach of the rule of law may yet come to redefine the approach of the courts to the provision of public services.

Conclusion

Authorities often emphasise the rule of law's 'importance' within the UK Constitution,[164] but they rarely define the term with any precision. Indeed, the Constitutional Reform Act 2005 went as far as to enshrine the rule of law as an 'existing constitutional principle' within the UK's legal systems, without explaining what this meant.[165] Whether the rule of

---

[157] See *R (Bailey)* v *London Borough of Brent Council* [2011] EWHC 2572 (Admin), [80] (Ouseley J).

[158] *R (McDonald)* v *Royal Borough of Kensington and Chelsea* [2011] UKSC 33; [2011] 4 All ER 881.

[159] Ibid., [61].

[160] Ibid., [77].

[161] Ibid., [79].

[162] Ibid., [27].

[163] *R (A and B)* v *Secretary of State for Health* [2017] UKSC 41, [95].

[164] See, for example, *X* v *Morgan Grampian* [1991] 1 AC 1, 48 (Lord Bridge).

[165] Constitutional Reform Act 2005, s. 1.

law denotes procedural elements which must, or should, be features of a legal system or serves as a synonym for a 'just' system which embodies a full range of social, economic, political, civil and cultural rights can seem to depend on how individual judges conceive of the issue. For all of this variation, a general trend is nonetheless discernible. From the 1960s onwards the frequent invocation of the rule of law as a constitutional principle has profoundly influenced the development of the UK's Constitution and, in particular, shaped the expansion of various heads of judicial review.[166] In *Alconbury Investments* Lord Hoffmann went so far as to explain the development of judicial review as a practical expression of the importance of the rule of law.[167] We will return to this thread of constitutional thought when we examine the operation of judicial review (Chapter 18).[168] For now, it suffices to acknowledge that whilst the rule of law is a very significant principle within the UK Constitution, its scope is by no means constant.

Practice questions

1. *'The Rule of Law . . . requires feasible limits on official power so as to constrain abuses on the part of even the most well-intentioned and compassionate of governments.'*

   (J. Jowell, 'The Rule of Law and its Underlying Values,' in J. Jowell and D. Oliver (eds), *The Changing Constitution,* (7ᵗʰ edn, OUP, 2011) 11, 34).

   How does the limitation imposed upon the state by the rule of law vary according to the different conceptions of the principle?

2. *'[A]t the very least, even in the case of cynical paeans on its behalf, the mere fact of its frequent repetition is compelling evidence that adherence to the rule of law is an accepted measure worldwide of government legitimacy.'*

   (B. Tamanaha, *On the Rule of Law* (CUP, 2004) 3).

   Discuss the meaning and relevance of the rule of law in the UK Constitution.

3. *'Access to a court to protect one's rights is the foundation of the rule of law.'*

   (*HM Treasury v Ahmed* [2010] UKSC 2, [146] (Lord Phillips)).

   Evaluate the operation of the principle of 'access to justice' under the UK Constitution.

Further reading

The rule of law remains as fundamental to an understanding of the UK Constitution as it is enigmatic. Each student of the constitution has to reach their own conclusion regarding the current content of the principle in UK jurisprudence and what they believe should be the content of the principle. Entire academic careers have been made for individuals with a confident response to these two questions, as such a response permits analysis of contemporary manifestations of the rule of law in light of the writer's ideal version of the principle. Jeffrey Jowell (**J. Jowell, 'The Rule of Law' in J. Jowell, D. Oliver and**

---

[166] See T. R.S. Allan, *The Sovereignty of Law: Freedom, Constitution, and Common Law* (OUP, 2013) 232.

[167] *R (Alconbury Investments)* v *Secretary of State for the Environment, Transport and the Regions* [2001] UKHL 23; [2003] 2 AC 295, [73].

[168] See pp. 507–16.

C. O'Cinneide (eds), *The Changing Constitution* (8th edn, OUP, 2015) 13–37) introduces these issues, giving a sweeping overview of the theoretical disputes between writers like Dicey and Jennings regarding the rule of law, and concluding with a detailed exposition on the relationship between the rule of law and judicial review.

With these foundations in place, the reader can turn to consider the different conceptions of the rule of law. Trevor Allan (**T. R. S. Allan, 'The Rule of Law as the Rule of Reason: Consent and Constitutionalism'** (1999) 115 *Law Quarterly Review* 221–44) examines what the rule of law requires in practice, and concluding that the principle requires that government officials not only be able to identify a legal basis for their actions but must also be able to explain how their decisions serve the common good. James Grant carefully unpicks the different and sometimes irreconcilable elements that different commentators impose upon the rule of law (**J. Grant, 'The Ideals of the Rule of Law'** (2017) 37 *Oxford Journal of Legal Studies* 383–405).

Readers must always realise that, even if they are confident in their vision of the constitutional role of the rule of law, the term remains politically contingent. Lord Bingham offers useful cautionary advice to anyone who considers that they have tamed the rule of law, in an article (**T. Bingham, 'The Rule of Law'** (2007) 66 *Cambridge Law Journal* 67–85) upon which his later book of the same name is based, grappling with the division between the rule of law as a legal concept and its use in political discourse. Finally, readers should beware of thinking that this chapter covers the only possible explanation of the different conceptions of the rule of law. Not as bleak as its title suggests, Timothy Endicott's article (**T. Endicott, 'The Impossibility of the Rule of Law'** (1999) 19 *Oxford Journal of Legal Studies* 1–18) challenges suggestions that the rule of law requires that law must govern every human interaction, recasting the concept instead as a balance between the twin evils of anarchy and overregulation.

Chapter 7
Separation of powers

'The accumulation of all powers, legislative, executive, and judiciary, in the same hands, whether of one, a few, or many, and whether hereditary, self-appointed, or elective, may be justly pronounced the very definition of tyranny . . . where the whole power of one department is exercised by the same hands which possess the whole power of another department, the fundamental principles of a free constitution are subverted.'

James Madison, Federalist No. XLVII.

Chapter outline

The constitutional doctrine of separation of powers seeks to divide governmental power between three arms, or branches, of government – the legislative, executive and judicial branches – with the aims of preventing arbitrary or oppressive government, and of promoting efficiency in the operation of government.

Separation of powers plays an uncertain role in the constitution of the United Kingdom as it is argued to be incompatible with the doctrine of parliamentary sovereignty. This chapter will examine how far the UK Constitution can be said to reflect an institutional and functional separation of powers, and how far the values of separation of powers can be seen in our constitutional arrangements.

Introduction

Imagine that *all* governmental functions under the UK Constitution were the responsibility of the Prime Minister. Imagine also that all such decisions were immune from challenge. In such a scenario, one individual would be responsible for designing policy, enacting legislation, ensuring that that legislation was enforced and for resolving any legal disputes which arose as a result. No body or group would have the ability to challenge decisions that were unreasonable, unjust, or otherwise flawed. In our hypothetical scenario, as *all* governmental matters would ultimately be decided upon by the Prime Minister, there would be no need for a separate judicial system, or for a legislative assembly made up of representatives of differing political persuasions able to voice the concerns of the electorate. Under such a system, legally enforceable rules would ultimately be implemented and policed by the person who had designed them, and the legislative power of the Prime Minister would – without a legislative assembly to scrutinise, revise or veto proposals – effectively be unfettered. While it could certainly be argued that such a regime would possess the simplicity that is often hard to find in the UK Constitution, it would almost certainly also amount to dictatorship; as the constitutional theorist M. C. J. Vile wrote in the 1960s in his seminal work, *Constitutionalism and the Separation of Powers,* 'the diffusion of authority among different centres of decision-making is the antithesis of totalitarianism or absolutism'.[1] The 'diffusion' of governmental authority 'among different centres of decision-making' is at the heart of separation of powers.

Separation of powers theories hold that governmental functions can be ascribed to three branches of government – the legislative, executive and judicial branches – and that there are three types of function which correspond with these three branches. A constitutional system which would effectively grant unfettered governmental power to the holder of one office or institution of government would therefore offend the doctrine of separation of powers. In fact, so important are the ideas associated with separation of powers to those of liberal democracy that it might be suggested that any governmental system which allocated power in such a way might not even be called 'constitutional' at all: as Art. 16 of the French Declaration of the Rights of Man holds, 'any society in which the safeguarding of rights is not assured, and the separation of powers is not established, has no constitution'. Separation of powers therefore holds a key place in liberal constitutional theory: as Eric Barendt has argued 'the separation of powers in some form is arguably the essence of constitutionalism'.[2]

This chapter examines the role and functions of the three branches of government in the constitution of the United Kingdom, and examines how far the dividing lines between the executive, legislature and judiciary can be said to reflect an understanding of the separation of powers doctrine in practice. We begin, however, with an outline of the origins, aims and objectives of separation of powers.

Key issues

- Separation of powers theories seek to divide governmental powers between distinct institutions of government. They do so in order to promote efficiency in government and, through the avoidance of concentrations of power, to promote liberty.

- The pure, or strict, approach to separation of powers advocates a complete separation of the personnel and functions of governmental institutions. The partial separation, or partial agency, variant of the theory contends that each branch of government should check and balance the powers of the other institutions of government.

---

[1] M. C. J. Vile, *Constitutionalism and the Separation of Powers* (Clarendon Press, 1967) p. 15.
[2] E. Barendt, 'Is There a United Kingdom Constitution?' (1997) 17(1) OLJS 137, 141.

The theory and aims of separation of powers

The history of separation of powers is a long one, traceable back as far as the ancient Greek philosophers.[3] For our purposes, the English philosopher John Locke's *Second Treatise on Civil Government* – published in the late seventeenth century – provides a neat introduction to the concept as it emerged in English political thought. Locke wrote:

> It may be too great a temptation to human frailty, apt to grasp at power, for the same persons who have the power of making laws, to have also in their hands the power to execute them, whereby they may exempt themselves from obedience to the laws they make, and suit the law, both in its making and execution, to their own private advantage.[4]

The desire to ensure the separation of legislative power (the power to make laws) and executive power (the power to administer their enforcement) is of course crucial to the idea of separation of powers. But for what ends is such separation regarded as being necessary?

Accounts of separation of powers theory can be seen, generally, to promote two main aims. First, separation of powers is described as being a restraint on governmental power; it avoids concentrations of power by dividing responsibilities between different branches of government and empowers each branch of government to exercise a degree of control over the actions of another. The degree of control exercised may differ depending on the circumstances; the legislature might exercise control over the implementation of executive policy by amending or rejecting legislative proposals, while the courts might review legislative measures for compatibility with, for example, human rights standards or those set down in the constitution. Second, separation of powers is also argued to promote efficient government through the allocation of specific governmental functions to the branch of government best equipped to undertake that particular activity.[5] It is perhaps uncontroversial, for example, to suggest that an independent judicial branch might be best equipped to determine disputes of law between the individual and the executive branch. Equally, the legislative branch might be said to be best placed to determine the form and content of rules of general applicability for the governance of the state.

Barendt, however, has downplayed the significance of the aim of governmental efficiency as a motivation for separated powers, asserting instead that the primary aim of the doctrine is the avoidance of tyrannical government.[6] Perhaps the most well-known endorsement of separation of powers in this regard was put forward by the French writer Montesquieu in the eighteenth century:

> When the legislative and executive powers are vested in the same person, or in the same body of magistrates, there can be no liberty; because apprehensions may arise, lest the same monarch or senates should enact tyrannical laws to execute them in a tyrannical manner . . . Again, there is no liberty if the power of judging is not separated from the legislative and executive. If it were joined with the legislative, the life and liberty of the subject would be exposed to arbitrary control; for the judge would then be the legislator. If it were joined to the executive power, the judge might behave with violence and oppression. There would be an end to everything, if the same

---

[3] For a survey, see: C. Munro, *Studies in Constitutional Law* (2nd edn) (Butterworths, 1999) Ch. 9, pp. 295–302.

[4] J. Locke, *Second Treatise on Civil Government* (1689), ch. XII.

[5] See, for example, Barber's analysis of Locke's conception of separation of powers: N. W. Barber, 'Prelude to the Separation of Powers' (2001) 60 CLJ 59, 63–4.

[6] E. Barendt, 'The Separation of Powers and Constitutional Government' [1995] PL 599, 602.

man, or the same body, whether of the nobles or of the people, were to exercise those three powers, that of enacting laws, that of executing public affairs, and that of trying crimes or individual causes.[7]

Described as such, separation of powers serves to protect the liberty of the individual from the oppressive, arbitrary or violent intentions of those who wield governmental power. For Montesquieu, the value of separated power lay not only in the avoidance of arbitrary or oppressive government, but also in the reduction of the perception that laws were administered in a partial or predetermined manner.

Montesquieu's espousal of separation of powers undoubtedly remains influential, and in particular is reflected in the views of James Madison, one of the authors of *The Federalist Papers* and founders of the United States, Constitution, whose quotation appears at the opening of this chapter.[8] In a similar vein to Montesquieu, Madison saw the separation of governmental power as one of the hallmarks of a liberal constitution and an 'essential precaution in favor of liberty'.[9] Perhaps consistently with the fact that separation of powers is said to promote multiple benefits, there is also some disagreement over the extent to which governmental powers should be separated in practice.

The pure theory

The 'pure' theory of separation of powers holds that there should be a strict separation of both personnel and functions between the legislative, executive and judicial branches; members of one branch of government should not also be members of one of the other two branches, and branches of government should not interfere with functions carried out by another branch.[10] There are, therefore, two dimensions to the idea of separation of powers; that of institutional separation, and that of functional separation. The pure theory of separation seeks to avoid concentrations of governmental power by dividing and allocating responsibilities between the three branches and by creating very clear dividing lines between governmental institutions and the functions that they discharge (see Figure 7.1).

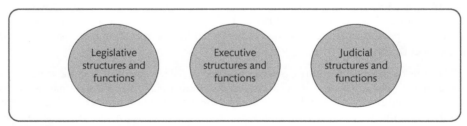

Figure 7.1 A pure separation of powers

---

[7] *l'Esprit des Lois (The Spirit of the Laws)*, Book XI, s. 6.
[8] Though for criticisms of Montesquieu see: I. Jennings, *The Law and the Constitution* (5th edn) (University of London Press, 1967) p. 23; C. Munro, *Studies in Constitutional Law* (2nd edn) (Butterworths, 1999) p. 299; M. Foley, *The Politics of the British Constitution* (Manchester University Press, 1999) p. 16.
[9] J. Madison, A. Hamilton and J. Jay, *The Federalist Papers* (Penguin Classics, 1987), No. XLVII.
[10] See: M. J. C. Vile, *Constitutionalism and the Separation of Powers* (Clarendon Press, 1967) p. 13.

Perhaps the most famous example of a pure *institutional* separation in practice can be found in Arts. I, II and III of the United States Constitution which, respectively, vest legislative power in Congress, executive power in the President, and judicial power in the Supreme Court.

The pure theory of separation seeks to ensure that governmental power is distributed amongst the three branches of government and does not seek to allow one branch of government to wield influence over another. However, the powers allocated to those institutions under the United States, Constitution have been said to infringe the pure version of separation of powers. Judicial review of primary legislation of the type exercised by the United States Supreme Court for example – where the court is empowered to strike down legislation which violates the constitution[11] – has been argued to be a violation of this pure theory of the separation of powers for the reason that it allows the judicial branch to interfere with the legislative autonomy of Congress. Similarly, parliamentary systems on the Westminster model[12] fail to satisfy the 'pure' theory of separation for the reason that in such a system the Cabinet – the executive branch – forms a part of the legislature.

The difficulty of this 'pure' theory of separation of powers lies in the fact that while it may be possible to comprise institutionally separate branches of government the strict approach also relies on each of those branches operating *entirely* independently of each other. The pure theory therefore treats the institutional and functional separation of the three branches of government as sufficient to effectively protect liberty and safeguard against oppressive or arbitrary exercises of governmental power. Under the pure theory, within their respective areas of competence the decisions and actions of the legislature, executive and judiciary are immune from challenge or from interference by one of the other branches. The pure approach is, therefore, arguably unsatisfactory as, while it disperses governmental power between three separate branches, it insulates the decisions of each of those branches from external challenge. Instead of establishing a system in which the exercise of governmental power can be restrained, the pure theory would simply seem to result in the concentration of unfettered governmental power in not one branch, but three.

The partial separation theory

By contrast with strict versions of separation of powers, the 'partial separation' or 'partial agency'[13] approach to the separation of powers allows a degree of interaction between the three branches of government. Instead of advocating independence of both function and personnel, the partial separation theory envisages that each of the branches should be able to exercise a degree of influence over the powers of the other branches. As such, the partial separation doctrine acts as a tool whereby the political and legal autonomy of one branch of government may be legitimately limited by one or more of the remaining branches. In *The Federalist Papers,* James Madison wrote that the separation of powers doctrine should not mean that each branch of government 'ought to have no partial agency in, or no control over,

---

[11] As, for example, carried out by the United States Supreme Court: *Marbury* v *Madison* 5 US (1 Cranch) 137 (1803).
[12] For example, the United Kingdom – after whose Parliament the system is named – Australia, New Zealand and Canada.
[13] For a more detailed analysis than space allows here, see M. J. C. Vile, *Constitutionalism and the Separation of Powers* (Clarendon Press, 1967); E. Barendt, 'The Separation of Powers and Constitutional Government' [1995] PL 599.

the acts of each other'.[14] By this, Madison meant that liberty would better be secured to the individual by branches of government able to exercise coercive powers over each other. Madison, therefore, rejected the idea that each branch of government exist and act entirely independently of each other and instead emphasised the ideas associated with what have become known as checks and balances. So, in spite of the apparent clear institutional divisions in the US Constitution, the power of each branch of government to wield a degree of influence over other branches is also clearly established. For example, the legislative power of Congress may be subject to presidential (executive) veto,[15] and is also subject to (judicial) review by the United States Supreme Court. Secondly, the executive powers of the President may require Congressional (legislative) endorsement.[16] And finally, judgments of the Supreme Court may be reversed by a process of constitutional amendment under Art. V of the Constitution.[17]

As a result, it can be seen that in practice separation of powers is as commonly invoked as a mechanism for restraining and limiting governmental power as it is relied upon as a mechanism for dividing and allocating governmental power. As Marshall has observed, this is particularly the case in Anglo-American conceptions of the doctrine which hold that, 'the branches of government, when "separated", may legitimately check or act upon each other and indeed are separated precisely so that they may exercise such checks'.[18] The ability of one branch of government to control or influence the activities of another branch is therefore seen as being central, rather than antithetical, to the partial agency model of separation of powers.

In advocating an idea of limited government and in endorsing the idea of an institutionally distinct judiciary, separation of powers clearly upholds values which are closely associated with the rule of law.[19] The two doctrines are mutually supportive, but separation of powers is to be distinguished by attempting to set down a particular mechanism by which individual liberty should be upheld, that is, by dividing and allocating specific powers amongst distinct branches of government rather than prescribing particular characteristics of 'good' law. It is to the question of which powers or functions should be exercised by which particular branch of government that we now turn.

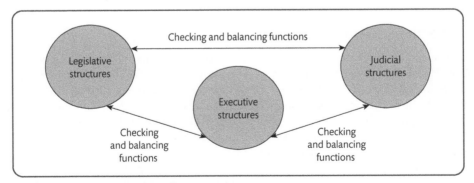

Figure 7.2 A partial separation of powers

[14] J. Madison, A. Hamilton and J. Jay, *The Federalist Papers* (Penguin Classics, 1987) p. 304.

[15] Article I, s. 7, Constitution of the United States.

[16] For example, Art. II, s. 2, Constitution of the United States (the Presidential power to enter into treaties).

[17] For example, the 14th Amendment to the US constitution – which extended provision for the due process and equal protection of laws to all citizens of the United States – overruled the Supreme Court's infamous decision in *Dred Scott* v *Sandford* 60 US 393 (1857).

[18] G. Marshall, *Constitutional Theory* (Clarendon Press, 1971) p. 99.

[19] See Chapter 6.

Governmental institutions and functions

Key issues

- Separation of powers theory holds that governmental functions are allocated to three branches of government: the executive, the legislature and the judiciary. In the United Kingdom Constitution, governmental functions are primarily carried out by the government of the day, Parliament and the courts.

- However, theories on the separation of powers are criticised on the ground that it is not possible to neatly allocate all governmental functions to one specific branch of government. This confusion is illustrated in the United Kingdom Constitution by the fact that while Parliament enjoys the ability to enact legislation, the executive and courts both carry out limited law-making functions (as a result of, respectively, delegated legislative powers and the common law).

Governmental institutions

The term 'Government' in the United Kingdom is often used to refer to those politicians, more accurately those Ministers of the Crown, who undertake much of the public business of governing the country. In its broader sense, however, the word 'government' encompasses each of the institutions engaged in the governance of the country: the legislature, the executive and the judicial branch.

Thinking Point . . .

The executive, legislature (Houses of Parliament) and judicial branches in the United Kingdom are considered more fully in Chapters 8–11. What follows only provides a snapshot for the purposes of illustrating the ideas associated with separation of powers.

The executive branch[20]

In the governance of the United Kingdom, the executive branch (or Government) administers the day-to-day business relating to the management of the state. The role of the executive branch – as Bagehot, author of *The English Constitution,* commented – is to 'rule the nation'.[21] The executive function includes the executing, or enforcing, of the criminal and civil law (through, for example, the Police, HM Revenue and Customs, and criminal prosecuting authorities), the maintenance of law and order, the design of public policy for the running of the state (including the drafting of legislative proposals), the defence of the realm, and the conduct of international relations (for example entering into treaties).[22]

---

[20] On which see Chapter 8.
[21] W. Bagehot, *The English Constitution* (Oxford World's Classics) (OUP, 2001) p. 12.
[22] See T. Daintith and A. Page, *The Executive in the Constitution: Structure, Autonomy and Internal Control* (OUP, 1999); P. Craig and A. Tomkins, *The Executive and Public Law: Power and Accountability in Comparative Perspective* (OUP, 2006).

In terms of personnel, the executive comprises the Cabinet – headed by the Prime Minister – and those Ministers who are responsible for the discharge of the functions of central government. The executive branch is also comprised of those officers of the state who exercise functions on behalf of the government of the day, including the civil service, the police and the armed forces. Since the 1980s at least, 'executive' functions have also been conducted by bodies which would not traditionally be thought of as being governmental as a result of privatisation, the contracting out of public services, and the establishment of quasi-autonomous non-governmental organisations (quangos).[23]

The legislative branch

Strictly speaking, the Parliament of the United Kingdom comprises the House of Commons, the House of Lords *and* the Queen in Parliament. In more practical terms, however, it is appropriate to say that the Westminster Parliament is bicameral, meaning it is composed of two distinct chambers or houses.

A. The House of Commons[24]

The House of Commons is made up of 650 directly elected Members of Parliament (MPs) representing the constituencies of England, Wales, Scotland and Northern Ireland. The vast majority of members of the Cabinet are drawn from the ranks of the House of Commons (with the remainder being drawn from the House of Lords). The disputed place of separation of powers in the United Kingdom is confirmed by Bagehot's famous remark that, far from being considered constitutionally problematic, this 'nearly complete fusion of the executive and legislative powers', should be regarded as the 'efficient secret' of the constitution.[25] A so-called 'parliamentary executive' – a 'fused' legislative and executive branch – is one of the hallmarks of the Westminster system of government; it also poses an immediate difficulty for any attempted principled application of separation of powers theory to the United Kingdom system.

B. The House of Lords[26]

The House of Lords is referred to as the 'upper' house of the United Kingdom Parliament and reflects the historical balance of powers between monarch, commoners and lords that continues to resonate in the United Kingdom system of government. The House of Lords is not elected by popular vote, and comprises a number of different types of peer, the vast majority of whom are appointed by the monarch on the recommendations of the main political parties. In spite of being referred to as the *upper* house, the House of Lords is not superior in either status or powers to the House of Commons.

The judiciary[27]

The highest court in the judicial branch of government is the United Kingdom Supreme Court, which – since its establishment in 2009[28] – hears appeals in criminal and civil cases

---

[23] On which see: R. A. W. Rhodes, 'The Hollowing Out of the State: The changing nature of the public service in Britain' (1994) 65 *Political Quarterly* 138. For a broader survey see: C. Harlow and R. Rawlings, *Law and Administration* (3rd edn) (CUP, 2009) Ch. 2.

[24] Chapter 9.

[25] W. Bagehot, *The English Constitution* (OUP, 2001) p. 11.

[26] Chapter 10.

[27] Chapter 11.

[28] Under the provisions of Part III of the Constitutional Reform Act 2005.

arising in England and Wales and Northern Ireland, and civil appeals from Scotland. Beneath the Supreme Court lies the Court of Appeal, which is split into civil and criminal divisions. Lying beneath the Court of Appeal is the High Court, which deals, *inter alia*, with chancery, family and administrative law cases. Certain matters may progress from the domestic court structures to either the European Court of Human Rights[29] or – until at least the United Kingdom's departure from the European Union and with any future role contingent on the outcome of the Brexit negotiations – the Court of Justice of the European Union.[30]

Thinking Point . . .

Prior to the establishment of the United Kingdom Supreme Court, the highest court in the United Kingdom had been the Appellate Committee of the House of Lords. As a committee of the House of Lords, the United Kingdom's apex court was institutionally linked to the upper house of Parliament being physically housed within, and drawing its membership from, the House of Lords.

The judicial branch of government fulfils a number of distinct roles within the constitution. It is the constitutional responsibility of the judiciary to interpret and apply the law as either passed by Parliament (statute law) or developed through prior judicial decisions (common law). In doing so, it is the task of the judiciary to adjudicate over criminal proceedings as the independent arbiter between the prosecuting authorities of the state and the accused individual(s). Similarly, in civil proceedings, it is the role of the judge to adjudicate between the parties involved in the case, applying the relevant law.

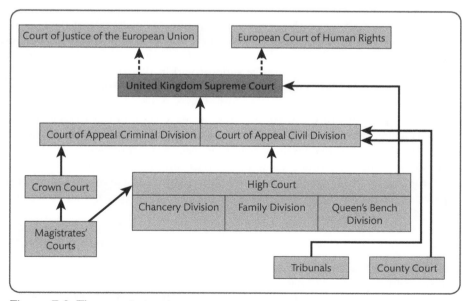

Figure 7.3 The court structure

---

[29] On which see pp. 609–16.
[30] On which see pp. 84–6.

Dividing governmental functions

What then of the suggestion that governmental functions can be easily defined as being legislative, executive or judicial? At first glance, this suggestion might appear uncontroversial. The legislature can be seen to make law by debating and amending legislative proposals through the House of Commons and House of Lords and enacting them as statutes. The executive can be seen to administer the functions of designing and implementing policy and of 'executing' the law, for example, via enforcement of the criminal law by the police. Finally, it might equally be seen as non-contentious to suggest that judges exercise peculiarly 'judicial' functions when they adjudicate over criminal trials and civil law causes of action. Making the law, executing the law, and adjudicating over the law are, it could be argued, the classic functions of the three branches, and Lord Mustill – in the *Fire Brigades Union* case – suggested that such a tripartite division *is* evident in our constitutional arrangements:

> It is a feature of the peculiarly British conception of the separation of powers that Parliament, the executive and the courts have each their distinct and largely exclusive domain. Parliament has a legally unchallengeable right to make whatever laws it thinks right. The executive carries on the administration of the country in accordance with the powers conferred on it by law. The courts interpret the laws, and see that they are obeyed.[31]

Lord Mustill's use of the word 'largely' is, however, telling; can all governmental functions be neatly categorised in this way? Does the legislature only legislate? Does the judiciary only adjudicate? Can one of the institutions of government exercise functions which might be said to belong to another?

As we have already seen, the sovereign authority of Parliament is 'the bedrock of the British constitution'.[32] Parliament is the dominant law-making body in the constitution. Law making, however, is not Parliament's sole function.[33] In addition to its legislative role, the functions of Parliament revolve around the scrutiny and endorsement (or otherwise) of the activities of the executive branch; without the support of a majority of parliamentarians the vast majority[34] of legislative proposals made by the executive will not come into force. Indeed, in the absence of effective support within Parliament the executive will effectively be hamstrung. For some commentators, this latter set of functions is as important – if not more so – than Parliament's technical power to enact legislation. As Bagehot commented, '[t]he legislature chosen, in name, to make laws, in fact finds its principal business in making and keeping an executive'.[35] As can even be seen from this brief analysis, it is clear that the legislature does more than simply enacting legislation.[36]

As a result of this, and other, complexities regarding the distribution of functions between the institutions of government, a number of writers have been particularly critical of separation of powers theories for the reason that all of the myriad functions of

---

[31] *R v Secretary of State for the Home Department, ex parte Fire Brigades Union* [1995] 2 AC 513, 567 (Lord Mustill).

[32] *Jackson v Attorney-General* [2005] UKHL 56, [9] (Lord Bingham). See Chapter 5.

[33] For a more detailed analysis see Chapters 9, 10 and 15. See also A. Tomkins, 'What is Parliament for?' in P. Leyland and N. Bamforth, *Public Law in a Multi-Layered Constitution* (Hart Publishing, 2003).

[34] Though see coverage of the Parliament Acts procedure at pp. 141–3.

[35] W. Bagehot, *The English Constitution* (Oxford World's Classics) (OUP, 2001) p. 12. See also A. Tomkins, *Our Republican Constitution* (Hart Publishing, 2005) p. 1.

[36] See also Chapters 9 and 10 on the respective functions of the House of Commons and House of Lords.

government cannot be categorised as neatly as the tripartite theory of separation of powers would suggest.[37] As a result, it is argued that separation of powers lacks coherence, and the division of functions – beyond those which can be said to comfortably fall within the competence of the executive, legislative and judicial branches – is largely arbitrary. Ivor Jennings, for one, argued that no principled lines could be draw between what governmental activities could be called executive, legislative and judicial, and suggested that while there were 'characteristics of various classes of functions which make it desirable that they should, for instance, be exercised by independent judges' there is nevertheless, 'no single characteristic or group of characteristics which enables the legislature to determine out of hand that a particular function should be assigned to the judges'.[38]

We turn now to two specific difficulties of a principled division of governmental functions in the United Kingdom; first, by examining the ability of the executive to make law, and secondly by looking at the law-making powers of the judicial branch.

The problem of delegated legislation

Due to the constraints of the parliamentary timetable, primary legislation frequently provides only a broad framework under which governmental activity should occur. As a result, such Acts of Parliament often also contain provisions allowing Ministers to make rules or regulations which specify in more detail how that Act is to apply. These rules or regulations are known as secondary, or delegated, legislation. Any strict separation of powers would preclude the delegation of legislative power from Parliament to the executive branch, yet in the United Kingdom delegated legislation has become an accepted – and arguably necessary – feature of governmental activity.[39]

For example, s. 130 of the Supreme Court Act 1981 – examined in the previous chapter in the context of the case of *R v Lord Chancellor, ex parte Witham*[40] – provided the Lord Chancellor with a power to set the fees to be charged in the event of a claimant issuing a writ to bring a case to court. Section 130, so far as is relevant, provided:

(1) The Lord Chancellor may by order under this section prescribe the fees to be taken in the Supreme Court, other than fees which he or some other authority has power to prescribe apart from this section . . .

(4) Any order under this section shall be made by statutory instrument which shall be laid before Parliament after being made.

Delegated legislation is often used to flesh out the bare bones of parliamentary legislation, and undoubtedly provides ministers with a significant, and frequently used, power to dictate the finer details of primary legislation.[41]

Delegated legislation is however subject to different types of control. First, the Statutory Instruments Act 1946 sets out two procedures for the coming into effect of delegated legislation which allow for parliamentary scrutiny of the legislative process. Under the affirmative resolution procedure, a statutory instrument will not come into effect until

---

[37] See in particular: E. Carolan, *The New Separation of Powers: A theory for the modern state* (OUP, 2009).

[38] I. Jennings, *The Law and the Constitution* (5th edn) (University of London Press, 1967) pp. 24–5.

[39] See: G. Ganz, 'Delegated Legislation: a Necessary Evil or a Constitutional Outrage?' in P. Leyland and T. Woods, *Administrative Law Facing the Future: Old Constraints and New Horizons* (Blackstone Press, 1997).

[40] *R v Lord Chancellor, ex parte Witham* [1995] QB 575. See pp. 140–41 above.

[41] See, for discussion, E. C. Page, *Governing by Numbers* (Hart Publishing, 2001).

endorsed by a parliamentary majority within 40 days. The appropriate minister will there-fore be under a responsibility to ensure that there is sufficient support in the house to carry the statutory instrument. Under the more commonly used negative resolution procedure a statutory instrument will come into force unless there are parliamentary objections within 40 days of the instrument being laid before Parliament. Under the negative resolution procedure, the onus is on the opposition parties to raise objections to the coming into force of the statutory instrument. Additional parliamentary scrutiny of this area of law making is provided by a number of dedicated parliamentary select committees,[42] but:

> Parliamentary scrutiny of delegated legislation is less intensive and arguably less effective than its scrutiny of primary legislation. Statutory instruments cannot be amended, so there is little scope or incentive for compromise. Far less time is spent debating delegated legislation than is spent debating primary legislation. And . . . it is established practice that the House of Lords does not vote down delegated legislation except in exceptional circumstances. The result is that the Government can pass legislative proposals with greater ease and with less scrutiny if it can do so as delegated, rather than primary, legislation.[43]

Thinking Point . . .

Occasionally, a specific form of delegated legislative power enables ministers to amend **primary** legislation – these powers are known as Henry VIII clauses (on which see pp. 32–4). Henry VIII clauses – for instance, s. 10 of the Human Rights Act 1998 (on which see pp. 672–3) – effectively permit Ministers, often acting with only minimal parliamentary scrutiny, to amend primary legislation. As such, Henry VIII powers are problematic for our understanding of parliamentary sovereignty, as well as for the separation of powers, for the reason that they test 'the boundaries of the constitutional principle that only Parliament may amend or repeal primary legislation' (House of Lords Select Committee on the Constitution, *Public Bodies Bill* (2010–11), HL 51, [4]).

Secondly, while it is accurate to say that a power to create delegated legislation may furnish Ministers with broad powers, it does not bestow upon them the powers of the sovereign legislature. As a result, the product of this ministerial law making is not of a similar nor-mative status to an Act of Parliament. Consequently, as in **Witham**, delegated legislation which is *ultra vires* the powers of the enabling, or parent, Act of Parliament can be struck down by the courts. It is for the reason that it is potentially subject to *both* parliamentary and judicial controls – as well as to the somewhat vague, convention-like, limitation that secondary legislation not involve 'great issues of principle'[44] – that this particular delegation of law-making power is generally regarded as constitutionally tolerable.

---

[42] The Joint Parliamentary Select Committee on Statutory Instruments, the House of Lords Delegated Power and Regulatory Reform Committee and the House of Lords Secondary Legislation Scrutiny Committee.

[43] House of Lords Select Committee on the Constitution, *Delegated Legislation and Parliament: A Response to the Strathclyde Review* (2015–16), HL 116, [36].

[44] Joint Committee on Conventions, *Conventions of the UK Parliament* (2005–2006), HL 265/HC 1212, [223] (quoting the evidence of Lord Norton of Louth).

Key debates

A fundamental realignment of the respective powers of Parliament and Executive?: The European Union (Withdrawal) Bill 2017

As we saw in Chapter 3, the draft legislation introduced in July 2017 intended to repeal the European Communities Act 1972 and address the status of European Union-derived laws post-Brexit seeks – in the first instance – to provide for legal certainty by transposing the entire corpus of EU Law onto the UK statute book. Following this transposition, on 'exit day', the ability of *Ministers* to amend 'retained EU law' is central to the scheme of the Bill, and therefore to the restoration of domestic 'control' over those areas of law previously governed by the institutions of the European Union. Via a series of delegating provisions and Henry VIII clauses, the Bill proposes to permit changes to be made to 'retained EU law' – potentially with substantive policy implications – by Government Ministers in order to address 'operational effectiveness' or other 'deficiency' in the retained law (clause 7 of the Bill, as introduced). Though the 2017 Queen's speech indicated that the Government would also ask Parliament to enact a series of specific statutes designed to facilitate the UK's transition out of the European Union, the potential for much detailed legislative amendment to take place in the absence of full and effective parliamentary scrutiny (and on the basis of a subjective test of 'deficiency') drew significant criticism.

The House of Lords Constitution Committee, in particular, was forthright in its criticisms of the breadth of the amendatory powers contained within the Bill:

> The number, range and overlapping nature of the broad delegated powers would create, in effect, an unprecedented and extraordinary portmanteau of effectively unlimited powers upon which the Government could draw. They would fundamentally challenge the constitutional balance of powers between Parliament and Government and would represent a significant – and unacceptable – transfer of legal competence. We stress the need for an appropriate balance between the urgency required to ensure legal continuity and stability, and meaningful parliamentary scrutiny and control of the executive (House of Lords Committee on the Constitution, *European Union (Withdrawal) Bill: Interim Report* (2017–2019), HL 19, [44].

As introduced, the Bill stands as an important corrective to those who hoped that Brexit would result in the restoration of law-making competence to the United Kingdom Parliament.

Judicial law making

What then of those occasions on which the judges formulate, or refine, the common law; are the judges, by making law, carrying out a legislative function? Is it permissible that they do so? In discharging their constitutional obligations, the judges have a 'creative', or law-making, role of their own.[45] Most obviously perhaps, the common law – that body of judicial decision-making which lies in areas outside those governed by statute law – is entirely judge-made. Again, such a body of law, created by a branch of government other than the legislature, would be incompatible with any strict separation of governmental functions.

Any recognition of a creative judicial role in respect of the common law must also naturally acknowledge that, unlike the theoretically unlimited law-making powers of Parliament, the creation of common law operates within limitations. Due to the case-by-case nature of common law adjudication, any change to be engineered will be incremental. Even if a suitable case makes its way before the courts, the common law is generally

---

[45] See the seminal article by Lord Reid, 'The Judge as Law-Maker' (1972–1973) 12 *Journal of the Society of Public Teachers of Law* 22.

regarded – not least by the judges – as an inappropriate mechanism by which to design and implement wholesale legal change.[46] It will also, of course, be subject to parliamentary override. So as Lord Devlin has written, even if it could be said that the judges possess a 'general warrant for judicial law-making' in the common law sphere:

> This warrant is an informal and rather negative one, amounting to a willingness to let the judges get on with their traditional work on two conditions – first, that they do it in the traditional way, i.e. in accordance with precedent, and second, that parliamentary interference should be regarded as unobjectionable.[47]

The general tenor of judicial restraint that permeates the development of this judge-made law is recognition that 'the common law is a process of law-making developed in a pre-democratic era, and maintained by a non-democratic form.'[48] As a result, the development of criminal offences at common law is regarded as being particularly controversial.[49] This tendency towards restraint has by no means, however, resulted in the stagnation of the common law:[50] there is a significant body of law in the fields of contract, tort and – most appropriately to this book – in the area of judicial review of executive action which ensures the continuing significance of the common law.[51]

Thinking Point . . .

The limits of the legitimate role of the courts in developing the law were discussed in *Malone* v *Metropolitan Police Commissioner* [1979] 1 Ch 344, 372, by Sir Robert Megarry VC. Megarry noted:

> [I]t is no function of the courts to legislate in a new field. The extension of the existing laws and principles is one thing, the creation of an altogether new right is another. At times judges must, and do, legislate; but . . . they do so only interstitially, and with molecular rather than molar motions . . . anything beyond that must be left for legislation. No new right in the law, fully-fledged with all the appropriate safeguards, can spring from the head of a judge deciding a particular case: only Parliament can create such a right.

More recently, the late Lord Bingham of Cornhill (in 'The way we live now: Human Rights in the New Millennium' in *The Business of Judging: Selected Essays and Speeches* (OUP, 2000), p. 167) employed a cricketing analogy to illustrate the incremental progress of common law development:

> . . . the common law scores its runs in singles: no boundaries, let alone sixes. The common law advances . . . in small, cautious steps.

---

[46] See e.g. *Malone* v *Metropolitan Police Commissioner* [1979] 1 Ch 344, 372 (Sir Robert Megarry VC).

[47] Lord Devlin 'Judges and Law-Makers' (1976) 39 MLR 1, 9.

[48] K.D. Ewing, 'A Theory of Democratic Adjudication: Towards a Representative, Accountable and Independent Judiciary' (2000) 38 *Alberta Law Review* 708, 711.

[49] For instance: *Shaw* v *Director of Public Prosecutions* [1962] AC 220 (conspiracy to corrupt public morals). For discussion see: H. Fenwick and G. Phillipson, *Media Freedom under the Human Rights Act* (OUP, 2006) pp. 443–7.

[50] Devlin, op. cit. (see note 47, above), 12: 'The judges who made the common law must not abrogate altogether their responsibility for keeping it abreast of the times.' As Dicey recognised, however, (A. V. Dicey, 'Judicial Legislation' in *Lectures on the Relationship between Law and Public Opinion in England during the Nineteenth Century* (Macmillan, 1914) p. 369) this responsiveness comes with clear limits: 'If a statute . . . is apt to reproduce the public opinion not so much of today as of yesterday, judge-made law occasionally represents the opinion of the day before yesterday.'

[51] On which, see Chapters 18 and 19.

Evidence of judicial creativity can also be found in the processes of statutory interpretation.[52] The most dramatic examples of this creative power can now be seen in adjudication under s. 3(1) of the Human Rights Act 1998 which requires that statutory provisions – whenever enacted – should be interpreted 'so far as is possible' to be compatible with the Convention rights given effect under s. 1(1) of that Act.[53] In the leading case on s. 3(1) of the Human Rights Act – the decision of the House of Lords in *Ghaidan* v *Godin-Mendoza*[54] – Lord Nicholls recognised that the courts are in effect able to 'modify the meaning and, hence, the effect, of primary and secondary legislation'.[55] To say that this is a departure from the traditional approach to the interpretation of statutory language, which gave effect to the sovereignty of Parliament through a close adherence to, and respect for, statutory language, is an understatement. As a result, a number of commentators agree that the application of s. 3(1) of the Human Rights Act 1998 provides the judges with an additional (albeit limited) law-making power.[56]

So just as the executive is permitted to exercise functions which would naturally attach to the legislative branch of government, it seems that the judges too undertake broader constitutional functions as a part of the processes of adjudication. If any separation of powers can be said to exist in the United Kingdom it would appear to be sufficiently fluid to permit not only a degree of institutional overlap, but also a degree of functional flexibility.

A partial separation of functions?

So while the United Kingdom Constitution provides numerous examples of infringements of a pure, or strict, separation of powers, a partial separation of functions might be said to exist. Munro, for one, has suggested that it *is* possible to make a general categorisation of the respective functions of the legislature, executive and judiciary, suggesting that:

> As the term is generally employed, the legislative activity involves the enactment of general rules for the individuals and groups in a society. The executive function is harder to define, but includes actions taken for the maintenance of order, in the implementation of the law, for the defence of the state, in the conduct of external affairs, and in the administration of internal policies. The judicial function involves the determination of issues of fact and the interpretation of the law, and dealing with crimes or civil causes by the application of the law to them.[57]

However, as important is the question of how to resolve disputes over which branch of government should exercise functions in a particular field. While any separation of functions must be underpinned by an allocation of those functions to the institutions expected to exercise them, Eric Barendt has argued that '[w]hat is crucial' is that the courts 'are entitled to take the final decision whether in practice a function is to be regarded as legislative, executive or judicial'.[58]

---

[52] On which, see pp. 144–52.

[53] For an analysis of the effects of this provision on the doctrine of parliamentary sovereignty, see pp. 165–7, for details and analysis of the Human Rights Act 1998 more broadly see Chapter 21.

[54] *Ghaidan* v *Godin-Mendoza* [2004] UKHL 30; [2004] 2 AC 557.

[55] Ibid., [32] (Lord Nicholls).

[56] See, for example, A. Kavanagh, 'The Elusive Divide between interpretation and legislation under the Human Rights Act' (2004) 24 OJLS 259, 261; A. Young, '*Ghaidan* v *Godin-Mendoza*: Avoiding the Deference Trap' [2004] PL 23, 27.

[57] C. Munro, *Studies in Constitutional Law* (2nd edn) (Butterworths, 1999) p. 294.

[58] E. Barendt, 'The Separation of Powers and Constitutional Government' [1995] PL 599, 605.

For Barendt then, the clear and principled division of functions is not the overriding concern of separation of powers; while it is important that functions are allocated – with a tolerable degree of flexibility – to the branches most competent to exercise them, it is *vital* that in instances of disagreement the courts have the determinative decision over where power should lie.[59] This view finds some support – at least insofar as the relationship between executive and judiciary is concerned – in the speech of Lord Nolan in *M* v *Home Office*:

> The proper constitutional relationship of the executive with the courts is that the courts will respect all acts of the executive within its lawful province, and that the executive will respect all decisions of the courts as to what its lawful province is.[60]

This finding raises two related points which are of relevance to our study of the United Kingdom Constitution. It should be noted that Lord Nolan's dictum applies only to the relationship between the courts and executive, whereas Barendt argues that the courts should possess the ability to determine with finality whether a certain decision falls within the powers of the courts, the executive or *Parliament*. If the judges are to have the final and determinative say over which governmental bodies should exercise what governmental functions, what does that tell us, first, about the status of the sovereignty of Parliament as a legal doctrine, and second, about the division of legal and political power in the United Kingdom Constitution? If the judges have the final say over where governmental power should – and does – lie, can Parliament be said to be truly sovereign?

Thinking Point . . .

In *R (Prolife Alliance)* v *BBC* [2004] 1 AC 185, at [75], Lord Hoffmann also found that determining which branch of government should exercise a particular function was a task which should be entrusted to the courts. Hoffmann said:

> In a country based on the rule of law and separation of powers, it is necessary to decide which branch of government has in any particular instance the decision-making power and what the limits of that power are. That is a question of law and must therefore be decided by the courts.

Separation of powers in the United Kingdom Constitution (I): a partial division of functions?

Key issues

- Governmental powers in the United Kingdom can perhaps, at best, only be described as being partially separated. A far bigger problem for those seeking to apply separation of powers theory to the United Kingdom Constitution is posed by the doctrine of parliamentary sovereignty under which – rather than being divided between equal branches of government – one, sovereign, institution is legally dominant.

- As a result, in its peculiarly British incarnation, separation of powers is argued to lack the required normative quality; it can only describe how powers are in fact divided, rather than *require* powers to be allocated in a specific way, to specific institutions.

---

[59]   Ibid.
[60]   *M* v *Home Office* [1992] QB 270, 314 (Lord Nolan).

Theories on the separation of powers clearly support a number of ideas which we would generally think of as being integral to the UK Constitution. For example, separation of powers supports the idea that disputes between the individual and the government should be legally determined by independent judges who are able to apply the law without concern for their popularity at the polls. The separation of powers also supports the idea the judges should have security of tenure, so that they might take (potentially unpopular) decisions against the government without fear of being removed from their posts. Both of these characteristics of a constitutional system – as we saw in Chapter 6 – are arguably also required by the rule of law and in this sense at least, in suggesting that separation of powers requires an independent judicial branch of government, the ideas of separation of powers and the rule of law are mutually supportive.

While most would agree that the rule of law holds an important place within the UK Constitution (though there is disagreement as to its scope), the precise relationship between the constitution and separation of powers theory is more hotly disputed. On the one hand Professor Hood Phillips, for instance, denounced separation of powers as a 'constitutional myth'[61] in the United Kingdom, while on the other, Lord Diplock was able to confidently assert in the **Duport Steel** case that, 'it cannot be too strongly emphasised that the British constitution, though largely unwritten, is firmly based on the separation of powers.'[62]

There are two immediate – and related – difficulties which are encountered when attempting to assess the relevance of separation of powers in the UK Constitution. First, without a constitutional document which prescribes that governmental power be allocated in a particular way, or to particular institutions, the constitution cannot be said to explicitly set down which branches of government should carry out a particular function, or that three branches of government should even exist. As a result, any separation of powers which can be said to exist in the UK cannot be said to be the consequence of any identifiable higher law or constitutional direction.

Secondly, as we have seen, the dominant principle in the UK remains the sovereignty of Parliament.[63] As a result, the sovereignty doctrine purports to ultimately vest all legal authority in *one* governmental institution: Parliament. If this is correct, as Dicey suggested, and Parliament's sovereign power remains the 'undoubted legal fact'[64] of the constitution, then legal authority would seem to be concentrated in one dominant body, rather than being divided between three co-equal branches of government.

Given that the doctrine of the sovereignty of Parliament remains the closest thing to a fundamental principle recognised in the UK constitution, it has been argued that separation of powers *cannot* regulate how powers should be dispersed between the institutions of government. Tomkins argues, therefore, that whatever separation of powers can be said

---

[61] O. Hood Phillips, 'A Constitutional Myth: Separation of Powers' (1977) 93 LQR 11. See also S. A. De Smith, 'The Separation of Powers in New Dress' (1966) 12 *McGill Law Journal* 491, 491.

[62] *Duport Steel* v *Sirs* [1980] 1 WLR 142, 157. See also *M* v *Home Office* [1994] 1 AC 377, 395 (Lord Templeman).

[63] Chapter 5.

[64] A. V. Dicey, *Introduction to the Study of the Law of the Constitution* (Liberty Fund, 1982) p. 24.

to exist is merely descriptive of the distribution of governmental power at a given time as determined by Parliament, rather than a constitutional determination that certain defined powers should be exercised by certain defined institutions in perpetuity:

> While we can as a matter of practice identify a distinct legislature, executive and judiciary, that is to say, we can say descriptively that there exist in England a Parliament, a government and a court structure, we cannot argue that the constitution prescribes that such a division should exist. To the limited extent that there is some separation along these lines, it is merely descriptive and not normative.[65]

Tomkins' account presents a significant obstacle to those who would seek to suggest that the UK Constitution is shaped by the doctrine of separation of powers; supporters of the doctrine as a requirement of liberal constitutionalism would suggest that separation of powers should not simply be the result of a division of governmental competence, but it should be a prerequisite of a constitution which prescribes that governmental powers be allocated in a specific way. In other words, separation of powers should be a normative – not merely a descriptive – characteristic of a constitutional system.

Is Tomkins' assessment correct? We can – as Tomkins acknowledges – identify a legislative branch, an executive branch and a judicial branch. Moreover, we can begin to suggest that each of these branches can be seen to exercise certain (potentially distinctive) functions. While there may exist a degree of uncertainty around the precise categorisation of certain disputed exercises of governmental power, we nevertheless can begin to say that certain functions should be carried out by certain branches of government. We can say that the conduct of criminal trials, for example, is a 'classic judicial function'[66] which should be carried out by a body which:

- is independent of the government and the parties to the case;
- is able to decide issues of law and of fact in a way which is seen to be objectively impartial; and
- is able to impose sanctions in the event of finding a breach of the law.

Tomkins' argument, taken to its logical extreme, would suggest that should Parliament wish to reallocate the power to conduct criminal trials, from the courts to, say, the executive branch, then it would be legally entitled to do so. That, of course, would be the natural consequence of parliamentary sovereignty as an unfettered legal doctrine. But we have already seen that the sovereignty doctrine sits in an uneasy relationship with both the rule of law, and those, related, 'political' restrictions on Parliament's power which dictate that, while Parliament might be legally entitled to act as it pleases, it might not necessarily do so due to the adverse political consequences which would result. It would be fair to suggest, therefore, based on the demands of the rule of law and the principle of legality[67] – not to mention the obligations of the state under Art. 6(1) of the European Convention on Human Rights – that Parliament would not legislate to completely abolish criminal

---

[65] A. Tomkins, *Public Law* (Clarendon, 2003) p. 38.

[66] *R v Secretary of State for the Home Department, ex parte Venables* [1998] AC 407, 526 (Lord Steyn).

[67] *R v Secretary of State for the Home Department, ex parte Simms* [2000] 2 AC 115, 131 (Lord Hoffmann): 'Parliamentary sovereignty means that Parliament can, if it chooses, legislate contrary to fundamental principles of human rights. The constraints upon . . . Parliament are ultimately political, not legal. But the principle of legality means that Parliament must squarely confront what it is doing and accept the political cost.'

trials and impose a system of executive-conducted 'adjudication'. If this is the case, it is not so straightforward to suggest that the separation of powers that can be said to exist in the United Kingdom is simply descriptive, for in this rudimentary example it can be seen to possess a degree of normative content. It is not, therefore, such a logical leap to suggest that Parliament would in fact be prevented from legislating on such a topic – for example, in a way which obviously and dramatically abrogated the right of the individual to be tried by a fair and independent procedure – because of the constitutional significance which separation of powers accords to an independent judicial system and process.

Moreover, when looking at the constitution in the light of the partial separation, or partial agency, reading of separation of powers, then it is arguable that a system of checks and balances can also be said to exist. While the sovereignty of Parliament remains the 'bedrock of the British constitution'[68] there nevertheless exists a system under which the three branches of government exercise a degree of control over the exercise of power by the other branches. For example, for the executive to ensure that a legislative proposal becomes an Act of Parliament, it must ordinarily seek and gain the support of the majority of the House of Commons and of the House of Lords. If the consent of Parliament cannot be obtained, the executive branch has no independent competence to enact primary legislation. Once that legislative proposal becomes law, the judiciary is then empowered to determine how – consistently with the intentions of Parliament and with obligations under the Human Rights Act and (at least until the UK exits the EU) EU law – that legislation is interpreted. Similarly, a member of the executive acting under a statutory power is subject to the judicial review jurisdiction of the courts and may be held to have acted *ultra vires* if he or she has acted beyond the power granted by the Act.[69] Checks and balances in the constitution are returned to below, but first it is necessary to examine the *institutional* difficulties of applying separation of powers theory to the United Kingdom.

Separation of powers in the United Kingdom (II): partially separated institutions?

Setting the scene
The overlapping of powers

- While separation of powers theory holds that they should be separated, there are, and have historically been, significant overlaps between the *personnel* who make up the various branches of government in the United Kingdom. The Cabinet – the core executive – is drawn from the ranks of Parliament, while the monarch retains a residual presence across all three branches of government. Historically, the Lord Chancellor enjoyed legislative, executive and judicial roles, while the Appellate Committee of the House of Lords (the predecessor to the United Kingdom Supreme Court) was a committee of the upper house of Parliament.
- The 'fusion' of the executive and legislative branches remains, perhaps, the defining characteristic of the Westminster model of government and one of the biggest institutional obstacles to the realisation of separation of powers in the United Kingdom. The judiciary, by contrast, is increasingly recognised to be institutionally separated and an independent branch of government.

---

[68] *R (Jackson)* v *Attorney-General* [2005] UKHL 56; [2006] 1 AC 262, [9] (Lord Bingham).
[69] See Chapter 19.

It has already been observed that at the heart of our constitutional arrangements lies 'the nearly complete fusion of the executive and legislative powers'.[70] The Cabinet is comprised of ministers drawn from the ranks of either the House of Commons or House of Lords. It has been suggested that such a significant institutional overlap would be seriously damaging to any claim that the UK Constitution was based on a pure, or strict, version of separation of powers. While the institutional overlap between executive and legislature is perhaps the most well known in the constitution, it by no means represents the only blurred boundary between the three branches of government to have been found in the United Kingdom.

The office of Lord Chancellor

The position of Lord Chancellor is one of the most long-standing in the UK Constitution. The office dates back to the medieval period, and holders of the office have been among some of the most notable in British history: Thomas Beckett, Cardinal Wolsey, Sir Thomas More, and Francis Bacon among them. The holder of the office of Lord Chancellor was – until the reforms to that office initiated in 2003[71] – effectively a member of all three branches of government. The holder of the office was not only the head of a government department responsible for the courts and legal policy and services – the Lord Chancellor's Department – but also acted as the speaker of the House of Lords, and further, as head of the judiciary in England and Wales, was able to sit as a judge and held responsibility for a wide range of judicial appointments.[72] The presence of an office which straddled all three branches of government – enabling the holder to exercise legislative, executive and judicial functions – would not appear to 'accord with even the weakest doctrine of the separation of powers',[73] and had accordingly been described by commentators as 'the living refutation of the doctrine of separation of powers in England'.[74] Prior to the reforms completed with the enactment of the Constitutional Reform Act 2005, the position of Lord Chancellor was defended on pragmatic, rather than principled, grounds; Lord Irvine of Lairg QC, holder of the office from 1997 to 2003, declared that the office was 'the natural conduit for communications between the judiciary and the executive, so that each fully understands the legitimate objectives of the other'.[75]

The Appellate Committee of the House of Lords

Prior to the creation of the United Kingdom Supreme Court in 2009, the United Kingdom's highest court – the Appellate Committee of the House of Lords – had also drawn criticism on separation of powers grounds.[76] The Appellate Committee of the House of Lords was technically a committee of the upper house of Parliament tasked with the

---

[70] W. Bagehot, *The English Constitution* (Oxford World's Classics) (OUP, 2001) p. 11.

[71] The reforms instituted by the Constitutional Reform Act 2005 are discussed more fully in Chapter 11. For an introduction see: A. Le Sueur, 'New Labour's Next (Surprisingly Quick) Steps in Constitutional Reform' [2003] PL 368.

[72] See generally, D. Woodhouse, *The Office of Lord Chancellor* (Hart Publishing, 2001).

[73] Ibid., p. 12.

[74] T. C. Hartley and J. A. G. Griffith, *Government and Law* (2nd edn) (Weidenfeld and Nicolson, 1981) p. 179.

[75] HL Debs, 25 November 1997, col. 934 (Lord Irvine of Lairg QC).

[76] R. Cornes, '*McGonnell v United Kingdom*, the Lord Chancellor and the Law Lords' [2000] PL 166.

administration of judicial functions. While the primary function of the Law Lords was to administer the judicial business of the House of Lords, the members of the Appellate Committee were appointed as peers on their elevation to the highest court. As a result, they were eligible to participate in the legislative and committee business of the House in the same way as other peers[77] and the Law Lords historically made a notable contribution to the legislative and committee business of the upper house.[78]

In keeping with the disputed position of the separation of powers in the United Kingdom the institutional overlap between judiciary and legislature was tolerated and defended by reference to the 'extensive judicial experience' with which the Law Lords were able to 'usefully clarify legal points or help identify issues which require decision'.[79] Equally, it was said that the Law Lords themselves gained benefit from 'a greater understanding of the problems of the legislator, of social trends, of the proper limits of judicial innovation' which would benefit them in their adjudicative role.[80] Nonetheless, in part due to increased awareness of the potential for confusion surrounding the Law Lords' exercise of this dual role, the Senior Law Lord in 2000 sought to clarify how the roles of legislator and adjudicator were to be kept distinct:

> First, the Lords of Appeal in Ordinary do not think it appropriate to engage in matters where there is a strong element of party political controversy; and secondly the Lords of Appeal in Ordinary bear in mind that they might render themselves ineligible to sit judicially if they were to express an opinion on a matter which might later be relevant to an appeal to the House.[81]

The creation of the United Kingdom Supreme Court was – alongside reform of the office of Lord Chancellor – one of the key reforms instituted by the Constitutional Reform Act 2005.[82] Both of these reforms considerably clarify the institutional separation at the apex of the United Kingdom's legal system, and are returned to and examined in further detail later (Chapter 11).

The monarch

Perhaps the most endemic institutional overlaps relate to the constitutional position of the monarch. The Queen retains a constitutional presence in respect of all three branches of government. In respect of the legislative branch, the Queen in Parliament is one of the constituent parts of the legislature, and as has already been seen, legislation cannot come into

---

[77] Appellate Jurisdiction Act 1876, s. 6: 'Every Lord of Appeal in Ordinary . . . shall by virtue and according to the date of his appointment be entitled during his life to rank as a Baron by such style as Her Majesty may be pleased to appoint, and shall be entitled to a writ of summons to attend, and to sit and vote in the House of Lords . . .'

[78] For a detailed (albeit dated) description of the Law Lords as legislators, see L. Blom-Cooper and G. Drewry, *Final Appeal* (Clarendon Press, 1972), ch. 10. For more recent examples, see Lord Hope, 'Voices from the Past – the Law Lords' Contribution to the Legislative Process' (2007) 123 LQR 547; Lord Hope, 'The Law Lords in Parliament' in L. Blom-Cooper, B. Dickson and G. Drewry (eds), *The Judicial House of Lords 1876–2009* (OUP, 2009); P. O'Brien, 'Judges and Politics: The Parliamentary Contributions of the Law Lords 1876–2009' (2016) 79 MLR 786.

[79] Royal Commission on Reform of the House of Lords, *A House for the Future,* Cm. 4534 (January 2000), Ch. 9, [9.6]. It is useful to note that the Royal Commission recognised that this role could be, and indeed is, also played by 'other members of the second chamber with legal expertise or experience' ([9.7]).

[80] Royal Commission on Reform of the House of Lords, op. cit., Evidence of Lord Wilberforce.

[81] HL Debs, cols 419–20, 22 June 2000.

[82] Constitutional Reform Act 2005, part III.

effect without obtaining the Royal Assent. It is the Queen who possesses the legal power to summon and prorogue Parliament. Members of the Cabinet – and other Ministers of the Crown – are appointed by the monarch and exercise executive power on behalf of the monarch. Similarly, the residual role of the monarch as fountain of justice is evident from the fact that the High Court and Court of Appeal are housed in the *Royal* Courts of Justice. Judicial review actions, for example, reflect the historical view that the function of controlling governmental activity – by way of the orders of *certiorari*, prohibition and mandamus[83] – was a matter for the Royal Prerogative.[84] As Peter Cane has explained, '[f]or this reason, the title of applications for prerogative orders took the form: *R* (*Regina*, the Crown, the nominal claimant) v *A* (defendant) *ex p.* (on behalf of) *B* (the real claimant)'.[85] Similarly, criminal trials are brought by the *Crown* Prosecution Service on behalf of the monarch and so will typically be recorded in the law reports in the following way – *R* v *A* (with *R* representing the prosecuting authority of the Crown and *A* being the defendant). It is undeniable, therefore, that – far from solely being a figurehead for the United Kingdom – the Crown has a pervasive influence on all three branches of the constitution of the United Kingdom.

It is also true that in many respects the role of the monarch in the day-to-day constitutional life of the United Kingdom is residual. This was certainly the view of Bagehot, for example, who declared that the Prime Minister was head of the 'efficient' part of the constitution and responsible for the day-to-day activities of government, while the monarch remained head of the constitution's 'dignified' arm.[86] Bagehot wrote:

> We have in England an elective first magistrate as truly as the Americans have an elective first magistrate. The Queen is only at the head of the dignified part of the constitution. The Prime Minister is at the head of the efficient part.

The role of the Crown, for example, as a nominal party to judicial review proceedings is wholly symbolic. Otherwise, in those areas where the monarch continues to exercise significant legal power – for example to appoint the Prime Minister – the discretion over when and how to exercise the authority is curtailed by convention. The most significant difficulty which results from the constitutional position of the monarch is the uncertainty and confusion which arises from the monarch effectively holding positions in all three branches of government. While it might be argued that the significant limitations placed on the abilities of the monarch to exercise legal power by convention render insignificant the separation of powers implications of the position of the monarch, the problem of constitutional coherence remains. Adam Tomkins has argued that this incoherence is reflected in particular in the case of *M* v *Home Office*.[87]

---

[83] *Certiorari,* prohibition and mandamus are the three 'prerogative orders' available on an application for judicial review. *Certiorari* has the effect of quashing an *ultra vires* act, prohibition would prohibit such an act and mandamus would make the performance of a certain act compulsory. They are now referred to as quashing, prohibiting and mandatory orders. See Chapter 18.

[84] Cane continues: '[t]his was nothing but form because the real claimant initiated the proceedings for a prerogative order, conducted them in their entirety, and was liable for the costs of the action. However, the form did serve as a reminder of uncertainty about the extent to which private citizens are the most appropriate persons to initiate action in the courts to challenge public decision-making. This uncertainty remains in the title of applications for quashing, prohibiting and mandatory orders: *R. (A)* v *B*, A being the real claimant.' (P. Cane, *Administrative Law* (4th edn) (Clarendon Press, 2004) pp. 33–4.

[85] Ibid.

[86] W. Bagehot, *The English Constitution* (Oxford World's Classics) (OUP, 2001) p. 11.

[87] *M* v *Home Office* [1994] 1 AC 377; 3 All ER 537. On which, see M. Gould, '*M* v *Home Office*: Government and the Judges' [1993] PL 568.

Key debates

The pervasive – and uncertain – constitutional influence of the Crown

M v *Home Office* arose out of an immigration dispute. M was a national of Zaire who had unsuccessfully applied for asylum in the United Kingdom. Prior to the hearing of an application to judicially review the decision to deport the applicant – during which time the judge had ordered that the deportation be stayed – M was put on a plane and flown back to Zaire. The judge issued an injunction requiring M's return. The Home Secretary, after taking legal advice, did not act upon the court order. The question for the House of Lords was whether, notwithstanding the effects of the Crown Proceedings Act 1947 (which allowed civil law actions – for example in contract and tort – to be brought against the Crown), a Minister of the Crown could be held in contempt of court for failing to abide by the court's order to bring M back to the United Kingdom. The question for the Law Lords was whether a Minister of the Crown could be held in contempt of court. At first glance, this issue appears to be phrased in relatively simple terms, however, as Tomkins suggests, this apparent simplicity masks the nature of the, altogether more confusing, problem:

> . . . can the Crown's courts find the Crown's Ministers in contempt of the Crown's courts? Can one branch of the Crown find that another branch of the Crown is in contempt of the Crown? Clearly, when phrased like this, the question becomes rather more problematic . . .[88]

The finding of the House of Lords in *M* v *Home Office* was that the courts *could* hold Ministers of the Crown to be in contempt of court. The case is a significant one as evidence of the ability of the courts to check and balance the powers of the executive, and, as we have seen, a landmark rule of law decision, yet it also resoundingly displays the vagueness and confusion surrounding the legal status of the Crown across the institutions of government.

The independence of the judiciary

While the UK Constitution cannot be said to have executive and legislative branches that are comprised of separate personnel, the judicial branch is, with limited and declining exceptions following the implementation of the Constitutional Reform Act 2005, both functionally and institutionally separate from the legislature and executive.

The notion of judicial independence is of course supported by the ideal of the rule of law. It is, in turn, the characteristic of separation of powers that can be seen most clearly in the UK Constitution. As Dicey observed, the rule of law requires that:

> . . . no man is punishable or can be lawfully made to suffer in body or goods except for a distinct breach of law established in the ordinary legal manner before the ordinary Courts of the land. In this sense the rule of law is contrasted with every system of government based on the exercise by persons in authority of wide, arbitrary, or discretionary powers of constraint.[89]

In Dicey's view, therefore, the rule of law requires the existence of an independent judiciary to ensure that general legal rules are applied fairly, and that legal sanctions may not be imposed capriciously by members of the executive branch. Hence, for Dicey, the rule of law – in seeking to restrain the exercise of executive powers – served much the same function as a constitutional separation of powers. While Dicey's views on the rule of law might

---

[88] A. Tomkins, *Public Law* (Clarendon Press, 2003) p. 53.
[89] A. V. Dicey, *Introduction to the Study of the Law of the Constitution* (Liberty Fund, 1982) p. 110.

be criticised on a number of grounds,[90] the presence of an independent judiciary can nevertheless be regarded as being central to his and more resonant accounts of the rule of law,[91] and to the UK's unique conception of separation of powers. Indeed, Hartley and Griffith have suggested that judicial independence is 'the one aspect of the separation of powers that is accepted in the British constitution'.[92] Similarly, Lord Hewart, in his polemic, *The New Despotism* wrote that in 'our Constitution, the "separation of powers" refers, and can refer only, to the principle that the judges are independent of the Executive'.[93]

Unlike those other aspects of separation of power which cannot be said to be clearly evident in the United Kingdom Constitution, support for an independent judiciary is evident in legislation of constitutional importance dating back hundreds of years. Magna Carta of 1215 contains the commitment that 'royal government must function both through judicial processes and with the counsel of the great men of the kingdom',[94] as well as to a number of guarantees of fair process, including that 'free men' accused of criminal offences should be tried by their 'peers' or, in other words, not by those who had levelled the accusations made.[95] The Act of Settlement 1701 – the Act which, along with the Bill of Rights 1689, cemented the transition from monarchical to parliamentary government – famously provides that 'judges' commissions be made *quamdiu se bene gesserint* (during good behaviour). The effect in practice of this arcane turn of Latin phraseology is to ensure that judges enjoy security of tenure, and that, as a result, they cannot therefore simply be removed on a whim by those against whom they may have made unpopular decisions. The Act of Settlement further provides that judges' salaries be ascertained and established, that is, established by statute and therefore immune from executive interference. And finally, the Act also provides that senior judges may only be lawfully removed from office 'upon the address of both houses of Parliament'. It is testament to the enduring influence of these provisions that not only have they been reinforced in more recent times in the Appellate Jurisdiction Act 1876, the Senior Courts Act 1981 and most recently in the Constitutional Reform Act 2005,[96] but that Parliament has not invoked the procedure to remove a serving judge from office during modern times. (And, in fact, the procedure has only *ever* been successfully invoked once, when in 1830 Sir Jonah Barrington was removed from the Irish High Court of Admiralty, after he was found guilty of committing embezzlement.) The cumulative effect of these provisions is that the senior judiciary possess security of tenure, allowing decisions to be taken in accordance with the law so as to 'do right to all manner of people after the laws and usages of this realm, without fear or favour, affection or ill will'.[97] This security of tenure forms the basis of judicial independence in the United Kingdom.

---

[90] Chapter 6.

[91] See e.g.: J. Raz, 'The Rule of Law and its Virtue' (1977) 93 *Law Quarterly Review* 195.

[92] T. C. Hartley and J. A. G. Griffith, *Government and Law* (2nd edn) (Weidenfeld and Nicolson, 1981) p. 175.

[93] Lord Hewart, *The New Despotism* (Ernest Benn Ltd, 1929) pp. 37–45.

[94] R. V. Turner, *Magna Carta through the Ages* (Pearson, 2003) p. 67 (cited in E. Wicks, *The Evolution of a Constitution: Eight Key Moments in British Constitutional History* (Hart Publishing, 2006) p. 5).

[95] For an outline, see E. Wicks, *The Evolution of a Constitution: Eight Key Moments in British Constitutional History* (Hart Publishing, 2006) pp. 3–6.

[96] See also: Supreme Court Act 1981, s. 11(3); Appellate Jurisdiction Act 1876, s. 6; Constitutional Reform Act 2005, s. 33.

[97] As per the judicial oath.

The independence of the judicial branch is supported by statute, by convention and at common law. The Constitutional Reform Act 2005 places Ministers of the Crown under an obligation to 'uphold the continued independence of the judiciary'.[98] Judges are disqualified from membership of the House of Commons by virtue of the House of Commons Disqualification Act 1975.[99] By convention, judges should insulate themselves from party politics by resigning any membership of a political party upon appointment, and are also by convention insulated from direct and personal criticism by ministers in respect of judicial decisions made.[100] In addition to these structural guarantees of judicial independence, the common law has also developed its own protections for the independence and impartiality of the judicial process. The common law on judicial bias, makes clear that a judge should be independent of the parties to a case, and may be automatically disqualified from sitting in the event of being found to have a financial interest in the outcome of the case[101] or in the event of having a non-pecuniary interest in the outcome of the case, for example, after having promoted a cause with which one of the parties is associated.[102]

While independence of the parties to a cause of action is one element of judicial independence, for our purposes it is judicial independence of the other branches of government which is materially important. The appearance of an independent and impartial judicial process is a maxim well established in the common law of England and Wales reflected in the well-known judicial dictum that 'justice should not only be done, but should manifestly and undoubtedly be *seen to be done*'.[103] Through the coming into force of the Human Rights Act 1998, this common law aphorism has been bolstered by Art. 6(1) of the European Convention on Human Rights which requires that:

> In the determination of his civil rights and obligations or of any criminal charge against him, everyone is entitled to a fair and public hearing within a reasonable time by an independent and impartial tribunal established by law.

The case law of the European Court of Human Rights indicates that the requirement of independence means that courts be independent of both the parties to the case *and* of the executive.[104] Further, the Art. 6(1) requirement of impartiality – that a court should possess the objectively-gauged appearance of impartiality – has been invoked to cast doubt on the propriety of judges exercising legislative functions.[105] The effect of Art. 6(1) is not that the European Convention on Human Rights requires signatories to the Convention to adhere to a general constitutional separation of powers.[106] However, the effect of the implementation of the Art. 6(1) case law has been to compel an effective

---

[98] Constitutional Reform Act 2005, s. 3(1).

[99] House of Commons Disqualification Act 1975, s. 1 and sch. 1.

[100] Although it should be noted that the effectiveness of this latter convention has occasionally been doubted in recent times: see the response of David Blunkett MP to the decision of Mr Justice Collins in *R (Q)* v *Secretary of State for the Home Department* [2003] EWCA Civ 364 (on which, see A. Bradley, 'Judicial Independence Under Attack' [2003] PL 397).

[101] *Dimes* v *Proprietors of the Grand Junction Canal* (1852) 3 HLC 759.

[102] *R* v *Bow Street Magistrate, ex parte Pinochet Ugarte (No. 2)* [2000] 1 AC 199.

[103] *R* v *Sussex Justices, ex parte McCarthy* [1924] 1 KB 256, 259 (emphasis added).

[104] *Ringeisen* v *Austria (No. 1)* (1971) 1 EHRR 455, [95]; *Campbell and Fell* v *United Kingdom* (1985) 7 EHRR 165, [78].

[105] See e.g. *Procola* v *Luxembourg* (1996) 22 EHRR 193.

[106] As the European Court of Human Rights noted in *McGonnell* v *United Kingdom* (2000) 30 EHRR 289, [51]: '. . . neither Art. 6(1) nor any other provision of the Convention requires states to comply with any theoretical constitutional concepts as such'.

separation of powers in a number of specific domestic instances,[107] and was one of the clear motivating factors behind stripping the Lord Chancellor of his judicial role, and behind the decision to remove the Law Lords from Parliament and establish an institutionally separate United Kingdom Supreme Court.[108]

Constitutional checks and balances

Key issues

Though there is some overlap in the allocation of governmental functions between institutions, and in the membership of the three branches of government, separation of powers is reflected in the United Kingdom in the sense that checks and balances do operate in practice. Parliament and the courts operate in tandem to check and balance the activities of the executive, and the courts – using, for instance, human rights norms – exercise a limited ability to temper the (theoretically unlimited) legislative power of Parliament.

So much for the requirement that separation of powers requires a clear separation of both governmental institutions and functions. However, examining separation of powers from the perspective of a constitutional guarantee ensuring the accountability of government, begins to reveal a slightly different picture. There is, it is suggested, evidence of a rudimentary separation of functions among the three branches of government in the United Kingdom. As Lord Templeman outlined in *M* v *Home Office*: 'Parliament makes the law, the executive carry the law into effect and the judiciary enforce[s] the law'.[109] As has been observed above, coming to a more principled separation of functions is particularly difficult due to the doctrine of parliamentary sovereignty. Nevertheless, even taking into account parliamentary sovereignty and the resulting difficulties of making a principle-based allocation of functions to the three branches of government, there is a well-established system of checks and balances operating at both the parliamentary and judicial levels. Governmental powers *are* therefore subject to constraints under our existing constitutional arrangements.

Parliamentary controls on the executive

Approaching separation of powers from a checks and balances perspective, the 'fusion' of executive and legislative branches is arguably not so troublesome as it would be if separation of powers required a definitive separation of governmental institutions. As outlined above, the executive cannot enact primary legislation without the agreement of Parliament; as a result, the executive is required to place its legislative proposals before Parliament, subject

---

[107] See e.g: *Davidson* v *Scottish Ministers* [2004] UKHL 34; [2004] HRLR 34 (requiring a separation of legislative and judicial functions); *R (Brooke)* v *Parole Board* [2008] EWCA Civ 29; [2008] 1 WLR 1950 (requiring a separation of judicial and executive functions).

[108] Chapter 11. See also R. Masterman, '*A Supreme Court for the United Kingdom*: Two Steps Forward but One Step Back on Judicial Independence' [2004] *Public Law* 48, 51–3.

[109] *M* v *Home Office* [1994] 1 AC 377, 395 (Lord Templeman).

them to revision and amendment by both the Commons and the Lords,[110] and ultimately try to persuade a majority of both Houses that the proposal deserves parliamentary endorsement. In addition, through parliamentary questions and debates and the activities of parliamentary committees, Parliament can hold the executive to account for the discharge of its functions and for the failings of its policies and its personnel. Due to the doctrine of individual ministerial responsibility, ministers are constitutionally obligated to explain and account for the activities of their departments, and ultimately may be required to resign in the event of severe failings.[111] Theoretically at least, therefore, Parliament is able to act as a constitutional check on the activities of the executive.

However, a number of commentators are of the view that the dominance of Parliament by the executive branch precludes effective parliamentary accountability.[112] It is certainly the case that a government with a substantial Commons majority will be able to effectively dominate the business of the House. It is a design feature of the electoral system used for elections to the Westminster Parliament[113] that it shows a tendency to elect strong governments, that is, governments with large majorities in the House of Commons. A strong government is institutionally well-placed – as a result of, *inter alia,* the whipping system, effective executive control of the parliamentary timetable and the primacy of the House of Commons – to achieve its manifesto commitments. For example, the first Blair administration – 1997–2001 – was elected with a majority of 179 seats, and was never defeated in a motion voted on in the House of Commons. Ditto the second Blair Government, elected in 2001 with a Commons majority of 167. In the 1970s, Lord Hailsham coined the term 'elective dictatorship' to describe the reality of executive power within our so-called parliamentary system,[114] and any assertion that the United Kingdom's separation of powers embraces an effective system of checks and balances must accept that Parliament's powers in the face of a particularly dominant executive branch may be limited. As Rodney Brazier has commented, the consequence of this may be that '[l]egal sovereignty is in practice exercised by – or at least at the request of – ministers'.[115] The effectiveness of these political limitations on government are examined in full below (see Chapters 14 and 15).

Judicial review

As a result of the supremacy of Parliament, and the accordant status of Acts of Parliament as the highest form of law in the jurisdiction, the courts are not entitled to strike down or otherwise invalidate legislation as a general rule. As we have seen, there has been a limited exception to this rule effective during the UK's membership of the EU in those spheres in which European Union law applies; in the event of an inconsistency between domestic and EU law, the courts might 'disapply' primary legislation to the strict extent required by the inconsistency.[116] Further, in the course of adjudication under the Human Rights

---

[110] Cf. those instances where the Parliament Acts 1911 and 1949 are invoked.

[111] *The Ministerial Code* (Cabinet Office, 2018). See Chapter 14.

[112] See, for example, E. Barendt, *An Introduction to Constitutional Law* (Clarendon Press, 1998) ch. 6. Cf. A. Tomkins, *Public Law* (Clarendon Press, 2003) ch. 5.

[113] The first-past-the-post system, further examined in Chapter 9.

[114] Lord Hailsham, *The Dilemma of Democracy: Diagnosis and Prescription* (Collins, 1978).

[115] R. Brazier, *Constitutional Reform: Reshaping the Political System* (3rd edn) (OUP, 2008) p. 43.

[116] *R v Secretary of State for Transport, ex parte Factortame (No. 2)* [1991] 1 AC 603.

Act 1998 the courts may declare parliamentary legislation to be incompatible with the Convention rights.[117] A declaration of incompatibility issued under the Human Rights Act does not, however, affect the 'validity, continuing operation or enforcement' of the provision(s) in respect of which it is made, and further action by either the executive or Parliament will be necessary to repeal or amend the contested section or sections.[118] As outlined above, the courts may also apply principles of statutory interpretation which require the use of express words to, for example, override a constitutional right existing at common law,[119] or to repeal a statutory provision regarded by the common law as being constitutional.[120] Each of these powers allows the judiciary to check the exercise of legislative power, to varying degrees, though none extends so far as to amount to a generally exercisable power to invalidate parliamentary legislation.

In respect of the powers exercised by the executive, however, the courts have a significant tool at their disposal. Judicial review of executive action allows the courts to review the legality of the exercise of administrative discretion and is the most significant check on executive power which is exercisable by the judiciary. Executive action may traditionally be challenged on the grounds of illegality, irrationality, or procedural impropriety.[121] In addition, s. 6 of the Human Rights Act 1998 makes it unlawful for public authorities to act in a way which is incompatible with the Convention rights given effect under that Act.

Judicial review is, however, a primarily procedural rather than a substantive check on executive power; judicial review is not a review of the merits of a particular decision.[122] Nor is the judicial power to review executive discretion a power of appeal – the court does not have the ability to replace the public authority's decision with its own. As Lord Greene MR indicated in the seminal *Wednesbury* case:

> The power of the court to interfere in each case is not as an appellate authority to override a decision of the local authority, but as a judicial authority which is concerned, and concerned only, to see whether the local authority have contravened the law by acting in excess of the powers which Parliament has confided in them.[123]

For this reason, the judicial review jurisdiction is described as being supervisory rather than appellate. The distinction between review and appeal therefore 'reflects a conception of limited judicial authority, recognising that in most cases a public authority may exercise a genuine choice between competing public policy objectives and contrasting methods of implementation'.[124] Judicial review is discussed in full below (see Chapters 18 and 19).

---

[117] Section 4(2) HRA. See also Chapter 21.

[118] Section 4(6) HRA.

[119] See for example: *R v Lord Chancellor, ex parte Witham* [1995] QB 575; *R v Secretary of State for the Home Department, ex parte Simms* [2000] 2 AC 115.

[120] *Thoburn v Sunderland City Council* [2003] QB 151.

[121] For the classic statement by Lord Diplock of the three heads of judicial review, *see Council of Civil Service Unions v Minister for the Civil Service* [1985] AC 374, 410–11.

[122] See: I. Leigh and R. Masterman, *Making Rights Real: the Human Rights Act in its First Decade* (Hart Publishing, 2008) ch. 6.

[123] *Associated Provincial Picture Houses Ltd v Wednesbury Corporation* [1948] 1 KB 223, 234.

[124] T. R. S. Allan, 'Human Rights and Judicial Review: a Critique of "Due Deference"' (2006) CLJ 671, 679.

Conclusion

In conclusion, while elements of the United Kingdom Constitution demonstrate an adherence to the demands of separation of powers, that adherence could certainly not be said to be the product of any constitutional or higher order law, nor could it be said to reflect a considered determination of how governmental powers ought to be allocated. The main obstacle to any principled separation of powers is parliamentary sovereignty, which would appear to suggest that one governmental institution in the United Kingdom holds legal powers which are disproportionate to those held by the courts and executive. Under a constitutional system in which one governmental branch is so clearly dominant, the relevance of separation of powers must be open to question.

Nevertheless, such is the importance which is attached to the notion of judicial independence – both as a fact of United Kingdom constitutional practice and as a requirement of the rule of law – that it may be argued that the independent judicial branch is the closest thing to an 'entrenched' feature of the United Kingdom's peculiar separation of powers. The separation between the powers of the executive and those of the judiciary in particular is quite clear – more so following the implementation of the Constitutional Reform Act 2005.[125] The House of Lords, in *ex parte Anderson*,[126] has explicitly endorsed this separation – in spite of the lack of explicit constitutional direction requiring it – with Lord Bingham stating that the 'complete functional separation of the judiciary from the executive' was '"fundamental" since the rule of law depends on it',[127] and Lord Hutton adding that such a separation is 'an essential part of a democracy'.[128] This structural independence obviously goes hand in hand with the abilities of the judges to exercise independent views over whether the executive branch has transgressed the law. The judicial review mechanism is arguably, therefore, the key check exercised by the judiciary over the powers of the executive branch.

In addition to the increased institutional independence of the judicial branch, it is certainly also arguable that the judiciary has gained increased functional autonomy in recent years. In *R v Secretary of State for the Home Department, ex parte Venables,* for example, the claim was made – and subsequently endorsed by the European Court of Human Rights[129] – that the Home Secretary, 'in fixing a tariff [the minimum sentence to be served by a convicted murder] . . . is carrying out, contrary to the constitutional principle of separation of powers, a classic judicial function.'[130] Recent years have seen a succession of activist judicial decisions in response to parliamentary attempts to curtail the exercise of judicial discretion.[131] So important to the ideal of the rule of law is the notion of judicial independence, that it has been suggested that some areas of judicial procedure are virtually

---

[125] Constitutional Reform Act 2005, s. 3(1). See also Chapter 11.

[126] *R v Secretary of State for the Home Department, ex parte Anderson* [2003] 1 AC 837. See also Lord Steyn, 'The Case for a Supreme Court' (2002) 118 LQR 382, 383.

[127] *R v Secretary of State for the Home Department, ex parte Anderson* [2003] 1 AC 837, 882.

[128] Ibid., 899.

[129] *V and T v United Kingdom* (1999) 30 EHRR 121.

[130] *R v Secretary of State for the Home Department, ex parte Venables* [1998] AC 407, 526 (Lord Steyn). See also *R v Secretary of State for the Home Department, ex parte Anderson* [2003] 1 AC 837.

[131] See, for discussion, I. Leigh and R. Masterman, *Making Rights Real: the Human Rights Act in its First Decade* (Hart Publishing, 2008) p. 128.

impervious to parliamentary interference. This view is certainly held by the academic T. R. S. Allan, who has suggested that:

> The separation and independence of judicial power would lose its point, as an essential safeguard against arbitrary power, if courts failed to observe the principles of natural justice: there would be no guarantee that people's rights would be upheld in practice. The integrity of appropriate standards of judicial procedure must therefore be regarded as constitutionally fundamental – substantially immune to legislative abrogation or abridgement, except perhaps in special cases where the courts may acknowledge the justification for departures from ordinary procedure.[132]

Judicial review does not (yet) extend so far as to afford the judiciary a generally exercisable power to invalidate legislative provisions. However, the core of the idea of separation of powers in the United Kingdom – the independence of the judiciary – is undoubtedly crucial to the rule of law, and such is the centrality of the independence of the judiciary that, as we have already seen, suggestions have been made that even parliamentary interference with judicial autonomy might be treated with scepticism by the courts.[133] Such is the importance attached to the independence of the judicial process in the contemporary constitution that it may now realistically be regarded as a key element of the United Kingdom Constitution's separation of powers. If this is accepted, then the independence of the judiciary should not simply be a description of the position of the judges in the constitution, but should rightly be regarded as a constitutional fundamental and pre-requisite of legitimate government in the United Kingdom.

Practice questions

1. *'Complete separation is impossible. There must be a point, however, at which partial separation is not worthy of the name. Where, then, should the lines be drawn? And how should the lines that are drawn be enforced?'*

   (C. Saunders, 'Separation of Powers and the Judicial Branch' [2006] *Judicial Review* 337, 338)

   Discuss.

2. Is it possible to reconcile the legal supremacy of Parliament with the requirements of separation of powers?

3. *'[T]he British constitution, though largely unwritten, is firmly based on the separation of powers.'*

   (*Duport Steel* v *Sirs* [1980] 1 WLR 142, 157)

   How far, if at all, is the veracity of this statement illustrated in the theory and practice of the United Kingdom Constitution?

---

[132] T. R. S. Allan, *Constitutional Justice: a Liberal Theory of the Rule of Law* (OUP, 2001) p. 133.

[133] See the discussion of *Jackson* v *Attorney-General* [2005] UKHL 56, at pp. 143–8.

Further reading

Two volumes in particular remain hugely influential to any contemporary discussion of the meaning and requirements of separation of powers and are worthy of consultation; **Montesquieu**'s, *l'Esprit des Lois* (The Spirit of the Laws) and *The Federalist Papers* by **James Madison, Alexander Hamilton and John Jay.** An outstanding study of the doctrine – with sections devoted to its operation in the United States, The United Kingdom and France – can be found in **M. C. J. Vile,** *Constitutionalism and the Separation of Powers* (Clarendon Press, 1967).

The tripartite doctrine itself has also been subject to significant criticism on the basis of its uncertain requirements (**G. Marshall,** *Constitutional Theory* (Clarendon Press, 1971) and, more recently, on the basis of its inability to accurately encapsulate and respond to the complexities of the modern administrative state (**E. Carolan,** *The New Separation of Powers: a theory for the Modern State* (OUP, 2009).

As has been made clear, the influence of the separation of powers doctrine in the United Kingdom Constitution is hotly contested. The debate is fully captured in the opposing contributions of Eric Barendt and Adam Tomkins (**E. Barendt, 'Separation of Powers and Constitutional Government'** [1995] PL 599; **E. Barendt,** *An Introduction to Constitutional Law* (Clarendon Press, 1998); **A. Tomkins, 'Of Constitutional Spectres'** [1999] PL 525; **A. Tomkins,** *Public Law* (Clarendon Press, 2003).

Following the enactment of the Constitutional Reform Act 2005, there has been a renewed interest in separation of powers scholarship in the United Kingdom. The doctrine is an underlying pillar of **Vernon Bogdanor's** *New British Constitution* (Hart Publishing, 2009) and is the focal point of **Roger Masterman's** book, *The Separation of Powers in the Contemporary Constitution: Judicial Competence and Independence in the United Kingdom* (CUP, 2011).

Part III
Central government in the United Kingdom

Chapter 8
The executive

'[T]he main work of Parliament is to raise supplies; – and, when that has been done with ease, when all the money wanted has been voted without a break-down, of course Ministers are very glad to get rid of the Parliament. It is as much a matter of course that a Minister should dislike Parliament now as that a Stuart King should have done so . . . '

Anthony Trollope, *The Prime Minister* (First published 1876, OUP, 1983), p. 184.

Chapter outline

In Chapter 2 we examined the sources of constitutional rules within the UK's governance order. We established the importance of Acts of Parliament, which can be used to override other rules and have not, in the UK's history as a polity, been challenged by the courts. But to examine only the theoretical relationship between constitutional sources provides a distorted picture of the UK Constitution. This chapter examines the actors who make up the executive branch of government in the UK and how they achieved a dominant position within the UK Constitution, in part in spite of and in part because of parliamentary sovereignty. We begin by charting how the modern executive managed to accrue powers shed by a declining monarchy and proceed to analyse how the executive branch was able to exert its control over Parliament through the control of the party system and the civil service.

Introduction

In legal theory, the UK Constitution seemingly accords little role to the executive. Today's government ministers are the inheritors of little more than the rump of the powers left to monarchs after the claims to absolute monarchy by the Stuart kings had been vanquished on the battlefields of the seventeenth century. Beyond these inherent Royal Prerogative powers, the executive is cast, in law, as the mere manager of the powers granted to it by a sovereign Parliament (to which ministers must return and persuade parliamentarians to pass legislation if they seek new powers). As the opening quote from Anthony Trollope's Victorian novel, *The Prime Minister,* makes clear, however, legal theory does not tell the whole story. Ministers, in the 1880s as now, regard Parliament as a creature to be harnessed to their own ends, be it raising finance or extending their powers. In order to explain how the extensive role of modern executive branch belies its theoretical weakness in law, this chapter must conduct an historical overview of some of the more convoluted constitutional arrangements governing the UK's executive branch. From the outset students must appreciate that these arrangements are amongst the least legalised aspects of the constitution. Where powers are laid down in law they are often bounded, in terms of their exercise, by a network of constitutional conventions.

From absolute monarchy to the modern executive

Key issues

- The monarchy's role within the UK Constitution has waned since Parliament took control of the supreme law-making power following the revolution of 1688. Nonetheless, the figure of the monarch remains symbolically central within the UK Constitution.

- The expression 'the Crown' can mean both the person of the monarch and central government under the UK Constitution. This can create confusion as to the powers and immunities enjoyed by the monarch and government.

- Some powers, at least formally, still rest with the figure of the monarch. Are there ever circumstances in which she could use these powers?

- Given the very limited constitutional role of the monarch, why is there not more pressure to abolish the institution of monarchy within the UK Constitution?

The Revolution of 1688

(i) The passing of sovereignty from the monarchy to Parliament

The civil wars that wracked the Britain and Ireland of the seventeenth century were in many respects localised off-shoots of the religious wars which swept across Europe during that period. But within these islands the conflicts were also driven by a dispute as to whether the legitimate source of law-making authority rested on the basis of the 'divine right of kings' or on the basis of the representative (although then, by no means democratic) nature of Parliament. Both the civil wars of the 1640s and the so-called 'Glorious Revolution' of 1688 were preceded by efforts of the Stuart monarchs to assert their primacy within the constitution.

In the 1630s, King Charles I tasked his legal advisers with finding a source of finance for his military adventures after Parliament refused his requests to levy taxes. They alighted upon the idea of 'ship money'. Under a long-unused prerogative power the monarch could request that English counties furnish him with ships and men when England was threatened with invasion. Better, they thought, that this power be used not as a reaction to threatened invasion but as a regular levy to provide for the defence of the realm. Opponents, such as John Hampden, MP, claimed that this exercise of the prerogative was a usurpation of Parliament's tax-raising role.[1] When Hampden was subsequently tried for refusing to pay the courts found in the King's favour, recognising that the collection of 'ship money' fell within his prerogative and refusing to question his assessment of threats to the realm. Several judgments addressed the relationship between Parliament's statutes and the prerogative, with Sir John Finch CJ asserting that '[t]hey are void Acts of Parliament [which seek] to bind the King not to command the subjects, their persons and goods, and I say their money too; for no Acts of Parliament make any difference'.[2]

The civil wars of the 1640s saw the conflict over whether the King or Parliament enjoyed supreme law-making power spill out of the courtroom and onto the battlefield. The struggle was not resolved with the victory of the parliamentarian forces, and the execution of Charles I in 1649. Instead, with the death of the parliamentary

---

[1] The Petition of Right 1628.
[2] *R v Hampden* (1637) 3 State Tr 825, 1235.

leader Oliver Cromwell, England restored the Stuart monarchy in 1660. The failure to settle the underlying constitutional struggle over the respective law-making powers of Parliament and the Crown ultimately doomed this political arrangement. Charles I's son King James II dissolved Parliament soon after he was crowned in 1685 and did not recall it during his reign. In 1688, as James became increasingly autocratic, and with the birth of a son who secured his Catholic dynasty, influential figures within England's Protestant nobility petitioned the Dutch leader Prince William of Orange, married to King James' daughter Mary, to invade. The success of this invasion, known to history as the Glorious Revolution, was coupled with Parliament's assumption of supreme law-making power.

Having displaced King James II from the throne, the influential figures who had instigated William III's invasion had no desire to see their new monarch, able to call upon his effective and loyal Dutch military, from imposing his will over Parliament. They therefore instituted what became known as a constitutional monarchy. In return for the Crown, and the strength this would bring him in his struggles against France, William III would reign as a limited monarch, subject to restraints which were symbolically imposed 'for ever' upon the monarchy. As we have seen, these restrictions were implemented under the Bill of Rights 1689, enacted 'for the further limitation of the Crown and better securing the rights and liberties of the subjects'.[3]

Thinking Point . . .

Statutory claims that circumstances will be maintained forever do not prevent them from being altered through the use of parliamentary sovereignty (see pp. 33–9). Nonetheless, this claim that the monarchy is permanently constrained does establish the primacy of Parliament over the Crown.

In the wake of this settlement, the monarchy could not make law, maintain an army or raise taxes without Parliament's permission. If Parliament granted such permission, the monarchy would not therefore derive its authority for actions taken under these powers from some inherent authority of the 'Crown', but from the position of Parliament as supreme law-maker. As the reactionary French political theorist Joseph de Maistre wrote in the early nineteenth century, the idea that sovereign law-making power was reposed in one body still held sway in the UK Constitution. The body in question was no longer the Crown, but Parliament:

> They say that in England sovereignty is limited. Nothing could be more false. It is Royalty which is limited in that famous country. But if the three powers which constitute sovereignty in England (Crown, Lords and Commons) are of one mind, what can they do? One must reply with Blackstone: Everything. And what can legally be undertaken against them? Nothing.[4]

The residual powers and immunities under the prerogative were all the inherent powers that remained in the hands of the monarch as head of state.

---

[3] Above pp. 127–8.

[4] J. de Maistre (1819), translated in F. Ridley, 'There is no British Constitution: A Dangerous Case of the Emperor's Clothes' (1988) 41 *Parliamentary Affairs* 340, 348.

> ## Thinking Point . . .
>
> Though de Maistre identifies the need for Royal Assent as one of the constituent elements of law making in the UK, it must be remembered that even at the time of his writing it had already been well over a century since legislation had been refused such assent.

(ii) Passing the remaining powers from the monarchy to government ministers

At the start of the eighteenth century the monarchy remained very important to political life in what, following the Act of Union in 1706, became the United Kingdom. The Privy Council, essentially a team of advisers, assisted the monarch with policy making and conducting the affairs of state. But under the post-1688 constitutional arrangements the monarch had to persuade Parliament to provide new powers or finance projects. This introduced new pressures into the UK's constitutional arrangements. The monarch had to rely upon representatives within the Commons and the Lords to persuade parliamentarians to agree to accept new laws. Monarchs such as George I and George II, neither of whom were native English speakers, relied heavily on a few trusted advisers.[5] For this combination of practical and constitutional reasons, a small group of advisers able to represent the Crown in Parliament began to supersede the Privy Council. This group of 'ministers' came to be known as the Cabinet.

Initially, these royal advisers were merely the monarch's assistants, exercising his or her wishes within particular policy areas such as financing or defence. Over time, however, the monarchy's role as policy maker declined. Nominally, in the UK's constitution, all executive power continued to rest in the hands of the monarch. In the mid-1700s Blackstone continued to claim that '[t]he King is considered in domestic affairs . . . as the fountain of justice, and general conservator of the peace of the kingdom'.[6] In reality, successive monarchs had placed increasing trust in their ministers to run complex affairs of state. Ministers were already directly responsible for exercising powers granted to the executive by Parliament and for the operation of many of the prerogative powers.[7] The policy-making input of the monarch continued to decline in the nineteenth century. Dicey, the late-Victorian chronicler of the UK's constitutional arrangements, revisited Blackstone's assertions regarding the monarch's constitutional role and poured scorn on them:

> The executive of England is in fact placed in the hands of a committee called the Cabinet. If there be any one person in whose single hand the power of the State is placed, that one person is not the King but . . . the Prime Minister.[8]

The development of the convention of collective ministerial responsibility (which we will examine in detail below) further undermined the monarch's ability to use the power to appoint or dismiss ministers against the Prime Minister's wishes. In a peculiar reversal of

---

[5] See D. Keir, *The Constitutional History of Modern Britain since 1485* (9th edn, Adam & Charles Black, 1975) pp. 318–19.

[6] W. Blackstone, *Commentaries on the Laws of England* (1st edn, Oxford: Clarendon Press, 1765–1769) vol. I., 267.

[7] Above, pp. 34–7.

[8] A. Dicey, *An Introduction to the Study of the Constitution* (8th edn, first published 1915, Liberty Fund, 1982) cxxx.

roles, rather than the Cabinet acting as the monarch's core advisers, Walter Bagehot came to describe the monarch as providing 'effectual and beneficial guidance' to the elected government.[9]

(iii) 'The Crown' as a brand name for the executive?

All of this suggests that, in Bagehot's arresting terms, in the UK '[a] republic has insinuated itself beneath the folds of a monarchy'.[10] Even in the Victorian era, Bagehot was willing to stake the claim that, when it came to key decisions such as choosing a government and dissolving Parliament (both of which remain, in legal terms, the monarch's personal prerogatives[11]), the monarch had no discernible impact upon the decision. But such assertions did not curtail debate over whether inherent constitutional functions rested with the monarchy, and monarchs continued to involve themselves in constitutional matters into the early 1900s.[12] Just prior to the First World War King George V personally involved himself in the Home Rule Crisis in Ireland, including implying that he might reject legislation if it was passed against the wishes of Unionist opposition.[13] Until the 1960s the Conservative Party continued to formally invite the monarch to choose its leader. However, as democratic governance became embedded within UK constitutional practice, it became apparent that 'parliamentary democracy, rather than the power of the sovereign, had become the prime engine of government'.[14] Writers like Blackburn summarily dismissed suggestions which cast the monarch as an independent constitutional actor:

> Certainly since the 1960s, if not earlier, talk of the 'personal prerogatives' as signifying personal discretionary constitutional rights of the sovereign, or the monarch's freedom from ministerial responsibility in exercising the prerogative, has become redundant in practice and an arcane academic red-herring.[15]

This suggests that 'the Crown' (when used in connection with day-to-day government functions) is little more than a 'brand name' applying to the executive branch of central government in the UK and confirms that the monarch has little bearing on how power is exercised. The name of institutions like the Crown Prosecution Service or the Royal Navy, for example, does not suggest that the monarch plays any operational role within their structures. Lord Diplock lamented the continued reliance on the concept of the Crown as evidence of the failure of the UK's constitutional terminology to keep pace with the realities of government:

> To use as a metaphor the symbol of royalty, 'the Crown', was no doubt a convenient way of denoting and distinguishing the monarch when doing acts of government in his political capacity from the monarch when doing private acts in his personal capacity, at a period when legislative and executive powers were exercised by him in accordance with his own will. But to continue nowadays to speak of 'the Crown' as doing legislative or executive acts of government, which, in reality as distinct from legal fiction, are decided on and done by human beings other than the Queen herself, involves risk of confusion.[16]

---

[9] See W. Bagehot, *The English Constitution* (2nd edn, first published 1872, OUP, 1961) p. 74.
[10] Ibid., p. 44.
[11] Above, pp. 35–6.
[12] See P. Hennessy, *The Hidden Wiring: Unearthing the British Constitution* (Victor Gollancz, 1995) p. 52–66.
[13] See V. Bogdanor, *The Monarchy and the Constitution* (OUP, 1995) pp. 122–35.
[14] R. Brazier, 'The Monarchy' in V. Bogdanor (ed.), *The British Constitution in the Twentieth Century* (OUP, 2003) 69, 73.
[15] R. Blackburn, 'Monarchy and the Personal Prerogatives' [2004] PL 546, 551.
[16] *Town Investments* v *Dept of the Environment* [1978] AC 359, 380–1 (Lord Diplock).

Lord Templeman traced much of the confusion surrounding the Crown to its dual meaning within the UK Constitution; 'The expression "the Crown" has two meanings; namely the monarch and the executive'.[17] To a large extent, therefore, Bagehot's view of the monarchy as providing a gloss upon the constitutional structure of the UK, without affecting the substantive operation of the UK's government institutions may not have been strictly accurate at the time of writing in the 1860s, but has gained considerable traction with the subsequent development of parliamentary democracy.

(iv) Crown immunity

The Queen, in her personal capacity as monarch cannot be prosecuted or sued within the UK's legal systems. The assumed perfection of the monarch is another throwback to the era of the divine right of kings and which remains difficult to square with the concept of equality before the law. Historically this immunity, and other advantages within the legal system were extended by the courts both to the monarch as an individual and, more problematically for the rule of law in the UK, to the executive operating under the 'brand name' of the Crown: 'The principle had been extended as a legal defence to deny remedies to citizens for wrongs committed by emanations of the Crown (or the state), whether they were breaches of contract, or tort, or minister' misdeeds'.[18] In one of the deeply unsatisfactory vagaries resulting from 'the use of the Crown as a synonym for the State' judges, conscious of their oath of allegiance to 'the Crown', maintained that they could not impose their jurisdiction over either the monarch or the executive.[19] Deep into the twentieth century these issues with the rule of law were only resolved by the Crown voluntarily submitting to the will of the courts.

Ultimately, the Crown Proceedings Act 1947 addressed this issue by subjecting the Crown to substantially the same liability in contract[20] and tort[21] as private individuals. Under contract law, the Crown retains the exceptional ability to respond to an action for breaches of contract committed in response to 'executive necessity', but this does not permit it to avoid contractual obligations simply on the basis of a change of government policy. The Act did, however, maintain that court orders such as damages cannot be enforced against the Crown under private law.[22] Nonetheless, in addition to this legislation, the courts have done their best to limit the immunities enjoyed under common law principles. In *M* v *Home Office*[23] Lord Templeman ruled that court orders finding a Minister of the Crown in contempt of court could bind such an executive officer even if they would not bind the monarch: 'The judges cannot enforce the law against the Crown as monarch because the Crown as monarch can do no wrong but judges enforce the law against the Crown as executive and against the individuals who from time to time represent the Crown'.[24] This judgment is both significant in extending the legal principle of the rule of

---

[17] *M* v *Home Office* [1994] 1 AC 377, 395.

[18] R. Brazier, 'The Monarchy' in V. Bogdanor (ed.), *The British Constitution in the Twentieth Century* (OUP, 2003) 69, 87.

[19] M. Loughlin, 'The State, the Crown and the Law' in M. Sunkin and S. Payne, (eds), *The Nature of the Crown* (OUP, 1999) 171, 190.

[20] Crown Proceedings Act 1947, s. 1.

[21] Ibid., s. 2.

[22] Ibid., s. 21.

[23] *M* v *Home Office* [1994] 1 AC 377.

[24] Ibid., 377, 395.

law and in displaying its limits.[25] Adam Tomkins, however, points out that such reasoning affirms that the monarch remains unanswerable to the courts and therefore, symbolically at least, 'the law struggles to keep the heart of British government (the Crown) within the rule of law'.[26]

The 'Magic' of monarchy

Today the monarch does not play any operative role in UK governance, but remains head of state and continues to play a formal role in all three branches of government:

Key debates
The functions of the monarch as head of state of the UK

To symbolise the nation – it is often said that the very limited power of the monarchy is the reason for their enduring role in the United Kingdom Constitution. The monarch and the royal family are, effectively, an entertaining rather than a functioning element of government.

To 'advise, encourage and to warn' the government – the Queen has met regularly with every Prime Minister since Winston Churchill. She is, therefore, in a privileged position to make her feelings on government policy known, but ministers have no duty to give weight to these views.

To perform formal functions – this role includes the Queen's responsibility for providing royal assent for legislation, issuing proclamations and Orders in Council, appointing the Prime Minister and summoning and proroguing Parliament. These roles are ordinarily performed in accordance with the wishes of ministers.

In all of these formal roles, the guiding precept behind the Queen's actions is one of 'strict political neutrality in her role as head of state'.[27] This begs the question of why the institution of monarchy has been retained within the UK's constitutional arrangements.

(i) The monarch as head of state

The Cabinet Manual, published in 2011 as an authoritative guide to the UK's rules of government, highlights the symbolism inherent in the position of the monarch; 'The Sovereign is the Head of State of the UK, providing stability, continuity and a national focus'.[28] But the Queen is also the head of state of many countries other than the UK, and of the Commonwealth of Nations. That one person, Queen Elizabeth II, is both Queen of Australia and the UK is not to say that these two Crowns are the same. The Crown is divisible, meaning that if Australia, for example, sought to become a republic the powers of the Crown in Australia would cease, but this would not affect the other Crowns held by Queen Elizabeth II.

The picture becomes even more complex when Crown Dependencies and British Overseas Territories are taken into consideration. In regard to the former (the Channel

---

[25] See pp. 242–3.
[26] A. Tomkins, 'Crown Privileges' in M. Sunkin and S. Payne (eds), *The Nature of the Crown* (OUP, 1999) 171, 190.
[27] R. Blackburn, 'Monarchy and the Personal Prerogatives' [2004] PL 546, 547.
[28] HM Government, *The Cabinet Manual: A Guide to Laws, Conventions and Rules on the Operation of Government* (Cabinet Office, 2011) 3.

Islands and the Isle of Man), UK ministers conduct international relations and defence. In regard to the latter (including Gibraltar), UK ministers exercise control over the territories in the name of the Crown. This means that ministers may be able to act with regard to these territories in a manner which would be unlawful within the UK:

Key case

R (Quark Fishing Ltd) v Secretary of State for Foreign and Commonwealth Affairs [2005] UKHL 57; [2006] 1 AC 529 (House of Lords)

The Foreign Secretary refused to grant a fishing licence to Quark Fishing, a firm operating out of South Georgia. This decision interfered with the firm's property rights under the Art. 1, First Protocol of the ECHR. However, the UK had not extended the ambit of the ECHR to cover the overseas territory of South Georgia. At issue, therefore, was whether the Foreign Secretary, when giving this instruction, was acting as Her Majesty's minister with regard to the UK or in regard to South Georgia.

The House of Lords held that a Secretary of State of the United Kingdom had no power under the South Georgia and South Sandwich Islands Order 1985 to instruct the Crown's representatives to withdraw the licence. The Foreign Secretary, therefore, had acted on behalf of the Queen in right of South Georgia and not in right of the United Kingdom. Lord Hope stated (at [79]) that:

> The reasons of policy that led to the giving of the instruction, or the motives that lay behind it, are irrelevant. The question is simply in what capacity was the instruction given by Her Majesty . . . it was in right of her position as Head of State of [South Georgia] that it was given by Her Majesty.

This meant that the Foreign Secretary did not have to have regard for the ECHR in his decision as he was acting on behalf of the Crown of South Georgia and not the Crown of the UK.

This multiplicity of roles can bring the monarch into direct conflict with her UK ministers, as the UK is just one member of the Commonwealth. The Commonwealth is an international organisation made up largely of states which formerly belonged to the British Empire. During the apartheid era in South Africa, many members of the Commonwealth sought to impose sanctions against South Africa in spite of the staunch opposition of the UK's Prime Minister, Margaret Thatcher. Ultimately, the issue was diffused, but it indicates how the Queen's role as Head of the Commonwealth is sometimes difficult to square with her political neutrality within the UK.[29]

Beyond the specific constitutional powers exercised by the monarchy (which we will address in the next sub-section) the day-to-day role of heads of state, in countries where they are not also head of the government, is to symbolise the nation:

> He or she may personify the state, and in the case of an old monarchy may personify the state's history and continuity. The head of state can represent the nation, both at home and overseas. He or she may be a focal point for national loyalty, and as such transcends party politics because in that role he or she is or strives to be above and outside partisan political rivalry. And a head of state may be expected to exemplify the values which it is assumed citizens may wish to see in themselves.[30]

---

[29] See S. Ramphal, 'Mrs Thatcher and the Commonwealth' (2013) 102 *The Round Table* 215, 216.
[30] R. Brazier, 'A British Republic' (2002) 61 CLJ 351, 362.

Arguably, a monarch like Queen Elizabeth II who has reigned for a considerable length of time is a potent force in this regard, especially in the context of occasions such as the State Opening of Parliament. This, however, does not detract from the fact that by its very nature a hereditary monarchy can undermine the symbolism of such occasions, for it conflicts with the core values of democracy. Moreover, particular legal rules surrounding the UK's monarchy long undermined the monarch's unifying role. Male progeny were preferred to female progeny in the order of succession. Under the Act of Settlement 1701, reflecting the prejudices of the time, any member of the Royal Family who married a Roman Catholic was excluded from the order of succession to the Crown.[31] Under the Coalition Government's Succession of the Crown Act 2013 gender was removed as a relevant factor in determining the order of succession[32] and the specific restriction on marrying Roman Catholics was repealed.[33] Even after this reform a member of the Royal Family who becomes a Roman Catholic is still legally removed from the order of succession.[34]

(ii) Extraordinary exercises of the monarch's formal roles within the UK Constitution

The Queen is one of the three constituent elements of the UK legislature. This can be seen in the standard enacting formula (the 'words of enactment') required to pass all Acts of Parliament:

> Be it enacted by the Queen's most Excellent Majesty, by and with the advice and consent of the Lords Spiritual and Temporal, and Commons, in this present Parliament assembled, and by the authority of the same, as follows . . . [35]

This leads to a question of whether the Queen (on advice from her ministers, perhaps when serving as part of a minority government) could ever reject legislation passed in Parliament. An Act of Parliament has not been refused Royal Assent since 1708,[36] and it seems clear that a convention has developed that the monarch's legislative role is merely to act as a 'rubber-stamp'. Even the judiciary have recognised this departure from the monarch's ability, as a matter of law, to block legislation:

> We very sensibly speak today of legislation being made by Act of Parliament – although the preamble to every statute still maintains the fiction that the maker was Her Majesty and that the participation of the members of the two Houses of Parliament had been restricted to advice and acquiescence.[37]

Similarly, in *Jackson* v *Attorney-General*,[38] Lord Rodger asserted that once legislation has completed its passage through Parliament 'the Bill [is] presented to His Majesty for the Royal Assent . . . The Royal Assent will follow automatically'.[39] These comments, however, have not cleared up the debate as to whether the monarch's legal power could ever be used

---

[31] Act of Settlement 1700, s. 2.
[32] Succession of the Crown Act 2013, s. 1.
[33] Ibid., s. 2.
[34] Act of Settlement 1700, s. 2.
[35] Sir W. McKay (ed.), *Erskine May's Treatise on the Law, Privileges, Proceedings and Usage of Parliament* (23rd edn, London: LexisNexis, 2004) 536.
[36] See A. Twomey, 'The Refusal or Deferral of Royal Assent' (2006) PL 580, 588.
[37] *Town Investments* v *Dept of the Environment* [1978] AC 359, 381 (Lord Diplock).
[38] *Jackson* v *Attorney-General* [2005] UKHL 56.
[39] Ibid., [134].

because, as Rodney Brazier has commented, royal prerogative powers 'do not become extinct merely through lack of use'.[40] Twomey therefore considers whether the constitutional convention restricting the monarch's role would be set aside if Parliament sought to act in a manner which threatened democracy within the UK:

> Constitutional principles of responsible and representative government would appear to constrain the formal exercise of the power to refuse assent. The elected representatives of the people are entitled to enact bad legislation and the remedy for such acts is held in the hands of the voters at the ballot box. However, the issue becomes more complicated if the effect of a Bill is to constrain or prevent the people from casting their judgment at the ballot box.[41]

Commentators continue to conjecture that, should democracy within the UK be under threat, the monarch may disregard the conventional restraints upon her powers. Intriguingly, the civil servants responsible for drafting the *Cabinet Manual,* which reveals some of the previously 'behind-closed-doors' government arrangements under the UK Constitution, defined the Crown Prerogative as 'the residual power inherent in the Sovereign, and now exercised *mostly* on the advice of the Prime Minister and Ministers of the Crown'.[42] Indeed, the draft version of this document envisaged a continued role of the monarch as a safeguard of democracy in time of constitutional crisis. In such circumstances it asserted that 'the Sovereign retains reserve powers to dismiss the Prime Minister or make a personal choice of successor'.[43] This presents us with the incongruous scenario of an unelected monarch, who inherited her position, exercising a role as the 'champion of democracy' or the UK's ultimate 'guardian of the constitution'. As Blackburn suggests, this is deeply unsatisfactory; 'If any such ground for vetoing legislation did exist, such a weighty matter should be for a Constitutional Court to determine, not a politically neutral, hereditary monarch'.[44] In the final version of the *Cabinet Manual* such claims are omitted. Instead, the document describes the historical operation of the personal prerogatives, but emphasises, in line with Blackburn, that '[i]n modern times the convention has been that the Sovereign should not be drawn into party politics'.[45]

(iii) The symbolic value of monarchy

Having examined how the modern executive structure of government departments and ministers, under the ultimate control of the Cabinet and the Prime Minister, succeeded to the political role and residual powers of the Crown, it is worth pausing to consider why this institution continues to exist. After all, the development of a constitutional monarchy, retaining some prerogative powers and immunities which ultimately derive their authority from the medieval Christian doctrine of the divine right of kings, provides for a rather messy set of constitutional arrangements. Any justification which did exist for these

[40] R. Brazier, 'The Monarchy' in V. Bogdanor (ed.), *The British Constitution in the Twentieth Century* (OUP, 2003) 69, 81.
[41] A. Twomey, 'The Refusal or Deferral of Royal Assent' [2006] PL 580, 590.
[42] HM Government, *The Cabinet Manual: A Guide to Laws, Conventions and Rules on the Operation of Government* (Cabinet Office, 2011) 6 (emphasis added).
[43] HM Government, *The Cabinet Manual – Draft: A Guide to Laws, Conventions and Rules on the Operation of Government* (Cabinet Office, 2010) 29.
[44] R. Blackburn, 'Monarchy and the Personal Prerogatives' [2004] PL 546, 553.
[45] HM Government, *The Cabinet Manual: A Guide to Laws, Conventions and Rules on the Operation of Government* (Cabinet Office, 2011) 14.

arrangements was surely further undermined as ministers took over the operation of large areas of the prerogative and, into the twentieth century, even the 'personal' prerogatives came to operate without reference to the monarch's own opinions.

Despite the limitations upon the monarch's constitutional role, the pageantry and romance of monarchy continued to have its uses for ministers long after Parliament had established its sovereignty. Into the twentieth century the UK remained a country where a small educated class ruled over a largely uneducated populace. The ostensibly politically neutral monarchy could therefore be used to generate nationalism in time of crisis and to deflect attention from legislative programmes weighted towards the interests of the ruling classes. Bagehot openly admitted that monarchy provided 'a visible symbol of unity to those still so imperfectly educated as to need a symbol'.[46] The apparent significance of the monarchy in the nineteenth-century constitution amounted to little more than a 'dignified' smokescreen, cloaking the 'efficient' reality of the workings of government and thereby distracting the majority of the populace from their lack of political power. Without this distraction, Bagehot believed that the self-interest of the political classes would be exposed and the Constitution would be overthrown; 'The use of the Queen, in a dignified capacity, is incalculable. Without her in England, the present English government would fail and pass away'.[47]

Prior to the First World War, better education and franchise reform ensured a gradual political awakening of the working classes. The terrible effects of that conflict, however, ultimately stripped much of the dignity from the 'dignified constitution':

> As others have often observed, the break-up of the nineteenth-century world in Britain was manifest in the years before 1914 and indeed it is arguable that the war prevented outbreaks and uprisings led by the Irish, the industrial working class and the suffragettes which might have changed the course of history in these islands. But the war of 1914–18 seriously damaged the concept of legitimate authority.[48]

Put simply, after the First World War there were very few people left who would go blindly 'over the top' for slogans like 'For King and Country'. With the magic of monarchy so profoundly shaken, a process exacerbated by numerous scandals involving senior members of the royal family as the twentieth century wore on, the continued 'dignified' role of the Crown rests on precarious foundations, beyond the fact that it would take a monumental legislative effort to replace it.[49]

Thinking Point . . .

The value of sentiment in the context of the monarchy should not be underestimated. In 2012, the year of the Queen's Diamond Jubilee, national affection for the long-serving Queen Elizabeth II (and the extra public holiday provided to allow for jubilee celebrations) saw public support for the monarchy reach a recent high in public opinion polls.

---

[46] W. Bagehot, *The English Constitution* (2nd edn, first published 1872, OUP, 1961) 40.
[47] Ibid., 30.
[48] J. Griffith, 'The Political Constitution' (1979) 42 MLR 1, 4.
[49] See P. Hennessy, *The Hidden Wiring: Unearthing the British Constitution* (Victor Gollancz, 1995) 71.

The composition and role of the modern executive

Key issues

- The Prime Minister is able to appoint all other ministers and is able to use this power to ensure personal dominance over the policy-making process.
- The Cabinet is made up of the most senior ministers in the government, most of whom have responsibility for management of major government departments. This managerial focus, however, further concentrates policy making in the hands of the Prime Minister.
- Cabinet ministers are assisted in their roles by junior ministers, who may exercise powers on behalf of their Cabinet minister.
- The convention of 'collective responsibility', which initially helped Cabinet develop as the central policy-making body in the UK Constitution, has more recently solidified the Prime Minister's dominance within the executive branch.
- Much of the work involved in implementing government policy rests in the hands of the civil service. These politically neutral officials are 'permanent', in that they serve different administrations and do not lose their position when a government leaves office.

Composition of the political executive

The politically accountable elements of the executive are ordinarily chosen as a result of general elections. Dissolutions of Parliament occur at the end of the five-year maximum term of Parliament,[50] or if one of the special votes under the Fixed-Term Parliaments Act 2011[51] is secured, as took place in April 2017.[52] Once Parliament reconvenes, the new executive is confirmed on the basis of its ability to persuade the House of Commons to support its legislative agenda. The UK Government is headed by the Prime Minister, at the time of writing Theresa May, who leads her Cabinet of senior ministers. These Cabinet ministers are supported by more junior ministers and by the politically neutral civil service.

(i) The Prime Minister

In the UK's constitutional arrangements a distinction between the head of state (the monarch) and the head of government (the 'Prime Minister') clearly emerged during Sir Robert Walpole's period as senior adviser to George I and George II from 1721–42. At the time, Walpole's political opponents used 'Prime Minister' as a term of derision, implying that cronyism underpinned the emerging Cabinet system. Walpole himself denied that he was the most important minister to the Crown.[53] The office did not begin to develop into its modern guise until the mid-nineteenth century, with Benjamin Disraeli being the first Prime Minister to formally adopt the title in the 1870s. The role is therefore not established by, nor is it enshrined in, statute.[54]

---

[50] Fixed-Term Parliaments Act 2011, s. 1.
[51] Ibid., s. 2.
[52] See pp. 289–90.
[53] See P. Hennessy, *The Prime Minister, The Office and its Holders Since 1945* (Penguin, 2001) p. 39.
[54] See I. Ward, *The English Constitution: Myths and Realities* (Hart, 2004) p. 71.

> **Thinking Point . . .**
>
> Legislation such as the Chequers Estate Act 1917 does recognise the existence of the office of Prime Minister, providing for a country residence.

There is a constitutional convention that the head of the majority block in the House of Commons after an election (usually the leader of the largest party in the Commons, but occasionally the designated head of a coalition of parties) is called upon by the monarch to become the head of 'her' government. The will of the electorate, as expressed in the make-up of the Commons, is therefore the determining factor in the choice of Prime Minister and is also the source of her 'unique position of authority'.[55] Because of the importance of the Commons within the UK Constitution (being the elected element of Parliament) Prime Ministers must by convention always be members of the Commons. Historically, before the advent of democracy in the UK, Prime Ministers were as likely to be members of the House of Lords.[56]

As for the resignation of a Prime Minister, this can be triggered by a failure to command the support of the Commons during motions of no confidence; defeat in such a motion brought down James Callaghan's Government in 1979. Alternately a Prime Minister may no longer command the backing of her own parliamentary party, as seen in the leadership struggle that deposed Margaret Thatcher in 1990. A defeat over a high-profile policy can also drive a Prime Minister to resignation. In 2016 David Cameron resigned as Prime Minister having invested his personal authority into his failed effort to secure support for the UK's continued EU membership in the Brexit referendum. These circumstances have different results. Loss of a vote of no confidence required Callaghan to seek the dissolution of Parliament and a general election,[57] whereas Thatcher and Cameron's resignations saw a new leader continuing their terms in office.

Prime Ministers have control of the appointment or dismissal of all other ministers (even if all are nominally advisers to the monarch). Political factors may influence how this power is exercised, for certain ministers may be particularly popular with the general public or may command the support of substantial sections of the governing parliamentary party. Tony Blair, when Prime Minister, found it impossible for the latter reason to dismiss or sideline his Chancellor of the Exchequer, Gordon Brown. Ironically, when Brown himself became Prime Minister, the weakness of his position from 2008 onwards, largely as a result of public perceptions of his mismanagement of the economy, prevented him from promoting his allies to key positions in the Cabinet. The bigger a Prime Minister's majority in Parliament, the more flexibility he or she will have to exercise powers of appointment.

(ii) Other government ministers

In order to understand how a Prime Minister can exert a substantial degree of control over the executive branch under the UK Constitution, we need to understand the relationship between this office and those of other ministers. By constitutional convention,

---

[55] HM Government, *The Cabinet Manual: A Guide to Laws, Conventions and Rules on the Operation of Government* (Cabinet Office, 2011) 21.
[56] See I. Jennings, *Cabinet Government* (3rd edn, CUP, 1965) p. 23.
[57] This is now a legal obligation under the Fixed-Term Parliaments Act 2011, s. 2.

to ensure that Parliament can hold ministers to account, all ministers must be members of either the House of Commons or the House of Lords (although they can be appointed for a short period in advance of joining either House).[58] For example, Gordon Brown appointed Peter Mandelson to his Cabinet in October 2008, despite the fact that Mandelson was not at the time a member of either House of Parliament. Ten days after his appointment, Mandelson took up a seat in the House of Lords. All ministers are expected to respect the standards set out in the Ministerial Code[59] and can be obliged to resign from office if they breach these standards.[60] By statute, a maximum of 95 ministers can sit in the House of Commons[61] and the overall number of paid ministers across both chambers cannot exceed 109.[62]

1. Senior (or 'Cabinet') ministers

The most senior ministers, 'Her Majesty's Principal Secretaries of State',[63] make up 'the Cabinet'. Like the office of Prime Minister, the Cabinet traces its origins in the UK Constitution to the small knot of advisers first preferred by George I during his reign in the early-eighteenth century. The term was also initially one of derision, implying that the body consisted of a small group of 'yes-men' whom the monarch met in his Cabinet (an anteroom adjacent to the royal bedchamber). And again, like the office of Prime Minister, the Cabinet is not statutory in nature (although its existence is noted in statutes, such as the Freedom of Information Act 2000 exemptions relating to Cabinet[64]) but is a product of constitutional conventions and centuries of political practice. This allows a great deal of flexibility in the organisation of the Cabinet; although it ordinarily consists of just over 20 senior ministers, the number varies between administrations.[65] During the two World Wars, for example, the 'War Cabinet' consisted of fewer than 10 ministers, each tasked with directing particular elements of the war effort.

In order to maintain this flexibility, where a statute allocates powers to the government, they are almost always simply allocated to 'the Secretary of State'. This allows any Cabinet minister to assume any such government functions; 'As powers generally rest with the Secretary of State and departments do not have their own legal personality, the structure of government departments tends to change to reflect the allocation of functions to ministers'.[66] Some functions, by statute, rest with particular offices, necessitating their inclusion in Cabinet. For example, particular duties with regard to protecting judicial independence rest with the Lord Chancellor under the Constitutional Reform Act 2005.[67] Beyond such legal requirements, over the last century, peace-time Cabinets have always included the important positions of Chancellor of the Exchequer, Secretary of State for Foreign Affairs (the 'Foreign Secretary') and Secretary of State for the Home Department (the 'Home

---

[58] HM Government, *The Cabinet Manual: A Guide to Laws, Conventions and Rules on the Operation of Government* (Cabinet Office, 2011) 22.

[59] HM Government, *The Ministerial Code* (Cabinet Office, 2018).

[60] Below, pp. 442–9.

[61] House of Commons Disqualification Act 1975.

[62] Ministerial and Other Salaries Act 1975.

[63] Interpretation Act 1978, sch. 1.

[64] For further information, see 489–500.

[65] See R. Brazier, *Ministers of the Crown* (OUP, 1997) pp. 15–17.

[66] HM Government, *The Cabinet Manual: A Guide to Laws, Conventions and Rules on the Operation of Government* (Cabinet Office, 2011) 26.

[67] Constitutional Reform Act 2005, s. 3(1).

Secretary'). These positions represent the 'core functions' of the government, respectively responsible for maintaining national finances, maintaining relations with the governments of other countries and international organisations and maintaining law and order within the UK. Beyond these offices, other secretaries of state are responsible for important areas of government activity, such as education, healthcare, transport and the environment. Ministers only exercise those functions within the portfolio to which they are appointed.[68]

This flexibility gives a great deal of power to the Prime Minister who, as the figure responsible for organising the Cabinet, can exert control over the careers of other prominent figures in her political party. She can promote or demote ministers by 'reshuffling' her Cabinet team. In this way, in response to a number of crises at the Home Office in 2006, Tony Blair sacked Charles Clarke as Home Secretary and replaced him with John Reid. The Prime Minister can also, if she wishes to place an issue 'above' party politics, appoint politically neutral figures as ministers. Gordon Brown, on becoming Prime Minister, attempted to shed his image as a politically polarised figure by appointing Lord Jones (the former Director-General of the Confederation of British Industry, a cross-bench peer) as Minister of State for Trade (admittedly a non-Cabinet post). The Prime Minister can also move responsibility for functions between members of the Cabinet, making certain Cabinet positions more powerful at the expense of others:

Key debates
Changing departmental responsibility for higher education

The repeated changes in ministerial responsibility for higher education in the UK illustrate how Prime Ministers can shift responsibilities to favour certain colleagues. For much of Tony Blair's time as Prime Minister, responsibility for universities rested within the portfolio of the Secretary of State for Education and Skills, alongside responsibilities for schools and vocational training. When Gordon Brown became Prime Minister, he overhauled these arrangements, separating research, vocational training and higher education from other aspects of education by creating a new Cabinet position of Secretary of State for Innovation, Universities and Skills. But the post lasted less than two years before it was merged into the portfolio of the Secretary of State for Business, Innovation and Skills.

This decision not only created a new and powerful Cabinet post, with a remit previously held by two Cabinet ministers (signifying the importance of Lord Mandelson, who was the first minister to fill the role of Secretary of State for Business, Innovation and Skills, within Gordon Brown's Cabinet), it also underlined a change in the Government's view of the role of universities, from providing education to providing graduate employees to serve the demands of business. This position continued unchanged under the 2010–15 Coalition Government, but responsibility for universities ultimately became shared between the Department for Education and the new Department for Business, Energy and Industrial Strategy under Theresa May's premiership.

The Cabinet historically functioned as the executive's policy-making forum. At twice-weekly Cabinet meetings in the early 1900s, ministers would meet to debate important national affairs, agree policy and even draft legislation. But as the responsibilities of government grew over the century, requiring ministers to attain ever more specialist

---

[68] HM Government, *The Cabinet Manual: A Guide to Laws, Conventions and Rules on the Operation of Government* (Cabinet Office, 2011) 24.

knowledge of the workings of their departments, this activity became unsustainable. Smaller 'Cabinet committees', made up of relevant ministers, began to oversee the bulk of policy development, presenting their proposals to Cabinet. With ministers predominantly occupied with the day-to-day task of running their departments, the Prime Minister became central to steering these Cabinet committees and policy making. Margaret Thatcher's tenure as Prime Minister, from 1979–90, saw new levels of centralisation of policy making. In this era the number of Cabinet meetings dropped to one two-hour meeting a week, with meetings even more intermittent when Parliament was not in session. Tony Blair, Prime Minister from 1997–2007, preferred to make policy in informal 'sofa' meetings with his ministers, by-passing Cabinet and Cabinet committees altogether (with Cabinet meetings sometimes lasting only 30 minutes).[69] And yet, despite the apparent draining of its power by Prime Ministers across the twentieth century, the Cabinet continues to meet around 40 times a year. Looking back over the historic status of Cabinet, Anthony Seldon concluded that it still played a vital role within the machinery of government:

> Cabinet's main focus and justification . . . was that of the one and only forum where the government's most senior ministers and heads of department met, where issues could be aired and where disagreements not settled outside could be vented. By meeting together, a sense of teamwork was engendered [and] ownership offered.[70]

These Cabinet activities assumed renewed importance in the era of coalition government ushered in by the 2010 general election. David Cameron, in contrast to his recent predecessors, had to develop policies which enjoyed the support not simply of his Conservative Party but also of his Liberal Democrat partners, relying upon Cabinet as a forum for deliberation. The Coalition also restricted Cameron's ability to dismiss ministers, as a balance between the coalition partners in Cabinet had to be retained.[71] Even after the 2015 and 2017 general elections, David Cameron and Theresa May found it difficult to restore the previous level of prime ministerial dominance in light of their relatively weak positions in Parliament.

2. Junior ministers

Most Cabinet ministers run government departments, also known as ministries. In this role they are assisted by teams of junior ministers who are responsible for particular aspects of the running of departments and who do not attend Cabinet meetings. Figure 8.1 shows the ministerial team running the Home Department (often colloquially known as the Home Office) in November 2017. Amber Rudd, MP, the Home Secretary is directly responsible for a team of five ministers. Four of these ministers, Brandon Lewis, MP, Ben Wallace, MP, Nick Hurd, MP, and Baroness Williams, are Ministers of State. This is the more senior of the two ranks of junior ministers. As a mark of their seniority, these ministers, like Cabinet ministers, are able to draw on the assistance of Parliamentary Private Secretaries.[72] These are Members of Parliament belonging to the governing party

---

[69] R. Heffernan, 'Prime Ministerial Predominance? Core Executive Politics in the UK' (2003) 5 *British Journal of Politics & International Relations* 347, 358.

[70] A. Seldon, 'The Cabinet System' in V. Bogdanor (ed.), *The British Constitution in the Twentieth Century* (OUP, 2003) 97, 127.

[71] See M. Bennister, and R. Heffernan, 'The Limits to Prime Ministerial Autonomy: Cameron and the Constraints of Coalition (2015) 68 *Parliamentary Affairs* 25.

[72] HM Government, *The Cabinet Manual: A Guide to Laws, Conventions and Rules on the Operation of Government* (Cabinet Office, 2011) 23.

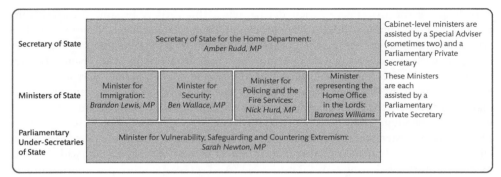

Figure 8.1 The Ministerial Structure of the Home Office in November 2017

(or parties) who are under consideration as future ministers but who are not yet members of the government and who do not draw any ministerial salary. The most junior government ministers, Parliamentary Under-Secretaries of State (with one in the Home Office, Sarah Newton), are not entitled to such support. Parliamentary Under-Secretaries of State often oversee less high-profile or contentious aspects of departmental policy than Ministers of State.

The internal workings of government departments are insulated from legal scrutiny by the *Carltona* principle. This, however, is not a constitutional convention but a deliberate decision by the judiciary to remain aloof from issues relating to how official functions, allocated by law to the Secretary of State, are implemented in practice. In the wartime case of *Carltona* v *Commissioners of Works* a factory was requisitioned by civil servants within the Ministry of Works. The company which owned the factory complained that the Minister of Works himself, to whom the requisition power was granted under the Defence of the Realm Regulations, was required by law to authorise the requisition. The Court of Appeal, however, refused to accept that a requisition carried out without the direct permission of the minister was invalid. Lord Greene MR, recognising the complexity of modern government, asserted that '[t]he duties imposed upon ministers and the powers given to ministers are normally exercised under the authority of ministers by responsible officials of the department. Public business could not be carried on if that were not the case'.[73] The principle has general effect in relation to functions granted to the Secretary of State by Parliament, unless it is explicitly excluded by a legislative provision.[74]

3. Law officers and whips

Two groups of government ministers operate separately from the ministerial hierarchy set out above: the law officers and the government whips. The law officers are the government's senior legal advisers. The senior law officer for England and Wales is the Attorney-General (currently Jeremy Wright, QC MP), who oversees the operations of the Treasury Solicitor's Department (responsible for providing legal advice to public bodies),[75] the Crown Prosecution Service (responsible for prosecuting most criminal offences in

---

[73] *Carltona* v *Commissioners of Works* [1943] 2 All ER 560, 563.
[74] See, for example, Immigration and Asylum Act 1999, s. 60(9)(a).
[75] See HM Government, *The Cabinet Manual: A Guide to Laws, Conventions and Rules on the Operation of Government* (Cabinet Office, 2011) 53.

England and Wales) and the Serious Fraud Office (responsible for prosecuting complex and high value cases of fraud in England, Wales and Northern Ireland).[76] He is also given specific responsibility under some statutes for authorising prosecutions of particular types of offence (often where criminal charges raise potential issues of public interest),[77] and can also intervene to halt prosecutions or criminal investigations on broad public interest grounds.

Thinking Point . . .

The process by which the Attorney-General assesses whether legal proceedings are in the public interest is known as a 'Shawcross exercise' (after former Attorney-General, Sir Hartley Shawcross). This involves seeking 'the views of any ministerial colleague who may have an interest in the case . . . so that I can be informed of their views of the public interest considerations of the case'. Lord Goldsmith, HL Deb., vol. 658, col. 339 (26 February 2004).

This role, therefore, presents a possible avenue for political interference in the administration of justice. Few recent Attorneys-General have faced allegations of undertaking a politically motivated prosecution, with one Independent Reviewer of counter-terrorism legislation declaring it all-but inconceivable that a prosecution would be based on political motives.[78] Parliament's Justice Committee nonetheless continues to warn of 'the difficulty of combining the political and legal duties of the Attorney-General',[79] for the office holder must not simply avoid political considerations in making prosecutorial judgments, but be able to publically demonstrate that this was the case.[80] In one prominent example, pressure groups investigating the arms trade alleged that political motivations contributed to ministerial pressure upon the Serious Fraud Office to stop investigating a major arms deal between BAE Systems and Saudi Arabia, although the House of Lords ultimately rejected such claims.[81] A further problem is that the office of Attorney-General unsatisfactorily combines the role of providing confidential legal advice to government with ministerial responsibility to Parliament. This duality in the role is difficult to sustain when Parliament seeks to know the content of the Attorney-General's advice to government:

Key debates
Legal advice on the Iraq War

On 20 March 2003 the UK joined a US-led coalition in the invasion of Iraq, ostensibly to prevent the risk posed by weapons of mass destruction supposedly possessed by Saddam Hussein's despotic regime. On 17 March 2003, the Attorney-General, Lord Goldsmith, advised

→

---

[76] Ibid., 49.
[77] See, for example, Serious Organised Crime and Police Act 2005, s. 128.
[78] Lord Carlile, *The Definition of Terrorism* (2007) Cm. 7052, para. 61.
[79] Justice Committee, *Draft Constitutional Renewal Bill (provisions relating to the Attorney General)* (2008) HC 698, para. 39.
[80] N. Walker, 'The Antinomies of the Law Officers' in M. Sunkin and S. Payne (eds), *The Nature of the Crown* (OUP, 1999) 135, 149.
[81] *R (Corner House Research)* v *Director of the Serious Fraud Office* [2008] UKHL 60.

→ Tony Blair's Government that military action against Iraq would not contravene international law. A summary of this advice was presented to Parliament and was instrumental in securing Parliament's support for the invasion in a vote on 18 March. In the aftermath of the war, as the conflict in Iraq continued and no weapons of mass destruction were found, parliamentarians repeatedly questioned the Attorney-General on the basis of this advice but it was not until the Chilcot Report of 2016 that the shortcomings in the Attorney General's performance (and indeed of the Cabinet Government in the UK) were fully exposed (Sir John Chilcot, *The Report of the Iraq Inquiry* (6 July 2016)).

The first section of volume 5 of the Report details the Attorney-General's doubts and concerns over the legality of the proposed invasion over a period of many months. But Lord Goldsmith found himself excluded from most Cabinet meetings and was repeatedly asked to reconsider advice which expressed caveats over the legality of the invasion. In any event, most of the important discussions on Iraq policy were conducted in one-to-one meetings between Tony Blair and his ministers which kept Cabinet in the dark about the big picture (see Chilcot Report, vol. 3, paras 269–73). Having been marginalised, Lord Goldsmith seems to have been determined not to undermine his precarious access (acutely aware of how easily Government could get a new, compliant, lawyer). He therefore decided that the question he needed to advise Tony Blair on was whether there was a reasonably arguable basis for war.

Goldsmith remains defiant that the advice which he gave to the Prime Minister on this question was correct (See T. Bingham, *The Rule of Law* (Penguin, 2011) p. v125). So limited was his frame of reference, however, that it would be difficult to dissuade him of this notion. He concluded that there was a reasonably arguable case for war, and because he was the sole official arbiter of the issue of lawfulness question within the UK Constitution this meant that he could convince himself that the action could be justified on this scant basis. As Jeffrey Jowell concluded, 'the dual political and legal role of the Attorney inevitably lends itself to charges of political bias in legal decisions' (Constitutional Affairs Committee, *Constitutional Role of the Attorney General* (2007) HC 306, para. 37).

In short, Lord Goldsmith presented all-but 'last minute' advice to the Prime Minister, which was subsequently made more widely available in digested form to the Cabinet, and thereafter only in summary to MPs. This process of delaying and truncating advice obscured the weaknesses in the legal basis for war. Far from strengthening and enforcing UN Security Council Resolutions Chilcot concluded that 'in the absence of a majority in support of military action . . . the UK was, in fact, undermining the Security Council's authority.'

The whips operate in all main parties in both Houses of Parliament and have the role of maintaining party discipline and ensuring that the government has sufficient support in Parliament to pass legislation. In this role they are aided by the strength of political parties in Westminster, allowing the whips to threaten Members of Parliament who refuse to follow the party line with de-selection for their parliamentary seat.[82] Government Whips, in consultation with Opposition Whips, also have the responsibility for scheduling government business in Parliament.[83] Like so many aspects of the executive we have examined so far the operation of these officers remains almost entirely governed by constitutional conventions.

---

[82] For further information. see pp. 53–61.
[83] See HM Government, *The Cabinet Manual: A Guide to Laws, Conventions and Rules on the Operation of Government* (Cabinet Office, 2011) 23.

The constitutional convention of collective responsibility

Two key constitutional conventions underpin the role of ministers, collective responsibility (by which ministers agree to speak with one voice in support of agreed government policies in public) and individual ministerial responsibility (by which ministers are responsible for explaining the activities of their departments to Parliament and may have to resign if they are personally responsible for departmental failings or if they mislead Parliament). This latter convention will be examined later, alongside the other political mechanisms for holding government to account for its actions. For now, it is essential to understand how collective Cabinet responsibility binds all ministers together into a cohesive unit.

(i) Collective responsibility: unanimity and confidentiality

When the Cabinet system was in its infancy in the eighteenth century, a time when monarchs retained the capacity to involve themselves in the day-to-day running of government, individual ministers risked their position if they were associated with policies which raised royal objections. As a defence mechanism, ministers therefore agreed that once a policy had been settled upon and gained the approval of Cabinet, they would all support it publically.[84] The *Cabinet Manual* defines the convention which emerged:

> The Cabinet system of government is based on the principle of collective responsibility. All government ministers are bound by the collective decisions of Cabinet, save where it is explicitly set aside, and carry joint responsibility for all the Government's policies and decisions.[85]

This definition focuses upon the need for unanimity in government action which the early Cabinets found so useful. But it tells only part of the story of collective responsibility, for government ministers are free to disagree with each other on a policy within Cabinet. This confidentiality in Cabinet discussion allows ministers to voice their opinion on the direction of policy in the knowledge that, if most Cabinet colleagues disagree, they can thereafter publically back the majority position without losing face:

> Ministers should be able to express their views frankly in the expectation that they can argue freely in private while maintaining a united front when decisions have been reached. This in turn requires that the privacy of opinions expressed in Cabinet and Ministerial Committees, including in correspondence, should be maintained.[86]

Only if ministers seek to *publically* repudiate a policy agreed in Cabinet, by speaking out against it or failing to support it in a parliamentary vote, will they be in breach of the convention. This convention therefore helps prime ministers to keep their cabinet colleagues 'on message', but it also fosters consultative decision-making within government and enables Parliament to hold ministers to account against a government's agreed position.[87]

The convention ultimately obliges wayward ministers to either resign or vote to support government policy (not simply abstain), but how rigorously it is enforced is often a matter for the Prime Minister, who in any event can explicitly set aside the convention with regard

---

[84] See R. Pares, *King George III and the Politicians* (OUP, 1953) pp. 148–9.
[85] See HM Government, *The Cabinet Manual: A Guide to Laws, Conventions and Rules on the Operation of Government* (Cabinet Office, 2011) 31.
[86] HM Government, *The Ministerial Code* (Cabinet Office, 2018) para. 2.1.
[87] Constitution Committee, *Constitutional Implications of Coalition Government* (2014) HL 130, para. 66.

to particular issues.[88] A 'free vote' takes place on an issue when the UK Government does not adopt an official position, thereby allowing ministers to vote as they choose. This mechanism is often employed where divisions involve issues of conscience or to head off party splits. It was employed by the 2010–15 Coalition Government when it legislated to introduce same-sex marriage, with David Cameron finding himself in a minority amongst Conservative MPs.[89] An 'Agreement to Differ', by contrast, suspends the operation of collective responsibility for a period of time on a particular issue. The Prime Minister is the key player in such an Agreement. As James Callaghan enigmatically explained during his time as Prime Minister, 'I certainly think that the doctrine should apply, except in cases where I announce that it does not'.[90]

Thinking Point . . .

As Prime Ministers control the Cabinet's composition they also determine how the conventions surrounding ministerial office operate. In the EU referendum campaigns of 1975 and 2016 both Harold Wilson and David Cameron suspended the operation of collective Cabinet responsibility by an 'Agreement to Differ' to allow ministers to depart from the government line, as not doing so would have risked irrevocably splitting their parties; 'there will be a clear Government position, but it will be open to individual Ministers to take a different personal position while remaining part of the Government' (D. Cameron, MP, HC Debs, vol. 604, col. 28 (5 January 2016)).

(ii) Resignations because of collective responsibility

If ministers find that they are unable to support a policy agreed by Cabinet then they are obliged to resign and oppose the policy out of office rather than attempting to remain in office and weakening the government from within. Should they choose not to resign, the Prime Minister (who controls the composition of the Cabinet) can dismiss renegade ministers.[91] A government's credibility can be threatened when policy disagreements are laid bare in the revelations of departing ministers in their resignation speeches to Parliament. Prior to the US-led invasion of Iraq in 2003 Parliament was convulsed over the Government's proposal to involve UK military forces. Robin Cook resigned from his ministerial post on the basis that he was unable to support the government's foreign policy:

> It has been a favourite theme of commentators that this House no longer occupies a central role in British politics. Nothing could better demonstrate that they are wrong than for this House to stop the commitment of troops in a war that has neither international agreement nor domestic support. I intend to join those tomorrow night who will vote against military action now. It is for that reason, and for that reason alone, and with a heavy heart, that I resign from the government.[92]

---

[88] See HM Government, *The Cabinet Manual: A Guide to Laws, Conventions and Rules on the Operation of Government* (Cabinet Office, 2011) 4.

[89] See P. Cowley and D. Kavanagh, *The British General Election of 2015* (Palgrave Macmillan, 2016) pp. 48–50.

[90] HC Debs, vol. 933, col. 552 (19 June 1977).

[91] See I. Jennings, *Cabinet Government* (3rd edn, CUP, 1965) p. 277.

[92] HC Deb., vol. 401, col. 728 (17 March 2003).

This excerpt demonstrates that even though Robin Cook publically disagreed over a single area of government policy, collective responsibility obliged him to leave office. Another minister, Clare Short, who had publically described military action against Iraq as 'reckless' in the preceding weeks, refused to follow Cook's lead when Cabinet reached its decision.[93] The pressures of the convention often constrain ministers with regard to their defence of their departmental interests. For as long as they remain ministers, for example, they cannot speak out against cuts to their departmental budgets. Only if they resign can they publically resist; in early 2016 Iain Duncan Smith resigned as Work and Pensions Secretary claiming that his flagship welfare-to-work policy had been undermined by budget cuts.[94] This resignation, it should be noted, also allowed him to immediately begin campaigning against the UK's continued EU membership, whereas ministers could only do so when the "Agreement to Differ" on this issue entered operation at the official start of the referendum campaign.[95]

Less dramatic than ministerial resignations, but no less corrosive for collective responsibility, are leaks to the press concerning confidential Cabinet deliberations. Ministers who leak in this way are, of course, breaching the convention of confidentiality surrounding Cabinet discussions, but, given how difficult it remains to establish the source of a leak amongst the ranks of ministers and advisers, leaking can occur with impunity. The positions taken by ministers in John Major's Cabinet, for example, riven by disputes over the UK's relationship with the EU, were frequently subject to leaks.[96] If the confidentiality aspects of collective responsibility are so difficult to secure, the value of this convention is dubious. Collective responsibility can thus be seen as having shrunk to the requirement that ministers maintain a unanimous public voice, meaning that a convention that helped to develop the independence of the Cabinet from the monarch now serves to strengthen Prime Ministerial dominance. When Clare Short did, belatedly, resign from government amidst the failures of post-invasion planning in Iraq, she disputed whether the convention now benefitted good governance; 'There is no real collective responsibility because there is no collective; just diktats in favour of increasingly badly thought through policy initiatives that come from on high'.[97] The Prime Minister's control of the agenda in Cabinet, the lack of time for lengthy Cabinet discussion of any policy and her power over the careers of her colleagues often serve to bind ministers to policies which they feel they have little say over.[98]

(iii) Coalition government and collective responsibility

Some Cabinets are better at constraining Prime Ministerial power than others. In the context of a coalition government in particular, the strictures of collective responsibility can be too rigid to accommodate policy differences between government ministers of different parties. As exemplified by the negotiations between senior Conservatives and Liberal Democrats following the inconclusive general election of May 2010, coalitions will struggle to agree upon every aspect of government policy. The solution, therefore, is to

---

[93] See I. Ward, *The English Constitution: Myths and Realities* (Hart, 2004) 67.

[94] See 'In Full: Iain Duncan Smith Resignation Letter' *BBC News* (18 March 2016).

[95] See C. Oliver, *Unleashing Demons: The Inside Story of Brexit* (Hodder & Stoughton, 2016).

[96] See P. Hennessy, *The Prime Minister, The Office and its Holders Since 1945* (Penguin, 2001) p. 470.

[97] HC Deb, vol. 405, col. 38, (12 May 2003).

[98] See C. Brady, 'Collective Responsibility of the Cabinet: An Ethical, Constitutional or Managerial Tool?' (1999) 52 *Parliamentary Affairs* 214, 218.

agree certain issues upon which collective responsibility is set aside, permitting public disagreement between ministers on these particular issues, but maintain cohesion with regard to the remainder of government policy. For example, the Coalition Agreement struck between the Conservatives and Liberal Democrats explicitly permitted Liberal Democrat ministers to abstain over increases to university tuition fees and permitted government ministers to campaign against each other on the referendum regarding the introduction of the alternative vote system for parliamentary elections in the UK.[99] When a Prime Minister requires the support of another political party to govern even such explicit agreements might be insufficient; having failed to gain Conservative backing for their Lords-reform proposals the Liberal Democrats voted to stymie the boundary changes required by the Parliamentary Voting System and Constituencies Act 2011. Even though ministers were involved in this action David Cameron could not require their resignation and maintain the Coalition.[100]

The civil service

(i) The role of the modern civil service

The civil service is made up of around 420,000 officials who help to administer public policy. They are distinct as a group from the remainder of the public sector workforce, set apart both by their role and by their terms of employment. Civil servants do not change with the election of a new government and have the role of assisting the government, regardless of its politics, 'in developing and implementing its policies, and in delivering public services'.[101] The concept of a politically neutral civil service, recruited by competitive examination and in which advancement depends upon ability and not upon political nepotism, is deep-rooted

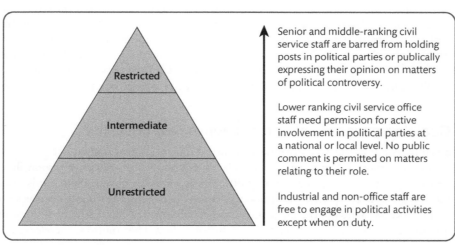

Figure 8.2 Civil service in order of seniority

---

[99] See HM Government, *The Coalition Agreement for Stability and Reform* (May 2010).

[100] See Constitution Committee, *Constitutional Implications of Coalition Government* (2014) HL 130, para. 71.

[101] HM Government, *The Cabinet Manual: A Guide to Laws, Conventions and Rules on the Operation of Government* (Cabinet Office, 2011) 57.

within the UK's constitutional history, being first set out in the Northcote-Trevelyan Report of 1854.[102] In order to secure this principle, restrictions are placed on the public expression of political opinion of civil servants, including statutory restrictions preventing civil servants from serving as Members of Parliament.[103] The extent of the applicable restrictions depends upon the seniority of the civil servant in question (Figure 8.2).

This system, of course, leaves many civil servants restricted in their ability to express their political opinions and participate in the political process to the same degree as private individuals. In one case, challenging whether the system of restriction by pay grade (as opposed to a system based upon the particular responsibilities of a civil servant) was compatible with the right to freedom of expression,[104] the Northern Ireland Court of Appeal recognised the importance of maintaining public confidence in the political neutrality of the civil service.[105] Dismissing the appeal, the court upheld the system of political restrictions even though they covered broad classes of civil servants:

> Fashioning restrictions on the engagement of civil servants in political activity cannot be conducted on an individual basis. It is unrealistic to suggest that examination of the particular duties of a civil servant can provide the inevitable answer to the extent of the necessary restriction on political activities within the group.[106]

The civil service also performs the function of constitutional 'ballast', ensuring that the government of the country receives sound advice even if new and inexperienced ministers take office.[107] By convention, civil servants are allowed to engage in pre-election discussions with opposition leaders to facilitate any change of government,[108] although such discussions can be truncated or even negated if a Parliament does not run to full term.[109] As one former minister, looking back to the moment he took office in 1970 recalled:

> It was thought by the pundits that the Conservatives would lose that election. Therefore I was agreeably surprised when I reached that department to find the amount of work that civil servants had done on what Conservatives had been saying in Opposition. The papers were prepared for us on day one.[110]

Because departmental civil servants are Crown servants, they are responsible to the ministers in charge of their department, rather than Parliament. Vernon Bogdanor explains that the rationale behind insulating civil servants from parliamentary scrutiny is that, 'if civil servants are to serve different political masters [after changes of government], they must be protected from attack, both in Parliament and in the country. Thus, the responsibility of civil servants is subsumed in that of ministers.'[111] As with junior ministers, efforts by civil servants to exercise functions statutorily authorised to a Secretary of State are

---

[102] Northcote-Trevelyan Report (23 November 1853) (Parliamentary Papers, 1854, vol. xxvii).
[103] House of Commons (Disqualification) Act 1975, s. 1(1)(b).
[104] ECHR, Article 10.
[105] See *Re McKinney's Application* [2006] NICA 15, [35] (Lord Kerr CJ).
[106] Ibid., [37].
[107] C. Vincenzi, *Crown Powers, Subjects and Citizens* (Continuum, 1998) p. 170.
[108] HM Government, *The Cabinet Manual: A Guide to Laws, Conventions and Rules on the Operation of Government* (Cabinet Office, 2011) 16.
[109] See Political and Constitutional Reform Committee, *Fixed-term Parliaments: The Final Year of a Parliament* (2014) HC 971, paras 63–64.
[110] Lord Dean of Harptree, HL Deb, vol. 560, col. 1532 (1 February 1995).
[111] V. Bogdanor, 'The Civil Service' in V. Bogdanor (ed.), *The British Constitution in the Twentieth Century* (OUP, 2003) 237, 238.

covered by the ***Carltona*** principle,[112] again on the basis that the Secretary of State will ultimately be responsible for all activities undertaken within his or her remit.

(ii) Changes threatening the role and ethos of the civil service

The 'permanency' of civil servants, when governments come and go with elections, has attracted criticism. For some commentators (and even ministers), it enables civil servants to delay reforms as they have no inherent commitment to a government's proposals.[113] Moreover, the lack of accountability of civil servants to the electorate has produced frequent attacks on the civil service for being less responsive to the needs of the general public than private enterprise. From the Thatcher Government on, successive ministers have sought to reform the civil service to respond to these challenges whilst supposedly maintaining the core principles on which the service is based (often explicitly criticising previous reforms):

> Too often in recent years the service has been marginalised, either through the spread of special advisers or the over-use of expensive consultants. Complicated delivery arrangements, sometimes through a myriad of public bodies, have also impaired the flexibility and agility of the Service.[114]

1. The development of executive agencies

One of the biggest shake-ups of the organisation of government in the second half of the twentieth century was the development of executive agencies which operate at 'arm's length' from government departments. Today, fewer than 50,000 civil servants work within the central government departments (known collectively as 'Whitehall' after the location of most central government buildings in London). Instead, from the early 1980s onwards, large sections of the civil service were separated from central departments and instead organised into quasi-autonomous agencies (known colloquially as quangos), such as the Driver and Vehicle Licensing Agency and the Environment Agency. The process was accelerated by the Deregulation and Contracting Out Act 1994, by which ministers became able to authorise other bodies, including private actors out side the civil service, to exercise their statutory functions.[115] The intention behind these reforms was that the agencies would concentrate on the implementation of government policy, thereby leaving slimmed-down departments to focus upon policy development. This distinction, however, is difficult to maintain, for the senior civil servants in charge of such agencies play a key role in developing the role of the agencies. As Bogdanor concludes, it is difficult 'to reconcile executive leadership by officials with the doctrine that responsibility for the actions of a civil servant working in an agency is located uniquely in the office of the minister'.[116]

Thinking Point . . .

Because these delegations are broader than those permitted under the ***Carltona*** principle, they are instead based on the statutory authority of legislation including the Deregulation and Contracting Out Act 1994.

---

[112] See HM Government, *The Cabinet Manual: A Guide to Laws, Conventions and Rules on the Operation of Government* (Cabinet Office, 2011) 25–6.
[113] See Public Administration Committee, *Lessons for Civil Service Impartiality from the Scottish Independence Referendum* (2015) HC 111, para. 37.
[114] Francis Maude, 'Speech to the Civil Service' (6 July 2010).
[115] Deregulation and Contracting Out Act 1994, Part 2.
[116] V. Bogdanor, 'The Civil Service' in V. Bogdanor (ed.), *The British Constitution in the Twentieth Century* (OUP, 2003) 237, 270.

These concerns drove the Coalition Government's efforts to reduce the number of quangos within the UK's public sector. The Public Bodies Act 2011 gave ministers the power to abolish or merge many public bodies, although maintained almost 200 quangos which had been under review.[117] In spite of these cuts quangos remain an established feature of the UK's executive arrangements. Although responsibility for quangos ultimately lies with the relevant minister (for example, the Legal Aid Agency operates under the responsibility of the Secretary of State for Justice), they help to insulate ministers from the political consequences of all but the most serious failings within the agencies. These arrangements are also, conversely, part of the reason why quangos 'lack democratic legitimacy and popular respect'.[118]

2. Civil servants and select committee investigations

Ministers are responsible to Parliament for any activities undertaken within their remit. But in the course of their investigations into the operation of government, parliamentary select committees (first established in 1979) often request oral evidence from named civil servants. These requests are ordinarily acceded to in the wake of controversy surrounding efforts by ministers in John Major's Government to stymie select committee investigations into the 'Arms to Iraq' scandal in the early 1990s.[119] Requiring senior civil servants to account for government actions before Parliament has changed the nature of the role of civil servants. Although select committees are not supposed to act in a disciplinary fashion with regard to the conduct of particular civil servants,[120] ministers might seek to facilitate the questioning of civil servants, thereby deflecting criticism away from their own ultimate responsibility.

This accusation was levelled against Geoff Hoon when, as Defence Secretary in 2003, and against the advice of his senior departmental civil servant, he agreed to the request of the Foreign Affairs Committee (FAC) to question the civil servant Dr David Kelly. This request followed revelations that Dr Kelly had informed the BBC of his doubts about the government's claims regarding Iraqi weapons of mass destruction prior to the Iraq War. Two days later, Dr Kelly committed suicide. In the subsequent Report of the Hutton Inquiry into Dr Kelly's death, Geoff Hoon's decision was not criticised, with Lord Hutton noting that 'there would have been a serious political storm if Mr Hoon had refused to permit Dr Kelly to appear before the FAC'.[121] This conclusion highlights the current weakness of the safeguards which once ensured that responsibility for government actions rested with ministers.

3. Civil service job security and external appointments

Civil servants were, until the enactment of the Constitutional Reform and Governance Act 2010, legally regarded as Crown servants appointed under the royal prerogative and with terms of service subject internally to the Civil Service Management Code (although they have long had recourse to many of the protections of employment law[122]). Under the 2010

---

[117] See Public Bodies Act 2011, sch. 1 and sch. 2.
[118] Public Administration Committee, *Quangos* (1999) HC 209-I, para. 2.
[119] HM Government, *Guidance on Departmental Evidence and Response to Select Committees* (Cabinet Office, 2009) para. 44.
[120] Ibid., para. 46.
[121] Lord Hutton, *Report of the Inquiry into the Circumstances Surrounding the Death of Dr David Kelly CMG* (2004) HC 247, para. 430.
[122] Employment Rights Act 1996, s. 191.

Act government retains the ability to dismiss civil servants without notice,[123] a power which appears to have the potential to undermine the politically neutral role of civil servants, opening them up to political reprisal, especially at a time of spending cuts within government departments. In reality, this power is exercised only in exceptional circumstances with the Management Code separating ministers from disciplinary procedures. One change since the 1990s which has affected the ethos of the civil service has been the opening up of many senior appointments to external competition, with one parliamentary report finding that roughly 20 per cent of all senior civil servants were recruited from outside civil-service ranks.[124] That said, pressure to slim the civil service has been relentless, with overall numbers falling by a fifth in the lifetime of the Coalition Government.

Thinking Point . . .

A Spending Review in 2010 required some departments to reduce their spending by 25 per cent, with one focus being cutting civil servant posts. Several commentators have noted that these cuts could undermine civil service performance. In an editorial in the aftermath of Department for Transport procurement errors regarding the West Coast Mainline railway contract (which cost over £40 million to rectify), the *Independent* noted that 'the Department for Transport was subject to some of the most rapid and swingeing staffing cuts of any government department; that a large number of senior officials – including 30 directors – lost their jobs, and that the directors of rail strategy and rail contracts were among those whose posts were abolished' (Editorial, 'Cut in haste – repent on the West Coast Main Line', *Independent* (15 October 2012)).

---

4. Special advisers

In the long run the increasing influx of senior 'outsiders' is likely to affect how the civil service advises the government, a trend reinforced by the increasing role played by 'special advisers' to Cabinet ministers. The *Cabinet Manual* explains their remit:

> Special advisers are employed as temporary civil servants to help ministers on matters where the work of government and the work of the party, or parties, of government overlap and where it would be inappropriate for permanent civil servants to become involved. They are an additional resource for the minister, providing assistance from a standpoint that is more politically committed and politically aware than would be available to a minister from the permanent Civil Service.[125]

These advisers are personal appointments by ministers (approved by the Prime Minister), and their term of appointment runs until a general election.[126] Although as of December 2016 there are only 83 special advisers in post across government, they play an established role within UK governments. Some prominent special advisers, such as Alastair Campbell (Tony Blair's first Director of Communications), Jonathan Powell (Tony Blair's Chief of Staff) and Andy Coulson (David Cameron's first Director of Communications), became

---

[123] See *McLaren* v *Home Office* [1990] IRLR 338, [38] (Woolf LJ).

[124] Public Administration Committee, *Outsiders and Insiders: External Appointments to the Senior Civil Service* (2010) HC 241, Table 2.

[125] HM Government, *The Cabinet Manual: A Guide to Laws, Conventions and Rules on the Operation of Government* (Cabinet Office, 2011) 58.

[126] Constitutional Reform and Governance Act 2010, s. 15.

much more recognisable government figures than many ministers. Some of these advisers, like Jonathan Powell, were given the power to direct civil servants.[127] As a result, the policy-making role of the senior civil service was further marginalised, leading former civil servant Sir Christopher Foster to conclude that Tony Blair 'treated [civil servants] as subordinates and excluded them from central policymaking unless ready to be politicised'.[128] Ministers are responsible to Parliament for the conduct of their special advisers.[129]

Thinking Point . . .

The Coalition Government attempted to distinguish itself from Labour by cutting the number of special advisers when it entered office in 2010. By the end of that year, numbers had dropped as low as 64. By 2012, however, amid concerns over frequent government 'u-turns' arising from unpopular policies, numbers again rose, ballooning to 104 in 2014. This suggests that modern governments find special advisers' political input into policy making indispensable. See Public Administration Committee, *Special Advisers* (2012) HC 134-ii.

(iii) To reaffirm or overhaul the foundations of the civil service?

Whilst the long-standing traditions of the civil service continue to imbue the institution with a shared ethos, successive governments have sought to respond to charges that their reforms have undermined these values. The Civil Service Code, first published in 1996, was the response of John Major's government to the accusations that, through the creation of numerous executive agencies, it was drawing civil servants directly into policy-making roles beyond their remit. In its current guise, the Code provides that civil servants exercise their duties on the basis of honesty and impartiality. It also provides that, if ministers direct civil servants to act in a manner contrary to these values (for example, involving civil servants in party political activities or in efforts to mislead Parliament), civil servants have the ultimate ability to raise the issue with the Civil Service Commissioners (although crucially, not the right to attempt a public release of material).[130]

Thinking Point . . .

Civil servants who leak information to the opposition or media risk their careers and even prosecution for misconduct in public office or breaches of the Official Secrets Acts. Christopher Galley, was a civil servant who was sacked and arrested (but not charged) in 2008 for leaking documents to Damian Green, MP, then a shadow minister. See Public Administration Committee, *Leaks and Whistleblowing in Whitehall* (2009) HC 83.

When Gordon Brown took office as Prime Minister he immediately sought to distance himself from his predecessor Tony Blair by revoking the power of any special advisers to direct the actions of civil servants, making it clear that he regarded this as an inappropriate intrusion

---

[127] Civil Service (Amendment) Order in Council 1995, Art. 3(3) (as amended in 1997).
[128] C. Foster, *British Government in Crisis* (Hart, 2005) p. 207.
[129] HM Government, *The Ministerial Code* (Cabinet Office, 2018) para. 3.3.
[130] HM Government, *The Civil Service Code* (Cabinet Office, 2015).

into the political impartiality of the civil service.[131] Under the Constitutional Reform and Governance Act 2010 the requirement for a Civil Service Code was ultimately enshrined in law,[132] with the Act providing that at a minimum the Code must require that civil servants serving either central government or the devolved administrations 'carry out their duties for the assistance of the administration as it is duly constituted for the time being, whatever its political complexion'.[133] The Act also affirmed in statute that special advisers were appointed for the sole purpose of assisting ministers and could not give instructions to civil servants.[134]

Thinking Point . . .

The resignation of Theresa May's Special Advisers Nick Timothy and Fiona Hill in the aftermath of the 2017 general election indicates the importance of some special advisers. They were so central to the management of government policy and the general election campaign that they were blamed by many within the party when it lost seats.

Cumulatively, these measures seemed to reaffirm rather than overhaul the traditional basis of the civil service. Nonetheless, the Coalition Government embarked on a programme of reforms intended 'to be disruptive and challenge the old orthodoxies'.[135] As we have already seen, the Coalition began by streamlining the UK's 'arms-length' public bodies, ending a trend that had seen an expansion in their number and remit under the Labour Governments in office from 1997–2010. These reforms were driven by a cost-cutting agenda, but concerns regarding the accountability of quangos made these bodies a soft target. Proposals for extensive performance management of civil servants sought to end practices which supposedly render the civil service 'cautious and slow-moving, focused on process not outcomes, bureaucratic, hierarchical and resistant to change'.[136] The civil service, however, proved adept at deflecting such calls for radical reform. Instead, the continued reliance of ministers upon special advisers to supplement, and often to by-pass, the advice of the permanent civil service looks set to continue, potentially to the detriment of long-term policy making.[137]

Conclusion

The culmination of all the conventions and legal rules we have examined in this chapter places the executive in the UK Constitution's driving seat. In theory, Parliament operates to restrict the executive. Indeed, as we have seen, it wrestled its law-making powers away from the monarchy (the historic 'working' executive and still symbolic focus of government activity) during the upheavals of the seventeenth century. In practice, however, almost all legislation is proposed to Parliament by ministers who are usually able to impose their will due to the party system and consequent loyalty of the largest block of MPs in the House of Commons. Such legislation can be skeletal in nature and allow for considerable

---

[131] See HM Government, *The Governance of Britain* (2007) Cm. 7170, 22.
[132] Constitutional Reform and Governance Act 2010, s. 5(5).
[133] Ibid., s. 7(2).
[134] Ibid., s. 8(5).
[135] F. Maude, MP, 'Key-note speech at the World-Class Public Services Conference' (11 June 2012).
[136] HM Government, *The Civil Service Reform Plan* (Cabinet Office, 2012) 9.
[137] See *Good Government: Reforming Parliament and the Executive* (Better Government Initiative).

delegation of authority to ministers.[138] As we shall see, these powers are often enhanced by the regular inflation of largest party representation through the 'first-past-the-post' electoral system and by government's ability to use its majority to control parliamentary procedure and curtail debate.[139] If it can command a stable parliamentary majority then the executive, which on paper appears unusually weak in the UK's system of government, will in reality be able to harness the power of Parliament to make laws and disburse funds in accordance with its purposes, and even, in the words of Lord Hailsham, to act as an 'elective dictatorship' subject to little by the way of parliamentary constraint.[140]

Even with the passing of the Fixed-Term Parliaments Act 2011 (which, as we will see in the next chapter, theoretically restricts the Prime Minister's ability to call elections at a time of her choosing), the Prime Minister remains the central figure of both Parliament and the government, being able to appoint, reshuffle or dismiss all other ministers. She is the arbiter of the careers of all other MPs in her party and can use her patronage to maintain discipline within the governing party. Although the Prime Minister sits at the centre of the policy making machinery of government, it would be wrong to regard her actions as unconstrained. Even Prime Ministers such as Tony Blair, possessing a strong parliamentary majority through-out his time in office, had to share his policy-making role with his advisers and senior figures in his party.[141] Policy making nonetheless becomes an increasingly collegial affair when a governing party's majority is small or a coalition of parties is in office.[142] Such constraints are, however, almost entirely political in nature; the internal workings of the executive remain amongst the least legalised aspects of the UK Constitution.

Practice questions

1. '[T]he powers of the prime minister . . . have been wrestled away from the Throne.'

   (A. Benn, *Arguments for Democracy* (Penguin, 1982) p. 20)

   Consider whether Tony Benn is suggesting that the office of Prime Minister has assumed the role once performed by the monarch under the UK Constitution.

2. 'Collective Cabinet responsibility is, as your Lordships well know, crucial to our system of government in Parliament. Without it, day-to-day executive decision making would simply break down.'

   (Lord Kingsland, HL Deb, vol. 708, col. 134 (24 February 2009))

   Would executive decision making 'break down' without collective Cabinet responsibility, or does the supposed importance of this convention disguise the weakness of the Cabinet within the UK Constitution?

3. 'Law would be too clumsy an instrument for regulating the conduct of Ministers of the Crown and the permanent Civil Servants of the State in their relations to each other. This is now far more effectually and far more safely accomplished by the power of public opinion.'

   (Earl Grey, *Parliamentary Government Considered with Reference to Reform* (John Murray, 1864) 326–7)

   →

---

[138] Above pp. 31–4.

[139] For further information, see pp. 463–5.

[140] Q. Hogg, *The Dilemma of Democracy, Diagnosis and Prescription* (Collins, 1978) p. 9.

[141] See R. Heffernan, 'Prime Ministerial Predominance? Core Executive Politics in the UK' (2003) 5 *British Journal of Politics & International Relations* 347, 359.

[142] See R. Fox, 'Five Days in May: A New Political Order Emerges' (2010) 63 *Parliamentary Affairs* 607.

Evaluate whether the lack of legal protections relating to the civil service prior to the enactment of the Constitutional Reform and Governance Act 2010 allowed practices to develop which have undermined the traditional role of the civil service.

Further reading

Efforts to understand the role of the executive branch in the UK's system of government must begin with an analysis of how the modern executive came into being, with the rise in the importance of elected politicians and the waning of the monarchy's power. This historical analysis allows the reader to form an opinion on whether the monarch does, and indeed, should, play any meaningful constitutional role today. In a thorough evaluation of the role (or lack of role) of the monarch in the legislative process, drawing on examples from both the UK and Australia, Anne Twomey (**A. Twomey, 'The Refusal or Deferral of Royal Assent'** [2006] *Public Law* 580–602) advances the argument that the monarch may still enjoy some discretion (albeit heavily restricted by convention) to refuse to assent to Acts of Parliament. Robert Blackburn (**R. Blackburn, 'Monarchy and the Personal Prerogatives'** [2004] *Public Law* 546–63), by contrast, carefully embarks upon an effort to 'bury' the idea of personal prerogatives of the monarch as an existing feature of the UK Constitution. His views should be contrasted with the *Cabinet Manual,* which seems to indicate that some of these prerogatives are still operable in time of constitutional crisis. Finally, Rodney Brazier (**R. Brazier, 'A British Republic'** (2002) 61 *Cambridge Law Journal* 351–85), a self-confessed monarchist, examines the difficulties which would beset attempts to reform the monarchy and in particularly efforts to turn the UK into a republic. He does suggest that any reform might be preceded by a referendum, allowing the people of the UK to express their opinion on the monarchy and thereby vesting a level of popular legitimacy in the institution.

Turning to the modern executive, Richard Heffernan (**R. Heffernan, 'Prime Ministerial Predominance? Core Executive Politics in the UK'** (2003) 5 *British Journal of Politics & International Relations* 347–72) dismisses the traditional idea of 'Cabinet government' as an outdated explanation of the operation of the executive in the UK, and examines instead the power relations in what he calls the 'core executive', the actors at the centre of government policy making. He analyses why some Prime Ministers are better able to exert their influence over the direction of executive policy than others, and the interplay of Prime Ministerial power with other key actors. Turning to the role of the civil service Richard Mulgan (**R. Mulgan, 'Truth in Government and the Politicization of Public Service Advice'** (2007) 85 *Public Administration* 569–86), in a study which overarches both Australia and the UK, examines the pressures upon historically politically neutral departmental officials to, at the very least, conform their advice to the wishes of the government of the day. He focuses not simply upon the demands of governments for advice that supports their policies but also examines the effect of freedom of information legislation on the role of the civil service in both countries.

Chapter 9
Parliament (I): the House of Commons

'Without any separation of powers, one party controls the legislature and forms the executive; while another party wants to.'

T. Wright, 'What are MPs for?' (2010) 81 *Political Quarterly* 298, 304.

Chapter outline

Parliament is the dominant legal force in the constitution of the United Kingdom. The Parliament of the United Kingdom, situated at Westminster, is also the hub of the United Kingdom's political system. Our system, therefore, is one of *parliamentary* – not constitutional – government. But government in the United Kingdom is largely conducted *through* rather than *by* Parliament. Behind the idea of parliamentary government lie two important features of the United Kingdom's legislature and therefore of the constitution itself: the pre-eminence within Parliament of the House of Commons and the dominance of the House of Commons by the government of the day. This chapter examines both features, in the context of the role, functions and composition of the House of Commons.

Introduction: Parliament

The origins of the United Kingdom Parliament are traceable back to medieval times. While the origins of the House of Commons can be found in the thirteenth century, those of the House of Lords reach back yet further to twelfth century Anglo-Saxon *Witenagemot*.[1] Over time, the ability of the monarch to raise taxes, make laws, and otherwise administer the realm became increasingly dependent on the advice, latterly consent, of those governed. Gradually the monarch's advisers (later ministers) – initially summoned only when required – began to convene regularly. It is in the formalisation of these arrangements for consultation between monarch and advisers, and for the provision of advice – and, importantly, resources – to the Crown that the development

---

[1] See: P. Norton, *Parliament in British Politics* (2ⁿᵈ edn) (Palgrave Macmillan, 2013) Ch. 2; A. Tomkins, 'What is Parliament for?' in N. Bamforth and P. Leyland, *Public Law in a Multi-Layered Constitution* (Hart Publishing, 2003) pp. 55–8.

of our parliamentary system can be found. As we have seen, the slow transition from monarchical to parliamentary government enhanced the autonomy of Parliament and culminated in the events of the Glorious Revolution and emergence of Parliament as the highest legal authority in the constitution.[2]

Key issues

- The United Kingdom Parliament is comprised of two houses – the House of Commons and the House of Lords – and is, therefore, a bicameral legislature.
- The House of Commons is the pre-eminent House of Parliament, both politically and legally.

Thinking Point . . .

According to Bagehot's distinction those 'dignified' elements of the constitution were those which 'excite and preserve the reverence of the population' (or as David Feldman has put it, 'those with traditional authority to which people feel a special loyalty' ('One, None or Several? Perspectives on the UK's Constitution(s)' [2005] CLJ 329, 339). The 'efficient' parts meanwhile were those under which the constitution actually operated in practice, in other words, where the real business of government took place.

The Parliament of the United Kingdom is bicameral. Parliament, therefore, comprises two houses or chambers – the House of Commons and the House of Lords – as well as the monarch or Queen in Parliament. This relationship between the three component parts of Parliament continues to be reflected in the passing of legislation; the monarch must grant assent before a Bill which has been passed by the Commons and Lords can become law. The composition of Parliament, therefore, theoretically continues to reflect the three historical bases of political power and influence within the constitution – the monarch, nobility, and commoners – but in practice this division is increasingly misleading as to the locus of political power in the modern constitution. For the most part, the role of the monarch in relation to the business of Parliament is – to adopt Bagehot's terminology – 'dignified' rather than 'efficient'.[3] The contemporary House of Lords is no longer dominated by hereditary peers – members of the nobility whose right to sit and vote has been passed down from generation to generation – and its influence (*vis-à-vis* that of the House of Commons) has since the early twentieth century at least been limited by both law and convention.[4] Of the three entities that, combined, make up Parliament, it is the House of Commons that is dominant; the Commons, as the Wright Committee Report noted, is 'the central institution in British democracy, in both real and symbolic terms'.[5] As a result,

---

[2] Chapter 5, pp. 127–8.
[3] W. Bagehot, *The English Constitution* (Oxford World's Classics, 2001).
[4] Chapter 10. Compare: P. Seaward and P. Silk, 'The House of Commons' and R. Walters, 'The House of Lords' both in V. Bogdanor (ed.), *The British Constitution in the Twentieth Century* (Oxford University Press, 2003).
[5] House of Commons Reform Committee, *Rebuilding the House* (2008–09) HC 1117, [3].

the epithets frequently attached to the House of Commons and House of Lords – respectively the 'Lower' and 'Upper' Houses of Parliament – while descriptive of the historic social status of the members of the two chambers, are now almost entirely inaccurate as indicators of the Houses' respective political and legal powers.

The Parliament of the United Kingdom is – applying the terminology of separation of powers – the legislative branch of government. The passage of legislation is, however, but one of the tasks for which Parliament is responsible. It also falls to Parliament to ensure that the government is held to account for its policies and the conduct of its administration. Parliament is not only therefore a legislator, but is also a 'scrutineer, or . . . a regulator, of government.'[6] Each House of Parliament makes a distinctive contribution to the carrying out of these core tasks; this chapter and the next examine the role, functions and composition of both. We begin with the House of Commons.

The composition of the House of Commons

Key issues

- The House of Commons is comprised of 650 directly elected Members of Parliament (MPs) representing constituencies in England, Northern Ireland, Scotland and Wales.
- MPs are elected at intervals regulated by the Fixed-Term Parliaments Act 2011 at a general election.
- A general election will determine how many seats within the House of Commons will be allocated to each political party and, in turn, which political party (or parties) will be in a position to form the government of the United Kingdom.
- Elections to the House of Commons are conducted under the first-past-the-post system.

The modern House of Commons is comprised of 650 members, each of whom is directly elected – under the first-past-the-post system (considered below) – from one of the 650 constituencies in England, Northern Ireland, Scotland and Wales.[7]

Territory	Number of constituencies
England	533
Scotland	59
Wales	40
Northern Ireland	18

---

[6] A. Tomkins, 'What is Parliament for?' in N. Bamforth and P. Leyland, *Public Law in a Multi-Layered Constitution* (Hart Publishing, 2003) p. 54.

[7] The Parliamentary Voting System and Constituencies Act 2011, s.11, proposes reducing the size of the House of Commons to 600 MPs. See pp. 312–13.

By law, certain persons are ineligible to stand for election to the House of Commons; they include persons holding judicial office, members of the armed forces, police officers and civil servants.[8]

The franchise

Until the nineteenth century, the membership of the House of Commons was linked to the ownership of land. The Great Reform Act of 1832 sparked the beginnings of the movement towards universal adult suffrage.

Setting the scene
Development of the general franchise

1832	*Reform Act*: significantly increased the size of the electorate – by some 49%[9] – in response to the pressures of industrialisation.
1884	*Representation of the People Act*: effectively established the one-member constituency method of parliamentary representation.
1918	*Representation of the People Act*: franchise extended to women over the age of 30.
1928	*Representation of the People (Equal Franchise) Act*: franchise extended to women over the age of 21.
1969	*Representation of the People Act*: voting age lowered from 21 to 18.

To be eligible to cast a vote in a UK parliamentary election, an individual must be registered to vote – in other words, must appear on the register of electors – must be over 18 years of age,[10] should be resident in the United Kingdom and either be a British citizen, a Commonwealth citizen eligible to vote in the UK or a citizen of the Republic of Ireland.[11]

Certain persons are, however, ineligible to vote in a general election. The most obvious, and largest, category is all those under the age of 18. A number of further exceptions to the general principle of universal adult suffrage also exist. Persons other than British, Irish and those Commonwealth citizens who are eligible to vote are not eligible to vote in a general election; citizens of other EU countries who are ordinarily resident in the UK for instance cannot vote at a general election. Members of the House of Lords may not vote in general elections.[12] Those who are detained on the basis of their mental health are denied the right to vote,[13] as are persons convicted of a criminal offence who may not vote during the term of their sentence.[14] The latter exception is perhaps the most controversial, with

---

[8] House of Commons Disqualification Act 1975, s. 1 and sch. 1.

[9] P. Norton, *Parliament in British Politics* (2nd edn) (Palgrave Macmillan, 2013) p. 20.

[10] The voting age for elections to the Scottish Parliament was set at 16 years of age as a result of the Scottish Elections (Reduction of Voting Age) Act 2015.

[11] Section 1, Representation of the People Act 1983.

[12] *Earl Beauchamp* v *Madresfield* [1872] LR 8 CP 245. Cf. House of Lords Act 1999, s. 3, which provides that hereditary peers *not* entitled to sit and vote in the House of Lords are not disqualified from voting in elections to the House of Commons.

[13] Section 3A, Representation of the People Act 1983.

[14] Ibid.

the continuing validity of the United Kingdom's ban underpinning a decade-long stand-off between the UK Government and the European Court of Human Rights.[15]

General elections

Until the passing of the Fixed-Term Parliaments Act 2011, elections to the House of Commons – general elections – ordinarily[16] took place once every five years[17] following the dissolution of Parliament by the monarch. By convention, the monarch would exercise the prerogative power to dissolve Parliament upon the request of the Prime Minister. Despite the technical role of the monarch, effective control over dissolution – and thereby over when a general election would be held – therefore generally lay with the Prime Minister. The maximum lifetime of a Parliament was set at five years – by virtue of s. 7 of the Parliament Act 1911 – although a dissolution may have been sought at any time during this period, for instance, in order to exploit the popularity of the government. Although a general election may also have been triggered by a vote of no confidence causing the resignation of the government, the ability to call a general election at a time favourable to his or her party ensured that the Prime Minister held a 'huge tactical advantage' over the opposition parties.[18] One of the intentions behind the enactment of the Fixed-Term Parliaments Act 2011 was to deny this considerable political influence to future Prime Ministers.

Upon forming a government in 2010, the Conservative–Liberal Coalition Government pledged to introduce legislation to establish five-year fixed-term Parliaments. The proposed measure – it was anticipated – would take away much of the Prime Minister's power to prompt a general election when most politically convenient, putting the power to dissolve Parliament on a statutory footing (thereby abolishing the prerogative power to dissolve Parliament) and making an early dissolution conditional either on a lost vote of confidence or on a 55 per cent vote in favour of dissolution in the House of Commons.[19] The Fixed-Term Parliaments Act was enacted in September 2011.

The most important provision of the Act fixed the date of the next United Kingdom general election as 7 May 2015.[20] General elections were thereafter to be held at five-year intervals, with polling taking place on the first Thursday in May during the designated year.[21] This five-year cycle is not, however, as rigid as it might at first seem; two provisions of the Act are designed to permit early elections to be held. First (and in a departure from the intentions of the Coalition Government), s. 2(1) allows an early election to be held in response to a House of Commons resolution indicating that 'there shall be an early parliamentary election' which is endorsed by more than two-thirds of the membership of the

---

[15] *Hirst* v *United Kingdom (No. 2)* (2006) 42 EHRR 41; *Greens and MT* v *United Kingdom* (2011) 53 EHRR 21. See also *Smith* v *Scott* 2007 SC 345; 2007 SLT 137 and *R (on the application of Chester)* v *Secretary of State for Justice* [2010] EWCA Civ 1439; [2011] 1 WLR 1436. For commentary, see C. R. G. Murray, 'We Need to Talk: "Democratic Dialogue" and the Ongoing Saga of Prisoner Disenfranchisement' (2011) 62 NILQ 57.

[16] The life of Parliament was extraordinarily extended during both World Wars.

[17] Parliament Act 1911, s. 7 (amending the Septennial Act 1715).

[18] R. Blackburn, 'The prerogative power of dissolution of Parliament: law, practice and reform' [2009] PL 766, 766.

[19] *The Coalition: Our Programme for Government* (May 2010), p. 26.

[20] Fixed-Term Parliaments Act 2011, s. 2(1).

[21] Ibid., s. 1(3).

House.[22] The second mechanism which might prompt an early election is a vote of no confidence. Under the provisions of the Act, a motion of no confidence in the government marks the beginning of a two-week period during which the government might regain the confidence of the House or – the more likely outcome – during which a new government might be formed. At the end of the two-week period, should the House be unable to endorse a motion of confidence in the government, a general election will be called.

It is clear, however, that the implementation of the Fixed-Term Parliaments Act has not extinguished Prime Ministerial *influence* over the timing of a general election.[23] As much became clear following the announcement by Theresa May in April 2017 that she would seek to hold a general election – nominally justified on the ground that it would provide 'stability and strong leadership'[24] in the delivery of Brexit negotiations – in advance of that expected to be held in 2020. The consent of the House of Commons to hold an early election was sought under s. 2(1) of the Fixed-Term Parliaments Act, and duly obtained by a majority – well in excess of the required two-thirds of MPs – of 509.[25] A general election took place on 8 June 2017, returning the Conservatives as the largest party in a hung Parliament.[26]

Key debates

The summoning, prorogation and dissolution of Parliament

Summoning. Following the proclamation that a new Parliament is to be summoned, writs are issued to the returning officer of each parliamentary constituency (see generally: Representation of the People Act 1983, sch. 1) requiring a parliamentary election to be held. Members of the House of Commons are elected by popular vote at a general election. While members of the House of Lords are not currently elected to sit in Parliament, they receive a new writ of summons at the beginning of each new Parliament.

Prorogation. Parliament is prorogued at the end of each parliamentary session. Prorogation marks a suspension of parliamentary business – rather than the end of the life of a Parliament – and as a result some parliamentary business can be carried over into the next session.

Dissolution. The dissolution of Parliament marks the end of a parliament's life. Prior to the implementation of the Fixed-Term Parliaments Act 2011, dissolution was achieved by Royal Proclamation – made under the prerogative – following a request made by the Prime Minister. Following the enactment of the Fixed-Term Parliaments Act 2011, the dissolution of Parliament is a matter of statute (s. 3). Upon being dissolved, the House of Commons effectively has no membership, with members being required to vacate their offices prior to the general election. Government ministers, however, will remain in post until the outcome of the general election is determined.

---

[22] The specific wording of the resolution can be found in Fixed-Term Parliaments Act 2011, s. 2(2).

[23] The successful call for a 2017 general election prompted some critics to question the value of retaining the Fixed-Term Parliaments Act 2011 – for analysis see: R. Hazell, 'Is the Fixed-Term Parliaments Act a dead letter?' UK Const. L. Blog (26 April 2017).

[24] http://www.bbc.co.uk/news/uk-politics-39630009.

[25] HC Debs, vol. 624, cols 681–712 (19 April 2017).

[26] Though in the run-up to the 2017 general election the Conservative Party had promised to repeal the Fixed-Term Parliaments Act 2011, this commitment did not feature amongst the legislation promised in the 2017 Queen's Speech.

The independent Electoral Commission fulfils a role in the oversight and regulation of elections in the United Kingdom. The Electoral Commission holds the power to, *inter alia,* register political parties (and donations to those parties), to regulate spending on election campaigns, to report on the conduct of elections and to review electoral law and constituency boundaries.[27]

While the Electoral Commission may monitor, and report on, the conduct of elections, assessing the legality of an election is a task for the courts.[28] Section 123 of the Representation of the People Act 1983 makes provision for the constitution of an 'election court' having jurisdiction to examine the legality of parliamentary and local elections. In *Watkins* v *Woolas,*[29] for instance, a parliamentary election was held to have been unlawful and declared to be a nullity. The illegality resulted from the false allegations made during the course of the election campaign against the Liberal Democrat candidate Mr Watkins by the previous MP, and Labour candidate, Phil Woolas. The court ordered the election to be re-held, and Mr Woolas was precluded from standing for re-election for three years.[30]

The importance of a majority in the House of Commons

A party wishing to form a government enjoying a majority of seats in the House of Commons would be required to gain at least 326 (or 50 per cent+) of those 650 seats. The Labour Governments elected in 1997, 2001 and 2005 each enjoyed an overall majority in the House of Commons. However, following the 2010 general election, no single party obtained an overall majority. The Conservatives were the largest single political party in the House of Commons but, standing alone, could count only 47 per cent of the membership of the Commons among their ranks. An overall majority was achieved through the formulation of a coalition between the Conservatives and Liberal Democrats whose members (following the 2010 general election) together numbered 362 (56 per cent), taking them beyond the 326 required for a majority. And while the general election of 2015 returned a small Conservative majority administration, the election of 2017 – at which the Prime Minister sought to strengthen the position of the Conservatives in the run-up to the Brexit negotiations – saw the Conservatives win only 317 seats.

The importance of the party system

The vast majority of members of the House of Commons are members of either the Conservative or Labour Parties. As Table 9.1 illustrates, at June 2017, MPs from those two parties accounted for 89 per cent of the membership of the House. Of the smaller parties, Scottish National Party held the largest number of seats (35), with the Liberal Democrats, Plaid Cymru and the Northern Irish MPs from Sinn Fein and the Democratic Unionist Party making up the vast majority of the remainder. Independent

---

[27] Political Parties, Elections and Referendums Act 2000, part I.

[28] Representation of the People Act 1983, part III.

[29] *Watkins* v *Woolas* [2010] EWHC 2702 (QB). On which, see F. Hoar, 'Public or personal character in election campaigns: a review of the implications of the judgment in *Watkins* v *Woolas*' (2011) 74 MLR 607.

[30] A subsequent application for judicial review of the Electoral Court's decision by Mr Woolas was unsuccessful: *R (Woolas) v Parliamentary Electoral Court* [2010] EWHC 3169 (Admin); [2011] 2 WLR 1362.

Table 9.1 Composition of the House of Commons (following the general election on 8 June 2017)

Party	Number of MPs	Percentage of overall membership
Conservative	317	49%
Labour	262	40%
Scottish National Party	35	5%
Liberal Democrat	12	2%
Democratic Unionist	10	2%
Sinn Fein	7	1%
Plaid Cymru	4	<1
Green	1	<1
Independent	1	<1
Speaker	1	<1
Total	650	100%

candidates are very much a rarity – '[t]o be non-party most of the time in British politics is to be non-influential'[31] – but by no means completely out of the ordinary.[32]

The overwhelming majority of members of the House of Commons are associated with one political party or another. This association comes with benefits – political parties have the means to finance election campaigns for instance – but the inevitable consequence is that the House of Commons is a deeply 'tribal' place.[33] It is, of course, in the interests of the parties to see their policies carried into effect; the whip system supports this objective by seeking to ensure that MPs toe the party line (the most emphatic direction – the 'three line whip' – is regarded as an 'unbreakable commitment'[34]). So integral are the whips to the business of Parliament that free votes – votes in which the whips do not play a role – are somewhat unusual. One former member has lamented that:

> [t]he fact that the results of parliamentary votes are routinely known in advance, under the iron discipline of the party whips, gives a sterile quality to much debate. In fact, 'debate' is really a misnomer for what are usually prepared speeches served up to a largely empty chamber in which neither minds nor votes are likely to be changed by what is said.[35]

---

[31] A. King, 'Modes of Executive–Legislative Relations: Great Britain, France and West Germany' (1976) 1 *Legislative Studies Quarterly* 11, 20.

[32] Following one of the most memorable elections in recent years, the journalist Martin Bell served as MP for Tatton between 1997 and 2001, having stood in opposition to Neil Hamilton – MP for Tatton since 1983 – as a result of the latter's involvement in the cash-for-questions affair (on which see pp. 417–18). The Labour Party and Liberal Democrat candidates both withdrew from the election in order to allow Bell a clear run at deposing Hamilton. Bell won with a majority of more than 11,000 votes.

[33] T. Wright, *British Politics: A Very Short Introduction* (Oxford University Press, 2003) p. 105.

[34] R. Rogers and R. Walters, *How Parliament Works* (7th edn) (Routledge, 2015) p. 83.

[35] T. Wright, *British Politics: A Very Short Introduction* (Oxford University Press, 2003) pp. 86–7.

While a touch of hyperbole may be in evidence here, the basic point stands: the influence exerted by party system is one of the determining factors in understanding how MPs operate, and therefore how Parliament works.[36]

Government and opposition

Party lines are also inevitably drawn in the relationships between the component parts of the House of Commons: the government and the opposition. Relations between the government and the opposition are indeed reflected throughout politics in the United Kingdom:

> . . . the set-piece debates in Parliament, the confrontations on television, the competitions for votes in the constituencies . . . the House of Commons is merely one of the arenas, not necessarily the most important, in which the party battle is fought out.[37]

The basic geographical division between the opposing benches in the House of Commons is perhaps the most immediate indicator of the importance of government and opposition in Parliament; the seats on either side of the debating chamber provide the forum for much of the adversarial business of the House of Commons. The fact that Conservative and Labour Parties often find themselves in either sole government or opposition re-enforces the fact that party politics – and therefore parliamentary activity – in the UK is often confrontational and polarised, rather than deliberative and participatory.

It should be noted however that while government/opposition relations are most commonly at the fore of the government's relationship with Parliament, a series of equally complex relationships can also impact on the fortunes of a government.[38] The first of these is the government's relationship with its own backbenches: MPs who are routinely relied on for support in Parliament, and whose support may be crucial to the government's ability to sustain the confidence of the House of Commons. The second is the relationship of the government with the combined forces of Parliament's backbench MPs. This latter relationship is perhaps most obviously played out in the activities of the Select Committees, in which backbench MPs from all parties are united and charged with the task of scrutinising government departments.[39]

The role and functions of the House of Commons

Key issues

- The composition of the House of Commons will determine which political party (or parties) will be in a position to form a government. The ability of that government to realise its legislative and policy objectives will be dependent on obtaining the support of the House of Commons; a government may only remain in office for so long as it enjoys the confidence of the House of Commons.

→

---

[36] J. A. G. Griffith and M. Ryle, *Parliament: Functions, Practice and Procedures* (Sweet and Maxwell, 1989) p. 17. For discussion see: R. Rogers and R. Walters, *How Parliament Works* (7th edn) (Routledge, 2015) pp. 80–93.
[37] A. King, 'Modes of Executive–Legislative Relations: Great Britain, France and West Germany' (1976) 1 *Legislative Studies Quarterly* 11, 17.
[38] A. King, 'Modes of Executive–Legislative Relations: Great Britain, France and West Germany' (1976) 1 *Legislative Studies Quarterly* 11, especially at 15–20.
[39] On which, see Chapter 15, pp. 456–61.

- The functions of the House of Commons include holding the government to account, considering and endorsing the government's legislative agenda, and the allocation of finances.

- The responsibilities of individual members extend to addressing the complaints, and representing the interests, of their constituents.

The lack of a written constitutional document prescribing the specific roles and functions of the various components of the United Kingdom Government has doubtless contributed to the perception that the constitutional role of the House of Commons, compared to that of the executive role of the government or the legislative role of Parliament itself, is rather more difficult to describe. Some commentators have concluded that the role of the House of Commons, compared with either that of government or of Parliament as a whole, is unimportant. Anthony King, for instance, has written that while the range of constitutional reforms since Labour came to power in 1997 has revitalised the constitution, one 'feature of the traditional British constitution that remains unperturbed is the relatively insignificant role assigned to the House of Commons.'[40] Of course, it is *Parliament* that is legally supreme and it is the powers and political activities of the *government* that will generate headlines.[41] But the role of the House of Commons is central – if perhaps subsidiary – to both; the endorsement of the House of Commons is a vital aspect of the legislative process and the continued confidence of the House of Commons is necessary for government to govern. King's suggestion therefore that the role of the House of Commons is not constitutionally important, is something of an exaggeration.

The 'efficient secret' of the constitution – Walter Bagehot argued – is 'nearly complete fusion of the executive and legislative powers' in Parliament.[42] From an institutional perspective, this description holds true: the parliamentary executive – or government – remains a part of the United Kingdom legislature. This 'fusion' of executive and legislature is nowhere more obvious than in the House of Commons. But an overly close focus on the distinction between executive and legislature clouds examination of the particular constitutional tasks undertaken by the House of Commons itself. How then, are we to distinguish the specific functions of the House of Commons from those of the executive and of Parliament? Bagehot, in his famous work, *The English Constitution,* went on to categorise the five core functions of the House of Commons as follows:

- the 'elective' function: it is the membership of the House of Commons that determines the formation of a government;

- the 'expressive' function: the ability of its members to express the views of the electorate;

- the 'teaching' function: the power of the Commons to exercise an educative role;

- the 'informing' function: to inform the nation of the complaints and grievances of particular individuals and groups; and

- the 'legislative' function: the ability to assent to and – acting in accord with the House of Lords – to pass statutes.[43]

---

[40] Anthony King, *Does the United Kingdom Still Have a Constitution?* (Sweet and Maxwell, 2001) p. 76.
[41] Chapter 5.
[42] W. Bagehot, *The English Constitution* (Oxford World's Classics, 2001) p. 11.
[43] Ibid., pp. 100–2.

The House of Commons continues to exercise each of these functions, but – as Bagehot's famous work was first published in 1867 – some refinement is necessary in order to place the role and functions of the Commons in a firm, and contemporary, constitutional perspective. The widening of the franchise has, for instance, meant that it is in practice the electorate – and not the members of the Commons themselves – who determine which political party (or parties) will in practice find themselves in a position to form a government. While it might be suggested that the 'elective' role of the Commons extends to sustaining the government of the day in office – through the continued confidence of the House – the composition of the House of Commons is determined by popular vote at a general election. Dawn Oliver, therefore, has summarised the role and functions of the contemporary House of Commons as follows:

- to provide the government of the day (all ministers must by convention be members of one or other of the two Houses, and the Prime Minister and the Chancellor of the Exchequer must be members of the Commons);
- to sustain the government in power by passing its legislation;
- to give – or refuse – consent to taxation;
- to authorise and control public expenditure;
- to secure redress of constituents' grievances; and
- generally, to hold the executive to account for its policies and the conduct of government.[44]

The role of individual MPs – leaving to one side career aspirations, party responsibilities and so on – is to contribute to fulfilling the functions of the House as a whole. The House of Commons Modernisation Committee listed the most 'commonly recognised tasks' of MPs as follows:

- supporting their party in votes in Parliament (furnishing and maintaining the government and opposition);
- representing and furthering the interests of their constituency;
- representing individual constituents and taking up their problems and grievances;
- scrutinising and holding the government to account and monitoring, stimulating and challenging the executive;
- initiating, reviewing and amending legislation; and
- contributing to the development of policy whether in the chamber, committees or party structures and promoting public understanding of party politics.[45]

The formation and sustenance of a government

As we have already seen, the appointment of ministers, including the Prime Minister, is a prerogative power exercised personally by the monarch.[46] Convention dictates how this

---

[44] D. Oliver, 'Reforming the United Kingdom Parliament' in J. Jowell and D. Oliver (eds), *The Changing Constitution* (7th edn) (OUP, 2011) p. 171.

[45] House of Commons Modernisation Committee, *Revitalising the Chamber: the Role of the Backbencher* (2007), HC 337, [10]. Cf. T. Wright, 'What are MPs for?' (2010) 81 *Political Quarterly* 298.

[46] On which see p. 35.

power is to be exercised, with the composition of the House of Commons – determined by popular election – playing an important regulatory role. Following a general election, if one party in the House of Commons enjoys an overall majority the monarch will, by convention, invite the leader of that party to form a government. Experience demonstrates that, during the post-war period, the formation of a single-party majority government will be the most common result of a general election. In recent years, the governments formed by Margaret Thatcher (1979, 1983, 1987), John Major (1992), Tony Blair (1997, 2001, 2005) and David Cameron (2015) have all been underpinned by a majority of seats in the House of Commons.

In practice then, experience tells us that the leader of the largest single party in the House of Commons is often also the leader of a party with a majority in the Commons, but enjoying the support of a Commons majority is not a pre-requisite to becoming Prime Minister. The Prime Minister during the 2010–15 Parliament, David Cameron MP, did not enjoy the support of a majority of members of the House of Commons. His *party* – the Conservative Party – held only 47 per cent of the available seats. His *government,* however, a coalition between the Conservative Party and the Liberal Democrats, did enjoy a majority, cumulatively holding 56 per cent of the available seats. Similarly, following loss of the Conservatives' Commons majority at the 2017 general election, Theresa May's Party accounted for 49 per cent of MPs.

So while the position relating to a leader who commands a clear Commons majority is relatively clear, beyond this, however, exists something of a grey area.[47] Three possibilities exist: the first is the formation of a minority administration, the second requires a co-operative agreement between parties, the third a formal agreement to enter into a Coalition Government.

1. Minority government

Prior to 2010, the last time a United Kingdom general election resulted in a hung Parliament was February 1974. Following the February 1974 general election, the Labour Party held 301 seats, the Conservatives 296 seats and the Liberals 14. The incumbent Prime Minister, Edward Heath, entered into negotiations with the Liberals to form a coalition. The negotiations were unsuccessful. The leader of the Labour Party – the largest single party in the Commons – Harold Wilson was subsequently invited to form a government. The period of minority government was, however, short-lived. A further general election was held in October 1974, and the Wilson Government was re-elected with a majority of three seats in the House of Commons.

While the leader of a minority party might be invited to form a government by the monarch, the question of whether such an administration is sustainable falls to be answered in the House of Commons; ultimately a government must command its confidence. If that confidence is no longer enjoyed – demonstrated by a vote of no confidence as per the Fixed-Term Parliaments Act 2011 – then the government must stand down and a general election is triggered.

---

[47] For discussion, see R. Blackburn, 'The 2010 General Election Outcome and the Formation of the Conservative–Liberal Democrat Coalition Government' [2011] PL 30, 33–38. See also *The Cabinet Manual: a Guide to Laws, Conventions and Rules of the Operation of Government* (1ˢᵗ edn) (October 2011), ch. 2.

2. Co-operation

Short of entering into a full coalition agreement, an agreement between political parties to co-operate on certain issues might serve to underpin a government which lacks an overall majority. The Labour Callaghan Government for instance, was sustained in office in 1977 by entering into negotiations with David Steel's Liberal Party. In exchange for advancing a number of Liberal policies, the Liberals agreed to vote to support the Labour Government in any subsequent confidence motion in the Commons.

A confidence and supply agreement between the Conservative Party and the Democratic Unionist Party (DUP) was also one outcome of the 2017 general election. The agreement saw the DUP agree to support the minority government (for 'the length of the Parliament') in relation to motions of confidence, the Queen's speech and budgetary measures, and also in relation to a number of shared areas of policy priority:

> In line with the parties' shared priorities for negotiating a successful exit from the European Union and protecting the country in the light of recent terrorist attacks, the DUP also agrees to support the government on legislation pertaining to the United Kingdom's exit from the European Union; and legislation pertaining to national security.[48]

On the terms of the agreement, co-operation in other fields was to be agreed on an ad hoc basis. In return for the support of their 10 MPs – effectively ensuring that May's government could operate on the basis of a bare Commons majority – the DUP negotiated a significant commitment to additional investment in Northern Ireland (the 'supply' element of the agreement).

More informal co-operation between parties might also serve to sustain a government in office: John Major's Conservative administration, for example, was able to survive between 1996 and 1997 – following the evaporation of its majority as a result of by-election defeats and defections to other parties – through the support of Ulster Unionist MPs.

3. Coalition

The Conservative–Liberal Democrat Coalition Government formed in May 2010 was the first of its kind for more than a generation; the preceding coalition had governed during the Second World War under Winston Churchill. Coalition governments have therefore been an infrequent feature of the United Kingdom's recent constitutional landscape; as Bogdanor has noted: '[e]very previous hung parliament in the twentieth century – in 1910, 1923, 1929 and 1974 – . . . led to a minority government rather than a majority coalition'.[49] In part, this may be attributed to the adversarial nature of party politics in the United Kingdom and to the associated reluctance of competing politicians to co-operate with each other.[50] In part, it might be put down to the ability of the first-past-the-post electoral system to generate strong governments and relative infrequency of hung parliaments. Either way, the impression is given – as Disraeli is famously reported to have observed – that 'England does not love coalitions.'[51] Since 2010, however, that landscape has changed; the

---

[48] Available at: https://www.gov.uk/government/publications/conservative-and-dup-agreement-and-uk-government-financial-support-for-northern-ireland/agreement-between-the-conservative-and-unionist-party-and-the-democratic-unionist-party-on-support-for-the-government-in-parliament.

[49] V. Bogdanor, *The Coalition and the Constitution* (Hart Publishing, 2011) p. 10.

[50] A. King, *Does the United Kingdom Still Have a Constitution?* (Sweet and Maxwell, 2001) pp. 36–7.

[51] On which, see I. McLean, '"England Does Not Love Coalitions": the Most Misused Political Quotation in the Book' (2012) 47 *Government and Opposition* 3.

politics of coalition formulation[52] and the constitutional implications of coalition government[53] have become topics of intense – and often polarised – debate.

Legislation

The initiation of legislative proposals is an operation carried out by the government – or individual MPs – rather than by Parliament itself. The Queen's speech at the opening of the parliamentary year provides the occasion on which the government's legislative agenda for the coming session will be announced. While the label 'legislature' implies something of an active role, Parliament's function in this regard therefore is to assent to legislation, rather than to initiate it.[54]

Insight

Types of Bill

Public Bills. These are Bills of general application: in other words, they are Bills which, if passed into legislation, would apply to the population at large. Bills changing the criminal law, for example, would be classified as Public Bills.

Private Bills. These seek to affect specific bodies or individuals. A Bill which, for instance, gave statutory powers to a local authority or company would be a Private Bill.

Hybrid Bills. Hybrid Bills share characteristics of Public and Private Bills; they are applicable to the general public, but also would have a particular impact on specific individuals or groups.

Government Bills. Any of the above types of Bill, if introduced by a government minister, will be referred to as a Government Bill.

Private Members' Bills. These are Public Bills introduced by Members of Parliament who are not government ministers. As the parliamentary timetable affords a more generous provision to Government Bills, Private Members' Bills are less likely to become law.

Draft legislation can be initiated in either House of Parliament. By convention, most contentious legislative proposals – that is, Bills which pursue a party-political objective of the government – will be introduced into the House of Commons. Bills dealing with finance will also always be introduced in the Commons. Government Bills which are less contentious may be introduced in the House of Lords. However, regardless of the House in which the Bill is first introduced, each Bill must be approved at a series of 'readings' in both Houses prior to being approved for Royal Assent (Figure 9.1).[55]

---

[52] See R. Blackburn, 'The 2010 General Election Outcome and the Formation of the Conservative–Liberal Democrat Coalition Government' [2011] PL 30; M. Debus, 'Portfolio Allocation and Policy Compromises: How and Why the Conservatives and the Liberal Democrats Formed a Coalition Government' (2011) 82 *Political Quarterly* 293.

[53] See V. Bogdanor, *The Coalition and the Constitution* (Hart Publishing, 2011).

[54] P. Norton, *Parliament in British Politics* (2nd edn) (Palgrave Macmillan, 2013) ch. 5.

[55] For a forensic examination see: M. Zander, *The Law-Making Process* (7th edn) (Hart Publishing, 2015) chs 1 and 2.

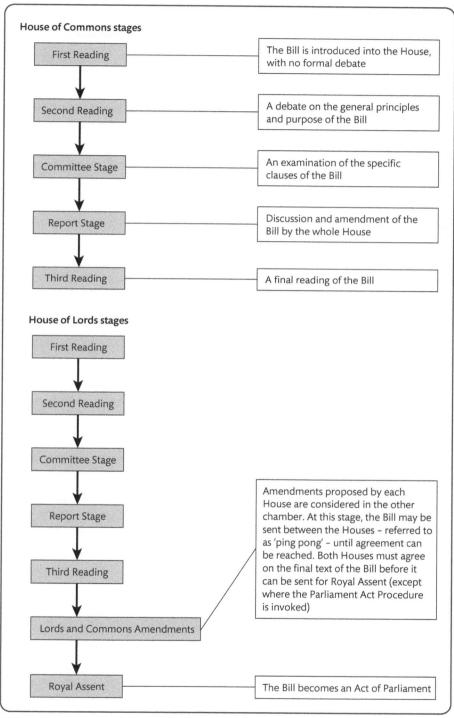

House of Commons stages

First Reading — The Bill is introduced into the House, with no formal debate

Second Reading — A debate on the general principles and purpose of the Bill

Committee Stage — An examination of the specific clauses of the Bill

Report Stage — Discussion and amendment of the Bill by the whole House

Third Reading — A final reading of the Bill

House of Lords stages

First Reading

Second Reading

Committee Stage

Report Stage

Third Reading

Lords and Commons Amendments — Amendments proposed by each House are considered in the other chamber. At this stage, the Bill may be sent between the Houses – referred to as 'ping pong' – until agreement can be reached. Both Houses must agree on the final text of the Bill before it can be sent for Royal Assent (except where the Parliament Act Procedure is invoked)

Royal Assent — The Bill becomes an Act of Parliament

Figure 9.1 The parliamentary progress of a public bill

Finance

The consent of Parliament is required for the levying of taxes; as outlined in Art. 4 of the Bill of Rights 1689:

> . . . levying money for or to the use of the Crown by pretence of prerogative, without grant of Parliament, for longer time, or in other manner than the same is or shall be granted, is illegal.

Parliamentary endorsement is therefore a pre-requisite of raising government finances, and authorising government expenditure. While this requirement is portrayed as parliamentary control of the purse, the ability of the House of Lords to influence matters of governmental revenue and expenditure is virtually non-existent as a result of the Parliament Acts,[56] while the authority of a government whose financial proposals did not enjoy the support of the Commons would be equally non-existent.[57]

Representation

The role of members of the House of Commons as representatives of their constituents is unique within Parliament; members of the House of Lords play no such role. There is a long-standing tradition of MPs acting on behalf of aggrieved constituents in order to obtain redress. For many, this is a pragmatic use of the influence of the House of Commons: 'MPs can demand, and get, responses from bureaucracies in ways that the individual citizen cannot, right up to ministers if necessary'.[58] MPs act on behalf of their constituents because, ultimately, constituents hold the power to re-elect them. The electoral link between MPs and their constituents represents a form of accountability,[59] albeit one which may only be formally exercised semi-frequently.

Insight

The Recall of MPs Act 2015

Accountability of MPs to their constituents is increased as a result of the Recall of MPs Act 2015. The 2015 Act was introduced into Parliament by the 2010–2015 Coalition Government and provided that – in the event of an MP being sentenced to serve a prison term or being suspended from the House of Commons for more than 21 sitting days – a recall petition would be issued. If, following an eight-week period, more than 10 per cent of registered voters in the relevant constituency had signed the recall petition, the seat would be declared vacant and a by-election would be held.

---

[56] Pages 141–3.
[57] For general discussion, see J. McEldowney, 'Public Expenditure and the Control of Public Finance' in J. Jowell, D. Oliver and C. O'Cinneide (eds), *The Changing Constitution* (8th edn) (Oxford University Press, 2015).
[58] T. Wright, 'What are MPs for?' (2010) 81 *Political Quarterly* 298, 304.
[59] HC Debs, vol. 493, col. 798, 10 June 2009 (Gordon Brown MP).

Key debates

The role of MPs – representatives of general or local interest?

The dilemma occasionally faced by the elected members of the House of Commons is whether to discharge their role by reference to their own judgement as to the interests of the state or by reference to the views of their constituents. Edmund Burke's famous *Speech to the Electors of Bristol* captured this distinction well:

> Parliament is not a *congress* of ambassadors from different and hostile interests; which interests each must maintain, as an agent and advocate, against other agents and advocates; but parliament is a *deliberative* assembly of *one* nation, with *one* interest, that of the whole; where, not local purposes, not local prejudices, ought to guide, but the general good, resulting from the general reason of the whole. You choose a member indeed; but when you have chosen him, he is not member of Bristol, but he is a Member of *Parliament*.

While Burke argued forcefully that the 'general good' should be the primary concern of an MP once elected, the aftermath of the Brexit referendum has highlighted that this is not necessarily a view that is widely shared, or – at the very least – that seeking the views of the electorate on a specific issue will be accompanied by an expectation that those views will be adhered to. It is well documented that a comfortable majority of serving MPs at the time of the June 2016 Brexit referendum were in favour of the United Kingdom's continued membership of the EU. Given that 52 per cent of the voting electorate indicated a preference to leave the EU, it was unsurprising to find that many sitting MPs had advocated a position with which a majority of their constituents disagreed. Writing later in 2016, Vernon Bogdanor commented that:

> The Commons is required, perhaps for the first time in its history, to follow a policy to which around three-quarters of its members are opposed. The sovereignty of Parliament is now to be constrained – not legally, of course, but for all practical purposes – not by Brussels but by the people.[60]

Scrutiny and accountability

The role of the House of Commons in scrutinising the operation of government is fundamental. The ability of elected representatives to hold government to account is one of the core ideas behind the notion of the political constitution. As Hartley and Griffith have succinctly put it:

> It is the job of the Government to govern: to make political and policy decisions; to put those decisions into practical effect. And it is the job of the remaining members of the Houses of Parliament to scrutinise those decisions and that administration.[61]

The scrutiny role of the House of Commons – and the mechanisms employed in the task of holding government to account – is the subject of more detailed coverage in Chapter 15. For present purposes, only a brief introduction is necessary. Ministers are both individually and collectively responsible to Parliament. It is a constitutional obligation of ministers to subject themselves to parliamentary scrutiny in order to be held to account for their decisions and policies. Collectively, the government must enjoy the confidence of

---

[60] V. Bogdanor, 'Europe and the Sovereignty of the People' (2016) *Political Quarterly* 348, 350.
[61] T. C. Hartley and J. A. G. Griffith, *Government and Law* (Wiedenfeld and Nicolson, 1975) p. 195.

Parliament in order to remain in office. The twin doctrines of individual ministerial responsibility[62] and of collective Cabinet responsibility[63] – the latter generally now referred to as collective responsibility – are central to the political processes of parliamentary accountability. In generating a culture in which ministers routinely provide full and accurate information to Parliament, however, these conventions provide only one side of the coin. The other side is Parliament's ability to extract information from government through questions to ministers, select committee enquiries and so on. The mechanisms of parliamentary scrutiny – the means by which MPs extract information from government – are examined in greater detail in Chapter 15.

Key issues

- The primacy of the House of Commons is a well-established feature of the relationship between the two Houses of Parliament.
- The House of Commons is dominant legally, as the Parliament Acts provide that certain legislative proposals might be put forward for Royal Assent notwithstanding the failure of the House of Lords to endorse them.
- The elected House of Commons is also democratically superior to the largely appointed House of Lords.

The pre-eminent House of Parliament

The House of Commons is the dominant House of Parliament. It is the more powerful house in legal terms; as a result of the Parliament Acts 1911 and 1949 the Commons enjoys the capacity to pass legislation that has been rejected by the House of Lords. The Commons is also politically dominant: as a result of the fact that its members are directly elected, the House of Commons can claim greater democratic legitimacy than the largely appointed House of Lords. As a result, as the academic and parliamentarian Lord Norton has observed, '[i]t is not uncommon for writers on British politics to use "Parliament" as a synonym for the House of Commons' before reminding us that '[t]he House of Lords may be a poor relation, but it is still part of the family'.[64] Our attentions will turn to the House of Lords in the following chapter. For present purposes, the legal and political pre-eminence of the House of Commons is amply illustrated in the provisions of the Parliament Acts 1911 and 1949 and in the Salisbury Convention.[65]

---

[62] pp. 436–49.

[63] pp. 273–6.

[64] P. Norton, *Parliament in British Politics* (2nd edn) (Palgrave Macmillan, 2013) p. 16.

[65] A full account of the conventions governing the relations between the House of Commons and House of Lords can be found in: Joint Committee on Conventions, *Conventions of the UK Parliament* (2005–2006), HL 265-I/HC 1212-I.

The Parliament Acts 1911 and 1949

The Parliament Acts and their effects have been considered in depth in an earlier chapter.[66] For present purposes, therefore, only a brief recap is necessary. The ability of the House of Lords to veto legislative proposals that have been approved by the House of Commons was effectively done away with by the passing of the Parliament Act 1911. First, the 1911 Act provided that the House of Lords should not be able to veto (or significantly delay) Bills certified by the Speaker of the House of Commons as Money Bills. The House of Lords, therefore, is powerless to oppose financial measures that have been endorsed by the House of Commons; as Jennings observed, 'in financial matters we have for all practical purposes a unicameral legislature'.[67]

The Parliament Act 1911 further provided that in respect of virtually all other Public Bills the Lords would only be able to delay – rather than veto – legislative proposals that had been initiated in, and approved by, the lower house. The maximum period of delay was initially set at two years, and was reduced further in 1949 – as a result of the Parliament Act 1949 – with the maximum period of delay effectively one year. The only exception to this rule – under s. 2(1) of the Acts – is in respect of a Bill which seeks to extend the life of a Parliament beyond five years (in other words, which purports to prolong the life of a government through the postponement of a general election). In respect of such a Bill, the House of Lords ultimate veto remains operative.

The Salisbury Convention[68]

The Salisbury Convention gives effect to the notion that the party holding a majority in the House of Commons does so as a result of the endorsement of its manifesto commitments at a general election. Its requirements preclude the House of Lords from wrecking or rejecting, at second or third reading, a Government Bill which purports to implement a manifesto commitment. While origins of the doctrine can be traced back to the 1880s, the modern-day understanding of the convention dates back to the 1945. At this point in time, the House of Lords was dominated by hereditary and Conservative peers. As a result, it lacked a democratic mandate, and a large number of its members were ideologically opposed to the policies of Clement Atlee's incoming Labour administration. The potential for conflict between the two Houses was significant. Realising that the obstruction of the government's agenda 'might invite a legislative assault on the position of the House of Lords',[69] a deal was brokered between Viscount Addison, then Leader of the House of Lords, and the Leader of the Opposition, Viscount Cranborne (the fifth Marquess of Salisbury) which would regulate the approach of the House of Lords to the Government's manifesto commitments and – in so doing – would minimise the potential for conflict between the two Houses.[70]

---

[66] Chapter 5, pp. 141–33.

[67] I. Jennings, *The Law and the Constitution* (4th edn) (University of London Press, 1956) p. 138.

[68] For a detailed account of the development of the convention, see G. Dymond and H. Deadman, *The Salisbury Doctrine* (House of Lords Library Note: LLN 2006/006), available at: www.parliament.uk/documents/lords-library/hllsalisburydoctrine.pdf.

[69] R. Brazier, 'Defending the Hereditaries: The Salisbury Convention' [1998] PL 371, 373.

[70] As a result, the convention is often referred to as the Salisbury–Addison convention.

Introducing the agreement, Viscount Cranborne outlined the opposition's view on the manifesto commitments of the incoming Labour Government in the following terms:

> Whatever our personal views, we should frankly recognise that these proposals were put before the country at the recent General Election and that the people of this country, with full knowledge of these proposals returned the Labour party to power. The Government may, therefore, I think, fairly claim that they have a mandate to introduce these proposals. I believe that it would be constitutionally wrong, when the country has so recently expressed its view, for this house to oppose proposals which have definitely been put before the electorate.[71]

The convention therefore acknowledges the inferior democratic legitimacy of the House of Lords, and seeks to give effect to the views of the electorate. It reflects the fact that it is 'not the duty of the House of Lords to make our system of government inoperable'[72] through routinely opposing change for which the government can claim an electoral mandate. While the circumstances which gave rise to the convention have since changed quite dramatically – the House of Lords is no longer dominated by either hereditary or Conservative peers[73] – there remains a parliamentary consensus that the Salisbury Convention should be retained in order to give effect to the superior democratic credentials of the House of Commons and its position as the pre-eminent chamber of Parliament.[74]

Thinking Point . . .

While the application of the Salisbury Convention is tolerably clear in respect of a government which can command a majority of MPs in the House of Commons, its operation in relation to coalition or minority administrations remains subject to debate (see Joint Committee on Conventions, *Conventions of the UK Parliament* (2005–06), HL 265/HC 1212, [101]–[113]).

The question of 'elective dictatorship'

Key issues

- While the House of Commons may be the dominant House of Parliament, it is the government that is generally dominant within the House of Commons.

- Not only does the British electoral system often produce single-party governments with significant parliamentary majorities, but the business of government is prioritised in almost every aspect of the parliamentary timetable.

- This phenomenon – whereby a nominally democratic process produces startling inequalities of power between government and opposition – has been labelled 'elective dictatorship'.

---

[71] HL Debs, vol. 137, col. 47 (16 August 1945).
[72] Lord Carrington, *Reflect on Things Past* (1988), pp. 77–8 (cited in R. Brazier, 'Defending the Hereditaries: the Salisbury Convention' [1998] PL 371, 373).
[73] Chapter 10, pp. 319–20.
[74] Joint Committee on Conventions, *Conventions of the UK Parliament* (2005–06), HL 265-I/HC 1212-I, paras 62–115 (esp. [99]).

> ## Thinking point . . .
>
> Government dominance of the activities of the House of Commons is nowhere more effectively summarised than in Standing Order 14(1) which reads, 'government business shall have precedence at every sitting'.

No one can realistically claim that the House of Lords is the constitutional co-equal of the House of Commons; the House of Commons is, both legally and politically, superior to the House of Lords. The UK's parliamentary system is therefore one of 'asymmetrical bicameralism'.[75] But behind the dominance of the Commons within Parliament, lies the fact that it is the government of the day that dominates the business of the Commons. In practice, therefore, the relative strength of the government within the House of Commons in turn gives rise to the, partially true, suggestion that the government will generally get its way no matter what decision is up for debate. The phrase coined by the former Conservative Lord Chancellor, Lord Hailsham, to describe the practical dominance of the House of Commons and its business by the government is 'elective dictatorship'.[76]

The constitutional consequences of 'elective dictatorship' are numerous. First, there are implications for our understanding of parliamentary sovereignty: a dominant government can dictate how Parliament's legislative power is exercised. As legal academic Rodney Brazier has surmised: '[l]egal sovereignty is in practice exercised by – or at least at the request of – ministers'.[77] Bagehot's suggestion that the Commons exercises a legislative function is therefore slightly misleading, for it is the *government* that is frequently in the position to dictate how this legislative function is exercised in practice.

As we will see in more detail in a later chapter,[78] the relative strength of a government *vis-à-vis* the House of Commons will have also have implications for the ability of the latter to hold the former to account. A government's policy initiatives may effectively be – within Parliament at least – insulated by the size of its majority. As the former MP and Chair of the Public Administration Committee, Tony Wright, has put it:

> Once the ceremonial veneer is stripped away, and the rhetorical fog of parliamentary sovereignty is allowed to clear, the fragility of accountability in a system in which the government controls the legislature . . . becomes abundantly clear.[79]

A vivid illustration is provided by the record of the first two administrations under the Labour Prime Minister, Tony Blair. Following the 1997 general election, the Labour Government was elected with a House of Commons majority of 179. In 2001, Labour was re-elected to government, this time with a majority of 167. As a result of these overwhelming majorities, it is perhaps unsurprising that between 1997 and 2005 the Labour Governments did not lose a single division (vote) in the House of Commons. This is not

---

[75] P. Norton, *Parliament in British Politics* (2nd edn) (Palgrave Macmillan, 2013) p. 17.

[76] Lord Hailsham, 'Elective Dictatorship', the Richard Dimbleby Lecture (1976). See also Lord Hailsham, *The Dilemma of Democracy: Diagnosis and Prescription* (Collins, 1978).

[77] R. Brazier, *Constitutional Reform: Reshaping the British Political System* (3rd edn) (Oxford University Press, 2008) p. 43.

[78] Chapter 15.

[79] Tony Wright, *British Politics: A Very Short Introduction* (Oxford University Press, 2003) p. 81.

to say that the government was not challenged in the House of Commons during this period. Far from it; debates over, *inter alia,* the imposition of higher education tuition fees in what became the Higher Education Act 2004, and opposition to military operations in Iraq from 2003 onwards ensured that during this period the government endured a series of uncomfortable episodes – made more uncomfortable by the involvement of the Labour backbenchers[80] – in the House of Commons. The sheer size of the government's majority, however, ensured that while serious opposition may have been provoked, this did not result in defeat for the government in *any* House of Commons vote between 1997 and 2005.

Thinking point . . .

By contrast with the Labour Governments led by Tony Blair, the position of the administration led – from June 2017 onwards – by Theresa May looks particularly precarious. Even with the support of the members of the DUP, the position in June 2017 was that the Prime Minister could only draw on the support of 327 MPs. As a result, a number of the more controversial measures promised in the Conservatives' 2017 election manifesto did not feature in the 2017 Queen's speech as – with only a paper-thin Commons majority – the Government could not be assured of their successful passage into law.

Towards a rebalancing of executive/legislative relations?

The hold often exercised by the government of the day over the House of Commons extends beyond the ability of the government to bring its objectives onto the statute book, reaching so far to influence the parliamentary timetable, procedures of the House, and so on. As the Wright Committee Report recorded: '[p]ut crudely, and subject to maintaining a majority, the government enjoys not merely precedence but exclusive domination of much of the House's agenda, and can stop others seeking similar control'.[81]

Despite the fact that it is not in the interest of government to empower those who are tasked with exposing their failings, weaknesses or wrongdoings, recent years have seen the coalescence of the idea that the adversarial politics of the effective two-party system has been damaging for parliamentary government, and for the image of Parliament.[82] The House of Commons Modernisation Committee had, between 1997 and 2010, prompted a number of changes to the working practices of the House of Commons. The *Governance of Britain* Green Paper, published by Gordon Brown's Labour Governments in 2007, spoke of the need to 'rebalance power between Parliament and the government, and give Parliament more ability to hold government to account'.[83] But it was not until the expenses scandal of 2009 – and the corresponding loss of public confidence in the House of Commons to regulate its own membership – that the movement towards wholesale reform of the House of Commons really gained momentum.

---

[80] On which, see P. Cowley and M. Stuart, 'Parliament: More Bleak House than Great Expectations' (2004) 57 *Parliamentary Affairs* 301.

[81] House of Commons Reform Committee, *Rebuilding the House* (2008–09) HC 1117, [126].

[82] M. Russell and A. Paun, *The House Rules?* (Constitution Unit, 2007), p. 7.

[83] *The Governance of Britain* (July 2007), Cm. 7170, p. 11.

The House of Commons Reform Committee (the Wright Committee[84]) – was appointed at the height of the expenses scandal,[85] when public confidence in Parliament and its MPs was reported to be at an all-time nadir. Its report – *Rebuilding the House* – was published in November 2009. The Committee's proposals sought to enhance the ability of the House of Commons to regulate and influence its own business, and in so doing, to loosen the grip of the government over a series of issues including the 'choice of topics for general debates, control over procedural reform, programming of government bills, [and] Private Members' Bills'.[86] The Wright Committee proposals included:

- elections to the chairs of departmental and other select committees;[87]
- elections within party groups to determine the membership of select committees;
- the creation of a backbench business committee;[88]
- increased public involvement in the parliamentary agenda (including allowing public input on the content of draft Bills, and e-Petitions).[89]

Implementation of the Wright proposals was interrupted by the 2010 dissolution of Parliament and general election.[90] Upon taking office in May 2010, The Conservative–Liberal Democrat Coalition Government subsequently pledged to implement the Wright reforms in full.[91] The Wright Committee reforms, and their implementation, are returned to in Chapter 15.

Key issues

- MPs are elected to the House of Commons from single-member constituencies using the first-past-the-post electoral system.
- First-past-the-post is a simple majority system and is ill-equipped to produce electoral results which reflect the proportion of votes cast across the constituencies which make up the United Kingdom.
- Following the adoption of proportional voting systems for elections to the devolved bodies, and significant criticisms of the inequalities caused by the first-past-the-post system, a national referendum was held in 2011 on the adoption of the *alternative-vote* mechanism. The referendum resulted in the resounding rejection of the proposed electoral reform.

Electoral systems and electoral reform

The House of Commons is a directly elected chamber; its members are returned from single-member constituencies on the basis of the first-past-the-post system. The

[84] Its chair was Dr Tony Wright MP, a political scientist and chair of the House of Commons Public Administration Committee between 1999 and 2010.
[85] The circumstances of which are outlined at p. 502.
[86] House of Commons Reform Committee, *Rebuilding the House* (2008–09) HC 1117, [19].
[87] Ibid., [80].
[88] Ibid., [180].
[89] Ibid., [276] and [254].
[90] For an interim progress report, see House of Commons Reform Committee, *Rebuilding the House: Implementation* (2009–10), HC 372.
[91] *The Coalition: Our Programme for Government* (May 2010), p. 27. See also Sir George Young MP, 'Parliamentary Reform: The Coalition Government's Agenda after Wright' Speech to the Hansard Society, 16 June 2010.

first-past-the-post system is, in fact, but one of a number of systems currently at use in elections in the United Kingdom.

Key debates
Electoral systems in the United Kingdom

1. First-past-the-post

First-past-the-post is the electoral system used in General Elections – elections to the House of Commons – and for local elections in England and Wales. First-past-the-post is a simple majority system of voting; the candidate securing the most votes in each constituency wins.

2. Additional member system (AMS)

The additional member system is currently employed in elections to the Scottish Parliament and National Assembly for Wales. Each voter is able to cast two votes; the first for a candidate, the second for a political party. Candidates are elected from single-member constituencies on a majority basis. The proportion of party votes is then used to determine the number of additional members from regional lists that will be elected.

3. Single transferrable vote (STV)

The single transferrable vote is used in elections to the Northern Ireland Assembly where multiple members are returned from each constituency. Under STV voters are able to rank candidates in order of preference. A quota is then generated following the formula:

Total votes cast ÷ number of candidates + 1

Each candidate achieving the required quota on the basis of first preference votes will be elected. First preference votes in excess of the quota will be allocated to second preference candidates. If seats remain to be filled then the candidates with fewest first preference votes are eliminated, and votes reallocated until the required number of members have met the quota.

4. Supplementary vote (SV)

Currently used for London – and other – mayoral elections, the supplementary vote is a variant of the alternative-vote mechanism (discussed at pp. 311-12 below). Electors are able to express a first and second preference by placing a 1 and 2 next to the respective candidates. Should one candidate receive >50 per cent first preference votes, he or she will be elected. If no one candidate receives >50 per cent, then the second preference votes are allocated to the two candidates receiving the most first preference votes. The candidate with the higher proportion of first and second preference votes wins.

5. Regional closed-list system

Used in England, Scotland and Wales for elections to the European Parliament (Northern Ireland uses STV). Members are elected from regions (rather than the smaller constituencies), with each region returning multiple members. Electors cast a vote for a party. The political parties themselves draw up lists of potential members, with their preferred candidates near the top of the list. The number of seats allocated to each party is calculated on the basis of a quota:

Total number votes received by party/independent candidate ÷ seats already won + 1

As the number of seats allocated to each party grows, the likelihood of further seats being gained decreases as the dividing factor increases.

First-past-the-post

Table 9.2 The disproportionate effect of the first-past-the-post system

Party	Election 1: proportion of votes cast	Election 2: proportion of votes cast
Labour	100%	35%
Conservative	0%	33%
Liberal Democrat	0%	32%
	Result: Labour wins	Result: Labour wins

The first-past-the-post system adopts a 'winner takes all' approach to elections. The person with the most votes wins. The losers get nothing. The outcome of fictitious elections held under the first-past-the-post system is demonstrated in Table 9.2.

In our hypothetical elections, the proportions of votes cast are radically different, yet the results are the same. In Election 1, with 100% of the vote secured, the Labour party would clearly, and justifiably, win the contested seat. In Election 2, the scenario is rather different; 65 per cent of electors would have voted for the Conservatives and Liberal Democrats, but Labour would still win the seat. The first-past-the-post system is therefore something of a blunt tool, which is unable to account for the overall proportion of votes cast.

Imagine that the results of Election 2 were replicated in other constituencies. The Labour party would win *all* of the available seats. The Conservatives and Liberal Democrats would win none. Labour would enjoy an overwhelming majority, despite 65 per cent of the electorate having voted for other parties. Presented in this way, such an outcome seems slightly unrealistic, yet the effect of the first-past-the-post system in practice can be seen to have generated similar results: in the 1997 general election the Labour Party won a landslide victory – gaining 419 seats (almost 64 per cent of the total) in the House of Commons – on the basis of only 42 per cent of the popular vote. In other words, 58% of the electorate voted against Labour, but Labour nonetheless gained an overwhelming Commons majority.

The system generally serves the main political parties well; in many ways the phenomenon of 'elective dictatorship' can be attributed to tendency of the first-past-the-post system to generate strong governments. First-past-the-post has the benefit of being easily understood, and frequently – although not always as the 2010 and 2017 general elections demonstrate – is 'decisive'.[92] The first-past-the-post system can often be seen to give rise to the very 'essence of the Westminster model'[93] of government, namely, single party majority governments. The experience between 1979 and 2010 is illustrative of this phenomenon; for 31 consecutive years the government of the United Kingdom was formed by either the Conservative (1979–97) or Labour (1997–2010) Parties. Only once during this thirty-year period – during 1996–97 under the Conservative Prime Minister, John Major – did the largest party lack an overall majority in the House of Commons (and this was not as a direct result of a general election).

---

[92] R. Brazier, *Constitutional Reform: Reshaping the British Political System* (3rd edn) (Oxford University Press, 2008) p. 46.
[93] V. Bogdanor, *The New British Constitution* (Hart Publishing, 2009) p. 121.

Smaller political parties are, however, generally not so well served by the first-past-the-post system. As Bogdanor has observed, 'the first-past-the-post electoral system allows an incipient multi-party system to be transmuted in the House of Commons into a two party system'.[94] Small parties are frequently the losers, with the Liberal Democrats historically the biggest losers of all. At the 2005 general election, for instance, the Liberal Democrats secured a 22 per cent share of the national vote, yet this translated into a mere 62 seats at Westminster (in other words, 9.5 per cent of the then total).[95] The Labour Party – with 35 per cent of the national vote – won a resounding 355 seats. A more recent illustration can be observed in the fortunes of UKIP at the 2015 general election where – despite receiving 12.6 per cent of votes cast nationally (almost 4 million votes) – only one UKIP MP was returned to Westminster. The reason for these discrepancies can be found in the first-past-the-post system. The first-past-the-post system serves generally to exaggerate the differential between the votes cast for the two main political parties and those cast in favour of other (smaller) parties. In so doing, it has tended to perpetuate the parliamentary duopoly of the Conservative and Labour Parties.

This is not to say, however, that hung parliaments – parliaments in which no single party can claim a majority – are an impossibility under first-past-the-post. The general elections of 2010 and 2017 both resulted in no single party enjoying an overall majority in the House of Commons. The general election of 2015 also demonstrated that significant transfers of power *away* from the two main political parties *can* take place under first-past-the-post. Such a transfer was most evident in the MPs returned in Scotland in May 2015 where a figure just short of 1.5 million votes – or 4.7 per cent of the national (UK-wide) share – resulted in 56 MPs for the SNP (all but three of the seats in Scotland). As a result of this, the SNP became the third largest party grouping in the House of Commons on the basis of significantly fewer votes than received by either the Liberal Democrats (who in 2015 returned 8 MPs following almost 2.5 million votes) or UKIP (one MP on the basis of almost 4 million votes).[96]

The pressure for electoral reform

As a result of its inability to reflect the complexity of voting patterns amongst the UK electorate, the first-past-the-post system has come under political pressure in recent years. Calls for the adoption of a more proportionate voting system have become increasingly common – and proportionate systems of voting have been adopted, and utilised, in elections to the European Parliament and elections to the devolved bodies in Northern Ireland, Scotland and Wales.[97] While electoral reform does not serve the interests of the main two political parties (the adoption of any system based on proportionality would reduce their numerical influence in the Commons), the first Blair Government's commitment to investigating the *prospect* of replacing the first-past-the-post system resulted in the – largely subsequently ignored – Jenkins Report.[98] In the aftermath of the 2009 expenses scandal,

---

[94] Ibid., p. 123.

[95] House of Commons Library Research Paper 05/33, *General Election 2005* (17 May 2005).

[96] This performance was not replicated in the 2017 general election, with the SNP returning 35 MPs.

[97] See Chapters 12 and 13.

[98] *The Report of the Independent Commission on the Voting System* (The Jenkins Commission), vols 1 and 2 (1998), Cm. 4090-I and Cm. 4090 II. The Commission recommended (Ch. 9) the adoption of a system described as 'AV top-up' under which the majority of members (80–85 per cent) would be elected by AV from single-member constituencies, with the remainder 'elected on a corrective top-up basis which would significantly reduce the disproportionality and . . . geographical divisiveness' associated with first-past-the-post (ch. 9.1).

Gordon Brown's Labour Government introduced clauses into the Constitutional Reform and Governance Bill 2009 which would have paved the way for a referendum on the adoption of the alternative vote system; those clauses were, however, removed from the Bill in order to secure its passage before the 2010 general election. The Liberal Democrats meanwhile, unsurprisingly, have long advocated the adoption of a proportional electoral system. In the run-up to the 2010 general election, only the Conservatives remained firmly committed to the retention of first-past-the-post, arguing that it provided a clear opportunity for the electorate to 'kick out a government that they are fed up with'.[99]

The Conservative–Liberal Democrat Coalition Government – in large part due to effective negotiations by the Liberal Democrats – promised upon taking office in May 2010 to hold a national referendum on the introduction of a new electoral system.[100] While the 2010 Liberal Democrat election manifesto indicated a preference for the single transferrable vote (STV) system,[101] the politics of coalition formation saw this preference amended in favour of a national referendum on the adoption of the alternative vote (AV) system for elections to the House of Commons.[102]

Key debates

What is the alternative vote (AV) system?

Under AV, voters are required to rank the available candidates (1, 2, 3 and so on) in order of preference. Voters may rank as many, or as few, candidates as they wish (it is in this respect that AV differs from SV; in the latter, voters may only express a maximum of two preferences).

In the first round of counting, all first preference votes are counted. If one candidate receives over 50 per cent of first preference votes then that candidate is elected. As a result, the 'yes' campaign argued that AV was preferential to first-past-the-post as it would ensure that each elected member would enjoy the support of >50 per cent of the electors in their constituency.

If no candidate has secured more than 50 per cent of first preference votes, a second round of counting takes place. The least popular candidate on the basis of first preference votes is eliminated, and the remaining candidates' second preference votes are considered. If, on the basis of first and second preference votes, one candidate has secured more votes than the combined total of the remaining candidates, that candidate is elected. If no one candidate emerges as winner after a second round of counting, the next least popular candidate is eliminated and the process repeated until one candidate secures a higher quantity of votes than the cumulative total of the remaining candidates.

AV is currently used as a mechanism to elect the chairs of a number of House of Commons select committees, the Lord Speaker of the House of Lords and those hereditary peers who are eligible to stand for election to the House of Lords (see pp. 319–20).

---

[99] Conservative Party, *Invitation to Join the Government of Britain* (2010) p. 67. The Labour Party promised a referendum on the adoption of AV (Labour Party, *A Future Fair for All* (2010) Ch. 9.2), while the Liberal Democrats preferred adoption of STV (*Liberal Democrat Manifesto* 2010) pp. 87–8).

[100] HM Government, *The Coalition: Our Programme for Government* (May 2010) p. 27.

[101] *Liberal Democrat Manifesto* 2010 pp. 87–8.

[102] *The Coalition: Our Programme for Government* (May 2010) p. 27. For a pre-2011 referendum analysis, see M. Threlfall, 'The Purpose of Electoral Reform for Westminster' (2010) 81 *Political Quarterly* 522.

Table 9.3 Results of the 2011 AV referendum

	Number of votes cast	Proportion of vote
'Yes'	6,152,607	32.1%
'No'	13,013,123	67.9%
	19,165,730	100%

The AV referendum – at that point in time the only national referendum held in the United Kingdom since 1975[103] – was held on 5 May 2011.[104] The question posed was: '[a]t present, the UK uses the "first-past-the-post" system to elect MPs to the House of Commons. Should the "alternative vote" system be used instead?'[105] The 2011 referendum resulted in the resounding rejection of the adoption of the AV system.

In the AV referendum, 19.1 million votes were cast, a relatively low turnout of some 42 per cent of the electorate. The result, however, was emphatic in its rejection of the adoption of AV and endorsement of the first-past-the-post system, with almost 68 per cent of the electorate voting in favour of its retention. The current prospects for electoral reform at Westminster, therefore, appear bleak. In the words of Rodney Brazier, 'the vote to keep the status quo was overwhelming, and the possibility of voting reform was thereby lost for decades'.[106]

The review of Westminster constituency boundaries

While the prospects for reform of the electoral *system* for general elections in the United Kingdom appears to be slim, the electoral *map* has undergone incremental change in recent years. In order to address the transfer of power from Westminster to Holyrood, one of the consequences of devolution for Westminster was the reduction in the number of Scottish MPs from 72 to 59.[107] In fact, the distribution of parliamentary constituencies is kept under periodic review by four permanent Boundary Commissions for England, Scotland, Wales and Northern Ireland. The Commissions are independent of government, established by statute[108] and currently charged with reviewing the boundaries of parliamentary constituencies at five-yearly intervals.[109] Reviews are held in order to ensure that – *inter alia* – each

---

[103] The 1975 referendum – on whether the UK should remain a part of the European Community – was called by Harold Wilson's Labour administration, and was the first ever national referendum to be held in the UK; 67 per cent voted in favour of the UK's continued membership, on a turnout of 65 per cent of the electorate. See generally: House of Lords Select Committee on the Constitution, *Referendums in the United Kingdom* (2009–10), HL 99.

[104] Parliamentary Voting System and Constituencies Act 2011, s. 1(3).

[105] Ibid., ss. 1(7), 1(8).

[106] R. Brazier, 'A Small Piece of Constitutional History' (2012) 128 LQR 315, 316.

[107] Scotland Act 1998, s. 86.

[108] Parliamentary Constituencies Act 1986, s. 2.

[109] Parliamentary Voting System and Constituencies Act 2011, s. 10. The previous regime had required reviews every 8–10 years (Boundary Commissions Act 1992, s. 2).

Table 9.4 Boundary review proposals to reduce number of Westminster MPs 2013

Territory	Proposed total of MPs	Reduction
England	502	−31
Scotland	52	−7
Wales	30	−10
Northern Ireland	16	−2

constituency[110] does not exceed a specified geographical area and consists of an approximately similar numbers of electors (effectively between 71,000 and 78,500).[111]

As well as making provision for the 2011 referendum on the adoption of the AV mechanism, the Parliamentary Voting System and Constituencies Act 2011 provided that the overall number of constituencies be reduced from 650 to 600.[112] The four Boundary Commissions, in 2013, proposed reductions in order to reduce the overall number of MPs in line with the 2011 Act (Table 9.4).

The implementation of the 2013 review was however postponed[113] and the recommendations and criteria laid down by the 2011 Act subject to parliamentary criticism on the ground that – *inter alia* – the requirements of relative uniformity in the size of constituencies imposed by the 2011 Act were overly restrictive.[114] Notwithstanding these criticisms, the Boundary Commission for England published proposals for the reconfiguration of the electoral map in England, reflecting the proposed reduction to 600 MPs, in October 2017. The final recommendations of the Commissions are due to be submitted to Parliament in September 2018, allowing an extended period – prior to an anticipated 2022 general election – for proposed changes to be confirmed.[115] In the absence of legislation amending the 2011 Act, the 2018 review will proceed on the basis that the size of the House of Commons be reduced to 600 MPs.

Conclusion

While the reform of the Westminster electoral system appears unlikely, the effects of the debates prompted by the 2009 expenses scandal continue to resound and are likely to impact on further reforms to the House of Commons. We return to the substance of those reforms – and their effects on the ability of the House of Commons to hold the government

---

[110] Excepting the two constituencies on the Isle of Wight, Orkney and Shetland, and Na h-Eileanan an lar (formerly Western Isles) (Parliamentary Voting System and Constituencies Act 2011, s. 11).

[111] Parliamentary Voting System and Constituencies Act 2011, s. 11.

[112] Ibid.

[113] Electoral Registration and Administration Act 2013, s. 6.

[114] House of Commons Political and Constitutional Reform Committee, *What Next on the Redrawing of Parliamentary Constituency Boundaries?* (HC600), March 2015, esp. [65]. See also: House of Lords Select Committee on the Constitution, *Parliamentary Voting Systems and Constituencies Bill* (HL58), November 2010.

[115] http://boundarycommissionforengland.independent.gov.uk/statement-on-the-general-election/.

to account – in a later chapter. While this chapter has sought to sketch some important aspects of the relationship between the executive and Parliament through an examination of the functions and composition of the House of Commons, a full appreciation can only be achieved through further consideration of those mechanisms which enable Parliament to exercise control over government and of the second chamber of Parliament, the House of Lords.

Practice questions

1. 'The idea that the United Kingdom has a functioning constitution is conclusively undermined by the fact that the unlimited legal power of Parliament can effectively be controlled by the Government of the day.'

   Discuss.

2. Given that reform of the electoral system for Westminster elections appears to be unlikely, how else can the difficulties associated with 'elective dictatorship' be addressed?

3. 'The premise that Parliaments should exist for fixed terms undermines the flexibility which has allowed the unwritten constitution to operate successfully for so long.'

   Discuss.

Further reading

The definitive work on the composition, workings and operation of Parliament is *Erskine May's Treatise on the Law, Privileges, Proceedings and Usage of Parliament* (24th edn) (LexisNexis, 2011). *Erskine May* is so well established and heavily relied upon that some commentators contend that it is a part of the fabric of the constitution itself.[116] Philip Norton's *Parliament in British Politics* (2nd edn) (Palgrave Macmillan, 2013) provides an authoritative and accessible alternative, replete with a parliamentarian's insights.

P. Seaward and P. Silk, 'The House of Commons' in V. Bogdanor (ed.), *The British Constitution in the Twentieth Century* (Oxford University Press, 2003) provides a detailed account of the development of the House of Commons – and its gradual rise to ascendency over the House of Lords – during the last century. **Tony Wright's** article **'What are MPs for?'** ((2010) 81 *Political Quarterly* 298) is an illuminating account of the role(s) of elected MPs in the aftermath of the 2009 expenses scandal.

Two pieces provide illuminating discussion of the Fixed-Term Parliaments Act 2011: **Mark Ryan's 'The Fixed-Term Parliaments Act 2011'** [2012] PL 214 provides a detailed and clear analysis of the Act's parliamentary progress and provisions while **Rodney Brazier's 'A Small Piece of Constitutional History'** (2012) 128 LQR 315 provides a robust critique of how the Act 'represents constitution-making at its worst'.

---

[116] For instance, A. Bradley and K. D. Ewing, *Constitutional and Administrative Law* (15th edn) (Harlow: Longman, 2011) pp. 30–1.

Chapter 10
Parliament (II): the House of Lords

'The House of Lords have only been tolerated all these years because they were thought to be in a comatose condition which preceded dissolution. They have got to dissolution now. That this body, utterly unrepresentative and utterly unreformed, should come forward and claim the right to make and unmake Governments, should lay one greedy paw . . . upon the long-established and most fundamental privileges of the House of Commons is a spectacle which a year ago no one would have believed could happen.'

Winston Churchill, *The People's Rights* (Jonathan Cape, 1909) 46.

Chapter outline

The House of Commons is the repository for elected legitimacy in the UK's national system of governance. Over the course of the twentieth century, this political fact relegated the House of Lords to the status of a subordinate chamber. This chapter examines the reason why the House of Commons came to dominate the UK Parliament by considering the problems with the composition of the House of Lords (it is a largely appointed House which still retains some hereditary membership) and the process by which the Commons came to strip the Lords of its equal role in the UK's law-making process (replacing the Lords' veto over legislation with a mere delaying power).

This chapter also considers the role that this subordinate chamber continues to play in the legislative process. Today, the work of the House of Lords largely revolves around scrutinising and, where necessary, revising legislation produced by the Commons. Nonetheless, the unelected nature of the UK's second chamber remains a contentious constitutional issue, one which has not been solved despite frequent reform proposals in the last two decades.

Introduction

The twentieth century was young when, in the speech quoted above, Winston Churchill thundered that the House of Lords constituted 'a lingering relic of a feudal order',[1] the reform of which had not to date 'received that priority of consideration which in the future it absolutely requires'.[2] And yet, over a century later, the House of Lords remains an integral unelected component of the UK Parliament. In the meantime, its powers have been reduced and its composition altered, but comprehensive reform of Westminster's upper house remains elusive. As we saw in the previous chapter, the House of Commons asserted its supremacy over the Lords in the Parliament Act 1911.[3] Following that reform successive governments largely lost interest in the upper chamber's function and composition. Lords reform was thereafter intermittently part of the political agenda, but was rarely accorded much priority. New Labour's overhaul of the UK Constitution brought the issue back to the forefront of political debate, but only partial reform was achieved. This chapter evaluates the composition, powers and role of the Lords, and investigates why more comprehensive reform has remained so elusive.

The composition of the House of Lords

Key issues

- For many centuries, the House of Lords played the role of providing a legislative forum through which members of the aristocracy played a role in law making in the UK. These 'hereditary peers' succeeded to their titles through family lines.

- In the pre-democratic era, the House of Lords also developed as a chamber through which important interest groups, the Church of England and the judiciary, could play a role in law making. These groups were represented by the Lords Spiritual and Lords of Appeal in the Ordinary (known as the 'Law Lords').

- In the middle of the twentieth century it was recognised that these groups did not provide the House of Lords with adequate expertise to fulfil its law-making function. 'Life peers' were created as a means of improving the functioning of the Lords. Following appointment to the Lords, such individuals could continue to take part in proceedings until their deaths, but thereafter the peerage was not passed to anyone else.

- Under the House of Lords Act 1999, the House of Lords was reformed to remove all but 92 of the hereditary peers (in an effort to cut the size of the House and to limit its connection with the aristocracy). Furthermore, under the Constitutional Reform Act 2005, the Law Lords were removed from the House in an effort to secure a better separation between the legislature and the judiciary.

---

[1] W. Churchill, *The People's Rights* (Jonathan Cape, 1909) p. 23.
[2] Ibid., p. 23.
[3] Above, pp. 302–4.

The chamber's historic composition

(i) Hereditary peers, Lords Spiritual and Law Lords

Churchill's complaint that the House of Lords was a 'feudal relic' applied deep into the twentieth century. Parliament had assumed its current two-chamber structure in the fourteenth century. Even in that era the members of the House of Commons had to be chosen to represent constituencies by election, if by no means on a modern democratic basis, whereas the Lords consisted of the most important church leaders ('Lords Spiritual') and landowners ('Lords Temporal') in the country. From the fourteenth century onwards, the Lords Temporal took their places in the House of Lords as a result of their status as senior members of the feudal aristocracy. No elections were ever held to the House, and members passed their entitlement to sit in the Lords to their eldest male heirs.

By the twentieth century, after successive generations of monarchs had granted peerages to their advisers and hangers-on, there were around 550 hereditary peers, but the reason for the House of Lords as a chamber representing large land-owning interests had diminished. Since the industrial revolution, land ownership had lost its status at the heart of the UK's economy.[4] In a rapidly changing country, most of the hereditary peers either took the Conservative whip or maintained a broadly conservative stance on political issues; as senior members of the aristocracy, few could see any personal gain in far-reaching societal or economic reform. Churchill's clash with the Lords occurred when peers rejected the Liberal Government's attempts to impose new taxes on wealthy landowners to fund such reforms. Moreover, despite the large number of peers, many were several centuries removed from predecessors who had played an active role in politics. If a matter did not affect their personal interests directly, or was not a prominent conservative cause, relatively few of these 'backwoodsmen' peers played any active role in the business of the chamber. The House of Lords was intermittently reactionary when its members felt threatened by an issue, but was otherwise moribund.

Alongside landed interests, the Church of England was represented in the House of Lords from its inception. By statute, up to 26 Church of England bishops may sit in the Lords as Lords Spiritual.[5] These bishops hold their place in Parliament by virtue of their high office within the established church, and their seat, therefore, is passed to another senior bishop on their death or retirement, rather than an heir. Their role of providing a voice for the Church in Parliament developed in an era of little religious diversity within England.[6] The Church was not, however, the only interest group represented in the House of Lords. The House had functioned historically as the highest appellate court for the UK legal systems other than for Scots criminal cases, and senior judges had frequently been granted hereditary peerages to enable them to sit in the House. Until the 1800s, however, no legal restrictions prevented other peers from taking part in the judicial work of the Lords' Appellate Committee.[7] The Appellate Jurisdiction Acts 1876 and 1887 provided

---

[4] See J. Harris, *Private Lives, Public Spirit: a Social History of Britain, 1870–1914* (OUP, 1993) 190.

[5] See Bishopric of Manchester Act 1847, s. 2 and Bishoprics Act 1878, s. 5.

[6] See A. Harlow, F. Cranmer and N. Doe, 'Bishops in the House of Lords: A Critical Analysis' [2008] PL 490, 492–3.

[7] See R. Stevens, 'Government and the Judiciary' in V. Bogdanor (ed.), *The British Constitution in the Twentieth Century* (OUP, 2003) 333, 334.

for the appointment of senior judges to the House of Lords as peers for life ('Lords of Appeal in Ordinary') and excluded other peers from undertaking judicial functions.[8] At most, around thirty sitting and retired senior judges sat in the Lords by virtue of this Act.

(ii) Life peers

By the middle of the twentieth century, the House of Lords was faltering. Having lost its fight against the Liberal Government prior to the First World War, and with it the power to veto legislation, the Lords became a backwater. When a Labour Government came into office in 1945, it commanded the support of 393 MPs in the Commons but just 16 peers. In response, as we shall see, Labour attempted to marginalise the Lords within the parliamentary system, further reducing its powers through law and constitutional convention. By the 1954–55 parliamentary session, the average daily attendance in the chamber had fallen to just 92. Nonetheless, most legislation still had to pass the House of Lords, and Labour therefore created 44 hereditary peers between 1945 and 1951 to handle government business. Such appointments, however, would in the long run see more apolitical peers succeeding to their family titles, rather than securing active members of the upper chamber.[9] The House was, in the words of one senior Conservative peer, 'perilously near a breakdown in its machinery'.[10]

In an attempt to address the political imbalance in the Lords and to inject much needed expertise into the chamber, the Conservative Government piloted the Life Peerages Act 1958 through Parliament. The Act enabled the Prime Minister to appoint members to sit in the upper chamber for life, but not pass on their title:

> What we want to achieve is the addition to the House of Lords of men and women of distinction from all main sectors of our national life, men and women who will strengthen it by their knowledge of affairs and their experience and widely varied interests, political, scientific, economic, cultural and religious.[11]

The expertise brought by such peers, and their willingness to contribute to the running of Parliament, were intended to reduce the legislative strain on the Commons. Labour Prime Ministers have tended to appoint more life peers than their Conservative counterparts, in an effort to redress the political imbalance of the Lords, and by 1999 the House contained almost 500 life peers. Membership of the House of Lords remains unpaid, although certain expenses and attendance allowances (of up to £300 per day) are provided.

Thinking Point . . .

In 2010/11, claims under the allowances and expenses scheme amounted to almost £24,000 per member of the House. Under this scheme of daily allowances, brought in following the parliamentary expenses scandal in 2009, daily average attendance in the House increased from 388 to 475 in one parliamentary session.

---

[8] Appellate Jurisdiction Act 1887, s. 2.
[9] D. Shell, *The House of Lords* (Philip Allan, 1988) pp. 13–14.
[10] Earl of Home, HL Debs, vol. 206, col. 610 (3 December 1957).
[11] R. A. Butler, MP, HC Debs, vol. 582, col. 408 (12 February 1958).

The reformed composition of the House of Lords

(i) The House of Lords Act 1999

By the time the New Labour Government took office in May 1997, the work of the House of Lords had indeed been transformed by the addition of life peers. The regular addition of new life peers over four decades and the constant recycling of hereditary peers had, however, seen membership of the upper chamber balloon to over 1,200. One of New Labour's concerns was that the large number of politically Conservative aristocrats who retained their seats in the Lords could stymie its legislative agenda. It proposed a 'quick fix' for this specific problem whilst its holistic Lords reform proposals were developed; all the hereditary peers would be stripped of their entitlement to sit in the House. In principle, there was little to stand in the way of such a reform. Churchill had contended back in 1909 that hereditary peerage was indefensible as someone's parents' achievements provided no firm evidence of their own abilities.[12] On the other hand, as the Conservative leadership in the House of Lords pointed out, some hereditary peers did play an active role in the work of the House. In order to smooth the passage of the reform, the Government reached an agreement with Viscount Cranborne, the Conservative leader in the Lords, whereby the House would retain a total of 92 hereditary peers, elected from amongst their number, until such time as full reform of the House could be undertaken.

(ii) The House of Lords Appointments Commission

The Prime Minister controls the appointment of peers, which is an exercise of the royal prerogative. This led to fears after the 1999 reforms that Tony Blair would pack the House of Lords full of his supporters (producing a House filled with 'Tony's cronies', according to opponents).[13] But appointments are made to the Lords within broad understandings between the political parties. Once the Prime Minister has decided how many peers should be appointed in any given year, an allocation within that total is provided to each of the main political parties, and the government accepts their nominations automatically. Some of these party nominees will be 'working peers' expected to actively contribute to the life of the Lords; others will receive their peerage essentially as an honour, with few expectations attached.

These understandings, however, did not stop the 'Tony's cronies' headlines, and in May 2000 the Labour Government sought to silence this criticism by forming a non-statutory Appointments Commission (consisting of representatives from the three main parties and a majority of independent members) with the remit of creating new 'crossbench' peers. Crossbench peers, who do not follow any particular party line, are a vital element of the current House of Lords, making up around a quarter of its overall membership. The Appointments Commission's mission is to recruit active legislators bringing diverse backgrounds, experiences and expertise to the chamber. Speaking for the Coalition Government, Lord Wallace set out the relationship between the Prime Minister's powers and the role of the Appointments Commission:

> [T]he House of Lords Appointments Commission recommends crossbench peers to the Prime Minister against an overall approach on numbers agreed by the Prime Minister. . . [O]nly in exceptional circumstances will he decline to pass on a recommendation to Her Majesty the Queen.[14]

---

[12] W. Churchill, *The People's Rights* (Jonathan Cape, 1909) p. 50.

[13] See A. Kelso, 'Stages and Muddles: The House of Lords Act 1999' (2011) 30 *Parliamentary History* 101, 104.

[14] HL Debs, vol. 734, col. WA133 (18 January 2012).

Although no Prime Minister has, to date, rejected any of the Appointments Commission's 67 nominees, the government continues to place strict limits on the number of proposals the Commission can make, and the number of 'political' appointees has outstripped the number of Commission appointees since 2000. For example, under the 2010–15 Coalition Government almost 200 new peers joined the upper chamber, but just eight were Appointments Commission nominees.

Thinking Point . . .

The Appointments Commission did not end complaints about cronyism in an appointed House of Lords; indeed these would re-emerge after both the Labour and Conservative Parties appointed large donors to the Lords after the 2005 general election (the 'cash for peerages' scandal), see N. Baldwin, 'The House of Lords – Into the Future? (2007) *Journal of Legislative Studies* 197, 202.

(iii) The Constitutional Reform Act 2005

As we saw when we considered the constitutional principle of the separation of powers,[15] the next piecemeal reform occurred when the Law Lords were removed from the chamber and a separate UK Supreme Court was created under the Constitutional Reform Act 2005. From the 1970s to 1990s, in particular, many Law Lords had made high-profile contributions to legislation through the Lords. According to one of these judges, Lord Hope, their work 'greatly strengthened the House's ability to perform its primary function as a revising Chamber'.[16] Such judicial interventions could not be considered apolitical, but nor were they party political. Instead these judges concentrated on pressing law-reform issues and ensuring the clarity and intelligibility of legislation. But this work raised serious concerns over their impartiality if cases later arose regarding provisions they had helped to enact.[17] The Law Lords' legislative interventions became infrequent, neutered by the recognition that speaking or voting on legislation would render them ineligible to hear appeals related to it.[18]

Thinking Point . . .

Lord Hoffmann was actively involved in passing the Defamation Act 1996, to the extent that he had to stand down from several libel cases which reached the House of Lords. See C. Dyer, 'Pinochet Law Lord Replaced Again as Judge' *Guardian* (8 July 1999).

The abolition of the Law Lords under the 2005 Act does not, however, mark the end of expert legal input into the Lords. Prominent barristers, such as Lord Pannick and Lord Lester, have been appointed to the House and use their position to promote law reform

---

[15] Above, pp. 228–9.
[16] D. Hope, 'Voices from the Past – the Law Lords' Contribution to the Legislative Process' (2007) 123 LQR 547, 570.
[17] For further information, see pp. 342–6.
[18] HL Debs, vol. 614, col. 419 (22 June 2000).

and scrutinise legislation. Moreover, as judges retire from the Supreme Court they become eligible to take their place in the House of Lords. A year after his retirement from the Bench Lord Hoffmann threw himself into libel reform debates in the House.[19] Another prominent reform of the House of Lords included in the 2005 Act was the limitation of the role of the Lord Chancellor, formally a government minister, a senior judge and the Speaker of the House of Lords. The Lord Chancellor lost all judicial functions in order to protect the separation of powers.[20] Similar concerns saw the introduction of a Lords Speaker, elected by the members of the House to fulfil the non-partisan role of presiding over debate in the House (currently Lord Fowler).[21]

(iv) The House of Lords Reform Act 2014 and House of Lords (Expulsion and Suspension) Act 2015

With the passage of the House of Lords Act 1999, the chamber was streamlined from roughly 1,200 to 666 members. Since then a steady stream of life peerage appointments saw membership of the House gradually expand to 835 members by 2013.[22] Although the growing membership was once again straining parliamentary resources, a second problem was that many peers in their 80s and 90s no longer played any role in the chamber, but held their place for life. The nature of a life peerage also prevented the expulsion of peers for misconduct. Two pieces of legislation, introduced as Private Members' Bills, have addressed these issues.

The House of Lords Reform Act 2014 permitted any peer to retire from their place in the Lords.[23] As of November 2017, 73 peers had used this provision to retire. Retiring peers are permitted to stand for election as MPs, sparking concerns that the major parties would start to use the Lords as a stepping stone for promising candidates.[24] Although such a development would undoubtedly make the chamber more partisan, no peer has yet made such an attempt.[25] The 2014 legislation also allowed for permanent expulsion of peers for non-attendance for an entire session (unless they have suspended their membership, for example because of illness or to enable them to hold an office)[26] or for conviction of a criminal offence carrying with it a sentence of more than one year's imprisonment.[27] The House of Lords (Expulsion and Suspension) Act 2015 augmented this legislation by giving the Lords the ability to suspend or expel a peer for misconduct.[28] These provisions enabled the enforced removal of inactive or unsuitable peers.

(v) The current composition of the House of Lords

Table 10.1 shows the number of Lords eligible to vote and their affiliations as of November 2017. Although the Prime Minister still controls the appointments process, a broad understanding remains at work between the Conservatives and Labour that each party will

---

[19] HL Debs, vol. 720, cols 430–4 (9 July 2010).
[20] See pp. 342–6.
[21] Constitutional Reform Act 2005, s. 18.
[22] See Lord Norton of Louth, HL Debs, vol. 750, cols 973–4 (12 December 2013).
[23] House of Lords Reform Act 2014, s. 1(1).
[24] Ibid., s. 4(5).
[25] Constitution Committee, *House of Lords Reform (No. 2) Bill* (2014) HL 155, para. 13–14.
[26] House of Lords Reform Act 2014, s. 2(1).
[27] Ibid., s. 3(1).
[28] House of Lords (Expulsion and Suspension) Act 2015, s. 1(1).

Table 10.1 Lords eligible to vote and their affiliations

Party	Life peers	Hereditary peers	Lords Spiritual	Total 'voting' peers	Percentage of total 'voting' peers
Conservative	201	49	—	250	31.3%
Labour	195	4	—	199	24.9%
Liberal Democrat	96	4	—	100	12.5%
Crossbench	152	32	—	184	23.0%
Other	41	2	—	43	5.4%
Bishops	—	—	24	24	3.0%
Total	685	91	24	800	

maintain comparable numbers of peers, with the balance of the House made up of Liberal Democrats and crossbench peers. The House, therefore, is controlled by no one political grouping (or in Vernon Bogdanor's description, it is 'permanently hung'[29]).

The combined impact of the Life Peerages Act 1958 and House of Lords Act 1999 has been to produce a much more active chamber with a more committed membership. In recent years, daily attendance has regularly averaged close to 500 peers when Parliament was in session. In other respects, however, the composition of the Lords remains far from perfect. Half of peers are over the age of 70 and the chamber is over-representative of London and the south of England and under-representative of other parts of the UK, particularly the Midlands and north of England.[30] Only a quarter of peers are women, and black and minority ethnic groups are under-represented. One argument frequently made in favour of the appointment of life peers is that individuals who would not normally enter politics are able to bring their experience into the legislative process.[31] A study conducted in March 2010 sheds some light on this claim. Deriving their data from sources such as *Who's Who* and operating on the basis that eight years' experience in a sector was sufficient for this to constitute a professional expertise, Meg Russell and Meghan Benton produced a break-down of the composition of the House of Lords by professional area (Table 10.2).[32] Taken as a whole, these figures tend to show that some professional interests are much better represented than others and, at worst, suggests that the House of Lords has become the preserve of semi-retired politicians.[33] If the House is to play an active role in the work of Westminster, however, experienced party-political figures remain an important asset:

---

[29] V. Bogdanor, *The New British Constitution* (Hart, 2009) p. 158.

[30] See M. Russell and M. Benton, 'Analysis of existing data on the breadth of expertise and experience in the House of Lords' (March 2010) 50, available at: http://lordsappointments.independent.gov.uk/media/17348/ucl_report.pdf.

[31] See Royal Commission on Reform of the House of Lords, *A House for the Future* (2000) Cm. 4534, para. 4.40.

[32] M. Russell and M. Benton, 'Analysis of Existing Data on the Breadth of Expertise and Experience in the House of Lords' (March 2010) 15.

[33] See H. Bochel and A. Defty '"A More Representative Chamber": Representation and the House of Lords' (2012) 18 *The Journal of Legislative Studies* 82, 88–90.

Table 10.2 Make-up of the House of Lords by professional area

Professional area	Number of peers with this primary professional area	Percentage of peers with this primary professional area
Representative politics	151	22%
Business and commerce	61	9%
Banking and finance	59	8%
Higher education	59	8%
Legal professions	54	8%
Clergy or religious leader	29	4%
Journalism, media and publishing	25	4%
Voluntary sector, NGOs and think tanks	25	4%
Other private sector	23	3%
Trade unions	21	3%
Agriculture and horticulture	20	3%
International affairs and diplomacy	18	3%
Culture, arts and sport	14	2%
Medical and healthcare	15	2%
Political staff and activists	15	2%
Armed forces	12	2%
Other public sector	12	2%
UK civil service	10	1%
Local authority administration	8	1%
Police	8	1%
Architecture, engineering and construction	5	1%
Education and training (not HE)	5	1%
Transport	5	1%
Royal family staff	2	0%
Manual and skilled trades	1	0%
Unclassified	42	6%
Total	699	100%

Following the 1999 reforms, commentators were divided over whether the new chamber had gained enhanced legitimacy as a result of the removal of the hereditary peers, or whether the Prime Minister now exerted such control over appointments to the House that its role in the UK's system of governance had been weakened.[34] With this dispute in mind, we can turn to consider the powers of the Lords and the chamber's workload since the 1999 reforms came into effect.

---

[34] See M. Russell, 'A Stronger Second Chamber? Assessing the Impact of House of Lords Reform in 1999 and the Lessons for Bicameralism' (2010) 58 *Political Studies* 866, 867–9.

The role of the House of Lords

Key issues

- From the creation of Parliament until 1911 both the House of Commons and the House of Lords had equal power over the creation of legislation and both had to approve all legislation before it could become law.

- In 1911, however, amid increasing recognition that the legitimacy that Parliament derived from elections to the Commons was not matched by the composition of the Lords, the two chambers became embroiled in a constitutional battle over taxation of large estates (many of them owned by members of the Lords). The Commons ultimately won the fight and, under the Parliament Act 1911, stripped the power to veto almost all legislation from the Lords and replaced it with a mere delaying power.

- The Lords, acutely aware of their lack of legitimacy, has used this delaying power on very few occasions in the last century. Instead, the unelected nature of the Lords allows it to function as a chamber primarily concerned with technical amendments to legislative proposals and, at times, has allowed it to counter balance the power of the dominant party in the Commons.

The formal powers of the House of Lords

(i) The House of Lords 1909–49: a chamber in decline

Prior to 1911, the Lords was a co-equal chamber to the Commons, with the power to veto any legislative proposals before Parliament. As a chamber, it had threatened, delayed or rejected swathes of the Liberal Government's legislative agenda from 1906 onwards. Then, in 1909, it over-reached. On the cusp of democracy in the UK, and at a time when representative politics had an established legitimacy, this aristocratic House blocked the Liberal's popular Finance Bill 1909. In doing so, it broke a constitutional convention that the elected House of Commons controlled financial legislation. Some breaches of constitutional conventions are so blatant that they trigger an almost instantaneous response. Churchill whipped up the electorate with an enraged pledge to 'smash the veto',[35] and after success at the polls the Liberals passed the Parliament Act 1911. Out manoeuvred, the Lords lost any power to reject or amend Money Bills (if these are not passed by the Lords within one month, they are deemed to have been passed).[36] Second, in relation to any other Bill, rejection by the Lords would no longer veto it, but merely delay its implementation for two parliamentary sessions (effectively two years).[37]

Having lost its equal status to the Commons and with its legitimacy undermined by its hereditary composition, the Lords could not resist further reductions in its powers by the Labour Government elected in 1945. Under the threat that the upper chamber would be abolished, Labour forced Lord Salisbury, the Conservative leader in the Lords, to accept that it would not seek to interfere with Labour's nationalisation agenda:

> Whatever our personal views, we should frankly recognise that these proposals were put before the country at the recent General Election and that the people of this country, with full knowledge of these proposals, returned the Labour Party to power . . . I believe that it would be

---

[35] W. Churchill, *The People's Rights* (Jonathan Cape, 1909) dedication.
[36] Parliament Act 1911, s. 1(2) and s. 2(1).
[37] Ibid., s. 2(1).

constitutionally wrong, when the country has so recently expressed its view, for this House to oppose proposals which have been definitely put before the electorate.[38]

This statement formed the basis of a new constitutional convention whereby the House of Lords will not obstruct legislation proposed in a government's election manifesto, on the basis that there was a popular mandate for such measures. As Labour's term in office continued, however, and its legislative agenda extended beyond its manifesto pledges, it once again feared that the Lords might use its powers to delay these plans. It consequently passed the Parliament Act 1949, a measure which reduced the Lords' maximum delaying power to one year. In other words, if the Commons passed the same proposals in two successive sessions then they would become law, regardless of their rejection by the Lords.[39]

(ii) The House of Lords 1949–99: a subordinate chamber

Following the 1949 reforms, Adam Tomkins talked of the 'impotence'[40] of the House of Lords within the UK's parliamentary system, and Vernon Bogdanor concluded that by the mid-1990s the UK in effect operated 'a unicameral system of government but with two chambers of parliament'.[41] The formal powers of the Lords were not, however, noticeably weaker than those of many second chambers in modern democracies. In Spain, for example, the second chamber can delay legislation for two months, whereas in Poland the second chamber has only 30 days to consider legislation and its objections can always be overridden by the first chamber.[42] Nonetheless, the Lords became reluctant to reject Bills supported by the elected House of Commons, 'whether a manifesto commitment or not'.[43] This deference to the primacy of the Commons was so strong that, in the half century between the 1949 and 1999 reforms, the Commons had to resort to the Parliament Act to pass legislation on just two occasions, the War Crimes Act 1991 and the European Parliamentary Elections Act 1999. For Rhodri Walters, the Lords' reluctance to use its legal powers came about 'because of the gradual evolution of the House from a chamber of veto to a chamber of scrutiny and amendment'.[44] This evolution would take on renewed vigour following the 1999 reforms.

The work of the House of Lords since 1999

(i) The transformation of the House of Lords

By the late 1990s the House of Lords was a busy chamber, sitting as frequently as the Commons. With its powers to veto legislation long removed, its role had changed. No longer was the Lords a rival to the Commons, instead it acted as a complementary chamber, as ministers have recognised:

> The House of Lords plays an important role in our legislature and, as a second chamber, is a vital part of our constitutional arrangements. The House of Lords shares responsibility for legislating with the House of Commons. Bills are debated and scrutinised in both Houses. The House of

---

[38] HL Debs, vol. 137, col. 47 (16 August 1945).
[39] Parliament Act 1949, s. 1.
[40] A. Tomkins, *Our Republican Constitution* (Hart, 2005) p. 126.
[41] V. Bogdanor, *Power to the People: a Guide to Constitutional Reform* (Victor Gollancz, 1997) p. 119.
[42] HM Government, *The House of Lords: Reform* (2007) Cm. 7027, 23.
[43] R. Walters, 'The House of Lords' in V. Bogdanor (ed.), *The British Constitution in the Twentieth Century* (OUP, 2003) 189, 211.
[44] Ibid., 211.

Lords has a reputation for the careful consideration of legislation and has the ability to delay and ask the government and House of Commons to think again and, in some cases, offer alternative amendments for further consideration. The House of Lords also plays a vital role in scrutinising the work of the government and holding it to account for its decisions and activities. It does this by members asking oral and written questions, responding to government statements and debating key issues. Select Committees of the House of Lords conduct inquiries into matters of public policy and publish their findings to Parliament.[45]

In other words, lacking the legitimacy to advance its own legislative agenda, the Lords must concentrate on reviewing the legislative output of the Commons and holding government to account. Although legislation can be initiated in the Lords, such Bills ordinarily do not relate to matters of party-political controversy.[46] In these roles, the Lords is arguably aided by its composition. As peers are appointed, they are freed from performing the constituency work required of MPs. Appointment, as we have seen, allows the composition of the Lords to be bolstered by experts who can contribute their specialist knowledge and experience to the law-making process. Furthermore, party loyalties do not bind members of the Lords as strongly as they do in the Commons. Not only do 'crossbench' peers, unaligned to particular parties, make up a large element of the House, but even peers who represent political parties are appointed for life and their parties therefore cannot threaten their place in Parliament as a means of controlling their loyalty.[47] Finally, House of Lords procedure has not historically involved guillotine or closure motions, mechanisms used by government to curtail Commons debates.

Thinking Point . . .

The lack of guillotine motions in the Lords changes the character of debates. In 2011 a determined group of Labour peers attempted to delay the passage of the Parliamentary Voting System and Constituencies Act 2011 by days of so-called filibustering through drawn-out speeches (a tactic which is ineffective in the Commons in most circumstances). Ministers ultimately threatened to employ a guillotine motion, and the peers backed down. See P. Wintour, 'Conservatives Act to Stop Labour Peers Derailing Voting Referendum Bill', *Guardian* (13 January 2011).

With the removal of the bulk of hereditary peers in 1999, and the introduction of the Appointment Commission process for crossbench peers in 2000, the Lords was freed from claims that it acted as the voice of aristocratic interests. With this drag on its legitimacy removed, the Lords was empowered to use its formal powers, and has supposedly found itself 'gaining in assertiveness and influence'.[48] To evaluate this claim, we need to consider how the upper chamber has performed its function since the reforms to its composition.

---

[45] HM Government, *House of Lords Reform Draft Bill* (2011) Cm. 8077, 10.
[46] B. Hadfield, 'Whither or Whether the House of Lords' (1994) 35 NILQ 320, 325.
[47] D. Oliver, 'Reforming the United Kingdom Parliament' in J. Jowell and D. Oliver (eds), *The Changing Constitution* (7th edn, OUP, 2011) 167, 182.
[48] M. Russell, 'A Stronger Second Chamber? Assessing the Impact of House of Lords Reform in 1999 and the Lessons for Bicameralism' (2010) 58 *Political Studies* 866, 880.

(ii) Revising legislation and statutory instruments

Much of the Lords' time is taken up by the scrutiny and revision of legislation. In this work, peers with specialist subject knowledge have the opportunity to contribute to the law-making process and scrutiny of government policy. Unless the Parliament Act procedure is used, Bills must ordinarily pass both the Lords and the Commons in the same form, sometimes 'ping-ponging' between both chambers until agreement is reached. In this way, a government facing a busy legislative agenda will often accept amendments to legislation from the Lords, particularly if they are technical in nature. In 2011, for example, the Coalition Government was engaged in attempting to reform the public sector by scrapping a large number of quangos.[49] Debate on the proposals was particularly robust in the House of Lords, fronted by peers with experience of the running of public sector organisations. By the conclusion of the committee stage in the Lords the government minister in charge of the Bill, Lord Taylor, reported to the chamber that the government would accept several key amendments preventing ministers from abolishing public bodies by delegated legislation:

> Progress on this Bill . . . has certainly been drawn out longer than I had hoped. However, I take comfort in the knowledge that the expert scrutiny of this House has improved and will continue to improve the Bill. Again, I thank all noble Lords who contributed to this process. In tabling the significant amendments that I described today . . . the Government have demonstrated their commitment to engage with and respond to your Lordships' House.[50]

Because of the expertise and independence of crossbench peers 'a crossbench amendment can be difficult for government'.[51] Even where high-profile legislation is at issue, such peers have been able to force ministers into concessions. In the aftermath of the 9/11 attacks on the US, the UK Government rushed the Anti-Terrorism, Crime and Security Bill 2001 before Parliament. The Commons, eager to be seen to respond quickly to the terrorist threat, passed the legislation in just 16 hours. In the weeks thereafter, however, the proposals met with much more thorough scrutiny in the Lords. In the course of these debates the former Master of the Rolls, Lord Donaldson, secured an amendment permitting judicial review of the detention without trial of suspected international terrorists.[52] The amendment, ultimately, allowed the Appellate Committee of the House of Lords to hear the *Belmarsh Detainees* case,[53] and to issue the Declaration of Incompatibility with human rights which spelt the end of detention without trial.[54]

Key debates

Legislative scrutiny in the House of Lords in practice

The Lords subjected the Welfare Reform Act 2012 to extensive scrutiny during its passage. The Act sought to reform welfare payments in the UK, introducing a universal credit to replace a range of means tested benefits. These proposals were particularly controversial, with Paralympian and disability-rights campaigner Baroness Grey-Thompson leading a campaign against disability benefit reforms. In all, the Lords returned 110 amendments to the Commons for consideration.

---

[49] Above, pp. 278–9.
[50] HL Debs, vol. 725, col. 800 (28 February 2011).
[51] M. Russell and M. Sciara, 'The Policy Impact of Defeats in the House of Lords' (2008) 10 BJPIR 571, 582.
[52] See HL Debs, vol. 629, cols 1440–2 (13 December 2001).
[53] *A v Secretary of State for the Home Department* [2004] UKHL 56; [2005] 2 AC 68.
[54] For further information, see p. 670.

→

> The Commons' response to these amendments indicates both the strength and the limits of the scrutiny role of the Lords. Of the amendments, the Commons found that 46 engaged its privilege relating to financial legislation. Whilst the Welfare Reform Act was not a 'money Bill' (had it been, the Parliament Act 1911 would have prevented the Lords from amending it), it was, in part, legislation relating to financial expenditure. Such provisions, by convention, fell within the exclusive remit of the Commons.
>
> A government minister, Lord Strathclyde, pointed out that under the previous Labour Government this mechanism had been frequently employed by the Commons with regard to 'Bills as varied as the Counter-Terrorism Bill and the Personal Care at Home Bill' (HL Debs, vol. 735, col. 483 (14 February 2012)). But this was not the end of the matter, for even where this convention applied the Government was willing to make compromises to ensure the passage of the legislation without further delay:
>
>> The Government asked the Commons to agree to 35 of those 46 amendments and to reject the remaining 11. In agreeing to those 35 Lords amendments, each a concession to this House, the Commons waived its financial privilege for more than £300 million of public expenditure. Therefore, we are really talking only about the remaining 11 Lords amendments, which, on policy grounds, the Government could not accept and which they asked the House of Commons to reject.
>
> As Dawn Oliver points out, '[c]onsent refusing activity carried out by . . . independent, unelected, expert bodies is a central part of the democratic arrangements in [many] countries' ('Reforming the United Kingdom Parliament' in J. Jowell and D. Oliver (eds), *The Changing Constitution* (7th edn, OUP, 2011) 167, 181). A very similar process can be seen at work in the activities of the House of Lords.

The Lords' legislative scrutiny does not stop with Bills, but extends to statutory instruments. Its Delegated Powers Scrutiny Committee frequently calls attention to flawed statutory instruments before they are formally proposed to Parliament.[55] Historically, however, the House of Lords almost never rejected delegated legislation once it was proposed; leading to claims that a convention had been developed preventing the Lords from doing so.[56] Soon after the compositional reforms to the Lords, however, the chamber began to flex its muscles in this regard, rejecting the Greater London Authority (Election Expenses) Order 2000 and the Gambling (Geographical Distribution of Casino Premises Licences) Order 2007.[57] Although a parliamentary committee on conventions concluded that 'the House of Lords should not regularly reject Statutory Instruments' it found no convention against the chamber doing so in exceptional cases.[58] In the autumn of 2015 the relationship between the Lords and the Commons was severely tested over proposed amendments to the system of tax credits. The 2015 Conservative Manifesto had not mentioned cuts to tax credits, but after that year's General Election David Cameron's Government moved to impose new restrictions on these benefits through a statutory instrument. Although this measure was accepted by the Commons the Lords refused to authorise it unless conditions were met, leading to the Government withdrawing the proposed regulations.

---

[55] R. Walters, 'The House of Lords' in V. Bogdanor (ed.), *The British Constitution in the Twentieth Century* (OUP, 2003) 189, 223.

[56] See Cabinet Office, *Strathclyde Review: Secondary Legislation and the Primacy of the House of Commons* (2015) Cm. 9177, 15.

[57] See M. Russell and R. Cornes, 'The Royal Commission on Reform of the House of Lords: A House for the Future?' (2001) 64 MLR 82, 87.

[58] Joint Committee on Conventions, *Conventions of the UK Parliament* (2006) HL 265, para. 227.

For Government ministers, the conventions securing the primacy of the Commons over financial matters had been sundered.[59] For recalcitrant peers, no manifesto commitment was at issue (therefore the Salisbury Convention did not apply), secondary legislation was at issue (thus there could be no application of the Money Bill rules under the Parliament Act 1911) and no convention restricted the powers of the Lords with regard to secondary legislation.[60] David Cameron turned to Lord Strathclyde to tackle this issue; as a senior Conservative peer he was not intended to neutrally officiate on the underlying causes of the dispute, but to find a way to prevent the Lords from acting in this way again. He insisted that a convention did exist whereby the Lords would 'not regularly' challenge statutory instruments and that the tax credits debacle 'broke new ground' in undermining this convention.[61] He therefore proposed that new legislation should restrict the Lords' powers over statutory instruments to mere delay.[62] In keeping with so many historic efforts at Lords' reform, however, other political priorities intervened. Amid the Brexit referendum campaign and its aftermath the Conservative Government quietly lost interest in this particular fight with the House of Lords, and the Strathclyde proposals have been shelved.[63]

Thinking Point . . .

The ability of ministers to portray the tax credits confrontation between the Lords and Commons as a 'constitutional crisis' on the basis of tenuous claims that constitutional conventions were at issue does flag up how a system which is reliant on conventions is open to manipulation. See Chris Bryant, MP, HC Deb, vol. 603, col. 1741 (17 December 2015).

(iii) Challenging legislation: a constitutional safeguard?

There is one exception to the removal of the Lords' veto under the Parliament Act 1911; the Commons cannot attempt to extend the life of Parliament without the Lords' consent.[64] This restriction on the power of the Commons was intended to prevent a government from using its Commons majority to extend its hold on power by delaying elections. This specific protection raises the issue of whether the UK's upper chamber should be conceived more broadly as providing a 'constitutional safeguard'. Although this term is difficult to apply in the context of the UK's uncodified constitution, it is worth noting that second chambers in many democracies have special powers over legislation of constitutional importance. With its somewhat depoliticised composition, Dawn Oliver finds it natural that the Lords' should be regarded as 'a kind of constitutional watchdog'.[65]

To assess the validity of this claim, we must consider instances in which the Lords have taken the ultimate step of rejecting a government's legislative proposals. Prior to the 1999 reforms, Labour Governments had sought to deflect criticism generated by defeats in the

---

[59] Chris Grayling, MP, HC Deb, vol. 601, col. 349 (28 October 2015).
[60] Baroness Hollis of Heigham, HL Deb, vol. 765, col. 991 (26 October 2015).
[61] Cabinet Office, *Strathclyde Review: Secondary Legislation and the Primacy of the House of Commons* (2015) Cm. 9177, 15.
[62] Ibid., 19.
[63] See Baroness Evans of Bowes Park, HL Deb, vol. 776, col. 1539 (17 November 2016).
[64] Parliament Act 1911, s. 2(1).
[65] D. Oliver, 'Reforming the United Kingdom Parliament' in J. Jowell and D. Oliver (eds), *The Changing Constitution* (7th edn, OUP, 2011) 167, 181.

Lords by alleging that the unreformed chamber was biased towards the Conservatives. As the then Home Secretary Jack Straw told the Commons in 1998:

> In an average Session when the Conservatives have been in power, there have been 13 defeats of Government business in the [Lords]. In an average Session when Labour has been in power the figure has been five times that – on average 60 defeats.[66]

Following the House of Lords Act 1999, however, no party controlled the chamber. Freed of accusations of party bias, the Lords began to use their powers much more assertively. Between 1999 and 2007 Tony Blair's Government suffered over 400 defeats at the hands of the Lords (many in the context of 'high-profile government bills'[67]). The Blair Government responded to only three of those defeats using the Parliament Act. In other instances it withdrew or revised legislation in light of the Lords' opposition. Overall, a study by Meg Russell and Maria Sciara established that in these clashes 'the Lords wins some concessions in six out of ten cases'.[68]

Many of the Lords' rejections of legislation related to constitutional issues, or concerns that some public interest had not been properly addressed by the Commons. The Criminal Justice (Mode of Trial) Bill 2000, for example, involved an attempt by the Labour Government to restrict the use of jury trials in England and Wales. The Lords rejected the proposals, and the legislation was abandoned. Under Gordon Brown's premiership, the Commons passed the Counter-Terrorism Bill 2008, permitting the police to hold terrorist suspects for up to 42 days without charge (a power which far exceeded maximum pre-charge detention periods for other criminal offences). Again, the Lords rejected these provisions and the Government, eager to enact the bulk of this legislation, abandoned these proposals. As Russell and Sciara point out, these defeats attracted 'unwelcome media attention' to government proposals, making it harder to fight these rejections in the Commons and thereby served to 'limit government flexibility'.[69]

Fighting defeats in the Lords can cost a government political capital and will also oblige it to invest further time on a piece of legislation (often upsetting a busy legislative schedule). The recent examples of the use of the Parliament Acts by the Government, therefore, give us a window into the limits of the Lords' power over legislation. The Sexual Offences (Amendment) Act 2000 was, in many respects, the last gasp of the unreformed House of Lords. During 1998 and 1999 a majority of MPs had voted for measures to equalise the homosexual and heterosexual age of consent. On both occasions the Lords, still a largely hereditary chamber, rejected the legislation. The rump of hereditary peers, together with other Conservative peers, continued their efforts to delay the legislation after the reforms, causing Labour to force the measure onto the statute book through the Parliament Act. Matthew Waites regarded this opposition as an abuse of the Lords' position:

> The Lords' legitimacy is often said to depend upon its recognition of itself as a revising chamber with secondary status, yet the alliance against the equal age of consent used every possible procedure to obstruct the will of the elected Commons, simultaneously showing disdain for the obligations of the UK under the European Convention on Human Rights.[70]

---

[66] HC Debs, vol. 321, cols 573–4 (30 November 1998).

[67] M. Russell and M. Sciara, 'The Policy Impact of Defeats in the House of Lords' (2008) 10 BJPIR 571, 578.

[68] Ibid., 574.

[69] Ibid., 573.

[70] See M. Waites, 'Regulation of Sexuality: Age of Consent, Section 28 and Sex Education' (2001) 54 *Parliamentary Affairs* 495, 507.

Once the hangover from the pre-reform era had cleared, such obstructionism became rare. Unfortunately for the Lords, however, the only other occasion since reform when a government has been obliged to use the Parliament Act to pass legislation occurred with regard to the fox-hunting ban under the Hunting Act 2004. Again, in opposing this measure the Lords seemed to affirm the degree to which particular sectional interests (in this case, rural interests) dominated the House. Too much emphasis, however, should not be placed on these examples. Protracted objection to proposed legislation, to the point where the Parliament Act is invoked, is uncommon and is merely 'the most visible sign of the chamber's intervention in policy'.[71] Moreover, if the government is determined to legislate, the one-year delay at most gives an opportunity for the public to consider the controversy surrounding the proposals.

Reform of the House of Lords

Key issues

- For the last two decades, political debate has frequently touched upon the necessity of Lords reform. With hereditary peers still sitting, and without any electoral mandate, the chamber's critics question whether its role in the UK's legislative process is legitimate.

- Notwithstanding these arguments, reform of the Lords has proven to be fraught with difficulty. Although the major political parties agree on the need for reform, all are riven by disagreements over the composition of a reformed House and the degree to which elections are necessary for it to undertake its limited role in the law-making process.

- Labour (at least once most hereditary peers had been removed) and the Conservatives have long given the issue a low priority, meaning that it has often remained an unfulfilled element of these parties' legislative agendas.

The purpose of Lords reform

(i) Lords reform: the never-ending story

Proposals for comprehensive Lords reform have waxed and waned in the political agenda since the Parliament Act 1911, which was explicitly stated to be a 'quick fix' Act until time could be found in Parliament's calendar to undertake further reform. Even before the House of Lords Act 1999 was passed, Tony Blair's Government hoped to build on the momentum for change by appointing a Royal Commission under the leadership of former Conservative minister Lord Wakeham to consider the future of the Lords. The arrangements under the 1999 Act were regarded as transitional by Labour ministers, so confident were they that the Wakeham Commission would deliver a blueprint for reform.[72] Instead the Commission could not agree on the composition of a reformed Lords and advanced three 'timid'[73] models for reform, proposing an elected element of either 12, 16 or 35 per cent of the House.[74] Following the 2001 general election, the Labour Government

---

[71] Ibid., 586.

[72] See Lord Irvine, HL Debs, vol. 606, col. 169 (26 October 1999).

[73] M. Russell and R. Cornes, 'The Royal Commission on Reform of the House of Lords: A House for the Future?' (2001) 64 MLR 82, 99.

[74] Royal Commission on Reform of the House of Lords, *A House for the Future* (2000) Cm. 4534.

responded to the Wakeham proposals with a White Paper proposing a reformed upper chamber of 600 members, 20 per cent of whom would be elected.[75] This proposal suggested that the Blair Government had lost its taste for transformational reform of the Lords and was content to maintain its powers to make political appointments. The proposed chamber retained such a high percentage of political appointees as to be 'derided as a giant quango, representing rule by an elite'.[76]

In February 2003, the potential for Lords reform seemed to evaporate when seven options for a reformed composition were put to the Commons and all were either rejected or not even voted upon.[77] All the while the supposedly transitional House of Lords seemed to have received a new lease of life, and commentators like Oliver began to recognise that the effect of the 1999 reforms had been 'very positive'.[78] Although another White Paper on Lords reform was produced in 2007, it again posed more questions over the shape of a reformed Lords than it provided answers, tentatively proposing a chamber which would be 50 per cent elected, 30 per cent politically appointed and 20 per cent independently appointed.[79] Yet another White Paper was issued by Gordon Brown's Government in 2008, but drew little attention.[80] Although pledges supporting Lords reform appeared in the 2010 manifestos of all three major parties, the urgency seemed to have left the issue. Had it not been for the Coalition Government following the 2010 general election, Lords reform may well have dropped to the bottom of the order of political priorities. The Liberal Democrats, however, were strongly committed to electing the second chamber by a form of proportional representation (which would likely increase their representation in Parliament). Once their flagship proposal for the introduction of the alternative vote system in general elections was rejected in a 2011 referendum,[81] their attention switched to the consolation prize of Lords reform.

(ii) Key issues affecting reform proposals

Many of the difficulties with Lords reform have stemmed from the failure of many proposals to address the interrelationship between a future second chamber's composition and its powers. Lords reform proposals since Wakeham, no matter the composition they have proposed, have all regarded a reformed upper chamber as playing essentially the same constitutional role as the present House. No proposal, by either Labour or the Coalition, envisaged substantial new powers for a reformed upper chamber. The Deputy Prime Minister, Nick Clegg, summed up the prevailing orthodoxy on reform:

> I do not think that there is an automatic link between composition and function. We are arguing that . . . the mandates and the constitutional role of the House of Lords as a revising chamber can remain intact notwithstanding the fact that the legitimacy of the members of the House of Lords would be different in a House of Lords that is wholly or largely elected.[82]

---

[75] HM Government, *House of Lords, Completing the Reform* (2001) Cm. 5291.
[76] G. Phillipson, '"The greatest quango of them all", "a Rival Chamber" or "a Hybrid Nonsense"? Solving the Second Chamber Paradox' [2004] PL 352, 353.
[77] See HM Government, *The House of Lords: Reform* (2007) Cm. 7027, 17.
[78] D. Oliver, 'The Parliament Acts, the Constitution, the Rule of Law, and the Second Chamber' [2012] *Statute Law Review* 1, 2.
[79] HM Government, *The House of Lords: Reform* (2007) Cm. 7027.
[80] HM Government, *An Elected Second Chamber: Further reform of the House of Lords* (2008) Cm. 7438.
[81] See pp. 307–12.
[82] Joint Committee, *Draft House of Lords Reform Bill* (2012) HL 284, para. 26.

The problem with such assertions is that the level of legitimacy invested in a chamber by an electoral process clearly impacts upon its role. Whereas the current unelected second chamber does not have a mandate to enable it to challenge the legislative agenda set by the Commons, the same cannot easily be said of a largely elected chamber, which would likely bridle at the limited role of the Lords. Moreover, although it may be possible to design an electoral system for a reformed upper house which preserves a greater mandate for the Commons, an elected upper chamber risks adding no distinctive element to the legislative process. The reformed chamber could gain legitimacy, and replicate the representative function of the Commons, but it has proven particularly difficult in the last decade to come up with an electoral system (or an appropriate elected/appointed balance in a reformed chamber) which retains the scrutiny capabilities of the current Lords' expert membership. Finally, if the reformed chamber is to be largely elected, then a question mark hangs over the quality of the candidates who will seek election to a chamber lacking in comparable powers to the Commons. Even if a case can be made for an elected upper chamber as a proving-ground for potential future MPs, such an ambitious membership would be inimical to the consensual scrutiny function currently undertaken by the Lords. With such concerns in mind, it seems inappropriate for Lords reform proposals to attempt to divorce consideration of powers from consideration of functions. Figure 10.1 posits a direct relationship between these elements of legislative chambers:

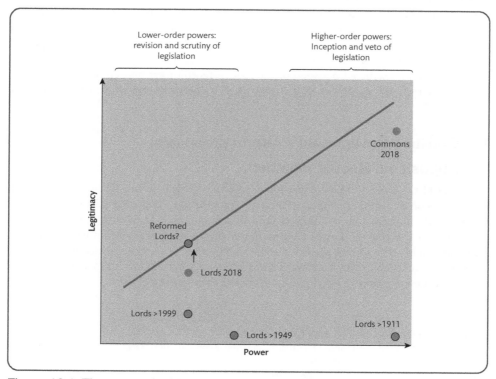

Figure 10.1 The power–legitimacy curve for legislation

This power–legitimacy curve provides for an ideal relationship between the composition of a legislative chamber and the powers it enjoys. The aim of proposals for parliamentary reform in the UK is to place the Lords (and perhaps also the Commons) on the power–legitimacy curve. At the moment, arguably, both chambers lack legitimacy commensurate with their role. As we have seen with the alternative-vote referendum, the main argument underpinning calls for electoral reform in the UK is that the first-past-the-post electoral system does not give the Commons a composition which reflects the intentions of the electorate sufficiently accurately to support the ultimate legislative power of a sovereign parliament which can be wielded through this chamber.[83]

The Lords has reached its present position on the graph through the reforms of the twentieth century. The Parliament Acts of 1911 and 1949, as we can see, reduced the powers of the Lords but did nothing to improve the legitimacy of its hereditary composition. The introduction of life peers from 1958 began to give the Lords a level of legitimacy because it could draw upon some expert members, but it was only after the 1999 reforms, and the removal of most hereditary peers, that considerable progress was made towards the Lords drawing upon this source of legitimacy. As the legitimacy of the Lords came more into line with its powers over the last decade, we have seen that the Lords became much more willing to use these powers (affirming the power–legitimacy link). Although these improvements lessened the urgency of further reform, the Lords remains under-legitimate for the powers that it wields. Most peers gaining their position through political patronage and not from the independent appointments process and hereditary peers continue to have a presence in the House. The challenge therefore lies in correctly assessing the degree of compositional reform needed to bring the powers and legitimacy of the Lords into alignment, whilst the danger lies in the government overshooting the optimal curve, and providing the reformed chamber with too much legitimacy for its powers. Such efforts are made more difficult by the subjective nature of legitimacy, and it is hardly surprising therefore that reform proposals since Wakeham have approached the concept differently, and indeed have 'oscillated between (often inadvertently) treating democratic legitimacy as the only type of legitimacy and declaring it to be only one route to institutional legitimacy'.[84]

The Coalition Government's reform proposals

(i) Composition: elected members

In May 2011 the Coalition Government published a draft Bill on Lords reform.[85] The draft Bill focused on reforming the upper chamber's composition, proposing a 300-seat chamber which would be either 80 or 100% elected by a single transferrable vote (STV) system operating on the basis of large, multiple-member constituencies. Members of the new chamber would serve fifteen-year, non-renewable, terms. Since general elections are fixed for five-year intervals under the Fixed-Term Parliaments Act 2011[86] this means that a third of seats in the upper house would be contested at each general election.

---

[83] For further information, see pp. 307–12.
[84] A. Kelso, 'Reforming the House of Lords: Navigating Representation, Democracy and Legitimacy at Westminster' (2006) 59 *Parliamentary Affairs* 563, 577.
[85] HM Government, *House of Lords Reform Draft Bill* (2011) Cm. 8077.
[86] Above pp. 287–93.

Thinking Point . . .

The electoral system for a reformed upper chamber is likely to be based upon the STV form of proportionate representation. This system allows electors to choose specific candidates from party lists, whereas closed-list systems simply permit votes for parties. The parties would control those named on the lists.

A reformed upper chamber would gain considerable legitimacy over the present House of Lords if such proposals are put into effect. Nonetheless, the reformed chamber would not necessarily, even if wholly elected, become a rival chamber to the House of Commons. Closed-list systems, for example, allow electors to control the number of seats available to each party but parties would decide the order of their preferred candidates on the list. Although the standing committee reviewing the draft Bill rejected this option,[87] such an approach would increase the legitimacy of the chamber, but not to a degree which would threaten the Commons. Furthermore, whereas MPs derive their legitimacy from regular elections (at least every five years), the proposed 15-year terms of members of the proposed upper chamber would prevent them from claiming the same level of legitimacy as MPs.

Notwithstanding the increased legitimacy of such a reformed chamber, it may be less well-equipped to perform its primary function of revising and reviewing legislation than the current Lords. As Oliver reminds readers, '[w]e depend entirely on intra-parliamentary scrutiny to protect us from ill-considered unconstitutional legislation and departures from the rule of law'.[88] A largely, and potential wholly-elected second chamber leaves little room for expert membership and seems to increase the grip of party politics on the Lords, as members 'may be reluctant to raise questions about bills that are against their party's interests'.[89] In answer to Oliver's concerns, the long, non-renewable terms of members of the reformed chamber do potentially make them less liable to the party whip than MPs, although in a wholly-elected House this would be at the expense of the independence of losing an unaligned block of crossbench peers. Moreover, the potential choice of a 'closed-list' electoral system for the House would allow such lists to be populated by members with diverse expertise and would not require active campaigning on any particular candidate's part. Such aspirations, however, are unlikely to survive hotly contested elections. Moreover, an elected chamber would not preclude experts from informing policy making; they would simply have to do so through engagement with select committees.

(ii) Composition: appointed members, ministers and bishops

Even taken together, those caveats provide cold comfort to commentators who see a wholly elected House as a risk to the scrutiny work of the upper chamber. Their concerns, however, dovetail with the government's desire that there should be an appointed element to the reformed chamber to forestall any threat it may pose to the primacy of the Commons.[90] The 20 per cent of appointed members would be selected by an Appointments Commission

---

[87] Joint Committee, *Draft House of Lords Reform Bill* (2012) HL 284, para. 129.

[88] D. Oliver, 'The Parliament Acts, the constitution, the rule of law, and the second chamber' [2012] *Statute Law Review* 1, 5.

[89] Ibid., 4.

[90] Joint Committee, *Draft House of Lords Reform Bill* (2012) HL 284, para. 99.

process, rather than continuing prime ministerial patronage. This proposal would produce a chamber of 'hybrid' composition. Some, including Vernon Bogdanor, have long maintained that such a House risks being riven by internal divisions, with elected members questioning the legitimacy of their appointed counterparts.[91] For others, such as Gavin Phillipson, this issue must be contextualised as the 'only real drawback in what is otherwise the best solution to a notoriously difficult problem'.[92]

The Coalition Government's proposal that it should be able to appoint ministers, who would be able to sit in the chamber as full members for the duration of their ministerial mandate, poses bigger questions for a reformed upper chamber's legitimacy. Ministerial appointments to an otherwise largely elected chamber give a government the opportunity to skew the balance of the chamber in its favour. The standing committee reviewing the proposals therefore made a strong case that the number of such appointments should be limited to no more than five, or that such ministers should be denied voting rights in the chamber.[93] The draft Bill also made provision for twelve Church of England bishops to remain in the Lords as ex-officio members. Although the Lords Spiritual were once thought of as representing the Church's interests in Parliament, in the reformed chamber they seem to be loosely conceived as providing 'spiritual leadership'. In such a role, however, they are hampered by a lack of reciprocal representation for other faith groups and for representatives of those with no religious faith. In the current House, the bishops do not take the whip of any political party. That said, they are not apolitical figures and frequently use their place in the Lords to criticise government policy.[94] At best, these proposals could be said to reflect 'a considerable amount of residual good-will towards the bishops who sit in the Lords'.[95] Nonetheless, retaining their privileged voice in Parliament remains a particularly conservative element of the reform proposals.

Thinking Point . . .

The mere fact that the Church of England is an established church does not, of itself, justify the inclusion of bishops in the Lords. Scotland's national church has no such formal representation in Westminster or Holyrood. See Royal Commission on Reform of the House of Lords, *A House for the Future* (2000) Cm. 4534, para. 15.8.

(iii) The powers of a reformed Lords

By formal powers, the current House of Lords remains 'one of the most powerful second chambers in the world'.[96] Ongoing concerns over legitimacy, however, keep the Lords from exercising these powers to their full extent. As one select committee report concluded, 'for all its expertise and experience, [the Lords] does not have enough confidence in its own

---

[91] See V. Bogdanor, 'Reform of the House of Lords: a Sceptical View' (1999) 70 *Political Quarterly* 375.

[92] G. Phillipson, '"The Greatest Quango of Them All", "a Rival Chamber" or "a Hybrid Nonsense"? Solving the Second Chamber Paradox' [2004] PL 352, 362.

[93] Joint Committee, *Draft House of Lords Reform Bill* (2012) HL 284, para. 267–8.

[94] A. Harlow, F. Cranmer and N. Doe, 'Bishops in the House of Lords: A Critical Analysis' [2008] PL 490, 508.

[95] Ibid., 509.

[96] Joint Committee, *Draft House of Lords Reform Bill* (2012) HL 284, para. 26.

legitimacy'.[97] Reconstituting the House as an entirely or largely elected chamber would dispel such concerns. Moreover, it would likely spell the end for conventions such as the Salisbury Convention (forbidding the Lords from rejecting legislation proposed in a governing party's manifesto) and the practice whereby the Lords only rejects statutory instruments in exceptional circumstances. As political commentator Peter Riddell told the standing committee considering the draft House of Lords Reform Bill, these conventions would become unsustainable if a reformed Lords gained elected legitimacy, likely giving rise to a 'bruising interlude' as the relationship between the reformed chamber and the Commons developed.[98]

Thinking Point . . .

Clause 2 of the Draft House of Lords Reform Bill included a provision stating that the present primacy of the Commons over the Lords will be retained under the new Act. The standing committee reviewing the proposals considered that this idea would likely be 'unworkable' and might result in undesirable litigation on the relationship between the Houses. Joint Committee, *Draft House of Lords Reform Bill* (2012) HL 284, para. 26.

Therefore, even if the proposed reforms make no substantive changes to the Lords' powers, the practical effect will likely be to increase the willingness of the reformed upper chamber to flex its muscles. As Oliver explains, the upper chamber's more frequent recourse to the power to delay legislation, which she terms a 'suspensory veto', could have a profound impact on government policy making:

> The existence of the suspensory veto in a house in which the government does not have a majority forces a government to anticipate the problems that are likely to arise in the House of Lords and seek to avoid them.[99]

The reform proposals, of course, do not guarantee that the party with a Commons majority might not also secure a majority in the new upper chamber, but the different electoral systems and electoral cycles for both chambers limit the possibility of such concurrence.

Second chambers around the world frequently have special powers over legislation likely to have an impact upon the constitution or fundamental rights. No special powers, such as an extended delaying power where legislation affects such issues, have been considered with regard to the reformed chamber. Framing such a role would be problematic, in the context of the uncodified UK constitution. As Phillipson points out, therefore, we might well have to rely on the reformed chamber using its powers particularly actively in such areas.[100]

---

[97] Public Administration Select Committee, *The Second Chamber: Continuing the Reform* (2002) HC 494, para. 60.

[98] Joint Committee, *Draft House of Lords Reform Bill* (2012) HL 284, para. 83.

[99] D. Oliver, 'The Parliament Acts, the Constitution, the Rule of Law, and the Second Chamber' [2012] *Statute Law Review* 1, 4.

[100] See G. Phillipson, '"The Greatest Quango of Them All", "a Rival Chamber" or "a Hybrid Nonsense"? Solving the Second Chamber Paradox' [2004] PL 352, 377–9.

Conclusion

Commending the Parliament Act 1949 to the Commons the Labour minister Hugh Dalton had considerable fun at the expense of Winston Churchill, then Leader of the Opposition. Throwing Churchill's speech from 1909 in his face, he asked why he now opposed a reduction in the Lords' delaying power when, decades earlier, he had championed Lords reform. Dalton's bravado, however, masked Labour's own lack of a comprehensive vision of Lords reform: 'Reform of the House of Lords can wait, in our view. Many alternative possibilities may be suggested . . . Certainly the reform of a Second Chamber is not urgent . . . and [can be] considered when we have a little leisure on our hands after the next Election'.[101] Many elections have passed since then, but comprehensive Lords reform remains unrealised.

The fundamental problem remains that no party has delivered a compelling vision of the role that a reformed House of Lords should play in the UK's system of government, and identified the composition and powers which correspond to that role. With this in mind it is unsurprising that the Coalition Government, riven by disagreement over the proposals in the Draft House of Lords Reform Bill (with back-bench Conservative MPs fearing that the Liberal Democrats and the UKIP would use the reform to boost their parliamentary presence at the Conservatives' expense), ultimately abandoned plans for comprehensive Lords reform in the 2010–15 Parliament.[102] The 2017 Conservative Manifesto put the matter bluntly: 'comprehensive reform is not a priority'.[103] The unpalatable truth remains that an entirely elected House would have the legitimacy to challenge the Commons as a law-making chamber, but that if a reviewing and scrutinising function is all that is envisaged for a reformed Lords, a high level of electoral legitimacy is unnecessary. Governments are left with the unappealing option of a hybrid House, which seems little more than one more piecemeal step towards Lords reform, or of once again delaying the issue's resolution.

Practice questions

1. *'[I]f, as we believe, the second chamber should remain essentially a revising chamber and if, as we also believe, the primacy of the House of Commons is to be maintained, the argument that such a chamber can only be effective and have proper legitimacy if it is wholly or mainly elected is no more than an assertion.'*

   (Archbishops of Canterbury and York, *Written Evidence to the Joint Committee on the Draft House of Lords Reform Bill* (2012), para. 12)

   In light of this argument, does a legislative chamber have to derive its legitimacy from democratic election?

2. *'[T]here is a real possibility that we could drift into House of Lords reform becoming our parliamentary equivalent of "Waiting for Godot", as it never arrives and some have become rather doubtful whether it even exists, but we sit around talking about it year after year.'*

   (Robin Cook, MP, HC Debs, vol. 399, col. 152 (4 February 2003))

   Why has the issue of House of Lords reform proved to be so intractable?

---

[101] HC Debs, vol. 469, col. 1812 (14 November 1949).
[102] See Nick Clegg, MP, HC Debs, vol. 548, cols 35–6 (3 September 2012).
[103] Conservative Party, *Forward, Together* (2017) 43.

Further reading

This chapter follows on from the last chapter on the House of Commons, and further reading on these chapters should be considered together with the aim of understanding Parliament's role and whether its composition is suitable to that role. In understanding the current role and composition of the House of Lords, readers should focus upon the shape of the chamber after the 1999 reforms. Writing at the time of these reforms and the subsequent Wakeham Commission, Meg Russell and Richard Cornes (**M. Russell and R. Cornes, 'The Royal Commission on Reform of the House of Lords: a House for the Future?'** (2001) 64 *Modern Law Review* 82–99) provide a comprehensive analysis of the Commission's reform proposals, exposing their timidity and ultimately why they were not acted upon. Whilst this article is now over a decade old and some of its analysis regarding, for example, the role of the Law Lords in the upper chamber, has been over-taken by the enactment of the Constitutional Reform Act 2005, it nonetheless serves as a good start point from which to review Lords reform proposals. Meg Russell (**M. Russell, 'A Stronger Second Chamber? Assessing the Impact of House of Lords Reform in 1999 and the Lessons for Bicameralism'** (2010) 58 *Political Studies* 866–85) provides a consistently informed opinion on the work of the second chamber. This more recent article sets out to review the operation of the Lords in the first decade since the reforms of 1999 and finds considerable evidence to support assertions that the chamber is a more effective element of the UK's law-making system than the unreformed House. This article also proves a window into the different models which political scientists have constructed to assess the effectiveness of second chambers.

Sometimes the different models for Lords' reform can seem difficult to entangle. Gavin Phillipson (**Gavin Phillipson, '"The Greatest Quango of Them all", "a Rival Chamber" or "a Hybrid Nonsense"? Solving the Second Chamber Paradox'** [2004] *Public Law* 352–79), however, offers an article which helps readers to navigate this confusion and explains why different compositional proposals seem to cancel each other out. Phillipson's solution is particularly interesting, as he is one of the few commentators to consider a special role for the upper chamber with regard to legislation which potentially breaches human rights. As the title suggests, Alexandra Kelso's article (**A. Kelso, 'Reforming the House of Lords: Navigating Representation, Democracy and Legitimacy at Westminster'** (2006) 59 *Parliamentary Affairs* 563–81) focuses on the frequently misunderstood concepts which stand at the heart of the Lords' reform debate. Any successful reform will have to answer concerns such as whether the Lords should have a representative function, what requirements are imposed by a democratic law-making process and the degree of legitimacy required by a revising chamber. Once these theoretical underpinnings have been digested, Dawn Oliver's comment piece (**D. Oliver, 'The Parliament Acts, the Constitution, the Rule of Law, and the Second Chamber'** [2012] *Statute Law Review* 1–6): delivers a powerful retort to the most recent reform proposals, explaining why reform of the composition of the Lords, and particularly proposals for a largely elected chamber, cannot be considered in isolation from the constitutional role of the Lords as a revising chamber and its limited powers.

Chapter 11
The United Kingdom Supreme Court and the office of Lord Chancellor: towards an independent judicial branch?

'The [Constitutional Reform] Act recognises that the judiciary is a third branch of the constitution, separate from Parliament and the executive, and it acknowledges the vital importance of the separation of powers in buttressing the independence of the judiciary.'

V. Bogdanor, *The New British Constitution* (Hart Publishing, 2009) p. 84.

Chapter outline

This chapter examines the structural reforms to the apex of the judicial branch implemented as a result of the Constitutional Reform Act 2005. By reforming the office of Lord Chancellor and establishing a Supreme Court for the UK, the Constitutional Reform Act severed the structural link between the executive, legislature and the senior judiciary in the UK. As a result, the Act has arguably cemented the idea of the institutional independence of the judiciary and has shown the contemporary relevance of ideas associated with separation of powers in achieving and implementing constitutional renewal.

Introduction

The third branch of government in the UK Constitution is the judiciary. On the basis of statute and common law and constrained by the doctrine of precedent, the judiciary is tasked with the resolution of legal disputes and with hearing criminal prosecutions. As with much in the UK Constitution, the functions of the courts are in many ways 'a matter of inference rather than express provision'.[1] Nonetheless, it might reasonably be suggested that it is a part of the constitutional functions of the courts to vindicate the rule of law[2] and to operate as a counterweight to the elected branches of government.[3] For the reason that the courts neither command the public purse nor dictate the direction of governmental policy, the judiciary is regarded as being the 'least dangerous' branch of government.[4] It is increasingly undeniable, however, that the judiciary exercises significant power. As a result, it is of fundamental importance that, although the judges are not elected or easily removable from office, there exists public confidence in the judicial process. In order to support this notion, the independence of the judiciary – the suggestion that '[t]he judiciary must . . . be secure from undue influence and autonomous within its own field'[5] – has underpinned the constitutional role of the courts since the passing of the Act of Settlement in 1701.[6] The gradual acknowledgment that the judiciary plays a vital role in the resolution of politically contentious disputes concerning, *inter alia*, the executive exercise of discretionary powers and the application of human rights norms has, in turn, prompted an increased focus on those measures designed to reinforce the independence of the courts. This reflection on the adequacy of measures designed to insulate the higher judiciary from the controversies of the political process culminated – with the passing of the Constitutional Reform Act 2005 – in significant structural reforms at the apex of the UK's legal system.

Key issues

Judicial independence – while having long been regarded as a constitutional fundamental – has traditionally lacked an institutional dynamic. As a result, the constitutional protections it affords have promoted the independence of the individual judge rather than a sense that the judiciary is an independent third branch of government. The development of a sense that the judiciary form a distinct branch of government was also hampered by historical institutional links with the executive and legislature at the apex of the judicial system.

The apex of the United Kingdom judicial system prior to the Constitutional Reform Act 2005

While we have already seen that the idea of individual judicial independence can be seen to have a long history in common and statute law in the UK,[7] meaningful discussion of the structural, or institutional, independence of the judicial branch has only become

---

[1] Dame Mary Arden, 'Judicial Independence and Parliaments' in Ziegler *et al.* (eds), *Constitutionalism and the Role of Parliaments* (Hart Publishing, 2007) p. 192.

[2] See, for instance, *R v Horseferry Road Magistrates' Court, ex parte Bennett* [1994] 1 AC 42, 61–62; *R (Corner House Research) v Director of the Serious Fraud Office* [2008] EWHC 714 (Admin), at [59], [62], [96] and [170].

[3] See pp. 346–8.

[4] J. Madison, A. Hamilton and J. Jay, *The Federalist Papers,* (Penguin Classics, 1987), No. LXXVIII; A. Bickel, *The Least Dangerous Branch: The Supreme Court at the Bar of Politics* (Bobbs-Merrill, 1962); J. Steyn, 'The Weakest and Least Dangerous Department of Government' [1997] PL 84.

[5] S. A. de Smith and R. Brazier, *Constitutional and Administrative Law* (7th edn) (Penguin, 1994) p. 395.

[6] See pp. 244–6.

[7] See pp. 244–6.

possible in more recent times. Commentators and judges alike have stressed the lack of an *'institutional* concept of judicial independence'[8] in the UK, instead placing emphasis on constitutional protections enabling the judge to exercise independent judgment in the context of the individual case.[9] So while legal and conventional mechanisms existed for maintaining the independence of individual judges, the idea of the judiciary as a distinct branch of government has been less well developed.[10]

In part at least this can be attributed to lasting – but now historic – institutional links between the judicial, legislative and executive branches embodied in the office of Lord Chancellor and in the Appellate Committee of the House of Lords. These institutional links were largely severed as a result of the reforms enacted in the Constitutional Reform Act 2005. The Act reformed the office of Lord Chancellor, created a Supreme Court for the UK and established a Judicial Appointments Commission which deprived the executive branch of much discretion in the appointment of members of the senior judiciary. In short, the structural reforms implemented by the Constitutional Reform Act did much to confirm the status of the judicial branch as an institutionally distinct 'third branch' of the UK Government.[11]

The unreformed office of Lord Chancellor

As we have already seen, the office of Lord Chancellor – as it existed prior to the reforms implemented in the Constitutional Reform Act 2005 – straddled the three branches of government.[12] The Lord Chancellor was the head of the judiciary of England and Wales – a position that allowed holders of the office to sit as a judge – speaker of the House of Lords and a high-ranking Cabinet minister. As a result of these combined judicial, legislative and executive roles, the office had been referred to as 'the living refutation of the doctrine of separation of powers' in the UK's Constitution.[13] Yet in this, as in many other respects, the UK Constitution had shown itself to be more pragmatic than principled and, as a result, the blurring of institutional roles inherent in the unreformed office of Lord Chancellor had been tolerated. The fact that the UK Constitution has always valued the independence of the judiciary above separation of powers more broadly construed made this particular institutional arrangement easier to defend. The Lord Chancellor was argued to be uniquely positioned to defend the judges and judicial independence as a result of his role as a Cabinet minister, forming a 'necessary link between Parliament and the executive on the one hand and the judges on the other'.[14] He (no woman had ever been appointed to the post) was said to be detached from the immediate pressures of party politics as a result of sitting in

---

[8] R. Stevens, *The English Judges: Their Role in the Changing Constitution* (Hart Publishing, 2005) p. 96. See also R. Stevens, 'A Loss of Innocence?: Judicial Independence and the Separation of Powers' (1999) OJLS 366; D. Woodhouse, 'Judicial Independence and Accountability in the UK' in G. Canivet, M. Andenas and D. Fairgrieve, *Indepdendence, Accountability and the Judiciary* (British Institute of International and Comparative Law, 2006) p. 122.

[9] HL Debs, 5 June 1996, col. 1308 (Lord Mackay of Clashfern).

[10] R. Stevens, *The English Judges: Their Role in the Changing Constitution* (Hart Publishing, 2005) p. 96.

[11] V. Bogdanor, *The New British Constitution* (Hart Publishing, 2009) p. 84.

[12] See p. 240.

[13] T. C. Hartley and J. A. G. Griffith, *Government and Law* (2nd edn) (Weideneld and Nicolson, 1981) p. 179.

[14] Lord Mackay, 'The Lord Chancellor in the 1990s' (1991) 44 *Current Legal Problems* 241, 250.

the House of Lords, rather than the House of Commons, and as a result of having taken the judicial oath (yet was at the same time bound by the convention of collective responsibility). That potential conflicts of interest might arise if the Lord Chancellor actually sat as a judge was also tolerated due to the relative lack of frequency with which it actually happened,[15] and the undertaking that the Lord Chancellor would not sit in any case 'where the interests of the executive were directly engaged'.[16] As Dawn Oliver has noted, these unique arrangements 'more or less worked'.[17]

Thinking Point . . .

Lord Woolf, then Master of the Rolls, appeared to offer support for the tripartite role of the Lord Chancellor, stating in a lecture originally published in 1997 that 'the Lord Chancellor of the day could . . . act as a safety valve avoiding undue tension between the judiciary and the government and possibly between the judiciary and Parliament as well' (Lord Woolf, 'Judicial Review – the Tensions between the Executive and the Judiciary' (1998) 114 LQR 579).

Yet, prior to the Constitutional Reform Act 2005 the pressure for reform had begun to mount. Lord Irvine – Lord Chancellor under Tony Blair and last holder of the office prior to its reform – had been a more overtly party-political Lord Chancellor then his immediate predecessors; Diana Woodhouse has commented that he was '[w]ithout doubt the Lord Chancellor who has exerted the greatest political influence in modern times'.[18] Irvine played a crucial role in piloting many of the significant constitutional reforms of the first Blair administration through Parliament, and influenced wider government policy through his involvement in a number of Cabinet Committees; such were the ministerial responsibilities of the holder of the office of Lord Chancellor that the holder of the position had become a 'pivotal figure in several aspects of public life extending beyond the law and the administration of justice'.[19] Irvine himself was also in many respects a controversial political figure, who drew – and perhaps even encouraged – unfortunate comparisons to Henry VIII's ambitious and influential Lord Chancellor, Cardinal Wolsey.[20] As the political role of the Lord Chancellor grew, the currency of continued claims that the holder of the office might effectively defend and promote judicial independence diminished in equal measure. In turn, those curious aspects of the Lord Chancellorship that had been tolerated despite their apparent defiance of constitutional principle began to be questioned more openly.[21]

---

[15] T. Bingham, 'The Old Order Changeth' (2006) 122 LQR 211, 216.

[16] HL Debs, 23 February 2000, col. WA33.

[17] D. Oliver, 'The Lord Chancellor as Head of the Judiciary' in L. Blom-Cooper, B. Dickson and G. Drewry (eds), The Judicial House of Lords 1876–2009 (OUP, 2009) p. 97.

[18] D. Woodhouse, *The Office of Lord Chancellor* (Hart Publishing, 2001) p. 80.

[19] Lord Windlesham, 'The Constitutional Reform Act 2005: Ministers, Judges and Constitutional Change: Part 1' [2005] PL806, 808.

[20] 'Where were Derry's brains when he needed them?', *Guardian*, 22 February 2001; 'Lord Irvine: The new Wolsey', *Telegraph*, 12 June 2003. On Cardinal Wolsey, see D. Starkey, *The Reign of Henry VIII: Personalities and Politics* (Vintage, 1985) chs 3 and 4.

[21] For an excellent account, see D. Woodhouse, *The Office of Lord Chancellor* (Hart Publishing, 2001).

> ## Thinking Point . . .
>
> Despite undertaking not to sit as a judge in cases where the executive had a direct interest in the outcome of the dispute, Lord Irvine nonetheless sat in two cases in which the wider interests of the executive might reasonably be said to have been engaged: *DPP* v *Jones* [1999] 2 AC 240 and *Boddington* v *British Transport Police* [1999] 2 AC 143 (both cases concerned criminal prosecutions).

The Appellate Committee of the House of Lords

> ## Thinking Point . . .
>
> The Appellate Jurisdiction Act 1876, section 6 (now repealed by the Constitutional Reform Act 2005), provided that: 'Every Lord of Appeal in Ordinary. . . shall by virtue and according to the date of his appointment be entitled during his life to rank as a Baron by such style as Her Majesty may be pleased to appoint, and shall. . . be entitled to a writ and summons to attend, and to sit and vote in the House of Lords. . . '

While the position of the Law Lords within Parliament was perhaps less controversial, similar arguments of principle applied as a result of the ability of the members of the country's highest court to discharge their judicial functions from within the legislature, and to participate in the legislative business of the House of Lords while so doing. Since the appellate functions of the House of Lords had been regulated by the Appellate Jurisdiction Act 1876, the Lords of Appeal in Ordinary had received the same writ of summons to the House of Lords as any other member. As a result, the position of the Law Lords could be argued to contravene the separation of the judicial and legislative branches. As with the office of Lord Chancellor, the overlap between judicial and legislative power was defended on the basis of efficiency and effectiveness; the Law Lords, it was said, took benefit from their direct exposure to the concerns of politicians and the practicalities of the legislative process, while Parliament derived benefit from the legal expertise of the Lords of Appeal in Ordinary. The 'extensive judicial experience' of the Law Lords, and 'their understanding of how law works in practice',[22] could be brought to legislative debates while the judges themselves were said to derive benefit from 'a greater understanding of the problems of the legislator, of social trends, of the proper limits of judicial innovation'.[23] The consequences for the separation of powers of this particular institutional overlap were therefore downplayed by some commentators, none perhaps more forcibly than the former Law Lord, Lord Lloyd of Berwick: 'it is sometimes said that for the Law

---

[22] Royal Commission on Reform of the House of Lords, *A House for the Future*, Cm. 4534 (January 2000), Ch. 9, [9.6]. On which see Lord Hope, 'Voices from the Past – the Law Lords' Contribution to the Legislative Process' (2007) 123 LQR 547; Lord Hope, 'The Law Lords in Parliament' in L. Blom-Cooper, B. Dickson and G. Drewry (eds), *The Judicial House of Lords 1876–2009* (OUP, 2009); P. O'Brien, 'Judges and Politics: The Parliamentary Contributions of the Law Lords 1876–2009' (2016) 79 MLR 786.

[23] Royal Commission on Reform of the House of Lords, *A House for the Future*, Cm. 4534 (2000), Evidence of Lord Wilberforce.

Lords to sit in the Upper House is contrary to the theory of the separation of powers. I regard that as a nonsense argument'.[24]

The contributions made by the Law Lords to the legislative process were nonetheless limited in practice by convention. As Lord Bingham, then Senior Law Lord, outlined in 2000 in response to a recommendation made by the Wakeham Commission on Reform of the House of Lords:[25]

> . . . the Lords of Appeal in Ordinary do not think it appropriate to engage in matters where there is a strong element of party political controversy; and. . . the Lords of Appeal in Ordinary bear in mind that they may render themselves ineligible to sit judicially if they were to express an opinion on a matter which might later be relevant to an appeal to the House.[26]

However, in spite of this conventional restraint, the dual role of the Law Lords was also seen to cause difficulties in practice. Woodhouse has recounted the confusion over the boundary between the Law Lords' legislative and judicial roles which became apparent during the *Pepper* v *Hart* appeal as, 'several of the Law Lords hearing the case, including Lord Mackay, had expressed strong feelings for or against the principle [that *Hansard* could be used as a tool of statutory interpretation where the intention of Parliament is unclear] in a debate in Parliament two years previously.'[27] In the *Fire Brigades Union* case,[28] Stevens notes, constituting a bench for the purposes of hearing the appeal proved problematic, 'since so many Law Lords had already spoken out, legislatively, against the proposals'[29] which were at the heart of that dispute. And following the *Pinochet* case – in which the House of Lords had to rehear one of its own decisions as a result of Lord Hoffmann's links to one of the parties to the case – Hoffmann was required to stand down from the libel proceedings involving Albert Reynolds,[30] the former Irish Taoiseach, and David Lange,[31] formerly Prime Minister of New Zealand, after counsel raised concerns about his prior (legislative) involvement in the passage of the Defamation Act 1996.[32]

---

[24] Lord Lloyd of Berwick, HL Debs, 21 January 2003, col. 615. For defences of the position of the Lords of Appeal in Ordinary, see Lord Cooke of Thorndon, 'The Law Lords: an Endangered Heritage' (2003) 119 LQR 49; Royal Commission on Reform of the House of Lords, *A House for the Future*, Cm. 4534 (2000), Evidence of Lord Wilberforce; HL Debs, 21 January 2003, col. 615, *per* Lord Lloyd of Berwick. For criticisms, see Lord Bingham of Cornhill, *A New Supreme Court for the United Kingdom* (Constitution Unit, 2002); Lord Steyn, 'The Case for a Supreme Court' (2002) 118 LQR 382.

[25] Royal Commission on Reform of the House of Lords, *A House for the Future*, Cm. 4534 (January 2000), recommendation 59. The full text of recommendation 59 is as follows: 'The Lords of Appeal should set out in writing and publish a statement of the principles which they intend to observe when participating in debates and votes in the second chamber and when considering their eligibility to sit on related cases.'

[26] HL Debs, cols 419–20, 22 June 2000. See also Judiciary of England and Wales, *Guide to Judicial Conduct* (2016), esp. [3.1]–[3.14], available at: https://www.judiciary.gov.uk/wp-content/uploads/2010/02/guidance-judicial-conduct-v2016-update.pdf.

[27] D. Woodhouse, 'The Office of Lord Chancellor: Time to Abandon the Judicial Role – the Rest will Follow' (2002) 22(1) LS 128, 138.

[28] *R* v *Secretary of State for the Home Department, ex parte Fire Brigades Union* [1995] 2 AC 513.

[29] R. Stevens, 'A Loss of Innocence?: Judicial Independence and the Separation of Powers' (1999) 19 OJLS 365, 399.

[30] *Reynolds* v *Times Newspapers* [2001] 2 AC 127.

[31] *Lange* v *Atkinson (No. 1)*, 28 October 1999, Privy Council (unreported).

[32] 'Pinochet Law Lord Replaced Again as Judge', *Guardian*, 8 July 1999.

The pressure for institutional reform of the judiciary

Key issues

- The domestic constitutional protections for judicial independence were bolstered by the implementation of the Human Rights Act 1998 which – as a result of Art. 6(1) of the European Convention on Human Rights – provided that legal disputes be resolved by an 'independent and impartial tribunal'.

- The Convention case law provided that an objectively-assessed appearance of judicial partiality would be sufficient to breach Art. 6(1), and that such an apprehension might arise out of structural links between the judiciary and executive or out of the ability of a judge to adjudicate over a dispute relating to matters with which he or she had previously been involved in a legislative capacity.

The implementation of the Human Rights Act 1998 brought with it the suggestion that the office of Lord Chancellor, and the Appellate Committee of the House of Lords, might have to be reformed in order to comply with the requirements of Art. 6(1) of the European Convention on Human Rights.[33] The Human Rights Act brought certain of the Convention rights into effect in domestic law, making those rights for the first time legally enforceable against public authorities in domestic courts.[34] For the purposes of present discussion, it is Art. 6(1) – the right to a fair trial – that is material. The text of Art. 6(1) of the Convention begins with the words:

> In the determination of his civil rights and responsibilities or of any criminal charge against him, everyone is entitled to a fair and public hearing within a reasonable time by an *independent and impartial tribunal* established by law.

Now, as we have already seen, wide-ranging protections for judicial independence do exist in the UK Constitution. The Act of Settlement, the Supreme Court Act 1981, various conventions and a range of decisions at common law all provide various protections for the independence of individual judicial proceedings.[35] Upon the implementation of the Human Rights Act, however, the suggestion was made that the more exacting standard of 'independence and impartiality' contained within Art. 6(1) would not be quite so tolerant of the institutional overlaps that existed between judicial and other governmental functions most evident in the office of Lord Chancellor and in the position of the Law Lords as a committee of the upper house of Parliament.[36]

The tests for 'independence' and 'impartiality' are closely linked in the case law of the Strasbourg court.[37] In *Findlay* v *United Kingdom*, the European Court of Human Rights outlined the requirements of independence and impartiality in the following terms:

> In order to establish whether a tribunal can be considered as 'independent', regard must be had inter alia to the manner of appointment of its members and their term of office, the existence of

---

[33] See, for example, R. Cornes, '*McGonnell* v *United Kingdom*, the Lord Chancellor and the Law Lords' [2000] PL 166.

[34] See Chapter 21.

[35] See pp. 244–6.

[36] See R. Cornes, '*McGonnell* v *United Kingdom*, the Lord Chancellor and the Law Lords' [2000] PL 166.

[37] *Findlay* v *United Kingdom* (1997) 24 EHRR 221, [73].

guarantees against outside pressures and the question whether the body presents an appearance of independence.

As to the question of 'impartiality', there are two aspects to this requirement. First, the tribunal must be subjectively free of personal prejudice or bias. Secondly, it must also be impartial from an objective viewpoint, that is, it must offer sufficient guarantees to exclude any legitimate doubt in this respect.[38]

Article 6(1) also requires that the court or tribunal be independent of the parties to the case and also of the *executive*[39] (given this requirement of Art. 6(1), and given also that the UK has been bound to adhere to the terms of the European Convention on Human Rights since 1953, it is perhaps miraculous that the office of Lord Chancellor managed to survive, unscathed, until the early twenty-first century). In order to assess whether a court is independent and impartial in practice, the court will therefore look to see what practical measures can be said to uphold the independence of the court: whether the judges have security of tenure, whether legal mechanisms protect the judicial process from external influences and so on.

But of *equal* importance is the question of whether the objective observer would apprehend a risk of bias arising out of the structure, composition, or functions of the court. It was as a result of questions relating to objectively assessed impartiality – could a court containing a member of the executive be regarded as independent of government? Could a court comprised of personnel who may have already expressed views on the merits (or otherwise) of the legislation they are being asked to apply appear impartial? – that the position of the Lord Chancellor and of the Law Lords appeared to be most under threat. The case of *McGonnell* v *United Kingdom* signalled the beginning of the end for the unreformed office of Lord Chancellor, and the position of the Law Lords within Parliament.

Insight

From packing shed to Supreme Court: *McGonnell* v *United Kingdom*

As with many cases of constitutional importance, *McGonnell* v *United Kingdom*[40] arose out of seemingly innocuous facts. McGonnell owned property in Guernsey, and applied for planning permission to convert a building that had been used as a packing shed into a house. The application was refused, following a hearing at which an official known as the Bailiff of Guernsey had presided. The position of Bailiff was – conveniently – not unlike the unreformed office of Lord Chancellor, with the holder being able to concurrently exercise both legislative and judicial functions.

In McGonnell's case, it transpired that the Bailiff had not only presided over the hearing at which McGonnell's application had been declined, but had also previously – in his legislative capacity – presided over the process by which the relevant planning legislation was passed through the island's legislature. The Bailiff, therefore, had acted as legislator, and subsequently as judge in respect of the design and application of the same set of rules.

The ground on which McGonnell complained to the European Court of Human Rights was that in sitting as a judge – after playing a role in the implementation of the rules under which

---

[38] *Findlay* v *United Kingdom* (1997) 24 EHRR 221, [73].

[39] See e.g. *Ringeisen* v *Austria* (1979–80) 1 EHRR 455, [95]; *De Wilde, Ooms and Versyp* v *Belgium (No. 1)* (1979–80) 1 EHRR 373, [78].

[40] *McGonnell* v *United Kingdom* (2000) 30 EHRR 289.

the case was to be decided – the Bailiff would give rise to an objectively assessed perception of bias, and, therefore, could not be regarded as being impartial for the purposes of Art. 6(1). The European Court found that, while Art. 6(1) did not require a strict, or pure, separation of judicial functions from those of the legislature,[41] circumstances may arise in which the ability of one person to exercise both legislative and judicial functions could give rise to perceptions of partiality. The court outlined that:

> . . . any direct involvement in the passage of legislation, or of executive rules, is likely to be sufficient to cast doubt on the judicial impartiality of a person subsequently called to determine a dispute over whether reasons exist to permit a variation from the wording of the legislation or rules at issue.[42]

As a result, the European Court found that Art. 6(1) had been breached, and McGonnell denied the right to a fair trial by an independent and impartial tribunal to which he was entitled. The findings of the European Court of Human Rights in **McGonnell** are broadly consistent with those of its earlier decision in *Procola* v *Luxembourg*.[43] In that case, the court made clear that the actual views of the persons exercising legislative and subsequent judicial functions will be irrelevant:

> . . . the mere fact that certain persons successively performed these two types of function in respect of the same decisions is capable of casting doubt on the institution's structural impartiality.[44]

The approach of the European Court of Human Rights to questions of judicial independence and impartiality is therefore much more structured, and more exacting, than domestic protections for judicial independence had traditionally been, and places a much greater emphasis on judicial independence and impartiality being *visibly* demonstrable. Perceived bias, in the view of the Strasbourg institutions, is as damaging to the ideal of judicial independence and impartiality as actual partiality, and judicial functions, when preceded by legislative activities undertaken by the same personnel in respect of the same, or similar, decisions, will give rise to a perception of bias sufficiently serious to violate Art. 6(1).

It did not take long for the influence of **McGonnell** to be felt in domestic law. Following the enactment of the Human Rights Act 1998 the influence of Art. 6(1) on the position of the judicial branch was demonstrated virtually immediately following a challenge to the appointment procedures for temporary sheriffs in Scotland. In the decision in *Starrs* v *Ruxton*, Lord Reed's explanation of the influence of the Convention on the procedures for protecting the independence of the judiciary is worth repeating in full:

> Conceptions of constitutional principle such as the independence of the judiciary, and of how these principles should be given effect in practice, change over time. Although the principle of judicial independence has found expression in similar language in Scotland and England since at least the late seventeenth century, conceptions of what it requires in substance – of what is necessary, or desirable or feasible – have changed greatly since that time. What was regarded as acceptable even as recently as 1971 may no longer be regarded as acceptable. The effect given to the European Convention by the Scotland Act and the Human Rights Act in particular represents,

---

[41] *McGonnell* v *United Kingdom* (2000) 30 EHRR 289, [51]: ' . . . neither Article 6 nor any other provision of the Convention requires States to comply with any theoretical constitutional concepts as such. The question is always whether, in a given case, the requirements of the Convention are met.'

[42] *McGonnell* v *United Kingdom* (2000) 30 EHRR 289, [55].

[43] *Procola* v *Luxembourg* (1996) 22 EHRR 193.

[44] Ibid., [45].

to my mind, a very important shift in thinking about the constitution. It is fundamental to that shift that human rights are no longer solely dependent on conventions, by which I mean values, customs and practices of the constitution which are not legally enforceable. Although the Convention protects rights which reflect democratic values and underpin democratic institutions, the Convention guarantees the protection of those rights through legal processes, rather than political processes. It is for that reason that Art. 6 guarantees access to independent courts. It would be inconsistent with the whole approach of the Convention if the independence of the courts itself rested upon convention rather than law.[45]

The significant difficulty highlighted by this finding, and of course those of the European Court of Human Rights in *McGonnell* and *Procola* among other cases, was that the notion of judicial independence at the apex of the domestic judicial structure was heavily reliant on both convention and understanding. The two most prominent structural infringements of the separation of judicial power from that of the executive and legislature – the office of Lord Chancellor and the position of the Lords of Appeal in Ordinary as a Committee of the House of Lords – relied on the operation of 'imprecise rules' rather than 'constitutional enactments' to ensure that judicial independence was not compromised through exposure to the day-to-day processes and pressures of executive and legislative politics.[46] Neither withstood the pressure exerted by Art. 6 for very long.

The Constitutional Reform Act 2005

Key issues

The enactment and coming into force of the Constitutional Reform Act 2005 saw the removal of the Lord Chancellor's judicial role, and the severing of institutional links between the UK's apex court and legislature. Alongside the creation of the UK Supreme Court, the Act prompted the creation of an independent Judicial Appointments Commission in order to reduce the degree of executive control over judicial appointments processes.

The reforms that were eventually enacted in the Constitutional Reform Act 2005 were initially announced by the Labour government, on the back of a Cabinet reshuffle, in June 2003, with the announcement made that the office of Lord Chancellor was to be abolished, a Supreme Court created and a Judicial Appointments Commission set up. The constitutional significance of the proposed reforms however appeared to be lost on the government, which was widely criticised for attempting significant amendment to the apex of the judicial structure with little or no prior consultation. A hastily arranged consultation process followed,[47] followed by a protracted parliamentary passage of the Constitutional Reform Bill.[48]

---

[45] *Starrs* v *Ruxton* 2000 JC 208, 250 (Lord Reed).

[46] D. Woodhouse, *The Office of Lord Chancellor* (Hart Publishing, 2001) p. 130.

[47] Department for Constitutional Affairs, *A New Way of Appointing Judges* (CP 10/03, July 2003); Department for Constitutional Affairs, *A Supreme Court for the United Kingdom* (CP 11/03, July 2003); Department for Constitutional Affairs, *Reforming the Office of Lord Chancellor* (CP 13/03, September 2003).

[48] For detailed accounts of the process, see Lord Windlesham, 'The Constitutional Reform Act 2005: Ministers, Judges and Constitutional Change: Part 1' [2005] PL 806; Lord Windlesham, 'The Constitutional Reform Act 2005: The Politics of Constitutional Reform: Part 2' [2006] PL 35; A. Le Sueur, 'From Appellate Committee to Supreme Court: A Narrative' in L. Blom-Cooper, B. Dickson and G. Drewry (eds), The Judicial House of Lords 1876–2009 (OUP, 2009).

The reformed office of Lord Chancellor

The Constitutional Reform Act saw the end of the Lord Chancellor's tripartite role as Cabinet minister, head of the judiciary in England and Wales and speaker of the House of Lords. While the government was persuaded of the necessity to retain the office itself, the reformed office of Lord Chancellor retains only the first of those three roles, with the Lord Chief Justice now head of the judiciary in England and Wales,[49] and the House of Lords now able to elect its own Lord Speaker.[50] The Lord Chancellor is no longer able to sit as a judge and – as a result – the Act stipulates that the holder of the post be 'qualified by experience'[51] rather than have prior legal knowledge or experience. Indeed, four of the most recent holders of the office – Chris Grayling MP (2012–15); Michael Gove MP (2015–16), Liz Truss MP (2016–17) and David Lidington MP (2017–18) – have not been lawyers by training.[52] As a result, the reformed position of Lord Chancellor is 'a conventional ministerial office'.[53] Even as a Cabinet Minister, however, the reformed office of Lord Chancellor has been shorn of a number of the responsibilities which had prompted calls for the abolition (or reform) of the office. The Lord Chief Justice became responsible for the administration of justice, judicial training and discipline and for representing the views of the judiciary to Parliament and to the Lord Chancellor,[54] while the powers of the Lord Chancellor in respect of judicial appointments have been severely limited.[55]

The Lord Chancellor remains responsible for upholding the independence of the judiciary.[56] Nowhere is the centrality of judicial independence to the new settlement more evident than in the specific direction in s. 3(1) of the Constitutional Reform Act that '[t]he Lord Chancellor, other Ministers of the Crown and all with responsibility for matters relating to the judiciary or otherwise to the administration of justice must uphold the continued independence of the judiciary'.[57] This provision in favour of the institutional independence of courts is buttressed by a supplementary provision in support of the individual independence of the judicial process – s. 3(5) provides: '[t]he Lord Chancellor and other Ministers of the Crown must not seek to influence *particular judicial decisions* through any special access to the judiciary'.[58] In discharging the functions of the office of Lord Chancellor, the holder is also given statutory directions to 'have regard to':

(a) the need to defend [judicial] independence;

(b) the need for the judiciary to have the support necessary to enable them to exercise their functions;

(c) the need for the public interest in regard to matters relating to the judiciary or otherwise to the administration of justice to be properly represented in decisions affecting those matters.[59]

---

[49] Section 7 CRA 2005.
[50] Section 18 and sch. 6 CRA 2005.
[51] Section 2(1) CRA 2005.
[52] For reflections on this point see: House of Lords Select Committee on the Constitution, *The Office of Lord Chancellor* (HL75), December 2014, [105]–[113].
[53] G. Gee, 'What are Lord Chancellors for?' [2014] PL 11, 14.
[54] Section 7(2) CRA 2005.
[55] See pp. 353–4.
[56] See, for instance, the Lord Chancellor's oath, s. 17 CRA 2005.
[57] Section 4 CRA 2005 makes similar provision in respect of Northern Ireland.
[58] Emphasis added.
[59] Section 3(6) CRA 2005.

The Lord Chancellorship is now essentially an executive position – albeit one with a specific responsibility for judicial affairs – and has been stripped of the judicial functions which made the office so difficult to defend on separation of powers grounds. The fact that the occupants of the reformed position have – since 2007 – each simultaneously held the 'more political'[60] position of Secretary of State for Justice has ensured that the role remains prominent within government and relevant to the administration of justice. The latter position adds Cabinet responsibility for prisons and the probation service, criminal law, sentencing policy, human rights policy and data protection and freedom of information to the postholders' responsibilities in relation to the administration of courts and legal services.[61] The Lord Chancellor and Secretary of State for Justice is therefore the head of a sizeable department that is 'subject to the same public management regime of accountability, efficiency and value for money as any other government department'.[62] These considerations have almost certainly brought into perspective tensions in the role that were not so evident prior to the implementation of the 2005 reforms.[63] While the House of Lords Select Committee on the Constitution has recognised the 'additional authority' wielded by the role of Lord Chancellor as effective head of a 'significant department of state' it has also cautioned that the new dual role of the office holder might precipitate 'a conflict of interests at the heart of the Ministry of Justice'.[64] In order to secure the longevity of the reformed position of Lord Chancellor current and future holders of the office will need to reassure that the tensions between financial efficiency and the effective and independent administration of justice can be reconciled with the 'political character of the new-style office'.[65]

Thinking Point . . .

The aftermath of the High Court decision in *R (Miller)* v *Secretary of State for Exiting the European Union* [2016] EWHC 2768 (Admin) – provided a litmus test of the Lord Chancellor's duty under s. 3(1) of the Constitutional Reform Act 2005 to 'uphold the continued independence of the judiciary'. Following a series of press reports which had, *inter alia*, branded the judges 'enemies of the people' (*Daily Mail*[66]), accused the court of 'frustrating the will of the people' (*Telegraph*[67]), and erroneously claimed that the court had 'blocked Brexit' (*The Express*[68]), the Lord Chancellor (then Liz Truss MP) was called upon – by the Bar Council, among others – to publicly support the independence of the judiciary. The response which came from Truss, simply stated that '[t]he independence of the judiciary is the foundation upon which our rule

---

[60] House of Lords Select Committee on the Constitution, *The Office of Lord Chancellor* (HL75), December 2014, [60].

[61] Ibid., [13].

[62] G. Gee, 'What are Lord Chancellors for?' [2014] PL 11, 18.

[63] See generally: 'Law in a time of austerity', *The Economist*, 27 February 2016. For coverage of the impact of efficiency and cost-saving measures on judicial review see: A. Mills, 'Reforms to judicial review in the Criminal Justice and Courts Act 2015: promoting efficiency or weakening the rule of law?' [2015] PL 583.

[64] House of Lords Select Committee on the Constitution, *The Office of Lord Chancellor* (HL75), December 2014, [133].

[65] G. Gee, 'What are Lord Chancellors for?' [2014] PL 11, 26.

[66] 'Enemies of the People', *Daily Mail*, 3 November 2016.

[67] 'The judges versus the people', *The Daily Telegraph*, 3 November 2016.

[68] 'Who are the three High Court judges who blocked Brexit?' *Daily Express*, 3 November 2016.

of law is built and our judiciary is rightly respected the world over for its independence and impartiality'. As it failed to address responses to the *Miller* decision explicitly the statement was, in turn, criticised for both its timidity and tardiness. Following the conclusion of the *Miller* litigation, in an appearance before the House of Lords Select Committee on the Constitution (22 March 2017), Lord Thomas LCJ – one of the three judges who had sat in *Miller* in the High Court – criticised Truss for failing to understand the difference between abuse and criticism, and for misunderstanding her constitutional duty to uphold judicial independence. Truss was replaced as Lord Chancellor following the 2017 general election.

The United Kingdom Supreme Court

The UK Supreme Court began hearing cases in October 2009. In many respects, the new court bears remarkable similarities to its predecessor, the Appellate Committee of the House of Lords, in terms of both its composition and jurisdiction. As regards the former, many of the Constitutional Reform Act's reforms are of terminology rather than substance. The judges who sit on the Supreme Court are now known as Justices of the Supreme Court, rather than as Lords of Appeal in Ordinary.[69] The court is comprised of 12 Justices[70] who generally sit in panels of five, though occasionally (and perhaps increasingly) – in cases of particular importance[71] – in panels of seven or nine, much as the Appellate Committee used to. Eleven of the Justices who were the first judges on the Supreme Court were previously Lords of Appeal in Ordinary in the Appellate Committee of the House of Lords.[72] Whereas the Appellate Committee had a Senior Law Lord and Second Senior Law Lord, the Supreme Court now has a President and Deputy President. The crucial difference between the two courts is of course that Justices of the Supreme Court are, during their judicial tenure, disqualified from sitting in Parliament.[73]

In terms of the court's jurisdiction, again, much remains the same.[74] While the new court is 'supreme' in name, this should not be taken to suggest that the concept of parliamentary sovereignty has been undermined by its creation; the Supreme Court does not have the power to invalidate statutes.[75] The Supreme Court therefore is the highest court of appeal in both civil and criminal matters for England and Wales, and for Northern Ireland, and will continue to only hear civil appeals from Scotland.[76] In the one significant addition to the jurisdiction of the UK's highest court, the Supreme Court will have responsibility for adjudication over 'devolution issues' arising under the Scotland Act 1998,

---

[69] Section 23(6) CRA 2005.

[70] Section 23(2) CRA 2005.

[71] A larger panel may be convened in the following circumstances: if the court is being asked to depart, or may depart from, a previous decision; if the case is one of 'high constitutional importance'; if the case is of 'great public importance'; if the case rests upon the reconciliation of 'conflict between decisions in the House of Lords, Judicial Committee of the Privy Council and/or Supreme Court'; or if the case raises an important point relating to the European Convention on Human Rights (see: https://www.supremecourt.uk/procedures/panel-numbers-criteria.html).

[72] Section 24(a) CRA 2005.

[73] Section 137 CRA 2005.

[74] Section 40 CRA 2005.

[75] Though for an assessment of the increasing 'constitutional' functions of the Supreme Court see: R. Masterman and J. E. K. Murkens, 'Skirting Supremacy and Subservience: The Constitutional Authority of the United Kingdom Supreme Court' [2013] PL 800.

[76] The highest court of appeal in matters of Scots criminal law is the High Court of Justiciary in Edinburgh.

Government of Wales Acts and Northern Ireland Act 1998.[77] When the devolution legislation was being debated prior to its enactment, it was felt that it would be inappropriate for the Appellate Committee of the House of Lords to have power to adjudicate over disputes concerning the devolved bodies and application and interpretation of Acts of the Westminster Parliament. As a result, the Judicial Committee of the Privy Council – which did not have the same institutional links to the UK Parliament – was initially chosen as the appropriate court. Other, more novel, jurisdictional developments were rejected at the outset of the consultation process,[78] with Le Sueur commenting that:

> . . . [i]n devising the new court, the government. . . rejected almost every innovation that could have been introduced: in terms of its personnel, jurisdiction, and powers, the UK Supreme Court will closely replicate its predecessor.[79]

The most significant difference between the Appellate Committee of the House of Lords and its successor court, is in terms of its location. Whereas the Appellate Committee was housed within the Houses of Parliament, the Supreme Court is housed in the Middlesex Guildhall on the opposite side of Parliament Square. As a result, the institutional link between legislature and judiciary has been severed and significant progress towards a structurally separate judicial branch made. The establishment of the Supreme Court therefore marks a significant strengthening of the separation of powers in the UK, especially as that concept extends to the structural independence of the higher judiciary. As Lord Phillips of Worth Matravers, the Supreme Court's first President, noted upon the opening of the new institution:

> For the first time, we have a clear separation of powers between the legislature, the judiciary and the executive in the United Kingdom. This is important. It emphasises the independence of the judiciary, clearly separating those who make the law, from those who administer it.[80]

The Judicial Appointments Commission

Prior to the enactment of the Constitutional Reform Act 2005 the powers of the Lord Chancellor in respect of judicial appointments were extensive. The Lord Chancellor advised the Prime Minister (who in turn advised the Queen) in respect of appointments to the following positions: Lord Chief Justice, Master of the Rolls, President of Family Division of the High Court, Vice Chancellor (Head of the Chancery Division of the High Court), Lords of Appeal in Ordinary and Lords Justices of Appeal. The Lord Chancellor also had a personal power of appointment to the High Court. Criticisms of the selection process – which was perceived to be closed, secretive and entrusting of too much power to one individual – had been widespread.[81]

---

[77] Section 40(4)(b) and sch. 9 CRA 2005. On which, see M. Walters and P. Craig, 'The Courts, Devolution and Judicial Review' [1999] PL 274, 371–8.

[78] Department for Constitutional Affairs, *A Supreme Court for the United Kingdom* (CP 11/03, July 2003), [23].

[79] A. Le Sueur, 'Judicial power in the Changing Constitution' in J. Jowell and D. Oliver (eds), *The Changing Constitution* (5ᵗʰ edn) (OUP, 2004) p. 331.

[80] Press Notice 01/09, 'Supreme Court of the United Kingdom comes into existence' (1 October 2009), available at: https://www.supremecourt.uk/docs/pr_0109__2_.pdf.

[81] D. Woodhouse, *The Office of Lord Chancellor* (Hart Publishing, 2001) Ch. 6.

The 2005 Act established a Judicial Appointments Commission which is comprised of 15 members, including five judges, representatives from the legal profession and a number of lay members. The Commission has taken on responsibility for the selection of candidates for each of the senior judicial positions named above. While the Lord Chancellor formally remains responsible for recommending a candidate to the Queen for appointment, in practice the discretion available to the holder of that position – and the personal influence able to be exercised in the appointment of judges – has been severely curtailed.[82]

Thinking Point . . .

Appointments to the UK Supreme Court are governed by ss. 25–31 of the Constitutional Reform Act 2005. Given the role of the court as the final court of appeal for the UK, the selection panel is required to consult representatives of the devolved administrations prior to recommending a candidate.

Upon a judicial vacancy arising, the Judicial Appointments Commission undertakes a process of selection.[83] The ground on which the Commission bases its decisions is 'merit'[84], though the Commission must also 'have regard to the need to encourage diversity in the range of persons available for selection for appointments'.[85] Following selection of a candidate by the Commission, the Lord Chancellor must then decide whether to accept the selection, reject it, or to ask the Commission to reconsider the selection of the candidate. Should the Lord Chancellor either reject the selection, or require reconsideration, then – following a subsequent selection process – the Lord Chancellor's options are limited; he or she may accept the selection, but can only reject the candidate if he did not reject the initial candidate, and may only require reconsideration if he did not require reconsideration in the first instance. If the Lord Chancellor rejects the candidate, or requires reconsideration, after a second selection process, then he or she must accept the candidate proposed after a third and final selection. If the Lord Chancellor requires reconsideration at any stage, it is open to the Appointments Commission to put forward the same candidate, following reconsideration. The rejection option is essentially one of absolute veto, and the rejected candidate may not be put forward again in the same appointments process. So while the Lord Chancellor would continue to play a crucial role in the appointments process, an early prediction was that the extent of the Lord Chancellor's individual discretion would be so limited that 'it seems in practice to be almost inevitable that he will accept the Judicial Appointments Commission's recommendations'.[86] This prediction appears to have been borne out in practice, with research published in 2014 finding that, 'successive new Lord Chancellors have not misused their limited discretion in appointments, accepting all but five of the 3,500 or so candidates recommended by the JAC since 2006.'[87]

---

[82] The Crime and Courts Act 2013, Sch. 13, Part 4 saw responsibility for appointments to courts below the level of the High Court and to tribunals pass from the Lord Chancellor to the Lord Chief Justice and Senior President of Tribunals.

[83] Part 4 CRA 2005.

[84] Section 63 CRA 2005.

[85] Section 64 CRA 2005.

[86] Lord Mance, 'Constitutional Reforms, the Supreme Court and the Law Lords' (2006) 25 CJQ 155.

[87] G. Gee, 'What are Lord Chancellors for?' [2014] PL 11, 24.

Conclusion

The reforms implemented under the Constitutional Reform Act 2005 have done much to clarify the previously confused boundaries between executive, legislative and judicial functions at the apex of the legal system in the UK. So marked have the changes been, that the judiciary can now be argued to be far more clearly positioned as an institutionally separate branch of government.[88] As a result, it can be suggested that the idea of judicial independence is now more securely protected in the UK Constitution as many of the structural links which might have given rise to an objectively assessed perception of bias have been removed or clarified.[89] It can also be suggested that the separation of powers more broadly construed is better respected as a result of the 2005 reforms. The Constitutional Reform Act 2005, however, is not perhaps the only constitutional reform in recent years to have demonstrated the guiding influence of the separation of powers in practice. As we will see in later chapters, for instance, recent reforms to the devolution settlement as it affects Wales established a 'Welsh Assembly Government'[90] to effect a clearer separation between executive functions and the legislative competence of the National Assembly for Wales.[91] So while many of the traditional obstacles to a complete separation of powers in the UK Constitution remain, it might be argued that constitutional developments continue to demonstrate the shaping influence that separation of powers exerts. The Constitutional Reform Act 2005 is the most clear indication given to date of an institutionally distinct judicial branch, and – perhaps – of the continuing development of a more fully formed separation of powers.

Practice questions

1. 'While the Constitutional Reform Act 2005 has enhanced the structural independence of the judiciary, this development should not be equated with the constitutional safeguards provided by a fully-fledged separation of powers.'
   Discuss.

2. What do the structural reforms to the office of Lord Chancellor and the establishment of a Supreme Court for the United Kingdom tell us about the relative strengths of law and convention in upholding constitutional principles?

---

[88] See A. W. Bradley, 'Relations between Executive, Judiciary and Parliament: an Evolving Saga?' [2008] PL 470, 487–8; K. Malleson, 'The Evolving Role of the Supreme Court' [2011] PL 754.

[89] See: R. Masterman, *The Separation of Powers in the Contemporary Constitution: Judicial Competence and Independence in the United Kingdom* (CUP, 2011) esp. Chs 8 and 9; R. Hazell, 'Judicial independence and accountability in the UK: have both emerged stronger as a result of the Constitutional Reform Act 2005?' [2015] PL 198.

[90] Government of Wales Act 2006, Part 2.

[91] Ibid., Parts 3 and 4. For commentary, see A. Trench, 'The Government of Wales Act 2006: the Next Steps on Devolution for Wales' [2006] PL 687; A. Sherlock, 'A New Devolution Settlement for Wales' (2008) 14 EPL 297.

Further reading

Perhaps the most readable account of the development of the constitutional role of the judiciary within the constitution can be found in **R. Stevens, *The English Judges: Their Role in the Changing Constitution*** (Hart Publishing, 2005). Stevens traces the relationships between politicians and courts across the twentieth century, examining the extent to which the emergence of the judiciary as a constitutional force requires us to reassess our understanding of the balance of powers between Parliament, executive and courts.

The life of the Appellate Committee of the House of Lords is covered, by an array of judges and academics, in **L. Blom-Cooper, B. Dickson and G. Drewry (eds), *The Judicial House of Lords 1876–2009*** (OUP, 2009). This significant and lengthy study, which was published to mark the replacement of the Law Lords by the UK Supreme Court, covers the creation and development of the court, the judges themselves, and the influence of the court across a range of legal spheres. The history and development of the position of Lord Chancellor can be found in **Diana Woodhouse**'s excellent – if now dated – book, ***The Office of Lord Chancellor*** (Hart Publishing, 2001).

The creation of the UK Supreme Court is traced in **A. Le Sueur, 'From Appellate Committee to Supreme Court: A Narrative,' L. Blom-Cooper, B. Dickson and G. Drewry (eds), The Judicial House of Lords 1876–2009** (OUP, 2009) and in two articles by **Lord Windlesham ('The Constitutional Reform Act 2005: Ministers, Judges and Constitutional Change'** [2005] *Public Law* 806 and **'The Constitutional Reform Act 2005: The Politics of Constitutional Reform'** [2006] *Public Law* 35). **Kate Malleson's** piece, **'The Evolving Role of the Supreme Court'** – [2011] *Public Law* 754 – provides a good introduction to the embryonic court, while the developing 'constitutional' role of the Supreme Court provides the focus to **Roger Masterman and Jo Murkens'** article, **'Skirting Supremacy and Subservience: The Constitutional Authority of the United Kingdom Supreme Court'** [2013] *Public Law* 800.

The implications of the Constitutional Reform Act 2005 for the separation of powers and judicial independence provide running themes of **Roger Masterman**'s book, **The Separation of Powers in the Contemporary Constitution: Judicial Competence and Independence in the United Kingdom** (CUP, 2011) and *The Politics of Judicial Independence in the UK's Changing Constitution* (CUP, 2015) by **Graham Gee, Robert Hazell, Kate Malleson and Patrick O'Brien**.

Part IV
Decentralised government in the United Kingdom

Chapter 12
The United Kingdom's devolution arrangements

'Devolution is a process, not an event.'

Ron Davies MP, HC Debs, vol. 304, col. 1108 (21 January 1998).

Chapter outline

The governance arrangements of the UK, and even its borders, have developed over many centuries and will continue to be subject to change. For a long period after its creation the UK maintained highly centralised governance arrangements based upon the sovereign Parliament in Westminster. Over the twentieth century these arrangements enabled central government to introduce far-reaching measures, from state pension provision to the National Health Service and comprehensive education. Nonetheless, because Westminster is dominated by MPs representing English constituencies, its legislative output was not always constrained by the wishes of MPs representing seats in Scotland, Wales or Northern Ireland. This chapter traces how discontent at the degree of centralisation in the UK has been answered by the devolution of law-making power to institutions in Scotland, Wales and Northern Ireland. Each of these sets of devolved institutions has different powers and functions, which will be explored in turn (including an evaluation of how these arrangements have changed since power was first devolved in 1998). Only then can we consider whether devolution has provided a solution to the difficulties of governance in the UK.

Introduction

Many European countries are nation states. In other words, the authority of the political mechanisms of a state extends over the area of predominance of a particular national group. The borders of modern France, for example, roughly extend over a national group which identifies itself as French. The UK, by contrast, is not a nation state, but a Union of different national groups within one country. This Union was not, at its inception, a marriage of equals, resulting instead from the military and economic dominance of England on the Atlantic archipelago. Nor has the Union been stable since its formation, with the UK's borders being subject to repeated changes in the 300-plus years since Scotland and England (including, as part of England, Wales) first combined to form one country. The current borders of the UK (and the population disparity in terms of residents in each part of the UK) are shown in Figure 12.1.

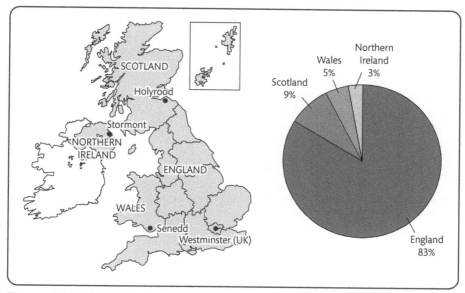

Figure 12.1 The countries of the UK: area and population

Devolution, one of New Labour's most ambitious constitutional reforms, can be seen as an attempt to address this instability by giving each of the smaller national groups within the UK some degree of legislative and administrative autonomy. In 1998, Parliament passed legislation establishing legislatures in Scotland, Wales and Northern Ireland, and granting each different degrees of law-making autonomy. These differences between the devolution arrangements in the various parts of the UK, together with the absence of comparable devolution arrangements in England, have imposed new stresses upon the Union. As devolution has matured, the devolved administrations have pushed for Westminster to grant them new powers. Hence the view of Ron Davies (the Secretary of State for Wales in 1998) in the above quote, that the devolution arrangements were not a final settlement of the constitutional relationship between the UK's different parts (an 'event') but instead the beginning of a 'process' which would transform that relationship over time. In this first chapter on devolution we will chart the development of this process to date. First, we will examine the foundations of the UK, to establish how this distinctive union of distinct national groups came into being and the pressures which resulted in the introduction of devolution. Thereafter we will investigate the operation of the devolution arrangements in Scotland, Wales and Northern Ireland respectively.

From union to devolution

Key issues

- The UK is the product of centuries of interaction between the major national groups resident on the Atlantic archipelago. The current geographical extent of the UK is only a century old.

- Prior to devolution, the UK was clearly a unitary state, with governmental power concentrated at Westminster. Unitary government system is different from federal systems of government (which maintain both regional and central government, and prevent one level of government from interfering in the functions of the other) and devolved systems of government (which divide regional and central government, but allow the latter the ultimate power to make decisions applicable throughout the country).

- Devolution was considered necessary in 1998 for Scotland, Northern Ireland and Wales for different reasons. In Scotland, devolution of some power to an elected institution was considered by the Labour Government as a potential answer to Scottish dissatisfaction with Westminster's ability to govern in Scotland's interest. In Northern Ireland, devolution was envisaged as a means by which to promote power sharing between the representatives of divided communities and thereby bring to an end decades of conflict. In Wales, however, there was no such compelling case for devolution, and the arrangements there emerged as an afterthought.

Unitary government in the United Kingdom

(i) The creation of the Union

Following the Norman victory at the Battle of Hastings in 1066, the invaders rapidly assumed control of much of what is now England. In the succeeding century the Normans extended their control into Wales, Scotland and Ireland. By the late-thirteenth century, through a combination of diplomacy, intermarriage and military campaigns, the islands of Great Britain and Ireland had largely fallen under Norman control.

Nonetheless, for much of the medieval era maintaining this control often involved compromises with the local populations in different parts of the islands, rather than directly asserting the authority of the English Crown over the entirety of Great Britain and Ireland. Following the conquest of Wales, Welsh princes were allowed to maintain local control, provided that they recognised their allegiance to the English Crown. This distinct arrangement, however, was extinguished after a failed rebellion by the Welsh in the late-thirteenth century. With his defeat of this rebellion King Edward I issued the Statute of Wales 1284, formally annexing Wales as part of England. Consequently, the common law was extended to Wales (providing the current jurisdiction of England and Wales).[1]

Scotland was added to Edward I's domains in 1291, after the Scottish King Alexander III and his heir died in quick succession. At the time, Scotland had neither a King to unite behind nor an army with which to resist Edward I. English control over Scotland, however, would be short-lived, being extinguished following the defeat of Edward II's army at the Battle of Bannockburn in 1314. The English Crown formally recognised Scotland's independence in 1328. For almost 400 years thereafter, Scotland remained an independent country, even after the Scottish Stuart Dynasty inherited the Crowns of Scotland and England in 1603. In the early years of the eighteenth century, however, Scotland was bankrupted by a combination of bad harvests and a failed attempt to found a colony in Panama. A treaty was signed between Scotland and England unifying the two countries in 1706, being accepted by the Parliaments of Scotland and England in the Acts of Union of 1706–07. Henceforth Scotland and England were simply parts of the new

---

[1] See Royal Commission on the Constitution, *Volume 1: Report* (1973) Cm. 5460, paras 109–122.

'United Kingdom', although both parts maintained separate established churches, education systems and legal systems.[2]

Even after union of Scotland and England, Ireland remained an anomaly. Following an invasion by the Normans in 1169, the Irish Kings recognised the 'Lordship' of King Henry II of England in 1171. Following this recognition, Ireland was divided between a combination of Irish and Norman lords for centuries. It was not until the Crown of Ireland Act 1542, however, during the reign of King Henry VIII, that a King of England also assumed the title of King of Ireland. Henry VIII, and his Protestant successors, attempted to strengthen their control over Ireland (still an overwhelmingly Catholic country) after this Act. These efforts provoked a rebellion by the Irish nobility, which was ultimately defeated in 1602. With this defeat, and with the rebellious Irish nobles dead or fleeing to Europe, Queen Elizabeth I took the opportunity to gift their lands to loyal (and Protestant) English nobles. Soon after, Protestant settlers were encouraged to take lands in the North-East of Ireland at the expense of the Catholic population. Into the eighteenth century, Ireland was therefore one of the countries subject to the English Crown, but otherwise independent from the UK. Its majority Catholic population was governed by Protestant landlords, who exercised power through a domestic Parliament for which only members of the established (Anglican Protestant) church could vote or stand. In 1798, at the height of the Napoleonic Wars, a major rebellion broke out. Although it was defeated, the UK faced the threat of further rebellion or French invasion. In 1800, a Treaty of Union was concluded between the UK and Ireland (and ratified in Westminster and in the Irish Parliament in the Acts of Union 1800). The Union was never stable, lacking the acceptance of the majority Catholic community in Ireland. Just 120 years later, following a short and vicious war of independence, the majority of Ireland left the UK to form an independent country. The six counties which today make up Northern Ireland remained within the Union.[3]

(ii) The operation of the Union

Given the unequal relationship between England and the other countries which joined the Union, the UK's system of government largely maintained the governance structures which existed in England prior to Union.[4] Law making, for example, was concentrated into a sovereign Parliament in Westminster. What had been the English Parliament simply accommodated additional representatives from first Scotland and later Ireland. In the mid-1950s one Scottish judge, Lord Cooper, questioned whether this approach to the UK's constitutional arrangements remained appropriate:

> Considering that the Union legislation extinguished the Parliaments of Scotland and England and replaced them by a new Parliament I have difficulty in seeing why it should have been supposed that the new Parliament of Great Britain must all inherit all the peculiar characteristics of the English Parliament but none of the Scottish Parliament.[5]

But post-Union Westminster was not an amalgam of its Scottish and English predecessors. Scotland's parliamentary tradition was not as deep rooted as England's, and the major

---

[2] Ibid., paras 66–79.
[3] Ibid., paras 145–152.
[4] See N. Aroney, 'Reserved Matters, Legislative Purpose and the Referendum on Scottish Independence' [2014] PL 422, 427.
[5] *MacCormick* v *Lord Advocate* 1953 SC 396, 411.

players supporting the Treaty of Union in Scotland had sought and achieved protections for its indigenous religious and legal institutions and education system.[6] Alongside English concepts such as parliamentary sovereignty, Scotland and Ireland had to accept Westminster as the hub of Cabinet government, with ministers having to pilot legislation through Parliament. The UK, by the nineteenth century, had developed a unitary system of government which, according to Dicey, involved 'the concentration of the strength of the state in the hands of one visible sovereign power'.[7]

Thinking Point . . .

One means of giving greater voice to the smaller national groups in the United Kingdom was over-representation in Parliament. Prior to devolution, for example, Scotland had 72 MPs (when proportionately it should have had fewer representatives). Since devolution became operational the number of Scots MPs at Westminster was reduced to 59 in 2005.

Alongside parliamentary sovereignty, however, as the Union developed Ireland, Scotland and eventually Wales were granted a level of 'executive autonomy'. Between the Act of Union and Irish independence in 1921, Irish administration was conducted primarily through the Chief Secretary for Ireland, a Cabinet minister. Scotland (in 1885) and Wales (in 1951) would also gain ministers (eventually with the status of Secretary of State) with the responsibility of overseeing the management of their budget and affairs. The holders of these offices enjoyed a particularly wide-ranging remit, especially after the development of the welfare state. By the end of the 1960s, executive autonomy meant that the remit of the Secretary of State for Scotland over Scotland's domestic affairs was extensive, covering 'a range of powers that in England are the responsibility of nine or ten departments of government including health, housing, education, industry and so on'.[8]

Pressure on unitary government

(i) Ireland and 'Home Rule'

Ireland's integration into the UK in 1801 may have fulfilled the then UK Government's goal by protecting against a French invasion during the Napoleonic wars, but this political union was particularly volatile. Impediments upon the political rights of the majority Catholic population continued until 1830 and thereafter the mismanagement of Irish affairs by successive UK Governments, most notably during the Great Famine of 1845–9, sustained nationalist sentiment in favour of separation from the UK. Through the late-nineteenth and early-twentieth centuries, however, the majority of Irish representatives in Westminster did not seek the immediate dissolution of the Union but 'Home Rule' for Ireland. Home Rule was essentially a form of devolution, allowing for a separate Irish legislature to manage Ireland's domestic

---

[6] H. Kearney, *The British Isles: A History of Four Nations* (CUP, 1995) p. 169.

[7] A. Dicey, *An Introduction to the Study of the Constitution* (8th edn, first published 1915, Liberty Fund, 1982) p. 87.

[8] J. Tomaney, 'End of the Empire State? New Labour and Devolution in the United Kingdom' (2000) 24 *International Journal of Urban and Regional Research* 675, 679.

affairs, whilst Westminster would continue to manage issues affecting the UK as a whole such as defence and currency.

Such plans were repeatedly thwarted, however, by Ireland's minority Protestant population, many of whom feared that Home Rule was a prelude to the dissolution of the Union (and that they would suffer discrimination under a majority-Catholic Irish state). They had powerful political backers within the UK. Dicey, in particular, prophesied drastic consequences should Ireland be granted Home Rule:

> [I]n the present state of the world it is inconceivable that Irish autonomy – if such be the proper term – should not excite or justify claims for local independence which would unloose the ties which bind together the huge fabric of the British Empire.[9]

In the event, failing to grant such autonomy exacerbated discontent with the Union in Ireland. With the repeated failures of Westminster to respond to demands for constitutional reform, opposition to the Union manifested itself in violence in the failed Easter Rising of 1916 and, following the First World War, in the Irish War of Independence of 1919–21. At the conclusion of this struggle, most of Ireland gained independence.

Only six counties in the North-East of Ireland with large Protestant populations remained within the Union. Ironically, given Unionist opposition to Home Rule on an all-Ireland basis, Northern Ireland was granted its own devolved Parliament and executive under the Government of Ireland Act 1920. Unionists dominated the Parliament of Northern Ireland from its creation, as a result of the deep sectarian divides in society in Northern Ireland and the ongoing identification of most of the majority Protestant community with Unionism. Most of the minority Catholic community, however, continued to identify themselves as Nationalists and sought reunification with Ireland. With Unionist politicians running the Parliament of Northern Ireland (based at Stormont) for the benefit of their own community, sectarian tensions erupted into violence from 1969 onwards. In 1972, in an effort to quell the rising levels of violence, the UK Government dissolved Northern Ireland's malfunctioning devolved arrangements and restored direct control from Westminster, administered by the Secretary of State for Northern Ireland. Political violence in Northern Ireland, known euphemistically as the 'Troubles', would continue for another 25 years and claim over 3,500 lives.

(ii) Following Ireland's lead

As Dicey recognised, nationalism in nineteenth-century Ireland would serve as a blue print for nationalist movements across the then British Empire. Such movements sought the creation of independent polities which would serve the interests of particular national groups more directly than the distant imperial Parliament at Westminster. Equally unsurprisingly, given Ireland's dramatic departure from the Union, was the emergence of organised nationalist politics in Wales and Scotland. Plaid Cymru ('The Party of Wales') was formed in 1925, followed almost a decade later in 1934 by the Scottish National Party (SNP). Both emphasised failings in the UK's unitary system of government in making their case for independence.

Deficiencies in the UK's unitary system of government contributed to the case of the nationalist parties from the mid-twentieth century onwards. The territorial Secretaries of State functioned essentially as 'London's viceroy' (a mocking label which denotes a leader

---

[9] A. Dicey, *England's Case Against Home Rule* (John Murray, 1886) p. 134.

imposed by imperial decree rather than a legitimate representative).[10] Despite their wide-ranging remit, these ministers were subject to insufficient scrutiny at Westminster as a result of the infrequent scheduling of Ministerial Questions. This compounded the lack of any separate forum in Scotland, Wales or Northern Ireland through which their political representatives could question ministers. Colin Munro, focusing on the oversight arrangements in place with regard to the Secretary of State for Scotland, highlights the nature of this problem:

> The Scottish Office's appearance on the parliamentary question rota once every three weeks was hardly commensurate with the scale of their activities, and more generally it was obvious that the House of Commons had insufficient time for scrutiny of Scottish administration.[11]

This lack of scrutiny was particularly problematic when the Conservative Party was in office. Since the Second World War, the Conservative Party has never controlled a majority of Scottish or Welsh seats in Parliament, but the scale of its general election victories in England (by far the largest part of the UK by population, and with the vast majority of seats in Westminster) frequently allowed it to govern in the UK as a whole. These victories allowed the nationalist parties, from the 1960s onwards, to argue that unitary government produced a 'democratic deficit' as the government in office in Westminster frequently did not reflect the wishes of the Scottish and Welsh electorates.

By the late-twentieth century international developments, most importantly '[t]he gradual dismantling of the British Empire . . . and the pooling of sovereignty of the United Kingdom with other Member States of the European Union',[12] bolstered the cases of the nationalist parties. The collapse of the Empire confirmed the importance of nationalism in the minds of ordinary voters, but the development of the EU perhaps became the most important element of their case. As the Labour Prime Minister James Callaghan recognised in 1976:

> As government has become bigger and more pervasive, operating internationally in ever larger groupings, components of the old sovereign States, and especially minority components, have become more conscious of a special individual identity and tradition.[13]

In joining the EU, the UK's political leaders had recognised that there were some functions that independent states cannot perform adequately in isolation from their neighbouring states. In transferring competences in these areas to the EU the UK was obliged to act in partnership with other European countries, including Ireland. Nationalist politicians were able to portray an independent Scotland and Wales working in partnership with England, countering suggestions that the disintegration of the UK would lead to acrimony. Furthermore, one of the guiding principles of the EU is subsidiarity, a concept which holds that centralised authority should be reserved for those functions which cannot adequately be exercised at lower levels of governance. At the European level, this means that the member states still have a say in how many EU provisions are transposed in domestic law. In the UK context, however, the principle of subsidiarity gave weight to nationalist claims that Westminster was overburdened and that separate institutions should be developed to serve the needs of the people of Scotland, Wales and Northern Ireland.

---

[10] M. O'Neill, 'Great Britain: From Dicey to Devolution' (2000) 53 *Parliamentary Affairs* 69, 70.
[11] C. Munro, *Studies in Constitutional Law* (Butterworths, 1999) p. 39.
[12] A. O'Neill, 'Stands Scotland Where it Did?' (2006) 57 NILQ 102, 103.
[13] HC Debs, vol. 922, col. 976 (13 December 1976).

Thinking Point . . .

EU membership could also be used to support claims for autonomy. Its structural funds are organised to provide support to areas, like Scotland and Wales, on the periphery of the EU single market, but were set up on the basis that they would be accessed by regional institutions.

(iii) Slow progress towards devolution

By the 1960s both Scotland and Wales were suffering from a downturn in their economically important heavy industries. This downturn, and the discovery of large reserves of oil off the coast of Scotland in the early 1970s, helped the nationalist parties to sell their agenda to a previously sceptical electorate.[14] In the face of electoral gains by the nationalist parties in the late 1960s, the then Labour Government created a Royal Commission on the Constitution. When the Commission reported back in 1973, it recommended that directly-elected assemblies with some law-making powers should be established in Wales and Scotland.[15] The Labour Party was, however, divided over these devolution plans. Much as the then Prime Minister, James Callaghan, proclaimed that his devolution proposals 'will be a new settlement among the nations that constitute the United Kingdom',[16] the reality was that the Scotland and Wales Acts provided for a watered-down form of devolution, even by comparison to the Royal Commission's modest proposals. Neither the proposed Scottish nor the Welsh legislatures would control their own finances or have the power to raise taxes. Instead, Westminster would control their funding, administering it via a block grant out of total UK tax revenues proportionate to the population of each part of the UK (a system known as the 'Barnett formula' after the civil servant who devised it). Finally, a group of English Labour back-benchers opposed to devolution introduced a provision into the legislation requiring that, in the referendums required in Scotland and Wales to bring devolution into effect, not only would a majority of those voting have to support devolution but they would have to total at least 40 per cent of the registered electorate. Amid apathy generated by the timid devolution proposals and dissatisfaction with Callaghan's administration, neither referendums met the requirement that 40 per cent of the registered electorate support devolution and the plans were scrapped.

Thinking Point . . .

In Scotland, a majority of those who voted in the 1979 referendum supported devolution (51.6 per cent), but, due to relatively low turn-out, this amounted to only 32.9 per cent of registered voters, resulting in the failure of the scheme.

In May 1979, two months after the failed devolution referendums, Margaret Thatcher's Conservative Party won a general election. The Conservatives would go on to win four general elections in a row, but their ranks included only a handful of parliamentarians representing Welsh and Scottish seats. Thatcher was not only opposed to devolution, but even came

---

[14] See M. O'Neill, 'Great Britain: From Dicey to Devolution' (2000) 53 *Parliamentary Affairs* 69, 72.

[15] Royal Commission on the Constitution, *Volume 1: Report* (1973) Cm. 5460, paras 1116–1124.

[16] HC Debs, vol. 922, col. 992 (13 December 1976).

to regard the executive autonomy of the Welsh and Scottish Offices as 'an extra level of bureaucracy', impeding her centralised reform agenda.[17] With sustained periods of high unemployment in Wales and Scotland during the Conservative period in office from 1979–1997, resentment against unitary government grew. In 1989 Labour, the Liberal Democrats, trade unions and church leaders formed a Constitutional Convention to discuss Scotland's future. The Conservative Party, committed to unitary government, refused to participate. As did the SNP, on the basis that the Convention's proposals would distract from pursuing full independence. Ultimately, the Convention's Report, *Scotland's Parliament, Scotland's Right,* would propose a 129-member Scottish Parliament which would serve as the blueprint for Labour devolution proposals issued in the wake of the 1997 general election.[18]

Thinking Point . . .

The attitudes of Conservative politicians, as much as their policies, fostered nationalist resentments. John Redwood, Secretary of State for Wales under John Major's Government, famously failed to learn the Welsh anthem and refused to sign documents prepared in Welsh.

(iv) Devolution and federalism compared

New Labour's adoption of devolution marked the closing of a highly centralised chapter of the UK's constitutional history, but O'Neill noted at the time that the UK's new constitutional arrangements were based upon 'sharing a degree of power, but far short of undermining the common authority'.[19] By this, he means that devolution was intended to preserve the authority of the Westminster Parliament. This is best explained by contrasting devolution with federalism, the system used for dividing governmental authority over particular functions employed in countries such as Canada, Germany, and the United States of America.

These countries maintain constitutional separations between functions within the remit of the central government (known as the federal government and often responsible for functions such as maintaining defence, foreign relations and currency which apply to the country as a whole) and the governments of particular regions, provinces and states (each of which maintaining institutions for managing its internal affairs). As the constitutions of federal countries divide up powers between 'state' and 'federal' institutions, so too must a supreme court be able to rule on instances where either of these sets of institutions have exceeded their remit. Given the UK's ongoing commitment to parliamentary sovereignty, no such restrictions apply to Westminster as a legislature. As Arden LJ has pointedly recognised, this serves to distinguish the UK's devolution arrangements from federalism:

> The United Kingdom devolution arrangements lack some of the characteristics of a federal system. The Westminster Parliament has not given up its sovereignty over the devolved administrations and that means that in theory, subject to constitutional conventions, it could restrict or revoke the powers that it has given to the devolved administrations. Furthermore, there is no provision for judicial review of legislation passed by the Westminster Parliament on the grounds that it deals with devolved matters. The only qualification to that principle is if the court decides that the legislation of the Westminster Parliament violates Community law.[20]

---

[17] M. Thatcher, *The Downing Street Years* (Harper Collins, 1993) p. 619.
[18] HM Government, *Scotland's Parliament* (1997) Cm. 3658.
[19] M. O'Neill, 'Great Britain: From Dicey to Devolution' (2000) 53 *Parliamentary Affairs* 69, 92.
[20] *R (Horvath) v Secretary of State for the Environment, Food and Rural Affairs* [2007] EWCA Civ 620, [57].

Moreover, devolution does not depend upon regional institutions all maintaining the same functions as each other (as is the norm in federal systems). Instead, in the UK, devolution operates 'asymmetrically', providing for what Dawn Oliver describes as 'lopsided decentralization under which some nations or regions enjoy a range of powers that is greater or less than the range enjoyed by others'.[21] In other words, very different devolution regimes were created in 1998 in Scotland, Wales and Northern Ireland, reflecting the differing levels of support for devolution in these areas. This differentiation requires us to consider, in turn, the different devolution regimes put in place in 1998 and their subsequent development.

Devolution in practice: Scotland

Key issues

- The composition of the Scottish Parliament is the product of an electoral system which fuses FPTP (for 73 constituency MSPs) and PR (for 56 regional MSPs). This mixed system is intended to secure the benefits of both electoral systems.
- The Scottish Parliament was granted extensive law-making powers under devolution. 'Transferred' competences under the Scotland Act cover most of the law making relevant to domestic issues affecting Scotland, whilst Westminster reserves the power to legislate in areas which affect the governance of the UK as a whole.
- The Scottish Government's composition, role and powers are based upon the Westminster model of an executive embedded within the legislature.
- The Scottish Parliament was able to make claims for extended tax altering competences in the Scotland Act 2012, and further new powers and competences were added after the 2014 independence referendum in the Scotland Act 2016.

The 1997 devolution referendum

Before putting its devolution proposals into effect, Labour sought the direct support of the people of Scotland. Under the Referendums (Scotland and Wales) Act 1997, over 60 per cent of the Scottish electorate turned out to vote on devolution in September 1997, and by a margin of nearly three to one the voters supported devolution. A large majority of those voting also supported the grant of tax-altering powers to the new Scottish Parliament, which was opened in May 1999. In 2004, the Parliament moved into a purpose-built building at Holyrood in Edinburgh. The Parliament is elected on the basis of a distinctive electoral system and from the start enjoyed extensive powers. Members of the Scottish Government exercise functions broadly similar to their counterparts at Westminster, but with notable differences. This section will chart the progress of devolution in Scotland since 1998, analysing the electoral system, the Scottish Parliament's powers and competences and the role of the Scottish Government.

---

[21] D. Oliver, *Constitutional Reform in the United Kingdom* (OUP, 2002) p. 245.

The electoral system for the Scottish Parliament

(i) Two types of MSP

Elections to the 129-seat, single-chamber Scottish Parliament ordinarily take place every four years.[22] Scotland encompasses a wide range of communities, from large urban areas such as Glasgow and Edinburgh in its central belt to its sparsely populated Highland region. The system used to elect Members of the Scottish Parliament (MSPs) was specifically designed to accommodate such a diverse polity and is more complicated than the system used to elect MPs to Westminster. Electors each have one first-past-the-post (FPTP) vote for a constituency MSP to represent their local area. Altogether Scotland is divided into 73 such constituencies,[23] which were based on the constituencies used for Westminster elections in Scotland up to 2004.[24] Electors also have a second vote, exercised using the additional-member system of proportional representation (PR). This vote is used to elect the 56 'regional' MSPs, with Scotland divided into eight regions, of widely varying size in light of different population densities, and seven such MSPs elected for each region.[25] The regions are mapped out in Figure 12.2.

The combination of PR and FPTP, modelled upon the electoral arrangements for the German Bundestag, allows Scotland to enjoy some of the advantages of both electoral systems. The 'constituency' MSPs represent local areas, facilitating a close connection between the representatives and their constituents, whilst the 'regional' MSPs help to ensure that the Scottish Parliament's composition more accurately reflects voter intentions than would be possible through the use of FPTP alone and allows parties with a level of support in a region (but which is not sufficiently concentrated in particular constituencies to win FPTP contests) to gain election.

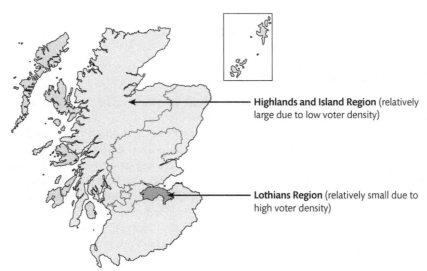

Highlands and Island Region (relatively large due to low voter density)

Lothians Region (relatively small due to high voter density)

Figure 12.2 Scottish Parliament regions

---

[22] Scotland Act 1998, s. 2(2).
[23] Ibid., s. 1(2).
[24] See the Scottish Parliament (Constituencies) Act 2004.
[25] Scotland Act 1998, s. 1(3).

(ii) The 2016 Scottish Parliament elections

The effect of the combination of these systems on the make-up of the Scottish Parliament can be appreciated by considering the outcome of the 2016 Scottish Parliament elections (Table 12.1).

After the 2016 election, the Scottish National Party was the largest party, but fell just short of controlling a majority of the Holyrood Parliament. Nicola Sturgeon has nonetheless continued to govern without a coalition. The addition of regional MSPs helps to limit the discrepancy between vote share and the composition of the Scottish Parliament. Had the Scottish Parliament consisted solely of its constituency MSPs elected on the basis of FPTP, as employed at Westminster, Table 12.1 shows that 47 per cent of the vote would have earned the SNP fully 81 per cent of MSPs. By contrast, given the geographical spread of Labour voters in Scotland, without regional MSPs that party would have gained a mere three seats, or 4 per cent of the total constituency seats, despite it achieving 23 per cent of the popular vote. With regional MSPs, the Labour Party makes up 19 per cent of the chamber, much more accurately reflecting voter intentions.

Table 12.1 Election results for the Scottish Parliament (2016)

Party	Constituency MSPs	Regional MSPs	Total MSPs
SNP	59	4	63
Conservatives	7	24	31
Labour	3	21	24
Greens	0	6	6
Liberal Democrats	4	1	5

The competence of the Scottish Parliament

(i) Reserved powers and transferred powers

The powers of the Scottish Parliament are defined *negatively*, meaning that the Scotland Act 1998 establishes the 'reserved' powers specifically retained within Westminster's competence.[26] All areas of law making not specifically reserved to Westminster under schedule 5 of the Scotland Act therefore lie within the Scottish Parliament's competence. This means that the powers 'transferred' to the Scottish Parliament's competence can be read in broad terms, but it does make it difficult to precisely list the Scottish Parliament's law-making competences. Table 12.2, therefore, highlights the main reserved and, by inference, transferred powers.

The reserved powers in this list can usually be distinguished from the transferred powers on the basis that they are essential to the governance of the UK as a whole (preventing Scotland, for example, from maintaining its own foreign policy or imposing tariffs on imports from other parts of the UK). As Lord Hope has put it, 'matters in which the United Kingdom as a whole has an interest should continue to be the responsibility of the UK Parliament at Westminster'.[27] Some reserved issues, however, are not so easily distin-

---

[26] Ibid., s. 30.
[27] *Imperial Tobacco Ltd* v *Lord Advocate* [2012] UKSC 61; 2013 SLT 2, [29].

Table 12.2 Competences of the Scottish Parliament in 1998

Reserved competences (sch. 5)	Transferred competences (implicit)
Matters relating to the constitution (including the monarchy, the UK Parliament, the rules regarding registration and funding of political parties and the Scottish civil service)	All areas of education and training
Foreign policy, defence and national security	Local government
Macro-economic issues (such as the fiscal, economic and monetary systems)	Land development, heritage and conservation, environmental regulation and planning policy
Trade and industry (including trade within and outside the UK and intellectual property)	Transport policy internal to Scotland
Employment, equal opportunities and social security	Health policy and the NHS
Consumer protection and competition law	The legal system (civil and criminal, including mots areas of substantive criminal law)
Transport safety and regulation of UK-wide transport networks	Agriculture, forestry and fisheries
Energy policy (including ownership and exploration of oil and gas)	Social work and social housing
Immigration and citizenship	Sports, arts and culture
Limited areas of criminal law, such as firearms offences	The emergency services
Miscellaneous matters (such as medical ethics, postal services, and broadcasting regulation)	Tourism and industrial development

guished on this basis, as they do not seem to touch upon important UK-wide issues. Why, for example, transfer competence over the Scottish NHS but reserve issues such as medical ethics? Parliament, in making this reservation, sought to ensure that there was a uniform UK law on controversial issues such as euthanasia, restricting the potential for movement around the different UK jurisdictions to take advantage of different regimes. Moreover, Westminster's sovereignty remains an important issue. Simply because an issue is not specifically reserved to Westminster under schedule 5 does not, as we will examine in depth in the next chapter, prevent Westminster from legislating. If it did, and there were clear distinctions in the competence of Westminster and Holyrood, then the UK's constitutional arrangements would be quasi-federal. Instead, by constitutional convention, Westminster ordinarily stops itself from legislating on domestic issues in Scotland unless it has permission from Holyrood to do so.[28]

---

[28] See above, pp. 394–8.

(ii) Altering the Scottish Parliament's powers

The Devolution Acts put in train a 'process' by which further powers may be transferred over time to devolved institutions. Embedded within the Scotland Act is provision for the UK Government to use Orders in Council to modify the list of reserved powers contained in schedule 5, allowing it to increase or decrease the legislative competence exercisable by the Scottish Parliament.[29] After a decade of devolution the UK Government appointed a Commission, headed by Sir Kenneth Calman, to consider the functioning of Scotland's Parliament and the balance between reserved and transferred powers. The Commission's Report, published in June 2009, highlighted the breadth of the competence transferred to Holyrood:

> The Scottish Parliament has very wide legislative powers. It can make law on anything that is not reserved to the UK Parliament. That enables it to deal with most domestic issues in Scotland – crime and justice, health, education, housing, transport and economic development, the environment, agriculture and fisheries and many other matters. Reserved issues include defence and foreign affairs, macro-economic management and social security.[30]

The Commission emphasised that this 'split between devolved and reserved areas is well drawn at present', but concluded that 'there will always be areas where the responsibilities of the different levels of government interact with one another'.[31]

Focusing on such areas, the Commission identified a series of minor changes to the Scottish Parliament's competence, fine tuning the devolution settlement. In the Scotland Act 2012, Westminster took up many of these recommendations, for example removing the ability to make law regarding air guns from the list of reserved competences under schedule 5.[32] With improving the relationship between devolved and centralised law making as its goal, the Calman Commission did suggest more widespread adjustments, including, in certain areas, *adding* to the list of reserved competences (on issues such as food labelling). Most of these recommendations were not followed.[33] In essence, Westminster attempted no more than tweaking Holyrood's competence in the 2012 Act, and this battle over competences highlights the friction between the two legislatures. Many of Calman's proposals to remove competences from Holyrood proved to be unacceptable to the SNP Executive in office in Scotland, whilst, with regard to welfare issues, the Coalition Government was reluctant to devolve further competences in an area which affected one of its key policies.

The limited nature of the reforms under the Scotland Act 2012 did nothing to stifle the independence movement, and as we shall see in the next chapter, the pro-Union parties would be obliged to promise more powers for Scotland in the 2014 referendum campaign to win over voters.[34] The Coalition Government promised to provide these new powers as swiftly as possible, recognising that 'the Scottish people did not vote for

---

[29] Scotland Act 1998, s. 30(2).

[30] Commission on Scottish Devolution, *Serving Scotland Better: Scotland and the United Kingdom in the 21st Century* (2009) 15.

[31] Ibid., 15.

[32] Scotland Act 2012, s. 10.

[33] Constitution Committee, *Scotland Bill* (2011) HL 184, para. 8.

[34] See pp. 406–10.

the status quo'.[35] After the hiatus imposed by the 2015 election the Scotland Act 2016 granted the Scottish Parliament powers to alter its own electoral arrangements and those applicable to local government in Scotland.[36] Indeed, the SNP's push on this issue was so strong that Westminster granted, by section 30 order, the Scottish Parliament the ability to enfranchise 16- and 17-year-olds ahead of the new legislation and in time for Holyrood to legislate ahead of the Scottish Parliament elections in 2016.[37] It also gained the power to legislate in a host of new policy areas from consumer advice,[38] to roads,[39] to abortion.[40] Particularly significantly, in light of the SNP's opposition to welfare cuts under the Coalition Government, the Scottish Parliament gained competence with regard to a wide range of benefit payments.[41] The net effect of these changes is to radically change the picture set out above in Table 12.2, increasing the range of transferred powers and reducing the number of reserved powers.

(iii) Financing devolution in Scotland

The Scottish Parliament's remit means that the Scottish Government is responsible for over half of the public expenditure which affects the people of Scotland. This means that, in order for the devolved competence to be meaningful, the Scottish Government must have control over the public finances necessary to exercise this competence. Instead, however, under the Scotland Act, the Scottish Parliament enjoyed a very limited capacity to raise funds to support distinct Scottish policies.

Following devolution, the Scottish Parliament gained a power to vary income tax rates in Scotland by up to three pence per pound earned by comparison to the national standard.[42] This meant that, on the standard rate of income tax of 20 pence in every pound earned over a minimum threshold, the Scottish Parliament could choose to lower that rate to 17 pence or raise it to 23 pence. Beyond this limited power, the devolved Scottish institutions received their funding on the basis of the 'Barnett formula', a system created to serve the proposed devolution scheme in the 1970s. Under the formula (named after the Chief Secretary to the Treasury in the late 1970s, Joel Barnett) each constituent part of UK received an allocation from total public funds (once shared expenditure, such as defence, has been allocated) based on their approximate population percentages of each nation, and not on the needs of each population. This system of allocating funding attracted numerous critics, especially as it did not build in recalibration in light of population shifts. For English-based critics of devolution, the formula amounts to the UK (and particularly England, as the UK's largest constituent element) subsidising the policies of the devolved administrations.[43] For the SNP in Scotland, the formula is instead regarded as a mechanism controlled by Westminster, which could always be altered by the UK Government to curtail particular Scottish policies. For the first decade of devolution's operation the Barnett Formula soldiered on, almost universally unloved, and Scotland's meagre tax-altering powers went unexercised.

---

[35] HM Government, *Scotland in the United Kingdom: An Enduring Settlement* (2015) Cm. 8990, 5.

[36] Scotland Act 2016, s. 3 to s. 10.

[37] Scottish Elections (Reduction of Voting Age) Act 2015.

[38] Scotland Act 2016, s. 50.

[39] Ibid., s. 40.

[40] Ibid., s. 53.

[41] Ibid., s. 22 to s. 35.

[42] Scotland Act 1998, s. 73.

[43] See B. Dickson, 'Devolution' in J. Jowell, D. Oliver and C. O'Cinneide (eds), *The Changing Constitution* (8th edn, OUP, 2015) 249, 251.

Thinking Point . . .

Even Lord Barnett eventually disowned the Formula he developed: 'It is a great embarrassment to have my name attached to so unfair a system. Especially as, when I introduced it, it was going to last only a year. It has now lasted more than 20 years, because successive governments have failed to deal with it for fear of upsetting the Scots'. See B. Brady, 'Unfair Formula? Not in My Name Says Barnett' *Scotland on Sunday* (11 January 2004).

Although the Calman Commission's recommendations on altering the competence of the Scottish Parliament were not all followed, the Scotland Act 2012 did implement its recommendation that a substantial part of its budget should be drawn from devolved taxation under its control and not from a grant controlled by Westminster:

> The Scottish Parliament should not be wholly dependent on grant, because that does not allow it to be accountable to the people of Scotland. Our recommendations will mean a big enough part of its budget will come from devolved taxation for it to be genuinely accountable.[44]

To bring this change into effect, the Scotland Act 2012 scrapped Holyrood's power to vary income tax rates and substituted a new section 80C into the Scotland Act 1998, which would allow MSPs to set a 'Scottish rate' of income tax which, above a minimum level necessary to pay for UK-wide expenditure administered by central government, would not by tied to the UK rates. The level of tax payable above this minimum level could be varied by the Scottish Parliament, and any tax receipts generated would be controlled by the Scottish Government.[45] The Scottish Parliament also received new powers to set Scottish taxes on landfill use and property transactions. When this measure came into effect in April 2016 the block grant was also reduced accordingly, placing the responsibility for a third of the Scottish budget into the hands of the Scottish Parliament.[46]

The Calman Commission made it clear that it regarded this change as only the first step in a potential move to reduce reliance on the block grant, and floated the possibility of permitting Scotland to directly administer a proportion of Scottish VAT receipts.[47] Again, after the independence referendum the issue of financing the devolution settlement gained considerable attention. Ahead of the Scotland Act 2016 the Coalition Government promised that, for the first time, 'the majority of money spent by the Scottish Parliament will come from revenues raised in Scotland'.[48] This meant that the Scottish Parliament could control an increasing range of tax rates and receive the receipts directly, as opposed to having the majority of its funding channelled through the block grant, over which it had no control. The Calman Commission proposal over VAT receipts was implemented, assigning the first 10 per cent of VAT revenues in Scotland direct to the Scottish Government,[49] and it gained new powers over the Air Passenger Duty[50] and Aggregates Levy.[51]

---

[44] Commission on Scottish Devolution, *Serving Scotland Better: Scotland and the United Kingdom in the 21st Century* (2009) 9.

[45] Amending the Income Tax Act 2007, s. 6(2).

[46] B. Dickson, 'Devolution' in J. Jowell, D. Oliver and C. O'Cinneide (eds), *The Changing Constitution* (8th edn, OUP, 2015) 249, 254.

[47] Commission on Scottish Devolution, *Serving Scotland Better: Scotland and the United Kingdom in the 21st Century* (2009) 9.

[48] HM Government, *Scotland in the United Kingdom: An Enduring Settlement* (2015) Cm. 8990, 5.

[49] Scotland Act 2016, s. 16.

[50] Ibid., s. 17.

[51] Ibid., s. 18.

The Scottish Government

(i) A parliamentary government

The Scottish Government operates as a parliamentary government under the Westminster model. One crucial difference in the executive's role, by comparison to its counterpart at Westminster, is that the Scotland Act prescribes in law many of the features of government activity that remain subject to constitutional conventions at the UK-level. For example, the Scottish Parliament's oversight of the Scottish Government's activities is enshrined in law, with MSPs having a legal power to summon Scottish ministers to appear before them[52] and with the Scottish Government being legally required to resign if defeated in a vote of no confidence.[53] In terms of the formation of the executive, the Scottish Parliament chooses the First Minister following an election or the post becoming vacant (for example, by resignation or death),[54] and this choice is (automatically) approved by the Queen.[55] The First Minister nominates all other ministers, who (in a break with Westminster tradition) must be approved by the Parliament and who are thereafter formally appointed by the Queen.[56] All ministers, with the exception of the Scottish Law Officers, must be members of the Scottish Parliament.[57]

(ii) The powers of the Scottish Government

Just as some of the Scottish Parliament's law-making competences were previously matters on which the Secretary of State for Scotland could make delegated legislation, so too did the Scottish Government derive a wide range of discretionary powers from the former remit of this Westminster minister.[58] Some specific functions were retained by the UK Government under the 1998 Act,[59] including the setting of speed limits and rail franchising, but many of these powers were transferred to the Scottish Government in the Scotland Acts 2012[60] and 2016 (allowing the Scottish Government to authorise public sector operators to bid to provide passenger railway services).[61] All of these functions are transferred to the extent that they are 'within the devolved competence',[62] meaning that although the Scottish Government can, for example, now set speed limits in Scotland, it has no power to extend these limits beyond Scotland's borders. In exercising these functions, the Scottish Government has no power to act in a manner which contravenes EU law or the ECHR.[63] One key role retained by the Secretary of State for Scotland is to oversee the activities of the devolved Executive, having the ability to step in and prevent or require actions where these would undermine the UK's international obligations.

---

[52] Scotland Act 1998, s. 23(1).

[53] Ibid., s. 45(2).

[54] Ibid., s. 46(3).

[55] Ibid., s. 46(4).

[56] Ibid., s. 47(2).

[57] Ibid., s. 47(3)(c).

[58] Ibid., s. 53(2).

[59] Ibid., s. 56.

[60] Scotland Act 2012, ss. 16–22.

[61] Scotland Act 2016, s. 57.

[62] Scotland Act 1998, s. 53(1).

[63] Ibid., s. 57(2).

Devolution in practice: Wales

Key issues

- Welsh devolution was an (ill-considered) afterthought to devolution in Scotland, largely because there was not an equivalent level of popular demand for devolution as existed in Scotland.

- Consequently, the powers granted to the Welsh Assembly under the Government of Wales Act 1998 did not compare favourably to those granted to the Scottish Parliament. The Welsh Assembly exercised secondary as opposed to primary law-making functions.

- Since devolution, the Welsh Assembly has become accepted as an established feature of governance in Wales and, consequently, it has been able to gain further powers, including, after a referendum in 2011, primary law-making powers.

The 1997 devolution referendum

Labour's devolution proposals were almost rejected by the Welsh electorate in the 1997 referendum, held on the same day as the referendum for devolution to Scotland. After a hard fought campaign, and on a turn-out of just 51 per cent, devolution was supported by the narrowest of majorities (50.3 per cent). Clearly the Welsh electorate was not nearly as enthusiastically supportive of devolution as the Scots, but then again, the powers offered to the proposed Welsh Assembly were far more limited than those proposed for the Scottish Parliament. In other words, there was little to excite the electorate in the 1997 proposals. They were an afterthought, developed not to answer any sustained demand for devolution, but because the Labour Party believed that if Scotland was granted devolution, Wales should be offered some superficially equivalent arrangements. Together, the Assembly's comparative lack of power and the at best apathetic attitude of the Welsh electorate posed a unique challenge for devolution in Wales. The direction of the devolution project depended upon developments in Welsh public opinion. If the Assembly was to gain more powers it would have to win over the electorate by being more responsive to their desires within devolved fields than Westminster had previously been.

The Government of Wales Act 1998

(i) The Welsh Assembly and Executive Committee

Following the first elections to the Welsh Assembly in 1999, the 60-seat body had to wait almost seven years before it was able to move into its purpose-built home, the Senedd Building was constructed in Cardiff. In the meantime, the Welsh electorate had become used to an electoral system for the Assembly which mirrors that employed in Scotland, with 40 Assembly Members (AMs) elected under FPTP to serve constituencies (the same constituencies used in Westminster elections) and 20 AMs elected to represent five regions under a party list form of proportional representation (with four AMs elected in this way for each region).[64] As with Scotland, this 'mixed' electoral system produces an Assembly in which the number of seats held by parties is closer to the proportion of the vote they attain than using FPTP only, and the regional representatives allow parties lacking in concentrated support in individual constituencies to gain seats. Table 12.3 sets out the 2016 Welsh Assembly election results:

---

[64] Government of Wales Act 1998, s. 2(1).

Table 12.3 Election results for the Welsh Assembly (2016)

Party	Constituency AMs	Regional AMs	Total AMs
Labour	27	2	29
Plaid Cymru	6	6	12
Conservatives	6	5	11
UKIP	0	7	7
Liberal Democrats	1	0	1

Following this election, Labour governs through holding almost 50 per cent of the Assembly seats. The Welsh Assembly, comprising just 60 representatives, is far smaller than the Scottish Parliament (or even, as we will see, the Northern Ireland Assembly). In 1998, however, such a small chamber was all that was required to administer the limited powers devolved to Wales under the Government of Wales Act. Moreover, under the 1998 Act the executive branch was simply a committee of the Assembly, headed by the First Secretary, rather than a separate entity with its own legal powers, in keeping with the Scottish Government.[65]

(ii) The Welsh Assembly's powers: 'Welsh Office Plus'

The Welsh Assembly established in 1998 was not, in truth, a law-making body equivalent to the Scottish Parliament. For a start, its areas of competence were set out in the Government of Wales Act, unlike the Scotland Act, which listed only those competences reserved to Westminster. The difference is not merely cosmetic. The Welsh Assembly *cannot* act outside the specified fields in which it has competence, whereas the Scottish Parliament can, by implication in the Scotland Act, act in any field not specifically reserved by Westminster. The Welsh Assembly's competences were listed in schedule 2 of the Government of Wales Act 1998 (Table 12.4).

The fields in which the Welsh Assembly exercises its competence are, as can be seen from this list, much more limited than those possessed by the Scottish Parliament. Policing and criminal justice, for example, are notable absences from the Assembly's remit. Even within the fields in which the Welsh Assembly could operate after 1998, its powers were more limited than those of the Scottish Parliament, for the Assembly could not make primary legislation for itself, but only subordinate legislation of specific relevance to Wales.[66] Essentially, the Welsh Assembly simply administered the executive function of making statutory instruments under a parent Westminster statute, a function previously performed by the Secretary of State for Wales. If a matter affected Wales specifically in one of the Assembly's areas of competence, and no current legal provisions existed, the 1998 Act required the Welsh Assembly to wait for Westminster to legislate granting it the scope to enact subordinate legislation. And if Westminster did not leave any scope for such subordinate legislation in its enactments, then under the 1998 Act the Welsh Assembly would be left with little meaningful scope for action. Furthermore, unlike the Scottish Parliament, the Assembly has no finance-raising power, and instead simply administers a block grant

---

[65] Ibid., s. 56(1).
[66] Government of Wales Act 1998, s. 22(1).

Table 12.4 Competences of the Welsh Assembly in 1998

Welsh Assembly competences (sch. 2)	Reserved competences (implicit)
Agriculture, forestry and fisheries	Any field of law making not specifically transferred to the Welsh Assembly
Ancient monuments and historic buildings	
Education and training	
Economic development and industry	
Local government	
Land development, planning and flood defence	
The environment	
Highways and transport policy	
Health and health services	
Tourism	
Social services and social housing	
Sports, arts and culture (including the Welsh language)	

provided under the Barnett formula.[67] Taking these provisions as a whole, Ian Loveland considered that under the 1998 Act 'the Assembly could sensibly be seen as a powerful instrument of *local* governance, but it could in no sense be seen as a structure of *national* governance'.[68] The limited nature of the Welsh Assembly's law-making competence also explained the embryonic nature of the Welsh Executive. In Scotland many of the Secretary of State's functions had been transferred to the Scottish Government. Given that the Welsh Assembly itself administered some of the powers previously held by the Welsh Secretary, there was thought to be no need for a fully-fledged executive branch.

The Government of Wales Act 2006

(i) Discontent with limited devolution

Although the Welsh Assembly's lack of powers under the 1998 Act prevented it from fashioning a unique legislative agenda for Wales, the mere fact that the Assembly had been created in 1998 was a significant first step. Once a chamber is invested with law-making authority, even mere power to make subordinate legislation, it tends to become a focal point for debate in the polity that it serves. By 2002, the Welsh Assembly was so embedded in Wales' national consciousness that Dawn Oliver felt able to conclude that 'it is now unthinkable that the Government of Wales Act 1998 could be repealed without being replaced by other measures acceptable in Wales'.[69]

In part the Assembly was successful because it has provided a distinctive Welsh voice in national governance. On issues from substance abuse to sexual health awareness the Welsh

---

[67] Ibid., s. 80(1).
[68] I. Loveland, *Constitutional Law, Administrative Law and Human Rights* (5th edn, OUP, 2009) p. 447.
[69] D. Oliver, *Constitutional Reform in the United Kingdom* (OUP, 2002) p. 274.

Assembly launched a series of high-profile campaigns and frequently concluded these campaigns with requests to the UK Parliament to grant secondary law-making power. These seeds often fell on fertile ground. Westminster was in theory able to leave the Assembly without a meaningful role, but this was unlikely to happen given that Labour had invested so much time in the devolution project and the early years of devolution in Wales coincided with an overlap in Labour control over the UK Parliament and the Assembly. As Chris Himsworth has recognised, soon after devolution began Westminster was frequently enacting legislation which permitted Wales considerable scope for subordinate measures (and which, in many instances, would not be operable without development by the Assembly):

> Some Acts of Parliament have been confined in their effect to Wales . . . [including] the Children's Commissioner for Wales Act 2001, the Health (Wales) Act 2003, the Public Services Ombudsman (Wales) Act 2005 and the Transport (Wales) Act 2006. Many other Acts have contained 'Wales-only' provisions and much delegated legislation has been made, since 1999 in large measure by the National Assembly, with application only to Welsh institutions.[70]

With its remit secure, as early as July 2002 the Welsh Assembly established the Richard Commission to consider whether the Assembly's powers and composition were adequate to the needs of the people of Wales. Following extensive public consultations the Commission concluded, in early 2004, that the Welsh electorate valued the Assembly's 'openness and responsiveness' and identified a widespread belief 'that the performance of the Assembly has been constrained by the present powers'.[71] Indeed, the Commission considered that although the Welsh Assembly's executive committee had enjoyed some success in promoting a Welsh agenda within Westminster legislation, its limited powers forced it to engage in horse trading.[72] The Commission concluded that for as long as the focus remained on Westminster and not on Cardiff, the Welsh Assembly would not be able to fulfil the growing expectations of the Welsh electorate. Two years after the Report, Parliament enacted a phased enhancement of the Assembly's powers under the Government of Wales Act 2006. The Act would also do away with the inadequate provisions for an executive committee within the Welsh Assembly. Part 2 of the Act created a Welsh Assembly Government headed by a First Minister (in keeping with the other devolved administrations),[73] although in truth the terms 'Executive Committee' and 'First Secretary' were rarely used in Assembly publications even between 1998 and 2006, given that they emphasised the limited nature of Welsh devolution in this era. In the Wales Act of 2014 the statute book finally caught up with common parlance, officially re-designating the Welsh Assembly Government as the Welsh Government.[74]

(ii) From subordinate legislation to enhanced legislative powers

Westminster's first extension of the Welsh Assembly's power predated the Government of Wales Act 2006 and required no new legislation. The UK Government came to accept that, if the Welsh Assembly was to fulfil its mandate it would have to be able to exercise a broad subordinate law-making competence. Prior to devolution, when Parliament had delegated

---

[70] C. Himsworth, 'Devolution and its jurisdictional asymmetries' (2007) 70 MLR 31, 35.
[71] Lord Richard, *The Report of the Richard Commission* (2004) 45.
[72] Ibid., 148.
[73] Government of Wales Act 2006, s. 45(1).
[74] Wales Act 2014, s. 4(1).

the ability to make secondary legislation to the Secretary of State for Wales, safeguards were often put in place in an effort to prevent such powers from being abused. But what was a sensible restraint over the executive's competence looked more like an unjustified restraint on the activity of the Welsh Assembly, which exercised its own oversight mechanisms. As Simon McCann, one of the Assembly's legal team, recognised, giving up this hang-over of the pre-devolution era enabled the Assembly to exercise its powers under the 1998 Act to their full extent:

> [W]hen primary legislation confers new powers on the Assembly, it may often be appropriate to draw those powers as widely as possible, leaving it to the democratic mechanisms in Cardiff to exercise the proper checks and balances over the use of the new powers. This is a format which is likely to be followed in future Bills where appropriate, thus expanding the legislative powers of the Assembly and conferring greater freedom on it to exercise those powers as the needs of Wales require.[75]

The presumption that the UK Government would draft primary legislation broadly in spheres of devolved competence (thereby permitting the Assembly to enact wide-ranging secondary legislation), was not accompanied by an extension of the areas of devolved competence under the Government of Wales Act 2006 (now found in schedule 5 of that Act). Instead, the 2006 Act allowed Wales' Government to request permission from the UK Government (by Order in Council) to make pieces of primary legislation within specified fields of its devolved competence, known as 'Assembly Measures'.[76]

Following the 2006 Act, the Welsh Assembly moved quickly to request the competence to make Assembly Measures in a number of fields, with Westminster providing 15 Legislative Competence Orders between 2007 and 2010. Under the National Assembly for Wales (Legislative Competence) (Agriculture and Rural Development) Order,[77] for example, Westminster granted the Assembly the power to make legislation in a number of areas relating to agriculture (Art. 2 on the Order, for example, allows the Assembly to pass legislation on a wide range of issues affecting the red meat industry). As each of these Legislative Competence Orders was enacted, the Welsh Assembly's scope for enacting primary legislation grew, but these powers remained patchy by comparison to the Scottish Parliament's wide-ranging law-making powers. This was, however, simply one stage in the incremental process of extending the Assembly's powers, allowing Assembly officials an opportunity to develop experience of legislative drafting.[78]

(iii) Primary legislative powers

The 2006 Act did not simply provide for Assembly Measures as a limited extension of the Assembly's powers, it also laid down how, in the future, wider powers to make primary legislation could be granted in the devolved fields of competence.[79] The 2006 Act provided

---

[75] S. McCann, 'Permissive Powers are Good for the Health: The Health Reforms in Wales' (2003) 2 *Wales Law Journal* 176, 178.

[76] Government of Wales Act 2006, ss. 93–102.

[77] National Assembly for Wales (Legislative Competence) (Agriculture and Rural Development) Order 2009 (SI 2009/1758).

[78] A. Trench, 'The Government of Wales Act 2006: the next steps on devolution for Wales' [2006] PL 687, 691.

[79] Government of Wales Act 2006, ss. 103–16.

that if two-thirds of AMs passed a resolution requesting that general primary law-making powers be devolved to Wales, and succeed in gaining the support of the Welsh electorate for such a proposal in a referendum, the Welsh Assembly would be granted such powers.

In February 2010, the First Minister, Carwyn Jones, gained the Assembly's permission (by a vote of 53–0) to trigger a referendum on primary legislative powers. In making his pitch for enhanced powers, the First Minister drew on the success of Assembly Measures:

> The Measures already passed – legislation which is making school transport safer, delivering integrated support for vulnerable children and their families, tackling child poverty, giving young people wider educational choices, and much more – have shown what we can achieve. However, we could do even more if all new laws on subjects which are already our responsibility as a government could be made here in Wales.[80]

In March 2011 the 63.5 per cent of Welsh voters, on a turn-out of 35.6 per cent, approved the proposal for primary law-making competence. Following the success of the referendum, the Assembly gained the power to make Acts of the Assembly in its areas of competence (set out in full, with exceptions, in schedule 7 of the 2006 Act). The transitional power to request 'Assembly Measures' became redundant and lapsed. Wales had gained a level of primary legislative competence.

The Wales Acts 2014 and 2017

Thereafter the 'process' of devolution in Wales accelerated. Once the Welsh people had accepted that the Assembly should have primary law-making functions efforts needed to be made to make its competences comparable to those of the Scottish institutions.[81] The Wales Act 2014 introduced fiscal powers to the Welsh institutions, devolving responsibility for stamp duty[82] and landfill taxes.[83] It also held out the possibility of powers to vary income tax, although only after another referendum.[84] Following the Scottish independence referendum and the passage of the Scotland Act 2016, a more profound shift was made. In the Wales Act 2017 the Wales Assembly also received powers to vary its electoral rules.[85] Furthermore, perhaps indicating a level of referendum fatigue, Westminster dropped the requirement for a referendum for the Welsh Assembly to gain powers to vary income tax (which will now enter force in 2019).[86] Of even greater significance is the profound shift in the nature of the Welsh Assembly's competences. Prior to this Act the Welsh scheme listed the competences possessed by the Assembly (a 'conferred powers' model), whereas the Scottish Parliament was instead able to legislate in any area not reserved to Westminster (a 'reserved powers' model).[87]

---

[80] C. Jones, AM, *Press Release: One Wales Government Announces Commitment to Seeking Referendum on New Powers* (2 February 2010).

[81] R. Rawlings, 'Riders on the Storm: Wales, the Union, and Territorial Constitutional Crisis' (2015) 42 JLS 471, 475–476.

[82] Wales Act 2014, s. 15.

[83] Ibid., s. 18.

[84] Ibid., s. 8 to s. 14.

[85] Wales Act 2017, s. 5 to s. 8.

[86] Wales Act 2017, s. 17.

[87] R. Rawlings, 'Riders on the Storm: Wales, the Union, and Territorial Constitutional Crisis' (2015) 42 JLS 471, 485.

As the Welsh Secretary, Alun Cairns, made clear to Parliament, the UK Government's major concern in this shift was to limit the restraint on law making in Wales (especially in light of UK Supreme Court cases which we will consider in the next chapter[88]):

> The Government's key aim in introducing the new reserved powers model is to deliver clarity on the boundary between the Assembly's competence and the competence of this Parliament, particularly in the light of the Supreme Court judgment on the Agricultural Wages Board settlement. Many amendments therefore either alter or remove altogether reservations contained in new schedule 7A to the Government of Wales Act 2006.[89]

Although Welsh devolution has therefore, in many respects, caught up with practice in Scotland (and also, as we shall see, Northern Ireland) the Welsh Assembly still lacks competences in areas such as crime and policing enjoyed by Holyrood and Stormont. Even with its new fiscal powers, the Welsh Assembly only controls a tenth of its income (making it much more reliant on the block grant than Scotland). Finally, the Assembly has not expanded in size in light of its new powers. As Trench asserts, '[i]f the Assembly becomes at all active as a legislature, it is hard to see how the issue of its size can be avoided, and so fresh Westminster legislation will be needed'.[90] Welsh devolution remains a work in progress.

Devolution in practice: Northern Ireland

Key issues

- Northern Ireland was the first part of the UK to experience devolved government, with a devolved Parliament of Northern Ireland sitting from June 1921 to March 1972. This Unionist-dominated Parliament was suspended amid the early years of the Northern Ireland conflict, having failed to address the needs of the nationalist community in Northern Ireland.

- In Northern Ireland devolution is one facet of the Good Friday/Belfast Agreement, a peace settlement intended to bring an end to years of political violence. As a result, devolution was not intended simply to improve standards of governance in Northern Ireland but to provide a forum in which nationalist and unionist politicians could co-operate.

- The Northern Ireland Assembly enjoys broad law-making powers equivalent to those of the Scottish Parliament, but in a more limited range of areas. The Northern Ireland Act 1998 makes provision for additional, currently 'reserved', areas of competence to be transferred to the Assembly provided that it is functioning satisfactorily.

The peace process and the 1998 referendum

Unlike Wales and Scotland, devolution was not a free-standing policy when it came to Northern Ireland. The devolution of power to an elected Northern Ireland Assembly was instead part of the peace process seeking a resolution which would end the intense period of political violence (the 'Troubles') which had affected Northern Ireland since 1969. When the Unionist-dominated Parliament of Northern Ireland was suspended by Westminster in

---

[88] See pp. 399–400.
[89] Alun Cairns, MP, HC Debs, vol. 620, col. 221 (24 January 2017).
[90] A. Trench, 'The Government of Wales Act 2006: the Next Steps on Devolution for Wales' [2006] PL 687, 696.

1972 (and formally abolished the following year), Westminster took over the governance of Northern Ireland. This re-imposition of 'direct rule' from Westminster marked a watershed in both the Troubles and the history of devolution in the UK. It provided a clear example of Westminster's ultimate sovereignty and prevented the Unionist Parties from maintaining policies and legislation which were discriminatory towards the minority Nationalist community in Northern Ireland. After 1972, however, all parties in Northern Ireland could blame Westminster directly for the ongoing governance failures in the province.

Following more than two decades of political violence, the 1990s saw progress towards a peace settlement. When Labour entered office in 1997, a ceasefire was established between the largest organisations involved in political violence, and negotiations commenced. Devolution was central to these negotiations, as it would involve Northern Ireland regaining responsibility for internal government affairs. A significant problem, however, lay in how to devise a system of devolution which avoided the entrenchment in power of parties representing the Unionist community, which continued to constitute the majority of the population of Northern Ireland, as had happened between 1921 and 1972. The aim of the 'Good Friday Agreement' (also known as the 'Belfast Agreement'),[91] which was accepted by most of the major political parties in Northern Ireland in April 1998, therefore, was not simply to devolve power from Westminster to institutions based in Northern Ireland, but to 'ensure that all sections of the community can participate and work together successfully in the operation of these institutions and that all sections of the community are protected'.[92] This guiding principle would mean that Northern Ireland's Assembly, operating under the Northern Ireland Act (NIA) 1998, would function very differently from the devolved legislatures in Wales and Scotland, as Lord Bingham recognised:

> The 1998 Act . . . was passed to implement the Belfast Agreement, which was itself reached, after much travail, in an attempt to end decades of bloodshed and centuries of antagonism. The solution was seen to lie in participation by the unionist and nationalist communities in shared political institutions, without precluding . . . a popular decision at some time in the future on the ultimate political status of Northern Ireland.[93]

Thinking Point . . .

The Good Friday/Belfast Agreement was not solely concerned with the establishment of devolution. Devolution was only part of a wider peace settlement which also included provisions for (amongst other issues) inter-governmental co-operation between the UK and Ireland, policing reform, decommissioning of paramilitary weapons, prisoner releases for individuals convicted of offences related to the Troubles and constitutional guarantees by the UK and Ireland on the status of Northern Ireland.

In May 1998, just over a month after the Agreement was concluded, its proposals formed the basis of a referendum. Of the major political parties in Northern Ireland, the Social Democratic and Labour Party and Sinn Féin (both Nationalist), supported the Agreement, as did the Ulster Unionist Party (Unionist) and the Alliance Party (non-aligned). Opposition to

---

[91] HM Government, *Agreement Reached in Multiparty Talks* (1998) Cm. 3883.
[92] Ibid., Strand One, para. 5.
[93] *Robinson v Secretary of State for Northern Ireland* [2002] UKHL 32; [2002] NI 390, [10].

the Agreement was led by the Democratic Unionist Party (Unionist). On a high turnout of 81 per cent of registered voters, the Agreement was approved by 71 per cent. This, however, left a vocal minority in Northern Ireland opposed to the settlement, which would prevent a smooth start to the operation of devolved governance.

The Northern Ireland Act 1998

(i) The Northern Ireland Assembly: composition and voting arrangements

In order to keep the momentum of the peace process going, the first elections to the new 108-seat Northern Ireland Assembly took place in June 1998, several months before the NIA 1998 was passed by Westminster. Therefore, despite Northern Ireland's referendum on devolution happening nearly nine months after those in Scotland and Wales, the Northern Ireland Assembly would be the first of the legislatures established in 1998 to convene. The rapid implementation of the Good Friday Agreement was aided by the existence of Parliament Buildings at Stormont (which had, up to 1972, housed the Parliament of Northern Ireland), meaning that no new accommodation needed to be found for the new legislature.

Few features of political life in Northern Ireland are uncontroversial, and the electoral system is no exception. Historically, in the era of the Parliament of Northern Ireland, the Unionists had artificially inflated their parliamentary majority by the use of a FPTP system, often in constituencies drawn up to maximise the Unionist vote (rather than to attempt to ensure comparable worth to each vote) and by permitting multiple votes to university graduates and business owners (a move which gave disproportion electoral weight to affluent members of the Unionist community). The electoral system adopted in the Northern Ireland Act 1998, therefore, had to counter this toxic legacy. The single transferable vote (STV) system was adopted, dividing Northern Ireland into 18 constituencies (the same constituencies used for electing MPs to Westminster), each returning six Members of the Legislative Assembly (MLAs).[94] If Wales had too few representatives this system gave Northern Ireland rather too many to serve a much smaller polity, and beginning with the 2017 Assembly election the number of MLAs was reduced to 90 (five for each of the 18 constituencies).[95]

As we saw in Chapter 9,[96] under such systems electors rank candidates in order of preference. Candidates who achieve more than one-sixth of the total votes cast are elected outright, and their additional votes over that quota are reallocated to other candidates. If all seats are not filled by this process, the candidate with the lowest number of votes is eliminated and his or her votes are reallocated according to second (and ultimately lower) preferences.[97] This process of elimination and reallocation continues until all seats are filled. In the context of Northern Ireland, STV has the particular merit of ensuring that candidates gain election in accordance to the proportion of votes cast for them, and, with multi-member constituencies, members of the minority community in a constituency will often be able to return at least some representation for their viewpoint (in contrast to single-member constituencies under FPTP, where only the electors supporting the candidate with the most votes may feel that their views are going to be represented in the legislature). The latest Assembly elections produced the chamber set out in Table 12.5:

---

[94] Northern Ireland Act 1998, s. 33.
[95] Assembly Members (Reduction of Numbers) Act (Northern Ireland) 2016, s. 1.
[96] See pp. 307–10.
[97] Northern Ireland Act 1998, s. 34.

Table 12.5 Election results for the Northern Ireland Assembly (2017)

Party	Designation	Number of seats	Percentage of seats	Percentage of first-preference votes
DUP	Unionist	28	31.1	28.1
Sinn Féin	Nationalist	27	30.0	27.9
SDLP	Nationalist	12	13.3	11.9
UUP	Unionist	10	11.1	12.9
Alliance	Other	8	8.9	9.1
Other	(2 Unionist, 3 other)	5	5.6	N/A

The electoral system for the Assembly may be distinctive, but unique arrangements govern how legislation is made. Under section 4(5) NIA 1998, all MLAs must officially be designated as 'Unionist', 'Nationalist' (or implicitly as 'other', where parties do not claim to represent either of the traditional national communities in Northern Ireland). Various measures, such as financial legislation[98] (and, indeed, any legislation which 30 or more MLAs express concern over[99]), can only be passed if they gain 'cross-community support'. For legislation to achieve cross-community support, where it is required, either of the following conditions must be fulfilled:

(a) the support of a majority of the members voting, a majority of the designated Nationalists voting and a majority of the designated Unionists voting; or

(b) the support of 60 per cent of the members voting, 40 per cent of the designated Nationalists voting and 40 per cent of the designated Unionists voting.[100]

The effect of this requirement, according to Richard Wilford, is to produce 'parliamentary life, but not quite as we know it'.[101] In other words, if we accept the workings of a majoritarian Parliament like Westminster as our paradigm legislature (having been, we have seen, largely reproduced in the operation of the Scottish Parliament and the Welsh Assembly), then Wilford would argue that the Northern Ireland Assembly is distinctive. In order to protect the minority community from abuses of power, the majority of MLAs is not free to impose their legislative wishes on the minority. Instead, if legislation touches on important issues, it will only be passed with the consent of a majority of both Nationalists and Unionists.

Table 12.5 shows the make-up of the Assembly in the summer of 2017 and reveals the close correlation between percentages of first-preference votes cast and seats won in the 2017 elections. The price of such protection is that, at times of tension between the communities, these provisions can be used to prevent legislation even if there is no good reason why it should not be decided by a simple-majority vote.[102] The DUP, for example, used this

---

[98] Ibid., s. 63(3).

[99] Ibid., s. 42(1).

[100] Ibid., s. 4(5).

[101] R. Wilford, 'Northern Ireland: The politics of constraint' (2010) 63 *Parliamentary Affairs* 134, 137.

[102] See A. Schwartz, 'How Unfair is Cross-Community Consent? Voting Power in the Northern Ireland Assembly' (2011) 61 NILQ 349, 360–1.

mechanism to block same-sex marriage proposals even though they were backed by a majority of MLAs in 2015. In rejecting a challenge to the lack of recognition of same-sex marriage in Northern Ireland, O'Hara J noted the mounting frustration with petitions of concern:

> To the frustration of supporters of same-sex marriage the Assembly has not yet passed into law any measure to recognise and introduce same sex marriage. Their frustration is increased by the fact that the Assembly has voted by a majority in favour of same sex marriage but by reason of special voting arrangements which reflect the troubled past of this State that majority has not been sufficient to give the vote effect in law.[103]

Although such measures may have been necessary as Northern Ireland made the transition from political violence to democratic politics, the longer provisions give special weight to parties which claim to be 'Nationalist' or 'Unionist' the harder it will become for Northern Ireland to escape political segregation into two communities, perpetually defined in opposition to each other.

(ii) The Northern Ireland Executive

The requirement of cross-community support in the functioning of Northern Ireland's devolved institutions does not stop with the passing of legislation, but extends into the functioning of the Northern Ireland Executive. The 'Nationalist' and 'Unionist' designations remain important. The largest party identifying itself with the larger of the two denominations in the Assembly nominates Northern Ireland's First Minister[104] and the largest party of the other denomination nominates the Deputy First Minister.[105] To date, the First Minister has always been Unionist and the Deputy First Minister has always been Nationalist. The titles, however, are largely symbolic, for in keeping with the power-sharing ideals of the Good Friday Agreement, if either of these office holders resigns, the other must also do so.[106] As with the Scottish Government, the Northern Ireland Executive inherited many of the administrative powers previously exercised by the Secretary of State for Northern Ireland.[107] These powers, of course, could be augmented through future legislation by the Assembly.[108] No power, however, can extend beyond the areas of competence transferred to the Assembly, necessitating a consideration of these competences.

The leading members of the Executive do not, however, choose the other Northern Ireland ministers at their discretion from within their parties. Instead they co-chair an Executive to which the 1998 Act requires that all of the major parties in the Assembly be entitled to nominate ministers.[109] The allocation of ministerial office takes place automatically, according to a mathematical formula known as the d'Hondt system. When it is the turn of a party to nominate a minister under this system, they can choose any ministerial

---

[103] *In re X* [2017] NIFam 12, [3].
[104] Northern Ireland Act 1998, s. 16A(5).
[105] Ibid., s. 16A(6).
[106] Ibid., s. 16B(2).
[107] Ibid., s. 23(2).
[108] Ibid., s. 22(1).
[109] Ibid., s. 18(2).

portfolio which has not already been filled.[110] The result was that for much of the life of the Assembly between 2007 and 2017 there was no meaningful opposition in the Assembly, with as many as five parties having a place in the Executive. The 1998 Act, therefore, established power sharing, but does so at the expense of the normal functions of government in a liberal democracy. Even when some of the major political parties in Northern Ireland lost large numbers of their Assembly seats in elections (as happened to the UUP and SDLP in 2007), they retained some representation in the Executive. After the 2016 Assembly elections the decision of the UUP and SDLP to co-operate within an official opposition for the first time seemed to offer an opportunity to move towards some form of adversarial politics.[111]

(iii) The Northern Ireland Assembly: competence and finance

Given the complex nature of Northern Ireland's political arrangements under the NIA 1998, it should be unsurprising that the competences devolved to the Assembly and its financing would also reflect the tentative nature of devolution. In terms of finance, no tax altering powers were granted to the Assembly. It would instead administer its functions using part of the Consolidated Fund of Northern Ireland, which was allocated from Westminster under the Barnett Formula.

Unlike Wales, the people of Northern Ireland had made a clear statement in the 1998 referendum that they were supportive of wide-ranging devolved power. On the other hand, Northern Ireland's political parties had yet to show that they could co-operate effectively under the power-sharing arrangements. Therefore, the Northern Ireland Assembly's powers are something of a compromise. In contrast to the Welsh Assembly, from the outset it enjoyed primary law-making competence. By comparison to the Scottish Parliament, however, relatively few areas of competence would automatically be transferred to Stormont under the NIA 1998. Instead, the Act set out two groups of functions that the Assembly could not exercise, those relating to reserved and excepted matters. The three classes of competence (with transferred powers being implied by the Act as covering all matters neither reserved nor excepted) are set out in Table 12.6.

Under schedule 2 of the NIA 1998, 'excepted' matters are issues of national importance to the UK as a whole (or are matters so sensitive in the Northern Ireland context as to require them to be governed by Westminster legislation). 'Reserved' matters, under schedule 3, are instead those areas of competence which would continue to be exercised by Westminster after 1998, until such time as the political parties in Northern Ireland established that they could share power responsibly. The eventual transfer of this category of competences, together with the powers already transferred, would make the Assembly's law-making remit broadly comparable to that of the Scottish Parliament. The NIA 1998's 'reserved' powers encapsulate the idea of devolution as a 'process' and not an 'event' in the Northern Ireland context, holding out the promise of new competences for the Assembly if devolution functioned effectively. For much of the first decade after devolution, however, the transfer of further powers seemed like a distant possibility.

---

[110] Ibid., s. 18(5).
[111] B. Dickson, 'Devolution' in J. Jowell, D. Oliver and C. O'Cinneide (eds), *The Changing Constitution* (8th edn, OUP, 2015) 249, 266.

Table 12.6 Competences of the Northern Ireland Assembly in 1998

Excepted competences	Reserved competences	Transferred competences
The Crown	Criminal law	Finance and personnel
Elections (including the franchise)	Policing	Health, social services and public safety
International relations	Prisons	Education
Defence and national security	Civil aviation	Agriculture and rural development
Honours	Navigation	Enterprise, trade and investment
Nationality	Post Office	Environment
National taxation	Disqualification from membership of the Assembly	Culture, arts and leisure
Appointment and removal of judges	Emergency powers	Learning and employment
Registration of political parties	Civil defence	Regional development
Coinage, etc.	Consumer protection	Social development
Nuclear energy and installations	Telecommunications and broadcasting	
Regulation of sea fishing outside Northern Ireland		
The provisions of the Northern Ireland Constitution Act 1973 and Northern Ireland Act 1998		

New hopes and false dawns

(i) From the collapse of the first Assembly to the St Andrews Agreement 2006

From the outset, devolution in Northern Ireland ran into difficulty. Disputes between the parties elected to the Assembly over controversial issues such as prisoner releases under the Good Friday Agreement 1998 prevented powers from being transferred to Stormont until December 1999. Over the next three years opposition to the Good Friday Agreement within the Unionist community strengthened and in October 2002 the Assembly was suspended amid allegations that Sinn Féin party officials were using their access to Stormont to gain information useful to the Provisional IRA (a banned organisation linked to Sinn Féin which was heavily involved in the Troubles).

The situation appeared to worsen with the 2003 Assembly elections, in which the hitherto anti-Agreement DUP eclipsed the pro-Agreement UUP as the Assembly's largest Unionist party. There seemed little chance of the DUP agreeing to enter government with Sinn Féin, the largest Nationalist party. Three years of stop–start negotiations ensued between the UK Government, the Irish Government and the Northern Ireland Parties. In

2005, these efforts received a boost when the decommissioning of Provisional IRA weapons was confirmed, and the following year the parties reached the St Andrews Agreement (with its provisions put into effect by Westminster in the Northern Ireland (St Andrews Agreement) Act 2006). The DUP agreed to return to power-sharing and Sinn Féin agreed to accept the Police Service of Northern Ireland. Fresh elections took place in March 2007 and the Assembly was restored on 8 May 2007.

(ii) New powers

The 2007 restoration of power-sharing paved the way for new powers to be transferred to the Assembly which had hitherto been 'reserved' to Westminster. The Northern Ireland Assembly passed legislation establishing a Department of Justice and in April 2010 powers over policing, prisons and criminal law were devolved amending Table 12.6 above.[112] With the transfer of policing competence, the Assembly's law-making competences began to look comparable to those of the Scottish Parliament. The Assembly, however, has no tax altering powers comparable to those of the Scottish Parliament. Following the 2010 general election the Coalition *Programme for Government* included a prominent pledge to promote 'economic prosperity' in Northern Ireland.[113] One of the major problems for the economy, during and even after the Troubles, is that Northern Ireland attracts little private-sector investment because of the perceived risk of terrorist violence. As a consequence, a higher percentage of jobs in Northern Ireland depend upon the public sector than in other parts of the UK.[114] The Executive therefore lobbied for the power to vary Northern Ireland's corporation tax rate from that of the rest of the UK to make it more attractive as a base for private companies (and to enable it to compete with the Republic of Ireland's low corporation tax rate).[115] Alongside the overhaul of devolution arrangements in the wake of the Scottish independence referendum Parliament passed the Corporation Tax (Northern Ireland) Act 2015.

(iii) The future of devolution in Northern Ireland

These new powers and the emergence of an official opposition within the Assembly might have suggested that devolution in Northern Ireland was moving on a comparable trajectory to Wales and Scotland. But day-by-day the devolved institutions were becoming ineffectual. The Executive was increasingly mired in procrastination and recriminations between the two major parties, which annual bouts of talks did little to alleviate.[116] After the 2016 Assembly elections the situation went from bad to worse. Brexit threatened to undermine the new strategy for attracting inward investment into Northern Ireland by lowering the corporation tax rate. Without the UUP, SDLP and Alliance in the Executive, the DUP and Sinn Féin found it increasingly difficult to co-operate. The collapse of the Assembly in early 2017 amid a scandal over the Renewable Heating Incentive scheme came before the UUP and SDLP had any meaningful opportunity to present themselves as an Executive in waiting. The result has been deadlock, with the major

---

[112] Northern Ireland Act 1998 (Amendment of Schedule 3) Order 2010, SI 2010/977.
[113] HM Government, *The Coalition: Our Programme for Government* (Cabinet Office, 2010) 28.
[114] See Northern Ireland Affairs Committee, *Corporation Tax in Northern Ireland* (2011) HC 558, para. 40.
[115] Ibid., para. 16.
[116] B. Dickson, 'Devolution' in J. Jowell, D. Oliver and C. O'Cinneide (eds), *The Changing Constitution* (8th edn, OUP, 2015) 249, 251.

parties unable or unwilling to co-operate in forming a new Executive. In just such circumstances the Secretary of State retains the important role of liaising between the Nationalist and Unionist blocs, and following the 2017 Northern Ireland Assembly election James Brokenshire was obliged to mediate upon so-far-fruitless efforts to restore power-sharing, all the while attempting to avoid the need for another election.[117] In November 2017, by which point Northern Ireland had been without functioning devolved institutions for nine months, the Northern Ireland Secretary informed the House of Commons that he would be proposing legislation to set out a budget for Northern Ireland in Westminster. He added, perhaps disingenuously, that this step 'does not mark a move to direct rule'.[118] A meaningful breakthrough, ending the cycle of crises in which devolution in Northern Ireland is mired, appears to be a distant possibility.

Conclusion

On the opening of the new Scottish Parliament in 1999, Donald Dewar, then Scotland's new First Minister, set out the reasoning behind devolution and his hopes for the new institution:

> Today, we reach back through the long haul to win this Parliament, through the struggles of those who brought democracy to Scotland, to that other Parliament dissolved in controversy nearly three centuries ago. Today, we look forward to the time when this moment will be seen as a turning point: the day when democracy was renewed in Scotland, when we revitalised our place in this our United Kingdom.[119]

He presented devolution as a solution to Scotland's lack of autonomy since it joined the Union, and one which would 'revitalise' Scotland's role within the UK. Since 1998, however, the powers enjoyed by the devolved institutions in Scotland, Wales and Northern Ireland have expanded. The changes we have charted in this chapter are illustrated in Figure 12.3.

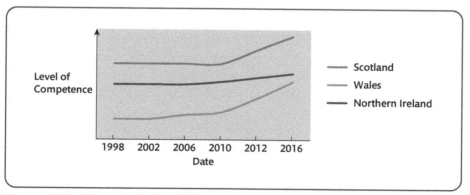

Figure 12.3 Changes in devolution arrangements since 1998

---

[117] Northern Ireland Act 1998, s. 32(3).
[118] James Brokenshire, MP, HC Debs, vol. 630, col. 994 (2 November 2017).
[119] D. Dewar, MP, 'The Voices of Scotland' *The Scotsman* (9 July 2008).

After the initial 'bedding-in' period of devolution, all of the institutions we have evaluated in this chapter have gained powers and competences, but these extensions have been far from uniform. In Scotland, where devolved powers were extensive to begin with, and matched by considerable public support for devolution, formal moves towards extending devolved law-making competences only began with the Calman Commission Report, which fed into the Scotland Act 2012. More importantly the offers of extended powers made by the pro-Union parties in the course of the 2014 independence referendum led to the enactment of the Scotland Act 2016. In Wales, by contrast, initial support for devolution was at best equivocal. As a result the 1998 devolution arrangements were constrained by comparison to Scotland, but have been extended in stages, as public acceptance of devolution grew, culminating in the referendum on the transfer of primary law-making competence in 2011 and the shift to a reserved-powers model in 2017. In Northern Ireland the consociational model of devolution means that the willingness of the major parties to engage in power-sharing is all important. When this willingness exists the pressure to extend new competences to Stormont has been as strong as in Wales and Scotland, as seen in the 2010 transfer of competence over policing and criminal justice. When the major parties have been unable to work together, however, the work of the Northern Ireland Assembly has had to be suspended for extended periods (meaning that the competence curve for Northern Ireland in Figure 12.3 has at times been at best notional).

This ongoing cycle of competence transfers is driven by two overarching factors. First, the pressure upon the three different sets of devolved institutions to respond to the needs of their constituents drives requests for more powers. Second, when Westminster accedes to some such requests the other devolved administrations often use the resultant transfers of powers as a pretext for demands of their own, as seen in efforts by Scottish Ministers to secure a deal comparable to Northern Ireland on corporation tax powers in 2016.[120] The asymmetry of devolution therefore sustains the process of further transfers of competence. Notwithstanding these shifts in power to the devolved bodies, nationalist sentiment remains unquenched by devolution, and, in Scotland in particular, the SNP has seen a surge in support during the devolution era. Devolution may have revitalised democratic engagement in the UK's 'Celtic fringe', but it is more difficult to make the case that it has secured the place of Scotland, Wales and Northern Ireland within the UK. In the next chapter we will therefore have to consider how the constitutional relationship between the devolved institutions and the UK as a whole is developing.

Practice questions

1. *'Does the Secretary of State [for Scotland] agree that Scotland's democratic Parliament does not need Westminster's permission for a self-determination referendum, although a generous spirit from the Westminster Government would indeed be welcome?'*

---

[120] See P. Gourtsoyannis, 'SNP warns May not to short-change Scotland in DUP Agreement' *The Scotsman* (16 June 2017).

(Angus MacNeil, MP, HC Deb., vol. 538, col. 71 (10 Jan 2012))

Advise the Secretary of State on how to respond to this question.

2. *'The UK has an asymmetric model of devolution, a model which in the words of the Ministry of Justice "catered for specific demands for new democratic institutions in those parts of the UK (Scotland, Wales and Northern Ireland), while maintaining the sovereignty of the UK Parliament in Westminster". The differing settlements not only reflect the differences in the historical and institutional background of Scotland, Wales and Northern Ireland, but have also had a key impact in the way in which devolution and devolved politics had developed in each of those places.'*

(Justice Committee, *Devolution: A Decade on* (2009) HC 529, para. 10)

Evaluate whether there remains a clear rationale for the different powers of the UK's devolved institutions.

Further reading

This chapter attempts to place devolution in its historic context, and in this regard Michael O'Neill (**M. O'Neill, 'Great Britain: From Dicey to Devolution'** (2000) 53 *Parliamentary Affairs* 69–95) offers a useful introduction not only to the forces driving the devolution debate prior to 1998 but also to the devolution arrangements adopted in Scotland, Wales and Northern Ireland in 1998. This article is especially helpful in explaining how these arrangements differ from federalism. From that point it is useful to assess the success of devolution in practice, and Bridget Hadfield (**B. Hadfield, 'Devolution: A National Conversation'** in **J. Jowell and D. Oliver (eds),** *The Changing Constitution* (7th edn, OUP, 2011) 213–37) challenging the idea that there has been a devolution 'settlement', instead sees an evolving process of devolution since the Devolution Acts of 1998. She charts the development in the devolution arrangements in Wales, Scotland and Northern Ireland, providing a useful comparative overview of these three approaches to devolution. Her work sits well alongside that of Peter Leyland (**P. Leyland, 'The Multi-faceted Constitutional Dynamics of UK Devolution'** (2011) 9 *International Journal of Constitutional Law* 251–73), who provides a fascinating overview of devolution in operation, arguing that factors such as the limitations on Scotland's revenue raising powers, limitations on Wales's ability to make primary legislation, the failure to devolve certain law-making competences to Northern Ireland and the absence of England in the devolution settlement introduced an instability into the workings of devolution which inevitably led to pressure for further change to the systems. Having considered devolution in the round, it is a good idea to focus on the powers of the specific devolved institutions and their environments. Murray Leith (**M. Leith, 'Governance and Identity in a Devolved Scotland'** (2010) 63 *Parliamentary Affairs* 286–301) examines the impact of the workings of devolution on a sense of 'Scottishness', and how the distinctive character of political discourse in Scotland plays a role in reinforcing national identity, perpetuating demands for greater transfers of power to Scotland. Richard Rawlings (**R. Rawlings, 'Riders on the Storm: Wales, the Union, and Territorial Constitutional Crisis'** (2015) 42 *Journal of Law in Society* 471–498) provides similar coverage of Wales, usefully putting developments there in the context of shifts in the UK's system of government as a whole. Finally,

Richard Wilford (**R. Wilford, 'Northern Ireland: The Politics of Constraint'** (2010) 63 *Parliamentary Affairs* 134–155) evaluates the extensive constraints imposed upon politics in Northern Ireland under devolution and the operation of the devolution settlement before and after the St Andrews Agreement. His work will help readers to assess whether the terms of the legislative mechanisms, or the restraint of political actors, is more important in the operation of devolution in Northern Ireland.

Chapter 13
Devolution and the United Kingdom Constitution

'For how long will English constituencies and English Honourable members tolerate . . . at least 119 Honourable Members from Scotland, Wales and Northern Ireland exercising an important, and probably often decisive, effect on British politics while they themselves have no say in the same matters in Scotland, Wales and Northern Ireland?'

Tam Dalyell, MP, HC Debs, vol. 939, cols 122–3 (14 November 1977).

Chapter outline

This chapter examines the impact of devolution upon the UK's constitutional arrangements. Firstly, devolution requires a major departure for the courts from their historic reluctance to review legislation. Devolution obliges the courts to become involved in politically contentious debates and, where necessary, to strike down legislation enacted by the devolved legislatures if it exceeds the terms of their remit under the devolution arrangements. As the devolved administrations push for increased autonomy, this may even require the courts to rule upon the legitimacy of legislation seeking independence. Thereafter, the chapter focuses upon the place of England within the United Kingdom following devolution to Scotland, Northern Ireland and Wales. England remains the only non-devolved territory within the United Kingdom and, as such, continues to be governed from Westminster. This gives rise to a number of representational, legislative and administrative difficulties. This chapter outlines the consequences of England lacking any meaningful devolved structures of government, and the proposed responses to the difficulties associated with the most obvious of devolution's asymmetries.

Introduction

The last chapter sought to explain why devolution was instituted in 1998 and how the devolved institutions function in Scotland, Wales and Northern Ireland. This chapter moves on to examine how devolution has affected our understanding of the UK

Constitution. We evaluate how the devolved institutions interact with the 'sovereign' Parliament in Westminster at the limits of their competences and how these limits are policed by the courts. As we saw in the last chapter, devolution arrangements have not stood still since 1998. The devolved institutions in Wales, Scotland and Northern Ireland have each succeeded in gaining new powers. This seemingly inherent instability within the UK's constitutional arrangements creates pressure for further devolution of powers and potentially even aids independence movements. This chapter evaluates the legal strictures which attempt to lock Wales, Scotland and Northern Ireland into the UK. The quote which opens this chapter also obliges us to consider another potential weakness in the operation of devolution in the UK, the lack of devolution arrangements in England (with the exception of the relatively weak London Assembly). Parliamentarians from Scotland, Wales and Northern Ireland continue to exercise voting rights in Westminster, even over legislation which only affects English constituencies. As Tam Dalyell recognised, this state of affairs has the potential to create general dissatisfaction with the operation of devolution, which has contributed to the development of the 'English Votes for English Laws' process in Westminster.

Key issues

- The Devolution Acts establish subordinate legislatures. In other words, Westminster remains the 'sovereign' Parliament and certain law-making powers have been delegated to the devolved legislatures.

- The Devolution Acts commit the devolved institutions to respect the UK's international legal commitments. This means, for example, that in contrast to the courts' limited powers with regard to Westminster statutes under the HRA 1998, they can strike down devolved legislation that conflicts with the ECHR.

- Under the Devolution Acts, the courts are obliged to police the competence of the devolved legislatures. The Acts permit the courts to engage in pre- and post-enactment scrutiny of devolved legislation in order to ensure that the limits of these competences are respected.

- When the courts examine the legislation created by devolved institutions, they are undertaking the review of measures passed by elected bodies with legislative competence. This role has long been denied to courts in the UK due to the operation of parliamentary sovereignty. This requires that the courts adopt a new approach to judicial review of devolved legislatures.

- The Devolution Acts seemingly prevent, in law, efforts by devolved bodies to attempt to gain independence from the UK. With the expansion in competence of devolved bodies in the last decade, can these legal strictures be circumvented?

The subordinate nature of the devolved legislatures

The devolved legislatures as limited legislatures

(i) The 'triple lock'

Devolution was intended to answer aspirations for autonomy over domestic affairs affecting Wales, Scotland and Northern Ireland. Once granted, however, autonomy can deliver so successfully for residents of a region that they come to question why more powers are not devolved, or even to consider independence. In Scotland, for example, the success of devolution in creating responsive governmental institutions, at least by comparison to earlier 'direct rule' from Westminster, may have provided additional impetus for the Scottish independence movement. The Conservative Party fought the 1997 general election on the basis of a manifesto expressly opposed to devolution, arguing that it would 'create a new layer of government which would be hungry for power' and that devolved institutions would be drawn into 'rivalry and conflict' with Westminster.[1]

Tony Blair's Government attempted to address these concerns in its devolution arrangements, protecting the current structure of the UK with a system of three 'locks'.[2] The *first lock* is that the devolution legislation acknowledges that all of the devolved institutions 'owe their authority and indeed their existence to the Parliament of the United Kingdom'.[3] The Scotland Act 1998, for example, maintained that Westminster delegated law-making powers to the Scottish Parliament, and expressly stated that devolution 'does not affect the power of the United Kingdom Parliament to make law for Scotland'.[4]

The *second lock* relates to the wording of the devolution legislation. The statutes enacted in 1998 are technical in nature, shorn of the high-flown 'constitutional' rhetoric which had been employed by the Scottish Constitutional Convention (see Chapter 12[5]). In Rodney Brazier's account of the Scotland Act 1998, '[e]ven passages of fundamental constitutional importance are not given the prominence which it may be said that they deserve, but are tucked away in the 132-section statute, leaving it to the assiduous reader to find them'.[6] This approach was intended not to spoil the image of devolution by prominently asserting the degree to which Holyrood remained subject to both Westminster and even to the judiciary. Of the three pieces of devolution legislation passed in 1998, only the Northern Ireland Act refers to the possibility of future independence for this part of the UK. The Act affirms that Northern Ireland will remain part of the UK unless the majority of the people of Northern Ireland vote to leave the UK in a referendum.[7] Even this provision approached the issue of independence in negative terms, as it was intended to assure Unionists in Northern Ireland that devolution could not be regarded as a stepping stone to removing Northern Ireland from the UK and that any such decision would require a popular vote. As we shall see, only after the 2014 independence referendum would Westminster be obliged to recognise the 'permanence' of devolution to Scotland.[8]

The *third lock* comes in the form of the express limitations on the competences of the devolved legislatures set out in the devolution legislation. Even with regard to the most

---

[1] I. Dale, *Conservative Party General Election Manifestos* 1900–1997 (Routledge, 2000) vol. 1, 459.
[2] R. Brazier, 'The Constitution of the United Kingdom' (1999) 58 CLJ 96, 102.
[3] Ibid., 100.
[4] Scotland Act 1998, s. 28(7).
[5] See p. 367.
[6] R. Brazier, 'The Constitution of the United Kingdom' (1999) 58 CLJ 96, 103.
[7] Northern Ireland Act 1998, s. 1(2).
[8] See pp. 406–10.

powerful of the devolved law-making institutions, the Scottish Parliament at Holyrood, the Scotland Act asserts that legislation passed by the Scottish Parliament is not valid law insofar as any provisions of that legislation are beyond the legislative competence of the Parliament.[9] The Scottish Parliament therefore cannot act *ultra vires* and since constitutional issues remain solely within the competence of the Westminster Parliament, it would have to authorise any legislative efforts by the Scottish Parliament which could affect the make-up of the UK.

(ii) Intergovernmental relations

Together, these locks imply that devolution has created legislatures of limited competence, and even within these competences Westminster can still make law as it chooses. In strict legal terms that view may be accurate, but the longer devolution operates, the more conventions and practices will emerge which will render it 'increasingly difficult' for Westminster to exercise its ultimate sovereignty to restrain (or even abolish) the devolved institutions.[10] As the devolution legislation passed through Parliament, Tam Dalyell, a parliamentarian with a long-standing interest in the constitutional relations between the different parts of the UK, sought to persuade Parliament that the safeguards built into the devolution legislation were inadequate. Claims that Westminster had not been restricted in its law-making powers by devolution for Dalyell were 'palpably misleading', and 'as true as it would be to say that the Queen can veto any legislation'.[11] This is because, just as with the royal assent to legislation, constitutional conventions have developed to reflect the day-to-day realities of intergovernmental relations between Westminster and the devolved legislatures.

The most important of these conventions is the Sewel Convention, named after one of the Labour ministers, Lord Sewel, responsible for piloting the devolution legislation through Parliament. Lord Sewel stated that the effect of section 28(7) of the Scotland Act 1998 would be tempered by a constitutional convention:

> We would expect a convention to be established that Westminster would not normally legislate with regard to devolved matters in Scotland without the consent of the Scottish Parliament.[12]

Thinking Point . . .

The then Secretary of State for Scotland (subsequently the Scottish First Minister), Donald Dewar, MP, spoke in 1998 during the passage of the Scotland Bill of the 'possibility, in theory, of the United Kingdom Parliament legislating across [devolved] areas, but it is not a possibility we anticipate or expect'. (HC Debs, vol. 305, cols 402–3 (28 January 1998)).

---

[9] Scotland Act 1998, s. 29.

[10] See V. Bogdanor, 'Review Article: The Evolution of a Constitution: Eight Key Moments in British Constitutional History' (2007) 123 LQR 480, 483.

[11] HC Deb., vol. 305, col. 366 (28 January 1998).

[12] HL Debs, vol. 592, col. 791 (21 July 1998).

This assertion was affirmed in the later Memorandum of Understanding concluded between the UK Government and the devolved administrations.[13] The Sewel Convention ensures, as a matter of practical politics, that even though Westminster could theoretically make law which relates to devolved competences, it will not ordinarily do so without first seeking the devolved legislature's permission. If Westminster continued to legislate without such agreement, its law making would be 'unconstitutional', in the sense of breaching a constitutional convention. Under section 2 of the Scotland Act 2016 and section 2 of the Wales Act 2017 the Convention was even recognised in statute, although as we have already seen this did not give it any legally binding force over Westminster procedure.[14] The Convention applies equally to other devolved jurisdictions, but in Northern Ireland the Executive, rather than the Assembly, usually consents to Westminster legislation.

Thinking Point . . .

The Calman Commission Report suggested joint meetings of legislators from the devolved institutions and Westminster as a way to firm up the consent process: Commission on Scottish Devolution, *Serving Scotland Better: Scotland and the United Kingdom in the 21st Century* (2009) 13.

Sewel motions (also known as Legislative Consent Motions) have helped to secure the co-operative governance between Westminster and the devolved legislatures on important issues, particularly in the early years of devolution. Batey and Page studied the operation of law making affecting Scotland in the first three years after devolution entered force and found that the Scottish Parliament permitted over 30 Acts of Parliament from Westminster to apply in supposedly devolved areas. They explained this as a result of 'the continuing pull towards uniformity in a devolved system of government, a pull which has sometimes been most easily accommodated by relying on Westminster'.[15] The frequent reliance on Sewel motions in the early days of devolution is unsurprising, as it took time for the devolved institutions to fully assert their law-making competences. Moreover, this was an era in which Labour was in office in Westminster and was the majority party in coalitions in office in Holyrood and Cardiff. As Tam Dalyell forewarned, this 'honeymoon' era of intergovernmental relations would not last:

> The difficulty lies in the assumption that there will be an eternally amiable relationship [between the Westminster and Holyrood Parliaments] . . . It will be relatively amiable to start with, but, once there is strife on delicate . . . subjects, one will get into a variety of difficulties.[16]

With regard to Scotland, since the SNP gained power in Holyrood in 2007, fewer Sewel motions have been passed permitting Westminster to legislate in devolved areas, with successive SNP administrations carefully guarding the areas of power transferred to Scotland. Sewel motions are often confined to pieces of legislation set apart from the party-political agenda:

---

[13] HM Government, *Memorandum of Understanding and Supplementary Agreements between the United Kingdom Government, Scottish Ministers and the Cabinet of the National Assembly of Wales* (1999) Cm. 4444, para. 14.

[14] See pp. 50–1.

[15] A. Batey and A. Page, 'Scotland's Other Parliament: Westminster Legislation about Devolved Matters in Scotland since Devolution' [2002] PL 501, 502.

[16] HC Debs, vol. 305, col. 367 (28 January 1998).

Key debates

The operation of the Sewel Convention

Sewel motions are always particularly useful with regard to certain types of legislation. The first type of legislation is where an issue is pressing and demands a UK-wide response which induces the devolved administrations to accept the need to consent to Westminster legislating. An example of such legislation is the Anti-Terrorism, Crime and Security Act 2001, which extended to Scotland despite the Scottish Parliament's devolved authority over criminal law. The Scottish administration was clear as to the need to accept this legislation from Westminster given the general terrorist threat to the UK as a whole:

> [T]he people of Scotland . . . would not appreciate the constitutional niceties of an approach that could leave Scotland behind in time or in the rigour of the measures. [They] would prefer us to compromise on our powers of legislation rather than risk compromise on their security. (Iain Gray, SP OR col. 3872 (15 November 2001))

At the opposite end of the spectrum is legislation which is necessary, but over which there is little political controversy, and for which administrations in Holyrood and Westminster are reluctant to make time in busy parliamentary schedules. The Scottish Government can free up some time in Holyrood's schedule by allowing Westminster to enact such legislation, even if the subject matter lies within devolved competences. The Duke of Montrose provides an example of just such legislation:

> A recent exercise [of the Sewel convention] which comes to mind was the Marine and Coastal Access Act 2009 where Scottish inshore waters were already devolved and the application of the Food and Environment Protection Act 1985 under Scottish jurisdiction was already devolved but the Bill had to encompass all these and therefore the Sewel convention was very appropriate. (HL Debs, vol. 730, col. 214 (6 September 2011))

The passage of the Coalition Government's Welfare Reform Act 2012 through Westminster highlights the complexities arising from the need for co-operation between legislatures. As Lord Freud, the minister piloting the legislation through the House of Lords was obliged to recognise:

> [T]he Scottish Parliament voted on a legislative consent Motion to the Bill. Legislative consent was given in relation to several provisions. However, the Scottish Parliament did not give consent in respect of the provisions of the Bill that give Scottish Ministers the power to make consequential, supplementary, incidental or transitional provisions by regulation in relation to universal credit and the personal independence payment. I indicated on Report that I intended to bring forward these amendments, removing the relevant provisions from the Bill, to ensure that the UK Government adhere to the principles of the Sewel convention. (HL Debs, vol. 734, col. 1482–3 (31 January 2012))

The Sewel Convention marks just one element of interaction between Westminster and Holyrood. As Lord Freud proceeded to acknowledge, social security is a reserved matter enabling the Coalition Government to apply most of its legislation to Scotland without the need for consent. Nonetheless, the amendments to the benefits system contained within the 2012 Act require references to benefits in devolved legislation to be changed by the Scottish Parliament.

Under the UK's devolution arrangements much of the burden of navigating competence disputes rests upon 'the relationships, both formal and informal, between

Governments, Parliaments and the other institutions of the state'.[17] Informal relationships are maintained at both ministerial level and within the civil service. The formal arrangements for maintaining good relations have, however, shifted alongside other aspects of the devolution settlement. In the early phases of devolution the Secretaries of State for Scotland, Wales and Northern Ireland and their departments were envisaged as the principle conduits for maintaining good intergovernmental relations.[18] But such channels became increasingly strained as the UK's devolution arrangements matured and as parties with politically divergent views have taken office in Westminster and in the devolved institutions. Since 2002 structured formal relationships have been maintained through the Joint Ministerial Council (JMC), and since 2013 this body has assumed a dispute-settlement function.[19] One example of a dispute referred to JMC mechanisms was the Northern Ireland Executive's complaints over funding arrangements and the impact of budget cuts.[20] The JMC's annual report, however, contains little detail on the role of the JMC in resolving this dispute. It often functions as little more than a public forum in which the devolved administrations grandstand for the consumption of their own constituencies, generating countervailing efforts by the UK Government to sanitise the agenda and to delay JMC sessions.[21] In the aftermath of the Brexit referendum the Welsh and Scottish administrations have expressed frustration with how little they were being involved in the process of forging a UK position on Brexit, and the European Negotiations sub-committee of the JMC has not been operative since the Northern Ireland Assembly collapsed in early 2017.[22] Given the evident problems with these political mechanisms for managing intergovernmental relations under devolution, legal mechanisms are playing an increasingly important part in the devolution process.

The courts: policing the devolution settlement

(i) Pre- and Post-enactment scrutiny mechanisms

With law-making competences divided across two legislatures, and given the complex interaction between many reserved and devolved/transferred fields, scope exists for mistakes over competence even if both Westminster and the devolved legislatures respect each other's remit. As the legislation passed by the devolved legislatures does not enjoy parliamentary sovereignty, any potential errors as to competence can be challenged in the courts and the Devolution Acts impose a duty on the courts to ensure that these legislatures do not step outside the limits of their powers.

---

[17] Commission on Scottish Devolution, *The Future of Scottish Devolution within the Union: A First Report* (2008) 75.

[18] See HM Government, *Devolution: Memorandum of Understanding and Supplementary Agreements* (2000) Cm. 4806 and HM Government, *Devolution Guidance Note 3: The Role of the Secretary of State for Scotland* (Cabinet Office, 2006).

[19] See HM Government, *Devolution: Memorandum of Understanding and Supplementary Agreements* (Cabinet Office, 2013) Part 2A.

[20] JMC, *Annual Report 2012–2013* (2013) 3.

[21] Constitution Committee, *The Union and Devolution* (2016) HL 149, para. 287.

[22] See Committee on Exiting the EU, *The Government's Negotiating Objectives: The White Paper* (2017) HC 1125, paras 65–74.

The role of the courts is essentially the same under each of the Devolution Acts, and since the most high-profile litigation on the issue of legislative competence has arisen in the context of Scotland, the provisions of the Scotland Act 1998 will serve as our example in examining these powers. Schedule 6 of the Scotland Act explains that the courts have the function of deciding upon 'devolution issues', which essentially cover any 'question about whether a function is exercisable within devolved competence'.[23] In other words, after the Scottish Parliament has enacted legislation, this provision allows individuals to challenge its competence to do so, just as they could challenge whether any other body established under statute had exceeded its powers under judicial review (see Chapter 18[24]). Given the importance of such cases, the Act includes a facility to refer devolution issues to the Supreme Court.[25]

Neither the UK Government, nor the devolved administrations, need wait until legislation is in force to test its validity. Under the Scotland Act 1998, both the Attorney-General and the Lord Advocate, the senior law officers for the UK Government and the Scottish Executive respectively, have a special power to refer Scottish Parliament Bills to the Supreme Court for an authoritative assessment of whether the proposals exceed legislative competence.[26] Where the UK Government reasonably believes that such a Bill breaches the Scottish Parliament's competence, it can suspend the legislation's entry into force pending the Supreme Court's decision.[27] Similar arrangements apply to Wales and Northern Ireland and it is in the context of Wales that this procedure has seen most use, with the complex arrangements for primary law making in Wales prior to the Wales Act 2017 proving 'a recipe for litigation at Supreme Court level'.[28] Some of the pre-legislative interventions to date have been initiated by the UK Attorney-General, attempting to restrict proposed law making by the Welsh Assembly,[29] whereas other cases have been referred to the Supreme Court by the Counsel General for Wales as a means of checking that high-profile legislative proposals are not left in limbo by protracted legal challenges over competence.[30]

Thinking Point . . .

The Attorney-General for Northern Ireland enjoys the same power to refer Assembly's legislation to the Supreme Court under section 11 of the Northern Ireland Act 1998. When the Welsh Assembly gained primary law-making competence in the Government of Wales Act 2006, section 99 granted the courts similar scrutiny powers over 'Assembly Measures' that Cardiff is able to pass (and section 112 similarly applies to Assembly legislation).

---

[23] Scotland Act 1998, sch. 6.1(f).

[24] See p. 520–1.

[25] Scotland Act 1998, sch. 6.10 and 6.22.

[26] Ibid., s. 33(1).

[27] Ibid., s. 35(1).

[28] R. Rawlings, 'Riders on the Storm: Wales, the Union, and Territorial Constitutional Crisis' (2015) 42 JLS 471, 475.

[29] See *Re Local Government Byelaws (Wales) Bill* [2012] UKSC 53; [2013] 1 AC 792 and *Re Agricultural Sector (Wales) Bill* [2014] UKSC 43; [2014] 1 WLR 2622.

[30] See *Re Recovery of Medical Costs for Asbestos Diseases (Wales) Bill* [2015] UKSC 3; [2015] 1 AC 1016.

(ii) Reviewing subordinate legislatures

In exercising their review powers over legislation passed by the devolved legislatures, the courts are in the novel position in UK constitutional law of being able to review legislative competence. Parliamentary sovereignty, historically, has denied the courts a similar function where Westminster's legislation is at issue. Parliament sought to guide the courts in their interpretation of devolved legislation. Under section 101 of the Scotland Act 1998, the courts are under a duty not to automatically invalidate legislation which exceeds the Scottish Parliament's competence, but to first attempt to read a provision 'as narrowly as is required for it to be within competence, if such a reading is possible'.[31]

Legislation rarely imposes such general duties upon the courts as to how to approach their task of statutory interpretation, and the existence of such duties in all of the Devolution Acts is therefore significant. Ian Loveland considers these provisions to be a statutory echo of a hitherto largely forgotten common law principle that the courts should interpret the competence of subordinate legislative bodies generously.[32] Loveland draws support for this proposition from the case of *Edwards* v *Attorney-General for Canada*, which concerned the interpretation of a UK Act of Parliament establishing the Canadian system of government whilst Canada was still a dominion of the UK, and therefore subordinate to Westminster's sovereignty. Lord Sankey LC declared that the Privy Council should not seek 'to cut down the provisions of the Act by a narrow and technical construction, but rather to give it a large and liberal interpretation so that the Dominion . . . may be mistress in her own house'.[33]

Thinking Point . . .

Again, section 101 Scotland Act 1998 is mirrored by section 83 Northern Ireland Act 1998 and section 154 Government of Wales Act 2006, both of which require that the courts read-down provisions of legislation passed by the Welsh and Northern Ireland Assemblies where a broad interpretation of such legislation would exceed their competences.

This idea that the courts should be reluctant to question the competence of devolved legislatures was reinforced by the House of Lords' decision in *Gallagher* v *Lynn*.[34] In 1934, the Stormont Parliament enacted legislation regulating milk sales in Northern Ireland. This devolved legislation, however, was applied by the authorities in Northern Ireland to cross-border trade in milk, and Donegal farmers affected by the legislation argued that it impinged upon a reserved matter (international trade). Lord Atkin dismissed such claims on the basis that, whatever the measure's incidental effect on trade, its 'pith and substance . . . is . . . to protect the health of the inhabitants of Northern Ireland'.[35] These authorities suggest a common law principle that devolved legislatures should be subject to

---

[31] Scotland Act 1998, s. 101(2).
[32] I. Loveland, *Constitutional Law, Administrative Law and Human Rights* (5th edn, OUP, 2009) pp. 439–40.
[33] *Edwards* v *Attorney-General for Canada* [1930] AC 124, 136.
[34] *Gallagher* v *Lynn* [1937] AC 863.
[35] Ibid., 870.

more limited standards of judicial review than ordinary public bodies.[36] But if this is the case, the provisions of the Devolution Acts do not simply affirm this jurisprudence. When the courts addressed the first litigation tackling the devolved legislation passed in Wales, Scotland and Northern Ireland after 1998, they found a statutory instruction to attempt to read devolved legislation in line with competence if possible (and only to strike down such legislation if this task could not be achieved). But they found no legislative affirmation of the *Edwards* principle that devolved law-making competence should be construed broadly. This issue was to become an early test for the courts' approach to the devolved bodies.

Key debates

Theoretical models underpinning the review of devolved legislation

There is an old saying that it is not possible to place a square peg in a round hole, a saying which can be applied to the legislative competence of devolved assemblies. Legislation which exceeds the limits of a devolved assembly's competence is a 'square peg' which the courts cannot fit within the 'round hole' of competence, and which, therefore, must be rejected. The saying, however, assumes that neither the size of the hole nor the dimensions of the peg are flexible. The common law principle contained in *Edwards* v *A-G for Canada* involves the courts reading the *competence* of a devolved legislature expansively (so as permit a wide range of law making), whereas section 101 of the Scotland Act requires the courts to interpret *legislation* restrictively (in place of striking down such legislation as incompatible). By contrast, the rule in *Gallagher* v *Lynn* allows the courts to consider whether the main purpose of a statute is within a devolved legislature's competence (effectively 'trimming off' incidental effects of a statute to allow it to fit within competence). The distinct effects of each of these rules can be visualised as follows in Figure 13.1:

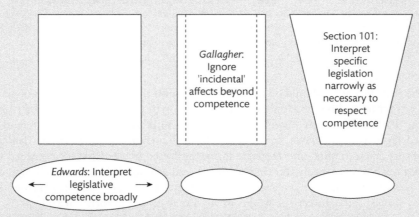

Gallagher. Ignore 'incidental' affects beyond competence

Section 101: Interpret specific legislation narrowly as necessary to respect competence

Edwards: Interpret ← legislative → competence broadly

Figure 13.1 Judicial management of devolved competences

---

[36] See also *Belfast Corporation* v *O.D. Cars* [1960] AC 490.

(iii) Legislative review in practice

Given the limited guidance within the Devolution Acts, several judges proposed different approaches to interpreting the legislative competence of the new institutions. In *Whaley* v *Lord Watson*[37] the claimant Whaley sought to prevent Watson, an MSP, from introducing legislation into the Scottish Parliament which would have banned fox hunting with hounds. The Court of Session dismissed the claim with little difficulty (the Scotland Act 1998 does not allow private individuals to request pre-enactment scrutiny of bills before the Scottish Parliament), but Lord Rodger did take the opportunity to consider how the courts should approach oversight of the Scottish Parliament's competences:

> [H]owever important its role [the Scottish Parliament] has been created by statute and derives its powers from statute. As such, it is a body which, like any other statutory body, must work within the scope of those powers. If it does not do so, then in an appropriate case the court may be asked to intervene and will be required to do so, in a manner permitted by the legislation.[38]

The Scottish Parliament proceeded to pass legislation, the Protection of Wild Mammals (Scotland) Act 2002, which did ban Hunting with Dogs in Scotland. In spite of their earlier rebuff in *Whaley*, the supporters of fox hunting made full use of the courts' jurisdiction to challenge this legislation. In *Adams* v *Scottish Ministers,* the Lord Justice Clerk, Lord Gill, accepted that the measures enacted by the Scottish Parliament constitute subordinate legislation. But, unlike Lord Rodger, he did not believe that the courts should treat the Scottish Parliament's competence in the same way they assessed the competences of ordinary public bodies because the legislative mandate of the devolved institutions made them exceptional.[39] Although Lord Gill's approach gained some academic support,[40] it would take the best part of a decade for this conflict to be resolved before the UK Supreme Court. In *Martin* v *Lord Advocate*[41] the majority in the Supreme Court expressly endorsed the application of the 'pith-and-substance test' first developed in *Gallagher* v *Lynn*. They did so, however, over a dissent led by Lord Rodger, in which he disavowed this test as overly generous to the devolved legislature and not supported by the language of the Scotland Act. Once again, he seemed intent on subjecting the Scottish Parliament to the same standards of judicial review as applied to ordinary public bodies. With argument on both sides finely poised, a special seven-judge panel of the Supreme Court was convened to consider the issue in the next case in which it arose.

Key case

AXA General Insurance Ltd v *Lord Advocate* (Scotland) [2011] UKSC 46; [2012] 1 AC 868 (Supreme Court)

This case concerned the Damages (Asbestos-related Conditions) (Scotland) Act 2009, which was enacted to ensure that insurance companies could be held responsible to pay claims arising out of asbestos-related conditions, in spite of earlier judicial decisions which denied

---

[37] *Whaley* v *Lord Watson* 2000 SC 340.
[38] Ibid., 348.
[39] *Adams* v *Scottish Ministers* 2004 SC 665, [48].
[40] B. Wintrobe, 'The Judge in the Scottish Parliament Chamber' [2005] PL 3, 11–12.
[41] *Martin* v *Lord Advocate* [2010] UKSC 10; 2010 SLT 412.

their liability. A number of insurers challenged this liability on the basis that it was outside the competence of the Scottish Parliament (as a breach of the ECHR's right to property, see below p. 594) or, as we will consider here, because such legislation was subject to judicial review on the grounds of irrationality, unreasonableness or arbitrariness. Lord Mance summarised the basis of the insurers' claims (at [96]):

> No doubt it was for financial reasons that the Scottish Parliament decided on this approach, rather than on an approach which would have imposed the resulting cost on Scottish taxpayers generally. One can have reservations about a policy framed . . . to avoid 'turning our backs on those who have contributed to the nation's wealth', when those whose backs were intended to bear the resulting burden were not the nation at large to whose wealth the contribution had been made, but employers and insurers who had, on a proper understanding of the common law and the relevant policies, never contracted to bear such cost.

Lord Hope accepted the insurers' assertion that Acts of the Scottish Parliament are subject to judicial review (at [46]):

> The Scottish Parliament takes its place under our constitutional arrangements as a self-standing democratically elected legislature. Its democratic mandate to make laws for the people of Scotland is beyond question. Acts that the Scottish Parliament enacts which are within its legislative competence enjoy, in that respect, the highest legal authority. The United Kingdom Parliament has vested in the Scottish Parliament the authority to make laws that are within its devolved competence. It is nevertheless a body to which decision making powers have been delegated . . . Sovereignty remains with the United Kingdom Parliament. The Scottish Parliament's power to legislate is not unconstrained. It cannot make or unmake any law it wishes.

As to the question of the approach the courts should take in exercising judicial review, Lord Reed (who delivered, alongside Lord Hope, one of the lead judgments in the court) was clear that the courts could not simply rely on the nineteenth-century case law which fed into decisions such as **Edwards** (at [141]):

> The question has arisen in the past in relation to overseas legislatures established by Parliament during the nineteenth century, but the context was not comparable to the devolution of legislative power within the United Kingdom, and the cases preceded modern developments in judicial review . . . [They offer], at best, an indirect way of approaching what seems to me to be the underlying question, which is the extent to which judicial review, having regard to its nature and purpose, can apply to the law-making functions of a devolved legislature. I prefer to approach that question directly.

Nonetheless, having disavowed the influence of cases such as **Edwards**, Lord Reed came to a remarkably similar conclusion as to the nature of the Scottish Parliament's competence as Lord Sankey had in the earlier case (at [146]):

> Within the limits set by section 29(2), however, [the Scottish Parliament's] power to legislate is as ample as it could possibly be: there is no indication in the Scotland Act of any specific purposes which are to guide it in its law-making or of any specific matters to which it is to have regard. Even if it might be said, at the highest level of generality, that the Scottish Parliament's powers had been conferred upon it for the purpose of the good government of Scotland, that would not limit its powers . . . The Act leaves it to the Scottish Parliament itself, as a democratically elected legislature, to determine its own policy goals. It has to decide for itself the purposes for which its legislative powers should be used, and the political and other considerations which are relevant to its exercise of those powers.

In essence, this left very little scope for 'traditional' judicial review. Beyond legislating upon reserved areas (or in some way transgressing the limits on competence set out in the Devolution Acts), the courts will only accept a challenge to devolved legislation if the assembly in question had acted fundamentally irrationally (see Lord Mance at [97], giving the example of 'a blatantly discriminatory decision directed at red-headed people') or in some way had breached common law fundamental rights in its legislation (for example, seeking to exclude judicial review; see Lord Hope at [43]).

If the hope was that the *AXA* case would provide a framework for seeing off competence disputes before they arose, the reality has been a flurry of litigation over devolved law making in Scotland and Wales.[42] Much as *AXA* attempted to lay down a framework of review that seeks to respect the mandate of the devolved administrations, as the devolved institutions gain new competences and move into new areas of law making litigation has been the inevitable result. And for all the courts might want to be flexible, as we shall see, the devolution legislation imposes particular red-lines with regard to EU and ECHR law. For example, in the pre-legislative review of the Welsh Assembly's Recovery of Medical Costs for Asbestos Diseases (Wales) Bill, Lord Thomas wanted to extend a great degree of law-making flexibility to the Assembly (in line with *AXA*):

> I have concluded that the view taken by the Welsh Assembly is a view which is reasonably open to it as a view of the public interest and of social justice on a matter of social and economic policy, I therefore consider great weight should be attached to the legislative choice made by the Welsh Assembly as expressed in the Bill enacted by it as primary legislation within its competence. It must follow therefore that the judgement of the Welsh Assembly as to the public interest and social justice should be preferred on matters of social and economic policy to a judicial view of what it regards as being in the public interest and representing social justice.[43]

But once he accepted that a provision of the proposed legislation infringed the right to property under A1P1 ECHR, he was obliged to conclude that the Welsh Assembly would exceed its competence if it enacted the measure.[44] The respect accorded by the courts to the democratic nature of devolved institutions nonetheless remains evident with regard to remedies. In *Christian Institute* the Supreme Court concluded that the information sharing provisions of Part 4 of the Children and Young People (Scotland) Act 2014 did not meet the requirements of Article 8 ECHR and were therefore outside the Scottish Parliament's competence.[45] The Court nonetheless accepted that the Scottish Parliament may need to have the opportunity to correct the defective provisions, under section 102(2)(b) of the Scotland Act 1998, and remitted this question to the consideration of the Scottish Courts.[46] Similarly in *Salvesen*, the Supreme Court suspended the effect of its judgment to allow for the Scottish Parliament to undertake remedial legislation.[47]

---

[42] See A. O'Neill, 'Back to the Future?: Judges, Politicians and the Constitution in the New Scotland' (2013) 18 JR 45.
[43] *Re Recovery of Medical Costs for Asbestos Diseases (Wales) Bill* [2015] UKSC 3; [2015] 1 AC 1016, [124].
[44] Ibid., [139].
[45] *Christian Institute* v *Scottish Ministers* [2016] UKSC 51; [2016] HRLR 19, [106].
[46] Ibid., [109].
[47] *Salvesen* v *Riddell* [2013] UKSC 22; [2013] HRLR 23, [58] (Lord Hope).

(iii) The devolved institutions and EU/ECHR law

The devolved institutions are bound by the UK's international commitments. Neither the Scottish Parliament[48] nor the Scottish Government[49] can use their powers in a manner which would breach EU law or the ECHR. With regard to EU law, this restriction mirrors the restriction on Westminster's own competence identified in the *Factortame* case (see Chapter 5[50]). But as Aidan O'Neill points out, the same is not true of the ECHR obligation imposed on the devolved legislatures. At a Westminster level, the HRA 1998 introduced, by mechanisms like declarations of incompatibility (see Chapter 21[51]), 'a delicate constitutional dialogue and a dance of deference between the judiciary and legislature but one where ultimately Parliament has the last word'.[52] By contrast, where devolved legislation conflicts with human rights, 'the courts are supreme and are required to strike down all and any "unconstitutional" acts of the devolved legislature'.[53]

In essence, the Devolution Acts create a distinct regime of rights protection, likened by Lord Rodger to an 'axe' by comparison to the HRA's 'scalpel'.[54] This axe can be used to strike down any legislation which conflicts with the ECHR:

> [I]n the case of acts or failures to act that are incompatible with the Convention rights, the Scotland Act contains its own system for dealing with the incompatibility in a way that gives effect to the Convention. The system is the same as that for any other act or failure to act that is said to be outside devolved competence. A statutory authority has no power to do anything that is outside its competence.[55]

This statement, made by Lord Hope, seems to run contrary to his decisions in *Martin* and in *AXA Insurance*. This only serves to emphasise, however, that the courts read the competence of the devolved legislatures broadly except, as in the case of human rights, where the sovereign Parliament in Westminster has ordered them not to do so. Nonetheless, when the courts have been obliged to bring the law in a devolved jurisdiction in line with human rights, the statutory requirement that the devolved legislatures and executives respect the ECHR has not lessened the political controversy raised by these decisions. In *Cadder* v *Her Majesty's Advocate*, the case concerned whether, under the Criminal Procedure (Scotland) Act 1995 (pre-devolution legislation passed by Westminster, but only applicable to Scotland's criminal justice system), evidence obtained during police interviews conducted in the absence of a solicitor could be admissible in court. The Supreme Court found that such interview practices were not compatible with Art. 6 ECHR and, noting the duty on members of the Scottish Government to respect human rights, ruled that the Lord Advocate had no power to rely on such evidence in criminal trials.[56] The decision provoked a storm of protest from Scotland's then First Minister, Alex Salmond, ostensibly on the basis that the UK Supreme Court should not have undermined such a distinct element of the Scottish criminal justice system. Nonetheless, once a breach of the ECHR was identified the decision was required by the Scotland Act's strictures with regard to human rights.

---

[48] Scotland Act 1998, s. 29.
[49] Ibid., ss. 167–176.
[50] See pp. 151–4.
[51] See pp. 660–72.
[52] A. O'Neill, 'Stands Scotland Where it Did?' (2006) 57 NILQ 102, 106.
[53] Ibid., 106.
[54] *R* v *HM Advocate* [2004] 1 AC 462; 2003 SC (PC) 21, [155].
[55] *Somerville* v *Scottish Ministers* [2007] UKHL 44; [2007] 1 WLR 2734, [18] (Lord Hope).
[56] *Cadder* v *Her Majesty's Advocate* (*Scotland*) [2010] UKSC 43; [2010] 1 WLR 2601, [55] (Lord Hope).

Alex Salmond's real problem with *Cadder* was that, in evidencing the courts' duty to police the boundaries of the devolution settlement, it highlighted the potential for the courts to undermine his quest for Scottish independence.

Thinking Point . . .

Following the **Cadder** controversy sections 35 and 36 of the Scotland Act 2012 limited the UK Supreme Court role in criminal appeals concerning 'devolution issues'. The Court now only has the power to determine the issue of compatibility with human rights, and appeals to the Supreme Court against the Scottish Parliament's criminal legislation and the actions of the Scottish Government in the criminal justice sphere are excluded.

From devolution to independence?

(i) Picking the triple lock

The 'triple lock' within the Devolution Acts places considerable emphasis on the safeguard that the courts will strike down devolved legislation which transgresses the limits of the devolved legislatures' competence. Nonetheless, these limits can be circumvented, as Lord Reed explained in *AXA*, if Westminster is persuaded to alter the devolved institutions' powers:

> As a result of the Scotland Act, there are thus two institutions with the power to make laws for Scotland: the Scottish Parliament and, as is recognised in section 28(7), the Parliament of the United Kingdom. The Scottish Parliament is subordinate to the United Kingdom Parliament: its powers can be modified, extended or revoked by an Act of the United Kingdom Parliament.[57]

All of the devolved legislatures have enjoyed considerable extensions of their competences since 1998. As Westminster assented to each new extension in the powers of the devolved bodies the concern emerged, even amongst the creators of the devolution project, that their scheme risked breaking up the UK. Even Tony Blair, considering devolution with the benefit of hindsight, declared in his memoirs that 'I was never a passionate devolutionist. It is a dangerous game to play. You can never be sure where nationalist sentiment ends and separatist sentiment begins'.[58] In such circumstances, supporters of the Union continue to put great stock in Westminster's ultimate sovereignty as a means of preventing the devolved legislatures from passing legislation seeking independence.

Key debates
Devolution and 'Balkanisation'

'Balkanisation' is a description used by pro-Union commentators to challenge Scottish, Welsh and Irish nationalists' claims in favour of the breakup of the UK. The term suggests that should the UK break up into its constituent units, like the former Yugoslavia, this will be the result of petty differences between the national groups which make up the UK (although without any

→

---

[57] Ibid., [146].
[58] T. Blair, *A Journey: My Political Life* (Hutchinson, 2010) p. 251.

meaningful implication that this process would be accompanied by the violence which erupted as Yugoslavia broke apart).

Balkanisation, a favourite term of former Welsh and Northern Ireland Secretary Peter Hain, amounts to an argument that replacing the UK with multiple countries will reduce the collective importance of all of those countries on the world stage. When so much shared history and culture unites the peoples of the UK, parochial differences should not be allowed to undermine the union. Nationalists counter that, if the UK is indeed made up of a number of distinct national groups no amount of overlap between their outlook should be allowed to thwart the aspirations of such groups to manage their own affairs. What these competing narratives highlight is really a clash of nationalisms, with pro-Union commentators asserting that an undivided UK provides the best basis for a successful polity and with Scottish, Welsh and Irish nationalists arguing that separate polities will better represent the wishes of their peoples.

Westminster's overall sovereignty, expressly declared in provisions such as section 28(7) of the Scotland Act 1998, is held up by pro-Union advocates as having the potential to avert Balkanisation. As Hain wrote in *The Guardian* ('The Balkanisation of Britain' (21 January 2004)):

The fundamental point is that the UK Parliament is sovereign. It has the power of decision over all legislation. The only exceptions are issues that Parliament has explicitly devolved.

This statement is poorly worded, as the Devolution Acts expressly preserve the Westminster Parliament's sovereignty over devolved matters. However, the term 'sovereignty' is not being used here in the lawyers' sense of the judicially-upheld 'supreme' status which attaches to an Act of Parliament, but as shorthand for the idea that the devolved legislatures cannot extend their remits without Westminster's permission.

If Westminster does not authorise an extension of power, the sovereignty argument goes, the courts will be obliged to strike down any legislation by which the devolved legislatures seek to grab such power for themselves. Hence, when the UK Supreme Court intervenes in cases like *Cadder*, it suits pro-independence politicians to portray the Court as meddling in Scotland's affairs. The SNP was, at the time of *Cadder*, acutely aware that its efforts to legislate for independence might be blocked in the Supreme Court; after all, 'the Scotland Act 1998 confers no legislative power on the Scottish Parliament to pass an Act purporting to authorise a referendum about independence'.[59] In attacking decisions like *Cadder* the SNP was laying the foundations of a political claim that the courts, should they strike down proposed referendum legislation as exceeding Holyrood's competence, are denying a voice to the Scottish people rather than performing the task required of them by the Scotland Act.

(ii) The 2014 Scottish Independence Referendum

Such posturing, however, proved unnecessary, for Westminster ultimately permitted the Scottish Parliament to call a referendum and test the will of the Scottish people on independence in 2014. Section 30 of the Scotland Act 1998 allows for the Scottish Parliament's competences to be altered by Order in Council in Westminster. Following the 2012 Edinburgh Agreement[60] between the Scottish Government and the UK Government this process was used to provide the Scottish Parliament the opportunity to legislate for a referendum on

---

[59] Constitution Committee, *Referendum on Scottish Independence* (2012) HL 263, para. 30.
[60] HM Government and the Scottish Government, *Agreement Between the United Kingdom Government and the Scottish Government on a Referendum on Independence for Scotland* (15 October 2012).

independence in 2014.[61] The legal structures of the 'triple lock' were picked by this political accommodation, circumventing legal challenges to the validity of the referendum.[62]

The referendum was a decisive moment in the UK's constitutional history. When much of Ireland broke away from the UK in 1922 it did so against a back-drop of civil war; now the future of the Union was being tested at the ballot box. Acceding to the SNP's demand for a referendum can be painted as a constitutional gamble by the Coalition Government,[63] but in some respects it had little choice in the matter. Had the UK Government attempted to use legal mechanisms to block efforts by the SNP to legislate for an independence referendum using the majority it enjoyed in the Scottish Parliament after the 2011 election it would have given credence to SNP charges that Westminster was bullying Scotland, and likely strengthened pro-independence sentiment. Nonetheless, acceding to the SNP's request was undoubtedly a risk, and not just with regard to the place of Scotland in the UK but in the long-run to the continuation of the UK as a pluri-national state; 'So long as Scotland and England remain under one Crown, then it has a magnetic effect on the other parts of the United Kingdom'.[64]

In 2013 the Scottish Parliament's legislative efforts were directed towards preparing for the referendum. The Scottish Independence Referendum (Franchise) Act 2013 was first passed which extended the franchise beyond that for general elections to include 16- and 17-year-olds.[65] This was followed by the Scottish Independence Referendum Act 2013, which set the question for the referendum as 'Should Scotland be an independent country?'[66] and the date as 18 September 2014.[67] Almost a year of campaigning followed. As the polls narrowed with the approach of the referendum date the pro-Union parties (the Conservatives, Labour and the Liberal Democrats) agreed a joint platform offering 'extensive new powers' to Scotland's institutions if Scotland remained in the UK.[68] This intervention could well have been decisive; in the referendum 55.3 per cent of voters opposed independence on a turn-out of almost 85 per cent. As we saw in the last chapter, this pledge was implemented in the Scotland Act 2016.[69] It might therefore be tempting to dismiss the referendum as a potential rupture in the UK Constitution which did not happen, but to do so would be to miss its profound importance. As Nicola McEwan notes, within a year of the vote moves were underway to extend powers in Scotland, Wales and Northern Ireland, to change the law-making process for England-only legislation at Westminster and to grant greater autonomy to cities across the UK.[70] In addition to transferring new powers, Westminster was obliged to recognise that the Scottish Parliament was a 'permanent' feature of the UK's governance structure which could only be removed by the will of the Scottish people

---

[61] The Scotland Act 1998 (Modification of Schedule 5) Order 2013 (SI 2013/242).

[62] A. Tickell, 'The Technical Jekyll and the Political Hyde' in A. McHarg, T. Mullen, A. Page and N. Walker (eds), *The Scottish Independence Referendum: Constitutional and Political Implications* (OUP, 2016) 325, 325.

[63] R. Rawlings, 'A Coalition Government in Westminster' in J. Jowell, D. Oliver and C. O'Cinneide (eds), *The Changing Constitution* (8th edn, OUP, 2015) 194, 213.

[64] P. Norton, 'Tony Blair and the Constitution' [2007] *British Politics* 269, 275–276.

[65] Scottish Independence Referendum (Franchise) Act 2013, s. 2.

[66] Scottish Independence Referendum Act 2013, s. 1(2).

[67] Ibid., s. 1(5).

[68] J. Mitchell, 'The Referendum Campaign' in A. McHarg, T. Mullen, A. Page and N. Walker (eds), *The Scottish Independence Referendum: Constitutional and Political Implications* (OUP, 2016) 75, 96.

[69] See pp. 372–5.

[70] N. McEwan, 'A Constitution in Flux' in A. McHarg, T. Mullen, A. Page and N. Walker (eds), *The Scottish Independence Referendum: Constitutional and Political Implications* (OUP, 2016) 225.

expressed in a referendum.[71] This brings us into the contested territory of whether restrictions on parliamentary sovereignty can ever be effective, with the House of Lords Constitution Committee opining that, because later Parliaments can override earlier legislation, this provision's significance was political rather than legal.[72] Even so, the territorial dimension of the UK Constitution has become increasingly prominent since the referendum.

Thinking Point . . .

It is very difficult to grant constitutional protections to one set of devolved institutions without coming under pressure to do the same for the others. Following the passage of the Scotland Act 2016 the Welsh Government sought similar assurances that Welsh institutions were 'permanent', which were introduced in section 1 of the Wales Act 2017.

The referendum result did not diminish the SNP's desire for independence, but it seemed in the immediate aftermath to have addressed the issue for the foreseeable future. After all, Alex Salmond had described the referendum as a once-in-a-generation opportunity in an effort to generate support in the run up to the vote.[73] A combination of the SNP's strong showing in the 2015 general election (winning 56 of Scotland's 59 seats) and Brexit, which arguably changed the basis of Scotland's relationship with the UK (given that 62 per cent of the Scottish electorate voted to remain in the EU) led the SNP's new leader Nicola Sturgeon to get the Scottish Parliament's permission to seek a second independence referendum.[74] Wags began calling the situation the Neverendum. Theresa May, however, ruled out granting permission for such a referendum, informing the Commons that 'now is not the time to be talking about a second independence referendum'.[75] If for a while in 2017 this position seemed to suggest that a new constitutional crisis was looming, the SNP's loss of 21 seats in the 2017 general election has put the issue on hold, at least until the SNP can again gain a clear mandate in support of another referendum.

The English/West Lothian question

Key issues

- How should the governance arrangements in the UK be adapted to tackle the 'English Question': should there be a place for England as a nation (or split into regions) within the devolution settlement?

- How should the governance arrangements in the UK be adapted to tackle the 'West Lothian Question': why should parliamentarians representing constituencies in Scotland, Wales and Northern Ireland retain the competence to vote in Westminster on matters solely affecting England?

- Why is the differentiation of public service provision in different parts of the UK resultant from devolution so controversial?

---

[71] Scotland Act 2016, s.1, inserting s.63A into the Scotland Act 1998.
[72] Constitution Committee, *Proposals for the devolution of further powers to Scotland* (2015) HL 145, para. 61.
[73] S. Johnson, 'Alex Salmond accused of rewriting history after he denies "once in a lifetime" referendum pledge' *The Telegraph* (19 March 2017).
[74] Scottish Parliament, 'Motion S5M-07410: Nicola Sturgeon' (20 March 2017).
[75] HC Debs, vol. 624, col. 244 (29 March 2017).

England and devolution

England remains the part of the UK without devolved institutions. Leaving local govern-ment structures aside, for all intents and purposes, England is governed from and by central government in Whitehall and the Parliament at Westminster. Robert Hazell considers that as a result:

> England is the gaping hole in the devolution settlement: some believe that devolution will not be complete, and the settlement will not stabilise, until the English Question has been solved; others believe that England can be left out indefinitely and devolution confined to the Celtic fringe.[76]

The lack of devolution to England unbalances and destabilises the UK's governance arrangements, giving rise to the 'West Lothian' question. In its most straightforward sense this asks, 'what contribution should be made by MPs representing a devolved nation (for example, Scotland) to matters which relate solely to a non-devolved nation (England)?'[77] As the quote introducing this chapter indicates, it questions why – after devolution – MPs representing seats in Wales, Scotland and Northern Ireland at Westminster retain the competence to influence votes which will impact only on England, when they are unable to exert the same influence over their own constituencies as a result of devolution. The question gets its name from the Scottish constituency represented by Tam Dalyell, who repeatedly raised the issue in Parliament during the course of the devolution debates of the 1970s. The legislative aspect of the question, as posed by Dalyell, is but one aspect of broader issues associated with the governance of England, post-devolution, concerning the representation of the devolved areas at Westminster, the Westminster's procedures when making law specific to England, and the much broader issue of how England should be governed post-devolution.

The West Lothian question explained

At the Westminster level, the West Lothian question possesses a number of distinct dynam-ics. For instance, should England be governed by a political party only able to muster a Commons majority by the votes of MPs representing seats in other parts of the UK? In other words, should a party which cannot command a majority of English MPs be able to form a government? The Labour Governments elected in 1950, 1964 and (October) 1974, for example, held a majority of seats in the House of Commons overall, but were in the minority in England.

Taking 1950 as our example, while Labour had an overall House of Commons major-ity of seven, in England the Conservatives and Liberals held a majority of one. Were that situation to be replicated after devolution entered effect, such a government would enjoy an overall majority for UK-wide business but would, in effect, be a minority adminis-tration in respect of the governance of England. The West Lothian question has long had a party political dimension; historically the Labour Party has enjoyed more support in Scotland and Wales than the Conservative Party, and therefore risks losing more if MPs representing non-English constituencies are marginalised. For example, when Labour formed a government following the 1997 general election, no Scottish or Welsh

---

[76] R. Hazell, 'Introduction: What is the English Question?' in R. Hazell (ed.), *The English Question* (Man-chester University Press, 2006) 1, 1.

[77] B. Hadfield, 'Devolution, Westminster and the English Question' [2005] PL 286, 286.

constituency was represented by a Conservative MP. Even taking into account the subsequent recovery in the Conservatives, electoral fortunes in Wales and Scotland, after the 2017 general election Labour held 35 Scottish and Welsh seats, compared to 21 held by the Conservatives.

The West Lothian question raises further issues about who should exercise governmental power. For example, should an MP who does not represent an English constituency be responsible for a ministerial portfolio which largely comprises devolved issues? Such was the case when Alistair Darling (MP for Edinburgh South West) held the post of Secretary of State for Transport between 2002 and 2006. Similar issues arose while John Reid (MP for Airdrie and Shotts) held the position of Secretary of State for Health from 2003 to 2005. Both health and transport are devolved issues meaning that initiatives taken by Westminster in those spheres extend, for the most part, to England alone. Yet in these instances policy was being devised and implemented by politicians with no direct line of accountability to the English electorate. The West Lothian question, therefore, asks whether it is constitutionally legitimate for UK ministers representing constituencies in devolved areas to exercise executive power over 'English' issues.

The West Lothian question is more frequently directed towards the fact that, following devolution to Scotland, Wales and Northern Ireland, Westminster no longer deals with the issues devolved to those territories on a day-to-day basis, but their MPs can continue to influence policy and legislation as it applies in England.[78] To give a brief example: education is a matter which, following the Scotland Act 1998, has been devolved to the Scottish Parliament. As a result, the Scottish Parliament legislates for the Scottish education system. MPs representing English constituencies therefore have no ability to influence, on a day-to-day basis, policy and legislation affecting educational affairs in Scotland. By contrast, education policy and legislation as it applies in England continue to be debated and passed by the Westminster Parliament, of which MPs representing Scottish constituencies continue to form a part. Scottish Members of the Westminster Parliament therefore possess the ability to influence the design and passage of legislation in which they have no direct constituency interests as a result of devolution.[79]

Questioning the West Lothian question

Arguments relating to the relative powers of Westminster MPs post-devolution are frequently couched in absolute terms. As Tam Dalyell's original exposition of the West Lothian question reproduced at the beginning of this chapter emphasises, following devolution, it was argued that English MPs would have 'no say' on matters devolved to the Scottish Parliament. More recently, William Hague, in a speech delivered in 1998 – which noticeably echoed the terms and pitch of Dalyell's famous question – asked:

> For how much longer will the English acquiesce to Scottish Members of the Westminster Parliament having a vote on health, education and other domestic matters in England, when English Members of Parliament . . . have *no* vote over similar matters in Scotland?[80]

---

[78] See B. Dickson, 'Devolution' in J. Jowell, D. Oliver and C. O'Cinneide (eds), *The Changing Constitution* (8th edn, OUP, 2015) 249, 268.
[79] A. King, *The British Constitution* (OUP, 2007) p. 201.
[80] W. Hague, 'Change and Tradition: Thinking Creatively about the Constitution' (Centre for Policy Studies, 24 February 1998).

Similarly, Brigid Hadfield has maintained that there is a 'lack of reciprocity' resultant from the current devolutionary arrangements.[81]

These iterations of the West Lothian question presuppose that Westminster's powers have in some way been diminished as a result of devolution, at least in terms of the day-to-day business of managing matters that fall within the remit of the devolved administrations. But as we have already seen, the Devolution Acts preserve the legal authority of the Westminster Parliament. As we have also already seen, the Sewel Convention has, contrary to predictions, operated with a degree of regularity.[82] In other words, Westminster continues to legislate with a degree of frequency in the devolved areas of competence. Some qualification of the West Lothian question, as it affects the relative competence of Westminster MPs, is therefore required. Claims that English MPs have *no* ability to influence legislation which affects a devolved area of power are therefore misleading; English MPs do have that power, as devolution, legally at least, does not 'affect the power of the Parliament of the United Kingdom to make laws for Scotland'[83] or any other devolved area. What was missing at the outset of devolution was an arrangement dealing with Scottish MPs' participation in 'English' affairs at Westminster.

When is the West Lothian question most pressing?

A second qualification of the West Lothian question is necessary: to imply that a majority of MPs representing English constituencies are being routinely overruled by a coalition of the remaining English MPs and those representing the devolved territories would be an exaggeration. In two decades of devolution legislative decisions in Parliament affecting England alone have rarely been taken against the wishes of a majority of English MPs as a result of votes cast by members representing constituencies in devolved areas. After all, parliamentarians representing English constituencies continue to dominate the Westminster Parliament. English MPs hold an overwhelming majority in the House of Commons, accounting for 533 of its 650 seats (82 per cent). Scottish MPs hold 59 seats, Welsh MPs 40 seats, while MPs from Northern Ireland hold just 18 seats.

Thinking Point . . .

While the issue of hunting with dogs had already been legislated on in the Scottish Parliament (see the Protection of Wild Mammals (Scotland) Act 2002), the participation of Scots MPs at Westminster in the passage of the Hunting Act 2004 (although controversial in that the Act would not extend to Scotland) did not impact on the outcome of any parliamentary votes.

The legislative dimension of the English question is most evident in two situations. The first is when a party, while holding an overall majority in the House of Commons, cannot command a majority of MPs representing English constituencies. In such circumstances,

---

[81] B. Hadfield, 'Devolution, Westminster and the English Question' [2005] PL 286, 286–7.
[82] See A. Page and A. Batey, 'Scotland's Other Parliament: Westminster Legislation about Devolved Matters in Scotland since Devolution' [2002] PL 501 and B. Winetrobe, 'A Partnership of the Parliaments? Scottish Law Making under the Sewel Convention at Westminster and Holyrood' in R. Hazell and R. Rawlings (eds), *Devolution, Law Making and the Constitution* (Imprint Academic, 2005) p. 39.
[83] Scotland Act 1998, s. 28(7).

the governing party would be forced to rely on the votes of MPs representing constituencies in Wales, Scotland and Northern Ireland to carry its legislative and policy decisions. There have only been three occasions in the last century when the party with the overall majority in the House of Commons has been reliant on MPs from Scotland, Wales and Northern Ireland to form that majority. Only the Labour Governments elected in 1950, 1964 and October 1974 were unable to command a majority among English MPs. In the aftermath of the 2017 general election the Conservative Government might by reliant upon the support of Northern Ireland's DUP for its overall Commons majority, but it does have a comfortable majority in English seats (see Table 13.1).

Nevertheless, as a result of divisions *within* as well as between the political parties, the problems associated with the West Lothian question have arisen since the devolved administrations in Edinburgh, Cardiff and Belfast were established in 1999. As a result of a rebellion by Labour MPs against the Labour Government during the parliamentary passage of two particularly controversial legislative proposals, the Health and Social Care (Community Health and Standards) Bill 2003 and the Higher Education Bill 2004, the Government was forced to rely on the support of its Scottish MPs to pass legislation which did not affect their constituents. During the passage of the first of those Bills, which provided the statutory basis of the Government's controversial Foundation Hospitals policy, two amendments were defeated in Parliament as a result of the votes of Scottish MPs. Needless to say, controversy arose out of the fact that the relevant provisions of the Bill did not apply in Scotland.[84] As Russell and Lodge have noted:

> At report stage an amendment tabled by David Hinchcliffe sought to remove the foundation hospitals provisions from the Bill. The amendment fell, by 286 votes to 251. However, on the votes of English MPs alone it would have passed, by 218 to 217 . . . Later, when the Bill returned from the House of Lords on 19 November [2003], the Government's majority was cut further, to just 17, with 62 Labour members voting against on the crucial amendment. On this occasion the Government would have lost by seventeen votes if only English MPs had voted.[85]

Table 13.1 Results of the 2017 general election (by country)

	Conservative	Labour	Liberal Democrat	Others	Total
United Kingdom	317	262	12	59	650
England	296	227	8	2	533
Wales	8	28	0	4	40
Scotland	13	7	4	35	59
Northern Ireland	0	0	0	18	18

---

[84] See B. Johnson, 'What has it got to do with the Scots?' *The Telegraph* (10 July 2003).
[85] M. Russell and G. Lodge, 'The Government of England by Westminster' in R. Hazell (ed.), *The English Question* (Manchester University Press, 2006) 64, 72.

Perhaps the more controversial of these pieces of legislation, at least for much of this book's readership, was the Higher Education Act 2004.

Key debates

The passage of the Higher Education Act 2004

The Higher Education Act 2004 introduced student top-up fees in England and made provision for their introduction in Wales. Subject to a number of provisions which applied to Scotland and Northern Ireland – none of which concerns the issue of student fees – the territorial extent of the Act is limited to England and Wales (Higher Education Act 2004, s. 53). The reasons for this territorial divide should, by now, be evident: education and related matters have been devolved from the Westminster Parliament to the Scottish Parliament, Northern Ireland Assembly and National Assembly for Wales. Hence, in simple terms, the large part of the Act would not apply in Scotland, the provisions of the Act would therefore not affect the Scottish electorate, and Members of Parliament from Scotland had no constituency interest in the Act's terms. Nonetheless, in the House of Commons divisions on the clauses of the Bill concerning student fees, Labour Members representing Scottish constituencies voted in favour of implementing top-up fees in England.

Had the proposed scheme of top-up fees been more popular, the participation of Scottish MPs in the Commons divisions would not have had a decisive impact (Labour enjoyed a Commons majority of 161). However, the Government's policy of top-up fees was deeply contested – not only as between the political parties, but within the governing Labour Party itself. Indeed, the very suggestion that top-up fees be introduced appeared to mark a departure from the Labour Party's 2001 election manifesto. As a result, many Labour MPs revolted and voted against the Labour Government. The Labour Government became reliant upon the support of its Scottish MPs to implement a policy which had divided its English representatives. In the end, the Higher Education Bill was passed by the House of Commons, by a mere five votes: 316 in favour, 311 against (HC Debs, vol. 417, cols 270–4 (27 January 2004)). Of those votes in favour of the Bill fully 46 came from Scotland; in other words, by MPs whose constituencies were largely unaffected by the Bill's most controversial clauses. Had the Scottish MPs not participated, the Government would have been defeated by 41, and top-up fees may not have been introduced.

It will be recalled that one of the arguments for devolution was that the Scottish electorate had – between 1979 and 1997 – been governed by a political party that had consistently been rejected by a majority of Scottish voters. The ironic consequence of devolution is that the settlement houses the potential for the English electorate to be subject to policies and legislation that have been rejected by a majority of English MPs, but that are carried into effect by reason of the support of MPs to whom they will not apply.

Tackling the English/West Lothian question

Key issues

- Could the English question be addressed by providing for an English Parliament (mirroring the arrangements for Scotland, Wales and Northern Ireland). The main problem with such an initiative is that England is so large (being home to over 83 per cent of the UK population) that it would not produce meaningful subsidiarity benefits.

- If it is impractical to devolve power to England as a whole, would it be possible to grant a level of devolution to different regions within the UK? The problem with this approach to the question is that there is apathy amongst the general public in England towards such regionalism.

- One potential solution to the West Lothian question is to limit the capacity of MPs sitting in Scotland, Wales and Northern Ireland to engage with matters solely affecting England. This approach is known as English Votes for English Laws (EVEL) and it would turn Westminster into the 'English' Parliament on certain issues.

An English Parliament

The response to the English/West Lothian question which would possess the most obvious symmetry would be the creation of an English legislature. Were England to be given its own legislature, exercising powers comparable to the Scottish Parliament, anxieties over England's place in the devolution settlement would be assuaged. As Tam Dalyell put it in 1998: 'some legislative entity is going to have to emerge in England to fill the vacuum left by Scottish home rule'.[86] And yet the possibility of what Bogdanor has called 'legislative devolution all round'[87] has not been seriously considered by any of the main political parties. There is little public support for an English legislature (in spite of the efforts of fringe movements such as the Campaign for an English Parliament and the English Democrats to harness English feelings of dissatisfaction with the current arrangements).[88] For Robert Hazell, 'those who demand [an English Parliament] are in effect demanding a full-blown federation, in which the four historic nations in the United Kingdom would form the component parts'.[89] Elsewhere he has noted that, 'in most federations no state represents more than one third of the whole'[90] yet 83 per cent of the UK's population resides in England.

It is therefore received-wisdom that an English Parliament would be unworkable in practice:

> A federation consisting of four units – England, Scotland, Wales and Northern Ireland – would be so unbalanced as to be unworkable. It would be dominated by . . . England. The English Parliament would rival the UK Federal Parliament; and in the Federal Parliament itself, the representation of England could hardly be scaled down in such a way as to enable it to be out-voted by Scotland, Wales and Northern Ireland, together representing less than one-fifth of the [UK] population.[91]

But perhaps objections based on potential political imbalance should be reappraised; the UK Parliament, after all, remains dominated by English MPs and it is at least debatable whether the creation of an English Parliament would *necessarily* mean that the United Kingdom had become a *de facto* federal state. As described in Chapter 12, the basic

---

[86] HC Debs, vol. 311, col. 741 (6 May 1998).

[87] V. Bogdanor, *Devolution in the United Kingdom* (OUP, 1999) 228.

[88] J. Curtice, 'What the people say – if anything', in R. Hazell (ed.), *The English Question* (Manchester University Press, 2006) 119, 121.

[89] R. Hazell, 'The English Question: Can Westminster Be a Proxy for an English Parliament?' [2001] PL 268, 268.

[90] R. Hazell, 'Reinventing the Constitution: Can the State Survive?' [1994] PL 84, 92.

[91] Royal Commission on the Constitution, *Volume 1: Report* (1973) Cmnd. 5460, para. 531.

characteristics of a federal state require a codified constitution outlining the exclusive areas of legal competence of the sub-national and federal legislatures, and a supreme – or constitutional – court able to review the legality of legislation passed by both sub-national and federal legislatures. Assuming that an English Parliament was established on the same model as the Scottish Parliament it would be a creature of statute. Flowing from this, it would be an inferior legal institution to the Westminster Parliament. Westminster would retain, at least in law, the same power to legislate on issues devolved to the English Parliament as operates in the current devolution legislation. Moreover, any hypothetical English Parliament would be subject to judicial review in contradistinction to Westminster.

The most significant objection to creation of an English Parliament is not, therefore, that it would be unworkable but that it would be pointless; devolving to a single institution powers over such a large populace and geographical area would provide little benefit in terms of subsidiarity:

> [A]n English Parliament would do nothing to remove the problems of over-centralization and lack of democratic accountability which comprise the dynamic behind devolution. Were an English Parliament to be set up, there would still be a need to disperse power within England. So an English Parliament . . . would not resolve the problem to which devolution is the answer.[92]

The natural response to this argument, of course, is that English devolution should take the form of regional assemblies, responsive to regional needs.

Decentralisation within England

(i) The London Mayor and Greater London Authority

If New Labour was not interested in an English Parliament it nonetheless had plans to decentralise governance in England, starting with the capital. As the 1997 Labour manifesto noted, London was the 'only Western capital' without an elected mayor.[93] It therefore proposed a directly-elected mayor to provide a figurehead to represent all of London and to co-ordinate policies in areas like transport, the environment and policing and emergency services which cut across all the individual local government areas within Greater London.[94] A referendum was held in May 1998 which saw 72 per cent of London's voters support an elected mayor, on a turnout of 34 per cent. The post of Mayor of London was subsequently introduced by the Greater London Authority Act 1999, which also established an Assembly to oversee the Mayor's performance.

A number of distinctive policies have been implemented in London as a result of this form of devolution, notably the congestion charge, championed by Ken Livingstone, and the cycle-hire scheme implemented by his successor, Boris Johnson. Nonetheless, despite the Mayor of London representing a larger population than the Welsh Assembly, the competence of the office looks limited by comparison. The Mayor, for example, has no power to implement distinct health or education policies for the capital. Some additional powers were added in the Greater London Authority 2007 (particularly in relation to planning policy), but since then there have been no moves to extend the Mayor's competence.

---

[92] V. Bogdanor, *Devolution in the United Kingdom* (OUP, 1999) pp. 267–8.
[93] Labour Party, *New Labour: Because Britain Deserves Better* (1997) 34.
[94] Department for the Environment, Transport and the Regions, *A Mayor and Assembly for London* (1998) Cm. 3897.

(ii) Regional Development Agencies and Regional Assemblies

London was supposed to be only the beginning of New Labour's 'regionalism' agenda for England. Elected Regional Assemblies were envisaged as operating at a level between local authorities and Westminster, and were to have exercised powers devolved from the latter. Regional Assemblies were intended to take over from the bodies established under the Regional Development Agencies Act 1998. Although they coordinated regional economic strategy, the eight Regional Development Agencies (RDAs) were 'regional outposts of central government'.[95] They nonetheless established the geographical footprint of regional governance, which the Blair Government sought to build upon with its 2002 White Paper *Your Region, Your Choice*. Legislation followed, in the form of the Regional Assemblies (Preparations) Act 2003, which made provision for ministers, following consideration of the level of interest in the proposals, to authorise referendums on the establishment of a Regional Assembly in a particular English Region. Each of the proposed Regional Assemblies was to have comprised between 25–35 members (elected by the additional-member system employed in Scottish Parliament and Welsh Assembly elections), from which would be drawn a leader and 'cabinet' of up to six members. They would be funded primarily by a central government grant, but would have powers to raise additional funds from a precept on the council tax. They were to have taken over the remit of the RDAs, as well as gaining new powers from central government over 'regeneration, improving housing and public transport, and developing tourism'.[96] Although the then-Deputy Prime Minister, John Prescott, led a campaign for Regional Assemblies the plans never gained traction. The first, and only, referendum on the establishment of a Regional Assembly, held in the North-East of England in November 2004, resulted in a resounding rejection. On a turnout of 48 per cent (in an all-postal ballot), 78 per cent voted against the proposals for a regional assembly, while only 22 per cent voted in support. The Regional Assemblies plans were subsequently abandoned in their entirety.

Regional Assemblies were not an enticing prospect for voters; they would have provided a watered-down version of the executive devolution provided under the Government of Wales Act 1998, rather than that established by the Scotland Act 1998. In the North-East, objectors successfully portrayed the proposed Assembly as an expensive additional layer of government with too few powers to make it worthwhile. Moreover, the proposed Regional Assemblies would not have addressed the legislative aspect of the West Lothian question; Westminster would have remained the legislature responsible for England and its regions. They might well, however, have addressed some of the representational inequalities caused by devolution by providing a second tier of government at a level closer to the local electorate. As such, Regional Assemblies could have increased subsidiarity and decentralisation, and as with devolution in Wales, Scotland and Northern Ireland further powers could have been transferred over time. But this was not to be; even the Regional Development Agencies were scrapped in 2012 as the Coalition Government (and its Conservative successors) attempted a new approach to decentralisation in England.[97]

---

[95] V. Bogdanor, *Devolution in the United Kingdom* (OUP, 1999) p. 269.
[96] HM Government, *Your Region, Your Choice: Revitalising the English Regions* (2002) Cm. 5511, para. 4.2.
[97] Public Bodies Act 2011, Sch. 1.

(iii) Building on London: elected mayors and 'city devolution'

The Local Government Act 2000 made provision for local councils to adopt an elected office of Mayor. Labour ministers often explicitly linked elected mayors into their wider devolution strategy, with Ruth Kelly once describing the policy as part of the 'theme of devolution to our cities, towns, counties and neighbourhoods throughout England'.[98] Take-up was, however, patchy. When, in May 2012, the Coalition Government imposed referendums for elected mayors in the 10 largest urban areas in England which had retained the traditional 'council' system, all but one of these referendums saw the proposal for an elected mayor was defeated. The offices were widely perceived as having insufficient power to effect meaningful political change at a local level[99] and very low turn-out rates in referendums suggested that 'the experiment has failed to revive significant public interest in local democracy'.[100] Moreover, concentrating the powers once exercised by a council's executive in the hands of an individual elected mayor does not amount to transferring powers away from central government; the offices do not, of themselves, address the over-centralisation of governance in England.

Having been unable to side-step local institutions by going directly to the electorate on the issue of elected mayors, the Conservatives returned to the issue after their 2015 General Election victory by trying to reach deals with local government in areas including Greater Manchester, the West Midlands, West Yorkshire and Sheffield. These deals were explicitly linked to the need to provide English counterweights to devolution to Wales, Scotland and Northern Ireland; as David Cameron announced immediately after the result of the Scottish independence referendum, further powers for Scotland would be balanced by renewed efforts to 'empower our great cities'.[101] Under the Cities and Local Government Devolution Act 2016, once these urban areas agreed to accept an elected-mayor model, the UK Government would grant them broad new powers in areas like housing and transport and a block grant in the form of an annual investment fund. For now, even though these deals have been described as 'city devolution' they are more closely equivalent to London than to the arrangements for Wales, Scotland and Northern Ireland. They are a form of enhanced local government, rather than autonomous bodies with law-making powers in broad areas of competence. This is not to say, however, that if these arrangements are successful there will not be pressure for further transfers of power.[102]

(iv) The 'localism' agenda

Throughout the latter half of the nineteenth century, local government played a vital role in the life of rapidly expanding towns and cities. Thereafter, however, central government came to dominate welfare provision and funding for major infrastructure projects. Local government mechanisms became, in large part, vehicles for the delivery of central

---

[98] Department for Communities and Local Government, *Devolution Agenda Pushed Forward with New Powers for London*, News Release 2006/0055 (13 July 2006).

[99] See A. Asquith, 'A Bullock, a Monkey and Robocop: An Assessment of the Directly Elected Mayor in English Local Government' (2008) 36 *Policy & Politics* 39, 48.

[100] I. Leigh, 'The New Local Government' in J. Jowell and D. Oliver (eds), *The Changing Constitution* (7th edn, OUP, 2011) 237, 252.

[101] D. Cameron, 'Scottish Independence Referendum: Statement by the Prime Minister' (19 September 2015).

[102] Communities and Local Government Committee, *Devolution: The Next Five Years and Beyond* (2016) HC 369, 49.

government schemes, and as a consequence became much less innovative. Amid this cycle of decline, public interest in local governance waned.[103] This is all the more concerning given that the 2017 Grenfell Tower disaster highlighted both the continuing importance of local government in the provision of services such as social housing, and the dangers inherent in a general lack of popular interest in its activities.

Before the 2010 general election the Conservative Party made great play of the dangers of centralisation of government functions; complaining that 'all too often decisions which affect local communities are taken by remote officials in Whitehall departments and unelected quangos and then simply implemented, with limited powers of variation, by officials in town halls'.[104] Although this amounted to railing against levels of centralisation to which Conservative Governments had contributed, it did point to enhancing the role of local government being on the national agenda. The Coalition Government subsequently endeavoured to reinvigorate, and supplement, existing local government structures. Two pieces of legislation were particularly important. The first was the Localism Act 2011, which granted local government the power to do 'anything that individuals generally may do'.[105] Historically, the courts have approached local government powers in line with the Diceyan view that all public authorities have to point to clear legal authority for their actions.[106] This provision was intended to free local government from the confines of this approach to public law, allowing councils to do anything that is not specifically prohibited in law. The general competence remains largely untested by litigation, but at least in theory marks 'a striking departure from more than a century of local government legislation and judicial practice'.[107]

Thinking Point . . .

For an example of how constrained local government was before the enactment of the general competence, see *R (National Secular Society)* v *Bideford Town Council* [2012] EWHC 175 (Admin); [2012] 2 All ER 1175, in which Ouseley J (at [80]) found that prayers ahead of a council meeting were unlawful because there was 'no statutory power permitting the practice'.

The second important piece of legislation is the Police Reform and Social Responsibility Act 2011, which replaced appointed police authorities with a directly elected Police and Crime Commissioners (PCC) for every English and Welsh police force outside London. This means that a Commissioner, elected for a four-year term of office, will now be responsible for ensuring efficient policing within each police force area and for holding chief constables to account. Ministers proclaimed that '[d]emocratic accountability will create a sharp incentive on Police and Crime Commissioners to cut bureaucracy, increase efficiency

---

[103] S. Bailey and M. Elliott, 'Taking Local Government Seriously: Democracy, Autonomy and the Constitution' (2009) 68 CLJ 436, 440.

[104] Conservative Party, *Control Shift: Returning Power to Local Communities* (2009) 4.

[105] Localism Act 2011, s. 1(1).

[106] *R v Cockerton* [1901] 1 QB 726.

[107] I. Leigh, 'The Changing Nature of the Local State' in J. Jowell, D. Oliver and C. O'Cinneide (eds), *The Changing Constitution* (8th edn, OUP, 2015) 279, 287.

and drive down costs, ensuring that forces focus on the policing the public want.[108] But turn-out in Police and Crime Commissioner elections in England and Wales remains below 20 per cent of the electorate and question marks remain as to whether the direct oversight of policing in a particular area should be conducted by a panel of politically impartial appointees, rather than politicians who may see political advantage in populist posturing over policing.[109] The PCCs might in some cases be a stop-gap measure; London, after all, needed no PCC because the Mayor already provided elected oversight of policing. As 'city devolution' becomes more widespread the new directly elected mayors are in a position to subsume the functions of some PCCs, with Greater Manchester leading the way in this regard.[110]

Even after these reforms, it must be remembered that local government remains in a poor position to counterbalance the power of Westminster and to negate the difficulties with centralisation highlighted by devolution. Local government often remains reliant on funding from central government to offset shortfalls in council tax revenues. For all of the Conservative Party's emphasis on localism, ministers maintain that 'it's up to local government leaders to use that freedom wisely'.[111] In other words, ministers often like to sound committed to localism, provided that central government continues to get its way. If localism is indeed going to bring about meaningful change to local government powers, central government ministers will have to accept that particular councils must be able to advance policies within their areas of competence, even if such policies run contrary to the central government's national agenda.

Westminster and the English/West Lothian Question

(i) Adapting Westminster to Devolution: The Early Steps

Devolution has resulted in a number of changes, of varying degrees of significance, at Westminster. Following the establishment of the devolved administrations, a number of procedural issues have, for instance, had to be attended to at the Westminster level. Questions to the territorial Secretaries of State – the Secretaries of State for Scotland, Wales and Northern Ireland – have been ruled out of order where they concern issues of devolved competence.[112] Departmental Select Committees had had to re-align the scope and range of their enquiries where matters previously falling within their remit have been devolved to Scotland, Wales and Northern Ireland.[113]

The most significant change at Westminster, perhaps, was the reduction in the number of Scottish MPs from 72 to 59 in 2005.[114] This reduction was designed to reduce the effec-

---

[108] HC Debs, vol. 529, col. 950W (16 June 2011).

[109] See M. Gilmore, 'Electing Police and Crime Commissioners' (2012) 157(5) *RUSI Journal* 6, 8–9.

[110] The Cities and Local Government Devolution Act 2016, s. 4 provided this power by adding the Local Democracy, Economic Development and Construction Act 2009, s. 107F.

[111] H. Fearn, 'Eric Pickles: Council Tax Rise a "Kick in the Teeth" for Cash-Strapped Residents', *Guardian* (26 January 2012).

[112] See HC Debs, vol. 335, cols 21–2 (12 July 1999). See generally, House of Commons Select Committee on Procedure, *The Procedural Consequences of Devolution* (1999) HC 185.

[113] See M. Russell and R. Hazell, 'Devolution and Westminster: Tentative Steps towards a More Federal Parliament' in R. Hazell (ed.), *The State and the Nations: the First Year of Devolution in the United Kingdom* (Imprint Academic, 2000) p. 183.

[114] Scotland Act 1998, s. 86.

tive over-representation, by head of population, that Scotland had enjoyed prior to devolution. Such a reduction reduces the chances of Scottish MPs being able to swing votes in the way seen during debates on the Health and Social Care (Community Health and Standards) Bill 2003 and the Higher Education Bill 2004. But did does not prevent Scottish MPs from voting on 'English' issues, and as such did not preclude the possibility of Scottish MPs influencing the determination of exclusively 'English' issues at Westminster.

Under Labour further efforts at the Westminster level to isolate and assess 'English' issues, and to provide specific mechanisms for the determination of such issues, were limited. Although Scotland, Wales and Northern Ireland continued to be represented in Parliament by the territorial Secretaries of State, England enjoyed no such privilege. Shortly after the establishment of the devolved administrations, the Blair Government resurrected the Standing Committee on English Regional Affairs – which had last met in the late 1970s – to provide a forum for the debate of English regional issues. The Committee met sporadically from 2001 onwards, but failed to make a significant impact, and last met in June 2004. Under Gordon Brown's premiership, attempts were made to revive the regionalism agenda within Westminster's processes. In June 2007, Brown appointed nine 'Ministers for the English Regions' with the responsibility to:

> [G]ive citizens a voice in central government, ensuring that government policy takes account of the differing needs of the nine English regions. Regional Ministers will make central government more visible in the regions, helping to raise its profile and generate awareness of the political system.[115]

Brown's *Governance of Britain* Green Paper also proposed Commons Select Committees for the English Regions to monitor and scrutinise the work of the regional ministers, and the various public bodies working (like the RDAs) in the English Regions.[116] In November 2008, eight new House of Commons select committees were established, each with the power to 'examine regional strategies and the work of regional bodies'. Another was added for London in June 2009. Each of the committees was supposed to comprise five members representing constituencies within the respective region. Labour, however, could not even generate interest in the regionalism agenda amongst parliamentarians. It took many months for representatives to be appointed to the regional select committees and meetings were infrequent in the run-up to the 2010 general election. Following Labour's defeat at that election, the Coalition Government scrapped regional ministers and select committees, banishing regionalism from Westminster's processes.[117]

(ii) English Votes for English Laws

Perhaps the appealingly simple response to the West Lothian question is that which would prevent MPs representing devolved constituencies from voting at Westminster on issues which would not apply to their constituents. This response has become popularly known as English votes for English laws (EVEL). The suggestion that English MPs alone should be able to vote on laws that would apply to England alone, however, is not a new one. Indeed the origins of the proposal of English votes on English laws predate the current arrangements for devolution by over 100 years. During the debates on Irish Home Rule in 1886, 1893 and 1914, the question of the role of Irish MPs in the Westminster

---

[115] HM Government, *The Governance of Britain* (2007) Cm. 7170, para. 116.
[116] Ibid., paras 119–120.
[117] See G. Young, MP, HC Debs, vol. 510, col. 173 (26 May 2010).

Parliament after the creation of an Irish legislature raised the same conundrum as to how a devolved nation 'was to be represented at Westminster after Home Rule'.[118]

New Labour refused to countenance EVEL, and instead sought to overlook the representational inequalities associated with the West Lothian/English questions. Lord Irvine, when Lord Chancellor, blithely concluded that 'now that we have devolution up and running, I think the best thing to do about the West Lothian Question is to stop asking it'.[119] Even if he followed this up with the assertion that preventing Scottish MPs from voting on English matters post-devolution would have the effect of creating two classes of MP,[120] the message was, undoubtedly, one of 'nothing to see here'. In 2007, Gordon Brown, new to the office of Prime Minister, included pledges to resist special arrangements covering the creation of English laws in his *Governance of Britain* agenda:

> [W]hile we will listen to all proposals to improve our constitution in the light of devolution, we do not accept the proposal for English votes for English laws, which would create two classes of Members of Parliament – some entitled to vote on all issues, some invited to vote only on some. We will do nothing to put at risk the Union.[121]

Such claims neglect the fact that devolution has *already* created a hierarchy of MPs, with some responsible to the Westminster Parliament, and their constituents, for a much wider range of governmental activities than others. To illustrate the point, Westminster MPs representing constituencies in Scotland, Wales and Northern Ireland have fewer constituency responsibilities than their English counterparts. As a result of devolution, MPs representing constituencies in Scotland, Wales, and Northern Ireland (unlike those in England) have no constituency responsibilities for health and education among other things. More realistically perhaps, the Labour Government's inertia prior to 2010 can be attributed to the fact that Labour derived considerable support from the devolved regions, and the government would have put itself at a considerable disadvantage if it precluded its own MPs from the devolved territories from voting on issues which did not apply outside of England.

The Conservative Party, which stood to gain from marginalising the role of parliamentarians from Scotland, Wales, and Northern Ireland (where they have in recent parliaments won few seats), refused to allow the issue to drop. Successive leaders mooted EVEL as a response to the West Lothian question, even though constitutional theorists pointed out that a strict application of the idea would have the potential effect of bifurcating the executive, if different parties could command a Commons majority depending on whether or not English-only issues were at stake.[122] In 2008 the Party's Democracy Task Force proposed a modified version of EVEL which, they argued, would avoid the absolutism of the strict policy, by allowing all members of a House of Commons to participate in debates at certain stages of the legislative process.[123] When the Conservatives took power after the 2015 general election these proposals formed the basis of instituting EVEL. One pressing problem, however, remained: just what exactly is an 'English' law?

---

[118] B. Hadfield, 'Devolution, Westminster and the English Question' [2005] PL 286, 287. See also V. Bogdanor, *Devolution in the United Kingdom* (OUP, 1999) 29.

[119] HL Debs, vol. 602, col. 1201 (25 June 1999).

[120] Ibid., cols 1201–2.

[121] HC Debs, vol. 462, col. 818 (3 July 2007).

[122] V. Bogdanor, *Devolution in the United Kingdom* (OUP, 1999) p. 231.

[123] Conservative Party Democracy Task Force, *Answering the Question: Devolution, the West Lothian Question and the Future of the Union* (2008).

Proposing that English MPs only are able to vote on laws that apply to England alone is dependent on the fact that we can readily identify such a thing as an English law. English issues, however, tend to have a knock-on effect, especially as a result of the arrangements for financing devolution. The Barnett Formula determines the amount of money to be allocated to the devolved institutions in Scotland, Wales and Northern Ireland, taking into account the level of public spending in England. As a result, the determination of English issues with resource implications will frequently have a knock-on effect in the devolved territories (effects which are often referred to as 'Barnett consequentials'[124]). Indirectly at least, English issues therefore become of concern to MPs representing devolved constituencies. As a result, it would not be equitable to entirely exclude MPs representing the devolved territories from what would nominally be called English proceedings, for the reason that those English issues may well have consequences for government in Scotland, Wales and Northern Ireland. As the Kilbrandon Commission recognised in the 1970s:

> Ability to vote [in the House of Commons] could not depend simply on whether the matter at issue related to a reserved or transferred subject. Any issue at Westminster involving expenditure of public money is of concern to all parts of the United Kingdom since it may directly affect the level of taxation and indirectly influence the level of a region's own expenditure.[125]

Even after transfers of power to the devolved institutions, Westminster continues to pass a significant body of legislation which applies across the entire UK, and legislation applicable to England and Wales is far more common than legislation that applies to England alone. Indeed, Robert Hazell has suggested that more Acts of Parliament which apply to England alone will eventually arise as a necessary consequence of devolution:

> English laws will come, not through popular demand, but simply as a by-product of devolution, as the residuum which Westminster is left with once much of Westminster's law-making is devolved to Scotland, Wales and Northern Ireland.[126]

Of course, once the Welsh Assembly gained the competence to pass primary legislation, then the likelihood of 'English laws' being passed by the Westminster Parliament increased; the National Assembly for Wales being no longer as reliant on the Westminster Parliament to pass legislative measures enabling it to give effect to specific policy initiatives.

In the aftermath of the Scottish independence referendum David Cameron faced a challenge. Many of his own Conservative MPs were already complaining that England was receiving a bad deal out of devolution, and he had pledged to extend the powers enjoyed by Scotland's devolved institutions as part of his effort to bolster the pro-Union campaign.[127] To counteract a potential parliamentary revolt he pledged a 'decisive answer' to

---

[124] C. Grayling, MP, HC Debs, vol. 598, col. 942 (15 July 2015).
[125] Royal Commission on the Constitution, *Volume 1: Report* (HMSO, 1973) Cmnd. 5460, para. 813.
[126] R. Hazell, 'The English Question: Can Westminster Be a Proxy for an English Parliament?' [2001] PL 268, 276.
[127] R. Rawlings, 'Riders on the Storm: Wales, the Union, and Territorial Constitutional Crisis' (2015) 42 JLS 471, 481.

the West Lothian question in the form of new arrangements for EVEL.[128] These arrangements would be adopted after the Conservative general election victory in 2015 through new House of Commons Standing Orders.[129] These Standing Orders introduced a new Legislative Grand Committee (LGC) stage to the Commons process for legislation affecting only England or England and Wales. The LGC stage of the legislative process takes place before a Bill receives its third reading in the Commons, if the Speaker certifies that a Bill contains provisions applicable to England or to England and Wales. Only MPs representing English constituencies can participate in the LGC (or English and Welsh MPs if provisions are applicable to England and Wales), effectively giving them the ability to block legislation at this phase if a majority of English MPs oppose it. But the measure does not exclude other MPs from the remainder of the legislative process; they can still vote and contribute to debate at all other stages of a Bill. There has yet to be a significant test of the procedure; for as long as the UK Government commands a healthy majority of English MPs the LGC stage is likely to be perfunctory. Moreover, for as long as the minority Conservative administration is reliant upon the support of the DUP (representing 10 Northern Ireland constituencies) to maintain its overall majority any Conservative enthusiasm for strengthening the EVEL arrangements is likely to cool.

Conclusion

Two decades on from the introduction of devolution and the territorial dimensions of the UK Constitution remain far from settled. The courts are still developing a jurisprudence of legislative review with regard to the devolved assemblies. The SNP's campaign for independence has only been paused after its defeat in the 2014 referendum. Should Brexit create economic hardship in Scotland or Northern Ireland, both parts of the UK in which a majority voted to remain in the EU, pressure on the Union could once again grow. The West Lothian question remains live; even after the introduction of EVEL parliamentarians from Scotland, Wales and Northern Ireland can all vote on matters in the Westminster Parliament which have no (direct) impact on their constituents. MPs representing devolved constituencies can hold ministerial positions which concern devolved areas of policy. And England remains without any meaningful structures of devolved regional government; Westminster remains a 'proxy for an English Parliament'.[130] Although these arrangements exacerbate devolution's asymmetry, there is no solution in sight. Indeed, it is not without irony that the Conservative Party, for so long the main proponent of English Votes for English Laws, found that it could only remain in government in the aftermath of the 2017 general election with the support of DUP MPs representing constituencies in Northern Ireland.

---

[128] D. Cameron, 'Scottish Independence Referendum: Statement by the Prime Minister' (19 September 2015).

[129] Standing Order 83J–83X (adopted 22 October 2015).

[130] R. Hazell, 'The English Question: Can Westminster be a Proxy for an English Parliament?' [2001] PL 268.

Practice questions

1. *'[D]evolution has been a real success. The last 10 years have shown that not only is it possible to have a Scottish Parliament inside the UK, but that it works well in practice. Having a Scottish Parliament is in general popular with the people of Scotland, and they welcome the scope to have Scottish issues debated and decided in Scotland. The Scottish Parliament has embedded itself in both the constitution of the United Kingdom and the consciousness of Scottish people. It is here to stay.'*

   (Commission on Scottish Devolution, Serving Scotland Better: Scotland and the United Kingdom in the 21st Century (2009) para. 14)

   Assess whether devolution is 'here to stay'.

2. *'This is a new model of governance and old procedural straight jackets may have to be modified so long as the parties have acted within the rule of law and the terms set down by Parliament.'*

   (Re Williamson's Judicial Review [2009] NIQB 63, [69] (Gillen J))

   How should the courts conduct their role of policing the devolution settlements?

3. *'[S]ome legislative entity is going to have to emerge in England to fill the vacuum left by Scottish home rule.'*

   (Tam Dalyell, MP, HC Debs, vol. 311, col. 741 (6 May 1998))

   Analyse this statement in the context of the operation of devolution in Scotland and the West Lothian question.

Further reading

Further reading with regard to this second chapter on devolution must be read alongside the further reading on the last chapter, for few works separate out the workings of devolution from the question of devolution's constitutional impact. On the issue of whether the devolved legislatures are sticking to their legislative competences, Chris Himsworth (**C. Himsworth, 'Devolution and its jurisdictional asymmetries'** (2007) 70 *Modern Law Review* 31–58) draws out the difference in judicial review competence and particularly the contrasts between human rights protection under the devolution legislation in Wales and Scotland and under the Human Rights Act. With regard to interaction between the devolved legislatures and Westminster, Alan Page and Andrea Batey (**A. Page and A. Batey, 'Scotland's Other Parliament: Westminster Legislation about Devolved Matters in Scotland since Devolution'** [2002] *Public Law* 501–23) provide a fascinating study of the degree to which, at a time when the Labour Party was the majority party in a coalition government in Scotland and was in office in Westminster, the UK Parliament frequently found itself legislating for Scotland. Their article offers an important insight into the operation of consent procedures allowing Westminster to legislate even in transferred areas of law making. Turning to the West Lothian question, Bridget Hadfield (**B. Hadfield, 'Devolution, Westminster and the English Question'** [2005] *Public Law* 286–305) provides an accessible catalogue of the different potential solutions to the issue of England's absence from the devolution settlement. She considers proposals that would involve differentiating powers of MPs from different parts of the UK, differentiating levels of representation and introducing devolution arrangements within England. Ultimately, in light of the problems with all of these potential solutions, she concludes that it may be better to simply accept the intractable nature of the problem. Once this key foundational article has been considered, readers should turn to Vernon Bogdanor (**V. Bogdanor, 'The West Lothian Question'** (2010) 63 *Parliamentary Affairs* 156–72), who rejects out-of-hand suggestions that tampering with levels of representation or MP competence at Westminster constitute effective ways of dealing with the West Lothian question. Instead, he emphasises the potential for efforts to address the West Lothian question to focus upon establishing English regional institutions. With so many different institutions pulling in distinct directions in the UK Constitution, Bogdanor recognises that devolution undermines efforts by central government to secure uniform provision of public services. Finally, with regard to efforts to counterbalance devolution's current asymmetries, readers will find a useful starting point in the work of Robert Hazell and Mark Sandford (**R. Hazell and M. Sandford, 'English question or Union question? Neither has easier answers'** (2015) 86 *Political Quarterly* 16–23). They provide an effective overview of the challenges facing both city devolution and English votes for English laws.

Part V
Accountability (I): responsibility, scrutiny, openness and good administration

Chapter 14
Principles of political accountability

'It is a distinguishing characteristic of Parliamentary Government that it requires the powers belonging to the Crown to be exercised through Ministers, who are held responsible for the manner in which they are used . . . and who are considered entitled to hold their office only while they hold the confidence of Parliament, and more especially the House of Commons.'

Earl Grey, 'Parliamentary Government 1858' in H. J. Hanham, *The Nineteenth Century Constitution: Documents and Commentary* (CUP, 1969).

Chapter outline

In the UK Constitution, Parliament provides the primary public forum in which the government is held to account on behalf of the electorate. The idea that the government and its ministers are, collectively and individually, responsible to Parliament for their policies, actions and inactions is perhaps the core principle on which accountability within the framework of the political constitution is based. This chapter opens by briefly contrasting the mechanisms of political and legal accountability within the constitution, before going on to examine the doctrine of ministerial responsibility to Parliament, considering its requirements, operation and effectiveness.

Introduction

Perhaps the most theatrical aspect of the UK's constitutional system is the weekly appearance, before an invariably packed House of Commons, of the Prime Minister for Prime Minister's Questions (PMQs). Every Wednesday during the sitting of Parliament, the Prime Minister (or his or her Deputy) will for half an hour answer questions posed by other members of the House of Commons. The Prime Minister will list his or her engagements for the day, and will then be questioned, first by the Leader of the Opposition and then by backbench Members of the House. The government does not set the agenda, and as such PMQs provides one of the better opportunities for the opposition parties to score political points against the government. This seemingly routine event is the most visible evidence of the constitutional responsibility owed by all Ministers of the Crown – not simply by the Prime Minister – to appear before Parliament in order to explain their policies and decisions, and in order to answer questions posed by members of the House. In other words, it is perhaps the most obvious evidence of the processes of political accountability in action.

It is from the understanding that Ministers of the Crown hold office for only so long as they enjoy the confidence of the House of Commons that the constitutional convention of ministerial responsibility to Parliament springs. As we have already seen, it is Parliament – and not the government – that is legally sovereign in the UK Constitution.[1] As a result, it is logical that the government of the day might be permitted to wield power (including of course the ability to influence the deployment of Parliament's legislative capability) for as long as it enjoys the confidence of the members of the House of Commons. For advocates of the democratic objectives of the political constitution, the doctrine of ministerial responsibility to Parliament is perhaps the central rule on which the constitution is founded.[2]

Earl Grey's classic encapsulation of the doctrine, reproduced at the beginning of this chapter, came at arguably the high point of Parliament's ability to effectively hold the government to account. Since the nineteenth century, a series of developments – most importantly the increasing influence of the party system and the growth in the relative powers of the government vis-á-vis those of Parliament (most particularly the House of Commons) – have led commentators to question whether the convention remains as forceful as Earl Grey suggested.[3] By the turn of the twenty-first century, Jeffrey Jowell and Dawn Oliver – editors of *The Changing Constitution* – wrote in the foreword to the fourth edition of that work that 'the doctrine of individual ministerial responsibility has been significantly weakened over the last ten years or so, so that it can no longer be said, in our view, that it is a fundamental doctrine of the constitution.'[4] During the late twentieth century, the doctrine of ministerial responsibility to Parliament undoubtedly came under threat. The ability of the doctrine to ensure the disclosure of full and frank information to Parliament itself came under scrutiny following the damaging series of episodes which prompted the establishment – in 1992 – of the Scott Inquiry into the sale of arms to Iraq; changes to the structure of government brought about by, *inter alia,* the creation of quangos and executive agencies blurred traditional lines of accountability between Parliament, Ministers and the Civil Service;[5] and judicial review steadily became a more potent force for acting as a check on governmental activity.[6] But to say that the doctrine of ministerial responsibility is no longer 'fundamental' is to question the effectiveness of the central doctrine of political accountability in the UK, and therefore to question the effectiveness of the political constitution itself. This chapter will begin by contrasting the ideas of legal and political accountability, before moving on to examine the meaning and requirements of the doctrine of ministerial responsibility to Parliament. A number of recent challenges to the doctrine will be assessed, and we will conclude by assessing the centrality of political accountability in the contemporary constitution.

---

[1] Chapter 5.

[2] A. Tomkins, *Our Republican Constitution* (Hart Publishing, 2005) p. 1.

[3] For discussion of the notion of 'elective dictatorship', see pp. 304–6.

[4] J. Jowell and D. Oliver (eds), *The Changing Constitution* (4th edn) (Oxford University Press, 2000) p. viii.

[5] Chapter 8, pp. 278–9.

[6] Chapter 4, pp. 247–8. And for detailed coverage of judicial review, see Chapters 18 and 19.

Political and legal accountability distinguished

Key issues

- Broadly speaking, the political constitution values the democratic characteristics of accountability structures, whereas the legal constitution emphasises the coercive powers of the courts.
- Political and legal mechanisms of accountability operate in parallel in the UK Constitution policing, respectively, constitutional propriety and legality, and potentially giving rise to sanctions.

In Chapter 4 we observed the complementary – or some would say competing – traditions of the political constitution and of legal, or common law, constitutionalism. Each provides structures which assist in the objective of holding government to account; as Peter Cane has written:

> In crude terms, the political constitution provides a framework of accountability to political institutions for policy failures, whereas the legal constitution provides a framework for accountability to courts and tribunals for breaches of public (and private) law.[7]

Each model places emphasis on different approaches to the processes of constitutional accountability. On the one hand, the political constitution regards the democratic credentials of the political process as paramount, as – ultimately – the electorate has the ability to remove those who govern on their behalf from office. On the other hand, the ideas associated with legalistic forms of constitutional regulation stress the value to be found in the independent oversight of judicial review, and find strength in the relatively stable doctrinal processes of common law decision-making.

There is clearly value in entrusting the political process, rather than appointed officials such as judges, to hold our elected officials to account. The political process is, of course, underpinned by democratic – and participatory – ideals.[8] As a result, many commentators show a clear normative preference for government to be held to account by politicians rather than courts.[9]

As we will see, however, there are reasons to doubt the effectiveness of the political process and the traditional conventions of constitutional accountability as a check on governmental power. The strength of the party system in the Houses of Parliament, for one, undermines the capability of politics to hold the government to account. The traditional systems of parliamentary accountability – and the more recent innovations in securing political accountability – will be examined in the chapters which follow.

---

[7] P. Cane, Administrative Law (4th edn) (Clarendon Press, 2004) p. 356.
[8] A. Tomkins, *Our Republican Constitution* (Hart, 2005) p. 10: 'Politics is able both democratically and effectively to stop government, to check the exercise of executive power, to hold it to account. The courts, no matter what their powers and what their composition, will always find it more difficult.'
[9] For instance, J. A. G. Griffith, 'The Political Constitution' (1979) 42 MLR 1; R. Bellamy, *Political Constitutionalism: a Republican Defence of the Constitutionality of Democracy* (CUP, 2007).

In the UK Constitution, the political and legal frameworks operate in parallel, with the context of the activities to be monitored determining the appropriate guarantor of accountability. A dispute concerning the legality of an exercise of a discretionary power by a minister might be appropriately regarded as a matter for the courts, while a dispute over whether a minister had knowingly provided misleading information to Parliament as a matter for the legislature. Constitutional regulation in this sense is broad enough to encapsulate both questions of legality, strictly construed, and questions of propriety, that is, questions relating to whether our public officials have acted in accordance with the standards expected of officials exercising power in a democratic state. The standards by which government can be held to account in the courts – primarily through recourse to judicial review – are examined in later chapters.[10] But in order to elaborate a little on exactly what type of conduct is expected of our public officials when we refer to issues of constitutional propriety, it is helpful to refer to the seven principles highlighted by the Committee on Standards in Public Life.[11]

Key debates

Committee on Standards in Public Life – the seven principles of public life

The Standing Committee on Standards in Public Life was established in 1994 under the chairmanship of Lord Nolan following a series of high-profile controversies relating to the conduct of MPs (a number of which are considered below). The Committee is an independent body charged with 'examining . . . concerns about the standards of conduct of all holders of public office . . . and mak[ing] recommendations as to any changes in present arrangements which might be required to ensure the highest standards of propriety in public life' (HC Debs, col. 758 (25 October 1994)).

The work of the Committee is informed by the following principles relating to the conduct of public officials:

1. *Selflessness.* Holders of public office should act solely in terms of the public interest. They should not do so in order to gain financial or other benefits for themselves, their family or friends.

2. *Integrity.* Holders of public office should not place themselves under any financial or other obligation to outside individuals or organisations that might seek to influence them in the performance of their official duties.

3. *Objectivity.* In carrying out public business, including making public appointments, awarding contracts, or recommending individuals for rewards and benefits, holders of public office should seek to make choices on merit.

4. *Accountability.* Holders of public office are accountable for their decisions and actions to the public and must submit themselves to whatever scrutiny is appropriate to their office.

5. *Openness.* Holders of public office should be as open as possible about all the decisions and actions that they take. They should give reasons for their decisions and restrict information only when the wider public interest clearly demands.

→

---

[10] Chapters 18 and 19.
[11] See: https://www.gov.uk/government/organisations/the-committee-on-standards-in-public-life.

6. *Honesty.* Holders of public office have a duty to declare any private interest relating to their public duties and to take steps to resolve any conflicts arising in a way that protects the public interest.

7. *Leadership.* Holders of public office should promote and support these principles by leadership and example.

Issues of legality should therefore be distinguished from issues of what might be called 'constitutional propriety'; the former are enforced by the courts, the latter by political institutions, such as Parliament (though it should be remembered that the two systems do not operate in complete isolation of each other and that the same set of facts might provoke a response from both political and legal actors). The principles on standards of conduct in public life attempt to set down rules of constitutional propriety, and provide a clear attempt to give meaning to the conventions governing the accountability of public officials to Parliament and the electorate. The most important convention in this regard is that of the responsibility of ministers to Parliament, otherwise known as the doctrine of individual ministerial responsibility. Before examining the content and operation of this particular constitutional doctrine, we turn our attention to an essential precursor to any effective system of accountability: information.

Open government and effective accountability[12]

Key issues

- Access to governmental information is an essential precursor to achieving effective accountability of government.

- The prevailing twentieth-century approach to official information in the UK was in favour of maintaining secrecy and confidentiality rather than in favour of openness and disclosure.

- Only by the end of the century were steps taken to change the constitutional culture regarding the disclosure of government documentation and records.

The availability of information is crucial to the ability of any body or institution to hold government – or, indeed, anyone else – to account. Without the provision of accurate information we cannot hope to formulate an informed assessment of how a particular government department is performing, of whether a particular policy has been shown to be a success or failure, or of whether the conduct of a particular official met the standards that are expected of someone holding public office. Hence, access to information is a prerequisite of accountability and a guarantor of effective participatory democracy, as Lord Bingham – echoing Abraham Lincoln's Gettysburg address – noted in the House of Lords decision in *R* v *Shayler*:

> Modern democratic government means government of the people by the people for the people. But there can be no government by the people if they are ignorant of the issues to be resolved, the arguments for and against different solutions and the facts underlying those arguments.

---

[12] For a more detailed coverage of access to government information, see Chapter 17.

The business of government is not an activity about which only those professionally engaged are entitled to receive information and express opinions. It is, or should be, a participatory process. But there can be no assurance that government is carried out for the people unless the facts are made known, the issues publicly ventilated.[13]

There is, however, a tension between the ideal of readily available access to information regarding the conduct of government, and the reality of government in practice. It should come as no surprise that, just as governments are keen to publicise their policy successes as widely as is possible, they are less eager to publicise their policy failures, and are keen to prevent some particularly sensitive information from reaching the public domain at all.

For the larger part of the twentieth century, the dominant trend in the UK was in favour of restricting, rather than permitting, access to official information. The Official Secrets Acts set the tone, with s. 2 of the 1911 Act – a 'catch all'[14] provision which made *all* unauthorised disclosures of information obtained in an official capacity unlawful – indicative of the prevailing attitude to the release of information relating to the conduct of government for much of the twentieth century. In consequence '[f]or most of the twentieth century, British government was conducted, if not in the dark, at least in very dim light.[15]

Thinking point . . .

Section 2(1) of the Official Secrets Act 1911 made it an offence punishable by imprisonment for '. . . *any* person having in his possession or control . . . *any* document or information . . . which has been entrusted in confidence to him by *any* person holding office under Her Majesty . . . [to] communicate . . . the . . . document or information to *any* person, other than a person to whom he is authorised to communicate it or a person to whom it is in the interests of the State his duty to communicate it' (emphasis added). Section 2(1) of the 1911 Act was repealed by the Official Secrets Act 1989.

It was only towards the end of the twentieth century that measures encouraging the routine disclosure of official information began to loosen the shroud of secrecy that surrounded much of government in the UK. The first of these were non-statutory initiatives implemented by John Major's Conservative Government in the early 1990s. First, the 1991 *Citizens' Charter* – a document outlining the standards of service the public should expect of government – held that '[t]here should be no secrecy about how public services are run, how much they cost, who is in charge, and whether or not they are meeting their standards.'[16] This was followed by the *Code of Practice on Access to Government Information*, first published in 1994,[17] which placed public bodies falling within the jurisdiction of the

---

[13] *R v Shayler* [2002] UKHL 11; [2003] 1 AC 247, [21] (Lord Bingham).

[14] *Departmental Committee on Section 2 of the Official Secrets Act 1911* (the Franks Committee), Cmnd. 5102 (1972), [17].

[15] P. Cane, *Administrative Law* (5th edn) (Clarendon Press, 2011) p. 127.

[16] *The Citizen's Charter* (1991) Cm. 1588.

[17] On which, see *Open Government* (1993) Cm. 2290. A revised second edition of the *Code of Practice on Access to Government Information* was published in 1997.

Parliamentary Ombudsman[18] under an obligation to publicise information on, *inter alia,* the background to government policy decisions, departmental dealings with the public and information on how services were administered. The Code of Practice also obliged public bodies to give reasons for individual administrative decisions to the affected parties, and required such bodies to respond to individual requests for information. The Code, of course, also contained wide-ranging exceptions to the general presumption in favour of disclosure, allowing information to be retained which, *inter alia,* related to Cabinet discussions and policy formulation, defence, security and international relations and communications between the government and royal household.

Most recently, at the initiation of the Labour Government under Tony Blair, Parliament enacted the Freedom of Information Act 2000 which provides a legal right to access to government information, again subject to exceptions. These mechanisms for enhancing openness in government will be discussed in more detail in Chapter 17. For present purposes, it is the occasional tension between the willingness of government to reveal information and the resulting ability of Parliament (and therefore the electorate) to hold government to account that is material.

Individual ministerial responsibility

Key issues

- The convention of *individual ministerial responsibility* requires that ministers provide Parliament with full and accurate information relating to the conduct of governmental business within their portfolio.

- While the notion of *collective responsibility* is linked to the suggestion that the government as a whole must enjoy the confidence of the House of Commons, individual ministerial responsibility emphasises that individual ministers must also enjoy parliamentary support.

- Individual ministerial responsibility requires that ministers explain to Parliament their policies and activities undertaken on their behalf, but also that errors and failures be addressed. The precise contours of what ministers are individually responsible for are, however, slightly unclear.

There is nothing unusual about ministers being called to account for, and give an account of, their decisions and actions in Parliament. It is part and parcel of the everyday business of government. This seeming routine activity should not however disguise the constitutional importance of what is taking place:

> The government is required to secure the support of a majority in Parliament . . . *every single day* . . . Parliament is the institution through which the government must legislate; Parliament is the institution that controls the government's purse strings; and Parliament is the institution that will continuously inquire into the 'expenditure, administration and policy, of every government department. It follows that in order for it to realise its legislative ambitions, the government will have to persuade a majority in Parliament that its policies are the right ones; that in order for the government to enjoy financial freedom, it will have to persuade a majority in Parliament that its spending plans are the right ones; and that in order for government departments to achieve success they will have to ensure that their expenditure, administration and policy are sustainable.[19]

---

[18] See Chapter 16.
[19] A. Tomkins, *Our Republican Constitution* (Hart, 2005) p. 2 (emphasis added).

In short then, the doctrine of individual ministerial responsibility to Parliament requires that – in order to remain in office – the government must obtain the support of a majority of members of the House of Commons, and in order to gain and sustain that continued support, ministers ought to offer justification for their policy choices, and should seek to persuade Parliament of the rightfulness of their preferred methods of achieving particular legislative aims. Such a view of ministerial responsibility is grounded in the idea that the government should remain in office for only so long as it enjoys the support of a majority of members of the House of Commons. However, such a view does *not* take account of the fact that in many instances the size of a government's overall majority and influence of the party whipping system mean that the business of persuading the House of Commons of the merits of a particular decision or legislative or policy initiative is not a particularly difficult exercise. Nevertheless, it remains the constitutional obligation of ministers to present themselves to Parliament to explain their reasons for taking a particular decision, to answer for failings, to reassure that faults will be rectified and to demonstrate that action has been taken to avoid further errors.[20]

The operation of the convention of individual ministerial responsibility displays in practice the tension between the need for openness (in order to secure accountability and legitimate government) and the desire of governments to prevent disclosure of embarrassing or damaging materials (in order to maintain political power and reputation). Before we examine how this tension is manifested in practice, we need to address two important questions. First, how do we distinguish individual ministerial responsibility from the related doctrine of collective responsibility? Secondly, what exactly are ministers individually responsible for?

Collective responsibility distinguished

While, taken together, the conventions on individual ministerial responsibility and collective responsibility both play a central role in regulating the relationship between the government and Parliament – and should be considered alongside each other in that respect – each also serves a distinctive purpose. The ideas associated with collective responsibility have been fully examined in Chapter 8,[21] but for the purposes of comparison a brief revision of the core principles of the doctrine is undertaken here. The primary objective of the convention of collective responsibility is to ensure that the Ministers of the Crown present a united front. This is done through the element of the doctrine which determines that decisions taken in Cabinet are supported publicly by all members of that Cabinet, regardless of whether they personally support the decision or not. Lord Salisbury is accredited with having formulated the classic statement on this element of collective responsibility:

> For all that passes in Cabinet each member of it who does not resign is absolutely and irretrievably responsible and has no right afterwards to say that he agreed in one case to a compromise, while in another he was persuaded by his colleagues.[22]

---

[20] G. Marshall, *Constitutional Conventions: the Rules and Forms of Political Accountability* (Clarendon Press, 1986) p. 65.

[21] See pp. 273–6.

[22] HC Debs, cols 833–4 (8 April 1878).

Should any minister be unable to support a policy adopted by, or a decision taken in, Cabinet, then he or she should resign from the government.[23] The result of this requirement of unanimity is the appearance, or perhaps the pretence, of strong government. From this, it follows that collective responsibility also requires that the content of Cabinet discussions also be confidential, for to reveal the internal reservations or divisions over a particular decision would undermine the appearance of solidarity.

Finally, and most importantly in any discussion of political accountability, is the requirement of collective responsibility that the government must enjoy the confidence of the House of Commons. Just as ministers are individually responsible to Parliament for their policies and decisions, the Cabinet is collectively responsible for the activities of government as a whole. Once the government loses the confidence of the House of Commons then – by convention – it should resign. In other words, collective responsibility requires that the Cabinet stand and fall together.

What is a minister individually responsible for?

The definitional difficulties associated generally with constitutional conventions have already been alluded to.[24] To briefly recap, conventions may be vague, with the difficulty of establishing whether particular conduct is prescribed by convention or simply a mere practice compounded by the fact that conventions are generally policed – and, therefore, defined in practice – by those to whom they are said to apply. The central conventions governing the relationship between the executive and Parliament – the conventions of collective responsibility and individual ministerial responsibility – have similarly and traditionally been open to interpretation, as Geoffrey Marshall memorably described:

> A clear and succinct account of the principle or convention of ministerial responsibility is not easy to give. One reason may be that the convention is, like most British conventions, somewhat vague and slippery – resembling (to borrow a phrase) the procreation of eels. Another reason is that collective and individual responsibility are two doctrines, not one, and each divides in turn into a series of disparate topics. The slipperiness shows itself when we see that propositions about both types of responsibility have to be formulated in some form such as: 'Ministers generally do or should do X in circumstances Y (but with various exceptions).' Thus:
>
> 1. The prerogatives of the Crown are exercised on the advice of ministers (except when they are not).
> 2. The government resigns when it loses the confidence of the House of Commons (except when it remains in office).
> 3. Ministers speak and vote together (except when they cannot agree to do so).
> 4. Ministers explain their policy and provide information to the House (except when they keep it to themselves).
> 5. Ministers offer their individual resignations if serious errors are made in their Departments (except when they retain their posts or are given peerages).
> 6. Every act of a civil servant is, legally speaking, the act of a minister (except those that are, legally speaking, his own).[25]

---

[23] For the most notable example in recent years, see the resignation speech of Robin Cook MP, over the 2003 decision of the UK Government to go to war in Iraq (HC Debs, cols 726–8 (17 March 2003)). See R. Cook, *The Point of Departure: Diaries from the Front Bench* (Simon and Schuster, 2003).

[24] For a detailed analysis, see Chapter 2.

[25] G. Marshall, *Constitutional Conventions: The Rules and Forms of Political Accountability* (Clarendon, 1984) p. 54.

Marshall's account vividly illustrates the potential disconnect in this area between constitutional principle and constitutional practice. Ideally, the former should govern the latter, but that is not always the case. The doctrine of individual ministerial responsibility has shown itself to be particularly susceptible to definitional uncertainty. In theory at least, a minister is responsible for 'everything done or left undone by his or her department' and owes an obligation to Parliament to explain '"what has happened and why" when failures occur.'[26] Ministerial accountability, in Colin Turpin's words, has two aspects: the obligation to provide information ('explanatory accountability') and the obligation to rectify administrative errors and faulty policy ('amendatory accountability').[27]

Accountability and/or responsibility

At its most basic, the doctrine of ministerial responsibility requires that government ministers provide Parliament with an account of actions undertaken in their official capacity. A minister will be responsible to provide Parliament with an explanation of activities undertaken by civil servants within their department, or of the activities of a quango or executive agency operating within the area of policy covered by the department of which they are head. The Home Secretary, for instance, is constitutionally obligated to account for the activities undertaken by the civil servants of the core Home Office, and those undertaken by the UK Border Agency and the Identity and Passport Service, for example. So while a minister should permit him or herself to be held to account by Parliament and should provide an account of activity in return, at what point does a minister become personally – or individually – responsible for the activity complained of? Does it necessarily follow that the Home Secretary, for example, should be held to be *personally* responsible in the event of serious failures in the work of the UK Border Agency or the Identity and Passport Service?

Historically, the position has been unclear. The resignation speech of Sir Thomas Dugdale, Minister for Agriculture and Fisheries, following the Crichel Down affair in 1954 appeared to indicate that ministers should take responsibility for *all* activity carried out within their departments, including activities undertaken by civil servants acting on their behalf. The Crichel Down affair concerned an area of land that had been compulsorily purchased by the government during the Second World War. Following the conclusion of the war, the land came under the responsibility of the Ministry of Agriculture and Fisheries. The scandal arose out of civil servants' alleged mismanagement of the land; instead of returning the land to its previous owners (as had been promised) the ministry retained ownership, leasing the property out to third parties. Dugdale announced his resignation with the following words:

> I, as Minister, must accept full responsibility to Parliament for any mistakes and inefficiency of officials in my department, just as, when my officials bring off any successes, I take full credit for them.[28]

Dugdale, therefore, appeared to indicate that ministers were under an obligation to not only provide Parliament with an account of the errors or misjudgements of civil servants, but also that they should take personal responsibility for those failures, even perhaps in

---

[26] C. Turpin, 'Ministerial Responsibility' in J. Jowell and D. Oliver (eds), *The Changing Constitution* (3rd edn) (OUP, 1994) p. 109.

[27] Ibid.

[28] HC Debs, vol. 530, col. 1186 (20 July 1954).

circumstances where the minister in question had no *personal* involvement whatsoever in the action held to be at fault. Dugdale's willingness to shoulder the blame for the civil servants personally responsible might in many ways be seen as a hangover from the Diceyan reading of the doctrine of ministerial responsibility under which the minister would 'relieve subordinates of public blame for their errors'.[29] If a minister were to accept responsibility for *all* official actions, then the anonymity and impartiality of the civil service would be preserved. Ultimately, however, such an extreme interpretation of 'responsibility' could not be sustained.

In the debate which followed Dugdale's resignation, the Home Secretary, Sir David Maxwell-Fyfe, sought to distinguish those circumstances in which a minister could be held personally blameworthy, and those in which he or she could not. Maxwell-Fyfe told the House of Commons:

> The Minister is not bound to defend action of which he did not know, or of which he disapproved. But . . . he remains constitutionally responsible to Parliament for the fact that something has gone wrong, and he alone can tell Parliament what has occurred and render an account of his stewardship.[30]

On Maxwell-Fyfe's contrasting account, therefore, in circumstances where the minister was not personally involved in the faulty decision or activity, he or she would remain responsible to provide Parliament with an account, but would not be held *personally* responsible for the failures of their civil servants. The more realistic position is that advanced by Maxwell-Fyfe, as summarised by Geoffrey Marshall: '[w]hen action is taken of which a minister disapproves and of which he has no prior knowledge, there is no obligation on his part to endorse it, to defend the errors of his officers, or to resign.'[31]

A contemporary variant on this distinction can be found in the suggestion that 'policy' matters fall within the responsibility of the relevant minister, while 'operations' or 'administration' are a matter for civil servants. If the system of parliamentary accountability permitted distinctions of this sort, then the result would be the equivalent of a minister being able to claim – in the words of Enoch Powell MP – that 'the policy was excellent and that was mine, but the execution was defective or disastrous and that was nothing to do with me.'[32] This particular distinction has been most evident in the claims made by a number of Home Secretaries attempting to circumvent criticism for failures in the management of prisons following the escape of prisoners.[33] During the 1990s the policy/operations distinction was famously invoked by the then Home Secretary Michael Howard following high-profile escapes from Whitemoor and Parkhurst prisons. The picture in this case was made more complex by the fact that by the mid-1990s management of prisons was the responsibility of the Prisons Service, an executive agency falling within the policy remit of, but simultaneously at one step removed from, the Home Office. As a result, Howard was able to claim responsibility for 'policy' on prisons, but to claim that responsibility for their operation lay, ultimately, with the Chief Executive of the Prisons Service. Thus Howard

---

[29] C. Turpin, 'Ministerial Responsibility' in J. Jowell and D. Oliver (eds), *The Changing Constitution* (3rd edn) (OUP, 1994) pp. 114–15.

[30] HC Debs, vol. 530, cols 1286–7 (20 July 1954).

[31] G. Marshall, *Constitutional Conventions: The Rules and Forms of Political Accountability* (Clarendon Press, 1986) p. 65.

[32] HC Debs, vol. 53, col. 1061 (9 February 1984).

[33] For instance, Kenneth Baker, following the 1991 escapes from Brixton prison.

sought to draw a distinction between his constitutional obligations to Parliament for matters of policy, and the 'internal, executive or management responsibility'[34] for execution of that policy which was owed by civil servants to the relevant minister. Howard survived, sacking the Chief Executive of the Prisons Service as a result of these 'operational' failures.

The truth, perhaps, is that it is difficult to neatly compartmentalise issues of 'responsibility' on the one hand, and 'accountability' on the other; the two run in parallel and together comprise the obligation owed by ministers to Parliament. This view was endorsed by the House of Commons Public Service Committee in 1994 in a report which indicated that it was not possible to separate the 'accountability' and 'responsibility' requirements of the doctrine of ministerial responsibility in the way that Dugdale's resignation – and a number of subsequent ministers[35] – had suggested. The Committee argued:

> It is not possible absolutely to distinguish an area in which a Minister is personally responsible, and liable to take blame, from one in which he is constitutionally accountable. Ministerial responsibility is not composed of two elements with a clear break between the two. Ministers have an obligation to Parliament which consists in ensuring that government explains its actions. Ministers also have an obligation to respond to criticism made in Parliament in a way that seems likely to satisfy it – which may include, if necessary, resignation.[36]

What is certain is that imprecision and uncertainty in the doctrine of ministerial responsibility has been compounded by modern developments in the machinery of government; as the House of Commons Liaison Committee observed in 2012: '[the] old doctrine of ministerial accountability (by which ministers alone are accountable to Parliament for the conduct of their department) is being stretched to implausibility by the complexity of modern government and by the increasing devolution of responsibility to civil servants and to arm's length bodies.'[37]

Is a minister responsible for personal indiscretions?

There is a school of thought which argues that activities undertaken by ministers in their personal capacity should not affect their ability to discharge their functions as a holder of public office. The difficulty here is not one of competence, but of judgment. And when questions of personal judgment bring embarrassment for the government as a whole, particularly if that government is facing political difficulties in other respects, then pressure will mount on the minister in question to resign. The fact that the indiscretion in question is not directly ruinous of their perceived competence may also serve to extend the period between the indiscretion coming to light and the resignation of the minister in question should 'such resistance sooner or later . . . prove futile'.[38] Going as far back as the Second World War – and illustrated in some of the examples in Table 14.1 below – it is arguably as common to find ministerial resignations as a result of some 'personal or moral scandal' as following on from official 'public or parliamentary criticism'.[39]

---

[34] A . Tomkins, *The Constitution After Scott: Government Unwrapped* (Clarendon Press, 1998) p. 47.
[35] Ibid., pp. 49–52.
[36] Public Service Committee, *Ministerial Accountability and Responsibility,* HC 313 (1995–1996), [21].
[37] House of Commons Liaison Committee, *Select Committee Effectiveness, Resources and Powers,* HC 697 (November 2012), [114].
[38] A. Tomkins, *Public Law* (Clarendon Press, 2003) p. 145.
[39] G. Marshall, *Constitutional Conventions: The Rules and Forms of Political Accountability* (Clarendon Press, 1986) p. 62.

Sanctions and effectiveness

Key issues

- Sanctions for breach of the convention of individual responsibility can range from an apology to resignation.
- Ministerial resignations, however, should not necessarily be seen as evidence of the effectiveness of the doctrine of ministerial responsibility, as history shows that various extraneous factors will in fact influence whether or not a minister resigns in the event of a breach of the convention.
- The successes of the doctrine are perhaps better gauged by the ability of Parliament to routinely extract information from government and to impose remedial measures in the event that doing so is necessary.
- The aftermath of the Scott Report saw Parliament reassert a degree of control over the responsibilities imposed by the doctrine, though doubts continue to exist over the effectiveness of the doctrine in practice.

As we have already seen, no legal remedy can be obtained in consequence of a breach of constitutional convention.[40] Sanctions for breaches of the convention of individual ministerial responsibility are therefore imposed only within the political realm. In response to an alleged failure, a minister will be expected to provide Parliament with information and an explanation of their conduct and/or that of officials within their remit. A minister should also provide an account of steps to be taken in order to avoid repetition of the alleged failure, and, if necessary, should offer an apology. In July 2010, for example, the then Education Secretary, Michael Gove, apologised to the House of Commons for releasing inaccurate information regarding a list of school building projects which (after being announced by the previous government) were to be shelved.[41]

The ultimate political sanction, of course, is that of resignation. However, it should not be assumed that resignation is a necessary consequence of even what might be seen as grave and flagrant breaches of the convention of ministerial responsibility. As we will see in our discussion of the circumstances which gave rise to the Scott inquiry – in which a number of ministers were found to have misled Parliament over an issue of government policy – no ministerial resignations resulted. Ministerial resignations are perhaps rather more an indicator of political climate or of the character of the individual concerned than a clear sign of an effective system of political accountability. As S. E. Finer wrote in the 1950s (in what is still regarded as the classic account of individual ministerial responsibility):

> . . . whether a Minister is forced to resign depends on three factors, on himself, on his Prime Minister and his party . . . For a Minister to resign all three factors have to be just so: the Minister compliant, the Prime Minister firm, the party clamorous. This conjuncture is rare, and is in fact fortuitous. Above all, it is indiscriminate – which Ministers escape and which do not is decided neither by the circumstances of the offence or its gravity . . .

---

[40] Chapter 2, pp. 46–8.
[41] HC Debs, vol. 513, cols 484–93 (7 July 2010). See also 'Michael Gove Apologises for Blunders in Cancelled School Project List,' *Guardian*, 8 July 2010.

> A remedy ought to be certain. A punishment, to be deterrent, ought to be certain. But whether the Minister should resign is simply the (necessarily) haphazard consequence of a fortuitous concomitance of personal, party and political temper.[42]

In cases of serious personal fault on the part of an individual minister, it is obviously correct that Parliament has the ability to call for a resignation. It is also obviously correct, in less serious circumstances or circumstances where the minister is not personally at fault, that the opportunity to apologise and take corrective action is available. The difficulty identified by Finer is that even in cases of clear and serious failings which can be directly attributed to the responsible minister, the resignation of that minister is by no means certain to follow. Even in cases of significant individual error, the support of the Prime Minister and a House of Commons dominated by the governing party may well be enough to repel political pressure for a resignation. If it is correct that 'ministerial resignations . . . are attributable to political and personal pressures rather than to the dictates of any constitutional principle',[43] then there is a clear disconnect between constitutional doctrine and constitutional practice (Table 14.1). The question we must ask ourselves then is, can this uncertainty be tolerated in a working and effective system of accountability? A red-light theorist might stress the necessity for the constitution to be able to put a stop to errors and misdemeanours committed by ministers. A green-light theorist might see the opportunity for remedial action – so long as effective – to be an adequate response.

However, history also demonstrates that in a number of linked cases of serious personal misconduct Parliament was unable to force the resignation of the ministers in question forcing a number of commentators to cast doubt upon the continuing effectiveness of the convention of individual ministerial responsibility and, as a result, of one of the central pillars of the political constitution.

Table 14.1 Notable ministerial resignations – some examples

Who?	When?	Why?
John Profumo	1963	Resigned from the Cabinet after misleading the House of Commons over the nature of his extra-marital relationship with Christine Keeler (a woman who was simultaneously involved with a Soviet attaché).
James Callaghan	1967	Resigned as Chancellor of the Exchequer following devaluation of the pound contrary to earlier assurances given to the House of Commons.
Cecil Parkinson	1983	Resigned as Secretary of State for Trade and Industry to Margaret Thatcher's government in 1983 when details of his affair with his secretary, and her pregnancy, emerged. The commentator Geoffrey Marshall noted that Parkinson's resignation gives some support to 'the conclusion that a constitutional convention or usage is emerging that ministers are not to be allowed to treat deviation from conventional sexual morality as a private matter that need not impinge upon their continuance and effectiveness in public office'.[44]

---

[42] S. E. Finer, 'The Individual Responsibility of Ministers' (1956) 34 *Public Administration* 377, 393.
[43] R. Scott, 'Ministerial Accountability' [1996] PL 410, 414.
[44] G. Marshall, *Constitutional Conventions: the Rules and Forms of Political Accountability* (Clarendon Press, 1986) p. 223.

Who?	When?	Why?
Edwina Currie	1988	Resigned as Health Minister after sparking food safety scare by claiming – incorrectly – that 'most of the egg production of this country, sadly, is now infected with salmonella'.
Norman Lamont	1992	Resigned as Chancellor of the Exchequer following the removal of Sterling from the ERM (Exchange Rate Mechanism) despite earlier assurances to the contrary.
David Mellor	1992	David Mellor resigned his post as Secretary of State for National Heritage (or 'Secretary of State for Fun' as the tabloids had dubbed the position) in 1992. Mellor, it was revealed, had been involved in an extra-marital affair with the actress Antonia de Sancha. A series of stories in the tabloid press detailing Mellor's foot-related peccadilloes brought embarrassment to John Major's, already faltering, government. The day following Mellor's resignation, *The Sun* newspaper gleefully ran the headline: 'From Toe Job to No Job'.[45]
Neil Hamilton and Tim Smith	1994	Neil Hamilton (Minister for Deregulation and Corporate Affairs) and Tim Smith (a Junior Minister in the Northern Ireland Office) both resigned from John Major's government in 1994 following allegations that they had accepted payments from the businessman Mohammed Al-Fayed in return for asking questions in Parliament in his behalf.[46] As news of the story broke, Smith resigned immediately. Hamilton protested his innocence, but resigned shortly after. The 'cash for questions affair', as it became known, led to the creation of the Committee on Standards in Public Life (the Nolan Committee) by the then Prime Minister, John Major.
Peter Mandelson	2001	Resigned from the position of Secretary of State for Northern Ireland following allegations regarding inappropriate attempts to influence the decision over whether to grant British citizenship to Indian businessman, Scrichand Hinduja.
Estelle Morris	2004	Resigned as Secretary of State for Education following government's failure to meet targets for literacy and numeracy in schools, admitting that she did not feel up to the task of holding ministerial office.
Hazel Blears	2009	Hazel Blears resigned the post of Communities Secretary following allegations of her failure to pay capital gains tax following the sale of a property. Despite Blears repaying some £13,000 of expenses, the then Prime Minister, Gordon Brown, was reported to have described Blears' claims as 'totally unacceptable'.[47]
Liam Fox	2011	Resigned as Defence Secretary following breaches of the ministerial code relating to the involvement of a friend and lobbyist in government business.

---

[45] 'From Toe Job to No Job', *Sun*, 25 September 1992.
[46] 'Tory MPs Were Paid to Plant Questions Says Harrods Chief', *Guardian*, 20 October 1994.
[47] 'Hazel Blears' Resignation Deepens Gordon Brown's Cabinet Crisis', *Telegraph*, 3 June 2009.

Who?	When?	Why?
Chris Huhne	2012	Resigned as Energy Secretary following criminal charges brought against him relating to a speeding offence.
Maria Miller	2014	Resigned as Culture Secretary following an expenses claim of £90,718 made in relation to costs on a second home in which her parents had been living. The claim was deemed – by the Parliamentary Commissioner for Standards – to be in breach of expenses rules, and Miller was ordered to repay £44,000. A subsequent report of the Cross-Party Standards Committee determined that there was no intentional wrong-doing, and ordered that Miller repay £5,800 and apologise to the House for her failure to fully co-operate with the parliamentary inquiry into her expenses claim. The terse apology which followed was described by the *Daily Mail* as 'an insult to Parliament'.
Michael Fallon	2017	Amid widespread allegations and rumours relating to sexual harassment at Westminster, Fallon resigned the position as Defence Secretary as a result of admitting to behaviour that had 'fallen below [the] high standards we require of the armed forces'.

Setting the scene

The failure of the political constitution? Arms to Iraq and the Scott Report

- Iran and Iraq were at war between 1980 and 1988. During this time, the UK Government's stated policy on the export of defence equipment to either country was that export licences should *not* be granted to British companies to allow the export of materials or equipment likely to 'prolong or exacerbate' the conflict or to strengthen the defence capability of either nation.

- In 1991, the directors of Matrix Churchill, a machine-tools manufacturing company, were prosecuted by Her Majesty's Customs and Excise as a result of having allegedly breached controls on the export of 'dual-use goods' (that is, goods that could be used in the manufacture of weapons) to Iraq. They were put on trial, and faced significant prison sentences if convicted.

- Prior to the trial, government ministers took steps to prevent certain documents from being put before the court, and signed Public Interest Immunity (PII) certificates on the ground that disclosure of information would be contrary to the public interest. The relevant documents contained information that the directors claimed would show that the government had relaxed its policy on selling arms to Iraq, and that Matrix Churchill – in exporting the so-called 'dual-use' goods – had acted with effective government sanction.

- The government had good reason to attempt to keep this documentation secret; the policy on weapons exports *had* been changed (though this information has been withheld by ministers from Parliament), and ministers *knew* of the activities of Matrix Churchill (but were seemingly prepared to see the directors of the company imprisoned in order to keep the policy change a secret). The trial collapsed as the inconsistencies in the government's evidence began to emerge. As Adam Tomkins records, '[i]t was this enticing cocktail of lying to Parliament, gagging the court, and legal controversy which generated such immense political pressure that the Prime Minister, John Major, felt that he had no alternative but to establish a full judicial inquiry to examine the entire matter'.[48]

---

[48] A. Tomkins, *The Constitution After Scott: Government Unwrapped* (Clarendon Press, 1998) p. 6.

- In 1992, following the collapse of the Matrix Churchill trial, the government appointed Lord Justice Scott to chair the inquiry into the circumstances surrounding the case.[49] The wide-ranging investigation examined a number of issues of some considerable constitutional importance, including the relationships between the responsible ministers, civil servants and security services, and the propriety (and legality) of the use of public interest immunity in the context of the aborted Matrix Churchill prosecution. For our purposes however, it is Scott's findings on the duty of ministers to provide information to Parliament, and the ability of Parliament to extract information from ministers, that are relevant.

- The Scott Report[50] was published in 1996 and provides a damning indictment of the governmental accounts provided to Parliament in respect of the policy on the sale of 'dual-use' goods to Iraq. Scott's report highlights multiple failures to provide full and accurate information to Parliament in respect of the changed policy; minister's responses to parliamentary questions ranged from the 'decidedly uninformative'[51] to 'inaccurate and potentially misleading'.[52] The government, Scott found, 'failed to inform Parliament of the current state of government policy on . . . arms sales to Iraq. This failure was deliberate.'[53]

- Scott's findings drew attention to systematic and collective action on the part of the government to prevent knowledge of the policy change reaching the public domain; 'Parliament and the public were designedly led to believe that a stricter policy towards non-lethal defence exports and dual-use exports to Iraq was being applied than was in fact the case.'[54] Government ministers had effectively colluded to act contrary to the expectations of the doctrine of ministerial responsibility to Parliament, and had been publicly exposed as having done so. Yet, no ministers resigned.

Individual responsibility defined? The parliamentary resolutions on individual responsibility and *The Ministerial Code*

In the aftermath of the Scott Inquiry, both Houses of Parliament passed resolutions which contained the substantive requirements of the doctrine of individual ministerial responsibility. The House of Commons resolution read as follows:

1. Ministers have a duty to Parliament to account, and to be held to account, for the policies, decisions and actions of their departments and next steps agencies.

2. It is of paramount importance that Ministers give accurate and truthful information to Parliament, correcting any inadvertent error at the earliest opportunity. Ministers who knowingly mislead Parliament will be expected to offer their resignation to the Prime Minister.

---

[49] The terms of reference for the Scott Inquiry were as follows: 'Having examined the facts in relation to the export from the United Kingdom of defence equipment and dual-use goods to Iraq between December 1984 and August 1990 and the decisions reached on the export licence applications for such goods and the basis for them, to report on which the relevant departments, agencies, and responsible ministers operated in accordance with the policies of her majesty's government; to examine and report on decisions taken by the prosecuting authority and by those signing public interest immunity certificates in *R* v *Henderson* and any other similar cases that he considers relevant to the issues of the inquiry; and to make recommendations.'

[50] *Report of the Inquiry into the Export of Defence Equipment and Dual-Use Goods to Iraq and Related Prosecutions* (HMSO, 1996).

[51] Ibid., [D3.107].

[52] Ibid., [D1.151].

[53] Ibid., [D4.42].

[54] Ibid., [D8.16].

3. Ministers should be as open as possible with Parliament, refusing to provide information only when disclosure would not be in the public interest, which should be decided in accordance with relevant statutes and the government's Code of Practice on Access to Government Information.

4. Similarly, Ministers should require civil servants who give evidence before parliamentary committees on their behalf and under their directions to be as helpful as possible in providing accurate, truthful and full information in accordance with the duties and responsibilities of civil servants as set out in the Civil Service Code.[55]

While the 1997 resolutions of the Houses of Parliament did much to clarify the obligations owed by ministers to Parliament, since then it has been a government document that has sought to define the content of ministerial responsibility. *The Ministerial Code* has been published by the Cabinet Office since 1997, replacing the previous guidance found in a document entitled *Questions of Procedure for Ministers*, and clearly taking its influence from the two parliamentary resolutions on individual ministerial responsibility. The most recent edition of *The Ministerial Code* was published in January 2018.[56] The relevant extract – outlining the core 'principles of ministerial conduct' – from *The Ministerial Code* is worth repeating in full:

(a) The principle of collective responsibility applies to all Government Ministers.

(b) Ministers have a duty to Parliament to account, and be held to account, for the policies, decisions and actions of their departments and agencies.

(c) It is of paramount importance that Ministers give accurate and truthful information to Parliament, correcting any inadvertent error at the earliest opportunity. Ministers who knowingly mislead Parliament will be expected to offer their resignation to the Prime Minister.

(d) Ministers should be as open as possible with Parliament and the public, refusing to provide information only when disclosure would not be in the public interest, which should be decided in accordance with the relevant statutes and the Freedom of Information Act 2000.

(e) Ministers should similarly require civil servants who give evidence before Parliamentary Committees on their behalf and under their direction to be as helpful as possible in providing accurate, truthful and full information in accordance with the duties and responsibilities of civil servants as set out in the *Civil Service Code.*

(f) Ministers must ensure that no conflict arises, or appears to arise, between their public duties and their private interests.

(g) Ministers should not accept any gift or hospitality which might, or might reasonably appear to, compromise their judgement or place them under an improper obligation.

(h) Ministers in the House of Commons must keep separate their roles as Minister and constituency member.

(i) Ministers must not use government resources for Party political purposes.

---

[55] HC Debs, vol. 292, cols 1046–7 (19 March 1997). See also HL Debs, vol. 579, col. 1057 (20 March 1997).

[56] *Ministerial Code* (Cabinet Office, January 2018), available at: https://www.gov.uk/government/uploads/system/uploads/attachment_data/file/672633/2018-01-08_MINISTERIAL_CODE_JANUARY_2018__FINAL___3_.pdf.

(j) Ministers must uphold the political impartiality of the civil service and not ask civil servants to act in any way which would conflict with the *Civil Service Code* as set out in the Constitutional Reform and Governance Act 2010.[57]

While the 'codification' of the doctrine of ministerial responsibility has resolved some of the definitional difficulties associated with that particular constitutional convention, another perhaps equally pressing difficulty remains. *The Ministerial Code* is published by the Cabinet Office, and includes a foreword written by the Prime Minister. It is manifestly a *government* document. Yet ministerial responsibility is not owed to the government; it is owed to Parliament.[58] As a result, treating *The Ministerial Code* as the authoritative statement on the duties owed by ministers to Parliament runs the risk of effectively allowing the government to dictate the terms on which they will allow itself to be held to account. Successive governments have, as a result, been able to unilaterally amend the terms in which the doctrine of ministerial responsibility is expressed.[59] The October 2015 iteration of the Code, for instance – in a move which was widely-interpreted as evidence of the then Conservative Government's growing antagonism towards decisions of the European Court of Human Rights[60] – removed explicit reference to Ministers' duty to act in accordance with 'international law and treaty obligations' leaving only a more general duty to 'comply with the law'.[61] This difficulty is exacerbated by the Code leaving to the Prime Minister the decision over whether an alleged breach of the Code should be investigated.[62] As Brazier has therefore correctly acknowledged, the effectiveness of individual ministerial responsibility in practice owes much to 'the personalities involved and their interpretation of what the doctrine of ministerial responsibility means'.[63] Treating *The Ministerial Code* as entirely synonymous with the convention of individual ministerial responsibility runs the risk of forgetting that ministerial responsibility is ultimately owed to Parliament.[64]

---

[57] See also the *Cabinet Manual* which endorses this section of *The Ministerial Code* in full (Cabinet Office, *The Cabinet Manual: a Guide to Laws, Convention and Rules on the Operation of Government* (1st edn) (October 2011), [5.6], available at: www.cabinetoffice.gov.uk/sites/default/files/resources/cabinet-manual.pdf.

[58] Cf. Public Administration Select Committee, *The Ministerial Code: Improving the Rule Book: The Government Response to the Committee's Third Report of Session 2001-02,* HC439 (December 2001): 'The Ministerial Code is the Prime Minister's guidance to his Ministers on how he expects them to undertake their official duties. *It is for the Prime Minister to determine the terms of the Code* (emphasis added).'

[59] For a summary see: E. Faulkner and M. Everett, *The Ministerial Code and the Independent Advisor on Ministers' Interests* (House of Commons Library Briefing Paper No. 03750, 21 October 2015), pp. 19–22.

[60] See for example: 'Cameron tells Tories they no longer have to follow international law', *The Spectator,* 21 October 2015.

[61] *The Ministerial Code* (Cabinet Office, October 2015), [1.2].

[62] Indeed a degree of controversy has resulted from Prime Ministerial decisions *not* to request investigations of alleged breaches of the Ministerial Code (for discussion see: E. Faulkner and M. Everett, *The Ministerial Code and the Independent Advisor on Ministers' Interests* (House of Commons Library Briefing Paper No. 03750, 21 October 2015), pp. 14–18.

[63] R. Brazier, *Ministers of the Crown* (Clarendon Press, 1997) p. 261.

[64] See generally: Public Administration Select Committee, *The Ministerial Code: Improving the Rule Book* (HC235), February 2001. Though see also: *The Ministerial Code* (Cabinet Office, December 2016), [1.6].

> **Thinking point . . .**
>
> It is helpful to consider the question of the enforcement of the obligations of ministerial respon-
> sibility in separation of powers terms. If responsibility is owed to, and policed by, Parliament
> then the enforcement of the convention is effectively separated from the obligations it imposes
> on members of the government. If the contours of the obligations imposed – and the ability
> to impose sanctions – are unduly shaped by those in government, such a clear separation
> cannot be achieved.

Conclusion

The resolutions of the House of Commons and House of Lords which were passed following publication of the Scott Report, and the frequent revision of *The Ministerial Code*
that has taken place since then seem to demonstrate the tacit acceptance – on the part of
both Parliament and successive governments – that the unwritten conventions of parliamentary accountability were inadequate. The 'codification' of ministerial responsibility that
has been the result is arguably demonstrative of the legalisation of the political process;
the creeping influence of more formalised regulation into areas previously governed by
unwritten convention and understanding. While this by no means signals the death of the
political constitution, it is indicative of both the growing influence of legalised regulation
on the UK's constitutional system, and, of course, of the continuing ability of that constitutional system to be reshaped over time. The 'codification' of the doctrine of ministerial
responsibility has certainly brought a degree of certainty to its core principles – it is clear
now for instance that ministers are as responsible to Parliament for the activities of executive agencies acting within their policy areas as they are for activities carried out by their
core Whitehall departments. However, while there is clear benefit in the added clarity
brought by this codification, we have also seen that doubts persist that the circumstances
in which the principles of ministerial responsibility will bite are as much a result of the
prevailing political climate as they a consequence of clear constitutional doctrine. Having
introduced the core principles of political accountability, over the following chapters we
turn our attentions to the mechanisms by which governmental accountability is achieved.
We begin with the processes of parliamentary accountability.

Practice questions

1. Why ought ministers be both individually and collectively responsible to Parliament?
2. 'The operation of the doctrine of individual ministerial responsibility to Parliament demonstrates the inherent weaknesses of conventions as regulatory tools.'
   Discuss.
3. 'The systems of political accountability in the United Kingdom Constitution are rendered
   ineffective by the structural links between executive and legislature and especially by the
   fact that – typically – the former controls the latter.'
   Discuss.

Further reading

The Ministerial Code (London: Cabinet Office, 2018) provides the governmental take on the standards of behaviour expected of members of the government. The most recent version can be found on the webpages of the Cabinet Office: https://www.gov.uk/government/organisations/cabinet-office.

While many of the academic assessments of ministerial responsibility are somewhat dated, a number remain worthy of note; they are: **S. E. Finer, 'The Individual Responsibility of Ministers'** (1956) 32 *Public Administration* 377; **G. Marshall,** *Constitutional Conventions: The Rules and Forms of Political Accountability* (Clarendon Press, 1987); and **D. Woodhouse,** *Ministers and Parliament: Accountability in Theory and Practice* (Clarendon Press, 1994). For an examination of the development of the doctrine of ministerial responsibility during the twentieth century, see **Diana Woodhouse, 'Ministerial Responsibility' in V. Bogdanor (ed.),** *The British Constitution in the Twentieth Century* (OUP/British Academy, 2003).

The five volumes of the Scott Report (*The Report of the Inquiry into the export of Defence Equipment and Dual-Use Goods to Iraq and Related Prosecutions*) provide a damning account of the failures of ministers – and Parliament – during the Arms to Iraq scandal. The Scott Report provoked a raft of analysis and commentary, among the best of which is **Adam Tomkins'** book, *The Constitution after Scott: Government Unwrapped* (Clarendon Press, 1998) which provides an excellent account of the Arms to Iraq affair and of the state of ministerial responsibility pre- and post-Scott

Chapter 15
Parliamentary scrutiny of government

'Parliamentary control of the executive – rightly conceived – is not the enemy of effective government, but its primary condition.'

Bernard Crick, *The Reform of Parliament (Weidenfeld and Nicolson,* 1970) p. 259.

Chapter outline

It is one of the central functions of Parliament to scrutinise the policies, administration and legislative proposals of the government of the day. This chapter examines the various mechanisms through which Parliament is able to extract information from, and monitor, members of the executive. Against the well-known backdrop of executive dominance of the business of Parliament, this chapter examines the effectiveness of these mechanisms and proposals for their reform.

Introduction

The 'Westminster model' of parliamentary democracy is intimately associated with the idea of the legally unlimited power of Parliament. The *legal* power of Parliament historically has been – and remains – the cornerstone of the UK Constitution. However, in a *political* sense, Parliament is relatively weak. As Brazier *et al.* have commented:

> The clarity of the stock constitutional phrase that 'Parliament makes the law' quickly blurs on the faintest of examinations, as it is the government that initiates and draws up legislative proposals.[1]

In many respects however, this is an understatement, for the influence of the executive over the business and activity of Parliament reaches well beyond the legislative process. Indeed, it is perhaps no exaggeration to say, as the former MP and Chair of the Public

---

[1] A. Brazier, S. Kalitowski, G. Rosenblatt and M. Korris, *Law in the Making: Influence and Change in the Legislative Process* (Hansard Society, 2008) p. 10. Though see M. Russell and D. Gover, *Legislation at Westminster: Parliamentary Actors and Influence in the Making of British Law* (OUP, 2017).

Administration Select Committee, Tony Wright, has done, that the government of the day effectively 'controls the legislature'.[2] As much is endorsed by Anthony King:

> So far as the House of Commons is concerned, the government of the day is still in charge most of the time. The vast majority of bills on important issues continue to be initiated by the government, and the vast majority of the bills initiated by the government continue to be passed by Parliament, even if amended in detail, sometimes in considerable detail (often, of course, by the government itself).[3]

Much as the Westminster model of government is associated with the notion of *parliamentary* sovereignty, behind this lies the idea of strong *government*.

Various constitutional characteristics have combined to produce, and sustain, the notion of strong government in the UK Constitution. The most obvious contender is the first-past-the-post electoral system which – as we examined in an earlier chapter – is arguably detrimental to the chances of victory of all but the candidates of the two largest political parties.[4] Should a government enjoy a majority in the House of Commons, then its power is consolidated by the tradition of robust party discipline which seeks to ensure that departures from the party line are as infrequent as possible. On top of this, however, government business is prioritised in the House of Commons; nowhere is this more clearly expressed than in the Standing Orders of the House, Order 14 of which contains the words 'government business shall have precedence in every sitting.'[5] These factors combine to support an important principle – 'that an elected government should have the means to implement the programme on which it has been elected'[6] – but in doing so they also place restrictions on the ability of Parliament to carry out one of its 'core functions';[7] to scrutinise and to hold the executive to account. As Matthew Flinders has written:

> The convention of ministerial responsibility provided the critical link in the Westminster/Whitehall model, and yet the executive's majority within the House insulated ministers from effective scrutiny. Moreover, the position of the executive allowed it to dictate the rules, resources and information flows through which it would be held to account.[8]

Discussion of executive 'dominance' of the House of Commons is most certainly misplaced in relation to the Conservative minority administration returned following the 2017 general election. However, the fact that the preceding general election to result in a minority administration was that held in February 1974[9] indicates a tendency towards the establishment of governments able to command a majority of votes in the House of Commons and it is against this imbalance that the respective power of Parliament to hold members of the executive to account should be considered.

---

[2] T. Wright, 'What Are MPs for?' (2010) 81 *Political Quarterly* 298, 304.

[3] A. King, *The British Constitution* (OUP, 2007) p. 340.

[4] See pp. 309–10.

[5] Standing Orders of the House of Commons, SO 14.

[6] T. Wright and A. Gamble, 'Reforming Parliament (Again)' (2010) 81 *Political Quarterly* 163, 164.

[7] D. Oliver, *Constitutional Reform in the United Kingdom* (OUP, 2003) p. 174.

[8] M. Flinders, 'Shifting the Balance? Parliament, the Executive and the British Constitution' (2002) 50 *Political Studies* 23, 26.

[9] While the 2010 general election resulted in a hung Parliament, the Conservative and Liberal Democrat Coalition Government did enjoy an overall majority.

Scrutiny in Parliament

Key issues

- The primary mechanisms through which Parliament is able to scrutinise the activities and legislative proposals of government are parliamentary debates, questions to ministers and through the work of select committees.
- Oral questions to ministers are often as concerned with political point-scoring as with the scrutiny of government policy, but detailed information is frequently extracted from government in answers to written questions and during select committee inquiries.

Parliamentary scrutiny of government is conducted, in both chambers of Parliament, through a number of mechanisms. The primary tools at the disposal of Parliament are questions to ministers, formal debates and parliamentary select committees. Each will be briefly introduced. In reading what follows, it should be remembered that the scrutiny functions of the House of Commons and those of the House of Lords are conditioned by their complementary role(s) and composition.[10] The elected membership of the House of Commons determines which political party, or parties, will form the government of the UK; as a result, it stands to reason that the democratic House of the UK Parliament should be the primary forum in which the peoples' representatives are called to account.[11] The House of Lords, by contrast, cannot make such a claim to democratic legitimacy, nor can it claim to be the legal equal of the House of Commons;[12] hence, its own particular scrutiny functions have come to focus on the detail and revision of legislative proposals, and are conditioned by the convention that bills seeking to implement government manifesto commitments will not be opposed in the upper house (as a result of the Salisbury Convention).[13]

Parliamentary debates

Parliamentary debates are the primary vehicle through which the business of the Houses of Parliament is carried out; indeed 'most proceedings in Parliament, whether on legislation or any other matter, take the form of debates.'[14] All debates proceed from an initial 'motion', that is, a premise around which the debate is centred. A typical motion might be that a particular bill is read and discussed, an atypical – but by no means out of the ordinary – motion might be centred on whether the government continues to enjoy the confidence of the House.

---

[10] On which, see Chapters 9 and 10.

[11] See pp. 302–4.

[12] As a result of the Parliament Acts 1911 and 1949. On which, see pp. 141–3.

[13] Although it should be noted that following the removal of the majority of the hereditary peers from the House of Lords (as a result of the House of Lords Act 1999), the Upper House has arguably become less deferential in its treatment of proposals endorsed by the House of Commons (on which, see pp. 325–31 and M. Russell, 'A Stronger Second Chamber? Assessing the Impact of House of Lords Reform in 1999 and the Lessons for Bicameralism' (2010) 58 *Political Studies* 866).

[14] R. Rogers and R. Walters, *How Parliament Works* (7th edn) (Routledge, 2015) p. 252.

Much of the policy and legislative scrutiny business of Parliament takes place in the context of parliamentary debates.[15] In either instance, due (typically) to a combination of party numbers and the influence of the whips, government defeats on a motion on the floor of the Commons are rare. During his period in office (1997–2007), Tony Blair's Government was defeated in the House of Commons a mere four times in 10 years. Gordon Brown's Government (2007–10) was defeated three times in three years. And even during the period of Coalition Government under David Cameron (2010–2015) the Government was defeated only six times. This amounts to a mere 13 defeats during the period 1997 to 2015. By contrast, during the same period those same governments were subject to in excess of 600 defeats in the House of Lords. The implications of these figures, however, should not be overstated; the House of Lords power over legislative proposals is, ultimately, only one of delay. As Norton observes, 'Parliament . . . rarely says no to government' outright, and is better placed to seek to encourage government to reconsider or to change its mind.[16]

The legislative scrutiny functions of the House of Commons, of course, display clear party political tendencies: '[s]crutiny tends to be highly politically partisan, aimed only partly towards improving the Bill and largely towards drawing attention to weaknesses in the Bill and opposing and harassing Ministers'.[17] Legislative scrutiny may also be perfunctory; the controversial Anti-Terrorism, Crime and Security Act 2001 – 'a bill some 124 pages long, which partially abrogated habeas corpus, and made the United Kingdom the only country in Europe to derogate from Art. 5 ECHR'[18] – was debated, and endorsed, by the House of Commons in a mere 16 hours. As we have already observed, in a number of instances, the House of Lords has shown itself to be well-equipped to engage in the expert, technical, revision and amendment of legislative proposals; as Norton comments, virtually all government defeats in the upper chamber are in respect of amendments to Bills.[19] Having said this, recent initiatives – including the increasing tendency of governments to publish legislative proposals in draft prior to their formal introduction into Parliament – have improved the overall capacity of Parliament to influence the formative stages of legislative design.[20]

Parliamentary questions (PQs)

Questions to ministers are also central to Parliament's routine business: '[t]he right of Members of the House of Commons to ask questions of Ministers . . . is an essential part of the process by which Parliament exercises its authority and holds the Government to account'.[21] Question time in the House of Commons takes place every day, except Fridays, while Parliament is sitting, with ministers from each government department questioned once every four weeks on the basis of a rota set by the government. The notable exception is Prime Minister's Question Time, which since 1997 has taken place for 30 minutes every Wednesday afternoon.

---

[15] For an introduction to the legislative process, see pp. 298–9.

[16] P. Norton, *Parliament in British Politics* (2nd edn) (Palgrave Macmillan, 2013) p. 105.

[17] D. Oliver, 'Reforming the United Kingdom Parliament' in J. Jowell and D. Oliver (eds), *The Changing Constitution* (7th edn) (OUP, 2011) p. 173.

[18] G. Phillipson, ' "The Greatest Quango of them all", "a Rival Chamber" or a "Hybrid Nonsense"? Solving the Second Chamber Paradox' [2004] PL 352, 369.

[19] P. Norton, *Parliament in British Politics* (2nd edn) (Palgrave Macmillan, 2013) pp. 103–4.

[20] House of Lords Constitution Committee, *Parliament and the Legislative Process*, 2003–2004, HL 173 (2004), [25].

[21] House of Commons Procedure Committee, *Parliamentary Questions,* 2001–2002, HC 622 (June 2002), [1].

> ## Thinking Point . . .
>
> Prior to 1997, Prime Minister's Questions was held twice every week while Parliament sat, for 15 minutes on Tuesdays and Thursdays. That Tony Blair was able to unilaterally determine that Prime Minister's Question Time should be held on Wednesdays only, gives some indication of the extent of government control over the scheduling of business in the House of Commons.

Parliamentary questions are – in the language of the parliamentary bible, *Erskine May* – asked in order to 'obtain information or to press for action'[22] and 'should relate to the public affairs with which [ministers] are officially connected, to proceedings pending in Parliament, or to matters of administration for which they are responsible'.[23] It follows that PQs relating to matters falling within the competence of one of the devolved administrations will, for instance, be out of order.[24] Further, PQs may not relate to matters currently before the courts, or to pending legal proceedings (the *sub judice* rule).[25] A PQ on a topic recently addressed by the relevant minister will also be out of order.

The notion of ministerial responsibility not only determines what questions may be asked, but also how those questions should be responded to; as we have already seen ministers are under a constitutional obligation to provide Parliament with full and accurate information relating to the discharge of their ministerial functions. It is worth recalling the terms of the 1997 House of Commons Resolution on individual ministerial responsibility, which provided that, in response to PQs, ministers should give 'accurate and truthful information' and 'be as open as possible with Parliament, refusing to provide information only when disclosure would not be in the public interest'.[26] This last point should be stressed; in spite of the requirements of openness imposed by the doctrine of ministerial responsibility to Parliament, 'the Government retains an ultimate right to decline to provide the information sought in questions'.[27] In the event that a minister refuses to answer a question, the Freedom of Information Act 2000 may *not* be used to compel disclosure of information where a minister has failed to do so; s. 34 of the Freedom of Information Act 2000 exempts information from the obligations imposed by the Act if disclosure would result in an infringement of parliamentary privilege. In practice, however, complete failure to answer a PQ is a relatively rare occurrence; in the period 2003–05 the Public Administration Select Committee reported that in excess of 98 per cent of PQs were answered.[28]

---

[22] *Erskine May's Treatise on the Law, Privileges, Proceedings and Usage of Parliament* (24th edn) (LexisNexis, 2011) p. 358.

[23] *Erskine May's Treatise on the Law, Privileges, Proceedings and Usage of Parliament* (24th edn) (LexisNexis, 2011) pp. 357, 360–63.

[24] House of Commons Procedure Committee, *The Procedural Consequences of Devolution*, 1998–1999, HC 185 (May 1999), [6]–[15].

[25] *Erskine May's Treatise on the Law, Privileges, Proceedings and Usage of Parliament* (24th edn) (LexisNexis, 2011) pp. 363–5.

[26] HC Debs, vol. 292, cols 1046–7 (19 March 1997). See also HL Debs, vol. 579, col. 1057 (20 March 1997). See: pp. 446–9.

[27] House of Commons Procedure Committee, *Parliamentary Questions*, 2001–2002, HC 622 (June 2002), [7].

[28] House of Commons Public Administration Select Committee, *Ministerial Accountability and Parliamentary Questions*, 2004–2005, HC 449-I (March 2005), [4].

It is important to remember that oral PQs are not solely posed for the purposes of extracting information from government or to place a minister in an awkward position; they may also play a role in the promotion of the government's agenda; as Anthony King pithily notes, during questions to ministers, '[s]upporters of the government seek to make the government look good, opponents of the government to make it look bad'.[29] Question Time is, therefore, as much a political 'duel' as it is an exercise in extracting information and securing accountability.[30] While ministerial question time may tell us much about whether a particular minister is evasive, quick-witted or fond of a sound bite, as Hartley and Griffith scathingly remarked in the 1970s, 'it is doubtful whether the procedure tests much else'.[31]

To arguably find better evidence of the ability of questions in Parliament to prompt ministers to release information, we should look to written questions rather than those PQs answered on the floor of the House. A brief assessment of the number of questions typically asked during a parliamentary session should provide an insight into the quantity of information revealed orally, and that released by way of written responses to questions. The House of Commons Procedure Committee has recorded that the number of oral PQs tabled in 1990–91 was 4,821. By 1999–2000, this number had reached 5,747.[32] By contrast, the annual figures for PQs tabled for *written* answer are significantly higher: 32,149 questions were tabled in 1998–9,[33] rising to 45,347 in 2013–14.[34]

Thinking Point . . .

During the 2008–2009 parliamentary session, some 56,000 questions were tabled by MPs for written answer by government ministers. While this increase in the volume of information released hints at greater transparency and openness, the Procedure Committee has warned that an increase in the *quantity* of information released may come at a cost to the *quality* and depth of that information (House of Commons Procedure Committee, *Parliamentary Questions,* 2001–2002, HC 622 (June 2002), at [67]–[68]).

The work of select committees

The parliamentary select committee system, as we understand it today, can be traced back to 1979. Though parliamentary committees were commonly used prior to this date,[35] 1979 was marked by the decision that there should exist a parliamentary select committee to monitor and scrutinise the work of each department of central government. Determining 'what departments have done, why and with what effect, constitutes a central part' of the activities of the departmental select committees.[36] The importance of this development – in terms of

---

[29] A. King, *The British Constitution* (OUP, 2007) p. 332.

[30] R. Rogers and R. Walters, *How Parliament Works* (7th edn) (Routledge, 2015) p. 281.

[31] T. C. Hartley and J. A. G. Griffith, *Government and Law* (Weidenfeld & Nicolson, 1975) p. 206.

[32] House of Commons Procedure Committee, *Parliamentary Questions,* 2001–2002, HC 622 (June 2002), [18].

[33] Ibid., [19].

[34] R. Rogers and R. Walters, *How Parliament Works* (7th edn) (Routledge, 2015) p. 291.

[35] Ibid., ch. 10.

[36] P. Norton, *Parliament in British Politics* (2nd edn) (Palgrave Macmillan, 2013) p. 126.

the development of parliamentary systems of dedicated and cross-party supervision – should not be understated; as Rogers and Walters have commented:

> [F]or the first time, the House of Commons now had at its disposal a means of systematic scrutiny of the government of the day potentially much more rigorous than the traditional methods of debate and question.[37]

In the words of the parliamentarian and academic Lord Norton of Louth, the formalisation of the select committee system was 'the most important [parliamentary] reform of the latter half of the twentieth century; possibly of the whole century'.[38]

Departmental select committees are appointed to 'examine the expenditure, administration and policy of the principle government departments . . . and associated public bodies'.[39] The focus of the work of the departmental select committees is, therefore, primarily executive, rather than legislative, oversight. But with this small proviso, the select committees enjoy considerable latitude as to what to inquire into, and how to go about doing it. Select committees, therefore, enjoy considerable autonomy of the collective will of both Parliament and government; they set their own agendas.[40] In conducting their inquiries, select committees have the power to send for 'persons, papers and records' and may appoint specialist advisers to provide expert guidance on issues within their areas of competence (Table 15.1).

Table 15.1 Departmental select committees (November 2017)

Business, Energy and Industrial Strategy Committee	Home Affairs Committee
Communities and Local Government Committee	International Development Committee
	International Trade Committee
Defence Committee	Justice Committee
Digital, Culture, Media and Sport Committee	Northern Ireland Committee
Education Committee	Scottish Affairs Committee
Environment, Food and Rural Affairs Committee	Transport Committee
	Treasury Committee
Exiting the European Union Committee	Welsh Affairs Committee
Foreign Affairs Committee	Work and Pensions Committee
Health Committee	

---

[37] R. Rogers and R. Walters, *How Parliament Works* (7th edn) (Routledge, 2015) p. 305.
[38] P. Norton, *Parliament in British Politics* (2nd edn) (Palgrave Macmillan, 2013) p. 30.
[39] Standing Orders of the House of Commons, SO 152(1). 'Associated Public Bodies' includes Executive Agencies, Quasi-Autonomous Non-Governmental Organisations (Quangos) and so on.
[40] Liaison Committee, Shifting the Balance: Select Committees and the Executive, 1999–2000, HC 300 (2000), [9].

Key debates

The core functions of the departmental select committees

In order to 'encourage a comprehensive and systematic approach to the scrutiny of government departments, without providing too prescriptive a model' (Liaison Committee, *The Work of Committees in 2008–9* (2009–10), HC 426, at [13]) the House of Commons Liaison Committee – comprising the chairs of each departmental select committee – has agreed a list of the core functions of departmental select committees. Those core functions are as follows:

Objective A: To examine and comment on the policy of the department

Task 1:   To examine policy proposals from the UK Government and the European Commission in Green Papers, White Papers, draft guidance etc, and to inquire further where the Committee considers it appropriate.

Task 2:   To identify and examine areas of emerging policy, or where existing policy is deficient, and make proposals.

Task 3:   To conduct scrutiny of any published draft bill within the Committee's responsibilities.

Task 4:   To examine specific output from the Department expressed in documents or other decisions.

Objective B: To examine the expenditure of the department

Task 5:   To examine the expenditure plans and out-turn of the department, its agencies and principal NDPBs.

Objective C: To examine the administration of the department

Task 6:   To examine the department's Public Service Agreements, the associated targets and the statistical measurements employed, and report if appropriate.

Task 7:   To monitor the work of the department's Executive Agencies, NDPBs, regulators and other associated public bodies.

Task 8:   To scrutinise major appointments made by the department.

Task 9:   To examine the implementation of legislation and major policy initiatives.

Objective D: To assist the House in debate and division

Task 10: To produce reports which are suitable for debate in the House, including Westminster Hall, or debating committees.

Departmental select committees comprise backbench MPs elected by the party groups within the House of Commons; frontbenchers – from either the government or opposition side of the House – will not be appointed. Most departmental select committees have eleven members.[41] In determining the balance of parties represented on each select committee, regard is had to the balance of parties within the House of Commons itself with membership of the departmental select committees being broadly proportionate to the overall balance of parties. Once appointed following a general election and formation of a government, MPs remain members of their respective select committee for the duration of the Parliament. Select committee chairs are elected by secret ballot by the membership of the Commons.

---

[41] The Northern Ireland Affairs Select Committee, with a maximum membership of 13 members, is one exception.

A number of House of Commons select committees are not specifically tied to the activities of any one government department. The Public Administration Committee and Public Accounts Committee – the latter of which has existed since 1861 – are two important examples. The Liaison Committee, comprising the Chairs of each of the House of Commons Select Committees and tasked with oversight of the work of those committees, is a third.

The House of Lords also has a select committee structure, including a number of committees whose task is to focus on particular areas of law and policy making; the Constitution Committee (first appointed in 2001), the more longstanding European Union Committee and the Delegated Powers and Regulatory Reform Committee are key examples. A number of select committees include a membership drawn from both Houses of Parliament with the Joint Committee on Human Rights (initially appointed in 2001) being amongst the most well known and highly regarded. These thematic committees undertake far more legislative (and pre-legislative) scrutiny than the oversight-focused departmental select committees of the House of Commons. The recent creation of committees with specific responsibility for the constitution and for human rights also gives credence to the suggestion that Parliament's function as a 'constitutional watchdog' has been significantly expanded in recent years.[42] Committees are also occasionally appointed to conduct an inquiry on a specific topic; the House of Commons Reform Committee (2009–2010, discussed below) and the Joint Committee on House of Lords Reform (2002–2003) are two such examples.

Thinking Point . . .

In addition to appearances at Prime Ministers' Questions, the Prime Minister has, since 2002, appeared bi-annually before the Liaison Committee. In addition to performing a cross-cutting role in relation to each commons select committee, the Liaison Committee performs an important prime ministerial scrutiny function.

Given the overt political point-scoring of ministerial question times, it is perhaps unsurprising to find that ministers are questioned 'more rigorously and more effectively'[43] in their appearances before parliamentary select committees than in the chamber of the House of Commons. As a mechanism of facilitating accountability, the select committee system has come to be regarded as a quietly effective, and efficient tool:

> . . . the 1979 select committee system has been a success . . . it has provided independent scrutiny of government . . . it has exposed mistaken and short-sighted policies and, from time to time, wrong-doing in both high places and low. It has been a source of unbiased information, rational debate, and constructive ideas. It has made the political process less remote, and more accessible to the citizen who is affected by that process – and who pays the bill. Its very existence has been a constant reminder to Ministers and officials, and many others in positions of power and influence, of the spotlight that may swing their way when least welcome.[44]

---

[42] On which see: R. Hazell, 'Who is the guardian of legal values in the legislative process: Parliament or the Executive?' [2004] PL 495; J. Simson Caird, R. Hazell and D. Oliver, *The Constitutional Standards of the House of Lords Select Committee on the Constitution* (Constitution Unit, 2014).

[43] A. King, *The British Constitution* (OUP, 2007) p. 333.

[44] Liaison Committee, *Shifting the Balance: Select Committees and the Executive* (1999–2000), HC 300, March 2000, [4].

However, in stressing the successes of the system of parliamentary select committees, we should be careful not to exaggerate their impact: '[s]elect committees exercise influence rather than power.'[45] Governments will ordinarily seek to respond to select committees' reports within two months of publication,[46] but they are not obligated to either agree with, or implement, their findings. As a result, King has observed that '[n]o one denies the committees' utility, but at the same time no one claims that they have had a more than marginal effect on the relations between government and Parliament'.[47]

Key debates

Commons v *Government* – Selecting select committee chairs

In 2001 a significant episode concerning the leadership of select committees provided a 'a classic example of the tussle between Parliament's right to scrutiny and the Executive's power of control' (R. Cook, *The Point of Departure: Diaries from the Front Bench* (Simon and Schuster, 2003), p. 23). At this point in time, select committee membership was the responsibility of the cross-party Committee of Selection. In practice, the whips exercised a 'covert and decisive influence' over those MPs put forward for selection (C. Turpin and A. Tomkins, *British Government and the Constitution* (7th edn) (CUP, 2012), p. 618). This influence was particularly evident when the two prominent and vocal Labour MPs – Gwyneth Dunwoody and Donald Anderson – were denied places on the Transport, Local Government and the Regions Committee and the Foreign Affairs Committee, respectively. Both had been members of the relevant committee prior to the 2001 election; both had – seemingly – been denied a committee position in the new Parliament on the basis of what the whips regarded as their track records of overly-enthusiastic scrutiny of government!

In response, the House of Commons voted to reject the list of committee members put forward by the Committee of Selection. Ordinarily, the approval of this list would have been a formality; the extraordinary response from the House of Commons was provoked by the apparent efforts of the Labour whips to neutralise critical voices within Parliament. Dunwoody and Anderson were both reinstated, and in turn were both re-elected as the chairs of their committees. As Adam Tomkins wrote in 2003, 'there is nothing unusual about the government, through its whips, seeking to control membership and chairmanship of select committees . . . What is unusual about the events of July 2001 was not that the whips tried it on, but that Parliament stood up to them, and won' (A. Tomkins, 'What is Parliament for?' in N. Bamforth and P. Leyland, *Public Law in a Multi-Layered Constitution* (Hart Publishing, 2003), pp. 62–3).

In the aftermath of this assertion of the collective power of the House of Commons, the House of Commons Modernisation Committee – under the chairmanship of the late Robin Cook MP – proposed a process of selection which would reduce the influence of the whips. When put to a vote, however, the proposals were defeated in the House of Commons by a mere 14 votes (209:195). As Russell wryly notes, '[t]here was clear evidence of collusion between Labour and Conservative whips to see [the] reform defeated' (M. Russell, '"Never Allow a Crisis to go to Waste": The Wright Committee Reforms to Strengthen the House of Commons' (2011) 64 *Parliamentary Affairs* 612, 616).

Reform in this area was not achieved until 2010, following the 2009 recommendations of the Wright Committee (considered below); select committee membership is now determined by election.

---

[45] R. Kelly, 'Select Committees: Powers and Functions' in A. Horne, G. Drewry and D. Oliver (eds), *Parliament and the Law* (Hart Publishing, 2013) p. 162.

[46] Cabinet Office, *Departmental Evidence and Response to Select Committees* (July 2005), [108].

[47] A. King, *The British Constitution* (OUP, 2007) p. 334.

Reforming parliamentary scrutiny: the Wright reforms

Key issues

- Attempts at reforming the scrutiny processes of the House of Commons, historically, have been difficult to implement for the reason that governments are reluctant to agree to proposals which might hamper their ability to carry their political agenda into effect.

- The expenses scandal of 2009, and subsequent collapse in popular confidence in the established practices of Parliament, prompted calls to reform the internal processes of parliamentary government (as well as the rules regarding members' expenditure) in order to restore faith in the legislature.

- The House of Commons Reform Committee (the Wright Committee) which reported in 2009 put forward a range of proposals designed to enhance the powers of the house of commons *vis-à-vis* those of the government, many of which have subsequently been implemented.

In a House of Commons traditionally dominated by the executive branch meaningful reform designed to improve the ability of the Commons to scrutinise government has been difficult to achieve;[48] as Russell has summarised, '[t]he contemporary view indicates that major Commons reform requires executive support, but also that this will not be forthcoming in the case of reforms to place greater restrictions upon the executive itself'.[49] Momentum for reform of the House of Commons, easy to generate while a party is in opposition, is difficult to carry into effect once in government when the consequence of implementation would be to limit that party's newly-found influence. However, such was the popular opprobrium generated by the 2009 expenses scandal that the parliamentary – and executive – resistance to change was temporarily suspended as 'both the government and reformers reached for solutions that could help restore Parliament's reputation'.[50]

In the aftermath of the parliamentary expenses scandal, the then Prime Minister, Gordon Brown MP, announced the appointment of a new committee to investigate reforms to the House of Commons. The committee was, Brown said, to be charged with advising on:

> . . . necessary reforms, including making Select Committee processes more democratic, scheduling more and better time for non-government business in the House, and enabling the public to initiate directly some issues for debate.[51]

Dr Tony Wright MP, the long-standing chair of the House of Commons Public Administration Select Committee, was to take up the chair of this new committee (hereafter referred to as the Wright Committee). The report of the Wright Committee, entitled *Rebuilding the House,* was published in November 2009.[52]

---

[48] See generally, P. Norton, 'Reforming Parliament in the United Kingdom: The Report of the Commission to Strengthen Parliament' (2000) 6 *Journal of Legislative Studies* 1.

[49] M. Russell, ' "Never Allow a Crisis to go to Waste": The Wright Committee Reforms to Strengthen the House of Commons' (2011) 64 *Parliamentary Affairs* 612, 615.

[50] Ibid., 612, 629. Russell reports, at 630, that one Labour MP, Martin Salter, in a letter to colleagues, wrote: 'There is no doubt that in the wake of the expenses scandal our constituents expect us to demonstrate that we are serious about putting reform of the House of Commons back on track . . . It is difficult to believe that any member of this, of all Parliaments, seriously thinks it is sensible to go into the forthcoming election having voted against reform.'

[51] HC Debs, vol. 493., col. 797 (10 June 2009).

[52] House of Commons Reform Committee, *Rebuilding the House,* 2008–2009, HC 1117 (24 November 2009).

Insight

The Wright reforms (House of Commons Reform Committee, Rebuilding the House, 2008–2009, HC 1117 (24 November 2009))

The Wright Committee proposed a range of reforms which were designed to 'enhance the House of Commons' control over its own agenda, timetable and procedures' in order to 'enhance the collective power of the Chamber as a whole' (at p. 83). The objectives which lay behind these proposals were to rejuvenate MPs' 'sense of ownership of their own institution' and to enhance public confidence in the House by ensuring that Commons' business is 'responsive to public concerns' (at [3]).

The major reforms proposed by the Wright Committee were as follows:

- Select committee chairs to be elected by secret ballot by the House of Commons using the AV system (at [80]) (implemented, 2010);
- Select committee members to be elected by secret ballot by political parties (at [87]–[88]) (implemented, 2010);
- Backbench Business Committee to be created in order to schedule non-government business in the House of Commons (at [180]) (implemented, 2010);
- House Business Committee (at [196]–[201]) (Coalition government initially proposed creation by the end of 2013 but the proposal was subsequently dropped).

The reforms implemented following the Wright report have gone some way towards increasing the independence of the House of Commons from the government, and of the party whips. The election of select committee members and chairs means that those appointed are representative of, and accountable to, the House itself, rather than to the party whips. The specific designation of backbench time in the Commons (allocated by the Backbench Business Committee), as Russell comments, 'ends the government's effective stranglehold over the Commons' agenda'[53] and facilitates the allocation of parliamentary time to issues which would otherwise have not been discussed formally (motions proposed by backbench MPs, select committees' reports, non-government Bills and so on). Following the recommendation of the Wright report, the Coalition Government also initially endorsed the creation of a House Business Committee, to consider the timetabling of *government* business, by the end of 2013.[54] This latter innovation was not however implemented, and the Coalition's successor government indicated in 2015 that it did not intend to bring forward proposals to establish a House Business Committee.[55]

---

[53] M. Russell, '"Never Allow a Crisis to go to Waste": The Wright Committee Reforms to Strengthen the House of Commons' (2011) 64 *Parliamentary Affairs* 612, 628.

[54] HM Government, *The Coalition: Our Programme for Government* (May 2010), p. 27. See also Sir George Young MP, 'Parliamentary reform: the Coalition Government's Agenda After Wright', Speech to the Hansard Society (16 June 2010).

[55] HC Debs, vol. 598, col. 448 (9 July 2015) (Dr Thérèse Coffey MP).

Assessing parliamentary scrutiny of government

Key issues

- As a result of ministers' constitutional obligations to account to Parliament, proceedings in the legislature clearly play a central role in the ability of opposition parties, and others, to scrutinise government.

- However, in spite of advances made as a result of the Wright reforms, a number of questions remain regarding the ability of Parliament to exercise autonomous control of, and extract meaningful information from, government. The limitations on Parliament's ability to effectively scrutinise government are procedural, structural and cultural.

Parliament, and the House of Commons in particular, clearly serves a vital constitutional purpose as far as the accountability of government is concerned:

> The existence of the House of Commons – and its presence when it is present – still forces ministers to explain and defend their actions; and it still forces them to think about their actions and to think about whether – and, if so, how – they can defend them.[56]

However, how we gauge the effectiveness of the legislature in holding the government to account may depend on what we conceive the function of Parliament to be. Is the primary function of Parliament the curtailment, or is it the sustenance, of government?[57] Is the role of Parliament – to adapt a metaphor introduced in Chapter 4 – to act as a red or green light for the policies and proposals of the elected government? The restraining and facilitative functions of the legislature are 'inherently contradictory'[58] and the tension between them provides at least a partial explanation as to why a fundamental rebalancing of the relationship between executive and Parliament has been difficult to achieve; it is simply not in the political interests of a government intent on realising its policy objectives to sacrifice or compromise its (potentially dominant) position within Parliament.

Regardless of what we understand the primary function of the legislature to be, concerns over Parliament's ability to exercise meaningful control over, and to carry out effective scrutiny of, government are perennial.[59] The imbalance of power in favour of government lay behind the 1979 reforms of the select committee system,[60] was the subject of the

---

[56] A. King, *The British Constitution* (OUP, 2007) p. 333.

[57] D. Oliver, 'Reforming the United Kingdom Parliament' in J. Jowell and D. Oliver (eds), *The Changing Constitution* (7th edn) (OUP, 2011) pp. 168–70.

[58] M. Flinders, 'Shifting the Balance? Parliament, the Executive and the British Constitution' (2002) 50 *Political Studies* 23, 23.

[59] See, for instance, Lord Hewart, *The New Despotism* (Ernest Benn Ltd, 1929); Lord Hailsham, *The Dilemma of Democracy: Diagnosis and Prescription* (Collins, 1978); M. Russell and A. Paun, *The House Rules? International Lessons for Enhancing the Autonomy of Parliament* (Constitution Unit, 2007).

[60] *First Report of the Select Committee on Procedure* (1977–1978), HC 588–I, p. viii: '. . .the balance of advantage between Parliament and Government in the day to day working of the constitution is now weighted in favour of the Government to a degree which arouses widespread anxiety and is inimical to the proper working of our parliamentary democracy . . . a new balance must be struck . . . with the aim of enabling the House as a whole to exercise effective control and stewardship over Ministers and the expanding bureaucracy of the modern state for which they are answerable, and to make the decisions of Parliament and Government more responsive to the wishes of the electorate.'

Liaison Committee's 2000 report – *Shifting the Balance: Select Committees and the Executive*[61] – and remained a running theme of the Wright Committee's 2009 Report.[62] The core limitations on Parliament's ability to subject the executive to effective scrutiny are threefold: procedural, structural and cultural.

Procedural change

The implementation of the Wright reforms has undoubtedly strengthened the position of the House of Commons *vis-à-vis* government, but the effects of these procedural changes should not be overstated; the Wright Committee was well aware of the need to preserve the ability of an elected government to seek to implement its legislative agenda.[63] Ultimately, the government's agenda will – for the most part – continue to take priority, even if the Wright reforms have seen increased the time and attention devoted to backbench business.

In assessing Parliament's ability to scrutinise government, we need also to consider the techniques of scrutiny employed. As a result, we might ask whether the combative exchanges frequently seen on the floor of the House of Commons are the most effective mechanism of extracting information. As Robin Cook, the former Labour MP and Leader of the House of Commons, has observed, '[t]he adversarial method is going out of fashion elsewhere as the means of establishing the truth, but it remains the animating principle of the Commons'.[64] Of course, the more investigative techniques of select committees and the less partisan debates in the House of Lords need to be included in any overall assessment of the ability of Parliament to obtain useful information from government; but the set-piece debates and PQs in the House of Commons – while serving deliberative and political ends perhaps – may not best facilitate the extraction of detailed information relating to policy delivery, legislative proposals and so on.

The 'fusion' of the elected branches

Structurally, Parliament's ability to control the activities of the government is arguably also hampered as a result of the 'fusion'[65] of legislative and executive branches that is the hallmark of the 'Westminster model' of government. As we noted in our earlier discussion of the separation of powers, the checking and balancing functions of institutions are enhanced by degree of autonomy between supervisor and supervisee.[66] The difficult question separation of powers theory poses for relations between the executive and legislature in the UK context is as follows:

> Can Parliament maintain, and be seen to maintain, a proper degree of autonomy while operating within a 'Westminster model' of governmental membership in, and practical control of, Parliament? Bagehot described the Cabinet as a committee of the legislature. Perhaps it would be more accurate nowadays, in some respects, to describe Parliament as a committee of the government.[67]

---

[61] Liaison Committee, Shifting the Balance: Select Committees and the Executive, 1999–2000, HC 300 (2000).

[62] House of Commons Reform Committee, *Rebuilding the House*, 2008–2009, HC 1117 (November 2009).

[63] Ibid., [20].

[64] R. Cook, *The Point of Departure: Diaries from the Front Bench* (Simon and Schuster, 2003) p. 26.

[65] W. Bagehot, *The English Constitution* (OUP, 2001) p. 11.

[66] See Chapter 7.

[67] B. K. Winetrobe, 'The Autonomy of Parliament' in D. Oliver and G. Drewry (eds), *The Law and Parliament* (Butterworths, 1998) p. 15.

At the micro-level this difficulty is reflected in the aspirations of many of the personnel who make up the Commons. It should also be borne in mind that being a Member of Parliament is, to the vast majority of MPs, a job. As a result, many members will seek to position themselves for career advancement. This presents us with a problem; can MPs with interests in re-election and promotion be effective agents of scrutiny: The realisation of both aspirations may be heavily reliant on the support of the political party – or government – meant to be under scrutiny. Yet, as Tony Wright has written, 'if you want to be picked to join a team, it is more sensible to be an enthusiastic cheerleader than a questioning critic'.[68]

The influence of political culture

Though the processes of parliamentary scrutiny of government have undergone some recent procedural changes, a number of commentators are less optimistic in respect of the prospects of broader cultural change; as one Labour MP is reported to have commented, '[y]ou can change the machine but you cannot change the culture of Parliament'.[69] While the immediate focus of the proposals of the Wright Committee Report was parliamentary procedure, it was an ambition of the report that procedural reform be a precursor to wholesale cultural change.[70] For the time being, the influence of the whips remains an obstacle to deliberation by representatives unburdened by party political concerns, the expectation remains that the government will get its way and the adversarial approach to much of Parliament's business remains questionable as a tool of legislative and policy development.

Recent events indicate that the tribal, adversarial, approach to party politics – and therefore to much of the business of the House of Commons – remains deeply entrenched. Upon taking office in 2010, the Coalition Government promised 'much greater co-operation along party lines'[71] and brought with it the prospect of collaboration between parties in the public interest. Yet, the experience of Coalition Government arguably revealed much more about intra-governmental tensions than about the ability of MPs to cross party divides and co-operate. Similarly, the failure of the main political parties to make concerted efforts to find common ground prior to the initiation and negotiation of the UK's departure from the European Union – perhaps the most momentous constitutional change for a generation – is a damning indictment of the ability of the parliamentary system to effectively promote anything other than a winner-takes-all approach to decision-making.

Conclusion

While the Wright Report led to significant procedural change in the House of Commons only time will tell whether the reforms will precipitate broader cultural change within Parliament. Additional reforms by the Coalition Government, in particular the enactment

---

[68] T. Wright, *British Politics: A Very Short Introduction* (OUP, 2003) p. 85.
[69] Comments attributed to an anonymous Labour MP in 1998 in M. Flinders, 'Shifting the Balance? Parliament, the Executive and the British Constitution' (2002) 50 *Political Studies* 23, 28.
[70] House of Commons Reform Committee, *Rebuilding the House*, 2008–2009, HC 1117 (November 2009), [3].
[71] HM Government, *The Coalition: Our Programme for Government* (May 2010), p. 26.

of the Fixed-Term Parliaments Act, sought to limit the ability of the Prime Minister to call an election at a time of his or her choosing, and thereby further reduce the control of the executive branch over at least one House of Parliament. But it is certainly arguable that through the passage of time, and the quiet abandonment of initiatives such as a House Business Committee, the momentum generated by Wright towards further rebalancing the relationship between government and Parliament has been lost. Events surrounding the calling of the 2017 general election illustrate the relative ease with which the 2011 Act can be sidestepped and the extent to which Prime Ministerial and Governmental authority within the Commons remains intact. However, the 2017 general election also illustrates the influence of one vital external influence on the relationship between government and Parliament – the electorate. Theresa May entered the 2017 general election campaign with a small, but workable, Commons majority, and – on the basis of favourable figures in the opinion polls – sought to increase her parliamentary majority as the UK entered the Brexit negotiations. Following a poor campaign, the results of that election saw her leading a minority government forced into a confidence and supply agreement with the Democratic Unionist Party in order to secure a working majority, and forced to drop flagship manifesto commitments in the process. Given the embedded nature of the UK's partisan politics, and in the continued absence of meaningful electoral reform, it is perhaps the volatility of electoral trends that – though imposing compositional change upon the House of Commons – holds the greatest potential to deny to governments the strength in numbers which exacerbates the sense of 'elective dictatorship'.[72]

Practice questions

1. *'The lack of a meaningful separation between executive and legislature is by far the biggest obstacle to holding government to account in the United Kingdom constitution.'*

   Discuss.

2. *'While the Wright reforms are a welcome advance, far deeper constitutional change will be required in order to loosen the grip of the executive on the business of Parliament, and facilitate greater democratic accountability.'*

   Discuss.

3. *'Parliament will – regardless of its shortcomings – always be better placed than courts, or indeed other constitutional actors, to secure effective accountability of government.'*

   How far do the checks and balances evident in the United Kingdom Constitution endorse this statement?

Further reading

The definitive work on the composition, workings and operation of Parliament is *Erskine May's Treatise on the Law, Privileges, Proceedings and Usage of Parliament* (24th edn) (LexisNexis, 2011). **R. Rogers and R. Walters,** *How Parliament Works* (7th edn) (Routledge, 2015) provides a detailed, lively and accessible alternative.

---

[72] See pp. 304–6.

The development of the imbalance of power between the House of Commons and the government is the subject of **Matthew Flinders'** article **'Shifting the Balance? Parliament, the Executive and the British Constitution'** (2002) 50 *Political Studies* 23. Flinders traces the recent difficulties faced by those seeking to reform Parliament, especially the House of Commons, by analysing the differing conceptions of the political role and functions of the legislature.

An empirically-informed examination of the effectiveness of the select-committee system can be found in **Meghan Benton and Meg Russell's** article **'Assessing the Impact of Parliamentary Oversight Committees: the Select Committees in the British House of Commons'** (2013) 66 *Parliamentary Affairs* 772.

Reform of the House of Commons is widely discussed in **House of Commons Reform Committee,** *Rebuilding the House* (The Wright Report), 2008–2009, HC 1117 (November 2009) and in **House of Commons Reform Committee,** *Rebuilding the House: Implementation,* 2009–2010, HC 372 (March 2010). For a detailed commentary on the Wright Reforms, placing the proposals in the context of earlier attempts to rebalance the House of Commons, see **Meg Russell's** article **'"Never Allow a Crisis to Go to Waste": The Wright Committee Reforms to Strengthen the House of Commons'** (2011) 64 *Parliamentary Affairs* 612.

Chapter 16
The Parliamentary Ombudsman

'. . . a new and powerful weapon with a sharp cutting edge to be added to the existing antiquated armoury of parliamentary questions and adjournment debates.'

Richard Crossman MP (HC Debs, vol. 734, col. 44 (18 October 1966)).

Chapter outline

This chapter examines the role, powers and effectiveness of the Parliamentary Commissioner for Administration, an officer of Parliament more frequently referred to as the Parliamentary Ombudsman. The Parliamentary Ombudsman plays an important role in helping to secure governmental accountability and also encourages continuing improvement in the standards of administrative decision-making. Alongside an assessment of the role, jurisdiction and powers of the Ombudsman, this chapter will consider the effectiveness of the office and possibilities for reform.

Introduction

Between the manifestly party-political structures of accountability present in Parliament, and the independent scrutiny of the courts, lies the office of the Parliamentary Commissioner for Administration, otherwise known as the Parliamentary Ombudsman. The Parliamentary Ombudsman was established by the Parliamentary Commissioner Act 1967 and was designed to investigate complaints of 'maladministration', that is, activity which might fall short of contravening the law but which could nonetheless be regarded as being faulty or lacking the standards of good administration expected of public officials. Inspired by similar offices in Sweden, Norway and New Zealand, the role of the Parliamentary Ombudsman is to investigate complaints, with the origins of the term 'ombudsman' coming from the Swedish post of *justitieombudsman* (a position originally established in the early nineteenth century). As a previous Parliamentary Ombudsman has explained: '[t]he etymology of the word entails for the Ombudsman a role as "representative of the people", implying an advocacy function in enforcing the rights of aggrieved citizens'.[1]

---

[1] A. Abraham, 'The Ombudsman as Part of the UK Constitution: a Contested Role?' (2008) 61 *Parliamentary Affairs* 206, 206.

Key issues

- The Parliamentary Ombudsman is one of the non-legal mechanisms of ensuring accountability and good administration within the constitution.
- The Ombudsman was established under the Parliamentary Commissioner Act 1967 with a remit to investigate 'maladministration'.
- The Parliamentary Ombudsman is now but one of a range of Ombudsmen across public services in the UK.

The Parliamentary Ombudsman – rather than being a direct representative of the people – is an officer of the House of Commons, whose appointment (following an open competition) is confirmed by the Queen on the advice of the Prime Minister.[2] As an officer of *Parliament* (rather than the executive), the Ombudsman fits within the framework of accountability provided by the political constitution;[3] as initially conceived, the primary role of the Parliamentary Ombudsman was to bolster *parliamentary* systems of accountability, with *individual* redress being only a supplementary objective.[4] In truth then, the position of the Parliamentary Ombudsman is perhaps better encapsulated as bridging the gap between traditional parliamentary and judicial mechanisms of accountability. Important factors, however, distinguish the Ombudsman from both parliamentary and judicial checking devices. First, although the Parliamentary Ombudsman is an officer of Parliament, 'the Commissioner's functions are manifestly not political'[5] – at least not in a party-political sense. Indeed, the Parliamentary Ombudsman is afforded statutory protections designed to insulate the holder of the office from political pressures: under s. 1(3) of the 1967 Act, the Parliamentary Ombudsman may only be removed following an address of both Houses of Parliament, as a result, the holder of the office is afforded much the same security of tenure as judges of the higher courts. In a further similarity with the higher judiciary, the Parliamentary Ombudsman's salary is paid out of the consolidated fund.[6] This parallel with the judiciary comes with some benefits for the perceived authority of the office of Parliamentary Ombudsman; as Peter Cane has suggested, 'the fact that the [Ombudsman] is in this way equated with High Court judges gives the office, by association, much of the moral authority which attaches to the judiciary'.[7]

If the office of Parliamentary Ombudsman might in certain respects be described as being 'quasi-judicial' then further parallels are visible in relation to its functions. There is, for instance, a degree of overlap between those circumstances which might result in a complaint to the Parliamentary Ombudsman and those which might result in judicial review proceedings:[8] 'maladministration encompasses both acting illegally and making incorrect

---

[2] Parliamentary Commissioner Act 1967, s. 1(2).

[3] The work of the Parliamentary Ombudsman falls within the scrutiny remit of the House of Commons Public Administration and Constitutional Affairs Select Committee.

[4] *The Parliamentary Ombudsman: Withstanding the Test of Time* (2007) HC 421.

[5] *R v Parliamentary Commissioner for Administration, ex parte Dyer* [1994] 1 WLR 621, 62.

[6] Parliamentary Commissioner Act 1967, s. 2.

[7] P. Cane, *Administrative Law* (4th edn) (Clarendon Press, 2004) p. 374.

[8] *R v Local Commissioner for Administration, ex parte Liverpool City Council* [2001] 1 All ER 462, [25].

decisions, but it is not confined to either.'[9] However, the Ombudsman was *not* designed to provide an alternative remedy to taking action to address administrative faults through the courts. Section 5(2) of the 1967 Act provides that the Ombudsman should not investigate matters where the complainant has a right of 'appeal, reference or review' before a tribunal, or where 'the person aggrieved has or had a remedy by way of proceedings in any court of law',[10] unless the Ombudsman deems it reasonable that other avenues of redress were not explored in the circumstances of the complaint.[11] There are also other crucial differences. By contrast with an action for judicial review, for instance, access to the Ombudsman is free of charge. Furthermore, in terms of the processes adopted, the role of the Parliamentary Ombudsman is investigative rather than adversarial. The task of the Ombudsman is, therefore, to investigate whether maladministration has occurred and why (with a view to improving standards in administrative decision-making), rather than determine which of competing positions is in accordance with the requirements of the law. Further, while the Parliamentary Ombudsman has no power to award enforceable remedies – the role of the Ombudsman is instead to 'facilitate redress'[12] – a finding of maladministration may frequently result in one remedy uncommonly awarded in judicial review proceedings: monetary compensation.

The Parliamentary Ombudsman was therefore designed to plug the gap between the existing politicised scrutiny procedures available through the parliamentary process and the legal remedies available through an action before the courts. Consequently, the Ombudsman is worthy of separate consideration for it has 'a distinct mandate, a distinctive style and a distinctive part to play' in the UK's systems of constitutional accountability and administrative justice.[13]

The work of the Parliamentary Ombudsman

Key issues

- The Parliamentary Ombudsman was designed to provide a more responsive mechanism for dealing with individual complaints concerning administrative decisions than Parliament, and a less formal and costly alternative to recourse to the courts.

- All central government bodies, and a wide range of quangos, fall within the Parliamentary Ombudsman's jurisdiction to investigate maladministration.

- Complaints are referred to the Parliamentary Ombudsman by MPs (a process referred to as the MP filter) as there is no right of direct access.

- Once an investigation is launched, the Ombudsman has extensive powers to compel disclosure of documentation and the examination of witnesses.

---

[9] P. Cane, *Administrative Law* (5th edn) (Clarendon Press, 2011) p. 378.

[10] Parliamentary Commissioner Act 1967, s. 5(2).

[11] Ibid.

[12] T. Buck, R. Kirkham and B. Thompson, *The Ombudsman: Enterprise and Administrative Justice* (Ashgate Publishing, 2010) p. 114 .

[13] A. Abraham, 'The Ombudsman as Part of the UK Constitution: a Contested Role?' (2008) 61 *Parliamentary Affairs* 206, 207.

Origins and growth

In our examination of the rule of law, we have already seen that for Dicey the idea of wide-ranging discretionary powers exercised by officials was anathema.[14] The growth of government – in terms of personnel and powers exercised – during the twentieth century saw the Diceyan ideal of the application of specific, predicable laws of general application suffer as the pressure for increased efficiency saw greater delegation of discretionary powers from Parliament to ministers and public officials. The growth of the administrative state in turn created a need for response mechanisms to be employed in the event of faulty decision-making. While the parliamentary structures of individual ministerial responsibility theoretically enabled the legislature to investigate and police the activities of the core executive, individuals adversely affected by routine administrative decision-making were left with few avenues for obtaining redress. As we will see in the chapters which follow, the focal point of administrative law – judicial review – developed in the latter part of the twentieth century to become arguably the most effective mechanism of ensuring the *legal* accountability of ministers and public officials. But judicial review cannot fully compensate for the failures of public officials which fall either short of, or outside, its doctrinal tests of legality. A non-legal mechanism for addressing issues of faulty administration was therefore created in the form of the Parliamentary Ombudsman, whose jurisdiction to investigate maladministration is wider in scope than the relatively narrow substantive grounds of judicial review[15] and comes with additional benefits for the complainant. The Parliamentary Ombudsman provides a mechanism for obtaining redress designed to be less formal, time-consuming and expensive than recourse to the courts, and more responsive than Parliament to individual concerns.[16]

Setting the scene
The Sachsenhausen Case (1967–1968) HC54[17]

- The *Sachsenhausen* case was one of the first high-profile investigations undertaken by the then newly established Parliamentary Ombudsman. The investigation arose out of the provision of £1 million compensation by the West German Government to British victims of Nazi persecution, specifically those who had been imprisoned in the Sachsenhausen concentration camp in Germany during the Second World War.

- The distribution of the compensation was undertaken by the UK Government. In attempting to determine eligibility to compensation, the criteria drawn up by the Foreign Office excluded a number of individuals who had in fact been imprisoned as prisoners of war. The relevant complaint was lodged by 12 people who argued that compensation had been denied to them, even though they had been detained in Sachsenhausen and should have been eligible to receive a payment.

- The Parliamentary Ombudsman found evidence of maladministration – on the basis that the 12 individuals had been unfairly excluded from the category of people who were eligible to receive compensation – and the UK Government made additional compensatory payments as a result.

---

[14] Chapter 6.

[15] *The Parliamentary Ombudsman: Withstanding the Test of Time* (2007) HC 421, pp. 11–12 .

[16] C. Clothier, 'The Value of an Ombudsman' [1986] PL 204, 204.

[17] *Third Report of the Parliamentary Commissioner for Administration* (1967–1968), HC 54.

The idea of an informal, responsive, complaint-resolution official has caught on across public service since the introduction of the Parliamentary Ombudsman in the 1960s.[18] There are now Ombudsmen with responsibility for, among other things, the three devolved administrations,[19] financial services,[20] prisons,[21] local government,[22] health services,[23] and housing.[24] One leading text has coined the term 'ombudsmania' to capture the speed at which the ombudsman idea spread across the range of governmental and regulatory activity.[25] However, the establishment of Ombudsmen across a range of governmental activities (broadly construed) has also led to accusations of fragmentation and incoherence across the system of complaints handling as a whole.[26] As a result, a significant Cabinet Office review of 2000 (the Collcutt Report) proposed the fusing of the Parliamentary Ombudsman, Local Government Ombudsman and Health Services Ombudsman under an umbrella body, the Ombudsman Commission.[27] Despite being received favourably by the Public Administration Select Committee, among others, the proposed reforms have not been fully implemented.

Thinking point . . .

The technically separate position of Health Services Ombudsman for England is also occupied by the Parliamentary Ombudsman, with the joint office often referred to as the Parliamentary and Health Services Ombudsman (PHSO) (see House of Commons Library Briefing Paper, *The Parliamentary Ombudsman: Role and Proposals for Reform* (March 2016), CBP7496).

The proliferation of Ombudsmen across various areas of governmental responsibility has resulted in persistent calls for consolidation,[28] and in March 2015 the Coalition Government announced an intention to combine the jurisdictions of the Parliamentary and Health Services Ombudsman with those of the Local Government Ombudsman and Housing Ombudsman in a new, unified, Public Service Ombudsman. Following a

---

[18] See M. Seneviratne, *Ombudsmen: Public Services and Administrative Justice* (Butterworths, 2002); T. Buck, R. Kirkham and B. Thompson, *The Ombudsman: Enterprise and Administrative Justice* (Ashgate Publishing, 2010).

[19] Separate ombudsmen have been created as a result of devolution: Scottish Public Services Ombudsman Act 2002; Public Services Ombudsman (Wales) Act 2005. See also the Ombudsman (Northern Ireland) Order 1996, Commissioner for Complaints (Northern Ireland) Order CSI 2007/1297 and the Commissioner for Complaints (Amendment) (Northern Ireland) Order 1997.

[20] Financial Services and Markets Act 2000.

[21] The Prisons and Probation Ombudsman is a non-statutory appointment made by the Secretary of State for Justice on the recommendation of the Justice Select Committee. The first appointment to the post was made in 1994.

[22] Originally established under the Local Government Act 1974. See now the Local Government and Public Involvement in Health Act 2007.

[23] National Health Service (Reorganisation) Act 1973.

[24] Housing Act 1996.

[25] C. Harlow and R. Rawlings, *Law and Administration* (3rd edn) (CUP, 2009) p. 480.

[26] P. Collcutt and M. Hourihan, *Review of the Public Sector Ombudsmen in England* (Cabinet Office, 2000). On which, see M. Elliott, 'Asymmetric devolution and ombudsman reform in England' [2006] PL 84.

[27] P. Collcutt and M. Hourihan, *Review of the Public Sector Ombudsmen in England* (Cabinet Office, 2000).

[28] See Public Administration Committee, *Time for a People's Ombudsman Service* (2014), HC 655.

consultation period, a Draft Public Service Ombudsman Bill was published in December 2016.[29] Progress on the proposal has stalled, however, and the Bill did not feature in the 2017 Queen's Speech.

Given its important role in ensuring the accountability of central government, our focus in this particular chapter will be on the Parliamentary Ombudsman.

Jurisdiction

Those bodies falling within the jurisdiction of the Parliamentary Ombudsman are listed in sch. 2 to the Parliamentary Commissioner Act 1967, as amended. The list includes all central government departments and a wide range of other public bodies and quangos. Actions which the Parliamentary Ombudsman might investigate relate to 'any action taken by or on behalf' of the listed bodies.[30] As a result, the jurisdiction of the Parliamentary Ombudsman extends to functions delegated to another body or contracted out by a government department or public body listed in sch. 2.

Insight

Sample of bodies falling within the jurisdiction of the Parliamentary Ombudsman[31]

- Central government departments
- Board of Trade
- Boundary Commissions for England, Northern Ireland, Scotland and Wales
- Civil Aviation Authority
- Commission for Equality and Human Rights
- Committee on Standards in Public Life
- Competition Commission
- Electoral Commission
- Environment Agency
- Health and Safety Executive
- Her Majesty's Revenue and Customs
- Office of Fair Trading
- Parole Board
- Public Records Office
- UK Atomic Energy Authority

A number of matters, however, are excluded from the remit of the Parliamentary Ombudsman. As already noted, where an individual might have had prior access to a judicial remedy, or has a right of 'appeal, reference or review' before a tribunal, then the Parliamentary Ombudsman may not begin an investigation.[32] Under sch. 3 to the 1967 Act, the Ombudsman is also precluded from investigating matters relating to a number of specific governmental functions.

---

[29] Draft Public Service Ombudsman Bill (2016), Cm. 9374.
[30] Parliamentary Commissioner Act 1967, s. 5(1).
[31] For the complete list of bodies falling within the jurisdiction of the Parliamentary Ombudsman, see Parliamentary Commissioner Act 1967, sch. 2.
[32] Parliamentary Commissioner Act 1967, s. 5(2).

Insight
Matters excluded from jurisdiction of the Parliamentary Ombudsman[33]

- Foreign affairs and diplomatic activity.
- The investigation of crime and protection of national security.
- Contractual and commercial transactions.
- The pay, removal and conditions of service of Crown servants.
- The grant of honours.

Maladministration and good administration

The remit of the Parliamentary Ombudsman is to investigate complaints made by individuals or groups[34] who have 'sustained injustice in consequence of maladministration'.[35] The function of the Ombudsman is to identify poor administrative decisions and practices, but also to seek to ensure the improvement of standards in public administration; it therefore provides a particularly good working example of both the 'red light' and 'green light' approaches to governmental activity that we outlined in Chapter 4.

Maladministration

'Maladministration' is not defined in the 1967 Act, and is something of an 'elastic' term.[36] The meaning given to the concept is, however, crucial, given that in the absence of 'maladministration' the Ombudsman has no jurisdiction to commence an investigation.[37] A number of attempts have therefore been made to define the term. Speaking in the parliamentary debates which preceded the passing of the 1967 Act, Richard Crossman MP indicated that maladministration might include decisions which displayed 'bias, neglect, inattention, delay, incompetence, ineptitude, perversity, turpitude, arbitrariness and so on'.[38] The first holder of the office, Sir Edmund Compton, was prepared to accept that maladministration might also extend to encompass decisions that were 'thoroughly bad in quality'.[39] More recently, Cane has noted that actual complaints made involve a range of activities from 'arrogance, inefficiency, or incompetence to deliberate misconduct such as lying, personal bias, and suppression of information'.[40] Since the conception of the office, the elasticity of

---

[33] For the full list of excluded matters see: Parliamentary Commissioner Act 1967, sch. 3.

[34] Parliamentary Commissioner Act 1967, s. 6(1).

[35] Ibid., s. 5(1)(a).

[36] C. Harlow and R. Rawlings, *Law and Administration* (3rd edn) (CUP, 2009) p. 534.

[37] Parliamentary Commissioner Act 1967, s. 12(3): '. . . nothing in this Act authorises or requires the Commissioner to question the merits of a decision taken without maladministration by a government department or other authority . . . '

[38] HC Debs, vol. 734, col. 51, 18 October 1966.

[39] Sir Edmund Compton held the office of Parliamentary Ombudsman between 1967 and 1971 (cited in W. B. Gwyn, 'The Ombudsman in Britain: a Qualified Success in Government Reform' (1982) *Public Administration* 177, 183).

[40] P. Cane, *Administrative Law* (5th edn) (Clarendon Press, 2011) p. 376.

the concept of maladministration has proved beneficial, allowing for incremental growth of the Ombudsman's remit.[41]

Though decisions of the Parliamentary Ombudsman are susceptible to judicial review, the courts have recognised that a degree of deference will be due to the Ombudsman's expertise and specific (statutory) responsibility for the investigation of faulty administration; as was recognised in *R (Doy)* v *Local Commissioner for Administration* 'the Ombudsman and not the court is the arbiter of what constitutes maladministration'.[42]

Bringing a complaint

In order for the Parliamentary Ombudsman to initiate an investigation into whether maladministration has occurred, a number of procedural steps must be taken. First, the individual concerned must have brought their complaint to the public body concerned in order to allow an opportunity for informal resolution. Then – within one year of the issue arising – a written complaint must be made to a Member of Parliament.[43] Following receipt of this complaint, the Member must then choose to refer the issue to the Parliamentary Commissioner.[44] The latter part of this process is referred to as the 'MP filter'. The MP filter was initially justified on the basis that 'constitutionally, the primary responsibility for defending the citizen against the executive is seen as resting with MPs.'[45] Constitutional developments since the 1960s, not least the development and expansion of the constitutional role of the courts, lend weight to the suggestion that this argument in favour of the MP filter is no longer as persuasive as it once might have been. It follows, and as will be seen below, that many now advocate removal of the MP filter and are in favour of allowing direct access to the Parliamentary Ombudsman.

Thinking point . . .

In a 2011 consultation undertaken by the Parliamentary and Health Service Ombudsman, 85 per cent of respondents were in favour of abolition of the MP filter and granting direct access to the Ombudsman (see Parliamentary and Health Service Ombudsman, *Report on the consultation on direct access to the Parliamentary Ombudsman* (November 2011)).

Once a complaint has been referred by a Member, an assessment will be undertaken to ascertain that the complaint falls within the jurisdiction of the Ombudsman and that there is prima facie evidence of injustice resulting from maladministration. The Parliamentary Ombudsman has discretion over whether or not to pursue investigation of a particular complaint and is not required to pursue all complaints that fall within jurisdiction.[46] This discretion is subject

---

[41] A. Abraham, Foreword to *The Parliamentary Ombudsman: Withstanding the Test of Time* (2007) HC 421; T. Buck, R. Kirkham and B. Thompson, *The Ombudsman: Enterprise and Administrative Justice* (Ashgate Publishing, 2011) pp. 108–12.

[42] *R (Doy)* v *Local Commissioner for Administration* [2001] EWHC Admin 361, 16.

[43] Parliamentary Commissioner Act 1967, s. 5(1)(a).

[44] Ibid., s. 5(1)(b).

[45] P. Cane, *Administrative Law* (5th edn) (Clarendon Press, 2011) p. 375. See also A. Abraham, 'The Ombudsman and the Executive: the Road to Accountability' (2008) 61 *Parliamentary Affairs* 535, 541.

[46] *Re Fletcher's Application* [1970] 2 All ER 527.

to judicial review, though – as Simon Brown LJ noted in the leading case on the topic – considering that the exercise of the Parliamentary Ombudsman's discretion 'inevitably involves a high degree of subjective judgment, it follows that it will always be difficult to mount an effective challenge on . . . the conventional ground of *Wednesbury* unreasonableness.'[47]

Investigations

The Parliamentary Ombudsman carries out investigations in private,[48] and affords the subject of the complaint the opportunity to comment on the allegations made.[49] Beyond this, however, the Ombudsman has considerable flexibility over how to conduct an investigation[50] and significant powers to force production of documents and persons:

> . . . the [Parliamentary] Commissioner may require any Minister, officer or member of the department or authority concerned or any other person who in his opinion is able to furnish information or produce documents relevant to the investigation to furnish any such information or produce any such document.[51]

The Parliamentary Ombudsman has the same powers as a court to compel the attendance and examination of witnesses.[52] Persons obstructing the Ombudsman in the course of an investigation or other duty under the 1967 Act may be subject to the law of contempt.[53]

Towards good administration?

The role of the Parliamentary Ombudsman is not simply to identify maladministration, but is also to encourage improvements to administrative processes.[54] To that end in 2007 the

---

Insight

The Parliamentary and Health Service Ombudsman's principles of 'good administration'

- Getting it right.
- Being customer focused.
- Being open and accountable.
- Acting fairly and proportionately.
- Putting things right.
- Seeking continuous improvement.[55]

---

[47] *R v Parliamentary Commissioner for Administration, ex parte Dyer* [1994] 1 WLR 621, 626. The grounds of judicial review – including so-called *Wednesbury* unreasonableness – are discussed in Chapter 19.

[48] Parliamentary Commissioner Act 1967, s. 7(2).

[49] Ibid., s. 7(1).

[50] Ibid., s. 7(2).

[51] Ibid., s. 8(1).

[52] Ibid., s. 8(2).

[53] Ibid., s. 9.

[54] A. Abraham, 'The Ombudsman and Individual Rights' (2008) 61 *Parliamentary Affairs* 370, 375.

[55] https://www.ombudsman.org.uk/sites/default/files/page/0188-Principles-of-Good-Administration-bookletweb.pdf.

Parliamentary Ombudsman published a series of principles of 'good administration'. The Parliamentary Ombudsman, therefore, has a clear preventative – or 'red light' – function, designed to avoid maladministration in government. The Ombudsman also can be seen to play a parallel role in encouraging continual improvement in the conduct of governmental activity and decision-making – in other words a facilitative, or 'green light', function.

Remedies and redress

Key issues

- The Parliamentary Ombudsman has no power to impose legal sanctions in response to a finding of maladministration, though may propose remedial action – ranging from an apology to the award of compensation – in order to provide restitution to the affected individual(s).
- The reports and findings of the Ombudsman carry significant political weight and are generally accepted and acted upon by the impugned department or public body.

One of the most valuable outcomes of litigation, for the successful litigant at least, is that the remedy imposed by the court is enforceable. In the event of the failure of the losing party to comply with the orders of the court, that party might be held to be in contempt of court and subject to further penalties. The Parliamentary Ombudsman has no power to impose similar legal sanctions.[56] Any suggestion, however, that the Parliamentary Ombudsman is entirely toothless as a result, would be misguided.

Following the conclusion of an investigation, the Ombudsman sends a report on the activity complained of to the referring MP and to the department, body or individual that was the subject of the complaint.[57] It has been the practice of successive holders of the office to propose remedial action, with the steps necessary to provide redress informed by the principle of *restitutio in integrum* (restored to the original condition). The remedial action suggested in practice is dependent on the circumstances giving rise to the complaint and can range from an apology, to an undertaking to amend practice so as to avoid repetition of the activity complained of, to the award of compensation. The report of the Parliamentary Ombudsman into the Barlow Clowes affair for instance – which found maladministration on the part of Department of Trade and Industry officials following the collapse of an investment group to which they had granted a licence – resulted in the government making *ex gratia* payments of some £150 million.[58] The award of the compensatory payments in this particular instance was all the more striking for the reason that the government actually rejected the Ombudsman's finding of maladministration.[59]

---

[56] Section 7(4) of the Parliamentary Commissioner Act 1967, as amended, reads: 'The conduct of an investigation under this Act shall not affect any action taken by the department or authority concerned or the person to whom the complaint relates, or any power or duty of that department, authority or person to take further action with respect to any matters subject to the investigation.'

[57] Section 10(1) and 10(2) Parliamentary Commissioner Act 1967.

[58] PCA, *The Barlow Clowes Affair* (1989–90), HC 76. On which, see G. Drewry and R. Gregory, 'Barlow Clowes and the Ombudsman: Part I' [1991] PL 192; G. Drewry and R. Gregory, 'Barlow Clowes and the Ombudsman: Part I' [1991] PL 408.

[59] HC Debs, vol. 164, cols 203–13, 19 December 1989 (Mr Nicholas Ridley MP).

Insight

The Barlow Clowes investigation

At the time it was conducted, the Barlow Clowes investigation was described by the Parliamentary Ombudsman, Sir Anthony Barrowclough, as 'the most complex, wide-ranging and onerous investigation' undertaken since the establishment of the office.[60] The investigation examined alleged maladministration on the part of officials working for the Department of Trade and Industry (DTI). The officials had granted licences to Barlow Clowes, an investment company, in order to permit the company to trade in government stock, despite the fact that significant doubts appeared to exist over the propriety of the company's business practices.

When Barlow Clowes collapsed in 1988 'a financial scandal on the grand scale'[61] was revealed, with some £190 million owed by the company to over 18,000 investors. Instead of investing money in government securities as advertised, it transpired that much of the money paid to Barlow Clowes 'was being secretly diverted into . . . high-risk business ventures', loaned to associates, or used to buy yachts and property.[62] Complaints were referred to the Parliamentary Ombudsman in respect of the conduct of the DTI officials by some 159 MPs.[63]

The Parliamentary Ombudsman reported on the affair in December 1989, making five separate findings of maladministration on the part of the DTI. The Ombudsman found that, in their investigation of Barlow Clowes prior to its collapse, the DTI officials had failed to adopt the 'sufficiently rigorous and enquiring approach' demanded in the light of continued and numerous doubts over the investment company's business practices,[64] and recommended that compensation was necessary in order to provide redress.[65]

The government – while refusing to accept the Ombudsman's findings of maladministration – made substantial payments of £150 million to those who had suffered loss 'out of respect for the office' of Parliamentary Ombudsman.[66]

In the event of a finding of maladministration by the Parliamentary Ombudsman, ministers or other relevant officials therefore find themselves under a 'strong political obligation' to accept the conclusions of the investigation and to 'take corrective action'.[67] In the event that no such action is taken – or the Ombudsman is of the view that any such action does not adequately address the concerns raised as a result of the investigation – then it is open to the Ombudsman to lay a special report before both Houses of Parliament drawing attention to the failure to remedy the injustice.[68] This political obligation has been bolstered by the suggestion of Bean J in *Bradley* that it would be unlawful for a public body to reject findings of fact in the investigations of the Ombudsman in the absence of objective evidence that the finding was flawed, irrational or peripheral or unless fresh evidence had rendered it obsolete.[69] The Court of Appeal in *Bradley* further found that a rejection of a

---

[60] *PCA Second Report 1988–1989: Annual Report for 1988* (1988–1989), HC 301, [62].

[61] G. Drewry and R. Gregory, 'Barlow Clowes and the Ombudsman: Part I ' [1991] PL 192, 194.

[62] Ibid., 192, 193 and 197.

[63] *PCA Second Report 1988–1989: Annual Report for 1988* (1988–1989), HC 301, [67].

[64] PCA, *The Barlow Clowes Affair* (1989–90), HC 76, [8.12]–[8.13].

[65] Ibid., [8.14]–[8.21].

[66] HC Debs, vol. 164, cols 203–13, 19 December 1989 (Mr Nicholas Ridley MP).

[67] M. Amos, 'The Parliamentary Commissioner for Administration, Redress and Damages for Wrongful Administrative Action' [2000] PL 21, 24.

[68] Section 10(3) Parliamentary Commissioner Act 1967.

[69] *R (on the application of Bradley)* v *Secretary of State for Work and Pensions* [2007] EWHC 242 (Admin), [58] (Bean J).

> ## Thinking point . . .
>
> The test for **Wednesbury** unreasonableness comes from the judgment of Lord Greene MR in *Associated Provincial Picture Houses* v *Wednesbury Corporation* [1948] 1 KB 223, 230 and will be considered in full in Chapter 19. For present purposes, a *Wednesbury* unreasonable decision is a decision 'so unreasonable that no reasonable [decision-maker] could ever have come to it'.

finding of maladministration must be accompanied by reasons, and must not be unreasonable in the **Wednesbury** sense.[70]

In practice then, though not bound to do so,[71] the relevant department, body or individual accepts findings of maladministration and adheres to the recommendations of the Ombudsman though on occasion, as seen in the Barlow Clowes case, acceptance of the Ombudsman's findings may well be 'grudging and qualified'.[72] A 'special report' to both Houses is nevertheless highly unusual, having only been resorted to by the Parliamentary Ombudsman only seven times since the introduction of the office over 50 years ago (Figure 16.1).[73]

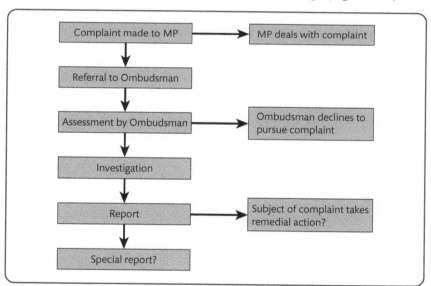

Figure 16.1 The complaint and investigation process

---

[70] *R (on the application of Bradley)* v *Secretary of State for Work and Pensions* [2008] EWCA Civ 36; [2009] QB 114.

[71] *R (on the application of Bradley)* v *Secretary of State for Work and Pensions* [2008] EWCA Civ 36; [2009] QB 114.

[72] R. Kirkham, 'Challenging the Authority of the Ombudsman: the Parliamentary Ombudsman's Special Report on Wartime Detainees' (2006) 69 MLR 792, 814.

[73] See *Rochester Way, Bexley: Refusal to Meet Late Claims for Compensation* (1977–1978), HC 598; *The Channel Tunnel Rail Link and Blight: Complaints against the Department of Transport* (1994–1995), HC 195; *A Debt of Honour: the Ex Gracia Scheme for British Groups Interned by the Japanese during the Second World War* (2004–2005), HC 324; *Trusting in the Pensions Promise: Government Bodies and the Security of Final Salary Occupational Pensions* (2005–2006), HC 984; *Injustice Unremedied: the Government's Response on Equitable Life* (2008–2009), HC 435; *Cold Comfort: The Administration of the 2005 Single Payment Scheme by the Rural Payments Agency* (2009), HC 81; *A Report by the Parliamentary Ombudsman on an Investigation into a Complaint about the Electoral Commission* (2014–2015), HC 540. And see generally, R. Kirkham, B. Thompson and T. Buck, 'When Putting Things Right Goes Wrong: Enforcing the Recommendations of the Ombudsman' [2008] PL 510.

Efficiency and effectiveness

Key issues

- The Parliamentary Ombudsman investigates injustice caused as a result of maladministration.
- Although the Ombudsman has no legal power to make enforceable remedies, it has wide investigative powers and its reports and findings carry political weight.
- Ultimately, however, the authority of the Ombudsman is dependent on parliamentary support.

Accessibility

The Parliamentary Ombudsman generally handles in the region of 6,000 complaints relating to government organisations each year.[74] The accessibility of the Parliamentary Ombudsman has however been called into question, with the suspicion raised that the MP filter amounts to an unnecessary obstruction which runs the risk of insulating the Ombudsman from the complainant.[75] An important Cabinet Office review published in 2000 found 'almost universal dissatisfaction'[76] with the MP filter and revealed that only a slight majority of MPs were prepared to advocate its retention.[77] By 2004, 66 per cent of MPs favoured its removal[78] and in 2009 the influential Public Administration Select Committee again voiced calls for its abolition.[79] A tension here is caused, in part at least, by the fact that part of the role of MPs is to address complaints and concerns made by their constituents themselves.[80] As a result, 'MPs deal personally with many more complaints than are referred by them to the [Ombudsman]'.[81] As Ann Abraham has summarised:

> The positive aspect of the MP filter was that it signified the close relationship between the Ombudsman and Parliament, and so reinforced the constitutional role of the Ombudsman as a check on the executive. However, when it comes to the practical relationship between the Ombudsman and the aggrieved citizen, the MP filter does rather interpose an unhelpful barrier and threaten to undermine the investigative and adjudicative authority of the Ombudsman.[82]

---

[74] Parliamentary and Health Service Ombudsman, *The Ombudsman's Annual Report and Accounts, 2015–2016* (2016), HC 779, p. 12 (in recent years the PHSO has additionally dealt with approximately 20,000 complaints per year relating to the NHS).

[75] J. A. G. Griffith, 'Comment' [1962] PL 1, 3. See also JUSTICE, *Our Fettered Ombudsman* (JUSTICE, 1977); W. B. Gwyn, 'The Ombudsman in Britain: a Qualified Success in Government Reform' (1982) *Public Administration* 177, 183–6.

[76] P. Collcutt and M. Hourihan, *Review of the Public Sector Ombudsmen in England* (Cabinet Office, 2000), [3.10].

[77] Ibid., [3.38].

[78] Public Administration Select Committee (cited in *The Parliamentary Ombudsman: Withstanding the Test of Time* (2007) HC 421, p. 12).

[79] Public Administration Select Committee, *Parliament and the Ombudsman* (2009–2010), HC 107, [9].

[80] A. Abraham, 'The Ombudsman as Part of the UK Constitution: a Contested Role?' (2008) 61 *Parliamentary Affairs* 206, 207.

[81] P. Cane, *Administrative Law* (5th edn) (Clarendon Press, 2011) p. 375.

[82] A. Abraham, 'The Ombudsman and Individual Rights' (2008) 61 *Parliamentary Affairs* 370, 375.

While links between the Parliamentary Ombudsman and Parliament itself can be argued to be of benefit to the processes of complaint resolution, they can also be seen as a source of weakness. Accordingly, proposals for the establishment of a Public Service Ombudsman have suggested that the MP filter be abolished in order that complainants can access the Ombudsman directly.[83]

Links with Parliament

The position of the Ombudsman as an officer of Parliament will affect the potency of the Parliamentary Ombudsman's role:

> As a result of the fact that the PO is a servant of Parliament, in cases of political sensitivity the work of the PO is bound to be affected by the relative weakness of Parliament as a check on the exercise of power by governments.[84]

The effectiveness of Parliament as a check is, in practice, conditioned by two related characteristics of the parliamentary system. The first is the perceived strength of the doctrine of ministerial responsibility. In the mid-1980s, for instance, one holder of the office of Parliamentary Ombudsman was able to attribute the successes of the office to the strong constitutional obligations owed by ministers to Parliament.[85] As we saw in Chapter 14, it is unlikely that similar claims could have been made by the mid-point of the following decade.[86] The second conditioning factor is the strength of the government *vis-à-vis* Parliament. The relative strength of governments in the period 1997–2010 was particularly marked, with the Blair administrations of 1997–2001 and 2001–05 enjoying working majorities of 179 and 167, respectively. It is perhaps no coincidence that these periods of particularly impressive government majorities coincided with a period in which the Public Administration Select Committee noted the increasing tendency of the government to contest the findings of the Ombudsman and to treat her reports 'less seriously than it should'.[87]

The parliamentary link has also been seen to create problems of a more practical nature. For instance, between the dissolution of Parliament and the holding of a general election there are, technically speaking, no Members of Parliament. As a result, there are periods during which there are no MPs to whom members of the public can refer their complaints. For any system of redress making claims to timeliness, this is clearly unsatisfactory.[88] Add to this the fact that every other Ombudsman within the UK allows direct access, and the abolition of the MP filter begins to appear long overdue.

---

[83] See Better to Serve the Public: Proposals to restructure, reform, renew and reinvigorate Public Services Ombudsmen (2014), [127]–[132]; Draft Public Service Ombudsman Bill (2016), Cm. 9374, cl. 5.

[84] P. Cane, *Administrative Law* (5th edn) (Clarendon Press, 2011) p. 374.

[85] C. Clothier, 'The Value of an Ombudsman' [1986] PL 204, 209.

[86] See p. 431.

[87] Public Administration Select Committee, *The Ombudsman in Question: the Ombudsman's Report on Pensions and Its Constitutional Implications* (2005–2006), HC 1081, [59] (for full discussion, see [59]–[79]).

[88] Public Administration Select Committee, *Parliament and the Ombudsman* (2009–2010), HC 107, [2]–[6]. The then Government declined – ironically in part due to the pending 2010 general election – to take action in response to this particular proposal (see Public Administration Select Committee, *Parliament and the Ombudsman: Further Report with Government Response* (2009–2010), HC 471).

Towards enforceable remedies?

The inability of the Ombudsman to impose enforceable remedies has been suggested to be a weakness of the position, making the efficacy of the Ombudsman's recommendations primarily reliant on publicity and parliamentary pressure. There are, however, at least two good reasons why the status quo in this regard should be maintained. The first relates to the more exacting standards of procedural fairness that would be the result of enforceable remedies. Were the Ombudsman able to impose enforceable remedies, then the Ombudsman's decisions would be likely to be considered 'determinative' of rights and obligations for the purposes of the European Convention on Human Rights and Human Rights Act 1998. As a result, Art. 6(1) of the Convention – which requires that obligations under the Convention are determined in public, by an independent and impartial tribunal – would apply. Should public hearings become a requirement of complaint investigation then process would become more adjudicative in nature, and a number of the valuable characteristics of the current process – informality, flexibility, lack of cost – would be placed at risk.[89]

Thinking point . . .

It is the lack of formal, coercive, enforcement powers that arguably makes the Parliamentary Ombudsman such a valuable agent of the political constitution. While the courts are able to effectively compel compliance with their decisions (often leading to the suggestion that the courts and executive are in perpetual conflict), the findings and remedial recommendations of the Ombudsman are more reliant on respect for the political authority of the office.

Secondly, a further strength of the Ombudsman system can be found in its ability to encourage and support, rather than *compel,* changes in administrative practice and decision-making. Were the Ombudsman able to impose enforceable remedies, then this valuable characteristic of the complaint resolution process – co-operation – might also be undermined. As Richard Kirkham has argued:

> Ombudsmen are given almost total access to information and people within public bodies, and possess a very broad remit with which to investigate public sector activity. Given the potential depth of such investigations, the consequences of an ombudsman's report can have a huge impact on the design of future policy. Recognition of the potentially sensitive nature of the ombudsman's work is one of the reasons why ombudsman schemes tend to leave the power of implementation in the hands of the public authority concerned. Political accountability between the decision-maker and the electorate for the consequences of an ombudsman's report is thereby maintained.[90]

As a result, maintaining lines of political accountability and responsibility for potentially wide-ranging policy issues provides – alongside maintenance of the facilitative, or 'green light', functions of the Parliamentary Ombudsman – a sound justification for maintaining

---

[89] P. Collcutt and M. Hourihan, *Review of the Public Sector Ombudsmen in England* (Cabinet Office, 2000), [6.75].

[90] *The Parliamentary Ombudsman: Withstanding the Test of Time* (2007) HC 421, p. 13.

the persuasive powers of the office. One final argument in favour of maintaining the status quo is worthy of mention: in practice the Parliamentary Ombudsman 'has an almost perfect record' of seeing its recommendations eventually taken to implementation.[91]

Conclusion

The work of the Parliamentary Ombudsman occupies a distinctive place in the UK's systems of constitutional accountability. The Ombudsman is less partisan than the traditional processes of accountability within Parliament, and more responsive to the concerns of individual complainants. Reinforced by the support of Parliament, specifically the Public Administration Select Committee (since 2015 the Public Administration and Constitutional Affairs Select Committee), the office and its reports carry real political weight (though they may also be susceptible to temporal fluctuations in the relative authority of Parliament and the executive). The operation of the MP filter, however, continues to pose questions of accessibility, with the suspicion that many would-be complainants do not in fact raise their concerns due to the additional procedural hurdle it presents.

By comparison with recourse to the courts, the Ombudsman also offers particular benefits for the individual adversely affected by faulty administrative decision-making:

> The formality, legalism and inflexibility that characterise the legal process are absent from the Ombudsman system, being instead replaced by relative informality, equitable principle and flexibility, all in the cause of producing a process of dispute resolution that is responsive to the needs of citizens, fair to both parties and effective in delivering appropriate remedies.[92]

Practice questions

1. 'The links between the legislature and the Parliamentary Commissioner for Administration are supporting and undermining of the effectiveness of the Ombudsman in equal measure.' Discuss.

2. Which aspects of the powers and jurisdiction of the Parliamentary Ombudsman are in most urgent need of reform?

3. 'It is the power of the Parliamentary Ombudsman to promote good administration, as well as to investigate maladministration, that makes it such a core component of the political constitution.' Discuss.

---

[91] T. Buck, R. Kirkham and B. Thompson, *The Ombudsman: Enterprise and Administrative Justice* (Ashgate Publishing, 2010) p. 118.

[92] A. Abraham, 'The Ombudsman as Part of the UK Constitution: A Contested Role?' (2008) 61 *Parliamentary Affairs* 206, 208.

Further reading

The **Public Administration and Constitutional Affairs Select Committee** monitors the activities of the Parliamentary Ombudsman and reports from time to time on specific aspects of the Ombudsman's work. Its **reports – and minutes of evidence** – can be found on the website of the UK Parliament: www.parliament.uk. **Richard Kirkham**'s report, *The Parliamentary Ombudsman: Withstanding the Test of Time* (2007) HC 421 provides an excellent, and accessible, account of the development of the office since its introduction and of its future challenges.

As the title of the work suggests, **C. Harlow and R. Rawlings,** *Law and Administration* (3rd edn) (CUP, 2009) examines the the Ombudsman within the broader context of the administrative state. More comprehensive accounts can be found in **M. Seneviratne,** *Ombudsmen: Public Services and Public Administration* (Butterworths, 2002) and **T. Buck, R. Kirkham and B. Thompson,** *The Ombudsman Enterprise and Administrative Justice* (Ashgate, 2011).

One previous holder of the position of Parliamentary Ombudsman, Ann Abraham, has written a series of useful articles examining the constitutional position of the post, discussing the role of the modern Parliamentary Ombudsman, its position as an agent of securing accountability and possible future directions for the Office:

- **Ann Abraham, 'The Ombudsman as a part of the UK Constitution: A Contested Role?'** (2008) 61 *Parliamentary Affairs* 206;

- **Ann Abraham, 'The Ombudsman and Individual Rights'** (2008) 61 *Parliamentary Affairs* 370;

- **Ann Abraham, 'The Ombudsman and the Executive: The Road to Accountability'** (2008) 61 *Parliamentary Affairs* 535;

- **Ann Abraham, 'The Future in International Perspective: The Ombudsman as Agent of Rights, Justice and Democracy'** (2008) 61 *Parliamentary Affairs* 681.

Chapter 17
Freedom of information

'Unnecessary secrecy in government leads to arrogance in governance and defective decision-making. The perception of excessive secrecy has become a corrosive influence in the decline of public confidence in government. Moreover, the climate of public opinion has changed: people expect much greater openness and accountability from government than they used to.'

'Your Right to Know: the Government's Proposals for a Freedom of Information Act', Cm. 3818 (December 1997), [1.1].

Chapter outline

The Freedom of Information Act 2000, which came into force in 2005, provides, for the first time, a legally enforceable right of access to official information. This chapter examines the benefits of freedom of information and the scheme and scope of the Freedom of Information Act, examining how it balances the competing interests in the disclosure and retention of official information. The enforcement mechanisms in the Act are outlined and the ministerial veto power discussed. The chapter concludes by examining the effectiveness of the openness regime imposed by the Freedom of Information Act.

Introduction

Freedom of information legislation enshrines in law the right of individuals to request disclosure of information held by public bodies.[1] Prior to the enactment of the Freedom of Information Act 2000 there was, in the UK Constitution, 'no legal concept of a right to official information.'[2] Indeed, as we have already seen,[3] for the greater part of the twentieth century the UK's system of government was widely perceived as being overly secretive, with the prevailing tone set by successive Official Secrets Acts rather than any legislative initiative *facilitating* access to governmental information. The trend towards the implementation of freedom of information initiatives in other comparable democratic systems

---

[1] P. Birkinshaw, *Freedom of Information: the Law, the Practice and the Ideal* (4th edn) (CUP, 2010) p. 29.
[2] P. Birkinshaw, 'Regulating Information' in J. Jowell, D. Oliver and C. O'Cinneide (eds), *The Changing Constitution* (8th edn) (OUP, 2015) p. 380.
[3] Chapter 14.

(Table 17.1) which had accelerated in the latter half of the twentieth century prompted the House of Commons Public Administration Select Committee to remark in 1997 that a UK Freedom of Information Act was 'long overdue'.[4]

Freedom of information was therefore a concept long-resisted in the UK's constitutional discourse.[5] As a result of the ministerial obligation of responsibility to the legislature,[6] the perception was that the 'primary recipient' of official information was – and should be – *Parliament,* rather than the public at large. The 1979 Green Paper on Open Government expressed this sentiment well:

> In the Government's judgement further steps designed to achieve greater openness must be fully in accord with our constitutional tradition and practice which has developed in this country. Nothing must be allowed to detract from the basic principle of Ministerial accountability to Parliament.[7]

As a result, a general right of access to official information was traditionally resisted on the ground that such a right would 'undermine the convention of ministerial responsibility', would compromise the candour with which officials provided advice to ministers and on the basis that giving effect to it would be too expensive.[8] The absence of freedom of information legislation was also, of course, politically convenient to those in power:

> Left to themselves, governments naturally tend to use their control over information to their own advantage. They disclose that which shows them and their policies in a positive light and withhold

Table 17.1 Freedom of information legislation overseas

Jurisdiction	Implemented	Measure
Finland	1951	Publicity of Documents Act
United States of America	1966	Freedom of Information Act
Netherlands	1978	Access to Official Information Act
Australia	1982	The Freedom of Information Act
Canada	1982	Access to Information Act
New Zealand	1983	Official Information Act
Ireland	1997	Freedom of Information Act

---

[4] House of Commons Public Administration Select Committee, *Your Right to Know: the Government's Proposals for a Freedom of Information Act* (1997–1998), HC 398-I, [4]. See also R. Hazell and D. Busfield-Birch, 'Opening the Cabinet Door: Freedom of Information and Government Policy Making' [2011] PL 260, 261–2.

[5] This is not to say, however, that pressure for greater access to official information was not evident; every Labour Party General Election Manifesto between 1974 and 1997 contained a commitment to greater openness in government.

[6] P. Birkinshaw, 'Regulating Information' in J. Jowell, D. Oliver and C. O'Cinneide (eds), *The Changing Constitution* (8th edn) (OUP, 2015) p. 379. See also D. Oliver, 'Freedom of Information and Ministerial Accountability' [1998] PL 171.

[7] *Open Government,* Cmnd. 7520 (1979), [2].

[8] P. Norton, *The Constitution in Flux* (Martin Robertson, 1982) p. 93.

information which suggests that mistakes may have been made, policies may have failed or commitments may have been broken, or which supports the arguments put forward by critics and opposition parties.[9]

But as – during the 1980s and 1990s[10] – the established, conventional, parliamentary lines of accountability were gradually exposed as being deficient, the movement for a right of access to official documentation steadily grew.[11] The Major Government's 1994 *Code of Practice on Access to Government information* provided a step in the right direction,[12] but in failing to provide a legally enforceable right of access to official information, the Government was still ultimately able to 'retain the initiative over the release of information'.[13] The 'arrogance . . . and defective policy decisions' which the Labour Party under Tony Blair associated with excessive secrecy in government – alluded to in the quote which opens this chapter – underpinned a 1997 manifesto commitment to freedom of information legislation and, ultimately, the passing of the Freedom of Information Act 2000 (hereafter 'FOIA').[14]

Following publication of the new Labour Government's White Paper in 1997, the House of Commons Public Administration Select Committee remarked that a legally enforceable right of access to official information would:

- make it easier for members of the public to find out what information government holds about themselves;

- make it easier for politicians, journalists and members of the public to hold the government to account by making government cover-ups more difficult;

- make it easier for members of the public to participate in an informed way in the discussion of policy issues, and improve the quality of government decision-making because those drafting policy advice know that they must be able, ultimately, to defend their reasoning before public opinion.[15]

As the then Lord Chancellor, Lord Falconer of Thoroton, succinctly summarised in 2004, 'the benefits of open government are clear: transparency, accountability, honesty'.[16]

---

[9] K. Gunderson, 'Freedom of Information' in P. Facey, B. Rigby and A. Runswick (eds), *Unlocking Democracy: 20 Years of Charter 88* (Politicos, 2008) p. 225.

[10] A period during which, as Rodney Austin wryly notes, '[i]ronically, the power of Parliament to extract information from the executive has declined as the volume of official information has expanded.' (R. Austin, 'Freedom of Information: The Constitutional Impact' in J. Jowell and D. Oliver (eds), *The Changing Constitution* (3rd edn) (OUP, 1994) p. 395.

[11] See, for instance, the influence exerted by groups such as the Campaign for Freedom of Information (www.cfoi.org.uk/), Charter 88 (www.unlockdemocracy.org.uk/pages/the-original-charter-88) and the Institute for Public Policy Research (*The Constitution of the United Kingdom* (IPPR, 1991)).

[12] Chapter 14, pp. 435–6.

[13] D. Woodhouse, *Ministers and Parliament: Accountability in Theory and Practice* (Clarendon Press, 1994) p. 276.

[14] *New Labour: Because Britain Deserves Better* (1997).

[15] House of Commons Public Administration Select Committee, *Your Right to Know: The Government's Proposals for a Freedom of Information Act* (1997–1998), HC 398-I, [3]. See also D. Oliver, *Constitutional Reform in the United Kingdom* (OUP, 2003), pp. 160–1; R. Austin, 'Freedom of Information: The Constitutional Impact' in J. Jowell and D. Oliver (eds), *The Changing Constitution* (3rd edn) (OUP, 1994) pp. 437–9.

[16] 26 November 2004 (cited in Ministry of Justice, *Memorandum to the Justice Select Committee: Post-Legislative Assessment of the Freedom of Information Act* 2000 (December 2011), [13].

There is, however, an inescapable tension between freedom of information and the realities of government. The effect of the FOIA 2000, as Jack Straw MP confidently outlined in 2009, was to 'profoundly change the relationship between citizens and their elected representatives and the media on the one hand, and the Government and public authorities on the other'. The result of this change was, he argued, to render the executive 'far more open and accountable' than ever before.[17] As much is undeniable; openness and accountability are clearly beneficial to the broad notion of good governance. But governments are also painfully aware of the necessity of information management and the damage that disclosures can do to political reputations and image.[18] As much has been acknowledged by the former Prime Minister Gordon Brown; freedom of information, he suggested, 'can be inconvenient, at times frustrating, and indeed embarrassing' for those in power.[19]

The Freedom of Information Act 2000

Key issues

- The Freedom of Information Act 2000 was designed to facilitate a move away from the culture of excessive secrecy that had blighted British Government during the twentieth century.

- The Freedom of Information Act provided, for the first time, a legally enforceable right of access to official information.

- The Act contains a number of exceptions designed to permit the non-disclosure of certain information, but also contains specifically-designed enforcement mechanisms (the Information Commissioner and Information Tribunal (now known as the Information Rights Tribunal) allowing applicants under the Act to challenge non-disclosure by public authorities.

- A ministerial veto may be exercised under the Freedom of Information Act, permitting politicians to override the determinations of the Information Commissioner and Information Rights Tribunal.

The Labour Government's White Paper – *Your Right to Know* – was published in December 1997. It hinted at a robust scheme providing a statutory right of access to official information which was 'bold and imaginative' and would have been 'more advanced than any comparable regimes' elsewhere.[20] As a result, the White Paper promised a freedom of information regime that had the potential to mark a significant departure from the excessive secrecy that had hitherto characterised British Government. Freedom of information campaigners, however, were to be disappointed. The White Paper's proposals were watered down considerably – 'emasculated' in the words of one commentator[21] – during the protracted period prior to the publication of the draft Freedom of Information Bill in May 1999. By contrast with the liberal scheme promised in *Your Right to Know,* the 1999 Freedom of Information Bill was

---

[17] HC Debates, vol. 488, cols 153–65 (24 February 2009), Jack Straw MP.

[18] B. Worthy, 'The Future of Freedom of Information in the United Kingdom' (2008) 79 *Political Quarterly* 100, 103.

[19] G. Brown, 'Speech on Liberty' (25 October 2007).

[20] P. Birkinshaw, 'An "All Singin' and All Dancin'" Affair: the New Labour Government's Proposals for Freedom of Information' [1998] PL 176, 187.

[21] H. Kennedy, *Just Law* (Vintage, 2004) p. 131.

'characterised by numerous devices whose targeted objective was the maintenance of secrecy'.[22] In spite of this, the Freedom of Information Act – which was subsequently passed in November 2000, becoming fully operative on 1 January 2005[23] – has been recognised as reflecting 'the value to be attached to transparency and openness in the workings of public authorities in a modern society'.[24] In that respect alone, the FOIA arguably amounts to a significant departure from British governmental traditions, and a progressive constitutional development.

Extent

The range of application of the FOIA is undoubtedly broad; the provisions of the Act apply to in excess of 100,000 public bodies.[25] The public authorities to which the FOIA applies are listed in sch. 1 to the Act, and include:

- the House of Commons;
- the House of Lords;
- almost all government departments;
- Local Authorities;
- the devolved institutions in Northern Ireland and Wales;[26]
- the National Health Service;
- police authorities; and
- maintained schools and educational institutions.

The Secretary of State may also, under s. 5 FOIA, issue an order designating that 'any person' who appears to be carrying out functions of a public nature, or who is under contract to carry out such functions on behalf of a public authority, be subject to the FOIA. However, a number of additional 'public' bodies fall outside the scope of the FOIA; they include the monarch and royal family, the security services and the banks taken into public ownership following the 2008 financial crisis.

The 'right' to information

The FOIA envisages two mechanisms through which official information can be released into the public domain. These can broadly be referred to as the 'proactive' and 'reactive' mechanisms. As the Ministry of Justice has outlined:

> Reactive openness and transparency suggests a system responsive to requests for information, while proactive openness and transparency suggests a system in which information is proactively released without the need for requests.[27]

---

[22] P. Birkinshaw, *Freedom of Information: the Law, the Practice and the Ideal* (4th edn) (CUP, 2010) p. 119.

[23] A delay apparently attributable to concerns – on the part of Tony Blair and his Director of Communications Alastair Campbell – as to the potential political damage implementation of the FOIA would cause (B. Worthy and R. Hazell, 'Disruptive, Dynamic and Democratic? Ten Years of FOI in the UK' (2017) 70 *Parliamentary Affairs* 22, 23).

[24] *Sugar* v *British Broadcasting Corporation* [2012] UKSC 4, [110].

[25] T. Pitt-Payne and R. Kamm, 'Freedom of Information: the Story So Far' [2009] JR 239, 239.

[26] Scottish public authorities – including the Scottish Parliament and Scottish Ministers – are subject to the Freedom of Information (Scotland) Act 2002.

[27] Ministry of Justice, *Memorandum to the Justice Select Committee: Post-Legislative Assessment of the Freedom of Information Act 2000* (December 2011), Cm. 8236, [11].

In order to facilitate 'proactive' openness and transparency, the FOIA requires that all public authorities devise a 'publication scheme'[28] under which certain information (relating to a body's purpose and role, expenditure, policies and procedures and so on[29]) be published as a matter of routine. Publication schemes are approved and monitored by the Information Commissioner,[30] whose functions include the promotion of good practice by public authorities in discharging their obligations under the Act and the dissemination of information relating to the operation of the Act.[31] Publication schemes are to be reviewed at regular intervals.[32]

The primary 'right' of access to official information is contained in s. 1(1) of the FOIA 2000. The duty imposed on public authorities under s. 1 is therefore 'reactive'. Section 1(1) states that:

. . . any person making a request for information to a public authority is entitled:

(a) to be informed in writing by the public authority whether it holds the information of the description specified in the request, and

(b) if that is the case, to have that information communicated to him.

The duty in s. 1(1)(a) of the FOIA is referred to as the 'duty to confirm or deny'.[33] A person requesting information is entitled to know whether or not the public body in question holds the information sought, and, if it does, to have the information provided to them (subject to the application of one of the Act's exemptions). On its face at least, the right to information – and the presumption in favour of disclosure – appears to be relatively strong.

The terminology employed by the FOIA is, however, important. The Act does not grant a right of access to 'documentation' or 'records', but to 'information'. The duty to disclose might in practice be satisfied by providing the applicant with either a copy of the relevant information, by allowing an opportunity to inspect a record containing the information or providing a summary or digest of the relevant documentation.[34] The consequence of this is that selective editing of the relevant documentation may be possible prior to disclosure. While the applicant may express a preference for the form in which the information is to be received, this need only be adhered to by the relevant public body 'so far as reasonably practicable' to do so.[35]

Exceptions

The duty to disclose information under the FOIA can, however, be displaced on a number of specific statutory grounds regardless of the nature of the information sought. First, information might be withheld should the cost of compliance exceed the relevant limit.[36]

---

[28] FOIA 2000, ss. 19, 20.

[29] See: P. Birkinshaw, 'Regulating Information' in J. Jowell, D. Oliver and O'Cinneide, *The Changing Constitution* (8th edn) (OUP, 2015) p. 392.

[30] FOIA 2000, s. 18.

[31] Ibid., s. 47.

[32] Ibid., s. 19(1)(c).

[33] Ibid., s. 1(6).

[34] Ibid., s. 11(1).

[35] Ibid., s. 11(1).

[36] Ibid., s. 12(1). The relevant limits are set by the Freedom of Information and Data Protection (Appropriate Limit and Fees) Regulations 2004. The maximum cost of compliance for those public authorities listed in sch. 1 to the FOIA is £600, while the maximum cost of compliance for all other public authorities is set at £450.

Secondly, information can be withheld by a public authority if a request is deemed to be 'vexatious'[37] or if it is 'identical or substantially similar' to a request previously made and granted.[38] But perhaps the most important exceptions to the duty to disclose are those which relate to the substance of the information requested. These exceptions take two forms: qualified exemptions, which require the weighing of the competing values of disclosure and non-disclosure, and absolute exemptions, which admit of no qualification whatsoever. Each will be addressed in turn.

Exceptions subject to a public interest test

So-called qualified exceptions to the duty to disclose under the FOIA require a balance to be struck between the public interest in disclosure and the public interest in non-disclosure on certain specified grounds. Section 2 FOIA provides that, in cases where a qualified exemption applies, the duty to disclose must take precedence unless 'in all the circumstances of the case, the public interest in maintaining the exemption outweighs the public interest in disclosing the information'.[39] As a result, public authorities are required to balance the public interests in disclosure and non-disclosure. As Lord Wilson has recognised in the Supreme Court decision in *Sugar* v *British Broadcasting Corporation,* even where a qualified exemption *might* apply, the Act displays a subtle preference in favour of disclosure:

> . . . the bias of the Act in favour of disclosure is visible in the requirement that the public interest in maintaining the exemption should 'outweigh' the public interest in disclosing the information.[40]

Qualified exemptions fall into one of two categories: so-called 'class based' exemptions and those which are subject to a test of prejudice. Class-based exemptions permit non-disclosure of information (subject to the application of a public interest test) without the need to demonstrate that harm of any sort would result were the information to be published. Exemptions relating to information intended for future publication,[41] national security,[42] the formulation and development of government policy[43] and communications with the royal family and royal household, and the honours system[44] are examples falling within this class-based category. Other qualified exemptions to the duty to disclose meanwhile are subject to a test of prejudice. This means that, prior to the application of the public interest test, the public body must consider that disclosure would be, or would be likely to be, prejudicial to the issue designed to be protected by the exemption. The exemptions relating

---

[37] Ibid., s. 14(1).

[38] Ibid., s. 14(2).

[39] Ibid., s. 2(2)(b).

[40] *Sugar* v *British Broadcasting Corporation* [2012] UKSC 4, [26]. See also P. Birkinshaw, 'Regulating Information' in J. Jowell, D. Oliver and C. O'Cinneide (eds), *The Changing Constitution* (8th edn) (OUP, 2015) p. 396 ('. . . where the interests are equal in weight, disclosure prevails'). Cf. K. Syrett, *The Foundations of Public Law: Principles and Problems of Power in the British Constitution* (Palgrave Macmillan, 2011) p. 275.

[41] FOIA 2000, s. 22.

[42] Ibid., s. 24.

[43] Ibid., s. 35.

[44] Ibid., s. 37 (amended as a result of the Constitutional Reform and Governance Act 2010, sch. 7).

to, for instance, defence,[45] international relations,[46] the economy,[47] law enforcement[48] and the effective conduct of public affairs[49] each require the application of such a test. The Information Tribunal has clarified that a 'real risk' of prejudice will be insufficient[50] and that a 'very significant and weighty chance of prejudice to the identified public interests' will be required in order to satisfy the requisite standard.[51]

Thinking Point . . .

It should be noted that, in the application of a bare test of prejudice, the FOIA is weaker than the proposals initially contained in *Your Right to Know* and in its Scottish counterpart; the former had proposed a test of 'substantial harm' while the latter (Freedom of Information (Scotland) Act 2002, s. 30) utilises a test of 'substantial prejudice'. As a consequence, as Syrett has observed, '. . . the test of "prejudice" is relatively easy to satisfy, meaning that non-disclosure is more likely than would have been the case if a test of "substantial prejudice" or "substantial harm" had been adopted' (K. Syrett, *The Foundations of Public Law: Principles and Problems of Power in the British Constitution* (Palgrave Macmillan, 2011) p. 275).

Perhaps the most difficult question relating to the qualified exemptions in the FOIA is how the balance between the public interest in disclosure and the public interest in non-disclosure should be struck. The FOIA itself provides no guidance on this particular issue. The Information Commissioner, however, has offered some assistance to public authorities carrying out this difficult task.[52] In a 2008 Decision Notice concerning a request that the Cabinet Office disclose papers relating to a meeting of the Asylum and Migration Working Group, the Information Commissioner provided illustrations of the public-interest factors that might weigh in favour of (and against) publication:

In favour of disclosure:

(i)   Promoting public understanding behind decisions taken.
(ii) Public participation and debate in policy issues, especially where the subject matter is controversial.
(iii) Accountability for decisions taken.
(iv) Transparency in decision-making.
(v)   Information contained within the papers which is already in the public domain.

Against disclosure:

(i)   The short period of time that has elapsed between the meeting in question and the complainant's request, and that the policy in question continues to be kept under review.

---

45 Ibid., s. 26.
46 Ibid., s. 27.
47 Ibid., s. 29.
48 Ibid., s. 31.
49 Ibid., s. 36.
50 *Hogan* v *Information Commissioner* (EA/2005/0026).
51 *C. Martin and Oxford City Council* v *Information Commissioner* (EA/2005/0026 and 0030).
52 See initially, The Information Commissioner, *Introduction to the Freedom of Information Act 2000* (cited in S. Holsen and J. Amos, *A Practical Guide to the Freedom of Information Act 2000* (Constitution Unit, 2004) p. 19).

(ii) Effects of the principle of collective responsibility for decisions by revealing interdepartmental considerations which may reveal disagreements between ministers and departments.

(iii) Revealing the policy options presented to ministers for collective discussion and decision-making could undermine the process of collective government and inhibit ministers from having frank and fully informed discussion in order to reach informed decisions.

(iv) Effects on the comprehensiveness of information provided for consideration in policy making.[53]

Perhaps the most discussed – and the frequently relied upon[54] – of all the exceptions contained within the FOIA is s. 35: information which relates to the formulation of government policy. This exception is only available to central government departments. It is regarded by those in government as being of fundamental importance as it is designed to permit free and candid discussions between ministers, policy advisers and civil servants that should be uninhibited by the potential threat of disclosure. As the former Prime Minister, Tony Blair, reflected in 2010:

> If you are trying to take a difficult decision and you're weighing up the pros and cons, you have frank conversations . . . And if those conversations then are put out in a published form that afterwards are liable to be highlighted in particular ways, you are going to be very cautious.[55]

The importance of this particular exception has also been recognised by the Information Tribunal:

> [D]isclosure of policy options, whilst policy is in the process of formulation, is highly unlikely to be in the public interest unless, for example, it would expose wrongdoing within government.[56]

Nonetheless, the perception is held by some that the FOIA imposes a 'chilling effect' on governmental deliberations in this particular regard, and hampers the formulation of policy as a result.[57]

Absolute exceptions

No duty to disclose arises if the information requested falls within one of the absolute exemptions listed in the FOIA. Release of the information requested can be denied on the basis of the absolute exemption alone; no public interest test applies. The following categories are regarded as being absolute exemptions to the duty of disclosure under the FOIA:

- information which is reasonably accessible to the applicant by other means;[58]

- information supplied to the public authority by, or relating to, bodies concerned with security issues;[59]

---

[53] See: Information Commissioner, *Freedom of Information Act 2000 (Section 50) Decision Notice* (5 August 2008), FS50126011. See also: *Department for Education and Skills* v *Information Commissioner and the Evening Standard* (EA/2006/0006), [75].

[54] P. Birkinshaw, *Freedom of Information: The Law, the Practice and the Ideal* (4th edn) (CUP, 2010) p. 196.

[55] *Guardian*, 1 September 2010.

[56] *Department for Education and Skills* v *Information Commissioner and Evening Standard* (EA/2006/0006), [75].

[57] Ministry of Justice, *Memorandum to the Justice Select Committee: Post-Legislative Assessment of the Freedom of Information Act 2000* (December 2011), Cm. 8236, [112], [212]–[218].

[58] FOIA 2000, s. 21.

[59] Ibid., s. 23.

- court records (including documents held by persons conducting an inquiry or arbitration);[60]
- information which would, on disclosure, infringe the privileges of Parliament;[61]
- information provided to the public authority under an obligation of confidence;[62]
- information which would be prevented from disclosure by other legal means (e.g. contempt of court).[63]

Should a public body decline to disclose the requested information, it should confirm which exemption applies and provide reasons for its application;[64] 'the onus of establishing an exception, or public interest in non-disclosure, lies on the authority, not the requester.'[65]

Enforcement

The first step for a dissatisfied applicant is to request an internal review of the public authority's decision not to disclose the information sought.[66] Should an internal review not address the request to the satisfaction of the applicant, the FOIA provides free access to specific bodies established to police the Act; the Information Commissioner[67] and the Information Rights Tribunal.[68]

The Information Commissioner

The office of Information Commissioner was created by the FOIA as the primary enforcement mechanism for the Act's provisions.[69] The general functions of the Information Commissioner are to:

- promote good practice by public authorities;
- provide information and advice to the public about the operation of the FOIA;
- assess whether public authorities are following good practice; and
- approve publication schemes.[70]

In short, the basic role of the Information Commissioner is to act as the independent[71] 'champion' of the FOIA.[72]

---

[60] Ibid., s. 32.

[61] Ibid., s. 34.

[62] Ibid., s. 41.

[63] Ibid., s. 44.

[64] Ibid., s. 17.

[65] P. Birkinshaw, 'Regulating Information' in J. Jowell, D. Oliver and C. O'Cinneide (eds), *The Changing Constitution* (8th edn) (OUP, 2015) p. 395.

[66] FOIA 2000, s. 45.

[67] Ibid., part IV.

[68] Ibid., part V.

[69] Ibid., s. 18. See also Protection of Freedoms Act 2012, ss. 105–108.

[70] Ibid., s. 47. See also Constitutional Affairs Committee, *Freedom of Information – One Year On* (2005–2006), HC 991, [47]–[50].

[71] The Information Commissioner reports annually to Parliament (FOIA 2000, s. 49).

[72] P. Birkinshaw, 'Freedom of Information and its impact in the United Kingdom' (2010) 27 *Government Information Quarterly* 312, 313.

In discharging its enforcement role, a number of avenues are open to the Information Commissioner. In response to a complaint, the Information Commissioner is able to determine whether the requirements of the FOIA have been met. Following investigation, notice of the Commissioner's findings is communicated to the complainant and public authority; this notification is referred to as a 'decision notice' and may specify action required to be taken in order to comply with the requirements of the FOIA. Under s. 51 FOIA, the Information Commissioner can also issue an 'information notice', requesting information in order to gauge whether or not a public body is discharging its responsibilities under the FOIA. If the Commissioner is of the view that the practices of the public authority have not been sufficient to fulfil its obligations under the Act, he or she may issue an 'enforcement notice' specifying the action necessary in order to comply with the FOIA.[73] Decision and enforcement notices issued by the Information Commissioner may be appealed against, with the appeal lying to the Information Tribunal.[74] Failure to comply with a notice issued by the Information Commissioner is treated as being a contempt of court.[75] In order to investigate the activities of public authorities under the FOIA, the Information Commissioner has significant powers to enter premises and inspect documents via judicial warrant.[76]

The Information Rights Tribunal

Appeals may be brought by either party to the Information Rights Tribunal on the basis that the notice issued was not in accordance with the law,[77] or on the basis that the notice was issued on the basis of a faulty exercise of discretion on the part of the Information Commissioner.[78] The Information Rights Tribunal may review the findings of fact on which the notice in question was issued.[79] Following consideration of the case by the Tribunal, a further appeal may lie to the High Court should the case disclose the need to clarify a point of law.[80] The dual-enforcement mechanisms provided by the FOIA can combine to great effect; as Worthy has noted, when the Information Commissioner and Information Rights Tribunal are in agreement 'they can create powerful legal precedents for openness.'[81]

The ministerial veto power

The inclusion of the ministerial veto had initially been ruled out of the Labour government's proposals for freedom of information legislation on the ground that it would 'undermine the authority of the Information Commissioner and erode public confidence

---

[73] FOIA 2000, s. 52.
[74] Ibid., s. 57.
[75] Ibid., s. 54(3).
[76] Ibid., s. 55 and sch. 3.
[77] Ibid., s. 58(1)(a).
[78] Ibid., s. 58(1)(b).
[79] Ibid., s. 58(2).
[80] Ibid., s. 59.
[81] B. Worthy, 'The Future of Freedom of Information in the United Kingdom' (2008) 79 *Political Quarterly* 100, 102.

in the Act'.[82] In spite of this, a ministerial veto power *was* included in s. 53 FOIA. Section 53(2) provides that:

> [A] decision notice or enforcement notice . . . shall cease to have effect if, not later than the twentieth working day following the effective date, the accountable person in relation to that authority gives the Commissioner a certificate signed by him stating that he has on reasonable grounds formed the opinion that, in respect of the request or requests concerned, there was no failure falling within subsection (1)(b).[83]

Austin, in a damning critique of the FOIA – in which he concludes that the FOIA is a 'fraud on democratic accountability'[84] – assessed the ministerial veto power in the following terms:

> . . . the right of ministerial veto undermines any credibility to the claim that the Act creates a legally enforceable individual right of access. The scope of the discretionary power is extraordinary: the minister need only certify that on reasonable grounds he has formed the opinion that there has been no failure to comply with the duty to grant access to the information requested. There is no obligation to give reasons for his opinion, nor to provide the information or grounds on which he formed the opinion.[85]

However, despite the undoubted stifling potential of this ministerial power, successive governments have confirmed that the veto should only be used in exceptional circumstances following a decision taken collectively by the Cabinet, and practice appears to have endorsed the predictions made by government ministers during the passage of the Freedom of Information Bill that reliance on the ministerial veto would be extraordinary.[86] Section 53 has only been employed on seven occasions since the FOIA came fully into force in 2005 (twice in relation to Cabinet minutes detailing the advice provided by the Attorney-General on the legality of the war in Iraq,[87] twice in respect of Cabinet Sub-Committee minutes concerning devolution to Scotland, Wales and the Regions,[88] to prevent publication of a risk assessment of proposed reforms to the NHS,[89] to prevent disclosure of letters

---

[82] *Your Right to Know: the Government's Proposals for a Freedom of Information Act,* Cm. 3818 (December 1997), [5.18].

[83] A comparable provision can be found in s. 52 Freedom of Information (Scotland) Act 2002.

[84] R. Austin, 'The Freedom of Information Act 2000 – A Sheep in Wolf's Clothing?' in J. Jowell and D. Oliver (eds), *The Changing Constitution* (5ᵗʰ edn) (OUP, 2000) p. 415. For a critique of the FOI Bill as originally introduced to Parliament, see N. Parry and P. Birkinshaw, 'Every trick in the book: the Freedom of Information Bill 1999' [1999] EHRLR 373.

[85] R. Austin, 'The Freedom of Information Act 2000 – a Sheep in Wolf's Clothing?' in J. Jowell and D. Oliver (eds), *The Changing Constitution* (5ᵗʰ edn) (OUP, 2000) p. 414.

[86] HC Debates, vol. 347, cols 918–23 (4 April 2000), Jack Straw MP; HL Debates, vol. 618, cols 441–3 (25 October 2000), Lord Falconer of Thoroton; House of Commons Library, *FoI and Ministerial Vetoes* (19 March 2014), SN/PC/05007, p. 4; *R (Evans)* v *Attorney-General* [2015] UKSC 21; [2015] 1 AC 1787, [20].

[87] See Information Commissioner, *Ministerial Veto on Disclosure of Cabinet Minutes Concerning Military Action Against Iraq* (2009), HC 622: https://www.gov.uk/government/uploads/system/uploads/attachment_data/file/60528/Statement_of_Reasons-31July2012_0.pdf.

[88] See Information Commissioner, *Ministerial Veto on Disclosure of the Minutes of the Cabinet Sub-Committee on Devolution for Scotland, Wales and the Regions* (2010), HC 218; Information Commissioner, *The Attorney-General's Veto on Disclosure of the Minutes of the Cabinet Sub-Committee on Devolution for Scotland, Wales and the Regions* (2012), HC 1850.

[89] Information Commissioner, *Ministerial Veto on Disclosure of the Department of Health's Transitional Risk Register* (2012), HC 77.

sent by the Prince of Wales to government ministers[90], and most recently to withhold disclosure of a review of the HS2 project[91]). As a point of comparison, Hazell and Bus-field-Birch record that – during the first five years of their FOI regimes – the equivalent veto power under the New Zealand freedom of information legislation was used 14 times, while the Australian veto was employed on a staggering 48 occasions.[92] In contrast. the ministerial veto was deployed only twice in the first five years following the FOIA's implementation. Although the ministerial veto may hold the potential to significantly undermine the effectiveness of the FOIA, its use in practice has therefore been relatively infrequent.

Key debate

Deployment of the ministerial veto – the Attorney-General's legal advice on the war in Iraq

In February 2009 (see: HC Debates, vol. 488, cols 153–65 (24 February 2009)), the veto power was employed for the first time in order to prevent disclosure of Cabinet minutes relating to discussions over the Attorney-General's advice as to the legality of the 2003 invasion of Iraq. Following a request made under the FOIA, the Cabinet Office had declined to disclose the minutes of the meetings – which were held in March 2003 – on the ground that the content of the minutes related to matters covered under s. 35 of the FOIA (the formulation or development of government policy) and that the public interest in maintaining the confidentiality of Cabinet proceedings outweighed the public interest in disclosure.

The applicant lodged a complaint with the Information Commissioner. The Commissioner acknowledged that the materials fell within the scope of s. 35, but found that such was the controversy over the information concerned that the public interest favoured disclosure (with a certain amount of redacted material). An information notice was issued to that effect. On appeal to the Information Tribunal, a majority decision found that the public interest favoured disclosure.

Announcing the use of the veto in the House of Commons, Jack Straw MP suggested that the balance struck by the Information Tribunal was 'not correct' (col. 154) and justified the use of the override power on the following grounds:

> The concomitant of collective responsibility is that debate is conducted confidentially. Confidentiality serves to promote thorough decision making. Disclosure of the Cabinet minutes in this case jeopardises that space for thought and debate at precisely the point where it has its greatest utility. In short, the damage that disclosure of the minutes in this instance would do far outweighs any corresponding public interest in their disclosure (col. 155).

Unfortunately, as Birkinshaw has observed, many observers felt that the use of the veto in this particular instance was 'not to protect sensitive information but to prevent the public seeing how little meaningful discussion on such a fateful decision took place' (P. Birkinshaw, 'Regulating Information' in J. Jowell, D. Oliver and C. O'Cinneide (eds), *The Changing Constitution* (8th edn) (OUP, 2015), p. 397).

---

[90] See *Evans* v *Information Commissioner* [2012] UKIT 340 (AAC) and the statement of reasons for use of the ministerial override provided by the Attorney-General: www.attorneygeneral.gov.uk/NewsCentre/Pages/AttorneyGeneralvetoesreleaseofPrinceofWalescorrespondence.aspx.

[91] See https://www.gov.uk/government/uploads/system/uploads/attachment_data/file/276159/mpa-statement-of-reasons.pdf. See also J. Milford, 'High Speed Trains and Black Spider Letters: Freedom of Information and the Ministerial Veto' [2015] *Judicial Review* 206.

[92] R. Hazell and D. Busfield-Birch, 'Opening the Cabinet Door: Freedom of Information and Government Policy Making' [2011] PL 260, 282–283.

Should the ministerial veto be exercised, the relevant minister must communicate the decision to the Information Commissioner, and lay a copy of the certificate before both Houses of Parliament.[93] The minister must give reasons for the decision to invoke the veto,[94] and must assert 'reasonable grounds' for adopting the view that the authority in question was not in breach of the requirements of the FOIA in refusing disclosure.

While the ministerial override power is regarded – in the words of the Independent Commission on Freedom of Information – as evidence 'that Parliament did intend the executive to have the last word when it came to whether information should be released under the Act',[95] the exercise of the s. 53 ministerial veto is nonetheless subject to judicial review. The decision in *R (Evans)* v *Attorney-General*,[96] in which the Supreme Court – by a majority – quashed the ministerial override used in order to withhold publication of correspondence between the Prince of Wales and various government ministers (the so-called 'Black Spider Memos') provides the most emphatic evidence to date of judicial review's ability to bolster the protections provided for by the FOIA. The Supreme Court quashed the decision of the Attorney-General to issue the veto on the bases that the reasons provided for its issue were inadequate,[97] and – as discussed above[98] – on the more expansive (and controversial) ground that the ability of the minister to effectively override the decision of a court[99] to order disclosure of the memos was effectively incompatible with the requirements of the rule of law.[100] The consequence of the decision – as seemingly subsequently acknowledged by the Government[101] – is that use of s. 53 to override disclosures ordered following a judicial review of the determination of the Information Commissioner will only be lawful in the event of 'a material change in circumstances since the tribunal decision' or if that decision was 'demonstrably flawed in fact or in law'.[102] As Lord Neuberger summarised:

> Where . . . a court has conducted a full open hearing into the question of whether, in the light of certain facts and competing arguments, the public interest favours disclosure of certain information and has concluded for reasons given in a judgment that it does, section 53 cannot be invoked effectively to overrule that judgment merely because a member of the executive, considering the same facts and arguments, takes a different view.[103]

---

[93] FOIA 2000, s. 53(3).

[94] Ibid., s. 53(6).

[95] *Report of the Independent Commission on Freedom of Information* (March 2016) p. 36.

[96] *R (Evans)* v *Attorney-General* [2015] UKSC 21; [2015] 1 AC 1787.

[97] In the words of Lord Mance (with whom Lady Hale was in agreement), the Attorney-General's statement of reasons failed to provide 'any real or adequate explanation' which would justify departure from the findings of the Upper Tribunal (*R (Evans)* v *Attorney-General* [2015] UKSC 21; [2015] 1 AC 1787, [145]).

[98] See p. 213.

[99] Prior to the issue of the s 53 certificate, release of the correspondence had been resisted by the various government departments (a decision upheld by the Information Commissioner), but ordered by the Upper Tribunal ([2012] UKUT 313 (AAC)).

[100] *R (Evans)* v *Attorney-General* [2015] UKSC 21; [2015] 1 AC 1787, [51]–[59].

[101] Written Statement, Matthew Hancock (Minister for the Cabinet Office and Paymaster General), 'Open and Transparent Government, HCWS566 (1 March 2016): '. . . the Government will in future only deploy the veto after an Information Commissioner decision.'

[102] *R (Evans)* v *Attorney-General* [2015] UKSC 21; [2015] 1 AC 1787, [71]–[85].

[103] *R (Evans)* v *Attorney-General* [2015] UKSC 21; [2015] 1 AC 1787, [59].

Given the extent to which the decision saw the judicial curtailment of a power conveyed upon the executive by primary legislation, assessments of *Evans* have been polarised.[104] For present purposes, *Evans* demonstrates that the FOIA and judicial review can together generate a powerful force supporting openness in government.

Insight

A common law principle of openness?

The Supreme Court decision in *Kennedy* v *Charity Commission* [2014] UKSC 20; [2015] AC 455 appeared to indicate that FOIA's provisions might be complemented at common law by a parallel right of access to information. The *Kennedy* decision was an appeal against the refusal of the Charity Commission to disclose information relating to an inquiry into a charitable appeal established by the former MP George Galloway, an application made under the FOIA by Kennedy having previously been rejected on the basis of s. 32 FOIA. Before the Supreme Court, Kennedy argued that even if s. 32 could provide prima facie justification for withholding the requested information (the inquiry into the charitable appeal having concluded) disclosure could be required on the basis that Article 10 ECHR (applicable via the interpretative means of s. 3(1) the Human Rights Act 1998) 'imposes a positive duty of disclosure on public authorities . . . in respect of material of genuine public interest.' The Supreme Court found that, as a matter of ordinary statutory construction, s. 32 provided an absolute exemption to disclosure under the FOIA, with a majority finding no clear support in the Strasbourg case law for an interpretation of Article 10 that would underpin the argued-for right of access to information.[105] In common with a number of broadly contemporaneous Supreme Court decisions (see p. 157), a majority of the justices in *Kennedy* sought to de-emphasise argument based around the Convention jurisprudence in favour of common law principle, here finding that the legal regulation of the Charity Commission was 'underpinned by a common law presumption in favour of openness in a context such as the present' (Lord Mance, [47]). Though Kennedy's claim was ultimately unsuccessful, the Supreme Court made plain that the FOIA is complemented by the common law's commitment to open justice (Lord Toulson, [110]).

Assessing the impact of the Freedom of Information Act

Initial reports on the impact of the FOIA were quietly positive. The House of Commons Constitutional Affairs Committee reported in 2006 that despite suffering from the 'inconsistency, delay and obfuscation that is typical of all early-stage FOI regimes':[106]

> [T]he implementation of the FOI Act has already brought about significant and new releases of information and that this information is being used in a constructive and positive way by a range of different individuals and organisations. We have seen many examples of the benefits resulting from this legislation and are impressed with the efforts made by public authorities to meet the demands of the Act. This is a significant success.[107]

---

[104] Compare, for instance, R. Ekins and C. Forsyth, *Judging the Public Interest: The Rule of Law vs. The Rule of Courts* (Policy Exchange, 2015) with M. Elliott, 'A Tangled Constitutional Web: The Black Spider Memos and the British Constitution's Relational Architecture' [2015] PL 539.

[105] Though see now *Magyar Helsinki Bizottság* v *Hungary,* Application No. 18030/11 (8 November 2016).

[106] B. Worthy, 'The Future of Freedom of Information in the United Kingdom' (2008) 79 *Political Quarterly* 100, 102.

[107] Constitutional Affairs Committee, *Freedom of Information – One Year On* (2005–2006), HC 991, [13].

During the first year following implementation of the FOIA the Information Commissioner estimated that between 100,000 and 130,000 requests for information were received by public authorities.[108] More recent experience suggests that the total number of requests for disclosure received annually by public authorities has shown an increase on these initial figures.[109] *Disclosure* rates are perhaps more difficult to gauge, and vary considerably across the affected organisations. As far as central government is concerned, the Ministry of Justice has recorded that the period 2005–10 saw a 'steady decrease' in the proportion of requests resulting in full disclosure of the information sought (from 66 per cent to 57 per cent). During the same period, the proportion of cases in which information was withheld in full increased (from 18 per cent to 25 per cent).[110] In spite of this, the Ministry of Justice was able to conclude in 2011 that 'public opinion on openness and transparency, and the trustworthiness of public authorities . . . clearly indicate that the FOIA has had significant success in opening up government.'[111] This assessment was endorsed in 2012 by the House of Commons Justice Committee.[112]

As the FOIA bedded down, reports from those falling in the full glare of FOI scrutiny were polarised. According to Gordon Brown's Labour Government, '[t]he Freedom of Information Act has established transparency as a mechanism for empowering the individual against the state'.[113] Brown's immediate predecessor in office was less positive about the changes brought about by the FOIA. Although freedom of information legislation had been a 'fundamental'[114] first-term objective of Blair's Labour Government, the FOIA came to be seen as an obstacle to frank policy deliberations. Writing in his autobiography – published in 2010 – Tony Blair lamented his government's support for freedom of information legislation, describing it as a 'folly' and as being 'utterly undermining of sensible government'.[115] Blair's comments are perhaps illustrative that one of the more lofty aims of the FOIA – the generation of a 'culture of openness' in government – remains elusive. Commenting on the implementation of comparable regimes in Commonwealth states, Roberts has written that:

> Governments have become more open; but this does not mean that they have acquired a 'culture of openness'. It means only that the rules that govern the conflict over information have shifted in favour of openness, and that government officials (as a rule) recognise their ultimate obligation to submit to the rule of law.[116]

Attempts to resist the development of such a 'culture of openness' were evident in the chain of events surrounding the 2009 parliamentary expenses scandal.

---

[108] Ibid., [5].

[109] Ministry of Justice, *Memorandum to the Justice Select Committee: Post-Legislative Assessment of the Freedom of Information Act 2000* (December 2011), Cm. 8236, [128].

[110] Ibid., [131].

[111] Ibid., [220].

[112] Justice Committee, *Post-Legislative Scrutiny of the Freedom of Information Act 2000,* First Report of Session 2012–2013 (July 2012), HC 96-I. See also *Report of the Independent Commission on Freedom of Information* (March 2016).

[113] Ministry of Justice, *Rights and Responsibilities: Developing our Constitutional Framework* (March 2009), Cm. 7577, p. 5.

[114] T. Blair, Speech to the Campaign for Freedom of Information Awards (1996) (cited in K. Gunderson, 'Freedom of Information' in P. Facey, B. Rigby and A. Runswick (eds), *Unlocking Democracy. 20 Years of Charter 88* (Politicos, 2008)).

[115] T. Blair, A *Journey* (Arrow Books, 2010) pp. 516–17.

[116] A. Roberts, 'Two Challenges in Administration of the Access to Information Act' (cited in Constitutional Affairs Committee, *Freedom of Information* – One Year On (2005–2006), HC 991, [112]).

Insight

The Freedom of Information Act and the MPs' expenses scandal

The 'extraordinary catalogue of revelations' associated with the parliamentary expenses scandal of 2009 can be seen as being 'directly related to [the] strong trend towards greater transparency which has followed in the wake of the Freedom of Information Act 2000' (P. Leyland, 'Freedom of Information and the 2009 Parliamentary Expenses Scandal' [2009] P.L. 675, 675). The scandal was the direct cause of the early resignation – for the first time since 1695 – of the Speaker of the House of Commons and the resignation of a number of other high-profile, office-holding MPs, and indirectly led to further MPs either standing down or losing their seats at the 2010 general election. Five Members of Parliament – three MPs and two peers – received prison sentences after being found guilty of offences relating to the scandal.

The roots of the scandal can be found in the disclosure of MPs' expenditure claims which were routinely made under the House of Commons FOIA publication scheme. A number of journalists sought disclosure of further details of the claims under the FOIA, a claim that was resisted (and which prompted a failed attempt to see Parliament excluded from the remit of the FOIA (See: Freedom of Information (Amendment) Bill 2007)).

The journalists then made a complaint to the Information Commissioner. The Information Commissioner determined that disclosure was merited in the public interest. The Corporate Officer of the House of Commons – supported by the Speaker of the House – appealed to the Information Tribunal (which upheld the notice issued by the Information Commissioner) and again to the High Court (which upheld the decision of the Information Tribunal). In the decision of the High Court, Sir Igor Judge suggested that:

> . . . it is inconceivable that MPs could expect to conduct their affairs on the basis that recently enacted legislation did not apply to them, or that the House, for its own purposes, was permitted to suspend or dispense with such legislation (*Corporate Officer of the House of Commons* v *Information Commissioner* [2008] EWHC 1084 (Admin), at [33]).

During May 2009, following a leak from a House of Commons employee, the *Daily Telegraph* published a succession of articles detailing the excessive and outlandish claims made by a number of MPs. In total, the expenses claims of some 173 MPs were revealed, detailing, *inter alia*, claims for mortgage repayments that had already been paid off in full, payments to family members for work that was never actually carried out and various claims for the maintenance and upkeep of property (including the now notorious claim relating to a 'floating duck island' (See *Guardian*, 'MP's Expenses: "Duck Island" Conservative Is Forced to Retire', 21 May 2009)).

The Speaker of the House of Commons, Michael Martin MP, was the most high-profile of the casualties of the parliamentary expenses affair. His stance was widely interpreted as an obstacle to opening up parliamentary procedures to public scrutiny and to the reforms of the expenses system that were so clearly needed.

The scandal resulted in the passing of the Parliamentary Standards Act 2009, which established the Independent Parliamentary Standards Authority (an independent regulator of MPs' allowances and pay (see: Parliamentary Standards Act 2009, and Constitutional Reform and Governance Act 2010)).

Further evidence of governmental antipathy towards the FOIA was arguably in evidence when – in the aftermath of the Supreme Court decision in *Evans* – David Cameron's Government initiated a process by which the Act would be subject to an extra-parliamentary review.[117] The appointment of the Independent Commission on Freedom of Information in July 2015 was widely interpreted as a step towards weakening the Act's protections, especially given that a number of the appointed commissioners had previously been critical of the Act.[118] The Commission's terms of reference mandated examination of whether the Act permitted an appropriate balance to be struck between 'transparency, accountability and the need for sensitive information to have robust protection', whether the Act recognised the need for a 'safe space' within which policy might be developed following frank discussion, and allowed the Commission to take into account the administrative burden placed by the FOIA on public authorities.

In spite of speculation that the Commission would be robustly critical of the FOIA, its March 2016 report found that the Act was 'generally working well', had 'enhanced openness and transparency' and found 'no evidence that the Act need[ed] to be radically altered'.[119] In spite of the proposal of a number of relatively modest recommendations designed to 'improve clarity and certainty around the operation of the Act'[120] – probably the most eye-catching of which was to recommend the introduction of legislation reiterating the executive ability to 'exercise a veto in those cases where it considers it appropriate'[121] – publication of the report indicated that governmental appetite for reform had dissipated even as the review concluded; a Cabinet Office statement issued upon publication of the report indicated that 'no legal changes' to the FOIA regime would result.[122]

Conclusion

Of the constitutional reforms implemented by the Blair administration during the 1997–2001 Parliament it is the FOIA 2000 that most clearly remains in its infancy. In part this can be attributed to the significant intervening period between the enactment and implementation of the Act in 2005, in part to the fact that freedom of information was not – in theory at least – as headline-grabbing as devolution, human rights legislation or even reform of the House of Lords (even in spite of the grand claim made by the Information Tribunal that s. 1 FOIA gives effect to a 'new fundamental right to information'[123]). In practice, however, the FOIA has been quietly effective, and has played a role in some significant exposures of questionable administration and in simply making the business of government more accessible to members of the electorate.[124] As we have seen, for some

---

[117] An earlier review by the House of Commons Justice Committee had found that the FOIA 'has enhanced the UK's democratic system and made our public bodies more open, accountable and transparent. It has been a success and we do not wish to diminish its intended scope, or its effectiveness (Justice Committee, *Post-Legislative Scrutiny of the Freedom of Information Act 2000,* First Report of Session 2012–2013 (July 2012), HC 96-I, p. 5).

[118] 'Freedom of Information Commission not very free with its information', *Guardian,* 9 October 2015.

[119] *Report of the Independent Commission on Freedom of Information* (March 2016), p. 3.

[120] Ibid., p. 3.

[121] Ibid., p. 37.

[122] See 'Review decides not to change Freedom of Information Act', *Guardian,* 1 March 2016; Written Statement, Matthew Hancock (Minister for the Cabinet Office and Paymaster General), 'Open and Transparent Government, HCWS566 (1 March 2016).

[123] *Department for Education and Skills* v *Information Commissioner and Evening Standard,* EA/2006/0006, [61].

[124] See generally: Justice Committee, *Post-Legislative Scrutiny of the Freedom of Information Act 2000,* First Report of Session 2012–2013 (July 2012), HC 96-I; *Report of the Independent Commission on Freedom of Information* (March 2016).

politicians, the FOIA is regarded as a hindrance rather than a tool of good governance; for so long as it continues to be so perceived the generation of a broader 'culture of openness' in government will remain an aspiration rather than reality. But having survived, unamended, following the report of the Independent Commission on Freedom of Information – widely-perceived as an attempt at destabilisation of the FOIA regime – the position of the Act on the statute book looks secure.

Practice questions

1. *'The Freedom of Information Act 2000 pursues laudable objectives but is rendered ineffectual by the breadth of its exception clauses and the inclusion of the ministerial veto power.'* Discuss.

2. *'FOIA 2000 is of assistance in meeting its identified objectives – openness, transparency, and access to information – but other procedures and opportunities need to be developed.'* (P. Birkinshaw, 'Regulating Information' in J. Jowell, D. Oliver and O'Cinneide (eds), *The Changing Constitution* (8th edn) (Oxford: OUP, 2015), p. 406) Discuss.

Further reading

The most comprehensive account of the provisions and operation of the FOIA can be found in **P. Birkinshaw, *Freedom of Information: the Law, the Practice and the Ideal*** (4th edn) (CUP, 2010). Shorter, and more accessible, summaries of the implementation of the FOIA can be found in **T. Pitt-Payne and R. Kamm, 'Freedom of Information: the Story So Far'** [2009] *Judicial Review* 239, **P. Birkinshaw, 'Freedom of Information and Its Impact in the United Kingdom** (2010) 27 *Government Information Quarterly* 312 and **B. Worthy and R. Hazell, 'Disruptive, Dynamic and Democratic? Ten Years of FOI in the UK'** (2017) 70 *Parliamentary Affairs* 22.

In relation to two of the specific controversies in which the FOIA played a prominent role **P. Leyland, 'Freedom of Information and the 2009 Parliamentary Expenses Scandal'** [2009] PL 675 provides a clear and readable account of the role of the FOIA in disclosing the extent of the MPs' expenses scandal, while **M. Elliott, 'A Tangled Constitutional Web: The Black Spider Memos and the British Constitution's Relational Architecture'** [2015] PL 539 examines the *Evans* decision and its implications for the constitutional principles of parliamentary sovereignty and the rule of law.

The **Campaign for Freedom of Information** website – www.cfoi.org.uk/ – provides regular updates and reports on the implementation of the FOIA and on freedom of information in the news. The website of the **Constitution Unit,** based at **University College London,** also provides a range of practical materials and research findings relating to freedom of information and its impact on government in the UK: www.ucl.ac.uk/constitution-unit/research/foiPages/AttorneyGeneralvetoesreleaseofPrinceofWalescorrespondence.aspx.

Part VI
Accountability (II): the courts

Chapter 18
Judicial review of administrative action – theory, procedure and remedies

'Since judges continue to develop the criteria for judicial review as they go along, administrators and litigants alike find themselves playing a complex game whose rules are liable to be adjusted by the umpire at the end of the match.'

Simon James, 'The Political and Administrative Consequences of Judicial Review' (1996) 74 *Public Administration* 613, 620.

Chapter outline

Much of this book has mapped the principles underpinning the UK Constitution. Judicial review provides an outlet by which those affected by government actions (including individuals, companies, pressure groups, and even other branches of government) can request that the courts check the lawfulness of such actions. It is the form of court procedure by which many of the most celebrated cases relating to the rule of law and separation of powers are decided. The exercise of this jurisdiction therefore defines the courts' relationship with other branches of government. This chapter assesses the basis for, and boundaries of, judicial review. It also examines the procedure by which judicial review is initiated and the remedies available for successful claimants.

Introduction

In the broadest possible terms, judicial review provides a mechanism by which those affected by government decisions can challenge the validity of those decisions in court. It therefore provides the main proving ground in which the courts can test the 'lawfulness' of official actions. In evaluating the validity of such actions the courts can test (specifically) whether legal authority existed for the decision, whether the proper procedure was followed in making the *decision,* and (more broadly) whether the manner in which it was made conflicts with constitutional principles like the rule of law and separation of powers. From the outset, it is important to realise that this judicial role, overseeing the public functions of public bodies (often under the direct or indirect authority of an elected decision maker), is inherently controversial. Unelected judges can use judicial review to invalidate ministerial decisions, on the basis that even elected decision makers must not be able to ignore the legal boundaries upon their authority if the rule of law is to remain a constitutional fundamental. This chapter explores these conflicting impulses, assessing how their changing relationship has altered the scope of judicial review. As the quote opening this chapter indicates, extensions to judicial review in recent decades have heightened tensions between ministers and judges; throughout the chapter we will be considering the impact of the Coalition Government's efforts to restrict judicial review, particularly through the Criminal Justice and Courts Act 2015. Having mapped judicial review's boundaries and examined the basis for its operation, this chapter will thereafter evaluate the procedural requirements which must be met if the courts are to review a decision and finally the remedies available when a claim succeeds. These elements of judicial review might sound mechanical and uncontroversial by comparison to the grounds on which the courts can accept a challenge to the exercise of a public function (considered in the next chapter), but they operate as levers which alter the scope of judicial review and which thereby influence its attractiveness for claimants.

Judicial review's constitutional role

Key issues

- A judicial review of a decision is conceptually different from an appeal against a decision. Judicial review does not determine whether a decision was right or wrong as a matter of public policy but instead allows the courts to supervise its lawfulness and the manner in which it was reached.

- Judicial review operates, in part, to improve the administration of governmental functions in the UK by securing the accountability of public bodies to their users and the electorate. The jurisdiction has two facets:

  1. supervising the exercise of powers granted to public bodies; and
  2. enhancing the efficiency of public administration.

- Judicial review cases often involve, and develop our understanding of, the principles underpinning the UK Constitution. The operation of the jurisdiction tells us much about the relationship between the separation of powers, rule of law and parliamentary sovereignty.

Judicial review: supervising public-authority decision-making

(i) Review, not appeal

Where a public authority breaks the rules of contracts to which it is party, the other affected party can ask the courts to enforce the contract or provide damages to compensate the breach, just as they could if the contract was with a private actor. Similarly, individuals employed within the public sector can be held responsible before courts for torts or criminal offences they commit. This is in keeping with the principle that the government is subject to the requirements of law, just as the law governs relations between private persons. But public authorities must additionally abide by the rules of administrative law in their decision-making. Owners of private businesses can, for example, give business to their family members without regard to their merit. Members of the executive, however, should not be able to exercise similar nepotism towards family members at the expense of taxpayers (see the discussion of the Nolan Principles in Chapter 14[1]). Administrative law provides a system of rules which apply specifically to decision making by public bodies, thereby securing the principle of government under the law (see Chapter 6). [2] Over time it developed as a means of preventing officials from using their public office for personal benefit, or to settle grudges against their rivals, or simply to act arbitrarily. The courts also used this jurisdiction to ensure that broader values of fairness (sometimes called the principles of 'natural justice') were embodied in public decision-making.

Much as the role of the courts in preventing public bodies from exceeding or abusing their powers is intended to improve the standard of governance in the UK, judicial review does not offer those aggrieved by a public body's activity an opportunity to appeal; the role of the courts under judicial review is limited. A court is not concerned with the merits of the decision (whether it represents good or bad public policy). The merits of a decision are the concern for primary decision makers on the basis of their expertise (be they town planners, NHS managers or senior police officers) or on the basis of the remit of their elected office (from local councillors to members of devolved administrations to UK government ministers). Instead, judicial review often evaluates procedural irregularities in decision-making or questions of whether a power was actually within the remit of a public body.

This distinction between review and appeal was considered in the decision in ***ex parte Evans.*** The Chief Constable of North Wales Police dismissed Evans, a probationary constable, as not fit for his position on the basis that he cohabited with an older woman and kept a large number of dogs in a property rented from the police. The Chief Constable's concerns regarding such behaviour were not, however, put to Evans prior to his dismissal, meaning that he could not offer any explanation for his conduct. When Evans sought a judicial review of his dismissal, the judges hearing the case made it clear that the Chief Constable was entitled to consider whether Evans' lifestyle choices impacted upon his fitness to serve in the police, but that taking a decision without providing Evans with a hearing was unfair. For Lord Brightman, this outcome accorded with the limited nature of judicial review:

> Judicial review is concerned, not with the decision, but with the decision-making process. Unless that restriction on the power of the court is observed, the court will in my view, under the guise of preventing the abuse of power, be itself guilty of usurping power.[3]

In other words, whether the judges approved or disapproved of Evans' lifestyle was irrelevant to the decision. The courts (not being experts in the management of a police force) made no effort to substitute their assessment of the merits for that of the Chief Constable. Nonetheless, the weaknesses in the way the decision was reached were a valid concern for the courts. This approach means that in many judicial review cases (at least where the public body is not found to be acting in excess of powers), the reviewing court's decision is not the end of the story. The decision maker can often react to an adverse judicial review by reassessing the dispute (in a procedurally fair manner) and reaching the same decision once again. Judges have traditionally accepted these limitations on the operation of judicial review for a number of reasons. Jeffrey Jowell categorised the most important of these as follows:[4]

---

[1] See pp. 433–4.
[2] See pp. 187–99.
[3] R v *Chief Constable of North Wales Police, ex parte Evans* [1982] 1 WLR 1155, 1173.
[4] See also J. Jowell, 'The Rule of Law' in J. Jowell, D. Oliver and C. O'Cinneide (eds), *The Changing Constitution* (8ᵗʰ edn, OUP, 2015) pp. 13–37.

Key debates

Judicial review and the courts' 'institutional capacity'

A judicial review action is not an appeal. The courts are under a constitutional duty to assess the validity of a decision, not to substitute their own decision for that of the reviewed body. Lord Bingham made this clear in his judgment in *R (Corner House Research)* v *Director of the Serious Fraud Office* [2008] UKHL 60; [2009] 1 AC 756 (see Chapter 6, pp. 210–11) in which he asserted, at [41], that '[t]he issue . . . is not whether his decision was right or wrong, nor whether the [court] agrees with it, but whether it was a decision which the Director was lawfully entitled to make'. Professor Jeffrey Jowell (J. Jowell, 'Of Vires and Vacuums: the Constitutional Context of Judicial Review' [1999] PL 448) considers that any effort to broaden judicial review beyond this basis would exceed the 'institutional capacity' of the courts, due to a triumvirate of 'functionalist' factors:

1. Democratic concerns and the need for specialist policy consideration

Jowell considers, at 451, that certain activities belong solely within the institutional competence of democratically elected bodies as in our society only they can allocate scarce resources or weigh opposing relevant considerations:

> [I]t is not the province of courts, when judging the administration, to make their own evaluation of the public good, or to substitute their personal assessment of the social and economic advantage of a decision. We should not expect judges therefore to decide whether the country should join a common currency, or to set a level of taxation. These are matters of policy and the preserve of other branches of government and courts are not constitutionally competent to engage in them.

Jowell contends, at 451, that there are 'inherent limitations to the process of adjudication', as the substantive reasonableness of certain decisions is not open to review by 'non-specialist' constitutional actors, including judges.

2. Institutional expertise of the courts

If Jowell's first proposition holds true, we must then consider the nature of the courts' constitutional role and their institutional competence and how these reflect upon their role in reviewing administrative decisions. Jowell notes, at 451, that the courts are well placed to evaluate the procedural fairness of decision-making processes:

> In respect of constitutional competence, the tenets of procedural fairness do not require an utilitarian evaluation of preferred outcomes. They are not based upon policy evaluations best suited to elected officials or their agents in a democracy.

By contrast, Jowell concludes that a lack of institutional competence makes the courts reluctant to engage with the merits of decisions.

3. Institutional comity

The courts, according to Jowell, have to co-operate with Parliament and the executive, because without such comity, public administration risks breaking down. The courts have historically accepted parliamentary sovereignty, for example, in order to preserve this relationship (at 458–9). If judges attempted to substitute their personal choices for those of other public bodies, the relationship between the courts and the other branches of government could collapse, and government would likely seek to restrict judicial oversight.

For a cogent critique of Jowell's view of the judiciary's constitutional role as overly formalist (meaning that the courts are reduced to policing formal rules laid down in statute), see T. R. S. Allan, 'The Constitutional Foundations of Judicial Review: Conceptual Conundrum or Interpretative Inquiry?' [2002] 61 CLJ 87, 93–97.

(ii) The benefits of judicial review: securing the rule of law and good governance

Despite these limits upon the jurisdiction, judicial review has performed from the 1960s onwards, a central function within the UK's system of government by facilitating the accountability of public bodies to their users and the electorate. In his dissenting speech in *ex parte Fire Brigades Union* Lord Mustill went some way towards mapping out the purpose behind judicial review and the reasons for its expansion. Having highlighted the weaknesses in parliamentary scrutiny of the executive, he asserted that the courts must exercise judicial review vigorously to ensure oversight of executive action:

> To avoid a vacuum in which the citizen would be left without protection against a misuse of executive powers the courts have had no option but to occupy the dead ground in a manner and in areas of public life, which could not have been foreseen 30 years ago.[5]

Thinking Point . . .

As discussed in Chapter 14, the factors weakening parliamentary scrutiny of the executive include the dominant position of the governing party, other demands upon parliamentary time restricting scrutiny and the difficulties MPs face in obtaining certain information from government (see pp. 442–9).

The primary motivation of the judges responsible for expanding judicial review was therefore to compensate for widely perceived failings in Parliament's control over executive functions. Lord Mustill proceeded to justify the scrutiny of public decision making by the courts:

> The executive carries on the administration of the country in accordance with the powers conferred on it by law. The courts interpret the laws and see that they are obeyed. This requires the courts to step into the territory which belongs to the executive, not only to verify that the powers asserted accord with the substantive law created by Parliament, but also that the manner in which they are exercised conforms with the standards of fairness which Parliament must have intended.[6]

Lord Mustill's statement provides the classic account of the relationship between the constitutional principle of the rule of law and judicial review. By launching a judicial review anyone affected by government action can employ rule of law principles to challenge that action on the basis that the public body lacks legal authority to pursue the policy (using judicial review 'to verify that the powers asserted accord with the substantive law created by Parliament') or has breached facets of the rule of law such as equality before the law (using judicial review to ensure that 'the manner in which [powers] are exercised conforms with the standards of fairness which Parliament must have intended'). Such proactive challenges to government action contrast markedly with other contexts, like defences against criminal charges, in which rule of law principles arise.

Judicial review might appear to be shaping up as the embodiment of the Diceyan idea of confining the executive within a strict conception of its powers in order to limit the scope of government activity (discussed in Chapter 6[7]). And executive actors rarely welcome the

---

[5] *R* v *Secretary of State for the Home Department, ex parte Fire Brigades Union* [1995] 2 All ER 244, 267.
[6] Ibid., 267.
[7] See pp. 177–81.

experience of being judicially reviewed, which 'has been likened to being struck by lightning—random, unpredictable and destructive'.[8] But modern administrative law is not intended to undermine the ability of government to function. In supplementing parliamentary oversight over the executive, the courts tackle areas of public administration that are malfunctioning, thereby improving the performance of government as a whole. Dawn Oliver therefore regards the courts as having a unique ability to inculcate the values of good governance (like fair and open administration) into executive activities.[9] In areas of decision-making such as resource allocation, however, judges have acknowledged the limits of their expertise and restricted judicial review accordingly.[10] Sir Stephen Sedley urges students of public law not to underestimate the importance of this function of judicial review:

> It is sometimes forgotten . . . that the protection of good government is as much the High Court's job as the castigation of misgovernment. Here, in fact, as much as in the criminal process, is where the communitarian dimension of law is displayed.[11]

The Office of the Independent Adjudicator is a relatively new public body, established under the Higher Education Act 2004 to assess student complaints regarding their course provision. Its decisions are regularly reviewed. In 2015 it published an account of the 'lessons learned' from this experience, the conclusion of which says much about the attitude of this particular public body to judicial review: 'Many of the judicial review challenges have tested or established significant principles and have provided useful and important clarification on the OIA's role, remit and approach. This has been immensely valuable, if a little painful at times'.[12]

The main reason why this capacity of judicial review to raise the standard of decision-making by the public sector as a whole is easily overlooked is that detecting its impact requires the analysis of administrative law as an aggregate of many decisions (and even its 'radiating' effect on decisions that do not come before the courts[13]), rather than assessing individual cases in isolation. For example, civil servants attending the National School of Government receive training (even if much of it is defensive[14]) on the potential for judicial review of government actions. As Sir Gus O'Donnell wrote of this training when Head of the Civil Service, the skill of public bodies in assessing the compatibility of their decisions with administrative law 'has become ever more important as we seek to ensure that we design and deliver effective services'.[15] If this training prevents decisions from being made which breach the principles of good governance laid down by judicial review, then administrative law will have improved the standard of decision-making without a case ever having to go to court. Judicial review, in short, checks the efficient running of public bodies and deters poor decision-making. Carol Harlow and Richard Rawlings therefore compared its role within the UK's governance order to a system of traffic lights controlled by the courts with the aim of permitting 'good governance' to flow:[16]

---

[8] T. Arvind and L. Stirton, 'The Curious Origins of Judicial Review' (2017) 133 LQR 91, 116.

[9] See D. Oliver, *Constitutional Reform in the United Kingdom* (OUP, 2002) 51–2.

[10] See, for example, *R v Cambridge Health Authority, ex parte B* [1995] 1 WLR 898.

[11] S. Sedley, *Freedom, Law and Justice* (Sweet and Maxwell, 1999) 14.

[12] F. Mitchell, 'The OIA and Judicial Review: Ten Principles from Ten Years of Challenges' (OIA, 2015) 11.

[13] R. Cranston, 'Reviewing Judicial Review' in G. Richardson and H. Genn (eds), *Administrative Law and Government Action* (OUP, 1994) 45, 74.

[14] See D. Oliver, 'The Judge Over Your Shoulder' (1989) 42 Parliamentary Affairs 302, 316.

[15] Treasury Solicitor's Office, *The Judge Over Your Shoulder* (4th edn, TSO, 2006) 3.

[16] C. Harlow and R. Rawlings, *Law and Administration* (CUP, 3rd edn, 2009) 22–40.

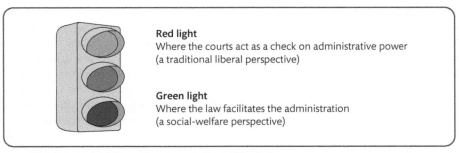

Red light
Where the courts act as a check on administrative power
(a traditional liberal perspective)

Green light
Where the law facilitates the administration
(a social-welfare perspective)

Figure 18.1 Administrative law as a traffic light

(iii) Judicial review and parliamentary sovereignty

The courts' acceptance of the doctrine of parliamentary sovereignty has historically prevented judges from accepting challenges to the contents of Acts of Parliament. As we saw when we explored parliamentary sovereignty, judges deciding cases such as *British Railways Board* v *Pickin* considered that the courts lacked the legitimacy to challenge the content of Acts of Parliament or to consider alleged irregularities in the manner of their enactment.[17] Even when judges moved to 'disapply' those provisions of the Merchant Shipping Act 1988 which conflicted with EU law in *ex parte Factortame (No. 2),* Lord Bridge was quick to assert that Parliament had placed limits upon itself in entering the EU and that the courts remained faithful to the parliamentary intention behind the European Communities Act 1972.[18] Although much of the discussion of judicial review in this and the following chapter will focus on the review of public functions derived from statute it is important to remember that other sources provide the basis for many public functions. If Parliament wanted to exclude judicial review of certain public authority actions, it would have to enact a specific 'ouster clause' excluding the jurisdiction of the courts. As we saw when we considered the rule of law, however, the courts will often attempt to circumvent such provisions if they regard them as a threat to administrative justice.[19]

Thinking Point . . .

The Criminal Justice and Courts Act 2015 provides an example of the UK Government introducing legislation which imposes more general restrictions on judicial review. In the words of Lord Neuberger, such reforms need to be treated with caution when they 'come from the very body which is at the receiving end of JR'; Lord Neuberger, *Tom Sargant Memorial Lecture: Justice in an Age of Austerity* (15 October 2013) 13.

(iv) Judicial review and the separation of powers

Despite the fact that the significance of judicial review has increased as a result of the weaknesses of ministerial responsibility before Parliament, politicians often fiercely resist judicial challenges to their authority. Notwithstanding the limitations to judicial review

---

[17] *British Railways Board* v *Pickin* [1974] AC 765.
[18] *R* v *Secretary of State for Transport, ex parte Factortame (No. 2)* [1991] 1 AC 603; [1991] 1 All ER 70.
[19] See pp. 187–99.

which we have already considered, with the courts respecting parliamentary sovereignty and largely confining themselves to the supervision (review of, as opposed to appeal over) executive functions, this jurisdiction remains a flash point of tension between the executive and judiciary. Some of this tension is inevitable, given that judicial review 'requires the courts to step into the territory which belongs to the executive'.[20] Ministers may, for example, face delays or be required to alter high-profile policies in light of even the threat of a judicial review.[21] As the former Lord Chancellor, Lord Mackay, points out, government ministers (whose position depends upon public perceptions of their competence) are only human when confronted by adverse judicial decisions; 'there are not many people who completely welcome their activities being judged, particularly if they are found to have failed'.[22] David Blunkett, as Home Secretary, had built his reputation on maintaining a 'tough' immigration policy.[23] When he perceived his policies to be under threat from judicial review, he attacked the judiciary for undermining public faith in government: 'If people believe that Parliament has no power or influence and that whatever promises we make will eventually fail, how can we persuade people to vote, stand for elections and be involved in democracy?'[24] This friction between the courts and government persisted, and a major policy focus of the Ministry of Justice under Chris Grayling's tenure as Lord Chancellor became 'the use of unmeritorious applications for judicial review to delay, frustrate or discourage legitimate executive action'.[25]

In the face of such resistance it is hardly surprising that for much of the twentieth century the judiciary were reluctant to develop administrative law, suffering what Robert Stevens identifies as a collective crisis in confidence as to the legitimacy of their challenging the actions of elected governments:

> As Britain moved from oligarchy to democracy, and as utilitarianism and then liberalism became the fashionable order of the day, the Reform Acts of 1832, 1867 and 1884 made it appear increasingly inappropriate for the judiciary to intrude into the public law arena.[26]

Even in the 1960s, in reviewing the dismissal of a police Chief Constable without providing him with any opportunity to first explain his position, Lord Evershed (in a dissenting judgment) continued to warn of the 'danger of usurpation of power on the part of the courts . . . under the pretext of having regard to the principles of natural justice'.[27] It was not until the courts began to appreciate that political scrutiny of government activity was 'falling short and sometimes well short, of what was needed'[28] to protect individuals against defective decision-making that the revival of judicial review gained pace.

---

[20] *R v Secretary of State for the Home Department, ex parte Fire Brigades Union* [1995] 2 All ER 244, 267 (Lord Mustill).

[21] S. James, 'The Political and Administrative Consequences of Judicial Review' (1996) 74 *Public Administration* 613, 620.

[22] Select Committee on the Constitution, *Relations between the Executive, the Judiciary and Parliament* (2007) HL 151-I, [35].

[23] See A. Bradley, 'Judicial Independence under Attack' [2003] PL 397.

[24] D. Blunkett, MP, 'I won't give in to the Judges' *Evening Standard* (12 May 2003).

[25] Ministry of Justice, *Judicial Review: Proposals for Further Reform* (TSO, 2013) Cm. 8703, para. 7.

[26] R. Stevens, 'Government and the Judiciary' in V. Bogdanor (ed.), *The British Constitution in the Twentieth Century* (OUP, 2003) 333, 335.

[27] *Ridge v Baldwin* [1964] AC 40, 96.

[28] *R v Secretary of State for the Home Department, ex parte Fire Brigades Union* [1995] 2 All ER 244, 267 (Lord Mustill).

Judicial expertise in fair procedure continues to provide the basis for this revival. In 2002 Lord Steyn confidently asserted that '[t]he claim that the courts stand between the executive and the citizen, and control all abuse of executive power, has been reinvigorated and become a foundation of our modern democracy'.[29] The growth of judicial review has been said to mark the 'emergence of the judiciary as the third branch of government'.[30] Nonetheless, as we explore judicial review we must remember that, whilst judicial scrutiny over executive action provides a necessary constitutional protection against the abuse of powers by government, judges exercising this jurisdiction must constantly grapple with the risks of usurping the decision-making function of the executive on the one hand and being overly deferential to public authorities on the other.

The source of the judicial review jurisdiction

Commentators upon administrative law can usually be identified as supporting one of two different theoretical explanations of the source of judicial review: the doctrine of *ultra vires* and common law theory. Understanding these different conceptions of judicial review, and applying them to the decisions of particular judges, can help us to appreciate how judges conceive of their role when deciding judicial review cases, and provides an insight into how the jurisdiction is changing.

(i) *Ultra vires* doctrine

Ultra vires doctrine provides the foundation of much post-Diceyan theory on the role of the courts when exercising judicial review. Its adherents, such as Christopher Forsyth, recognise that judicial review can be questioned on the basis of the lack of democratic legitimacy of the courts, and that such concerns undermined the courts' willingness to use their powers to supervise public decision-making for much of the twentieth century. Hence, they argue that the extension of judicial review can be explained by reference to the explicit and implicit intention of Parliament; given that an 'all-powerful' Parliament has not sought to restrict this role of the courts it must be taken to approve of it. The main problem with this approach is that even its supporters acknowledge that the 'constructive intention' of Parliament on which it relies is essentially fictional (existing to preserve constitutional 'decencies').[31] Moreover in the eagerness of *ultra vires* theorists to find a democratically legitimate basis for the exercise of judicial review, they struggle to account for the review of statutory powers being only one part (albeit the most important part) of the judicial review jurisdiction.[32] The courts' capacity to superintend non-statutory *de facto* powers[33] and prerogative powers does not easily fit this model. As a result, a rival theory emerged.

---

[29] J. Steyn, 'The Case for a Supreme Court' (2002) 118 LQR 382, 385.

[30] K. Malleson, 'Rethinking the Merit Principle in Judicial Selection' (2006) 33 JLS 126, 134. See also Chapter 11, pp. 353–4.

[31] C. Forsyth, 'Of Fig Leaves and Fairly Tales: The *Ultra Vires* Doctrine, the Sovereignty of Parliament and Judicial Review' (1996) 55 CLJ 122, 136–7.

[32] See J. Jowell, 'Of Vires and Vacuums: the Constitutional Context of Judicial Review' [1999] PL 448, 459–60.

[33] See below, pp. 522–4.

(ii) Common law theory

Common law theorists argue that public bodies must act in accordance with values of fairness, justice, respect for rights and rationality which are inherent within the common law. Judicial review therefore rests upon an inherent power of the courts to develop common law principles which are 'logically prior to the institution of democratic government'.[34] Under this theory the courts are able to act as constitutional 'principals' with regard to the common law; they are not merely the 'agents' of Parliament, as mapped out by *ultra vires* theory. For leading common law theorists like Trevor Allan, the judiciary's role as keepers of the common law and its underlying values allows the courts to displace or qualify the literal meaning of statutes 'in order to advance judicial conceptions of legality and administrative propriety'.[35] Leaving aside instrumentalist concerns as to the usefulness of these conceptions of what constitutes good governance, the intrinsic difficulty with common law theory is that it constitutes a 'provocative challenge to traditional British constitutional doctrine', under which Parliament is sovereign and statute law superior to common law.[36] Nonetheless, common law theorists like Paul Craig dispute the idea that their theory stands for 'unchecked judicial supremacism'[37] and counter that, even under the principle of legality (see Chapter 5[38]), the legislature simply has to make it clear that it seeks to modify these common law principles for them to be subordinated to statute.

(iii) Reformed *ultra vires* theory

Common law theorists had, in the late twentieth century, all but toppled some of the fundamental concepts underpinning *ultra vires* theory. No longer could *ultra vires* theorists argue that the role of the courts was effectively constrained by obedience to the legislative intent of Parliament, for numerous cases showed that 'legislative intent' was 'determined by the courts in accord with whatsoever they choose to include within it pursuant to the rule of law ideal'.[39]

Responding to this pressure, Mark Elliott endeavoured to recast *ultra vires* theory with a heavy emphasis upon the constitutional context of parliamentary authority. He acknowledges that the legislature rarely specifically asserts the rules by which the courts can consider the validity of administrative decisions, and that it can be presumed that a general set of standards is applied by the courts, but concludes that these 'judicially-created rules of good administration should nevertheless be viewed as having been made pursuant to a constitutional warrant granted by Parliament'.[40] These rules also apply to non-statutory bodies exercising a public function where these are operating in place of a statutory body, but are ultimately constrained by Parliament's sovereignty.

In response to this reformulation, opponents of *ultra vires* theory argue that in seeking Parliament's 'general' as opposed to 'specific' intent this approach hampers the evaluation

---

[34] J. Laws, 'The Constitution: Morals and Rights' (1996) PL 622, 629.
[35] T. Allan, 'Constitutional Dialogue and the Justification of Judicial Review' (2003) 23 OJLS 563, 574.
[36] J. Jowell, 'Of Vires and Vacuums: The Constitutional Context of Judicial Review' [1999] PL 448, 449.
[37] P. Craig, 'Competing Models of Judicial Review' [1999] PL 428, 447.
[38] See pp. 155–8.
[39] P. Craig, 'Competing Models of Judicial Review' [1999] PL 428, 431.
[40] M. Elliott, 'The Ultra Vires Doctrine in a Constitutional Setting: Still the Central Principle of Administrative Law' (1999) 58 CLJ 129, 143.

of judicial review by perpetuating 'fictional and misleading references to legislative intent'[41] which explain little of how the courts actually employ their powers. Moreover, the reformed theory does not maintain the centrality of judicial obedience to will of a democratically elected legislature that made the original conception of *ultra vires* such a compelling basis for administrative law for much of the twentieth century. Generalised ideas of legislative intent begin to sound a lot like common law constitutional principles.

Just as *ultra vires* theorists cannot be stereotyped as being opposed to the expanding remit of judicial review (but rather acknowledge parliamentary sovereignty as an ultimate restriction on the operation of judicial review), neither do common law theorists support an absence of constraints upon the jurisdiction (with leading common law constitutionalists recognising that common law principles provide a default position which can be supplemented or circumvented by specific legislative intent).[42] Indeed, the adaptation of *ultra vires* theory provides support for Trevor Allan's contention that 'opponents and defenders of the *ultra vires* doctrine have apparently moved closer together'.[43] With these developments, much of the heat has dissipated from the *ultra vires*/common law debate. As Tom Poole concluded, 'judicial review is better understood as a means of trying to ensure legitimacy in the making and application of laws'.[44]

Procedural elements of judicial review

Key issues

- Judicial review hearings are conducted by specialist judges, who are experts in the jurisdiction (ensuring that controversial aspects of judicial discretion are exercised in a considered manner).

- Judicial review applies to bodies exercising public functions (which are often powers specifically provided by statute). Other functions, covered by branches of private law, are not susceptible to judicial review.

- Standing ('*locus standi*') to seek judicial review is rarely questioned by the courts on the basis that a wide range of groups and individuals may have an interest in a decision.

- Time limits for challenging a decision through judicial review are very restrictive – the claimant must inform the public authority in question within three months (at most).

Controlling the Jurisdiction

(i) The Administrative Court

Judicial review emerges from the theoretical overview above as a dynamic jurisdiction, expanding and contracting in accordance with different conceptions of the judicial role within

---

[41] T. Allan, 'The Constitutional Foundations of Judicial Review: Conceptual Conundrum or Interpretative Inquiry?' (2002) 61 CLJ 87, 97.

[42] See J. Leslie, 'Vindicating Common Law Constitutionalism' (2010) 30 LS 301, 307–8.

[43] T. Allan, 'The Constitutional Foundations of Judicial Review: Conceptual Conundrum or Interpretative Inquiry?' (2002) 61 CLJ 87, 88. See also M. Elliott, 'The Ultra Vires Doctrine in a Constitutional Setting: Still the Central Principle of Administrative Law' (1999) 58 CLJ 129, 131.

[44] T. Poole, 'Legitimacy, Rights and Judicial Review' (2005) 25 OJLS 697, 725.

the constitution. Up until the late 1990s, critics of judicial review maintained that, even if the growth of administrative law had, up until that point, been incremental, any one High Court judge (and perhaps one who was relatively inexperienced in administrative law) hearing a judicial review had the ability to dramatically expand the jurisdiction.[45] To an extent, such concerns were mitigated by the ability of public bodies to appeal first-instance decisions which they disputed, but such appeals sapped public funds. The Administrative Court was therefore established in 2000 as the branch of the High Court responsible for hearing judicial review cases, placing the function of scrutinising executive action in the hands of a specialist panel of judges mindful of the particular responsibilities attaching to this jurisdiction.[46]

The Administrative Court quickly became a victim of its own success. From just over 4,000 judicial reviews being instituted annually in 2000, the figure skyrocketed to nearly 16,000 in 2013. In 2012 the Prime Minister complained that many of these claims were 'completely pointless' on the basis of their low success rate, and were needlessly clogging up government decision-making.[47] As Lord Chancellor, Chris Grayling vigorously promoted judicial review reform, a process which culminated in the controversial Criminal Justice and Courts Act 2015. Following these reforms the numbers of judicial review claims handled by the Administrative Court have dropped back to their level in 2000.[48] But there is a level of sleight of hand in claims that official statistics demonstrate that this policy produced a profound shift in the oversight of government action. Prior to 2013 the vast majority of judicial reviews heard by the Administrative Court related to Home Office immigration and asylum decisions, as no alternative judicial mechanism had been provided by government for challenging these decisions. The transfer of review of most of these decisions to the newly-created Immigration and Asylum Chamber of the Upper Tribunal in 2013 accounts for almost the entire shift in the number of judicial reviews.[49] There would therefore appear to be little immediate change in the overall volume of judicial review activity as a result of the 2015 reforms.

(ii) The cost of judicial review

Rather than attempting to radically restrict the ambit of judicial review by statute, provoking a constitutional clash with the courts, the main focus of the Criminal Justice and Courts Act 2015 was to make judicial review a less attractive option for claimants. The Government's presumption, taking a leaf out of Lord Denning's book, was that judicial review actions have become a means by which to 'harass innocent folk who have only been doing their duty'.[50] But if judicial review on a public interest basis is less likely to be initiated, public authorities could in turn become less focused upon such concerns in their decision-making. This might well curtail judicial review's ability to reinforce the standards of good governance.[51]

---

[45] See S. James, 'The Political and Administrative Consequences of Judicial Review' (1996) 74 *Public Administration* 613, 634.

[46] Lord Woolf CJ, Rougier and Bell JJ, *Practice Direction (Administrative Court: Establishment)* (20 July 2000).

[47] D. Cameron, MP, *Prime Minister's speech to CBI* (19 November 2012).

[48] See Ministry of Justice, *Civil Justice Statistics Quarterly* (TSO, 2017) 6.

[49] Crime and Courts Act 2013, s.22.

[50] *Neilson v Laugharne* [1981] QB 736, 749 (Lord Denning MR).

[51] See A. Mills, 'Reforms to Judicial Review in the Criminal Justice and Courts Act 2015: Promoting Efficiency or Weakening the Rule of Law?' [2015] PL 583, 590–591.

The costs of a judicial review usually fall on the losing party, but because there is a risk that such costs could dissuade public-interest claims the courts developed a system of protective costs orders to limit public-interest claimants' exposure to costs.[52] Under the 2015 legislation reformed costs capping orders were restricted to claims that had succeeded at permission stage, with the intention of making claimants less likely to initiate marginal claims.[53] These reforms followed restrictions upon legal aid to pursue a judicial review,[54] which have been vigorously contested and indeed had to be substantially reworked after the High Court quashed a first attempt.[55] Although the intention behind this legislation was to restrict the volume of judicial review proceedings the ultimate reforms were so watered down that this aim has not been realised.

(iii) The judicial review process

Judicial Review, as recast in 2000 under Part 54 of the Civil Procedure Rules (CPR) (the rules which govern civil claims), involves a three-stage process. The purpose of this extended process is to ensure that only the most 'deserving' claims proceed to full hearings in open court.

Table 18.1 The three stages of judicial review

Stage	Description
Pre-action protocol	Intended to allow the parties to avoid litigation, during this stage the claimant must inform the body being challenged of the decision in question and the reasons why this decision is alleged to breach administrative law.
	The body being challenged has 14 days in which to respond. If the claim is plainly unarguable or compelling then the claimant can withdraw without taking up court time or the respondent can take immediate steps to address the problem.
Permission stage	A judge of the Administrative Court conducts a preliminary examination of the basis of the claim and assessment of whether the procedural hurdles required to seek judicial review have been satisfied. This is a weeding exercise, designed to exclude unarguable claims (CPR 54.4).
	If a claim is rejected at permission stage, the claimant can seek that this decision be reconsidered after an oral hearing (CPR 54.12).
Full hearing	A full examination of whether evidence exists which establishes one or more of the grounds upon which the exercise of a public function can be successfully challenged.
	If a claim is rejected by the Administrative Court, its decisions can be appealed to the Court of Appeal and subsequently to the Supreme Court.

---

[52] *R (Corner House Research)* v *Secretary of State for Trade and Industry* [2005] EWCA Civ 192; [2005] 1 WLR 2600.

[53] Criminal Justice and Courts Act 2015, s. 88(3).

[54] Civil Legal Aid (Remuneration) (Amendment) Regulations 2015 (SI 2015/898).

[55] See *R (Ben Hoare Bell Solicitors)* v *Lord Chancellor* [2015] EWHC 523 (Admin); [2015] 1 WLR 4175.

This process enables the Administrative Court to receive, and quickly address, a large number of cases at 'permission stage'. The number of claims which subsequently gain permission to proceed to a full judicial review hearing remain relatively low (around 400–500 of the roughly 4,000 cases handled at permission stage). This indicates that the Administrative Court is open to hearing a large number of judicial review claims, to ensure that unlawful or procedurally improper decisions do not go unreviewed, but that its judges use the permission stage to filter out unmeritorious cases.[56] As this step can be performed quickly, the multi-stage process ensures that claims which have no hope of success are dismissed without costly and disruptive delays to the administration of public bodies. Five factors loom large during the permission stage:

(1) whether the activity at issue is judicially reviewable;

(2) whether the claimant has a sufficient interest in the case;

(3) whether the claimant challenges the public authority within a three-month time limit;

(4) whether any alternate bases for the challenge existed; and

(5) whether judicial review proceedings are likely to make any difference to the outcome.

We need to consider how the courts approach each of these procedural requirements in turn, and the impact of their choices for the jurisdiction as a whole. The Coalition Government's 2015 reforms sought to restrict judicial freedom of action under several of these headings, with the stated aim of preventing judicial review from 'being used for trivialities and technicalities in a way that causes cost to the public purse'.[57]

What activities can be judicially reviewed?

(i) The public/private divide

From the outset, students of administrative law must accept the uncomfortable truth, that, in the words of the then Woolf LJ, 'there is no universal test . . . which will indicate . . . beyond peradventure . . . when judicial review is or is not available'.[58] Instead, from the 1960s onwards, the courts outlined the scope of the jurisdiction and its boundaries with other civil proceedings. In 2000 Parliament made an effort to codify these developments, enacting a loose definition of the scope of judicial review within Part 54 of the CPR:

> a 'claim for judicial review' means a claim to review the lawfulness of –
>
> (i) an enactment; or
> (ii) a decision, action or failure to act in relation to the exercise of a public function.[59]

---

[56] See T. Hickman and M. Sunkin, 'Success in Judicial Review: The Current Position' *UK Constitutional Law Blog* (20 March 2015). Available at: https://ukconstitutionallaw.org/2015/03/20/tom-hickman-and-maurice-sunkin-success-in-judicial-review-the-current-position/.

[57] JCHR, *The Implications for Access to Justice of the Government's Proposals to Reform Judicial Review* (2014) HL 174/HC 868, para. 19.

[58] *R v Derbyshire CC, ex parte Noble* [1990] ICR 808, 814 (Woolf LJ).

[59] Civil Procedure Rules 2000 (SI 2000/2092) Rule 54.1(2)(a).

Table 18.2 outlines what these rules leave within the ambit of judicial review:

Table 18.2 The potential reach of judicial review

Acts of Parliament (Not reviewable unless in conflict with EU Law or on the basis provided by the Human Rights Act 1998)	
Exercises of public functions (Reviewable)	**Subordinate legislation** (Reviewable)
• Exercises of statutory public functions • Existence and exercises of the Royal Prerogative • Exercises of *de facto* public functions	• Legislation enacted by subordinate legislatures • Subordinate legislation enacted by Westminster

The above table lacks any mention of private functions. Judicial review is a special jurisdiction, imposing particular constraints upon exercises of public functions lest these special powers be abused. The recognition by the courts that public functions are special and therefore require special safeguards through administrative law is known as the public/private divide. This divide can be rather indistinct, requiring a careful appraisal of whether a function is public in nature before we can tell whether it will be reviewable.

(ii) Sources of public functions

Bodies exercising public functions which are subject to judicial review derive these powers from one of the following sources:

(a) Statute

Although the Act of Parliament which allows a body to undertake a particular public function is, in traditional constitutional theory, secure against review, the courts must still assess whether exercises of the public function under that statute conform to its requirements. Such exercises in decision-making could involve activities as diverse as the admissions processes of universities, the licensing of public houses by local authorities and the determination of an inmate's parole hearing. Lord Diplock summarised the range of powers subject to judicial review as follows in the *GCHQ* case:

> For a decision to be susceptible to judicial review the decision-maker must be empowered by public law (and not merely, as in arbitration, by agreement between private parties) to make decisions that, if validly made, will lead to administrative action or abstention from action by an authority endowed by law with executive powers . . . The ultimate source of the decision-making power is nearly always nowadays a statute or subordinate legislation made under the statute . . . [60]

(b) Subordinate legislation (including devolved legislation)

If a public function is contained in subordinate legislation then not only are the actions of the decision maker reviewable by the courts, the source of the power is also reviewable and can be struck down.[61] Delegated legislation (also known as secondary legislation) is open to review on the basis of incompatibility with the requirements of its parent legislation:

---

[60] *Council of Civil Service Unions* v *Minister for the Civil Service* [1985] AC 374, 409.
[61] See Civil Procedure Rules 2000 (SI 2000/2092) Rule 54.1(2)(a)(i).

That an attack can be made on a statutory instrument for want of power needs no demonstration, and I agree with your Lordships that it makes no difference, for this purpose, that the instrument has been laid before and approved by the two Houses of Parliament.[62]

The courts will evaluate whether Parliament has sanctioned, 'either in intention or by reason of the statutory words employed in the [parent Act]', the power to create a particular statutory instrument.[63] Even where regulations are within the scope of the parent legislation, the courts have been willing to consider challenges to them where they impose particularly grave restrictions of individual liberties, on the basis that serious restrictions should be imposed by a fully-considered Act of Parliament.[64]

Subordinate legislation includes enactments by the devolved legislatures in Scotland, Wales and Northern Ireland. Consider Lord Hope's matter-of-fact statement regarding the courts' jurisdiction to assess whether legislation passed by the Scottish Parliament conforms to the Scotland Act 1998:

> [The Scotland Act] provides that an Act of the Scottish Parliament is not law in so far as any provision is outside the legislative competence of the Parliament . . . It follows that the Protection of Wild Mammals (Scotland) Act 2002 . . . like any other enactment of the Scottish Parliament, is open to scrutiny . . . [65]

In every case executive actors seeking to exercise powers granted by such measures have to be able to show that the measures themselves are within the powers provided by the 'parent' Act of Parliament. As we saw in Chapter 13, however, the courts are cautious about applying the full rigour of judicial review, given that the enactments of representative legislatures are at issue.[66]

(c) Royal prerogative

Exercises of those powers that the executive by virtue of the prerogative are today recognised as generally reviewable. In *GCHQ* Lord Diplock recognised the prerogative as a continuing source of important public functions:

> [I]n the absence of any statute regulating the subject matter of the decision the source of the decision-making power may still be the common law itself, i.e., that part of the common law that is given by lawyers the label of 'the prerogative'. Where this is the source of decision-making power, the power is confined to executive officers of central as distinct from local government and in constitutional practice is generally exercised by those holding ministerial rank.[67]

Although exercises of prerogative powers are undoubtedly public functions, the courts continue to tread warily where these powers relate to defence or foreign relations. Even after the *GCHQ* case made it clear that prerogative powers were generally reviewable, some judges continued to consider such sensitive powers to be 'forbidden'[68] to the courts. In more recent decisions, however, courts have been willing to review prerogative powers

---

[62] *Hoffman-La Roche* v *Secretary of State for Trade and Industry* [1975] AC 295, 354 (Lord Wilberforce).
[63] *R* v *Halliday, ex parte Zadig* [1917] AC 260, 277 (Lord Shaw).
[64] *Chester* v *Bateson* [1920] 1 KB 829, 832–3 (Darling J).
[65] *Whaley* v *Lord Advocate* [2007] UKHL 53; 2007 SLT 1209, [6] (Lord Hope).
[66] See pp. 398–404.
[67] *Council of Civil Service Unions* v *Minister for the Civil Service* [1985] AC 374, 409.
[68] *R (Abbasi)* v *Secretary of State for Foreign and Commonwealth Affairs* [2002] EWCA Civ 1598; [2003] UKHRR 76, [106].

affecting defence and foreign relations, under the caveat that the government will not be held to a strict standard of review. In the ***Al Rawi*** case, for example, UK residents who were held without trial by the US Government at Guantánamo Bay brought a judicial review action seeking to oblige the UK Government to petition the US Government for their release. Such a petition would have involved an exercise of the prerogative. Laws LJ outlined the courts' approach in such cases:

> This case has involved issues touching both the Government's conduct of foreign relations, and national security: pre-eminently the former. In those areas the common law assigns the duty of decision upon the merits to the elected arm of government; all the more so if they combine in the same case . . . The court's role is to see that the government strictly complies with all formal requirements, and rationally considers the matters it has to confront. Here, because of the subject-matter, the law accords to the executive an especially broad margin of discretion.[69]

This approach is comparable to cases where the courts, reviewing the exercise of statutory powers which turn on the considered opinion of a senior government minister (such as the Home Secretary's power to exclude from the UK foreign nationals who are thought to pose a threat[70]), have asserted that such decisions are reviewable, but granted a broad measure of discretion to ministerial opinion.[71]

(d) De facto *public functions*

An ostensibly private body may be said to possess *de facto* public powers where the government has made the decision not to assume certain powers because of the private body's activities. Put simply, 'but for' the existence of this private body, a public body would have to operate in its place. An example of such a body is the Panel on Takeovers and Mergers, an independent body established in 1968 by the City of London to oversee takeovers and mergers between companies and to ensure that they are not anti-competitive. Although many of its powers are now provided under the Companies Act 2006,[72] historically it enforced the privately agreed City Code on Take-overs and Mergers. In the mid-1980s a company called Datafin plc complained to the Panel that its rival bidders for another company had breached the code. When the panel refused to intervene, Datafin sought a judicial review. The Court of Appeal accepted that the Panel's decision could be reviewed:

> As an act of government it was decided that, in relation to take-overs, there should be a central self-regulatory body which would be supported and sustained by a periphery of statutory powers and penalties wherever non-statutory powers and penalties were insufficient or non-existent or where [European Union] requirements called for statutory provisions. No one could have been in the least surprised if the panel had been instituted and operated under the direct authority of statute law, since it operates wholly in the public domain . . . As government increasingly accepted the necessity for intervention to prevent fraud, it built on City institutions and mores, supplementing and reinforcing them as appeared necessary.[73]

---

[69] See *R (Al Rawi)* v *Secretary of State for Foreign and Commonwealth Affairs* [2006] EWCA Civ 1279; [2007] 2 WLR 1219, [148].

[70] See the Immigration Act 1971, s. 3(5)(b).

[71] See *R (Farrakhan)* v *Secretary of State for the Home Department* [2002] EWCA Civ 606; [2002] QB 1391.

[72] See Companies Act 2006, Part 28.

[73] *R* v *Panel on Takeovers and Mergers, ex parte Datafin plc* [1987] QB 815, 835–836 (Sir John Donaldson MR)

Thinking Point . . .

The ***Datafin*** decision sparked the debate between those supporting *ultra vires* and common law conceptions of the rule of law when Dawn Oliver, noting that a body not created under statute was nonetheless subject to judicial review, concluded that *ultra vires* theory was insufficient to explain judicial review (D. Oliver 'Is *Ultra Vires* the Basis of Judicial Review?' [1987] PL 543, 567).

Such circumstances, in which an important sphere of public life is regulated by a private body, are by no means unique to the City of London. The activities of bodies such as sports associations (like the Football Association[74]) and religious organisations[75] suddenly seemed to be susceptible to review. Nonetheless, the courts stepped back from such an extreme extension of the scope of administrative law.

Key case

R v *Jockey Club, ex parte Aga Khan* [1993] 2 All ER 853 (Court of Appeal)

The Jockey Club exercises responsibility for the organisation of horse racing in the UK. The club's powers and duties did not derive from primary or secondary legislation and its control was maintained through the issue of licences and permits to racecourse managers, owners, trainers and jockeys. His Highness the Aga Khan, a racehorse owner registered with the club, sought a judicial review of the Jockey Club's decision to disqualify one of his horses after a race 'win' due to the presence of a banned substance in a urine sample.

The Divisional Court held that although the Jockey Club exercised dominant control over racing activities and was formed under a Royal Charter (and theoretically under the Royal Prerogative) its powers were in no sense governmental but derived from the contractual relationship between the club and those bound by its 'Rules of Racing'. As such powers gave rise to private rights enforceable by private action and allowing for private law remedies, the club's decision was private in nature and not susceptible to judicial review.

Sir Thomas Bingham MR elaborated upon the ***ex parte Datafin*** approach to *de facto* powers, explaining (at 866–867) why the Jockey Club's decisions could be distinguished from those of the Take-Over Panel:

> I have little hesitation in accepting the applicant's contention that the Jockey Club effectively regulates a significant national activity, exercising powers which affect the public and are exercised in the interest of the public. I am willing to accept that if the Jockey Club did not regulate this activity the government would probably be driven to create a public body to do so . . . It has not been woven into any system of governmental control of horseracing, perhaps because it has itself controlled horseracing so successfully that there has been no need for any such governmental system and such does not therefore exist. This has the result that while the Jockey Club's powers may be described as, in many ways, public they are in no sense governmental.

---

[74] See *R* v *Football Association, ex parte Football League* [1993] 2 All ER 833.
[75] See *R* v *Chief Rabbi, ex parte Wachmann* [1992] 1 WLR 1036.

A *de facto* public function therefore emerges as not simply a power exercised by a private body 'in place' of government activity, but one which is 'woven into' a system of regulation otherwise provided under legislation or the royal prerogative. This position was affirmed in *West,* in which the claimant argued that the regulatory role played by Lloyd's of London in relation to insurance markets could be reviewed. The Court of Appeal, noted that the decisions being challenged were concerned solely with the commercial relationship between West and Lloyd's managing agents, which was governed by the contracts. Brooke LJ held that:

> It seems to me that the functions of Lloyd's which are under review in this case are totally different from the functions of the Takeover Panel that were under consideration in *ex p Datafin*. The Panel exercised regulatory control in a public sphere where governmental regulatory control was absent. This case is concerned with the working out of private contractual arrangements at Lloyd's which is itself subject to external governmental regulation.[76]

(iii) The nature of public functions

Not all functions exercised by a public body, such as a government department or university, are public in nature. Contracts for stationery by the National Health Service (NHS), for example, remain the subject of contract law in spite of the legislative basis of NHS procurement powers. Conversely, if a private body like the Panel on Takeovers and Mergers performs some public functions, we have seen that these functions will be reviewable even though the body itself may not be maintained by public funds or staffed by civil servants. Lord Irvine, whilst Lord Chancellor, gave a good example of when the actions of such a body will be reviewable:

> A private security company would be exercising public functions in relation to the management of a contracted-out prison but would be acting privately when, for example, guarding commercial premises.[77]

The blurring of the distinction between public and private bodies has been exacerbated by government decisions, from the 1980s onwards, to privatise industries and services which were previously run by the public sector (including railways and telecommunications). Such private companies could even fulfil statutory functions. More recently, the public sector has once again assumed control over failing privatised companies such as Railtrack (responsible for railway maintenance and renationalised as Network Rail), and even assumed majority holdings in banks in danger of collapse during the 2008 financial crisis. The cumulative effect of these upheavals is that the nature of the body exercising a function is not conclusive of whether or not it is a public function. Instead, as Dyson LJ asserted in the Court of Appeal in *Beer,* we must consider the nature of the function in question in deciding whether it is susceptible to judicial review:

> It seems to me that the law has now been developed to the point where, unless the source of power clearly provides an answer, the question whether the decision of a body is amenable to judicial review requires a careful consideration of the nature of the power and function that has been exercised to see whether the decision has a sufficient public element, flavour or character to bring it within the purview of public law. It may be said with some justification that this criterion for amenability is very broad, not to say question-begging. But it provides the framework for the investigation that has to be conducted.[78]

---

[76] *R (West)* v *Lloyd's of London* [2004] EWCA Civ 506; [2004] 3 All ER 251, [32].
[77] HL Debs, vol. 583, col. 811 (24 November 1997).
[78] *R (Beer)* v *Hampshire Farmers' Market Ltd* [2003] EWCA Civ 1056; [2004] 1 WLR 233, [16] (Dyson LJ).

In identifying whether a decision is susceptible to review, we must therefore assess whether it 'has a sufficient public element, flavour or character'. This calculation depends on how several factors combine in a particular case, including the source and nature of the power, the degree of involvement of 'pure' public bodies (like government departments or local authorities) and the degree to which the power is publically funded.

Key case

YL v Birmingham City Council and Southern Cross [2007] UKHL 27; [2007] 3 WLR 112 (House of Lords)

YL was a resident of a care home run by a healthcare company, Southern Cross. Her placement had been arranged by the respondent local authority, Birmingham City Council, which provided the bulk of the funding for the placement. Following allegations about the conduct of YL's family during visits, the care home sought to transfer her to a different home. In an effort to retain her place, YL invoked her Article 8 ECHR right to family life. At issue was whether a privately owned care home, when providing care to a resident pursuant to agreements made with a local authority acting under statute, was performing functions of a public nature Human Rights Act 1998.

Despite this specific Human Rights Act context, the House of Lords' decision that the care home was not a public body (as an effective 'part' of Birmingham City Council) remains one of the leading decisions on the scope of public authorities in public law. Lord Scott, one of the judges in the majority, explained his reasons for recognising that the care home provider was not a public body as follows (at [26]):

> Southern Cross is a company carrying on a socially useful business for profit. It is neither a charity nor a philanthropist. It enters into private law contracts with the residents in its care homes and with the local authorities with whom it does business. It receives no public funding, enjoys no special statutory powers, and is at liberty to accept or reject residents as it chooses (subject, of course, to anti-discrimination legislation which affects everyone who offers a service to the public) and to charge whatever fees in its commercial judgment it thinks suitable. It is operating in a commercial market with commercial competitors.

When Lord Scott describes Southern Cross as receiving no public money, he means as separate from the money received in business contracts with local authorities. Lord Neuberger went on to note that the mere fact that the Council could have alternately placed YL in one of its own care homes did not mean that the care home she was placed in became a public body for that reason (at [144]):

> On the other hand, I would not accept that the mere fact that a core public authority, even where it is the body funding the activity, could carry out the activity concerned must mean that the activity is such a function. Apart from anything else, there must scarcely be an activity which cannot be carried out by some core public authority.

Despite the divide between the judges in *YL*, all were grappling with whether a function is public in nature on the basis of a matrix of factors. What made *YL* so difficult was the degree to which these factors pointed in different directions. Often the decision is easier. The following two cases (Table 18.3) involve attempts to have the decisions of ostensibly private bodies (a pub-watch scheme and a community development trust) reviewed:

Table 18.3 Deciding whether ostensibly private bodies are subject to judicial review

Case	Power in question	Source of power	Involvement of public bodies	Public funding	Reviewable?
R (Boyle) v Haverhill Pub Watch [2009] EWHC 2441 (Admin)	Banning an individual from a network of pubs	Private Agreement between licence holders (but Pub Watch member-ship usually required by licence)	Low: council was one of the licensees and the local police 'initiate, encourage and provide administrative support' (see [55])	No public funding	No
R (Jenkins) v Marsh Farm Community Develop-ment Trust [2011] EWHC 1097 (Admin)	Disbursement of public funds for the benefit of Marsh Farm Estate	Statutory: ss. 126 to 128 of the Hous-ing Grants, Construction and Regen-eration Act 1996	Body 'stepped' into the shoes of national or local govern-ment, dis-bursing funds in their stead (see [84])	Fully publicly funded	Yes

(iv) The 'public/private divide' as control mechanism

The courts have therefore been willing to conceive the scope of judicial review relatively broadly, extending it to cover decisions of private bodies tasked with carrying out public functions (even, in the case of *de facto* powers, where these powers have not been provided by statute). Although these aspects of the jurisdiction are bounded by the procedural rules contained in Part 54 of the CPR, these provisions amount to, at best, a loose framework which encourages the courts to focus on the nature of the power in question regardless of whether the body exercising the power is obviously public in nature. Nonetheless, as the boundaries between public and private functions become more blurred, especially with private bodies exercising public functions on behalf of public bodies through the 'contracting out' of statutory duties, this focus on functions has forced the courts to accept that a growing number of different bodies are reviewable, at least in terms of some of their functions. If judicial review is to remain concerned with scrutinising public powers because of the unique risks should such powers be abused, the courts will have to continue with this complex task.

Who can seek a judicial review?

(i) The statutory basis of standing requirements

The Senior Courts Act 1981 prevents anyone from applying for judicial review of any government decision they choose. An individual seeking to challenge the exercise of a public function using judicial review must have standing (or '*locus standi*') to do so:

No application for judicial review shall be made unless the leave of the High Court has been obtained in accordance with rules of court; and the court shall not grant leave to make such an application unless it considers that the applicant has a sufficient interest in the matter to which the application relates.[79]

The requirement that a claimant must display 'sufficient interest' in a decision is in theory one of the most important considerations for the court at the permission stage of judicial review proceedings: 'if the applicant has no interest whatsoever and is, in truth, no more than a meddlesome busybody', then the court will not allow a judicial review to proceed.[80]

(ii) Judicial interpretation of standing requirements

In spite of claims of using standing requirements to weed out 'meddlesome busybodies', the courts moved towards a position where a wide range of claimants potentially fulfil the 'sufficient interest' test. These extensions have drawn fire from ministers. In the consultation document which preceded the 2015 reforms to judicial review the Ministry of Justice suggested revising the statutory test to 'require a more direct and tangible interest in the matter to which the application for judicial review relates'.[81] Ultimately, the Coalition Government backed down from these particular suggestions; as we are about to see, a broad basis for standing is essential if judicial review is to have a role in improving general standards of governance.

(a) Individuals/legal persons

Individuals and legal persons can seek standing on either of two bases, with the former being much more commonly asserted:

(1) direct personal interest;

(2) 'public interest' standing.

Cases in which a person directly affected by decision seeks a judicial review are the least controversial in terms of standing. If such individuals could not bring a claim, then no one would be able to seek a judicial review. In the case of *ex parte Hindley*, for example, a murderer challenged the Home Secretary's decision that she would never be eligible for parole. In spite of public opprobrium towards Hindley the Court affirmed that there was no question as to her ability to mount such a challenge to a decision with such a serious affect upon her, she remained 'entitled to the full measure of the protection of the law'.[82] Nonetheless, if a decision relates primarily to a particular person (such as a refusal to admit a pupil to a particular state school) and another person, in no way affected by that decision, sought to mount a challenge, then the courts would likely regard such a challenger as a busy-body. The 'simple cases'[83] in which a direct personal interest is evident are so uncontroversial that the ultimate judgments rarely even mention standing. Standing on the basis of direct personal interest is not restricted to individuals. Legal persons, such as companies or trade unions, can also claim

---

[79] Senior Courts Act 1981, s. 31(3).

[80] *R v Monopolies and Mergers Commission, ex parte Argyll Group* [1986] 1 WLR 763, 773 (Donaldson MR).

[81] Ministry of Justice, *Judicial Review: Proposals for Further Reform* (TSO, 2013) Cm. 8703, para. 80.

[82] *R v Secretary of State for the Home Department, ex parte Hindley* [2000] UKHL 21; [2001] 1 AC 410, [414] (Lord Steyn).

[83] *Inland Revenue Commissioners v National Federation of Self-Employed and Small Businesses Ltd* [1982] AC 617, 630.

to have a direct personal interest in decisions that affect them. When a body has legal personality, it means that it is treated in law as being distinct from its members or employees. We have already encountered examples of legal persons being accorded standing in cases such as Datafin plc's challenge against a decision by the Panel on Takeovers and Mergers.[84]

Whilst granting standing to persons who are directly affected by a decision provides a necessary foundation for judicial review, the courts recognise that limiting standing to such individuals would mean that many government decisions would not be amenable to review. When ministers make a decision over the allocation of overseas development funding out of public funds to particular projects, for example, it is impossible to say that anyone in the UK is particularly affected by this decision. All taxpayers are concerned equally with such a disbursement of public funds. In such circumstances, given the focus of judicial review upon ensuring that all government decision making accords with certain basic standards, the courts have been willing to allow standing to almost any potential claimant. This can be seen in the case of *ex parte Smedley* in which an individual, with no more interest in the decision than his capacity as a taxpayer and elector, sought to challenge the UK's annual contribution to the EU budget. The Court of Appeal did not throw out his claim on the basis of lack of standing, indeed, Slade LJ stated that 'I do not feel much doubt that Mr Smedley, if only in his capacity as a taxpayer, has sufficient *locus standi* to raise this question'.[85] Similarly, in *ex parte Rees Mogg,* an individual was granted standing to challenge the UK's signing of the Maastricht Treaty on the basis of his 'sincere concern for the constitutional issues'.[86] Both challenges were ultimately unsuccessful, but not for want of standing.

These cases amount to the courts accepting that any claimant who is willing to seek judicial review has a sufficient interest in a decision in instances where the degree of public interest in the decision is high. The culmination of this process can be seen in *Evans.* The peace campaigner Maya Evans sought a judicial review of the UK's policy of transferring individuals detained in the course of operations in Afghanistan to the Afghan authorities, on the basis that there was a real risk in many cases that, subsequent to the transfer, such detainees could suffer torture or serious mistreatment. She had no particular personal interest in these decisions, and as the court noted:

> The claim itself is brought in the public interest, with the benefit of public funding. It raises issues of real substance concerning the risk to transferees and, although the claimant's standing to bring it was at one time in issue, the point has not been pursued by the Secretary of State.[87]

The court went on to detail how the government's resistance to standing 'came to an end . . . in June 2009, following the emergence of fresh allegations of mistreatment of UK transferees'.[88] From the facts it can be deduced, with such 'fresh allegations' generating a public interest in the conduct of the UK's armed forces in Afghanistan, and with no person in a better position to challenge the activity than Maya Evans, that the government appreciated that the courts were unlikely to reject her claim for want of standing.

---

[84] See above, p. 520.
[85] *R v Her Majesty's Treasury, ex parte Smedley* [1985] QB 657, 670.
[86] *R v Secretary of State for Foreign and Commonwealth Affairs, ex parte Rees Mogg* [1994] QB 552, 562 (Lloyd LJ).
[87] *R (Evans) v Secretary of State for Defence* [2010] EWHC (Admin) 1445; [2011] ACD 11, [2].
[88] Ibid., [4].

(b) Non-governmental organisations

The expansion of standing evidenced in cases from *ex parte Smedley* to *Evans* is mirrored by the extension of standing to cover groups of individuals (unincorporated associations) who act together to bring a judicial review. The case of *Inland Revenue Commissioners v National Federation of Self-Employed and Small Businesses* marks the first signs of the courts appreciating the significance of the activities of pressure groups (also known as non-governmental organisations) seeking judicial reviews for good public administration. Casual workers in the newspaper industry had historically been able to claim their pay under names like 'Mickey Mouse', thereby avoiding taxation. The Inland Revenue reached a deal ending the practice, on the condition that the workers would not be pursued for the tax owed to date. The applicants, an interest group made up of businessmen, challenged this tax 'amnesty'.

Whilst the court ultimately accepted that an individual's taxes were not amenable to review by another, the Law Lords devoted considerable attention to the question of standing. In *obiter dicta* comments which opened up the scope both for 'public interest' claims and claims fronted by pressure groups, Lord Diplock asserted that:

> It would, in my view, be a grave lacuna in our system of public law if a pressure group, like the federation, or even a single public-spirited taxpayer, were prevented by outdated technical rules of *locus standi* from bringing the matter to the attention of the court to vindicate the rule of law and get the unlawful conduct stopped.[89]

The liberal basis for pressure group standing evinced in *Inland Revenue Commissioners* took a long time to gain broad acceptance within the courts:

Key debates

The expansion of pressure-group standing

To illustrate the incremental acceptance by the judiciary that standing considerations should not get in the way of the courts tackling a decision which breaches the rules of administrative law, consider the following cases.

The first involved the discovery of the Elizabethan-era Rose Theatre during a development in London. When the government refused to list the site as a monument, a pressure group campaigning for the preservation of the site challenged this decision. Schiemann J rejected this application (*R v Secretary of State for the Environment, ex parte Rose Theatre Trust* [1990] 1 QB 504), finding (at 522) that the trust had no more standing than any of its individual members and that the decision could not therefore be reviewed:

> [T]he law does not see it as the function of the courts to be there for every individual who is interested in having the legality of an administrative action litigated. Parliament could have given such a wide right of access to the court but it has not done so . . . Since, in my judgment, no individual has the standing to move for judicial review it follows, from what I ruled earlier, that the company created by those individuals has no standing.

→

---

[89] *Inland Revenue Commissioners* v *National Federation of Self-Employed and Small Businesses Ltd* [1982] AC 617, 644.

Although Schiemann J also ruled that the decision was valid, his decision opened up the possibility that illegal decisions might remain in force for want of a claimant with standing. But ***ex parte Rose Theatre Trust*** has been described as 'the last twitch of a dying doctrine' (Simon James, 'The Political and Administrative Consequences of Judicial Review' (1996) 74 *Public Administration* 613, 630). In the aftermath of the 2009 Gaza conflict a Palestinian non-governmental organisation launched a judicial review of the UK Government's failure to condemn Israel's actions (*R (Al-Haq)* v *Secretary of State for Foreign & Commonwealth Affairs* [2009] EWHC 1910 (Admin)). Despite ultimately rejecting the claim, Cranston J (at [61]) clearly asserted the importance of granting standing:

> The issue of standing had to be approached on the premises that there was a justiciable issue of public law arising out of grave human rights abuses and imperatives recognised in customary international law, and that the claim may be well-founded on the facts and evidence. If the claim were to fail it should fail because the premises were flawed; it would be unthinkable for the claim to fail for want of standing.

A good illustration of just how far public interest standing for NGOs has developed since ***ex parte Rose Theatre Trust*** came in *R (Plantagenet Alliance)* v *Secretary of State for Justice* [2014] EWHC 1662; [2015] 3 All ER 261. The claimant not-for-profit group challenged the decision to bury the newly-rediscovered remains of King Richard III in Leicester Cathedral. The Government opposed any suggestion that this group had standing to mount this challenge. Although the group represented some of Richard III's indirect descendants, the court (Hallett LJ, at [82]) considered that this 'may not suffice for personal standing'. In any event, they did not need to decide on this issue, being satisfied that 'the points raised have a broader public interest sufficient for the Claimant to have standing in this case as a public interest litigant'.

Sometimes pressure groups use one of their members to challenge a decision (as, for example, Amnesty International and the Redress Trust did in ***ex parte Bull***[90]). Such instances reflect an uncertainty regarding standing which is now out of step with developing case law. Today, pressure groups can assert that they have a 'sufficient interest' in a case on either (or both) of two broad bases:

(1) 'Representative' standing;

(2) 'Expertise' standing.

The case of ***ex parte Greenpeace*** involved a challenge to a decision by the Inspectorate of Pollution to permit activity at the THORP (thermal oxide reprocessing plant) at Sellafield, Cumbria. Otton J granted standing to the group to challenge the decision, in part on the basis that it had a sizable membership in the local area and these individuals were liable to be personally directly affected by any radioactive discharge from the plant.[91] Even if a group cannot be said to be a representative amalgam of individuals with a sufficient interest in a decision, the courts will nonetheless 'apply a liberal standing test to responsible, expert groups'.[92] This is illustrated by a case in which the World Development Movement challenged a £306 million low-interest loan by the UK Government towards the construction

---

[90] *R* v *DPP, ex parte Bull* [1998] 2 All ER 755.
[91] *R* v *Inspectorate of Pollution, ex parte Greenpeace (No. 2)* [1994] 4 All ER 329, 350–1.
[92] *R (Al-Haq)* v *Secretary of State for Foreign & Commonwealth Affairs* [2009] EWHC (Admin) 1910, [61] (Cranston J).

of the Pergau Dam in Malaysia.[93] The government sought to have the claim dismissed on the basis that neither the group nor its individual members had an interest in the decision. Rose LJ instead flagged up factors which he considered made granting standing essential:

> [T]here seem to me to be a number of factors of significance in the present case: the importance of vindicating the rule of law, . . . the importance of the issue raised, . . . the likely absence of any other responsible challenger, . . . the nature of the breach of duty against which relief is sought . . . and the prominent role of these applicants in giving advice, guidance and assistance with regard to aid.[94]

(c) Other public authorities

Finally, even public bodies may seek to have decisions judicially reviewed, if it is within their powers to do so. In *ex parte Equal Opportunities Commission* the EOC (now part of the Equality and Human Rights Commission) sought to challenge provisions of the Employment Protection (Consolidation) Act 1978 which it believed conflicted with EU law on the basis that they discriminated against female employees with regard to redundancy pay and compensation for unfair dismissal. Noting that the EOC was under a statutory duty to 'work towards the elimination of discrimination', Lord Keith asserted that any 'steps taken by the EOC towards securing that these provisions are changed may very reasonably be regarded as taken in the course of working towards the elimination of discrimination. The present proceedings are clearly such a step'.[95] In 2004 the courts were confronted by the odd sight of the then Home Secretary David Blunkett, a figure who as we have seen was intensely critical of many judicial review decisions, actually mounting such a challenge. Following severe criticism of the performance of Humberside Police during a high-profile murder investigation, Blunkett issued a letter requiring the Police Authority to suspend the Chief Constable of Humberside. When the Police Authority refused to do so, claiming that this was not a valid exercise of the Home Secretary's statutory powers, Blunkett went to court. Stanley Burnton J decided that the Home Secretary had 'validly exercised his power' and clearly had an interest in seeing his instructions carried into effect.[96] Even Home Secretaries appreciate the importance of judicial review's oversight function, at least in some cases.

(iii) Standing as a control mechanism

In summary, the growing importance of judicial review in recent decades has therefore been facilitated by the willingness of the courts to conceive standing in judicial review proceedings very broadly. Although this aspect of jurisdiction is covered by seemingly restrictive statutory rules, contained in section 31 of the Senior Courts Act 1981, the courts have approached the requirement of 'sufficient interest' in a case flexibly, to allow claimants

---

[93] *R v Secretary of State for Foreign and Commonwealth Affairs, ex parte World Development Movement* [1995] 1 WLR 386.

[94] Ibid., 395.

[95] *R v Secretary of State for Employment, ex parte Equal Opportunities Commission* [1995] 1 AC 1, 26.

[96] *R (Secretary of State for the Home Department)* v *Humberside Police Authority* [2004] EWHC (Admin) 1642, [13].

to essentially mount challenges in the public interest where a decision may otherwise go unreviewed. The reason for this approach is ably summarised by Lord Diplock:

> The rules as to 'standing' for the purpose of [judicial review] . . . were made by judges, by judges they can be changed; and so they have been over the years to meet the need to preserve the integrity of the rule of law despite changes in the social structure, methods of government and the extent to which the activities of private citizens are controlled by governmental authorities, that have been taking place continuously, sometimes slowly, sometimes swiftly . . . Those changes have been particularly rapid since World War II.[97]

Having fended off the latest reform proposals the rules for standing remain substantially within the hands of the courts and they continue to use them, as Lord Diplock foresaw, to ensure that important decisions do not escape the ambit of legal control.

Time limits for judicial review

(i) The three-month (maximum) time limit

The time limits imposed upon judicial review claims are much stricter than the time limits in ordinary civil law cases, such as tort or contract, in which claimants enjoy up to six years from the breach of obligation to prepare their claim.[98] For judicial review proceedings Part 54 of the CPR mandates the following:

> A claim for permission must be filed –
>
> (a) promptly; and
> (b) in any event not later than 3 months after the grounds to make the claim first arose.[99]

The Coalition Government introduced even tighter time limits for reviews of planning (six weeks)[100] and public procurement decisions (30 days).[101] If either of these requirements is breached, the courts have the option to under the Senior Courts Act 1981 to refuse 'leave for the making of the application'[102] or 'any relief sought on the application'.[103] It should be noted, however, that these consequences for a late claim remain optional.[104] The courts can differentiate between particular claims in imposing these time limits on the basis of whether delayed judicial review proceedings 'would be detrimental to good administration'.[105] We therefore need to assess how strictly they have employed this control mechanism on the jurisdiction in practice.

(ii) The time limit as a control mechanism

A concern regarding the delay which judicial review imposes upon the exercise of public functions is a frequent concern amongst officials, including claims in the 1990s (which

---

[97] *Inland Revenue Commissioners* v *National Federation of Self-Employed and Small Businesses Ltd* [1982] AC 617, 639–40.
[98] See Limitation Act 1980, ss. 2 and 5.
[99] Civil Procedure Rules 2000 (SI 2000/2092) Rule 54.5(1).
[100] Ibid., Rule 54.5(5).
[101] Rule 54.5(6).
[102] Senior Courts Act 1981, s. 31(6)(a).
[103] Ibid., s. 31(6)(b).
[104] See D. Oliver, 'Public Law Procedures and Remedies: Do we need them?' [2002] PL 91, 98–9.
[105] Senior Courts Act 1981, s. 31(6).

were reheated ahead of the 2015 reforms) that '[s]ome environmental groups are making quite deliberate use of this tactic to delay the building of new roads'.[106] The courts seem to accept the potential for mischief should these time limits be set aside, even when a claim might otherwise be meritorious. In the wake of riots at Hull Prison a large number of inmates were disciplined. Several alleged that the Prison Board's disciplinary decisions against them had been reached as a result of unfair procedures, successfully seeking a judicial review.[107] Following this decision, other similarly affected prisoners attempted to challenge the disciplinary proceedings against them. However, because these prisoners had missed the judicial review time limit, they instituted a private law action against the prison governor. The House of Lords rejected this effort to circumvent judicial review time limits, with Lord Diplock asserting that:

> The public interest in good administration requires that public authorities and third parties should not be kept in suspense as to the legal validity of a decision . . . for any longer than is absolutely necessary in fairness to the person affected.[108]

In some cases, even a challenge brought within the three-month time limit has been rejected by the courts for being insufficiently 'prompt'.[109] When Swale Borough Council approved a land-reclamation scheme in a wetland area, the Royal Society for the Protection of Birds (RSPB) challenged this decision on the basis that it had been made without proper consideration for the environmental impact of the scheme. Although the RSPB sought permission just within the three-month time limit, the High Court found that it had delayed in making this challenge and refused permission for judicial review on the basis that, permitting a challenge at this late stage would have imposed large financial losses.[110]

Thinking Point . . .

By way of contrast to **ex parte RSPB,** consider *R (Buglife)* v *Natural England* [2011] EWHC 746 (Admin), [65], where Judge Anthony Thornton QC accepted that judicial review 520 proceedings initiated only two days short of the three-month time limit could continue in light of 'the limited prejudice shown to have resulted from the three-month delay and the public importance of this particular application'.

Judicial review and procedural exclusivity

The factors listed above explain the key features of judicial review procedure and when the jurisdiction can be accessed by claimants. But the distinctive nature of the

---

[106] S. James, 'The Political and Administrative Consequences of Judicial Review' (1996) 74 *Public Administration* 613, 619.

[107] *R v Board of Visitors of Hull Prison, ex parte St Germain (No. 2)* [1979] 1 WLR 1401.

[108] *O'Reilly* v *Mackman* [1983] 2 AC 237, 280–1.

[109] Civil Procedure Rules 2000 (SI 2000/2092) Rule 54.5(1)(a).

[110] *R v Swale Borough Council, ex parte Royal Society for the Protection of Birds* [1991] JPL 39.

jurisdiction, imposing particular standards on the exercise of a function because it is public in nature, gives rise to particular questions:

(1) Can a claimant seek judicial review even if other means of redress are available?

(2) Does judicial review have to be sought when available or can the claimant seek other means of redress?

At first glance, these questions appear very similar. The distinction lies in the position of the claimant. Under the first question, the claimant is seeking to pursue a claim before the administrative court even though they could make a claim within another forum. Under the second, the issue is whether a claimant using another forum should have instead pursued judicial review. We will consider each scenario in turn.

(i) Judicial review: a jurisdiction of last resort?

If another avenue is available by which to make a claim, for example through contract, tort, or employment law, the courts can refuse to hear a judicial review or grant remedies.[111] In the *YL* case,[112] considered above,[113] one of the factors which weighed heavily on the mind of the judges in the majority who found that Southern Cross, the care home provider, could not be subjected to judicial review for removing the claimant from its care home, was that 'it enters into private law contracts with the residents in its care homes and with the local authorities with whom it does business'.[114]

Even where a measure is 'public' in nature, Parliament can establish a specialist forum in which claims must be heard (to the exclusion of judicial review). For example, when the government proscribes a group as a terrorist organisation or for supporting terrorism, members of the group can appeal to the Proscribed Organisations Appeal Commission (POAC). As judicial review operates as a backstop, the courts have held that provided that such 'specialist' tribunals have an adequate remit to review executive actions, claimants cannot ignore them and seek instead to use judicial review.[115] In most cases in which a statutory right of appeal to a specific body exists, the courts will 'as a matter of discretion expect the right of appeal to be exercised and will consequently refuse relief'.[116] Nonetheless, it must be noted that public law powers relating to benefit claimants and prisoners lack effective alternative avenues for challenge and therefore constitute the bulk of the courts' judicial review workload. Rather than reject a claim outright on the basis that it was mistakenly made under judicial review, the court may, under Part 54 of the CPR, issue an order transferring the claim to another judicial body.[117] Reclassifying a case as a private law claim will, however, prevent a claimant from relying upon the special public law grounds of review which may have provided the basis of their case.

---

[111] See *R v Inland Revenue Commissioners, ex parte Preston* [1985] AC 835, 862 (Lord Templeman).

[112] *YL v Birmingham City Council* [2007] UKHL 27; [2007] 3 WLR 112.

[113] See p. 525.

[114] *YL v Birmingham City Council* [2007] UKHL 27; [2007] 3 WLR 112, [26] (Lord Scott).

[115] *R (PKK) v Secretary of State for the Home Department* [2002] EWHC (Admin) 644, [76] (Richards J).

[116] *R (DR) v Head Teacher of St George's Catholic School* [2002] EWCA Civ 1822; [2003] LGR 371, [54] (Keene LJ).

[117] Civil Procedure Rules 2000 (SI 2000/2092) Rule 54.20.

(ii) Judicial review as the exclusive jurisdiction for public law claims

On the other side of the coin, what of public law claims initiated in error through ordinary civil proceedings? Whilst theoretically the courts could simply transfer these into the more appropriate judicial review jurisdiction, it is unlikely that claimants who have made such an error will have acted within the strict three-month time limit required for a judicial review. Historically the courts have taken a very dim view of such actions. In *O'Reilly* v *Mackman* the House of Lords treated such a claim as an effort to evade 'the safeguards imposed in the public interest against groundless, unmeritorious or tardy attacks upon the validity of decisions made by public authorities in the field of public law',[118] and unceremoniously rejected it.

This, however, has proven a hard benchmark to follow in subsequent cases. The danger with conceiving of judicial review as an 'exclusive' jurisdiction is that meritorious claimants might be excluded from court. In many cases which should theoretically be heard in judicial review the divide between public and private law issues is not clear. Indeed, as Lord Lowry recognised in *Roy* v *Kensington and Chelsea FPC*, even in cases where judicial review is the theoretically preferable forum, private law interests may 'dominate the proceedings',[119] lulling all but the best prepared claimants down the path of ordinary civil proceedings. In this case a doctor brought an action against his Family Practitioner Committee after it withheld part of his allowance on the basis that he had failed to devote a sufficient amount of his time to general practice. Lord Bridge refused to invoke a strict divide between public and private law claims:

> Whatever remuneration [Dr Roy] is entitled to under the statement is remuneration he has duly earned by the services he has rendered. The circumstance that the quantum of that remuneration . . . is affected by a discretionary decision made by the committee cannot deny the doctor his private law right of recovery or subject him to the constraints which the necessity to seek judicial review would impose upon that right.[120]

Thereafter, in *Clark,* the Court of Appeal acknowledged that in such 'grey-area' cases (this particular case involved a student, who enjoyed a contractual relationship with her university, challenging an exercise of its discretionary powers to classify degrees), provided that the claimant did not set out to flout the procedural rules of judicial review and that public administration was not jeopardised as a result, a private law claim would not be rejected out-of-hand.[121]

Limiting judicial review: no prospect of changing outcomes

Section 84 of the Criminal Justice and Courts Act 2015 asserts that a court should refuse judicial review (or at least refuse a remedy) where it appears to be highly likely that the outcome for the claimant would not have been substantially different if the conduct

---

[118] *O'Reilly* v *Mackman* [1983] 2 AC 237, 282 (Lord Diplock).
[119] *Roy* v *Kensington and Chelsea Family Practitioner Committee* [1992] 1 AC 624, 654 (Lord Lowry).
[120] Ibid., 630.
[121] *Clark* v *University of Lincolnshire and Humberside* [2000] 1 WLR 1988, [39] (Lord Woolf MR).

complained of had not happened.[122] This is a controversial provision, for it seems to strike at the heart of the idea that judicial review is not simply focused on remedying a wrong done to a claimant but on improving standards of public administration. Resistance to the proposals in Parliament, however, seem to have neutered the effect of this provision, for the Government was obliged to concede that the courts could ignore this condition when it is appropriate to do so for reasons of public interest.[123]

Remedies available under judicial review

Key issues

- The public law remedies (mandatory orders, prohibiting orders and quashing orders) are only available when a claimant uses judicial review.
- The private law remedies (declarations and injunctions) may be sought through judicial review but have to be sought through judicial review if a claimant requests them alongside a public law remedy.
- Damages are very rarely issued under judicial review, and may only be sought alongside a public law remedy.
- All of these remedies are discretionary; a court does not have to provide a remedy where a public function is used wrongfully.

The public law remedies

Judicial review makes a variety of remedies available which claimants can pursue individually or in any combination. The correct remedy for a claimant to seek depends on the activity that he is seeking to challenge. As Part 54 of the CPR makes clear, these 'public law' remedies are only available where a claimant seeks judicial review: (a) a mandatory order; (b) a prohibiting order; (c) a quashing order.[124] In contrast to private law claims, however, none of these remedies has to be awarded to a successful claimant. These remedies may be awarded to a successful claimant at the discretion of the court, but they may be withheld where it is in the public interest to do so. Lord Bingham, writing extra-judicially, considered that this flexibility over remedies was a necessary feature of judicial review, because in certain cases 'adverse public consequences would ensue from the grant of the remedy' or the case may cover a sphere of government activity 'in which the courts are reluctant to intrude'.[125] Consider the following case, which demonstrates the courts refusing to provide a judicial review remedy despite recognising a claim's merits:

---

[122] Amending the Senior Courts Act 1981, s. 31.
[123] Ibid., s. 31(2B).
[124] Civil Procedure Rules 2000 (SI 2000/2092) Rule 54.2. See also the Senior Courts Act 1981, s. 31(1)(a).
[125] T. Bingham, 'Should Public Law Remedies be Discretionary?' [1991] PL 64, 74.

Key case

R (Hurley and Moore) v Secretary of State for Business Innovation & Skills [2012] EWHC (Admin) 201; [2012] HRLR 13 (High Court)

This case involved a challenge by two teenagers, Katy Moore and Callum Hurley, to the Higher Education (Higher Amount) Regulations 2010 (SI 2010/3020), which raised university tuition fees in England to a maximum of £9,000. They attempted to persuade the court (amongst other arguments) that the government had breached its Public Sector Equality Duty (PSEDs) under section 149 of the Equality Act 2010, which require that consideration be given to whether decisions have a disproportionate (and hence, potentially indirectly discriminatory) impact on groups within society protected on the basis of characteristics such as race, gender and disabilities.

The Court evaluated whether fee increases would have a discriminatory effect upon participation in university by protected groups (such as students from lower socio-economic backgrounds). Elias LJ concluded that general consideration of opportunities for access to higher education was not equivalent to conducting the range of Equality Impact Assessments required by law. The Government was therefore in breach of the PSED requirements (at [96]); 'I cannot discount the possibility that a more precise focus on the specific statutory duties might have led to the conclusion that some other requirements were potentially engaged and merited consideration'.

The court nonetheless refused to quash the Higher Education (Higher Amount) Regulations. Exemplifying the flexibility of remedies in administrative law, Elias LJ recognised that the requested remedy would have such far-reaching ramifications as to render it inappropriate (at [99]):

> [A]ll the parties affected by these decisions – Government, universities and students – have been making plans on the assumption that the fees would be charged. It would cause administrative chaos, and would inevitably have significant economic implications, if the regulations were now to be quashed.

The court, therefore, simply declared that a breach of PSED had occurred. Given that the decision was reached in February 2012 (just months before the first affected students entered university in September 2012), Elias LJ concluded that quashing the Regulations would result in more harm to public administration than good.

(i) Quashing orders – formerly *certiorari*

Quashing orders strike down a decision, rendering it void from inception, either because the decision itself, or the manner in which it is made, is unlawful. If the latter, this does not mean that the judge disputes the merits of the decision, but rather that she finds that there is something wrong with *how* it has been made. It is possible that the public body will reconsider its decision following adequate procedures and be able to reach the same conclusion. Having quashed a decision the court may:

(a) (i) remit the matter to the decision-maker; and
     (ii) direct it to reconsider the matter and reach a decision in accordance with the judgment of the court; or
(b) in so far as any enactment permits, substitute its own decision for the decision to which the claim relates.[126]

---

[126] Civil Procedure Rules 2000 (SI 2000/2092) Rule 54.19(2).

> ### Thinking Point . . .
>
> In *R (Ali)* v *Secretary of State for the Home Department* [2003] EWHC 899 (Admin), [31], Goldring J maintained that even after a decision had been quashed, 'dependent upon reconsideration on sufficient and proper evidence, the Secretary of State may reach exactly the same decision.'

(ii) Prohibiting orders – formerly *prohibition*

Where a decision has been reached wrongfully but not yet carried into effect, the courts can use a prohibiting order to prevent a public body from acting upon the decision.

(iii) Mandatory orders – formerly *mandamus*

Mandatory orders essentially function as the 'flip side' of prohibiting orders. They are concerned with preventing wrongful *inaction* by a public body, rather than stopping wrongful actions. Using these orders the courts can compel a public body to use its powers where it is found to have wrongfully decided not to do so. Mandatory orders cannot be used to compel a decision maker to use one of his discretionary powers, but only apply where a public body is failing to perform a statutory or common law duty.

The private law remedies

(i) Declarations and injunctions

Judicial review procedure may also be used where the claimant seeks the following remedies which historically developed in private actions: (a) a declaration; or (b) an injunction.[127] As these are private law remedies they do not have to be sought using judicial review, unless they are sought alongside a public law remedy. Injunctions serve like prohibiting orders; they stop a decision from being carried into effect. More usefully, they can be sought on an *interim* basis. This allows courts to temporarily suspend the operation of a decision (say for the duration of litigation). Such a suspension ensures that a claimant does not lose out whilst their challenge is on-going. Declarations, on the other hand, are non-coercive remedies. They simply amount to the court delivering an authoritative statement on the law at issue in a case. They may therefore be useful where a litigant seeks to persuade a public authority to act in a particular manner, without being so confrontational as to seek one of the public law remedies.

(ii) Damages

Under Part 54 of the CPR the courts have some scope to provide a claimant with damages when sought alongside the public law remedies: 'A claim for judicial review may include a claim for damages, restitution or the recovery of a sum due but may not seek such a remedy alone.'[128] Crucially, however, the Senior Courts Act 1981 lays down the additional requirement that for the courts to accede to a claim for damages in judicial review, a private law claim

---

[127] Ibid., Rule 54.3(1). See also the Senior Courts Act 1981, s. 31(1)(b).
[128] Ibid., Rule 54.3(2). See also the Senior Courts Act 1981, s. 31(4).

would have to succeed on the same facts.[129] The Law Commission postulated a scenario which flags up the inadequacies of this situation. It envisages a case in which a complainant successfully argues that a decision by a public body has prevented her from engaging in a commercial activity, and a court quashes this decision as the result of a judicial review action:

> On one view, the applicant has obtained what he or she wanted and will thus be content. On another view, the applicant will have been unable to pursue the commercial activity from the time of the original decision until the time of the later decision. That period may have been several weeks or months. The profits which the applicant could have made in that period had he or she not wrongfully been refused the licence might be significant.[130]

All that can be said, under the present law, is that such a claimant may be provided with some compensation by the public authority in question on an 'ex gratia' basis, but it will be under no legal obligation to do so.

Conclusion

This chapter has attempted to explain how, no matter the political controversies in which judicial review might embroil the courts, judges today generally accept that judicial oversight over whether a public function has been exercised lawfully and fairly is a requisite feature of a modern system of government: 'It is a commonplace of modern law that [public] bodies must act fairly and that the courts have power to redress unfairness'.[131] In their eagerness to exercise this oversight function, the courts have loosened many of the strictures, like standing requirements, which have historically constrained the exercise of judicial review. This process may have caused considerable ministerial discontent, culminating in the Criminal Justice and Courts Act 2015. But even this legislation did not attempt to challenge the core features of judicial review, it instead sought to make instituting a challenge a less attractive option for claimants. No Parliament, therefore, has sought to reverse the expansion of judicial review, and its general role within UK public administration has become increasingly secure.

Practice questions

1. 'Judicial review is the exercise of the court's inherent power at common law to determine whether action is lawful or not; in a word to uphold the rule of law.'

   (R v HM the Queen in Council, ex parte Vijayatunga [1988] QB 322, 343 (Simon Brown J))

   Evaluate whether this statement accurately summarises the function of the judicial review jurisdiction within the UK Constitution.

2. 'For the sake of promoting efficient public decision-making, judicial review has been weakened by the Criminal Justice and Courts Act 2015, and with it the protection of the rule of law.'

   (A. Mills, 'Reforms to Judicial Review in the Criminal Justice and Courts Act 2015: Promoting Efficiency or Weakening the Rule of Law?' [2015] PL 583, 593–594)

   Evaluate whether the Coalition Government's reforms of judicial review warrant such criticism.

---

[129] Senior Courts Act 1981, s. 31(4).
[130] Law Commission, *Monetary Remedies in Public Law: A Discussion Paper* (11 October 2004), para. 2.12.
[131] *HTV Ltd* v *Price Commission* [1976] ICR 170, 189 (Scarman LJ).

Further reading

This chapter aims to provide both an overview of the workings of judicial review and an explanation of the theory underpinning the jurisdiction. The suggested reading that follows mirrors this divide. With this chapter fresh in mind it is a good idea to get an administrator's view of judicial review, to get a flavour of how public bodies regard the work of the courts in this sphere. Simon James (**S. James, 'The Political and Administrative Consequences of Judicial Review'** (1996) 74 *Public Administration* 613–38) captures the fast moving nature of the jurisdiction, even if his overall account of the courts' oversight of the administrative process is generally negative. On the other side of the coin, judicial review claimants are often confronted by standing criteria which can seem very difficult to navigate. Edite Legere's short article (**E. Legere, '*Locus Standi* and the Public Interest: a Hotchpotch of Legal Principles'** [2005] *Judicial Review* 128–34) provides a useful overview of just how many different standing criteria now exist in various branches of public law beyond the ordinary judicial review test for standing. Where the controversial issue of whether a body is 'public' in nature is at issue (a factor determinative of whether its actions are reviewable), Colin Campbell's work (**C. Campbell, 'The Nature of Power as Public in English Judicial Review'** [2009] 68 *Cambridge Law Journal* 90–117) should be required reading. Noting that the courts have developed a number of tests for approaching the question of whether a particular function, as opposed to an organisation, is public in nature, Campbell investigates the centrality of the public–private divide to judicial review.

Once readers are comfortable with their understanding of the workings of judicial review, they should attempt to engage with the competing theories behind the jurisdiction. Justin Leslie (**J. Leslie, 'Vindicating Common Law Constitutionalism'** (2010) 30 *Legal Studies* 301–323) provides a detailed consideration of 'common law constitutionalism', deploying case law in support of the doctrine and attempting to establish that this doctrine best summarises how the courts perceive their role when undertaking judicial reviews. On the other hand, dismissing much of the debate between proponents of *ultra vires* and common law theories of judicial review as missing the most controversial aspects of the judiciary's constitutional role, T. R. S. Allan (**T. Allan, 'The Constitutional Foundations of Judicial Review: Conceptual Conundrum or Interpretative Inquiry?'** [2002] 61 *Cambridge Law Journal* 87–125) sets out to examine the nature and legitimacy of the judicial function. Allan's critique is worth reading as an argument which builds upon the underlying *ultra vires*/common law debate.

Chapter 19
Judicial review of administrative action – grounds for review

'To the famous question . . . "Is it not lawful for me to do what I will with mine own?" . . . the modern answer would be clear: "Yes, subject to such regulatory and other constraints as the law imposes." But if the same question were posed by a [public body] the answer would be different. It would be: "No, it is not lawful for you to do anything save what the law expressly or impliedly authorises. You enjoy no unfettered discretions. There are legal limits to every power you have".'

Sir Thomas Bingham in *R* v *Somerset County Council, ex parte Fewings* [1995] 1 WLR 1037, 1042

Chapter outline

In the last chapter, we saw that judicial review is not the same as an appeal against a lower court's decision. The courts will only intervene in the operation of a public function on the basis of particular criteria. The longest-established and least controversial of these criteria is illegality, which at its most limited involves the courts checking that lawful authority exists for a decision maker's actions (fundamental to even the most limited conceptions of the rule of law). The courts, however, have developed further grounds for judicial review beyond this core function. Even if a decision maker has lawful authority for an action, the courts may still scrutinise its activity on the basis that there was no rational basis for the action (controversially requiring the courts to consider the reasoning behind a decision) or on the basis that adequate procedural safeguards where not operative within the decision-making process (which can, controversially, involve the courts introducing procedural requirements upon exercises of a power beyond those imposed by Parliament). Finally, in recent decades judicial review has extended to protecting the interests of claimants who received specific promises from a decision maker, preventing the decision maker from reneging upon those promises without good reason.

Introduction

As Lord Bingham makes clear in the opening quotation, judicial review remains a limited jurisdiction in which the courts supervise the operation of a public function to ensure that key requirements of good governance are met. From the outset, we have to remember that it would be beyond the constitutional remit of the courts to substitute their own opinion of a policy for that of elected decision makers or the officials subordinate to them simply because they did not approve of a decision. Instead, the courts test a decision's validity against various 'heads' of judicial review which they have developed under this jurisdiction. As judicial review expanded from the late twentieth century onwards, several judges attempted to classify the heads of judicial review then available in public law. Lord Templeman provided a traditional account of the heads of review in *ex parte Preston:* 'Judicial review is available where a decision-making authority exceeds its powers, commits an error of law, commits a breach of natural justice, reaches a decision which no reasonable tribunal could have reached, or abuses its powers'.[1] Although these concepts remain features of judicial review, in the **GCHQ** case[2] Lord Diplock recast the heads of review to better describe the modern operation of the jurisdiction:

> Judicial review has I think developed to a stage today when . . . one can conveniently classify under three heads the grounds upon which administrative action is subject to control by judicial review. The first ground I would call 'illegality', the second 'irrationality' and the third 'procedural impropriety'.[3]

This approach rolls acting in excess of powers, abuse of powers and committing errors of law into the 'illegality' head of review. It provides a flexible platform which has seen new sub-headings develop within these main heads of review. Nonetheless, because the older terms are employed in cases up to the mid-1980s and are occasionally still used, we need to be able to map them to Lord Diplock's taxonomy:

Traditional terminology	Lord Diplock's GCHQ terminology
Ultra vires	Illegality
Unreasonableness	Irrationality
Breach of natural justice	Procedural impropriety

In this chapter we will consider each of these heads in turn, together with a fourth head, based on the 'legitimate expectations' of the claimant which remained nascent at the time Lord Diplock set out his list of grounds.

These heads of judicial review do not operate in isolation from each other. When the facts allow, multiple heads can be raised in a single judicial review action. Together they give the courts a relatively broad scope on which to intervene in the decision-making process. The relationship between review and appeal is best conceived as a continuum, with full appellate jurisdiction and simple review of legality at opposite ends of the spectrum (see Figure 19.1). When, as we saw in the last chapter, the judicial review jurisdiction lay

---

[1] *R* v *Inland Revenue Commissioners, ex parte Preston* [1985] AC 835, 862.
[2] *Council of Civil Service Unions* v *Minister for the Civil Service* [1985] AC 374.
[3] Ibid., 410.

Setting the scene

Although the heads of review together expand the jurisdiction along the Review/Appeal continuum, judicial review remains much more limited than appeal against a decision:

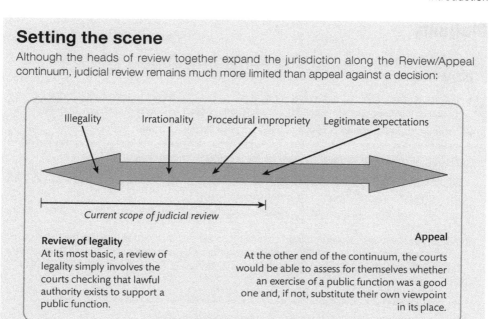

Illegality   Irrationality   Procedural impropriety   Legitimate expectations

Current scope of judicial review

Review of legality
At its most basic, a review of legality simply involves the courts checking that lawful authority exists to support a public function.

Appeal
At the other end of the continuum, the courts would be able to assess for themselves whether an exercise of a public function was a good one and, if not, substitute their own viewpoint in its place.

Figure 19.1 The review/appeal continuum

virtually idle for much of the twentieth century,[4] the courts retreated along the continuum to the point where they were satisfied that the requirements of administrative law were met simply on the basis that a decision was not illegal. In the old judicial review terminology a decision would have to be *'ultra vires'*, literally beyond the powers of the decision maker, before the courts would intervene (on the basis that the actions of decision makers were legitimated by the democratic process and the courts lacked similar legitimacy to intervene).

Since the 1960s the rise of modern judicial review has seen the courts testing the compatibility of public functions against long-moribund concepts such as unreasonableness (now called irrationality) and the principles of natural justice (the requirements of procedural propriety) and developing new restraints upon decision makers (the doctrine of legitimate expectations). The combined operation of these heads pushed judicial review further along the spectrum towards appeal as the courts sought to compensate for inadequacies in the political oversight of the decision-making process. As we will see in Chapter 21, this shift has been reinforced by the enactment of the Human Rights Act 1998, which has provided the courts with new grounds on which to challenge the operation of public functions.[5] For now, it is important to recognise that the further judicial review expands along this spectrum, the more executive actors will object that the courts lack the legitimacy to challenge their decisions.

---

[4] See pp. 507–10.
[5] See pp. 651–60.

Illegality

Key issues

- Administrative actions can be *ultra vires* for a number of different reasons, which can be grouped together under the headings of acting in excess of power and abuse of power.

- Where a decision maker is found to have acted in excess of power, the courts have assessed the scope of the power in question and determined that the decision maker has lacked the authority to make a decision, for one of the following reasons:

  (i)   exceeding the limits of a public function;

  (ii) unauthorised delegation of a public function;

  (iii) the decision maker has committed errors of law or fact.

- More controversially, the courts can also find that the decision maker abused their power. This means that even though the decision maker did possess a sufficient power to reach a certain decision, its lawfulness is thrown into question by considerations of how the power has been used, such as:

  (i)   exercising a public function on the basis of irrelevant considerations;

  (ii) exercising a public function to further improper purposes;

  (iii) the decision maker has fettered its discretion.

The concept of illegality/*ultra vires*

Having famously reclassified the heads of judicial review in the *GCHQ* case, Lord Diplock proceeded to succinctly define what was involved in review under each head. His first head of review, 'illegality', is the bedrock on which the rest of the jurisdiction is built:

> By 'illegality' as a ground for judicial review I mean that the decision-maker must understand correctly the law that regulates his decision-making power and must give effect to it. Whether he has or not is *par excellence* a justiciable question to be decided, in the event of dispute, by those persons, the judges, by whom the judicial power of the state is exercisable.[6]

In other words, assessing whether there is a legal basis for a public authority's actions is essential to the 'core' rule of law (discussed in Chapter 6[7]). Without illegality as a head of review the courts could not hope to ensure government by law. The central importance of this head of review to even a core (Diceyan) conception of the rule of law meant that even when the courts operated a very restricted version of judicial review from the First World War until the 1960s, they continued to test government decisions for illegality. During litigation arising out of slum clearance schemes in the 1920s Lord Thankerton continued to maintain that 'unless Parliament expressly excludes the jurisdiction of the Court, the Court has the right and duty to decide whether the Minister has acted within the limits of his delegated power'.[8] The courts have since expanded the concept of illegality to encompass not only situations where a public authority clearly exceeds its mandate, but also circumstances in which otherwise lawful powers are exercised improperly.

---

[6] *Council of Civil Service Unions* v *Minister for the Civil Service* [1985] AC 374, 410.
[7] See pp. 187–99.
[8] *Minister of Health* v *The King (on the Prosecution of Yaffe)* [1931] AC 494, 532.

Thinking Point . . .

For much of the twentieth century, a basic conception of illegality was not simply central to judicial review, it was all there was to the jurisdiction. In *Theodore* v *Duncan* [1919] AC 696, 706, the House of Lords held that, in relation to the discretion of the ministers, 'no Court of law can interfere so long as no provision enacted by the Legislature is infringed. The ministers are responsible for the exercise of their functions to the Crown and to Parliament only, and cannot be controlled by any outside authority, so long as they do nothing that is illegal'.

Acting in excess of powers

(i) Exceeding the limits of a public function

If illegality is the core of judicial review, then the rule that public bodies cannot exceed the limits of their power is central to the concept of illegality. Finding these limits is often a matter of evaluating the statutory provisions which grant a power but this head of judicial review, as with the others, applies equally to powers derived from the royal prerogative or secondary legislation. When a judicial review involves statutory powers the courts are not challenging the legality of those statutory rules but assessing the compatibility of the actions of a public body with those rules:

> The common law does not control Parliament, and if Parliament confers on a Minister a power to make regulations, how can the court enquire into these regulations beyond ascertaining whether they are within the power?[9]

This statement by Lord Greene MR, made in the immediate aftermath of the Second World War, indicates that even at a time when the courts approached judicial review restrictively judges remained willing to supervise whether a public body was acting 'within [its] power'.

(a) Express limitations upon a public function must be respected

The proposition that a public body's decision can be found unlawful if it acted on the basis of a power which it did not possess is relatively straightforward. For example, under section 74 of the Housing Act 1936, local authorities were granted authority to compulsorily acquire land for the provision of houses for the working classes. Section 75, however, created a specific exception; the Act did not authorise the compulsory acquisition of land 'which at the date of the compulsory purchase forms part of any park, garden or pleasure ground'. Ripon Borough Council attempted to use this power to purchase land which included part of Highfield park. In *White & Collins* v *Minister of Health* this purchase was found to be unlawful:

> I am satisfied that there was no evidence . . . sufficient to entitle the local authority or the Minister to come to a conclusion that the land in question was not part of the park of Highfield . . . In these circumstances it seems to me plain that there was no jurisdiction in the Ripon Borough Council to make or in the Minister to confirm the order for compulsory purchase.[10]

---

[9] *Taylor* v *Brighton Borough Council* [1947] KB 736, 739 (Lord Greene MR).
[10] *White & Collins* v *Minister of Health* [1939] 2 KB 838, 859 (Luxmoore LJ).

Other cases are more complex. *Attorney-General* v *Fulham Corporation* concerned whether a power to run a washhouse (to allow people to wash their clothes) under the Baths and Washhouses Acts 1846 and 1847 permitted the local authority in Fulham to establish a home-delivery laundry service. Sargant J ruled that all public authorities must identify some affirmative powers which provide authority for their actions:

> [I]n every case it is for a corporation of this kind to show that it has affirmatively an authority to do particular acts; but that in applying that principle, the rule is not to be applied too narrowly, and the corporation is entitled to do not only that which is expressly authorized but that which is reasonably incidental to or consequential upon that which is in terms authorized. And it is, of course, for the defendant corporation to point out the authority under which it has acted in what it has done.[11]

Although the laundrette service was not directly authorised by the Washhouse Acts, could it be said to be incidental to that power? Sargant J held that a loss-making home-delivery laundry service subsidised by taxpayers (and in competition with private firms) could not be covered by these Acts. Decisions such as this opened up the scope for the courts to look beyond statutes' express terms when assessing the legality of a public body's actions.

(b) Implicit requirements upon public functions

A public body acting beyond its statutory powers is often said to act beyond the 'four corners' of its authority.[12] Using a similar metaphor Laws LJ once declared that, when it came to judicial consideration of the scope of authorising provisions, such provisions 'may be a very large tapestry, but every tapestry has a border'.[13] In other words, the first duty of the courts in conducting a judicial review is to assess the limits of a power (its 'four corners') and whether a public authority's exercise of the power conforms to these limits. The 'four corners' metaphor, however, can lead to confusion, as it attributes a degree of regularity and clarity to the scope of statutory powers that is often lacking.

Statutory requirements upon the exercise of a public body's power fall into two groups; those expressly imposed by the legislation and those which the courts infer are necessarily incidental. In Figure 19.2 exercise of a public function 'X' lies squarely within the four corners of the authorising power. Exercise Z, by contrast, although seemingly within the four corners of the power, might not be if the courts identify implicit restrictions upon its operation. Exercise Y, although seemingly outside the four corners of the statute, might be accepted by the courts as 'reasonably incidental to or consequential' upon the terms of the power (to borrow Sargant J's phrase in *Attorney-General* v *Fulham Corporation*).

We have encountered implicit restrictions identified by the courts before. When we considered the 'principle of legality' (see Chapter 5[14]) espoused by the courts in cases such as *ex parte Simms,* for example, we saw Lord Hoffmann declare that '[f]undamental rights cannot be overridden by general or ambiguous words'.[15] No matter how broadly a statutory power seems to be worded, therefore, the courts may declare that an exercise of a public function like Z above falls foul of implicit restrictions protecting civil liberties which could

---

[11] *Attorney-General* v *Fulham Corporation* [1921] 1 Ch. 440, 450.
[12] See, for example, *R (Edison First Power Ltd)* v *Secretary of State For Environment, Transport & Regions* [2000] EWHC (Admin) 317, [37] (Carnwarth J).
[13] *R (Bancoult)* v *Secretary of State for the Foreign and Commonwealth Office* [2001] QB 1067, 1103.
[14] See pp. 155–8.
[15] *R v Secretary of State for the Home Department, ex parte Simms* [2000] 2 AC 115, 131.

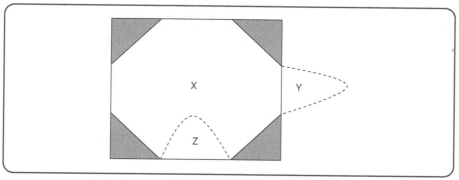

Figure 19.2 The four corners rule (and implicit powers/requirement)

only be overridden by a direct assertion by Parliament that this statutory power overrides such liberties. In the principle of legality we see the courts trying to adopt an approach to parliamentary sovereignty which allows them to protect civil liberties. This readiness to 'find' implicit restrictions on the operation of public functions became one of the hallmarks of judicial review's expansion in the last decades of the twentieth century.

One prominent, and often controversial, group of implicit restrictions on public functions relates to sound economic management of public funds. In the early 1980s the Labour-dominated Greater London Council (GLC, a forerunner of the London Assembly discussed in Chapter 13[16]) announced the 'Fares Fair' scheme, a plan to use money raised from rates payments to subsidise public-transport fares. To justify this action, the GLC pointed to legislation which gave it the authority to administer public transport in London in an 'economic, efficient and integrated' manner.[17] The Conservative-run Bromley Council challenged this exercise of discretion, claiming that although the GLC had the authority to run public transport in London (and to set rates), it did not have the authority to run a loss-making transport service subsidised by rate-payers. The House of Lords ultimately acknowledged the GLC's broad power over transport in London, but ruled that the reference to 'economic' in the statue obliged the GLC to run the service at break-even point.[18]

The Foreign Secretary once enjoyed a legislative power to provide funding for overseas development projects.[19] As we saw in the last chapter,[20] in the early 1990s Douglas Hurd exercised this power to part fund the economically unviable and environmentally destructive Pergau Dam in Malaysia. The Divisional Court ruled this decision illegal by identifying an implicit requirement that overseas development grants be must economically sound:

> As to the absence of the word 'sound' from section 1(1), it seems to me that, if Parliament had intended to confer a power to disburse money for unsound developmental purposes, it could have been expected to say so expressly . . . the contemplated development is, on the evidence, so economically unsound that there is no economic argument in favour of the case . . .[21]

---

[16] See p. 417.
[17] Transport (London) Act 1969, s.1.
[18] See *Bromley London Borough Council* v *Greater London Council* [1983] 1 AC 768, 815 (Lord Wilberforce).
[19] Overseas Development and Co-operation Act 1980, s.1.
[20] See p. 531.
[21] *R* v *Secretary of State for Foreign and Commonwealth Affairs, ex parte World Development Movement* [1995] 1 WLR 386, 402 (Rose LJ).

The quest to identify implicit features of an authorising provision with which public bodies must comply leads the courts into uncertain territory. Both the decisions in the *Fares Fair* and *Pergau Dam* cases were criticised as evidence of the judiciary accepting challenges to decisions on the basis of their personal preferences, rather than respecting the decisions of elected decision makers.[22] Nonetheless, because 'the four corners' of a power are seldom fully mapped out in legislation, the courts will continue to be drawn into such grey areas.

(ii) Unauthorised delegation of a public function

Illegality also places limits upon the ability of a decision maker, when designated by a statute as the actor tasked with exercising a power, to pass on such a function to a third party. Unless Parliament has permitted it, such a delegation would be contrary to Parliamentary intention and therefore illegal. Whereas the courts' willingness to recognise implicit restrictions upon the exercise of statutory powers evidences the increasingly close judicial oversight of governance functions, the courts have treated delegations of authority more flexibly than a simple assertion of the rule would suggest. At least where central and devolved government is at issue, the courts' approach to this form of illegality demonstrates an on-going concern not to obstruct effective decision-making.

A good example of the ordinary operation of the unauthorised delegation rule came in the case of *Barnard* v *National Dock Labour Board*. In the course of industrial action, a port manager suspended several dock workers. In the 1950s many ports were nationalised, and Parliament had placed the employment of individuals in the docks in the hands of a national scheme, the National Dock Labour Board. The claimant dock workers argued that the power had to be exercised by the Board and could not be exercised by individual port managers. Denning LJ, as he then was, held that it was irrelevant that the port manager had suspended the workers with good reason. Nor could a power to delegate the Board's authority to a senior manager be said to be necessarily implied by its statutory powers (even if this would have saved time and money). The port manager had illegally exercised powers that he should not have been given:

> The port manager . . . has assumed a mantle which was not his, but that of another. This is not a case of a tribunal which has a lawful jurisdiction and exercises it; it is a case of a man acting as a tribunal when he has no right to do so.[23]

But what of the many thousands of public functions placed in the hands of 'the Secretary of State' by statutes? If the approach adopted in *Barnard* were applied to such provisions then Cabinet-level ministers would have to exercise all of those powers personally or face action against them for unlawful delegation. As we saw in Chapter 8,[24] however, the courts created an exception to the rule against unauthorised delegation when central-government decision-making is at issue. In *Carltona*, Lord Greene MR accepted that civil servants acting under the authority of a minister could exercise requisitioning powers vested in the minister personally. Justifying this leniency, Lord Greene pointed to the political controls over such decision-making:

> The whole system of departmental organisation and administration is based on the view that ministers, being responsible to Parliament, will see that important duties are committed to

---

[22] See J. Griffith, *The Politics of the Judiciary* (5th edn, Fontana, 1997) 119–33.
[23] *Barnard* v *National Dock Labour Board* [1953] 2 QB 18, 42.
[24] See pp. 270.

experienced officials. If they do not do that, Parliament is the place where complaint must be made against them.[25]

In other words, no delegation at all is at issue in such cases; 'a decision made on behalf of a minister by one of his officials is constitutionally the decision of the minister himself'.[26] Lord Greene's reliance upon ministerial responsibility to exclude the possibility of judicial review seems out of step with the current judicial acceptance that political control mechanisms are insufficient to fully secure good governance.[27] And yet the courts have maintained the **Carltona** doctrine. In **ex parte Doody,** the House of Lords affirmed that 'whether statutory discretion is capable of delegation, and if so to what degree, principally depends upon the interpretation of the statute'.[28] Although this ruling affirmed that, in theory, the courts evaluate whether delegations of a statutory power are within its terms, the special rule of interpretation introduced in **Carltona** was not called into question.

Indeed, the **Carltona** doctrine might even be expanding. **Chief Constable of the West Midlands Police** saw the Divisional Court approve the Chief Constable's delegation to his subordinates of his statutory power to apply for anti-social behaviour orders. Comparing the position of Chief Constable to a government minister, Sedley LJ asserted that:

> A chief constable similarly is not the employer of the officers under his or her command but is legally answerable for them. The **Carltona** principle appears to apply readily in such a situation, with two well established qualifications. One is that some functions are such that they cannot, consistently with the statutory purpose, be delegated at all . . . The other is that delegation has to be to somebody suitable. As the **Carltona** case demonstrates, who is suitable is primarily for the office-holder to decide. Today, however, it is clear that an improper delegation will be a matter for the courts, at least where the discharge of a statutory office is in issue.[29]

This decision has been followed in subsequent cases, with Lord Phillips acknowledging in **Haw** that '[w]here the responsibilities of the office created by statute are such that delegation is inevitable, there will be an implied power to delegate'.[30] Judicial acceptance of an implicit ability of many officials to delegate their functions seems out of step with a general trend towards increased judicial oversight over the executive. One possible explanation requires us to return to red and green light theories of judicial review (see Chapter 18[31]). Whereas other judicial review constraints are maintained to prevent illegal exercises of power, this flexible approach to delegation allows public bodies to manage their own decision-making processes. The courts nonetheless remain able to find such processes illegal if junior officials are left in charge of decisions they are not competent to make.

(iii) Errors of law and errors of fact

(a) Errors of law

Since a public body's mistake as to an aspect of its jurisdiction often leads it to exceed its legal powers, claims that an error of law has been committed have often been tackled under

---

[25] *Carltona Ltd v Commissioners of Works* [1943] 2 All ER 560, 563.
[26] *R (Bourgass) v Secretary of State for Justice* [2015] UKSC 54; [2016] AC 384, [49] (Lord Reed).
[27] See *R v Secretary of State for the Home Department, ex parte Fire Brigades Union* [1995] 2 All ER 244, 267 (Lord Mustill).
[28] *R v Secretary of State for the Home Department, ex parte Doody* [1994] 1 AC 531, 566 (Lord Mustill).
[29] *R (Chief Constable of the West Midlands Police) v Birmingham Justices* [2002] EWHC (Admin) 1087, [10].
[30] *Director of Public Prosecutions v Haw* [2007] EWHC (Admin) 1931; [2008] 1 WLR 379, [33].
[31] See pp. 511–12.

'acting in excess of powers', leaving this ground for review in the shadows. Nonetheless, since *Anisminic Ltd* v *Foreign Compensation Commission,* the courts have in principle accepted that 'all relevant errors of law are open to challenge'.[32] In *Anisminic* statute had established the Foreign Compensation Commission (FCC) to compensate UK nationals and companies whose property was seized or damaged by acts of foreign governments. The Egyptian Government seized Anisminic Ltd's property, but the FCC refused compensation on the basis that its jurisdiction did not cover purchases of UK-owned property by foreign governments. This interpretation of the FCC's powers would have excluded most of the cases it was established to deal with, leading the House of Lords to treat the FCC's approach as an error of law:

> But if [a decision-making tribunal] reach a wrong conclusion as to the width of their powers, the court must be able to correct that – not because the tribunal has made an error of law, but because as a result of making an error of law they have dealt with and based their decision on a matter with which, on a true construction of their powers, they had no right to deal. If they base their decision on some matter which is not prescribed for their adjudication, they are doing something which they have no right to do and . . . their decision is a nullity.[33]

Justifying such interventions, Yeats recognises that the courts are responsible for providing definitive interpretations of statutory provisions and that 'it is this technical expertise which legitimises their activities in suppressing the rival interpretations of lesser bodies in an administrative hierarchy'.[34]

(b) Errors of fact

Although the courts have long accepted that a decision maker's error as to the legal limits of its role is reviewable, they have historically been much more circumspect where errors of fact are at issue, for fear that permitting review on this basis would oblige judges to assess the merits of the decision maker's choices. The courts therefore made strident efforts to deal with these questions using other grounds for review. In the case of *ex parte A* the claimant challenged, as an error of fact, the Criminal Injuries Compensation Board's refusal to compensate her despite medical evidence that she had been raped. The House of Lords nonetheless preferred to deal with the case under other grounds, as seen in this excerpt from Lord Slynn's judgment:

> For my part, I would accept that there is jurisdiction to quash on that ground [error of fact] in this case, but I prefer to decide the matter on the alternative basis argued, namely that what happened in these proceedings was a breach of the rules of natural justice and constituted unfairness.[35]

As Williams nonetheless explains, cases exist in which there is an objectively right answer to questions of fact (such as whether the age of a child in a household entitles an individual to maintenance payments). In such circumstances, '[i]f a decision maker wrongly assesses an individual's age and fails to make a grant, it does not matter who points that mistake

---

[32] P. Craig, '*Ultra Vires* and the Foundations of Judicial Review' [1998] 57 CLJ 63, 66.

[33] *Anisminic Ltd* v *Foreign Compensation Commission* [1969] 2 AC 147, 174 (Lord Reid).

[34] I. Yeats, 'Findings of Fact: The Role of the Courts', in G. Richardson and H. Genn (eds), *Administrative Law and Government Action* (OUP, 1994) 131, 153.

[35] *R* v *Criminal Injuries Compensation Board, ex parte A* [1999] 2 AC 330, 345.

out . . . ; the mistake is undeniable and must be corrected'.[36] These can be described as facts which are directly relevant to a decision maker's jurisdiction. This meant that, by the time the House of Lords decided the case of **Begum,** Lord Bingham was willing to assert that illegality applied where 'there is no evidence to support factual findings made or they are plainly untenable or . . . if the decision-maker is shown to have misunderstood or been ignorant of an established and relevant fact'.[37]

Thinking Point . . .

White & Collins, considered above (pp. 545–6), exemplifies a case in which the public authorities in question exceeded their powers by attempting to purchase park land, but this could equally have been treated as an error of fact relevant to their jurisdiction.

Following on from this lead, the Court of Appeal has since fleshed out the conditions on the basis of which a claimant can assert that a public authority has reached a decision based upon an error of fact in the case of **E,** which involved immigration claims:

> First, there must have been a mistake as to an existing fact, including a mistake as to the availability of evidence on a particular matter. Secondly, the fact or evidence must have been 'established', in the sense that it was uncontentious and objectively verifiable. Thirdly, the [claimant] (or his advisers) must not have been responsible for the mistake. Fourthly, the mistake must have played a material (not necessarily decisive) part in the [decision maker's] reasoning.[38]

Challenges under these grounds for review can involve mixtures of fact and law. *R (Ghai)* v *Newcastle City Council* provides a good example of such a case, involving the factual elements of a structure and the legal definition of a building. When Newcastle City Council informed Ghai, a Hindu resident of the city, that it would not make provision for open-air cremation of his body on death (on the basis that regulations on cremations required that they be held inside a building), he sought a judicial review. The Court of Appeal sidestepped the complex questions of religious liberty raised by the case by instead considering whether the council had committed an error of fact in failing to consider whether a cremation pyre constructed inside a walled, but not roofed, structure would constitute a building for the purposes of the regulations on cremations. In declaring that such a structure *could* satisfy these regulations, the court was able to remit the issue for the council to reconsider its decision.[39] Therefore, much as errors of fact are often covered by other aspects of illegality, **Ghai** indicates that in some cases the concept remains useful for the courts.

Abuse of powers

During judicial review's slumber throughout the early and mid-twentieth century *ultra vires* illegality was the only viable basis on which the courts would question administrative

---

[36] R. Williams, 'When is an Error Not an Error? Reform of Jurisdictional Review of Error of Law and Fact' [2007] PL 973, 978.

[37] *Begum* v *London Borough of Tower Hamlets* [2003] UKHL 5; [2003] 2 AC 430, [7].

[38] *E* v *Secretary of State for the Home Department* [2004] EWCA Civ 49; [2004] 2 WLR 1351, [66] (Carnwath LJ).

[39] *R (Ghai)* v *Newcastle City Council* [2010] EWCA Civ 59; [2010] 3 WLR 737, [39] (Lord Neuberger MR).

decisions. For decades the courts clung to this limited conception of illegality even where parties before them attacked the four corners doctrine and contended that a public body's actions should 'be construed to include the general purposes of the [authorising statute]'.[40] In the 1960s, alongside expanding the concept of acting in excess of powers, the courts opened up the possibility of challenges to abuses of powers. An abuse of powers takes place when a public body, which will often have gained powers from a statute, uses these powers in a way which conflicts with the purpose of that enactment. This sub-species of illegality is therefore concerned with uses of powers which are contrary not to the *wording* but to the *spirit* of an authorising statute.

Thinking Point . . .

Roberts v *Hopwood* [1925] AC 578 – discussed at p. 113 – provides a good example of the potential for the courts to abuse this ground for review to advance their own political opinions. Lord Atkinson (at 594), struck down a council's efforts to equalise wages between male and female employees as being guided by 'some eccentric principles of socialistic philanthropy'.

Lord Reid was one of the first judges to declare that, with regard to any given discretionary power, 'Parliament must have conferred the discretion with the intention that it should be used to promote the policy and objects of the Act'.[41] The controversy with this proposition is that the courts thereby lay claim to the ability to identify Parliament's intention concerning discretionary powers, regardless of how the decision makers using the powers conceive of them. By accepting that they could undertake 'purposive' interpretation of statutes the courts extended the reach of judicial review and opened themselves to accusations that they are imposing their political viewpoint on decision makers. Nonetheless, judges have justified this extension on the basis that public authorities have to be held to higher standards than private persons:

> If the allegation is of abuse of power the courts should, in general, hear the complaint. Public law bodies should not be free to abuse their power by invoking the principle that private individuals can act unfairly or abusively without legal redress.[42]

Public bodies can abuse their statutory powers in three ways. They can take into account irrelevant (or fail to take into account relevant) considerations in exercising their power, they can use the power for a purpose unintended by the statute, or they can fetter their discretion. Each type of abuse of power will be considered in turn.

(i) The relevance of the pubic authority's considerations

Once a court has evaluated the purposes behind Parliament's grant of discretionary powers to a decision maker, it can then examine the considerations used by this actor to reach a

---

[40] *Attorney-General* v *London and Home Counties Joint Electricity Authority* [1929] 1 Ch 513, 528–9 (Astbury J).
[41] *Padfield* v *Minister of Agriculture, Fisheries and Food* [1968] AC 997, 1030.
[42] *R (Molinaro)* v *The Royal Borough of Kensington and Chelsea* [2001] EWHC (Admin) 896; [2002] BLGR 336, [69] (Elias J).

decision, and assess whether the two align. If a decision maker has acted on the basis of irrelevant considerations or has failed to take relevant factors into account, then the decision is open to challenge. Conversely, if it has not acted in this way (for example, where the judge 'can find no evidence that he failed to consider anything that he ought to have considered or that he took into account anything that he ought not to have taken into account'[43]) then a decision cannot be challenged on this basis.

The case of *Wheeler* v *Leicester City Council* provides a good illustration of the approach of the courts to irrelevant considerations. When, during the apartheid era, the England rugby team toured South Africa, three members of Leicester RUFC were included in the squad. Despite requests from the Leicester City Council, which was opposed to dealings with apartheid South Africa, the club refused to withdraw its team members from the tour. In response, the council revoked the rugby club's permission to use council-owned sports grounds, justifying this decision on the basis of its statutory duty to promote good race relations.[44] The House of Lords ruled that this exercise of the council's managerial powers over its sports grounds was an abuse of powers. In the absence of any infringement of the law or any improper conduct by the club, whether it supported the council's goals was not relevant to a concern for good race relations: 'A private individual or a private organisation cannot be obliged to display zeal in the pursuit of an object sought by a public authority and cannot be obliged to publish views dictated by a public authority'.[45] By contrast, in *ex parte Fewings,* a local authority's failure to take relevant considerations into account was at issue. Somerset County Council used control over council land, exercisable for purposes which would benefit the area,[46] to ban fox hunting. The council's concern for animal welfare, whilst not irrelevant to the exercise of this power, could not be justified in light of the Council's failure to consider other factors, with Sir Thomas Bingham MR declaring that, '[i]n the absence of legal guidance, it was not, I think, appreciated that personal views, however strongly held, had to be related to the benefit of the area'.[47]

Even where Parliament does not clearly explain the purposes behind a statutory power, the courts remain able to intervene on the basis that particular considerations are irrelevant in the context of the statute as a whole. The flexibility in this rule, however, can lead to accusations that the courts are categorising considerations as relevant or irrelevant to suit their own attitude towards a decision, rather than upholding the will of Parliament. One controversial challenge under this head of review came in the *Fares Fair* case. As we saw above,[48] the GLC's 'Fares Fair' scheme was found to be illegal on the basis that running an uneconomic transport system exceeded its statutory powers. The GLC had claimed that its statutory powers should be considered in light of the policy implementing an electoral promise to Londoners. Lord Wilberforce, however, discounted the relevance of such concerns:

> It makes no difference on the question of legality . . . whether the impugned action was or was not submitted to or approved by the relevant electorate: that cannot confer validity upon *ultra*

---

[43] *R (Mayor and Citizens of the City of Westminster)* v *The Mayor of London* [2002] EWHC (Admin) 2440, [90] (Maurice Kay J).
[44] Race Relations Act 1976, s. 17.
[45] *Wheeler* v *Leicester County Council* [1985] AC 1054, 1080 (Lord Templeman).
[46] Local Government Act 1972, s. 120(1)(b).
[47] *R* v *Somerset County Council, ex parte Fewings* [1995] 1 WLR 1037, 1046.
[48] See p. 547.

vires action. Indeed, it forms part of Bromley's argument, that the GLC in so far as it considered that it has a commitment to bring about the reduction in fares, regardless of other considerations, misdirected itself in law.[49]

Key debates
When is public opinion an irrelevant consideration?

The courts have come to accept that public officials (and especially elected representatives) will often have regard to public opinion in their decision-making and are no longer as quick as Lord Wilberforce was in **Fares Fair** to forbid such considerations, unless they are manifestly inappropriate in a particular case or excluded by statute.

One case which provides a useful example of when a decision maker should exclude any considerations based on public opinion is *R v Secretary of State for the Home Department, ex parte Venables* [1998] AC 407 (see above p. 238), which involved the power, then possessed by the Home Secretary, to vary the tariff which prisoners sentenced to life would have to serve before they would be eligible for parole. Michael Howard, when Home Secretary, had used this power to extend the sentences of the murderers of the toddler Jamie Bulger, given public outcry in this case. Lord Goff explained (at 490–1) that in reaching such a decision, analogous to a judicial sentencing power, 'should [the Home Secretary] take into account public clamour directed towards the decision . . . he will be having regard to an irrelevant consideration which will render the exercise of his discretion unlawful'.

Likewise, when the Education Secretary, then Ed Balls, involved himself in the removal from office of Sharon Shoesmith, Director of Children's Services at the London Borough of Haringey, after a child protection plan devised by her department failed to prevent the death, in 2007, of the baby Peter Connolly, he considered a petition organised by *The Sun* newspaper demanding her dismissal. In *R (Shoesmith) v OFSTED* [2011] EWCA Civ 642; [2011] IRLR 679, the Court of Appeal held that it was not impermissible to take this petition into account (Maurice Kay LJ, [68]):

> I have little to say about the Secretary of State's regard to *The Sun*'s petition. For my part, I do not consider that it was necessarily unlawful for the Secretary of State to have taken it into account . . . . He was legitimately concerned about public confidence and the petition may have had some modest value in that respect.

The crucial difference between the cases is the sentencing context of the first decision, which required the Home Secretary to ignore public opinion so as to ensure the sentencing process amounted to a fair hearing. Outside such limited circumstances public bodies have much more scope to consider public opinion in contexts such as the level of confidence in public officials.

If the above cases map the limits of when public opinion can be considered, *Porter v Magill* [2001] UKHL 67; [2002] 2 AC 357 (see also below pp. 573–4), indicates when the weight attributed to this factor in decision-making will be considered impermissible. This case involved an effort by Westminster Council (then led by Shirley Porter) to sell off council housing in marginal wards on the basis that the new homeowners would be more likely to vote Conservative. The House of Lords considered that the centrality of gaining political advantage to this policy was impermissible (Lord Bingham, at [21]):

> Elected politicians of course wish to act in a manner which will commend them . . . to the electorate. Such an ambition is the life blood of democracy and a potent spur to responsible

---

[49] *Bromley London Borough Council* v *Greater London Council* [1983] 1 AC 768, 814.

decision-taking and administration. Councillors do not act improperly or unlawfully if, exercising public powers for a public purpose for which such powers were conferred, they hope that such exercise will earn the gratitude and support of the electorate and thus strengthen their electoral position . . . But a public power is not exercised lawfully if it is exercised not for a public purpose for which the power was conferred but in order to promote the electoral advantage of a political party.

(ii) Exercising a power for improper purposes

There is no bright dividing line between illegality on the basis of 'irrelevant consider-ations' or on the basis of 'improper purposes'. In *Porter* v *Magill*, the Council could be described as taking account of irrelevant electoral considerations in its sell off of council houses (whereas the Court styled these actions as seeking to achieve the improper pur-pose of securing electoral advantage). Nonetheless, in some cases it remains necessary to consider these sub-headings of illegality separately. In *ex parte Fewings*, for example, the Court of Appeal accepted that the council's ban on hunting for the purpose of promoting animal welfare fitted within the statutory direction that the land should be managed for the benefit of the area. Nonetheless, because the council failed to take into account the broad range of considerations relevant to the benefit of the area, its decision was illegal.

Lord Bridge summed up the essence of the courts' approach to improper purposes as follows: 'Statutory power conferred for public purposes is conferred as it were upon trust, not absolutely – that is to say, it can validly be used only in the right and proper way which Parliament when conferring it is presumed to have intended'.[50] In other words, a public body must establish a 'rational connection' between its purposes and those of the authorising legislation.[51] The first modern example of the courts applying this requirement to an action by central government came in *Padfield* v *Minister of Agriculture, Fisheries and Food*, one of the cases by which the courts began to consciously expand the reach of judicial review. The Agricultural Marketing Act 1958 gave the government the discretion to alter milk market-ing tariffs and also to constitute a Committee of Investigation where there were complaints that these tariffs were unfair. Farmers in the south east of England claimed that the trans-porting costs factored into milk prices were unfair, but the minister refused to establish a committee to investigate these claims. Lord Reid found that this decision conflicted with the purpose of the statute. By failing to refer genuine complaints the minister was circum-venting the statutory safeguards which Parliament had intended to operate:

When these provisions were first enacted in 1931 it was unusual for Parliament to compel people to sell their commodities in a way to which they objected and it was easily foreseeable that any such scheme would cause loss to some producers. Moreover, if the operation of the scheme was put in the hands of the majority of the producers, it was obvious that they might use their power to the detriment of consumers, distributors or a minority of the producers. So it is not surprising that Parliament enacted safeguards.[52]

---

[50] *R* v *Tower Hamlets London Borough Council, ex parte Chetnik Developments Ltd* [1988] AC 858, 872.
[51] *R (Ben Hoare Bell Solicitors)* v *Lord Chancellor* [2015] EWHC 523 (Admin); [2015] 1 WLR 4175, [59] (Beatson LJ).
[52] *Padfield* v *Minister of Agriculture, Fisheries and Food* [1968] AC 997, 1030.

Unfortunately, it is often possible for a public body to mask improper purposes by paying lip service to the proper statutory purpose. When the courts came to consider the 'Homes-for-Votes' scandal in *Porter* v *Magill,* for example, the council leaders had justified their plan to sell off council houses on the basis that this would simply be a normal sale of properties (keeping secret their plan to use the targeted sell-off to change the political complexion of areas). Lord Scott prevented them from availing of this ruse:

> [T]here is all the difference in the world between a policy adopted for naked political advantage but spuriously justified by reference to a purpose which, had it been the true purpose, would have been legitimate, and a policy adopted for a legitimate purpose and seen to carry with it significant political advantage.[53]

The task of the courts, therefore, is to assess whether a prohibited purpose underpins a decision. If, under this test, the decision maker's dominant purpose is out of line with the statutory purpose, then the courts will intervene. The test was coined by Glidewell J in *ex parte Westminster City Council*:

> [I]f a local authority resolves to expend its ratepayers' money in order to achieve two purposes, one of which it is authorised to achieve by statute but for the other of which it has no authority, is that decision invalid?[54]

In this case, the Inner London Education Authority opposed government policies which it believed would reduce education spending. It therefore used its statutory power to provide information to the public to campaign against education cuts. Westminster City Council, which, like central government, was then under the control of the Conservative Party, accused the Education Authority of exercising its power not on an information campaign but to galvanise opposition to government policy. Glidewell J agreed, stating that although the campaign might have had some informative value, the 'major purpose' of poster slogans like 'Education Cuts Never Heal' was to influence public opinion.[55] Ironically, *ex parte Westminster City Council* was coterminous with the efforts of the same council's leadership to 'buy' votes exposed in *Porter* v *Magill*. As the head of a public body, Shirley Porter both exploited, and was ultimately constrained by, the expansion of judicial control over administrative action, indicating the potential of the 'abuse of powers' ground to draw the courts into politically charged issues.

(iii) Fettering of discretion

Where a statute grants a public body discretion over its exercise of a particular power, attempts by that body to limit the circumstances in which it will exercise that discretion may be illegal. This does not mean that public bodies cannot make rules as to how a power will be used, simply that the requirement of equality before the law means that they must give some consideration to affected parties whose circumstances are in some way distinctive. The **British Oxygen** case provides a good example of this basis of review in action. Parliament passed statute allowing the government to provide grants to support UK industry. However, the government department managing these grants imposed a rule

---

[53] *Porter* v *Magill* [2001] UKHL 67; [2002] 2 AC 357, [144].
[54] *R* v *Inner London Education Authority, ex parte Westminster City Council* [1986] 1 WLR 28, 46–47.
[55] Ibid., 49–50.

whereby it would only provide funding where individual products in question were worth more than £25. The British Oxygen's application for a grant to purchase a large volume of compressed gas cylinders (costing on an average just under £20 each) was rejected. The company challenged this decision on the basis that the department had simply applied its general policy without properly considering the particular circumstances of its request. Lord Reid mapped out the rule against fettering discretion as follows:

> [A] Ministry or large authority may have had to deal with a multitude of similar applications and then they will almost certainly have evolved a policy so precise that it could well be called a rule. There can be no objection to that, provided that the authority is always willing to listen to anyone with something new to say.[56]

In this case, in which the evidence indicated careful consideration of British Oxygen's application despite the terms of the general policy, the government had done all that was required to show that it had not unduly 'fettered' its discretion. Nonetheless, this ground for review supports good governance, requiring that all public authorities do not unthinkingly apply general policies but consider claims made by parties raising special individual circumstances.

Thinking Point . . .

The rule against fettering discretion applies, for example, to university admissions. Universities cannot simply reject an application when a prospective student does not achieve the required grades for a course (the general policy); because of this rule they must consider any explanation an applicant offers for their failure to achieve the required grades (such as taking assessments affected by adverse personal circumstances).

That public authorities only have to show that they were reasonably receptive to individual cases circumvents claims that the fettering-of-discretion rule undermines public administration. A good example of the limits on the concept of fettering discretion arose when the Home Secretary retained responsibility over the length of sentence criminals sentenced to life imprisonment had to serve before they could be considered for parole. One of the notorious 'Moors Murderers', Myra Hindley, was informed that she would serve a whole life tariff, meaning that a parole board would never be able to consider her for release. Hindley claimed that this decision amounted to a fettering of discretion. In *ex parte Hindley,* however, the Home Secretary was able to show that he did not consider this position final and was prepared to reconsider in light of pertinent factors. The House of Lords ruled that this was sufficient to satisfy the rule against fettering discretion:

> The Secretary of State envisages the possibility of release in the event of exceptional progress in prison; and, even in absence of such progress, the Secretary of State is prepared to reconsider any whole life tariff decision from time to time . . . I would hold that it is impossible to say that the Secretary of State has unlawfully fettered his discretion.[57]

---

[56] *British Oxygen Co. v Minister of Technology* [1971] AC 610, 625.
[57] *R v Secretary of State for the Home Department, ex parte Hindley* [2000] UKHL 21; [2001] 1 AC 410, 417 (Lord Steyn).

Irrationality

Key issues

- Administrative actions may be irrational if no valid reasons support the exercise of a power. In short, irrationality applies to arbitrary as opposed to illegal exercises of power. Irrationality is a very limited head of review which the courts have historically been reluctant to expand as it involves examining the merits of a public body's decision.

- Where a decision falls within the particular expertise of the decision maker the courts will generally be even more reluctant to intervene (the 'super' *Wednesbury* test). Nonetheless, where a decision involves particularly important interests of affected individuals the courts will generally be more willing to intervene than usual (the 'sub' *Wednesbury* test).

- Irrationality, although still a head of review in the legal systems of the UK, is a much narrower basis for judicial oversight than the comparable basis for review in much of European administrative law, proportionality. Considerable speculation surrounds the future of this head of review.

The meaning of *Wednesbury* irrationality

(i) Formulating the test for irrationality

Irrationality, as a head of judicial review, allows the courts to step in to prevent irrational (also known as unreasonable) public body decisions. The modern test for such a review was provided by Lord Greene MR in his famous decision in *Wednesbury Corporation v Associated Provincial Picture Houses*. Wednesbury's local council sought to limit the use of the town's cinema (run by Associated Provincial Picture Houses) on Sundays by using their licensing power over local cinemas to require that any child under the age of fifteen would have to be accompanied by an adult. Associated Provincial Picture Houses sought to have what it regarded as an arbitrary restriction on its licence quashed. Lord Greene MR asserted that even if a decision falls within the authority's legitimate discretion the courts may still intervene if it involved: 'something so absurd that no sensible person could ever dream that it lay within the powers of the authority'.[58]

Irrationality and illegality are not necessarily related. A decision can be sensibly arrived at on the basis of a clear policy objective, but nonetheless be illegal on the basis that the decision maker has misunderstood its power. On the other hand, a decision can be legally within an authority's powers, for example, using a power to appoint staff to appoint only people with red hair, but could nonetheless be irrational.[59] As Lord Greene MR stated:

> [T]he task of the court is not to decide what it thinks is reasonable, but to decide whether what is *prima facie* within the power of the local authority is a condition which no reasonable authority, acting within the four corners of their jurisdiction, could have decided to impose.[60]

This statement makes it clear that although an exercise of a power does not fall under the illegality head of review (as it is '*prima facie* within the power of the local authority'), it may

---

[58] *Associated Provincial Picture Houses v Wednesbury Corporation* [1948] 1 KB 223, 229.
[59] See *Short v Poole Corporation* [1926] Ch. 66, 91 (Warrington LJ).
[60] *Associated Provincial Picture Houses v Wednesbury Corporation* [1948] 1 KB 223, 233.

nonetheless be challenged if it represents a use of a power which 'no reasonable authority' would have undertaken. Associated Provincial Picture Houses, however, failed in their effort to challenge this licence condition. In the late 1940s, when **Wednesbury** was decided, administrative law remained in a deep slumber. Lord Greene's decision, in the words of Sir Stephen Sedley, 'invented nothing and clarified little'.[61] Instead, it perpetuated the reluctance of the courts to consider the merits of public authority decisions, on the basis that questioning a public body's substantive decision amounted to substituting a court's evaluation for that of the decision maker. The judges were so concerned by the potential to overstep the limits of their constitutional authority under this heading of review that even when Lord Diplock came to restate the grounds for judicial review in the **GCHQ** case, his formulation of 'irrationality' tracked closely to Lord Greene's approach, requiring 'a decision which is so outrageous in its defiance of logic or of accepted moral standards that no sensible person who had applied his mind to the question to be decided could have arrived at it'.[62]

Thinking Point . . .

As a measure of how far administrative law has developed since **Wednesbury,** similar licensing restrictions would today likely be challenged as an abuse of power. When Lord Greene found the decision to be legal, he did so on the basis of a narrow *'ultra vires'* approach to this head of review (because abuse of powers had yet to develop as a ground).

(ii) The *Wednesbury* test in action

For the courts to accept a challenge to a public body's decision as irrational, the claimant will have to establish that a decision is not simply unwise, or even misguided. The problems undermining a decision need to be of a different order of magnitude. Under the **Wednesbury** test, the claimant will have to show that a decision was arbitrary or perverse before they will succeed.

Over the years, many claimants have attempted to argue that a decision is irrational, but few have succeeded. For example, in *ex parte Croydon LBC,* a court found that the Croydon Council Education Committee's decision not to allow a child to join an already oversubscribed school could not be **Wednesbury** unreasonable. Even though the parents involved in the case were able to establish that classes that should have held 30 children already held 36, the council's 'drawing the line' against further admissions at this point was found not to be arbitrary.[63] Similarly, in *ex parte Tameside MBC* not even the Secretary of State for Education was able to rely on this head of review. Tameside was, by the mid-1970s, one of the few areas in England that had not replaced its secondary and grammar schools with comprehensive schools following education reforms in the 1960s. The Secretary of State claimed that in light of the nationwide move to comprehensive education, Tameside Council's efforts to maintain selective education were irrational, and directed the council to implement a scheme for comprehensive schools. But much as central government did not like the council's choice, and much as it conflicted with national policy,

---

[61] S. Sedley, 'Governments, Constitutions and Judges', in G. Richardson and H. Genn (eds), *Administrative Law and Government Action* (OUP, 1994) 35, 38.
[62] *Council of Civil Service Unions* v *Minister for the Civil Service* [1985] AC 374, 410–11.

the House of Lords did not find this a sufficient basis to conclude that the council was acting unreasonably. As Lord Wilberforce concluded:

> [I]f [the minister] had exercised his judgment on the basis of the factual situation in which this newly elected authority was placed – with a policy approved by its electorate, and massively supported by the parents – there was no ground – however much he might disagree with the new policy, and regret such administrative dislocation as was brought about by the change – upon which he could find that the authority was acting or proposing to act unreasonably.[64]

So the courts will not readily intervene to find a decision irrational, on the basis that doing so challenges the merits of a decision. The *Wednesbury* test sets a high bar for claimants to clear; a public authority under review will satisfy the test if it is able to show some good reason for its decision (Figure 19.3). Nonetheless, even on this exacting basis, some claimants have managed to clear the *Wednesbury* standard, especially in recent years as the courts have become steadily more active in expanding judicial review principles. After all, as Lord Bingham (then Lord Chief Justice) pointed out in *ex parte Manning*, 'the standard of review should not be set too high, since judicial review is the only means by which the citizen can seek redress . . . and if the test were too exacting an effective remedy would be denied'.[65]

A good example of a successful *Wednesbury* claim came when the Home Secretary challenged a decision by the Mental Health Review Tribunal to conditionally discharge a patient from a secure hospital. The tribunal, exercising its statutory function, had concluded that the patient was not suffering from any mental illness requiring his

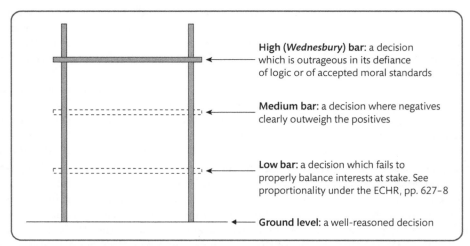

High (*Wednesbury*) bar: a decision which is outrageous in its defiance of logic or of accepted moral standards

Medium bar: a decision where negatives clearly outweigh the positives

Low bar: a decision which fails to properly balance interests at stake. See proportionality under the ECHR, pp. 627–8

Ground level: a well-reasoned decision

Figure 19.3 The *Wednesbury* test: a high jump for claimants

---

[63] *R v Commissioner for Local Administration, ex parte Croydon London Borough Council* [1989] 1 All ER 1033, 1045 (Woolf LJ).

[64] *R v Secretary of State for Education, ex parte Tameside MBC* [1977] AC 1014, 1052.

[65] *R v Director of Public Prosecutions, ex parte Manning* [2001] QB 330, [23].

hospitalisation.[66] Nonetheless, the Tribunal sought to impose conditions on the patient's discharge, which Sullivan J described as 'a powerful indication' that it could not be confident that he was not suffering from a mental illness.[67] With the merits of the decision to discharge thereby undermined, Sullivan J accepted that the Tribunal had acted irrationally. The House of Lords clarified its approach to irrationality in *In re Duffy*:

Key case

In re Duffy [2008] UKHL 4 (House of Lords)

As Lord Carswell observed parades in Northern Ireland have long provided a flash-point for sectarian violence (at [34]):

> In many countries throughout the world parades constitute no more than a colourful and enjoyable diversion. In Northern Ireland, sadly, they have been for many years the focus of hostility, aggressiveness and misunderstanding between different sections of the community.

In this case the applicant, a member of the Garvaghy Road Residents' Coalition (which opposes Orange Order marches through part of Portadown), challenged the appointment, by the Secretary of State for Northern Ireland, of two members of the Orange Order to the Parades Commission of Northern Ireland. This body, established in the wake of violent clashes surrounding parades in the 1990s, exercised a statutory duty (under the Public Processions (Northern Ireland) Act 1998) to attempt to resolve disputes over contentious parades by mediation and to make determinations over whether parades could proceed, and if so under what conditions, if such disputes could not be resolved.

The House of Lords unanimously accepted that these appointments were irrational. Lord Bingham was insistent that no reasonable minister should have reached such a decision (at [27]):

> It was one thing to ensure that the loyalist interest was represented within the commission, but quite another to recruit two hardline members of the very lodges whose activities had been a focus, probably the main focus, of the serious problems which had caused widespread disorder and led to establishment of the commission.

Baroness Hale's short concurrence emphasises indicates how little merit the Law Lords found in the decision to appoint these Commissioners (at [33]):

> [T]here is no indication that the appointing panel or the Secretary of State understood this, or how little there would be left for them usefully to do, or how their membership would affect the credibility of the Commission as a whole. No doubt both men had something to bring to the Commission, but they could never have been perceived as impartial adjudicators or mediators by the public at large.

(iii) The variable *Wednesbury* test

The standard *Wednesbury* approach is not, however, good for all seasons. In certain cases, involving specific expertise on the part of decision makers and the allocation of scarce resources by public bodies, the courts are even more reluctant than usual to examine the merits of decisions. Such decisions *require* democratic legitimacy and the courts have freely

---

[66] Mental Health Act 1983, s. 72(1)(b).
[67] *R (Secretary of State for the Home Department)* v *Mental Health Review Tribunal* [2007] EWHC (Admin) 2224; [2008] MHLR 212, [21].

admitted that their lack of expertise and legitimacy regarding such questions prevents the operation of a normal irrationality standard. Instead, the already high bar that applicants have to clear is replaced by an even more daunting 'super-*Wednesbury*' standard.

The courts expressed their reluctance to consider such cases in *ex parte Nottinghamshire County Council,* in which the Council sought to challenge the government's allocation of grants to local authorities under a system which penalised high-spending councils, arguing that its spending targets had been set at an unfairly low level. The council claimed that the combination of low spending targets and heavy penalties for breach were irrational. Rejecting this claim, Lord Scarman held that the *Wednesbury* test would be strictly applied in the field of public financial administration:

> [A]n examination by a court would be justified only if a *prima facie* case were to be shown for holding that the Secretary of State had acted in bad faith, or for an improper motive, or that the consequences of his guidance were so absurd that he must have taken leave of his senses.[68]

This restricted role for irrationality as a head of judicial review in the financial context (and thereafter applied to decisions involving political or expert judgement) was subsequently explained by Lord Bridge on the basis of the judiciary's constitutional role:

> Both the constitutional propriety and the good sense of this restriction seem to me to be clear enough. The formulation and the implementation of national economic policy are matters depending essentially on political judgment. The decisions which shape them are for politicians to take and it is in the political forum of the House of Commons that they are properly to be debated and approved or disapproved on their merits. If the decisions have been taken in good faith within the four corners of the Act, the merits of the policy underlying the decisions are not susceptible to review by the courts and the courts would be exceeding their proper function if they presumed to condemn the policy as unreasonable.[69]

Lord Bridge seems to be suspicious of irrationality as a head of judicial review which extends basic review of whether a decision is legal (within the 'four corners' of a power). With such concerns at the forefront of some judges' minds, it is not surprising that the courts also expressed their reluctance to review the reasonableness of decisions by expert decision makers. In the *ex parte B* case, Cambridge Health Authority refused to fund a series of operations on a seriously ill child on the basis of their expense and the low probability of success. When her family sought a judicial review the Court of Appeal refused to find that the Health Authority's decision was irrational. Sir Thomas Bingham, then Master of the Rolls, acknowledged that '[d]ifficult and agonising judgments have to be made as to how a limited budget is best allocated to the maximum advantage of the maximum number of patients'.[70] In this context, he recognised that:

> The courts are not, contrary to what is sometimes believed, arbiters as to the merits of cases of this kind. Were we to express opinions as to the likelihood of the effectiveness of medical treatment, or as to the merits of medical judgment, then we should be straying far from the sphere which under our constitution is accorded to us. We have one function only, which is to rule upon the lawfulness of decisions. That is a function to which we should strictly confine ourselves.[71]

---

[68] *R v Secretary of State for the Environment, ex parte Nottinghamshire County Council* [1986] AC 240, 247.
[69] *R v Environment Secretary, ex parte Hammersmith London Borough Council* [1991] 1 AC 521, 597.
[70] *R v Cambridge Health Authority, ex parte B* [1995] 1 WLR 898, 906.
[71] Ibid., 905.

He would later recognise that '[w]here decisions of a policy-laden, esoteric or security-based nature are in issue even greater caution than normal must be shown in applying the [*Wednesbury*] test'.[72] These cases indicate that there is now no 'uniform . . . rigid test' for irrationality under administrative law.[73] The standard is variable and context specific. Just as the 'bar' claimants face can be raised when expert decision-making and resource allocation are at issue, the courts have also acknowledged that 'the graver the impact of the decision upon the individual the more substantial the justification that will be required'.[74]

Thus, beginning with *ex parte Smith,* the courts developed a sub-*Wednesbury* test extending the scope for judicial review in such cases. In the 1990s personnel continued to be discharged from the armed forces on the basis that they were homosexual. This official policy, which had been affirmed by a House of Commons Select Committee just four years before the case, was consistent with the current advice received from senior members of the services (ostensibly concerned with morale, but not then known for adopting a positive position on gay-rights issues). Under a simple *Wednesbury* test, this would have been sufficient for the courts to dismiss the challenge to this policy in *ex parte Smith.* However, given the importance of the personal interests at issue, the Court of Appeal contrasted the policy with the decisions of several countries allied to the UK under the North Atlantic Treaty Organisation (NATO) to end similar bans, and subjected the ban to careful scrutiny:

> The present cases . . . concern innate qualities of a very personal kind and the decisions of which the [claimants] complain have had a profound effect on their careers and prospects . . . This does not of course mean that the court is thrust into the position of the primary decision-maker. It is not the constitutional role of the court to regulate the conditions of service in the armed forces of the Crown, nor has it the expertise to do so. But it has the constitutional role and duty of ensuring that the rights of citizens are not abused by the unlawful exercise of executive power.[75]

Thinking Point . . .

The claimants would take their case to the European Court of Human Rights (*Smith and Grady* v *United Kingdom* (2000) 29 EHRR 493). Because, under Art. 8 ECHR interferences with an individual's private and family life must be proportionate, and not simply rational (see Chapter 20, pp. 627–8), this claim ultimately succeeded.

Notwithstanding this heightened standard of review and despite the Court's clear desire that the policy be re-evaluated,[76] the policy was not struck down as irrational (in large measure because of Parliament's recent consideration of the issue).

---

[72] *R* v *Ministry of Defence, ex parte Smith* [1996] QB 517, 556.
[73] *Kennedy* v *Charity Commission* [2014] UKSC 20, [2015] 1 AC 455, [51] (Lord Mance).
[74] *R (Mahmood)* v *Secretary of State for the Home Department* [2000] EWCA Civ 315; [2001] 1 WLR 840, [19] (Laws LJ).
[75] *R* v *Ministry of Defence, ex parte Smith* [1996] QB 517, 556 (Sir Thomas Bingham MR).
[76] Ibid., 564 (Henry LJ).

The future of *Wednesbury*

(i) Responding to criticisms of the *Wednesbury* test

The super- and sub-*Wednesbury* tests, by varying review according to the context of the decision under consideration by the courts, responded to criticisms that the original test was a blunt instrument. In *Daly,* Lord Cooke explained that he thought it likely that *Wednesbury* would come to be regarded as:

> [A]n unfortunately retrogressive decision in English administrative law, in so far as it suggested that there are degrees of unreasonableness and that only a very extreme degree can bring an administrative decision within the legitimate scope of judicial invalidation. The depth of judicial review and the deference due to administrative discretion vary with the subject matter.[77]

Figure 19.4 symbolises the different approaches of the courts to reasonableness/irrationality from the 1940s onwards. Line A represents the classic *Wednesbury* standard, a fixed low level of reviewability applied by the courts regardless of the subject matter at issue. The level of reviewability under *Wednesbury* is low, as we have seen, as a result of the high degree of irrationality claimants have to make out before this head of review is triggered. By contrast, Line B represents the variable standard of reviewability, with the courts exercising 'anxious scrutiny'[78] where the most important personal interests of an individual (such as life and liberty) are affected by a decision, but applying a much lower degree of oversight where expert decisions on national security or resource allocation are at issue.

> The evolution of *Wednesbury* away from a strict standard of review does not, however, provide clear guidance as to how the courts will navigate hard cases, which raise 'policy-laden' decisions affecting significant personal interests.

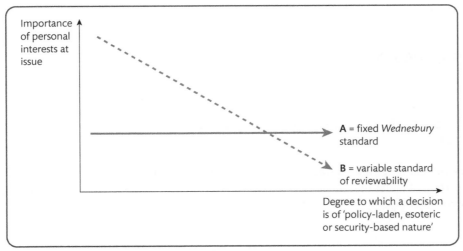

Figure 19.4 Variable versus fixed standard of review

---

[77] *R (Daly)* v *Secretary of State for the Home Department* [2001] 2 AC 532, 549.
[78] *R* v *Secretary of State for the Home Department, ex parte Bugdaycay* [1987] AC 514, 531 (Lord Bridge).

Key case

R (Rogers) v Swindon NHS Primary Care Trust [2006] EWCA Civ 392; [2006] 1 WLR 2649 (Court of Appeal)

The claimant was a breast cancer patient denied the drug Herceptin by Swindon NHS Primary Health Care Trust (PCT) on the basis that it had not yet been authorised (licensed) by the National Institute for Clinical Excellence (NICE) for the treatment of early-stage breast cancer. She led a campaign to see this drug authorised on the NHS, including a judicial review of the rationality of the decision to deny her this treatment. The PCT countered this challenge on the basis that safety concerns surrounded the drug and that there were cost implications for other services.

The court accepted that due to the potential impact on the patient's life expectancy, a 'rigorous scrutiny' standard of review was at issue (at [56]). It acknowledged, however, this alone could not overcome concerns regarding the allocation of scarce resources, if these were indeed at issue in the case (at [58]):

> [T]his case would be very different if the PCT had decided that as a matter of policy it would adopt the Secretary of State's guidance that applications should not be refused solely on the grounds of cost but that, as a hard-pressed authority with many competing demands on its budget, it could not disregard its financial restraints and that it would have regard both to those restraints and to the particular circumstances of the individual patient in deciding whether or not to fund Herceptin treatment in a particular case. In such a case it would be very difficult, if not impossible, to say that such a policy was arbitrary or irrational.

Nonetheless, in this case the court was able to disregard these concerns, because the PCT had accepted that there might be cases where it would permit the prescription of Herceptin. For Sir Anthony Clarke MR, this fact was determinative (at [63]):

> The essential question is whether the policy was rational; and, in deciding whether it is rational or not, the court must consider whether there are any relevant exceptional circumstances which could justify the PCT refusing treatment to one woman within the eligible group but granting it to another. And to anticipate, the difficulty that the PCT encounters in the present case is that while the policy is stated to be one of exceptionality, no persuasive grounds can be identified, at least in clinical terms, for treating one patient who fulfils the clinical requirements for Herceptin treatment differently from others in that cohort.

The Court of Appeal therefore accepted that the policy of rejecting applications without considering clinical need in individual cases was irrational.

(ii) Proportionality: a potential head of review

Even with this evolution in the courts' approach to the *Wednesbury* test, critics still insist that in most cases a variable standard still imposes too high a burden upon claimants. They instead identify the standard of proportionality, developed in continental administrative law, as a preferable approach to cases which call for an assessment of the merits of a public body's policy. Proportionality has long been waiting in the wings of UK administrative law, and was even considered as a potential head of review as long ago as Lord Diplock's judgment in *GCHQ*:

The first ground I would call 'illegality,' the second 'irrationality' and the third 'procedural impropriety'. That is not to say that further development on a case by case basis may not in course of time add further grounds. I have in mind particularly the possible adoption in the future of the principle of 'proportionality' which is recognised in the administrative law of several of our fellow members of the [European Union]; but to dispose of the instant case the three already well-established heads that I have mentioned will suffice.[79]

Thinking Point . . .

Adopting a proportionality test will not necessarily make a difference to the outcome of some cases. As Lord Steyn noted, in *R* v *Chief Constable of Sussex, ex parte International Trader's Ferry Ltd* [1999] 2 AC 418 (at 439): 'the distinction between the two tests in practice is . . . much less than is sometimes suggested'. Moreover, as Lord Mance recognised in *Kennedy* v *Charity Commission* [2014] UKSC 20, [2015] 1 AC 455 (at [54]), 'both reasonableness review and proportionality involve considerations of weight and balance, with the intensity of the scrutiny and the weight to be given to any primary decision maker's view depending on the context'.

The tenor of Lord Diplock's judgment suggests that he was simply waiting for the right case to usher this new standard into our administrative law. However, the introduction of the concept of proportionality would potentially transform administrative law. Rather than focusing on whether a public authority had *some* valid reason for acting (under the basic *Wednesbury* test), proportionality instead requires the courts to examine how a decision is reached, and in particular the decision maker's efforts to balance the claimant's interests against the public interest. If decision makers fail in their performance of this task, they may have imposed disproportionate burdens upon the claimant in pursuit of a policy. Putting this in the context of the 'high jump' diagram above (Figure 19.3),[80] this standard will often amount to a lower bar for claimants to clear.

Lord Diplock's judicial colleagues, however, were unwilling to follow his lead. In the early 1990s his successors as Law Lords closed off any suggestion that the courts should adopt a proportionality standard of review in *ex parte Brind*. The case involved a challenge to the operation of a ban on the broadcasting interviews with, or statements by, representatives of proscribed terrorist organisations. One of the arguments by the journalists bringing the case was that even if the ban was not *Wednesbury*-irrational (the government insisted that it was a valuable counter-terrorism measure), then it could still disproportionately affect their ability to present balanced news reports. This argument was rejected out of hand by Lord Lowry, who regarded proportionality as an unjustifiable extension to judicial review: '[T]here can be very little room for judges to operate an independent judicial review proportionality doctrine in the space which is left between the conventional judicial review doctrine and the admittedly forbidden appellate approach'.[81] He concluded that judges had 'a much better chance of reaching the right answer where the question is put in a *Wednesbury* form'.[82] Nonetheless, in spite of these efforts to cling to the *Wednesbury* test, the influence of European law within the UK's legal systems threatens to eclipse this standard.

---

[79] *Council of Civil Service Unions* v *Minister for the Civil Service* [1985] AC 374, 410.
[80] See Figure 19.3, p. 560.
[81] *R* v *Secretary of State for the Home Department, ex parte Brind* [1991] 1 AC 696, 767.
[82] Idem.

Thinking Point . . .

For the application of a proportionality standard by the House of Lords in an EU law context, see *R v Chief Constable of Sussex, ex parte International Trader's Ferry Ltd* [1999] 2 AC 418. Where doubt is expressed as to whether EU law applies, the Supreme Court have emphasised that proportionality does not necessarily lead to a different outcome from irrationality; *Pham v Secretary of State for the Home Department* [2015] UKSC 19, [2015] 1 WLR 1591, [116] (Lord Sumption). We will cover the approach of the courts to proportionality with regard to the ECHR in detail in Chapter 20, pp. 627–8.

Under both European Union (EU) and European Convention on Human Rights (ECHR) rules decision makers' choices are tested against a proportionality standard. Following the incorporation of these legal orders into the UK's domestic legal systems (through the European Communities Act 1972 and the Human Rights Act 1998), in so far as EU or ECHR provisions apply in a case before the UK courts, judges are obliged to apply a proportionality standard of review. The Court of Appeal has nonetheless maintained that, in the absence in a change in approach by the Supreme Court, the irrationality test will continue to 'apply in a case such as the present which does not involve [EU] law, and does not engage any question of rights under the ECHR'.[83] The Supreme Court, for its part, has vacillated. In *Keyu*, the claimants argued that the Foreign Secretary's refusal to institute a public inquiry into the conduct of the UK's armed forces in colonial-era Malaya had a disproportionate impact upon them (even though EU and ECHR issues were not arguable). The Supreme Court refused to consider this claim, with Lord Neuberger recognising that it 'potentially has implications which are profound in constitutional terms and very wide in applicable scope'.[84] He noted that only a nine-judge Supreme Court panel would have the authority to approve this shift, or once again reject a general proportionality doctrine.

Procedural impropriety

Key issues

- When exercising statutory powers public bodies must respect any express statutory rules on the exercise of the power (failure to do so will render a decision illegal). Beyond such explicit requirements, administrative law also presumes that when a body exercises public powers it will do so in a manner which is fair.

- The standards of fairness (or procedural propriety) which public bodies must observe vary according to the circumstances of the case. Two long-established principles lie at the heart of the concept of fair decision-making:

  (a) *Nemo judex in causa sua* ('no one may judge in his own cause', which imposes a rule against bias).

  (b) *Audi alterem partem* (the requirement 'to hear the other side').

→

---

[83] *Association of British Civilian Internees Far Eastern Region* v *Secretary of State for Defence* [2003] EWCA Civ 473; [2003] 3 WLR 80, [37] (Dyson LJ).

[84] *R (Keyu)* v *Secretary of State for Foreign and Commonwealth Affairs* [2015] UKSC 69, [2015] 3 WLR 1665, [131].

> - These principles are not immutable – their application has been changed as a result of the incorporation of Art. 6 ECHR into UK law and they operate alongside a nascent common law duty upon decision makers to give reasons for their actions.

The meaning of procedural impropriety

Procedural impropriety, as a head of judicial review, seeks to ensure that public bodies' decision-making processes are fair. This is a deceptively simple idea, for as Lord Reed has noted, there are many reasons for the courts to challenge procedural impropriety:

> There is no doubt that one of the virtues of procedurally fair decision-making is that it is liable to result in better decisions, by ensuring that the decision-maker receives all relevant information and that it is properly tested . . . [but] the purpose of a fair hearing is not merely to improve the chances of the tribunal reaching the right decision. At least two other important values are also engaged . . . . The first . . . [is] the avoidance of the sense of injustice which the person who is the subject of the decision will otherwise feel . . . justice is intuitively understood to require a procedure which pays due respect to persons whose rights are significantly affected by decisions taken in the exercise of administrative or judicial functions . . . The second value is the rule of law. Procedural requirements . . . promote congruence between the actions of decision-makers and the law which should govern their actions.[85]

(i) Breach of express statutory procedural rules

At its least controversial, this head of review involves the courts checking that a public authority has adhered to the procedural rules imposed by Parliament in an authorising statute. Many legislative provisions impose specific procedural requirements upon the powers they grant to public bodies. The Mental Health Act 1983 (as amended by the Mental Health Act 2007), for example, sets out the tests which medical professionals are obliged to carry out before an individual can be detained as a result of their mental health[86] and establishes the procedure whereby detention decisions are reviewed.[87] Breach of such rules is therefore as much an example of illegality as procedural impropriety, despite Lord Diplock's insistence that procedural impropriety encompasses a public body's failure to follow statutory processes.[88]

(ii) Breach of the rules of 'natural justice'

Although some statutes do explain the procedural rules by which public authority powers should be employed, much legislation does not state the procedure to be followed in exercising the powers it grants, or provides mere guidelines which cannot found a claim for illegality. During the nineteenth century, as the role of public authorities expanded, the courts required them to respect basic common law principles of fair process. At a time when

---

[85] *R (Osborn)* v *Parole Board* [2013] UKSC 61; [2014] 1 AC 1115, [67]–[71] (Lord Reed).
[86] Mental Health Act 1983, s. 3.
[87] Ibid., ss. 65–79.
[88] See *Council of Civil Service Unions* v *Minister for the Civil Service* [1985] AC 374, 411.

the professional civil service remained in its infancy (see Chapter 8[89]) such oversight was intended to promote what judges considered to be good decision-making. As one nine-teenth-century Lord Chancellor, Lord Selbourne, declared in one of the earliest plan-ning-regulation decisions to reach the House of Lords:

> No doubt, in the absence of special provisions as to how the person (a Board of Works' official) who is to decide is to proceed, the law will imply no more than that the substantial requirements of justice shall not be violated. He is not a judge in the proper sense of the word; but he must give the parties an opportunity of being heard before him and stating their case and their view. . . . There would be no decision within the meaning of the statute if there were anything of that sort done contrary to the essence of justice.[90]

In other words, the courts were willing to impose procedural obligations regarding the exercise of statutory powers, here requiring that a Board of Works gave claimants subject to its powers a hearing ('an opportunity of being heard before him and stating their case') before it could exercise those powers.

By the turn of the twentieth century, however, rising standards of professionalism within public bodies and the authority of a popularly elected Parliament to set such procedural rules as it chose led to a crisis of confidence amongst the judiciary. A then highly politicised generation of Law Lords, eager to restrict judicial interference with social legislation, paid no more than lip service to the principles of natural justice[91] and actively encouraged the courts to respect the remit of decision makers. As late as the 1950s, in *Nakkuda Ali* v *Jayaratne,*[92] the Privy Council refused to imply rules of procedural fairness into the process by which the claimant's licence was cancelled, even though his livelihood was at issue.[93] At this point, a new generation of judges mounted a fight back against the constraints imposed by their predecessors on this head of judicial review. They were spurred into action by events like the Crichel Down affair (discussed in Chapter 14[94]), which caused many to question the lack of judicial oversight over what seemed to have become an 'excessively autonomous bureaucratic apparatus' constrained only by inadequate 'hierarchical political controls'.[95] In *Ridge* v *Baldwin,* which will be considered in detail below, Lord Reid re-eval-uated *Nakuda Ali.* Noting that the Privy Council had considered no nineteenth-century case law in its decision, and had therefore neglected important cases on implicit rules of procedural fairness, he concluded that this decision 'cannot be regarded as authoritative'.[96]

---

[89] See pp. 276–7.

[90] *Spackman* v *Plumstead Board of Works* (1885) 10 App Cas 229, 240. See also *Cooper* v *Wandsworth Board of Works* (1863) 143 ER 414, 420 (Byles J).

[91] See *Board of Education* v *Rice* [1911] AC 179, 182 (Lord Loreburn LC) and *Local Government Board* v *Arlidge* [1915] AC 120, 132 (Lord Haldane LC).

[92] *Nakkuda Ali* v *Jayaratne* [1951] AC 66. See also *R* v *Metropolitan Police Commissioner, ex parte Parker* [1953] 1 WLR 1150.

[93] See H. W. R. Wade, 'The Twilight of Natural Justice' (1951) 67 LQR 103, 106 and H. W. R. Wade, 'Law, Opinion and Administration' (1962) 78 LQR 188, 199.

[94] See pp. 439–40.

[95] P. Lindseth, 'Reconciling with the Past: John Willis and the Question of Judicial Review in Inter-War and Post-War England' (2005) 55 UTLJ 657, 688.

[96] *Ridge* v *Baldwin* [1964] AC 40, 78–9 (Lord Reid).

The rules of procedural fairness (historically known as the rules of natural justice) quickly regained their place as a key feature of judicial review. Just over two decades after *Ridge* v *Baldwin*, Lord Bridge was able to declare that procedural impropriety was a 'well established' basis upon which a claimant could challenge an administrative decision:

> [I]t is well established that when a statute has conferred on any body the power to make decisions affecting individuals, the courts will not only require the procedure prescribed by the statute to be followed, but will readily imply so much and no more to be introduced by way of additional procedural safeguards as will ensure the attainment of fairness.[97]

These additional procedural safeguards fall into two established categories (the rule against bias and the right to a fair hearing) and one emergent category (the requirement to give reasons for a decision). Each will be examined in turn.

The rule against bias

(i) Bias (or the appearance of bias)

A decision can be challenged on the basis that decision makers did not approach their task with the necessary degree of impartiality, resulting in procedural unfairness towards the claimant. From the outset, it is important to acknowledge that this type of procedural impropriety bears some relation to acting with improper purposes and taking into account irrelevant considerations (both facets of illegality as a head of review). The rule against bias, however, is in many cases easier for the claimant to make out than these forms of illegality; the claimant does not have to establish actual bias on the part of the decision maker but simply that a decision was tainted by the appearance of bias. This principle was set out in the decision in *ex parte McCarthy*. A solicitor involved in criminal proceedings against McCarthy following a road traffic accident sat as a clerk in a civil case arising out of the same accident. McCarthy lost the civil action and sought a judicial review of the decision, claiming that the clerk's role had undermined the impartiality of the hearing. Although the clerk had not taken an active role in the proceedings, Lord Hewart CJ trumpeted that 'justice must not only be done but must manifestly and undoubtedly be seen to be done'.[98] He proceeded to explain the application of this aphorism to the case at hand:

> The question . . . is not whether in this case the deputy clerk made any observation or offered any criticism which he might not properly have made or offered; the question is whether he was so related to the case in its civil aspect as to be unfit to act as clerk to the justices in the criminal matter. The answer to that question depends not upon what actually was done but upon what might appear to be done. Nothing is to be done which creates even a suspicion that there has been an improper interference with the course of justice.[99]

Lord Hewart ruled that the clerk's role was sufficient to cast the suspicion of impropriety over these proceedings, and he therefore quashed the Sussex Justices' decision. That this case dates from the inter-war period, in which the courts were least activist in applying the rules of judicial review, indicates the fundamental nature of this rule. In its modernised form, it applies in two scenarios; when decision makers show themselves to have personal

---

[97] *Lloyd* v *McMahon* [1987] AC 625, 702–3.
[98] *R* v *Sussex Justices, ex parte McCarthy* [1924] 1 KB 256, 259.
[99] Ibid.

or financial interests in a decision which should have disqualified them from reaching the decision; and, when decision makers show that they have prejudged the issue at stake.

(ii) A disqualifying personal or financial interest in a decision

The most straightforward (and long-settled) application of this rule is that a decision maker with a financial interest in the outcome of a decision will appear to be biased. In the mid-nineteenth century the then Lord Chancellor, Lord Cottenham, sat in a case in which he owned £1,000 in shares in the defendant canal company. When the claimant sought to have his decision quashed on this basis, Lord Cottenham claimed to have forgotten about his shareholding and that it had not influenced his decision. The House of Lords panel hearing *Dimes* accepted that Lord Cottenham had not actually been influenced by his shareholding, but nonetheless decided that his behaviour had created the appearance of bias. In the words of Lord Campbell:

> No one can suppose that Lord Cottenham could be, in the remotest degree, influenced by the interest he had in this concern; but, my Lords, it is of the last importance that the maxim that no man is to be a judge in his own cause should be held sacred. And that is not to be confined to a cause in which he is a party, but applies to a cause in which he has an interest.[100]

In short, justice will never 'be seen to be done' where a decision maker has a financial interest in the decision. But more challenging cases arise when a decision maker's alleged interest is personal, rather than financial, in nature. In *Gough* a defendant was convicted of robbery and appealed on the basis that a juror on his trial had been his brother's neighbour. The House of Lords dismissed this claim without difficulty; the alleged personal bias was so speculative as to be insignificant. Nonetheless, Lord Goff took the opportunity to reformulate the common law test for personal bias:

> [H]aving ascertained the relevant circumstances, the court should ask itself whether, having regard to those circumstances, there was a real danger of bias on the part of the relevant member of the tribunal in question, in the sense that he might unfairly regard (or have unfairly regarded) with favour, or disfavour, the case of a party to the issue . . . [101]

Within a matter of years, the test would be employed against a decision by one of Lord Goff's fellow Law Lords, Lord Hoffmann, in the course of the *Pinochet* litigation. As we saw when we considered the relationship between the UK and international legal orders, the courts had to consider a request to extradite General Augusto Pinochet (the former Chilean President) to Spain on the basis of allegations that he had orchestrated a campaign of torture against political opponents during his time in office (discussed in Chapter 3[102]). By a bare majority, the House of Lords decided to extradite Pinochet. Pinochet, however, sought to have this decision reviewed on the basis that Lord Hoffmann, one of the majority judges, had sat in the case despite an intervention by Amnesty International, an organisation in which Lord Hoffmann acted as a sub-Director.

A reconstituted House of Lords panel decided that his links to Amnesty should have disqualified Lord Hoffmann from sitting. Lord Browne-Wilkinson ruled that:

> If the absolute impartiality of the judiciary is to be maintained, there must be a rule which automatically disqualifies a judge who is involved, whether personally or as a director of a company,

---

[100] *Dimes* v *Proprietors of the Grand Junction Canal* (1852) 2 HL Cas 759, 793.
[101] *R* v *Gough* [1993] 2 All ER 724, 738.
[102] See pp. 72–3.

in promoting the same causes in the same organisation as is a party to the suit. There is no room for fine distinctions if Lord Hewart CJ's famous dictum is to be observed: it is 'of fundamental importance that justice should not only be done, but should manifestly and undoubtedly be seen to be done'.[103]

In the wake of *Pinochet,* a glut of claimants attempted to argue that a variety of family interests, distant connections to employers and links through solicitors' firms biased decision makers in their particular cases. Given the common legal issues at stake these claims where rolled together into the *Locabail* litigation. A heavyweight Court of Appeal panel dismissed many of these cases, but listed factors which would suggest an appearance bias by personal interest (with the passage of time between any supposedly bias-inducing events lessening such connections):

> [A] real danger of bias might well be thought to arise if there were personal friendship or animosity between the judge and any member of the public involved in the case; or if the judge were closely acquainted with any member of the public involved in the case, particularly if the credibility of that individual could be significant in the decision of the case . . .[104]

The Court further clarified that a claim regarding a decision maker's personal bias was extremely unlikely to be accepted if it related to societal factors such as 'the religion, ethnic or national origin, gender, age, class, means or sexual orientation of the judge' or the 'social or educational or service or employment background or history, nor that of any member of the judge's family; or previous political associations; or membership of social or sporting or charitable bodies; or Masonic associations; or previous judicial decisions; or extra-curricular utterances'.[105]

(iii) Predetermination of an issue

The Court of Appeal dismissed all but one of the *Locabail* claims as fanciful and disclosing no real danger of bias. One successful claim, however, was against a decision in which a judge had awarded a particularly large sum in personal-injury damages in line with his well-documented views on the issue at stake.[106] The Court accepted that the judge had given the appearance of predetermining this issue before considering the case. This ground for bias would be raised:

> [If] on any question at issue in the proceedings before him the judge had expressed views, particularly in the course of the hearing, in such extreme and unbalanced terms as to throw doubt on his ability to try the issue with an objective judicial mind . . . or if, for any other reason, there were real grounds for doubting the ability of the judge to ignore extraneous considerations, prejudices and predilections and bring an objective judgment to bear on the issues before him.[107]

This quotation highlights the distinction between prejudgement and predisposition (an issue we have also discussed in Chapter 6[108]). No judge or decision maker can approach a case entirely free of predispositions (all decision makers possess human sympathies on certain issues), but decision makers must avoid the appearance of having predetermined a

---

[103] *R v Bow Street Metropolitan Stipendiary Magistrate, ex parte Pinochet (No. 2)* [2000] 1 AC 119, 135.
[104] *Locabail (UK) Ltd* v *Bayfield Properties* [2000] 2 WLR 870, [25].
[105] Ibid.
[106] Ibid., [75].
[107] Ibid., [25].
[108] See pp. 207–9.

decision (by following their sympathies without regard to pertinent facts or rules). *Cole* demonstrates a decision maker employing such 'extreme and unbalanced terms' as to cast doubt upon his impartiality. A trial judge repeatedly intervened during the course of a defence counsel's submissions in a dangerous driving case, culminating in his passing a note to the barrister stating 'Prior Planning Prevents Piss Poor Performance'. Latham LJ ruled that the resultant conviction was unsafe due to these interventions, concluding that the note 'helps us to understand whether or not this appellant can have felt that he was getting a fair trial in front of this judge'.[109]

The bulk of cases we have examined to date in the context of bias have involved judges. Today, however, the rule against bias has a general application to all public decision makers, not just to those making judicial decisions. This poses particular difficulties for the rule against predetermination of an issue, for elected decision makers often appear to have prejudged particular issues, having attained office on the basis of their 'publicly stated views on a variety of policy issues'.[110] Historically, the courts simply avoided applying this aspect of the bias test beyond judicial actors.[111] Nonetheless, in *ex parte Kirkstall Valley Campaign*, Sedley J recognised a broad rule that 'the decision of a body, albeit composed of disinterested individuals, will be struck down if its outcome has been predetermined . . . by effective surrender of the body's independent judgment'.[112] In the *Condron* case, the decision makers in question were the Planning Committee of the National Assembly of Wales. When the Committee granted permission for a company to conduct opencast mining operations, the complainant objected that its members had predetermined the issue by deciding to follow a report into the operation's viability and had not properly considered objections. The Court of Appeal was willing to assess such claims:

> [I]t is necessary to look beyond pecuniary or personal interests and to consider in addition whether . . . some of its members were biased in the sense of approaching the decision with a closed mind and without impartial consideration of all relevant planning issues.[113]

The Court identified no evidence of bias on this basis, concluding that policy statements and manifesto commitments differed from instances when a decision maker had predetermined an issue because '[t]he former is consistent with a preparedness to consider and weigh relevant factors in reaching the final decision; the latter involves a mind that is closed to the consideration and weighing of relevant factors'.[114] This indicates that the bias test is flexible, and, with regard to the appearance of bias by predetermination at least, will be applied more strictly in relation to judicial proceedings than to the actions of other decision makers.[115]

(iv) The *Porter* v *Magill* reformulation of the test for bias

Article 6 ECHR imposes a requirement that when the civil rights and obligations of individuals are at issue, or when they face criminal charges, they are 'entitled to a fair and public hearing within a reasonable time by an independent and impartial tribunal established by

---

[109] *R* v *Cole* [2008] EWCA Crim 3234; (2009) 173 CL & J 39, [22].

[110] *R* v *Secretary of State for the Environment, ex parte Kirkstall Valley Campaign* [1996] 3 All ER 304, 325 (Sedley J).

[111] See *Franklin* v *Minister of Town and Country Planning* [1948] AC 87, 103 (Lord Thankerton).

[112] *R* v *Secretary of State for the Environment, ex parte Kirkstall Valley Campaign* [1996] 3 All ER 304, 321.

[113] *R* *(Condron)* v *National Assembly for Wales* [2006] EWCA Civ 1573, [31] (Richards LJ).

[114] Ibid., [43].

[115] See *R* *(Lewis)* v *Persimmon Homes* [2008] EWCA Civ 746; [2009] 1 WLR 83, [71] (Pill LJ).

law'.[116] After the Human Rights Act 1998 incorporated this provision of the ECHR into domestic law, the UK courts were obliged to consider whether the 'real danger' test for bias established in *Gough* ensured a sufficient standard of impartiality within the decision-making process to meet these requirements.

We have already considered *Porter* v *Magill* in the context of abuse of powers by a decision maker.[117] The claimant former leaders of Westminster Council alleged that an auditor's decision that they had been involved in misconduct in office had been tainted by procedural impropriety, on the basis that the auditor had predetermined his decision when he outlined preliminary findings against them at a press conference before his report had been completed. The House of Lords concluded that this press conference might have appeared to observers to constitute an 'exercise in self-promotion', but it had not created the appearance of bias.[118] In reaching this conclusion, Lord Hope made a 'modest adjustment'[119] to the *Gough* test to better align the rule against bias with the requirements of European Court of Human Rights' Article 6 ECHR case law. Whereas the *Gough* test had required the court to ask itself if there was a real danger of bias, Lord Hope instead asserted that judges should consider: '[W]hether the fair-minded and informed observer, having considered the facts, would conclude that there was a real possibility that the tribunal was biased'.[120] The adjustment of the *Gough* test was not the ECHR's only impact upon administrative law, but the speed of this reaction to the HRA 1998 was striking.

Although this reformulation seemingly replaces the subjective view of events by the judges under *Gough* with an objective test, Olowofoyeku considers that the notion of an 'informed' observer requires the courts to attribute to this figure a considerable degree of specialist knowledge. He uses the case of *Lewis*,[121] involving a claim of bias on the basis of predetermination by a council, as an example. In that decision Jackson J stated that:

> In the context of decisions reached by a council committee, the notional observer is a person cognisant of the practicalities of local government. He does not take it amiss that councillors have previously expressed views on matters which arise for decision.[122]

With such a degree of knowledge imputed, Olowofoyeku concludes that the new test is really a more complicated version of the *Gough* test, in which the informed observer 'might as well be a judge'.[123]

The right to a fair hearing

(i) The flexible standard of fairness

If, in the words of Longmore LJ, '[i]t is axiomatic that no person making a decision which is subject to judicial review should in fact be biased [and] in most cases it is axiomatic that

---

[116] ECHR, Article 6(1).

[117] See above pp. 554–6.

[118] *Porter* v *Magill* [2001] UKHL 67; [2002] 2 AC 357, [105] (Lord Hope).

[119] Ibid., [103].

[120] Ibid.

[121] *R (Lewis)* v *Redcar & Cleveland BC* [2007] EWHC (Admin) 3166; [2008] ACD 38.

[122] Ibid., [76]. This decision was successfully appealed in *R (Lewis)* v *Persimmon Homes* [2008] EWCA Civ 746; [2009] 1 WLR 83, but Pill LJ, at [70], expressly approved this statement.

[123] A. Olowofoyeku, 'Bias and the Informed Observer: a Call for a Return to *Gough*' (2009) 68 CLJ 388, 404.

there should also be no appearance of bias',[124] modern administrative law attributes scarcely less importance to the notion that anyone affected by a decision should have the opportunity to put their point of view to the decision maker. What amounts to a fair hearing, however, is context specific; the minimum requirements for a hearing to be fair vary according to the interests of the affected party which are at stake. As Lord Bridge declared in *Lloyd* v *McMahon*:

> [T]he so-called rules of natural justice are not engraved on tablets of stone. To use the phrase which better expresses the underlying concept, what the requirements of fairness . . . [demand] depends on the character of the decision-making body, the kind of decision it has to make and the statutory or other framework in which it operates.[125]

Using this statement as a base it is possible to divide the requirements of a right to a fair hearing into two categories. First, there is the irreducible core to the right, made up of those requirements which cannot be excluded from any decision-making process (except by express statutory provision). Second, there are 'optional extra' features which the courts will require only in cases where the affected party's interests are sufficiently serious to warrant them. Imposing such protections in every single case would burden public administration, so the courts have attempted, in line with the green-light theory of judicial review, to develop a legal heuristic (rule of thumb) which enables them to balance the individual interest in due process against society's interest effective administration. Judges seek to reconcile 'fairness to an adversely affected class with the principles of public administration that are also part of the common law'.[126] The features of the right to a fair hearing can therefore be categorised as follows:

	Features of the right to a fair hearing
Core requirements	• Notice of the decision/information as to the case to be met
	• An opportunity to make out a case
Optional extras	• An oral hearing
	• An appeal process
	• Legal representation
	• Cross-examination of witnesses
	• Reasons for a decision

(ii) The core requirements

There are basic standards of procedural fairness that the common law imposes upon administrative decision-making. Although, in certain cases, a public body might be able to establish that the denial of these basic standards did not result in any material unfairness for an affected party, such cases are 'of great rarity'.[127] In other words, given the value in promoting the principles of fair decision-making throughout the activities of public bodies, the

---

[124] *R (Lewis)* v *Persimmon Homes* [2008] EWCA Civ 746; [2009] 1 WLR 83, [102].
[125] *Lloyd* v *McMahon* [1987] AC 625, 702.
[126] *R (BAPIO Action Ltd)* v *Secretary of State for the Home Department* [2008] UKHL 27; [2008] 1 AC 1003; affirming [2007] EWCA Civ 1139; [2008] ACD 7, [43] (Sedley LJ).
[127] *R* v *Chief Constable of the Thames Valley Police, ex parte Cotton* [1990] IRLR 344, 352 (Bingham LJ).

courts will almost always remedy breaches of these core requirements of fairness. In *Ridge* v *Baldwin,* the case in which the House of Lords 'rediscovered' the right to a fair hearing, Lord Hodson sought to demark the limits of natural justice/procedural impropriety as a head of review:

> No one, I think, disputes that three features of natural justice stand out – (1) the right to be heard by an unbiased tribunal; (2) the right to have notice of charges . . . ; (3) the right to be heard in answer to those charges.[128]

The latter two elements of procedural impropriety relate to the right to a fair hearing. In the 1960s, when *Ridge* was decided, the right to have notice of a potential decision and to be able to respond to it were the only common law procedural rules that the courts were prepared to recognise. Today, after several decades of growth in the concept of procedural impropriety as a head of review, they still represent the core requirements of a fair hearing.

(a) Notice of the decision

If affected parties are not notified of pending administrative decisions applicable to them, they will find it impossible to resist those decisions. In *Anufrijeva,* at issue was whether the claimant should have received income support as an asylum seeker over a five-month period. The answer depended upon whether, at the start of this period, she had ceased to be an asylum seeker. The government argued that at the start of this period a decision had been reached on the claimant's status, and it was irrelevant for the purpose of the payments that the claimant had not been notified of this decision. The House of Lords followed Lord Steyn in asserting that a decision could not affect claimants prior to notification:

> Counsel for the Home Secretary submits that before a 'determination' can be 'notified' there must be a determination. This is legalism and conceptualism run riot. One can readily accept that in this case there must have been a decision as reflected in the file note. That does not mean that the statutory requirement of a 'determination' has been fulfilled. On the contrary, the decision is provisional until notified.[129]

The requirement that an affected party must receive notice of an impending decision is bolstered by the requirement that they receive sufficient detail regarding the decision to enable them to respond (described by Lord Mustill as receiving 'the gist of the case which he has to answer'[130]). In *ex parte Benaim and Khaida* the body responsible for licensing gambling refused the claimants' licence applications. Lord Denning MR made it clear that in such circumstances the requirement of notice extended to providing details regarding the refusal:

> [T]he Board ought in every case to be able to give to the applicant sufficient indication of the objections raised against him such as to enable him to answer them. That is only fair. And the Board must at all costs be fair. If they are not these courts will not hesitate to interfere.[131]

Likewise, in the *Shoesmith* case which we considered above,[132] the Court of Appeal recognised the procedural unfairness inherent in the Secretary of State for Education's failure to provide Sharon Shoesmith with an opportunity to consider even the gist of the

---

[128] *Ridge* v *Baldwin* [1964] AC 40, 132.
[129] *R (Anufrijeva)* v *Secretary of State for the Home Department* [2003] UKHL 36, [32].
[130] *R* v *Secretary of State for the Home Department, ex parte Doody* [1994] 1 AC 531, 560.
[131] *R* v *Gaming Board for Great Britain, ex parte Benaim and Khaida* [1970] 2 QB 417, 431.
[132] See p. 554.

allegations against her before dismissing her from her post.[133] In doing so, the Court emphasised the fundamental importance of this procedural right, notwithstanding the fact that the need for urgency when the protection of vulnerable children is at issue can restrict other aspects of procedural fairness.[134]

(b) Opportunity to make a case

Since *Ridge* v *Baldwin* the courts have maintained that parties affected by administrative action must have the opportunity to make their case before a final decision is reached. Ridge, the Chief Constable of Sussex Police, was severely criticised by a judge in a corruption trial, even though he was acquitted of the charges he faced. He was subsequently dismissed from his post by the constabulary's Watch Committee, the body which oversaw police activity. Given the judicial criticism of Ridge, this dismissal was neither illegal nor irrational – the Committee had legal authority and a good reason for its action. However, Ridge was given no opportunity to provide the Watch Committee with an explanation of his conduct before it dismissed him. Giving the lead judgment in the House of Lords, Lord Reid considered that the dismissal power 'could not then have been exercised and cannot now be exercised until the watch committee have informed the constable of the grounds on which they propose to proceed and have given him a proper opportunity to present his case in defence'.[135] The courts have accepted that the opportunity to make a case can acceptably arise 'either before the decision is taken with a view to producing a favourable result' or, in some cases 'after it is taken, with a view to procuring its modification'.[136]

When a decision has wider effects than a specific individual or group of individuals, government can provide for a consultation before a final decision is reached. Requirements to consult can be imposed by statute and in such instances the courts can treat decisions made in the absence of mandatory consultations as *ultra vires*.[137] The scope of such consultations is thus determined by the statutory context; where statutory duties upon local government to consult over benefit provision are at issue, as they were in *Moseley,* the requirements of an objective consultation are driven by the statutory purpose to 'ensure public participation in the local authority's decision-making process'.[138]

General consultation requirements are not imposed by the common law rule that affected parties must have an opportunity to make their case. This was established in *BAPIO,* in which the Home Secretary abolished the system which allowed junior doctors with no right of abode to train in the UK without a permit. The Court of Appeal accepted that '[i]t is not unthinkable that the common law could recognise a general duty of consultation in relation to proposed measures which are going to adversely affect an identifiable interest group or sector of society'.[139] But Sedley LJ retreated from any attempt to introduce such a requirement into administrative law, on the basis that it would be impossible to constrain such a duty:

---

[133] *R (Shoesmith)* v *OFSTED* [2011] EWCA Civ 642; [2011] IRLR 679, [67] (Maurice Kay LJ).
[134] Ibid., [60] (Maurice Kay LJ).
[135] *Ridge* v *Baldwin* [1964] AC 40, 69.
[136] *R* v *Secretary of State for the Home Department, ex parte Doody* [1994] 1 AC 531, 560 (Lord Mustill).
[137] *R (Moseley)* v *Haringey LBC* [2014] UKSC 56; [2014] 1 WLR 3947, [23] (Lord Wilson).
[138] Ibid., [38] (Lord Reed).
[139] *R (BAPIO Action Ltd)* v *Secretary of State for the Home Department* [2007] EWCA Civ 1139; [2008] ACD 7, [43].

The appellants have not been able to propose any limit to the generality of the duty. Their case must hold good for all such measures, of which the state at national and local level introduces certainly hundreds, possibly thousands, every year. If made good, such a duty would bring a host of litigable issues in its train: is the measure one which is actually going to injure particular interests sufficiently for fairness to require consultation? If so, who is entitled to be consulted? Are there interests which ought not to be consulted? How is the exercise to be publicised and conducted? Are the questions fairly framed? Have the responses been conscientiously taken into account? The consequent industry of legal challenges would generate in its turn defensive forms of public administration.[140]

This restrictive approach was affirmed by the House of Lords.[141] As a result, a common law duty to consult will only arise as a result of specific promises or practice by the public body (amounting to a legitimate expectation) or where the claimant can establish that 'a failure to consult would lead to conspicuous unfairness'.[142]

(iii) The 'optional extra' requirements of fairness

Beyond the core requirements of fairness, Lord Mustill has emphasised that '[t]he principles of fairness are not to be applied by rote identically in every situation'.[143] The courts will impose additional requirements on a decision-making process dependent upon the circumstances of the case. Key factors amongst these circumstances include the impact of a decision upon important interests of affected individuals (the more significant the interest at stake, the more additional elements of the right to a fair hearing will be engaged), the policy context of the decision (the courts are less likely to impose requirements if a decision involves policy concerns such as foreign relations or national security) and the terms on which a discretion is granted to the decision maker.

(a) Oral hearings

Where interests as important as an individual's livelihood or property are at issue, the courts have established that the right to a fair hearing will ordinarily require that such an individual be able to make their case in an oral hearing before the decision maker and not merely in writing. In *ex parte Hook,* for example, Barnsley Council banned a stallholder from its markets for life after he got into an argument with a security guard who found him urinating in the street. At no stage in the process of revoking Hook's licence was he able to appear in person before the relevant council committees. Lord Denning MR led the Court of Appeal in declaring that this failure (contrasted with the participation of the market manager in all the proceedings) breached the requirements of natural justice.[144] To quote the then Scarman LJ, the stallholder 'was on trial not for his life but for his livelihood'.[145]

This decision can be contrasted with the outcome of cases involving less important interests. In *McInnes* v *Onslow-Fane,* the British Boxing Board of Control refused McInnes'

---

[140] Ibid., [44].
[141] *R (BAPIO Action Ltd)* v *Secretary of State for the Home Department* [2008] UKHL 27; [2008] 1 AC 1003.
[142] *R (Plantagenet Alliance)* v *Secretary of State for Justice* [2014] EWHC 1662 (QB), [2015] 3 All ER 261, [98] (Hallett LJ).
[143] *R v Secretary of State for the Home Department, ex parte Doody* [1994] 1 AC 531, 560.
[144] *R v Barnsley MBC, ex parte Hook* [1976] 1 WLR 1052, 1057.
[145] Ibid., 1062.

application for a management licence without giving him an oral hearing. Unlike Hook, McInnes did not currently hold a licence, so his livelihood could not be said to be at stake. Megarry VC therefore concluded that, beyond an honest consideration of the application, no additional requirements need be imposed in this case for a hearing to be considered fair.[146] Similarly, when a council revoked a licence for a market stall being used to distribute political material without providing cause or a hearing, the High Court recognised that 'there was no question of the claimant earning his living'[147] from the stall and consequently accepted that administrative law provided no additional protections beyond the contractual terms of stall-holding.

Thinking Point . . .

R (Smith) v *Parole Board* [2005] UKHL 1; [2005] 1 WLR 350 indicates the degree to which common law rules of procedural fairness align with the ECHR's requirements. At [37], Lord Bingham noted that the Parole Board's review of those issues would 'satisfy the requirements of Art. 5(4) [ECHR] provided it is conducted in a manner that meets the requirements of procedural fairness'.

Where more important interests than livelihood are at stake it is even more likely that an oral hearing will be required. In *Smith* the revocation of the claimants' release from prison under licence was at issue. With the claimant's liberty at stake the requirements of procedural fairness were particularly high. Indeed, as Lord Slynn noted, when the affected individual disputes the factual basis of the decision, the courts will usually insist upon an oral hearing.[148] In the absence of such hearings, the House of Lords found a breach of procedural fairness. Facing numerous time-consuming oral proceedings in the aftermath of *Smith* the Parole Board subsequently restricted oral hearings by requiring that the prisoner make a case as to why one was necessary. When this approach was once again challenged before the Supreme Court in *Osborn,* Lord Reed spelled out why oral hearings were so important where liberty is at stake:

> The board should also bear in mind that the purpose of holding an oral hearing is not only to assist it in its decision-making, but also to reflect the prisoner's legitimate interest in being able to participate in a decision with important implications for him, where he has something useful to contribute. An oral hearing should therefore be allowed where it is maintained on tenable grounds that a face to face encounter with the board . . . is necessary to enable him or his representatives to put their case effectively or to test the views of those who have dealt with him.[149]

(b) Witnesses and cross-examination

If an oral hearing is intended to allow an affected individual to better explain his perspective upon the facts at issue, resolving such factual disputes will also likely require the

---

[146] *McInnes* v *Onslow-Fane* [1978] 3 All ER 211, 219.
[147] *Horsnell* v *Boston BC* [2005] EWHC (QB) 1311, [22] (Mowschenson QC).
[148] *R (Smith)* v *Parole Board* [2005] UKHL 1; [2005] 1 WLR 350.
[149] *R (Osborn)* v *Parole Board* [2013] UKSC 61; [2014] 1 AC 1115, [82] (Lord Reed).

involvement of witnesses and the ability of the affected individual to cross examine opposing witnesses.[150] Therefore, in cases involving a factual dispute and a personal interest sufficient to require an oral hearing, parties should ordinarily be able to call witnesses. The case of *ex parte St Germain* exemplifies this relationship between oral hearings and calling witnesses. In the wake of riots at Hull Prison in 1976 many prisoners had their terms in prison increased, in St Germain's case by a disciplinary board revoking two years of expected sentence remission. St Germain launched a judicial review, claiming that he should have had the ability to call witnesses before this board. In the Court of Appeal, Lane LJ recognised that the disciplinary process had fulfilled the core requirements of a fair hearing, allowing St Germain to 'know what evidence has been given and what statements have been made effecting him' and giving him 'an opportunity to correct or contradict them'.[151] Nonetheless, he recognised that these arrangements were insufficient to provide a fair hearing where the claimant's liberty was at stake:

> [T]he right to be heard will include, in appropriate cases, the right to call evidence. It would in our judgment be wrong to attempt an exhaustive definition as to what are appropriate cases, but they must include proceedings whose function is to establish the guilt or innocence of a person charged with serious misconduct. In the instant cases, what was being considered was alleged serious disciplinary offences, which . . . did result in a very substantial loss of liberty.[152]

As with oral hearings, however, in cases with less serious consequences for affected individuals the courts will be less likely to require such an examination of the evidence. *Maxwell* v *Department of Trade and Industry* involved an official investigation of the dealings of the media tycoon Robert Maxwell. When officials questioned Maxwell on the basis of evidence received from people involved in these dealings, Maxwell brought an action seeking the opportunity to cross examine these individuals. Lord Denning, finding that the investigation had been conducted with 'conspicuous fairness',[153] concluded that there were no interests at stake in this investigation requiring such adversarial proceedings.

(c) Legal representation

The 'optional extra' requirements of procedural fairness often overlap, as the principle linking the importance of the interest at stake and the level of procedural protection applies to all of these requirements. Granting individuals whose liberty is at stake with an oral hearing and the opportunity to call and cross examine witnesses, for example, provides hollow safeguards if they do not also have the support of a legal representative capable of using these opportunities to advance her case. This interrelationship can be seen at work in cases like *Roose,* in which Keith J affirmed that cases involving deprivation of liberty require the highest standards of procedural fairness.[154] Nonetheless, where lesser interests are at stake, and in circumstances which do not involve formal court or tribunal proceedings, requiring legal representation can stymie important administrative processes.[155] In *Kulkarni* the claimant was a junior doctor who was excluded from work following allegations that he had conducted a sexually inappropriate examination of a patient. Although he was due to be represented by a professional representative at a disciplinary hearing

---

[150] Ibid.
[151] *R* v *Board of Visitors of Hull Prison, ex parte St Germain (No. 2)* [1979] 1 WLR 1401, 1404.
[152] Ibid., 1408.
[153] *Maxwell* v *Department of Trade and Industry* [1974] 2 All ER 122, 129.
[154] *Roose* v *Parole Board* [2010] EWHC (Admin) 1780, [21] (Keith J).
[155] See *R* v *Secretary of State for the Home Department, ex parte Tarrant* [1985] 1 QB 251, 278.

concerning these allegations, given the quasi-criminal nature of the allegations and the threat to his livelihood, Dr Kulkarni sought an injunction preventing the hearing from proceeding unless he received legal representation. Penry-Davey J found that no aspect of the case, in which an effective NHS procedure was in place, required that the claimant receive the additional protection of legal representation.[156]

(d) Facility to appeal

Where the most important interests are at stake, an appeal process can be a vital procedural safeguard. The courts have recognised that when an independent appeals process is in place this can negate the importance of procedural impropriety at earlier stages of the decision-making process. This provides an instrumental incentive for decision makers to put such procedures in place, as it insulates them from the threat of judicial review on grounds of procedural impropriety. *Porter* v *Magill* indicates the value in appeal processes. In this case, discussed above,[157] the claimant contended that the decision maker, a district auditor, was not independent and had predetermined her wrongdoing before completing his report on her conduct whilst leader of Westminster City Council. Although Lord Hope accepted that there was some force to the claim that the auditor's role required him 'to act not only as an investigator but also as prosecutor and as judge',[158] the House of Lords ruled that these arrangements were acceptable in light of the ability of the subjects of a report to appeal to an independent tribunal.[159]

(e) Providing reasons for decisions

Beyond the requirement that individuals must have sufficient notice of administrative measures which may affect them to enable them to make a response,[160] there is no general common law duty upon public bodies to provide reasons for decisions they make.[161] Many public bodies, listed in sch. 1 of the Tribunals and Inquiries Act 1992, however, are required to do so by statute.[162]

Nonetheless, as the then Sedley J has recognised, 'inability to know whether [a decision] has been arrived at in reliance on irrelevant factors is universal in unreasoned decisions, except where such factors are revealed by chance'.[163] Such a failure to provide reasons for a decision, in circumstances where it appears questionable on the basis of abuse of powers or irrationality, could undermine potential challenges under judicial review. Indeed, the civil service training guide on judicial review recognises that '[t]he need to record reasons when the decision is made with a view to their disclosure may be onerous, but it encourages careful decision-making'.[164] Therefore, the courts have established that 'the decision-maker (in so far as this had not already been done) owes to the court a duty to provide the court with the reasons for its decision which are relevant to the grounds of challenge'.[165]

---

[156] *Kulkarni* v *Milton Keynes Hospital NHS Trust* [2008] EWHC (QB) 1861; [2008] IRLR 949, [20].

[157] See pp. 554–6.

[158] *Porter* v *Magill* [2001] UKHL 67; [2002] 2 AC 357, [92].

[159] See also *Kingsley* v *United Kingdom* (2002) 35 EHRR 10, [41].

[160] See above, p. 576.

[161] *R* v *Higher Education Funding Council, ex parte Institute of Dental Surgery* [1994] 1 All ER 651, 671 (Sedley J).

[162] See Tribunals and Inquiries Act 1992, s. 10.

[163] *R* v *Higher Education Funding Council, ex parte Institute of Dental Surgery* [1994] 1 All ER 651, 668.

[164] Treasury Solicitor, *The Judge Over Your Shoulder: A Guide to Judicial Review for UK Government Administrators* (4th edn, TSO, 2006) 25.

[165] *R* v *Secretary of State for Transport, ex parte Richmond upon Thames LBC (No. 4)* [1996] 1 WLR 1005, 1019 (Jowitt J).

> ## Thinking Point . . .
>
> Although there is no general duty on a public authority to provide reasons it must be remembered that judicial review is just one element of administrative law. As we saw in Chapter 17, pp. 489–500, in many cases affected individuals can use the Freedom of Information Act 2000 to gain reasons for a decision.

Beyond these circumstances, a *duty* to give reasons only arises where the subject matter of the decision at issue constitutes a sufficiently important interest. For example, in *ex parte Doody,* the Home Secretary exercised the power he then possessed to increase the minimum 'tariff' element of the claimant prisoner's life sentence without providing him with a reason for this decision. In striking down this approach as unfair given that the claimant's liberty was at stake, Lord Mustill identified an increasing judicial willingness to require reasons for a decision in order to foster 'greater openness, or if one prefers the contemporary jargon "transparency", in the making of administrative decisions'.[166] Conversely, however, in *ex parte Institute of Dental Surgery,*[167] Sedley J held that there was no obligation on the Higher Education Funding Council to provide the reasons behind its decision to reduce the research rating of the claimant institute, as the interests at stake were not sufficiently serious to trigger the common law duty.[168] Despite complaints that 'the fuzziness of the law in this area obliges administrators in most cases to play safe and give reasons anyway',[169] this test does not appear more difficult to apply than it does with regard to other aspects of procedural fairness.

These decisions explain when reasons are required as an element of procedural fairness, but they do not indicate the level of detail required to satisfy this duty when it does arise. In *South Bucks DC v Porter* the claimant Council challenged a decision by a planning inspector to allow a Romany Gypsy to remain in a residential mobile home erected without permission on a green-field site, arguing that it had been given insufficient reasons for this decision in light of the resultant environmental harm. The inspector had explained that in reaching this decision he had taken into account that Porter was a 62-year-old woman in serious ill health with a rooted fear of being put into permanent housing, with no alternative site to go to, whose displacement would imperil her continuing medical treatment and probably worsen her condition. The House of Lords accepted that these reasons were sufficient, with Lord Brown explaining that:

> Reasons can be briefly stated, the degree of particularity required depending entirely on the nature of the issues falling for decision. The reasoning must not give rise to a substantial doubt as to whether the decision-maker erred in law, for example by misunderstanding some relevant policy or some other important matter or by failing to reach a rational decision on relevant grounds. But such adverse inference will not readily be drawn. The reasons need refer only to the main issues in the dispute, not to every material consideration.[170]

---

[166] *R v Secretary of State for the Home Department, ex parte Doody* [1994] 1 AC 531, 561.
[167] *R v Higher Education Funding Council, ex parte Institute of Dental Surgery* [1994] 1 All ER 651.
[168] Ibid., 671–672 (Sedley J).
[169] S. James, 'The Political and Administrative Consequences of Judicial Review' (1996) 74 *Public Administration* 613, 632.
[170] *South Bucks DC v Porter* [2004] UKHL 33; [2004] 1 WLR 1953, [36].

Similarly, where a consultation process is at issue, the High Court has confirmed that procedural propriety requires 'sufficient reasons for the proposal in hand to enable consultees to respond intelligently'.[171] When Lord Brown states that reasons, in certain cases, can be 'briefly stated', this is exemplified by *Asha Foundation,* in which the claimant charity challenged the decision of the Millennium Commission not to provide it with funding. Lord Woolf CJ explained that the Commission's response to the funding request, which acknowledged that although the Asha Foundation was eligible for funding other applications were preferred, was entirely sufficient given the limited interests at stake.[172]

(iv) Statutory exceptions

Procedural impropriety is generally recognised as introducing minimum standards from which decision makers must not deviate. It is possible for a statute to introduce procedural rules which exceed these minimum common law standards. More controversially, however, it is possible for sufficiently clearly drafted statutes to deny the application of even these basic standards to particular decisions. Given the primacy of parliamentary sovereignty, this exception has been recognised from the earliest stages of procedural impropriety's development. As Lord Reid recognised in *Wiseman* v *Borneman,* for the courts to impose procedural rules, 'it must be clear that the statutory procedure is insufficient to achieve justice and that to require additional steps would not frustrate the apparent purpose of the legislation'.[173]

Nonetheless, under the principle of legality (discussed in Chapter 5[174]), the courts will presume that, unless there is the clearest wording of a statutory provision to the contrary, it was not the intention of Parliament to exclude the common law rules of procedural propriety.[175] In *ex parte Fayed,* concerning an application for UK citizenship, statutory rules expressly excluded any obligation upon the Home Secretary to give reasons for refusing to grant citizenship.[176] The Home Secretary, however, claimed that these rules also impliedly allowed him to withhold notice of possible reasons for rejecting a citizenship application. The Court of Appeal rejected this contention, with Lord Woolf MR asserting that it would be 'surprising' if Parliament had intended such a broad restriction upon the common law rules of fair process.[177] This suggests that the courts will be reluctant to read all but the clearest statutory terms as excluding requirements of a fair hearing.

By contrast, in rejecting any general requirement for public consultation before particular decisions are reached in *BAPIO,* Maurice Kay LJ recognised that 'in these circumstances, primary legislation has prescribed a well-worn, albeit often criticised procedure and I attach some significance to the fact that it has not provided an express duty of prior consultation, as it has on many other occasions'.[178] In this case the relatively low threshold that the Court of Appeal required to exclude the requirement for consultation relates

---

[171] *R (Evans)* v *Lord Chancellor* [2011] EWHC (Admin) 1146; [2012] 1 WLR 838, [32].
[172] *R (Asha Foundation)* v *Millennium Commission* [2003] EWCA Civ 88, [34].
[173] *Wiseman* v *Borneman* [1971] AC 297, 308.
[174] See pp. 155–8.
[175] See *R (Anufrijeva)* v *Secretary of State for the Home Department* [2003] UKHL 36; [2004] 1 AC 604, [57] (Lord Scott).
[176] British Nationality Act 1981, s. 44.
[177] *R* v *Secretary of State for the Home Department, ex parte Fayed* [1998] 1 WLR 763, 774.
[178] *R (BAPIO Action Ltd)* v *Secretary of State for the Home Department* [2007] EWCA Civ 1139; [2008] ACD 7, [58].

directly to its difficulty in identifying the scope of any such common law requirement. No such difficulties were in issue in *Bank Mellat,* which concerned the core procedural requirement that affected parties be able to make representations to decision makers. In this case the Treasury had used its statutory powers to issue an order excluding Bank Mellat from the UK financial market on the basis that it was involved in financing Iran's nuclear and ballistic weapons programmes.[179] A nine-judge Supreme Court panel assessed whether these circumstances permitted the closed hearing of some of the security-related material (excluding the claimant bank), even if such a hearing risked undermining common law rules of procedural fairness. The majority accepted that Parliament had struck a balance between competing public interests in security and open justice and authorised a closed hearing on this basis. But a three-judge minority vociferously maintained that in circumstances in which the counter-terrorism legislation in question did not explicitly authorise such a procedure the Court should not abrogate 'fundamental' common law rules regarding a fair hearing.[180] The rules of fair hearing clearly go to the heart of many judges' conception of their constitutional role.

Key issues

- Legitimate expectations arise where a public body, by representations or conduct, promises to exercise its discretionary powers in line with a particular policy. There are two types:

   1. *Procedural legitimate* expectations arise where the courts conclude that, because of its promises to affected parties, a public body cannot change a policy without first putting in place procedural arrangements (often consultations) with regard to these parties.

   2. *Substantive legitimate* expectations arise where the courts conclude that, because of its promises to affected parties, restrictions must be placed on a public body's ability to change that policy.

- Before the courts will accept that a legitimate expectation exists, individuals claiming to enjoy such an expectation have to show that they are relying upon a representation or course of conduct by the public body which amounts to a clear promise regarding its policy.

- Even where a claimant can show that such a promise exists, the public body will not have to fulfil that expectation when it can establish that doing so would conflict with an important public interest.

Legitimate expectations

The meaning of legitimate expectations

As we saw when we considered illegality, it is lawful for public bodies to establish policies concerning the use of their discretionary powers provided that they do not approach these policies in such a strict manner as to exclude a claimant with something new to say. Once such policies are published, however, affected parties are likely to order their affairs to

---

[179] Counter-Terrorism Act 2008, sch. 7.
[180] *Bank Mellat* v *HM Treasury* [2013] UKSC 38; [2014] AC 700, [81] (Lord Hope).

conform to their requirements. If a government department, for example, announces that it is going to use its discretion to extend eligibility criteria for a benefit (say, by shifting the age at which it is payable from 60 to 55), affected individuals may alter their spending patterns as a result. If the government subsequently abandons this policy as too expensive and does not make payments to this group, they could suffer hardship as a result. The courts have therefore justified holding public authorities to account on the basis of legitimate expectations which they have generated as maintaining 'fairness'[181] in the decision-making process and ensuring that public bodies 'deal straightforwardly and consistently with the public'.[182] Under this head of review the courts must decide whether, for affected parties, a public body created a legitimate expectation which it cannot now neglect. Nonetheless, even if such a legitimate expectation does exist, this does not mean that the claimant will gain a remedy if it is breached. As Lord Hope has explained, '[p]olicy is not law, so it may be departed from if a good reason can be shown'.[183]

(i) Procedural legitimate expectations

The concept of legitimate expectations is a comparatively recent addition to the heads of judicial review (as can be seen from their omission from Lord Diplock's famous taxonomy of the heads of review in **GCHQ**). This omission is unsurprising given that, only two years before **GCHQ**, Lord Fraser had complained that the concept was 'somewhat lacking in precision'.[184] The first form of this head of review to emerge was 'procedural' legitimate expectations. As the name suggests, these are expectations regarding process generated by decision makers. Procedural legitimate expectations developed because of growing concerns amongst the courts in the 1960s over how the common law fair-process rules applied to decision-making. They are thus, as Lord Woolf MR has acknowledged, an offshoot of the 'historic jurisdiction of the courts over issues of procedural justice'.[185] In *ex parte Schmidt*, the claimants were a group of scientologists who were US citizens. The Home Secretary refused to consider renewing their residence permits on the basis of a new policy seeking to curb the growth of scientology in the UK. Lord Denning stated that whether this issue could be challenged by judicial review 'depends on whether [the claimant] has some right or interest or, I would add, some legitimate expectation of which it would not be fair to deprive him without hearing what he has to say'.[186] He concluded that such expectations would arise if the government attempted to revoke an individual's residence permit before its time limit elapsed (on the basis that she would have ordered her affairs with the expectation of staying in the UK up to the end of her permit), but did not apply to renewals.[187]

However the recognition of an individual's genuine expectation did not mean, under this new doctrine, that she would be able to remain for the duration of her permit. At most, the affected individual would gain a *procedural* claim, by which 'the law recognises that the interest cannot properly be withdrawn (or denied) without the claimant being given an opportunity to comment and without the authority communicating rational grounds

---

[181] *R (A) v Secretary of State for the Home Department* [2006] EWHC (Admin) 526, [29] (Collins J).
[182] *Abdi and Nadarajah v Secretary of State for the Home Department* [2005] EWCA Civ 1363, [68] (Laws LJ).
[183] *R (Kambadzi) v Secretary of State for the Home Department* [2011] UKSC 23; [2011] 1 WLR 1299, [36].
[184] *Attorney-General of Hong Kong v Ng Yuen Shiu* [1983] 2 All ER 346, 350.
[185] *R v North and East Devon Health Authority, ex parte Coughlan* [2001] QB 213, [62] (Lord Woolf CJ).
[186] *Schmidt v Secretary of State for Home Affairs* [1969] 1 All ER 904, 909.
[187] Ibid.

for any adverse decision'.[188] A clear example of procedural legitimate expectations in practice came in *ex parte Asif Mahmood Khan.* The Home Secretary issued a circular (a letter to concerned parties) detailing the criteria which had to be fulfilled in order to allow UK nationals to adopt children from overseas. Mr Khan sought to adopt a relative living in Pakistan. He fulfilled all of the criteria stipulated in the circular, but his application was nonetheless refused. He sought a review of this proposal on the basis of his expectations arising out of the circular. The Court of Appeal accepted this claim, and Parker LJ outlined the scope of Khan's procedural expectations:

> *Vis-à-vis* the recipient of such a letter, a new policy can only be implemented after such recipient has been given a full and serious consideration whether there is some overriding public interest which justifies a departure from the procedures stated in the letter.[189]

(ii) Substantive legitimate expectations

The *Khan* decision showed that official policy statements could create procedural rights. More controversial was whether or not public bodies could be obliged to keep *substantive* promises. Taking *Khan* as an example, could the claimant successfully claim that he had a legitimate expectation to be able to adopt on the basis that he fulfilled the conditions of the circular, rather than merely gaining the right to have his case reconsidered by the Home Office?

Substantive expectations may seem superficially similar to procedural expectations, but the courts have shown themselves to be much more reluctant to assert such requirements. It is one thing for the courts to require decision makers to reconsider the cases of parties particularly affected by changes in policy but quite another to prevent a changed policy from applying to such parties. This reluctance is illustrated by *ex parte United States Tobacco International,* in which the claimant company, which had invested in its business in the UK on the basis of the government's policy of permitting the sale of oral snuff, sought to challenge a subsequent decision to ban the product. Although the Divisional Court was willing to accept that the company had a sufficient interest to require the government to consider its position before bringing its new policy into effect, it refused to countenance any restriction on the government's ultimate ability to adopt the policy.[190] Administrative law had reached a position where:

> [T]he propriety of a breach by a public authority of a legitimate expectation . . . of a procedural benefit – typically a promise of being heard or consulted – is a matter for full review by the court. The court has, in other words, to examine the relevant circumstances and to decide for itself whether what happened was fair . . . But in relation to a legitimate expectation of a substantive benefit . . . doubt has been cast upon whether the same standard of review applies.[191]

To further extend the jurisdiction the courts would have to recognise that the breach of some expectations did not simply produce procedural unfairness, but amounted to an abuse of power. Only in the late 1990s did the courts begin to recognise substantive legitimate expectations, and even then only in extraordinary cases. In *ex parte Hamble Fisheries,*

---

[188] *R v Devon County Council, ex parte Baker and Johns* [1995] 1 All ER 73, 89 (Simon Brown LJ).
[189] *R v Secretary of State for the Home Department, ex parte Asif Mahmood Khan* [1985] 1 All ER 40, 48.
[190] *R v Secretary of State for Health, ex parte United States Tobacco International Inc* [1992] QB 353, 370–1 (Taylor LJ).
[191] *R v North and East Devon Health Authority, ex parte Coughlan* [2001] QB 213, [62] (Lord Woolf CJ).

Sedley J first asserted that 'it is the court's task to recognise the constitutional importance of ministerial freedom to formulate and to reformulate policy; but it is equally the court's duty to protect the interests of those individuals whose expectation of different treatment has a legitimacy which in fairness outtops the policy choice which threatens to frustrate it'.[192] The case involved a policy change preventing the transfer of fishing licences, and Hamble Fisheries sought that it should be allowed to proceed with its transfer. Although Sedley J ultimately rejected this claim (given the transitional arrangements the government put in place), his statements in favour of the possibility of substantive legitimate expectations caused something of an outcry. Hirst LJ went as far as to condemn them as 'heresy', for imposing substantive restrictions on the decision maker which ignored the limits of the judicial review jurisdiction.[193]

The dispute was not resolved until the case of *ex parte Coughlan,* in which, having already informed a small group of patients affected by a care home closure that they would not be moved again from their new residence, the North and East Devon Health Authority sought to close Mardon House, the residential home into which they had been moved. Lord Woolf MR accepted that substantive expectations can arise and where they do the courts must decide 'whether to frustrate the expectation is so unfair that to take a new and different course will amount to an abuse of power'.[194] The Health Authority's assurances in this case created just such an expectation and the Court of Appeal accepted that the decision to close the home was unlawful as it constituted 'an unjustified breach of a clear promise given by the health authority's predecessor to Miss Coughlan that she should have a home for life at Mardon House'.[195]

Thinking Point . . .

Affirming the links between abuse of powers and legitimate expectations, in *R (A)* v *Secretary of State for the Home Department* [2006] EWHC 526 (Admin), at [29], Collins J stated that ignoring a legitimate expectation will 'mean that the decision maker has failed to have regard to a material consideration'.

Following *Coughlan,* the possibility of substantive legitimate expectations is now generally accepted, to the point where Laws LJ has suggested that continuing to distinguish between substantive and procedural expectations is unnecessary, as '[t]he dichotomy between procedure and substance has nothing to say about the reach of the duty of good administration'.[196] Nonetheless, given the different basis of each of these claims (procedural expectations having their roots in the rule against procedural impropriety and substantive expectations developing out of the rule against abuse of powers) and the stricter limits upon the scope for substantive expectations, it remains necessary to consider them separately.

---

[192] *R* v *Ministry of Agriculture Fisheries and Food, ex parte Hamble (Offshore) Fisheries Ltd* [1995] 2 All ER 714, 731.

[193] *R* v *Secretary of State for the Home Department, ex parte Hargreaves* [1997] 1 WLR 906, 921.

[194] *R* v *North and East Devon Health Authority, ex parte Coughlan* [1999] EWCA Civ 1871; [2001] QB 213, [57].

[195] Ibid., [118].

[196] *Abdi and Nadarajah* v *Secretary of State for the Home Department* [2005] EWCA Civ 1363, [69] (Laws LJ).

Creating legitimate expectations

(i) Legitimate expectations arise from official representations or conduct

Legitimate expectations arise from promises or agreements made by a public body, either expressly (contained, for example, within specific advice to an individual, more generally circulated official circulars, or publically stated policies) or as a result of the body's past conduct (official practice in equivalent previous situations). It must be remembered that the actions of the public body, and not the affected party, create legitimate expectations. We have already encountered different examples of the manner in which an expectation is formed. In *Coughlan,* for example, the expectation arose from a specific promise to the claimant and a small group of other residents. In *Khan,* by contrast, an official circular dispatched to everyone who had notified the Home Office of their intention to adopt a foreign national sufficed. *Abbasi* turned upon whether a UK national detained at Guantánamo Bay could rely on policy statements by the UK Government concerning how it would exercise its power to make diplomatic representations where UK nationals are detained overseas. Lord Phillips MR accepted that in these circumstances the UK Government 'has indicated . . . what a British citizen may expect of it . . . [and] there is no reason why its decision or inaction should not be reviewable if it can be shown . . . [to be] contrary to legitimate expectation'.[197]

Legitimate expectations do not only arise from express promises. They can be implied from the conduct of public bodies. Much of this chapter has considered Lord Diplock's taxonomy of the heads of review in the *GCHQ* case. The case itself provides an important authority regarding the emergence of legitimate expectations by conduct. Under a new government policy, civil servants who were members of trade unions were reassigned from posts at the UK's communications surveillance centre, GCHQ. Prior changes to working conditions had been made after consultation with the unions. The House of Lords accepted that this body of past practice gave rise to a legitimate expectation on the part of the civil servants, with Lord Fraser declaring that '[l]egitimate, or reasonable, expectation may arise either from an express promise given on behalf of a public authority or from the existence of a regular practice which the claimant can reasonably expect to continue'.[198]

(ii) The representations/conduct must be sufficiently clear to create an expectation

The actions of a public body can only give rise to legitimate expectations where those actions are official and constitute a clear promise. The first of these conditions is illustrated by the case of *ex parte Begbie*. Begbie had taken a place at an independent school under a state-funded assisted places scheme. The Labour Party, when in opposition, had resolved to abolish this scheme, but had given undertakings that children already holding school places under the scheme would continue to receive funding. Once in office after the election victory of 1997, Labour abolished the scheme and did not allow those with places to continue. The Court of Appeal held that pre-election statements could not be treated as

---

[197] *R (Abbasi)* v *Secretary of State for Foreign and Commonwealth Affairs* [2002] EWCA Civ 1598; [2003] UKHRR 76, [106].
[198] *Council of Civil Service Unions* v *Minister for the Civil Service* [1985] AC 374, 401.

having legal consequences and, if made by a party in opposition, did not arise from a public authority so as to fall within the ambit of judicial review. As Gibson LJ stated:

> An opposition spokesman, even the Leader of the Opposition, does not speak on behalf of a public authority. A further difficulty relates to the effect in law of a pre-election promise by politicians anxious to win the votes of electors. . . . It is obvious that a party in opposition will not know all the facts and ramifications of a promise until it achieves office. To hold that the pre-election promises bound a newly-elected government could well be inimical to good government.[199]

If the context in which a statement which potentially creates an expectation is made is therefore important, the clarity of the pledge made by a public body is ordinarily determinative of whether the doctrine of legitimate expectations is even at issue in a case. Some of the successful cases discussed above indicate the level of detail required for the courts to find that a legitimate expectation exists, but to fully understand this requirement we must consider some unsuccessful cases. In *Association of British Civilian Internees* the government published a policy leaflet detailing that compensation payments of £10,000 would be made to 'surviving British civilians who were interned by the Japanese in the Far East during the Second World War'. Subsequently, the Government clarified that this policy did not extend to individuals who lacked very strong links to the UK (either as their birthplace or the birthplace of their parents). The Association brought an action on behalf of these excluded individuals, asserting that the policy statement had created the legitimate expectation that they would receive a payment. The Court of Appeal found that the statements contained in the leaflet were insufficiently clear to create an expectation, noting that 'anyone reading the announcement and the specimen claim form carefully should have realised that the scheme did not, or might not, entitle all those who were British subjects at the time of their internment to compensation without qualification'.[200]

A further example of the refusal of the courts to accept that a representation was sufficiently clear to give rise to an expectation arose in *Bancoult,* when the House of Lords considered the Chagos Islanders' (the Ilois) case to be allowed to return to their home islands (having been removed from these islands in the 1960s to allow the construction of a military airbase). Following earlier court defeats the Government had stated that it would allow 'the Ilois to return to the outer islands [in the Chagos archipelago]' subject to an ongoing study 'on the feasibility of resettling the Ilois'. The House of Lords rejected assertions that such conditional statements could create legitimate expectations, with Lord Hoffmann declaring that:

> As we have seen, [the Ilois] tried to persuade the government that the press statement amounted to the adoption of a policy of resettlement . . . But the question is what the statement unambiguously promised and in my opinion it comes nowhere near a promise that, even if there could be no resettlement, immigration control would not be reimposed.[201]

---

[199] *R v Secretary of State for Education and Employment, ex parte Begbie* [2000] 1 WLR 1115, 1126.
[200] *Association of British Civilian Internees – Far Eastern Region v Secretary of State for Defence* [2003] EWCA Civ 473; [2003] 3 WLR 80, [60] (Dyson LJ).
[201] *R (Bancoult) v Secretary of State for Foreign and Commonwealth Affairs (No. 2)* [2008] UKHL 61; [2009] 1 AC 453, [62].

(iii) The importance of detrimental reliance

The courts have historically been unclear as to whether the reaction of the individual or group subject to a pledge by a public body will have any bearing on whether that pledge will give rise to legitimate expectations. In cases like *Abbasi* there was no evidence to suggest that the claimant, when detained by US forces, had any knowledge of the UK Government's policy regarding diplomatic protection of UK nationals overseas. Nonetheless, the Court of Appeal accepted that this general policy created the procedural expectation that the claimant's request for protection would be considered.[202] By contrast, in *Association of British Civilian Internees,* the Court of Appeal drew attention to the Association's response to the policy statement on compensation payments to show that its leading members did not, when the statement was made, believe that it constituted a promise to all its members sufficient to give rise to a substantive expectation that they would receive payment.[203]

These cases can be distinguished on the basis that whereas the first related merely to procedural expectations, the latter related to substantive expectations. This allows us to conclude that the more serious an impediment to policy changes by public bodies that a legitimate expectation would involve, the more likely parties claiming an expectation will have to show that they actively relied upon the body's promise or past conduct. This supposition was affirmed in *Begbie,* where Gibson LJ acknowledged that when parties seek to enforce substantive expectations the courts will ordinarily expect them to demonstrate detrimental reliance upon the public body's policy.[204]

(iv) The importance of the size of the group to which a promise is made

When the courts were developing the concept of legitimate expectations, they were slow to explain the importance of the breadth of a promise, in terms of the number of individuals potentially covered by it. As late as *Coughlan,* Lord Woolf MR continued to ponder the significance of this factor:

> May it be . . . that, when a promise is made to a category of individuals who have the same interest, it is more likely to be considered to have binding effect than a promise which is made generally or to a diverse class, when the interests of those to whom the promise is made may differ or, indeed, may be in conflict?[205]

Nonetheless, in *Coughlan,* the Court did stress that the pledge not to move residents from the care home in question applied only to eight individuals,[206] and this fact seems to have influenced its recognition of a substantive expectation in this case. By contrast, in cases we have considered in which a general policy extending to many individuals was found to give rise to legitimate expectations, such expectations were procedural in nature.

---

[202] *R (Abbasi)* v *Secretary of State for Foreign & Commonwealth Affairs* [2002] EWCA Civ 1598; [2003] UKHRR 76, [92].

[203] See *Association of British Civilian Internees – Far Eastern Region* v *Secretary of State for Defence* [2003] EWCA Civ 473; [2003] 3 WLR 80, [64]–[65] (Dyson LJ).

[204] *R* v *Secretary of State for Education and Employment, ex parte Begbie* [2000] 1 WLR 1115, 1124.

[205] *R* v *North and East Devon Health Authority, ex parte Coughlan* [1999] EWCA Civ 1871; [2001] QB 213, [80].

[206] Ibid., [3].

Laws LJ's decision in **Bhatt Murphy** sheds some light on this issue. The case concerned an effort by the Government to withdraw a discretionary compensation scheme for victims of miscarriages of justice. Although the Court of Appeal found that no legitimate expectations existed on the facts of the case, Laws LJ took the opportunity to explain that substantive legitimate expectations would likely be accepted only when the pledge related to (at most) a small group:

> Though in theory there may be no limit to the number of beneficiaries of a promise for the purpose of such an expectation, in reality it is likely to be small, if the court is to make the expectation good. There are two reasons for this . . . First, it is difficult to imagine a case in which government will be held legally bound by a representation or undertaking made generally or to a diverse class . . . The second reason is that the broader the class claiming the expectation's benefit, the more likely it is that a supervening public interest will be held to justify the change of position complained of.[207]

Countering a legitimate expectation claim

(i) Fulfilling an expectation

Even when a legitimate expectation is found to exist, this does not mean that parties enjoying such expectations will succeed. Legitimate expectations arise as a result of promises regarding policies and the courts have recognised that public bodies can do enough to fulfil expectations by taking steps that do not necessarily involve providing claimants with the procedural or substantive benefits they seek. In **Coughlan,** Lord Woolf MR recognised that the public body will in many cases be found to have discharged an expectation by putting transitional policies in place for the benefit of expectation-holders:

> The court's task [is] . . . limited to asking whether the application of the policy to an individual who has been led to expect something different is a just exercise of power. In many cases the authority will already have considered this and made appropriate exceptions . . . or resolved to pay compensation where money alone will suffice. But where no such accommodation is made, it is for the court to say whether the consequent frustration of the individual's expectation is so unfair as to be a misuse of the authority's power.[208]

Only where no such transitional measures are put in place, or they are inadequate, will the courts act upon an individual's expectations. Moreover the courts will not lightly dismiss official efforts to soften the transition between two policies, with Sedley LJ acknowledging that '[s]uch provision may take the simple form of giving prior warning that the change is coming'.[209]

(ii) Individual interests must be balanced against the public interest

Despite the above discussion of the importance of factors such as detrimental reliance in the courts' recognition of legitimate expectations, the doctrine does not, in contrast to some statements in early legitimate expectations cases,[210] operate in the same way as the private law

---

[207] *R (Bhatt Murphy)* v *Independent Assessor* [2008] EWCA Civ 755, [46].
[208] Ibid., [80].
[209] Ibid., [70].
[210] See, for example, *R* v *IRC, ex parte MFK Underwriting Agencies Ltd* [1990] 1 WLR 1545, 1569 (Bingham LJ).

doctrine of estoppel.[211] The public body making a promise is not, in all circumstances, prevented from resiling from it; it is simply prevented from going back on its promise where it has no good reason for doing so. As Lord Woolf made clear in ***Coughlan,*** '[o]nce the legitimacy of the expectation is established, the court will have the task of weighing the requirements of fairness against any overriding interest relied upon for the change of policy'.[212]

Especially in the context of substantive legitimate expectations, the courts have made it clear that these will not constrain a decision maker's freedom of action where it can show some sound reason why a policy needed to be changed in spite of parties relying upon that policy. This was well expressed by Gibson LJ in ***Begbie*** when he recognised that:

> In some cases a change of tack by a public authority, though unfair from the applicant's stance, may involve questions of general policy affecting the public at large or a significant section of it (including interests not represented before the court); here the judges may well be in no position to adjudicate save at most on a bare ***Wednesbury*** basis, without themselves donning the garb of policy-maker, which they cannot wear.[213]

Often such public interest considerations can transform what may have been a substantive expectation into mere procedural expectations in the court's eyes. Indeed, not even procedural expectations, such as expectations of consultation, are immune from being rejected when the courts recognise 'an overriding public interest'.[214] The ***GCHQ*** case provides an example of such public interests at work overriding a legitimate expectation. As we saw above, on the basis of past conduct an expectation had developed amongst the civil service trade unions that they would be consulted on changes in working conditions for civil servants at GCHQ. No such consultations took place when the government banned union members from working at GCHQ in the 1980s. Nonetheless, the House of Lords concluded that the national security concerns at issue in this case were sufficiently serious to 'trump' this particular expectation. As Lord Roskill stated:

> My Lords, if no question of national security were involved I cannot doubt that the evidence and the whole history of the relationship between management and staff since 1919 shows that there was a legitimate expectation of consultation before important alterations in the conditions of service of civil servants were made.[215]

Conclusion

Rather than simply attempting to provide a snap-shot of the current state of judicial review, this chapter has sought to highlight the changing nature of the jurisdiction in recent decades. The approach demonstrates the flexibility of the jurisdiction and flags up just how easily and quickly emerging concepts, like legitimate expectations, have become accepted features of judicial review. Moreover, as we will see when we come to examine the concept of human rights and the incorporation of the ECHR, this flexibility made it possible for legislators to graft aspects of the HRA 1998's enforcement arrangements onto the structure of judicial review.

---

[211] See P. Sales, 'Legitimate Expectations' [2006] JR 186, 186–187.
[212] *R v North and East Devon Health Authority, ex parte Coughlan* [1999] EWCA Civ 1871; [2001] QB 213, [57].
[213] *R v Secretary of State for Education and Employment, ex parte Begbie* [2000] 1 WLR 1115, 1130.
[214] *R v North and East Devon Health Authority, ex parte Coughlan* [1999] EWCA Civ 1871; [2001] QB 213, [80].
[215] *Council of Civil Service Unions v Minister for the Civil Service* [1985] AC 374, 419.

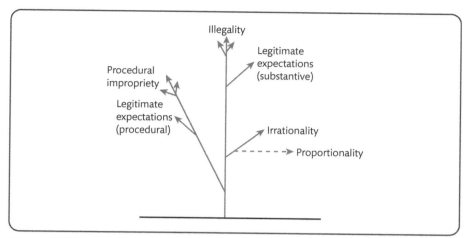

Figure 19.5 The tree of judicial review

The grounds for judicial review can be likened, in Figure 19.5 above, to a maturing tree. At the centre, illegality forms the jurisdiction's main trunk, supporting the core constitutional idea that public bodies must be able to be held account on the basis of whether or not they can show legal authority for their actions. No matter how savagely judicial review was pruned back for much of the twentieth century, the core *ultra vires* conception of illegality remained operative, for without it the whole jurisdiction would collapse.

Beyond illegality, procedural impropriety and irrationality are nineteenth-century growths in the concept of judicial review. These branches of judicial review were constrained, and in the case of procedural impropriety, almost completely cut back during the long period from the start of the twentieth century until the mid-1960s in which the courts were extremely reluctant to challenge exercises of executive power. Since then, procedural impropriety has probably grown more rapidly than any of the other branches of judicial review. Irrationality, by contrast, remains a relatively weak branch, stunted by the judiciary's reluctance to face accusations of challenging decisions on their merits. In this context, proportionality remains a tantalising prospect, with the potential to extend the courts' oversight of administrative decisions only realised to-date in relation to EU and ECHR Law. Together, these different branches create the image of a jurisdiction in a state of flux, with recent cases tending towards further extensions of judicial oversight for so long as Parliament allows this organic development to continue.

Practice questions

1. *'Public law has grown to meet the needs of justice on the one hand and of good government on the other by holding public administration to as much of its public undertakings – its policies – as is necessary and fair.'*

(R (Bhatt Murphy) v Independent Assessor [2008] EWCA 755, [67] (Sedley LJ))

Evaluate whether the concept of legitimate expectations has developed to such a degree that it fulfils Sedley LJ's goal.

2. *'[Whether the Supreme Court] should authorise a general move from the traditional judicial review tests to one of proportionality . . . is a subject which continues to attract intense academic debate. It is to be hoped that an opportunity can be found in the near future for an authoritative review in this court of the judicial and academic learning on the issue, including relevant comparative material from other common law jurisdictions. Such a review might aim for rather more structured guidance for the lower courts than such imprecise concepts as "anxious scrutiny" and "sliding scales".'*

(Youssef v Secretary of State for Foreign and Commonwealth Affairs [2016] AC 1457; [2016] UKSC 3, [55] (Lord Carnwath))

Evaluate why the UK Supreme Court has been so reluctant to introduce a general proportionality standard within administrative law.

Further reading

Given the diverse nature of the different 'heads of review' considered in this chapter, it is worth focusing some further reading on each of the different heads. One of the most difficult concepts within illegality, as a head of review, is fettering of discretion and Adam Perry (**A. Perry, 'The Flexibility Rule in Administrative Law'** (2017) 76 *Cambridge Law Journal* 375–398) diagnoses conceptual weaknesses in the way in which courts are handling this rule. With regard to irrationality, Paul Daly (**P. Daly, 'Wednesbury's Reason and Structure'** [2011] *Public Law* 238–259) provides a thorough overview of the main criticisms of *Wednesbury* unreasonableness, coupled with a useful attempt to draw out the factors which will lead a court to consider whether a decision is unreasonable (by Daly's account, illogicality, disproportionality and inconsistency with statute). Some of the most controversial irrationality cases have involved when the judiciary should challenge the merits of a public body's decisions regarding the allocation of scarce resources. Jeff King (**J. King, 'The Justiciability of Resource Allocation'** (2007) 70 *Modern Law Review* 197–224) provides an important contribution to this debate, examining how the Human Rights Act 1998 is changing the approach of the judiciary to these questions. Within the procedural impropriety head of review many students feel that they instinctively grasp the concept of bias. To gain a deeper understanding of this deceptively difficult concept, however, readers should consider Abimbola Olowofoyeku's excellent overview (**A. Olowofoyeku, 'Bias and the Informed Observer: a Call for a Return to *Gough*'** (2009) 68 *Cambridge Law Journal* 388–409) of the cases related to the rival tests for bias which have existed in UK public law, examining how, far from placing the *Gough* test on an objective basis, the test propounded in *Porter* v *Magill* leaves considerable room for judges to take their subjective view of the circumstances surrounding a bias claim into account. Finally, highlighting the complexity which has inevitably accompanied the rapid growth of the concept of legitimate expectations in administrative law, Rebecca Williams' article (**R. Williams, 'The Multiple Doctrines of Legitimate Expectations'** (2016) 132 LQR 639–663) posits that there are three different varieties of legitimate expectation, each with a different conceptual and normative base and different working elements for claimants to make out.

Chapter 20
The European Convention on Human Rights

'[T]ill some way be invented to regulate the motions of the people's maliminous body, I think arbitrary rule was the most safe for the world.'

Henry Parker, *Observations upon Some of his Majesties late Answers and Expresses,* 2 July 1642, E. 153, 10.

Chapter outline

This first part of this chapter examines what is meant by the term 'human rights' and the role of this concept in twenty-first century public law. The concept of human rights is intended to protect those civil, political, social and economic interests vital to maintaining human autonomy. Human rights law, in its modern guise, came to the forefront of public thought across Europe in the aftermath of the Second World War, an era which produced the European Convention on Human Rights (ECHR). The institutions established by the ECHR and the rights enumerated therein continue to evolve, providing the basis for some of the UK's commitments in international law. The ECHR regime is designed to provide a framework not only for protecting human rights but, where necessary, for balancing competing rights against each other and against other important societal interests. The concept of human rights therefore provides a basis both for enumerating the most fundamental interests enjoyed by individuals within the UK and for restraining the actions of public authorities which conflict with those interests.

Introduction

With civil war looming over Great Britain and Ireland in the mid-seventeenth century, Henry Parker wrote an 'original and brilliant'[1] tract in defence of the concept of parliamentary sovereignty, quoted above. But even Parker, focused on the immediate issue of substituting Parliament's authority for that of King Charles I, saw dangers in the

---

[1] T. Pease, *The Leveller Movement: a Study in the History and Political Theory of the English Great Civil War* (OUP, 1916) p. 23.

concept. The 'maliminous' body of public opinion (put another way, the strength reposed in the majority by representative government) needed to be regulated or minority groups would suffer from abuses of this power. Parker was one of the first of a new generation of political philosophers, collectively known as the enlightenment thinkers, to wrestle with the issue of preventing the abuse of majoritarian power inherent within representative systems of government. Over the succeeding centuries many of his successors strove to 'invent' the solution to this problem. After many false starts and painful reverses, across the countries of Europe, the concept of human rights has, from the late twentieth century onwards, come to occupy a central place amongst the control mechanisms over majority power.

Some writers conclude that human rights are no more, and no less, than what internationally agreed human rights treaties say that they are.[2] Nonetheless, even though this chapter focuses on what, within the UK's constitutional arrangements, is the most important international human rights treaty, the European Convention on Human Rights (ECHR), the concept of human rights cannot be reduced to the provisions set out in any one document. The first section of this chapter therefore introduces the theoretical underpinnings of human rights and the development of the concept. These underpinnings allow us to put the ECHR in context as an important milestone in the development of human rights but also serve to remind us that the terms of the ECHR do not provide the definitive boundaries of the concept. Thereafter, successive sections of the chapter explain the institutional arrangements operating under the ECHR and provide a summary of the rights enumerated within the treaty. Finally, this chapter concludes with an examination of the different mechanisms employed under the ECHR to balance, or reconcile, human rights with other important community interests. A word of caution is, however, necessary. This is a general public law textbook and much more detailed appraisals of human rights[3] and the law of the European Convention on Human Rights[4] can be found in subject specific texts.

The nature of human rights

Key issues

- The modern concept of human rights has developed out of earlier attempts to accord rights on the basis of religion or citizenship. The concept has gone through several stages of development since it emerged during the seventeenth century (during the 'Enlightenment'), resulting in very different systems and degrees of human rights protection across the world.

- Human rights are best understood as very important interests which are essential to the autonomous personhood of individuals. However, few of these values are absolute and

---

[2] See: C. Beitz, *The Idea of Human Rights* (OUP, 2009) pp. 209–12.

[3] For instance: C. Tomuschat, *Human Rights: Between Idealism and Realism* (3rd edn) (OUP, 2014); A. Clapham, *Human Rights: A Very Short Introduction* (2nd edn) (OUP, 2015).

[4] For instance: D. Harris, M. O'Boyle, E. Bates and C. Buckley, *Law of the European Convention on Human Rights* (3rd edn) (OUP, 2014); B. Rainey, E. Wicks and C. Ovey, *The European Convention on Human Rights* (6th edn) (OUP, 2014).

human rights regimes often make allowance for most rights to be traded-off against other important public policy concerns.

- Sceptics criticise human rights on a number of grounds:

   1. The vision of human rights' advocates has not been universally realised.
   2. Human rights promote undesirable values.
   3. Human rights change the relationship between law and politics.
   4. Human rights do not constrain private power.
   5. Human rights constitute 'Western' impositions.

The developing concept of human rights

(i) Human rights: a contested concept

When, as set out in the quote that opens this chapter, Parker identified the difficulty in constraining majoritarian power, he was grappling with the problem of whether a constitutional order would ever be able to contain the extremes of unrestricted individual liberty and unlimited authority of government over the people.[5] Advocates usually present the concept of human rights as achieving just such an accommodation by identifying certain 'rights' as particularly important individual interests and placing them outside the ordinary reach of the political process. As Conor Gearty asserts, this separation of human rights from ordinary politics imbues the concept with a kind of 'moral magic':

> The phrase 'human rights' is a strong one, epistemologically confident, ethically assured, carrying with it a promise to the hearer to cut through the noise of assertion and counter-assertion, of cultural practices and relativist perspectives, and thereby to deliver truth. To work its moral magic, human rights needs to exude this kind of certainty, this old-fashioned clarity.[6]

Such 'old-fashioned clarity' is, unfortunately, illusory. For one thing, as Gearty recognises, '*uncertainty* rather than *certainty* is, perhaps more than anything else, the key defining feature of our culture today'.[7] Political ideologies and religion, once dominant within public life, are today restricted to the margins of public discourse in the UK. Secondly, the concept of human rights is itself shrouded in uncertainty. Many frequently-asserted rights, such as the right to liberty and privacy, and even the right to life, are often contested concepts. For example, different commentators may be able to invoke 'the right to life' to support very different arguments. Some would argue that respect for the right to life precludes a state's use of the death penalty (such arguments regard the right as a superior interest to criminal justice concerns such as retribution). Others would argue that any state which claims to uphold the right to life should prohibit abortion, on the basis that life begins from the moment of conception (such arguments regard the right as a superior interest to conflicting rights, such as women's reproductive rights). Still others conceive of legitimate exceptions to the right to life permitting a state, for example, to kill a suspected terrorist where it is believed that he poses an imminent danger to civilian life. Seemingly turning the right to life upon its head, some

---

[5] See: B. Wilson, *What Price Liberty? How Freedom Was Won and is Being Lost* (Faber & Faber, 2010) pp. 16–17.

[6] C. Gearty, *Can Human Rights Survive?* (CUP, 2006) p. 19.

[7] Ibid.

would argue that it encompasses the ability of individuals to control their lives and therefore a right to decide when life ends (permitting practices such as euthanasia). Still others emphasise that the right to life does not simply require a state not to take life, it also implies that a state is under a positive obligation to protect the lives of individuals living within its territory (potentially extending to a right to state provision of life-preserving medical treatment).

For legal theorists such as Tom Campbell, these different conceptions of the right to life flow from 'differing philosophical and political views, none of which exclude endorsing human rights as the basis of humane treatment and political legitimacy and none of which contravenes the standard catch phrases of "human dignity" or "equal concern and respect"'.[8] Different attempts to translate human rights from moral standards to legal rules, either through domestic legislation or international human rights treaties, can therefore arrive at very different definitions of rights dependent on the philosophical assumptions underpinning the legal document. With regard to international human rights treaties in particular, where differences of opinion regarding the content of a right mean that its terms in law are often vague and brief, such textual ambiguity can give considerable scope for judges to bring their personal political and philosophical opinions to bear on human rights questions.

The existence of human rights treaties has therefore failed to resolve debates on issues such as euthanasia, pornography and hate crime; all remain politically contentious.[9] Each of these issues involves clashes between different human rights or between rights and other important societal interests. Vague drafting of rights instruments (often essential to gain broad acceptance of the existence of a right) can allow different courts to accept very different interpretations of rights. Campbell describes this phenomenon as the potential for 'ideological capture'[10] of human rights, in that, rather than rights being inviolable, judges can emphasise different elements of rights or their in-built limitations to reach the outcome of a case which they desire. Unless courts and decision makers understand, and apply, the philosophical underpinnings embodied within particular human rights in their decisions, the concept amounts to little more than a smoke screen disguising the real basis for decision making from public attention.

(ii) Decoupling rights from religion

The idea that humanity shares common values and interests is not novel. As Paul Lauren asserts at the outset of his account of the history of human rights, '[t]houghtful and insightful visionaries in many different times and places have seen in their mind's eye a world in which all people might enjoy certain basic and inherent rights simply by virtue of being human beings'.[11] These visionaries, however, did not produce legally enforceable human rights documents. The roots of modern human rights are better traced to the French and American revolutions of the late-eighteenth century and to the 'Enlightenment' thinkers writing during this era. Previously, the acceptability of a state's treatment of individuals had often been assessed on the basis of whether or not it conformed with the strictures of the dominant religion in the state.[12] Enlightenment thinkers approached

---

[8] T. Campbell, 'Human Rights: A Culture of Controversy' (1999) 26 JLS 6, 15–16.
[9] Ibid., 14.
[10] Ibid.
[11] P. Lauren, *The Evolution of International Human Rights: Visions Seen* (2nd edn) (University of Pennsylvania Press, 2003) p. 1.
[12] See J. Shestack, 'The Philosophic Foundations of Human Rights' (1998) 20 *Human Rights Quarterly* 200, 204–5.

human relationships (including those between the individual and the state) differently, seeking to ground them in something other than religion. The seventeenth-century philosopher John Locke, for example, began the process of seeking to define 'natural rights' to life, liberty, and property enjoyed by individuals living in a state of nature (a situation without any governance structures), concluding that these could not ultimately be removed by any system of government later produced by humans.[13]

Locke's writings, and those of French philosopher Jean-Jacques Rousseau,[14] would provide the philosophical backbone for the US and French revolutions in the late eighteenth century. Nonetheless, in many respects the 'rights' documents produced in this transitional era differ greatly from more modern formulations of human rights. The Declaration of Independence issued by the colonies set to form the United States in 1776 may have given a prominent place to the 'inalienable' rights of individuals to 'life, liberty, and the pursuit of happiness', but it did so on the basis that these were rights granted to individuals by their creator. By contrast, the rights advanced in the French Declaration of the Rights of Man and of the Citizen of 1789 and the United States' Bill of Rights of 1792 were not expressed as being 'God-given', extending their rights on the basis of common humanity. This marked a crucial turning-point in the development of modern human rights, extending the concept's attractiveness beyond the adherents of a particular faith.

(iii) The evolution of human rights

The United States' Bill of Rights therefore marks the first generation of human rights document, theoretically extending its protections to individuals within the jurisdiction of the United States by virtue of their humanity and not their citizenship, religion or race. Nonetheless, by failing to protect against infringements of human rights such as slavery, the Bill of Rights had to be supplemented by additions through the nineteenth and twentieth centuries. Even with such updating, the Bill of Rights remains very different in structure and content to human rights documents drafted in the twentieth century. It contains a more limited number of rights than many later rights documents, but these rights often provide for fewer acceptable qualifications by the US Government. Francesca Klug explains such discrepancies as being the product of different generations of thinking on the concept of human rights:

Key debates

Three 'waves' of human rights thinking

Francesca Klug (F. Klug, 'The Human Rights Act – a "Third Way" or a "Third Wave" Bill of Rights' (2001) EHRLR 361) divides human rights documents into three generations, which can be divided on the basis of the rights included, the terms of those rights and the geographical reach of the document.

→

---

[13] See J. Locke, *Two Treatises of Civil Government* (first published 1690, Everyman's Library, 1961) Book II, Ch. II, para. 5–6.

[14] See J.-J. Rousseau, *On the Social Contract* (First published 1762, J. Masters (trans.), St. Martin's Press, 1978).

1. 'First wave' document (e.g. US Bill of Rights 1792)

Human rights documents produced in the late-eighteenth century focus on securing protections for individuals living within particular states. The rights included within the US Bill of Rights were limited to those thought necessary to prevent a government from acting as a tyranny and were used to emphasise the freedoms secured within the United States in contrast to the restrictions previously endured under colonial rule by the UK.

2. 'Second wave' document (e.g. European Convention on Human Rights and Fundamental Freedoms, 3 September 1953, 213 UNTS 222)

As Klug writes, at 364, if the eighteenth-century rights documents had been intended 'to set people free', the aim of the regional and international rights documents which were developed after the Second World War 'was to create a sense of moral purpose for all humankind'. Although lists of rights continued to be included within national constitutions these were frequently developed to conform to international documents. Human rights continued to be thought of primarily as a counterweight to the potential excesses of state power, but the horrors of Nazi and Soviet abuses of office resulted in the framers of these documents introducing more extensive lists of rights. Nonetheless, these documents were conscious of the need to limit certain rights and the conflicts between certain rights. Very few of the rights contained within them are cast in absolute terms.

3. 'Third wave' document (e.g. International Covenant on Economic, Social and Cultural Rights, 16 December 1966, 993 UNTS 3)

Torture can be eliminated without any financial burden on the state. Regulation simply needs to be put in place ensuring that agents of the state adhere to minimum standards of conduct. By contrast 'third-generation' social and economic rights require the state to maintain provisions such as healthcare and education, in proportion to the resources available to society. These rights remain very controversial, with some arguing that the interests they protect are insufficiently important to be classed as rights and that their enforcement unduly constrains public finances. In the UK, in particular, concerns that judges would adjudicate upon the allocation of scarce public resources have restricted the impact of these rights.

The focus of human rights has also shifted to the international plain since the Second World War. After this conflict it was recognised that it was no longer desirable for states not to comment on the domestic policies of other states where these involved human rights abuses. Starting with the statement of human rights found in the UN's Universal Declaration on Human Rights (UDHR),[15] states began to agree on minimum standards of rights protection that applied across borders. Klug again captures the revolutionary nature of this development:

> It is easy to forget that until the UDHR was adopted, virtually *any* criticism – let alone interference – by one government with the treatment of the citizens of another, was considered a breach of the principle of national sovereignty. Human rights abuses were perfectly lawful if they complied with a country's domestic law.[16]

Today, many countries have ratified international human rights treaties with some, like the ECHR, being superintended by international institutions. This international focus of human rights enforcement helps to offset majoritarian power in particular polities,

---

[15] UN General Assembly Resolution 217 A (III), UN Doc. A/810 (10 December 1948).
[16] F. Klug, 'The Universal Declaration of Human Rights: 60 Years on' [2009] PL 205, 207.

requiring governments to look to international responsibilities and not simply to domestic electoral considerations in formulating policies which affect human rights.

Assessing the philosophical basis of human rights

A large body of human rights law has therefore developed in the international and domestic spheres, particularly since the end of the Second World War. If we can point to the fact of a law's existence, this can tempt us as lawyers into thinking that we no longer have to engage with the reasons behind its creation on the basis that such concerns are part of the political process that brought the law into being. We must avoid this temptation with regard to human rights. Firstly, the philosophical basis of human rights is, as we have seen, open to dispute (producing wide variations in how particular rights can be interpreted). Moreover, the concept is itself subject to continuing evolution (through the various phases of human rights instrument identified above). Human rights treaties simply claim to *proclaim* human rights, rather than purporting to *create* rights.[17]

This capacity for rapid evolution seems to preclude some of the traditional explanations for the nature of human rights. For example, writers such as John Finnis have argued that human rights amount to basic moral norms common across a range of established human value-structures. Arguably, for example, the vast majority of human groups (which can, for example, be based on their members' shared nationality, religion or culture) prohibit torture, rape or murder.[18] But there is far less evidence of such synergy over, say, the minimum requirements of due process, freedom of expression or privacy. Some commentators, therefore, have claimed that the breadth of rights contained within modern human rights documents exceeds the philosophical basis of rights as being 'self-evidently' fundamental to human society and therefore 'inherently uncontroversial amongst reasonable people'.[19] Nonetheless, states continue to agree to such broad human rights treaties in spite of the lack of any agreement common amongst humanity over many of the rights in question, arguably highlighting a weakness in the coherence of the 'consensus' explanation of human rights rather than with the concept of human rights itself.

This is not to argue, however, that the concept of human rights does not, in part, derive strength from consensus. Instead, as Tom Campbell identifies, the focus of this consensus lies less in the detailed content of rights, but in their primary purpose of constraining government action:

> The moral power of the human rights ideology derives from the consensus that there are certain things that people have done to each other in the course of human history which are atrocious and ought not to be repeated.[20]

In other words, human rights exist not to create a moral code for governing all human relations but to protect human beings from arbitrary exercises of government power. Therefore, in common with James Griffin's analysis of the underpinnings of the concept of human rights,[21] it is possible to see all rights as existing to protect valuable aspects of human autonomy, but that systems of rights can allow such autonomy to be traded-off against other important societal concerns (at least to a degree).

---

[17] J. Harris, 'Human Rights and Mythical Beasts' (2004) 120 LQR 428, 430.
[18] See J. Finnis, *Natural Law and Natural Rights* (OUP, 1980) p. 83–4.
[19] T. Campbell, 'Human Rights: a Culture of Controversy' (1999) 26 JLS 6, 18.
[20] Ibid., 18.
[21] J. Griffin, *On Human Rights* (OUP, 2008).

(i) Normative agency (or 'personhood')

Normative agency is essentially the ability of humans to act as autonomous individuals. Under Griffin's definition, it represents 'our capacity to choose and to pursue our conception of a worthwhile life'.[22] Griffin's approach owes much to the writings of Immanuel Kant who, in the late-eighteenth century, recognised the centrality of the capacity of individuals to act autonomously to the then nascent concept that individuals should enjoy freedom on the basis that they are rational beings.[23] Kant considered that our own personhood allowed us to choose to lead our lives in a way which we considered to be good and that no government should constrain our personhood unless we seek to use it in a manner which would infringe the personhood of others.[24] As Griffin recognises, personhood is the key factor underpinning many of the commonly accepted human rights:

> We have a right to life (without it, personhood is impossible), to security of person (for the same reason), to a voice in political decision (a key exercise of autonomy), to free expression, to assembly and to a free press (without them, exercise of autonomy would be hollow), to worship (a key exercise of what one takes to be the point of life). It also generates, I should say (though this is hotly disputed), a positive freedom: namely, a right to basic education and minimum provision needed for existence as a person – something more, that is, than mere physical survival. It also generates a right not to be tortured, because, among its several evils, torture destroys one's capacity to decide and to stick to the decision. And so on. It should already be quite clear that the generative capacities of the notion of personhood are quite great.[25]

Normative agency is therefore, on most accounts, the engine room driving the creation of human rights. The concept owes much to earlier efforts by Locke and Rousseau to derive a system of natural rights, but does not require us to imagine a state of nature to be able to work out what these rights are. Nonetheless, as Griffin notes, at the outer edges of the concept of human rights the focus on personhood has not lessened debate as to when an interest should be elevated to the status of a human right.

(ii) Trade-offs: practical considerations

By protecting personhood as an end in itself, the concept of human rights is intended to prevent governments from advancing policies which ride rough-shod over interests of such 'paramount importance'. Even where a democratically elected government is seeking to maximise the wellbeing of the majority of individuals within a state (in accordance with the utilitarian principle that government exists to secure the greatest good for the greatest number of individuals) the possibility exists that it will seek to do so by denying resources or access to institutions to particular individuals or minority groups within the state (and thereby advantaging the majority). This 'sinister side'[26] of utilitarian policy making resulted in legal scholars led by Ronald Dworkin championing human rights as 'trumps' which override countervailing community interests. Under this conception, human rights

---

[22] Ibid., 45.

[23] See: I. Kant, *Groundwork of the Metaphysics of Morals* (first published 1797, M. Gregor trans., CUP, 1996) pp. 37, 95.

[24] Ibid., pp. 100–1.

[25] J. Griffin, *On Human Rights* (OUP, 2008) p. 33.

[26] J. Shestack, 'The Philosophic Foundations of Human Rights' (1998) 20 *Human Rights Quarterly* 200, 213.

represent the irreducible core of individual interests which cannot be infringed no matter what the policy arguments in favour of their limitation.[27]

For Griffin, however, the need for human rights to act as a bulwark against state encroachments upon the interests essential to personhood does not mean that all (or even most) rights represent absolute values which cannot in any circumstances be curtailed in pursuit of community interests. Instead, a much greater range of human rights can be envisioned, and rights will much more readily be acceptable to policy makers, if such rights are flexible enough to accommodate other particularly serious policy concerns. In Griffin's opinion, human rights have 'special importance' but not 'uniquely great importance',[28] allowing such trade-offs. Griffin describes this process as considering personhood in light of 'practicalities'.[29] For example, curtailing exercises of expression which incite violence infringe an individual's personhood less than the infringement of the potential victim's personhood. Practicalities, however, do not always affect the equation. Griffin in particular argues that torture, for example, amounts to such a serious infringement of personhood that it can *never* be validated by practical considerations such as the value of any information gained.[30]

As we shall see, Griffin's approach to human rights closely adheres to the ECHR's system of rights protection, permitting certain *prima facie* rights infringements where the rights at issue are outweighed by other concerns or held in balance by countervailing rights. This potential for trade-offs may be one of the hallmarks of modern human rights documents (potentially providing a more pragmatic realisation of the world than the enlightenment thinkers envisaged), but critics argue that this flexibility dilutes the assurance that individuals can successfully call upon human rights.[31] As the philosopher Isaiah Berlin cautioned, 'some among the Great Goods cannot live together',[32] and the debate on the interaction between human rights and other public policy values (and, in some cases, the clashes between different rights) highlights the fact that systems of government will often have to make difficult choices between such values.

(iii) Human rights scepticism

Even if we accept the conceptual coherence of Griffin's account of human rights, many critics seek to portray human rights advocates as idealists trapped in an unrealisable or undesirable quest for what Conor Gearty describes as 'Heaven on earth and for all not just (or even mainly) for themselves or the chosen few'.[33] Such 'rights scepticism' would exist even if the concept's philosophical roots were uncontroversial, requiring us to consider the arguments advanced by sceptics even if we accept Griffin's explanation of the concept. Although human rights advocates are often able to respond to the arguments advanced by rights sceptics in isolation, cumulatively they at the very least require us to treat with caution some of the transformative claims made in favour of human rights.

---

[27] R. Dworkin, *Taking Rights Seriously* (Duckworth, 1977) pp. 184–205.
[28] J. Griffin, *On Human Rights* (OUP, 2008) p. 36.
[29] Ibid., p. 37.
[30] Ibid.
[31] See R. Mullender, 'Review: *On Human Rights,* by James Griffin' (2010) 30 LS 151, 154–5.
[32] I. Berlin, *The Crooked Timber of Humanity: Chapters in the History of Ideas* (Pimlico, 2003) 13.
[33] C. Gearty, *Can Human Rights Survive?* (CUP, 2006) p. 18.

1. The vision of human rights advocates has not been realised

Although human rights standards have been widely heralded in recent decades, historian Reza Afshari points to the 'apparent disparity between the often-celebrated normative global achievements in codifying human rights values among the UN member states and the often lamented failures to enforce them'.[34] Even as the concept of human rights has secured a central place within international legal discourse, widespread examples of serious human rights abuses by many regimes (even regimes which claim to be 'rights respecting', such as the United States, whilst engaged in its Cold War struggle with the Soviet Union) prompted Alasdair MacIntyre to proclaim that belief in human rights 'is as one with belief in witches and in unicorns'.[35] Criticising human rights standards on the basis that they are not at present respected within all legal systems, however, is not the same as claiming that they cannot be realised as such in the future. The strength of human rights can be seen by what has been described as the 'soft law' value of its compliance-pull.[36] Even states which systematically infringe human rights often seek to conceal this fact, and value being accepted as 'rights respecting' to maintain their status within the international community.

2. The concept of human rights promotes undesirable values

Human rights remain a difficult concept to market to any community. The safeguards they provide exist to protect individual/minority interests against the will of the majority, as expressed in democratic countries by the government in office. This often draws opposition, especially where deeply unpopular individuals such as serious criminals invoke human rights to challenge their treatment by the state (as press coverage in the UK frequently attests).

Key debates

Human rights scepticism amongst some UK politicians and sections of the UK media

Human rights are frequently attacked by sections of the UK media. In July 2006, the then Department of Constitutional Affairs (the forerunner to the Ministry of Justice), sought to address some of the criticisms, publishing its *Review of the Implementation of the Human Rights Act.* This review noted (at 29) a number of common misperceptions and agendas underpinning criticisms that human rights existed 'for giving undeserving people a means of jumping the queue and getting their interests placed ahead of those of decent hardworking folk'.

Such misperceptions frequently arise from inaccurate reporting of cases. For example, the *Review* highlighted the case of Barry Chambers, who sought to avoid arrest by refusing to leave the roof of a house in Gloucester to which he had fled. The police, as part of their strategy to resolve the stand-off peacefully, brought Chambers food during negotiations. As a result of off-hand comments by a police officer, the tabloid press reported (J. Coles, 'A Finger Nickin' Good Farce', *Sun* (7 June 2006)) that food (specifically from a popular fried chicken chain) had been brought to Chambers as a result of his human rights.

From the opposite end of the political spectrum, Marxist theorists have argued that human rights are undesirable not because they impose excessive constraints upon the

---

[34] R. Afshari, 'On Historiography of Human Rights Reflections on Paul Gordon Lauren's the Evolution of International Human Rights: Visions Seen' (2007) 29 *Human Rights Quarterly* 1, 1.

[35] A. MacIntyre, *After Virtue: a Study in Moral Theory* (2nd edn, Duckworth, 1985) p. 69.

[36] C. Douzinas, *The End of Human Rights* (Hart, 2000) p. 9.

The *Review* concluded that such misreporting was often intended to further two viewpoints. The first was that, as they were derived from a 'European' Convention (despite the ECHR not being a creation of the EU), human rights provisions in UK law were 'a target for criticism by those who urge withdrawal from the European Union' (at 30). Secondly, when 'vulnerable and excluded groups' did win cases using human rights claims, opponents of such groups' interests often paint human rights as advancing a 'compensation culture' (at 30). Such factors indicate that much of the 'mainstream' opposition to human rights targets the ECHR as a proxy for other concerns.

The findings of the *Review,* in this regard were underlined by the events at the 2011 Conservative Party Conference. Theresa May MP, then the Coalition Government's Home Secretary, sought to score some points with rank-and-file members of her party by highlighting a deportation case in which the government's efforts to remove a Bolivian national from the UK were blocked 'because – I am not making this up – he had a pet cat' (see N. Watt and A. Travis, 'Tory Conference Cat-Fight: Clarke and May Clash Over Human Rights Act story', *Guardian* (4 October 2011)). The Asylum and Immigration Tribunal decision in question (IA/14578/2008), however, had focused upon the Home Office's failure to follow its policy towards immigrants with unmarried spouses in the UK, with the couples' ownership of a cat forming the basis of some light-hearted judicial asides.

It is no accident that in the immediate aftermath of the Home Secretary's comments both the then Attorney-General, Dominic Grieve, MP, and the then Justice Secretary, Kenneth Clarke, MP, reaffirmed the Government's commitment to human rights, with the Attorney-General attacking the 'hysterical untruths' often printed about the Human Rights Act 1998 in the UK media (see N. Morris, 'Dominic Grieve: Stop Spreading Lies About Human Rights Act', *Independent* (6 October 2011)). Perhaps the final point regarding public debate on human rights should go to the former President of the Supreme Court, who warns of the dangers of anti-human rights 'propaganda' (Lord Neuberger, 'Open Justice Unbound' (Judicial Studies Board Annual Lecture 2011, 16 March 2011) 16):

> It is a sign of a healthy democracy that there are different views within society and that the outcome of individual cases, and the balance struck between individual rights, can be vigorously debated. But such debates must be based on fact not misconception, deliberate or otherwise. Persuasion should be based on truth rather than propaganda.

government of a country but because they envisage very limited societal change and constitute a bar to transformative efforts to bring about a more equal society.[37] Indeed, it is possible to argue that the concept of human rights has absorbed much of the energy of groups seeking to oppose the status quo:

> With the end of the Cold War and the consequent failure of socialism to maintain (for the time being at least) an ideological challenge to capitalism, 'human rights' has been able for the first time to step fully onto the centre-stage that the Universal Declaration [of Human Rights] had erected for it.[38]

The problem with this growing importance is that the most widely accepted human rights (civil and political rights) are, by and large, freedoms *from* abuse by the state, born out of a desire not to allow the majority to impose its will on the minority. The issue is whether this conception of the government's role in society actually undermines its ability to act

---

[37] For an introduction to the differing 'socialist' and 'bourgeois' conceptions of rights see: I. Markovits, 'Socialist vs. Bourgeois Rights – An East-West German Comparison' (1977–1978) 45 *University of Chicago Law Review* 612, esp. at 614–625.

[38] C. Gearty, *Can Human Rights Survive?* (CUP, 2006) p. 27.

positively for the benefit of a country's citizens. Griffin counters such suggestions, arguing that a proper conception of human rights does not prevent such government action:

> Grounding human rights in personhood imposes an obvious constraint on their content: they are rights not to do anything that promises human *good* or *flourishing*, but merely to what is needed for human *status*.[39]

In this claim, Griffin is suggesting that human rights establish basic conditions necessary for meaningful human life, rather than promoting any ultimate vision of what constitutes a 'good life'.

Human rights are intended to safeguard the basic requirement that no one should be prevented from pursuing their chosen conception of what constitutes a good life unless it harms others, but, provided that this basic standard is secure, a government should be able to organise a community's energies and resources in accordance with the wishes of the majority. In other words, human rights must not be portrayed as the sole marker of good governance. If the concept of human rights is indeed 'utopian', it appears to constitute an appropriately minimal utopia which is within human capacity to realise.

Thinking Point . . .

Consider Gearty's claims, above at p. 603, that human rights advocates seek 'Heaven on earth'. Griffin (*On Human Rights* (OUP, 2008), p. 34) suggests, by contrast, that 'at most we have a right to the *pursuit* of happiness, to the base on which one might construct a happy life, not to happiness itself'.

---

3. The concept of human rights changes the relationship between law and politics

A danger exists that human rights, as part of the legal process, do not benefit individuals within a society equally but can instead be harnessed by organised and wealthy groups to secure their interests. Rather than such a group having to secure the backing of the majority in a society to advance its interests through the democratic process, human rights instead permit a small, unelected cadre of judges to adjudicate upon such interests. Lord Devlin, one of the most prominent judges of the post-war era, cautioned against placing such important interests within the purview of the judiciary in the starkest possible terms:

> It is a great temptation to cast the judiciary as an elite which will bypass the traffic-laden ways of the democratic process. But it would only apparently be a bypass. In truth it would be a road that would never rejoin the highway but would lead inevitably, however long and winding the path, to the authoritarian state.[40]

Campbell, less starkly, highlights the risk that requiring judges to adjudicate on broadly drafted rights could lead to a 'juridification of politics',[41] reducing the importance of political decision-making and public faith in the ability of the political process to improve standards of living. Juridification may indeed lead to more groups seeking to advance claims in court which have failed in the political arena, with litigation by those in favour

---

[39] J. Griffin, *On Human Rights* (OUP, 2008) p. 34.
[40] P. Devlin, *The Judge* (OUP, 1970) p. 17.
[41] T. Campbell, 'Human Rights: A Culture of Controversy' (1999) 26 JLS 6, 6.

of fox hunting offering a good example of this development. The response to suggestions that this weakens the democratic process, however, is that to be a modern liberal democracy a state cannot permit a government absolute power to undermine individual rights simply on the basis that it accords with the wishes of the majority. Moreover, simply pointing to an upsurge in such cases does not mean that the political process is under threat. The courts, as we have seen in previous chapters, refused to recognise that anti-fox hunting legislation infringed any of the human rights of claimant hunt supporters.[42]

4. Human rights do not constrain private power

As we have seen above, 'to engage human rights, conduct must be in some sense official'.[43] Some critics therefore see human rights as at best an incomplete doctrine for protecting human interests as our most important interests as human beings can be threatened by other private individuals and bodies as easily as they can be threatened by the state. As Tom Campbell recognises, the fixation of human rights with state abuses is largely a product of the history of the concept.[44] Nonetheless, human rights advocates respond that courts adjudicating upon particular rights increasingly recognise that these rights can impose duties on states to maintain adequate systems to regulate *private* conduct. We will consider rights which give rise to such 'positive obligations' below, but for now the capacity of human rights to require states to regulate private conduct is evidenced by the following example:

> Suppose a government announces, truthfully, that none of its employees ever tortures anyone, but also that it knows of widespread torture perpetrated by its supporters and in family life and it proposes not to interfere. It would, of course, be condemned for 'infringing' or (in worst cases) 'violating' the right not to be tortured.[45]

5. Human rights constitute 'Western' impositions

When human rights are presented as precepts common amongst major moral and religious codes, this narrows the scope of the concept. As Harris states, given the vast differences in the 'individual aspirations and cultural expectations' of humans, 'how could it be supposed that there are interests which are of value to them all?'.[46] If it is accepted that there are few such interests and that they form the basis of human rights, then human rights becomes a search for such existing consensus rather than a vehicle by which to reform government practices. Nonetheless, efforts to ground human rights in the normative agency of individuals (such as Griffin's personhood thesis) run the risk, according to writers such as John Rawls, that they will be rejected by groups which see this conception of the person as 'distinctive of the Western political tradition'.[47] These concerns stem from an idea called 'cultural relativism', which views all cultural standards as independently valuable and rejects attempts to assert the superiority of one set of moral norms.[48] This concept gained

---

[42] See: *R (Countryside Alliance)* v *Attorney-General* [2007] UKHL 52; [2008] 1 AC 719.
[43] T. Pogge, 'The International Significance of Human Rights' (2000) 4 *Journal of Ethics* 45, 47.
[44] T. Campbell, 'Human Rights: a Culture of Controversy' (1999) 26 JLS 6, 11.
[45] J. Harris, 'Human Rights and Mythical Beasts' (2004) 120 LQR 428, 447.
[46] Ibid., 451.
[47] J. Rawls, *Law of Peoples* (Harvard University Press, 1999) p. 68.
[48] For a critique of such 'Westernised' visions of human rights law see: M. Matua, 'Savages, Victims and Saviors: The Metaphor of Human Rights' (2001) 42 *Harvard International Law Journal* 201.

prominence in the aftermath of the Second World War as movements opposed to the Western colonisation of large parts of the globe flourished. The central place given in many independence struggles to the dominant culture of the colonised group often translated into independent countries in which governments pursued policies to strengthen that cultural identity, to the detriment of minority groups and individual rights.

Thinking Point . . .

John Rawls considered that the concept of human rights should be restricted to a very limited group of values which are intended to prevent government practices which are 'equally condemned by both reasonable liberal peoples and decent hierarchical peoples' (*Law of Peoples* (Harvard University Press, 1999), p. 68). In this, his vision of human rights is closer to *jus cogens* norms under customary international law (see Chapter 3).

Griffin counters the arguments of cultural relativism by recognising that not all countries which gained their independence after the Second World War adopted constitutional systems which sidelined the role of human rights. When India gained its independence, in spite of role of the caste structure in Hindu tradition (effectively denying rights simply on the basis of humanity), human rights concepts found a prominent role in the Indian Constitution of 1950.[49] It helps in this regard that human rights does not attempt to provide a doctrine for ordering all human relations, but simply a 'floor' of minimum protections above which governments can seek to encourage or discourage certain behaviour in line with their cultural or ideological beliefs. If that floor is to hold, preventing rights from being infringed, human rights must reflect certain universally applicable ideas. By doing so, Conor Gearty notes, human rights is able to act as a set of globally understood standards against which government actions can be compared: 'a language that speaks for people and that manages, by forcing people to be visible to everyone, first to make it possible for others to speak for themselves'.[50]

The continuing importance of human rights

And yet, in spite of this scepticism, the concept of human rights continues to play a growing role in legal discourse and in constraining the powers of governments, particularly across Europe. One reason for the concept's resilience in the face of criticism is simply the lack of an alternative; human rights, in the words of Samuel Moyn, offer humanity 'the last utopia'.[51] Much of twentieth-century history charts the rise and collapse of ideologies from fascism through to communism, failing to deliver on their promises of freedom from capitalism or colonisation without attendant misery. As Moyn recognises, in this environment where other utopian visions have failed, 'internationalism revolving around individual rights surged, and it did so because it was defined as a pure alternative in an era of ideological betrayal and political collapse.'[52]

---

[49] J. Griffin, *On Human Rights* (OUP, 2008) pp. 141–2.
[50] C. Gearty, *Can Human Rights Survive?* (CUP, 2006) p. 42.
[51] S. Moyn, *The Last Utopia: Human Rights in History* (Belknap Press, 2010).
[52] Ibid., p. 8.

If the lack of a viable alternative sees advocates turn to human rights as a vision for improving models of government almost by default, worldwide concerns over population growth and lack of resources nonetheless add urgency to efforts to bolster the role of human rights in governance structures across the globe. Gearty offers a particularly bleak prognosis:

> I see the . . . war on terror as a dismal harbinger of an even greater war over natural resources that the West looks as though it is getting ready to fight, but which it will want to do without losing its label as a human-rights-respecting culture.[53]

Human rights therefore either constitute the ropes with which we seek to bind policy makers against impending temptations when faced with difficult policy choices or a smoke-screen, flexible enough to allow policy makers to pay lip service to the importance of human autonomy whilst subverting the principle in practice. Much depends on the robustness of human rights treaties and jurisprudence and the mechanisms in place to defend them, the subjects to which we now turn.

The development of the ECHR and associated institutions

Key issues

- The ECHR was agreed in 1950 and entered into force in 1953. However, the system of rights protection that it created was slow to develop. The first cases were not heard by the ECHR institutions until the mid-1960s, with the UK only permitting individuals to bring cases against it in 1966.

- Today the ECHR has 47 member states (a dramatic increase from the initial 10). This increase in the pool of potential claimants, together with increasing rights-consciousness across Europe, placed considerable workload pressures upon the ECHR institutions. Protocols 11 and 14 ECHR were introduced as a result, streamlining the original Convention processes to help them to cope with this caseload.

- The European Court of Human Rights (hereafter 'the European Court') is made up of one judge from each member state. Cases are normally filtered by one- or three-judge panels (rejecting the vast majority of applications as inadmissible). Cases which do not simply involve applying settled case law are then heard in full by a seven-judge panel (a 'chamber'). If a case is of exceptional importance, the court may agree to convene a seventeen-judge 'Grand Chamber' to consider the chamber's decision.

The development of the ECHR

(i) The creation of the ECHR

The creation of the ECHR, an international treaty concluded in November 1950 and which entered into force in September 1953, has been mythologised by later generations of rights advocates. Looking back, modern commentators, including judges such as Lord Steyn,

---

[53] C. Gearty, *Can Human Rights Survive?* (CUP, 2006) p. 8.

invest the ECHR's creation by the Council of Europe with momentous symbolism, with the states of Western Europe following on from the lead of the United Nations and its UDHR:

> During the Second World War a new idea took root. Previously there had been an assumption that however outrageously a government treated individuals it was not properly the concern of other governments. The Third Reich and the Holocaust changed that perception. Out of the ashes of the war came the creation in 1945 of the United Nations committed by its charter to uphold 'the dignity and worth of the human person'.[54]

The reality was less grandiose. Fearful of the rise of communism and eager to set out a statement of what Winston Churchill described as 'common spiritual values' which the peoples of Western Europe could unite behind,[55] the statesmen and diplomats who concluded the ECHR valued the symbolism of the treaty and little more.[56] In one crucial respect, however, the ECHR differed from the UDHR. It made provision for state parties and individuals who claimed their rights had been violated to bring claims against the states allegedly responsible for a violation before an independent adjudication mechanism. Over the decades since the ECHR's ratification this system has allowed the judges of the European Court of Human Rights, based in Strasbourg, to develop the specific legal content of what had previously been moral proscriptions. In other words, the Court's judgments turned the ECHR's broadly-worded aspirations into positive law.

Thinking Point . . .

Today's Council of Europe and the European Union are distinct bodies, emerging out of different ideas of how to strengthen Western European countries shattered by the Second World War. Whilst the drafting of the ECHR by the Council of Europe was a minimalist effort to identify common values, the bodies which grew into the European Union were established as efforts to integrate the European countries, starting with their economies.

(ii) The increasing importance of the ECHR

Many of the governments of the countries which signed the ECHR were profoundly sceptical of human rights and with good reason, given that many of the first signatory states maintained profoundly illiberal regimes within their colonised territories (Art. 56 ECHR even permits states to exclude overseas territories from the Convention's remit).[57] It is therefore unsurprising that the UK permitted claimants unable to secure a remedy before the courts of the UK's domestic legal systems to bring cases before the ECHR only after 1966, by which time most of its colonies had gained independence. Up to the mid-1960s the European Court's case load was negligible (it delivered only two judgments before 1965) and its mechanisms for adjudicating upon human rights claims remained largely

---

[54] J. Steyn, 'Guantánamo Bay: the Legal Black Hole,' (2004) 53 ICLQ 1, 5.

[55] R. James (ed.), *Winston S. Churchill: His Complete Speeches, 1897–1963* (Chelsea House Publishers, 1974) pp. 7635–9.

[56] A. Simpson, *Human Rights and the End of Empire: Britain and the Genesis of the European Convention* (OUP, 2001) pp. 639–40.

[57] See W. Osiatynski, 'Are Human Rights Universal in an Age of Terrorism', in R. Wilson (ed.), *Human Rights in the 'War on Terror'* (CUP, 2005) pp. 295, 297–8.

untested. From this point onwards, however, the Court's case load slowly began to rise, in part due to countries such as the UK permitting individuals to petition the ECHR institutions to hear their claims and in part due to the increasing number of countries that acceded to the ECHR. By 1990, the Convention covered 22 states.

Thinking Point . . .

When the ECHR came into force only three of the original ten states then party to the Convention permitted individuals to bring cases. By 1990, all states then party to the ECHR permitted individual petitions, and acceptance of the right of individual petition has, since 1998, been a requirement of membership of the Convention regime.

Although, by 1982, the Court had delivered a mere sixty one judgments, these had included a number of high-profile cases, such as Ireland's successful claim that the UK's security policies in Northern Ireland had included the inhuman and degrading treatment of terrorism suspects.[58] Taking a lead from such decisions, which suggested that the Court would indeed be willing to rule against states even in high-profile and politically-contentious cases, claimants across Europe began to pursue litigation before the ECHR mechanisms which would previously have been abandoned once they failed before domestic courts. Very quickly, the ECHR would lurch from being an under-used tool to a victim of its own success.

(iii) Institutional development

By the mid-1990s, the existing ECHR mechanisms were beginning to come under increasing case-load pressure. Until this time, all complaints were screened by the European Commission on Human Rights, which considered whether the complaint was admissible and reached a preliminary finding on whether a violation had occurred. States could either accept this decision or bring the case before the (still part-time) Court for final adjudication. With the increasing number of states covered by the ECHR and the willingness of claimants to turn to the Commission, this cumbersome system, which duplicated the work of evaluating claims, was overdue for replacement.

The states party to the ECHR took action to respond to the growing workload of the ECHR institutions by drafting new procedural rules (although, more seriously, chronic underfunding continued).[59] These new rules, contained in Protocol 11 ECHR (a protocol being an international legal instrument used to change the terms of, or add new terms to, an existing treaty), replaced the Convention's existing institutional arrangements in November 1998. The Commission was scrapped and the European Court made into a full-time body. Moreover, individuals in any contracting state gained the right to petition the Court. Whilst these changes better equipped the Court to deal with the changes in case patterns experiences in the early 1990s, it failed to take into account a looming problem. With the collapse of communism, most of the countries of eastern Europe signed and ratified the ECHR, expanding the number of contracting states from 22 in 1990 to 47 today (covering in excess of 800 million individuals). From the late 1990s onwards, the

---

[58] *Ireland* v *United Kingdom* (1979–80) 2 EHRR 25.
[59] G. Ress, 'The Effect of Decisions and Judgments of the European Court of Human Rights in the Domestic Legal Order' (2005) 40 *Texas Int'l LJ* 359, 363.

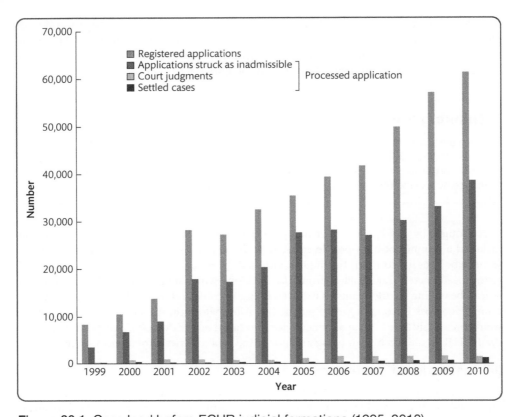

Figure 20.1 Case load before ECHR judicial formations (1995–2010)

Source: statistics derived from ECHR Annual Reports 2010 and 2004, available at: www. echr.coe.int/echr/en/header/reports+and+statistics/reports/annual+reports/.

number of new cases from these fledgling democracies, with their government officials still adapting their approach to public policy to accord with human rights standards, dramatically outstripped the Court's ability to manage its case load. Figure 20.1 displays the increasing case load of the Court and the mounting backlog of unprocessed claims.

In Figure 20.1, a processed application includes registered applications which are struck out as inadmissible, on which a friendly settlement is reached or on which the Court reached a decision. Even though Protocol 11 had streamlined the process of bringing a claim before the ECHR institutions, and had thereby allowed the Court to increase its capacity, its capacity had failed to keep pace with demand. By the end of 2011, a backlog of 160,000 cases which had been allocated to the panels of judges deciding admissibility awaited a decision. Further reform was clearly needed.

As early as May 2004, Protocol 14 ECHR was drafted, which proposed changes which would enhance the Court's filtering capacity regarding the admissibility of claims, add additional admissibility requirements, streamline the process of dealing with repetitive claims from particular states and facilitate friendly settlements between claimants and states. This enhanced ability to terminate inadmissible and process repetitive claims would leave the Court with more time to devote to cases involving serious human rights infringements. A Protocol making such radical procedural changes, however, can only come into effect when all states party to the ECHR have agreed to it. Only four states (Russia, Turkey, Romania and Ukraine), accounted for nearly 56 per cent of the case backload,[60] meaning that these states had an incentive to stall reform of the Court's procedure and admissibility rules, thereby delaying these claims against them. Ultimately, in early 2010, Russia became the final state to ratify Protocol 14, which came into effect in June of that year. By 2011, with this new system in place, the Court was able to slow the rate at which a backlog of cases developed, reducing the total figure to 84,515 cases by July 2014, and 64,850 by December 2015.

The ECHR's adjudication and enforcement framework

There follows a brief summary of the process for bringing a case before the ECHR institutions, as amended under Protocol 14. The ECHR mechanisms for rights protection can be called into action in two ways. Firstly, as we noted above, under Art. 33 states are able to bring 'inter-state' claims against other states party to the ECHR. This mechanism is a product of the experience of the drafters of the ECHR, who in the aftermath of the Second World War were alive to the fact that, prior to that conflict, states possessed no formal process by which to challenge other European states regarding widespread human rights abuses. In recent years, however, given the diplomatic rupture involved in bringing such a case and the success of the individual petition process, the Art. 33 process has been turned to very rarely, often arising in the context of wider disputes between ECHR states (such as the *Cyprus* v *Turkey*[61] case, in which Cyprus complained to the Court about on-going human rights abuses[62] arising out of the aftermath of Turkish military operations in Northern Cyprus in 1974).

(i) Individual petitions to the court

1. Admissibility

Under Art. 34 ECHR, the Court is able to hear cases brought by 'any person, non-governmental organisation or group of individuals claiming to be the victim of a violation by one of the High Contracting Parties of the rights set forth in the Convention or the protocols thereto'. Before the Court considers such a claim, however, it must fulfil the admissibility criteria set out in Art. 35 ECHR. These require that:

- Claims must be made within six months of the conclusion of the domestic legal process regarding an alleged infringement.

- Claims must not be anonymous (to ensure the openness of court proceedings, although the Court may subsequently prevent the publication of the names of claimants).

- Claims must not be 'substantially the same as a matter that has already been examined by the Court' or which has been submitted to other international mechanisms for resolving human rights disputes.

- Claims must not be 'manifestly ill founded' or an 'abuse of the right of individual application' (allowing the Court to reject vexatious or unwarranted claims at the earliest possible stage).

---

[60] J.-P. Costa, 'Speech on the Occasion of the Opening of the Judicial Year' (29 January 2010), *ECHR Annual Report 2010,* 37.
[61] *Cyprus* v *Turkey* (2002) 35 EHRR 30.
[62] Ibid., [18].

- As amended by Protocol 14, claims can also be dismissed where 'the applicant has not suffered a significant disadvantage' (in order to allow the Court to devote its time to more serious cases). The Court can only reject cases on this basis where they have already been addressed by a domestic tribunal.

In order to determine whether a claim meets these requirements, following Protocol 14 it is first considered by a judge (known, under Art. 27 as 'single judge' procedure) who has the capacity to reject it outright if all of the admissibility requirements are not met. This process allows for a more efficient assessment of admissibility criteria than existed prior to Protocol 14, when all cases had to be considered by a panel of judges.

2. Hearing the merits of a case

Where a case is admissible (disclosing a potential breach of human rights, involving a victim of that breach and meeting the admissibility criteria), it is passed by the single judge to one of two bodies. If the single judge believes that the claim falls clearly within existing case law, then under Art. 28 a three-judge panel (known as a 'committee') will consider the case. If it is agreed that the case 'is already the subject of well-established case-law of the Court', the committee can issue a judgment on the merits of the case on the basis of the existing law, allowing uncontroversial cases to be expedited. If the judge deciding admissibility, or a committee to which a claim is passed, conclude that a claim is in some way novel or is not the subject of the Court's settled case law, then the case is passed under Art. 29 to a seven-judge panel (known as a 'chamber'), which will include the judge from the country in question.

3. Referrals to the Grand Chamber

Decisions by chambers of the Court are binding on the state against which they are delivered unless, under Art. 43, they are referred by one of the parties to the 'Grand Chamber' (a panel of 17 judges) on the basis of the exceptional seriousness of the alleged rights infringement or because 'the case raises a serious question affecting the interpretation or application of the Convention'. The Grand Chamber does not have to accept referrals and given the workload of the Court often reserves this final stage of the ECHR adjudication machinery for exceptional cases. In a number of very high-profile cases from the UK, including *Gillan and Quinton* v *United Kingdom*[63] on the politically sensitive subject of whether the UK's counter-terrorism stop-and-search powers infringed the right to privacy (Art. 8 ECHR), efforts by the UK Government to refer the matter to the Grand Chamber (thereby delaying the need to address a breach) have been rejected by the Court.

Thinking point . . .

Subsequent to the Strasbourg Court's decision in *Gillan and Quinton* v *United Kingdom* the UK repealed stop-and-search powers, available to the police involved in counter-terrorism, which required police officers to show no reason why an individual was stopped (no 'basis for suspicion'). Replacement powers (see the Terrorism Act 2000 (Remedial) Order 2011 (SI 631/2011)) placed tighter restraints on the police. See B. Dickson, 'The Record of the House of Lords in Strasbourg' (2012) 128 LQR 354, 379.

---

[63] *Gillan and Quinton* v *United Kingdom* (2010) 50 EHRR 45.

4. Overview of the court process and future reform proposals

Figure 20.2 outlines the basic process of hearing a claim before the European Court. These processes, however, are not fixed, as the European Court continues to face a backload of cases even with the streamlining of its procedures (by the end of 2016, this backlog had crept back up to around 80,000 cases). In the spring of 2012, as the culmination of the UK's period chairing the Council of Europe, the Brighton Declaration[64] was agreed, which envisages future reforms (under a new protocol to the Convention[65]) including cutting the time limits for an application to the Court from six months to four.[66] The UK, had been the driving force behind these reform proposals, but it did not succeed in

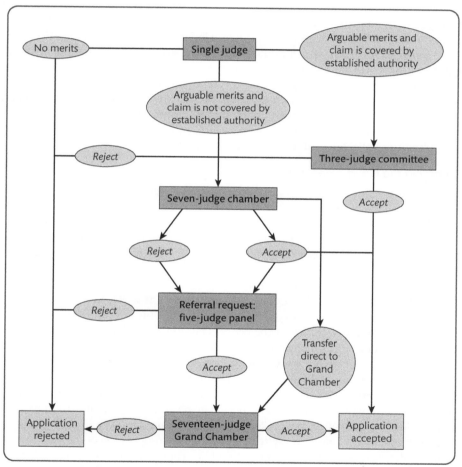

Figure 20.2 The stages a claim may go through in adjudication by the ECHR

---

[64] Council of Europe, *Brighton Declaration* (19 April 2012), available at: http://hub.coe.int/20120419-brighton-declaration.

[65] Protocol 15 to the ECHR, available at: http://www.echr.coe.int/Documents/Protocol_15_ENG.pdf.

[66] Ibid., [15a]. See also: Article 4, Protocol 15 to the ECHR.

persuading other Council of Europe members to act more radically to restrict the European Court's jurisdiction where domestic courts had already considered the ECHR implications of a case.[67]

(ii) The European Court of Human Rights and the Council of Europe

1. The composition of the court

The European Court of Human Rights is composed of one judge from each of the 47 states members of the Council of Europe, ensuring that the Court includes expertise from the different legal systems from which cases arise. Although there is one judge from each state, Art. 21 affirms that each judge sits in an independent capacity and not as a representative of their state. The Parliamentary Assembly of the Council of Europe selects one judge from a shortlist of three candidates proposed by a state as being of high moral character and qualified for high judicial office. Under Art. 23 the term of office for the selected judge is nine years, which cannot be renewed (so as to secure the impartiality of judges from their own states). Even if this term is not finished, a judge must retire from the Court when they reach the age of 70. In recent years critics of the Court have raised concerns over the qualifications of some judges, particularly in newer Convention states.[68] An advisory panel has therefore been established to ensure 'full satisfaction of the Convention's criteria for office as a judge of the court' amongst potential candidates before their applications are submitted to the Parliamentary Assembly.

2. Enforcing the Court's decisions

Article 1 ECHR requires that all state parties 'secure to everyone within their jurisdiction the rights and freedoms defined in . . . this Convention'. This 'commitment clause' binds all 47 members of the Council of Europe to uphold the European Convention as a matter of international law. Rather than leaving remedying breaches of human rights and compensating victims entirely to the states responsible for those breaches, Art. 46 ECHR gives the Committee of Ministers (a body of government representatives from all of the Council of Europe member states) the role of monitoring the execution of court decisions by the respondent State. Prior to the adoption of Protocol 14, the Committee was largely toothless in enforcing provisions against a state that refused to rectify its breach. This was evident in the repeated findings of the Committee that, over the period since 2005, the UK was failing to address a breach of the right to vote inherent in its blanket ban on prisoners voting.[69] Such examples of extended delay in complying with a ruling, however, remain exceptional. Such delaying tactics will be increasingly difficult in future because, under Protocol 14's amendments to Art. 46, the Committee can refer a failure to execute a judgment back to the Court, and – in the event that an ongoing violation is found – may result in the Committee of Ministers requiring additional measures to be taken to address the breach. Even in the light of this, the extent to which the Convention system rests upon the co-operation of the member states and their willingness to act to address identified breaches of the Convention's protections remains a potential weakness in the ability of the Court to compel legal change at the domestic level.

---

[67] See M. Elliot, 'After Brighton: between a Rock and a Hard Place' [2012] PL 619, 622–3.

[68] M. Pinto-Duschinsky, *Bringing Rights Back Home: Making Human Rights Compatible with Parliamentary Democracy in the UK* (Policy Exchange, 2011) p. 66.

[69] *Hirst* v *United Kingdom (No. 2)* (2006) 42 EHRR 41 (GC).

The rights and freedoms protected under the ECHR

Key issues

- ECHR rights primarily apply to the territorial jurisdiction of the Convention states. However, in limited circumstances where the agents of a Convention state are effectively in control of a situation outside its borders the Court has ruled that its jurisdiction is similarly extended.

- Absolute rights require the application of a one-stage test in determining whether a breach has occurred:

  1. Is the conduct of the state prohibited under the terms of the protected right?

- Limited rights require the application of a two-stage test in determining whether a breach has occurred:

  1. Is the conduct of the state prohibited under the terms of the protected right?

  2. Does the conduct fall within the terms of one of the stated exceptions to the right?

- Qualified rights require the application of a three-stage test in determining whether a breach has occurred:

  1. Is the conduct of the state prohibited under the terms of the protected right?

  2. Does the conduct fall within the terms of one of the categories of permissible restrictions upon the right?

  3. Is the conduct proportionate to the aims being pursued?

Rights protection under the ECHR

(i) The ECHR rights

The basic ECHR rights have stood for over 60 years, being augmented over time by a series of additional protocols to the ECHR which, although not part of the original treaty, have been agreed to by some or all of its state parties. Today, in the UK, the ECHR is often taken (particularly amongst lawyers) as being synonymous with the concept of human rights. Instead, we must recognise that it represents a *choice* of how to legalise the moral precepts embodied by the philosophical concept of human rights and that it could have looked very different. It emphasises civil and political rights and largely ignores social and economic interests, in part for fear that including the latter would draw 'judges into areas with which they are not equipped to deal and give them power over resources for which they are not responsible'.[70] Within the context of our examination of UK public law, we will focus on the ECHR, and in particular on those provisions which the UK incorporated into the domestic legal systems through the Human Rights Act 1998 (which we will consider in the next chapter). Nonetheless we should, from the outset, appreciate that the rights enjoyed within domestic law could in the future be changed, either by the drafting of a UK Bill of Rights (as recently proposed by the Conservative party) or be the incorporation of other international treaties (such as the European Social Charter[71] or the International Covenant on Economic, Social and Cultural Rights[72]).

---

[70] T. Campbell, 'Human Rights: A Culture of Controversy' (1999) 26 JLS 6, 22.
[71] European Social Charter (1965) 529 UNTS 89.
[72] International Covenant on Economic, Social and Cultural Rights (1976) 999 UNTS 3.

Rather than examine the ECHR rights in the order in which they appear in the treaty we will divide them into different classes of right, in accordance with the manner in which these measures are approached by the European Court of Human Rights. Given that we will not be addressing each right in turn, and because exploring every right in depth would be beyond the scope of this book, each section on the different classes of ECHR right will open with a brief explanation of the rights covered by that class.

(ii) The geographic reach of the ECHR rights

A casual reading of Art. 1 ECHR might suggest that, whilst member states must respect the human rights contained therein, these rights only apply to 'everyone within their jurisdiction', thereby, excluding the conduct of states outside their territories from the remit of the Convention. This provision, however, has been interpreted by the Court to mean only that the ECHR applies *primarily* to the conduct of contracting states within their borders, and that, in exceptional cases, acts of the contracting states producing effects outside their territory can fall within their 'jurisdiction' for the purposes of the Convention.[73]

The Court has to date recognised three exceptional circumstances of expanded jurisdiction. Firstly, if one Convention state invades another Convention state (such as Turkey's invasion of Cyprus in 1974), its actions will be subject to the ECHR as, if this was not the case, the inhabitants of the invaded area would lose the Convention's protection.[74] Secondly, where the agents of a Convention state are in control of a situation (even if it is beyond the state's borders) the Convention applies. For example, when a fugitive Kurdish separatist leader was handed over to Turkish officials in Kenya the Court held that:

> [D]irectly after being handed over to the Turkish officials by the Kenyan officials, the applicant was effectively under Turkish authority and therefore within the 'jurisdiction' of that State for the purposes of Article 1 of the Convention, even though in this instance Turkey exercised its authority outside its territory.[75]

This extension of jurisdiction ensures that Convention states cannot simply avoid the ECHR by removing individuals beyond the territorial remit of the Convention, preventing the states from being tempted to employ practices such as 'extraordinary rendition', practised by the United States during the 'War on Terror' to circumvent domestic legal restraints on the treatment of individuals in custody by transporting individuals to third countries which do not respect international human rights standards.[76]

More controversial, however, have been efforts to persuade the European Court to employ the ECHR to constrain the activity of states engaged in military operations outside the territory of any Convention state. Recent decades have seen frequent examples of such military interventions, from NATO-led operations in the former Yugoslavia, Afghanistan and Libya to the involvement of several Convention states in the invasion of Iraq. Where such military interventions occur, the Court has ruled that only if a Convention state exercises effective control of territory within another state are its actions subject to the ECHR. In *Banković* the applicants before the Court were individuals injured or killed by the NATO bombing of the Serbian television and radio centre during operations in April 1999. The

---

[73] *Banković and Others v Belgium and Others* (2007) 44 EHRR SE5, [67] (GC).
[74] *Loizidou v Turkey* (1997) 23 EHRR 513, [78].
[75] *Öcalan v Turkey* (2005) 41 EHRR 45, [91] (GC).
[76] See J. Boys, 'What's So Extraordinary About Rendition?' (2011) 15 IJHR 589.

Court concluded that the Convention could not be interpreted to equate high-level bombing of a target in a non-Convention state with having 'effective control' over the area.[77]

By contrast, following the invasion of Iraq in 2003, the UK helped to administer large areas of southern Iraq. In *Al-Skeini*[78] and *Al-Jedda*[79] the applicants argued that deaths and injuries caused by the actions of UK forces operating in south-eastern Iraq were therefore subject to the ECHR, because the UK's presence in the region amounted to 'effective control'. When the House of Lords considered the case it accepted that deaths in UK custody in Iraq did fall within the ECHR's scope (on the basis, as in *Öcalan* above, that the agents of a Convention state controlled the situation), it refused to recognise that the ECHR applied to all activity by UK forces in southern Iraq. Lord Carswell asserted that 'it would . . . require a high degree of control by the agents of the state of an area in another state before it could be said that that area was within the jurisdiction of the former'.[80] In essence, the House of Lords rejected expansive interpretations of 'effective control', recognising the limitations of the ECHR as a regional, and not global, human rights treaty, reliant upon the respect of the Convention states.

When the cases progressed to Strasbourg, the European Court refused to follow the House of Lords' approach. The Court noted that 'the United Kingdom (together with the United States) assumed in Iraq the exercise of some of the public powers normally to be exercised by a sovereign government', and:

> In these exceptional circumstances, the Court considers that the United Kingdom, through its soldiers engaged in security operations in Basrah during the period in question, exercised authority and control over individuals killed in the course of such security operations, so as to establish a jurisdictional link between the deceased and the United Kingdom.[81]

Given that the ECHR rights are indivisible for the purposes of Art. 1, the UK would have had the duty to uphold not simply the right to life but also freedom of expression and association in its time in 'effective control' in Iraq. This seems far removed from the *Banković* decision's cautious focus on the European structure of the ECHR and seems reckless towards the fact that the Court's operations remain 'to a large extent dependent on the support of the Contracting States themselves'.[82] The concurring judgments in *Al-Skeini*, however, give us some idea of the motivation behind the Court's decision to recognise jurisdiction. Judge Bonello was scathing in his dismissal of the UK Government's accusations that the court was engaged in 'human rights imperialism', declaring that 'ill behoves a State that imposed its military imperialism over another sovereign State without the frailest imprimatur from the international community, to resent the charge of having exported human rights imperialism to the vanquished enemy'.[83] By extending the nature of 'effective control' in this way, the Court was eager to ensure that if ever Convention states were again tempted to act as an invading and occupying power, they would know that their actions would be subject to the Court's watchful jurisdiction. The extra-territorial application of the Convention in such circumstances remains a contentious issue in the

---

[77] *Banković and Others* v *Belgium and Others* (2007) 44 EHRR SE5, [75] (GC).
[78] *Al-Skeini* v *United Kingdom* (2011) 53 EHRR 18.
[79] *Al-Jedda* v *United Kingdom* (2011) 53 EHRR 23.
[80] *R (Al-Skeini)* v *Secretary of State for Defence* [2007] UKHL 26, [97].
[81] *Al-Skeini* v *United Kingdom* (2011) 53 EHRR 18, [149].
[82] G. Ress, 'The Effect of Decisions and Judgments of the European Court of Human Rights in the Domestic Legal Order', (2005) 40 *Texas International Law Journal* 359, 364–5.
[83] *Al-Skeini* v *United Kingdom* (2011) 53 EHRR 18, Concurring Opinion, [37].

Table 20.1 Absolute rights in the ECHR

ECHR provision	Right	Coverage
Article 3	The prohibition of torture	People must not be subjected to torture or inhuman and degrading treatment
Article 4	The prohibition of slavery and forced labour	People must not be enslaved or compelled to perform forced labour
Article 5 (some elements)	Right to liberty and security	People who are arrested must be promptly informed of the charges against them and must promptly have the lawfulness of their detention confirmed by a judge
Article 6 (some elements)	Right to a fair trial	People facing criminal charges must have time to prepare their defence, access to legal representation and the ability to call witnesses

UK[84] with the Government proposing in 2016 to derogate (under Art. 15 ECHR[85]) from the Convention's protections in future military conflicts on the basis that the operation of the ECHR rights inhibits the operational effectiveness of the armed forces.[86]

'Absolute' rights

(i) The absolute rights

Absolute rights, as the name suggests, are rights which cannot be justifiably or excusably infringed by a state. Often, they are easily identifiable as the shortest rights in the ECHR, as the terms of the rights provide no circumstances in which the right can be infringed without the state being found in breach of its ECHR commitments (Table 20.1).

(ii) Engaging these rights

Article 3 ECHR's prohibition of torture provides a good basis from which to analyse the Court's approach to the 'absolute' rights. The right is one sentence long: 'No one shall be subjected to torture or to inhuman or degrading treatment or punishment'. Lacking any caveats or exceptions, it is clear that the task of the European Court where an individual claims that her Art. 3 right has been infringed is primarily to assess whether the actions of the state actually constitute 'torture or inhuman or degrading treatment or punishment'. If they do, then the state has breached its duty. The case turns on how the Court interprets these terms. The Court has emphasised that for a state's activity to fall within the scope of Art. 3, the 'ill-treatment must attain a minimum level of severity', with factors such as the

---

[84] See: R. Ekins, J. Morgan and T. Tugendhat, *Clearing the Fog of War: Saving our Armed Forces from Defeat by Judicial Diktat* (Policy Exchange, 2015).

[85] See below pp. 642–3.

[86] See: P. Walker and O. Bowcott, 'Plan for UK Military to opt out of European Convention on Human Rights', *Guardian*, 4 October 2016.

age, health and sex of the victim affecting this threshold.[87] In terms of the types of ill treatment that exceed this minimum threshold, it is necessary to consider the case law of the Court. Where children are the victims, corporal punishment can be sufficiently severe to breach this right.[88] Where the victims are healthy adult males, the European Court addressed the threshold in its ground-breaking decision in *Ireland* v *United Kingdom*.[89] In the 1970s, amid high levels of violence in Northern Ireland, the UK Government authorised the use of five interrogation techniques to attempt to gain information from suspected terrorists. The 'five techniques' were (i) forcing suspects to stand in stress positions (awkward positions which rapidly cause individuals tiredness and pain), (ii) hooding (thereby preventing individuals from seeing their surroundings), (iii) subjection to loud noise, (iv) deprivation of sleep and (v) deprivation of food and drink. The Court concluded that such acts were sufficiently severe to infringe Art. 3:

> The five techniques were applied in combination, with premeditation and for hours at a stretch; they caused, if not actual bodily injury, at least intense physical and mental suffering to the persons subjected thereto and also led to acute psychiatric disturbances during interrogation. They accordingly fell into the category of inhuman treatment within the meaning of Article 3. The techniques were also degrading since they were such as to arouse in their victims feelings of fear, anguish and inferiority capable of humiliating and debasing them and possibly breaking their physical or moral resistance.[90]

Where provisions such as the prohibition of slavery or torture are at issue, the Court has repeatedly affirmed that these constitute 'fundamental values of the democratic societies making up the Council of Europe'.[91] As such, the Court does not simply consider whether the Convention states have been responsible for conducting torture or inhuman and degrading treatment. It approaches the right more broadly, applying it to any steps taken by a Convention state which expose individuals to a risk of torture or inhuman and degrading treatment, such as extraditing a person to a state where he is at risk of such treatment or colluding with a non-Convention state in its ill-treatment of an individual. This approach is followed on the basis that:

> It would hardly be compatible with the underlying values of the Convention, that 'common heritage of political traditions, ideals, freedom and the rule of law' to which the Preamble refers, were a Contracting State knowingly to surrender a fugitive to another State where there were substantial grounds for believing that he would be in danger of being subjected to torture, however heinous the crime allegedly committed. Extradition in such circumstances, while not explicitly referred to in the brief and general wording of Article 3, would plainly be contrary to the spirit and intendment of the Article, and in the Court's view this inherent obligation not to extradite also extends to cases in which the fugitive would be faced in the receiving State by a real risk of exposure to inhuman or degrading treatment or punishment proscribed by that Article.[92]

The Court's acknowledgement that the breath of a right depends on the spirit and not simply the wording of the relevant ECHR provision makes it clear that in considering any Convention rights we cannot simply rely on a literal interpretation. Instead, the Court is responsible for safeguarding and if necessary developing the ECHR rights in light of the philosophical underpinnings of the rights. This approach to Art. 3, first established in

---

[87] *A, B and C* v *Ireland* (2011) 53 EHRR 13, [164].
[88] See *Costello-Roberts* v *United Kingdom* (1995) 19 EHRR 112.
[89] *Ireland* v *United Kingdom* (1978) 2 EHRR 25.
[90] Ibid., [167].
[91] *Soering* v *United Kingdom* (1989) 11 EHRR 439, [88].
[92] Ibid., [88].

the late 1980s, would become extremely important in the aftermath of the September 11 attacks, for it allowed the Court to emphasise that the absolute nature of the right was long-settled, in the face of pressure from states, including the UK, to allow for national-security exceptions:

> The Court notes first of all that States face immense difficulties in modern times in protecting their communities from terrorist violence . . . It cannot therefore underestimate the scale of the danger of terrorism today and the threat it presents to the community. That must not, however, call into question the absolute nature of Article 3.[93]

'Limited' rights

(i) The limited rights

Limited rights are rights so important that they can only be restricted under explicit and finite circumstances (Table 20.2). These circumstances are explicitly provided for in the ECHR itself and cannot be altered without amending the treaty.

Table 20.2 Limited rights in the ECHR

ECHR provision	Right	Coverage	Specific limitations
Article 2	Right to life	People cannot ordinarily be deprived of their life	1 Defending another from violence 2 Effecting a lawful arrest/preventing an escape from lawful detention 3 Quelling a riot or insurrection
Article 5 (some elements)	Right to liberty and security	People cannot ordinarily be deprived of their liberty	1 Lawfully detaining convicted criminals 2 Detaining individuals who fail to comply with a court order 3 Detaining individuals prior to a court appearance 4 Detaining children (in limited circumstances) 5 Detaining individuals with serious mental illness or to prevent the spread of infectious disease 6 Detaining foreign nationals believed to have entered the country illegally pending deportation/extradition
Article 7	No punishment without law	People cannot be prosecuted for acts/omissions which were not criminal offences when committed; similarly punishments cannot be increased after an act	Prosecution remains possible if the act was criminal 'according to the general principles of law recognised by civilised nations'

---

[93] *Saadi* v *Italy* (2009) 49 EHRR 30, [137].

As with the absolute rights (indeed, any of the ECHR rights), the first task is to assess whether the impugned activity actually engages the right in question. The question of whether the right is engaged can be very difficult with many of the limited rights, with the Court having to consider questions such as when life begins for the purposes of the Art. 2 right to life[94] and whether certain restrictions on a person's freedom amount to deprivations of liberty under Art. 5 or mere restrictions on freedom of movement.[95] However, for the purpose of this overview of the ECHR system of rights protection, we will concentrate our analysis on the distinguishing features of each class of rights, which in this instance means the limitations to those rights. The existence of such limitations does not reduce the day-to-day importance of these rights for individuals protected by the ECHR, rather they show how even important rights must in limited circumstances be curtailed to protect the interests of others.

(ii) Triggering the specific limitations

The right to life will serve as our example for examining the specific limitations associated with the limited rights. This right also provides a good example of how major changes to the content of, or exceptions to, a right require a new protocol to be agreed amongst the Convention states. The original terms of Art. 2 ECHR allowed for states to maintain the death penalty as a sanction for serious crimes. Starting with Protocol 6, introduced in 1983, the Convention states began to restrict this exception. States which ratified Protocol 6 agreed that the death penalty would not be used outside wartime. Later, under Protocol 13, most member states agreed not to use the death penalty even within wartime. Only Russia has yet to agree to either of these Protocols, but for the UK's purposes the exception was closed during the passage of the Human Rights Act 1998.[96]

With the removal of the death penalty exception, the killing of an individual by the state will only be justified if it took place within one of three situations (the limitations set out within Art. 2):

(a) in defence of any person from unlawful violence (including self-defence);

(b) in order to effect a lawful arrest or to prevent the escape of a person lawfully detained;

(c) in action lawfully taken for the purpose of quelling a riot or insurrection.

To trigger one of these exceptions, the state must show not only that the case before the Court fits within the terms of the exception but also, because of the importance of the right to life, that its actions were no more than necessary to fulfil this aim. This introduces a proportionality requirement into the test (a concept we will examine in detail below[97]). For now, all we need to recognise is that this requirement allows the Court to interpret the limitations upon the right restrictively, as seen in the following decision.

---

[94] See *Vo v France* (2005) 40 EHRR 259.
[95] See *Guzzardi v Italy* (1981) 3 EHRR 333.
[96] Human Rights Act 1998, s. 21(1) as amended.
[97] See pp. 627–8.

Key case

McCann v United Kingdom (1996) 21 EHRR 97 (European Court of Human Rights)

In this case SAS soldiers shot and killed three Provisional IRA members who had been preparing a bomb attack on Gibraltar. The European Court found that the actions of the soldiers responsible for firing the fatal shots constituted a justified effort to save lives from what they believed to be an imminent bomb attack, thereby fitting within the first exception to Art. 2 (at [200]):

> The Court accepts that the soldiers honestly believed, in the light of the information that they had been given, as set out above, that it was necessary to shoot the suspects in order to prevent them from detonating a bomb and causing serious loss of life . . . The actions which they took, in obedience to superior orders, were thus perceived by them as absolutely necessary in order to safeguard innocent lives. It considers that the use of force by agents of the State in pursuit of one of the aims delineated in paragraph 2 of Article 2 (Art. 2-2) of the Convention may be justified under this provision (Art. 2-2) where it is based on an honest belief which is perceived, for good reasons, to be valid at the time but which subsequently turns out to be mistaken. To hold otherwise would be to impose an unrealistic burden on the State and its law-enforcement personnel in the execution of their duty, perhaps to the detriment of their lives and those of others.

The same, however, could not be said for the way in which the operation was planned. The UK authorities had deliberately spurned the opportunity to arrest the IRA team at Gibraltar's border and had presented as fact to the SAS soldiers flawed intelligence that the IRA members were at the time in possession of a bomb. As a result of these facts, the European Court found (at [211]) the UK had failed in its obligation 'to exercise the greatest of care in evaluating the information at their disposal before transmitting it to soldiers whose use of firearms automatically involved shooting to kill'.

McCann is one of the cases where the European Court has found that establishing a breach is sufficient remedy and has refused to award damages resultant from the breach to the families of the deceased (over and above legal costs). As the majority concluded (at [219]), 'having regard to the fact that the three terrorist suspects who were killed had been intending to plant a bomb in Gibraltar, the court does not consider it appropriate to make an award'.

The strict approach to the 'protection from unlawful violence' exception adopted in *McCann* feeds into the other exceptions to the right to life. The approach of the Court suggests that, whilst circumstances may arise in which people are killed in the course of an arrest or during the response to a riot, this will not be justified under the limitations to Art. 2 unless the authorities had made meaningful efforts to minimise the risk to life.

'Qualified' rights

(i) The qualified rights

Qualified rights do allow for interference by the state, and the rights focus on arriving at a 'fair balance' between the interests of individuals against society.[98] The qualifications to these rights are public policy concerns which can be raised by the state to justify actions by public authorities that would otherwise constitute an infringement of the right in question (Table 20.3).

---

[98] G. Letsas, 'Two Concepts of the Margin of Appreciation' (2006) 26 OJLS 705, 711.

Table 20.3 Qualified rights in the ECHR

ECHR provision	Right	Coverage	Qualifications
Article 6 (some elements)	Right to a fair trial	Both criminal and civil cases must be subject to fair and public hearing before an independent and impartial tribunal	The public (including the press) may be excluded from all or part of the trial in the interests of morals, public order or national security in a democratic society, where the interests of juveniles or the protection of the private life of the parties so require, or where publicity would prejudice the interests of justice
Article 8	Right to respect for private and family life	People have a right to respect for private and family life, home and correspondence	Public authorities can intervene in spite of this right 'in the interests of national security, public safety or the economic well-being of the country, for the prevention of disorder or crime, for the protection of health or morals, or for the protection of the rights and freedoms of others'
Article 9	Freedom of thought, conscience and religion	People have the right to freedom of thought, conscience and religion (with the latter including changing religion and manifesting religious belief)	Public authorities can intervene in spite of this right 'in the interests of public safety, for the protection of public order, health or morals, or for the protection of the rights and freedoms of others'
Article 10	Freedom of expression	People have the right to freedom of expression, including the freedom to hold opinions and to receive and impart information and ideas	Public authorities can intervene in spite of this right 'in the interests of national security, territorial integrity or public safety, for the prevention of disorder or crime, for the protection of health or morals, for the protection of the reputation or rights of others, for preventing the disclosure of information received in confidence, or for maintaining the authority and impartiality of the judiciary'

ECHR provision	Right	Coverage	Qualifications
Article 11	Freedom of assembly and association	People have the right to freedom of peaceful assembly and to freedom of association with others, including the right to form and to join trade unions	Public authorities can intervene in spite of this right 'in the interests of national security or public safety, for the prevention of disorder or crime, for the protection of health or morals or for the protection of the rights and freedoms of others'
Article 12	Right to marry	'Men and women' have the right to marry	The couple must be of marriageable age and the marriage must conform to the state's marriage laws
Protocol 1, Article 1	Protection of property	Both natural or legal persons (e.g.: companies) are entitled to the peaceful enjoyment of their possessions	No one shall be deprived of his possessions except in the public interest and in accordance with law

As well as being 'qualified' in the sense that they can be restricted to meet public policy objectives, these rights, moreover, can also conflict with each other, obliging the Court to make a decision as to which right prevails in given circumstances.

(ii) Triggering the qualifications

In assessing whether a state has, *prima facie,* infringed any of the qualified rights, the European Court has ordinarily interpreted the basic rights very broadly. Thereafter, the text of the qualified rights allows Convention states to interfere with these rights where specified classes of important public objectives are at issue. Only the types of such permissible policy objectives are provided by the text of the qualified rights, rather than the tightly defined list of exceptional circumstances found in the limited rights. If a state seeks to restrict a qualified right in light of one of these types of public-policy objectives it must also ensure that this restriction on the right is provided for in law and, furthermore, that the restriction must be 'necessary in a democratic society'. This means that it must represent a proportionate restriction of the right in question. We will examine these requirements in relation to Art. 10 ECHR, which provides for freedom of expression.

1. The aim must constitute a listed public policy objective

As we can see from Table 20.3, Art. 10 ECHR details nine legitimate purposes for which a state may take steps to restrict freedom of expression. This contrasts with the five purposes for which freedom of thought, conscience and religion can be justifiably curtailed. A state seeking to restrict any of the qualified rights must first show that the restriction is 'relevant and sufficient' to at least one of these categories of legitimate purpose.[99] Under Art. 10, these purposes have permitted, for example, restrictions to prevent or rectify damage to reputation under libel law, restricting the sale of pornography to protect public morals and

---

[99] *Sunday Times* v *United Kingdom* (1979) 2 EHRR 245, [62].

the criminalisation of the release of official secrets and the glorification of acts of terrorism in the interests of national security. The different restrictions arise from the nature of the rights themselves. For example, whilst freedom of expression may need to be curtailed to protect national security (for example, preventing the dissemination of plans of military equipment), there is no comparable need to restrict freedom of religion on the basis of security concerns. If the reason for which a qualified right is restricted is not part of the list of legitimate purposes associated with that right, then the restriction will not be justified.

2. The restriction must be lawful

Even if the state's aim in restricting a right is acceptable under the terms of the ECHR, the Court will still find that one of the qualified rights has been infringed unless the restriction in question is prescribed by law. This means that statutory or common law rules restricting a right must be sufficiently clear to guide the conduct of individuals affected by the restriction. Even if the scope of a restriction is not clear on the terms of the law in question, it will still pass this test if it has been clarified by subsequent judicial decisions and its scope can be ascertained with legal advice.[100]

3. The restriction must be proportionate

Where qualified rights are restricted in the interests of a permissible public policy objective, the restriction must be 'necessary in a democratic society'. The Court has interpreted this requirement of the qualified rights as meaning that restrictions must be proportionate in light of the aims pursued and the rights at issue. In relation to freedom of expression under Art. 10, this means that the Court will have to first consider the nature of the expression in question. It will 'have particular regard to the words used . . . the context in which they were made public and the case as a whole'.[101] Particular expression within, for example, a heated interview might be restricted by a state for the protection of public morals, but the Court will have to consider whether it was appropriate in the context of the interview as a whole. Considering the wider context might also disclose a political purpose to the expression, making its protection particularly important, as Lord Bingham has noted:

> Freedom of thought and expression is an essential condition of an intellectually healthy society. The free communication of information, opinions and argument about the laws which a state should enact and the policies its government at all levels should pursue is an essential condition of truly democratic government. These are the values which article 10 exists to protect, and their importance gives it a central role in the Convention regime, protecting free speech in general and free political speech in particular.[102]

Given the importance of the right at issue, what must states do to show that their restrictions upon freedom of expression are not disproportionate? The Court fleshed out the meaning of 'necessary in a democratic society' in *Handyside* v *United Kingdom*,[103] in which the European Court ruled that the prosecution of the publisher of a book, *The Little Red Schoolbook*, did not breach Art. 10. The book could be banned on the basis of its

---

[100] *Open Door and Dublin Well Woman* v *Ireland* (1993) 15 EHRR 244, [60].
[101] *Fuentes Bobo* v *Spain* (2001) 31 EHRR 50, [46].
[102] *R (Animal Defenders International)* v *Secretary of State for Culture, Media and Sport* [2008] UKHL 15; [2008] 1 AC 1312, [27].
[103] *Handyside* v *United Kingdom* (1976) 1 EHRR 737.

encouraging indecent and illegal activity amongst children (on the basis that such content had the risk of corrupting public morals). The Court accepted that a state did not have to show that the restriction of a right was indispensible for the protection of public morals:

> The Court notes . . . that, whilst the adjective 'necessary', within the meaning of Article 10 para. 2 (Art. 10–2), is not synonymous with 'indispensable' . . . neither has it the flexibility of such expressions as 'admissible', 'ordinary' . . . 'useful' . . . 'reasonable' . . . or 'desirable'. Nevertheless, it is for the national authorities to make the initial assessment of the reality of the pressing social need implied by the notion of 'necessity' in this context.[104]

In order not to overstep the limits of an acceptable restriction, the Court has since emphasised the importance of the state taking steps to ensure the public policy objective is realised by the means least harmful to the protected right:

> States are required to minimise, as far as possible, the interference with these rights, by trying to find alternative solutions and by generally seeking to achieve their aims in the least onerous way as regards human rights.[105]

Nonetheless, even if a state is able to show that the restrictions it has established are not arbitrary in their effect and have been carefully drafted to meet a permitted objective, this does not necessarily mean that the restrictions are proportionate. The Court has made it clear that, even where the qualified rights are at issue, there is an essential core to such rights which cannot simply be balanced away.[106]

(iii) Weighing one qualified right against others

The qualified rights exist in a relationship of tension. Although the Court nominally accords freedom of expression, freedom of religion and the right to privacy 'equal respect',[107] difficult choices often have to be made as to the relationship between these rights in particular cases, with Lord Steyn acknowledging that 'an intense focus on the comparative importance of the specific rights being claimed in the individual case is necessary'.[108] Lord Steyn made this statement in a case which provides a classic example of the incommensurability of privacy rights and freedom of expression. A child's mother was charged with murdering his brother and his representatives sought to protect the surviving child's privacy (under Art. 8) by preventing the publication of the names and details of his mother or brother. Newspapers brought an action to allow them to name the family (citing their Art. 10 right) on the basis that not doing so would stifle the public debate in relation to a serious trial. In this case the House of Lords found that the requirement of protecting privacy was outweighed by the needs of open reporting of court proceedings:

> [I]t is important to bear in mind that from a newspaper's point of view a report of a sensational trial without revealing the identity of the defendant would be a very much disembodied trial. If the newspapers choose not to contest such an injunction, they are less likely to give prominence to reports of the trial. Certainly, readers will be less interested and editors will act accordingly. Informed debate about criminal justice will suffer.[109]

---

[104] Ibid., [48].
[105] *Hatton* v *United Kingdom* (2002) 34 EHRR 1, [97].
[106] *Sheffield and Horsham* v *United Kingdom* (1999) 27 EHRR 163, [66].
[107] *Mosley* v *United Kingdom* (2011) 53 EHRR 30, [111].
[108] *Re S (A Child) (Identification: Restriction on Publication)* [2004] UKHL 47; [2005] 1 AC 593, [17].
[109] Ibid., [34].

The conflict between these two rights came to a head in the recent case of *Mosley* v *United Kingdom*.[110] The applicant, a former FIA President, had won an action for damages from the *News of the World's* publisher for the unauthorised disclosure of personal information which infringed his rights of privacy as protected by Art. 8, following the publication of an article and pictures claiming that he hosted Nazi-themed sex parties.[111] He argued before the European Court, however, that whilst damages were sufficient to compensate for his loss of reputation they did not adequately compensate his loss of privacy under Art. 8 and that the UK should have put in place regulations requiring that newspapers notify the subjects of their stories in advance to enable them to seek an injunction before the courts if their privacy had been violated. The Court addressed the balance between the Arts 8 and 10 rights in this case as follows:

> The publication of news about [celebrities] contributes to the variety of information available to the public and, although generally for the purposes of entertainment rather than education, undoubtedly benefits from the protection of Article 10. However, as noted above, such protection may cede to the requirements of Article 8 where the information at stake is of a private and intimate nature and there is no public interest in its dissemination.[112]

Whilst this suggests that the Court considered that Art. 10 had a lower priority than Art. 8 in the instant case, it thereafter took great pains to emphasise the broader 'chilling effect' which a pre-notification requirement would likely have on investigative journalism which was in the public interest, and so refused to interpret Art. 8 as encompassing such a requirement.[113]

A similar act of balance is involved where expression is said to impinge upon freedom of religion under Art. 9 ECHR. The famous case of *Otto-Preminger-Institut* v *Austria*[114] involved the Austrian Government's decision to ban the institute from showing a film satirising Christianity and to prosecute its distributors. The Court acknowledged that:

> The issue before the Court involves weighing up the conflicting interests of the exercise of two fundamental freedoms guaranteed under the Convention, namely the right of the applicant association to impart to the public controversial views and, by implication, the right of interested persons to take cognisance of such views, on the one hand, and the right of other persons to proper respect for their freedom of thought, conscience and religion, on the other hand.[115]

In a controversial decision, the Court accepted that Austria had not breached Art. 10, on the basis that the authorities' action to 'ensure religious peace' lay within the ability to restrict expression to protect public morals.[116] In later cases the Court has maintained that, 'in the context of religious opinions and beliefs' the Convention states remain able to restrict expressions 'that are gratuitously offensive to others . . . and which . . . do not contribute to any form of public debate capable of furthering progress in human affairs'.[117]

---

[110] *Mosley* v *United Kingdom* (2011) 53 EHRR 30.
[111] *Mosley* v *News Group Newspapers Ltd* [2008] EWHC (QB) 1777; [2008] EMLR 20.
[112] Ibid., [131].
[113] Ibid., [132].
[114] *Otto-Preminger-Institut* v *Austria* (1995) 19 EHRR 34.
[115] Ibid., [55].
[116] Ibid., [56].
[117] *Gunduz* v *Turkey* (2005) 41 EHRR 5, [37].

'Under-developed' rights

When the ECHR was being drafted in the late 1940s, some rights were acknowledged by the drafters as too important to leave out of the Convention, but conversely, were found to be too controversial to develop in full. Only with the Court's jurisprudence have these rights been developed, and some have yet to reach their full potential.

(i) Non-discrimination

Today, especially after the passing of the Equality Act 2010, it seems remarkable that the place of a prohibition on discrimination within a human rights framework would be overly controversial. In the drafting of the ECHR, however, the Convention states would only agree to a provision, Art. 14 ECHR, which prevented discrimination 'on any ground such as sex, race, colour, language, religion, political or other opinion, national or social origin, association with a national minority, property, birth or other status' where other Convention rights were at issue. Subsequently, 'other status' has allowed the right to apply to discrimination on the basis of sexual orientation.

This approach meant that the Art. 14 right was not 'free standing' but rather parasitic, in that the enjoyment of other Convention rights had to be at issue before the right to non-discrimination could be claimed. Despite this handicap this right has been subject to intense litigation and judicial development, with the Court arriving at the following definition of discrimination:

> [D]iscrimination means treating differently, without an objective and reasonable justification, persons in similar situations. 'No objective and reasonable justification' means that the distinction in issue does not pursue a 'legitimate aim' or that there is not a 'reasonable relationship of proportionality between the means employed and the aim sought to be realised.'[118]

Under Art. 1 of Protocol 12, which entered into force in 2005, a freestanding prohibition against discrimination now applies in states which have accepted the Protocol with regard to 'any right set forth by law'. The same test developed with regard to Art. 14 applies to this provision,[119] but at the time of writing only 20 Convention states (not including the UK) have ratified the Protocol.

(ii) Education

Education is essential to human flourishing, in that for any individual to pursue their vision of a good life they must be sufficiently educated to enable them to make the choices that this entails. Therefore, it might seem particularly surprising that the ECHR makes no provision for a 'right' to education, only, in Art. 2 of Protocol 1, a right *not to be denied* such educational provision (including primary, secondary, further and higher education[120]) as a state chooses to make available and ensuring that the state will respect the rights of parents to access that education provision 'in conformity with their own religious and philosophical convictions'. These limitations can only be understood on the basis that a full right to education amounts to a social right, which could only be secured by public expenditure by the Convention states. At the time of the ECHR's drafting there was (and,

---

[118] *Sejdić and Finci* v *Bosnia and Herzegovina* [2009] ECHR 2122, [42].
[119] Ibid., [55].
[120] *Bahin* v *Turkey* (2007) 44 EHRR 5, [137] (GC).

in the UK in particular, remains) considerable reluctance amongst politicians to accord judges the ability to oversee public spending decisions required by such rights.

Given this controversy we should not be surprised that the Court's interpretation of the right, from its early jurisprudence to the modern day, has closely reflected the limitations in the wording of Art. 2 of Protocol 1. The guiding authority remains the 1960s decision in *Belgian Linguistics (No. 2),*[121] which involved a failed challenge to the adequacy of Belgium's language requirements for education. The Court found, and has since maintained, that the right merely guarantees 'persons subject to the jurisdiction of the Contracting Parties the right, in principle, to avail themselves of the means of instruction existing at a given time'.[122]

(iii) Free and fair elections

Like the 'right' to education, the terms of Art. 3 of Protocol 1 ECHR on 'free elections' does not seem on its face to provide for a 'right' to vote or to stand in elections. When the Convention was concluded the contracting states had, and still maintain, diverse electoral systems and there was concern amongst the drafters that a more explicit right would see the Court require a uniform electoral system based on proportional representation for elections across Europe (see Chapter 9[123]). Whilst such fears have not been borne out by the European Court's jurisprudence, by contrast to Art. 2 of Protocol 1, however, the Court has in recent decades taken active steps to develop individual rights under Art. 3 of Protocol 1:

> The Court observes that, while this might not be obvious from its wording, Art. 3 of Protocol No. 1 enshrines a characteristic principle of an effective democracy and is accordingly of prime importance in the Convention system. Democracy constitutes a fundamental element of the 'European public order', and the rights guaranteed under art. 3 of Protocol No. 1 are crucial to establishing and maintaining the foundations of an effective and meaningful democracy governed by the rule of law.[124]

The Court's acceptance of the importance of the ECHR's protection of free elections has allowed it to develop *qualified* rights to vote and stand in elections in cases such as *Hirst,*[125] drawing upon the preparatory materials that contributed to Art. 3 of Protocol 1.[126] The most important qualification is the degree to which the Court permits some leeway to enable states to disenfranchise prisoners (particularly those who have engaged in crimes which threaten democracy, such as electoral fraud), although it has ruled that this qualification is not sufficiently broad to allow states to remove the vote from all serving prisoners.[127] Such developments show that even if some ECHR rights appear to be underdeveloped the Court controls their interpretation, supporting the maxim that the Convention is a 'living instrument which . . . must be interpreted in the light of present-day conditions.'[128]

---

[121] *Belgian Linguistic Case* (1979–80) 1 EHRR 252.
[122] Ibid., 281.
[123] See pp. 308–9.
[124] *Frodl* v *Austria* (2011) 52 EHRR 5, [22].
[125] *Hirst* v *United Kingdom (No. 2)* (2006) 42 EHRR 41 (GC).
[126] Ibid., [57].
[127] Ibid., [62].
[128] *Tyrer* v *United Kingdom* (1979-80) 2 EHRR 1, [31].

Human rights and trade-offs under the ECHR

Key issues

- The European Court has historically imposed human rights standards in a manner sensitive to the demands upon states to trade-off these interests against each other and against other important public policy concerns. It, therefore, has developed several strategies to achieve this accommodation (in addition to accommodation provisions in the ECHR itself).

- A margin of appreciation is employed by the court to emphasise the primary responsibility of the institutions of the member states for the protection of human rights. The doctrine allows the Court to give leeway to the interpretation of these rights by state institutions where a particular application of the rights is controversial.

- The European Court has been very cautious in recognising positive obligations as inherent within particular rights. Positive obligations require states to take active steps to protect an individual's rights and not simply to refrain from infringing them, requiring regulatory systems to be put in place by the states.

- Under Art. 15, the ECHR makes provision for the states to suspend the operation of some of the ECHR rights in circumstances of war or serious public emergency. These derogations are subject to the scrutiny of the European Court.

Myths surrounding human rights

Listening only to Prime Minister David Cameron's speeches in the wake of the riots which took place across English cities in August 2011, casual observers would assume that human rights were not predominantly flexible standards which can be traded-off against other important public interests (as outlined under James Griffin's writings, assessed at the start of this chapter). According to the then Prime Minister, 'phoney human rights concerns'[129] would jeopardise efforts to bring rioters to justice. Similarly, in the wake of the July 7 bomb attacks on London in 2005, Cameron's predecessor Tony Blair railed against judgments under the ECHR that had restricted his Government's counter-terrorism policy and promised that if more 'legal obstacles arise, we will legislate further, including, if necessary, amending the Human Rights Act in respect to the interpretation of the European Convention on Human Rights'.[130] This trend can be recently observed in Theresa May's reported comments – in the aftermath of terrorist incidents in Manchester and London in 2017 – that, if the fight against terrorism was impeded by human rights laws, then those laws would be amended.[131]

Such comments feed a perception amongst the general public that all human rights are absolute, providing for no exceptions. Instead, as we have seen, very few human rights are absolute and most provide either specific or broad circumstances in which infringements are acceptable. As Gearty recognises:

> It is both inevitable and right that all legally enforceable human rights instruments in a democracy should allow for exceptions and derogations in the interests of national survival: the values that

---

[129] HC Debs, vol. 531, col. 1052 (11 August 2011).
[130] T. Blair, Downing Street Press Conference (5 August 2005).
[131] 'May: I'll rip up human rights laws that impede new terror legislation' *Guardian*, (6 June 2017).

give rise to such legal human rights may be absolute but their expression in legal form cannot be held to be such without descending into incoherence.[132]

We have already seen how most human rights under the ECHR are limited or qualified in nature. In this section we will look at how *additional* 'safety valves', provided by the ECHR or developed by the European Court's jurisprudence, operate to ensure that human rights concerns do not undermine effective decision-making.

The subsidiary role of the European Court

Within the Convention system, the European Court of Human Rights is designed to provide a secondary, or supervisory, layer of protection. National authorities provide the primary layer of rights protection within the Convention system, and the Court 'can and should intervene *only* where the domestic authorities fail in that task'.[133] As such, the role of the Court is subsidiary to that of the member states; as the European Court noted in its judgment in the ***Handyside*** case:

> . . . the machinery of protection established by the Convention is subsidiary to the national systems regarding human rights . . . by reason of their direct and continuous contact with the vital forces of their countries, State authorities are in principle in a better position than the international judge to give an opinion on the exact content of these requirements as well as on the 'necessity' of a 'restriction' or 'penalty' intended to meet them.[134]

Consistently with this, and in acknowledgement that the realisation of rights involves the balancing of competing rights and interests, the European Court has sought to recognise that the member states enjoy a degree of policy autonomy in upholding the Convention's protections.

(i) The margin of appreciation doctrine

In some circumstances, often when the qualified rights are at issue, the European Court permits what it describes as a 'margin of appreciation' to a state's national authorities. The margin of appreciation doctrine acknowledges that across the 47 member states different approaches will often be adopted towards already qualified rights in light of factors specific to particular territories. In the context of such pluralism, the margin of appreciation arguably operates to 'tip' the proportionality balance between the qualified rights and the public interests weighed against them in favour of the public interests asserted by a state:

> This is because [l]egally, politically, and culturally heterogeneous national governments can develop divergent but not necessarily incompatible approaches to common legal problems that the Court has afforded them a context-based zone of discretion when reviewing compliance with their treaty obligations and in balancing those obligations against other important interests.[135]

---

[132] C. Gearty, 'Terrorism and Human Rights' (2007) 42 *Government and Opposition* 340, 349.

[133] Jurisconsult of the European Court of Human Rights, *Interlaken Follow-up: Principle of Subsidiarity* (8 July 2010), available at: http://www.echr.coe.int/Documents/2010_Interlaken_Follow-up_ENG.pdf.

[134] *Handyside* v *United Kingdom* (1979-1980) 1 EHRR 737, at [48].

[135] L. Helfer, 'Adjudicating Copyright Claims under the TRIPs Agreement: the Case for a European Human Rights Analogy' (1998) 39 *Harvard Int'l LJ* 357, 396.

Equally, use of the doctrine could be seen as code for the Court refusing to engage in the difficult task of testing the proportionality of a state's actions. It is therefore a controversial doctrine, not least because it is a jurisprudential tool that is 'not found in the text of the Convention'.[136]

(ii) Factors relevant to the margin of appreciation

From the case law we can identify a number of factors that feed into the European Court's decision as to whether or not to grant a state a sufficiently broad margin of appreciation to negate what would otherwise amount to a rights infringement.

1. Importance of the right/restrictions in question

In the case of *Connors v United Kingdom*,[137] which involved an Art. 8 ECHR claim by a family of travellers evicted from their plot in a council-run caravan park, the Court undertook a particularly thorough evaluation of the margin of appreciation available to the state. The Court emphasised that the most important concern in assessing the margin would be the importance of the interests at stake in a case:

> This margin will vary according to the nature of the Convention right in issue, its importance for the individual and the nature of the activities restricted, as well as the nature of the aim pursued by the restrictions. The margin will tend to be narrower where the right at stake is crucial to the individual's effective enjoyment of intimate or key rights . . . On the other hand, in spheres involving the application of social or economic policies, there is authority that the margin of appreciation is wide . . . [138]

In this case the Court emphasised the importance of the Art. 8 right at issue, as the applicants were being forced from their home which meant that 'the margin of appreciation to be afforded to the national authorities must be regarded as correspondingly narrowed'.[139] This indicates the Court's reluctance to employ the margin of appreciation where it would restrict *core* exercises of a right and led to its conclusion that summary eviction was an unacceptable means of controlling anti-social behaviour on the caravan site in question, outside any margin of appreciation ordinarily due to the management of public housing.

2. 'On the ground' experience

In *Connors,* one of the main reasons why the European Court considered granting a margin of appreciation to the UK authorities was on the basis that they were better placed to weigh up any rights concerns at issue than an international court:

> [A] margin of appreciation must, inevitably, be left to the national authorities, who by reason of their direct and continuous contact with the vital forces of their countries are in principle better placed than an international court to evaluate local needs and conditions.[140]

The Court will regularly rely on this justification for invoking the margin of appreciation where a case is politically sensitive in nature, such as cases involving Art. 15 ECHR, the

---

[136] G. Letsas, 'Two Concepts of the Margin of Appreciation' (2006) 26 OJLS 705, 705.
[137] *Connors v United Kingdom* (2005) 40 EHRR 9.
[138] Ibid., [82].
[139] Ibid., [86].
[140] Ibid., [82].

Convention provision which allows states to temporarily suspend the operation of particular rights because of an emergency situation.[141]

3. Lack of consensus amongst Convention states

The Court ordinarily invokes the margin of appreciation on the basis that there is a 'lack of consensus' across the Convention states as to how to address a particular issue regarding the balance between individual rights and public interests.[142] The Court extends such a margin of appreciation on the basis that Convention state institutions are better placed than an international court to address this balance in their local context. The Court's consideration of the degree of consensus as a factor expanding the margin of appreciation has a long pedigree in its case law, as can be seen by the late-1970s case of *Tyrer* v *United Kingdom*:[143]

> The Court must also recall that the Convention is a living instrument which . . . must be interpreted in the light of present-day conditions. In the case now before it the Court cannot but be influenced by the developments and commonly accepted standards in the penal policy of the member States of the Council of Europe in this field.[144]

Letsas notes how this focus on consensus has been criticised for 'lending weight to the idea of moral relativism and compromising the universality of human rights'.[145] Nonetheless, the 'consensus' amongst states is not frozen in time and in many cases the Court has been able to use Europe-wide changes in law regarding certain rights to justify denying a margin of appreciation. *Tyrer*, for example, involved a schoolboy from the Isle of Man who was sentenced to be hit three times by a birch rod after being found guilty of assault. In finding a violation of Art. 3 ECHR, the Court noted how in many Convention states judicial corporal punishment had 'never existed in modern times'.[146]

4. Whether the state has thoroughly considered ECHR rights

The margin of appreciation must be recognised as a doctrine that applies *only* to the European Court. The domestic institutions (judiciary, legislature or executive) may freely return to an issue within the margin of appreciation and increase levels of rights protection. Indeed, a state's failure to do so, especially if the consensus across Europe regarding a particular right is shifting, can be one reason for the Court to deny that the margin of appreciation applies in a case.[147] For example, in *Hirst* v *United Kingdom*,[148] when the Court's Grand Chamber found that the UK's denial of the vote to prisoners breached Art. 3 of Protocol 1, one of the factors which militated against awarding a margin of appreciation was that there had been no proper consideration of this policy since 1870.[149]

---

[141] See below, pp. 642–3. For a good example see *Ireland* v *United Kingdom* (1979–80) 2 EHRR 25, [207].
[142] On which see generally K. Dzehtsiarou, *European Consensus and the Legitimacy of the European Court of Human Rights* (CUP, 2016).
[143] *Tyrer* v *United Kingdom* (1979–80) 2 EHRR 1.
[144] Ibid., [31].
[145] G. Letsas, 'Two Concepts of the Margin of Appreciation' (2006) 26 OJLS 705, 723.
[146] *Tyrer* v *United Kingdom* (1979–80) 2 EHRR 1, [38].
[147] *Cf. Animal Defenders International* v *United Kingdom* (2013) 57 EHRR 21, [114]–[116].
[148] *Hirst* v *United Kingdom (No. 2)* (2006) 42 EHRR 41 (GC).
[149] Ibid., [79].

This decision can be contrasted with the judgment in *A, B and C v Ireland*,[150] which concerned whether Ireland's prohibition of abortion, even for reasons related to the health and well-being of the pregnant woman, violated Art. 8 ECHR. Even though the Court accepted that Ireland's law was now out of step with the European consensus,[151] the Court considered that Ireland's repeated legislative discussion and referenda upon the issue of abortion sufficed to maintain the margin of appreciation:

> From the lengthy, complex and sensitive debate in Ireland . . . as regards the content of its abortion laws, a choice has emerged. Irish law prohibits abortion in Ireland for health and well-being reasons but allows women, in the first and second applicants' position who wish to have an abortion for those reasons . . . , the option of lawfully travelling to another State to do so.[152]

(iii) Controversy over the margin of appreciation

To its critics, the Court developed the margin of appreciation as a means of restricting the transformative effect of human rights, with the effect that rights do not always guarantee the same level of protection across all of the Convention states.[153] Even those closely tied to the operation of the Court, such as its former Registrar, Michael O'Boyle, have highlighted the risk that the doctrine can often seem like an excuse on the part of the Court not to become involved in a dispute:

> The concept of margin of appreciation remains ill-defined and its application is not differentiated according to the individual situation. There is a risk that this standard is being trotted out as a substitute for rational review.[154]

Others, by contrast, recognise that the Court relies on the support of the Convention states to ensure that its judgments are upheld, meaning that '[c]areful attention to national sensitivities and differences still is an essential key to success'.[155] Whilst the Court recognises its own *ultimate* responsibility for policing the enforcement of ECHR provisions, it often casts itself in the role of a constitutional institution serving Europe as a whole, and therefore only stepping in where domestic rights protection has failed:

> [T]he main purpose of the Convention is to lay down certain international standards to be observed by the Contracting States in their relations with persons under their jurisdiction. This does not mean absolute uniformity is required and, indeed, since the Contracting States remain free to choose the measures which they consider appropriate, the Court cannot be oblivious of the substantive or procedural features of their respective domestic laws.[156]

Indeed, as we have seen in the context of case load, no one court could hope to deal with all human rights claims across the 47 Convention states.[157] By according a margin of appreciation to the human rights decisions of domestic institutions, the Court encourages these

---

[150] *A, B and C v Ireland* (2011) 53 EHRR 13.

[151] Ibid., [235].

[152] Ibid., [239]. See also: *Animal Defenders International v United Kingdom* [2013] 57 EHRR 21, [95].

[153] See P. Mahoney, 'Marvellous Richness of Diversity or Invidious Cultural Relativism?' (1998) 19 HRLJ 1, 12.

[154] M. O'Boyle, 'The Margin of Appreciation and Derogation under Article 15: Ritual Incantation or Principle?' (1998) 19 HRLJ 23, 29.

[155] J. Gerards, 'Pluralism, Deference and the Margin of Appreciation Doctrine' (2011) 17 ELJ 80, 104.

[156] *Sunday Times v United Kingdom* (1979–80) 2 EHRR 245, [61].

[157] L. Helfer, 'Redesigning the European Court of Human Rights: Embeddedness as a Deep Structural Principle of the European Human Rights Regime' (2008) 19 EJIL 125, 128.

institutions to take *primary* responsibility for safeguarding human rights.[158] But flexibility might also come at a cost; in affording an overly-wide margin, as it has been suggested that the Court has occasionally done in order to avoid conflict with critical states,[159] the Court runs the risk of weakening its standing as a pan-European defender of human rights.[160]

The margin of appreciation doctrine is only one part of a wider tapestry of approaches adopted by the European Court to ensure rights protection is primarily a concern for national institutions. For example, historically the Court did not specify the measures which states must take to comply with its rulings. This approach can be traced to the earliest decisions of the Court:

> The national authorities remain free to choose the measures which they consider appropriate in those matters which are governed by the Convention. Review by the Court concerns only the conformity of these measures with the requirements of the Convention.[161]

Thinking point . . .

One of the factors suggesting the 'harmonising' factions amongst the Court are gaining in strength is its recent willingness to set out the minimum requirements necessary to bring a state's law in line with the ECHR's requirements in its judgments (particularly where it faces repeated applications on an issue). See *Broniowski* v *Poland* (2006) 43 EHRR 1 (GC).

Judicial approaches which emphasise the subsidiary nature of the ECHR adjudication and enforcement mechanisms frequently come into conflict with approaches seeking to harmonise standards of rights protection across the Convention states. The impact of this clash can be seen in cases on prisoner voting rights in the wake of *Hirst* v *United Kingdom*,[162] in which, despite many different approaches to prisoner voting across Europe, chambers of the European Court refused to extend any margin of appreciation to states including Austria.[163] This approach caused considerable dissatisfaction amongst Convention states and, in *Scoppola* v *Italy (No. 3)*,[164] Italy referred a judgment to the Grand Chamber which threatened its law banning prisoners serving more than three years' imprisonment from voting. The Grand Chamber reaffirmed that automatic disenfranchisement of all prisoners was incompatible with the right to free and fair elections provided by Art. 3, Protocol 1 of the ECHR.[165] Nonetheless, turning to Italy's more limited restrictions on voting, the Grand Chamber concluded that, because 'the restrictions imposed on the applicant's right to vote did not "thwart the free expression of the people in the choice of the legislature", and maintained "the integrity and effectiveness of an electoral procedure

---

[158] *Tomašic* v *Croatia* [2012] MHLR 167, [73]–[74].

[159] On which see: P. Popelier, S. Lambrecht and K. Lemmens, *Criticism of the European Court of Human Rights: Shifting the Convention System – Counter-Dynamics at the National and EU Levels* (Intersentia, 2016).

[160] Concerns raised in the dissenting judgment of Judge Pinto De Albuquerque in *Hutchinson* v *United Kingdom* (5759208/08), 17 January 2017 (GC).

[161] *Belgian Linguistic Case* (1979–80) 1 EHRR 252, [10].

[162] Above, p. 635.

[163] See: *Frodl* v *Austria*, (2011) 52 EHRR 5, [23].

[164] *Scoppola* v *Italy (No. 3)* [2012] ECHR 868.

[165] Ibid., [96].

aimed at identifying the will of the people through universal suffrage"', in these circumstances '[t]he margin of appreciation afforded to the respondent government in this sphere has therefore not been overstepped'.[166]

In decisions like *Scoppola,* even though it was decided by a Grand Chamber majority of sixteen to one, the tensions between different views of the European Court's role are evident. Moreover, whilst *Scoppola* points towards the Court accepting a diversity of approaches to elements of the qualified rights, some commentators believe the long-term trend in the Court's jurisprudence tends towards harmonisation. Lord Hoffmann, for example, accuses the Court of seeking 'to aggrandise its jurisdiction and to impose uniform rules on Member States'.[167] The applicability and scope of margin of appreciation doctrine remains a key indicator of the extent to which the Court continues to view itself as playing a subsidiary role within the Convention system.

Positive and negative obligations

The ECHR provides a list of civil and political rights and at the time of its creation it was widely thought that these rights at most required non-interference by the state. Non-interference is a relatively easy proposition to sell to governments managing scarce resources. It costs nothing, in financial terms, for a government not to torture its opponents. Nonetheless, this amounted to a very limited vision of human rights as primarily intended to restrict the activities of states. The push for such 'negative rights' amounted, for Campbell, to 'a form of extreme libertarianism', concerned with pushing the state out of large areas of human life.[168] In some respects, the ECHR is locked into this limited role, for, as we have seen, the Convention and its Protocols make no meaningful room for social and economic rights.[169] Nonetheless, although the right to private and family life under Art. 8 ECHR has not been interpreted by the Court in such a way as to require Convention states to provide universal access to social housing, the Court has moved to recognise that some 'positive rights' are included within the terms of the ECHR.

Thinking Point . . .

Positive obligations often involve the state taking responsibility for not adequately regulating the activities of private individuals and bodies (for example, requiring governments to maintain a system of press regulation to protect privacy rights). See *Von Hannover* v *Germany* (2006) 43 EHRR 7, [57].

(i) Positive obligations regarding the right to life/freedom from torture

In our examination of Art. 2 ECHR above, we assumed that the Convention provides for a negative right; the state must not take the life of an individual within its jurisdiction (outside certain exceptional circumstances). The exact wording of Art. 2, however, provides that '[e]veryone's right to life shall be protected by law'. The European Court has used the

---

[166] Ibid., [110].
[167] L. Hoffmann, 'The Universality of Human Rights' (2009) 125 LQR 416, 424.
[168] T. Campbell, 'Human Rights: A Culture of Controversy' (1999) 26 JLS 6, 10.
[169] See above, pp. 617–18.

flexibility inherent in this formulation to ensure that the right not only provides for the duty on the state not to kill people, but also to require an adequate independent investigation of circumstances where agents of the state kill an individual. Without such positive obligations on the state the negative right would be undermined as there would be no official mechanism for establishing the circumstances of a death.[170] This right to an investigation of all the circumstances surrounding a killing (including what safeguards the authorities put in place during operational planning) applies even where the killing takes place in the context of a conflict, and it was on this basis that the killings of individuals by UK forces in Iraq were found to breach Art. 2 in *Al-Skeini*:[171]

> It is clear that where the death to be investigated under Article 2 occurs in circumstances of generalised violence, armed conflict or insurgency, obstacles may be placed in the way of investigators and . . . concrete constraints may compel the use of less effective measures of investigation or may cause an investigation to be delayed . . . Nonetheless, the obligation under Article 2 to safeguard life entails that, even in difficult security conditions, all reasonable steps must be taken to ensure that an effective, independent investigation is conducted into alleged breaches of the right to life.[172]

Ultimately, the investigation will only be recognised as effective if it has the means to determine whether the use of force by state agents was justified and, where it was not, the investigation must form the basis of action to bring those involved to justice.[173]

More onerous positive obligations exist under Arts 2 and 3 ECHR in circumstances where the state is in a position to intervene to stop the killing of, or serious injury to, a person or the infliction of torture or inhuman and degrading treatment by another private individual. Where the authorities know, or ought to have knowledge, of such a serious threat to an individual they are under an obligation to use the resources of the state to take 'reasonable steps' to tackle that threat.[174] The boundaries of this duty can be seen in the next case.

Key case

PF and EF v United Kingdom, Application No. 28326/09 [2010] ECHR 2015 (European Court of Human Rights)

During the summer and autumn of 2001, tensions between the loyalist and nationalist communities in North Belfast were particularly high. The most serious flash point was the Holy Cross Girl's Primary School, where children and their parents were subject to sustained abuse and physical attack for several months. Police mounted an operation to ensure children could reach their school by their preferred route using Perspex screens lined by police and soldiers. The police did not take steps to arrest the groups throwing stones, urine-filled balloons and even explosive devices at the children and their protective screen, concerned that such action would spark even more widespread disorder. The applicant parent and child brought an action claiming that their Articles 2 and 3 ECHR rights had not been adequately protected.

---

[170] *McCann* v *United Kingdom* [1995] 21 EHRR 97, [161] (GC).
[171] *Al-Skeini* v *United Kingdom* (2011) 53 EHRR 18.
[172] Ibid., [164].
[173] Ibid., [166].
[174] *Z* v *United Kingdom* [2001] 34 EHRR 3, [73].

➜

> The European Court accepted (at [38]) that the loyalists' actions had interfered with the applicant's Art. 3 rights and that the police were forewarned of this situation:
>
> > The Court observes that the behaviour of the loyalist protesters was premeditated, it continued for two months, it was designed to cause fear and distress to young children and their parents making their way to school, and it clearly resulted in considerable mental suffering. The Court would therefore agree that the actions of the loyalist protesters reached the minimum level of severity required to fall within the scope of Article 3.
>
> This finding required the Court to address whether the actions of the police fulfilled their duty to take all reasonable steps to uphold these rights. Noting that 41 officers sustained injury in their efforts to protect the children, the Court (at [43]) found that the duty had been fulfilled in this case:
>
> > [T]he police followed a course of action which they reasonably believed would end the protest with minimal risk to the children, their parents and the community at large. The risks which concerned the police were not, in fact, purely speculative. Violence had been erupting through-out the city over the summer, often at great speed and with little prior warning. Moreover, the police had intelligence which suggested that a more direct approach could increase the risk to the parents and children walking to the Holy Cross School, lead to further attacks on Catholic schools and also result in increased violence in north Belfast.
>
> This case emphasises that, when it comes to the positive obligation to protect individuals under Articles 2 and 3, the Court will look for evidence of a considered and meaningful response by authorities but once that standard is met, the Court will not be drawn into the operational choices confronting police.

(ii) Positive obligations regarding the right to private and family life

Whilst the primary focus of Art. 8 remains on preventing interferences with an individual's private and family life, the European Court has acknowledged, in cases like *A, B and C v Ireland*[175] (which we considered above[176]), circumstances in which this provision gives rise to positive obligations.[177] Just as with the negative obligations in the context of this qualified right, when the Court comes to consider imposing such obligations, it considers the fair balance between 'the competing interests of the individual and of the community as a whole'.[178] This balancing process, where positive obligations are at issue, was explored by the Court when one of the claimants asserted that Art. 8 ECHR obliged the Irish state to have in place an adequate procedure by which applicants could find out whether they qualified for an abortion on the basis that a pregnancy endangered their life. The Court considered the relevant factors weighing upon the decision as follows:

> Some factors concern the applicant: the importance of the interest at stake and whether 'funda-mental values' or 'essential aspects' of private life are in issue . . . and the impact on an applicant of a discordance between the social reality and the law, the coherence of the administrative and legal practices within the domestic system being regarded as an important factor in the assessment carried out under Article 8 . . . Some factors concern the position of the State: whether the alleged

---

[175] *A, B and C v Ireland* (2011) 53 EHRR 13.
[176] See above p. 636.
[177] *A, B and C v Ireland* (2011) 53 EHRR 13, [244].
[178] Ibid., [247].

obligation is narrow and defined or broad and indeterminate . . . and the extent of any burden the obligation would impose on the State . . . [179]

In this case, the failure of Ireland to maintain any effective regulatory regime by which abortion could be sought if a woman's life was in danger did breach the positive obligations required by Art. 8. Nonetheless, such a regime is not a particularly large financial burden on the state; it is necessary to ensure a woman's *access* to treatment when a pregnancy is life-threatening and stops short of requiring that the state funds such treatment. Only in cases involving particularly vulnerable groups has the Court gone further towards requiring benefits provision by the state. For example, in the **Connors** case[180] we saw the Court declare the removal of a gypsy family from their pitch on a council-run caravan site breached Art. 8. In this context, the Court noted a broader positive obligation to this particular group:

> The vulnerable position of gypsies as a minority means that some special consideration should be given to their needs and their different lifestyle both in the relevant regulatory framework and in reaching decisions in particular cases . . . To this extent, there is thus a positive obligation imposed on the Contracting States by virtue of Article 8 to facilitate the gypsy way of life.[181]

These examples indicate the caution with which the Court has approached the question of positive obligations under Art. 8 ECHR. The Court has proceeded on the basis that the level of funding which a state allocates towards social housing and healthcare remains a political issue best left to the ultimate responsibility of elected decision makers. Nonetheless, as cases such as **Connors** indicate, this approach has not prevented the Court from actively asserting positive obligations towards particularly vulnerable groups.

(iii) Can positive rights be 'hijacked' by government?

Where positive rights are at issue, Toulson LJ has observed that '[h]uman rights law is sometimes in danger of becoming over complicated'.[182] Indeed, in some of the cases we have examined the European Court seems to have been straining the wording of the ECHR rights to ensure their usefulness to claimants outside a narrow range of cases. In essence, the Court has considered the relationship between the ECHR's narrow range of rights and the public interest and has undertaken to shift that balance by its judgments towards a broader conception of rights protection.

Arguably, this process is necessary. The ECHR, as the Court frequently notes, is a 'living instrument' developing to enhance rights protection across Europe. But once the Court recognised positive rights, one additional complexity is that states begin to argue that, in the balance between rights, their interference with certain rights is necessary to ensure that they fulfil their positive obligations. For example, in seeking to defend the system of counter-terrorism 'control orders'[183] in force in the UK from 2005 to 2011 (which could impose strict curfews on individuals) against claims that it amounted to an infringement of the Art. 5 ECHR right to liberty, the UK Government sought to claim that it was obliged to take such action to fulfil its positive obligations under Art. 2 ECHR to protect the right to life of people threatened by terrorist violence. Whilst the House of

---

[179] Ibid., [248].
[180] *Connors* v *United Kingdom* (2005) 40 EHRR 9.
[181] Ibid., [84].
[182] *R (Condliff)* v *North Staffordshire Primary Care Trust* [2011] EWCA Civ 910; (2011) 121 BMLR 192, [34].
[183] Prevention of Terrorism Act 2005, s. 2.

Lords ultimately rejected this proposition,[184] it does highlight the additional complexity positive obligations bring to systems of rights protection.

Derogations from the ECHR

(i) The nature of derogations

Derogations are essentially temporary suspensions of most of the human rights contained in the ECHR (although not absolute rights) to enable a state to address an ongoing crisis situation. For example, the UK has relied on derogations from the right to liberty (Art. 5 ECHR) to enable it to tackle terrorism in Northern Ireland and in the aftermath of September 11. By permitting derogations under Art. 15 ECHR, the drafters of the Convention intended that states would be able to tackle emergency situations without being restricted by ordinarily applicable human rights standards (thereby acknowledging that the need for decision makers to weigh up such concerns could at least delay action). Nonetheless, the terms of Art. 15 ensure that derogations are only available in the most extreme circumstances and that any effort to derogate can be assessed by the European Court: 'In time of war or other public emergency threatening the life of the nation any High Contracting Party may take measures derogating from its obligations under this Convention to the extent strictly required by the exigencies of the situation'.

(ii) 'An emergency threatening the life of the nation'

One of the problems with the notion of an 'emergency threatening the life of the nation' is that it is not immediately obvious when a situation reaches the required level of seriousness to trigger the ability to derogate:

> [Article 15] does not stipulate whether the threat has to be to the whole of the nation or whether a threat to a part can suffice, it does not say how imminent, or how durable, any such threat needs to be and above all it does not elaborate upon the meaning of the phrase 'life of the nation' – does it presuppose a threat to the stability of the government, to the lives of a significant number of people or to the continuity of essential services?[185]

The Court has historically granted states wide latitude in determining when a sufficiently serious threat to warrant derogation exists. In one of the very first cases to come before the Court, *Lawless* v *Ireland* (which involved a challenge to the Republic of Ireland's introduction of internment – detention without trial – to tackle a campaign of political violence),[186] the judges asserted that a derogation requires 'an exceptional situation or emergency which affects the whole population and constitutes threat to the organised life of the community of which the State is composed'.[187] Nonetheless, the Court has long accepted that the assertion of a state of emergency is primarily a political decision, often made on the basis of incomplete facts in the midst of a rapidly developing situation and not at the remove of a courtroom. In *Lawless,* for example, the absence of widespread violence did not preclude Ireland maintaining a derogation allowing it to intern suspected members of the IRA.

---

[184] See *Secretary of State for the Home Department* v *AF* [2009] UKHL 28; [2010] 2 AC 269, [76] (Lord Hope).
[185] B. Dickson, 'Law versus Terrorism: Can Law Win?' (2005) 1 EHRLR 11, 20–1.
[186] *Lawless* v *Ireland (No. 3)* (1979–80) 1 EHRR 15.
[187] Ibid., [28].

Although in many respects the Convention has outgrown the earliest jurisprudence of the Court, states still enjoy much of the extensive leeway to issue derogations provided by the *Lawless* decision. When the European Court came to consider the derogation from Art. 5 ECHR adopted by the UK in response to the September 11 attacks it accepted that, although the UK was the only state to derogate in response to the Al-Qaeda threat, 'it was for each government, as the guardian of their own people's safety, to make their own assessment on the basis of the facts known to them'.[188] Even though there had, at the time of the derogation, been no Al-Qaeda attack against the UK, the Court emphasised that Art. 15 did not require 'a State to wait for disaster to strike before taking measures to deal with it' and that the attacks on London of July 2005 showed that the threat faced by the UK was 'very real'.[189]

(iii) 'Strictly required by the exigencies of the situation'

Nonetheless, if the European Court is generous to states in terms of when they can seek a derogation, it has been much more strict on the second requirement in Art. 15, that measures enacted under a derogation must be 'strictly required' to respond to the emergency in question. This rule introduces a proportionality requirement, meaning that any interference with an ECHR right should be carefully designed to meet the objective in question and must not be arbitrary or unfair. Even if a particular interference supposedly serves a purpose as important as protecting national security, it will not be justified if it is arbitrary or discriminatory in its operation or amounts to a greater infringement than is necessary to tackle the threat in question.

The effect of this requirement is best illustrated by the UK's derogation after September 11, which permitted the Home Secretary to designate certain foreign nationals as suspected international terrorists and to detain them without trial (ordinarily a breach of Art. 5, as this practice did not fit within the limitations to the right to liberty) in Belmarsh Prison. The European Court concluded that, even though it had accepted that some derogation may have been permissible, 'where a derogating measure encroaches upon a fundamental Convention right, such as the right to liberty, the Court must be satisfied that it was a genuine response to the emergency situation, that it was fully justified by the special circumstances of the emergency and that adequate safeguards were provided against abuse'.[190] Following the position adopted by the House of Lords,[191] the European Court accepted that this requirement had not been fulfilled. The UK's derogation affected only foreign nationals, even though there was no evidence that such individuals posed more of a threat of launching an Al-Qaeda attack than UK nationals:

> The choice by the Government and Parliament of an immigration measure to address what was essentially a security issue had the result of failing adequately to address the problem, while imposing a disproportionate and discriminatory burden of indefinite detention on one group of suspected terrorists.[192]

In the absence of a valid derogation, the UK was therefore in breach of the claimants' Article 5 and 14 rights. Nonetheless, the Court noted that, even when released from Belmarsh, the claimants were subject to control orders restricting their activities. As a result, and in

---

[188] *A* v *United Kingdom* (2009) 49 EHRR 29, [180] (GC).
[189] Ibid., [177].
[190] Ibid., [184].
[191] *A* v *Secretary of State for the Home Department* [2004] UKHL 56; [2005] 2 AC 68.
[192] *A* v *United Kingdom* (2009) 49 EHRR 29, [186] (GC).

a concession to the UK's counter-terrorism policy, none of the applicants was awarded damages of more than 3,900 Euros.

Conclusion

This chapter has examined human rights both as moral precepts and as codified legal rules under the ECHR. To conclude, we must remember that even though the ECHR has assumed the important status of 'a constitutional instrument of European public order',[193] this does not mean that it, and its associated jurisprudence, can be regarded as providing us with the last word on human rights. The ECHR is instead an effort to codify *some* of those rights and to provide a legal framework to support their enforcement on a particular continent. As George Letsas notes, human rights claims under the ECHR draw both on the moral strength of human rights principles and on the legal obligations assumed by the Convention states:

> The ruling of a violation of the ECHR is thus a mixture of two kinds of claims: a claim about the moral rights that individuals are entitled to by virtue of being human and a claim about the nature of obligations that states have undertaken by joining the ECHR. These two claims need not be identical. The power of the European Court to hold Contracting States accountable under the ECHR may not give full effect to the rights that individuals have by virtue of being human.[194]

At vital junctures in Convention jurisprudence, such as the decision in *Al-Skeini* to recognise that the Court had the jurisdiction to hear cases brought by Iraqis tortured or killed by UK forces during the occupation of Iraq, the Court's judges return to the moral principles (and historical roots) underpinning the ECHR for guidance. Hence, Judge Bonello's powerful assertion in *Al-Skeini* that 'I believe that those who export war ought to see to the parallel export of guarantees against the atrocities of war'.[195]

Being rooted in moral principles provides the ECHR's provisions with particular strength to resist political attack. In upholding human rights, Sir John Laws considers that the courts 'protect values which no democratic politicians could honestly contest: values which, therefore, may be described as apolitical, since they stand altogether above the rancorous but vital dissensions of party politicians'.[196] Nonetheless, even where such important interests are at stake Lord Bingham reminds us that 'inherent in the whole of the Convention is a search for balance between the rights of the individual and the wider rights of the society to which he belongs, neither enjoying any absolute right to prevail over the other'.[197] Only the most ardent human rights zealots and sceptics refuse to recognise the trade-offs between rights and the public interest which are inherent to the concept of human rights, and both groups undermine the usefulness of the concept in the process.

---

[193] *Al-Skeini* v *United Kingdom* (2011) 53 EHRR 18, [141].
[194] G. Letsas, 'Two Concepts of the Margin of Appreciation' (2006) 26 OJLS 705, 709.
[195] *Al-Skeini* v *United Kingdom* (2011) 53 EHRR 18, Concurring Opinion, [38].
[196] J. Laws, 'Law and Democracy' [1995] PL 72, 93.
[197] *Kay* v *Lambeth BC* [2006] UKHL 10; [2006] 2 AC 465, [32].

Practice questions

1. *'Human rights will be the weaker if they are seen as the impositions of controversial inter-pretations of basic rights outwith the scope of democratic accountability.'*

(T. Campbell, 'Human Rights: A Culture of Controversy' (1999) 26 *Journal of Law and Society* 6, 6)

Consider whether, as Campbell suggests, the most controversial aspect of human rights is the constraints which the concept imposes upon democratic politics.

2. *'The results so far achieved within the framework of Protocol No. 14 are encouraging, par-ticularly as a result of the measures taken by the Court to increase efficiency and address the number of clearly inadmissible applications pending before it. However, the growing number of potentially well-founded applications pending before the Court is a serious prob-lem that causes concern . . . Protocol No. 14 alone will not provide a lasting and comprehen-sive solution to the problems facing the Convention system. Further measures are therefore also needed to ensure that the Convention system remains effective and can continue to protect the rights and freedoms of over 800 million people in Europe.'*

(Council of Europe, *Brighton Declaration* (19 April 2012), [6])

Assess why it has proven so difficult to design an operating procedure which allows the European Court to effectively manage its case load.

3. *'[I]n this country we are proud to stand up for human rights, at home and abroad. It is part of the British tradition. But what is alien to our tradition – and now exerting such a corrosive influence on behaviour and morality – is the twisting and misrepresenting of human rights in a way that has undermined personal responsibility . . . The truth is, the interpretation of human rights legislation has exerted a chilling effect on public sector organisations, leading them to act in ways that fly in the face of common sense, offend our sense of right and wrong, and undermine responsibility.'*

(David Cameron, MP, 'PM's speech on the fightback after the riots' (15 August 2011) (www.number10. gov.uk/news/pms-speech-on-the-fightback-after-the-riots/))

Evaluate whether the operation of human rights under the ECHR really does force public authorities to 'act in ways that fly in the face of common sense'.

Further reading

Just as this chapter begins with an attempt to understand the philosophical underpinnings of human rights, so too should further reading be directed towards this key issue. Jerome Shestack (**J. Shestack, 'The Philosophic Foundations of Human Rights'** (1998) 20 *Human Rights Quarterly* 200–34) efficiently examines the philosophical justifications employed to explain human rights and explains why, even amid an increasing number of positive treaties it remains important to understand the basis of these rights. His approach offers an accessible start point from which to understand the philosophical underpinnings of human rights, examining the strengths and weaknesses of different theories in turn. James Griffin (**J. Griffin, 'Discrepancies between the Best Philosophical Account of Human Rights and the International Law of Human Rights'** (2001) 101 *Proceedings of the Aristotelian Society* 1–28) details what he regards as the best philosophical approach to human rights, grounded in the idea of personhood (as explored in this chapter). He then proceeds to outline the manner in which many international treaties go beyond the requirements of human rights grounded on personhood (and questions whether they therefore outrun their philosophical foundations). Tom Campbell's writing (**T. Campbell, 'Human Rights: A Culture of Controversy'** (1999) 26 *Journal of Law and Society* 6–26), at the beginning of the Human Rights Act era, remains a devastating critique of dogmatic assertions of the utility of human rights. He examines the nature of human rights as an idea, what it means to institutionalise the concept and proceeds to evaluate the particular form of institutionalisation encapsulated by the Human Rights Act (giving the reader a useful window onto the next chapter of this book). Campbell provides an excellent start point from which to begin a theoretical consideration of the modern human rights debate. Whilst Conor Gearty's short book (**C. Gearty, *Can Human Rights Survive?*** (CUP, 2006) 17–59) is worth reading in its entirety, Chapter 2 focuses upon what he describes as the 'crisis' threatening to engulf the authoritative basis of human rights. He evaluates rights scepticism and, whilst he does concede that human rights may be largely grounded in superstitions, he concludes that this does not necessarily mean that they should be dismissed as fictions.

Having considered the intersection between legal and philosophical debates on human rights, the reader should focus on gaining a more thorough understanding of the ECHR regime. Formerly one of the most prominent European Court judges, Lucius Caflisch (**L. Caflisch, 'The Reform of the European Court of Human Rights: Protocol No. 14 and Beyond'** (2006) 6 *Human Rights Law Review* 403–415) delivers an illuminating analysis of the need for reform of the European Court under Protocol 14 ECHR and how some states, eager to curtail the effectiveness of the Court, stymied even more radical reform proposals. To provide this account with more recent reform of the Convention regime, readers should also consider Mark Elliott's comment piece on the Brighton Declaration (**M. Elliott, 'After Brighton: Between a Rock and a Hard Place'** [2012] *Public Law* 619–628). The margin of appreciation remains one of the most contested jurisprudential concepts we have considered in the course of this chapter. To explore the concept in greater depth, consider George Letsas's work (**G. Letsas, 'Two Concepts of the Margin of Appreciation'** (2006) *Oxford Journal of Legal Studies* 705–732), which focuses on the margin of appreciation and the nature of qualified rights. Letsas recognises that the Court employs a *substantive* margin of appreciation when it decides that an interference with a qualified right is justified by the public interests asserted by states. He also recognises that the Court employs a *structural* margin of appreciation when it recognises that because of the international nature of the ECHR states are better placed to decide certain issues (the sense in which the term is used in this chapter).

Chapter 21
The Human Rights Act 1998

'[T]he senior judges are now required to police constitutional boundaries and determine sensitive human rights issues in a way which would have been unthinkable forty years ago. This new judicial role is still developing, but . . . the effect of this trend will be to reshape the relationship between the judiciary and the other branches of government.'

House of Lords Select Committee on the Constitution, *Relations between the Executive, the Judiciary and Parliament* (2007) HL 151-I, [33].

Chapter outline

Throughout the latter half of the twentieth century UK policy makers and constitutional lawyers grappled with how to incorporate human rights concerns into a constitution based upon the theoretically unlimited legislative power of Parliament. This chapter charts progress towards this goal, examining first the inadequacies of the protection of 'civil liberties' in the UK under common law and statute. We then consider how other countries have attempted to reconcile majoritarian democratic politics with legal protections for individual rights, and how these efforts influenced the UK in the development of the Human Rights Act 1998 (HRA). The remainder of the chapter examines the scheme of the HRA 1998, considering what rights were incorporated under the Act and the powers that the courts gained over legislation and over the activities of public bodies.

Introduction

The Human Rights Act 1998 (HRA) profoundly changed the role of the UK judiciary by 'incorporating'[1] the ECHR rights that we considered in the last chapter into UK law. At a stroke, it removed many of the long-standing constraints upon the judicial role within the UK Constitution. Almost two decades since the Act entered force, the courts and constitutional commentators are still trying to assess where the new boundaries lie. At the

---

[1] *R v Director of Public Prosecutions, ex parte Kebilene* [2000] 2 AC 326, 374 (Lord Hope).

heart of the above quote, taken from evidence given by Professor Kate Malleson to a parliamentary select committee in 2007, is the recognition that the 'new judicial role is still developing'. The Act shook the constitutional kaleidoscope and we are still waiting for the image of this new judicial role to come clearly into focus.

The implementation of the HRA should be seen as a significant point in the ongoing evolution of the judicial function within the UK Constitution. Even before the HRA 1998 came into force, many judges sensed that a constitutional turning point had been reached, recognising 'common law fundamental rights' and novel constitutional concepts like the principle of legality (on which, see Chapter 5[2]). The HRA 1998, however, held the promise of a clearly enumerated set of rights with both remedial backbone and the jurisprudential underpinnings of decades of case law from the European Court of Human Rights. As Lord Bingham recognised on the eve of the Act's entry into force, it 'has assumed something of the character of a religious event: an event eagerly sought and long-awaited but arousing feelings of apprehension as well as expectation, the uncertainty that accompanies any new and testing experience'.[3] Even after the Act entered into force, other judges were decidedly reluctant to enter what has been called the 'age of human rights'.[4] Throughout this chapter it is important to remember that the judiciary is not a monolith, with a uniform attitude towards human rights. Indeed, there is not one judiciary, but many judges, and after an enactment like the HRA 1998, it can take a considerable amount of time for the work of these judges to be distilled into a coherent body of legal authority.[5] This chapter will consider how the HRA 1998 came into being, its major provisions and the direction of the UK's burgeoning human rights jurisprudence, before considering the potential for its repeal and replacement with a UK Bill of Rights.

From civil liberties to human rights

Key issues

- Prior to the enactment of the Human Rights Act 1998, civil liberties were regarded as being residual; individuals were free to act as they wished, so long as their conduct was not prohibited by law. Rights and freedoms were indirectly supported by decisions of the courts at common law, but these liberties were susceptible to encroachment by primary legislation.

- Though the UK was, for the latter part of the twentieth century, a signatory to the European Convention on Human Rights, the influence of the Convention on domestic legal proceedings was slight at best, and individuals were forced to pursue litigation to the European Court of Human Rights at Strasbourg in order to vindicate the positive rights contained in the Convention.

---

[2] See pp. 154–7.
[3] T. Bingham 'Foreword' in R. Clayton and H. Tomlinson, *The Law of Human Rights* (1st edn, OUP, 2000) v.
[4] C. Warbrick, 'The European Response to Terrorism in an Age of Human Rights' (2004) 15 EJIL 989, 989.
[5] Nonetheless, the HRA – and the attendant ability of courts to contribute to the enforcement of human rights standards – remains a focal-point for those concerned by the expansion of judicial power at the expense of the powers of the elected branches of government. The work of the 'Judicial Power Project' – administered by the (right-leaning) think tank Policy Exchange – seeks to critically explore these concerns (see: https://judicialpowerproject.org.uk/).

The historic conception of 'negative' civil liberties

Prior to the enactment and implementation of the HRA, civil liberties were conceived of negatively; as the former Law Lord, Lord Brown-Wilkinson, noted in *Wheeler* v *Leicester City Council*:

> Basic constitutional rights in this country such as freedom of the person and freedom of speech are based not upon any express provision conferring such a right but on freedom of an individual to do what he will save to the extent that he is prevented from so doing by the law . . . These fundamental freedoms therefore are not positive rights but an immunity from interference by others.[6]

In short, so long as activity was not prohibited by legislation or at common law, an individual was free to engage in it. Individual liberty was not, as Dicey noted, 'a special privilege but the outcome of the ordinary law of the land enforced by the Courts'[7] and many felt able to dismiss the case for enforceable, positive rights, on the basis of this *laissez-faire* approach; as John Major, the Conservative Prime Minister between 1990 and 1997, is reported to have said, 'we have no need of a Bill of Rights because we have freedom'.[8]

Enforceable, positive, human rights were therefore slightly alien to the UK Constitution, and – in the absence of incorporation of the European Convention on Human Rights into domestic law – attempts to assert such 'rights' in litigation before the courts had met with failure.[9] While Parliament had indeed passed legislation supporting what we would now recognise as human rights,[10] and while the rights of individuals received, at common law, indirect support from court decisions,[11] the UK Constitution lacked a systematic internal system of protection for individual freedoms. As a result, Doyle and Wells highlighted two specific limitations of the pre-HRA state of affairs:

> The first is a matter of law – the principle of parliamentary sovereignty. Any legislation can override rights recognised and protected by the common law. The second is a matter of technique and attitude. By and large the common law courts have not reasoned from the premise of specific rights. Our boast, that we are free to do anything not prohibited by law, and that official action against our will must have the support of law, reflects the fact that our rights are residual – what is left after the law (and in particular legislation) is exhausted. Our thinking does not proceed from rights to results – rather, our rights are the result.[12]

The 'residue' of freedom was, in the eyes of many, being slowly eroded by the steady expansion of legislative regulation; by 1990, additionally faced with mounting evidence of the UK's poor record before the European Court of Human Rights,[13] the legal philosopher Ronald Dworkin was able to make the claim that 'liberty is ill in Britain'.[14] In the absence of statutory recognition of human rights, the common law was virtually powerless to fight back.

---

[6] *Wheeler* v *Leicester City Council* [1985] AC 1054, 1065.

[7] A. Dicey, *An Introduction to the Study of the Constitution* (8th edn, first published 1915, Liberty Fund, 1982) p. 124.

[8] Lord Irvine, HL Debs, vol. 582, col. 1228 (3 November 1997).

[9] For example, *Malone* v *Metropolitan Police Commissioner (No. 2)* [1979] Ch 344; *Kaye* v *Robertson* [1991] FSR 62.

[10] For example, the Habeas Corpus Act 1679.

[11] For example, *Entick* v *Carrington* (1765) 19 St Tr 1030; *Beatty* v *Gillbanks* (1882) 9 QBD 308.

[12] J. Doyle and B. Wells, 'How Far Can the Common Law Go towards Protecting Human Rights?' in P. Alston (ed.), *Promoting Human Rights through Bills of Rights* (OUP, 1999) p. 17.

[13] See: P. Boateng and J. Straw, 'Bringing Rights Home: Labour's plans to incorporate the European Convention on Human Rights into UK law' [1997] EHRLR 71, 73–75.

[14] See: R. Dworkin, *A Bill of Rights for Britain* (Chatto and Windus, 1990). See also K. Ewing and C. Gearty, *Freedom under Thatcher* (OUP, 1990).

The domestic effect of the Convention pre-HRA

(i) The impact of the Convention upon domestic law

The UK had, of course, been a signatory to the European Convention on Human Rights since 1951, and had permitted the right of individual petition to the European Court of Human Rights – following the exhaustion of domestic remedies – since 1966. A number of significant legal changes had been implemented after claimants had taken their case through the domestic judicial hierarchy and up to the European Court of Human Rights in Strasbourg.[15] The cost and time implications of this method of realising individual rights were, however, significant (and would eventually underpin the Labour case for enactment of the HRA[16]). Judicial remedies at the *domestic* level were hard to come by. As a result of the UK's dualist system[17] reliance in domestic courts on the unincorporated provisions of the European Convention was permitted in only very limited circumstances; as Starmer and Klug observed in research published in 1997, despite being raised in argument in some 316 cases in domestic courts between 1973 and 1996 the rights contained in the Convention could only be said to have influenced the outcome of the case in a mere 16 of those decisions.[18]

(ii) The limits of the Convention's role

Direct reliance on the Convention rights in legal proceedings prior to the implementation of the HRA was not possible.[19] This is not, however, to say that the Convention rights did not have a – strictly limited – influence in domestic litigation. Prior to the enactment of the HRA, the courts had articulated a number of ways in which the Convention might be relied upon as an interpretative aid. In the event of an ambiguity in a statute, the courts would presume Parliament to have legislated in a way which would be compatible with the UK's treaty obligations under the European Convention (this presumption would have clear additional force in those instances where the UK Parliament had legislated in response to a specific decision of the European Court of Human Rights against the UK).[20] The Convention might also be used as an aid to the interpretation and clarification of the requirements of the common law.[21] However, as the House of Lords made clear in the then leading decision of *R v Secretary of State for the Home Department, ex parte Brind*, for the courts to give *direct* effect to the Convention rights in domestic law – where Parliament had failed to do so – would be to cross the constitutional Rubicon and to engineer the incorporation of the European Convention via the back door.[22]

---

[15] See, for example, the Contempt of Court Act 1981, enacted following the European Court of Human Rights decision in *Sunday Times* v *United Kingdom* (1979–80) 2 EHRR 245.

[16] See P. Boateng and J. Straw, *Bringing Rights Home: Labour's Plans to Incorporate the European Convention on Human Rights into United Kingdom Law* (Labour Party, 1996) and HM Government, *Rights Brought Home: the Human Rights Bill* (Stationery Office, 1997), Cm. 3782.

[17] See Ch. 3.

[18] K. Starmer and F. Klug, 'Incorporation through the Back Door' [1997] PL 223, 225.

[19] See for instance, *Malone* v *Metropolitan Police Commissioner (No. 2)* [1979] Ch 344; *Kaye* v *Robertson* [1991] FSR 62.

[20] *R v Secretary of State for the Home Department, ex parte Brind* [1991] 1 AC 696, 760 (Lord Ackner).

[21] For instance, *Derbyshire County Council* v *Times Newspapers* [1992] QB 770.

[22] *R v Secretary of State for the Home Department, ex parte Brind* [1991] 1 AC 696, 718 (Lord Donaldson of Lymington), 762–3 (Lord Ackner).

(iii) Fundamental human rights at common law

Prior to the implementation of the HRA, the interpretative influence of the ECHR was complemented by the development of an embryonic jurisprudence of fundamental rights recognised by the common law.[23] This judicially-developed body of rights included the right of access to a court, to legal advice, to confidential communications with a legal adviser and to freedom of expression.[24] As we have already seen, however, the emergence of this common law jurisprudence of rights amounted only to a presumption that Parliament could not be taken to inadvertently legislate to constrain the exercise of certain fundamental rights; this presumption is most famously articulated by Lord Hoffmann in the House of Lords decision in *ex parte Simms* as the 'principle of legality':

> Parliamentary sovereignty means that Parliament can, if it chooses, legislate contrary to fundamental principles of human rights . . . But the principle of legality means that Parliament must squarely confront what it is doing and accept the political cost. Fundamental rights cannot be overridden by general or ambiguous words. This is because there is too great a risk that the full implications of their unqualified meaning may have passed unnoticed in the democratic process. In the absence of express language or necessary implication to the contrary, the courts will therefore presume that even the most general words were intended to be subject to the basic rights of the individual.[25]

In spite of this bold rhetorical defence of the importance of individual freedoms, so-called fundamental common law rights could be trumped by evidence of clear parliamentary intent. Parliamentary sovereignty therefore remained the most significant obstacle to placing human rights beyond the reach of temporary majorities in the UK's Constitution.

Thinking point . . .

The UK Supreme Court has confirmed that fundamental rights recognised by the common law retain credence in the HRA era. Despite the – perhaps unavoidable – tendency towards human rights disputes being framed in the context of the extensive Strasbourg jurisprudence which attaches to the Convention rights, the Supreme Court has reiterated – in *R (Osborn) v Parole Board* [2013] UKSC 61; [2014] AC 1115 – that while '[t]he importance of the Act is unquestionable', '[i]t does not however supersede the protection of human rights under the common law or statute, or create a discrete body of law based on the judgments of the European court. Human rights continue to be protected by our domestic law, interpreted and developed in accordance with the Act when appropriate.'

Incorporating the Convention

Key issues

- The UK found it very difficult to incorporate the ECHR rights into its domestic law because of the effect of the foundational principle of parliamentary sovereignty. If the Convention

→

---

[23] See pp. 154–7.

[24] See *R v Secretary of State for the Home Department, ex parte Leech (No. 2)* [1994] QB 198; *R v Lord Chancellor, ex parte Witham* [1998] QB 575; *R v Secretary of State for the Home Department, ex parte Simms* [2000] 2 AC 115; R. Cooke, 'The Road Ahead for the Common Law' (2004) 53 ICLQ 273, 276–7.

[25] *R v Secretary of State for the Home Department, ex parte Simms* [2000] 2 AC 115, 131.

→

> was supposed to set out fundamental rights that should not be violated, how can such rights be built into a system which permits Parliament to enact any law it chooses?
>
> - The HRA does not incorporate the whole of the ECHR, but a selection of the rights contained therein (HRA 1998, s. 1). The Act also requires the UK courts to consider Strasbourg jurisprudence when interpreting these rights (HRA 1998, s. 2).
>
> - The HRA attempted to set out that certain interests, such as freedom of expression (HRA 1998, s. 12) and freedom of religion (HRA 1998, s. 13), are of particular importance when the courts consider competing rights claims. The courts have regarded this provision as simply declaratory, and have not used it to, for example, depart from interpretations of rights set by Strasbourg.

Reconciling parliamentary sovereignty with human rights

(i) Comparative rights protection regimes

For decades, successive UK governments faced down calls for them to institute a UK Bill of Rights, responding that it would be impossible to place human rights on a pedestal, beyond the reach of parliamentary control, in a constitution that values the political system as a mechanism for addressing society's concerns above all others. Others, like Lord Scarman, saw the UK's fixation with parliamentary sovereignty and the 'political constitution' as an obstacle standing in the path of meaningful rights protection in the UK:

> It is the helplessness of the law in face of the legislative sovereignty of Parliament which makes it difficult for the legal system to accommodate the concept of fundamental and inviolable human rights.[26]

Throughout the 1980s, Lord Scarman argued that the 'helpless' state of rights and liberties in the face of parliamentary sovereignty necessitated not simply a codification of these rights but their protection against even the encroachments of parliamentary sovereignty. In effect, he was advocating 'entrenched' human rights protections, equivalent to the US Constitution's Bill of Rights. The rights included within the US Constitution have superior status to ordinary legislation, and therefore incompatible legislation enacted by the legislature can be struck down by the US courts (as considered in Chapter 1).[27] This power to invalidate unconstitutional legislation did not develop in a vacuum, but can be attributed to the particular historical context in which the US gained its independence from the UK in the late eighteenth century. As Sir Igor Judge has noted, one of the factors which caused the War of Independence was the UK Parliament's attempt, in the Duties in American Colonies Act 1765, to tax the American colonies. A sovereign Parliament 'was the problem',[28] or at least one of the problems, which the fledgling country had sought to address in creating its new system of government.

---

[26] L. Scarman, *English Law – the New Dimension* (Steven & Sons, 1974) p. 15.

[27] See p. 11.

[28] I. Judge, "'No Taxation without Representation": A British Perspective upon Constitutional Arrangements' (28 August 2010) 9–10, available at: www.judiciary.gov.uk/media/speeches/2010/lcj-speech-no-representation-without-taxation.

Other countries with deep historical ties to the UK and the Westminster model of government did not abandon political constitutionalism so completely when human rights are at issue. The Canadian Charter of Rights and Freedoms, enacted in 1982, acts as a constitutional safeguard on human rights, which, like its US equivalent, allows the judiciary to invalidate contrary legislation. Built into the Charter, however, was a mechanism designed to allow for 'democratic override' of the judicial role, the 'notwithstanding' clause.[29] Invoking one of these clauses when an enactment of either Canada's Federal or a Provincial Legislature is passed renders that legislation immune from judicial invalidation on the basis of the Charter's rights. This provision was useful in the context in which the Charter was passed, in the face of opposition from the Quebec legislature, which between 1982 and 1987 protected *all* of its legislation by invoking the notwithstanding clause. Although some commentators now claim that the clause is falling into disuse, as Stephen Gardbaum points out, if the Canadian courts were to adopt an expansive interpretation of rights in a controversial case, they are aware that 'the relevant legislature would seriously consider and, perhaps, use the override'.[30]

The New Zealand Bill of Rights Act 1990 established an alternative approach to incorporating fundamental rights into a system of government under the Westminster model. The Bill of Rights Act enumerated a list of rights and imposed a duty on the courts to interpret the provisions of legislation so that, where possible, it would not conflict with these rights. Beyond this power to reinterpret legislation, however, the courts could not invalidate legislation which clearly conflicted with human rights. New Zealand and Canada had taken the first steps towards what Gardbaum has labelled 'the new Commonwealth model of constitutionalism':

> This model is new in that it attempts to straddle the previous dichotomous choice between parliamentary sovereignty as traditionally conceived in these countries and constitutional or judicial supremacy as in jurisdictions such as . . . the United States.[31]

These approaches indicated that human rights and parliamentary democracy are not mutually exclusive and, indeed, affirmed that the protection of minority rights from abuse by the majority is a recognised facet of liberal democracies' constitutions, even those based upon the Westminster model (see Figure 21.1). New Zealand's approach, in particular, would exert considerable influence over the UK's HRA 1998.

Thinking point . . .

Lord Woolf provides a good indication of the influence of the so-called 'commonwealth' approach to rights protection – that is, a model of rights protection which seeks to track a mid-way between parliamentary and judiciary supremacy – in UK constitutional thinking during the mid-1990s in Lord Woolf 'Droit Public – English Style' [1995] PL 57.

---

[29] Canadian Charter of Rights and Freedoms 1982, s. 33.
[30] S. Gardbaum, 'Reassessing the New Commonwealth Model of Constitutionalism' [2010] IJCL 167, 180.
[31] S. Gardbaum, 'How Successful and Distinctive Is the Human Rights Act? An Expatriate Comparatist's Assessment' (2011) 74 MLR 195, 195.

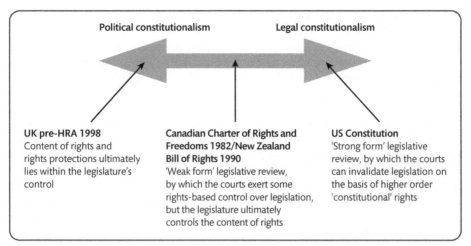

Figure 21.1 Political and legal protections for individual rights

(ii) The UK model of incorporation

Prior to the 1997 general election, the Tony Blair-led Labour Party made a firm pledge to incorporate the ECHR into domestic law. Canada and New Zealand had already pointed the way to reconciling human rights with parliamentary sovereignty and in a White Paper released just a few months after it entered office, the Labour Government recognised that rights protection in the UK was inadequate, and proposed to incorporate the ECHR into the UK's legal systems:

> The effect of non-incorporation on the British people is a very practical one. The rights, originally developed with major help from the United Kingdom Government, are no longer actually seen as British rights. And enforcing them takes too long and costs too much . . . Bringing these rights home will mean that the British people will be able to argue for their rights in the British courts – without this inordinate delay and cost.[32]

Nonetheless, the White Paper made it clear that the government did *not* intend to give domestic judges a power of legislative review comparable with that exercised by the United States Supreme Court:

> The Government has reached the conclusion that courts should not have the power to set aside primary legislation, past or future, on the ground of incompatibility with the Convention. This conclusion arises from the importance which the Government attaches to Parliamentary sovereignty . . . In enacting legislation, Parliament is making decisions about important matters of public policy. The authority to make those decisions derives from a democratic mandate.[33]

Instead of being able to strike down legislation, the HRA gave the courts an interpretive power modeled upon the system in place in New Zealand, and the ability to declare that legislation was incompatible with human rights.[34] In constitutional matters the UK often

---

[32] HM Government, *Rights Brought Home: The Human Rights Bill* (Stationary Office, 1997), [1.14].
[33] Ibid., [2.13].
[34] See below, pp. 668–72.

adopts compromise positions, and the HRA is no exception. As with all half-way houses, the HRA 1998 has provoked controversy amongst constitutional commentators. Keith Ewing, for example, has lambasted the 'futility' of the Act, for even when the courts identify failings with legislation in light of the ECHR rights, they are powerless to invalidate such measures.[35] Others, like Adam Tomkins, consider that the judiciary has gained too much power under the HRA, placing the UK 'on the high road to juristocracy'.[36]

This controversy does not, however, diminish the international influence of the Act. Ireland's European Convention on Human Rights Act 2003 owes much to the HRA,[37] as does legislation passed by two Australian territories (the Australian Capital Territory's Human Rights Act 2004 and the Victorian Charter of Human Rights and Responsibilities 2006[38]). Moreover, returning the complement that the HRA 1998 paid to the Bill of Rights 1990, the New Zealand Court of Appeal has subsequently asserted that it can indicate that legislation was inconsistent with the Bill of Rights, mirroring the HRA's declarations of incompatibility.[39]

What elements of the ECHR were incorporated into UK law?

(i) The incorporated rights

The HRA's first provision sets out which ECHR rights are incorporated into the UK's legal systems, listing Articles 2 to 12 and 14 of the Convention, Articles 1 to 3 of the First Protocol, and Art. 1 of the Thirteenth Protocol.[40] Dicey had lauded the UK's model of civil liberties protection in the nineteenth century by comparison to statements regarding rights protection issued by other European countries, because civil liberties were backed up by judicial remedies, but the statements of rights were often little more than unenforceable rhetoric.[41] The irony of this list, therefore, is that it omits Art. 13 ECHR, which provides the right to an effective remedy.

The omission, however, was required because of the UK Government's desire to protect parliamentary sovereignty.[42] As the HRA did not give the courts the ability to strike down legislation incompatible with the ECHR, in some cases – should government and Parliament choose not to address a declaration of incompatibility[43] – a rights abuse would be

---

[35] K. Ewing, 'The Futility of the Human Rights Act' [2004] PL 829; K. Ewing and J.-C. Tham, 'The Continuing Futility of the Human Rights Act' [2008] PL 668.

[36] A. Tomkins, 'The Role of the Courts in the Political Constitution' (2010) 60 UTLJ 1, 2.

[37] On which see: F. de Londras and C. Kelly, *The European Convention on Human Rights Act: Operation, Impact and Analysis* (Round Hall/Thomson Reuters, 2010).

[38] On which see: C. Evans and S. Evans, *Australian Bills of Rights: The law of the Victorian Charter and ACT Human Rights Act* (LexisNexis Butterworths, 2008). And for a comparison between the HRA and Victorian Charter of Rights and Responsibilities see: R. Masterman, 'Interpretations, Declarations and Dialogue: Rights Protections under the Human Rights Act and Victorian Charter of Rights and Responsibilities' [2009] PL 112.

[39] See: *Moonen v Board of Film and Literature Board* [2000] 2 NZLR 9; *R v Hansen* [2007] NZSC 7; *Attorney-General v Taylor* [2017] NZCA 215; A. Geddis, '"Declarations of Inconsistency" under the New Zealand Bill of Rights Act 1990', UK Const. L. Blog, 19 June 2017.

[40] HRA 1998, s. 1.

[41] See A. Dicey, *An Introduction to the Study of the Constitution* (8th edn, first published 1915, Liberty Fund, 1982) pp. 123–5.

[42] See K. Ewing, 'The Human Rights Act and Parliamentary Democracy' (1999) 62 MLR 79, 84–5.

[43] As has – to date – been the case in relation to the declaration of incompatibility issued in relation to the statutory ban on prisoner voting (see *Smith v Scott* [2007] CSIH 9; 2007 SC 345).

perpetuated in spite of being identified by the courts. In these circumstances, it is hardly surprising that the European Court has refused to recognise that the system of remedies in place under the HRA is not sufficient to satisfy Art. 13 in all cases.[44]

(ii) The status of Strasbourg jurisprudence

By incorporating the ECHR, the HRA 1998 does not provide the UK with a 'fresh-out-of-the-box' Bill of Rights that the domestic courts are free to develop for themselves. Decades of Strasbourg jurisprudence has developed around the ECHR rights, providing for 'what is widely considered the strongest and most powerful international human rights regime in the world'.[45] If the UK courts were free to develop the ECHR rights as they chose, without reference to the European Court's jurisprudence, domestic decisions would be subject to a high proportion of appeals to Strasbourg, negating the reasoning behind the legislation. Therefore, the HRA incorporates not only the main body of ECHR rights, but also requires that the courts 'must take into account' the European Court's decisions 'so far as, in the opinion of the court or tribunal, it is relevant to the proceedings in which that question has arisen'.[46]

Under s. 2, all courts, from lowly Magistrates' Courts to the UK Supreme Court, are obliged to consider relevant Strasbourg case law in reaching their decisions on the application of law. The obligation to 'take into account' such case law, however, does not on its face amount to a binding obligation to follow Strasbourg's approach. Indeed, as the White Paper which provided the basis for the HRA explained, 'British judges will be enabled to make a distinctively British contribution to the development of the jurisprudence of human rights in Europe'.[47] The HRA therefore seemed to invite the UK courts to embark upon their own jurisprudential journey, guided by Strasbourg's interpretation of the ECHR, but not bound by it. If this was the intention behind the HRA, however, the courts would prove slow to accept the invitation.

Thinking point . . .

Compare s. 2 HRA 1998 to s. 3 ECA 1972 (Chapter 3). The obligation with regard to Strasbourg case law seems, on its face, to be less strict than the obligation towards ECJ case law.

The case of *Ullah* exemplifies the early jurisprudence of the UK courts under section 2(1) HRA.[48] The claimant attempted to prevent his deportation to his home country, Pakistan, claiming that if he were returned he would face religious discrimination (contrary to Art. 9 ECHR). The Court of Appeal rejected his appeal on the basis that Strasbourg had, to date, only restricted the ability of states to deport individuals when deportation exposed them to a real risk of a violation of the absolute prohibition of torture (under Art.

---

[44] *Burden* v *United Kingdom* (2008) 47 EHRR 38, [41].

[45] S. Gardbaum, 'How Successful and Distinctive is the Human Rights Act? An Expatriate Comparatist's Assessment' (2011) 74 MLR 195, 200.

[46] HRA 1998. s. 2(1).

[47] HM Government, *Rights Brought Home: the Human Rights Bill* (Stationery Office, 1997) Cm. 3782, [1.14].

[48] *R (Ullah)* v *Special Adjudicator* [2004] UKHL 26; [2004] 2 AC 323.

3 ECHR). Ullah appealed this decision to the House of Lords, asking the court to develop new grounds for preventing deportation on the basis of the qualified rights. The Law Lords refused to do so, with Lord Bingham explaining that, in his view, the HRA 1998 required the courts to apply the ECHR rights within the domestic legal systems, but not to develop them:

> It is of course open to member states to provide for rights more generous than those guaranteed by the Convention, but such provision should not be the product of interpretation of the Convention by national courts, since the meaning of the Convention should be uniform throughout the states party to it. The duty of national courts is to keep pace with the Strasbourg jurisprudence as it evolves over time: no more, but certainly no less.[49]

Lord Bingham considered that the HRA incorporated the ECHR into domestic law, but that it did not require the courts to give a national flavour to these rights. The following year, Lord Hope echoed this sentiment in deciding that deporting an AIDs sufferer to her home country of Uganda, and thereby denying her access to treatment under the NHS, would not constitute inhuman and degrading treatment (contrary to Art. 3 ECHR) on the basis of Strasbourg jurisprudence:

> Our task, then, is to analyse the jurisprudence of the Strasbourg court and, having done so and identified its limits, to apply it to the facts of this case. We must not allow sympathy for the appellant to divert us from this task. It is not for us to search for a solution to her problem which is not to be found in the Strasbourg case law.[50]

This approach, by which the UK courts 'mirror'[51] Strasbourg interpretations, had advantages for the UK judiciary. In making controversial decisions in the early years of the HRA's operation, the judges hoped that by pointing to an obligation to follow Strasbourg's interpretations of ECHR rights they might be able to deflect political criticism of their decisions.[52] Strasbourg, however, is an international court deciding cases from 47 countries. Its judgments are interpretations of how a treaty, the ECHR, applies in particular cases, not generalised rulings which necessarily apply in the same way in the legal systems of every member state.[53]

Eventually, conflicts developed between the UK courts and Strasbourg in cases where the latter's decisions did not seem to apply adequately within the UK context. The *Horncastle* case,[54] one of the first decisions by the UK's Supreme Court, exemplifies just such a divergence. The appellants had been convicted of serious criminal offences, and appealed against their convictions on the basis that in each case a key witness against them had provided their evidence to the court by witness statements, and had therefore not been subject to cross examination. The appellants claimed that this breached their right to a fair trial (Art. 6 ECHR), and pointed to the Strasbourg ruling in *Al-Khawaja* that such

---

[49] Ibid., [20].
[50] *N v Secretary of State for the Home Department* [2005] UKHL 31; [2005] 2 AC 296, [25].
[51] See: J. Lewis, 'The European Ceiling on Human Rights' [1997] PL 720; R. Masterman, 'Section 2(1) of the Human Rights Act: Binding Domestic Courts to Strasbourg?' [2004] PL 725.
[52] See N. Krisch, 'The Open Architecture of European Human Rights Law' (2008) 71 MLR 183, 205–6.
[53] On which see: R. Masterman, 'Taking the Strasbourg Jurisprudence into Account: Developing a "Municipal Law of Human Rights" under the Human Rights Act' (2005) 54 ICLQ 907, 915–921.
[54] *R v Horncastle* [2009] UKSC 14; [2010] 2 AC 373.

'hearsay' evidence should not form the basis of a prosecution.[55] The Supreme Court in *Horncastle* declined to follow the decision in *Al-Khawaja*. Lord Phillips said that although the requirement to 'take into account' the Strasbourg jurisprudence would 'normally result' in the domestic court applying principles that are clearly established by the Strasbourg Court:

> There will, however, be rare occasions where the domestic court has concerns as to whether a decision of the Strasbourg court sufficiently appreciates or accommodates particular aspects of our domestic process. In such circumstances, it is open to the domestic court to decline to follow the Strasbourg decision, giving reasons for adopting this course.[56]

Lord Phillips explained that this was just such a case, asserting that if Art. 6 always precluded such witness statements, then it would prove impossible to prosecute some individuals, particularly in instances where a witness has died between making their statement and the trial.[57]

While the *Ullah* approach remains influential in judicial reasoning under the HRA, judicial interpretation of s. 2(1) can increasingly be seen to permit a degree of flexibility in the translation of Strasbourg case law into the national context. As such, the courts have found that Strasbourg jurisprudence should not necessarily be followed, *inter alia*, if:

- It is 'reasonably foreseeable' that the European Court of Human Rights would now come to a different conclusion than in the available authorities;[58]
- A margin of appreciation would be likely to be afforded, rendering the question to be resolved as one for domestic authorities to 'decide for themselves';[59]
- The area is governed by common law and the court is minded to exercise its discretion to depart from the Strasbourg line;[60]
- The court attaches 'great weight' to a parliamentary (legislative) decision which determines the balance to be struck between rights and interests in a way which might be interpreted as being inconsistent with Strasbourg authority;[61]
- The Strasbourg case law is outdated;[62]
- The Strasbourg authority is 'inconsistent with some fundamental substantive or procedural aspect of our law';[63]
- The Convention case law 'appear[s] to overlook or misunderstand some argument or point of principle';[64]
- The Strasbourg case law discloses no 'clear and constant' line of jurisprudence.[65]

---

[55] *Al-Khawaja and Tahery* v *United Kingdom* (2009) 49 EHRR 1.
[56] *R* v *Horncastle* [2009] UKSC 14; [2010] 2 AC 373, [11].
[57] Ibid., [91].
[58] *R (Gentle)* v *Prime Minister* [2008] UKHL 20; [2008] 1 AC 1356, [53].
[59] *Re P* [2008] UKHL 38; [2009] 1 AC 173, [31].
[60] *Rabone* v *Pennine Care Foundation NHS Trust* [2012] UKSC 2; [2012] 2 AC 72, [113].
[61] *R (Animal Defenders International)* v *Secretary of State for Culture, Media and Sport* [2008] UKHL 15; [2008] 1 AC 1312, [33].
[62] *R (Quila)* v *Secretary of State for the Home Department* [2011] UKSC 48; [2012] 1 AC 621, [43].
[63] *Manchester City Council* v *Pinnock* [2010] UKSC 45; [2011] 2 AC 104, [48].
[64] *Manchester City Council* v *Pinnock* [2010] UKSC 45; [2011] 2 AC 104, [48].
[65] *R (Keyu)* v *Secretary of State for Foreign and Commonwealth Affairs* [2015] UKSC 69; [2016] AC 1355, [291].

The Supreme Court decision in **Pinnock** provides, in summary, clear evidence of this more nuanced approach. In that decision, Lord Neuberger, with whom the eight other Justices agreed, said:

> This court is not bound to follow every decision of the European Court. Not only would it be impractical to do so: it would sometimes be inappropriate, as it would destroy the ability of the court to engage in the constructive dialogue with the European court which is of value to the development of Convention law . . . Of course, we should usually follow a clear and constant line of decisions by the European court . . . but we are not actually bound to do so or (in theory, at least) to follow a decision of the Grand Chamber . . . section 2 of the HRA requires our courts to 'take into account' European court decisions, not necessarily to follow them. Where, however, there is a clear and constant line of decisions whose effect is not inconsistent with some fundamental substantive or procedural aspect of our law, and whose reasoning does not appear to overlook or misunderstand some argument or point of principle, we consider that it would be wrong for this Court not to follow that line.[66]

Recent experience suggests that it is not simply the role of the courts under s. 2(1) to 'mirror' the requirements of the Strasbourg jurisprudence in the domestic context, but rather it is beholden on the domestic judges to 'work out for themselves where the answer lies, taking into account not only the principles developed in Strasbourg, but also the legal, social and cultural traditions of the United Kingdom'.[67]

Section 2 also creates potential issues for the hierarchy of domestic courts. The requirement that the UK courts must consider a Strasbourg 'judgment . . . whenever made or given' gives rise to the possibility that later Convention jurisprudence may render earlier domestic precedents outdated. If s. 2 were applied rigidly, to mean that domestic law was always developed in light of Strasbourg authorities, the county court would seemingly have to disregard a relevant Supreme Court authority if an intervening Strasbourg judgment had developed the rights in question. Perhaps recognising that cases like **Horncastle** would likely arise in which 'mirroring' Strasbourg would produce an inadequate result, in **Kay**[68] the House of Lords affirmed that s. 2 could not serve as a basis for ignoring the common law rules of precedent. Lord Bingham concluded that when a binding precedent conflicted with a Strasbourg authority, the first-instance court should apply the domestic precedent, giving leave to appeal as necessary to pass the matter to a court with sufficient authority to address the conflict.[69]

(iii) Human rights and special interests

The passage of the HRA caused concern in a number of quarters, notably from the media and the Church of England. Ironically, both groups felt that there was a possibility that the Act would actually threaten their respective rights to freedom of expression and freedom of religion, even though these interests are protected by Arts 9 and 10 ECHR. In essence, they believed that the courts might develop other rights, such as freedom from discrimination (under Art. 14 ECHR) and the right to privacy (under Art. 10 ECHR) in

---

[66] *Manchester City Council* v *Pinnock* [2010] UKSC 45; [2011] 2 AC 104, [48].
[67] *R (Keyu)* v *Secretary of State for Foreign and Commonwealth Affairs* [2015] UKSC 69; [2016] AC 1355, [291]. For a helpful judicial summary of the developing approach to the interpretation and application of s. 2(1) see: *Moohan* v *Lord Advocate* [2014] UKSC 67; [2015] AC 901, [104] (Lord Wilson).
[68] *Kay* v *Lambeth LBC* [2006] UKHL 10; [2006] 2 AC 465.
[69] Ibid., [43].

a manner inimical to their interests. Their 'special pleading' seemed to pay off.[70] Two provisions were added to the HRA 1998 requiring that the courts, in applying the Act, must have 'particular regard' to freedom of religion[71] and to freedom of expression[72] when a public interest is at issue. With regard to the latter, Jack Straw informed Parliament that:

> [Section 12 should] send a powerful signal to the United Kingdom courts that they should be at least as circumspect as judgments of the European Court of Human Rights have been about any action that would give the article 8 rights any supremacy over the freedom of expression rights in Article 10. I hope and believe that an amendment along those lines will deal satisfactorily with the concerns of the press.[73]

Since the HRA came into effect, however, the impact of these provisions has been difficult to discern. Although the courts have accepted under s. 12(3) that no interim injunctions will be granted against a publication on the basis of human rights concerns unless the applicant establishes that they are likely to succeed in a full hearing,[74] this has actually proven to be a relatively low bar for applicants to cross. As we saw in the last chapter, for example, the courts have continued to develop individual privacy interests at the expense of (generally relatively low value) freedom of expression, and they have done so with little reference to the requirement to have particular regard to this interest under section 12, on the basis that this provision cannot, in the context of the ECHR system of rights protection, give Article 10 'presumptive priority' over other rights.[75] Similarly, section 13 is widely regarded as being purely symbolic in nature and no judgments have placed strong emphasis on its influence.[76]

Thinking point . . .

Adam Tomkins notes that political constitutionalists have particular difficulty with 'those qualified political claims that are elevated to the status of substantive rights' (A. Tomkins, 'The Role of the Courts in the Political Constitution' (2010) 60 UTLJ 1, 3). In ss. 12 and 13 HRA, Parliament was attempting to give guidance on how conflicts between human rights should be resolved. Political constitutionalists have the greatest concerns with the lack of adherence to these provisions.

The HRA and legislation

Key issues

- The HRA 1998 embeds the consideration of ECHR rights into the legislative process, requiring that Government certify to Parliament that all legislation conforms to the requirements of the ECHR before it is passed into law.

---

[70] K. Ewing, 'The Human Rights Act and Parliamentary Democracy' (1999) 62 MLR 79, 93–5.
[71] HRA 1998, s. 13.
[72] Ibid., s. 12.
[73] HC Debs, vol. 306, col. 775 (16 February 1998).
[74] *Cream Holdings* v *Bannerjee and Others* [2004] UKHL 44.
[75] *Douglas* v *Hello! Ltd* [2000] EWCA Civ 353; [2001] QB 967, [137] (Sedley LJ).
[76] See P. Cumper, 'The Protection of Religious Rights under Section 13 of the Human Rights Act 1998' [2000] PL 265.

- The HRA imposes a broad obligation on the courts, as public bodies, to respect human rights (HRA 1998, s. 6). This means that, in developing the common law or addressing measures not protected by parliamentary sovereignty, they have a duty to undertake such tasks in the light of human rights concerns.
- Where the courts are faced with a statute which raises human rights concerns the courts have two specific powers:

  1. The duty to reinterpret the statute (if it is possible to do so) to comply with the ECHR (HRA 1998, s. 3).

  2. The ability to issue a 'declaration of incompatibility' where it proves impossible to reinterpret a statute to comply with the ECHR (HRA 1998, s. 4).

- Declarations of incompatibility do not affect the validity of a statute, but they flag up serious inconsistencies between a statute and ECHR standards, allowing the government to fast-track amendments to rectify the inconsistency (HRA 1998, s. 10).

Developing the law in light of human rights

(i) Pre-legislative checks

The HRA does not operate with the sole purpose of rectifying breaches of ECHR rights in existing law, it was intended to influence the legislative process of all legislation passed after it entered into force. Since 1998, the HRA has required that each new enactment passed by Parliament be subjected to a process of pre-legislative review in order to assess whether it conforms to the requirements of the Convention rights. First, though the HRA preserves the ability of Parliament to legislate incompatibly with the Convention rights, s. 19 obliges the ministerial team piloting legislation through Parliament to issue a statement either confirming that they have considered the ECHR and have taken steps to ensure that the Bill is compatible (s. 19(1)(a)) or explaining why Parliament should, in the government's view, proceed with the Bill in spite of an identified incompatibility (s. 19(1)(b).

Thinking Point . . .

The ability of Parliament to legislate in apparent contravention of the Convention rights is illustrated by the passage of the Communications Bill 2005. In recognition of an anticipated inconsistency between the Bill – specifically the potential inconsistency with the right to freedom of expression arising out of its provisions relating to the prohibition of the broadcast of 'political advertisements' – the relevant minister was unable to provide a statement of compatibility under s. 19 of the HRA. The minister nonetheless indicated that the Bill should proceed, and it was duly enacted as the Communications Act 2005. (Fears as to the potential incompatibility of the relevant provisions were eventually allayed; the House of Lords – in its decision in *R (Animal Defenders International)* v *Secretary of State for Culture, Media and Sport* [2008] UKHL 15; [2008] 1 AC 1312 – declined to declare the contested provisions incompatible with Art. 10 of the Convention.)

Moreover, the Joint Committee of Human Rights (JCHR) will frequently issue detailed reports on whether legislative proposals conform to the requirements of the Convention rights, on governmental responses to human rights decisions in the courts and on a range of topical or thematic issues besides.[77] So important has the role of the Joint Committee on Human Rights become that it has been described as playing a 'quasi-judicial' role in the legislative process.[78] As Murray Hunt, former Legal Adviser to the JCHR has observed, 'reports of the JCHR are playing an increasingly important role in parliamentary debate about human rights, and . . . parliamentarians are becoming more literate in human rights as a result of the Committee's work.'[79] Moreover, the HRA obliges the ministerial team piloting legislation through Parliament to issue a statement confirming that they have considered the ECHR and have taken steps to ensure that the Bill is compatible or to explain why Parliament should, in the government's view, proceed with the Bill in spite of an identified incompatibility.[80]

These mechanisms seem to embed human rights within the political constitution, preventing the courts from becoming the sole branch of the state concerned with rights protection. Nonetheless, the work of the JCHR and the certification system has not always stopped breaches of human rights in legislation passed since the HRA became fully operational in October 2000. As Danny Nicol notes, all too often the government has 'sidelined' the JCHR's concerns, particularly when it is eager to pass legislation quickly in response to an emergency (as occurred with counter-terrorism legislation in the aftermath of the attack of 11 September 2001).[81] Furthermore, no minister who has certified the compliance of legislation subsequently found to be in breach of the ECHR has faced calls to resign from office on the basis of having misled Parliament. The certification requirement is sufficiently broad to permit ministers to state that an inaccurate certification was made in good faith, on the basis of advice from parliamentary counsel and departmental law officers. Indeed, sometimes a potential ECHR infringement will only come to light after legislation has been considered by the courts in light of the circumstances of a particular case. The political constitution does not, therefore, prevent the enactment of legislation detrimental to human rights, obliging us to consider the courts' role under the HRA 1998.

Thinking Point . . .

The JCHR exemplifies the role of select committees within the UK's system of government (Chapter 15). It draws on members from the Commons and Lords and therefore its membership includes prominent human rights specialists from the upper chamber, such as the former Master of the Rolls and Lord Chief Justice Lord Woolf. This expertise allows it to conduct very detailed analysis of legislative proposals and wider human rights issues.

---

[79] See for instance: Joint Committee on Human Rights, *The Human Rights Implications of Brexit* (5th Report of session 2016–2017), HL88/HC695, December 2016; Joint Committee on Human Rights, *Counter-Extremism* (2nd Report of session 2016–2017), HL39/HC105, July 2016.

[78] F. Klug and H. Wildbore, 'Breaking New Ground: the Joint Committee on Human Rights and the Role of Parliament in Human Rights Compliance' [2007] EHRLR 231, 243.

[79] M. Hunt, 'The Joint Committee on Human Rights' in A. Horne, G. Drewry and D. Oliver (eds), *Parliament and the Law* (Hart Publishing, 2013) p. 245.

[80] HRA 1998, s. 19(1).

[81] D. Nicol, 'The Human Rights Act and the Politicians' (2004) 24 LS 451, 464.

(ii) The Courts and the Human Rights Act 1998

Courts and tribunals are explicitly listed as public authorities under the HRA.[82] It is therefore 'unlawful' for the courts 'to act in a way which is incompatible with a Convention right'.[83] As Tom Campbell recognised following the HRA's enactment, this responsibility would likely 'encourage judicial creativity . . . in the development of the common law in line with European Human Rights jurisprudence'.[84] Indeed, soon after the HRA entered force, the courts came to consider whether the equitable remedy of breach of confidence adequately protected the right to privacy (Art. 8 ECHR). In *Campbell* v *MGN*,[85] Naomi Campbell claimed that stories published in *The Mirror* newspaper, concerning her attendance at Narcotics Anonymous meetings, breached her privacy, despite no right to privacy having to date been recognised in English law. The courts, following their responsibility under the HRA, adapted breach of confidence to apply to such unauthorised disclosures of personal information. As Lord Hope explains, the 'language' by which this new tort of 'misuse of private information' was defined had to change after the HRA's entry into force, with Art. 8 giving 'new breadth and strength . . . to the action for breach of confidence'.[86]

Beyond developments of the common law under the general duty on the courts to respect the ECHR, the HRA imposes two specific duties on the courts with regard to both primary and secondary legislation. Under s. 3 the courts are obliged to attempt to reinterpret legislation to exclude meanings which would undermine the incorporated ECHR rights. This duty interacts with a second power, imposed under s. 4, whereby the courts might formally notify Parliament of any primary legislation which cannot be reconciled with ECHR rights by process of reinterpretation. Before we look at these provisions in detail, their operation is summarised in Figure 21.2.

The interpretive duty

(i) The duty to interpret legislation compatibly with the Convention rights

Prior to the HRA, the Convention rights could only be employed to consider the interpretation of ambiguous legislation, particularly where it had been enacted in response to the UK's ECHR obligations (likely as a result of an adverse ruling by Strasbourg). Following the HRA's incorporation of the ECHR into the UK's domestic legal systems, all primary and subordinate legislation (whether enacted before or after the HRA entered force) must be 'read and given effect in a way which is compatible with the Convention rights'.[87] This duty is, however, subject to an important caveat. All courts may be under the obligation to attempt to reinterpret legislation when its plain meaning conflicts with incorporated rights, but this duty only extends '[s]o far as it is possible to do so'.[88] Much of the jurisprudence on s. 3 considers the issue of the boundary between 'interpreting' legislation and the judiciary so radically altering a provision's meaning that it is 'legislating' for itself.

---

[82] HRA 1998, s. 6(3)(a).

[83] Ibid., s. 6(1).

[84] T. Campbell, 'Human Rights: a Culture of Controversy' (1999) 26 JLS 6, 7.

[85] *Campbell* v *MGN Ltd* [2004] UKHL 22; [2004] 2 AC 457.

[86] Ibid., [86] (Lord Hope). For an exhaustive coverage of the field see: N. Moreham and M. Warby, *Tugend-hat and Christie: The Law of Privacy and the Media* (3rd edn) (OUP, 2016).

[87] HRA 1998, s. 3(1).

[88] Ibid., s. 3(1).

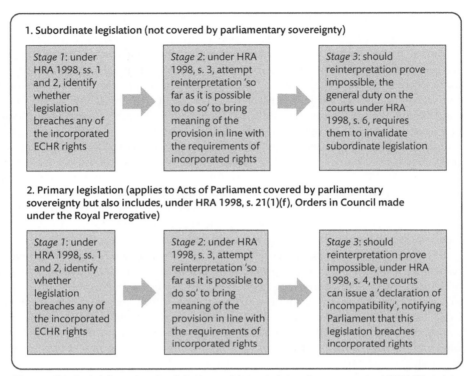

Figure 21.2 Addressing legislation which violates incorporated ECHR rights

One important factor to remember is that, in the words of Labour's manifesto for the 1997 general election, the HRA provides 'a floor, not a ceiling, for human rights'.[89] Legislation in the UK can provide for rights that are not covered by the ECHR (such as the right, albeit with exceptions, to trial by jury for indictable criminal offences), and the UK Parliament is free to set higher standards of rights protection than are contained within any of the ECHR rights. Therefore, where UK legislation *exceeds* ECHR requirements, the courts are not subject to a duty to read down its provisions to the level of protection contained in the ECHR.[90]

(ii) Case law on the interpretive duty

Section 3 changes the nature of judicial interpretation when a human rights concern is raised regarding legislation. No longer do the judges seek, as an overarching goal, to straightforwardly give effect to the intention of Parliament under the impugned statute. Instead, judges must consider such legislation in light of the incorporated rights. This duty does not reinvent the judicial function where individual rights are concerned – as we have seen when we considered parliamentary sovereignty in Chapter 5,[91] under the principle of legality the courts were willing, before the HRA entered force, to depart from literal

---

[89] Labour Party, *New Labour: Because Britain Deserves Better* (1997).
[90] HRA 1998, s. 11.
[91] See pp. 155–7.

interpretations of legislation which adversely affected individual rights. Nor does Parliament's legislative intention become unimportant following the HRA; as Aileen Kavanagh points out,[92] the purpose of legislation must be considered when the courts evaluate whether an infringement of a qualified right is 'necessary in a democratic society' (considered in Chapter 20[93]). Furthermore, in line with the other cautious elements of the HRA, the duty imposed upon the courts under s. 3 is limited by what it is possible to do within the concept of interpretation.

Despite all of these caveats, the impact of section 3 was felt almost immediately. In *Poplar Housing*,[94] decided only a few months after the HRA entered force, the claimant tenant challenged her eviction from social housing under the Housing Act 1988. This Act required that the tenant be removed from social housing as she became homeless by choice, which the claimant argued did not comply with the requirements of the right to private and family life (Art. 8 ECHR). The claimant argued in favour of a reinterpretation of the Housing Act which would have not detrimentally affected her Art. 8 rights. The Court of Appeal rejected this claim, with Lord Woolf concluding that this provision was necessary to protect the human rights of others seeking housing. In *obiter dicta,* however, he proceeded to consider how the interpretive duty should operate, warning the courts that:

> The most difficult task which courts face is distinguishing between legislation and interpretation . . . if it is necessary in order to obtain compliance [with an ECHR right] to *radically alter* the effect of the legislation this will be an indication that more than interpretation is involved.[95]

Even where a reinterpretation of a provision was possible under section 3, Lord Woolf considered that the courts must 'limit the extent of the modified meaning to what is necessary to achieve compliance'.[96] Notwithstanding these warnings, other judges seemed eager to test the limits of this duty. Less than a month after the *Poplar Housing* decision, Lord Steyn led the House of Lords in a major reworking of the 'rape shield' provisions of the Youth Justice and Criminal Evidence Act 1999, which prohibited defendants from cross examining complainants about their sexual history in rape cases.[97] Whilst complainant fears over such intrusive cross-examinations are often cited as a reason why comparatively few rape cases are brought to trial, Lord Steyn was concerned that this provision hampered a defendant's ability to conduct his defence, thereby prejudicing the right to a fair hearing (Art. 6 ECHR). He set out his opinion of s. 3:

> The interpretative principle under section three of the 1998 Act is a strong one. It applies even if there is no ambiguity in the language in the sense of the language being capable of two different meanings . . . Under ordinary methods of interpretation a court may depart from the language of the statute to avoid absurd consequences: section 3 goes much further . . . In accordance with the will of Parliament as reflected in section three it will sometimes be necessary to adopt an interpretation which linguistically may appear strained.[98]

---

[92] A. Kavanagh, 'The Role of Parliamentary Intention in Adjudication under the Human Rights Act 1998' (2006) 26 OJLS 179, 204.

[93] See pp. 626–8.

[94] *Poplar Housing and Regeneration Community Association Limited* v *Donoghue* [2001] EWCA Civ 595; [2001] 3 WLR 183.

[95] Ibid., [76] (emphasis added).

[96] Ibid., [75].

[97] Youth Justice and Criminal Evidence Act 1999, s. 41.

[98] *R* v *A* [2001] UKHL 25; [2002] 1 AC 45, [44].

Having emphasised the potential scope of s. 3, Lord Steyn created an exception to the rape shield law, permitting evidence and cross-examination when these would be 'so relevant to the issue of consent that to exclude it would endanger the fairness of the trial under Article 6'.[99] This reinterpretation was particularly controversial, essentially cutting out large sections of the shield Parliament had provided to rape complainants. Two months later, the same panel of Law Lords issued another bold reinterpretation under s. 3, recasting a reverse burden of proof contained in the Misuse of Drugs Act 1971 as being merely evidential in nature.[100]

These cases are often considered to be the high watermark in the courts' use of s. 3 with such 'activist' uses of the interpretative power less clearly seen in more recent decisions.[101] Division crept into decisions as to when 'interpreting' became 'legislating', forcing judges to carefully consider the limits of this provision as much as its creative potential.

Key case

Ghaidan v Godin-Mendoza [2004] UKHL 30; [2004] 2 AC 557 (House of Lords)

On the death of a protected tenant of a dwelling-house, his or her surviving spouse, if then living in the house, becomes a statutory tenant by succession. Under the Rent Act 1977 a person who was living with the original tenant 'as his or her wife or husband' is treated as the spouse of the original tenant. In *Fitzpatrick* v *Sterling Housing Association Ltd* [2001] 1 AC 27 the Law Lords decided this provision did not include persons in same-sex relationships. In **Fitzpatrick** the original tenant had died in 1994. In **Ghaidan,** however, the spouse's death came after the HRA 1998 entered force. The question raised in *Ghaidan* v *Godin-Mendoza* was therefore whether this interpretation of the Rent Act 1977 could be sustained in light of the entry into force of the HRA.

By a margin of 4:1, the House of Lords departed from its earlier judgment, ruling that a literal interpretation of the Rent Act violated the right not to be discriminated against in the exercise of private and family life (Art. 14 in conjunction with Art. 8). There was no justification for the difference in treatment of heterosexual and homosexual couples. Under s. 3 HRA 1998, the relevant provisions of the 1977 Act were re-interpreted to comply with the 1998 Act by eliminating the difference in treatment. For the majority, Lord Nicholls explained ([32]) that:

> Section 3 enables language to be interpreted restrictively or expansively. But section 3 goes further than this. It is also apt to require a court to read in words which change the meaning of the enacted legislation, so as to make it Convention-compliant. In other words, the intention of Parliament in enacting section 3 was that, to an extent bounded only by what is 'possible', a court can modify the meaning, and hence the effect, of primary and secondary legislation.

By contrast, Lord Millet (dissenting) asserted ([57]) that:

> Sections 3 and 4 of the Human Rights Act were carefully crafted to preserve the existing constitutional doctrine, and any application of the ambit of section 3 beyond its proper scope subverts it. This is not to say that the doctrine of Parliamentary supremacy is sacrosanct, but only that

---

[99] Ibid., [46].

[100] *R* v *Lambert* [2001] UKHL 37; [2002] 2 AC 545.

[101] See: A. Wagner and G. Barth, 'Judicial Interpretation or Judicial Vandalism? Section 3 of the Human Rights Act 1998' [2016] JR 99. Though see: *Secretary of State for the Home Department* v *AF (No. 3)* [2010] 2 AC 269.

> any change in a fundamental constitutional principle should be the consequence of deliberate legislative action and not judicial activism, however well meaning.
>
> In other words, Lord Millet was sympathetic to the plight of the surviving partner, but considered that 'fixing' this breach of human rights was a job for Parliament, enacting new legislation. According to Nicol (Danny Nicol, 'Law and Politics after the HRA' (2006) PL 722, 747–8) this case gives us a clear indication of the limits of the s. 3 HRA duty:
>
> As Lords Nicholls . . . demonstrate[s] in *Ghaidan* v *Godin-Mendoza*, strained interpretation is a matter of degree. While it is nothing new for judges to 'add words' to a statute, such interpretation must be compatible with the statute's underlying thrust: it must 'go with the grain of the legislation'. There would be judicial vandalism if courts removed the very core and essence, the pith and substance, of the measure Parliament had enacted. Indeed, such judicial vandalism can be conceived as a form of constitutional anti-social behaviour, with judges ushering the rights dispute away from the gaze of media and polity and hogging the legislative function to themselves.

Following *Ghaidan* v *Godin-Mendoza*, the courts have more readily asserted some of the limitations on s. 3 by comparison to their earlier jurisprudence; Lord Reed has reminded, for instance, that unless ordinary methods of interpretation reveal a potential breach of the Convention rights, s. 3(1) need not be employed by the courts at all.[102] The Supreme Court has otherwise adhered to the view that s. 3(1) 'interpretation' which would run contrary to 'essential principles' of the challenged legislation will not be possible.[103] Lord Hoffmann offers the following summary of the prevailing judicial attitude towards reinterpretation in light of the ECHR:

> I do not believe that section 3 of the 1998 Act was intended to have the effect of requiring the courts to give the language of statutes acontextual meanings. That would be playing games with words . . . There is a strong presumption, arising from the fundamental nature of Convention rights, that Parliament did not intend a statute to mean something which would be incompatible with those rights . . . But . . . the question is still one of *interpretation*, i.e. the ascertainment of what, taking into account the presumption created by section 3, Parliament would reasonably be understood to have meant by using the actual language of the statute.[104] In the final analysis, s. 3 imposes a duty on the courts which has the *potential* to alter the meaning of large swathes of legislation; as Lord Hope observed shortly before the Act became fully operational, the HRA has the potential to 'subject the *entire legal system* to a fundamental process of review and, where necessary, reform *by the judiciary*'.[105]

The Act's effects have been by no means as far reaching, and the feared transfer of power from political institutions to courts less extensive than Lord Hope predicted. In spite of this, the HRA remains subjected to anti-democratic critiques, with s. 3(1) a particular target.[106] But, as Conor Gearty recognises, Parliament imposed this duty on the

---

[102] *S* v *L (No. 2)* [2012] UKSC 30; 2013 SC (UKSC) 20, [15].

[103] *McDonald* v *McDonald* [2016] UKSC 28; [2016] 3 WLR 45, [65].

[104] *R (Wikinson)* v *Inland Revenue Commissioners* [2005] UKHL 30; [2005] 1 WLR 1718, [17].

[105] *R* v *Director of Public Prosecutions, ex parte Kebeline* [2000] 2 AC 326, 374–375 (emphasis added).

[106] A Conservative Party commitment to repeal the HRA and replace it with a British Bill of Rights aims to limit the powers presently conveyed by s. 3(1) in order to prevent legislation from being 're-written through interpretation' (*The Conservative Party, Protecting Human Rights in the United Kingdom – The Conservatives' Proposals for Changing Britain's Human Rights Laws* (October 2014)).

courts, and the judges 'have neither assumed it [for themselves] nor smuggled it into the law camouflaged as a longstanding principle of interpretation'.[107] The very fact that the interpretive duty is imposed by Parliament provides a source of legitimacy for judicial actions.[108] Section 3, moreover, cannot be applied in all cases. The duty of the courts is to interpret, and the process of interpretation should preclude radical alterations to the meaning of legislation.[109] Finally, it must always be remembered that the HRA 1998 was designed to *preserve* parliamentary sovereignty. As Jack Straw informed Parliament during the legislative process:

> If the higher courts come up with an interpretation that makes the intention of Parliament risible and means that legislation is applied in a way that is unreasonable and has ridiculous results, it is open to the House to change the decision.[110]

In doing so, however, Parliament would need to carefully consider the potential for further litigation before Strasbourg. Therefore, having examined s. 3 and its limitations, we must consider what powers the HRA provides to courts when interpretation is inadequate to address a statutory provision which infringes incorporated ECHR rights.

Declarations of incompatibility

(i) The power to affirm that legislation breaches human rights

Where it is impossible to re-interpret legislation so as to reconcile it to an ECHR right, any court or tribunal of equivalent or higher standing to the High Court in the hierarchy of courts has the option, under s. 4 of the HRA, to issue a 'declaration of incompatibility'.[111] Such a declaration 'does not affect the validity, continuing operation or enforcement of the provision in respect of which it is given'.[112] It is instead, in Gearty's view, 'little more than a cry for action'.[113] When a court issues a declaration, it is warning the government and Parliament that legislation needs to be reconsidered in light of human rights concerns. It is, moreover, providing lobbying groups and the media with an authoritative basis on which to campaign for law reform.

But a declaration, of itself, does not provide any protection to a claimant whose rights have been infringed. This factor influences the relationship between ss. 3 and 4, with the courts eager to use the former power to enable them to provide some redress to the victims

---

[107] C. Gearty, 'Reconciling Parliamentary Democracy and Human Rights' (2002) LQR 248, 251.

[108] As Lord Bingham famously noted in *A v Secretary of State for the Home Department* [2004] UKHL 56; [2005] 2 AC 68, [42], characterising judicial power under the HRA as 'undemocratic' is misguided as 'Parliament has expressly legislated in section 6 of the 1998 Act to render unlawful any act of a public authority, including a court, incompatible with a Convention right, has required courts (in section 2) to take account of relevant Strasbourg jurisprudence, has (in section 3) required courts, so far as possible, to give effect to Convention rights and has conferred a right of appeal on derogation issues. The effect is not, of course, to override the sovereign legislative authority of the Queen in Parliament, since if primary legislation is declared to be incompatible the validity of the legislation is unaffected (section 4(6)) and the remedy lies with the appropriate minister (section 10), who is answerable to Parliament. The 1998 Act gives the courts a very specific, wholly democratic, mandate.'

[109] *HM's application for Judicial Review* [2014] NIQB 43, [53].

[110] HC Debs, vol. 313, col. 423 (3 June 1998).

[111] HRA 1998, s. 4(2).

[112] Ibid., s. 4(6)(a).

[113] C. Gearty, 'Revisiting Section 3(1) of the Human Rights Act' (2003) 119 LQR 551, 552.

of rights abuses.[114] As Lord Steyn observed in *Ghaidan* v *Godin-Mendoza,* as a declaration of incompatibility cannot of itself provide a remedy to the claimant whose rights have been interfered with, 'rights could only effectively be brought home if section 3(1) was the prime remedial measure, and section 4 a measure of last resort.'[115] Despite concerns relating to the remedial capacity of s. 4, and the fact that the terms of the HRA accord precedence to the interpretive duty, the approach of the courts to these provisions has acted as a fault line for constitutional commentators. Legal constitutionalists tend to promote active reinterpretation by the courts under s. 3, whereas political constitutionalists have, to date, criticised the courts for undertaking reinterpretations in cases where they would have preferred the question to be transferred to political actors using declarations.[116]

(ii) Case law on declarations of incompatibility

From the earliest cases under the HRA, some judges have shown considerable scepticism towards s. 4. Lord Hutton, for example, in preferring a radical reinterpretation of the 'rape shield' law in *R* v *A,* declared that it was 'clearly desirable that a court should seek to avoid having to make a declaration of incompatibility under s. 4 of the 1998 Act unless the clear and express wording of the provision makes this impossible'.[117]

Nonetheless, the courts soon recognised that some cases could not be resolved through re-interpretation. In *Bellinger* v *Bellinger*[118] the claimant, a post-operative male-to-female transsexual, attempted to persuade the courts to use s. 3 of the HRA to reinterpret the Matrimonial Causes Act 1973, which defined marriage as between a man and a woman, so as to uphold the validity of her marriage. Rejecting this course of action, Lord Hobhouse declared that permitting transsexuals to come within the scope of the terms man or woman under the 1973 Act would involve 'making a legislative choice as to what precise amendment was appropriate', which was a task for Parliament.[119] Lord Nicholls explained that Mrs Bellinger's claim raised broad issues which could not be adequately addressed on a case-by-case basis:

> The recognition of gender reassignment for the purposes of marriage is part of a wider problem which should be considered as a whole and not dealt with in a piecemeal fashion. There should be a clear, coherent policy.[120]

For these reasons, and even though 'the interpretation proposed by Mrs Bellinger under [s. 3] may have been linguistically and legally possible',[121] the House of Lords issued a declaration of incompatibility. Under the Gender Recognition Act 2004, Parliament responded by creating a mechanism by which transsexuals could gain a legal recognition of their acquired gender.

---

[114] S. Gardbaum, 'Reassessing the New Commonwealth Model of Constitutionalism' [2010] IJCL 167, 200.
[115] *Ghaidan* v *Godin-Mendoza* [2004] UKHL 30; [2004] 2 AC 557, [46].
[116] For an excellent examination of the political positions reflected in this debate see: T. Hickman, 'Constitutional Dialogue, Constitutional Theories and the Human Rights Act 1998' [2005] PL 306.
[117] *R* v *A* [2001] UKHL 25; [2002] 1 AC 45, [162].
[118] *Bellinger* v *Bellinger* [2003] UKHL 21; [2003] 2 WLR 1174.
[119] Ibid., [78].
[120] Ibid., [45].
[121] A. Kavanagh, 'Statutory Interpretation and Human Rights after *Anderson*: a More Contextual Approach' [2004] PL 537, 541.

The most high-profile declaration of incompatibility to have been issued by the courts, however, came with regard to the UK's counter-terrorism provisions, and in particular the power to detain terrorism suspects without trial in Belmarsh Prison:

Key case

A v Secretary of State for the Home Department [2004] UKHL 56; [2005] 2 AC 68 (House of Lords)

The House of Lords had to assess whether the Home Secretary's power, under Part IV of the Anti-Terrorism, Crime and Security Act 2001 (ATCSA), to impose unlimited detention without trial on suspected international terrorists, was a proportionate response to the threat posed by these individuals, thereby justifying a derogation (Art. 15) from the right to liberty (Art. 5). Seven of the nine judges hearing the case decided that although the security situation in the aftermath of the terrorist attacks on 9/11 amounted to an 'emergency', a power of indefinite detention applicable only to foreign nationals constituted a disproportionate infringement of human rights.

Lord Bingham, giving the lead judgment for the majority concluded ([43]), that 'the choice of an immigration measure to address a security problem had the inevitable result of failing adequately to address that problem'. Nonetheless, none of the nine Law Lords gave serious consideration to employing s. 3 HRA to reinterpret the relevant provisions of the ATCSA. Its provisions expressly stated that they applied only to foreign nationals and there was therefore no way to read into this provision a power applicable to anyone, irrespective of nationality. Therefore, Lord Bingham issued ([73]):

> [A] declaration under section 4 of the Human Rights Act 1998 that section 23 of the Anti-Terrorism, Crime and Security Act 2001 is incompatible with articles 5 and 14 of the European Convention insofar as it is disproportionate and permits detention of suspected international terrorists in a way that discriminates on the ground of nationality or immigration status.

The problem with this solution is that, as s. 4(6) HRA makes clear, declarations do not affect the validity of the legislation they cover. It was left to Parliament to rectify the breach by repealing the ATCSA and enacting new legislation in its place. As sceptical commentators (K. Ewing and J.-C. Tham, 'The Continuing Futility of the Human Rights Act' [2008] PL 668, 670) have noted:

> Far from vindicating a human rights culture under the HRA, the response to *A* provides evidence the other way. It did not lead to the immediate release of the detainees, who despite the Lords' ruling on December 16, 2004 were not 'liberated' from their internment until March 10 and 11, 2005, once the Prevention of Terrorism Act 2005 had eventually been rushed through.

On the other hand, s. 4 of the HRA did operate as intended. The House of Lords judgment gave sufficient support to the ATCSA's opponents to oblige the government to alter its most high-profile counter-terrorism power.

Declarations of incompatibility therefore have the character of a measure of 'last resort' under the HRA, operating, in Kavanagh's opinion, when re-interpretation would be an abuse of the judicial function:

> Rights have to be balanced against institutional reasons pertaining to the limits of the judicial role, the propriety of judicial intervention in certain contexts, and the degree to which an innovative judicial decision will be accepted either by politicians or the populace at large.[122]

---

[122] A. Kavanagh, 'Judicial Restraint in the Pursuit of Justice' (2010) 60 UTLJ 23, 31–32.

Whilst declarations are, therefore, a less controversial route for judges to take than reinterpretation, this is not to say that they are uncontroversial. Simply because a court issues a declaration, and does not undertake reinterpretation of the law for itself, this does not immunise its decision from a political backlash. This fact is exemplified by the Supreme Court's decision in *F and Thompson*.[123] Both claimants had committed sexual offences and were therefore included on the sex offenders register for life. They argued that this permanent sanction, with no opportunity to seek a review, amounted to a disproportionate infringement of their right to private and family life (Art. 8), F's offence having been committed when he was 11 years old and Thompson not having reoffended in over a decade. Focusing on the lack of a facility for review, the Court declared that the relevant provisions of the Sexual Offences Act 2003 were incompatible with Art. 8. Prime Minister David Cameron told Parliament that he found the ruling 'offensive' and made it clear that he would take 'the minimum possible approach'[124] to compliance.[125]

The important factor, however, is that even in light of a supposedly 'offensive' declaration of incompatibility, the Prime Minister is not talking of non-compliance. To date, none of the governments in office since the HRA was passed have refused to respond to a declaration. Only in the case of prisoner voting rights[126] has government dragged its heals to a serious degree over law reform.[127] In such a situation, some commentators might be tempted to suggest that, if Parliament 'almost certainly' responds to declarations,[128] then the HRA provides for US-style legislative review in all but name. Such a conclusion, however, neglects the co-operative aspect of s. 4. As a matter of UK constitutional law, it remains for the *political branches of government* to draft law reform in response to a declaration as it chooses, and as the prisoner voting rights saga shows, to take as much time over doing so as they may choose.[129]

The prisoner voting saga also reminds us that the issue of a declaration of incompatibility will not inevitably follow a judicial finding that s. 3(1) may not be utilised. A declaration of incompatibility is a *discretionary* remedy. In the 2013 decision in *R (Chester) v Secretary of State for Justice*, the Supreme Court declined to issue a second declaration of incompatibility in relation to the legislation prohibiting convicted prisoners from voting (Representation of the People Act 1983, s. 3) following the failure of the government and/or Parliament to address the incompatibility previously identified in 2007 in *Smith v Scott*.[130] In spite of the fact that the 2007 declaration had not been acted upon, the Supreme Court found that as the issue remained under 'active consideration' by the elected branches there would be 'no point in making any further declaration of incompatibility'.[131]

---

[123] *R (F and Thompson) v Secretary of State for the Home Department* [2010] UKSC 17; [2011] 1 AC 331.

[124] HC Debs, vol. 523, col. 955 (16 February 2011).

[125] The incompatibility was addressed via the Sexual Offences Act 2003 (Remedial) Order 2012.

[126] *Smith v Scott* [2007] CSIH 9; 2007 SC 345.

[127] See C. Murray, 'We Need to Talk: "Democratic Dialogue" and the Ongoing Saga of Prisoner Disenfranchisement' (2011) 62 NILQ 57.

[128] HM Government, *Rights Brought Home: The Human Rights Bill* (London: Stationery Office, 1997) Cm. 3782, [2.10].

[129] Correspondence between the UK Government and the Committee of Ministers dated 25 October 2016 indicates that action to address the incompatibility confirmed in *Hirst v United Kingdom (No. 2)* (2006) 42 EHRR 41 is still being considered but is unlikely to involve the amendment of s. 3 of the Representation of the People Act 1983 (see: https://rm.coe.int/CoERMPublicCommonSearchServices/DisplayDCTMContent?documentId=09000016806b63f9, [10]).

[130] *Smith v Scott* [2007] CSIH 9; 2007 SC 345.

[131] *R (Chester) v Secretary of State for Justice* [2013] UKSC 63; [2014] AC 271, [39].

The Supreme Court also declined to issue a declaration of incompatibility in the *Nicklinson* decision.[132] *Nicklinson* was a case brought by a number of applicants who – as a result of profound physical disabilities – wished to, with assistance, bring their lives to an end. The primary objective of the applicants was to seek declarations that any assistance provided by third parties would not incur criminal sanctions.[133] A secondary line of argument challenged the existing laws criminalising assisted suicide on the basis of their incompatibility with Art. 8 ECHR (the right to a private and family life). A nine-judge Supreme Court found that a law prohibiting assisted suicide was likely to fall within the margin of appreciation granted to states within the Convention system. A majority of the court held that the Court *could* issue a declaration of incompatibility in relation to the Suicide Act 1961, with Lords Neuberger, Mance and Wilson finding that in the present case it would be inappropriate to do so (Lady Hale and Lord Kerr dissented on the latter point[134]). The remaining four Justices considered that the case raised complex issues relating to the balancing of individual rights and the interests of society as a whole that the court was ill-positioned to assess (Lord Sumption, for instance, described a society's response to assisted dying as an 'inherently legislative issue'[135]). A majority of the Court determined that issuing a declaration of incompatibility would not be appropriate as, *inter alia,* Parliament had considered the state of the law relatively recently and had declined to make any change,[136] an Assisted Dying Bill was contemporaneously being considered by Parliament,[137] and on the basis of the Court's (lack of) institutional competence on the issue.[138] However, in coming to its conclusion, a number of the Justices also noted the possibility that – should a similar case arise in the future in the absence of further legislative deliberation of the complex issues raised by the prospect of assisted dying – a declaration of incompatibility could be issued.[139]

(iii) Remedial orders in response to declaration of incompatibility

Under s. 10 of the HRA, where the courts find legislation incompatible with incorporated rights,[140] or where Strasbourg makes a ruling which seems to the government to raise issues of the compatibility of UK legislation with the ECHR,[141] the government has the power to issue a 'fast-track' order to remedy the breach without having to pass a new Act of Parliament.[142] Ewing explains that these orders were intended to expedite reform, by-passing busy legislative schedules in Parliament.[143] But many parliamentarians were concerned that such measures would allow government to reshape legislation with the minimum of parliamentary scrutiny and they have in practice been neglected in favour of using primary

---

[132] *R (Nicklinson)* v *Ministry of Justice* [2014] UKSC 38; [2015] AC 657.

[133] On the basis of the Suicide Act 1961, s. 2.

[134] Lady Hale ([300]) and Lord Kerr ([326]) would have issued a declaration of incompatibility in the instant case.

[135] *R (Nicklinson)* v *Ministry of Justice* [2014] UKSC 38; [2015] AC 657, [234].

[136] Ibid., [51].

[137] Ibid., [190], [197].

[138] Ibid., [166]–[170], [234], [267].

[139] Ibid., [118], [190], [293].

[140] HRA 1998, s. 10(1)(a).

[141] Ibid., s. 10(1)(b).

[142] Ibid., s. 10(2).

[143] K. Ewing, 'The Human Rights Act and Parliamentary Democracy' (1999) 62 MLR 79, 92.

legislation to rectify breaches;[144] of the 22 declarations of incompatibility which had become final (i.e. not subject to an appeal) by July 2016 only three had been addressed by way of a remedial order under s. 10 HRA.[145]

Employing the Convention rights under the HRA

Key issues

- The ECHR was an international treaty designed to constrain abuses of power by states. Unsurprisingly, the HRA, in incorporating the ECHR, maintains its focus on obligations on 'public authorities' to uphold human rights (s. 6 HRA). This provision also extends the reach of the HRA to cover private bodies exercising public functions.

- Individuals are able to rely on the incorporated ECHR rights in two sets of circumstances:

  1. in bringing action against public authorities; and

  2. in defending legal actions brought against them.

- Different standing requirements apply in each of these types of action before ECHR rights can be raised.

- Despite the HRA's express focus upon public bodies, several of its provisions allow for private bodies and individuals to become the focus of rights-based claims.

The HRA and public authorities

(i) The obligations upon public authorities

To date, we have considered the new powers which the HRA granted to the courts over legislation. Just as significant, in terms of rights protection in the UK, is how the HRA grafts the regime of human rights protection onto the existing system of judicial oversight of public authorities in the UK's domestic legal systems. In a dramatic departure from the approach adopted in cases such as *ex parte Brind*,[146] where the House of Lords concluded that the courts could not hold public authorities to account under the ECHR standards, s. 6 of the HRA forbids public authorities from acting (or failing to act[147]) 'in a way which is incompatible with a Convention right'.[148]

As an exception to this general duty, the HRA provided that a public authority would not be acting in breach of this duty if it was required to act in a particular manner 'as the result of one or more provisions of primary legislation'.[149] This exception would clearly apply if the Act in question mandated a particular action, but not if it simply gave the public authority discretion to act in a number of ways, only some of which conflicted with the incorporated ECHR rights. The purpose of this exception is to protect parliamentary

---

[144] S. Gardbaum, 'Reassessing the New Commonwealth Model of Constitutionalism' [2010] IJCL 167, 200.

[145] Ministry of Justice, *Responding to Human Rights Judgments: Report to the Joint Committee on Human Rights on the Government's Response to Human Rights Judgments 2014–2016*, Cm. 9360 (November 2016), p. 45.

[146] *R v Secretary of State for the Home Department, ex parte Brind* [1991] 1 AC 696.

[147] HRA 1998, s. 6(6).

[148] Ibid., s. 6(1).

[149] Ibid., s. 6(2)(a).

sovereignty. Clearly, all of Parliament's efforts not to undermine sovereignty in the carefully calibrated power under s. 4 of the HRA would be for naught if the judiciary could prevent public authorities from employing a statute subject to a declaration of incompatibility even though it remains valid law until Parliament effects reform.

Thinking Point . . .

The scheme of protections under the HRA interact. Should the courts use s. 3(1) of the HRA to reinterpret a statute placing certain obligations on public authorities, and thereby remove any rights incompatibility, a public authority will not be able to point to that statute as requiring it act in a manner which infringes human rights, under s. 6(2). If the court cannot employ s. 3(1), and therefore cannot reject a public body's action under s. 6(2), it can still enter a declaration of incompatibility over the statute under s. 4(2).

This obligation could, in many cases, be characterised as a 'bolt-on upgrade' to judicial review. When we considered the grounds on which judicial review can be sought, for example, we saw examples of how irrationality had been expanded to incorporate a proportionality test when human rights were at issue (see Chapter 19[150]) and how the right to a fair hearing had influenced the procedural impropriety head of review (see Chapter 19[151]). Rather than cover this ground again, the 'bolt on' theory is neatly summarised by Lord Rodger in *In re McKerr*:

> Over the years, Parliament has passed many Acts, and public authorities have taken many steps, to secure that, under our domestic law, people should enjoy the rights and freedoms guaranteed by the Convention . . . In 1998 Parliament adopted a more elegant and comprehensive solution. The [Human Rights] Act reproduces as rights in our domestic law the rights that are to be found in certain specified articles in the Convention . . . It then makes it unlawful for public authorities to act or to fail to act in a way which is incompatible with those rights: section 6(1) and (6) . . . In any given situation, therefore, a person may rely not only on all the pre-existing rights and remedies afforded by the common law and statute, but also on the relevant new domestic rights . . . [152]

The bolt-on thesis does not, however, capture the full change that the HRA brought about in judicial oversight of public bodies. Whilst the existing heads of judicial review were largely focused (irrationality notwithstanding) on the process by which a public authority arrives at a decision, the same cannot always be said of the public authority duty under s. 6. David Mead summarised the question at issue for the courts in cases like *Begum*:[153]

> If a public authority decision . . . is challenged under the HRA as being disproportionate, for it to be upheld as lawful is it enough that the reviewing court adjudges that decision to be proportionate or must the council show it considered the impact or the proportionality of that decision at the time?[154]

---

[150] See pp. 565–7.

[151] See pp. 573–4.

[152] *In re McKerr* [2004] UKHL 12; [2004] 1 WLR 807, [77].

[153] *R (Begum)* v *Governors of Denbigh High School* [2006] UKHL 15; [2007] 1 AC 100. See also *Belfast City Council* v *Miss Behavin' Ltd* [2007] UKHL 19; [2007] 1 WLR 1420 and *R (Nasseri)* v *Secretary of State for the Home Department* [2009] UKHL 23; [2010] 1 AC 1.

[154] David Mead, 'Outcomes Aren't All: Defending Process-Based Review of Public Authority Decisions under the Human Rights Act' [2012] PL 61, 62.

In these cases the courts adopted the former approach to human rights claims, testing the proportionality of the decision itself, rather than the Convention compliance of the process by which the decision was taken. But why did the House of Lords, in deciding these cases, seemingly abandon judicial review's focus on process? In *Begum*, the claimant was a female Muslim pupil of a state-run school, who argued that the school's policy preventing the wearing of the *jilbab* (but permitting Muslim pupils to instead wear the *shalwar kameez*) interfered with her freedom of religion (Art. 9). The House of Lords agreed that this case did involve a *prima facie* interference, and it was noted that the school did not arrive at its policy after a full consideration of human rights concerns. For the Court of Appeal, this factor had been significant in rejecting the policy, but the House of Lords instead looked at the narrower issue of whether the policy's outcome constituted a disproportionate infringement on Begum's right. As Lord Hoffmann pithily concluded, '[h]ead teachers and governors cannot be expected to make such decisions with textbooks on human rights law at their elbows'.[155] The House of Lords' focus on whether the correct outcome had been reached in the eyes of the court was therefore a less expansive approach than would have been possible under the HRA. Essentially, the courts adopted a minimal, outcome-based, approach to proportionality cases under s. 6, because not doing so would have amounted to 'a recipe for judicialisation' of the policy-making process.[156]

Thinking Point . . .

The outcome-based focus of cases, like **Begum**, means that public authorities do not necessarily have to grapple with human rights concerns in their decision-making, provided the outcome is nonetheless proportionate. This approach could be criticised for not embedding a human rights culture in public authority decision-making.

(ii) What amounts to a public authority?

Having imposed a duty on public authorities to respect human rights, the HRA provided much less guidance on the question of what constitutes a public body. As we have seen, courts and tribunals are expressly included.[157] At the other extreme, Parliament (despite its pivotal role in both the executive and legislative branches of government) is expressly excluded from the Act's definition of a public authority.[158] If it were not, it would be *obliged* to respect human rights in its legislative output.

Beyond these extremes, the HRA provides no definitive list of what constitutes a public authority for the purpose of s. 6.[159] Instead, this provision covers 'any person certain of whose functions are functions of a public nature'.[160] This circular definition provides no

---

[155] *R (Begum)* v *Governors of Denbigh High School* [2006] UKHL 15; [2007] 1 AC 100, [68].
[156] T. Poole, 'Of Headscarves and Heresies: the Denbigh High School Case and Public Authority Decision Making under the Human Rights Act' [2005] PL 685, 695.
[157] HRA 1998, s. 6(3)(a).
[158] Ibid., s. 6(3).
[159] Cf. Freedom of Information Act 2000, s 3 and Schedule 1 (which lists the public bodies to which the Act applies).
[160] HRA 1998, s. 6(3)(b).

meaningful guidance of itself, unhelpfully proclaiming that bodies are 'public' when they act in a public way. Therefore, the public authority duty largely depends upon the approach adopted by the courts under judicial review. Public authorities, as under the common law approach to judicial review, can therefore be 'core' public bodies which are created, often under statutory authority, to exercise public functions (for example, the police, prisons and state-run schools). The HRA also extends, to a degree, to 'hybrid' bodies. These are often private bodies in terms of their legal composition, such as companies or charities, but part of their activity is to exercise a public function. Lord Nicholls provided the following explanation of what is meant by a public function under the HRA:

> What, then, is the touchstone to be used in deciding whether a function is public for this purpose? Clearly there is no single test of universal application. There cannot be, given the diverse nature of governmental functions and the variety of means by which these functions are discharged today. Factors to be taken into account include the extent to which in carrying out the relevant function the body is publicly funded, or is exercising statutory powers, or is taking the place of central government or local authorities, or is providing a public service.[161]

Hybrid bodies are only covered by the HRA when an act is part of their public function, and not when 'the nature of the act is private'.[162] The aim of basing the HRA on the common law definition of public authorities was, in light of the complexity of what is meant by 'public bodies' (highlighted by Lord Nicholl's speech), to enable the courts to apply nuanced evaluation to this issue, rather than providing a blunt list of bodies which would require regular updating. As we have seen with regard to judicial review, human rights cases like *YL* v *Birmingham City Council*[163] have played an important role in developing the common law approach to public authorities (see Chapter 18[164]). Rather than repeat this analysis, it suffices to note that Parliament can always use legislation to expressly override a judicial authority on the public/private divide. On the question of whether private care homes under contract with local authorities constituted public bodies, answered by the House of Lords in the negative in *YL*, Parliament quickly enacted legislation to reverse this conclusion.[165]

(iii) Remedies against public authorities under the HRA

Within the legal systems of the UK, the courts' long-standing approach has been to permit awards of damages against public authorities in response to public law claims only in exceptional cases. As we saw when we considered the judicial review remedies, the courts prefer to address claims by quashing a decision or mandating or prohibiting particular actions (see Chapter 18[166]). Again, 'the approach taken to compensation in the HRA fits squarely within this tradition'.[167] 'Within its powers' and where 'just and appropriate',[168] under s. 8

---

[161] *Aston Cantlow and Wilmcote with Billesley Parochial Church Council* v *Wallbank* [2003] UKHL 37; [2004] 1 AC 546, [12] (Lord Nicholls).

[162] HRA 1998, s. 6(5).

[163] *YL* v *Birmingham City Council* [2007] UKHL 27; [2007] 3 WLR 112.

[164] See p. 525.

[165] Health and Social Care Act 2008, s. 145.

[166] See pp. 536–9.

[167] I. Leigh and L. Lustgarten, 'Making Rights Real: the Courts, Remedies and the Human Rights Act' (1999) 58 CLJ 509, 527.

[168] HRA 1998, s. 8(2).

of the HRA a court may award damages for the breach of a public authority's duty to respect rights under s. 6, but only where such damages would be 'necessary to afford just satisfaction'.[169] In other words, the HRA is intended to remedy a rights abuse suffered by an individual, and if the problem with a public authority's behaviour is rectified, that will usually suffice.

Few cases under the HRA, therefore, have made an extensive evaluation of the question of damages. One of the cases to do so is ***Anufrijeva***, in which the claimant asylum seekers claimed that their respective local authorities had, as a result of maladministration, failed to comply with their statutory public law duty to provide benefits to which they were entitled, and that as a result their family life had been seriously affected (Art. 8).[170] The Court of Appeal dismissed the claim, and also noted that damages were not recoverable as of right where Convention rights had been breached. Lord Woolf confirmed that the concern in such cases was usually to bring the infringement to an end and compensation was of secondary importance:

> In considering whether to award compensation and, if so, how much, there is a balance to be drawn between the interests of the victim and those of the public as a whole . . . In essence this involves determining the 'appropriate' remedy in the light of the particular circumstances of an individual victim whose rights have been violated, having regard to what would be 'just', not only for that individual victim, but also for the wider public who have an interest in the continued funding of a public service. Damages are not an automatic entitlement but . . . a remedy of 'last resort'.[171]

Again, the stated purpose of the HRA was to incorporate particular ECHR rights into domestic law. As Strasbourg ordinarily treats rectification of a breach as a sufficient remedy, and is itself 'slow' to award compensation,[172] this approach to damages should come as little surprise.

Standing to claim Convention rights

(i) General standing requirements

When individuals seek to employ the ECHR rights incorporated under the ECHR in an action before the domestic courts, they must first establish that they qualify as a 'victim' of the breach of human rights. This provides a clear example of the purpose behind the HRA being to bring the ECHR 'home' in the UK, rather than to advance an indigenous human rights regime. Section 7 of the HRA ties human rights actions to the reach of the ECHR:

> For the purposes of this section, a person is a victim of an unlawful act only if he would be a victim for the purposes of Article 34 of the Convention if proceedings were brought in the European Court of Human Rights in respect of that act.[173]

Article 34 ECHR establishes that only a 'person, non-governmental organisation or group of individuals claiming to be the victim of a violation' enjoy standing to bring an action

---

[169] Ibid., s. 8(3).
[170] *Anufrijeva* v *Southwark LBC* [2003] EWCA Civ 1406; [2004] 2 WLR 603.
[171] Ibid., [56].
[172] *R (Greenfield)* v *Secretary of State for the Home Department* [2005] UKHL 14; [2005] 1 WLR 673, [11].
[173] HRA 1998, s. 7(7).

before the Strasbourg Court. Strasbourg's case law explains that this requires that applicants must have been personally affected by the action they are challenging and that they lose victim status if the public authority acknowledges its breach of ECHR rights and provides adequate redress.[174] This standard is narrower than the rules developed by the domestic courts regarding when an individual can seek judicial review (especially after the expansion in standing to claim judicial review in recent decades, considered in Chapter 18[175]). This means that when a party to a judicial review action seeks to raise human rights grounds as part of their challenge to a public authority action, they can only 'bolt-on' such elements to their claim if they also satisfy the victim standard.[176]

The *Rabone* case illustrates these conditions.[177] The claimants were the parents of a twenty-four-year-old woman who hospital staff allowed to return home despite being a suicide risk. When the woman committed suicide, the hospital trust admitted negligence and made a settlement in the case. The parents subsequently brought an action under the HRA, claiming that the hospital had failed to fulfil its positive duty to protect their daughter's right to life (Art. 2). The hospital responded that the Rabones could not bring this action as they were not victims for the purpose of Art. 34, and even if they had been, they lost this status when they accepted a compensation settlement. The Supreme Court dismissed both of these claims. Lord Dyson first recognised that Strasbourg case law accepted that family members of a deceased individual were personally affected for the purposes of Art. 34.[178] As for the compensation settlement already made, Lord Dyson asserted:

> [I]f (i) the domestic law claim that is settled was made by the same person as seeks to make an Article 2 claim and (ii) the head of loss embraced by the settlement broadly covers the same ground as the loss which is the subject of the Article 2 claim, then I would expect the ECtHR to say that, by settling the former, the claimant is to be taken to have renounced any claim to the latter.[179]

In this case the Supreme Court accepted that the claimants had settled a negligence action but not a claim under Art. 2 ECHR and that there had been no express acceptance by the hospital trust of its breach of Art. 2. The claim was permitted to proceed.

(ii) Using Convention rights as a 'sword'

There are two forms of action under the HRA. From the date that the HRA entered force,[180] as we have seen, public authorities owe a s. 6 duty to respect incorporated rights. From October 2000 onwards, therefore, any public authority action which infringed an individual's rights provided the basis of a claim under the HRA. Thus, individuals can use the HRA as a 'sword', taking it upon themselves to challenge public authorities by bringing 'proceedings against the authority under this Act in the appropriate court or tribunal'.[181] Such actions must be brought against the public authority within one year of the impugned

---

[174] See *Eckle* v *Germany* (1983) 5 EHRR 1, [66].
[175] See pp. 527–532.
[176] HRA 1998, s. 7(3).
[177] *Rabone* v *Pennine Care NHS Trust* [2012] UKSC 2; [2012] 2 AC 72.
[178] Ibid., [46].
[179] Ibid., [57].
[180] HRA 1998, s. 22(3).
[181] Ibid., s. 7(1)(a).

action or omission.[182] This time limit, however, does not supplant the three-month time limit under judicial review actions, so if a human rights claim is conjoined alongside other public law causes of action, it will have to meet this stricter time limit.

(iii) Using Convention rights as a 'shield'

Human rights may also be relied upon as a 'shield' where a public authority has commenced 'any legal proceedings' against an individual and the individual argues that such proceedings amount to an action breaching the public authority duty to respect human rights.[183] Not looking beyond the criminal justice context bodies such as the police, the Crown Prosecution Service, prisons, parole boards and the probation service might all be involved in actions against an individual. Such proceedings can be defended on the basis of the HRA if such individuals can show that they have been the victim of human rights abuses.

Using the Human Rights Act against private individuals: 'horizontal rights'

(i) Vertical and horizontal conceptions of rights

Just as the ECHR focuses on rights abuses by states, the HRA (aiming to bring many of the ECHR's provisions into effect in domestic law) focuses on the responsibilities of public authorities. This is known as 'vertical' human rights protection, impacting as it does upon the relationship between the individual and the state. By contrast, actions between private individuals are 'horizontal' in nature. This does not imply that all private individuals, from asylum seekers to multi-national corporations are equal in their ability to affect the rights of others, but that private bodies do not have the same access to coercive means, like the police, military and security services, as are enjoyed be the state. Support for a vertical conception of human rights is premised, according to Murray Hunt, 'on a rigid distinction between the public and the private sphere and presupposes that the purpose of fundamental rights protection is to preserve the integrity of the private sphere against coercive intrusion by the state'.[184]

(ii) Horizontal applications of human rights under the HRA

The primary focus of the Convention rights – as has been recognised in the UK Supreme Court – is 'to protect citizens from having their rights infringed *by the State*'.[185] As such, s. 6 of the HRA seems focused upon 'public authorities' and there is an 'absence of any references to private individuals or organisations anywhere in the Act'.[186] Several features of the HRA, however, make it possible for the Convention rights to impact upon relations between private individuals.

The first avenue by which private bodies can be affected by human rights claims is where they are not private bodies at all, but hybrid bodies exercising some public functions. On that basis organisations such as Hampshire Farmers Markets, nominally a private company,

---

[182] Ibid., s. 7(5)(a).
[183] Ibid., s. 7(1)(b).
[184] M. Hunt, 'The "Horizontal Effect" of the Human Rights Act' [1998] PL 423, 424.
[185] *McDonald* v *McDonald* [2016] UKSC 28; [2016] 3 WLR 45, [41] (emphasis added).
[186] M. Hunt, 'The "Horizontal Effect" of the Human Rights Act' [1998] PL 423, 438.

have been found to actually be subject to the HRA.[187] Secondly, courts and tribunals are public bodies under the HRA, which means that whenever a court exercises discretion, perhaps with regards to the rules of evidence, even when a case involves two private parties, this constitutes an 'act' under s. 6.[188] But, as Hunt explains, the horizontalist effect of the duty on the courts to respect rights under s. 6 extends beyond court discretion over its own procedure:

> [O]nce it is recognised that relations between private individuals as well as relations between individuals and the state are moulded by both legislation and common law, and that the state lurks behind both forms of law, it becomes artificial and dishonest to constrain the reach of fundamental rights protection by limiting it to the so-called public sphere.[189]

In other words, when the courts interpret statutes or develop common law which governs the relationship between private individuals, they can do so using the HRA. We have seen examples of such cases throughout this chapter. In *Ghaidan* v *Godin-Mendoza*, neither of the parties were emanations of the state.[190] Nonetheless, as Lord Nicholls explained, the case took on a human rights dimension not because of the status of the parties but because the courts, under their duty to respect human rights, were prepared to reinterpret the key statute which overarched the landlord–tenant relationship:

> [T]he social policy underlying the 1988 extension of security of tenure under [the Rent Act] to the survivor of couples living together as husband and wife is equally applicable to the survivor of homosexual couples living together in a close and stable relationship. In this circumstance I see no reason to doubt that application of section 3 to [the Rent Act] has the effect that [the Rent Act] should be read and given effect to as though the survivor of such a homosexual couple were the surviving spouse of the original tenant.[191]

This case produced a 'horizontal' outcome; a reinterpretation under the HRA changed private responsibilities. Nonetheless, this horizontal effect is indirect. The target of Godin-Mendoza's human rights claim was not his landlord but the statute which failed to protect his rights, and therefore the UK Government for not maintaining a legal regime which provided for adequate rights protection. Similarly, in cases in which the common law which affects relationships between parties provides inadequate rights protections, the courts will be able to develop it in line with incorporated rights. In cases such as *Campbell* v *MGN*,[192] for example, both Naomi Campbell and the publisher of *The Mirror* were private bodies, and yet, as we have seen, Campbell was able to successfully argue that the common law cause of action of breach of confidence did not adequately protect her Art. 8 right.[193] Once the courts accepted this argument, and expanded breach of confidence action, her claim against *The Mirror* succeeded on the basis that the exercise of *The Mirror*'s countervailing right of freedom of expression came at disproportionate cost to Campbell's right to privacy.[194]

---

[187] *R (Beer (t/a Hammer Trout Farm))* v *Hampshire Farmers Markets* [2003] EWCA Civ 1056; [2004] 1 WLR 233.

[188] *Kay* v *Lambeth London Borough Council; Leeds City Council* v *Price* [2006] UKHL 10; [2006] 2 AC 465, [61].

[189] M. Hunt, 'The "Horizontal Effect" of the Human Rights Act' [1998] PL 423, 425.

[190] Above, pp. 666–7.

[191] *Ghaidan* v *Godin-Mendoza* [2004] UKHL 30; [2004] 2 AC 557, [35].

[192] *Campbell* v *MGN Ltd* [2004] UKHL 22; [2004] 2 AC 457.

[193] Above, p. 663.

[194] For commentary see: G. Phillipson, 'Clarity Postponed: Horizontal Effect after *Campbell*' in H. Fenwick, G. Phillipson and R. Masterman (eds), *Judicial Reasoning under the UK Human Rights Act* (CUP, 2007).

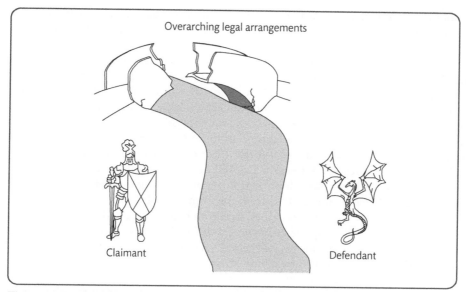

Figure 21.3 Bridging the public–private divide under the HRA

Figure 21.3 attempts to visualise how such cases bridge the public–private divide in human rights law. On the left bank of the river, which represents the public–private divide under the HRA, stands a private individual seeking to rely on incorporated human rights (either as a sword or a shield) in an action against another private individual (here represented by the dragon on the right bank) whose behaviour, it is claimed, has infringed the claimant's human rights.

Ordinarily, the focus of the HRA on public authority actions, would preclude such an action. The claimant must use the HRA not directly against the defendant, but against the overarching legal arrangements (be they statute or common law). If the claimant succeeds in persuading the court that his legal interests are not adequately protected, the effect will be to bridge the public–private divide, providing the claimant with a new legal basis on which to challenge the defendant.

Towards A Bill of Rights for the United Kingdom?

While the HRA has undoubtedly improved the protections for, and standing of, human rights in the UK Constitution,[195] and has been influential in the development of similar instruments overseas,[196] political opposition to the Act has ensured that it does not enjoy the symbolic importance, and stability, of Bills of Rights in other jurisdictions. Even the

---

[195] See: British Institute for Human Rights, *The Human Rights Act: Changing Lives* (2ⁿᵈ edn) (British Institute for Human Rights, 2014).

[196] See above p. 655. And for literature placing the HRA in a comparative context see: S. Gardbaum, *The New Commonwealth Model of Constitutionalism: Theory and Practice* (CUP, 2013); R. Leckey, *Bills of Rights in the Common Law* (CUP, 2015); K. Gledhill, *Human Rights Acts: The Mechanisms Compared* (Hart Publishing, 2015).

senior figures in the Labour Party responsible for introducing the Act have been lukewarm as to its impact;[197] as Anthony Lester notes, the HRA is scarcely mentioned in Tony Blair's memoir.[198] This is at least in part for the reason that the HRA presented an obstacle to the successful delivery of government policies in the contested fields of counter-terrorism and criminal justice. As such, the HRA quickly began to bear 'the hallmark of a proposal conceived in opposition that comes to be viewed differently in the cold harsh light of government'.[199] In addition, as we saw in the last chapter, large sections of the UK media, and the Conservative Party, have stated their ongoing opposition to the HRA 1998. Since at least 2006, there have been Conservative calls to reform or repeal the HRA, and in 2010 the Conservatives approached the General Election with a manifesto commitment to 'replace the Human Rights Act with a UK Bill of Rights'. Following the 2010 election, David Cameron was unable to deliver on this promise (having formed a coalition government with the Liberal Democrats). Instead, the formation of the Commission on A Bill of Rights effectively saw the issue consigned to the long grass for the duration of the 2010–2015 Parliament.[200] Following the 2015 general election – and the return of a Conservative majority administration – Cameron said that plans to repeal the HRA would be published within the first 100 days of the new administration.[201] And while the Queen's Speeches in 2015 and 2016 promised *proposals* to introduce a UK Bill of Rights, no such proposals emerged, and Cameron resigned as Prime Minister in the immediate aftermath of the 2016 Brexit referendum.

Following the subsequent appointment of Theresa May as Prime Minister, the then Secretary of State for Justice and Lord Chancellor (Liz Truss MP) again reiterated the Government's intention to replace the HRA with a UK Bill of Rights,[202] with the Conservatives' 2017 election manifesto duly promising a re-examination of the UK's human rights framework on completion of the Brexit negotiations.[203] In spite of repeated policy promises, the precise shape of the proposed replacement instrument remains unclear. However, a Conservative Party policy document published in October 2014 indicates a number of perceived deficiencies in the HRA regime that a new Bill of Rights would seek to address.[204] Core amongst these concerns is limiting the influence of the European Court of Human Rights in the domestic sphere. As a result, while the proposed Bill of Rights would – it is indicated – be structured around the text of the ECHR rights, the influence

---

[197] Cf. Lord Irvine, 'The Impact of the Human Rights Act: Parliament, the Courts and the Executive' [2003] PL 308.

[198] A. Lester, 'Human Rights and the British Constitution' in J. Jowell and D. Oliver (eds), *The Changing Constitution* (7th ed) (OUP, 2011) pp. 70, 97.

[199] J. Croft, *Whitehall and the Human Rights Act 1998* (Constitution Unit, 2000) p. 27.

[200] See: Commission on a Bill of Rights, *The Choice Before Us? The Report of the Commission on a Bill of Rights* (2012).

[201] See e.g.: Oliver Wright, 'Unshackled from coalition partners, Tories get ready to push radical agenda', *The Independent* 9 May 2015.

[202] House of Commons Justice Committee, Oral Evidence, 'The Work of the Secretary of State' HC620, 7 September 2016, Q78–Q91.

[203] HC Debates, vol. 618, col. 355, 8 December 2016 (Jeremy Wright QC MP).

[204] See: 'The Conservative Party, Protecting Human Rights in the United Kingdom – The Conservatives' Proposals for Changing Britain's Human Rights Laws' (October 2014), available at: https://www.google.co.uk/url?sa=t&rct=j&q=&esrc=s&source=web&cd=3&ved=0ahUKEwiEjOWO3rvYAhVMJVAKHcaCCCwQFggxMAI&url=https%3A%2F%2Fwww.conservatives.com%2F~%2Fmedia%2Ffiles%2Fdownloadable%2520files%2Fhuman_rights.pdf&usg=AOvVaw0-swi17xHJ3AONxoBU2K49.

of the Strasbourg court and the Strasbourg case law would be reduced through removal of the requirement that domestic courts 'take into account' the Convention case law. It is further suggested that the proposals will seek to ensure that decisions of the European Court of Human Rights against the UK are regarded as being advisory only (a proposal which would seem to run counter to the UK's obligation – under Article 46 ECHR – to abide by judgments of the Strasbourg court to which it is a party). In addition, the Bill of Rights would seek to engineer a 'proper balance between rights and responsibilities in UK law' through 'clarification' of the Convention rights. The Bill of Rights would also limit the powers of UK courts under s. 3(1) to prevent statute law from being 're-written through interpretation' and would further seek to ensure that employment of human rights laws would be possible in only the 'most serious cases' in relation to potential breaches within the jurisdiction (therefore ensuring that the armed forces overseas are not 'subject to persistent human rights claims' that are argued to inhibit their operational effectiveness). Though the influence of the HRA and the Convention case law will undoubtedly be hard to displace in the event of the enactment of a UK Bill of Rights – 'the rights that exist are generally better and more widely known and understood than under the pre-HRA regime of common law rights supplemented by various specific statutory protections'[205] – the general tenor of these proposals clearly points towards a proposed weakening of the UK's human rights regime through seeking to reduce the ability of the Strasbourg Court and domestic courts to influence the shape of domestic human rights protections, and through a narrowing of the circumstances in which human rights laws will bite.[206]

It is by no means clear, however, that the reform or repeal of the HRA is a foregone conclusion. First, proposals to repeal the HRA are by no means assured of a smooth (Westminster) parliamentary process. In the House of Commons, the current Conservative administration does not enjoy a majority and a number of Conservatives are known to be sympathetic to the HRA and suspicious of attempts to water-down its protections.[207] The House of Lords may also pose an obstacle to the straightforward legislative implementation of a UK Bill of Rights; one influential House of Lords Committee observed in 2016 that the proposal for a new Bill of Rights would amount to a 'constitutional change of the greatest significance'[208] and was unpersuaded by the Government's arguments in favour of such a change.[209] Secondly, significant constitutional obstacles will also need to be navigated in order to see a Bill of Rights replace the HRA. This is for the reason that the protections currently afforded by the HRA are woven into the fabric of the three sets of devolutionary arrangements effective in Scotland, Wales and Northern Ireland[210]

---

[205] S. Gardbaum, 'How Successful and Distinctive is the Human Rights Act? An Expatriate Comparatist's Assessment' (2011) 74 MLR 195, 198.

[206] For critical assessment see: S. Greer and R. Slowe, 'The Conservatives' Proposals for a British Bill of Rights: Mired in Muddle, Misconception and Misrepresentation' [2015] EHRLR 372.

[207] For instance, the former Attorney-General, Dominic Grieve QC MP (see: 'Why Human Rights Should matter to Conservatives', Speech at the Constitution Unit, University College London, 3 December 2014).

[208] House of Lords European Union Committee, *The UK, the EU and a British Bill of Rights* (HL139), 9 May 2016, [47].

[209] Ibid., [46].

[210] See: ss. 29, 57 Scotland Act 1998; ss. 81, 94, 108, 158 Government of Wales Act 2006; ss. 6, 24, 81, 83 Northern Ireland Act 1998.

(in the latter amounting to a 'critical part of the Belfast-Good Friday Agreement'[211] upon which the Northern Ireland Act 1998 rests[212]). The extent to which the protections afforded by the Convention rights are 'entrenched'[213] in the UK's three schemes of devolution means that proposals to amend the devolutionary arrangements in relation to the legal protection of human rights would be unlikely to command widespread support in the devolved territories.[214]

Conclusion

If the approach of the domestic courts to the adoption of human rights has at times appeared hesitant, this must be considered in light of two factors. First, and from a practical perspective given that its effects on government policy loom large, the HRA has long been seen as an obstacle to effective policy delivery. As we have seen in this chapter, where a government persuades Parliament to enact what it admits to be 'draconian' powers over individuals, often with scant regard for due process, it will frequently be challenged before the courts. The HRA operates as a parliamentary decree applicable to public body decision-making and all legislation, tasking the courts to read such legislation compatibly with the Convention rights where it is possible to do so, and to flag up breaches where it is not. In this sense of course, the HRA could be seen as functioning exactly as it should do, as a mechanism by which legislation and public body decision-making which unjustifiably interferes with human rights standards might be challenged.

Second, the HRA has operated – for much of its lifespan – in a critical political environment, under threat of repeal or replacement. Scepticism of the HRA and Convention rights is both grounded in the roots of the UK Constitution's traditional tendency towards empowering the institutions of 'the political constitution'[215] and overtly driven by the partisan concerns of party politics. There remains a body of opinion that is mistrustful of judicial determination of the controversial questions that can often be found at the heart of human rights adjudication.[216] The HRA's emphasis on a model of constitutional collaboration – requiring the input of *all three* core branches of government – has often done little to mollify such concerns.[217] Further, and consistently with the Brexit era's apparently prevailing tendency towards Euro-scepticism, the ECHR roots of the HRA – rather than its enforcement by domestic courts – provide a susceptible target for critics. For the

---

[211] House of Lords European Union Committee, *The UK, the EU and a British Bill of Rights* (HL139), 9 May 2016, [168].

[212] Belfast Good Friday Agreement (10 April 1998), s. 6 (available at: https://www.gov.uk/government/uploads/system/uploads/attachment_data/file/136652/agreement.pdf). And see: M.H. Murphy, 'Repealing the Human Rights Act: Implications for the Belfast Agreement' (2015) 26 KLJ 335.

[213] House of Lords European Union Committee, *The UK, the EU and a British Bill of Rights* (HL139), 9 May 2016, [180].

[214] Ibid., [146]–[183].

[215] On which see Ch. 4.

[216] See generally: K. D. Ewing, 'The Futility of the Human Rights Act' [2004] PL 829; A. Tomkins, 'The Role of Courts in the Political Constitution' (2010) 60 *University of Toronto Law Journal* 1.

[217] See for instance: R. Ekins, *The Dynamics of Judicial Power in the New British Constitution* (Policy Exchange, 2017) (available at: http://judicialpowerproject.org.uk/wp-content/uploads/2017/02/Ekins-text-final.pdf).

Conservatives, the 'mission creep' evidenced in the European Court of Human Rights living instrument doctrine is increasingly perceived as an unjustifiable encroachment upon national sovereignty.[218] Even Jack Straw, who as Labour Home Secretary had piloted the HRA into law, could only mount a qualified defence of the measure when Parliament debated judgments under the ECHR which required the UK to end its absolute ban on prisoners exercising the right to vote:

> [T]he tension and conflict that we have to resolve today can in no sense be laid at the door of the Human Rights Act or, in my judgment, at that of the plain text of the Convention . . . Rather, the problem has arisen because of the judicial activism of the Court in Strasbourg . . .[219]

Here Straw brings us face-to-face with an important factor shaping the role of human rights within the UK Constitution, the guiding hand of the European Court of Human Rights. In the first instance, the Convention jurisprudence has provided 'real normative force'[220] to the HRA's otherwise relatively weak scheme of judicial review. Secondly, if the domestic authorities have not provided adequate protection for human rights concerns in their decisions, the European Court fulfils the role of a 'back stop', a last line of defence protecting the rights enshrined in the ECHR. In the HRA era, the Strasbourg Court has continued to play this role, upholding a higher standard of rights protection than UK national authorities would have done in a number of important decisions.[221] In the first edition of this text, we were able to claim that 'no matter the degree of rights scepticism in the UK media, or amongst UK politicians, there appears to be little serious appetite amongst the mainstream parties for complete withdrawal from the ECHR'. Given that in the run-up to the 2016 Brexit referendum Theresa May openly advocated withdrawal from the Convention system[222] (and that subsequent reports have indicated such a course as a potential future Conservative manifesto commitment[223]) the UK's long-term membership of the ECHR system did not appear to be completely secure. But the 2017 general election has left the Conservatives without the necessary political weight to pilot controversial measures through Parliament. As a result, the place of the HRA within the UK's constitutional firmament – and of the UK within the ECHR regime – would appear to be secure for the time being.

---

[218] See: 'The Conservative Party, Protecting Human Rights in the United Kingdom – The Conservatives' Proposals for Changing Britain's Human Rights Laws' (October 2014), available at: https://www.google.co.uk/url?sa=t&rct=j&q=&esrc=s&source=web&cd=3&ved=0ahUKEwiEjOWO3rvYAhVMJVAKH-caCCCwQFggxMAI&url=https%3A%2F%2Fwww.conservatives.com%2F~%2Fmedia%2Ffiles%2Fdownload-able%2520files%2Fhuman_rights.pdf&usg=AOvVaw0-swi17xHJ3AONxoBU2K49.

[219] HC Debs, vol. 523, cols 501–2 (10 February 2011).

[220] M. Elliott, 'After Brighton: Between a Rock and a Hard Place' [2012] PL 619, 621.

[221] See for instance: *Gillan* v *United Kingdom* (2010) 50 EHRR 45; *S and Marper* v *United Kingdom* (2008) 48 EHRR 1169; *A* v *United Kingdom* (2009) 49 EHRR 29.

[222] 'UK must leave the European Convention on Human Rights, says Theresa May', *Guardian*, 25 April 2016.

[223] 'Theresa May to fight 2020 election on plans to take Britain out of the European Convention on Human Rights', *The Telegraph*, 28 December 2016.

Practice questions

1. *'Human rights is a cause that runs deep in the British heart and long in British history.'*

   (David Cameron, MP, 'Speech on the European Court of Human Rights', *Guardian* (25 January 2012))

   To what extent and in what ways does the HRA 1998 constitute a clean break from earlier efforts to protect 'civil liberties' under the UK Constitution?

2. *'[I]f you were to take away the Human Rights Act now, all that jurisprudence is there . . . and the right of individual petition will be there. And we will still have to recognise that if we take a decision which is contrary to the Human Rights Convention, somebody is going to complain to Strasbourg and that may cause trouble for the UK. So it's very difficult to see how simply wiping out the Human Rights Act is really going to change anything until we withdraw from the convention – which, personally, I don't think is conceivable.'*

   (Lord Hope, reported in J. Rozenberg, 'Are Supreme Court justices More Assertive Than They Were as Law Lords?', *Law Society Gazette* (5 August 2010))

   To what extent do you agree with Lord Hope?

3. Given that the HRA scheme seemingly contemplates legislative and governmental inaction in the face of a declaration of incompatibility, how can the Supreme Court's failure to issue such a declaration in Nicklinson be rationalised?

4. *'Political constitutionalists privilege political forms and institutions of accountability; legal constitutionalists privilege legal forms and institutions of accountability.'*

   (A. Tomkins, 'The Role of the Courts in the Political Constitution' (2010) 60 UTLJ 1, 2)

   Evaluate whether the HRA 1998 has extinguished political constitutionalism in favour of legal constitutionalism.

Further reading

In conducting further reading on the HRA 1998, readers may wish to consider the extent to which the HRA has impacted upon institutional relationships within the constitution, particularly those between judges and politicians. **Aileen Kavanagh's** article, **'The Elusive Divide between Interpretation and Legislation under the HRA 1998'** (2004) 24 *Oxford Journal of Legal Studies* 259–85, focuses on the limits of the judicial role under the interpretive duty contained within s. 3 of the HRA and the factors which tip interpretation, required under the Act, into 'legislation', which would amount to a judicial usurpation of Parliament's function. Kavanagh's work – including her excellent monograph, **Constitutional Review under the UK Human Rights Act** (CUP, 2009) – should be regarded as required reading to understand the relationship between when the use of s. 3 is appropriate and when the courts should issue a declaration of incompatibility under s. 4. Partly written as a response to Kavanagh, Danny Nicol's article (**D. Nicol, 'Law and Politics after the Human Rights Act'** [2006] *Public Law* 722) is not focused solely on the HRA, but on what he regards as the changed relationship between the courts and the 'political' branches of government in recent decades. The HRA, however, is a key driver behind this changed role, and this article examines how the judges, once the sole arbiters of lawfulness, have been drawn into issuing politically contestable remedies under this Act.

Beyond the interpretative/legislative divide, a number of other thorny issues – such as the relationship between the UK courts and Strasbourg and the definition of public bodies under the HRA – have spawned significant bodies of scholarship. In regard to the former issue, Philip Sales (**P. Sales, 'Strasbourg Jurisprudence and the Human Rights Act: a Response to Lord Irvine'** [2012] *Public Law* 253–67) makes the case for continuing to regard the 'mirror principle' as the basis for the interaction between the UK's domestic courts and Strasbourg jurisprudence. Given that the avowed intention behind the HRA was to tie the UK's domestic legal systems more closely into the Strasbourg system of rights protection, Sales considers the process of mirroring Strasbourg to be justified. This article also features a useful overview of Lord Irvine's contrary contention that the UK courts should play a more active role in developing an indigenous approach to ECHR rights. **Roger Masterman's, *Supreme, Submissive or Symbiotic? UK Courts and the European Court of Human Rights*** (Constitution Unit, 2015) provides an overview of the developing approach to the interpretation and application of the Strasbourg jurisprudence under the HRA in the light of the potential implementation of a UK Bill of Rights.

In considering what amounts to a public authority under the HRA, numerous works are available to the reader. Building upon the debate as to whether the HRA's reach is vertical or horizontal (between the individual and the state or extending to cases between private bodies), Alex Williams (**A. Williams, 'A Fresh Perspective on Hybrid Public Authorities under the Human Rights Act 1998: private contractors, rights-stripping and "chameleonic" horizontal effect'** [2011] *Public Law* 139–63) examines the impact of this debate on 'hybrid' public bodies. He concludes that such bodies are neither private nor public in nature, but 'chameleons' which change their status according to whether they are claiming rights protections or facing claims that they have breached rights. Finally, in considering the manner in which the courts police the decisions of public authorities, David Mead (**D. Mead, 'Outcomes Aren't All: Defending Process-Based Review of Public Authority Decisions under the Human Rights Act'** [2012] *Public Law* 61–84) contrasts the outcomes-driven approach to proportionality in cases where public authorities have been accused of failing to fulfil their s. 6 obligation with the process-driven focus of other aspects of public law. Whilst judicial review's expansion was long driven by a desire amongst judges to improve the quality of decision-making processes, he concludes that the courts' refusal to consider the adequacy of the rights-reasoning in public authority decision-making weakens the degree to which human rights values are inculcated within such bodies.

For those interested in placing the HRA in a comparative context, the work of **Stephen Gardbaum** examines the HRA in the context of other systems of rights protection, grouping it alongside the Canadian Charter and the New Zealand Bill of Rights Act as adhering to the 'commonwealth model' of reconciling political and legal authority on questions of rights. His article, **'How Successful and Distinctive is the Human Rights Act? An Expatriate Comparatist's Assessment'** (2011) 74 *Modern Law Review* 195–215 provides an accessible way into his work, with **The New Commonwealth Model of Constitutionalism: Theory and Practice** (CUP, 2013) providing a fuller account.

Chapter 22
Political freedoms and democratic participation

'. . . there has always arisen the problem of maintaining a balance between, on the one hand, the necessity of maintaining public order and, on the other, the need to preserve and protect the classic civil liberties of the subject: the right to freedom of speech and of lawful protest, the right of public assembly and of procession, all the hallmarks of a democratic society.'

Lord Elwyn-Jones (HL Debates, Vol. 481, Col. 749, 29 October 1986).

Chapter outline

This chapter introduces those rights and freedoms that are considered core to the democratic process. Those freedoms (including those often labelled 'civil liberties') ensure that individuals are able to circulate and obtain information freely, are able to participate in the election of representatives (and governments) and are able to peacefully – and collectively – make public demonstrations of political viewpoints without incurring criminal sanctions. In turn this chapter will therefore consider freedom of expression, freedom of assembly, the liberty and security of the person, and the right to vote.

Introduction

Certain core rights and liberties are 'inextricably bound up with representative government'.[1] These rights can provide a basis for the composition of elected government (the right to vote), facilitate membership of political parties or groupings (freedom of association), enable participation in debate (freedom of expression) and permit unimpeded peaceful political action (the freedom of assembly and the liberty and security of the person). This chapter sketches a number of those rights and freedoms – often collectively referred to as 'civil liberties' – that are regarded as being integral to the political process, as well as providing illustrations of their operation and of the extent to which they might yield in the face of collective (broader societal) interests. Civil liberties have a long – and occasionally chequered[2] – history within the common law, with many prominent judicial

---

[1] C. A. Gearty, *Civil Liberties* (OUP, 2007) p. 3.
[2] C. A. Gearty and K. D. Ewing, *The Struggle for Civil Liberties: Political Freedom and the Rule of Law in Britain, 1914–1945* (OUP, 2000).

decisions providing support for the notion that individuals should enjoy freedom to act without state interference provided that their conduct was not otherwise unlawful.[3] As we saw however in Chapter 20, this liberty was residual. For Dicey, writing in the late nineteenth and early twentieth century, '[t]he security . . . for personal freedom does not really depend upon or originate in any general proposition contained in any written document'.[4] Such civil liberties were later conceptualised in the common law as 'an immunity from interference by others',[5] and indeed narrowed over time as statutes extended the powers through which the government and its officials might exercise coercive influence over individuals.[6]

The protection of liberties via the common law was hampered by two specific aspects of the UK's constitutional culture:

> The first is a matter of law – the principle of parliamentary sovereignty. Any legislation can override rights recognised and protected by the common law. The second is a matter of technique and attitude. By and large the common law courts have not reasoned from the premise of specific rights. Our boast, that we are free to do anything not prohibited by law, and that official action against our will must have the support of law, reflects the fact that our rights are residual – what is left after the law (and in particular, legislation) is exhausted. Our thinking does not proceed from rights to results – rather, our rights are the result.[7]

The latter point in particular – the suggestion that '*legal* rights were derivative not foundational'[8] – is consistent with notions of a political constitution in which rights are conceived of not as overriding imperatives, but as claims – potentially in competition with counter-claims – made by political actors. In the absence of a written constitution, or Bill of Rights, such rights or liberties as were recognised by Parliament or the courts were inevitably both fluid and susceptible to erosion. Though the common law's protection for those freedoms which are essential to effective participation in the political process is now bolstered by the (broader) positive protections afforded by the Human Rights Act 1998 (as well as potentially by the willingness of the courts to deploy the principle of legality in defence of constitutional rights recognised by the common law[9]) the heritage of civil liberties protection via the courts continues to shape political freedom within the UK Constitution. This chapter does not attempt a comprehensive review of the rights to expression, to association, to liberty and to vote as they operate in the UK Constitution today. Instead it explains why these rights have particular constitutional importance by illustrating some of the most important linkages between them and the democratic process.

---

[3] For instance: *Beatty* v *Gillbanks* (1882) 9 QBD 308.

[4] A. V. Dicey, *Introduction to the Study of the Law of the Constitution* (8th edn, Liberty Fund, 1982) p. 123.

[5] *Wheeler* v *Leicester City Council* [1985] AC 1054, 1065 (Lord Browne-Wilkinson).

[6] For a sample of the literature examining the consequences of this expansion of governmental powers see: K. D. Ewing and C. A. Gearty, *Freedom under Thatcher: Civil Liberties in Modern Britain* (OUP, 1990); G. Robertson, *Freedom, The Individual and the Law* (7th edn, Penguin, 1993); K. D. Ewing, *The Bonfire of the Liberties: New Labour, Human Rights and the Rule of Law* (OUP, 2010).

[7] J. Doyle and B. Wells, 'How far can the Common Law go towards Protecting Human Rights?' in P. Alston (ed), *Promoting Human Rights Through Bills of Rights* (OUP, 1999) p. 17.

[8] A. McHarg, 'Rights and Democracy in UK Public Law' in M. Elliott and D. Feldman (eds), *The Cambridge Companion to Public Law* (CUP, 2015), p. 118.

[9] See pp. 155–8.

Thinking Point . . .

For J. A. G. Griffith ('The Political Constitution' (1979) 42 MLR 1, 17), 'it is misleading to speak of certain rights of the individual, as being fundamental in character and inherent in the person of the individual. As an individual I make claims on the authorities who control the society in which I live. If I am strong enough – and I shall have to join with others to be so – my claim may be recognised within certain limits. It may even be given legal status.'

Freedom of expression

Key issues

- Freedom of expression is essential to democratic participation; without the ability to exchange ideas and information it is impossible for individuals to make meaningful decisions in a democratic process.

- This means that in a liberal democracy freedom of expression is particularly important in the context of political expression. Protections for freedom of expression have varied over time within the UK Constitution, but at times the weight attributed to these concerns in law has not matched its importance as a foundation stone for democracy.

- Even today, under the Human Rights Act 1998 (and through it Article 10 of the ECHR), freedom of expression remains a qualified right. Even where political expression is at issue the authorities are able to curtail the exercise of this right in responding to countervailing societal interests.

The contours of free expression

Freedom of expression is essential to the maintenance of a democratic system,[10] and to the ability of actors within that system – whether they be politicians or members of the electorate – to effectively participate. As such, the authors of one of the leading texts on the law of the European Convention on Human Rights have noted that the 'marked importance attached to [freedom of expression] is readily explicable by its close linkage to democracy's political process and its role as an indispensible vehicle for minorities, political opponents, and civil society to foster public debates.'[11] The right to free expression supports democratic government in two core ways: (i) as an enabler of informed participation in government and the processes of selecting a government and (ii) as providing the flow of information through which governmental accountability can be secured.[12] On the basis that is essentially one of the pillars on which democratic government rests, freedom of

---

[10] See: S. Kentridge, 'Freedom of Speech: Is it the primary right?' (1996) 45 ICLQ 253.

[11] D. J. Harris, M. O'Boyle, E. P. Bates and C. M. Buckley, *Law of the European Convention on Human Rights* (3rd edn, OUP, 2014) p. 613.

[12] Broader arguments for freedom of expression also concern the quest for truth – see expressive rights as being inherent in an individual's ability to develop in E. Barendt, *Freedom of Speech* (2nd edn, OUP, 2005) ch. 1.

expression is 'invariably' guaranteed and protected against state intrusion by constitutional instruments and bills of rights across the world.[13]

Despite lacking a written constitution or a constitutional Bill of Rights, the fundamental importance of freedom of expression is also recognised in the UK. As Lord Steyn outlined in the decision *R* v *Secretary of State for the Home Department, ex parte Simms*:

> [F]reedom of speech is the lifeblood of democracy. The free flow of information and ideas informs political debate. It is a safety valve: people are more ready to accept decisions that go against them if they can in principle seek to influence them. It acts as a brake on the abuse of power by public officials. It facilitates the exposure of errors in the governance and administration of justice of the country . . . [14]

The linkage between expression and the democratic process was made plain by Lord Bingham, in the decision of the House of Lords in *R* v *Shayler*, which is worth quoting at length:

> Modern democratic government means government of the people by the people for the people. But there can be no government by the people if they are ignorant of the issues to be resolved, the arguments for and against different solutions and the facts underlying those arguments. The business of government is not an activity about which only those professionally engaged are entitled to receive information and express opinions. It is, or should be, a participatory process. But there can be no assurance that government is carried out for the people unless the facts are made known, the issues publicly ventilated. Sometimes, inevitably, those involved in the conduct of government, as in any other walk of life, are guilty of error, incompetence, misbehaviour, dereliction of duty, even dishonesty and malpractice. Those concerned may very strongly wish that the facts relating to such matters are not made public. Publicity may reflect discredit on them or their predecessors. It may embarrass the authorities. It may impede the process of administration. Experience however shows, in this country and elsewhere, that publicity is a powerful disinfectant. Where abuses are exposed, they can be remedied. Even where abuses have already been remedied, the public may be entitled to know that they occurred. The role of the press in exposing abuses and miscarriages of justice has been a potent and honourable one. But the press cannot expose that of which it is denied knowledge.[15]

Common law protections for freedom of expression include a bar on political parties,[16] or institutions of central or local government,[17] bringing actions in defamation, and 'public interest' defences have been operable as responses to actions in defamation[18] and breach of confidence.[19] Statute law has also afforded support for openness in government and freedom of expression. As we have already seen, the Freedom of Information Act 2000 has become a powerful tool through which the press can extract information from government.[20] Similarly, s. 10 of the Contempt of Court Act 1981 protects journalists from being required to disclose their sources, while the Public Interest Disclosure Act 1998

---

[13] Ibid., p.1.

[14] *R* v *Secretary of State for the Home Department, ex parte Simms* [2000] 2 AC 115, 126 (Lord Steyn). See also: *Attorney-General* v *Guardian Newspapers Ltd* [1987] 1 WLR 1248, 1286.

[15] *R* v *Shayler* [2002] UKHL 11; [2003] 1 AC 247, [21].

[16] *Goldsmith* v *Bhoyrul* [1998] QB 489.

[17] *Derbyshire Council Council* v *Times Newspapers* [1993] AC 534.

[18] *Reynolds* v *Times Newspapers* [2001] 2 AC 127 (and see now Defamation Act 2013, s. 4).

[19] *Lion Laboratories* v *Evans* [1985] QB 526.

[20] Chapter 17. See also P. Leyland, 'Freedom of Information and the 2009 Parliamentary Expenses Scandal' [2009] PL 675.

offers protection to 'whistleblowers' who reveal detail of dangerous or illegal practices on the part of their employers. Parliamentary speech in particular has long attracted special protections.

Key debates

Speech in Parliament

Freedom of speech in parliamentary proceedings is recognised – and protected – by Article IX of the Bill of Rights 1689 which provides that 'the freedom of speech and debates or proceedings in Parliament ought not to be impeached or questioned in any court or place out of Parliament'. As a result – and in the words of *Erskine May* – 'a Member may state whatever he thinks fit in debate, however offensive it may be to the feelings, or injurious to the character, of individuals; and he is protected by parliamentary privilege from any action in defamation, as well as from any other question or molestation' (*Erskine May's Treatise on the Law, Privileges, Proceedings and Usage of Parliament* (24th edn, LexisNexis, 2011) p. 222). MPs' and peers' speech is therefore privileged; it is held to be of fundamental importance to the maintenance of full and frank debate and in turn therefore the effective functioning of the legislature. As the 1999 report of the Joint Committee on Parliamentary Privilege found, 'without this protection members would be handicapped in performing their parliamentary duties, and the authority of Parliament itself in confronting the executive and as a forum for expressing the anxieties of citizens would be correspondingly diminished (Joint Committee on Parliamentary Privilege, *Parliamentary Privilege: First Report* (1999) HL43-I/HC214-I, [3])'. While the Bill of Rights may protect against externally imposed sanctions resulting from things said in the course of parliamentary business, the Speaker may nonetheless ask a member to withdraw 'unparliamentary language'.

Numerous examples can nonetheless be found of legislative and other restrictions on expression in the UK. The exercise of expressive rights has given rise to sanctions where, for instance, it has been defamatory, given rise to a breach of confidentiality, or amounted to a contempt of court. In each instance, the right to freedom of expression is essentially pitched against the countervailing objective in, respectively, protecting the reputation of individuals[21] or companies,[22] protecting against the disclosure of information revealed in confidence,[23] and avoiding interference with the course of justice in particular legal proceedings.[24] Similarly, expression which could incite racial hatred[25] or encourage terrorism[26] may give rise to criminal sanctions on the basis that it is damaging to public order and safety.

Perhaps the most notorious examples of the legislative limitation of free expression can be found in the Official Secrets Acts which – as we have already touched on[27] – did

---

[21] e.g. *Sim* v *Stretch* [1936] 2 All ER 1237.
[22] e.g. *South Hetton Coal Co.* v *North Eastern News Association Ltd* [1894] 1 QB 133.
[23] e.g. *Lion Laboratories* v *Evans* [1985] QB 526.
[24] See the Contempt of Court Act 1981.
[25] Public Order Act 1986, Part III.
[26] Terrorism Act 2006, s. 1.
[27] See p. 435.

much to emphasise that much of the business of government in the UK was not for public consumption. The breadth of the offence under s. 2 of the Official Secrets Act 1911 was particularly problematic. It was an offence punishable by up to two years' imprisonment if:

> *any* person having . . . *any* document or information . . . entrusted in confidence to him by any person holding office under Her Majesty . . . communicates the . . . document or information to *any* person, other than a person to whom he is authorised to communicate it or a person to whom it is in the interests of the State his duty to communicate it.[28]

Though s. 2 of the 1911 Act was repealed by the Official Secrets Act 1989,[29] subsequent governments have sought to resist, or limit, disclosure of information – and therefore to restrict freedom of expression – via a number of other means. Breach of confidence provided the cause of action by which the government (unsuccessfully) sought to prevent publication of the diaries of the former Cabinet Minister Richard Crossman in *Attorney-General* v *Jonathan Cape*.[30] An action in breach of confidence was similarly integral to the *Spycatcher* saga, which saw the UK Government (again, ultimately unsuccessfully) pursue legal actions in Australia, Ireland and the UK in order to prevent publication of a book written by a former MI5 official that contained various revelations about the activities of the British Security Services.[31]

The decision of the House of Lords in *Brind* well illustrates the limitations of the pre-HRA common law protections for expression in the face of legislative or executive incursion. As well as being the leading case on the pre-HRA status of the Convention rights in domestic law,[32] the circumstances underpinning *Brind* are also illustrative of the ability of government to subtly influence the communication of political messages:

Key case

R v *Secretary of State for the Home Department, ex parte Brind* [1991] 1 AC 696; [1991] 4 All ER 720

A challenge by way of judicial review was brought by members of the National Union of Journalists against directives issued by the Home Secretary (under the Broadcasting Act 1981) requiring broadcasters not to transmit 'any matter' containing words spoken by members of various proscribed organisations who were either engaged in, or supportive of, terrorist activity (the organisations concerned were those which had been proscribed under the Prevention of Terrorism (Temporary Provisions) Act 1984 and the Northern Ireland (Emergency

---

→

[28] Emphasis added.

[29] On which see: S. Palmer, 'Tightening Secrecy Law: The Official Secrets Act 1989' [1990] PL 243.

[30] *Attorney-General* v *Jonathan Cape* [1976] QB 572 (although the government lost this case, the willingness of the court to extend the breach of confidence action beyond personal confidences paved the way for its deployment in the later *Spycatcher* decisions).

[31] See – for the most relevant decisions of the House of Lords – *Attorney-General* v *Guardian Newspapers Ltd* [1987] 1 WLR 1248; *Attorney-General* v *Observer Ltd* [1990] 1 AC 109. An accessible summary of the *Spycatcher* affair can be found in K. D. Ewing and C. A. Gearty, *Freedom under Thatcher: Civil Liberties in Modern Britain* (OUP, 1990) pp. 152–69.

[32] See p. 650.

→
Provisions) Act 1978 – including the Irish Republican Army and the Ulster Volunteer Force – but also included the non-proscribed political groups Sinn Fein, Republican Sinn Fein and the Ulster Defence Association). The directives did not allow the transmission of the actual words spoken by the members of the relevant organisations – but did allow a verbatim transcript to be read by an actor over pictures of the actual speaker. Denying representatives of the affected organisations direct access to the broadcast press would, the then Home Secretary argued, deprive them of the 'support and sustenance' that can be derived from free access to broadcast media.

The applicant journalists contended that the directives were *ultra vires* on the ground that they disproportionately infringed Article 10 of the European Convention on Human Rights (the right of freedom of expression). Their application was dismissed by the High Court, and Court of Appeal. On appeal to the House of Lords it was held that to require an executive discretion to be exercised in accordance with the European Convention on Human Rights would have the effect of importing the Convention into the domestic law of judicial review without the authority of Parliament. As such, it would have the effect of 'incorporating the Convention into English domestic law by the back door' (Lord Ackner, p. 762) and would be, in the words of Lord Bridge, a 'judicial usurpation of the legislative function' (at p. 748).

Brind is best known for providing the definitive pre-HRA statement on the status of the (then) unincorporated ECHR rights in domestic law. The circumstances giving rise to the case also illustrate that governments can subtly influence the deployment of expressive rights via means that fall short of fully restraining expression. As Brian Thompson argued, the Home Secretary's directives '. . . affect[ed] the freedom of expression of people who belong to, or are supporters of, lawful organisations as well as members of proscribed organisations. It should not be thought that the ban affect[ed] only members of the specified organisations, or the broadcasters. It also affect[ed] the citizens of the United Kingdom, because it interfere[d] with their freedom to be informed directly by participants in events in Northern Ireland' (B. Thompson, 'Broadcasting and Terrorism' [1989] PL 527, 539).

Though freedom of expression was acknowledged as a 'constitutional right with attendant high normative force' prior to the enactment of the Human Rights Act 1998,[33] it was undoubtedly vulnerable to both legislative and executive incursion. It is the Human Rights Act that now provides the core means by which freedom of expression is legally recognised in the UK Constitution. Article 10 of the ECHR – given effect via s. 1(1) of the Human Rights Act 1998 – provides:

> Everyone has the right to freedom of expression. This right shall include freedom to hold opinions and to receive and impart information and ideas without interference by public authority and regardless of frontiers . . .

The influence of Article 10 via ss. 3, 4 and 6 of the HRA[34] is also apparently bolstered by a specific provision in the HRA – s. 12 – which requires that a court, when considering granting relief which might interfere with freedom of expression, have 'particular regard

---

[33] *McCartan Turkington Breen* v *Times Newspapers Ltd* [2001] 2 AC 277, 297 (Lord Steyn). For commentary, see E. Barendt, *Freedom of Speech* (2nd edn, OUP, 2005) pp. 40–2. See also now: *Kennedy* v *Information Commissioner* [2014] UKSC 20; [2015] AC 455, [46].

[34] For a survey see H. Fenwick and G. Phillipson, *Media Freedom under the Human Rights Act* (OUP, 2006) ch. 3.

to the importance' of that right. As we saw above,[35] though, it stands as an important marker as to the value of expression – and to the extent to which those seeking to stymie the development of judicially-developed privacy protections were able to influence the legislative process – section 12 has *not* in practice seen Article 10 concerns routinely elevated above those protected by other Convention rights.[36]

In common with domestic courts, the European Court of Human Rights has also acknowledged freedom of expression as being foundational to a democratic society and 'one of the basic conditions for its progress'.[37] Free expression is therefore integral to the ability of electors to make decisions about government and governance on the basis – it is to be hoped – of accurate and openly available information relating to politicians' and political parties' policies and positions. Recognising this, the case law of the European Court of Human Rights has stressed the importance of expression (and of a free press) to the political process, noting that 'freedom of political debate is at the very core of the concept of a democratic society which prevails throughout the Convention'.[38] As a result, the European Court of Human Rights has accorded a priority to *political* expression that is not necessarily reflected in its jurisprudence concerning challenged limitations on artistic, commercial or other forms of expression.[39]

Thinking Point . . .

Alinak v Turkey (Application no. 40287/98 [2005]) saw the Strasbourg Court explain the importance of artistic expression (at [42]): 'Article 10 includes freedom of artistic expression – notably within freedom to receive and impart information and ideas – which affords the opportunity to take part in the public exchange of cultural, political and social information and ideas of all kinds . . . Those who create, perform, distribute or exhibit works of art contribute to the exchange of ideas and opinions which is essential for a democratic society. Hence there is an obligation on the State not to encroach unduly on the author's freedom of expression.'

In spite of the lofty claim by the Strasbourg Court that the protections afforded to expression should extend to information and ideas which might 'offend, shock or disturb'[40] it is apparent that the courts regard some expression as contributing little to the life of a democratic society. As Baroness Hale recognised in *Campbell* v *Mirror Group Newspapers* – in the context of a (successful) privacy claim made by the model Naomi Campbell – '[t]he political and social life of the community, and the intellectual, artistic or personal development of individuals, are not obviously assisted by pouring over the intimate details of a fashion model's private life.'[41]

---

[35] See p. 660.
[36] *Douglas* v *Hello! Ltd* [2000] EWCA Civ 353; [2001] QB 967, [137] (Sedley LJ).
[37] *Lingens* v *Austria* (1986) 8 EHRR 407, [41].
[38] Ibid., [42]; *Oberschlick* v *Austria* (1995) 19 EHRR 389, [58].
[39] *Casado Coca* v *Spain* (1994) 18 EHRR 1.
[40] *Handyside* v *United Kingdom* (1979–1980) 1 EHRR 737, [49]; *Lingens* v *Austria* (1986) 8 EHRR 407, [41].
[41] *Campbell* v *Mirror Group Newspapers Ltd* [2004] UKHL 22; [2004] 2 AC 457, [149].

Thinking Point . . .

Freedom of expression is valued in a democracy as the basis upon which members of the electorate might make informed choices about the future leadership and political direction of their communities. The making of informed political choices is, to some extent at least, dependent on the availability of reliable information on which judgments might be based. While a degree of information management – or 'spin' – is of course a common tool of political campaigning, the questionable veracity of much of the campaigning material circulated in the run-up to the June 2016 referendum on the UK's membership of the EU provided considerable cause for concern. (See 'Both Remain and Leave are Propagating Falsehoods at Public Expense', *The Telegraph* (14 June 2016)).

Limiting expression

Article 10(2) ECHR provides the following, detailed, illustration of how the right to freedom of expression might be legitimately restricted in the pursuance of similar objectives:

> The exercise of these freedoms . . . may be subject to such formalities, conditions, restrictions or penalties as are prescribed by law and are necessary in a democratic society, in the interests of national security, territorial integrity or public safety, for the prevention of disorder or crime, for the protection of health or morals, for the protection of the reputation or rights of others, for preventing the disclosure of information received in confidence, or for maintaining the authority and impartiality of the judiciary.

Thinking Point . . .

The First Amendment to the United States' Constitution does *not* make explicit the grounds on which free speech might be limited, instead simply stating that 'Congress shall make no law . . . abridging the freedom of speech, or of the press'. The right to freedom of speech cannot, however, be regarded as being as absolute as the text of the Bill of Rights would suggest. As Holmes J observed in the Supreme Court decision in *Schenck* v *United States* (1919) 249 US 47, 52:

> The most stringent protection of free speech would not protect a man in falsely shouting fire in a theatre and causing a panic . . . The question in every case is whether the words used are used in such circumstances and are of such a nature as to create a clear and present danger that they will bring about the substantive evils that Congress has a right to prevent.

The range of grounds on which expression might be legitimately limited under Article 10(2) is undoubtedly broad. As a counter-balance, given the importance that attaches to freedom of expression, the European Court of Human Rights has held that – not only should any limitation be proportionate to the legitimate aim pursued but – exceptions to the right should be restrictively construed, and the necessity of any purported restriction convincingly established.[42] Nonetheless, freedom of political expression may still be restricted in practice, even in circumstances in which a compelling case for maintaining political expression exists. One pertinent illustration can be found in the ***ProLife Alliance*** case.

---

[42] *Vereinigung Demokratischer Soldaten Österreichs and Gubi* v *Austria* (1994) 20 EHRR 56, [37]; *Mouvement Raëlien Suisse* v *Switzerland* (2013) 56 EHRR 14, [48].

The ProLife Alliance was a political party, entitled – on account of the number of candidates it was supporting – to a political broadcast to be transmitted, in Wales, in the run-up to the 2001 UK general election. As its name suggests, the ProLife Alliance was an anti-abortion movement. The BBC however, declined to transmit the ProLife Alliance's election broadcast – which included graphic images of aborted foetuses – on taste and decency grounds (relying on the terms of the Broadcasting Act 1990 and the BBC Agreement). Given the emphasis which free speech theory places on the importance of making informed political choices, and the proximity to an important national election, Laws LJ – giving the lead judgment in the Court of Appeal – began by noting that '[i]t is difficult to think of a context in which the claims of free expression are more pressing.'[43] The Court of Appeal duly found in favour of the ProLife Alliance, with Laws LJ finding that the BBC's approach amounted to 'censorship' inconsistent with the requirements of Article 10 ECHR and indicating that 'considerations of taste and decency cannot prevail over free speech by a political party at election time save wholly exceptionally.'[44]

On appeal to the House of Lords, the Court of Appeal's decision was overturned by a majority of 4:1. Instead of focusing – as the Court of Appeal had done – on a Human Rights Act-driven assessment of the proportionality of the limitation placed on the ProLife Alliance's freedom of expression, the House of Lords asked (i) whether Parliament was entitled to require broadcasters to adhere to standards of taste and decency? And if so (ii) whether those standards had been properly applied in the context of the case? The majority answered both questions in the affirmative. The speech of Lord Hoffmann (in the majority) is illustrative of two important points: first, that – even in the light of the implementation of the Human Rights Act – it remains possible to conceive of free expression in negative, rather than positive, terms ('the primary right protected by Article 10 is the right of every citizen not to be prevented from expressing his opinions'[45]); second, that even a credible claim as to the importance of political speech might be undermined by 'deference' to the determination of a primary decision maker.[46]

Freedom of expression has – so far in this chapter – been portrayed as being constructive, or facilitative, of democratic government. It is clear however, that some speech may be inimical to, and therefore damaging, of the democratic process. Speech which runs contrary to the Convention's 'underlying values' – which threatens the democratic order on which the Convention rests[47] – has duly been held to fall outside of the scope of protection afforded by Article 10. On such a basis, for instance, extreme forms of speech including holocaust denial[48] and incitement to racial[49] and/or religious[50] hatred have been found to not benefit from Article 10 protection. The European Court of Human Rights has also determined that limitations on less extreme political expression may be Convention-compliant only if proportionate to the legitimate aim pursued:

---

[43] *R (ProLife Alliance)* v *British Broadcasting Corporation* [2002] EWCA Civ 297; [2002] 3 WLR 1080, [1].
[44] Ibid., [44].
[45] *R (ProLife Alliance)* v *British Broadcasting Corporation* [2003] UKHL 23; [2004] 1 AC 185, [55] (emphasis in the original).
[46] See for discussion: A. Macdonald, '*R (on the application of ProLife Alliance)* v *British Broadcasting Corporation* [2013] EHRLR 651; J. Jowell, 'Judicial Deference: Servility, Civility or Institutional Capacity?' [2003] PL 592.
[47] *Communist Party of Germany* v *Federal Republic of Germany*, Application No. 250/57 (1957).
[48] *Marais* v *France*, Application No. 31159/96 (1996).
[49] *Glimmerveen and Hagenbeek* v *The Netherlands* (1982) 4 EHRR 260.
[50] *Pavel Ivanov* v *Russia*, Application No. 35222/04 (2007); *Norwood* v *United Kingdom* (2005) 40 EHRR SE11.

[T]olerance and respect for the equal dignity of all human beings constitute the foundations of a democratic, pluralistic society. That being so, as a matter of principle it may be considered necessary in certain democratic societies to sanction or even prevent all forms of expression which spread, incite, promote or justify hatred based on intolerance . . . provided that any 'formalities', 'conditions', 'restrictions' or 'penalties' imposed are proportionate to the legitimate aim pursued.[51]

The UK's ban on the broadcasting of political advertisements provides a study in point:

Key debates

Limiting political expression in defence of democracy? The Communications Act 2003

Section 321(2) of the Communications Act 2003 prohibits the broadcast of political advertisements (on both television and radio) in the UK. The provision reads as follows:

> For the purposes of section 319(2)(g) [under which the role of the relevant regulator – OFCOM – is outlined] an advertisement contravenes the prohibition on political advertising if it is — (a) an advertisement which is inserted on or behalf of a body whose objects are wholly or mainly of a political nature; (b) an advertisement which is directed towards a political end; or (c) an advertisement which has a connection with an industrial dispute.

Given that – upon its introduction into Parliament – the Secretary of State was unable to certify that the Communications Bill was compliant with the rights protected via the Human Rights Act 1998 (the Minister instead making a statement under s. 19(1)(b) of the Act), the Government was alert to the potential for conflict between the provision and the requirements of Article 10 ECHR. As separate arrangements existed for the permissible broadcast of public service information and party political or referendum campaign broadcasts (s. 321(7)), the general ban was enacted in pursuance of the objective of otherwise maintaining a level playing field in relation to the broadcasting of political messages. As Lewis and Cumper ('Balancing Freedom of Political Expression against Equality of Political Opportunity: The Courts and the UK's Broadcasting Ban on Political Advertising' [2009] PL 89, 90–91) have summarised, in the absence of such a prohibition:

> [T]hose organisations willing and/or able to purchase air time will be at a significant advantage in the game of political persuasion as compared to those organisations unwilling and/or unable to afford such expenditure. There will be a tendency for the field of political discourse to be tilted in favour of the wealthiest players, and this will create a risk that equality of opportunity in the democratic process will be undermined.

The Government's doubt as to the Convention-compatibility of s. 321(2)(g) arose as a result of the European Court of Human Rights decision in *VgT Verein gegen Tierfabriken* v *Switzerland* (2001) 34 EHRR 159. In that decision, the European Court found that – in the light of the narrow margin of appreciation applicable in relation to political speech – a comparable ban on political broadcasting amounted to a disproportionate interference with the applicant's ECHR rights.

A challenge was brought against the UK ban, on the basis of its alleged incompatibility with Article 10 ECHR, by Animal Defenders International, a non-profit group opposed to cruelty towards animals. Following a decision not to broadcast an advertisement produced by Animal Defenders International on the basis that it would fall within the s. 321 prohibition, the group brought judicial review proceedings, seeking a declaration that the section was incompatible with Article 10 ECHR, as given effect by the Human Rights Act. The High Court ([2006] EWHC 3069; [2007] EMLR 6) did not provide the remedy sought, but permitted a leap-frog appeal to the House of Lords.

---

[51] *Erbakan* v *Turkey*, Application No. 59405/00 (2006), [56].

In *R (Animal Defenders International)* v *Secretary of State for Culture, Media and Sport* [2008] UKHL 15; [2008] 1 AC 1312 a unanimous House of Lords declined to hold the ban on political advertising to be incompatible with the right to freedom of expression under Article 10. Drawing on the authority of *Murphy* v *Ireland* (2003) 38 EHRR 212 – a decision of the European Court of Human Rights which had found that a limitation on the televisual broadcast of *religious* advertising was Article 10 compliant – Lord Bingham (giving the lead speech) found that the provisions of the 2003 Act did not give rise to an incompatibility. On the basis that the **Murphy** decision pointed towards a lack of a European consensus as to the regulation of politicised advertising, Bingham found that a wider margin of appreciation than that suggested by the **VgT** case would apply. On the basis of this, he was able to place 'great weight' [33] on the determination by Parliament of the 'checks and balances necessary to safeguard, consistently with Article 10, the integrity of [the UK's] democracy' [37].

On a subsequent application to the European Court of Human Rights it was narrowly found – by nine votes to eight – that the Communications Act 2003 did not violate Article 10 (*Animal Defenders International* v *United Kingdom* (2013) 57 EHRR 21). This brief sketch has illustrated that freedom of expression is both foundational to democracy, and in practice susceptible to limitations that may be framed as being both inhibiting to and facilitative of democratic government. That our concern in this chapter has been on 'hard cases' – those cases in which freedom of speech is pitched against some countervailing imperative (for instance the need to protect national security) – is in one sense an indicator of the maturity of the system and the seriousness with which expressive rights are treated. But it should also be recalled that – in practical terms – the realisation of freedom of expression is symbiotic with the prior vindication of other political freedoms. The relationship between free expression and other of the guarantees provided by democratic government is, in reality, somewhat circular; as Conor Gearty has written: 'it is only when other entitlements have been secured, when it is possible to vote and engage in political activity without fear of death, disappearance, torture or incarceration, that the civil libertarian has the time and freedom to be exercised by inhibitions on his or her power of communication.'[52]

Freedom of assembly

Key issues

- Political life is by its very nature communal. In a liberal democracy like-minded individuals can choose to come together in political parties, trade unions or protest movements with the explicit aim of using their collective voice to influence public policy.

- But over centuries of political life in the UK political assemblies have also been raucous affairs with the potential to raise passions both amongst adherents and detractors to a political viewpoint.

- As with the other rights we are considering in this chapter, freedom of association (under Article 11 ECHR) is not only a political right (it covers the broad swathe of humanity's social life), but it is a right which can be particularly valuable (and also particularly controversial) in the context of political participation.

---

[52] C. A. Gearty, *Civil Liberties* (OUP, 2007) p. 122. See also: *Attorney-General* v *Guardian Newspapers Ltd* [1987] 1 WLR 1248, 1286 (Lord Bridge).

Freedom of assembly at common law

Dicey wrote of freedom of assembly – or the right of public meeting – that '[n]o better instance . . . can be found of the way in which in England the constitution is built up upon individual rights than our rules as to public assemblies.'[53] In keeping with the common law's recognition of a space – untouched by the criminal and other laws – within which individuals could lawfully act without hindrance, 'the right of assembling is nothing more than a result of the view taken by the courts as to individual liberty of the person and individual liberty of speech.'[54] Freedom of assembly (which includes meetings held in public and private, as well as processions and marches) provides an important means by which free expression may be exercised,[55] and an important safety valve for the expression of political views that might complement, and potentially compensate for, the relative infrequency of participation in elections. Public protest marches and assemblies (representing both widely-held and minority political viewpoints) have long been a part of political life in the UK and features of – *inter alia* – campaigns for nuclear disarmament (in particular the Women's Peace Camp at Greenham Common 1981–2000), against the so-called Poll Tax (1989–1990), against the Iraq War (2003), against globalisation and capitalism, including the activities of the Occupy movement (2011), and for the UK to remain an EU member state (People's March for Europe, 2017). As the Joint Committee on Human Rights has recognised, '[p]eaceful protest has a long history in the United Kingdom and is a cornerstone of democracy'.[56]

The liberty to lawfully assemble in public has therefore been long recognised in some of the leading cases in the common law canon, even – as seen in *Beatty* v *Gillbanks*[57] – where those assembling are able to apprehend that their doing so will provoke opposition, and potentially also public disturbance.

Key case
Beatty v *Gillbanks* (1882) 9 QBD 308

Members of the Salvation Army assembled and marched in Weston-super-Mare, knowing that their so doing was likely to be the cause of a disturbance (previous marches had resulted in clashes with a group known as the Skeleton army and various other people hostile to the Salvation army). Local magistrates issued notices attempting to prevent the Salvationists assembling, and in the light of these notices, the police attempted to disperse their assembly. When Beatty – one of the leaders of the Salvation Army – refused to obey the notice, he was arrested, subsequently convicted by the magistrates of unlawful assembly in breach of the peace and bound over for 12 months. Appealing his conviction to the Queen's Bench Division, Field J (with whom Cave J agreed) said the following (at 314):

> What has happened here is that an unlawful organization [the Skeleton Army] has assumed to itself the right to prevent the appellants and others from lawfully assembling together, and the

---

[53] A. V. Dicey, *Introduction to the Study of the Law of the Constitution* (8ᵗʰ edn, Liberty Fund, 1982) pp. 169–170.

[54] Ibid., p. 170.

[55] *R (Laporte)* v *Chief Constable of Gloucestershire* [2006] UKHL 55; [2007] 2 AC 105, [93].

[56] Joint Committee on Human Rights, 'Demonstrating respect for rights? A Human Rights Approach to Policing Protest' (2009) HL47/HC320, para. 1.

[57] *Beatty* v *Gillbanks* (1882) 9 QBD 308.

> finding of the justices amounts to this, that a man may be convicted for doing a lawful act if he knows that his doing it may cause another to do an unlawful act. There is no authority for such a proposition.

While *Beatty* v *Gillbanks* retains its position amongst the most revered decisions in the common law library, during the course of the twentieth century its protections for the right of public assembly were demonstrated to be insubstantial. Two cases in particular – *Thomas* v *Sawkins* [58] and *Duncan* v *Jones*,[59] both of which were decided in 1936 – in employing an expansive reading of the duty of the police to prevent breaches of the peace made significant inroads into the ability of the common law to protect freedom of assembly.

Thinking Point . . .

For a well-known attempt to define breach of the peace see *R* v *Howell* [1982] QB 416, 427: 'there is a breach of the peace whenever harm is actually done or is likely to be done to a person or in his presence to his property or a person is in fear of being so harmed through an assault, an affray, a riot, unlawful assembly or other disturbance. It is for this breach of the peace when done in his presence or the reasonable apprehension of it taking place that a constable, or anyone else, may arrest an offender without warrant.' See also: *R (Laporte)* v *Chief Constable of Gloucestershire* [2006] UKHL 55; [2007] 2 AC 105.

Thomas v *Sawkins* concerned whether police officers were able to lawfully enter and remain present at a private meeting on the basis of a reasonable apprehension that seditious speeches would be made and that a breach of the peace would occur. Police officers attended a meeting organised by communists protesting against a bill then before Parliament, and demanding the removal from office of the local Chief Constable. The organisers of the meeting attempted to deny the officers entry, but the officers entered the meeting nonetheless, seating themselves in the front row. The appellant (Thomas) requested that the officers leave, and – when they refused to do so – stated that the police officers would be ejected, and . . . laid his hand upon [one of them] to eject him'.[60] The appellant's hand was pushed away by Sergeant Sawkins, and the officers remained in the hall for the remainder of the meeting. The police pursued no further action, but Thomas brought a private prosecution against Sergeant Sawkins claiming he had been assaulted by the police officer while seeking to legitimately remove 'trespassers' from his private meeting. It was argued on the behalf of Sawkins that the reasonable belief that the meeting would result in a breach of the peace entitled them to attend and remain at the assembly. Both the magistrates and the King's Bench division found in favour of Sergeant

---

[58] *Thomas* v *Sawkins* [1936] 1 KB 249.
[59] *Duncan* v *Jones* [1936] 1 KB 218.
[60] *Thomas* v *Sawkins* [1936] 1 KB 249, 251.

Sawkins. Giving the lead judgment in the latter, and drawing on Blackstone's Commentaries, Lord Hewart CJ was able to conclude that:

> [I]t is part of the preventative power, and, therefore, part of the preventative duty, of the police, in cases where there are such reasonable grounds of apprehension as the justices have found here, to enter and remain on private premises.[61]

On the basis of this – and a subjective test of the reasonableness of the belief of the relevant police officer – a significant inroad was made into the right to lawfully and peacefully assemble as recognised by the common law.[62]

The decision in *Duncan* v *Jones*[63] further illustrates the occasional ambivalence – some would say contempt[64] – of the courts towards the freedom to assemble. Katherine Duncan had attempted to address a meeting outside a training centre for the unemployed. William Jones, a police inspector, told Duncan that the meeting could not be held, and asked her to relocate the meeting to a nearby street. Duncan said 'I'm going to hold it', began to address the crowd (some 30 people), and was arrested on the basis that Jones apprehended that a breach of the peace would occur if the meeting were to take place. Jones' apprehension was based on the knowledge that a meeting in the same place, over a year prior to Duncan's arrest, had resulted in a disturbance. On the basis of *Beatty* v *Gillbanks*, it could be suggested that an otherwise peaceful assembly should not have been dispersed on the basis of the potential disruption caused by others (indeed, it was conceded that neither Duncan, nor any persons involved in the meeting, had either 'committed, incited or provoked any breach of the peace'[65]). The court did not agree. Lord Hewart CJ (again) set the tone, beginning his judgment with the following admonition:

> There have been moments during the argument in this case when it appeared to be suggested that the Court had to do with a grave case involving what is called the right of public meeting. I say 'called' because English law does not recognise any special right of public meeting for political or other purposes.[66]

Instead, the court conceived of the issue at hand as relating to the 'duty' of the police officer to prevent the holding of a meeting which he reasonably apprehended might lead to a breach of the peace. As Jones' apprehension was found to be reasonable – in the light of the previous disturbance – the court agreed that Duncan's arrest was lawful. In the view of Hewart CJ therefore, the decision in *Beatty* v *Gillbanks* was not only 'somewhat unsatisfactory' but irrelevant to the facts of the case. Humphreys J was in agreement, noting that the case had 'nothing to do with the law of unlawful assembly'.[67]

---

[61] Ibid., 254.

[62] A similar statutory power is now contained in the Police and Criminal Evidence Act 1984, s. 17(6). For commentary on the case, see A. L. Goodhart, '*Thomas* v *Sawkins*: A Constitutional Innovation' (1936–1938) 6 CLJ 22; C. A. Gearty and K. D. Ewing, *The Struggle for Civil Liberties: Political Freedom and the Rule of Law in Britain, 1914–1945* (OUP, 2000) pp. 289–95.

[63] *Duncan* v *Jones* [1936] 1 KB 218.

[64] Ewing and Gearty comment that *Duncan* v *Jones* is 'a decision which is as noteworthy today for the vacuity of its reasoning as for its long term deleterious effect on civil liberties'; C. A. Gearty and K. D. Ewing, *The Struggle for Civil Liberties: Political Freedom and the Rule of Law in Britain, 1914–1945* (OUP, 2000) p. 265.

[65] *Duncan* v *Jones* [1936] 1 KB 218, 219.

[66] Ibid., 221–222.

[67] Ibid., 223.

The potential stifling effect of these two decisions is highlighted by the fact that – before the interventions of the police – no unlawful conduct had actually taken place in either instance. In the absence of any unlawful conduct prior to the involvement of the state officials it is difficult to conclude that the residual liberty afforded by the common law was sufficient to provide effective protection for peaceful assembly. As E. C. S. Wade subsequently commented of *Duncan v Jones*: '[i]t would thus appear that the Common Law of England . . . has ceased to protect the speaker who merely desires to give expression to his opinions without causing any obstruction or committing, inciting or provoking any breach of the peace'.[68]

Statutory management of assembly

The tendency towards maintenance of order and avoidance of public disturbance – as opposed to the facilitation of the freedom to assemble – is also reflected in the statutory framework relevant to freedom of assembly.[69] The opening provisions of the primary piece of legislation in the field, the Public Order Act 1986, for instance, are directed towards the creation of offences which may result from non-peaceful protest – including riot, violent disorder and affray[70] – and are complemented by a series of provisions creating offences relating to the fear or provocation of violence and the (likely or intentional) causing of harassment, alarm or distress.[71]

Part II of the 1986 Act is specifically directed towards the regulation of public processions and assemblies. As to the former (defined by the Act as 'a procession in a public place'[72]), section 11(1) directs that advance written notice be given (to a police station in proximity of the route (section 11(4)) of an intended procession, unless it is not reasonably practicable to do so.[73] The notice must specify the date and time of the proposed procession, its intended course, and include the details of the organiser(s).[74] An offence may be committed if the requirements of section 11 are not met, or if the timing or route of the procession deviates from that specified in the organiser's notice.[75] Following receipt of the notice, if the senior police officer reasonably believes that the procession might result in serious disorder, damage to property or disruption to the life of the community, or the intimidation of others in order to prevent them undertaking lawful activity, then:

> [H]e may give directions imposing on the persons organising or taking part in the procession such conditions as appear to him necessary to prevent such disorder, damage, disruption or intimidation, including conditions as to the route of the procession or prohibiting it from entering any public place specified in the directions.[76]

---

[68] E. C. S. Wade, 'Police Powers and Public Meetings' (1936–1938) 6 CLJ 175, 178.

[69] On which see generally: H. Fenwick, *Fenwick on Civil Liberties and Human Rights* (5th edn, Routledge, 2017) ch. 9.

[70] Public Order Act 1986, ss. 1, 2 and 3.

[71] Ibid., ss. 4, 4A, and 5.

[72] Ibid., s. 16.

[73] On the latter point see: *Kay v Commissioner of Police for the Metropolis* [2008] UKHL 69; [2008] 1 WLR 2723.

[74] Public Order Act 1986, s. 11(3).

[75] Ibid., s. 11(7).

[76] Ibid., s. 12(1). On the frequency with which conditions are imposed via ss. 12 and 14 of the 1986 Act see: Joint Committee on Human Rights, *Demonstrating Respect for Rights? A Human Rights Approach to Policing Protest* (2009) HL47/HC320, paras 47–48.

Knowing failure to comply with a condition imposed is an offence.[77] In the event that the senior police officer believes that public order cannot be maintained through the imposition of conditions on the proposed procession, then he or she may – with the consent of the relevant local authority (or, in the case of the City of London, the Secretary of State) – prohibit the proposed procession.[78]

In relation to public assemblies,[79] while there is no comparable requirement that advance notice be provided to the local police, conditions may also be imposed on the assembly in the name of public order.[80] Those conditions may relate to – *inter alia* – the location of the assembly, its maximum duration, and/or the maximum number of people who may be present. Similarly to the above, failure to comply with a specified condition may be an offence.[81] Though *public* assemblies cannot be banned, amendments were made to the 1986 Act as a result of the Criminal Justice and Public Order Act 1984 in order to make provision for the prohibition of *trespassory* assemblies (assemblies held on land to which the public have no (or only a limited) right of access).[82] Such assemblies may be prohibited (with the consent of the local authority[83]) where the permission of the landowner is not obtained *and* the assembly would either seriously disrupt the life of the community or cause significant damage to any building or monument of historical, architectural, archaeological or scientific importance.[84] Organisation of, participation in, and incitement to participate in, prohibited trespassory assemblies are all made offences under Public Order Act 1986, section 14B. The Act also furnishes the police with a power to prevent people from travelling to assemblies prohibited, or likely to be prohibited, under section 14A.[85] Given that the power to prohibit such an assembly amounts to a greater incursion into the freedom to assemble than the imposition of one or more conditions, it is only exercisable in relation to groups of 20 or more people,[86] on land to which the public has no or only limited access, and when the impact of the assembly itself is likely to be significant.

Key debates
Demonstrations in the vicinity of Parliament

While it is commonly the role of Parliament to enact legislation of general applicability, instances can be found of legislative action targeting a highly specific perceived mischief. A pertinent example can be found in sections 132–138 of the Serious Organised Crime and Police Act 2005. The 'primary target' (I. Loveland, 'Public Protest in Parliament Square' [2007] EHRLR 251, 252) of these provisions was a Mr Brian Haw, a lone protestor against economic sanctions imposed upon Iraq and the subsequent involvement of the UK military in the conflict there. Haw's one-man protest had – since June 2001 – taken the form of a constant, small

---

[77] Public Order Act 1986, s. 12(4).

[78] Ibid., s. 13.

[79] Ibid., s. 16: 'an assembly of 2 or more persons in a public place which is wholly or partly open to the air'.

[80] Public Order Act 1986, s. 14(1).

[81] Ibid., s. 14(4).

[82] Ibid., s. 14A. See: *Director of Public Prosecutions* v *Jones* [1999] 2 AC 240; [1999] 2 WLR 625.

[83] The relevant provision applicable to such assemblies held within London is Public Order Act 1986, s. 14A(4).

[84] Ibid., s. 14A(1).

[85] Ibid., s. 14C.

[86] Ibid., s. 14A(9).

but visible, encampment in Parliament Square. An attempt by Westminster Council to have the encampment removed was rejected on the basis that to do so would disproportionately interfere with Haw's freedom of expression as guaranteed by Article 10 ECHR.

The relevant provisions of the 2005 Act permitted the Home Secretary to 'designate' an area within which any demonstration must be authorised (potentially subject to conditions) by the Metropolitan Police Commissioner. An unauthorised demonstration carried the potential for a prison sentence (of – under section 136 – up to 51 weeks). Following the enactment of the legislation, the Home Secretary duly designated the area surrounding Parliament Square, and Haw's demonstration – following an unsuccessful judicial review application (*R (Haw)* v *Secretary of State for the Home Department* [2006] EWCA Civ 532; [2006] QB 780) – was removed in May 2006.

The relevant provisions of the 2005 Act were controversial (see Joint Committee on Human Rights, *Demonstrating Respect for Rights? A Human Rights Approach to Policing Protest* (2009) HL47/HC320) and were repealed by the Police Reform and Social Responsibility Act 2011. Part III of the 2011 Act – which is no more supportive of public protest than the 2005 legislation, and appears to be as motivated by the wish to prevent anything other than fleeting demonstrations – prohibits a series of activities, including unauthorised use of loudspeakers, erecting a tent, sleeping overnight and so on (section 143(2)), within the 'controlled area of Parliament square' (section 142).

The statutory framework regulating freedom of assembly has not, however, completely replaced the common law powers of the police to keep the peace. These powers – as we have seen in this chapter and elsewhere in this book[87] – remain somewhat ill-defined. As Helen Fenwick has commented, the concept of breach of the peace is '[b]reathtakingly broad, bewilderingly imprecise in scope, [and] it provides the police with such wide powers to use against protestors as to render the statutory powers almost redundant'.[88] As such, and given the availability of specific statutory powers to regulate assemblies and processions in the Public Order Act (as well as the statutory codification of broader police powers[89]), it is unsurprising to encounter periodical calls for the abolition of the breach of the peace doctrine.[90]

Freedom of Assembly in the Human Rights Act Era

The right of assembly is protected, via the Human Rights Act 1998, in Article 11 EHCR. Article 11(1) reads:

Everyone has the right to freedom of peaceful assembly and to freedom of association with others, including the right to form and join trade unions for the protection of his interests.

As with freedom of expression, Article 11(2) also provides for grounds upon which the exercise of the right can be justifiably restricted:

No restrictions shall be placed on the exercise of these rights other than such as are prescribed by law and are necessary in a democratic society in the interests of national security or public safety,

---

[87] *R* v *Secretary of State for the Home Department, ex parte Northumbria Police Authority* [1989] QB 26 (discussed at p. 35).

[88] H. Fenwick, *Fenwick on Civil Liberties and Human Rights* (5th edn, Routledge, 2017) p. 554.

[89] See pp. 709–10.

[90] H. Fenwick, 'Marginalising Human Rights: Breach of the Peace, "Kettling", the Human Rights Act and Public Protest' [2009] PL 737, 757–758.

for the prevention of disorder or crime, for the protection of health or morals or for the protection of the rights and freedoms of others.

As a result of the Human Rights Act, statute law regulating assemblies and processions should be interpreted – in so far as possible – in a way which is compatible with the Convention rights (or else may be declared to be incompatible with those rights),[91] while the common law rules applicable to assemblies may be influenced by the Convention by way of the applicability of the Human Rights Act to the judges themselves.[92] The protection afforded by Article 11 for 'peaceful' assembly would appear to be consistent with the general tenor of domestic law towards controlling, and potentially criminalising, involvement in assemblies with potentially disruptive consequences. The protection of Article 11 should also be seen, however, as a notable departure (a 'constitutional shift'[93]) for the existing law, amounting to a right capable of regulating the proportionality of public authority conduct as well as the interpretation of legislation. By contrast with the common law, Article 11, as well as permitting public interest limitations on the freedom to assemble, emphasises the positive role of the state in facilitating peaceful assemblies.[94]

Given that – as the cases discussed above illustrate – much of the pre-HRA case law on freedom of assembly was characterised by a judicial deference to police officers' operational judgments as to the steps necessary to maintain the peace,[95] the recognition of a positive right to assemble was a welcome addition to the uneven law on public protest. The House of Lords decision in *R (Laporte)* v *Chief Constable of Gloucestershire* provided one of the first significant indicators of the impact of the Human Rights Act regime. The facts of the case concerned a decision taken by Gloucestershire Constabulary to divert a coach carrying anti-war protesters away from RAF Fairford, an air force base from which American B52 bombers had mounted operations in Iraq. RAF Fairford had been the site of previous protests, and had seen incidents of mass trespass onto the base, damage to equipment and – on one occasion – 'serious disorder' following the forcing open of the main gate.[96] A protest demonstration had been organised by a number of anti-war groups for 22 March 2003. Gloucester Constabulary, aware of the proposed march and demonstration, decided not to exercise powers under the Public Order Act to prohibit the procession (section 13) and instead planned to manage the event through – *inter alia* – conditions on the route of the proposed march.[97] Laporte was travelling from London on one of the three coaches of protestors headed for RAF Fairford. The coaches also contained a small number (eight) of members of a group known as Wombles who were suspected of planning to gain unlawful access to the air base. The coaches were stopped by the police a short distance from the RAF Fairford, and a number of items – including face masks, spray paint, scissors and a flare – were seized. Passengers who were due to speak at the event were allowed to proceed. Apprehending that

---

[91] Human Rights Act 1998, ss. 3 and 4.
[92] Human Rights Act 1998, s. 6(3)(a). For an early assessment of the impact of the Human Rights Act in this sphere see H. Fenwick and G. Phillipson, 'Public Protest, the Human Rights Act and Judicial Responses to Political Expression' [2000] PL 627.
[93] *Redmond-Bate* v *Director of Public Prosecutions* [2000] HRLR 249, 256 (Sedley LJ).
[94] *Plattform 'Ärzte für das Leben'* v *Austria* (1988) 13 EHRR 204, [34].
[95] H. Fenwick, 'Marginalising Human Rights: Breach of the Peace, "Kettling", the Human Rights Act and Public Protest' [2009] PL 737, 740–741.
[96] *R (Laporte)* v *Chief Constable of Gloucestershire* [2006] UKHL 55; [2007] 2 AC 105, [5].
[97] Ibid., [8].

a breach of the peace would become 'imminent' and would likely occur *if* the Wombles were allowed to reach RAF Fairford, the Chief Constable directed that all the remaining passengers be redirected back to London under police escort.[98]

Laporte brought judicial review proceedings, challenging the decision to prevent her travelling to RAF Fairford and forcing her return to London. Laporte contended that the actions taken by the Chief Constable amounted to interferences with her rights under Articles 10 and 11 of the ECHR, and that those interferences were neither prescribed by law (for the reason that a breach of the peace was not 'imminent') nor proportionate (on the basis that the preventative actions of the police were both premature and indiscriminate given the number of non-Womble protestors).[99] The House of Lords agreed unanimously. Lord Bingham summarised the general duty of the police officers as follows:

> Every constable . . . enjoys the power and is subject to a duty to seek to prevent, by arrest or other action short of arrest, any breach of the peace occurring in his presence, or any breach of the peace which (having occurred) is likely to be renewed, or any breach of the peace which is about to occur.[100]

The relevant test to be applied in the apprehension of a breach of the peace was that of imminence (where it could be said that there 'is a reasonable apprehension of imminent danger of a breach of the peace.')[101] However, as Lord Bingham noted:

> There is nothing in domestic authority to support the proposition that action short of arrest may be taken when a breach of the peace is not so imminent as would be necessary to justify an arrest.[102]

On the basis that no breach of the peace was about to occur when the coaches were stopped, the test of imminence was not met, and the Chief Constable's actions were not, therefore, prescribed by law.[103] As to the proportionality of the measures taken – in a statement reminiscent of *Beatty* v *Gillbanks* – Lord Bingham noted that as Laporte was a 'peaceful demonstrator' it was 'wholly disproportionate to restrict her exercise of her rights under Articles 10 and 11 because she was in the company of others some of whom might, at some time in the future, breach the peace'.[104]

Laporte brought welcome precision to the temporal requirement of imminence in relation to a future breach of the peace; the finding that a breach of the peace is on the verge of occurring effectively narrows the extent to which prior restraints can operate in relation to freedom of assembly at common law. This finding was reinforced by the requirement that measures taken by the police also meet the standard of proportionality as required by Article 11 ECHR. As the subsequent case of *Austin* v *Commissioner of Police for the Metropolis* demonstrates, however, where the standard of imminence *is* met, the police retain significant powers at common law to control public assemblies in practice.[105] We will return to *Austin* below.

---

[98] Ibid., [13].

[99] Ibid., [38].

[100] Ibid., [29]. See also: *Steel* v *United Kingdom* (1998) 28 EHRR 603, [29]: 'A person may be arrested without warrant by exercise of the common law power of arrest, for causing a breach of the peace or where it is reasonably apprehended that he is likely to cause a breach of the peace.'

[101] Ibid., [30]. See also: *R* v *Howell* [1982] QB 416, 426.

[102] Ibid., [39].

[103] Ibid., [45]–[52].

[104] Ibid., [55].

[105] *Austin* v *Commissioner of Police for the Metropolis* [2009] UKHL 5; [2009] 1 AC 564.

Liberty

Key issues

- Liberty of the person is an important political freedom; it prevents the authorities from using the forces at their disposal to lock up political opponents. This concept was long protected in the UK's domestic legal systems by the law of habeas corpus, and is now protected under Article 5 ECHR.

- Again, however, the right to liberty is not an absolute right and we need to assess how the courts have approached this concept in controversial cases to understand how it operates to protect political agency under the UK Constitution.

Liberty of the person

For Dicey, 'freedom of person is not a special privilege but the outcome of the ordinary law of the land enforced by the courts'.[106] In this statement he is not denying the importance of protections for freedom of the person to prevent the arbitrary detention by the authorities of the UK Government's political opponents, but is instead claiming that there is no special constitutional right at play where the authorities abuse their powers for political reasons; the law that protects opposition activists and political protestors from arbitrary arrest and detention is the same that protects against abuses of these powers in more every-day contexts. As Dicey proceeded to elaborate:

> The right to personal liberty . . . means in substance a person's right not to be subjected to imprisonment, arrest or other physical coercion in any manner that does not admit of legal justification.[107]

Once again, however, current legal protections for this right developed in the context of highly-charged political disputes. Habeas corpus is perhaps the most famous writ in common law legal history. Initiating such an action informs a court of a suspicion that a person is being held unlawfully by the authorities and compels them to show that they have legal justification for detaining the person in question. It was a lightning-rod issue in the tumults of the seventeenth century, as successive Stuart monarchs sought to silence political opponents by locking them up. This led to Parliament passing two Habeas Corpus Acts, in 1640 and 1679, the latter providing legal protections which remain in place to this day.

Insight
Habeas Corpus

The writ of habeas corpus – meaning 'that you have the body' – will procure the release of a person 'detained without authority or purported authority or [where] the purported authority is beyond the powers of the person authorising the detention and so is unlawful' (*R v Secretary of State for the Home Department, ex parte Cheblak* [1991] 1 WLR 890, 894). The purpose of

---

[106] A. V. Dicey, *Introduction to the Study of the Law of the Constitution* (8th edn, Liberty Fund, 1982) p. 124.
[107] Ibid., p. 124.

the writ is to require that the detained person be brought before a court in order that the legality of their detention can be examined. Originally a tool by which a person's attendance in court might be ensured, the writ became an important tool for guaranteeing individual liberty and a potent symbol of the ability of the common law to act as a 'bulwark against executive oppression and arbitrary detention' (S. Brown, 'Habeas Corpus – A New Chapter' [2000] PL 31, 32).

In spite of habeas corpus being hailed as 'the most effective remedy against executive lawlessness that the world has ever seen' (T. Bingham, *The Rule of Law* (Penguin, 2011) p. 14), it has not been immune from legislative abrogation. Habeas corpus has been suspended on numerous occasions during times of military conflict (for instance, as a result of the Defence of the Realm Act 1914), and was substantially abridged by the indefinite detention provisions of the Anti-Terrorism, Crime and Security Act 2001.

Contemporary recourse to the writ of habeas corpus is relatively uncommon as a result of – among other things – statutory limitations on periods of pre-charge detention and the availability of judicial review as an alternative avenue by which administrative decisions can be challenged. Notwithstanding this, a substantially parallel guarantee remains an integral aspect of Article 5(4) ECHR:

> Everyone who is deprived of his liberty by arrest or detention shall be entitled to take proceedings by which the lawfulness of his detention shall be decided speedily by a court and his release ordered if his detention is not lawful.

Police powers of arrest and detention

Habeas corpus is now very much relegated to the background in terms of protection of liberty. In essence, it requires that the authorities be able to show a legal basis justifying a particular detention. Where Parliament passes a statute authorising detentions (or other restrictions upon liberty, such as curfews) in particular circumstances the authorities can meet a habeas corpus claim to show that the conditions of that statute have been met. In most circumstances this would involve the police demonstrating that they had a warrant issued by a magistrate authorising an arrest (and subsequent detention for questioning).[108] The preventative tenor of the common law jurisprudence covered above in relation to assemblies which have the potential to cause breaches of the peace is also found in primary legislation which grants police officers arrest powers without a warrant in circumstances in which the officer reasonably suspects that an offence is being or is about to be committed.[109] Even broader arrest powers exist in the counter-terrorism context (enabling the police to make arrests when they suspect some conduct linked to terrorism, even if they cannot ascertain a particular offence).[110] The police are permitted to use reasonable force to effect a lawful arrest.[111]

Police powers of arrest are often at their most political in the context of public protests. Given the framing of arrest powers their scope often depends upon the terms of the offence in question. The broader the terms of the offence, the more likely the police are going to be able to effect an arrest. In protest situations, police concerns over an ongoing or potential breach of the peace were historically used (as we have seen) to justify arrests.[112] But under

---

[108] Magistrates' Courts Act 1980, s. 1.
[109] Police and Criminal Evidence Act 1984, s. 24.
[110] Terrorism Act 2000, s. 41.
[111] Criminal Law Act 1967, s. 3.
[112] Public Order Act 1936, s. 5. See *Marsh* v *Arscott* (1982) 75 Cr App Rep 211.

statutory provisions introduced in the 1980s the link to a breach of the peace was eroded. The offence of wilful obstruction of the public highway provides one useful pretext for arrest.[113] Under the Public Order Act 1986 (as enacted), police officers gained the power to arrest an individual for the offence of using threatening, insulting or abusive words/ behaviour or disorderly behaviour within the hearing or sight of a person likely to be caused harassment, alarm or distress.[114] In a protest situation, in which groups with opposing opinions on highly charged issues of public policy meet, insulting words are almost inevitable and gave the police considerable scope to make arrests. But the power could be used in circumstances beyond confrontations between rival groups of protesters. The courts accepted that under the terms of the 1986 Act police officers could use themselves as the person 'likely to be caused harassment, alarm or distress' to trigger this offence.[115] The combination of arrest powers and such a broad offence effectively gave the police the opportunity to stifle political protests.[116] Concerns over (potential or actual) breaches of the peace have also been used by the police to undertake the controversial practice of 'kettling' (a means of crowd control involving forming a cordon around a procession or demonstration, which leads to people held therein being detained for extended periods).

Deprivations of liberty under the Human Rights Act

The Human Rights Act contributed to a major re-evaluation of the police use of detention and arrest in dealing with protests. The change was not immediate; indeed it was only really felt after the crisis in public confidence in protest policing following the G20 protests in 2009 triggered a re-evaluation of whether the police approaches to public order situations really were human rights compliant.[117] Serious questions were raised over whether long-standing policies and legislation could still be justified under Article 5 of the ECHR, which protects the liberty of the person.

Considerable attention was directed towards the police use of section 5 of the Public Order Act 1986. For David Mead, whether the offence 'will be applied on the beat in a proportionate, rights-sensitive fashion seems open to question'.[118] Under Article 5 of the ECHR lawful arrests are one of the circumstances in which deprivations of liberty by the authorities are, on their face, human rights compatible.[119] But if the power of arrest under s. 5 is so broad as to cover the prevention of insults causing offence, then the proportionality of this power also needs to be considered in terms of the chilling effect that its use can impose on freedom of expression. The Joint Committee of Human Rights noted the following concerns with this power:

> There is an inextricable and fundamental link between the right to protest and free speech. We are concerned by the evidence that section 5 has, on occasions, been used to prevent people from freely expressing their views on matters of concern to them, and thereby has stifled otherwise legal, peaceful protest. Whilst we agree that people should be protected by existing laws

---

[113] Highways Act 1980, s. 137.
[114] Public Order Act 1986, s. 5.
[115] See *DPP* v *Orum* [1989] 1 WLR 88.
[116] See Joint Committee on Human Rights, *Demonstrating Respect for Rights? A Human Rights Approach to Policing Protest* (2009) HL47/HC320, [80].
[117] See J. Gilmore, 'Policing Protest: An Authoritarian Consensus' (2010) 82 Criminal Justice Matters 21.
[118] D. Mead, *The New Law of Public Protest: Rights and Regulation in the Human Rights Act Era* (Hart, 2010) p. 223.
[119] ECHR, Article 5(1)(c).

preventing incitement on a number of grounds, free speech in the context of protest and dissent has long been protected by the common law because of its importance for the functioning of a democratic society. It is inevitable that some protests will cause others to be offended.[120]

In light of this pressure, the 2010–15 Coalition Government introduced reforms to the terms of section 5 to make it more obviously human-rights compliant, removing reference to insulting words.[121] This reform means that words or behaviour have to be threatening or abusive before the police will be able to make an arrest. This remains an offence which allows the police considerable scope for intervening in a protest, but does constitute a higher hurdle than the unreformed law.

Arrests, as we have seen, are not the only circumstances in which the police can detain individuals. This brings us back to the case of *Austin,* which concerned the use of kettling by the police in an effort to prevent potential breaches of the peace. For the UK authorities, such cases (even if individuals were held in a cordon for hours) involved restrictions upon freedom of movement, but not liberty. The UK has not accepted the optional protocol on freedom of movement under the ECHR, in part to allow for such police tactics, and for the authorities this precluded a human rights challenge to kettling.[122] This case would nonetheless contribute to the reexamination of police powers of detention in protest situations which began in 2009.

Key case

Austin v *Commissioner of Police for the Metropolis* [2009] UKHL 5; [2009] 1 AC 564

In the course of the policing of May Day protests in 2001, Lois Austin was detained in a police cordon in central London, known as a 'kettle', for roughly seven hours. The cordon covered 2,000 square metres and enclosed roughly 3,000 people. Austin had been taking part in the protest entirely lawfully, but a number of others caught in the kettle were just bystanders in the wrong place when the police established their cordon. The police had established this cordon on grounds of public protection, in light of a belief that some protestors might have violent intent and in the hope of dispersing people slowly. Although the case undoubtedly concerned an assembly within the meaning of Article 11 ECHR, because of these facts Austin's challenge proceeded on the basis of the deprivation of liberty pursuant to Article 5 ECHR.

In response to this challenge, the House of Lords refused to address Article 5 arguments. In his lead judgment, Lord Hope concluded that crowd control measures did not immediately raise Article 5 issues (at [34]):

[T]here is room, even in the case of fundamental rights as to whose application no restriction or limitation is permitted by the Convention, for a pragmatic approach to be taken which takes full account of all the circumstances. No reference is made in article 5 to the interests of public safety or the protection of public order as one of the cases in which a person may be deprived of his liberty. This is in sharp contrast to article 10(2), which expressly qualifies the right to freedom of expression in these respects. But the importance that must be attached in the context of article 5 to measures taken in the interests of public safety is indicated by article 2 of the Convention,

→

---

[120] Joint Committee on Human Rights, *Demonstrating Respect for Rights? A Human Rights Approach to Policing Protest* (2009) HL47/HC320, para. 84.
[121] The Crime and Courts Act 2013, s. 57(2).
[122] ECHR, Protocol 4, Article 2.

➜

> as the lives of persons affected by mob violence may be at risk if measures of crowd control cannot be adopted by the police. This is a situation where a search for a fair balance is necessary if these competing fundamental rights are to be reconciled with each other. The ambit that is given to article 5 as to measures of crowd control must, of course, take account of the rights of the individual as well as the interests of the community. So any steps that are taken must be resorted to in good faith and must be proportionate to the situation which has made the measures necessary. This is essential to preserve the fundamental principle that anything that is done which affects a person's right to liberty must not be arbitrary. If these requirements are met however it will be proper to conclude that measures of crowd control that are undertaken in the interests of the community will not infringe the article 5 rights of individual members of the crowd whose freedom of movement is restricted by them.

> In other words, Lord Hope was willing to read qualifications into the operation of Article 5 which did not exist in the wording of the provision or in the jurisprudence of the Strasbourg Court. For some commentators Austin summarises many of the flawed presumptions which characterise approaches to protest under the UK Constitution. David Mead offers the following rhetorical question in response to this decision (*The New Law of Public Protest: Rights and Regulation in the Human Rights Act Era* (Hart, 2010) p. 351):

> > What persuaded the House to conclude that being held for seven hours in a police cordon without food or water, without shelter or suitable clothing on a wet, windy day unable to leave even though, of most members individually, there was no suspicion that they themselves had done anything wrong, was not in fact a deprivation of liberty?

Austin subsequently took her challenge to the European Court of Human Rights. At Strasbourg, the Grand Chamber's 14:3 majority began by recognising the importance of the principle of subsidiarity (which would make it particularly reluctant to question the findings of fact) established in the domestic courts. This set the tone for a judgment which cleaved closely to the position of the House of Lords:

> In these circumstances, where the police kept the situation constantly under close review, but where substantially the same dangerous conditions which necessitated the imposition of the cordon at 2 p.m. continued to exist throughout the afternoon and early evening, the Court does not consider that those within the cordon can be said to have been deprived of their liberty within the meaning of Article 5 s. 1. Since there was no deprivation of liberty, it is unnecessary for the Court to examine whether the measure in question was justified . . .[123]

The Court did emphasise that its conclusion that there was no deprivation of liberty 'is based on the specific and exceptional facts of this case'.[124] But even stripped of value as a precedent this judgment seems to be an acknowledgement from the court that the structure of Article 5 is problematic; if it had recognised that the right to liberty was engaged then none of the limitations contained in Article 5 could have been used to justify the actions of the police. The effect of its judgment is to tacitly establish an exception to the ordinary operation of the right to liberty where public order is at issue.[125]

---

[123] *Austin* v *United Kingdom* (2012) 55 EHRR 14 (GC), [67].
[124] Ibid., [68].
[125] See also *R (McClure)* v *Commissioner of Police for the Metropolis* [2012] EWCA Civ 12, [95].

Voting rights

Key issues

- Universal suffrage, as we have seen in earlier chapters, is the legitimating force which underpins the exercise of power by public authorities in a liberal democracy.
- The right to vote is a positive right, constructed out of the obligation on ECHR states to hold free and fair elections (ECHR, Article 3 of Protocol 1).
- The transformation of the UK into a liberal democracy took many generations, and some legal restrictions on the franchise (particularly upon the voting rights of prisoners) call into question whether the UK has yet to fully assimilate the principle of universal suffrage into its constitutional order.

Democratic participation

It has sometimes been claimed that a system of government can be liberal without necessarily being democratic. In the late nineteenth century, for example, at a time when the UK had yet to fully embrace democracy within its political order (and substantially less than half of adult citizens enjoyed the vote) writers like Henry Maine saw no conflict in presenting the UK as a liberal, but not democratic, state.[126] So the right to vote became a relatively recent addition to the pantheon of human rights, and one which looks very different from some of the other rights we have examined in this chapter as supporting the UK's political order. By contrast with the traditional negative, or residual, approach to the conception of political freedoms in the UK, the ability to participate in elections is 'realizable *only* through positive state action'.[127] As Gearty explains:

> [O]ur right to vote cannot exist in the abstract; it requires a large state machinery to make it work. To be effective it also needs to be by way of a secret ballot and to be a right capable of being exercised at regular intervals and, in combination with the use of the right by others, to have the capacity to produce a legislature to make laws on behalf of the community over which it presides which body is broadly speaking representative of that community.[128]

For the European Court of Human Rights the right to free and fair elections[129] pointed towards a presumption that all states party to the ECHR would base their political systems on the basis of universal suffrage:

> [T]he right to vote is not a privilege. In the twenty-first century, the presumption in a democratic state must be in favour of inclusion, as may be illustrated . . . by the parliamentary history of the United Kingdom and other countries where the franchise was gradually extended over the centuries from select individuals, elite groupings or sections of the population approved of by those in power. Universal suffrage has become the basic principle.[130]

The right to vote puts 'the people' at the heart of a governance order.[131] Indeed, for Martin Loughlin, it is impossible today to explain the nature of 'sovereign authority' within the

---

[126] H. Maine, *Popular Government* (John Murray, 1886) p. 98.
[127] C. A. Gearty, *Principles of Human Rights Adjudication* (OUP, 2004) p. 34 (emphasis added).
[128] Ibid., p. 34.
[129] ECHR, Article 3, Protocol 1.
[130] *Hirst* v *United Kingdom (No. 2)* (2006) 42 EHRR 41 (GC), [59].
[131] See T. Paine, *The Rights of Man: Part II* (1st edn, J. S. Jordan, 1792) p. 93.

UK without appreciating that it is 'a product of the relation between the people and the state' (not something which rests in Parliament, but which is generated by the electorate as constituent power holders giving authority to their representatives as constituted power holders through the electoral process).[132] As one parliamentary committee put it, '[i]n a democracy all citizens possess a presumptive right to vote, thereby having a say in the making of the laws that govern them'.[133]

The right to vote connects with the rights which we have already considered. The freedom to associate under Article 11 of the ECHR, now protected via the Human Rights Act 1998, is the right of individuals to form groups to pursue collective goals and is closely related to the right to participate in the electoral process. Clear linkages can be traced, for instance, between the formation, and engagement, of political parties and systems of democratic governance. Such linkages have not, however, prevented limitations being placed on the right to associate in the public interest, though – as with legitimate limitations on freedom of political speech – such actions have tended towards upholding democracy or democratic government. In our coverage of the **GCHQ**[134] decision we have already seen how the government (in the name of safeguarding national security) prevented employees of GHCQ participating in trade union activity.[135] As we have also already seen, judges – by convention – should not be members of political parties in order that the independence of the judiciary be upheld. Similarly, police officers[136] and civil servants[137] should not be involved in party political activities in order that they can be seen to be politically impartial. At the more extreme end of the scale, certain political groupings whose aims and objectives are held to be damaging to democratic government have been proscribed. Current groups banned under the Terrorism Act 2000 include those known to be supportive or involved in international terrorist activity (including Al Qaeda, Islamic State and Boko Haram) and a number of domestic organisations associated with violent or paramilitary activities (for instance, the Irish Republican Army, the Ulster Defence Association and the neo-Nazi group National Action).[138]

Democracy as a constitutional principle

As we have seen in earlier sections of this book, the UK was gradually reformed over the course of the nineteenth and early twentieth centuries from being a constitutional monarchy in which only elite groups in society could contribute to supposedly representative institutions like the House of Commons, to a liberal democracy which prized a conception of universal suffrage for adult citizens.[139] It might therefore be tempting to claim that pre-existing constitutional principles, including parliamentary sovereignty, the rule of law and the separation of powers simply accommodated democracy in the twentieth century (after all, this textbook has not set out a separate chapter on the principle of democracy within our section on constitutional principles). But it is impossible to underplay how significantly this adaptation altered how important actors saw their role within the system

---

[132] M. Loughlin, *The Idea of Public Law* (OUP, 2003) pp. 63–64.

[133] Joint Committee on the Draft Voting Eligibility (Prisoners) Bill, *Draft Voting Eligibility (Prisoners) Bill* (2013) HL103/HC924, para. 154.

[134] *Council of Civil Service Unions* v *Minister for the Civil Service* [1985] AC 374.

[135] See pp. 588 and 592. The ban was effective until reversed by the Labour Government in 1997.

[136] *Champion* v *Chief Constable of Gwent* [1990] 1 WLR 1.

[137] Civil Service Code (March 2015); Constitutional Reform and Governance Act 2010, Part I.

[138] See C. R. G. Murray, 'Convergences and Divergences: Countering Terrorist Organisations in the United States and the United Kingdom' (2017) 28 King's Law Journal 745–770.

[139] For detail of the extensions of the franchise in the UK, see above p. 288.

of government. As Lord Sumption has explained, the courts saw their relationship with the other branches of government as changed by the advent of democracy, and it changed how they approached public law cases:

> The immense powers exercised by modern governments over their own citizens have arisen almost entirely from the collective aspirations of the population at large, aspirations which depend for their fulfilment on persistent intervention by the state in many areas of our national life . . . It is no longer sensible to view this as a power-grab by ambitious ministers and officials, as the opponents of the Crown did in the simpler world of seventeenth century England and some commentators still do. The truth is that a powerful executive is inherent in the democratic character of the modern state.[140]

We have seen many decisions in the context of this book in which the courts have, in the final analysis, adopted a decision with regard to statutory interpretation which carefully acknowledges Parliament's democratic legitimacy.[141] Decisions which seem to minimise this issue have often drawn anguished dissenting judgments.[142] If concerns over the effectiveness of the UK's democratic processes did eventually spur the development of judicial review[143] and the principle of legality,[144] these developments only marginally offset the focus upon democratic legitimacy inherent in current approaches to parliamentary sovereignty.

Denying the right to vote

By the late twentieth century, however, a new current had entered judicial thinking. If democracy underpinned and justified parliamentary sovereignty, then surely the courts have a special duty to protect against legislation which attempts to erode the principle of universal suffrage. For Sir John Laws, writing extra-judicially:

> It is . . . a condition of democracy's preservation that the power of a democratically elected government – or Parliament – be not absolute. The institution of free and regular elections . . . has to be vindicated by a higher order law; very obviously, no government can tamper with it, if it is to avoid the mantle of tyranny; no government, therefore, must be allowed to do so.[145]

If the courts' commitment to the suggestion that they have a special role as guardians of democracy has been tested, this has most clearly come in the context of the prisoner voting cases. The issue of whether prisoners should be disenfranchised during (and sometimes even after) their incarceration is one which divides liberal democracies.[146] Nonetheless, once the European Court of Human Rights recognised in *Hirst* v *United Kingdom* that the UK's 'blanket ban' on prisoners voting breached Article 3 of Protocol 1 of the ECHR,[147] the issue was always likely to require consideration by the UK courts, especially when successive UK Governments dragged their heels on introducing law reform:

---

[140] J. Sumption, 'Judicial and political decision-making: the uncertain boundary' (2011) 16 JR 301, 301.

[141] See, for example, *R v IRC, ex parte Rossminster* [1980] AC 952, 998 (Lord Wilberforce).

[142] See, for example, *R (Evans)* v *Attorney General* [2015] UKSC 21; [2015] 2 WLR 813, [168] (Lord Wilson).

[143] See, for example, *R v Secretary of State for the Home Department, ex parte Fire Brigades Union* [1995] 2 All ER 244, 267 (Lord Mustill).

[144] See, for example, *R v Secretary of State for the Home Department, ex parte Simms* [1999] 3 All ER 400, 412 (Lord Hoffmann).

[145] J. Laws, 'Law and Democracy' [1995] PL 72, 84.

[146] See *R (Chester and McGeoch)* v *Secretary of State for Justice* [2013] UKSC 63; [2014] 1 AC 271, [114] (Lord Sumption).

[147] See above pp. 637–8.

Key debates

Prisoner voting and the democratic foundations of the UK Constitution

The UK's domestic courts have found themselves caught in the clash between the European Courts of Human Rights and the UK Government over prisoner voting. With such a highly charged issue at stake even the UK Supreme Court has attempted to play a low-profile role. In *R (Chester and McGeoch)* v *Secretary of State for Justice* [2013] UKSC 63; [2014] 1 AC 271 two long-term prisoners convicted of murder challenged their exclusion from the franchise whilst incarcerated. The Supreme Court acknowledged that the automatic bar on prisoners voting under s. 3(1) of the Representation of the People Act 1983 breaches Article 3 of Protocol 1 of the ECHR (see [34] (Lord Mance)), but refused to countenance any further use of the remedies available under the Human Rights Act 1998 given that Scotland's Registration Appeal Court has already issued a declaration of incompatibility in *Smith* v *Scott* 2007 SC 345 (see [39] (Lord Mance)).

This does not mean, however, that these judgments have not provided a window onto how different judges conceive of their role when it comes to protecting democracy and the specific position of prisoner voting. In the Court of Appeal Laws LJ regarded this issue as not being simply a matter of an unjustified interference with voting rights; the issue of prisoner voting provokes 'deep philosophical differences of view between reasonable people' ([2010] EWCA Civ 1439, [2011] 1 WLR 1436, [32]). Lord Mance recognised that the European Court's jurisprudence did not require all prisoners to be enfranchised where their offences are 'sufficiently serious' to warrant disenfranchisement (at [30]). In other words, under the ECHR, universal suffrage for adult citizens remains a presumption, not a rule.

Of all the judges deciding the case, Baroness Hale went furthest in noting the particular role of the courts to protect democracy (at [88]):

> [I]n any modern democracy, the views of the public and Parliamentarians cannot be the end of the story. Democracy is about more than respecting the views of the majority. It is also about safeguarding the rights of minorities, including unpopular minorities. 'Democracy values everyone equally even if the majority does not': *Ghaidan* v *Godin-Mendoza* [2004] 2 AC 557, [132]. It follows that one of the essential roles of the courts in a democracy is to protect those rights.

She nonetheless noted that the courts looked on the question of prisoner disenfranchisement differently from restrictions on the vote affecting other groups in society (at [91]):

> [T]he exclusion of prisoners from voting is of a different order from the exclusion of women, African-Caribbeans or homosexuals. It is difficult to see how any elected politician would have a vested interest in excluding them (save just possibly from local elections in places where there are very large prisons). The arguments for and against their exclusion are quite finely balanced. On the one hand, unlike women, African-Caribbeans and homosexuals, prisoners share a characteristic which many think relevant to whether or not they should be allowed to vote: they have all committed an offence deemed serious enough to justify their removal from society for at least a while and in some cases indefinitely. While clearly this does not mean that all their other rights are forfeited, why should they not for the same time forfeit their right to take part in the machinery of democracy?

In particular, where the rights of two murderers were at issue, Baroness Hale recognised that there are very powerful justifications for withdrawing the right to participate in elections (at [99]).

For Lord Sumption, by contrast, this was not a case in which he saw the courts as having a role to play, and he would not have questioned the UK's law had he not been obliged to do so in light of settled Strasbourg jurisprudence (at [137]):

> Without the decisions in *Hirst* and *Scoppola,* I would have held that the question how serious an offence has to be to warrant temporary disenfranchisement is a classic matter for political and

legislative judgment, and that the United Kingdom rule is well within any reasonable assessment of a Convention state's margin of appreciation. However, the contrary view has now been upheld twice by the Grand Chamber of the European Court of Human Rights, and is firmly established in the court's case-law. It cannot be said that the Grand Chamber overlooked or misunderstood any relevant principle of English law. The problems about the view which the court ultimately came to were fairly pointed out in both cases in the course of argument. Whatever parliamentary consideration may or may not have been given to the issue in 1969, it has undoubtedly received a great deal of parliamentary attention more recently, in debates which were drawn to the Grand Chamber's attention in *Scoppola* but made no difference to its view. There is no realistic prospect that further dialogue with Strasbourg will produce a change of heart.

This was not the end of the story. The later case of *Moohan* v *Lord Advocate* [2014] UKSC 67; [2015] AC 901 also saw a judicial refusal to act on prisoner claims (this time with regard to the Scottish independence referendum) but once again the idea of the courts playing a special role in upholding democracy (even against parliamentary sovereignty) was raised by Lord Hodge (at [35]):

> While the common law cannot extend the franchise beyond that provided by parliamentary legislation, I do not exclude the possibility that in the very unlikely event that a parliamentary majority abusively sought to entrench its power by a curtailment of the franchise or similar device, the common law, informed by principles of democracy and the rule of law and international norms, would be able to declare such legislation unlawful.

Conclusion

The context in which citizens exercise their political freedoms has changed significantly in recent years. Though civil liberties were long-cherished as a by-product of judicial decisions, there existed 'no space in the common law for political liberty as an end in itself'.[148] The Human Rights Act 1998 has seen the positively enforceable Convention rights provide additional backbone to the common law's powerful rhetorical support for political freedoms. It has triggered debate, and sometimes profound change, in the protections of political rights. While the Human Rights Act adds positive recognition, and enforceability, to many political rights, this has not seen the occasional deference of the courts to legislative, executive and operational decisions impacting upon democratic participation consigned to history. Just as the occasional limitation of political freedoms attempts to strike a democratically defensible balance between individual rights and community interests, the role of courts within the UK's political constitution is also conditioned by their own 'counter-majoritarian' position within the constitutional order. Civil liberties remain – in common with much of the UK Constitution – subject to the ebb and flow of political tides. This much is evident in the all-too-swift transition between the relative liberalism of the late 1990s – a period which spawned the Human Rights Act 1998 – and the raft of restrictive anti-terrorism, security and crime-combatting initiatives of the twenty-first century.[149]

---

[148] K. D. Ewing, 'The Politics of the British Constitution' [2000] PL 405, 408.

[149] For a highly critical survey see: K. D. Ewing, *The Bonfire of the Liberties: New Labour, Human Rights and the Rule of Law* (OUP, 2010).

Practice questions

1. *'[F]reedom of speech and freedom of association are essential to the Constitution. Without free elections the people cannot make a choice of policies. Without freedom of speech the appeal to reason which is the basis of democracy cannot be made. Without freedom of association, electors and elected representatives cannot bind themselves into parties for the formulation of common policies and the attainment of common ends.'*

   (I. Jennings, *Cabinet Government* (3rd edn, CUP, 1969) p. 14.)

   Critically analyse this statement, reflecting on the extent to which these political freedoms are reflected in the UK Constitution.

2. *'A consequence of thinking about liberty, expression, assembly and so on, and also the entitlement to vote, as civil liberties rather than human rights is to focus attention away from the possibility of these being absolute entitlements vested in human beings as such and to divert the analytical spotlight instead on to their utility as part of the essential fabric that goes into the making of our democratic tapestry.'*

   (C. A. Gearty, 'Civil Liberties and Human Rights' in N. Bamforth and P. Leyland (eds), *Public Law in a Multi-Layered Constitution* (Hart, 2003) p. 373)

   Discuss.

3. *'In spite of advances made in response to decisions of the European Court of Human Rights and under the Human Rights Act, the deference of courts to legislative and executive decisions means that the extent of political freedom in the UK remains an issue of serious concern.'*

   Discuss.

Further reading

Conor Gearty's *Civil Liberties* (OUP, 2007) provides an accessible account of the core liberties which underpin democratic participation. **Geoffrey Robertson QC's** important, but sadly dated, *Freedom, the Individual and the Law* (7th edn, Penguin, 1993) remains an important reference point with a broad coverage, while **Gearty and Ewing's** *The Struggle for Civil Liberties: Political Freedom and the Rule of Law in Britain, 1914–1945* (OUP, 2000) charts the somewhat chequered history of the legal protection of democratic rights during the first half of the twentieth century. **Helen Fenwick's** *Fenwick on Civil Liberties and Human Rights* (Routledge-Cavendish, 2017) provides an extensive, authoritative, treatment of the freedoms covered in this chapter in their broader context. A short, incisive, account of the interplay between rights adjudication and democracy in the UK – albeit with a focus on the HRA – can be found in **A. McHarg, 'Rights and Democracy in UK Public Law' in M. Elliott and D. Feldman (eds),** *The Cambridge Companion to Public Law* (CUP, 2015) 116.

One of the best studies of the law of freedom of speech – including valuable comparisons between the UK, Germany and the United States – remains **Eric Barendt's** *Freedom of Speech* (OUP, 2005). The House of Lords decision in *Animal Defenders International* remains a controversial confirmation of the UK's ban on political advertising, and its essential endorsement by the European Court of Human Rights is similarly contentious. An illuminating assessment of the latter can be found in **T. Lewis, '***Animal Defenders International* v *United Kingdom*: **Sensible Dialogue or a Bad Case of the Strasbourg**

Jitters?' (2014) 77 MLR 460. **David Mead's** *The New Law of Public Protest: Rights and Regulation in the Human Rights Act Era* (Hart, 2010) provides an excellent survey of the law of freedom of assembly as a tool of collective, political, action. **Helen Fenwick's** article **'Marginalising Human Rights: Breach of the Peace, "Kettling", and Human Rights Act and Public Protest'** [2009] PL 737 is an excellent account of the cumulative effect of the House of Lords decisions in *Laporte* and *Austin* framed within a discussion of the, still controversial, concept of breach of the peace.

Index

Access to courts 206–207
Accountability 430–450
    ministerial responsibility, and 439–441
    open government, and 434–436
Acts of Parliament 22, 23–29 *see also* Statutes
    altering geographical extent of UK 27
    bringing UK into other legal orders 27
    constitutionally significant 23–29
    legal status 23–24
    organising government institutions 25–26
    regulating relationship between individual
        and state 24–25
    regulating relationship between private
        individuals 26–27
Act of Settlement 1701
    key features 128
Adams, Gerry
    resignation as MP 45
Administrative Court
    judicial review, and 516–517
Administrative law
    traffic light, as 512
Ancient constitution
    end of 37–38
Appellate Committee of the House of Lords
    344–345
    separation of powers, and 240–241
Arms to Iraq 445–446
Asset-freezing orders 30–31

Bagehot, Walter
    conventions, on 41
    UK constitution, on 22
Balkanisation
    devolution, and 407–408
Banking crisis 2008 31–32
Bill of Rights 9, 24–25, 681–684
Bill of Rights 1689
    key features 128
Black-spider memos 43–44
Brexit 89–96
    aftermath of referendum 91–93
    European Union (Withdrawal) Bill 93–94
    Henry VIII powers 94
    key issues 89

    on-going process 93–95
    Parliamentary sovereignty, and 176–179
    referendum 89–91
    sovereignty, and 91–93
    Supreme Court, and 92–93
    'take back control' 89–91
Brown, Gordon
    international law, on 56

Cabinet ministers 267–269
Case law
    source of constitutional rules, as 38–39
    source of interpretative principles, as 39–40
City devolution 419
Civil liberties 648–649
    negative 649
Civil service 276–282
    changes threatening role and ethos 278–281
    executive agencies, and 278–279
    external appointments 279–280
    job security 279–280
    order of seniority 276
    reaffirming or overhauling foundations
        281–282
    role 276–278
    select committee investigations 279
    special advisers 280–281
Clarity and stability of law
    rule of law, and 204–206
Coalition 297–298
Coalition government
    collective responsibility, and 275–276
Collective cabinet responsibility 47–48
Collective responsibility 273–278
    coalition government, and 275–276
    confidentiality 273–274
    individual ministerial responsibility
        distinguished 437
    resignations because of 274–275
    unanimity 273–274
Committee on Standards in Public Life
    433–434
Common law 37–40
    ancient constitution, end of 37–38
    freedom of assembly, and 700–703

human rights, and 651
non-retroactivity, and 202–204
principle of openness 499
residual limitation of Parliamentary
sovereignty 161–163
Common law constitutionalism 105–107
Comparative human rights protection regimes
652–653
Competing ideas of constitutionalism 102–103
Competing schools of constitutional thought
108
Constituency boundaries
review of 312–313
Constitutional checks and balances 246–248
judicial review 267–268
Parliamentary controls on executive
246–247
Constitutional conventions *see* Conventions
Constitutional law
nature of 2–3
Constitutional principle
primary legislation, and 151–152
Constitutional Reform Act 2005 349–354
Constitutional Reform and Governance Act
2010 60
Constitutional statutes 158–161
common law, and 158
definition 158–159
implied repeal, and 159
Constitutions
allocations of governmental power 3
amendment 13–14
characteristics 4–8
contents 8–11
defining and delimiting powers exercisable
by government 10–11
defining relationships between individuals
and state 11
elections, and 6
entrenched 6
entrenchment 13–14
establishing central structures of government
10
forms 12–15
interpretation 14–15
length 9
nature 2–4
notion of constituent power 5
prior to government 5
purpose 2–4
superior to ordinary law 5
typical types 12–13

UK 4–8
unwritten norms 14–15
written, advantages of 12–13
Conventions 40–51
codifying 48–51
collective cabinet responsibility 47–48
courts, and 46–48
elections, length of time between 45
government ministers 41–412
interpretation of statutes 47
judicial recognition 46–48
laws, and 42–44
laws, turning into 49–51
Money Bills 50
nature of 41
practices, and 44–45
prerogative powers of monarch 41
Prime Minister as MP 46
Prince Charles 43–44
relationship between executive and
legislative 42
replacement with statutory rules 49–51
respect for rule over period of time 46
risks associated with 48–49
role 41–42
US electoral college 49
Council of Ministers 81–82
key roles 82
Council of the European Union 81–82
key roles 82
Countries of the UK 359
Court of Justice of the European Union 84–86
key roles 85
main types of case 86
pivotal role of 85
Court proceedings
judicial immunity relating to 191–192
Courts
conventions, and 46–48
Human Rights Act 1998, and 663
Crown
brand name for executive 258–259
Crown immunity 259–260
Crown Prerogative 22–23, 34–37 *see also* Royal
Prerogative
Customary international law 66–70
courts as gatekeepers 67–70
distinct role 67
historical approach 66–67
incorporation model 66–67
jus cogens norms under 72–73
legal effect within UK 66–70

Customary international law (*continued*)
    state immunity, and 68
    transformation model 67–70

Damages
    judicial review, and 538–539
Declarations
    judicial review, and 538
Delegated legislation 29–34 *see also* Secondary
        legislation
    positive resolution procedure 32
    primary legislation, and 29–31
    separation of powers, and 231–232
Democracy
    constitutional principle, as 714–715
Democratic participation 688–719
Devolved administrations
    statutes establishing 26
Devolution 358–392, 393–427
    adapting Westminster to 421–425
    Balkanisation, and 407–408
    devolved legislation as limited legislation
        394
    EU/ECHR law, and 406–407
    federalism, and 366–367
    from union to 359
    Higher Education Act 2004 415
    independence, and 407–410
    intergovernmental relations 396–397
    legislative review in practice 403–405
    Northern Ireland *see* Northern Ireland
    Parliamentary sovereignty, and 130–131
    picking triple lock 407
    Scotland 367–374 *see also* Scotland
    Scottish independence referendum 408–410
    Sewel Convention 398
    slow progress towards 365–366
    subordinate nature of devolved legislatures
        394–399
    triple lock 394–396
    UK constitution, and 393–427
    UK courts, and 399–405
        judicial management of devolved
            competences 402
        policing devolution settlement 399–405
        pre-and post-enactment scrutiny
            mechanisms 399–400
        reviewing subordinate legislatures
            401–402
        theoretical models underpinning review
            of devolved legislation 402
    Wales *see* Wales

Westminster Parliament, and 394
Dicey, A.V.
    conventions, on 41, 42–43, 51–52
    rule of law, on 184–185
Diceyan orthodoxy
    Parliamentary sovereignty, and 123–126
Diplomatic immunity 189–190
Directives
    EU 87
Discrimination statutes 26–27
Dividing governmental functions 230–231
Domestic law
    treatment of international law as separate
        from 56
Domestic policy prerogative 36
Dualism
    international law, and 59–61

Elected mayors 419
Elections
    length of time between 45
Elective dictatorship 304–306
Electoral reform 307–312
Electoral systems 307–312
    AMS 308
    AV 311–312
    first past the post 308, 309–310
    pressure for 310–311
    regional closed-list system 308
    STV 308
    SV 308
English Parliament 416–417
English votes for English laws 422–425
Equality before the law 188–192
    diplomatic immunity 189–190
    exceptional privileges 189–192
    immunity relating to parliamentary
        proceedings 190–191
    judicial immunity relating to court
        proceedings 191–192
    no inherent privileges for public officials
        188–189
    re-evaluating 197–198
European Commission 84
    key roles 84
European Convention on Human Rights
        (ECHR) 595–646 *see also* Human
        Rights
    absolute rights 620–622
    adjudication and enforcement 613–616
    controversy over margin of appreciation
        636–638

creation 609–610
derogations 642–643
    emergency threatening life of nation
        642–643
    nature of 642
    strictly required by exigencies of situation
        643
development 609–610
education 630–631
factors relevant to margin of appreciation
    634–636
free and fair elections 631
geographical reach of rights 618–619
human rights and trade offs 632–642
impact on domestic law 650
incorporation of 651–660
increasing importance 610–611
individual petitions to court 613–616
    admissibility 613–614
    court process 615
    hearing merits of case 614
    referrals to Grand Chamber 614
    reform proposals 615
institutional development 611–613
limited rights 622–624
limits of role 650
margin of appreciation doctrine 633–634
myths surrounding human rights 632–633
non-discrimination 630
positive and negative obligations 638–642
positive obligations 638–642
    freedom from torture 638–640
    hijacking by government 641–642
    right to life 638–640
    right to private and family life 640–641
qualified rights 624–629
    lawful restriction 627
    listed public policy objective 626–627
    proportionate restrictions 627–628
    triggering 626
    weighing one against others 628–629
rights 637
rights and freedoms 617–631
subsidiary role of European Court 633
UK model of incorporation 654–655
under-developed rights 630–631
European Council 81
    key roles 81
European Court of Human Rights
    composition 616
    enforcing decisions 616
European Court of Justice 84

European General Court 84
European legal system 87–89
    diversity amidst harmonisation 88–89
    UK judges as EU judges 87–88
European Parliament 82–83
    key roles 83
European Union 74–96
    current operation 79
    current structure 79
    development 74–79
    Directives 87
    expanding competence 77
    expansion 76
    history of 75–78
    institutions 80
    key issues 74
    legal measures 86–87
    Parliamentary sovereignty, and 167–179
    regulations 86–87
    role under Lisbon Treaty 79–80
    UK judges as EU judges 87–88
    UK withdrawal from see Brexit
    UKs accession to 78–79
European Union (Withdrawal) Bill 93–94
    separation of powers, and 233
Executive 3, 254–284
    absolute monarchy, and 255–260
    changing department responsibility for
        higher education 268
    composition 265–282
    Crown as brand name for 258–259
    Crown immunity 259–260
    Parliamentary controls on 246–247
    passing of sovereignty from monarchy to
        Parliament 255–257
    passing remaining powers from monarchy to
        government ministers 257–258
    Revolution of 1688 255–257
    role 254, 265–282
    separation of powers, and 227–228
Executive agencies
    civil service, and 278–279
External sources of constitutional law 55–57

Factortame litigation 169–175
    application of rules of separate and distinct
        legal jurisdiction 173–174
    controlling influence of common law
        174–175
    European Union Act 2011 175
    European Court of Justice, response from
        171

Factortame litigation (*continued*)
  evolution of rule of statutory constitution
    173
  law, questions of 170
  legal revolution, whether 172
  No. 1 170
  No. 2 171–175
  relevant domestic legislation 169–170
Fairness of legal process 206–211
  access to courts 206–207
  consistent operation of official discretion
    210–211
  impartial and open adjudication 207–209
Federalism
  devolution, and 366–367
Federalist Papers 52
Foreign policy prerogatives 36
Freedom of assembly 699–707
  common law 700–703
  demonstrations in vicinity of Parliament
    704–705
  Human Rights Act era 705–707
  statutory management 703–705
Freedom of expression 690–699
  contours 690–692
  limiting 696–699
  speech in Parliament 692–696
Freedom of information 485–504
  absolute exceptions 493–494
  Act of 2000 485, 488–502
  advantages 488
  Attorney-General's legal advice on war in
    Iraq 497
  common law principle of openness 499
  enforcement 494
  exceptions 490–491
  exceptions subject to public interest test
    491–493
  extent 489
  impact of 2000 Act 499–500
  key issues 488–489
  legislation overseas 486
  ministerial veto power 495–497
  MPs expenses scandal 501
  right to information 489–490

General elections 289–290
Government by law 193–197
  government actions require authority
    193–194
  limitations 194–197
Government minsters
  conventions 41–42

Government under the law 200
Greater London Authority 417
Green light approach
  legal power, and 107–108
Grey, Earl
  political accountability, on 431
Griffith, J.A.G
  constitution, on 7–8
  political constitution, on 103–105

Habeas corpus 708–709
Henry VIII clauses 32–34
Henry VIII powers
  Brexit, and 94
Hierarchies of norms within international law
  70–73
  treaties 70–71
Higher education
  changing department responsibility
    for 268
Hobbs, Thomas
  common law, on 37
Home Office
  ministerial structure 270
House of Commons 285–314
  accountability 301–302
  composition 287–293, 292
  finance 300
  formation and sustenance of government
    295–298
    coalition 297–298
    co-operation 297
    minority government 296
  franchise 288–289
  functions 293–302
  general elections 289–290
  government and opposition 293
  legislation 298
  majority, importance of 291
  party system 291–293
  pre-eminent House 302
  rebalancing of executive/legislative relations
    306–307
  Recall of MPs Act 2015 300
  representation 300
  role 293–302
  scrutiny 301–302
  separation of powers, and 228
  types of Bill 298
House of Lords 315–339
  challenging legislation 329–331
  composition 316–323
  Constitutional Reform Act 2005 320–321

current composition 321–323
formal powers 324–331
hereditary peers 317–318
House of Lords Act 1999 319
House of Lords Appointments Commission
    319–320
House of Lords (Expulsion and Suspension)
    Act 2015 321
House of Lords Reform Act 2014 321
Law Lords 317–318
legislative scrutiny 327–329
life peers 318
Lords Spiritual 317–318
make-up by professional area 323
reform 331–337
reformed composition 319–323
revising legislation and statutory instruments
    327
role 324
separation of powers, and 228
transformation 325–326
Hunting Act 2004
legal battles over 28–29
Human rights 595–646
common law 651
comparative rights protection regimes
    652–653
concept 596
contested concept 597–598
continuing importance 608–609
developing concept 597
evolution 599
individual, political and legal protections for
    654
nature of 596–597
normative agency 602
parliamentary sovereignty, and 652–655
personhood 602
philosophical basis 601
practical considerations 602–603
private power, and 607
promotion of undesirable values 604
relationship between law and politics, and
    606–607
religion, and 598–599
scepticism 603–606
special interests, and 659–660
three waves of thinking 599–601
trade-offs 602–603
vision of advocates not realised 604
UK media, and 604–606
Western impositions 607–608

Human Rights Act 1998 25, 163–167,
    647–687
addressing legislation which violates
    incorporated ECHR rights 664
bridging public-private divide 681
case law on interpretive duty 664–668
civil liberties, and 648–649
courts, and 663
declarations of incompatibility 668–673
    case law 669–672
    power to affirm that legislation breaches
        human rights 668–669
    remedial orders 672–673
domestic effect of Convention prior to
    650–651
duty to interpret legislation compatibly with
    Convention rights 663–664
effect 647–648
employing Convention rights under
    673–681
horizontal applications of human rights
    679–681
importance 647–648
incorporated rigts 655–656
incorporating statute, as 62
influence over primary legislation 166–167
legislation, and 660
parliamentary sovereignty, and 163–167
    basic account 165–166
    implied repeal, and 166
pre-legislative checks 661–662
public authorities 673–677
    meaning 675–676
    obligations 673–675
    remedies against 676–677
standing 677–678
Strasbourg jurisprudence, status of 656–659
using Convention rights as shield 679
using Convention rights as sword 678–679
vertical and horizontal conceptions of rights
    679

Impartial and open adjudication 207–209
Independence of the judiciary
separation of powers, and 243–246
Individual ministerial responsibility 436
accountability, and 439–441
collective responsibility distinguished 437
definition 446–449
effectiveness 442–445
Ministerial Code 446
parliamentary resolutions 446–449

Individual ministerial responsibility (*continued*)
    personal indiscretions 441
    sanctions 442–445
    scope 438–439
Information Commissioner 494–495
Information Rights Tribunal 495
Injunctions
    judicial review, and 538
Intergovernmental relations
    devolution, and 396–397
International law 55–97
    common law superiority, and 60
    Constitutional Reform and Governance Act
        2010 60
    customary *see* Customary international law
    dualism 59–61
    hierarchies of norms 70–73 *see also*
        Hierarchies of norms within
        international law
    importance of 57
    international obligations contextualising
        rights and obligations 66
    monism 58
    primary legislation, and 150–151
    rival approaches within domestic legal
        systems 57–61
    statute enacted in light of UK's international
        obligations 65–66
    treatment as separate from domestic law 56
International obligations
    contextualising rights and obligations 66
Interpretation of primary legislation 152–158
    common law rights 154–158
    interpretative presumptions 152–154
    interpretative technique 152–154
    legality, principle of 154–158
Interpretation of statutes
    conventions, and 47
Iraq War
    Attorney-General's legal advice on 498
    legal advice on 271–272
Ireland
    following lead of 363–365
    Home Rule, and 362–364

Jackson v Attorney-General 143–148
    arguments 143–144
    courts' jurisdiction 144–145
    House of Lords decision 145
    implications 146–148
    reach of Parliament Acts procedure 145–146
Jennings, Sir Ivor

conventions, on 42–43
Judges
    political questions, and 108–115
Judicial Appointments Commission 353–354
Judicial identification of private interests 198
Judicial immunity
    court proceedings, relating to 191–192
Judicial independence 340–341
Judicial law-making
    separation of powers, and 233–235
Judicial review 267–268, 506–540, 541–594
    abuse of powers 551–557
        public authority's considerations
            552–555
    Administrative Court 516–517
    appearance of bias 570–584
    benefits 510–512
    bias 570–584
        disqualifying personal or financial interest
            571–572
        Porter v *Magill* reformulation of test
            573–574
        predetermination of issue 572–573
    breach of express statutory procedural rules
        568
    breach of rules of natural justice 568–570
    classification of grounds 542
    common law theory 515
    constitutional role 507–514
    controlling 516–519
    cost of 517–518
    courts 'institutional capacity', and 509
    damages 538–539
    deciding whether ostensibly private bodies
        are subject to 526
    declaration 538
    errors of fact 550–551
    errors of law 549–550
    exceeding limits of public function 545–548
    exclusive jurisdiction for public law claims
        535
    exercising power for improper purposes
        555–556
    fair hearing, right to 574–583
        core requirements 575–578
        facility to appeal 581
        flexible standard of fairness 574–575
        legal representation 580–581
        notice of decision 576–577
        opportunity to make case 577–578
        optional extra requirements 578–583
        oral hearings 578–579

providing reasons for decisions 581–283
witnesses and cross-examination 579–580
fettering of discretion 556–557
four corners rule 547
grounds 541–594
illegality 544–557
implicit powers/requirement 547
injunctions 538
irrationality 558–565
jurisdiction of last resort 534
key issues 507
legitimate expectations 584–592
 countering claim 591–592
 creating 588–589
 detrimental reliance, importance of 590
 importance of size of group to which
  promise mode 590–591
 meaning 584
 procedural 585–586
 substantive 586–588
limiting 535–536
mandatory orders 538
nature of 506–507
nature of public functions 524–526
parliamentary sovereignty, and 512
political dimension 100
potential reach 520
procedural elements 516
procedural exclusivity, and 533–534
procedural impropriety 567–584
 meaning 568
 statutory exceptions 583–584
process 518–519
prohibiting orders 538
proportionality 565–567
public law remedies 536–538
public/private divide 519–520
public/private divide as control mechanism
 526
quashing orders 537–538
reformed *ultra vires* theory 515–516
remedies 536
review/appeal continuum 543
review, not appeal 507–508
securing rule of law and good governance
 510–512
separation of powers, and 512–514
source of jurisdiction 514–516
sources of public functions 520–524
 de facto public functions 522
 royal prerogative 521–522
 statute 520

subordinate legislation 520–521
standing requirements 526–532
 control mechanism, as 531–532
 individuals/legal persons 527–528
 judicial interpretation 527–531
 non-governmental organisations 529
 pressure group 529–531
 public authorities 531
 supervising public authority decision making
  507
 terminology 542
 three stages 518
 time limits 532–533
 tree of 593
 ultra vires doctrine 514, 544
 unauthorised delegation of public function
  548–549 *Wednesbury see Wednesbury*
Judiciary 4, 111–115
 composition by ethnicity 112
 composition by gender 112
 determination of political questions
  113–115
 independence 111
 lack of diversity 111
 politics of 111–115
 pressure for institutional reform 346–349
 separation of powers, and 228–229
Jus cogens norms
 customary international law, under 72–73

King, Anthony
 constitutions, on 7

Law and politics 98–120
 differing responses 115–118
 forms 101
 relationships between 98–102
Law officers 270–271
Laws
 conventions, and 42–44
Legal accountability
 political accountability distinguished
  432–434
Legal constitutionalism
 six tenets 106
Legal power
 green light approach 107–108
 red light approach 107–108
Legalisation of UK constitutions 118–119
Legislative branch
 separation of powers, and 228
Legislative reform orders 32–34

Legislature 3
Liberty 708–712
   deprivation under Human Rights Act
      710–712
Liberty of the person 708
Limitations upon Parliamentary competence
      133–138
   express repeal 134
   future repeal 135–136
   implied repeal 134–135
   orthodox responses 134–136
   self-embracing sovereignty 136–139
Lisbon Treaty
   EU role under 79–80
Localism agenda 419–421
London Mayor 417
Lord Chancellor
   reformed office 350–352
   separation of powers, and 240
   unreformed office 342–344

Magna Carta 24, 25
Mandatory orders 538
Ministerial resignations 443–445
Ministers 266–272
   Cabinet 267–269
   junior 269–270
   senior 267–269
Monarch
   separation of powers, and 241–243
Monarchy 260–264
   extraordinary exercise of roles within UK
      Constitution 262–263
   monarch as Head of State 260–262
   symbolic value 263–264
Money Bills convention 50
Monism
   international law, and 58
MPs
   role 301
MPs' expenses scandal 501

Natural justice
   breach of rules 568–570
Non-retroactivity of law 200–204
   common law, and 202–204
   legislation, and 200–202
Northern Ireland 381–389
   St Andrews Agreement 2006 387–388
   collapse of 387
   devolution 381–389
   future of devolution 388–389

   peace process 381–383
   referendum 1998 381–383
Northern Ireland Assembly 383–385
   competence 386–387
   finance 386–387
   new powers 388
Northern Ireland Executive 385–386

Official discretion
   consistent operation 210–211

Parliament 285–287
   development 285–286
   dissolution 290
   key issues 286
   preliminary progress of public bill 299
   prorogation 290
   summoning 290
   supreme legal authority 99
Parliament Act 1911
   Acts passed under 142, 143
   enactment of 141
Parliament Acts 26, 303
Parliament Acts procedure
   Jackson v Attorney-General *see* Jackson v
      Attorney-General
   validity of 143–148
Parliamentary controls on executive
      246–247
Parliamentary debates 453–454
Parliamentary Ombudsman 468–484
   accessibility 480–481
   Barlow Clowes investigation 478–479
   bringing on complaint 475–476
   complaint and investigation process 480
   effectiveness 480–483
   efficiency 480–483
   enforceable remedies 482
   growth 471
   investigations 476–477
   jurisdiction 473–474
   links with Parliament 481
   maladministration, and 468, 474–475
   maladministration and good administration
      474–475
   matters excluded from jurisdiction 474
   origins 471
   principles of good administration 477
   quasi-judicial 469
   redress 477
   remedies 477
   Sachsenhausen Case 471

towards good administration 476
work of 470
Parliamentary proceedings
immunity relating to 190–191
Parliamentary questions 454–456
Parliamentary scrutiny of government 451–467
assessing 463–465
fusion of elected branches 464–465
mechanisms 453
political culture, influence of 465
procedural change 464
reforming 461–462
Wright reforms 461–462
Parliamentary sovereignty 122–181
amendment of primary legislative process
139–140
Brexit, and 176–179
constitutional principle, and 151–152
constitutional statutes 158–161
Diceyan orthodoxy 123–126
democratic foundation 126–127
devolution, and 130–131
extended rule of law, and 211–214
European Union, and 167–179
key issues 167
membership 167–168
reconciliation through interpretation
168–169
Factortame litigation *see* Factortame
litigation
fundamental nature of 122
human rights, and 652–655
Human Rights Act 1998, and 163–167
judicial review, and 512
legal and political distinguished 129–133
legal device, as 129
legal or political construct, whether
126–128
legally unlimited power of Parliament
123–126
limitations upon own legislative competence
133–138
monarch versus Parliament 127
negative aspect 124–126
origins of doctrine 126
Parliament can make or unmake any law 124
Parliament redesigning itself 141
positive aspect 124
power relationships between courts and
Parliament 179
primary legislation and international law
150–151

primary legislation and prerogative 149–150
relationships between primary legislation and
other sources of law 148–161
residual common law limitation 161–163
Paulson plan 31–32
Police powers of arrest and detention
709–710
Political accountability 430–450 *see also*
Accountability
legal accountability distinguished 432–434
Political constitution 103–105
Political freedoms 688–719
Political questions 108–115
determination by judiciary 113–115
nature of 109
Political understandings 40
Politics of the judiciary 111–115
Ponsonby Rule 59
Positive resolution procedure 32
Practices
conventions, and 44–45
primary legislation, and 149–150
Pressure groups
judicial review, and 529–531
Primary legislation
constitutional principle, and 151–152
international law, and 150–151
interpretation *see* Interpretation of primary
legislation 152–158
prerogative, and 149–150
Prime Minister 265–266
MP, as 46
Prime Minister's Questions 430
Prince Charles
conventions, and 43–44
Prisoner voting 716–717
Private interests
judicial identification 198
Prohibiting orders 538
Public authorities
Human Rights Act 1998, and 673–677
Public international law 57–73
Public officials
no inherent privileges for 188–189

Quashing orders 537–538

Red light approach
legal power, and 107–108
Referendums
status in UK constitutional law 131–132
Regional assemblies 418

Regional development agencies 418
Regulations
    EU 86–87
Religion
    human rights, and 598–599
Representation of the People Acts 25
Revolution of 1688 255–257
Ridley, F.F.
    characteristics of constitutions, on 4–7
Royal Prerogative 22–23, 34–373
    domestic policy 36
    foreign policy 36
    government, exercised by 35–37
    monarch's historic powers, and 34–35
    monarch's personal prerogatives 35
Rule of law 182–220
    clarity and stability of law 204–206
    core 187
    core, continued significance of 199
    Dicey's account 184–185
    different conceptions 187
    domain 183–187
    equality before the law 188–192 *see also*
        Equality before the law
    extended 199
        increasing role in UK Constitution
            214–215
        overturning statutes in conflict with 214
        Parliamentary sovereignty, and 211–214
    government by law 193–197 *see also*
        Government by law
    government under the law 200
    importance 218–219
    judicial identification of private interests 198
    key issues 183
    legal process must be fair *see also* Fairness of
        legal process
    limitations of procedural conceptions 215
    modern conceptions 185–187
    narrow conceptions
        formal equality, and 215–216
    nature of 182
    non-retroactivity of law 200–204
    one label, many ideas 183
    range of ideas, as 182–183
    re-evaluating equality before the law 197–198
    substantive 215–218
    substantive equality, and 216–218
    tackling limitations of core 197

Salisbury Convention 303–304
Scotland 367–374

competence of Parliament 369–373
    altering powers 371–372
    financing devolution 372–373
    reserved powers 369–370
    transferred powers 369–370
devolution 367–374
devolution referendum 1997 367
electoral system 368–369
executive 374
Parliament elections 2016 369
Parliament regions 368
two types of MSP 368
Scott Report 445–446
Secondary legislation 29–34 *see also* Delegated
    legislation
    asset-freezing orders 30–31
    creation 31–32
    First World War, and 29–30
    primary legislation, and 29–31
Select Committee investigations
    civil service, and 279
Select Committees 456–460
    core functions 458
    departmental 457
    selecting chairs 460
    work of 456–457
Self-embracing sovereignty 136–139
    departure from orthodoxy 136–139
    limitations on form of future
        legislation 137
    limitations on manner of enactment of
        future legislation 137
    limitations on substance or content of future
        legislation 138
    practice 138–139
Senior ministers 267–269
Separation of powers 221–251
    aim of doctrine 221
    aims 223
    Appellate Committee of the House of Lords
        240–241
    constitutional checks and balances
        see Constitutional checks and balances
    delegated legislation 231–232
    dividing governmental functions
        230–231
    European Union (Withdrawal) Bill 2017
        233
    executive branch 227–228
    governmental institutions 227
    history 223
    House of Commons 228

House of Lords 228
independence of the judiciary 243–246
judicial law-making 233–235
judicial review, and 512–514
judiciary 228–229
key issues 222
legislative branch 228
Lord Chancellor 240
monarch, and 241–243
overlapping of powers 239
Parliamentary sovereignty, and 236–239
partial division of functions 236–239
partial separation of functions, and 235–236
partial separation theory 225–226
partially separated institutions 239–246
pure theory 224–225
theory 223
three branches 222
Sewel Convention 50–51, 398
Sources of UK constitution 21–54
    Acts of Parliament 22, 23–29 *see also* Acts of
        Parliament
    common law 37–40 *see also* Common Law
    Crown Prerogative 22–23
    legal rules 23
    legal sources 22–40
    non-legal sources 40–51
    organic constitution 22
    Royal Prerogative 22–23
Special advisers
    civil service, and 280–281
State immunity
    customary international law, and 68
Statutes *see also* Acts of Parliament
    constitutional 27–28
    ordinary 27–28
Strasbourg jurisprudence
    status of 656–659
Supreme Court 352–353

Tomkins, Adam
    Our Republican Constitution 106
Treaties 62–66
    dualist approach 62
    hierarchies between 70–71
    incorporated 62
    legal effect within UK Constitution 62–64
    presumption against enforceability 63–64
        exceptions to 64

private parties assuming obligations under
        64–65
    unincorporated 63–64
Treaty approval
    process of 61

UK Constitution 4–8, 15–19
    central features of government, and 18
    characteristics 18
    constitutional landmarks 16–17
    definition 17
    domestic sources 21–54 *see also* Sources of
        UK constitution
    key debates 16–17
    organic development 15–16
UK judicial system
    apex prior to Constitutional Reform Act
        2005 341–345
Ultra vires doctrine 514
Union, creation of 360–361
Union, operation of 361–362
Unitary government 360
    pressure on 362
US Electoral College
    conventions, and 49

Voting rights 713–717
    denying 715
    prisoners 716–717

Wales 375–381
    devolution referendum 1997 375
    discontent with limited devolution 377–378
    from subordinate legislation to enhanced
        legislative powers 378–379
    Government of Wales Act 2006 327
    Wales Act 2014 and 2017 380–381
    Welsh Assembly 375–377
Wednesbury 558–565
    future of 564
    meaning 558
    responding to criticisms 564–565
    test for irrationality 558–559
    test in action 559–561
    variable test 561–563
Welsh Assembly 375–377
    competences 1998 377
    election results 2016 376
    powers 376
    primary legislative powers 379–380

Welsh Office Plus 376
West Lothian question 410–415
    decentralisation within England 417–421
    English Parliament 416–417
    key issues 415–416
    tackling 415–425
    Westminster, and 421–425
Whips 270–271
Wright reforms 461–462